THE OXFORD FRENCH MINIDICTIONARY

THE OXFORD FRENCH MINIDICTIONARY

French-English
English-French

Français-anglais
Anglais-français

MICHAEL JANES

Oxford New York
OXFORD UNIVERSITY PRESS

Oxford University Press, Walton Street, Oxford OX2 6DP

Oxford New York Toronto
Delhi Bombay Calcutta Madras Karachi
Petaling Jaya Singapore Hong Kong Tokyo
Nairobi Dar es Salaam Cape Town
Melbourne Auckland

and associated companies in
Berlin Ibadan

Published in the United States
by Oxford University Press, New York

First Published 1986
Reprinted 1987, 1988 (twice), 1989

British Library Cataloguing in Publication Data

Janes, Michael
The Oxford French minidictionary: French-English, English-French.—(Dictionaries—English)
1. French language—Dictionaries-English
2. English language—Dictionaires—French
I. Title
443v.21 PC2640

ISBN 0-19-864145-1

Library of Congress Cataloging in Publication Data

The Oxford French minidictionary.
1. French language—Dictionaries—English.
2. English language—Dictionaries—French.
I. Janes, Michael.
PC2640.08 1986 443v.21 86-12438

ISBN 0-19-864145-1 (pbk.)

Printed in Great Britain
by Courier International
Tiptree, Essex

Contents · Table des matières

Preface

This work is one of the first of a new range of bilingual dictionaries in the format of *The Oxford Minidictionary*. It is written with speakers of both English and French in mind, and contains the most useful words and expressions of the English and French languages of today.

Indicators in brackets marking different uses of the same word together with a wide range of style and field labels guide the user towards the appropriate translation.

Common abbreviations, names of countries, and other useful geographical names are included.

Pronunciation is given by means of the International Phonetic Alphabet for all headwords and for those derived words whose pronunciation cannot easily be deduced from that of a headword.

For their valuable help and advice, I am grateful to Dr J. B. Sykes, Miss J. M. Hawkins, and Mrs J. Andrews, and to Mr H. Ferrar, Dr J. A. Hutchinson, and Professor J. Leblon who made many useful suggestions.

M. J.

March 1986

Préface

Cet ouvrage fait partie d'une nouvelle série de dictionnaires bilingues qui ont pour modèle *The Oxford Minidictionary*. Il s'adresse à tous ceux, francophones et anglophones, qui désirent connaître les mots et les expressions les plus courants du français et de l'anglais d'aujourd'hui.

Des indications en italique placées entre parenthèses distinguent chaque sens différent d'un même mot et guident l'usager dans son choix de la traduction juste. L'usager trouvera également dans ce dictionnaire les abréviations et les sigles les plus courants, et les noms géographiques les plus utiles.

La prononciation, qui est celle de l'Alphabet Phonétique International, est donnée pour chaque mot principal—ou mot vedette—d'un article et pour un mot dérivé lorsque la prononciation de celui-ci ne résulte pas de celle du mot principal.

Je tiens à remercier ici les personnes qui ont accepté de me faire profiter de leur compétence: le Dr J. B. Sykes, Miss J. M. Hawkins et Mrs J. Andrews, Mr H. Ferrar et le Dr J. A. Hutchinson, ainsi que le Professeur J. Leblon à qui je dois maintes suggestions.

M. J.

Mars 1986

Introduction

A swung dash (~) is used within entries to represent a headword or that part of a headword preceding a vertical bar (|).

An obelisk (†) immediately following a verb headword in the French into English section indicates that the verb is listed in the tables of irregular verbs on p. 643. In English, the past tense and past participle are usually formed by the addition of *ed* to the infinitive (e.g. *jump, jumped*), although only *d* is added to a verb ending in a silent *e* (e.g. *move, moved*), and in a verb ending in *y* the *y* changes to *i* before the addition of *ed* (e.g. *carry, carried*). Irregular English past tenses and participles are given in the English into French text.

An asterisk immediately following a French word (e.g. qu'*) shows the form of that word used before a vowel or mute h.

In French, the plural of a noun is usually formed by the addition of *s* to the singular, whereas a noun ending in *s, x*, or *z* remains unchanged. In English, the plural is also formed by the addition of *s*, although *es* is added to form the plural of a noun ending in *ch, s, sh, ss, us, x*, or *z* (e.g. *sash, sashes*). In the case of a noun ending in *quy*, or *y* preceded by a consonant, *y* becomes *ies* (e.g. *baby, babies*). French and English plurals are listed when they do not follow these rules.

In general, the feminine of a French adjective is formed by the addition of *e* to the masculine, except that a masculine ending in *e* remains unchanged. In the English into French section, only the masculine form of a French adjective is shown. In the French headword list, the feminine of an adjective is given when the addition of *e* to the masculine affects pronunciation (e.g. *petit*, *petite*; *fatigant*, *fatigante*) or when there is some other change besides the addition of *e*, whether or not pronunciation is affected (e.g. *ambigu*, *ambiguë*; *dû*, *due*; *heureux*, *heureuse*).

Proprietary Terms

This dictionary includes some words which are, or are asserted to be, proprietary names or trade marks. Their inclusion does not imply that they have acquired for legal purposes a non-proprietary or general significance, nor is any other judgement implied concerning their legal status. In cases where the editor has some evidence that a word is used as a proprietary name or trade mark this is indicated by the letter (P.), but no judgement concerning the legal status of such words is made or implied thereby.

Introduction

Un *s* couché (~) figurant à l'intérieur d'un article remplace le mot vedette de cet article ou la partie de ce mot qui précède une ligne verticale (|).

Le symbole † placé après un verbe français renvoie le lecteur aux tableaux des conjugaisons, page 643. En anglais, on forme généralement le passé simple et le participe passé d'un verbe régulier en ajoutant *ed* à l'infinitif (par exemple *jump, jumped*), ou en ajoutant *d* à un infinitif se terminant par un *e* muet (par exemple *move, moved*). Si l'infinitif se termine par un *y*, on change le *y* en *ied* (par exemple *carry, carried*). Les passés simples et participes passés irréguliers sont indiqués.

En français, le pluriel d'un nom se forme généralement par le simple ajout d'un *s*; un nom qui se termine par *s*, *x*, ou *z* reste toutefois invariable. En anglais aussi, on forme le pluriel en ajoutant un *s*; toutefois, un nom se terminant par *ch*, *s*, *sh*, *ss*, *us*, *x*, ou *z* prend *es* au pluriel (par exemple *sash, sashes*); et un nom se terminant par *quy*, ou *y* précédé d'une consonne, change le *y* en *ies* (par exemple *baby, babies*). En français et en anglais, sont indiqués les pluriels qui ne suivent pas les règles précédentes.

En général, on forme le féminin d'un adjectif français en ajoutant un *e* au masculin; toutefois, un adjectif masculin se terminant par *e* ne varie pas. Dans la partie anglais-français, figure seulement la forme masculine de l'adjectif français. Dans la partie français-anglais, le féminin d'un adjectif est indiqué lorsque l'ajout d'un *e* modifie la prononciation (par exemple *petit, petite*; *fatigant, fatigante*) ou lorsque la forme masculine subit un changement autre que celui du simple ajout d'un *e* (par exemple *ambigu*, *ambiguë*; *dû*, *due*; *heureux*, *heureuse*).

Marques déposées
Ce dictionnaire contient des termes qui sont ou qui ont été désignés comme des marques déposées. La présence ou l'absence de cette désignation ne peut toutefois être considérée comme ayant valeur juridique.

Pronunciation of French

Phonetic symbols

Vowels

i	v*i*e	y	vêt*u*
e	pr*é*	ø	p*eu*
ɛ	l*ai*t	œ	p*eu*r
a	pl*a*t	ə	d*e*
ɑ	b*a*s	ɛ̃	mat*in*
ɔ	m*o*rt	ɑ̃	s*an*s
o	m*o*t	ɔ̃	b*on*
u	gen*ou*	œ̃	l*un*di

Consonants and semi-consonants

p	*p*ayer	ʒ	*j*e
b	*b*on	m	*m*ain
t	*t*erre	n	*n*ous
d	*d*ans	l	*l*ong
k	*c*ou	r	*r*ue
g	*g*ant	ɲ	a*gn*eau
f	*f*eu	ŋ	campi*ng*
v	*v*ous	j	*y*eux
s	*s*ale	w	*ou*i
z	*z*éro	ɥ	h*u*ile
ʃ	*ch*at		

Note: ' before the pronunciation of a word beginning with *h* indicates no liaison or elision.

Prononciation de l'anglais

Symboles phonétiques

Voyelles et diphtongues

iː	*see*	ə	*ago*
ɪ	s*i*t	eɪ	p*a*ge
e	t*e*n	əʊ	h*o*me
æ	h*a*t	aɪ	f*i*ve
ɑː	*ar*m	aɪə	f*ire*
ɒ	g*o*t	aʊ	n*ow*
ɔː	s*aw*	aʊə	fl*our*
ʊ	p*u*t	ɔɪ	j*oi*n
uː	t*oo*	ɪə	n*ear*
ʌ	c*u*p	eə	h*air*
ɜː	f*ur*	ʊə	p*oor*

Consonnes

p	*p*en	s	*s*o
b	*b*ad	z	*z*oo
t	*t*ea	ʃ	*sh*e
d	*d*ip	ʒ	mea*s*ure
k	*c*at	h	*h*ow
g	*g*ot	m	*m*an
tʃ	*ch*in	n	*n*o
dʒ	*J*une	ŋ	si*ng*
f	*f*all	l	*l*eg
v	*v*oice	r	*r*ed
θ	*th*in	j	*y*es
ð	*th*en	w	*w*et

Note: ˈ précède la syllabe accentuée.

Abbreviations · Abréviations

abbreviation	*abbr., abrév.*	abréviation
adjective(s)	*a. (adjs.)*	adjectif(s)
adverb(s)	*adv(s).*	adverbe(s)
American	*Amer.*	américain
anatomy	*anat.*	anatomie
approximately	*approx.*	approximativement
archaeology	*archaeol., archéol.*	archéologie
architecture	*archit.*	architecture
motoring	*auto.*	automobile
auxiliary	*aux.*	auxiliaire
aviation	*aviat.*	aviation
botany	*bot.*	botanique
commerce	*comm.*	commerce
conjunction(s)	*conj(s).*	conjonction(s)
cookery	*culin.*	culinaire
electricity	*electr., électr.*	électricité
feminine	*f.*	féminin
familiar	*fam.*	familier
figurative	*fig.*	figuré
geography	*geog., géog.*	géographie
geology	*geol., géol.*	géologie
grammar	*gram.*	grammaire
humorous	*hum.*	humoristique
interjection(s)	*int(s).*	interjection(s)
invariable	*invar.*	invariable
legal, law	*jurid.*	juridique
language	*lang.*	langue
masculine	*m.*	masculin
medicine	*med., méd.*	médecine
military	*mil.*	militaire
music	*mus.*	musique
noun(s)	*n(s).*	nom(s)
nautical	*naut.*	nautique
oneself	*o.s.*	se, soi-même
proprietary term	P.	marque déposée
pejorative	*pej., péj.*	péjoratif
philosophy	*phil.*	philosophie

photography	*photo.*	photographie
plural	*pl.*	pluriel
politics	*pol.*	politique
possessive	*poss.*	possessif
past participle	*p.p.*	participe passé
prefix	*pref., préf.*	préfixe
preposition(s)	*prep(s)., prép(s).*	préposition(s)
present participle	*pres. p.*	participe présent
pronoun	*pron.*	pronom
relative pronoun	*pron. rel.*	pronom relatif
psychology	*psych.*	psychologie
past tense	*p.t.*	passé
something	*qch.*	quelque chose
someone	*qn.*	quelqu'un
railway	*rail.*	chemin de fer
religion	*relig.*	religion
relative pronoun	*rel. pron.*	pronom relatif
school, scholastic	*schol., scol.*	scolaire
singular	*sing.*	singulier
slang	*sl.*	argot
someone	*s.o.*	quelqu'un
something	*sth.*	quelque chose
technical	*techn.*	technique
television	*TV*	télévision
university	*univ.*	université
auxiliary verb	*v. aux.*	verbe auxiliaire
intransitive verb	*v.i.*	verbe intransitif
pronominal verb	*v. pr.*	verbe pronominal
transitive verb	*v.t.*	verbe transitif

FRANÇAIS-ANGLAIS
FRENCH-ENGLISH

A

a /a/ *voir* **avoir.**

à /a/ *prép.* (*à* + *le* = *au*, *à* + *les* = *aux*) in, at; (*direction*) to; (*temps*) at; (*jusqu'à*) to, till; (*date*) on; (*époque*) in; (*moyen*) by, on; (*prix*) for; (*appartenance*) of; (*mesure*) by. **donner**/*etc.* **~,** give/*etc.* to. **apprendre**/*etc.* **~,** learn/*etc.* to. **l'homme ~ la barbe,** the man with the beard. **~ la radio,** on the radio. **c'est ~ moi**/*etc.*, it is mine/*etc.* **c'est ~ vous**/*etc.* **de,** it is up to you/*etc.* to; (*en jouant*) it is your/*etc.* turn to. **dix km ~ l'heure,** ten km. an *ou* per hour.

abaissement /abɛsmɑ̃/ *n.m.* (*baisse*) drop, fall.

abaisser /abese/ *v.t.* lower; (*levier*) pull *ou* push down; (*fig.*) humiliate. **s'~** *v. pr.* go down, drop; (*fig.*) humiliate o.s. **s'~ à,** stoop to.

abandon /abɑ̃dɔ̃/ *n.m.* abandonment; desertion; (*sport*) withdrawal; (*naturel*) abandon. **à l'~,** in a state of neglect. **~ner** /-ɔne/ *v.t.* abandon, desert; (*renoncer à*) give up, abandon; (*céder*) give (**à,** to). **s'~ner à,** give o.s. up to.

abasourdir /abazurdir/ *v.t.* stun.

abat-jour /abaʒur/ *n.m. invar.* lampshade.

abats /aba/ *n.m. pl.* offal.

abattement /abatmɑ̃/ *n.m.* dejection; (*faiblesse*) exhaustion; (*comm.*) allowance.

abattis /abati/ *n.m. pl.* giblets.

abattoir /abatwar/ *n.m.* slaughterhouse.

abattre† /abatr/ *v.t.* knock down; (*arbre*) cut down; (*animal*) slaughter; (*avion*) shoot down; (*affaiblir*) weaken; (*démoraliser*) dishearten. **s'~** *v. pr.* come down, fall (down).

abbaye /abei/ *n.f.* abbey.

abbé /abe/ *n.m.* priest; (*supérieur d'une abbaye*) abbot.

abcès /apsɛ/ *n.m.* abscess.

abdi|quer /abdike/ *v.t./i.* abdicate. **~cation** *n.f.* abdication.

abdom|en /abdɔmɛn/ *n.m.* abdomen. **~inal** (*m. pl.* **~inaux**) *a.* abdominal.

abeille /abɛj/ *n.f.* bee.

aberrant, ~e /abɛrɑ̃, -t/ *a.* absurd.

aberration /abɛrɑsjɔ̃/ *n.f.* aberration; (*idée*) absurd idea.

abêtir /abetir/ *v.t.* make stupid.

abhorrer /abɔre/ *v.t.* loathe, abhor.

abîme /abim/ *n.m.* abyss.

abîmer /abime/ *v.t.* damage, spoil. **s'~** *v. pr.* get damaged *ou* spoilt.

abject /abʒɛkt/ *a.* abject.

abjurer /abʒyre/ *v.t.* abjure.

ablation /ablɑsjɔ̃/ *n.f.* removal.

ablutions /ablysjɔ̃/ *n.f. pl.* ablutions.

abnégation /abnegɑsjɔ̃/ *n.f.* self-sacrifice.

aboiement /abwamɑ̃/ *n.m.* bark(ing). **~s,** barking.

abois (aux) /(oz)abwa/ *adv.* at bay.
abol|ir /abɔlir/ *v.t.* abolish. **~ition** *n.f.* abolition.
abominable /abɔminabl/ *a.* abominable.
abond|ant, ~ante /abɔ̃dɑ̃, -t/ *a.* abundant, plentiful. **~amment** *adv.* abundantly. **~ance** *n.f.* abundance; (*prospérité*) affluence.
abonder /abɔ̃de/ *v.i.* abound (**en,** in).
abonn|er (s') /(s)abɔne/ *v. pr.* subscribe (**à,** to). **~é, ~ée** *n.m., f.* subscriber; season-ticket holder. **~ement** *n.m.* (*à un journal*) subscription; (*de bus, théâtre, etc.*) season-ticket.
abord /abɔr/ *n.m.* access. **~s,** surroundings. **d'~,** first.
abordable /abɔrdabl/ *a.* (*prix*) reasonable; (*personne*) approachable.
abordage /abɔrdaʒ/ *n.m.* (*accident: naut.*) collision. **prendre à l'~,** (*navire*) board, attack.
aborder /abɔrde/ *v.t.* approach; (*lieu*) reach; (*problème etc.*) tackle. —*v.i.* reach land.
aborigène /abɔriʒɛn/ *n.m.* aborigine, aboriginal.
aboutir /abutir/ *v.i.* succeed, achieve a result. **~ à,** end (up) in, lead to. **n'~ à rien,** come to nothing.
aboutissement /abutismɑ̃/ *n.m.* outcome.
aboyer /abwaje/ *v.i.* bark.
abrasi|f, ~ve /abrazif, -v/ *a.* & *n.m.* abrasive.
abrégé /abreʒe/ *n.m.* summary.
abréger /abrèʒe/ *v.t.* (*texte*) shorten, abridge; (*mot*) abbreviate, shorten; (*visite*) cut short.
abreuv|er /abrœve/ *v.t.* water; (*fig.*) overwhelm. **s'~er** *v. pr.* drink. **~oir** *n.m.* watering-place.
abréviation /abrevjɑsjɔ̃/ *n.f.* abbreviation.
abri /abri/ *n.m.* shelter. **à l'~,** under cover. **à l'~ de,** sheltered from.
abricot /abriko/ *n.m.* apricot.
abriter /abrite/ *v.t.* shelter; (*recevoir*) house. **s'~** *v. pr.* (take) shelter.
abroger /abrɔʒe/ *v.t.* repeal.
abrupt /abrypt/ *a.* steep, sheer; (*fig.*) abrupt.
abruti, ~e /abryti/ *n.m., f.* (*fam.*) idiot.
abrutir /abrytir/ *v.t.* make *ou* drive stupid, dull the mind of.
absence /apsɑ̃s/ *n.f.* absence.
absent, ~e /apsɑ̃, -t/ *a.* absent, away; (*chose*) missing. —*n.m., f.* absentee. **~éisme** /-teism/ *n.m.* absenteeism. **~éiste** /-teist/ *n.m./f.* absentee.
absenter (s') /(s)apsɑ̃te/ *v. pr.* go *ou* be away; (*sortir*) go out, leave.
absinthe /apsɛ̃t/ *n.m.* absinthe.
absolu /apsɔly/ *a.* absolute. **~ment** *adv.* absolutely.
absolution /apsɔlysjɔ̃/ *n.f.* absolution.
absor|ber /apsɔrbe/ *v.t.* absorb; (*temps etc.*) take up. **~bant, ~bante** *a.* (*travail etc.*) absorbing; (*matière*) absorbent. **~ption** *n.f.* absorption.
absoudre /apsudr/ *v.t.* absolve.
absten|ir (s') /(s)apstənir/ *v. pr.* abstain. **s'~ir de,** refrain from. **~tion** /-ɑ̃sjɔ̃/ *n.f.* abstention.
abstinence /apstinɑ̃s/ *n.f.* abstinence.
abstr|aire /apstrɛr/ *v.t.* abstract. **~action** *n.f.* abstraction. **faire ~action de,** disregard. **~ait, ~aite** *a.* & *n.m.* abstract.
absurd|e /apsyrd/ *a.* absurd. **~ité** *n.f.* absurdity.
abus /aby/ *n.m.* abuse, misuse; (*injustice*) abuse.
abuser /abyze/ *v.t.* deceive. —*v.i.* go too far. **s'~** *v. pr.* be mistaken. **~ de,** abuse, misuse; (*profiter de*)

take advantage of; (*alcool etc.*) over-indulge in.

abusi|f, ~ve /abyzif, -v/ *a.* excessive, improper.

acabit /akabi/ *n.m.* ilk.

académicien, ~ne /akademisjɛ̃, -jɛn/ *n.m., f.* academician.

académ|ie /akademi/ *n.f.* academy; (*circonscription*) educational district. **A~ie,** Academy. **~ique** *a.* academic.

acajou /akaʒu/ *n.m.* mahogany.

acariâtre /akarjɑtr/ *a.* cantankerous.

accablement /akɑbləmɑ̃/ *n.m.* despondency.

accabl|er /akɑble/ *v.t.* overwhelm. **~er d'impôts,** burden with taxes. **~er d'injures,** heap insults upon. **~ant, ~ante** *a.* (*chaleur*) oppressive.

accalmie /akalmi/ *n.f.* lull.

accaparer /akapare/ *v.t.* monopolize; (*fig.*) take up all the time of.

accéder /aksede/ *v.i.* **~ à,** reach; (*pouvoir, requête, trône, etc.*) accede to.

accélér|er /akselere/ *v.i.* (*auto.*) accelerate. —*v.t.*, **s'~er** *v. pr.* speed up. **~ateur** *n.m.* accelerator. **~ation** *n.f.* acceleration; speeding up.

accent /aksɑ̃/ *n.m.* accent; (*sur une syllabe*) stress, accent; (*ton*) tone. **mettre l'~ sur,** stress.

accent|uer /aksɑ̃tɥe/ *v.t.* (*lettre, syllabe*) accent; (*fig.*) emphasize, accentuate. **s'~uer** *v. pr.* become more pronounced, increase. **~uation** *n.f.* accentuation.

accept|er /aksɛpte/ *v.t.* accept. **~er de,** agree to. **~able** *a.* acceptable. **~ation** *n.f.* acceptance.

acception /aksɛpsjɔ̃/ *n.f.* meaning.

accès /aksɛ/ *n.m.* access; (*porte*) entrance; (*de fièvre*) attack; (*de colère*) fit; (*de joie*) (out)burst. **les ~ de,** (*voies*) the approaches to.

accessible /aksesibl/ *a.* accessible; (*personne*) approachable.

accession /aksɛsjɔ̃/ *n.f.* **~ à,** accession to.

accessit /aksesit/ *n.m.* honourable mention.

accessoire /akseswar/ *a.* secondary. —*n.m.* accessory; (*théâtre*) prop.

accident /aksidɑ̃/ *n.m.* accident. **~ de train/d'avion,** train/plane crash. **~é** /-te/ *a.* damaged *ou* hurt (in an accident); (*terrain*) uneven, hilly.

accidentel, ~le /aksidɑ̃tɛl/ *a.* accidental.

acclam|er /aklame/ *v.t.* cheer, acclaim. **~ations** *n.f. pl.* cheers.

acclimat|er /aklimate/ *v.t.*, **s'~er** *v. pr.* acclimatize; (*Amer.*) acclimate. **~ation** *n.f.* acclimatization; (*Amer.*) acclimation.

accolade /akɔlad/ *n.f.* embrace; (*signe*) brace, bracket.

accommodant, ~e /akɔmɔdɑ̃, -t/ *a.* accommodating.

accommodement /akɔmɔdmɑ̃/ *n.m.* compromise.

accommoder /akɔmɔde/ *v.t.* adapt (**à,** to); (*cuisiner*) prepare; (*assaisonner*) flavour. **s'~ de,** put up with.

accompagn|er /akɔ̃paɲe/ *v.t.* accompany. **s'~er de,** be accompanied by. **~ateur, ~atrice** *n.m., f.* (*mus.*) accompanist; (*guide*) guide. **~ement** *n.m.* (*mus.*) accompaniment.

accompli /akɔ̃pli/ *a.* accomplished.

accompl|ir /akɔ̃plir/ *v.t.* carry out, fulfil. **s'~ir** *v. pr.* be carried out, happen. **~issement** *n.m.* fulfilment.

accord /akɔr/ *n.m.* agreement; (*harmonie*) harmony; (*mus.*) chord. **être d'~,** agree (**pour,** to). **se mettre d'~,** come to an agreement, agree. **d'~!,** all right!, OK!

accordéon /akɔrdeɔ̃/ *n.m.* accordion.
accord|er /akɔrde/ *v.t.* grant; (*couleurs etc.*) match; (*mus.*) tune. **s'~er** *v. pr.* agree. **s'~er avec,** (*s'entendre avec*) get on with. **~eur** *n.m.* tuner.
accoster /akɔste/ *v.t.* accost; (*navire*) come alongside.
accotement /akɔtmɑ̃/ *n.m.* roadside, verge; (*Amer.*) shoulder.
accoter (s') /(s)akɔte/ *v.pr.* lean (**à,** against).
accouch|er /akuʃe/ *v.i.* give birth (**de,** to); (*être en travail*) be in labour. —*v.t.* deliver. **~ement** *n.m.* childbirth; (*travail*) labour. (**médecin**) **~eur** *n.m.* obstetrician. **~euse** *n.f.* midwife.
accoud|er (s') /(s)akude/ *v. pr.* lean (one's elbows) on. **~oir** *n.m.* armrest.
accoupl|er /akuple/ *v.t.* couple; (*faire copuler*) mate. **s'~er** *v. pr.* mate. **~ement** *n.m.* mating; coupling.
accourir /akurir/ *v.i.* run up.
accoutrement /akutrəmɑ̃/ *n.m.* (strange) garb.
accoutumance /akutymɑ̃s/ *n.f.* habituation; (*méd.*) addiction.
accoutum|er /akutyme/ *v.t.* accustom. **s'~er** *v. pr.* get accustomed. **~é** *a.* customary.
accréditer /akredite/ *v.t.* give credence to; (*personne*) accredit.
accroc /akro/ *n.m.* tear, rip; (*fig.*) hitch.
accroch|er /akrɔʃe/ *v.t.* (*suspendre*) hang up; (*attacher*) hook, hitch; (*déchirer*) catch; (*heurter*) hit; (*attirer*) attract. **s'~er** *v. pr.* cling, hang on; (*se disputer*) clash. **~age** *n.m.* hanging; hooking; (*auto.*) collision; (*dispute*) clash; (*mil.*) encounter.
accroissement /akrwasmɑ̃/ *n.m.* increase (**de,** in).
accroître /akrwatr/ *v.t.*, **s'~** *v. pr.* increase.
accroup|ir (s') /(s)akrupir/ *v. pr.* squat. **~i** *a.* squatting.
accueil /akœj/ *n.m.* reception, welcome.
accueill|ir† /akœjir/ *v.t.* receive, welcome; (*aller chercher*) meet. **~ant, ~ante** *a.* friendly.
acculer /akyle/ *v.t.* corner. **~ à,** force *ou* drive into *ou* against *ou* close to.
accumul|er /akymyle/ *v.t.*, **s'~er** *v. pr.* accumulate, pile up. **~ateur** *n.m.* accumulator. **~ation** *n.f.* accumulation.
accus /aky/ *n.m. pl.* (*fam.*) battery.
accusation /akyzɑsjɔ̃/ *n.f.* accusation; (*jurid.*) charge. **l'~,** (*magistrat*) the prosecution.
accus|er /akyze/ *v.t.* accuse; (*blâmer*) blame; (*jurid.*) charge; (*fig.*) show, emphasize. **~er réception,** acknowledge receipt. **~ateur, ~atrice** *a.* incriminating; *n.m., f.* accuser. **~é, ~ée** *a.* marked; *n.m.,f.* accused.
acerbe /asɛrb/ *a.* bitter.
acéré /asere/ *a.* sharp.
achalandé /aʃalɑ̃de/ *a.* **bien ~,** well-stocked.
acharn|é /aʃarne/ *a.* relentless, ferocious. **~ement** *n.m.* relentlessness.
acharner (s') /(s)aʃarne/ *v. pr.* **s'~ sur,** set upon; (*poursuivre*) hound. **s'~ à faire,** struggle to do.
achat /aʃa/ *n.m.* purchase. **~s,** shopping. **faire l'~ de,** buy.
acheminer /aʃmine/ *v.t.* dispatch. **s'~ vers,** head for.
achet|er /aʃte/ *v.t.* buy, purchase. **~er à,** buy from; (*pour*) buy for. **~eur, ~euse** *n.m., f.* buyer; (*client de magasin*) shopper.
achèvement /aʃɛvmɑ̃/ *n.m.* completion.
achever /aʃve/ *v.t.* finish (off). **s'~** *v. pr.* end.

acid|e /asid/ *a.* acid, sharp. —*n.m.* acid. **~ité** *n.f.* acidity. **~ulé** *a.* slightly acid.
acier /asje/ *n.m.* steel. **aciérie** *n.f.* steelworks.
acné /akne/ *n.f.* acne.
acolyte /akɔlit/ *n.m.* (*péj.*) associate.
acompte /akɔ̃t/ *n.m.* deposit, part-payment.
à-côté /akote/ *n.m.* side-issue. **~s,** (*argent*) extras.
à-coup /aku/ *n.m.* jolt, jerk. **par ~s,** by fits and starts.
acoustique /akustik/ *n.f.* acoustics. —*a.* acoustic.
acqu|érir† /akerir/ *v.t.* acquire, gain; (*biens*) purchase, acquire. **~éreur** *n.m.* purchaser. **~isition** *n.f.* acquisition; purchase.
acquiescer /akjese/ *v.i.* acquiesce, agree.
acquis, ~e /aki, -z/ *n.m.* experience. —*a.* acquired; (*fait*) established; (*faveurs*) secured. **~ à,** (*projet*) in favour of.
acquit /aki/ *n.m.* receipt. **par ~ de conscience,** for peace of mind.
acquitt|er /akite/ *v.t.* acquit; (*dette*) settle. **s'~er de,** (*promesse, devoir*) carry out. **s'~er envers,** repay. **~ement** *n.m.* acquittal; settlement.
âcre /ɑkr/ *a.* acrid.
acrobate /akrɔbat/ *n.m./f.* acrobat.
acrobatie /akrɔbasi/ *n.f.* acrobatics. **~ aérienne,** aerobatics.
acrobatique /-tik/ *a.* acrobatic.
acte /akt/ *n.m.* act, action, deed; (*théâtre*) act; (*de naissance, mariage*) certificate. **~s,** (*compte rendu*) proceedings. **prendre ~ de,** note.
acteur /aktœr/ *n.m.* actor.
acti|f, ~ve /aktif, -v/ *a.* active. —*n.m.* (*comm.*) assets. **avoir à son ~f,** have to one's credit *ou* name. **~vement** *adv.* actively
action /aksjɔ̃/ *n.f.* action; (*comm.*) share; (*jurid.*) action. **~naire** /-jɔnɛr/ *n.m./f.* shareholder.
actionner /aksjɔne/ *v.t.* work, activate.
activer /aktive/ *v.t.* speed up; (*feu*) boost. **s'~** *v. pr.* hurry, rush.
activiste /aktivist/ *n.m./f.* activist.
activité /aktivite/ *n.f.* activity. **en ~,** active.
actrice /aktris/ *n.f.* actress.
actualiser /aktɥalize/ *v.t.* update.
actualité /aktɥalite/ *n.f.* topicality; (*événements*) current events. **~s,** news. **d'~,** topical.
actuel, ~le /aktɥɛl/ *a.* present; (*d'actualité*) topical. **~lement** *adv.* at the present time.
acuité /akɥite/ *n.f.* acuteness.
acupunct|ure /akypɔ̃ktyr/ *n.f.* acupuncture. **~eur** *n.m.* acupuncturist.
adage /adaʒ/ *n.m.* adage.
adapt|er /adapte/ *v.t.* adapt; (*fixer*) fit. **s'~er** *v. pr.* adapt (o.s.); (*techn.*) fit. **~ateur, ~atrice** *n.m., f.* adapter; *n.m.* (*électr.*) adapter. **~ation** *n.f.* adaptation.
additif /aditif/ *n.m.* (*note*) rider; (*substance*) additive.
addition /adisjɔ̃/ *n.f.* addition; (*au café etc.*) bill; (*Amer.*) check. **~nel, ~nelle** /-jɔnɛl/ *a.* additional. **~ner** /-jɔne/ *v.t.* add; (*totaliser*) add (up).
adepte /adɛpt/ *n.m./f.* follower.
adéquat, ~e /adekwa, -t/ *a.* suitable.
adhérent, ~e /aderɑ̃, -t/ *n.m., f.* member.
adhé|rer /adere/ *v.i.* adhere, stick (**à,** to). **~rer à,** (*club etc.*) be a member of; (*s'inscrire à*) join. **~rence** *n.f.* adhesion. **~sif, ~sive** *a.* & *n.m.* adhesive. **~sion** *n.f.* membership; (*accord*) adherence.
adieu (*pl.* **~x**) /adjø/ *int.* & *n.m.* goodbye, farewell.

adipeu|x, ~se /adipø, -z/ *a.* fat; (*tissu*) fatty.
adjacent, ~e /adʒasɑ̃, -t/ *a.* adjacent.
adjectif /adʒɛktif/ *n.m.* adjective.
adjoindre /adʒwɛ̃dr/ *v.t.* add, attach; (*personne*) appoint. **s'~** *v. pr.* appoint.
adjoint, ~e /adʒwɛ̃, -t/ *n.m.*, *f.* & *a.* assistant. **~ au maire,** deputy mayor.
adjudant /adʒydɑ̃/ *n.m.* warrant-officer.
adjuger /adʒyʒe/ *v.t.* award; (*aux enchères*) auction. **s'~** *v. pr.* take.
adjurer /adʒyre/ *v.t.* beseech.
admettre† /admɛtr/ *v.t.* let in, admit; (*tolérer*) allow; (*reconnaître*) admit; (*candidat*) pass.
administrati|f, ~ve /administratif, -v/ *a.* administrative.
administr|er /administre/ *v.t.* run, manage; (*justice, biens, etc.*) administer. **~ateur, ~atrice** *n.m., f.* administrator, director. **~ation** *n.f.* administration. **A~ation,** Civil Service.
admirable /admirabl/ *a.* admirable.
admirati|f, ~ve /admiratif, -v/ *a.* admiring.
admir|er /admire/ *v.t.* admire. **~ateur, ~atrice** *n.m., f.* admirer. **~ation** *n.f.* admiration.
admissible /admisibl/ *a.* admissible; (*candidat*) eligible.
admission /admisjɔ̃/ *n.f.* admission.
adolescen|t, ~te /adɔlesɑ̃, -t/ *n.m., f.* adolescent. **~ce** *n.f.* adolescence.
adonner (s') /(s)adɔne/ *v. pr.* **s'~ à,** devote o.s. to; (*vice*) take to.
adopt|er /adɔpte/ *v.t.* adopt. **~ion** /-psjɔ̃/ *n.f.* adoption.
adopti|f, ~ve /adɔptif, -v/ *a.* adopted.
adorable /adɔrabl/ *a.* delightful, adorable.
ador|er /adɔre/ *v.t.* adore; (*relig.*) worship, adore. **~ation** *n.f.* adoration; worship.
adosser /adɔse/ *v.t.*, **s'~** *v. pr.* lean back (**à, contre,** against).
adoucir /adusir/ *v.t.* soften; (*boisson*) sweeten; (*personne*) mellow; (*chagrin*) ease. **s'~** *v. pr.* soften; mellow; ease; (*temps*) become milder.
adresse /adrɛs/ *n.f.* address; (*habileté*) skill.
adresser /adrese/ *v.t.* send; (*écrire l'adresse sur*) address; (*remarque etc.*) address. **s'~ à,** address; (*aller voir*) go and ask *ou* see; (*bureau*) enquire at; (*viser, intéresser*) be directed at.
adroit, ~e /adrwa, -t/ *a.* skilful, clever. **~ement** /-tmɑ̃/ *adv.* skilfully, cleverly.
aduler /adyle/ *v.t.* adulate.
adulte /adylt/ *n.m./f.* adult. **—*a.*** adult; (*plante, animal*) fully-grown.
adultère /adyltɛr/ *a.* adulterous. —*n.m.* adultery.
advenir /advənir/ *v.i.* occur.
adverbe /advɛrb/ *n.m.* adverb.
adversaire /advɛrsɛr/ *n.m.* opponent, adversary.
adverse /advɛrs/ *a.* opposing.
adversité /advɛrsite/ *n.f.* adversity.
aérateur /aeratœr/ *n.m.* ventilator.
aér|er /aere/ *v.t.* air; (*texte*) lighten. **s'~er** *v. pr.* get some air. **~ation** *n.f.* ventilation. **~é** *a.* airy.
aérien, ~ne /aerjɛ̃, -jɛn/ *a.* air; (*photo*) aerial; (*câble*) overhead; (*fig.*) airy.
aérodrome /aerɔdrom/ *n.m.* aerodrome.
aérodynamique /aerɔdinamik/ *a.* streamlined, aerodynamic.
aérogare /aerɔgar/ *n.f.* air terminal.

aéroglisseur /aerɔglisœr/ *n.m.* hovercraft.

aérogramme /aerɔgram/ *n.m.* airmail letter; (*Amer.*) aerogram.

aéronautique /aerɔnotik/ *a.* aeronautical. —*n.f.* aeronautics.

aéronavale /aerɔnaval/ *n.f.* Fleet Air Arm; (*Amer.*) Naval Air Force.

aéroport /aerɔpɔr/ *n.m.* airport.

aéroporté /aerɔpɔrte/ *a.* airborne.

aérosol /aerɔsɔl/ *n.m.* aerosol.

aérospat|ial (*m. pl.* **~iaux**) /aerɔspasjal, -jo/ *a.* aerospace.

affable /afabl/ *a.* affable.

affaibl|ir /afeblir/ *v.t.*, **s'~ir** *v. pr.* weaken. **~issement** *n.m.* weakening.

affaire /afɛr/ *n.f.* matter, affair; (*transaction*) deal; (*occasion*) bargain; (*firme*) business; (*jurid.*) case. **~s**, affairs; (*comm.*) business; (*effets*) belongings. **avoir ~ à**, (have to) deal with. **c'est mon ~, ce sont mes ~s**, that is my business.

affair|er (s') /(s)afere/ *v. pr.* bustle about. **~é** *a.* busy.

affaiss|er (s') /(s)afese/ *v. pr.* (*sol*) sink, subside; (*poutre*) sag; (*personne*) collapse. **~ement** /-ɛsmɑ̃/ *n.m.* subsidence.

affaler (s') /(s)afale/ *v. pr.* slump (down), collapse.

affam|er /afame/ *v.t.* starve. **~é** *a.* starving.

affect|é /afɛkte/ *a.* affected. **~ation**[1] *n.f.* affectation.

affect|er /afɛkte/ *v.t.* (*feindre, émouvoir*) affect; (*destiner*) assign; (*nommer*) appoint, post. **~ation**[2] *n.f.* assignment; appointment, posting.

affecti|f, ~ve /afɛktif, -v/ *a.* emotional.

affection /afɛksjɔ̃/ *n.f.* affection; (*maladie*) ailment. **~ner** /-jɔne/ *v.t.* be fond of.

affectueu|x, ~se /afɛktɥø, -z/ *a.* affectionate.

affermir /afɛrmir/ *v.t.* strengthen.

affiche /afiʃ/ *n.f.* (public) notice; (*publicité*) poster; (*théâtre*) bill.

affich|er /afiʃe/ *v.t.* post up, announce; (*sentiment etc.*) display. **~age** *n.m.* billposting; (*électronique*) display.

affilée (d') /(d)afile/ *adv.* in a row, at a stretch.

affiler /afile/ *v.t.* sharpen.

affil|ier (s') /(s)afilje/ *v. pr.* become affiliated. **~iation** *n.f.* affiliation.

affiner /afine/ *v.t.* refine.

affinité /afinite/ *n.f.* affinity.

affirmati|f, ~ve /afirmatif, -v/ *a.* affirmative. —*n.f.* affirmative.

affirm|er /afirme/ *v.t.* assert. **~ation** *n.f.* assertion.

affleurer /aflœre/ *v.i.* appear on the surface.

affliction /afliksjɔ̃/ *n.f.* affliction.

afflig|er /afliʒe/ *v.t.* grieve. **~é de**, afflicted with.

affluence /aflyɑ̃s/ *n.f.* crowd(s).

affluent /aflyɑ̃/ *n.m.* tributary.

affluer /aflye/ *v.i.* flood in; (*sang*) rush.

afflux /afly/ *n.m.* influx, flood; (*du sang*) rush.

affol|er /afɔle/ *v.t.* throw into a panic. **s'~er** *v. pr.* panic. **~ement** *n.m.* panic.

affranch|ir /afrɑ̃ʃir/ *v.t.* stamp; (*à la machine*) frank; (*esclave*) emancipate; (*fig.*) free. **~issement** *n.m.* (*tarif*) postage.

affréter /afrete/ *v.t.* charter.

affreu|x, ~se /afrø, -z/ *a.* (*laid*) hideous; (*mauvais*) awful. **~sement** *adv.* awfully, hideously.

affriolant, ~e /afrijɔlɑ̃, -t/ *a.* enticing.

affront /afrɔ̃/ *n.m.* affront.

affront|er /afrɔ̃te/ *v.t.* confront. **s'~er** *v. pr.* confront each other. **~ement** *n.m.* confrontation.

affubler /afyble/ *v.t.* rig out.

affût /afy/ *n.m.* **à l'~,** on the watch (**de,** for).

affûter /afyte/ *v.t.* sharpen.

afin /afɛ̃/ *prép.* & *conj.* **~ de/que,** in order to/that.

africain, ~e /afrikɛ̃, -ɛn/ *a.* & *n.m., f.* African.

Afrique /afrik/ *n.f.* Africa. **~ du Sud,** South Africa.

agacer /agase/ *v.t.* irritate, annoy.

âge /ɑʒ/ *n.m.* age. **quel ~ avez-vous?,** how old are you? **~ adulte,** adulthood. **~ mûr,** middle age. **d'un certain ~,** past one's prime.

âgé /ɑʒe/ *a.* elderly. **~ de cinq ans**/*etc.*, five years/*etc.* old.

agence /aʒɑ̃s/ *n.f.* agency, bureau, office; (*succursale*) branch.

agenc|er /aʒɑ̃se/ *v.t.* organize, arrange. **~ement** *n.m.* organization.

agenda /aʒɛ̃da/ *n.m.* diary; (*Amer.*) datebook.

agenouiller (s') /(s)aʒnuje/ *v. pr.* kneel (down).

agent /aʒɑ̃/ *n.m.* agent; (*fonctionnaire*) official. **~ (de police),** policeman. **~ de change,** stockbroker.

agglomération /aglɔmerɑsjɔ̃/ *n.f.* built-up area, town.

aggloméré /aglɔmere/ *n.m.* (*bois*) chipboard.

agglomérer /aglɔmere/ *v.t.*, **s'~** *v. pr.* pile up.

agglutiner /aglytine/ *v.t.*, **s'~** *v. pr.* stick together.

aggraver /agrave/ *v.t.*, **s'~** *v. pr.* worsen.

agil|e /aʒil/ *a.* agile, nimble. **~ité** *n.f.* agility.

agir /aʒir/ *v.i.* act. **il s'agit de,** it is a matter of; (*il faut*) it is necessary to. **dans ce livre il s'agit de,** this book is about. **dont il s'agit,** in question.

agissements /aʒismɑ̃/ *n.m. pl.* (*péj.*) dealings.

agité /aʒite/ *a.* restless, fidgety; (*troublé*) agitated; (*mer*) rough.

agit|er /aʒite/ *v.t.* (*bras etc.*) wave; (*liquide*) shake; (*troubler*) agitate; (*discuter*) debate. **s'~er** *v. pr.* bustle about; (*enfant*) fidget; (*foule, pensées*) stir. **~ateur, ~atrice** *n.m., f.* agitator. **~ation** *n.f.* bustle; (*trouble*) agitation.

agneau (*pl.* **~x**) /aɲo/ *n.m.* lamb.

agonie /agɔni/ *n.f.* death throes.

agoniser /agɔnize/ *v.i.* be dying.

agraf|e /agraf/ *n.f.* hook; (*pour papiers*) staple. **~er** *v.t.* hook (up); staple. **~euse** *n.f.* stapler.

agrand|ir /agrɑ̃dir/ *v.t.* enlarge. **s'~ir** *v. pr.* expand, grow. **~issement** *n.m.* extension; (*de photo*) enlargement.

agréable /agreabl/ *a.* pleasant. **~ment** /-əmɑ̃/ *adv.* pleasantly.

agréer /agree/ *v.t.* accept. **~ à,** please.

agrég|ation /agregɑsjɔ̃/ *n.f.* agrégation (*highest examination for recruitment of teachers*). **~é, ~ée** /-ʒe/ *n.m., f.* agrégé (*teacher who has passed the agrégation*).

agrément /agremɑ̃/ *n.m.* charm; (*plaisir*) pleasure; (*accord*) assent.

agrémenter /agremɑ̃te/ *v.t.* embellish (**de,** with).

agrès /agrɛ/ *n.m. pl.* (gymnastics) apparatus.

agress|er /agrese/ *v.t.* attack. **~eur** /-ɛsœr/ *n.m.* attacker; (*mil.*) aggressor. **~ion** /-ɛsjɔ̃/ *n.f.* attack; (*mil.*) aggression.

agressi|f, ~ve /agresif, -v/ *a.* aggressive. **~vité** *n.f.* aggressiveness.

agricole /agrikɔl/ *a.* agricultural; (*ouvrier etc.*) farm.

agriculteur /agrikyltœr/ *n.m.* farmer.

agriculture /agrikyltyr/ *n.f.* agriculture, farming.

agripper /agripe/ *v.t.*, **s'~ à,** grab, clutch.

agrumes /agrym/ *n.m. pl.* citrus fruit(s).
aguerrir /agerir/ *v.t.* harden.
aguets (aux) /(oz)agɛ/ *adv.* on the look-out.
aguicher /agiʃe/ *v.t.* entice.
ah /ɑ/ *int.* ah, oh.
ahur|ir /ayrir/ *v.t.* dumbfound. **~issement** *n.m.* stupefaction.
ai /e/ *voir* **avoir.**
aide /ɛd/ *n.f.* help, assistance, aid. *—n.m./f.* assistant. **à l'~ de,** with the help of. **~ familiale,** home help. **~-mémoire** *n.m. invar.* handbook of facts. **~ sociale,** social security; (*Amer.*) welfare. **~ soignant, ~ soignante** *n.m., f.* auxiliary nurse. **venir en ~ à,** help.
aider /ede/ *v.t./i.* help, assist. **s'~ de,** use.
aïe /aj/ *int.* ouch.
aïeul, ~e /ajœl/ *n.m., f.* grandparent.
aïeux /ajø/ *n.m. pl.* forefathers.
aigle /ɛgl/ *n.m.* eagle.
aigr|e /ɛgr/ *a.* sour, sharp; (*fig.*) sharp. **~e-doux, ~e-douce** *a.* bitter-sweet. **~eur** *n.f.* sourness; (*fig.*) sharpness. **~eurs d'estomac,** heartburn.
aigrir /egrir/ *v.t.* embitter; (*caractère*) sour. **s'~** *v. pr.* turn sour; (*personne*) become embittered.
aigu, ~ë /egy/ *a.* acute; (*objet*) sharp; (*voix*) shrill.
aiguillage /egɥijaʒ/ *n.m.* (*rail.*) points; (*rail., Amer.*) switches.
aiguille /egɥij/ *n.f.* needle; (*de montre*) hand; (*de balance*) pointer.
aiguill|er /egɥije/ *v.t.* shunt; (*fig.*) steer. **~eur** *n.m.* pointsman; (*Amer.*) switchman. **~eur du ciel,** air traffic controller.
aiguillon /egɥijɔ̃/ *n.m.* (*dard*) sting; (*fig.*) spur. **~ner** /-jɔne/ *v.t.* spur on.
aiguiser /eg(ɥ)ize/ *v.t.* sharpen; (*fig.*) stimulate.
ail (*pl.* **~s**) /aj/ *n.m.* garlic.
aile /ɛl/ *n.f.* wing.
ailé /ele/ *a.* winged.
aileron /ɛlrɔ̃/ *n.m.* (*de requin*) fin.
ailier /elje/ *n.m.* winger; (*Amer.*) end.
aille /aj/ *voir* **aller**[1].
ailleurs /ajœr/ *adv.* elsewhere. **d'~,** besides, moreover. **par ~,** moreover, furthermore. **partout ~,** everywhere else.
ailloli /ajɔli/ *n.m.* garlic mayonnaise.
aimable /ɛmabl/ *a.* kind. **~ment** /-əmɑ̃/ *adv.* kindly.
aimant [1] /ɛmɑ̃/ *n.m.* magnet. **~er** /-te/ *v.t.* magnetize.
aimant[2], **~e** /ɛmɑ̃, -t/ *a.* loving.
aimer /eme/ *v.t.* like; (*d'amour*) love. **~ bien,** quite like. **~ mieux** *ou* **autant,** prefer.
aine /ɛn/ *n.f.* groin.
aîné, ~e /ene/ *a.* eldest; (*entre deux*) elder. *—n.m., f.* eldest (child); elder (child). **~s** *n.m. pl.* elders. **il est mon ~,** he is my senior.
ainsi /ɛ̃si/ *adv.* thus; (*donc*) so. **~ que,** as well as; (*comme*) as. **et ~ de suite,** and so on.
air /ɛr/ *n.m.* air; (*mine*) look, air; (*mélodie*) tune. **~ conditionné,** air-conditioning. **avoir l'~,** look (**de,** like). **avoir l'~ de faire,** appear to be doing. **en l'~,** (up) in the air; (*promesses etc.*) empty.
aire /ɛr/ *n.f.* area. **~ d'atterrissage,** landing-strip.
aisance /ɛzɑ̃s/ *n.f.* ease; (*richesse*) affluence.
aise /ɛz/ *n.f.* joy. *—a.* **bien ~ de/que,** delighted about/that. **à l'~,** (*sur un siège*) comfortable; (*pas gêné*) at ease; (*fortuné*) comfortably off. **mal à l'~,** uncomfortable; ill at ease. **aimer ses ~s,** like one's comforts.

aisé /eze/ *a.* easy; (*fortuné*) well-off. **~ment** *adv.* easily.
aisselle /ɛsɛl/ *n.f.* armpit.
ait /ɛ/ *voir* **avoir.**
ajonc /aʒɔ̃/ *n.m.* gorse.
ajourn|er /aʒurne/ *v.t.* postpone; (*assemblée*) adjourn. **~ement** *n.m.* postponement; adjournment.
ajout /aʒu/ *n.m.* addition.
ajouter /aʒute/ *v.t.*, **s'~** *v. pr.* add (**à,** to). **~ foi,** lend credence.
ajust|er /aʒyste/ *v.t.* adjust; (*coup*) aim; (*cible*) aim at; (*adapter*) fit. **s'~er** *v. pr.* fit. **~age** *n.m.* fitting. **~é** *a.* close-fitting. **~ement** *n.m.* adjustment. **~eur** *n.m.* fitter.
alambic /alɑ̃bik/ *n.m.* still.
alanguir (s') /(s)alɑ̃gir/ *v. pr.* grow languid.
alarme /alarm/ *n.f.* alarm.
alarmer /alarme/ *v.t.* alarm. **s'~** *v. pr.* become alarmed (**de,** at).
albâtre /albɑtr/ *n.m.* alabaster.
albatros /albatros/ *n.m.* albatross.
albinos /albinos/ *n.m.*/*f.* albino.
album /albɔm/ *n.m.* album.
alcali /alkali/ *n.m.* alkali.
alchim|ie /alʃimi/ *n.f.* alchemy. **~iste** *n.m.* alchemist.
alcool /alkɔl/ *n.m.* alcohol; (*eau de vie*) brandy. **~ à brûler,** methylated spirit. **~ique** *a.* & *n.m.*/*f.* alcoholic. **~isé** *a.* (*boisson*) alcoholic. **~isme** *n.m.* alcoholism.
alcootest /alkɔtɛst/ *n.m.* (P.) breath test; (*appareil*) breathalyser.
alcôve /alkov/ *n.f.* alcove.
aléa /alea/ *n.m.* hazard.
aléatoire /aleatwar/ *a.* uncertain.
alentour /alɑ̃tur/ *adv.* around. **~s** *n.m. pl.* surroundings. **aux ~s de,** round about.
alerte /alɛrt/ *a.* agile. —*n.f.* alert.
alerter /alɛrte/ *v.t.* alert.
algarade /algarad/ *n.f.* altercation.
alg|èbre /alʒɛbr/ *n.f.* algebra. **~ébrique** *a.* algebraic.
Alger /alʒe/ *n.m.*/*f.* Algiers.
Algérie /alʒeri/ *n.f.* Algeria.
algérien, ~ne /alʒerjɛ̃, -jɛn/ *a.* & *n.m., f.* Algerian.
algue /alg/ *n.f.* seaweed.
alias /aljɑs/ *adv.* alias.
alibi /alibi/ *n.m.* alibi.
aliéné, ~e /aljene/ *n.m., f.* insane person.
alién|er /aljene/ *v.t.* alienate; (*céder*) give up. **s'~er** *v. pr.* alienate. **~ation** *n.f.* alienation.
aligner /aliɲe/ *v.t.* (*objets*) line up, make lines of; (*chiffres*) string together. **~ sur,** bring into line with. **s'~** *v. pr.* line up. **s'~ sur,** align o.s. on. **alignement** /-əmɑ̃/ *n.m.* alignment.
aliment /alimɑ̃/ *n.m.* food. **~aire** /-tɛr/ *a.* food.
aliment|er /alimɑ̃te/ *v.t.* feed; (*fournir*) supply; (*fig.*) sustain. **~ation** *n.f.* feeding; supply(ing); (*régime*) diet; (*aliments*) groceries.
alinéa /alinea/ *n.m.* paragraph.
aliter (s') /(s)alite/ *v. pr.* take to one's bed.
allaiter /alete/ *v.t.* feed, suckle.
allant /alɑ̃/ *n.m.* verve, drive.
allécher /aleʃe/ *v.t.* tempt.
allée /ale/ *n.f.* path, lane; (*menant à une maison*) drive(way). **~s et venues,** comings and goings.
allégation /alegɑsjɔ̃/ *n.f.* allegation.
alléger /aleʒe/ *v.t.* make lighter; (*poids*) lighten; (*fig.*) alleviate.
allégor|ie /alegɔri/ *n.f.* allegory. **~ique** *a.* allegorical.
allègre /alɛgr/ *a.* gay; (*vif*) jaunty.
allégresse /alegrɛs/ *n.f.* gaiety.
alléguer /alege/ *v.t.* put forward.
alléluia /aleluja/ *n.m.* & *int.* alleluia.
Allemagne /almaɲ/ *n.f.* Germany. **~ de l'Ouest,** West Germany.
allemand, ~e /almɑ̃, -d/ *a.* & *n.m., f.* German. —*n.m.* (*lang.*) German.
aller[1]† /ale/ *v.i.* (*aux. être*) go. **s'en**

~ *v. pr.* go away. **~ à,** (*convenir à*) suit; (*s'adapter à*) fit. **~ faire,** be going to do. **comment allez-vous?, (comment) ça va?,** how are you? **ça va!,** all right! **il va bien,** he is well. **allez-y!,** go on! **allez!,** come on!

aller² /ale/ *n.m.* outward journey; (*billet*) single (ticket); (*Amer.*) one-way (ticket). **~ et retour,** return journey; (*Amer.*) round trip; (*billet*) return (ticket); (*Amer.*) round trip (ticket).

allerg|ie /alɛrʒi/ *n.f.* allergy. **~ique** *a.* allergic.

alliage /aljaʒ/ *n.m.* alloy.

alliance /aljɑ̃s/ *n.f.* alliance; (*bague*) wedding-ring; (*mariage*) marriage.

allié, ~e /alje/ *n.m., f.* ally; (*parent*) relative (by marriage).

allier /alje/ *v.t.* combine; (*pol.*) ally. **s'~** *v. pr.* combine; (*pol.*) become allied; (*famille*) become related (**à,** to).

alligator /aligatɔr/ *n.m.* alligator.

allô /alo/ *int.* hallo, hello.

allocation /alɔkasjɔ̃/ *n.f.* allowance. **~ de chômage,** unemployment benefit. **~s familiales,** family allowance.

allocution /alɔkysjɔ̃/ *n.f.* speech.

allongé /alɔ̃ʒe/ *a.* elongated.

allongement /alɔ̃ʒmɑ̃/ *n.m.* lengthening.

allonger /alɔ̃ʒe/ *v.t.* lengthen; (*bras, jambe*) stretch (out). **s'~** *v. pr.* get longer; (*s'étendre*) stretch (o.s.) out.

allouer /alwe/ *v.t.* allocate.

allum|er /alyme/ *v.t.* light; (*radio, lampe, etc.*) switch on; (*pièce*) switch the light(s) on in; (*fig.*) arouse. **s'~er** *v. pr.* (*lumière*) come on. **~age** *n.m.* lighting; (*auto.*) ignition. **~e-gaz** *n.m. invar.* gas lighter.

allumette /alymɛt/ *n.f.* match.

allure /alyr/ *n.f.* speed, pace; (*démarche*) walk; (*prestance*) bearing; (*air*) look. **à toute ~,** at full speed. **avoir de l'~,** have style.

allusion /alyzjɔ̃/ *n.f.* hint (**à,** at), allusion (**à,** to). **faire ~ à,** hint at, allude to.

almanach /almana/ *n.m.* almanac.

aloi /alwa/ *n.m.* **de bon ~,** sterling; (*gaieté*) wholesome.

alors /alɔr/ *adv.* then. *—conj.* so, then. **~ que,** when, while; (*tandis que*) whereas.

alouette /alwɛt/ *n.f.* lark.

alourdir /alurdir/ *v.t.* weigh down.

aloyau (*pl.* **~x**) /alwajo/ *n.m.* sirloin.

alpage /alpaʒ/ *n.m.* mountain pasture.

Alpes /alp/ *n.f. pl.* **les ~,** the Alps.

alpestre /alpɛstr/ *a.* alpine.

alphab|et /alfabɛ/ *n.m.* alphabet. **~étique** *a.* alphabetical.

alphabétiser /alfabetize/ *v.t.* teach to read and write.

alpin, ~e /alpɛ̃, -in/ *a.* alpine.

alpinis|te /alpinist/ *n.m./f.* mountaineer. **~me** *n.m.* mountaineering.

altér|er /altere/ *v.t.* falsify; (*abîmer*) spoil; (*donner soif à*) make thirsty. **s'~er** *v. pr.* deteriorate. **~ation** *n.f.* deterioration.

alternati|f, ~ve /altɛrnatif, -v/ *a.* alternating. *—n.f.* alternative. **~vement** *adv.* alternately.

altern|er /altɛrne/ *v.t./i.* alternate. **~ance** *n.f.* alternation. **en ~ance,** alternately. **~é** *a.* alternate.

Altesse /altɛs/ *n.f.* Highness.

alt|ier, ~ière /altje, -jɛr/ *a.* haughty.

altitude /altityd/ *n.f.* altitude, height.

alto /alto/ *n.m.* viola.

altruiste /altrɥist/ *a.* altruistic. *—n.m./f.* altruist.

aluminium /alyminjɔm/ *n.m.* aluminium; (*Amer.*) aluminum.

alvéole /alveɔl/ *n.f.* (*de ruche*) cell.

amabilité /amabilite/ *n.f.* kindness.

amadouer /amadwe/ *v.t.* win over.

amaigr|ir /amegrir/ *v.t.* make thin(ner). **~issant, ~issante** *a.* (*régime*) slimming.

amalgam|e /amalgam/ *n.m.* combination. **~er** *v.t.* combine, amalgamate.

amande /amɑ̃d/ *n.f.* almond; (*d'un fruit à noyau*) kernel.

amant /amɑ̃/ *n.m.* lover.

amarr|e /amar/ *n.f.* (mooring) rope. **~es,** moorings. **~er** *v.t.* moor.

amas /amɑ/ *n.m.* heap, pile.

amasser /amɑse/ *v.t.* amass, gather; (*empiler*) pile up. **s'~** *v. pr.* pile up; (*gens*) gather.

amateur /amatœr/ *n.m.* amateur. **~ de,** lover of. **d'~,** amateur; (*péj.*) amateurish. **~isme** *n.m.* amateurism.

amazone (en) /(ɑ̃n)amazon/ *adv.* side-saddle.

ambages (sans) /(sɑ̃z)ɑ̃baʒ/ *adv.* in plain language.

ambassade /ɑ̃basad/ *n.f.* embassy.

ambassa|deur, ~drice /ɑ̃basadœr, -dris/ *n.m., f.* ambassador.

ambiance /ɑ̃bjɑ̃s/ *n.f.* atmosphere.

ambiant, ~e /ɑ̃bjɑ̃, -t/ *a.* surrounding.

ambidextre /ɑ̃bidɛkstr/ *a.* ambidextrous.

ambigu, ~ë /ɑ̃bigy/ *a.* ambiguous. **~ïté** /-ɥite/ *n.f.* ambiguity.

ambitieu|x, ~se /ɑ̃bisjø, -z/ *a.* ambitious.

ambition /ɑ̃bisjɔ̃/ *n.f.* ambition. **~ner** /-jɔne/ *v.t.* have as one's ambition (**de,** to).

ambivalent, ~e /ɑ̃bivalɑ̃, -t/ *a.* ambivalent.

ambre /ɑ̃br/ *n.m.* amber.

ambulanc|e /ɑ̃bylɑ̃s/ *n.f.* ambulance. **~ier, ~ière** *n.m., f.* ambulance driver.

ambulant, ~e /ɑ̃bylɑ̃, -t/ *a.* itinerant.

âme /ɑm/ *n.f.* soul. **~ sœur,** soul mate.

amélior|er /ameljɔre/ *v.t.*, **s'~er** *v. pr.* improve. **~ation** *n.f.* improvement.

aménag|er /amenaʒe/ *v.t.* (*arranger*) fit out; (*transformer*) convert; (*installer*) fit up; (*territoire*) develop. **~ement** *n.m.* fitting out; conversion; fitting up; development; (*modification*) adjustment.

amende /amɑ̃d/ *n.f.* fine. **faire ~ honorable,** make an apology.

amend|er /amɑ̃de/ *v.t.* improve; (*jurid.*) amend. **s'~er** *v. pr.* mend one's ways. **~ement** *n.m.* (*de texte*) amendment.

amener /amne/ *v.t.* bring; (*causer*) bring about. **s'~** *v. pr.* (*fam.*) come along.

amenuiser (s') /(s)amənɥize/ *v. pr.* dwindle.

amer, amère /amɛr/ *a.* bitter.

américain, ~e /amerikɛ̃, -ɛn/ *a.* & *n.m., f.* American.

Amérique /amerik/ *n.f.* America. **~ du Nord/Sud,** North/South America.

amerrir /amerir/ *v.i.* land (on the sea).

amertume /amɛrtym/ *n.f.* bitterness.

ameublement /amœbləmɑ̃/ *n.m.* furniture.

ameuter /amøte/ *v.t.* draw a crowd of; (*fig.*) stir up.

ami, ~e /ami/ *n.m., f.* friend; (*de la nature, des livres, etc.*) lover. —*a.* friendly.

amiable /amjabl/ *a.* amicable. **à l'~** *adv.* amicably; *a.* amicable.

amiante /amjɑ̃t/ *n.m.* asbestos.

amic|al (*m. pl.* **~aux**) /amikal, -o/

a. friendly. **~alement** *adv.* in a friendly manner.
amicale /amikal/ *n.f.* association.
amidon /amidɔ̃/ *n.m.* starch. **~ner** /-ɔne/ *v.t.* starch.
amincir /amɛ̃sir/ *v.t.* make thinner. **s'~** *v. pr.* get thinner.
amir|al (*pl.* **~aux**) /amiral, -o/ *n.m.* admiral.
amitié /amitje/ *n.f.* friendship. **~s,** kind regards. **prendre en ~,** take a liking to.
ammoniac /amɔnjak/ *n.m.* (*gaz*) ammonia.
ammoniaque /amɔnjak/ *n.f.* (*eau*) ammonia.
amnésie /amnezi/ *n.f.* amnesia.
amnistie /amnisti/ *n.f.* amnesty.
amoindrir /amwɛ̃drir/ *v.t.* diminish.
amollir /amɔlir/ *v.t.* soften.
amonceler /amɔ̃sle/ *v.t.*, **s'~** *v. pr.* pile up.
amont (en) /(ɑ̃n)amɔ̃/ *adv.* upstream.
amorc|e /amɔrs/ *n.f.* bait; (*début*) start; (*explosif*) fuse, cap; (*de pistolet d'enfant*) cap. **~er** *v.t.* start; (*hameçon*) bait; (*pompe*) prime.
amorphe /amɔrf/ *a.* (*mou*) listless.
amortir /amɔrtir/ *v.t.* (*choc*) cushion; (*bruit*) deaden; (*dette*) pay off; (*objet acheté*) make pay for itself.
amour /amur/ *n.m.* love. **pour l'~ de,** for the sake of. **~-propre** *n.m.* self-respect.
amouracher (s') /(s)amuraʃe/ *v. pr.* become infatuated (**de,** with).
amoureu|x, ~se /amurø, -z/ *a.* (*ardent*) amorous; (*vie*) love. —*n.m., f.* lover. **~x de qn.,** in love with s.o.
amovible /amɔvibl/ *a.* removable.
ampère /ɑ̃pɛr/ *n.m.* amp(ere).
amphibie /ɑ̃fibi/ *a.* amphibious.
amphithéâtre /ɑ̃fiteɑtr/ *n.m.* amphitheatre; (*d'université*) lecture hall.
ample /ɑ̃pl/ *a.* ample; (*mouvement*) broad. **~ment** /-əmɑ̃/ *adv.* amply.
ampleur /ɑ̃plœr/ *n.f.* extent, size; (*de vêtement*) fullness.
amplif|ier /ɑ̃plifje/ *v.t.* amplify; (*fig.*) expand, develop. **s'~ier** *v. pr.* expand, develop. **~icateur** *n.m.* amplifier.
ampoule /ɑ̃pul/ *n.f.* (*électrique*) bulb; (*sur la peau*) blister; (*de médicament*) phial.
ampoulé /ɑ̃pule/ *a.* turgid.
amput|er /ɑ̃pyte/ *v.t.* amputate; (*fig.*) reduce. **~ation** *n.f.* amputation; (*fig.*) reduction.
amuse-gueule /amyzgœl/ *n.m. invar.* appetizer.
amus|er /amyze/ *v.t.* amuse; (*détourner l'attention de*) distract. **s'~er** *v. pr.* enjoy o.s.; (*jouer*) play. **~ement** *n.m.* amusement; (*passe-temps*) diversion. **~eur** *n.m.* (*péj.*) entertainer.
amusette /amyzɛt/ *n.f.* petty amusement.
amygdale /amidal/ *n.f.* tonsil.
an /ɑ̃/ *n.m.* year. **avoir dix**/*etc.* **~s,** be ten/*etc.* years old.
anachronisme /anakrɔnism/ *n.m.* anachronism.
anagramme /anagram/ *n.f.* anagram.
analogie /analɔʒi/ *n.f.* analogy.
analogue /analɔg/ *a.* similar.
analphabète /analfabɛt/ *a.* & *n.m.*/*f.* illiterate.
analy|se /analiz/ *n.f.* analysis; (*de sang*) test. **~ser** *v.t.* analyse. **~ste** *n.m.*/*f.* analyst. **~tique** *a.* analytical.
ananas /anana(s)/ *n.m.* pineapple.
anarch|ie /anarʃi/ *n.f.* anarchy. **~ique** *a.* anarchic. **~iste** *n.m.*/*f.* anarchist.
anatom|ie /anatɔmi/ *n.f.* anatomy. **~ique** *a.* anatomical.

ancestr|al (*m. pl.* **~aux**) /ɑ̃sɛstral, -o/ *a.* ancestral.
ancêtre /ɑ̃sɛtr/ *n.m.* ancestor.
anche /ɑ̃ʃ/ *n.f.* (*mus.*) reed.
anchois /ɑ̃ʃwa/ *n.m.* anchovy.
ancien, ~ne /ɑ̃sjɛ̃, -jɛn/ *a.* old; (*de jadis*) ancient; (*meuble*) antique; (*précédent*) former, ex-, old; (*dans une fonction*) senior. —*n.m., f.* senior person; (*par l'âge*) elder. **~ combattant,** ex-serviceman. **~nement** /-jɛnmɑ̃/ *adv.* formerly. **~neté** /-jɛnte/ *n.f.* age; seniority.
ancr|e /ɑ̃kr/ *n.f.* anchor. **jeter/lever l'~e,** cast/weigh anchor. **~er** *v.t.* anchor; (*fig.*) fix. **s'~er** *v. pr.* anchor.
andouille /ɑ̃duj/ *n.f.* sausage filled with chitterlings; (*idiot: fam.*) nitwit.
âne /ɑn/ *n.m.* donkey, ass; (*imbécile*) ass.
anéantir /aneɑ̃tir/ *v.t.* destroy; (*exterminer*) annihilate; (*accabler*) overwhelm.
anecdot|e /anɛkdɔt/ *n.f.* anecdote. **~ique** *a.* anecdotal.
anémi|e /anemi/ *n.f.* anaemia. **~ié, ~ique** *adjs.* anaemic.
ânerie /ɑnri/ *n.f.* stupidity; (*parole*) stupid remark.
ânesse /ɑnɛs/ *n.f.* she-ass.
anesthés|ie /anɛstezi/ *n.f.* (*opération*) anaesthetic. **~ique** *a.* & *n.m.* (*substance*) anaesthetic.
ang|e /ɑ̃ʒ/ *n.m.* angel. **aux ~es,** in seventh heaven. **~élique** *a.* angelic.
angélus /ɑ̃ʒelys/ *n.m.* angelus.
angine /ɑ̃ʒin/ *n.f.* sore throat, tonsillitis.
anglais, ~e /ɑ̃glɛ -z/ *a.* English. —*n.m., f.* Englishman, Englishwoman. —*n.m.* (*lang.*) English.
angle /ɑ̃gl/ *n.m.* angle; (*coin*) corner.
Angleterre /ɑ̃glətɛr/ *n.f.* England.
anglicisme /ɑ̃glisism/ *n.m.* anglicism.
angliciste /ɑ̃glisist/ *n.m./f.* English specialist.
anglo- /ɑ̃glɔ/ *préf.* Anglo-.
anglophone /ɑ̃glɔfɔn/ *a.* English-speaking. —*n.m./f.* English speaker.
anglo-saxon, ~ne /ɑ̃glɔsaksɔ̃, -ɔn/ *a.* & *n.m., f.* Anglo-Saxon.
angoiss|e /ɑ̃gwas/ *n.f.* anguish. **~ant, ~ante** *a.* harrowing. **~é** *a.* anguished. **~er** *v.t.* cause anguish to.
anguille /ɑ̃gij/ *n.f.* eel.
anguleux, ~se /ɑ̃gylø, -z/ *a.* (*figure*) angular.
anicroche /anikrɔʃ/ *n.f.* snag.
anim|al (*pl.* **~aux**) /animal, -o/ *n.m.* animal. —*a.* (*m. pl.* **~aux**) animal.
anima|teur, ~trice /animatœr, -tris/ *n.m., f.* organizer, leader; (*TV*) compère; (*TV, Amer.*) master of ceremonies.
anim|é /anime/ *a.* lively; (*affairé*) busy, (*être*) animate. **~ation** *n.f.* liveliness; (*affairement*) activity; (*cinéma*) animation.
animer /anime/ *v.t.* liven up; (*mener*) lead; (*mouvoir, pousser*) drive; (*encourager*) spur on. **s'~** *v. pr.* liven up.
animosité /animozite/ *n.f.* animosity.
anis /anis/ *n.m.* (*parfum, boisson*) aniseed.
ankylos|er (s') /(s)ɑ̃kiloze/ *v. pr.* go stiff. **~é** *a.* stiff.
annales /anal/ *n.f. pl.* annals.
anneau (*pl.* **~x**) /ano/ *n.m.* ring; (*de chaîne*) link.
année /ane/ *n.f.* year.
annexe /anɛks/ *a.* attached; (*bâtiment*) adjoining. —*n.f.* annexe; (*Amer.*) annex.
annex|er /anɛkse/ *v.t.* annex; (*document*) attach. **~ion** *n.f.* annexation.

annihiler /aniile/ *v.t.* annihilate.

anniversaire /anivɛrsɛr/ *n.m.* birthday; (*d'un événement*) anniversary. —*a.* anniversary.

annonc|e /anɔ̃s/ *n.f.* announcement; (*publicitaire*) advertisement; (*indice*) sign. **~er** *v.t.* announce; (*dénoter*) indicate. **s'~er bien/mal,** look good/bad. **~eur** *n.m.* advertiser; (*speaker*) announcer.

Annonciation /anɔ̃sjɑsjɔ̃/ *n.f.* **l'~,** the Annunciation.

annot|er /anɔte/ *v.t.* annotate. **~ation** *n.f.* annotation.

annuaire /anɥɛr/ *n.m.* year-book. **~ (téléphonique),** (telephone) directory.

annuel, ~le /anɥɛl/ *a.* annual, yearly. **~lement** *adv.* annually, yearly.

annuité /anɥite/ *n.f.* annual payment.

annulaire /anylɛr/ *n.m.* ring-finger.

annul|er /anyle/ *v.t.* cancel; (*contrat*) nullify; (*jugement*) quash. **s'~er** *v. pr.* cancel each other out. **~ation** *n.f.* cancellation.

anodin, ~e /anɔdɛ̃, -in/ *a.* insignificant; (*blessure*) harmless.

anomalie /anɔmali/ *n.f.* anomaly.

ânonner /ɑnɔne/ *v.t./i.* mumble, drone.

anonymat /anɔnima/ *n.m.* anonymity.

anonyme /anɔnim/ *a.* anonymous.

anorak /anɔrak/ *n.m.* anorak.

anorm|al (*m. pl.* **~aux**) /anɔrmal, -o/ *a.* abnormal.

anse /ɑ̃s/ *n.f.* handle; (*baie*) cove.

antagonis|me /ɑ̃tagɔnism/ *n.m.* antagonism. **~te** *n.m./f.* antagonist; *a.* antagonistic.

antan (d') /(d)ɑ̃tɑ̃/ *a.* of long ago.

antarctique /ɑ̃tarktik/ *a.* & *n.m.* Antarctic.

antécédent /ɑ̃tesedɑ̃/ *n.m.* antecedent.

antenne /ɑ̃tɛn/ *n.f.* aerial; (*Amer.*) antenna; (*d'insecte*) antenna; (*succursale*) agency; (*mil.*) outpost; (*auto., méd.*) emergency unit. **à l'~,** on the air. **sur l'~ de,** on the wavelength of.

antérieur /ɑ̃terjœr/ *a.* previous, earlier; (*placé devant*) front. **~ à,** prior to. **~ement** *adv.* earlier. **~ement à,** prior to. **antériorité** /-jɔrite/ *n.f.* precedence.

anthologie /ɑ̃tɔlɔʒi/ *n.f.* anthology.

anthropolo|gie /ɑ̃trɔpɔlɔʒi/ *n.f.* anthropology. **~gue** *n.m./f.* anthropologist.

anthropophage /ɑ̃trɔpɔfaʒ/ *a.* cannibalistic. —*n.m./f.* cannibal.

anti- /ɑ̃ti/ *préf.* anti-.

antiaérien, ~ne /ɑ̃tiaerjɛ̃, -jɛn/ *a.* anti-aircraft. **abri ~,** air-raid shelter.

antiatomique /ɑ̃tiatɔmik/ *a.* **abri ~,** fall-out shelter.

antibiotique /ɑ̃tibjɔtik/ *n.m.* antibiotic.

anticancéreu|x, ~se /ɑ̃tikɑ̃serø, -z/ *a.* (anti-)cancer.

antichambre /ɑ̃tiʃɑ̃br/ *n.f.* waiting-room, antechamber.

anticipation /ɑ̃tisipɑsjɔ̃/ *n.f.* **d'~,** (*livre, film*) science fiction. **par ~,** in advance.

anticipé /ɑ̃tisipe/ *a.* early.

anticiper /ɑ̃tisipe/ *v.t./i.* **~ (sur),** anticipate.

anticonceptionnel, ~le /ɑ̃tikɔ̃sɛpsjɔnɛl/ *a.* contraceptive.

anticorps /ɑ̃tikɔr/ *n.m.* antibody.

anticyclone /ɑ̃tisyklon/ *n.m.* anticyclone.

antidater /ɑ̃tidate/ *v.t.* backdate, antedate.

antidote /ɑ̃tidɔt/ *n.m.* antidote.

antigel /ɑ̃tiʒɛl/ *n.m.* antifreeze.

antillais, ~e /ɑ̃tijɛ, -z/ *a.* & *n.m., f.* West Indian.

Antilles /ɑ̃tij/ *n.f. pl.* **les ~,** the West Indies.

antilope /ɑ̃tilɔp/ *n.f.* antelope.
antimite /ɑ̃timit/ *n.m.* moth repellent.
antipath|ie /ɑ̃tipati/ *n.f.* antipathy. **~ique** *a.* unpleasant.
antipodes /ɑ̃tipɔd/ *n.m. pl.* antipodes. **aux ~ de,** (*fig.*) poles apart from.
antiquaire /ɑ̃tikɛr/ *n.m./f.* antique dealer.
antiqu|e /ɑ̃tik/ *a.* ancient. **~ité** *n.f.* antiquity; (*objet*) antique.
antisémit|e /ɑ̃tisemit/ *a.* anti-Semitic. **~isme** *n.m.* anti-Semitism.
antiseptique /ɑ̃tisɛptik/ *a.* & *n.m.* antiseptic.
antithèse /ɑ̃titɛz/ *n.f.* antithesis.
antivol /ɑ̃tivɔl/ *n.m.* anti-theft lock *ou* device.
antre /ɑ̃tr/ *n.m.* den.
anus /anys/ *n.m.* anus.
anxiété /ɑ̃ksjete/ *n.f.* anxiety.
anxieu|x, ~se /ɑ̃ksjø, -z/ *a.* anxious. —*n.m., f.* worrier.
août /u(t)/ *n.m.* August.
apais|er /apeze/ *v.t.* appease, calm, soothe; (*douleur, colère*) soothe. **s'~er** *v. pr.* (*tempête*) die down. **~ement** *n.m.* appeasement; soothing. **~ements** *n.m. pl.* reassurances.
apanage /apanaʒ/ *n.m.* **l'~ de,** the privilege of.
aparté /aparte/ *n.m.* private exchange; (*théâtre*) aside. **en ~,** in private.
apath|ie /apati/ *n.f.* apathy. **~ique** *a.* apathetic.
apatride /apatrid/ *n.m./f.* stateless person.
apercevoir† /apɛrsəvwar/ *v.t.* see. **s'~ de,** notice. **s'~ que,** notice *ou* realize that.
aperçu /apɛrsy/ *n.m.* general view *ou* idea; (*intuition*) insight.
apéritif /aperitif/ *n.m.* aperitif.
à-peu-près /apøprɛ/ *n.m. invar.* approximation.
apeuré /apœre/ *a.* scared.
aphone /afɔn/ *a.* voiceless.
aphrodisiaque /afrɔdizjak/ *a.* & *n.m.* aphrodisiac.
aphte /aft/ *n.m.* mouth ulcer.
apit|oyer /apitwaje/ *v.t.* move (to pity). **s'~oyer sur,** feel pity for. **~oiement** *n.m.* pity.
aplanir /aplanir/ *v.t.* level; (*fig.*) smooth out.
aplatir /aplatir/ *v.t.* flatten (out). **s'~** *v. pr.* (*s'allonger*) lie flat; (*s'humilier*) grovel; (*tomber: fam.*) fall flat on one's face.
aplomb /aplɔ̃/ *n.m.* balance; (*fig.*) self-possession. **d'~,** (*en équilibre*) steady, balanced.
Apocalypse /apɔkalips/ *n.f.* Apocalypse. **apocalyptique** /-tik/ *a.* apocalyptic.
apogée /apɔʒe/ *n.m.* peak.
apologie /apɔlɔʒi/ *n.f.* vindication.
a posteriori /apɔsterjɔri/ *adv.* after the event.
apostolat /apɔstɔla/ *n.m.* proselytism; (*fig.*) calling.
apostroph|e /apɔstrɔf/ *n.f.* apostrophe; (*appel*) sharp address. **~er** *v.t.* address sharply.
apothéose /apɔteoz/ *n.f.* final triumph.
apôtre /apotr/ *n.m.* apostle.
apparaître† /aparɛtr/ *v.i.* appear. **il apparaît que,** it appears that.
apparat /apara/ *n.m.* pomp. **d'~,** ceremonial.
appareil /aparɛj/ *n.m.* apparatus; (*électrique*) appliance; (*anat.*) system; (*téléphonique*) phone; (*dentier*) brace; (*auditif*) hearing-aid; (*avion*) plane. **~(-photo),** camera. **~ électroménager,** household electrical appliance.
appareiller[1] /apareje/ *v.i.* (*navire*) cast off, put to sea.
appareiller[2] /apareje/ *v.t.* (*assortir*) match.
apparemment /aparamɑ̃/ *adv.* apparently.

apparence /aparɑ̃s/ *n.f.* appearance. **en ~,** outwardly; (*apparemment*) apparently.
apparent, ~e /aparɑ̃, -t/ *a.* apparent; (*visible*) conspicuous.
apparenté /aparɑ̃te/ *a.* related; (*semblable*) similar.
appariteur /aparitœr/ *n.m.* (*univ.*) attendant, porter.
apparition /aparisjɔ̃/ *n.f.* appearance; (*spectre*) apparition.
appartement /apartəmɑ̃/ *n.m.* flat; (*Amer.*) apartment.
appartenance /apartənɑ̃s/ *n.f.* membership (**à,** of), belonging (**à,** to).
appartenir† /apartənir/ *v.i.* belong (**à,** to). **il lui/vous/***etc.* **appartient de,** it is up to him/you/ *etc.* to.
appât /apɑ/ *n.m.* bait; (*fig.*) lure. **~er** /-te/ *v.t.* lure.
appauvrir /apovrir/ *v.t.* impoverish. **s'~** *v. pr.* grow impoverished.
appel /apɛl/ *n.m.* call; (*jurid.*) appeal; (*mil.*) call-up. **faire ~ à,** (*recourir à*) call on; (*invoquer*) appeal to; (*évoquer*) call up; (*exiger*) call for. **faire l'~,** (*scol.*) call the register; (*mil.*) take a roll-call.
appelé /aple/ *n.m.* conscript.
appel|er /aple/ *v.t.* call; (*nécessiter*) call for. **s'~er** *v. pr.* be called. **~é à,** (*désigné à*) marked out for. **en ~er à,** appeal to. **il s'appelle,** his name is. **~lation** /apelɑsjɔ̃/ *n.f.* designation.
appendic|e /apɛ̃dis/ *n.m.* appendix. **~ite** *n.f.* appendicitis.
appentis /apɑ̃ti/ *n.m.* lean-to.
appesantir /apzɑ̃tir/ *v.t.* weigh down. **s'~** *v. pr.* grow heavier. **s'~ sur,** dwell upon.
appétissant, ~e /apetisɑ̃, -t/ *a.* appetizing.
appétit /apeti/ *n.m.* appetite.
applaud|ir /aplodir/ *v.t./i.* applaud. **~ir à,** applaud. **~issements** *n.m. pl.* applause.
applique /aplik/ *n.f.* wall lamp.
appliqué /aplike/ *a.* painstaking.
appliquer /aplike/ *v.t.* apply. **s'~** *v. pr.* apply o.s. (**à,** to). **s'~ à,** (*concerner*) apply to. **applicable** /-abl/ *a.* applicable. **application** /-ɑsjɔ̃/ *n.f.* application.
appoint /apwɛ̃/ *n.m.* contribution. **d'~,** extra. **faire l'~,** give the correct money.
appointements /apwɛ̃tmɑ̃/ *n.m. pl.* salary.
apport /apɔr/ *n.m.* contribution.
apporter /apɔrte/ *v.t.* bring.
apposer /apoze/ *v.t.* affix.
appréciable /apresjabl/ *a.* appreciable.
appréc|ier /apresje/ *v.t.* appreciate; (*évaluer*) appraise. **~iation** *n.f.* appreciation; appraisal.
appréhen|der /apreɑ̃de/ *v.t.* dread, fear; (*arrêter*) apprehend. **~sion** *n.f.* apprehension.
apprendre† /aprɑ̃dr/ *v.t./i.* learn; (*être informé de*) hear of. **~ qch. à qn.,** teach s.o. sth.; (*informer*) tell s.o. sth. **~ à faire,** learn to do. **~ à qn. à faire,** teach s.o. to do. **~ que,** learn that; (*être informé*) hear that.
apprenti, ~e /aprɑ̃ti/ *n.m., f.* apprentice.
apprentissage /aprɑ̃tisaʒ/ *n.m.* apprenticeship.
apprêter /aprete/ *v.t.,* **s'~** *v. pr.* prepare.
apprivoiser /aprivwaze/ *v.t.* tame.
approba|teur, ~trice /aprɔbatœr, -tris/ *a.* approving.
approbation /aprɔbɑsjɔ̃/ *n.f.* approval.
approchant, ~e /aprɔʃɑ̃, -t/ *a.* close, similar.
approche /aprɔʃ/ *n.f.* approach.
approché /aprɔʃe/ *a.* approximate.
approcher /aprɔʃe/ *v.t.* (*objet*) move near(er) (**de,** to); (*roi,*

artiste, etc.) approach. *—v.i.* **~ (de),** approach. **s'~ de,** approach, move near(er) to.
approfond|ir /aprɔfɔ̃dir/ *v.t.* deepen; (*fig.*) go into thoroughly. **~i** *a.* thorough.
approprié /aprɔprije/ *a.* appropriate.
approprier (s') /(s)aprɔprije/ *v. pr.* appropriate.
approuver /apruve/ *v.t.* approve; (*trouver louable*) approve of; (*soutenir*) agree with.
approvisionn|er /aprɔvizjɔne/ *v.t.* supply. **s'~er** *v. pr.* stock up. **~ement** *n.m.* supply.
approximati|f, ~ve /aprɔksimatif, -v/ *a.* approximate. **~vement** *adv.* approximately.
approximation /aprɔksimɑsjɔ̃/ *n.f.* approximation.
appui /apɥi/ *n.m.* support; (*de fenêtre*) sill; (*pour objet*) rest. **à l'~ de,** in support of.
appuyer /apɥije/ *v.t.* lean, rest; (*presser*) press; (*soutenir*) support, back. *—v.i.* **~ sur,** press (on); (*fig.*) stress. **s'~ sur,** lean on; (*compter sur*) rely on.
âpre /ɑpr/ *a.* harsh, bitter. **~ au gain,** grasping.
après /aprɛ/ *prép.* after; (*au-delà de*) beyond. *—adv.* after(wards); (*plus tard*) later. **~ avoir fait,** after doing. **~ qu'il est parti,** after he left. **~ coup,** after the event. **d'~,** (*selon*) according to. **~-demain** *adv.* the day after tomorrow. **~-guerre** *n.m.* postwar period. **~-midi** *n.m./f. invar.* afternoon. **~-ski** *n.m.* snow-boot (*worn when not skiing*).
a priori /aprijɔri/ *adv.* in principle, without going into the matter.
à-propos /aprɔpo/ *n.m.* timeliness; (*fig.*) presence of mind.
apte /apt/ *a.* capable (**à,** of).
aptitude /aptityd/ *n.f.* aptitude, ability.
aquarelle /akwarɛl/ *n.f.* watercolour, aquarelle.
aquarium /akwarjɔm/ *n.m.* aquarium.
aquatique /akwatik/ *a.* aquatic.
aqueduc /akdyk/ *n.m.* aqueduct.
arabe /arab/ *a.* Arab; (*lang.*) Arabic; (*désert*) Arabian. *—n.m./f.* Arab. *—n.m.* (*lang.*) Arabic.
Arabie /arabi/ *n.f.* **~ Séoudite,** Saudi Arabia.
arable /arabl/ *a.* arable.
arachide /araʃid/ *n.f.* peanut.
araignée /areɲe/ *n.f.* spider.
arbitraire /arbitrɛr/ *a.* arbitrary.
arbitr|e /arbitr/ *n.m.* referee; (*cricket, tennis*) umpire; (*maître*) arbiter; (*jurid.*) arbitrator. **~age** *n.m.* arbitration; (*sport*) refereeing. **~er** *v.t.* (*match*) referee; (*jurid.*) arbitrate.
arborer /arbɔre/ *v.t.* display; (*vêtement*) sport.
arbre /arbr/ *n.m.* tree; (*techn.*) shaft.
arbrisseau (*pl.* **~x**) /arbriso/ *n.m.* shrub.
arbuste /arbyst/ *n.m.* bush.
arc /ark/ *n.m.* (*arme*) bow; (*voûte*) arch. **~ de cercle,** arc of a circle.
arcade /arkad/ *n.f.* arch. **~s,** arcade, arches.
arc-boutant (*pl.* **arcs-boutants**) /arkbutɑ̃/ *n.m.* flying buttress.
arc-bouter (s') /(s)arkbute/ *v. pr.* lean (for support), brace o.s.
arceau (*pl.* **~x**) /arso/ *n.m.* hoop; (*de voûte*) arch.
arc-en-ciel (*pl.* **arcs-en-ciel**) /arkɑ̃sjɛl/ *n.m.* rainbow.
archaïque /arkaik/ *a.* archaic.
arche /arʃ/ *n.f.* arch. **~ de Noé,** Noah's ark.
archéolo|gie /arkeɔlɔʒi/ *n.f.* archaeology. **~gique** *a.* archaeological. **~gue** *n.m./f.* archaeologist.
archer /arʃe/ *n.m.* archer.
archet /arʃɛ/ *n.m.* (*mus.*) bow.

archétype /arketip/ *n.m.* archetype.
archevêque /arʃəvɛk/ *n.m.* archbishop.
archi- /arʃi/ *préf.* (*fam.*) tremendously.
archipel /arʃipɛl/ *n.m.* archipelago.
architecte /arʃitɛkt/ *n.m.* architect.
architecture /arʃitɛktyr/ *n.f.* architecture.
archiv|es /arʃiv/ *n.f. pl.* archives. **~iste** *n.m./f.* archivist.
arctique /arktik/ *a.* & *n.m.* Arctic.
ardemment /ardamɑ̃/ *adv.* ardently.
ard|ent, ~ente /ardɑ̃, -t/ *a.* burning; (*passionné*) ardent; (*foi*) fervent. **~eur** *n.f.* ardour; (*chaleur*) heat.
ardoise /ardwaz/ *n.f.* slate.
ardu /ardy/ *a.* arduous.
are /ar/ *n.m.* are (= *100 square metres*).
arène /arɛn/ *n.f.* arena. **~(s)**, (*pour courses de taureaux*) bullring.
arête /arɛt/ *n.f.* (*de poisson*) bone; (*bord*) ridge.
argent /arʒɑ̃/ *n.m.* money; (*métal*) silver. **~ comptant,** cash.
argenté /arʒɑ̃te/ *a.* silver(y); (*métal*) (silver-)plated.
argenterie /arʒɑ̃tri/ *n.f.* silverware.
argentin, ~e /arʒɑ̃tɛ̃, -in/ *a.* & *n.m., f.* Argentinian, Argentine.
Argentine /arʒɑ̃tin/ *n.f.* Argentina.
argil|e /arʒil/ *n.f.* clay. **~eux, ~euse** *a.* clayey.
argot /argo/ *n.m.* slang. **~ique** /-ɔtik/ *a.* (*terme*) slang; (*style*) slangy.
arguer /argɥe/ *v.i.* **~ de,** put forward as a reason.
argument /argymɑ̃/ *n.m.* argument. **~er** /-te/ *v.i.* argue.
aride /arid/ *a.* arid, barren.
aristocrate /aristɔkrat/ *n.m./f.* aristocrat.
aristocrat|ie /aristɔkrasi/ *n.f.* aristocracy. **~ique** /-atik/ *a.* aristocratic.
arithmétique /aritmetik/ *n.f.* arithmetic. —*a.* arithmetical.
armateur /armatœr/ *n.m.* shipowner.
armature /armatyr/ *n.f.* framework; (*de tente*) frame.
arme /arm/ *n.f.* arm, weapon. **~s,** (*blason*) arms. **~ à feu,** firearm.
armée /arme/ *n.f.* army. **~ de l'air,** Air Force. **~ de terre,** Army.
armement /armәmɑ̃/ *n.m.* arms.
armer /arme/ *v.t.* arm; (*fusil*) cock; (*navire*) equip; (*renforcer*) reinforce. **~ de,** (*garnir de*) fit with. **s'~ de,** arm o.s. with.
armistice /armistis/ *n.m.* armistice.
armoire /armwar/ *n.f.* cupboard; (*penderie*) wardrobe.
armoiries /armwari/ *n.f. pl.* (coat of) arms.
armure /armyr/ *n.f.* armour.
arnica /arnika/ *n.f.* (*méd.*) arnica.
aromate /arɔmat/ *n.m.* herb, spice.
aromatique /arɔmatik/ *a.* aromatic.
aromatisé /arɔmatize/ *a.* flavoured.
arôme /arom/ *n.m.* aroma.
arpège /arpɛʒ/ *n.m.* arpeggio.
arpent|er /arpɑ̃te/ *v.t.* pace up and down; (*terrain*) survey. **~eur** *n.m.* surveyor.
arqué /arke/ *a.* arched; (*jambes*) bandy.
arraché (à l') /(al)araʃe/ *adv.* with a struggle, after a hard struggle.
arrache-pied (d') /(d)araʃpje/ *adv.* relentlessly.
arracher /araʃe/ *v.t.* pull out; (*plante*) pull *ou* dig up; (*cheveux, page*) tear *ou* pull out; (*par une explosion*) blow off. **~ à,** (*enlever*

à) snatch from; (*fig.*) force *ou* wrest from. **s'~ qch.,** fight over sth. **arrachage** /-aʒ/ *n.m.* pulling *ou* digging up.

arraisonner /arɛzɔne/ *v.t.* inspect.

arrangeant, ~e /arɑ̃ʒɑ̃, -t/ *a.* obliging.

arrangement /arɑ̃ʒmɑ̃/ *n.m.* arrangement.

arranger /arɑ̃ʒe/ *v.t.* arrange, fix up; (*réparer*) put right; (*régler*) sort out; (*convenir à*) suit. **s'~** *v. pr.* (*se mettre d'accord*) come to an arrangement; (*se débrouiller*) manage (**pour,** to).

arrestation /arɛstɑsjɔ̃/ *n.f.* arrest.

arrêt /arɛ/ *n.m.* stopping (**de,** of); (*lieu*) stop; (*pause*) pause; (*jurid.*) decree. **~s,** (*mil.*) arrest. **à l'~,** stationary. **faire un ~,** (make a) stop. **~ de travail,** (*grève*) stoppage. **rester** *ou* **tomber en ~,** stop short.

arrêté /arete/ *n.m.* order.

arrêter /arete/ *v.t./i.* stop; (*date, regard*) fix; (*appréhender*) arrest. **s'~** *v. pr.* stop. **(s')~ de faire,** stop doing.

arrhes /ar/ *n.f. pl.* deposit.

arrière /arjɛr/ *n.m.* back, rear; (*football*) back. *—a. invar.* back, rear. **à l'~,** in *ou* at the back. **en ~,** behind; (*marcher*) backwards. **en ~ de,** behind. **~-boutique** *n.f.* back room (of the shop). **~-garde** *n.f.* rearguard. **~-goût** *n.m.* aftertaste. **~-grand-mère** *n.f.* great-grandmother. **~-grand-père** (*pl.* **~-grands-pères)** *n.m.* great-grandfather. **~-pensée** *n.f.* ulterior motive. **~-plan** *n.m.* background.

arriéré /arjere/ *a.* backward. *—n.m.* arrears.

arrimer /arime/ *v.t.* rope down; (*cargaison*) stow.

arrivage /arivaʒ/ *n.m.* consignment.

arrivant, ~e /arivɑ̃, -t/ *n.m., f.* new arrival.

arrivée /arive/ *n.f.* arrival; (*sport*) finish.

arriver /arive/ *v.i.* (*aux. être*) arrive, come; (*réussir*) succeed; (*se produire*) happen. **~ à,** (*atteindre*) reach. **~ à faire,** manage to do. **en ~ à faire,** get to the stage of doing. **il arrive que,** it happens that. **il lui arrive de faire,** he (sometimes) does.

arriviste /arivist/ *n.m./f.* self-seeker.

arrogan|t, ~te /arɔgɑ̃, -t/ *a.* arrogant. **~ce** *n.f.* arrogance.

arroger (s') /(s)arɔʒe/ *v. pr.* assume (without justification).

arrondir /arɔ̃dir/ *v.t.* (make) round; (*somme*) round off. **s'~** *v. pr.* become round(ed).

arrondissement /arɔ̃dismɑ̃/ *n.m.* district.

arros|er /aroze/ *v.t.* water; (*repas*) wash down; (*victoire*) celebrate with a drink. **~age** *n.m.* watering. **~oir** *n.m.* watering-can.

arsen|al (*pl.* **~aux)** /arsənal, -o/ *n.m.* arsenal; (*naut.*) dockyard.

arsenic /arsənik/ *n.m.* arsenic.

art /ar/ *n.m.* art. **~s et métiers,** arts and crafts. **~s ménagers,** domestic science.

artère /artɛr/ *n.f.* artery. **(grande) ~,** main road.

artériel, ~le /arterjɛl/ *a.* arterial.

arthrite /artrit/ *n.f.* arthritis.

artichaut /artiʃo/ *n.m.* artichoke.

article /artikl/ *n.m.* article; (*comm.*) item, article. **à l'~ de la mort,** at death's door. **~ de fond,** feature (article). **~s d'ameublement,** furnishings. **~s de voyage,** travel requisites *ou* goods.

articul|er /artikyle/ *v.t.,* **s'~er** *v. pr.* articulate. **~ation** *n.f.* articulation; (*anat.*) joint.

artifice /artifis/ *n.m.* contrivance.

artificiel, ~le /artifisjɛl/ *a.* artificial. **~lement** *adv.* artificially.
artill|erie /artijri/ *n.f.* artillery. **~eur** *n.m.* gunner.
artisan /artizɑ̃/ *n.m.* artisan, craftsman. **l'~ de,** (*fig.*) the architect of. **~al** (*m. pl.* **~aux**) /-anal, -o/ *a.* of *ou* by craftsmen, craft. **~at** /-ana/ *n.m.* craft; (*classe*) artisans.
artist|e /artist/ *n.m.*/*f.* artist; (*musicien, acteur*) performer. **~ique** *a.* artistic.
as[1] /a/ *voir* **avoir.**
as[2] /ɑs/ *n.m.* ace.
ascendant[1], **~e** /asɑ̃dɑ̃, -t/ *a.* ascending, upward.
ascendan|t[2] /asɑ̃dɑ̃/ *n.m.* influence. **~ts,** ancestors. **~ce** *n.f.* ancestry.
ascenseur /asɑ̃sœr/ *n.m.* lift; (*Amer.*) elevator.
ascension /asɑ̃sjɔ̃/ *n.f.* ascent. **A~,** Ascension.
ascète /asɛt/ *n.m.*/*f.* ascetic.
ascétique /asetik/ *a.* ascetic.
aseptique /asɛptik/ *a.* aseptic.
asiatique /azjatik/ *a.* & *n.m.*/*f.*, **Asiate** /azjat/ *n.m.*/*f.* Asian.
Asie /azi/ *n.f.* Asia.
asile /azil/ *n.m.* refuge; (*pol.*) asylum; (*pour malades, vieillards*) home.
aspect /aspɛ/ *n.m.* appearance; (*fig.*) aspect. **à l'~ de,** at the sight of.
asperge /aspɛrʒ/ *n.f.* asparagus.
asper|ger /aspɛrʒe/ *v.t.* spray. **~sion** *n.f.* spray(ing).
aspérité /asperite/ *n.f.* bump, rough edge.
asphalt|e /asfalt/ *n.m.* asphalt. **~er** *v.t.* asphalt.
asphyxie /asfiksi/ *n.f.* suffocation.
asphyxier /asfiksje/ *v.t.*, **s'~** *v. pr.* suffocate, asphyxiate.
aspic /aspik/ *n.m.* (*serpent*) asp.
aspirateur /aspiratœr/ *n.m.* vacuum cleaner.
aspir|er /aspire/ *v.t.* inhale; (*liquide*) suck up. *—v.i.* **~er à,** aspire to. **~ation** *n.f.* inhaling; suction; (*ambition*) aspiration.
aspirine /aspirin/ *n.f.* aspirin.
assagir /asaʒir/ *v.t.*, **s'~** *v. pr.* sober down.
assaill|ir /asajir/ *v.t.* assail. **~ant** *n.m.* assailant.
assainir /asenir/ *v.t.* clean up.
assaisonn|er /asɛzɔne/ *v.t.* season. **~ement** *n.m.* seasoning.
assassin /asasɛ̃/ *n.m.* murderer; (*pol.*) assassin.
assassin|er /asasine/ *v.t.* murder; (*pol.*) assassinate. **~at** *n.m.* murder; (*pol.*) assassination.
assaut /aso/ *n.m.* assault, onslaught. **donner l'~ à, prendre d'~,** storm.
assécher /aseʃe/ *v.t.* drain.
assemblée /asɑ̃ble/ *n.f.* meeting; (*gens réunis*) gathering; (*pol.*) assembly.
assembl|er /asɑ̃ble/ *v.t.* assemble, put together; (*réunir*) gather. **s'~er** *v. pr.* gather, assemble. **~age** *n.m.* assembly; (*combinaison*) collection; (*techn.*) joint.
assener /asene/ *v.t.* (*coup*) deal.
assentiment /asɑ̃timɑ̃/ *n.m.* assent.
asseoir† /aswar/ *v.t.* sit (down), seat; (*affermir*) establish; (*baser*) base. **s'~** *v. pr.* sit (down).
assermenté /asɛrmɑ̃te/ *a.* sworn.
assertion /asɛrsjɔ̃/ *n.f.* assertion.
asservir /asɛrvir/ *v.t.* enslave.
assez /ase/ *adv.* enough; (*plutôt*) quite, fairly. **~ grand/rapide/** *etc.*, big/fast/*etc.* enough (**pour,** to). **~ de,** enough.
assid|u /asidy/ *a.* (*zélé*) assiduous; (*régulier*) regular. **~u auprès de,** attentive to. **~uité** /-ɥite/ *n.f.* assiduousness; regularity. **~ûment** *adv.* assiduously.
assiéger /asjeʒe/ *v.t.* besiege.

assiette /asjɛt/ *n.f.* plate; (*équilibre*) seat. ~ **anglaise,** assorted cold meats. ~ **creuse/plate,** soup-/dinner-plate. **ne pas être dans son** ~, feel out of sorts.

assiettée /asjete/ *n.f.* plateful.

assigner /asiɲe/ *v.t.* assign; (*limite*) fix.

assimil|er /asimile/ *v.t.*, **s'~er** *v. pr.* assimilate. **~er à,** liken to; (*classer*) class as. **~ation** *n.f.* assimilation; likening; classification.

assis, ~e /asi, -z/ *voir* **asseoir.** —*a.* sitting (down), seated.

assise /asiz/ *n.f.* (*base*) foundation. **~s,** (*tribunal*) assizes; (*congrès*) meeting.

assistance /asistɑ̃s/ *n.f.* audience; (*aide*) assistance. **l'A~ (publique),** government child care service.

assistant, ~e /asistɑ̃, -t/ *n.m., f.* assistant; (*univ.*) assistant lecturer. **~s,** (*spectateurs*) members of the audience. ~ **social, ~e sociale,** social worker.

assister /asiste/ *v.t.* assist. —*v.i.* ~ **à,** attend, be (present) at; (*scène*) witness.

association /asɔsjɑsjɔ̃/ *n.f.* association.

associé, ~e /asɔsje/ *n.m., f.* partner, associate. —*a.* associate.

associer /asɔsje/ *v.t.* associate; (*mêler*) combine. ~ **qn. à,** have s.o. become involved with *ou* in. **s'~** *v. pr.* become associated, join forces (**à,** with); (*s'harmoniser*) combine (**à,** with). **s'~ à,** (*joie de qn.*) share in; (*opinion de qn.*) share.

assoiffé /aswafe/ *a.* thirsty.

assombrir /asɔ̃brir/ *v.t.* darken; (*fig.*) make gloomy. **s'~** *v. pr.* darken; become gloomy.

assommer /asɔme/ *v.t.* knock out; (*tuer*) kill; (*animal*) stun; (*fig.*) overwhelm; (*ennuyer: fam.*) bore.

Assomption /asɔ̃psjɔ̃/ *n.f.* Assumption.

assorti /asɔrti/ *a.* matching; (*objets variés*) assorted.

assort|ir /asɔrtir/ *v.t.* match (**à,** with, to). **~ir de,** accompany with. **s'~ir (à),** match. **~iment** *n.m.* assortment.

assoup|ir (s') /(s)asupir/ *v. pr.* doze off; (*s'apaiser*) subside. **~i** *a.* dozing.

assouplir /asuplir/ *v.t.* make supple; (*fig.*) make flexible.

assourdir /asurdir/ *v.t.* (*personne*) deafen; (*bruit*) deaden.

assouvir /asuvir/ *v.t.* satisfy.

assujettir /asyʒetir/ *v.t.* subject, subdue. ~ **à,** subject to.

assumer /asyme/ *v.t.* assume.

assurance /asyrɑ̃s/ *n.f.* (self-) assurance; (*garantie*) assurance; (*contrat*) insurance. **~s sociales,** National Insurance.

assuré, ~e /asyre/ *a.* certain, assured; (*sûr de soi*) (self-) confident, assured. —*n.m., f.* insured. **~ment** *adv.* certainly.

assurer /asyre/ *v.t.* ensure; (*fournir*) provide; (*exécuter*) carry out; (*comm.*) insure; (*stabiliser*) steady; (*frontières*) make secure. ~ **à qn. que,** assure s.o. that. ~ **qn. de,** assure s.o. of. **s'~ de/que,** make sure of/that. **s'~ qch.,** (*se procurer*) secure *ou* ensure sth. **assureur** /-œr/ *n.m.* insurer.

astérisque /asterisk/ *n.m.* asterisk.

asthm|e /asm/ *n.m.* asthma. **~atique** *a.* & *n.m./f.* asthmatic.

asticot /astiko/ *n.m.* maggot.

astiquer /astike/ *v.t.* polish.

astre /astr/ *n.m.* star.

astreignant, ~e /astrɛɲɑ̃, -t/ *a.* exacting.

astreindre /astrɛ̃dr/ *v.t.* ~ **qn. à qch.,** force sth. on s.o. ~ **à faire,** force to do.

astringent, ~e /astrɛ̃ʒɑ̃, -t/ *a.* astringent.

astrolo|gie /astrɔlɔʒi/ *n.f.* astrology. **~gue** *n.m.*/*f.* astrologer.

astronaute /astrɔnot/ *n.m.*/*f.* astronaut.

astronom|ie /astrɔnɔmi/ *n.f.* astronomy. **~e** *n.m.*/*f.* astronomer. **~ique** *a.* astronomical.

astuce /astys/ *n.f.* smartness; (*truc*) trick; (*plaisanterie*) wisecrack.

astucieu|x, ~se /astysjø, -z/ *a.* smart, clever.

atelier /atəlje/ *n.m.* workshop; (*de peintre*) studio.

athé|e /ate/ *n.m.*/*f.* atheist. —*a.* atheistic. **~isme** *n.m.* atheism.

athl|ète /atlɛt/ *n.m.*/*f.* athlete. **~étique** *a.* athletic. **~étisme** *n.m.* athletics.

atlantique /atlɑ̃tik/ *a.* Atlantic. —*n.m.* **A~**, Atlantic (Ocean).

atlas /atlɑs/ *n.m.* atlas.

atmosph|ère /atmɔsfɛr/ *n.f.* atmosphere. **~érique** *a.* atmospheric.

atome /atom/ *n.m.* atom.

atomique /atɔmik/ *a.* atomic.

atomiseur /atɔmizœr/ *n.m.* spray.

atout /atu/ *n.m.* trump (card); (*avantage*) great asset.

âtre /ɑtr/ *n.m.* hearth.

atroc|e /atrɔs/ *a.* atrocious. **~ité** *n.f.* atrocity.

atroph|ie /atrɔfi/ *n.f.* atrophy. **~ié** *a.* atrophied.

attabler (s') /(s)atable/ *v. pr.* sit down at table.

attachant, ~e /ataʃɑ̃, -t/ *a.* likeable.

attache /ataʃ/ *n.f.* (*agrafe*) fastener; (*lien*) tie. **à l'~,** (*chien*) on a leash.

attach|é, ~ée /ataʃe/ *a.* **être ~é à,** (*aimer*) be attached to. —*n.m., f.* (*pol.*) attaché. **~ement** *n.m.* attachment.

attacher /ataʃe/ *v.t.* tie (up); (*ceinture, robe, etc.*) fasten; (*étiquette*) attach. **~ à,** (*attribuer à*) attach to. —*v.i.* (*culin.*) stick. **s'~ à,** (*se lier à*) become attached to; (*se consacrer à*) apply o.s. to.

attaque /atak/ *n.f.* attack. **~ à main armée,** armed attack.

attaqu|er /atake/ *v.t.*/*i.*, **s'~er à,** attack; (*problème, sujet*) tackle. **~ant, ~ante** *n.m., f.* attacker; (*football*) striker; (*football, Amer.*) forward.

attardé /atarde/ *a.* backward; (*idées*) outdated; (*en retard*) late.

attarder (s') /(s)atarde/ *v. pr.* linger.

atteindre† /atɛ̃dr/ *v.t.* reach; (*blesser*) hit; (*affecter*) affect.

atteint, ~e /atɛ̃, -t/ *a.* **~ de,** suffering from.

atteinte /atɛ̃t/ *n.f.* attack (**à,** on).

attel|er /atle/ *v.t.* (*cheval*) harness; (*remorque*) couple. **s'~er à,** get down to. **~age** *n.m.* harnessing; coupling; (*bêtes*) team.

attenant, ~e /atnɑ̃, -t/ *a.* **~ (à),** adjoining.

attendant (en) /(ɑ̃n)atɑ̃dɑ̃/ *adv.* meanwhile.

attendre /atɑ̃dr/ *v.t.* wait for, await; (*escompter*) expect. —*v.i.* wait. **~ que qn. fasse,** wait for s.o. to do. **s'~ à,** expect.

attendr|ir /atɑ̃drir/ *v.t.* move (to pity). **s'~ir** *v. pr.* be moved to pity. **~issant, ~issante** *a.* moving.

attendu /atɑ̃dy/ *a.* (*escompté*) expected; (*espéré*) long-awaited. **~ que,** considering that.

attentat /atɑ̃ta/ *n.m.* murder attempt. **~ (à la bombe),** (bom[illegible] attack.

attente /atɑ̃t/ *n.f.* wa[illegible] (*espoir*) expectation.

attenter /atɑ̃te/ *v.i.* [illegible] an attempt on; (*fig.*) [illegible]

attenti|f, ~ve /at[illegible] tive; (*scrupuleux*) [illegible] mindful of; (*soucieux*) careful of. **~vement** *adv.* attentively.

attention /atɑ̃sjɔ̃/ *n.f.* attention. **~ (à)!**, watch out (for)! **faire ~ à**, pay attention to; (*veiller à*) be careful of. **~né** /-jɔne/ *a.* considerate.

attentisme /atɑ̃tism/ *n.m.* wait-and-see policy.

atténuer /atenɥe/ *v.t.* (*violence*) tone down; (*douleur*) ease; (*faute*) mitigate. **s'~** *v. pr.* subside.

atterrer /atere/ *v.t.* dismay.

atterr|ir /aterir/ *v.i.* land. **~issage** *n.m.* landing.

attestation /atɛstɑsjɔ̃/ *n.f.* certificate.

attester /atɛste/ *v.t.* testify to. **~ que**, testify that.

attifé /atife/ *a.* (*fam.*) dressed up.

attirail /atiraj/ *n.m.* (*fam.*) gear.

attirance /atirɑ̃s/ *n.f.* attraction.

attirant, ~e /atirɑ̃, -t/ *a.* attractive.

attirer /atire/ *v.t.* draw, attract; (*causer*) bring. **s'~** *v. pr.* bring upon o.s.; (*amis*) win.

attiser /atize/ *v.t.* (*feu*) poke; (*sentiment*) stir up.

attitré /atitre/ *a.* accredited; (*habituel*) usual.

attitude /atityd/ *n.f.* attitude; (*maintien*) bearing.

attraction /atraksjɔ̃/ *n.f.* attraction.

attrape-nigaud /atrapnigo/ *n.m.* (*fam.*) con.

attraper /atrape/ *v.t.* catch; (*habitude, style*) pick up; (*duper*) take in; (*gronder: fam.*) tell off.

attrayant, ~e /atrɛjɑ̃, -t/ *a.* attractive.

attrib|uer /atribɥe/ *v.t.* award; (*donner*) assign; (*imputer*) attribute. **s'~uer** *v. pr.* claim. **~ution** *n.f.* awarding; assignment. **~utions** *n.f. pl.* attributions.

[at]trister /atriste/ *v.t.* sadden.

[attr]oup|er (s') /(s)atrupe/ *v. pr.* [gath]er. **~ement** *n.m.* crowd.

au /o/ *voir* **à**.

aubaine /obɛn/ *n.f.* (stroke of) good fortune.

aube /ob/ *n.f.* dawn, daybreak.

aubépine /obepin/ *n.f.* hawthorn.

auberg|e /obɛrʒ/ *n.f.* inn. **~e de jeunesse,** youth hostel. **~iste** *n.m./f.* innkeeper.

aubergine /obɛrʒin/ *n.f.* aubergine, egg-plant.

aucun, ~e /okœ̃, okyn/ *a.* no, not any; (*positif*) any. —*pron.* none, not any; (*positif*) any. **~ des deux,** neither of the two. **d'~s,** some. **~ement** /okynmɑ̃/ *adv.* not at all.

audace /odas/ *n.f.* daring; (*impudence*) audacity.

audacieu|x, ~se /odasjø, -z/ *a.* daring.

au-delà /odla/ *adv.*, **~ de** *prép.* beyond.

au-dessous /odsu/ *adv.*, **~ de** *prép.* below.

au-dessus /odsy/ *adv.*, **~ de** *prép.* above.

au-devant (de) /odvɑ̃(də)/ *prép.* **aller ~ de qn.,** go to meet s.o.

audience /odjɑ̃s/ *n.f.* audience; (*d'un tribunal*) hearing; (*intérêt*) attention.

audiotypiste /odjɔtipist/ *n.m./f.* audio typist.

audio-visuel, ~le /odjɔvizɥɛl/ *a.* audio-visual.

audi|teur, ~trice /oditœr, -tris/ *n.m., f.* listener.

audition /odisjɔ̃/ *n.f.* hearing; (*théâtre, mus.*) audition. **~ner** /-jɔne/ *v.t./i.* audition.

auditoire /oditwar/ *n.m.* audience.

auditorium /oditɔrjɔm/ *n.m.* (*mus., radio*) recording studio.

auge /oʒ/ *n.f.* trough.

augment|er /ɔgmɑ̃te/ *v.t./i.* increase; (*employé*) increase the pay of. **~ation** *n.f.* increase. **~ation (de salaire),** (pay) rise; (*Amer.*) raise.

augure /ogyr/ *n.m.* (*devin*) oracle. **de bon/mauvais ~,** of good/ill omen.
augurer /ogyre/ *v.t.* predict (**de,** from).
auguste /ogyst/ *a.* august.
aujourd'hui /oʒurdɥi/ *adv.* today.
aumône /omon/ *n.f.* alms.
aumônier /omonje/ *n.m.* chaplain.
auparavant /oparavɑ̃/ *adv.* before(hand).
auprès (de) /oprɛ(də)/ *prép.* by, next to; (*comparé à*) compared with; (*s'adressant à*) to.
auquel, ~le /okɛl/ *voir* **lequel.**
aura, aurait /ora, orɛ/ *voir* **avoir.**
auréole /oreɔl/ *n.f.* halo.
auriculaire /orikylɛr/ *n.m.* little finger.
aurore /orɔr/ *n.f.* dawn.
ausculter /ɔskylte/ *v.t.* examine with a stethoscope.
auspices /ospis/ *n.m. pl.* auspices.
aussi /osi/ *adv.* too, also; (*comparaison*) as; (*tellement*) so. —*conj.* (*donc*) therefore. **~ bien que,** as well as.
aussitôt /osito/ *adv.* immediately. **~ que,** as soon as. **~ arrivé/levé**/*etc.*, as soon as one has arrived/got up/*etc.*
aust|ère /ostɛr/ *a.* austere. **~érité** *n.f.* austerity.
austral (*m. pl.* **~s**) /ostral/ *a.* southern.
Australie /ostrali/ *n.f.* Australia.
australien, ~ne /ostraljɛ̃, -jɛn/ *a.* & *n.m., f.* Australian.
autant /otɑ̃/ *adv.* (*travailler, manger, etc.*) as much (**que,** as). **~ (de),** (*quantité*) as much (**que,** as); (*nombre*) as many (**que,** as); (*tant*) so much; so many. **~ faire,** one had better do. **d'~ plus que,** all the more since. **en faire ~,** do the same. **pour ~,** for all that.
autel /otɛl/ *n.m.* altar.
auteur /otœr/ *n.m.* author. **~ de,** (*action*) person who carried out *ou* caused.
authentifier /otɑ̃tifje/ *v.t.* authenticate.
authenti|que /otɑ̃tik/ *a.* authentic. **~cité** *n.f.* authenticity.
auto /oto/ *n.f.* car. **~s tamponneuses,** dodgems, bumper cars.
auto- /oto/ *préf.* self-, auto-.
autobiographie /otɔbjɔgrafi/ *n.f.* autobiography.
autobus /otɔbys/ *n.m.* bus.
autocar /otɔkar/ *n.m.* coach.
autochtone /ɔtɔktɔn/ *n.m./f.* native.
autocollant, ~e /otɔkɔlɑ̃, -t/ *a.* self-adhesive. —*n.m.* sticker.
autocratique /otɔkratik/ *a.* autocratic.
autodéfense /otɔdefɑ̃s/ *n.f.* self-defence.
autodidacte /otɔdidakt/ *a.* & *n.m./f.* self-taught (person).
auto-école /otɔekɔl/ *n.f.* driving school.
autographe /otɔgraf/ *n.m.* autograph.
automate /otɔmat/ *n.m.* automaton.
automatique /otɔmatik/ *a.* automatic. **~ment** *adv.* automatically.
automat|iser /otɔmatize/ *v.t.* automate. **~ion** /-mɑsjɔ̃/ *n.f.*, **~isation** *n.f.* automation.
automne /otɔn/ *n.m.* autumn.
automobil|e /otɔmɔbil/ *a.* motor, car. —*n.f.* (motor) car. **l'~e,** (*sport*) motoring. **~iste** *n.m./f.* motorist.
autonom|e /otɔnɔm/ *a.* autonomous. **~ie** *n.f.* autonomy.
autopsie /otɔpsi/ *n.f.* post-mortem, autopsy.
autorail /otɔrɑj/ *n.m.* railcar.
autorisation /otɔrizɑsjɔ̃/ *n.f.* permission, authorization; (*permis*) permit.

autoris|er /otɔrize/ *v.t.* authorize, permit; (*rendre possible*) allow (of). **~é** *a.* (*opinions*) authoritative.

autoritaire /otɔritɛr/ *a.* authoritarian.

autorité /otɔrite/ *n.f.* authority. **faire ~,** be authoritative.

autoroute /otɔrut/ *n.f.* motorway; (*Amer.*) highway.

auto-stop /otɔstɔp/ *n.m.* hitch-hiking. **faire de l'~,** hitch-hike. **prendre en ~,** give a lift to. **~peur, ~peuse** *n.m., f.* hitch-hiker.

autour /otur/ *adv.*, **~ de** *prép.* around. **tout ~,** all around.

autre /otr/ *a.* other. **un ~ jour/***etc.*, another day/*etc.* —*pron.* **un ~, une ~,** another (one). **l'~,** the other (one). **les autres,** the others; (*autrui*) others. **d'~s,** (some) others. **~ chose/part,** sth./somewhere else. **qn./rien d'~,** s.o./nothing else. **d'~ part,** on the other hand. **vous ~s Anglais,** you English. **d'un jour/***etc.* **à l'~,** (*bientôt*) any day/*etc.* now.

autrefois /otrəfwa/ *adv.* in the past.

autrement /otrəmɑ̃/ *adv.* differently; (*sinon*) otherwise; (*plus*) far more.

Autriche /otriʃ/ *n.f.* Austria.

autrichien, ~ne /otriʃjɛ̃, -jɛn/ *a.* & *n.m.,f.* Austrian.

autruche /otryʃ/ *n.f.* ostrich.

autrui /otrɥi/ *pron.* others.

auvent /ovɑ̃/ *n.m.* canopy.

aux /o/ *voir* **à.**

auxiliaire /oksiljɛr/ *a.* auxiliary. —*n.m./f.* (*assistant*) auxiliary. —*n.m.* (*gram.*) auxiliary.

auxquel|s, ~les /okɛl/ *voir* **lequel.**

aval (en) /(ɑ̃n)aval/ *adv.* downstream.

avalanche /avalɑ̃ʃ/ *n.f.* avalanche.

avaler /avale/ *v.t.* swallow.

avance /avɑ̃s/ *n.f.* advance; (*sur un concurrent*) lead. **~ (de fonds),** advance. **à l'~, d'~,** in advance. **en ~,** early; (*montre*) fast. **en ~ (sur),** (*menant*) ahead (of).

avancement /avɑ̃smɑ̃/ *n.m.* promotion.

avanc|er /avɑ̃se/ *v.t./i.* move forward, advance; (*argent*) advance; (*montre*) be *ou* go fast; (*faire saillie*) jut out. **s'~er** *v. pr.* move forward, advance; (*se hasarder*) commit o.s. **~é, ~ée** *a.* advanced; *n.f.* projection.

avanie /avani/ *n.f.* affront.

avant /avɑ̃/ *prép.* & *adv.* before. —*a. invar.* front —*n.m.* front; (*football*) forward. **~ de faire,** before doing. **~ qu'il (ne) fasse,** before he does. **en ~,** (*mouvement*) forward. **en ~ (de),** (*position, temps*) in front (of). **~ peu,** before long. **~ tout,** above all. **bien ~ dans,** very deep(ly) *ou* far into. **~-bras** *n.m. invar.* forearm. **~-centre** *n.m.* centre-forward. **~-coureur** *a. invar.* precursory, foreshadowing. **~-dernier, ~-dernière** *a.* & *n.m., f.* last but one. **~-garde** *n.f.* (*mil.*) vanguard; (*fig.*) avant-garde. **~-goût** *n.m.* foretaste. **~-guerre** *n.m.* pre-war period. **~-hier** /-tjɛr/ *adv.* the day before yesterday. **~-poste** *n.m.* outpost. **~-première** *n.f.* preview. **~-veille** *n.f.* two days before.

avantag|e /avɑ̃taʒ/ *n.m.* advantage; (*comm.*) benefit. **~er** *v.t.* favour; (*embellir*) show off to advantage.

avantageu|x, ~se /avɑ̃taʒø, -z/ *a.* attractive.

avar|e /avar/ *a.* miserly. —*n.m./f.* miser. **~e de,** sparing of. **~ice** *n.f.* avarice.

avarié /avarje/ *a.* (*aliment*) spoiled.

avaries /avari/ *n.f. pl.* damage.

avatar /avatar/ *n.m.* (*fam.*) misfortune.

avec /avɛk/ *prép.* with; (*envers*) towards. *—adv.* (*fam.*) with it *ou* them.

avenant, ~e /avnɑ̃, -t/ *a.* pleasing.

avenant (à l') /(al)avnɑ̃/ *adv.* in a similar style.

avènement /avɛnmɑ̃/ *n.m.* advent; (*d'un roi*) accession.

avenir /avnir/ *n.m.* future. **à l'~,** in future. **d'~,** with (future) prospects.

aventur|e /avɑ̃tyr/ *n.f.* adventure; (*sentimentale*) affair. **~eux, ~euse** *a.* adventurous; (*hasardeux*) risky. **~ier, ~ière** *n.m., f.* adventurer.

aventurer (s') /(s)avɑ̃tyre/ *v. pr.* venture.

avenue /avny/ *n.f.* avenue.

avérer (s') /(s)avere/ *v. pr.* prove (to be).

averse /avɛrs/ *n.f.* shower.

aversion /avɛrsjɔ̃/ *n.f.* aversion.

avert|ir /avɛrtir/ *v.t.* inform; (*mettre en garde, menacer*) warn. **~i** *a.* informed. **~issement** *n.m.* warning.

avertisseur /avɛrtisœr/ *n.m.* (*auto.*) horn. **~ d'incendie,** fire-alarm.

aveu (*pl.* **~x**) /avø/ *n.m.* confession. **de l'~ de,** by the admission of.

aveugl|e /avœgl/ *a.* blind. *—n.m./f.* blind man, blind woman. **~ement** *n.m.* blindness. **~ément** *adv.* blindly. **~er** *v.t.* blind.

aveuglette (à l') /(al)avœglɛt/ *adv.* (*à tâtons*) blindly.

avia|teur, ~trice /avjatœr, -tris/ *n.m., f.* aviator.

aviation /avjɑsjɔ̃/ *n.f.* flying; (*industrie*) aviation; (*mil.*) air force. **d'~,** air.

avid|e /avid/ *a.* greedy (**de,** for); (*anxieux*) eager (**de,** for). **~e de faire,** eager to do. **~ité** *n.f.* greed; eagerness.

avilir /avilir/ *v.t.* degrade.

avion /avjɔ̃/ *n.m.* (aero)plane, aircraft. **~ à réaction,** jet.

aviron /avirɔ̃/ *n.m.* oar. **l'~,** (*sport*) rowing.

avis /avi/ *n.m.* opinion; (*renseignement*) notification; (*comm.*) advice. **être d'~ que,** be of the opinion that.

avisé /avize/ *a.* sensible. **bien/mal ~ de,** well-/ill-advised to.

aviser /avize/ *v.t.* notice; (*informer*) advise. *—v.i.* decide what to do (**à,** about). **s'~ de,** suddenly realize. **s'~ de faire,** take it into one's head to do.

aviver /avive/ *v.t.* revive.

avocat[1], ~e /avɔka, -t/ *n.m., f.* barrister; (*Amer.*) attorney; (*fig.*) advocate. **~ de la défense,** counsel for the defence.

avocat[2] /avɔka/ *n.m.* (*fruit*) avocado (pear).

avoine /avwan/ *n.f.* oats.

avoir† /avwar/ *v. aux.* have. *—v.t.* have; (*obtenir*) get; (*duper: fam.*) take in. *—n.m.* assets. **~ à faire,** have to do. **~ chaud/faim/***etc.*, be hot/hungry/*etc.* **~ dix/***etc.* **ans,** be ten/*etc.* years old. **~ lieu,** take place. **~ lieu de,** have good reason to. **en ~ à** *ou* **contre,** have a grudge against. **en ~ assez,** have had enough. **en ~ pour une minute/***etc.*, be busy for a minute/*etc.* **il en a pour cent francs,** it will cost him one hundred francs. **qu'est-ce que vous avez?,** what is the matter with you?

avoisin|er /avwazine/ *v.t.* border on. **~ant, ~ante** *a.* neighbouring.

avort|er /avɔrte/ *v.i.* (*projet etc.*) miscarry. **(se faire) ~er,** have an abortion. **~é** *a.* abortive. **~ement** *n.m.* (*méd.*) abortion.

avorton /avɔrtɔ̃/ *n.m.* runt.

avou|er /avwe/ *v.t.* confess (to). —*v.i.* confess. **~é** *a.* avowed; *n.m.* solicitor; (*Amer.*) attorney.

avril /avril/ *n.m.* April.

axe /aks/ *n.m.* axis; (*essieu*) axle; (*d'une politique*) main line(s), basis. **~ (routier),** main road.

axer /akse/ *v.t.* centre.

axiome /aksjom/ *n.m.* axiom.

ayant /ɛjɑ̃/ *voir* **avoir.**

azimuts /azimyt/ *n.m. pl.* **dans tous les ~,** (*fam.*) all over the place.

azote /azɔt/ *n.m.* nitrogen.

azur /azyr/ *n.m.* sky-blue.

B

baba /baba/ *n.m.* **~ (au rhum),** rum baba.

babil /babi(l)/ *n.m.* babble. **~ler** /-ije/ *v.i.* babble.

babines /babin/ *n.f. pl.* chops.

babiole /babjɔl/ *n.f.* knick-knack; (*bagatelle*) trifle.

bâbord /bɑbɔr/ *n.m.* port (side).

babouin /babwɛ̃/ *n.m.* baboon.

bac[1] /bak/ *n.m.* (*fam.*) = **baccalauréat.**

bac[2] /bak/ *n.m.* (*bateau*) ferry; (*récipient*) tub; (*plus petit*) tray.

baccalauréat /bakalɔrea/ *n.m.* school leaving certificate.

bâch|e /bɑʃ/ *n.f.* tarpaulin. **~er** *v.t.* cover (with a tarpaulin).

bachel|ier, ~ière /baʃəlje, -jɛr/ *n.m., f.* holder of the *baccalauréat.*

bachot /baʃo/ *n.m.* (*fam.*) = **baccalauréat. ~er** /-ɔte/ *v.i.* cram (for an exam).

bâcler /bɑkle/ *v.t.* botch (up).

bactérie /bakteri/ *n.f.* bacterium.

badaud, ~e /bado, -d/ *n.m., f.* (*péj.*) onlooker.

baderne /badɛrn/ *n.f.* **(vieille) ~,** (*péj.*) old fogey.

badigeon /badiʒɔ̃/ *n.m.* whitewash. **~ner** /-ɔne/ *v.t.* whitewash; (*barbouiller*) daub.

badin, ~e /badɛ̃, -in/ *a.* light-hearted.

badine /badin/ *n.f.* cane.

badiner /badine/ *v.i.* joke **(sur, avec,** about).

baffe /baf/ *n.f.* (*fam.*) slap.

bafouer /bafwe/ *v.t.* scoff at.

bafouiller /bafuje/ *v.t./i.* stammer.

bâfrer /bɑfre/ *v.t./i.* (*fam.*) gobble.

bagage /bagaʒ/ *n.m.* bag; (*fig.*) (store of) knowledge. **~s,** luggage, baggage. **~s à main,** hand luggage.

bagarr|e /bagar/ *n.f.* fight. **~er** *v.i.*, **se ~er** *v. pr.* fight.

bagatelle /bagatɛl/ *n.f.* trifle; (*somme*) trifling amount.

bagnard /baɲar/ *n.m.* convict.

bagnole /baɲɔl/ *n.f.* (*fam.*) car.

bagou(t) /bagu/ *n.m.* glib tongue.

bagu|e /bag/ *n.f.* (*anneau*) ring. **~er** *v.t.* ring.

baguenauder (se) /(sə)bagnode/ *v. pr.* (*fam.*) stroll *ou* loaf about.

baguette /bagɛt/ *n.f.* stick; (*de chef d'orchestre*) baton; (*chinoise*) chopstick; (*magique*) wand; (*pain*) stick of bread. **~ de tambour,** drumstick.

bahut /bay/ *n.m.* chest.

baie /bɛ/ *n.f.* (*géog.*) bay; (*fruit*) berry. **~ (vitrée),** picture window.

baign|er /beɲe/ *v.t.* bathe; (*enfant*) bath. —*v.i.* **~er dans,** soak in; (*être enveloppé dans*) be steeped in. **se ~er** *v. pr.* go swimming *ou* bathing. **~é de,** bathed in; (*sang*) soaked in. **~ade** /bɛɲad/ *n.f.* bathing, swimming. **~eur, ~euse** /bɛɲœr, -øz/ *n.m., f.* bather.

baignoire /bɛɲwar/ *n.f.* bath(-tub).

bail (*pl.* **baux**) /baj, bo/ *n.m.* lease.

bâill|er /baje/ *v.i.* yawn; (*être ouvert*) gape. **~ement** *n.m.* yawn.
bailleur /bajœr/ *n.m.* **~ de fonds,** (*comm.*) backer.
bâillon /bajɔ̃/ *n.m.* gag. **~ner** /bajɔne/ *v.t.* gag.
bain /bɛ̃/ *n.m.* bath; (*de mer*) bathe. **~(s) de soleil,** sunbathing. **~-marie** (*pl.* **~s-marie**) *n.m.* double boiler. **dans le ~,** (*compromis*) involved; (*au courant*) in the picture. **prendre un ~ de foule,** mingle with the crowd.
baïonnette /bajɔnɛt/ *n.f.* bayonet.
baiser /beze/ *n.m.* kiss. —*v.t.* (*main*) kiss; (*duper: fam.*) con.
baisse /bɛs/ *n.f.* fall, drop. **en ~,** falling.
baisser /bese/ *v.t.* lower; (*radio, lampe, etc.*) turn down. —*v.i.* go down, fall; (*santé, forces*) fail. **se ~** *v. pr.* bend down.
bajoues /baʒu/ *n.f. pl.* chops.
bal (*pl.* **~s**) /bal/ *n.m.* dance; (*habillé*) ball; (*lieu*) dance-hall.
balad|e /balad/ *n.f.* stroll; (*en auto*) drive. **~er** *v.t.* take for a stroll. **se ~er** *v. pr.* (go for a) stroll; (*excursionner*) wander around. **se ~er (en auto),** go for a drive.
balafr|e /balafr/ *n.f.* gash; (*cicatrice*) scar. **~er** *v.t.* gash.
balai /balɛ/ *n.m.* broom. **~-brosse** *n.m.* garden broom.
balance /balɑ̃s/ *n.f.* scales; (*équilibre*) balance.
balancer /balɑ̃se/ *v.t.* swing; (*doucement*) sway; (*lancer: fam.*) chuck; (*se débarrasser de: fam.*) chuck out. —*v.i.*, **se ~** *v. pr.* swing; sway. **se ~ de,** (*fam.*) not care about.
balancier /balɑ̃sje/ *n.m.* pendulum; (*de montre*) balance-wheel.
balançoire /balɑ̃swar/ *n.f.* swing; (*bascule*) see-saw.
balay|er /baleje/ *v.t.* sweep (up); (*chasser*) sweep away; (*se débarrasser de*) sweep aside. **~age** *n.m.* sweeping. **~eur, ~euse** *n.m., f.* road sweeper. **~ures** *n.f. pl.* sweepings.
balbut|ier /balbysje/ *v.t./i.* stammer. **~iement** *n.m.* stammering.
balcon /balkɔ̃/ *n.m.* balcony; (*théâtre*) dress circle.
baldaquin /baldakɛ̃/ *n.m.* canopy.
baleine /balɛn/ *n.f.* whale.
balis|e /baliz/ *n.f.* beacon; (*bouée*) buoy; (*auto.*) (road) sign. **~er** *v.t.* mark out (with beacons); (*route*) signpost.
balistique /balistik/ *a.* ballistic.
balivernes /balivɛrn/ *n.f. pl.* balderdash.
ballade /balad/ *n.f.* ballad.
ballant, ~e /balɑ̃, -t/ *a.* dangling.
ballast /balast/ *n.m.* ballast.
balle /bal/ *n.f.* (*projectile*) bullet; (*sport*) ball; (*paquet*) bale.
ballerine /balrin/ *n.f.* ballerina.
ballet /balɛ/ *n.m.* ballet.
ballon /balɔ̃/ *n.m.* balloon; (*sport*) ball. **~ de football,** football.
ballonné /balɔne/ *a.* bloated.
ballot /balo/ *n.m.* bundle; (*nigaud: fam.*) idiot.
ballottage /balɔtaʒ/ *n.m.* second ballot (*due to indecisive result*).
ballotter /balɔte/ *v.t./i.* shake about, toss.
balnéaire /balneɛr/ *a.* seaside.
balourd, ~e /balur, -d/ *n.m., f.* oaf. —*a.* oafish. **~ise** /-diz/ *n.f.* (*gaffe*) blunder.
balustrade /balystrad/ *n.f.* railing(s).
bambin /bɑ̃bɛ̃/ *n.m.* tiny tot.
bambou /bɑ̃bu/ *n.m.* bamboo.
ban /bɑ̃/ *n.m.* round of applause. **~s,** (*de mariage*) banns. **mettre au ~ de,** cast out from.
banal (*m. pl.* **~s**) /banal/ *a.* commonplace, banal. **~ité** *n.f.* banality.
banane /banan/ *n.f.* banana.
banc /bɑ̃/ *n.m.* bench; (*de poissons*)

shoal. ~ **des accusés,** dock. ~ **d'essai,** test bed; (*fig.*) testing-ground.

bancaire /bɑ̃kɛr/ *a.* banking; (*chèque*) bank.

bancal (*m. pl.* **~s**) /bɑ̃kal/ *a.* wobbly; (*personne*) bandy.

bandage /bɑ̃daʒ/ *n.m.* bandage. ~ **herniaire,** truss.

bande[1] /bɑ̃d/ *n.f.* (*de papier etc.*) strip; (*rayure*) stripe; (*de film*) reel; (*radio*) band; (*pansement*) bandage. ~ **(magnétique),** tape. ~ **dessinée,** comic strip. ~ **sonore,** sound-track. **par la ~,** indirectly.

bande[2] /bɑ̃d/ *n.f.* (*groupe*) bunch, band, gang.

bandeau (*pl.* **~x**) /bɑ̃do/ *n.m.* headband; (*sur les yeux*) blindfold.

bander /bɑ̃de/ *v.t.* bandage; (*arc*) bend; (*muscle*) tense. ~ **les yeux à,** blindfold.

banderole /bɑ̃drɔl/ *n.f.* banner.

bandit /bɑ̃di/ *n.m.* bandit. **~isme** /-tism/ *n.m.* crime.

bandoulière (en) /(ɑ̃)bɑ̃duljɛr/ *adv.* (slung) across one's shoulder.

banjo /bɑ̃(d)ʒo/ *n.m.* banjo.

banlieu|e /bɑ̃ljø/ *n.f.* suburbs. **de ~e,** suburban. **~sard, ~sarde** /-zar, -zard/ *n.m., f.* (suburban) commuter.

bannière /banjɛr/ *n.f.* banner.

bannir /banir/ *v.t.* banish.

banque /bɑ̃k/ *n.f.* bank; (*activité*) banking. ~ **d'affaires,** merchant bank.

banqueroute /bɑ̃krut/ *n.f.* (fraudulent) bankruptcy.

banquet /bɑ̃kɛ/ *n.m.* dinner; (*fastueux*) banquet.

banquette /bɑ̃kɛt/ *n.f.* seat.

banquier /bɑ̃kje/ *n.m.* banker.

bapt|ême /batɛm/ *n.m.* baptism; christening. **~iser** *v.t.* baptize, christen; (*appeler*) christen.

baquet /bakɛ/ *n.m.* tub.

bar /bar/ *n.m.* (*lieu*) bar.

baragouin /baragwɛ̃/ *n.m.* gibberish, gabble. **~er** /-wine/ *v.t./i.* gabble; (*langue*) speak a few words of.

baraque /barak/ *n.f.* hut, shed; (*boutique*) stall; (*maison: fam.*) house. **~ments** *n.m. pl.* huts.

baratin /baratɛ̃/ *n.m.* (*fam.*) sweet *ou* smooth talk. **~er** /-ine/ *v.t.* (*fam.*) chat up; (*Amer.*) sweet-talk.

barbar|e /barbar/ *a.* barbaric. —*n.m./f.* barbarian. **~ie** *n.f.* (*cruauté*) barbarity.

barbe /barb/ *n.f.* beard. ~ **à papa,** candy-floss; (*Amer.*) cotton candy. **la ~!,** (*fam.*) blast (it)! **quelle ~!,** (*fam.*) what a bore!

barbecue /barbəkju/ *n.m.* barbecue.

barbelés /barbəle/ *n.m. pl.* barbed wire.

barber /barbe/ *v.t.* (*fam.*) bore.

barbiche /barbiʃ/ *n.f.* goatee.

barbiturique /barbityrik/ *n.m.* barbiturate.

barboter[1] /barbɔte/ *v.i.* paddle, splash.

barboter[2] /barbɔte/ *v.t.* (*voler: fam.*) pinch.

barbouiller /barbuje/ *v.t.* (*peindre*) daub; (*souiller*) smear; (*griffonner*) scribble; (*estomac: fam.*) upset.

barbu /barby/ *a.* bearded.

barda /barda/ *n.m.* (*fam.*) gear.

barder /barde/ *v.i.* **ça va ~,** (*fam.*) sparks will fly.

barème /barɛm/ *n.m.* list, table; (*échelle*) scale.

baril /bari(l)/ *n.m.* barrel; (*de poudre*) keg.

bariolé /barjɔle/ *a.* motley.

barman /barman/ *n.m.* barman; (*Amer.*) bartender.

baromètre /barɔmɛtr/ *n.m.* barometer.

baron, ~ne /barɔ̃, -ɔn/ *n.m., f.* baron, baroness.

baroque /barɔk/ *a.* weird; (*archit.*, *art*) baroque.
baroud /barud/ *n.m.* **~ d'honneur,** gallant last fight.
barque /bark/ *n.f.* (small) boat.
barrage /baraʒ/ *n.m.* dam; (*sur route*) road-block.
barre /bar/ *n.f.* bar; (*trait*) line, stroke; (*naut.*) helm.
barreau (*pl.* **~x**) /baro/ *n.m.* bar; (*d'échelle*) rung. **le ~,** (*jurid.*) the bar.
barrer /bare/ *v.t.* block; (*porte*) bar; (*rayer*) cross out; (*naut.*) steer. **se ~** *v. pr.* (*fam.*) hop it.
barrette /barɛt/ *n.f.* (hair-)slide.
barreur /barœr/ *n.m.* (*sport*) coxswain.
barricad|e /barikad/ *n.f.* barricade. **~er** *v.t.* barricade. **se ~er** *v. pr.* barricade o.s.
barrière /barjɛr/ *n.f.* (*porte*) gate; (*clôture*) fence; (*obstacle*) barrier.
barrique /barik/ *n.f.* barrel.
baryton /baritɔ̃/ *n.m.* baritone.
bas, basse /bɑ, bɑs/ *a.* low; (*action*) base. —*n.m.* bottom; (*chaussette*) stocking. —*n.f.* (*mus.*) bass. —*adv.* low. **à ~,** down with. **en ~,** down below; (*dans une maison*) downstairs. **en ~ de,** at the bottom of. **plus ~,** further *ou* lower down. **~-côté** *n.m.* (*de route*) verge; (*Amer.*) shoulder. **~ de laine,** nest-egg. **~-fonds** *n.m. pl.* (*eau*) shallows; (*fig.*) dregs. **~-relief** *n.m.* low relief. **~-ventre** *n.m.* lower abdomen.
basané /bazane/ *a.* tanned.
bascule /baskyl/ *n.f.* (*balance*) scales. (**jeu de**) **~,** see-saw. **cheval/fauteuil à ~,** rocking-horse/-chair.
basculer /baskyle/ *v.t./i.* topple over; (*benne*) tip up.
base /bɑz/ *n.f.* base; (*fondement*) basis; (*pol.*) rank and file. **de ~,** basic.
baser /bɑze/ *v.t.* base. **se ~ sur,** base o.s. on.
basilique /bazilik/ *n.f.* basilica.
basket(-ball) /baskɛt(bol)/ *n.m.* basketball.
basque /bask/ *a.* & *n.m./f.* Basque.
basse /bɑs/ *voir* **bas.**
basse-cour (*pl.* **basses-cours**) /bɑskur/ *n.f.* farmyard.
bassement /bɑsmɑ̃/ *adv.* basely.
bassesse /bɑsɛs/ *n.f.* baseness; (*action*) base act.
bassin /basɛ̃/ *n.m.* bowl; (*pièce d'eau*) pond; (*rade*) dock; (*géog.*) basin; (*anat.*) pelvis. **~ houiller,** coalfield.
basson /bɑsɔ̃/ *n.m.* bassoon.
bastion /bastjɔ̃/ *n.m.* bastion.
bat /ba/ *voir* **battre.**
bât /bɑ/ *n.m.* pack-saddle.
bataill|e /bataj/ *n.f.* battle; (*fig.*) fight. **~er** *v.i.* fight. **~eur, ~euse** *n.m., f.* fighter; *a.* fighting.
bataillon /batajɔ̃/ *n.m.* battalion.
bâtard, ~e /bɑtar, -d/ *n.m., f.* bastard. —*a.* (*solution*) hybrid.
bateau (*pl.* **~x**) /bato/ *n.m.* boat. **~-mouche** (*pl.* **~x-mouches**) *n.m.* river-boat, sightseeing boat.
bâti /bɑti/ *a.* **bien ~,** well-built. —*n.m.* frame.
batifoler /batifɔle/ *v.i.* fool about.
bâtiment /bɑtimɑ̃/ *n.m.* building; (*navire*) vessel; (*industrie*) building trade.
bâtir /bɑtir/ *v.t.* build; (*coudre*) baste.
bâtisse /bɑtis/ *n.f.* (*péj.*) building.
bâton /bɑtɔ̃/ *n.m.* stick. **à ~s rompus,** jumping from subject to subject. **~ de rouge,** lipstick.
battage /bataʒ/ *n.m.* (*publicité: fam.*) (hard) plugging.
battant /batɑ̃/ *n.m.* (*vantail*) flap. **porte à deux ~s,** double door.
battement /batmɑ̃/ *n.m.* (*de cœur*) beat(ing); (*temps*) interval.
batterie /batri/ *n.f.* (*mil.*, *électr.*)

battery; (*mus.*) drums. **~ de cuisine,** pots and pans.
batteur /batœr/ *n.m.* (*mus.*) drummer; (*culin.*) whisk.
battre† /batr/ *v.t./i.* beat; (*blé*) thresh; (*cartes*) shuffle; (*parcourir*) scour; (*faire du bruit*) bang. **se ~** *v. pr.* fight. **~ des ailes,** flap its wings. **~ des mains,** clap. **~ en retraite,** beat a retreat. **~ la semelle,** stamp one's feet. **~ pavillon,** fly a flag. **~ son plein,** be in full swing.
baume /bom/ *n.m.* balm.
bavard, ~e /bavar, -d/ *a.* talkative. *—n.m., f.* chatterbox.
bavard|er /bavarde/ *v.i.* chat; (*jacasser*) chatter, gossip. **~age** *n.m.* chatter, gossip.
bav|e /bav/ *n.f.* dribble, slobber; (*de limace*) slime. **~er** *v.i.* dribble, slobber. **~eux, ~euse** *a.* dribbling; (*omelette*) runny.
bav|ette /bavɛt/ *n.f.*, **~oir** *n.m.* bib.
bavure /bavyr/ *n.f.* smudge; (*erreur*) mistake. **sans ~,** flawless(ly).
bazar /bazar/ *n.m.* bazaar; (*objets: fam.*) clutter.
bazarder /bazarde/ *v.t.* (*vendre: fam.*) get rid of, flog.
béant, ~e /beɑ̃, -t/ *a.* gaping.
béat, ~e /bea, -t/ *a.* (*hum.*) blissful; (*péj.*) smug. **~itude** /-tityd/ *n.f.* (*hum.*) bliss.
beau *ou* **bel*, belle** (*m.pl.* **~x**) /bo, bɛl/ *a.* fine, beautiful; (*femme*) beautiful; (*homme*) handsome; (*grand*) big. *—n.f.* beauty; (*sport*) deciding game. **au ~ milieu,** right in the middle. **bel et bien,** well and truly. **de plus belle,** more than ever. **faire le ~,** sit up and beg. **on a ~ essayer/insister/***etc.*, however much one tries/insists/*etc.*, it is no use trying/insisting/*etc.* **~x-arts** *n.m. pl.* fine arts. **~-fils** (*pl.* **~x-fils**) *n.m.* son-in-law; (*remariage*) stepson. **~-frère** (*pl.* **~x-frères**) *n.m.* brother-in-law. **~père** (*pl.* **~x-pères**) *n.m.* father-in-law; stepfather. **~x-parents** *n.m. pl.* parents-in-law.
beaucoup /boku/ *adv.* a lot, very much. *—pron.* many (people). **~ de,** (*nombre*) many; (*quantité*) a lot of. **pas ~ (de),** not many; (*quantité*) not much. **~ plus/***etc.*, much more/*etc.* **~ trop,** much too much. **de ~,** by far.
beauté /bote/ *n.f.* beauty. **en ~,** magnificently.
bébé /bebe/ *n.m.* baby.
bec /bɛk/ *n.m.* beak; (*de plume*) nib; (*de bouilloire*) spout; (*de casserole*) lip; (*bouche: fam.*) mouth. **~-de-cane** (*pl.* **~s-de-cane**) door handle. **~ de gaz,** gas lamp (*in street*).
bécane /bekan/ *n.f.* (*fam.*) bike.
bécasse /bekas/ *n.f.* woodcock.
bêche /bɛʃ/ *n.f.* spade.
bêcher /beʃe/ *v.t.* dig.
bécoter /bekɔte/ *v.t.*, **se ~** *v. pr.* (*fam.*) kiss.
becquée /beke/ *n.f.* **donner la ~ à,** feed.
becqueter /bɛkte/ *v.t.* peck (at).
bedaine /bədɛn/ *n.f.* paunch.
bedeau (*pl.* **~x**) /bədo/ *n.m.* beadle.
bedonnant, ~e /bədɔnɑ̃, -t/ *a.* paunchy.
beffroi /befrwa/ *n.m.* belfry.
bégayer /begeje/ *v.t./i.* stammer.
bègue /bɛg/ *n.m./f.* stammerer. **être ~,** stammer.
bégueule /begœl/ *a.* prudish.
béguin /begɛ̃/ *n.m.* **avoir le ~ pour,** (*fam.*) be sweet on.
beige /bɛʒ/ *a.* & *n.m.* beige.
beignet /bɛɲɛ/ *n.m.* fritter.
bel /bɛl/ *voir* **beau.**
bêler /bele/ *v.i.* bleat.
belette /bəlɛt/ *n.f.* weasel.
belge /bɛlʒ/ *a.* & *n.m./f.* Belgian.

Belgique /bɛlʒik/ *n.f.* Belgium.
bélier /belje/ *n.m.* ram.
belle /bɛl/ *voir* **beau.**
belle|-fille (*pl.* **~s-filles**) /bɛlfij/ *n.f.* daughter-in-law; (*remariage*) stepdaughter. **~-mère** (*pl.* **~s-mères**) *n.f.* mother-in-law; stepmother. **~-sœur** (*pl.* **~s-sœurs**) *n.f.* sister-in-law.
belligérant, ~e /beliʒerɑ̃, -t/ *a.* & *n.m.* belligerent.
belliqueu|x, ~se /belikø, -z/ *a.* warlike.
belote /bəlɔt/ *n.f.* belote (*card game*).
belvédère /bɛlvedɛr/ *n.m.* (*lieu*) viewing spot, viewpoint.
bémol /bemɔl/ *n.m.* (*mus.*) flat.
bénédiction /benediksjɔ̃/ *n.f.* blessing.
bénéfice /benefis/ *n.m.* (*gain*) profit; (*avantage*) benefit.
bénéficiaire /benefisjɛr/ *n.m.*/*f.* beneficiary.
bénéficier /benefisje/ *v.i.* **~ de,** benefit from; (*jouir de*) enjoy, have.
bénéfique /benefik/ *a.* beneficial.
Bénélux /benelyks/ *n.m.* Benelux.
benêt /bənɛ/ *n.m.* simpleton.
bénévole /benevɔl/ *a.* voluntary.
bén|in, ~igne /benɛ̃, -iɲ/ *a.* mild, slight; (*tumeur*) benign.
bén|ir /benir/ *v.t.* bless. **~it, ~ite** *a.* (*eau*) holy; (*pain*) consecrated.
bénitier /benitje/ *n.m.* holy-water stoup.
benjamin, ~e /bɛ̃ʒamɛ̃, -in/ *n.m.*, *f.* youngest child.
benne /bɛn/ *n.f.* (*de grue*) scoop; (*amovible*) skip. **~ (basculante),** dump truck.
benzine /bɛ̃zin/ *n.f.* benzine.
béotien, ~ne /beɔsjɛ̃, -jɛn/ *n.m.*, *f.* philistine.
béquille /bekij/ *n.f.* crutch; (*de moto*) stand.
bercail /bɛrkaj/ *n.m.* fold.
berceau (*pl.* **~x**) /bɛrso/ *n.m.* cradle.
bercer /bɛrse/ *v.t.* (*balancer*) rock; (*apaiser*) lull; (*leurrer*) delude.
berceuse /bɛrsøz/ *n.f.* lullaby.
béret /berɛ/ *n.m.* beret.
berge /bɛrʒ/ *n.f.* (*bord*) bank.
berg|er, ~ère /bɛrʒe, -ɛr/ *n.m.*, *f.* shepherd, shepherdess. **~erie** *n.f.* sheep-fold.
berline /bɛrlin/ *n.f.* (*auto.*) saloon; (*auto.*, *Amer.*) sedan.
berlingot /bɛrlɛ̃go/ *n.m.* boiled sweet; (*emballage*) carton.
berne (en) /(ɑ̃)bɛrn/ *adv.* at half-mast.
berner /bɛrne/ *v.t.* hoodwink.
besogne /bəzɔɲ/ *n.f.* task, job, chore.
besogneu|x, ~se /bəzɔɲø, -z/ *a.* needy.
besoin /bəzwɛ̃/ *n.m.* need. **avoir ~ de,** need. **au ~,** if need be.
best|ial (*m. pl.* **~iaux**) /bɛstjal, -jo/ *a.* bestial.
bestiaux /bɛstjo/ *n.m. pl.* livestock.
bestiole /bɛstjɔl/ *n.f.* creepy-crawly.
bétail /betaj/ *n.m.* farm animals.
bête[1] /bɛt/ *n.f.* animal. **~ noire,** pet hate, pet peeve. **~ sauvage,** wild beast.
bête[2] /bɛt/ *a.* stupid. **~ment** *adv.* stupidly.
bêtise /betiz/ *n.f.* stupidity; (*action*) stupid thing.
béton /betɔ̃/ *n.m.* concrete. **~ armé,** reinforced concrete. **~nière** /-ɔnjɛr/ *n.f.* cement-mixer, concrete-mixer.
betterave /bɛtrav/ *n.f.* beetroot. **~ sucrière,** sugar-beet.
beugler /bøgle/ *v.i.* bellow, low; (*radio*) blare.
beurr|e /bœr/ *n.m.* butter. **~er** *v.t.* butter. **~ier** *n.m.* butter-dish.
bévue /bevy/ *n.f.* blunder.
biais /bjɛ/ *n.m.* expedient; (*côté*)

angle. **de ~, en ~,** at an angle. **de ~,** (*fig.*) indirectly.
biaiser /bjeze/ *v.i.* hedge.
bibelot /biblo/ *n.m.* curio.
biberon /bibrɔ̃/ *n.m.* (feeding-) bottle.
bible /bibl/ *n.f.* bible. **la B~,** the Bible.
bibliobus /biblijɔbys/ *n.m.* mobile library.
bibliograph|e /biblijɔgraf/ *n.m./f.* bibliographer. **~ie** *n.f.* bibliography.
bibliophile /biblijɔfil/ *n.m./f.* book-lover.
biblioth|èque /biblijɔtɛk/ *n.f.* library; (*meuble*) bookcase; **~écaire** *n.m./f.* librarian.
biblique /biblik/ *a.* biblical.
biceps /bisɛps/ *n.m.* biceps.
biche /biʃ/ *n.f.* doe.
bichonner /biʃɔne/ *v.t.* doll up.
bicoque /bikɔk/ *n.f.* shack.
bicyclette /bisiklɛt/ *n.f.* bicycle.
bide /bid/ *n.m.* (*ventre*: *fam.*) belly; (*théâtre*: *argot*) flop.
bidet /bidɛ/ *n.m.* bidet.
bidon /bidɔ̃/ *n.m.* can. —*a. invar.* (*fam.*) phoney. **ce n'est pas du ~,** (*fam.*) it's the truth.
bidonville /bidɔ̃vil/ *n.f.* shanty town.
bidule /bidyl/ *n.m.* (*fam.*) thing.
bien /bjɛ̃/ *adv.* well; (*très*) quite, very. —*n.m.* good; (*patrimoine*) possession. —*a. invar.* good; (*passable*) all right; (*en forme*) well; (*à l'aise*) comfortable; (*beau*) attractive; (*respectable*) nice, respectable. —*conj.* **~ que,** (al)though. **~ du,** (*quantité*) a lot of, much. **~ des,** (*nombre*) many. **il l'a ~ fait,** (*intensif*) he did do it. **ce n'est pas ~ de,** it is not right to. **~ sûr,** of course. **~s de consommation,** consumer goods. **~-aimé, ~-aimée** *a.* & *n.m., f.* beloved. **~-être** *n.m.* well-being. **~-fondé** *n.m.* soundness.
bienfaisan|t, ~te /bjɛ̃fəzɑ̃, -t/ *a.* beneficial. **~ce** *n.f.* charity.
bienfait /bjɛ̃fɛ/ *n.m.* (kind) favour; (*avantage*) benefit.
bienfai|teur, ~trice /bjɛ̃fɛtœr, -tris/ *n.m., f.* benefactor.
bienheureu|x, ~se /bjɛ̃nœrø, -z/ *a.* blessed.
bienséan|t, ~te /bjɛ̃seɑ̃, ~t/ *a.* proper. **~ce** *n.f.* propriety.
bientôt /bjɛ̃to/ *adv.* soon. **à ~,** see you soon.
bienveillan|t, ~te /bjɛ̃vɛjɑ̃, -t/ *a.* kind(ly). **~ce** *n.f.* kind(li)ness.
bienvenu, ~e /bjɛ̃vny/ *a.* welcome. —*n.f.* welcome. —*n.m., f.* **être le ~, être la ~e,** be welcome. **souhaiter la ~e à,** welcome.
bière /bjɛr/ *n.f.* beer; (*cercueil*) coffin. **~ blonde,** lager. **~ brune,** stout, brown ale. **~ pression,** draught beer.
biffer /bife/ *v.t.* cross out.
bifteck /biftɛk/ *n.m.* steak.
bifur|quer /bifyrke/ *v.i.* branch off, fork. **~cation** *n.f.* fork, junction.
bigam|e /bigam/ *a.* bigamous. —*n.m./f.* bigamist. **~ie** *n.f.* bigamy.
bigarré /bigare/ *a.* motley.
bigot, ~e /bigo, -ɔt/ *n.m., f.* religious fanatic. —*a.* over-pious.
bigoudi /bigudi/ *n.m.* curler.
bijou (*pl.* **~x**) /biʒu/ *n.m.* jewel. **~terie** *n.f.* (*boutique*) jeweller's shop; (*bijoux*) jewellery. **~tier, ~tière** *n.m., f.* jeweller.
bikini /bikini/ *n.m.* bikini.
bilan /bilɑ̃/ *n.m.* outcome; (*d'une catastrophe*) (casualty) toll; (*comm.*) balance sheet. **faire le ~ de,** assess.
bile /bil/ *n.f.* bile. **se faire de la ~,** (*fam.*) worry.
bilieu|x, ~se /biljø, -z/ *a.* bilious; (*fig.*) irascible.
bilingue /bilɛ̃g/ *a.* bilingual.

billard /bijar/ *n.m.* billiards; (*table*) billiard-table.
bille /bij/ *n.f.* (*d'enfant*) marble; (*de billard*) billiard-ball.
billet /bijɛ/ *n.m.* ticket; (*lettre*) note. **~ (de banque),** (bank)note. **~ d'aller et retour,** return ticket; (*Amer.*) round trip ticket. **~ de faveur,** complimentary ticket. **~ simple,** single ticket; (*Amer.*) one-way ticket.
billion /biljɔ̃/ *n.m.* billion (= 10^{12}); (*Amer.*) trillion.
billot /bijo/ *n.m.* block.
bimensuel, ~le /bimɑ̃sɥɛl/ *a.* fortnightly, bimonthly.
bin|er /bine/ *v.t.* hoe. **~ette** *n.f.* hoe.
biochimie /bjɔʃimi/ *n.f.* biochemistry.
biograph|ie /bjɔgrafi/ *n.f.* biography. **~e** *n.m./f.* biographer.
biolog|ie /bjɔlɔʒi/ *n.f.* biology. **~ique** *a.* biological. **~iste** *n.m./f.* biologist.
bipède /bipɛd/ *n.m.* biped.
bique /bik/ *n.f.* (nanny-)goat.
bis¹, bise /bi, biz/ *a.* greyish brown.
bis² /bis/ *a.invar.* (*numéro*) A, a. —*n.m.* & *int.* encore.
bisbille (en) /(ɑ̃)bisbij/ *adv.* (*fam.*) at loggerheads.
biscornu /biskɔrny/ *a.* crooked; (*bizarre*) weird.
biscotte /biskɔt/ *n.f.* rusk.
biscuit /biskɥi/ *n.m.* (*salé*) biscuit; (*Amer.*) cracker; (*sucré*) biscuit; (*Amer.*) cookie. **~ de Savoie,** sponge-cake.
bise¹ /biz/ *n.f.* (*fam.*) kiss.
bise² /biz/ *n.f.* (*vent*) north wind.
bison /bizɔ̃/ *n.m.* (American) buffalo, bison.
bisser /bise/ *v.t.* encore.
bistouri /bisturi/ *n.m.* lancet.
bistre /bistr/ *a.* & *n.m.* dark brown.
bistro(t) /bistro/ *n.m.* café, bar.
bitume /bitym/ *n.m.* asphalt.
bizarre /bizar/ *a.* odd, peculiar. **~ment** *adv.* oddly. **~rie** *n.f.* peculiarity.
blafard, ~e /blafar, -d/ *a.* pale.
blagu|e /blag/ *n.f.* joke. **~e à tabac,** tobacco-pouch. **~er** *v.i.* joke; *v.t.* tease. **~eur, ~euse** *n.m., f.* joker; *a.* jokey.
blaireau (*pl.* **~x**) /blɛro/ *n.m.* shaving-brush; (*animal*) badger.
blâm|e /blɑm/ *n.m.* rebuke, blame. **~able** *a.* blameworthy. **~er** *v.t.* rebuke, blame.
blanc, blanche /blɑ̃, blɑ̃ʃ/ *a.* white; (*papier, page*) blank. —*n.m.* white; (*espace*) blank. —*n.m., f.* white man, white woman. —*n.f.* (*mus.*) minim. **~ (de poulet),** breast, white meat (of the chicken). **le ~,** (*linge*) whites. **laisser en ~,** leave blank.
blancheur /blɑ̃ʃœr/ *n.f.* whiteness.
blanch|ir /blɑ̃ʃir/ *v.t.* whiten; (*linge*) launder; (*personne*: *fig.*) clear. **~ir (à la chaux),** whitewash. —*v.i.* turn white. **~issage** *n.m.* laundering. **~isserie** *n.f.* laundry. **~isseur, ~isseuse** *n.m., f.* laundryman, laundress.
blas|er /blɑze/ *v.t.* make blasé. **~é** *a.* blasé.
blason /blazɔ̃/ *n.m.* coat of arms.
blasph|ème /blasfɛm/ *n.m.* blasphemy. **~ématoire** *a.* blasphemous. **~émer** *v.t./i.* blaspheme.
blatte /blat/ *n.f.* cockroach.
blazer /blɛzœr/ *n.m.* blazer.
blé /ble/ *n.m.* wheat.
bled /blɛd/ *n.m.* (*fam.*) dump, hole.
blême /blɛm/ *a.* (sickly) pale.
bless|er /blese/ *v.t.* injure, hurt; (*mil.*) wound; (*offenser*) hurt, wound. **se ~er** *v. pr.* injure *ou* hurt o.s. **~ant, ~ante** /blɛsɑ̃, -t/ *a.* hurtful. **~é, ~ée** *n.m., f.* casualty, injured person.

blessure /blesyr/ *n.f.* wound.
blet, ~te /blɛ, blɛt/ *a.* over-ripe.
bleu /blø/ *a.* blue; (*culin.*) very rare. —*n.m.* blue; (*contusion*) bruise. **~(s),** (*vêtement*) overalls. **~ir** *v.t./i.* turn blue.
bleuet /bløɛ/ *n.m.* cornflower.
bleuté /bløte/ *a.* slightly blue.
blind|er /blɛ̃de/ *v.t.* armour (-plate). **~é** *a.* armoured; *n.m.* armoured car, tank.
blizzard /blizar/ *n.m.* blizzard.
bloc /blɔk/ *n.m.* block; (*de papier*) pad; (*système*) unit; (*pol.*) bloc. **à ~,** hard, tight. **en ~,** all together. **~-notes** (*pl.* **~s-notes**) *n.m.* note-pad.
blocage /blɔkaʒ/ *n.m.* (*des prix*) freeze, freezing; (*des roues*) locking.
blocus /blɔkys/ *n.m.* blockade.
blond, ~e /blɔ̃, -d/ *a.* fair, blond. —*n.m., f.* fair-haired *ou* blond man *ou* woman. **~eur** /-dœr/ *n.f.* fairness.
bloquer /blɔke/ *v.t.* block; (*porte, machine*) jam; (*freins*) slam on; (*roues*) lock; (*prix, crédits*) freeze; (*grouper*) put together. **se ~** *v. pr.* jam; (*roues*) lock.
blottir (se) /(sə)blɔtir/ *v. pr.* snuggle, huddle.
blouse /bluz/ *n.f.* smock.
blouson /bluzɔ̃/ *n.m.* lumber-jacket; (*Amer.*) windbreaker.
blue-jean /bludʒin/ *n.m.* jeans.
bluff /blœf/ *n.m.* bluff. **~er** *v.t./i.* bluff.
boa /bɔa/ *n.m.* boa.
bobard /bɔbar/ *n.m.* (*fam.*) fib.
bobine /bɔbin/ *n.f.* reel; (*sur machine*) spool; (*électr.*) coil.
bocage /bɔkaʒ/ *n.m.* grove.
boc|al (*pl.* **~aux**) /bɔkal, -o/ *n.m.* jar.
bock /bɔk/ *n.m.* beer glass; (*contenu*) glass of beer.
bœuf (*pl.* **~s**) /bœf, bø/ *n.m.* ox; (*viande*) beef. **~s,** oxen.
bohème /bɔɛm/ *a.* & *n.m./f.* bohemian.
bohémien, ~ne /bɔemjɛ̃, -jɛn/ *n.m., f.* gypsy.
boire† /bwar/ *v.t./i.* drink; (*absorber*) soak up. **~ un coup,** have a drink.
bois¹ /bwa/ *voir* **boire.**
bois² /bwa/ *n.m.* (*matériau, forêt*) wood. **de ~, en ~,** wooden.
boisé /bwaze/ *a.* wooded.
bois|er /bwaze/ *v.t.* (*chambre*) panel. **~eries** *n.f. pl.* panelling.
boisson /bwasɔ̃/ *n.f.* drink.
boit /bwa/ *voir* **boire.**
boîte /bwat/ *n.f.* box; (*de conserves*) tin, can; (*firme: fam.*) firm. **~ à gants,** glove compartment. **~ aux lettres,** letter-box. **~ de nuit,** night-club. **~ postale,** post-office box.
boiter /bwate/ *v.i.* limp; (*meuble*) wobble.
boiteu|x, ~se /bwatø, -z/ *a.* lame; (*meuble*) wobbly.
boîtier /bwatje/ *n.m.* case.
bol /bɔl/ *n.m.* bowl. **un ~ d'air,** a breath of fresh air.
bolide /bɔlid/ *n.m.* racing car.
Bolivie /bɔlivi/ *n.f.* Bolivia.
bolivien, ~ne /bɔlivjɛ̃, -jɛn/ *a.* & *n.m., f.* Bolivian.
bombance /bɔ̃bɑ̃s/ *n.f.* **faire ~,** (*fam.*) revel.
bombard|er /bɔ̃barde/ *v.t.* bomb; (*par obus*) shell; (*nommer: fam.*) appoint unexpectedly (as). **~er qn. de,** (*fig.*) bombard s.o. with. **~ement** *n.m.* bombing; shelling. **~ier** *n.m.* (*aviat.*) bomber.
bombe /bɔ̃b/ *n.f.* bomb; (*atomiseur*) spray, aerosol.
bombé /bɔ̃be/ *a.* rounded; (*route*) cambered.
bomber /bɔ̃be/ *v.t.* **~ la poitrine,** throw out one's chest.
bon, bonne /bɔ̃, bɔn/ *a.* good; (*qui convient*) right; (*prudent*) wise. **~ à/pour,** (*approprié*) fit to/for.

—*n.m.* (*billet*) voucher, coupon; (*comm.*) bond. **du ~,** some good. **à quoi ~?,** what's the good *ou* point? **bonne année,** happy New Year. **~ anniversaire,** happy birthday. **~ appétit/voyage,** enjoy your meal/trip. **bonne chance/nuit,** good luck/night. **bonne femme,** (*péj.*) woman. **bonne-maman** (*pl.* **bonnes-mamans**) *n.f.* (*fam.*) granny. **~-papa** (*pl.* **~s-papas**) *n.m.* (*fam.*) grand-dad. **~ sens,** common sense. **~ vivant,** jolly fellow. **de bonne heure,** early.

bonasse /bɔnas/ *a.* weak.

bonbon /bɔ̃bɔ̃/ *n.m.* sweet; (*Amer.*) candy. **~nière** /-ɔnjɛr/ *n.f.* sweet box; (*Amer.*) candy box.

bond /bɔ̃/ *n.m.* leap.

bonde /bɔ̃d/ *n.f.* plug; (*trou*) plug-hole.

bondé /bɔ̃de/ *a.* packed.

bondir /bɔ̃dir/ *v.i.* leap.

bonheur /bɔnœr/ *n.m.* happiness; (*chance*) (good) luck. **au petit ~,** haphazardly. **par ~,** luckily.

bonhomme[1] (*pl.* **bonshommes**) /bɔnɔm, bɔ̃zɔm/ *n.m.* fellow. **~ de neige,** snowman.

bonhom|me[2] /bɔnɔm/ *a. invar.* good-hearted. **~ie** *n.f.* good-heartedness.

boni /bɔni/ *n.m.* surplus.

boniment /bɔnimɑ̃/ *n.m.* smooth talk.

bonjour /bɔ̃ʒur/ *n.m.* & *int.* hallo, hello, good morning *ou* afternoon.

bon marché /bɔ̃marʃe/ *a. invar.* cheap. —*adv.* cheap(ly).

bonne[1] /bɔn/ *a.f. voir* **bon.**

bonne[2] /bɔn/ *n.f.* (*domestique*) maid. **~ d'enfants,** nanny.

bonnement /bɔnmɑ̃/ *adv.* **tout ~,** quite simply.

bonnet /bɔnɛ/ *n.m.* cap; (*de femme*) bonnet.

bonneterie /bɔnɛtri/ *n.f.* hosiery.

bonsoir /bɔ̃swar/ *n.m.* & *int.* good evening; (*en se couchant*) good night.

bonté /bɔ̃te/ *n.f.* kindness.

bonus /bɔnys/ *n.m.* (*auto.*) no claims bonus.

boom /bum/ *n.m.* (*comm.*) boom.

bord /bɔr/ *n.m.* edge; (*rive*) bank. **à ~ (de),** on board. **au ~ de la mer,** at the seaside. **au ~ des larmes,** on the verge of tears. **~ de la route,** roadside. **~ du trottoir,** kerb; (*Amer.*) curb.

bordeaux /bɔrdo/ *n.m. invar.* Bordeaux (wine). —*a. invar.* maroon.

bordée /bɔrde/ *n.f.* **~ d'injures,** torrent of abuse.

bordel /bɔrdɛl/ *n.m.* (*désordre: fam.*) shambles.

border /bɔrde/ *v.t.* line, border; (*tissu*) edge; (*personne, lit*) tuck in.

bordereau (*pl.* **~x**) /bɔrdəro/ *n.m.* (*liste*) note, slip; (*facture*) invoice.

bordure /bɔrdyr/ *n.f.* border. **en ~ de,** on the edge of.

borgne /bɔrɲ/ *a.* one-eyed; (*fig.*) shady.

borne /bɔrn/ *n.f.* boundary marker. **~ (kilométrique),** (*approx.*) milestone. **~s,** limits.

borné /bɔrne/ *a.* narrow; (*personne*) narrow-minded.

borner /bɔrne/ *v.t.* confine. **se ~** *v. pr.* confine o.s. (**à,** to).

bosquet /bɔskɛ/ *n.m.* grove.

bosse /bɔs/ *n.f.* bump; (*de chameau*) hump. **avoir la ~ de,** (*fam.*) have a gift for.

bosseler /bɔsle/ *v.t.* emboss; (*endommager*) dent.

bosser /bɔse/ *v.i.* (*fam.*) work (hard). —*v.t.* (*fam.*) work (hard) at.

bossu, ~e /bɔsy/ *n.m., f.* hunchback.

botani|que /bɔtanik/ *n.f.* botany. —*a.* botanical. **~ste** *n.m./f.* botanist.

bott|e /bɔt/ *n.f.* boot; (*de fleurs,*

légumes) bunch; (*de paille*) bundle, bale; (*coup d'épée*) lunge. **~ier** *n.m.* boot-maker.
botter /bɔte/ *v.t.* kick, boot.
bottillon /bɔtijɔ̃/ *n.m.* ankle boot.
Bottin /bɔtɛ̃/ *n.m.* (P.) phone book.
bouc /buk/ *n.m.* (billy-)goat; (*barbe*) goatee. **~ émissaire,** scapegoat.
boucan /bukɑ̃/ *n.m.* (*fam.*) din.
bouche /buʃ/ *n.f.* mouth. **~ bée,** open-mouthed. **~ d'égout,** manhole. **~ d'incendie,** (fire) hydrant. **~ de métro,** entrance to the underground *ou* subway (*Amer.*).
bouché /buʃe/ *a.* (*temps*) overcast; (*personne*: *fam.*) dense.
bouchée /buʃe/ *n.f.* mouthful.
boucher[1] /buʃe/ *v.t.* block; (*bouteille*) cork. **se ~** *v. pr.* get blocked. **se ~ le nez,** hold one's nose.
bouch|er[2], **~ère** /buʃe, -ɛr/ *n.m., f.* butcher. **~erie** *n.f.* butcher's (shop); (*carnage*) butchery.
bouche-trou /buʃtru/ *n.m.* stopgap.
bouchon /buʃɔ̃/ *n.m.* stopper; (*en liège*) cork; (*de bidon, tube*) cap; (*de pêcheur*) float; (*de circulation*: *fig.*) traffic jam.
boucle /bukl/ *n.f.* (*de ceinture*) buckle; (*forme*) loop; (*de cheveux*) curl. **~ d'oreille,** ear-ring.
boucl|er /bukle/ *v.t.* fasten; (*terminer*) finish off; (*enfermer*: *fam.*) shut up; (*encercler*) seal off; (*budget*) balance. *—v.i.* curl. **~é** *a.* (*cheveux*) curly.
bouclier /buklije/ *n.m.* shield.
bouddhiste /budist/ *a.* & *n.m./f.* Buddhist.
boud|er /bude/ *v.i.* sulk. *—v.t.* steer clear of. **~erie** *n.f.* sulkiness. **~eur, ~euse** *a.* & *n.m., f.* sulky (person).
boudin /budɛ̃/ *n.m.* black pudding.
boudoir /budwar/ *n.m.* boudoir.
boue /bu/ *n.f.* mud.
bouée /bwe/ *n.f.* buoy. **~ de sauvetage,** lifebuoy.
boueu|x, ~se /bwø, -z/ *a.* muddy. *—n.m.* dustman; (*Amer.*) garbage collector.
bouff|e /buf/ *n.f.* (*fam.*) food, grub. **~er** *v.t./i.* (*fam.*) eat; (*bâfrer*) gobble.
bouffée /bufe/ *n.f.* puff, whiff; (*méd.*) flush; (*d'orgueil*) fit.
bouffi /bufi/ *a.* bloated.
bouffon, ~ne /bufɔ̃ -ɔn/ *a.* farcical.
bouge /buʒ/ *n.m.* hovel; (*bar*) dive.
bougeoir /buʒwar/ *n.m.* candlestick.
bougeotte /buʒɔt/ *n.f.* **la ~,** (*fam.*) the fidgets.
bouger /buʒe/ *v.t./i.* move; (*agir*) stir. **se ~** *v. pr.* (*fam.*) move.
bougie /buʒi/ *n.f.* candle; (*auto.*) spark(ing)-plug.
bougon, ~ne /bugɔ̃, -ɔn/ *a.* grumpy. **~ner** /-ɔne/ *v.i.* grumble.
bougre /bugr/ *n.m.* (*fam.*) fellow. **ce ~ de,** (*fam.*) that devil of a.
bouillabaisse /bujabɛs/ *n.f.* fish soup.
bouillie /buji/ *n.f.* porridge, baby food. **en ~,** crushed, mushy.
bouill|ir† /bujir/ *v.i.* boil. *—v.t.* (**faire**) **~ir,** boil. **~ant, ~ante** *a.* boiling.
bouilloire /bujwar/ *n.f.* kettle.
bouillon /bujɔ̃/ *n.m.* bubble; (*aliment*) broth. **~ner** /-jɔne/ *v.i.* bubble.
bouillotte /bujɔt/ *n.f.* hot-water bottle.
boulang|er, ~ère /bulɑ̃ʒe, -ɛr/ *n.m., f.* baker. **~erie** *n.f.* bakery. **~erie-pâtisserie** *n.f.* baker's and confectioner's shop.
boule /bul/ *n.f.* ball. **~s,** (*jeu*) bowls. **~ de neige,** snowball. **faire ~ de neige,** snowball.
bouleau (*pl.* **~x**) /bulo/ *n.m.* (silver) birch.
bouledogue /buldɔg/ *n.m.* bulldog.

boulet /bulɛ/ *n.m.* (*de canon*) cannon-ball; (*de forçat*) ball and chain.
boulette /bulɛt/ *n.f.* (*de papier*) pellet; (*aliment*) meat ball.
boulevard /bulvar/ *n.m.* boulevard.
boulevers|er /bulvɛrse/ *v.t.* turn upside down; (*pays, plans*) disrupt; (*émouvoir*) distress, upset. **~ement** *n.m.* upheaval.
boulier /bulje/ *n.m.* abacus.
boulimie /bulimi/ *n.f.* compulsive eating.
boulon /bulɔ̃/ *n.m.* bolt. **~ner** /-ɔne/ *v.t.* bolt.
boulot[1] /bulo/ *n.m.* (*travail*: *fam.*) work.
boulot[2], **~te** /bulo, -ɔt/ *a.* (*rond*: *fam.*) dumpy.
boum /bum/ *n.m.* & *int.* bang. —*n.f.* (*réunion*: *argot*) party.
bouquet /bukɛ/ *n.m.* (*de fleurs*) bunch, bouquet; (*d'arbres*) clump. **c'est le ~!**, (*fam.*) that's the last straw!
bouquin /bukɛ̃/ *n.m.* (*fam.*) book. **~er** /-ine/ *v.t.*/*i.* (*fam.*) read. **~iste** /-inist/ *n.m.*/*f.* second-hand bookseller.
bourbeu|x, **~se** /burbø, -z/ *a.* muddy.
bourbier /burbje/ *n.m.* mire.
bourde /burd/ *n.f.* blunder.
bourdon /burdɔ̃/ *n.m.* bumble-bee.
bourdonn|er /burdɔne/ *v.i.* buzz. **~ement** *n.m.* buzzing.
bourg /bur/ *n.m.* (market) town.
bourgade /burgad/ *n.f.* village.
bourgeois, **~e** /burʒwa, -z/ *a.* & *n.m.*, *f.* middle-class (person); (*péj.*) bourgeois. **~ie** /-zi/ *n.f.* middle class(es).
bourgeon /burʒɔ̃/ *n.m.* bud. **~ner** /-ɔne/ *v.i.* bud.
bourgogne /burgɔɲ/ *n.m.* burgundy. —*n.f.* **la B~**, Burgundy.
bourlinguer /burlɛ̃ge/ *v.i.* (*fam.*) travel about.
bourrade /burad/ *n.f.* prod.
bourrage /buraʒ/ *n.m.* **~ de crâne**, brainwashing.
bourrasque /burask/ *n.f.* squall.
bourrati|f, **~ve** /buratif, -v/ *a.* filling, stodgy.
bourreau (*pl.* **~x**) /buro/ *n.m.* executioner. **~ de travail**, workaholic.
bourrelet /burlɛ/ *n.m.* weather-strip, draught excluder; (*de chair*) roll of fat.
bourrer /bure/ *v.t.* cram (**de**, with); (*pipe*) fill. **~ de**, (*nourriture*) stuff with. **~ de coups**, thrash. **~ le crâne à qn.**, fill s.o.'s head with nonsense.
bourrique /burik/ *n.f.* ass.
bourru /bury/ *a.* surly.
bours|e /burs/ *n.f.* purse; (*subvention*) grant. **la B~e**, the Stock Exchange. **~ier**, **~ière** *a.* Stock Exchange; *n.m.*, *f.* holder of a grant.
boursoufler /bursufle/ *v.t.*, **se ~** *v. pr.* puff up, swell.
euscul|er /buskyle/ *v.t.* (*pousser*) jostle; (*presser*) rush; (*renverser*) knock over. **~ade** *n.f.* rush; (*cohue*) crush.
bouse /buz/ *n.f.* (cow) dung.
bousiller /buzije/ *v.t.* (*fam.*) mess up.
boussole /busɔl/ *n.f.* compass.
bout /bu/ *n.m.* end; (*de langue, bâton*) tip; (*morceau*) bit. **à ~**, exhausted. **à ~ de souffle**, out of breath. **à ~ portant**, point-blank. **au ~ de**, (*après*) after. **~ filtre**, filter-tip. **venir à ~ de**, (*finir*) manage to finish.
boutade /butad/ *n.f.* jest; (*caprice*) whim.
boute-en-train /butɑ̃trɛ̃/ *n.m. invar.* joker, live wire.
bouteille /butɛj/ *n.f.* bottle.
boutiqu|e /butik/ *n.f.* shop; (*de mode*) boutique. **~ier**, **~ière** *n.m.*, *f.* (*péj.*) shopkeeper.

bouton /butɔ̃/ *n.m.* button; (*pustule*) pimple; (*pousse*) bud; (*de porte, radio, etc.*) knob. **~ de manchette,** cuff-link. **~-d'or** *n.m.* (*pl.* **~s-d'or**) buttercup. **~ner** /-ɔne/ *v.t.* button (up). **~nière** /-ɔnjɛr/ *n.f.* buttonhole. **~-pression** (*pl.* **~s-pression**) *n.m.* press-stud; (*Amer.*) snap.

boutonneu|x, ~se /butɔnø, -z/ *a.* pimply.

bouture /butyr/ *n.f.* (*plante*) cutting.

bovin, ~e /bɔvɛ̃, -in/ *a.* bovine. **~s** *n.m. pl.* cattle.

bowling /bɔliŋ/ *n.m.* bowling; (*salle*) bowling-alley.

box (*pl.* **~** *ou* **boxes**) /bɔks/ *n.m.* lock-up garage; (*de dortoir*) cubicle; (*d'écurie*) (loose) box; (*jurid.*) dock.

box|e /bɔks/ *n.f.* boxing. **~er** *v.t./i.* box. **~eur** *n.m.* boxer.

boyau (*pl.* **~x**) /bwajo/ *n.m.* gut; (*corde*) catgut; (*galerie*) gallery; (*de bicyclette*) tyre; (*Amer.*) tire.

boycott|er /bɔjkɔte/ *v.t.* boycott. **~age** *n.m.* boycott.

bracelet /braslɛ/ *n.m.* bracelet; (*de montre*) strap.

braconn|er /brakɔne/ *v.i.* poach. **~ier** *n.m.* poacher.

brad|er /brade/ *v.t.* sell off. **~erie** *n.f.* open-air sale.

braguette /bragɛt/ *n.f.* fly, flies.

brailler /brɑje/ *v.t./i.* bawl.

braire /brɛr/ *v.i.* bray.

braise /brɛz/ *n.f.* embers.

braiser /breze/ *v.t.* braise.

brancard /brɑ̃kar/ *n.m.* stretcher; (*bras*) shaft. **~ier** /-dje/ *n.m.* stretcher-bearer.

branch|e /brɑ̃ʃ/ *n.f.* branch. **~ages** *n.m. pl.* (cut) branches.

branch|er /brɑ̃ʃe/ *v.t.* connect; (*électr.*) plug in. **~ement** *n.m.* connection.

branchies /brɑ̃ʃi/ *n.f. pl.* gills.

brandir /brɑ̃dir/ *v.t.* brandish.

branle /brɑ̃l/ *n.m.* **mettre en ~, donner le ~ à,** set in motion. **~-bas** *n.m. invar.* commotion.

branler /brɑ̃le/ *v.i.* be shaky. *—v.t.* shake.

braquer /brake/ *v.t.* aim; (*regard*) fix; (*roue*) turn; (*personne*) antagonize. *—v.i.* (*auto.*) turn (the wheel).

bras /bra/ *n.m.* arm. *—n.m. pl.* (*fig.*) labour, hands. **à ~-le-corps** *adv.* round the waist. **~ dessus bras dessous,** arm in arm. **~ droit,** (*fig.*) right-hand man. **en ~ de chemise,** in one's shirt-sleeves.

brasier /brɑzje/ *n.m.* blaze.

brassard /brasar/ *n.m.* arm-band.

brasse /bras/ *n.f.* (breast-)stroke; (*mesure*) fathom.

brassée /brase/ *n.f.* armful.

brass|er /brase/ *v.t.* mix; (*bière*) brew; (*affaires*) handle a lot of. **~age** *n.m.* mixing; brewing. **~erie** *n.f.* brewery; (*café*) brasserie. **~eur** *n.m.* brewer. **~eur d'affaires,** big businessman.

brassière /brasjɛr/ *n.f.* (baby's) vest.

bravache /bravaʃ/ *n.m.* braggart.

bravade /bravad/ *n.f.* bravado.

brave /brav/ *a.* brave; (*bon*) good. **~ment** *adv.* bravely.

braver /brave/ *v.t.* defy.

bravo /bravo/ *int.* bravo. *—n.m.* cheer.

bravoure /bravur/ *n.f.* bravery.

break /brɛk/ *n.m.* estate car; (*Amer.*) station-wagon.

brebis /brəbi/ *n.f.* ewe. **~ galeuse,** black sheep.

brèche /brɛʃ/ *n.f.* gap, breach.

bredouille /brəduj/ *a.* empty-handed.

bredouiller /brəduje/ *v.t./i.* mumble.

bref, brève /brɛf, -v/ *a.* short, brief. *—adv.* in short. **en ~,** in short.

Brésil /brezil/ *n.m.* Brazil.

brésilien, ~ne /breziljɛ̃, -jɛn/ *a.* & *n.m., f.* Brazilian.
Bretagne /brətaɲ/ *n.f.* Brittany.
bretelle /brətɛl/ *n.f.* (shoulder-) strap; (*d'autoroute*) access road. **~s,** (*pour pantalon*) braces; (*Amer.*) suspenders.
breton, ~ne /brətɔ̃, -ɔn/ *a.* & *n.m., f.* Breton.
breuvage /brœvaʒ/ *n.m.* beverage.
brève /brɛv/ *voir* **bref.**
brevet /brəvɛ/ *n.m.* diploma. **~ (d'invention),** patent.
brevet|er /brəvte/ *v.t.* patent. **~é** *a.* (*diplômé*) qualified.
bréviaire /brevjɛr/ *n.m.* breviary.
bribes /brib/ *n.f. pl.* bits, scraps.
bric-à-brac /brikabrak/ *n.m. invar.* bric-à-brac.
bricole /brikɔl/ *n.f.* trifle.
bricol|er /brikɔle/ *v.i.* do odd (do-it-yourself) jobs. —*v.t.* fix (up). **~age** *n.m.* do-it-yourself (jobs). **~eur, ~euse** *n.m., f.* handyman, handywoman.
brid|e /brid/ *n.f.* bridle. **tenir en ~e,** keep in check. **~er** *v.t.* (*cheval*) bridle; (*fig.*) keep in check, bridle.
bridge /bridʒ/ *n.m.* (*cartes*) bridge.
briève|ment /brijɛvmɑ̃/ *adv.* briefly. **~té** *n.f.* brevity.
brigad|e /brigad/ *n.f.* (*de police*) squad; (*mil.*) brigade; (*fig.*) team. **~ier** *n.m.* (*de police*) sergeant.
brigand /brigɑ̃/ *n.m.* robber. **~age** /-daʒ/ *n.m.* robbery.
briguer /brige/ *v.t.* seek (after).
brill|ant, ~ante /brijɑ̃, -t/ *a.* (*couleur*) bright; (*luisant*) shiny; (*remarquable*) brilliant. —*n.m.* (*éclat*) shine; (*diamant*) diamond. **~amment** *adv.* brilliantly.
briller /brije/ *v.i.* shine.
brim|er /brime/ *v.t.* bully; (*contrarier*) annoy. **~ade** *n.f.* bullying; annoyance.
brin /brɛ̃/ *n.m.* (*de corde*) strand; (*de muguet*) sprig. **~ d'herbe,** blade of grass. **un ~ de,** a bit of.
brindille /brɛ̃dij/ *n.f.* twig.
bringuebaler /brɛ̃gbale/ *v.i.* (*fam.*) wobble about.
brio /brijo/ *n.m.* brilliance.
brioche /brijɔʃ/ *n.f.* brioche (*small round sweet cake*); (*ventre: fam.*) tummy.
brique /brik/ *n.f.* brick.
briquer /brike/ *v.t.* polish.
briquet /brikɛ/ *n.m.* (cigarette-) lighter.
brisant /brizɑ̃/ *n.m.* reef.
brise /briz/ *n.f.* breeze.
bris|er /brize/ *v.t.* break; (*fatiguer*) exhaust. **se ~er** *v. pr.* break. **~e-lames** *n.m. invar.* breakwater. **~eur de grève** *n.m.* strike-breaker.
britannique /britanik/ *a.* British. —*n.m./f.* Briton. **les B~s,** the British.
broc /bro/ *n.m.* pitcher.
brocant|e /brɔkɑ̃t/ *n.f.* second-hand goods. **~eur, ~euse** *n.m., f.* second-hand goods dealer.
broche /brɔʃ/ *n.f.* brooch; (*culin.*) spit.
broché /brɔʃe/ *a.* paperback(ed).
brochet /brɔʃɛ/ *n.m.* (*poisson*) pike.
brochette /brɔʃɛt/ *n.f.* skewer.
brochure /brɔʃyr/ *n.f.* brochure, booklet.
brod|er /brɔde/ *v.t.* embroider. —*v.i.* (*fig.*) embroider the truth. **~erie** *n.f.* embroidery.
broncher /brɔ̃ʃe/ *v.i.* falter.
bronch|es /brɔ̃ʃ/ *n.f. pl.* bronchial tubes. **~ite** *n.f.* bronchitis.
bronze /brɔ̃z/ *n.m.* bronze.
bronz|er /brɔ̃ze/ *v.i.,* **se ~er** *v. pr.* get a (sun-)tan. **~age** *n.m.* (sun-)tan. **~é** *a.* (sun-)tanned.
brosse /brɔs/ *n.f.* brush. **~ à dents,** toothbrush. **~ à habits,** clothes-brush. **en ~,** (*coiffure*) in a crew cut.

brosser /brɔse/ *v.t.* brush; (*fig.*) paint.
brouette /bruɛt/ *n.f.* wheelbarrow.
brouhaha /bruaa/ *n.m.* hullabaloo.
brouillard /brujar/ *n.m.* fog.
brouille /bruj/ *n.f.* quarrel.
brouill|er /bruje/ *v.t.* mix up; (*vue*) blur; (*œufs*) scramble; (*radio*) jam; (*amis*) set at odds. **se ~er** *v. pr.* become confused; (*ciel*) cloud over; (*amis*) fall out. **~on**[1], **~onne** *a.* disorderly.
brouillon[2] /brujɔ̃/ *n.m.* (rough) draft.
broussailles /brusɑj/ *n.f. pl.* undergrowth.
brousse /brus/ *n.f.* **la ~,** the bush.
brouter /brute/ *v.t./i.* graze.
broutille /brutij/ *n.f.* (*bagatelle*) trifle.
broyer /brwaje/ *v.t.* crush; (*moudre*) grind.
bru /bry/ *n.f.* daughter-in-law.
bruin|e /brɥin/ *n.f.* drizzle. **~er** *v.i.* drizzle.
bruire /brɥir/ *v.i.* rustle.
bruissement /brɥismɑ̃/ *n.m.* rustling.
bruit /brɥi/ *n.m.* noise; (*fig.*) rumour.
bruitage /brɥitaʒ/ *n.m.* sound effects.
brûlant, ~e /brylɑ̃, -t/ *a.* burning (hot); (*sujet*) red-hot; (*ardent*) fiery.
brûlé /bryle/ *a.* (*démasqué: fam.*) blown. —*n.m.* burning.
brûle-pourpoint (**à**) /(a)brylpurpwɛ̃/ *adv.* point-blank.
brûl|er /bryle/ *v.t./i.* burn; (*essence*) use (up); (*signal*) go through *ou* past (without stopping); (*dévorer: fig.*) consume. **se ~er** *v. pr.* burn o.s. **~eur** *n.m.* burner.
brûlure /brylyr/ *n.f.* burn. **~s d'estomac,** heartburn.
brum|e /brym/ *n.f.* mist. **~eux, ~euse** *a.* misty; (*idées*) hazy.
brun, ~e /brœ̃, bryn/ *a.* brown, dark. —*n.m.* brown. —*n.m., f.* dark-haired person. **~ir** /brynir/ *v.i.* turn brown; (*se bronzer*) get a tan.
brusque /brysk/ *a.* (*soudain*) sudden, abrupt; (*rude*) abrupt. **~ment** /-əmɑ̃/ *adv.* suddenly, abruptly.
brusquer /bryske/ *v.t.* rush.
brut /bryt/ *a.* (*diamant*) rough; (*soie*) raw; (*pétrole*) crude; (*comm.*) gross.
brut|al (*m. pl.* **~aux**) /brytal, -o/ *a.* brutal. **~aliser** *v.t.* treat roughly *ou* violently, manhandle. **~alité** *n.f.* brutality.
brute /bryt/ *n.f.* brute.
Bruxelles /brysɛl/ *n.m./f.* Brussels.
bruy|ant, ~ante /brɥijɑ̃, -t/ *a.* noisy. **~amment** *adv.* noisily.
bruyère /bryjɛr/ *n.f.* heather.
bu /by/ *voir* **boire.**
bûche /byʃ/ *n.f.* log. **ramasser une ~,** (*fam.*) come a cropper.
bûcher[1] /byʃe/ *n.m.* (*supplice*) stake.
bûch|er[2] /byʃe/ *v.t./i.* (*fam.*) slog away (at). **~eur, ~euse** *n.m., f.* (*fam.*) slogger.
bûcheron /byʃrɔ̃/ *n.m.* woodcutter.
budg|et /bydʒɛ/ *n.m.* budget. **~étaire** *a.* budgetary.
buée /bɥe/ *n.f.* mist, condensation.
buffet /byfɛ/ *n.m.* sideboard; (*table, restaurant*) buffet.
buffle /byfl/ *n.m.* buffalo.
buis /bɥi/ *n.m.* (*arbre, bois*) box.
buisson /bɥisɔ̃/ *n.m.* bush.
buissonnière /bɥisɔnjɛr/ *a.f.* **faire l'école ~,** play truant; (*Amer.*) play hooky.
bulbe /bylb/ *n.m.* bulb.
bulgare /bylgar/ *a.* & *n.m./f.* Bulgarian.

Bulgarie /bylgari/ *n.f.* Bulgaria.
bulldozer /buldozœr/ *n.m.* bulldozer.
bulle /byl/ *n.f.* bubble.
bulletin /byltɛ̃/ *n.m.* bulletin, report; (*scol.*) report; (*billet*) ticket. **~ (de vote),** ballot-paper. **~ de salaire,** pay-slip.
buraliste /byralist/ *n.m./f.* tobacconist; (*à la poste*) clerk.
bureau (*pl.* **~x**) /byro/ *n.m.* office; (*meuble*) desk; (*comité*) board. **~ de location,** booking-office; (*théâtre*) box-office. **~ de poste,** post office. **~ de tabac,** tobacconist's (shop).
bureaucrate /byrokrat/ *n.m./f.* bureaucrat.
bureaucrat|ie /byrokrasi/ *n.f.* bureaucracy. **~ique** /-tik/ *a.* bureaucratic.
bureautique /byrotik/ *n.f.* office automation.
burette /byrɛt/ *n.f.* (*de graissage*) oilcan.
burlesque /byrlɛsk/ *a.* ludicrous; (*théâtre*) burlesque.
bus /bys/ *n.m.* bus.
busqué /byske/ *a.* hooked.
buste /byst/ *n.m.* bust.
but /by(t)/ *n.m.* target; (*dessein*) aim, goal; (*football*) goal. **avoir pour ~ de,** aim to. **de ~ en blanc,** point-blank.
butane /bytan/ *n.f.* butane, Calor gas (P.).
buté /byte/ *a.* obstinate.
buter /byte/ *v.i.* **~ contre,** knock against; (*problème*) come up against. —*v.t.* antagonize. **se ~** *v. pr.* (*s'entêter*) become obstinate.
buteur /bytœr/ *n.m.* striker.
butin /bytɛ̃/ *n.m.* booty, loot.
butiner /bytine/ *v.i.* gather nectar.
butoir /bytwar/ *n.m.* **~ (de porte),** doorstop.
butor /bytɔr/ *n.m.* (*péj.*) lout.
butte /byt/ *n.f.* mound. **en ~ à,** exposed to.
buvard /byvar/ *n.m.* blotting-paper.
buvette /byvɛt/ *n.f.* (refreshment) bar.
buveu|r, ~se /byvœr, -øz/ *n.m., f.* drinker.

C

c' /s/ *voir* **ce**[1].
ça /sa/ *pron.* it, that; (*pour désigner*) that; (*plus près*) this. **~ va?,** (*fam.*) how's it going? **~ va!,** (*fam.*) all right! **où ~?,** (*fam.*) where? **quand ~?,** (*fam.*) when?
çà /sa/ *adv.* **~ et là,** here and there.
caban|e /kaban/ *n.f.* hut; (*à outils*) shed; (*à lapins*) hutch. **~on** *n.m.* hut; (*en Provence*) cottage.
cabaret /kabarɛ/ *n.m.* night-club.
cabas /kabɑ/ *n.m.* shopping basket.
cabillaud /kabijo/ *n.m.* cod.
cabine /kabin/ *n.f.* (*à la piscine*) cubicle; (*à la plage*) (beach) hut; (*de bateau*) cabin; (*de pilotage*) cockpit; (*de camion*) cab; (*d'ascenseur*) cage. **~ (téléphonique),** phone-booth, phone-box.
cabinet /kabinɛ/ *n.m.* (*de médecin*) surgery; (*Amer.*) office; (*d'avocat*) office; (*clientèle*) practice; (*pol.*) Cabinet; (*pièce*) room. **~s,** (*toilettes*) toilet. **~ de toilette,** toilet.
câble /kɑbl/ *n.m.* cable; (*corde*) rope.
câbler /kɑble/ *v.t.* cable.
cabosser /kabɔse/ *v.t.* dent.
cabot|age /kabɔtaʒ/ *n.m.* coastal navigation. **~eur** *n.m.* coaster.
cabotin, ~e /kabɔtɛ̃, -in/ *n.m., f.* (*théâtre*) ham; (*fig.*) play-actor. **~age** /-inaʒ/ *n.m.* ham acting; (*fig.*) play-acting.
cabrer /kabre/ *v.t.*, **se ~** *v. pr.*

(*cheval*) rear up. **se ~ contre,** rebel against.
cabri /kabri/ *n.m.* kid.
cabriole /kabrijɔl/ *n.f.* caper; (*culbute*) somersault.
cabriolet /kabrijɔlɛ/ *n.m.* (*auto.*) convertible.
cacahuète /kakaɥɛt/ *n.f.* peanut.
cacao /kakao/ *n.m.* cocoa.
cachalot /kaʃalo/ *n.m.* sperm whale.
cachemire /kaʃmir/ *n.m.* cashmere.
cach|er /kaʃe/ *v.t.* hide, conceal (**à,** from). **se ~er** *v. pr.* hide; (*se trouver caché*) be hidden. **~e-cache** *n.m. invar.* hide-and-seek. **~-nez** *n.m. invar.* scarf.
cachet /kaʃɛ/ *n.m.* seal; (*de la poste*) postmark; (*comprimé*) tablet; (*d'artiste*) fee; (*fig.*) style.
cacheter /kaʃte/ *v.t.* seal.
cachette /kaʃɛt/ *n.f.* hiding-place. **en ~,** in secret.
cachot /kaʃo/ *n.m.* dungeon.
cachott|eries /kaʃɔtri/ *n.f. pl.* secrecy. **~ier, ~ière** *a.* secretive.
cactus /kaktys/ *n.m.* cactus.
cadavérique /kadɑverik/ *a.* (*teint*) deathly pale.
cadavre /kadɑvr/ *n.m.* corpse.
cadeau (*pl.* **~x**) /kado/ *n.m.* present, gift.
cadenas /kadnɑ/ *n.m.* padlock. **~ser** /-ase/ *v.t.* padlock.
cadenc|e /kadɑ̃s/ *n.f.* rhythm, cadence; (*de travail*) rate. **en ~e,** in time. **~é** *a.* rhythmic(al).
cadet, ~te /kadɛ, -t/ *a.* youngest; (*entre deux*) younger. —*n.m., f.* youngest (child); younger (child). **il est mon ~,** he is my junior.
cadran /kadrɑ̃/ *n.m.* dial. **~ solaire,** sundial.
cadre /kɑdr/ *n.m.* frame; (*milieu*) surroundings; (*limites*) scope; (*contexte*) framework. —*n.m./f.* (*personne: comm.*) executive. **les ~s,** (*comm.*) the managerial staff.
cadrer /kɑdre/ *v.i.* **~ avec,** tally with. —*v.t.* (*photo*) centre.
cadu|c, ~que /kadyk/ *a.* obsolete.
cafard /kafar/ *n.m.* (*insecte*) cockroach. **avoir le ~,** (*fam.*) be feeling low.
caf|é /kafe/ *n.m.* coffee; (*bar*) café. **~é au lait,** white coffee. **~etier, ~etière** *n.m., f.* café owner; *n.f.* coffee-pot.
caféine /kafein/ *n.f.* caffeine.
cafouiller /kafuje/ *v.i.* (*fam.*) bumble, flounder.
cage /kaʒ/ *n.f.* cage; (*d'escalier*) well; (*d'ascenseur*) shaft.
cageot /kaʒo/ *n.m.* crate.
cagibi /kaʒibi/ *n.m.* storage room.
cagneu|x, ~se /kaɲø, -z/ *a.* knock-kneed.
cagnotte /kaɲɔt/ *n.f.* kitty.
cagoule /kagul/ *n.f.* hood.
cahier /kaje/ *n.m.* notebook; (*scol.*) exercise-book.
cahin-caha /kaɛ̃kaa/ *adv.* **aller ~,** (*fam.*) jog along.
cahot /kao/ *n.m.* bump, jolt. **~er** /kaɔte/ *v.t./i.* bump, jolt. **~eux, ~euse** /kaɔtø, -z/ *a.* bumpy.
caïd /kaid/ *n.m.* (*fam.*) big shot.
caille /kɑj/ *n.f.* quail.
cailler /kɑje/ *v.t./i.,* **se ~** *v. pr.* (*sang*) clot; (*lait*) curdle.
caillot /kajo/ *n.m.* (blood) clot.
caillou (*pl.* **~x**) /kaju/ *n.m.* stone; (*galet*) pebble. **~teux, ~teuse** *a.* stony. **~tis** *n.m.* gravel.
caisse /kɛs/ *n.f.* crate, case; (*tiroir, machine*) till; (*guichet*) pay-desk; (*bureau*) office; (*mus.*) drum. **~ enregistreuse,** cash register. **~ d'épargne,** savings bank.
caiss|ier, ~ière /kesje, -jɛr/ *n.m., f.* cashier.
caisson /kɛsɔ̃/ *n.m.* (little) box.
cajol|er /kaʒɔle/ *v.t.* coax. **~eries** *n.f. pl.* coaxing.
cake /kɛk/ *n.m.* fruit-cake.
calamité /kalamite/ *n.f.* calamity.

calcaire /kalkɛr/ *a.* (*sol*) chalky; (*eau*) hard.
calciné /kalsine/ *a.* charred.
calcium /kalsjɔm/ *n.m.* calcium.
calcul /kalkyl/ *n.m.* calculation; (*scol.*) arithmetic; (*différentiel*) calculus.
calcul|er /kalkyle/ *v.t.* calculate. **~ateur** *n.m.* (*ordinateur*) computer, calculator. **~atrice** *n.f.* (*ordinateur*) calculator.
cale /kal/ *n.f.* wedge; (*de navire*) hold. **~ sèche,** dry dock.
calé /kale/ *a.* (*fam.*) clever.
caleçon /kalsɔ̃/ *n.m.* underpants. **~ de bain,** (bathing) trunks.
calembour /kalɑ̃bur/ *n.m.* pun.
calendrier /kalɑ̃drije/ *n.m.* calendar; (*fig.*) timetable.
calepin /kalpɛ̃/ *n.m.* notebook.
caler /kale/ *v.t.* wedge; (*moteur*) stall. *—v.i.* stall.
calfeutrer /kalføtre/ *v.t.* stop up the cracks of.
calibr|e /kalibr/ *n.m.* calibre; (*d'un œuf, fruit*) grade. **~er** *v.t.* grade.
calice /kalis/ *n.m.* (*relig.*) chalice.
califourchon (**à**) /(a)kalifurʃɔ̃/ *adv.* astride. *—prép.* **à ~ sur,** astride.
câlin, ~e /kɑlɛ̃, -in/ *a.* endearing, cuddly. **~er** /-ine/ *v.t.* cuddle.
calmant /kalmɑ̃/ *n.m.* sedative.
calm|e /kalm/ *a.* calm *—n.m.* calm(ness). **~er** *v.t.*, **se ~er** *v. pr.* (*personne*) calm (down); (*diminuer*) ease.
calomn|ie /kalɔmni/ *n.f.* slander; (*écrite*) libel. **~ier** *v.t.* slander; libel. **~ieux, ~ieuse** *a.* slanderous; libellous.
calorie /kalɔri/ *n.f.* calorie.
calorifuge /kalɔrifyʒ/ *a.* (heat-) insulating. *—n.m.* lagging.
calot /kalo/ *n.m.* (*mil.*) forage-cap.
calotte /kalɔt/ *n.f.* (*relig.*) skull-cap; (*tape: fam.*) slap.
calqu|e /kalk/ *n.m.* tracing; (*fig.*) exact copy. **~er** *v.t.* trace; (*fig.*) copy. **~er sur,** model on.
calvaire /kalvɛr/ *n.m.* (*croix*) calvary; (*fig.*) suffering.
calvitie /kalvisi/ *n.f.* baldness.
camarade /kamarad/ *n.m.*/*f.* friend; (*pol.*) comrade. **~ de jeu,** playmate. **~rie** *n.f.* good companionship.
cambouis /kɑ̃bwi/ *n.m.* (engine) oil.
cambrer /kɑ̃bre/ *v.t.* arch. **se ~** *v. pr.* arch one's back.
cambriol|er /kɑ̃brijɔle/ *v.t.* burgle. **~age** *n.m.* burglary. **~eur, ~euse** *n.m., f.* burglar.
cambrure /kɑ̃bryr/ *n.f.* curve.
camée /kame/ *n.m.* cameo.
camelot /kamlo/ *n.m.* street vendor.
camelote /kamlɔt/ *n.f.* junk.
camembert /kamɑ̃bɛr/ *n.m.* Camembert (cheese).
caméra /kamera/ *n.f.* (*cinéma, télévision*) camera.
caméra|man (*pl.* **~men**) /kameraman, -mɛn/ *n.m.* cameraman.
camion /kamjɔ̃/ *n.m.* lorry, truck. **~-citerne** *n.m.* tanker. **~nage** /-jɔnaʒ/ *n.m.* haulage. **~nette** /-jɔnɛt/ *n.f.* van. **~neur** /-jɔnœr/ *n.m.* lorry *ou* truck driver; (*entrepreneur*) haulage contractor.
camisole /kamizɔl/ *n.f.* **~ (de force),** strait-jacket.
camoufl|er /kamufle/ *v.t.* camouflage. **~age** *n.m.* camouflage.
camp /kɑ̃/ *n.m.* camp; (*sport*) side.
campagn|e /kɑ̃paɲ/ *n.f.* country(side); (*mil., pol.*) campaign. **~ard, ~arde** *a.* country; *n.m., f.* countryman, countrywoman.
campanile /kɑ̃panil/ *n.m.* bell-tower.
camp|er /kɑ̃pe/ *v.i.* camp. *—v.t.* plant boldly; (*esquisser*) sketch. **se ~er** *v. pr.* plant o.s. **~ement** *n.m.* encampment. **~eur, ~euse** *n.m., f.* camper.

camping /kɑ̃piŋ/ *n.m.* camping. **(terrain de) ~,** campsite.

campus /kɑ̃pys/ *n.m.* campus.

camus, ~e /kamy, -z/ *a.* (*personne*) pug-nosed.

Canada /kanada/ *n.m.* Canada.

canadien, ~ne /kanadjɛ̃, -jɛn/ *a.* & *n.m., f.* Canadian. —*n.f.* fur-lined jacket.

canaille /kanɑj/ *n.f.* rogue.

can|al (*pl.* **~aux**) /kanal, -o/ *n.m.* (*artificiel*) canal; (*bras de mer*) channel; (*techn., TV*) channel. **par le ~al de,** through.

canalisation /kanalizɑsjɔ̃/ *n.f.* (*tuyaux*) main(s).

canaliser /kanalize/ *v.t.* (*eau*) canalize; (*fig.*) channel.

canapé /kanape/ *n.m.* sofa.

canard /kanar/ *n.m.* duck.

canari /kanari/ *n.m.* canary.

cancans /kɑ̃kɑ̃/ *n.m. pl.* malicious gossip.

canc|er /kɑ̃sɛr/ *n.m.* cancer. **~éreux, ~éreuse** *a.* cancerous; *n.m., f.* cancer victim.

cancre /kɑ̃kr/ *n.m.* dunce.

cancrelat /kɑ̃krəla/ *n.m.* cockroach.

candélabre /kɑ̃delabr/ *n.m.* candelabrum.

candeur /kɑ̃dœr/ *n.f.* naïvety.

candidat, ~e /kɑ̃dida, -t/ *n.m., f.* candidate; (*à un poste*) applicant, candidate (**à,** for). **~ure** /-tyr/ *n.f.* application; (*pol.*) candidacy.

candide /kɑ̃did/ *a.* naïve.

cane /kan/ *n.f.* (female) duck. **~ton** *n.m.* duckling.

canette /kanɛt/ *n.f.* (*de bière*) bottle.

canevas /kanva/ *n.m.* canvas; (*plan*) framework, outline.

caniche /kaniʃ/ *n.m.* poodle.

canicule /kanikyl/ *n.f.* hot summer days.

canif /kanif/ *n.m.* penknife.

canin, ~e /kanɛ̃, -in/ *a.* canine.

caniveau (*pl.* **~x**) /kanivo/ *n.m.* gutter.

canne /kan/ *n.f.* (walking-)stick. **~ à pêche,** fishing-rod. **~ à sucre,** sugar-cane.

cannelle /kanɛl/ *n.f.* cinnamon.

cannibale /kanibal/ *a.* & *n.m./f.* cannibal.

canoë /kanɔe/ *n.m.* canoe; (*sport*) canoeing.

canon /kanɔ̃/ *n.m.* (big) gun; (*d'une arme*) barrel; (*principe, règle*) canon. **~nade** /-ɔnad/ *n.f.* gunfire. **~nier** /-ɔnje/ *n.m.* gunner.

cañon /kaɲɔ̃/ *n.m.* canyon.

canoniser /kanɔnize/ *v.t.* canonize.

canot /kano/ *n.m.* boat. **~ de sauvetage,** lifeboat. **~ pneumatique,** rubber dinghy.

canot|er /kanɔte/ *v.i.* boat. **~age** *n.m.* boating.

cantate /kɑ̃tat/ *n.f.* cantata.

cantatrice /kɑ̃tatris/ *n.f.* opera singer.

cantine /kɑ̃tin/ *n.f.* canteen.

cantique /kɑ̃tik/ *n.m.* hymn.

canton /kɑ̃tɔ̃/ *n.m.* (*en France*) district; (*en Suisse*) canton.

cantonade (à la) /(ala)kɑ̃tɔnad/ *adv.* for all to hear.

cantonner /kɑ̃tɔne/ *v.t.* (*mil.*) billet. **se ~ dans,** confine o.s. to.

cantonnier /kɑ̃tɔnje/ *n.m.* roadman, road mender.

canular /kanylar/ *n.m.* practical joke.

caoutchou|c /kautʃu/ *n.m.* rubber; (*élastique*) rubber band. **~c mousse,** foam rubber. **~ter** *v.t.* rubberize. **~teux, ~teuse** *a.* rubbery.

cap /kap/ *n.m.* cape, headland; (*direction*) course. **doubler** *ou* **franchir le ~ de,** go beyond (the point of). **mettre le ~ sur,** steer a course for.

capable /kapabl/ *a.* able, capable. **~ de qch.,** capable of sth. **~**

de faire, able to do, capable of doing.
capacité /kapasite/ *n.f.* ability; (*contenance*) capacity.
cape /kap/ *n.f.* cape.
capillaire /kapilɛr/ *a.* (*lotion, soins*) hair.
capilotade (en) /(ɑ̃)kapilɔtad/ *adv.* (*fam.*) reduced to a pulp.
capitaine /kapitɛn/ *n.m.* captain.
capit|al, ~ale (*m. pl* **~aux**) /kapital, -o/ *a.* major, fundamental; (*peine, lettre*) capital. —*n.m.* (*pl.* **~aux**) (*comm.*) capital; (*fig.*) stock. **~aux,** (*comm.*) capital. —*n.f.* (*ville, lettre*) capital.
capitalis|te /kapitalist/ *a.* & *n.m./f.* capitalist. **~me** *n.m.* capitalism.
capiteu|x, ~se /kapitø, -z/ *a.* heady.
capitonner /kapitɔne/ *v.t.* pad.
capitul|er /kapityle/ *v.i.* capitulate. **~ation** *n.f.* capitulation.
capor|al (*pl.* **~aux**) /kapɔral, -o/ *n.m.* corporal.
capot /kapo/ *n.m.* (*auto.*) bonnet; (*auto., Amer.*) hood.
capote /kapɔt/ *n.f.* (*auto.*) hood; (*auto., Amer.*) (convertible) top.
capoter /kapɔte/ *v.i.* overturn.
câpre /kɑpr/ *n.f.* (*culin.*) caper.
capric|e /kapris/ *n.m.* whim, caprice. **~ieux, ~ieuse** *a.* capricious; (*appareil*) temperamental.
capsule /kapsyl/ *n.f.* capsule; (*de bouteille, pistolet*) cap.
capter /kapte/ *v.t.* (*eau*) tap; (*émission*) pick up; (*fig.*) win, capture.
captieu|x, ~se /kapsjø, -z/ *a.* specious.
capti|f, ~ve /kaptif, -v/ *a.* & *n.m., f.* captive.
captiver /kaptive/ *v.t.* captivate.
captur|e /kaptyr/ *n.f.* capture. **~er** *v.t.* capture.
capuch|e /kapyʃ/ *n.f.* hood. **~on** *n.m.* hood; (*de stylo*) cap.
caquet /kakɛ/ *n.m.* cackle.
caquet|er /kakte/ *v.i.* cackle. **~age** *n.m.* cackle.
car[1] /kar/ *conj.* because, for.
car[2] /kar/ *n.m.* coach; (*Amer.*) bus.
carabine /karabin/ *n.f.* rifle.
caracoler /karakɔle/ *v.i.* prance.
caract|ère /karaktɛr/ *n.m.* (*nature, lettre*) character. **~ères d'imprimerie,** block letters. **~ériel, ~érielle** *a.* character; *n.m., f.* disturbed child.
caractérisé /karakterize/ *a.* well-defined.
caractériser /karakterize/ *v.t.* characterize. **se ~ par,** be characterized by.
caractéristique /karakteristik/ *a.* & *n.f.* characteristic.
carafe /karaf/ *n.f.* decanter.
carambol|er (se) /(sə)karɑ̃bɔle/ *v. pr.* (*voitures*) smash into each other. **~age** *n.m.* multiple smash-up.
caramel /karamɛl/ *n.m.* caramel.
carapace /karapas/ *n.f.* shell.
carat /kara/ *n.m.* carat.
caravane /karavan/ *n.f.* (*auto.*) caravan; (*auto., Amer.*) trailer; (*convoi*) caravan.
carbone /karbɔn/ *n.m.* carbon. **(papier) ~,** carbon (paper).
carboniser /karbɔnize/ *v.t.* burn (to ashes).
carburant /karbyrɑ̃/ *n.m.* (motor) fuel.
carburateur /karbyratœr/ *n.m.* carburettor; (*Amer.*) carburetor.
carcan /karkɑ̃/ *n.m.* (*contrainte*) yoke.
carcasse /karkas/ *n.f.* carcass; (*d'immeuble, de voiture*) frame.
cardiaque /kardjak/ *a.* heart. —*n.m./f.* heart patient.
cardin|al (*m. pl.* **~aux**) /kardinal, -o/ *a.* cardinal. —*n.m.* (*pl.* **~aux**) cardinal.
Carême /karɛm/ *n.m.* Lent.
carence /karɑ̃s/ *n.f.* inadequacy; (*manque*) deficiency.

carène /karɛn/ *n.f.* hull.
caressant, ~e /karɛsɑ̃, -t/ *a.* endearing.
caress|e /karɛs/ *n.f.* caress. **~er** /-ese/ *v.t.* caress, stroke; (*espoir*) cherish.
cargaison /kargɛzɔ̃/ *n.f.* cargo.
cargo /kargo/ *n.m.* cargo boat.
caricatur|e /karikatyr/ *n.f.* caricature. **~al** (*m. pl.* **~aux**) *a.* caricature-like.
car|ie /kari/ *n.f.* cavity. **la ~ie (dentaire),** tooth decay. **~ié** *a.* (*dent*) decayed.
carillon /karijɔ̃/ *n.m.* chimes; (*horloge*) chiming clock. **~ner** /-jɔne/ *v.i.* chime, peal.
carlingue /karlɛ̃g/ *n.f.* (*d'avion*) cabin.
carnage /karnaʒ/ *n.m.* carnage.
carnass|ier, ~ière /karnasje, -jɛr/ *a.* flesh-eating.
carnaval (*pl.* **~s**) /karnaval/ *n.m.* carnival.
carnet /karnɛ/ *n.m.* notebook; (*de tickets, chèques, etc.*) book. **~ de notes,** school report.
carotte /karɔt/ *n.f.* carrot.
carotter /karɔte/ *v.t.* (*argot*) swindle. **~ qch. à qn.,** (*argot*) wangle sth. from s.o.
carpe /karp/ *n.f.* carp.
carpette /karpɛt/ *n.f.* rug.
carré /kare/ *a.* (*forme, mesure*) square; (*fig.*) straightforward. —*n.m.* square; (*de terrain*) patch.
carreau (*pl.* **~x**) /karo/ *n.m.* (window) pane; (*par terre, au mur*) tile; (*dessin*) check; (*cartes*) diamonds. **à ~x,** check(ed).
carrefour /karfur/ *n.m.* crossroads.
carrel|er /karle/ *v.t.* tile. **~age** *n.m.* tiling; (*sol*) tiles.
carrelet /karlɛ/ *n.m.* (*poisson*) plaice.
carrément /karemɑ̃/ *adv.* straight; (*tout à fait: fam.*) definitely.
carrer (se) /(sə)kare/ *v. pr.* settle firmly.
carrière /karjɛr/ *n.f.* career; (*terrain*) quarry.
carrossable /karɔsabl/ *a.* suitable for vehicles.
carrosse /karɔs/ *n.m.* (horse-drawn) coach.
carross|erie /karɔsri/ *n.f.* (*auto.*) body(work). **~ier** *n.m.* (*auto.*) body-builder.
carrousel /karuzɛl/ *n.m.* (*tournoiement*) merry-go-round.
carrure /karyr/ *n.f.* build.
cartable /kartabl/ *n.m.* satchel.
carte /kart/ *n.f.* card; (*géog.*) map; (*naut.*) chart; (*au restaurant*) menu. **~s,** (*jeu*) cards. **à la ~,** (*manger*) à la carte. **~ blanche,** a free hand. **~ des vins,** wine list. **~ grise,** (car) registration card. **~ postale,** postcard.
cartel /kartɛl/ *n.m.* cartel.
cartilage /kartilaʒ/ *n.m.* cartilage.
carton /kartɔ̃/ *n.m.* cardboard; (*boîte*) (cardboard) box. **~ à dessin,** portfolio. **faire un ~,** (*fam.*) take a pot-shot. **~nage** /-ɔnaʒ/ *n.m.* cardboard packing.
cartonné /kartɔne/ *a.* (*livre*) hardback.
cartouch|e /kartuʃ/ *n.f.* cartridge; (*de cigarettes*) carton. **~ière** *n.f.* cartridge-belt.
cas /kɑ/ *n.m.* case. **au ~ où,** in case. **~ urgent,** emergency. **en aucun ~,** on no account. **en ~ de,** in the event of, in case of. **en tout ~,** in any case. **faire ~ de,** set great store by.
casan|ier, ~ière /kazanje, -jɛr/ *a.* home-loving.
casaque /kazak/ *n.f.* (*de jockey*) shirt.
cascade /kaskad/ *n.f.* waterfall; (*fig.*) spate.
cascadeur /kaskadœr/ *n.m.* stuntman.

case /kɑz/ *n.f.* hut; (*compartiment*) pigeon-hole; (*sur papier*) square.
caser /kaze/ *v.t.* (*mettre*) put; (*loger*) put up; (*dans un travail*) find a job for; (*marier*) marry off.
caserne /kazɛrn/ *n.f.* barracks.
casier /kɑzje/ *n.m.* pigeon-hole, compartment; (*meuble*) cabinet; (*à bouteilles*) rack. **~ judiciaire**, criminal record.
casino /kazino/ *n.m.* casino.
casqu|e /kask/ *n.m.* helmet; (*chez le coiffeur*) (hair-)drier. **~e (à écouteurs)**, headphones. **~é** *a.* wearing a helmet.
casquette /kaskɛt/ *n.f.* cap.
cassant, ~e /kɑsɑ̃, -t/ *a.* brittle; (*brusque*) curt.
casse /kɑs/ *n.f.* (*objets*) breakages. **mettre à la ~**, scrap.
cass|er /kɑse/ *v.t./i.* break; (*annuler*) annul; (*dégrader*) demote. **se ~er** *v. pr.* break. **~er la tête à**, (*fam.*) give a headache to. **~e-cou** *n.m. invar.* daredevil. **~e-croûte** *n.m. invar.* snack. **~e-noisettes** *ou* **~e-noix** *n.m. invar.* nutcrackers. **~e-pieds** *n.m./f. invar.* (*fam.*) pain (in the neck). **~e-tête** *n.m. invar.* (*problème*) headache.
casserole /kasrɔl/ *n.f.* saucepan.
cassette /kasɛt/ *n.f.* casket; (*de magnétophone*) cassette.
cassis /kasis/ *n.m.* black currant; (*sur une route*) dip.
cassoulet /kasulɛ/ *n.m.* stew (of beans and meat).
cassure /kɑsyr/ *n.f.* break.
caste /kast/ *n.f.* caste.
castor /kastɔr/ *n.m.* beaver.
castr|er /kastre/ *v.t.* castrate. **~ation** *n.f.* castration.
cataclysme /kataklism/ *n.m.* cataclysm.
catalogu|e /katalɔg/ *n.m.* catalogue. **~er** *v.t.* catalogue; (*personne: péj.*) label.
catalyseur /katalizœr/ *n.m.* catalyst.
cataphote /katafɔt/ *n.m.* reflector.
cataplasme /kataplasm/ *n.m.* poultice.
catapult|e /katapylt/ *n.f.* catapult. **~er** *v.t.* catapult.
cataracte /katarakt/ *n.f.* cataract.
catastroph|e /katastrɔf/ *n.f.* disaster, catastrophe. **~ique** *a.* catastrophic.
catch /katʃ/ *n.m.* (all-in) wrestling. **~eur, ~euse** *n.m., f.* (all-in) wrestler.
catéchisme /kateʃism/ *n.m.* catechism.
catégorie /kategɔri/ *n.f.* category.
catégorique /kategɔrik/ *a.* categorical.
cathédrale /katedral/ *n.f.* cathedral.
cathode /katɔd/ *n.f.* cathode.
catholi|que /katɔlik/ *a.* Catholic. **~cisme** *n.m.* Catholicism.
catimini (en) /(ɑ̃)katimini/ *adv.* on the sly.
cauchemar /koʃmar/ *n.m.* nightmare.
cause /koz/ *n.f.* cause; (*jurid.*) case. **à ~ de**, because of. **en ~**, (*en jeu, concerné*) involved. **pour ~ de**, on account of.
caus|er /koze/ *v.t.* cause. —*v.i.* chat. **~erie** *n.f.* talk. **~ette** *n.f.* **faire la ~ette**, have a chat.
caustique /kostik/ *a.* caustic.
cauteleu|x, ~se /kotlø, -z/ *a.* wily.
caution /kosjɔ̃/ *n.f.* surety; (*jurid.*) bail; (*appui*) backing. **sous ~**, on bail.
cautionn|er /kosjɔne/ *v.t.* guarantee; (*soutenir*) back. **~ement** *n.m.* (*somme*) guarantee.
cavalcade /kavalkad/ *n.f.* (*fam.*) stampede, rush.
cavalerie /kavalri/ *n.f.* (*mil.*) cavalry; (*au cirque*) horses.
caval|ier, ~ière /kavalje, -jɛr/ *a.* offhand. —*n.m., f.* rider; (*pour*

danser) partner. —*n.m.* (*échecs*) knight.
cave[1] /kav/ *n.f.* cellar.
cave[2] /kav/ *a.* sunken.
caveau (*pl.* **~x**) /kavo/ *n.m.* vault.
caverne /kavɛrn/ *n.f.* cave.
caviar /kavjar/ *n.m.* caviare.
cavité /kavite/ *n.f.* cavity.
ce[1], **c'*** /sə, s/ *pron.* it, that. **c'est,** it *ou* that is. **ce sont,** they are. **c'est un chanteur/une chanteuse/** *etc.*, he/she is a singer/*etc.* **ce qui, ce que,** what. **ce que c'est bon/** *etc.***!**, how good/*etc.* it is! **tout ce qui, tout ce que,** everything that.
ce[2] *ou* **cet***, **cette** (*pl.* **ces**) /sə, sɛt, se/ *a.* that; (*proximité*) this. **ces,** those; (*proximité*) these.
ceci /səsi/ *pron.* this.
cécité /sesite/ *n.f.* blindness.
céder /sede/ *v.t.* give up. —*v.i.* (*se rompre*) give way; (*se soumettre*) give in.
cédille /sedij/ *n.f.* cedilla.
cèdre /sɛdr/ *n.m.* cedar.
CEE *abrév.* (*Communauté économique européenne*) EEC.
ceinture /sɛ̃tyr/ *n.f.* belt; (*taille*) waist; (*de bus, métro*) circle (line). **~ de sauvetage,** lifebelt. **~ de sécurité,** seat-belt.
ceinturer /sɛ̃tyre/ *v.t.* seize round the waist; (*entourer*) surround.
cela /səla/ *pron.* it, that; (*pour désigner*) that. **~ va de soi,** it is obvious.
célèbre /selɛbr/ *a.* famous.
célébr|er /selebre/ *v.t.* celebrate. **~ation** *n.f.* celebration (**de,** of).
célébrité /selebrite/ *n.f.* fame; (*personne*) celebrity.
céleri /sɛlri/ *n.m.* (*en branches*) celery. **~(-rave),** celeriac.
céleste /selɛst/ *a.* celestial.
célibat /seliba/ *n.m.* celibacy.
célibataire /selibatɛr/ *a.* unmarried. —*n.m.* bachelor. —*n.f.* unmarried woman.
celle, celles /sɛl/ *voir* **celui.**
cellier /selje/ *n.m.* store-room (*for wine*).
cellophane /selɔfan/ *n.f.* (P.) Cellophane (P.).
cellul|e /selyl/ *n.f.* cell. **~aire** *a.* cell. **fourgon** *ou* **voiture ~aire,** prison van.
celui, celle (*pl.* **ceux, celles**) /səlɥi, sɛl, sø/ *pron.* the one. **~ de mon ami,** my friend's. **~-ci,** this (one). **~-là,** that (one). **ceux-ci,** these (ones). **ceux-là,** those (ones).
cendr|e /sɑ̃dr/ *n.f.* ash. **~é** *a.* (*couleur*) ashen.
cendrier /sɑ̃drije/ *n.m.* ashtray.
censé /sɑ̃se/ *a.* **être ~ faire,** be supposed to do.
censeur /sɑ̃sœr/ *n.m.* censor; (*scol.*) assistant headmaster.
censur|e /sɑ̃syr/ *n.f.* censorship. **~er** *v.t.* censor; (*critiquer*) censure.
cent (*pl.* **~s**) /sɑ̃/ (*generally* /sɑ̃t/ *pl.* /sɑ̃z/ *before vowel*) *a.* & *n.m.* (a) hundred. **~ un** /sɑ̃œ̃/ a hundred and one.
centaine /sɑ̃tɛn/ *n.f.* hundred. **une ~ (de),** (about) a hundred.
centenaire /sɑ̃tnɛr/ *n.m.* (*anniversaire*) centenary.
centième /sɑ̃tjɛm/ *a.* & *n.m./f.* hundredth.
centigrade /sɑ̃tigrad/ *a.* centigrade.
centilitre /sɑ̃tilitr/ *n.m.* centilitre.
centime /sɑ̃tim/ *n.m.* centime.
centimètre /sɑ̃timɛtr/ *n.m.* centimetre; (*ruban*) tape-measure.
centr|al, ~ale (*m. pl.* **~aux**) /sɑ̃tral, -o/ *a.* central. —*n.m.* (*pl.* **~aux**). **~al (téléphonique),** (telephone) exchange. —*n.f.* power-station. **~aliser** *v.t.* centralize.
centr|e /sɑ̃tr/ *n.m.* centre. **~e-ville** *n.m.* town centre. **~er** *v.t.* centre.

centupl|e /sɑ̃typl/ *n.m.* **le ~e (de),** a hundredfold. **au ~e,** a hundredfold. **~er** *v.t./i.* increase a hundredfold.

cep /sɛp/ *n.m.* vine stock.

cépage /sepaʒ/ *n.m.* (variety of) vine.

cependant /səpɑ̃dɑ̃/ *adv.* however.

céramique /seramik/ *n.f.* ceramic; (*art*) ceramics.

cerceau (*pl.* **~x**) /sɛrso/ *n.m.* hoop.

cercle /sɛrkl/ *n.m.* circle; (*cerceau*) hoop. **~ vicieux,** vicious circle.

cercueil /sɛrkœj/ *n.m.* coffin.

céréale /sereal/ *n.f.* cereal.

cérébr|al (*m. pl.* **~aux**) /serebral, -o/ *a.* cerebral.

cérémonial (*pl.* **~s**) /seremɔnjal/ *n.m.* ceremonial.

cérémon|ie /seremɔni/ *n.f.* ceremony. **~ie(s),** (*façons*) fuss. **~ieux, ~ieuse** *a.* ceremonious.

cerf /sɛr/ *n.m.* stag.

cerf-volant (*pl.* **cerfs-volants**) /sɛrvɔlɑ̃/ *n.m.* kite.

ceris|e /sriz/ *n.f.* cherry. **~ier** *n.m.* cherry tree.

cerne /sɛrn/ *n.m.* ring.

cern|er /sɛrne/ *v.t.* surround; (*question*) define. **les yeux ~és,** with rings under one's eyes.

certain, ~e /sɛrtɛ̃, -ɛn/ *a.* certain; (*sûr*) certain, sure (**de,** of; **que,** that). *—pron.* **~s,** certain people. **d'un ~ âge,** past one's prime. **un ~ temps,** some time.

certainement /sɛrtɛnmɑ̃/ *adv.* certainly.

certes /sɛrt/ *adv.* indeed.

certificat /sɛrtifika/ *n.m.* certificate.

certif|ier /sɛrtifje/ *v.t.* certify. **~ier qch. à qn.,** assure s.o. of sth. **~ié** *a.* (*professeur*) qualified.

certitude /sɛrtityd/ *n.f.* certainty.

cerveau (*pl.* **~x**) /sɛrvo/ *n.m.* brain.

cervelas /sɛrvəla/ *n.m.* saveloy.

cervelle /sɛrvɛl/ *n.f.* brain.

ces /se/ *voir* **ce**².

césarienne /sezarjɛn/ *n.f.* Caesarean (section).

cessation /sɛsɑsjɔ̃/ *n.f.* suspension.

cesse /sɛs/ *n.f.* **n'avoir de ~ que,** have no rest until. **sans ~,** incessantly.

cesser /sese/ *v.t./i.* stop. **~ de faire,** stop doing.

cessez-le-feu /seselfø/ *n.m. invar.* cease-fire.

cession /sɛsjɔ̃/ *n.f.* transfer.

c'est-à-dire /setadir/ *conj.* that is (to say).

cet, cette /sɛt/ *voir* **ce**².

ceux /sø/ *voir* **celui.**

chacal (*pl.* **~s**) /ʃakal/ *n.m.* jackal.

chacun, ~e /ʃakœ̃, -yn/ *pron.* each (one), every one; (*tout le monde*) everyone.

chagrin /ʃagrɛ̃/ *n.m.* sorrow. **avoir du ~,** be distressed. **~er** /-ine/ *v.t.* distress.

chahut /ʃay/ *n.m.* row, din. **~er** /-te/ *v.i.* make a row; *v.t.* be rowdy with. **~eur, ~euse** /-tœr, -tøz/ *n.m., f.* rowdy.

chaîn|e /ʃɛn/ *n.f.* chain; (*de télévision*) channel. **~e de montage/fabrication,** assembly/production line. **~e hi-fi,** hi-fi system. **en ~e,** (*accidents*) multiple. **~ette** *n.f.* (small) chain. **~on** *n.m.* link.

chair /ʃɛr/ *n.f.* flesh. **bien en ~,** plump. **~ à saucisses,** sausage meat. **la ~ de poule,** goose-flesh.

chaire /ʃɛr/ *n.f.* (*d'église*) pulpit; (*univ.*) chair.

chaise /ʃɛz/ *n.f.* chair. **~ longue,** (*siège pliant*) deck-chair.

chaland /ʃalɑ̃/ *n.m.* barge.

châle /ʃɑl/ *n.m.* shawl.

chalet /ʃalɛ/ *n.m.* chalet.

chaleur /ʃalœr/ *n.f.* heat; (*moins intense*) warmth; (*d'un accueil, d'une couleur*) warmth. **~eux, ~euse** *a.* warm.

challenge /ʃalɑ̃ʒ/ *n.m.* contest.
chaloupe /ʃalup/ *n.f.* launch, boat.
chalumeau (*pl.* **~x**) /ʃalymo/ *n.m.* blowlamp; (*Amer.*) blowtorch.
chalut /ʃaly/ *n.m.* trawl-net. **~ier** /-tje/ *n.m.* trawler.
chamailler (se) /(sə)ʃamɑje/ *v. pr.* squabble.
chambarder /ʃɑ̃barde/ *v.t.* (*fam.*) turn upside down.
chambre /ʃɑ̃br/ *n.f.* (bed)room; (*pol., jurid.*) chamber. **~ à air,** inner tube. **~ à coucher,** bedroom. **~ à un lit/deux lits,** single/double room. **~ forte,** strong-room.
chambrer /ʃɑ̃bre/ *v.t.* (*vin*) bring to room temperature.
chameau (*pl.* **~x**) /ʃamo/ *n.m.* camel.
chamois /ʃamwa/ *n.m.* chamois.
champ /ʃɑ̃/ *n.m.* field. **~ de bataille,** battlefield. **~ de courses,** racecourse.
champagne /ʃɑ̃paɲ/ *n.m.* champagne.
champêtre /ʃɑ̃pɛtr/ *a.* rural.
champignon /ʃɑ̃piɲɔ̃/ *n.m.* mushroom.
champion, ~ne /ʃɑ̃pjɔ̃, -jɔn/ *n.m., f.* champion. **~nat** /-jɔna/ *n.m.* championship.
chance /ʃɑ̃s/ *n.f.* (good) luck; (*possibilité*) chance. **avoir de la ~,** be lucky. **une ~,** a stroke of luck.
chanceler /ʃɑ̃sle/ *v.i.* stagger; (*fig.*) falter.
chancelier /ʃɑ̃səlje/ *n.m.* chancellor.
chanceu|x, ~se /ʃɑ̃sø, -z/ *a.* lucky.
chancre /ʃɑ̃kr/ *n.m.* canker.
chandail /ʃɑ̃daj/ *n.m.* sweater.
chandelier /ʃɑ̃dəlje/ *n.m.* candlestick.
chandelle /ʃɑ̃dɛl/ *n.f.* candle.
change /ʃɑ̃ʒ/ *n.m.* (foreign) exchange.
changeant, ~e /ʃɑ̃ʒɑ̃, -t/ *a.* changeable.
changement /ʃɑ̃ʒmɑ̃/ *n.m.* change.
changer /ʃɑ̃ʒe/ *v.t./i.* change. **se ~** *v. pr.* change (one's clothes). **~ de nom/voiture,** change one's name/car. **~ de place/train,** change places/trains. **~ de direction,** change direction. **~ d'avis** *ou* **d'idée,** change one's mind.
changeur /ʃɑ̃ʒœr/ *n.m.* **~ automatique,** (money) change machine.
chanoine /ʃanwan/ *n.m.* canon.
chanson /ʃɑ̃sɔ̃/ *n.f.* song.
chant /ʃɑ̃/ *n.m.* singing; (*chanson*) song; (*religieux*) hymn.
chantage /ʃɑ̃taʒ/ *n.m.* blackmail.
chant|er /ʃɑ̃te/ *v.t./i.* sing. **si cela vous ~e,** (*fam.*) if you feel like it. **~eur, ~euse** *n.m., f.* singer.
chantier /ʃɑ̃tje/ *n.m.* building site. **~ naval,** shipyard. **mettre en ~,** get under way, start.
chantonner /ʃɑ̃tɔne/ *v.t./i.* hum.
chanvre /ʃɑ̃vr/ *n.m.* hemp.
chao|s /kao/ *n.m.* chaos. **~tique** /kaɔtik/ *a.* chaotic.
chaparder /ʃaparde/ *v.t.* (*fam.*) filch.
chapeau (*pl.* **~x**) /ʃapo/ *n.m.* hat; (*techn.*) cap.
chapelet /ʃaplɛ/ *n.m.* rosary; (*fig.*) string. **dire son ~,** tell one's beads, say the rosary.
chapelle /ʃapɛl/ *n.f.* chapel. **~ ardente,** chapel of rest.
chapelure /ʃaplyr/ *n.f.* breadcrumbs.
chaperon /ʃaprɔ̃/ *n.m.* chaperon. **~ner** /-ɔne/ *v.t.* chaperon.
chapiteau (*pl.* **~x**) /ʃapito/ *n.m.* (*de cirque*) big top; (*de colonne*) capital.
chapitre /ʃapitr/ *n.m.* chapter; (*fig.*) subject.
chapitrer /ʃapitre/ *v.t.* reprimand.
chaque /ʃak/ *a.* every, each.
char /ʃar/ *n.m.* (*mil.*) tank; (*de*

carnaval) float; (*charrette*) cart; (*dans l'antiquité*) chariot.

charabia /ʃarabja/ *n.m.* (*fam.*) gibberish.

charade /ʃarad/ *n.f.* (*jeu*) charade.

charbon /ʃarbɔ̃/ *n.m.* coal. **~ de bois,** charcoal. **~nages** /-ɔnaʒ/ *n.m.pl.* coal-mines. **~nier** /-ɔnje/ *n.m.* coal-merchant.

charcut|erie /ʃarkytri/ *n.f.* pork-butcher's shop; (*aliments*) (cooked) pork meats. **~ier, ~ière** *n.m., f.* pork-butcher.

chardon /ʃardɔ̃/ *n.m.* thistle.

charge /ʃarʒ/ *n.f.* load, burden; (*mil., électr., jurid.*) charge; (*mission*) responsibility. **~s,** expenses; (*de locataire*) service charges. **être à la ~ de,** be the responsibility of. **~s sociales,** social security contributions. **prendre en ~,** take charge of; (*transporter*) give a ride to.

chargé /ʃarʒe/ *a.* (*arbre*) laden; (*journée*) busy; (*langue*) coated.

charger /ʃarʒe/ *v.t.* load; (*attaquer*) charge; (*batterie*) charge. —*v.i.* (*attaquer*) charge. **se ~ de,** take charge *ou* care of. **~ qn. de,** weigh s.o. down with; (*tâche*) entrust s.o. with. **~ qn. de faire,** instruct s.o. to do. **chargement** /-əmɑ̃/ *n.m.* loading; (*objets*) load.

chariot /ʃarjo/ *n.m.* (*à roulettes*) trolley; (*charrette*) cart.

charitable /ʃaritabl/ *a.* charitable.

charité /ʃarite/ *n.f.* charity. **faire la ~,** give to charity. **faire la ~ à,** give to.

charlatan /ʃarlatɑ̃/ *n.m.* charlatan.

charmant, ~e /ʃarmɑ̃, -t/ *a.* charming.

charm|e /ʃarm/ *n.m.* charm. **~er** *v.t.* charm. **~eur, ~euse** *n.m., f.* charmer.

charnel, ~le /ʃarnɛl/ *a.* carnal.

charnier /ʃarnje/ *n.m.* mass grave.

charnière /ʃarnjɛr/ *n.f.* hinge. **à la ~ de,** at the meeting point between.

charnu /ʃarny/ *a.* fleshy.

charpent|e /ʃarpɑ̃t/ *n.f.* framework; (*carrure*) build. **~é** *a.* built.

charpentier /ʃarpɑ̃tje/ *n.m.* carpenter.

charpie (en) /(ɑ̃)ʃarpi/ *adv.* in(to) shreds.

charretier /ʃartje/ *n.m.* carter.

charrette /ʃarɛt/ *n.f.* cart.

charrier /ʃarje/ *v.t.* carry.

charrue /ʃary/ *n.f.* plough.

charte /ʃart/ *n.f.* charter.

charter /ʃartɛr/ *n.m.* charter flight.

chasse /ʃas/ *n.f.* hunting; (*au fusil*) shooting; (*poursuite*) chase; (*recherche*) hunt. **~ (d'eau),** (toilet) flush. **~ sous-marine,** underwater fishing.

châsse /ʃɑs/ *n.f.* shrine, reliquary.

chass|er /ʃase/ *v.t./i.* hunt; (*faire partir*) chase away; (*odeur, employé*) get rid of. **~e-neige** *n.m. invar.* snow-plough. **~eur, ~euse** *n.m, f.* hunter; *n.m.* pageboy; (*avion*) fighter.

châssis /ʃɑsi/ *n.m.* frame; (*auto.*) chassis.

chaste /ʃast/ *a.* chaste. **~té** /-əte/ *n.f.* chastity.

chat, ~te /ʃa, ʃat/ *n.m., f.* cat.

châtaigne /ʃɑtɛɲ/ *n.f.* chestnut.

châtain /ʃɑtɛ̃/ *a. invar.* chestnut (brown).

château (*pl.* **~x**) /ʃɑto/ *n.m.* castle; (*manoir*) manor. **~ d'eau,** water-tower. **~ fort,** fortified castle.

châtelain, ~e /ʃatlɛ̃, -ɛn/ *n.m., f.* lord of the manor, lady of the manor.

châtier /ʃɑtje/ *v.t.* chastise; (*style*) refine.

châtiment /ʃɑtimɑ̃/ *n.m.* punishment.

chaton /ʃatɔ̃/ *n.m.* (*chat*) kitten.
chatouill|er /ʃatuje/ *v.t.* tickle. **~ement** *n.m.* tickling.
chatouilleu|x, ~se /ʃatujø, -z/ *a.* ticklish; (*susceptible*) touchy.
chatoyer /ʃatwaje/ *v.i.* glitter.
châtrer /ʃɑtre/ *v.t.* castrate.
chatte /ʃat/ *voir* **chat.**
chaud, ~e /ʃo, ʃod/ *a.* warm; (*brûlant*) hot; (*vif: fig.*) warm. —*n.m.* heat. **au ~,** in the warm(th). **avoir ~,** be warm; be hot. **il fait ~,** it is warm; it is hot. **~ement** /-dmɑ̃/ *adv.* warmly; (*disputé*) hotly.
chaudière /ʃodjɛr/ *n.f.* boiler.
chaudron /ʃodrɔ̃/ *n.m.* cauldron.
chauffage /ʃofaʒ/ *n.m.* heating. **~ central,** central heating.
chauffard /ʃofar/ *n.m.* reckless driver.
chauff|er /ʃofe/ *v.t./i.* heat (up). **se ~er** *v. pr.* warm o.s. (up). **~e-eau** *n.m. invar.* water-heater.
chauffeur /ʃofœr/ *n.m.* driver; (*aux gages de qn.*) chauffeur.
chaum|e /ʃom/ *n.m.* (*de toit*) thatch. **~ière** *n.f.* thatched cottage.
chaussée /ʃose/ *n.f.* road(way).
chauss|er /ʃose/ *v.t.* (*chaussures*) put on; (*enfant*) put shoes on (to). **se ~er** *v. pr* put one's shoes on. **~er bien,** (*aller*) fit well. **~er du 35**/ *etc.*, take a size 35/*etc.* shoe. **~e-pied** *n.m.* shoehorn. **~eur** *n.m.* shoemaker.
chaussette /ʃosɛt/ *n.f.* sock.
chausson /ʃosɔ̃/ *n.m.* slipper. **~ (aux pommes),** (apple) turnover.
chaussure /ʃosyr/ *n.f.* shoe.
chauve /ʃov/ *a.* bald.
chauve-souris (*pl.* **chauves-souris**) /ʃovsuri/ *n.f.* bat.
chauvin, ~e /ʃovɛ̃, -in/ *a.* chauvinistic. —*n.m., f.* chauvinist. **~isme** /-inism/ *n.m.* chauvinism.
chaux /ʃo/ *n.f.* lime.
chavirer /ʃavire/ *v.t./i.* (*bateau*) capsize.
chef /ʃɛf/ *n.m.* leader, head; (*culin.*) chef; (*de tribu*) chief. **~ d'accusation,** (*jurid.*) charge. **~ d'équipe,** foreman; (*sport*) captain. **~ d'État,** head of State. **~ de famille,** head of the family. **~ de file,** (*pol.*) leader. **~ de gare,** station-master. **~ d'orchestre,** conductor. **~ de service,** department head. **~-lieu** (*pl.* **~s-lieux**) *n.m.* county town.
chef-d'œuvre (*pl.* **chefs-d'œuvre**) /ʃɛdœvr/ *n.m.* masterpiece.
cheik /ʃɛk/ *n.m.* sheikh.
chemin /ʃmɛ̃/ *n.m.* path, road; (*direction, trajet*) way. **beaucoup de ~ à faire,** a long way to go. **~ de fer,** railway. **en** *ou* **par ~ de fer,** by rail. **~ de halage,** tow-path. **~ vicinal,** by-road. **se mettre en ~,** start out.
cheminée /ʃmine/ *n.f.* chimney; (*intérieure*) fireplace; (*encadrement*) mantelpiece; (*de bateau*) funnel.
chemin|er /ʃmine/ *v.i.* plod; (*fig.*) progress. **~ement** *n.m.* progress.
cheminot /ʃmino/ *n.m.* railway-man; (*Amer.*) railroad man.
chemis|e /ʃmiz/ *n.f.* shirt; (*dossier*) folder; (*de livre*) jacket. **~e de nuit,** night-dress. **~erie** *n.f.* (*magasin*) man's shop. **~ette** *n.f.* short-sleeved shirt.
chemisier /ʃmizje/ *n.m.* blouse.
chen|al (*pl.* **~aux**) /ʃənal, -o/ *n.m.* channel.
chêne /ʃɛn/ *n.m.* oak.
chenil /ʃni(l)/ *n.m.* kennels.
chenille /ʃnij/ *n.f.* caterpillar.
chenillette /ʃnijɛt/ *n.f.* tracked vehicle.
cheptel /ʃɛptɛl/ *n.m.* livestock.
chèque /ʃɛk/ *n.m.* cheque. **~ de voyage,** traveller's cheque.

chéquier /ʃekje/ *n.m.* cheque-book.
cher, chère /ʃɛr/ *a.* dear, expensive; (*aimé*) dear. —*adv.* (*coûter, payer*) a lot (of money). —*n.m., f.* **mon ~, ma chère,** my dear.
chercher /ʃɛrʃe/ *v.t.* look for; (*aide, paix, gloire*) seek. **aller ~,** go and get *ou* fetch, go for. **~ à faire,** attempt to do. **~ la petite bête,** be finicky.
chercheu|r, ~se /ʃɛrʃœr, -øz/ *n.m., f.* research worker.
chèrement /ʃɛrmɑ̃/ *adv.* dearly.
chéri, ~e /ʃeri/ *a.* beloved. —*n.m., f.* darling.
chérir /ʃerir/ *v.t.* cherish.
cherté /ʃɛrte/ *n.f.* high cost.
chéti|f, ~ve /ʃetif, -v/ *a.* puny.
chev|al (*pl.* **~aux**) /ʃval, -o/ *n.m.* horse. **~al (vapeur),** horse-power. **à ~al,** on horseback. **à ~al sur,** straddling. **faire du ~al,** ride (a horse).
chevaleresque /ʃvalrɛsk/ *a.* chivalrous.
chevalerie /ʃvalri/ *n.f.* chivalry.
chevalet /ʃvalɛ/ *n.m.* easel.
chevalier /ʃvalje/ *n.m.* knight.
chevalière /ʃvaljɛr/ *n.f.* signet-ring.
chevalin, ~e /ʃvalɛ̃, -in/ *a.* (*boucherie*) horse; (*espèce, regard*) equine.
chevauchée /ʃvoʃe/ *n.f.* (horse) ride.
chevaucher /ʃvoʃe/ *v.t.* straddle. —*v.i.*, **se ~** *v. pr.* overlap.
chevelu /ʃəvly/ *a.* hairy.
chevelure /ʃəvlyr/ *n.f.* hair.
chevet /ʃvɛ/ *n.m.* **au ~ de,** at the bedside of.
cheveu (*pl.* **~x**) /ʃvø/ *n.m.* (*poil*) hair. **~x,** (*chevelure*) hair.
cheville /ʃvij/ *n.f.* ankle; (*fiche*) peg, pin; (*pour mur*) (wall) plug.
chèvre /ʃɛvr/ *n.f.* goat.
chevreau (*pl.* **~x**) /ʃəvro/ *n.m.* kid.
chevreuil /ʃəvrœj/ *n.m.* roe (-deer); (*culin.*) venison.
chevron /ʃəvrɔ̃/ *n.m.* (*poutre*) rafter. **à ~s,** herring-bone.
chevronné /ʃəvrɔne/ *a.* experienced, seasoned.
chevroter /ʃəvrɔte/ *v.i.* quaver.
chewing-gum /ʃwiŋgɔm/ *n.m.* chewing-gum.
chez /ʃe/ *prép.* at *ou* to the house of; (*parmi*) among; (*dans le caractère ou l'œuvre de*) in. **~ le boucher/** *etc.*, at the butcher's/*etc.* **~ soi,** at home; (*avec direction*) home. **~-soi** *n.m. invar.* one's own house.
chic /ʃik/ *a. invar.* smart; (*gentil*) decent. —*n.m.* style. **avoir le ~ pour,** have the knack of. **~ (alors)!,** great!
chicane /ʃikan/ *n.f.* zigzag; (*querelle*) quarrel.
chiche /ʃiʃ/ *a.* mean (**de,** with). **~ (que je le fais)!,** (*fam.*) I bet you I will, can, *etc.*
chichis /ʃiʃi/ *n.m. pl.* (*fam.*) fuss.
chicorée /ʃikɔre/ *n.f.* (*frisée*) endive; (*à café*) chicory.
chien, ~ne /ʃjɛ̃, ʃjɛn/ *n.m.* dog. —*n.f.* dog, bitch. **~ de garde,** watch-dog. **~-loup** *n.m.* (*pl.* **~s-loups**) wolfhound.
chiffon /ʃifɔ̃/ *n.m.* rag.
chiffonner /ʃifɔne/ *v.t.* crumple; (*préoccuper: fam.*) bother.
chiffonnier /ʃifɔnje/ *n.m.* rag-and-bone man.
chiffre /ʃifr/ *n.m.* figure; (*code*) code. **~s arabes/romains,** Arabic/Roman numerals. **~ d'affaires,** turnover.
chiffrer /ʃifre/ *v.t.* set a figure to, assess; (*texte*) encode. **se ~ à,** amount to.
chignon /ʃiɲɔ̃/ *n.m.* bun, chignon.
Chili /ʃili/ *n.m.* Chile.
chilien, ~ne /ʃiljɛ̃, -jɛn/ *a.* & *n.m., f.* Chilean.
chim|ère /ʃimɛr/ *n.f.* fantasy. **~érique** *a.* fanciful.

chim|ie /ʃimi/ *n.f.* chemistry. **~ique** *a.* chemical. **~iste** *n.m./f.* chemist.

chimpanzé /ʃɛ̃pɑ̃ze/ *n.m.* chimpanzee.

Chine /ʃin/ *n.f.* China.

chinois, ~e /ʃinwa, -z/ *a.* & *n.m., f.* Chinese. —*n.m.* (*lang.*) Chinese.

chiot /ʃjo/ *n.m.* pup(py).

chiper /ʃipe/ *v.t.* (*fam.*) swipe.

chipoter /ʃipɔte/ *v.i.* (*manger*) nibble; (*discuter*) quibble.

chips /ʃips/ *n.m. pl.* crisps; (*Amer.*) chips.

chiquenaude /ʃiknod/ *n.f.* flick.

chiromanc|ie /kirɔmɑ̃si/ *n.f.* palmistry. **~ien, ~ienne** *n.m., f.* palmist.

chirurgic|al (*m. pl.* **~aux**) /ʃiryrʒikal, -o/ *a.* surgical.

chirurg|ie /ʃiryrʒi/ *n.f.* surgery. **~ie esthétique,** plastic surgery. **~ien** *n.m.* surgeon.

chlore /klɔr/ *n.m.* chlorine.

choc /ʃɔk/ *n.m.* (*heurt*) impact, shock; (*émotion*) shock; (*collision*) crash; (*affrontement*) clash; (*méd.*) shock.

chocolat /ʃɔkɔla/ *n.m.* chocolate. **~ au lait,** milk chocolate.

chœur /kœr/ *n.m.* chorus; (*chanteurs, nef*) choir. **en ~,** in chorus.

chois|ir /ʃwazir/ *v.t.* choose, select. **~i** *a.* carefully chosen; (*passage*) selected.

choix /ʃwa/ *n.m.* choice, selection. **au ~,** according to preference. **de ~,** choice. **de premier ~,** top quality.

choléra /kɔlera/ *n.m.* cholera.

chômage /ʃomaʒ/ *n.m.* unemployment. **en ~,** unemployed. **mettre en ~ technique,** lay off.

chôm|er /ʃome/ *v.i.* be unemployed; (*usine*) lie idle. **~eur, ~euse** *n.m., f.* unemployed person. **les ~eurs,** the unemployed.

chope /ʃɔp/ *n.f.* tankard.

choquer /ʃɔke/ *v.t.* shock; (*commotionner*) shake; (*verres*) clink.

choral, ~e (*m. pl.* **~s**) /kɔral/ *a.* choral. —*n.f.* choir, choral society.

chorégraph|ie /kɔregrafi/ *n.f.* choreography. **~e** *n.m./f.* choreographer.

choriste /kɔrist/ *n.m./f.* chorister.

chose /ʃoz/ *n.f.* thing. **(très) peu de ~,** nothing much.

chou (*pl.* **~x**) /ʃu/ *n.m.* cabbage. **~ (à la crème),** cream puff. **~x de Bruxelles,** Brussels sprouts. **mon petit ~,** (*fam.*) my little dear.

choucas /ʃuka/ *n.m.* jackdaw.

chouchou, ~te /ʃuʃu, -t/ *n.m., f.* pet, darling.

choucroute /ʃukrut/ *n.f.* sauerkraut.

chouette[1] /ʃwɛt/ *n.f.* owl.

chouette[2] /ʃwɛt/ *a.* (*fam.*) super.

chou-fleur (*pl.* **choux-fleurs**) /ʃuflœr/ *n.m.* cauliflower.

choyer /ʃwaje/ *v.t.* pamper.

chrétien, ~ne /kretjɛ̃, -jɛn/ *a.* & *n.m., f.* Christian. **~nement** /-jɛnmɑ̃/ *adv.* in a Christian way.

Christ /krist/ *n.m.* **le ~,** Christ.

christianisme /kristjanism/ *n.m.* Christianity.

chrom|e /krom/ *n.m.* chromium, chrome. **~é** *a.* chromium-plated.

chromosome /krɔmozom/ *n.m.* chromosome.

chroniqu|e /krɔnik/ *a.* chronic. —*n.f.* (*rubrique*) column; (*nouvelles*) news; (*annales*) chronicle. **~eur** *n.m.* columnist; (*historien*) chronicler.

chronolog|ie /krɔnɔlɔʒi/ *n.f.* chronology. **~ique** *a.* chronological.

chronom|ètre /krɔnɔmɛtr/ *n.m.* stop-watch. **~étrer** *v.t.* time.

chrysanthème /krizɑ̃tɛm/ *n.m.* chrysanthemum.

chuchot|er /ʃyʃɔte/ *v.t./i.* whisper. **~ement** *n.m.* whisper(ing).

chuinter /ʃwɛ̃te/ *v.i.* hiss.
chut /ʃyt/ *int.* shush.
chute /ʃyt/ *n.f.* fall; (*déchet*) scrap. **~ (d'eau)**, waterfall. **~ du jour**, nightfall. **~ de pluie**, rainfall.
chuter /ʃyte/ *v.i.* (*fam.*) fall.
Chypre /ʃipr/ *n.f.* Cyprus.
-ci /si/ *adv.* (*après un nom précédé de ce, cette, etc.*) **cet homme-ci**, this man. **ces maisons-ci**, these houses.
ci- /si/ *adv.* here. **ci-après**, hereafter. **ci-contre**, opposite. **ci-dessous**, below. **ci-dessus**, above. **ci-gît**, here lies. **ci-inclus**, **ci-incluse**, **ci-joint**, **ci-jointe**, enclosed.
cible /sibl/ *n.f.* target.
ciboul|e /sibul/ *n.f.*, **~ette** *n.f.* chive(s).
cicatrice /sikatris/ *n.f.* scar.
cicatriser /sikatrize/ *v.t.*, **se ~** *v. pr.* heal (up).
cidre /sidr/ *n.m.* cider.
ciel (*pl.* **cieux, ciels**) /sjɛl, sjø/ *n.m.* sky; (*relig.*) heaven. **cieux**, (*relig.*) heaven.
cierge /sjɛrʒ/ *n.m.* candle.
cigale /sigal/ *n.f.* cicada.
cigare /sigar/ *n.m.* cigar.
cigarette /sigarɛt/ *n.f.* cigarette.
cigogne /sigɔɲ/ *n.f.* stork.
cil /sil/ *n.m.* (eye)lash.
ciller /sije/ *v.i.* blink.
cime /sim/ *n.f.* peak, tip.
ciment /simɑ̃/ *n.m.* cement. **~er** /-te/ *v.t.* cement.
cimetière /simtjɛr/ *n.m.* cemetery. **~ de voitures**, breaker's yard.
cinéaste /sineast/ *n.m.*/*f.* film-maker.
ciné-club /sineklœb/ *n.m.* film society.
cinéma /sinema/ *n.m.* cinema. **~tographique** *a.* cinema.
cinémathèque /sinematɛk/ *n.f.* film library; (*salle*) film theatre.
cinéphile /sinefil/ *n.m.*/*f.* film buff.
cinétique /sinetik/ *a.* kinetic.
cinglant, ~e /sɛ̃glɑ̃, -t/ *a.* biting.
cinglé /sɛ̃gle/ *a.* (*fam.*) crazy.
cingler /sɛ̃gle/ *v.t.* lash.
cinq /sɛ̃k/ *a.* & *n.m.* five. **~ième** *a.* & *n.m.*/*f.* fifth.
cinquantaine /sɛ̃kɑ̃tɛn/ *n.f.* **une ~ (de)**, about fifty.
cinquant|e /sɛ̃kɑ̃t/ *a.* & *n.m.* fifty. **~ième** *a.* & *n.m.*/*f.* fiftieth.
cintre /sɛ̃tr/ *n.m.* coat-hanger; (*archit.*) curve.
cintré /sɛ̃tre/ *a.* curved; (*chemise*) fitted.
cirage /siraʒ/ *n.m.* (wax) polish.
circoncision /sirkɔ̃sizjɔ̃/ *n.f.* circumcision.
circonférence /sirkɔ̃ferɑ̃s/ *n.f.* circumference.
circonflexe /sirkɔ̃flɛks/ *a.* circumflex.
circonscription /sirkɔ̃skripsjɔ̃/ *n.f.* district. **~ (électorale)**, constituency.
circonscrire /sirkɔ̃skrir/ *v.t.* confine; (*sujet*) define.
circonspect /sirkɔ̃spɛkt/ *a.* circumspect.
circonstance /sirkɔ̃stɑ̃s/ *n.f.* circumstance; (*occasion*) occasion.
circonstancié /sirkɔ̃stɑ̃sje/ *a.* detailed.
circonvenir /sirkɔ̃vnir/ *v.t.* circumvent.
circuit /sirkɥi/ *n.m.* circuit; (*trajet*) tour, trip.
circulaire /sirkylɛr/ *a.* & *n.f.* circular.
circul|er /sirkyle/ *v.i.* circulate; (*train, automobile, etc.*) travel; (*piéton*) walk. **faire ~er**, (*badauds*) move on. **~ation** *n.f.* circulation; (*de véhicules*) traffic.
cire /sir/ *n.f.* wax.
ciré /sire/ *n.m.* oilskins.
cir|er /sire/ *v.t.* polish, wax. **~eur** *n.m.* bootblack. **~euse** *n.f.* (*appareil*) floor-polisher.
cirque /sirk/ *n.m.* circus; (*arène*)

amphitheatre; (*désordre*: *fig.*) chaos.
cisaill|e(s) /sizaj/ *n.f.* (*pl.*) shears. **~er** *v.t.* prune.
ciseau (*pl.* **~x**) /sizo/ *n.m.* chisel. **~x,** scissors.
ciseler /sizle/ *v.t.* chisel.
citadelle /sitadɛl/ *n.f.* citadel.
citadin, ~e /sitadɛ̃, -in/ *n.m., f.* city dweller. —*a.* city.
cité /site/ *n.f.* city. **~ ouvrière,** (workers') housing estate. **~ universitaire,** (university) halls of residence.
cit|er /site/ *v.t.* quote, cite; (*jurid.*) summon. **~ation** *n.f.* quotation; (*jurid.*) summons.
citerne /sitɛrn/ *n.f.* tank.
cithare /sitar/ *n.f.* zither.
citoyen, ~ne /sitwajɛ̃, -jɛn/ *n.m., f.* citizen. **~neté** /-jɛnte/ *n.f.* citizenship.
citron /sitrɔ̃/ *n.m.* lemon. **~nade** /-ɔnad/ *n.f.* lemon squash *ou* drink, (still) lemonade.
citrouille /sitruj/ *n.f.* pumpkin.
civet /sivɛ/ *n.m.* stew. **~ de lièvre/lapin,** jugged hare/rabbit.
civette /sivɛt/ *n.f.* (*culin.*) chive(s).
civière /sivjɛr/ *n.f.* stretcher.
civil /sivil/ *a.* civil; (*non militaire*) civilian; (*poli*) civil. —*n.m.* civilian. **dans le ~,** in civilian life. **en ~,** in plain clothes.
civilisation /sivilizɑsjɔ̃/ *n.f.* civilization.
civiliser /sivilize/ *v.t.* civilize. **se ~** *v. pr.* become civilized.
civi|que /sivik/ *a.* civic. **~sme** *n.m.* civic sense.
clair /klɛr/ *a.* clear; (*éclairé*) light, bright; (*couleur*) light; (*liquide*) thin. —*adv.* clearly. —*n.m.* **~ de lune,** moonlight. **le plus ~ de,** most of. **~ement** *adv.* clearly.
claire-voie (à) /(a)klɛrvwa/ *adv.* with slits to let the light through.
clairière /klɛrjɛr/ *n.f.* clearing.
clairon /klɛrɔ̃/ *n.m.* bugle. **~ner** /-ɔne/ *v.t.* trumpet (forth).
clairsemé /klɛrsəme/ *a.* sparse.
clairvoyant, ~e /klɛrvwajɑ̃, -t/ *a.* clear-sighted.
clamer /klame/ *v.t.* utter aloud.
clameur /klamœr/ *n.f.* clamour.
clan /klɑ̃/ *n.m.* clan.
clandestin, ~e /klɑ̃dɛstɛ̃, -in/ *a.* secret; (*journal*) underground
clapet /klapɛ/ *n.m.* valve.
clapier /klapje/ *n.m.* (rabbit) hutch.
clapot|er /klapɔte/ *v.i.* lap. **~is** *n.m.* lapping.
claquage /klakaʒ/ *n.m.* strained muscle.
claque /klak/ *n.f.* slap.
claqu|er /klake/ *v.i.* bang; (*porte*) slam, bang; (*fouet*) snap, crack; (*se casser*: *fam.*) conk out. —*v.t.* (*porte*) slam, bang; (*gifler*) slap; (*fatiguer*: *fam.*) tire out. **~er des doigts,** snap one's fingers. **~er des mains,** clap one's hands. **il claque des dents,** his teeth are chattering. **~ement** *n.m.* bang(ing); slam(ming); snap(ping).
claquettes /klakɛt/ *n.f. pl.* tap-dancing.
clarifier /klarifje/ *v.t.* clarify.
clarinette /klarinɛt/ *n.f.* clarinet.
clarté /klarte/ *n.f.* light, brightness; (*netteté*) clarity.
classe /klɑs/ *n.f.* class; (*salle*: *scol.*) class(-room). **aller en ~,** go to school. **~ ouvrière/moyenne,** working/middle class. **faire la ~,** teach.
class|er /klɑse/ *v.t.* classify; (*par mérite*) grade; (*papiers*) file; (*affaire*) close. **se ~er premier/dernier,** come first/last. **~ement** *n.m.* classification; grading; filing; (*rang*) place, grade; (*de coureur*) placing.
classeur /klɑsœr/ *n.m.* filing cabinet; (*chemise*) file.

classif|ier /klasifje/ *v.t.* classify. **~ication** *n.f.* classification.
classique /klasik/ *a.* classical; (*de qualité*) classic(al); (*habituel*) classic. —*n.m.* classic; (*auteur*) classical author.
clause /kloz/ *n.f.* clause.
claustration /klostrɑsjɔ̃/ *n.f.* confinement.
claustrophobie /klostrɔfɔbi/ *n.f.* claustrophobia.
clavecin /klavsɛ̃/ *n.m.* harpsichord.
clavicule /klavikyl/ *n.f.* collarbone.
clavier /klavje/ *n.m.* keyboard.
clé, clef /kle/ *n.f.* key; (*outil*) spanner; (*mus.*) clef. —*a. invar.* key. **~ anglaise,** (monkey-) wrench. **~ de contact,** ignition key. **~ de voûte,** keystone.
clémen|t, ~te /klemɑ̃, -t/ *a.* (*doux*) mild; (*indulgent*) lenient. **~ce** *n.f.* mildness; leniency.
clémentine /klemɑ̃tin/ *n.f.* clementine.
clerc /klɛr/ *n.m.* (*d'avoué etc.*) clerk; (*relig.*) cleric.
clergé /klɛrʒe/ *n.m.* clergy.
cléric|al (*m. pl.* **~aux**) /klerikal, -o/ *a.* clerical.
cliché /kliʃe/ *n.m.* cliché; (*photo.*) negative.
client, ~e /klijɑ̃, -t/ *n.m., f.* customer; (*d'un avocat*) client; (*d'un médecin*) patient; (*d'hôtel*) guest. **~èle** /-tɛl/ *n.f.* customers, clientele; (*d'un avocat*) clientele, clients, practice; (*d'un médecin*) practice, patients; (*soutien*) custom.
cligner /kliɲe/ *v.i.* **~ des yeux,** blink. **~ de l'œil,** wink.
clignot|er /kliɲɔte/ *v.i.* blink; (*lumière*) flicker; (*comme signal*) flash. **~ant** *n.m.* (*auto.*) indicator; (*auto., Amer.*) directional signal.
climat /klima/ *n.m.* climate. **~ique** /-tik/ *a.* climatic.
climatis|ation /klimatizɑsjɔ̃/ *n.f.* air-conditioning. **~é** *a.* air-conditioned.
clin d'œil /klɛ̃dœj/ *n.m.* wink. **en un ~,** in a flash.
clinique /klinik/ *a.* clinical. —*n.f.* (private) clinic.
clinquant, ~e /klɛ̃kɑ̃, -t/ *a.* showy. —*n.m.* (*lamelles*) tinsel.
clique /klik/ *n.f.* clique; (*mus., mil.*) band.
cliquet|er /klikte/ *v.i.* clink. **~is** *n.m.* clink(ing).
clivage /klivaʒ/ *n.m.* cleavage.
clochard, ~e /klɔʃar, -d/ *n.m., f.* tramp.
cloch|e[1] /klɔʃ/ *n.f.* bell. **~ette** *n.f.* bell.
cloche[2] /klɔʃ/ *n.f.* (*fam.*) idiot.
cloche-pied (à) /(a)klɔʃpje/ *adv.* hopping on one foot.
clocher[1] /klɔʃe/ *n.m.* bell-tower; (*pointu*) steeple. **de ~,** parochial.
clocher[2] /klɔʃe/ *v.i.* (*fam.*) be wrong.
cloison /klwazɔ̃/ *n.f.* partition; (*fig.*) barrier. **~ner** /-ɔne/ *v.t.* partition; (*personne*) cut off.
cloître /klwatr/ *n.m.* cloister.
cloîtrer (se) /(sə)klwatre/ *v. pr.* shut o.s. away.
clopin-clopant /klɔpɛ̃klɔpɑ̃/ *adv.* hobbling.
cloque /klɔk/ *n.f.* blister.
clore /klɔr/ *v.t.* close.
clos, ~e /klo, -z/ *a.* closed.
clôtur|e /klotyr/ *n.f.* fence; (*fermeture*) closure. **~er** *v.t.* enclose; (*festival, séance, etc.*) close.
clou /klu/ *n.m.* nail; (*furoncle*) boil; (*de spectacle*) star attraction. **~ de girofle,** clove. **les ~s,** (*passage*) zebra *ou* pedestrian crossing. **~er** *v.t.* nail down; (*fig.*) pin down. **~er qn. au lit,** keep s.o. confined to his bed.
clouté /klute/ *a.* studded.
clown /klun/ *n.m.* clown.
club /klœb/ *n.m.* club.

coaguler /kɔagyle/ *v.t./i.*, **se ~** *v. pr.* coagulate.
coaliser (se) /(sə)kɔalize/ *v. pr.* join forces.
coalition /kɔalisjɔ̃/ *n.f.* coalition.
coasser /kɔase/ *v.i.* croak.
cobaye /kɔbaj/ *n.m.* guinea-pig.
cocaïne /kɔkain/ *n.f.* cocaine.
cocarde /kɔkard/ *n.f.* rosette.
cocard|ier, ~ière /kɔkardje, -jɛr/ *a.* chauvinistic.
cocasse /kɔkas/ *a.* comical.
coccinelle /kɔksinɛl/ *n.f.* ladybird; (*Amer.*) ladybug.
cocher[1] /kɔʃe/ *v.t.* tick (off), check.
cocher[2] /kɔʃe/ *n.m.* coachman.
cochon, ~ne /kɔʃɔ̃, -ɔn/ *n.m.* pig. —*n.m., f.* (*personne: fam.*) pig. —*a.* (*fam.*) filthy. **~nerie** /-ɔnri/ *n.f.* (*saleté: fam.*) filth; (*marchandise: fam.*) rubbish.
cocktail /kɔktɛl/ *n.m.* cocktail; (*réunion*) cocktail party.
cocon /kɔkɔ̃/ *n.m.* cocoon.
cocotier /kɔkɔtje/ *n.m.* coconut palm.
cocotte /kɔkɔt/ *n.f.* (*marmite*) casserole. **~ minute,** (P.) pressure-cooker. **ma ~,** (*fam.*) my sweet, my dear.
cocu /kɔky/ *n.m.* (*fam.*) cuckold.
code /kɔd/ *n.m.* code. **~s, phares ~,** dipped headlights. **~ de la route,** Highway Code. **se mettre en ~,** dip one's headlights.
coder /kɔde/ *v.t.* code.
codifier /kɔdifje/ *v.t.* codify.
coéquip|ier, ~ière /kɔekipje, -jɛr/ *n.m., f.* team-mate.
cœur /kœr/ *n.m.* heart; (*cartes*) hearts. **à ~ ouvert,** (*opération*) open-heart; (*parler*) freely. **avoir bon ~,** be kind-hearted. **de bon ~,** with a good heart. **par ~,** by heart.
coexist|er /kɔɛgziste/ *v.i.* coexist. **~ence** *n.f.* coexistence.
coffre /kɔfr/ *n.m.* chest; (*pour argent*) safe; (*auto.*) boot; (*auto., Amer.*) trunk. **~-fort** (*pl.* **~s-forts**) *n.m.* safe.
coffrer /kɔfre/ *v.t.* (*fam.*) lock up.
coffret /kɔfrɛ/ *n.m.* casket, box.
cognac /kɔɲak/ *n.m.* cognac.
cogner /kɔɲe/ *v.t./i.* knock. **se ~** *v. pr.* knock o.s.
cohabit|er /kɔabite/ *v.i.* live together. **~ation** *n.f.* living together.
cohérent, ~e /kɔerɑ̃, -t/ *a.* coherent.
cohésion /kɔezjɔ̃/ *n.f.* cohesion.
cohorte /kɔɔrt/ *n.f.* troop.
cohue /kɔy/ *n.f.* crowd.
coi, coite /kwa, -t/ *a.* silent.
coiffe /kwaf/ *n.f.* head-dress.
coiff|er /kwafe/ *v.t.* do the hair of; (*chapeau*) put on; (*surmonter*) cap. **~er qn. d'un chapeau,** put a hat on s.o. **se ~er** *v. pr.* do one's hair. **se ~er d'un chapeau,** put a hat on. **~é de,** wearing. **bien/mal ~é,** with tidy/untidy hair. **~eur, ~euse** *n.m., f.* hairdresser; *n.f.* dressing-table.
coiffure /kwafyr/ *n.f.* hairstyle; (*chapeau*) hat; (*métier*) hairdressing.
coin /kwɛ̃/ *n.m.* corner; (*endroit*) spot; (*cale*) wedge; (*pour graver*) die. **au ~ du feu,** by the fireside. **dans le ~,** locally. **du ~,** local.
coincer /kwɛ̃se/ *v.t.* jam; (*caler*) wedge; (*attraper: fam.*) catch. **se ~** *v. pr.* get jammed.
coïncid|er /kɔɛ̃side/ *v.i.* coincide. **~ence** *n.f.* coincidence.
coing /kwɛ̃/ *n.m.* quince.
coite /kwat/ *voir* **coi.**
coke /kɔk/ *n.m.* coke.
col /kɔl/ *n.m.* collar; (*de bouteille*) neck; (*de montagne*) pass. **~ roulé,** polo-neck; (*Amer.*) turtleneck.
coléoptère /kɔleɔptɛr/ *n.m.* beetle.
colère /kɔlɛr/ *n.f.* anger; (*accès*) fit of anger. **en ~,** angry. **se mettre en ~,** lose one's temper.

colér|eux, ~euse /kɔlerø, -z/, **~ique** *adjs.* quick-tempered.
colifichet /kɔlifiʃɛ/ *n.m.* trinket.
colimaçon (en) /(ɑ̃)kɔlimasɔ̃/ *adv.* spiral.
colin /kɔlɛ̃/ *n.m.* (*poisson*) hake.
colique /kɔlik/ *n.f.* diarrhoea. **~s,** colic.
colis /kɔli/ *n.m.* parcel.
collabor|er /kɔlabɔre/ *v.i.* collaborate (**à,** on). **~er à,** (*journal*) contribute to. **~ateur, ~atrice** *n.m., f.* collaborator; contributor. **~ation** *n.f.* collaboration (**à,** on); contribution (**à,** to).
collant, ~e /kɔlɑ̃, -t/ *a.* skin-tight; (*poisseux*) sticky. —*n.m.* (*bas*) tights; (*de danseur*) leotard.
collation /kɔlɑsjɔ̃/ *n.f.* light meal.
colle /kɔl/ *n.f.* glue; (*en pâte*) paste; (*problème: fam.*) poser; (*scol., argot*) detention.
collect|e /kɔlɛkt/ *n.f.* collection. **~er** *v.t.* collect.
collecteur /kɔlɛktœr/ *n.m.* (*égout*) main sewer.
collecti|f, ~ve /kɔlɛktif, -v/ *a.* collective; (*billet, voyage*) group. **~vement** *adv.* collectively.
collection /kɔlɛksjɔ̃/ *n.f.* collection.
collectionn|er /kɔlɛksjɔne/ *v.t.* collect. **~eur, ~euse** *n.m., f.* collector.
collectivité /kɔlɛktivite/ *n.f.* community.
coll|ège /kɔlɛʒ/ *n.m.* (secondary) school; (*assemblée*) college. **~égien, ~égienne** *n.m., f.* schoolboy, schoolgirl.
collègue /kɔlɛg/ *n.m./f.* colleague.
coll|er /kɔle/ *v.t.* stick; (*avec colle liquide*) glue; (*affiche*) stick up; (*mettre: fam.*) stick; (*scol., argot*) keep in; (*embarrasser: fam.*) stump. —*v.i.* stick (**à,** to); (*être collant*) be sticky. **~er à,** (*convenir à*) fit, correspond to. **être ~é à,** (*examen: fam.*) fail.
collet /kɔlɛ/ *n.m.* (*piège*) snare. **~ monté,** prim and proper. **prendre qn. au ~,** collar s.o.
collier /kɔlje/ *n.m.* necklace; (*de chien*) collar.
colline /kɔlin/ *n.f.* hill.
collision /kɔlizjɔ̃/ *n.f.* (*choc*) collision; (*lutte*) clash.
colloque /kɔlɔk/ *n.m.* symposium.
colmater /kɔlmate/ *v.t.* seal; (*trou*) fill in.
colombe /kɔlɔ̃b/ *n.f.* dove.
Colombie /kɔlɔ̃bi/ *n.f.* Colombia.
colon /kɔlɔ̃/ *n.m.* settler; (*enfant*) child staying at a holiday camp.
colonel /kɔlɔnɛl/ *n.m.* colonel.
colon|ial, ~iale (*m. pl.* **~iaux**) /kɔlɔnjal, -jo/ *a.* & *n.m., f.* colonial.
colon|ie /kɔlɔni/ *n.f.* colony. **~ de vacances,** children's holiday camp.
coloniser /kɔlɔnize/ *v.t.* colonize.
colonne /kɔlɔn/ *n.f.* column. **~ vertébrale,** spine. **en ~ par deux,** in double file.
color|er /kɔlɔre/ *v.t.* colour; (*bois*) stain. **~ant** *n.m.* colouring; stain. **~ation** *n.f.* (*couleur*) colour(ing).
colorier /kɔlɔrje/ *v.t.* colour (in).
coloris /kɔlɔri/ *n.m.* colour.
coloss|al (*m. pl.* **~aux**) /kɔlɔsal, -o/ *a.* colossal.
colosse /kɔlɔs/ *n.m.* giant.
colport|er /kɔlpɔrte/ *v.t.* hawk. **~eur, ~euse** *n.m., f.* hawker.
colza /kɔlza/ *n.m.* rape(-seed).
coma /kɔma/ *n.m.* coma. **dans le ~,** in a coma.
combat /kɔ̃ba/ *n.m.* fight; (*sport*) match. **~s,** fighting.
combati|f, ~ve /kɔ̃batif, -v/ *a.* eager to fight; (*esprit*) fighting.
combatt|re† /kɔ̃batr/ *v.t./i.* fight. **~ant, ~ante** *n.m., f.* fighter; (*mil.*) combattant.
combien /kɔ̃bjɛ̃/ *adv.* **~ (de),** (*quantité*) how much; (*nombre*) how many. **~ il a changé!,** (*comme*) how he has changed! **~ y**

a-t-il d'ici à . . .?, how far is it to . . .?
combinaison /kɔ̃binɛzɔ̃/ *n.f.* combination; (*manigance*) scheme; (*de femme*) slip; (*bleu de travail*) boiler suit; (*Amer.*) overalls. **~ d'aviateur,** flying-suit.
combine /kɔ̃bin/ *n.f.* trick; (*fraude*) fiddle.
combiné /kɔ̃bine/ *n.m.* (*de téléphone*) receiver.
combiner /kɔ̃bine/ *v.t.* (*réunir*) combine; (*calculer*) devise.
comble[1] /kɔ̃bl/ *a.* packed.
comble[2] /kɔ̃bl/ *n.m.* height. **~s,** (*mansarde*) attic, loft. **c'est le ~!,** that's the last straw!
combler /kɔ̃ble/ *v.t.* fill; (*perte, déficit*) make good; (*désir*) fulfil; (*personne*) gratify. **~ qn. de cadeaux**/*etc.*, lavish gifts/*etc.* on s.o.
combustible /kɔ̃bystibl/ *n.m.* fuel.
combustion /kɔ̃bystjɔ̃/ *n.f.* combustion.
comédie /kɔmedi/ *n.f.* comedy. **~ musicale,** musical. **jouer la ~,** put on an act.
comédien, ~ne /kɔmedjɛ̃, -jɛn/ *n.m., f.* actor, actress.
comestible /kɔmɛstibl/ *a.* edible. **~s** *n.m. pl.* foodstuffs.
comète /kɔmɛt/ *n.f.* comet.
comique /kɔmik/ *a.* comical; (*genre*) comic. —*n.m.* (*acteur*) comic; (*comédie*) comedy; (*côté drôle*) comical aspect.
comité /kɔmite/ *n.m.* committee.
commandant /kɔmɑ̃dɑ̃/ *n.m.* commander; (*armée de terre*) major. **~ (de bord),** captain. **~ en chef,** Commander-in-Chief.
commande /kɔmɑ̃d/ *n.f.* (*comm.*) order. **~s,** (*d'avion etc.*) controls.
command|er /kɔmɑ̃de/ *v.t.* command; (*acheter*) order. —*v.i.* be in command. **~er à,** (*maîtriser*) control. **~er à qn. de,** command s.o. to. **~ement** *n.m.* command; (*relig.*) commandment.
commando /kɔmɑ̃do/ *n.m.* commando.
comme /kɔm/ *conj.* as. —*prép.* like. —*adv.* (*exclamation*) how. **~ ci comme ça,** so-so. **~ d'habitude, ~ à l'ordinaire,** as usual. **~ il faut,** proper(ly). **~ pour faire,** as if to do. **~ quoi,** to the effect that. **qu'avez-vous ~ amis**/*etc.*?, what have you in the way of friends/*etc.*?
commémor|er /kɔmemɔre/ *v.t.* commemorate. **~ation** *n.f.* commemoration.
commenc|er /kɔmɑ̃se/ *v.t.* begin, start. **~er à faire,** begin *ou* start to do. **~ement** *n.m.* beginning, start.
comment /kɔmɑ̃/ *adv.* how. **~?,** (*répétition*) pardon?; (*surprise*) what? **~ est-il?,** what is he like?
commentaire /kɔmɑ̃tɛr/ *n.m.* comment; (*d'un texte*) commentary.
comment|er /kɔmɑ̃te/ *v.t.* comment on. **~ateur, ~atrice** *n.m., f.* commentator.
commérages /kɔmeraʒ/ *n.m. pl.* gossip.
commerçant, ~e /kɔmɛrsɑ̃, -t/ *a.* (*rue*) shopping; (*nation*) trading; (*personne*) business-minded. —*n.m., f.* shopkeeper.
commerce /kɔmɛrs/ *n.m.* trade, commerce; (*magasin*) business. **faire du ~,** trade.
commerc|ial (*m. pl.* **~iaux**) /kɔmɛrsjal, -jo/ *a.* commercial. **~ialiser** *v.t.* market.
commère /kɔmɛr/ *n.f.* gossip.
commettre† /kɔmɛtr/ *v.t.* commit.
commis /kɔmi/ *n.m.* (*de magasin*) assistant; (*de bureau*) clerk.
commissaire /kɔmisɛr/ *n.m.* (*sport*) steward. **~ (de police),** (police) superintendent. **~-**

priseur (*pl.* **~s-priseurs**) *n.m.* auctioneer.

commissariat /kɔmisarja/ *n.m.* **~ (de police),** police station.

commission /kɔmisjɔ̃/ *n.f.* commission; (*course*) errand; (*message*) message. **~s,** shopping. **~naire** /-jɔnɛr/ *n.m.* errand-boy.

commod|e /kɔmɔd/ *a.* handy; (*facile*) easy. **pas ~e,** (*personne*) a difficult customer. —*n.f.* chest (of drawers). **~ité** *n.f.* convenience.

commotion /kɔmosjɔ̃/ *n.f.* **~ (cérébrale),** concussion. **~né** /-jɔne/ *a.* shaken.

commuer /kɔmɥe/ *v.t.* commute.

commun, ~e /kɔmœ̃, -yn/ *a.* common; (*effort, action*) joint; (*frais, pièce*) shared. —*n.f.* (*circonscription*) commune. **~s** *n.m. pl.* outhouses, outbuildings. **avoir** *ou* **mettre en ~,** share. **~al** (*m. pl.* **~aux**) /-ynal, -o/ *a.* of the commune, local. **~ément** /-ynemɑ̃/ *adv.* commonly.

communauté /kɔmynote/ *n.f.* community.

commune /kɔmyn/ *voir* **commun.**

communiant, ~e /kɔmynjɑ̃, -t/ *n.m., f.* (*relig.*) communicant.

communicati|f, ~ve /kɔmynikatif, -v/ *a.* communicative.

communication /kɔmynikɑsjɔ̃/ *n.f.* communication; (*téléphonique*) call. **~ interurbaine,** long-distance call.

commun|ier /kɔmynje/ *v.i.* (*relig.*) receive communion. **~ion** *n.f.* communion.

communiqué /kɔmynike/ *n.m.* communiqué.

communiquer /kɔmynike/ *v.t.* pass on, communicate; (*mouvement*) impart. —*v.i.* communicate. **se ~ à,** spread to.

communis|te /kɔmynist/ *a.* & *n.m./f.* communist. **~me** *n.m.* communism.

commutateur /kɔmytatœr/ *n.m.* (*électr.*) switch.

compact /kɔ̃pakt/ *a.* dense; (*voiture*) compact.

compagne /kɔ̃paɲ/ *n.f.* companion.

compagnie /kɔ̃paɲi/ *n.f.* company. **tenir ~ à,** keep company.

compagnon /kɔ̃paɲɔ̃/ *n.m.* companion; (*ouvrier*) workman. **~ de jeu,** playmate.

comparaître /kɔ̃parɛtr/ *v.i.* (*jurid.*) appear (**devant,** before).

compar|er /kɔ̃pare/ *v.t.* compare. **se ~er** *v. pr.* be compared. **~able** *a.* comparable. **~aison** *n.f.* comparison; (*littéraire*) simile. **~atif, ~ative** *a.* & *n.m.* comparative. **~é** *a.* comparative.

comparse /kɔ̃pars/ *n.m./f.* (*péj.*) stooge.

compartiment /kɔ̃partimɑ̃/ *n.m.* compartment. **~er** /-te/ *v.t.* divide up.

comparution /kɔ̃parysjɔ̃/ *n.f.* (*jurid.*) appearance.

compas /kɔ̃pa/ *n.m.* (pair of) compasses; (*boussole*) compass.

compassé /kɔ̃pɑse/ *a.* stilted.

compassion /kɔ̃pɑsjɔ̃/ *n.f.* compassion.

compatible /kɔ̃patibl/ *a.* compatible.

compatir /kɔ̃patir/ *v.i.* sympathize. **~ à,** share in.

compatriote /kɔ̃patrijɔt/ *n.m./f.* compatriot.

compens|er /kɔ̃pɑ̃se/ *v.t.* compensate for. **~ation** *n.f.* compensation.

compère /kɔ̃pɛr/ *n.m.* accomplice.

compéten|t, ~te /kɔpetɑ̃, -t/ *a.* competent. **~ce** *n.f.* competence.

compétiti|f, ~ve /kɔ̃petitif, -v/ *a.* competitive.

compétition /kɔ̃petisjɔ̃/ *n.f.* competition; (*sportive*) event. **de ~,** competitive.

compiler /kɔ̃pile/ *v.t.* compile.

complainte /kɔ̃plɛ̃t/ *n.f.* lament.

complaire (se) /(sə)kɔ̃plɛr/ *v. pr.* **se ~ dans,** delight in.

complaisan|t, ~te /kɔ̃plɛzɑ̃, -t/ *a.* kind; (*indulgent*) indulgent. **~ce** *n.f.* kindness; indulgence.

complément /kɔ̃plemɑ̃/ *n.m.* complement; (*reste*) rest. **~ (d'objet),** (*gram.*) object. **~ d'information,** further information. **~aire** /-tɛr/ *a.* complementary; (*renseignements*) supplementary.

compl|et[1], ~ète /kɔ̃plɛ, -t/ *a.* complete; (*train, hôtel, etc.*) full. **~ètement** *adv.* completely.

complet[2] /kɔ̃plɛ/ *n.m.* suit.

compléter /kɔ̃plete/ *v.t.* complete; (*agrémenter*) complement. **se ~** *v. pr.* complement each other.

complex|e[1] /kɔ̃plɛks/ *a.* complex. **~ité** *n.f.* complexity.

complex|e[2] /kɔ̃plɛks/ *n.m.* (*sentiment, bâtiments*) complex. **~é** *a.* inhibited, hung up.

complication /kɔ̃plikɑsjɔ̃/ *n.f.* complication; (*complexité*) complexity.

complic|e /kɔ̃plis/ *n.m.* accomplice. **~ité** *n.f.* complicity.

compliment /kɔ̃plimɑ̃/ *n.m.* compliment. **~s,** (*félicitations*) congratulations. **~er** /-te/ *v.t.* compliment.

compliqu|er /kɔ̃plike/ *v.t.* complicate. **se ~er** *v. pr.* become complicated. **~é** *a.* complicated.

complot /kɔ̃plo/ *n.m.* plot. **~er** /-ɔte/ *v.t./i.* plot.

comporter[1] /kɔ̃pɔrte/ *v.t.* contain; (*impliquer*) involve.

comport|er[2] (se) /(sə)kɔ̃pɔrte/ *v. pr.* behave; (*joueur*) perform. **~ement** *n.m.* behaviour; (*de joueur*) performance.

composé /kɔ̃poze/ *a.* compound; (*guindé*) affected. —*n.m.* compound.

compos|er /kɔ̃poze/ *v.t.* make up, compose; (*chanson, visage*) compose; (*numéro*) dial. —*v.i.* (*scol.*) take an exam; (*transiger*) compromise. **se ~er de,** be made up *ou* composed of. **~ant** *n.m.*, **~ante** *n.f.* component.

composi|teur, ~trice /kɔ̃pozitœr, -tris/ *n.m., f.* (*mus.*) composer.

composition /kɔ̃pozisjɔ̃/ *n.f.* composition; (*examen*) test, exam.

composter /kɔ̃pɔste/ *v.t.* (*billet*) punch.

compot|e /kɔ̃pɔt/ *n.f.* stewed fruit. **~e de pommes,** stewed apples. **~ier** *n.m.* fruit dish.

compréhensible /kɔ̃preɑ̃sibl/ *a.* understandable.

compréhensi|f, ~ve /kɔ̃preɑ̃sif, -v/ *a.* understanding.

compréhension /kɔ̃preɑ̃sjɔ̃/ *n.f.* understanding, comprehension.

comprendre† /kɔ̃prɑ̃dr/ *v.t.* understand; (*comporter*) comprise. **ça se comprend,** that is understandable.

comprimé /kɔ̃prime/ *n.m.* tablet.

compr|imer /kɔ̃prime/ *v.t.* compress; (*réduire*) reduce. **~ession** *n.f.* compression; reduction.

compris, ~e /kɔ̃pri, -z/ *a.* included; (*d'accord*) agreed. **~ entre,** (contained) between. **service (non) ~,** service (not) included, (not) including service. **tout ~,** (all) inclusive. **y ~,** including.

compromettre /kɔ̃prɔmɛtr/ *v.t.* compromise.

compromis /kɔ̃prɔmi/ *n.m.* compromise.

comptab|le /kɔ̃tabl/ *a.* accounting. —*n.m.* accountant. **~ilité** *n.f.* accountancy; (*comptes*) accounts; (*service*) accounts department.

comptant /kɔ̃tɑ̃/ *adv.* (*payer*) (in) cash; (*acheter*) for cash.

compte /kɔ̃t/ *n.m.* count; (*facture, comptabilité*) account; (*nombre exact*) right number. **~s,** (*justifications*) explanation. **à bon ~,**

cheaply. **à son ~,** (*travailler*) for o.s., on one's own. **faire le ~ de,** count. **pour le ~ de,** on behalf of. **sur le ~ de,** about. **~ à rebours,** countdown. **~-gouttes** *n.m. invar.* (*méd.*) dropper. **~ rendu,** report; (*de film, livre*) review.

compter /kɔ̃te/ *v.t.* count; (*prévoir*) reckon; (*facturer*) charge for; (*avoir*) have; (*classer*) consider. —*v.i.* (*calculer, importer*) count. **~ avec,** reckon with. **~ faire,** expect to do. **~ parmi,** (*figurer*) be considered among. **~ sur,** rely on.

compteur /kɔ̃tœr/ *n.m.* meter. **~ de vitesse,** speedometer.

comptine /kɔ̃tin/ *n.f.* nursery rhyme; (*pour compter*) counting rhyme.

comptoir /kɔ̃twar/ *n.m.* counter; (*de café*) bar.

compulser /kɔ̃pylse/ *v.t.* examine.

comt|e, ~esse /kɔ̃t, -ɛs/ *n.m., f.* count, countess.

comté /kɔ̃te/ *n.m.* county.

con, conne /kɔ̃, kɔn/ *a.* (*argot*) bloody foolish. —*n.m., f.* (*argot*) bloody fool.

concave /kɔ̃kav/ *a.* concave.

concéder /kɔ̃sede/ *v.t.* grant, concede.

concentr|er /kɔ̃sɑ̃tre/ *v.t.,* **se ~er** *v. pr.* concentrate. **~ation** *n.f.* concentration. **~é** *a.* concentrated; (*lait*) condensed; (*personne*) absorbed; *n.m.* concentrate.

concept /kɔ̃sɛpt/ *n.m.* concept.

conception /kɔ̃sɛpsjɔ̃/ *n.f.* conception.

concerner /kɔ̃sɛrne/ *v.t.* concern.

concert /kɔ̃sɛr/ *n.m.* concert. **de ~,** in unison.

concert|er /kɔ̃sɛrte/ *v.t.* organize, agree, prepare. **se ~er** *v. pr.* confer. **~é** *a.* (*plan etc.*) concerted.

concerto /kɔ̃sɛrto/ *n.m.* concerto.

concession /kɔ̃sesjɔ̃/ *n.f.* concession; (*terrain*) plot.

concessionnaire /kɔ̃sesjɔnɛr/ *n.m./f.* (authorized) dealer.

concevoir† /kɔ̃svwar/ *v.t.* (*imaginer, engendrer*) conceive; (*comprendre*) understand.

concierge /kɔ̃sjɛrʒ/ *n.m./f.* caretaker.

concil|ier /kɔ̃silje/ *v.t.* reconcile. **se ~ier** *v. pr.* (*s'attirer*) win (over). **~iation** *n.f.* conciliation.

concis, ~e /kɔ̃si, -z/ *a.* concise. **~ion** /-zjɔ̃/ *n.f.* concision.

concitoyen, ~ne /kɔ̃sitwajɛ̃, -jɛn/ *n.m., f.* fellow citizen.

concl|ure† /kɔ̃klyr/ *v.t./i.* conclude. **~ure à,** conclude in favour of. **~uant, ~uante** *a.* conclusive. **~usion** *n.f.* conclusion.

concombre /kɔ̃kɔ̃br/ *n.m.* cucumber.

concorde /kɔ̃kɔrd/ *n.f.* concord.

concord|er /kɔ̃kɔrde/ *v.i.* agree. **~ance** *n.f.* agreement; (*analogie*) similarity. **~ant, ~ante** *a.* in agreement.

concourir /kɔ̃kurir/ *v.i.* compete. **~ à,** contribute towards.

concours /kɔ̃kur/ *n.m.* competition; (*examen*) competitive examination; (*aide*) aid; (*de circonstances*) combination.

concr|et, ~ète /kɔ̃krɛ, -t/ *a.* concrete. **~ètement** *adv.* in concrete terms.

concrétiser /kɔ̃kretize/ *v.t.* give concrete form to. **se ~** *v. pr.* materialize.

conçu /kɔ̃sy/ *a.* **bien/mal ~,** (*appartement etc.*) well/badly planned.

concurrenc|e /kɔ̃kyrɑ̃s/ *n.f.* competition. **faire ~e à,** compete with. **~er** *v.t.* compete with.

concurrent, ~e /kɔ̃kyrɑ̃, -t/ *n.m., f.* competitor; (*scol.*) candidate. —*a.* competing.

condamn|er /kɔ̃dane/ *v.t.* (*censurer, obliger*) condemn; (*jurid.*) sentence; (*porte*) block up.

~ation *n.f.* condemnation; (*peine*) sentence. **~é** *a.* (*fichu*) without hope, doomed.
condens|er /kɔ̃dɑ̃se/ *v.t.*, **se ~er** *v. pr.* condense. **~ation** *n.f.* condensation.
condescendre /kɔ̃desɑ̃dr/ *v.i.* condescend (**à,** to).
condiment /kɔ̃dimɑ̃/ *n.m.* condiment.
condisciple /kɔ̃disipl/ *n.m.* classmate, schoolfellow.
condition /kɔ̃disjɔ̃/ *n.f.* condition. **~s,** (*prix*) terms. **à ~ de** *ou* **que,** provided (that). **sans ~,** unconditional(ly). **sous ~,** conditionally. **~nel, ~nelle** /-jɔnɛl/ *a.* conditional.
conditionner /kɔ̃disjɔne/ *v.t.* condition; (*emballer*) package.
condoléances /kɔ̃dɔleɑ̃s/ *n.f. pl.* condolences.
conduc|teur, ~trice /kɔ̃dyktœr, -tris/ *n.m., f.* driver.
conduire† /kɔ̃dɥir/ *v.t.* lead; (*auto.*) drive; (*affaire*) conduct. —*v.i.* drive. **se ~** *v. pr.* behave. **~ à,** (*accompagner à*) take to.
conduit /kɔ̃dɥi/ *n.m.* (*anat.*) duct.
conduite /kɔ̃dɥit/ *n.f.* conduct; (*auto.*) driving; (*tuyau*) main. **~ à droite,** (*place*) right-hand drive.
cône /kon/ *n.m.* cone.
confection /kɔ̃fɛksjɔ̃/ *n.f.* making. **de ~,** ready-made. **la ~,** the clothing industry. **~ner** /-jɔne/ *v.t.* make.
confédération /kɔ̃federɑsjɔ̃/ *n.f.* confederation.
conférenc|e /kɔ̃ferɑ̃s/ *n.f.* conference; (*exposé*) lecture. **~e au sommet,** summit conference. **~ier, ~ière** *n.m., f.* lecturer.
conférer /kɔ̃fere/ *v.t.* give; (*décerner*) confer.
confess|er /kɔ̃fese/ *v.t.*, **se ~er** *v. pr.* confess. **~eur** *n.m.* confessor. **~ion** *n.f.* confession; (*religion*) denomination. **~ionnal** (*pl.* **~ionnaux**) *n.m.* confessional. **~ionnel, ~ionnelle** *a.* denominational.
confettis /kɔ̃feti/ *n.m. pl.* confetti.
confiance /kɔ̃fjɑ̃s/ *n.f.* trust. **avoir ~ en,** trust.
confiant, ~e /kɔ̃fjɑ̃, -t/ *a.* (*assuré*) confident; (*sans défiance*) trusting. **~ en** *ou* **dans,** confident in.
confiden|t, ~te /kɔ̃fidɑ̃, -t/ *n.m., f.* confidant, confidante. **~ce** *n.f.* confidence.
confidentiel, ~le /kɔ̃fidɑ̃sjɛl/ *a.* confidential.
confier /kɔ̃fje/ *v.t.* **~ à qn.,** entrust s.o. with; (*secret*) confide to s.o. **se ~ à,** confide in.
configuration /kɔ̃figyrɑsjɔ̃/ *n.f.* configuration.
confiner /kɔ̃fine/ *v.t.* confine. —*v.i.* **~ à,** border on. **se ~** *v. pr.* confine o.s. (**à, dans,** to).
confins /kɔ̃fɛ̃/ *n.m. pl.* confines.
confirm|er /kɔ̃firme/ *v.t.* confirm. **~ation** *n.f.* confirmation.
confis|erie /kɔ̃fizri/ *n.f.* sweet shop. **~eries,** confectionery. **~eur, ~euse** *n.m., f.* confectioner.
confis|quer /kɔ̃fiske/ *v.t.* confiscate. **~cation** *n.f.* confiscation.
confit, ~e /kɔ̃fi, -t/ *a.* (*culin.*) candied.
confiture /kɔ̃fityr/ *n.f.* jam.
conflit /kɔ̃fli/ *n.m.* conflict.
confondre /kɔ̃fɔ̃dr/ *v.t.* confuse, mix up; (*consterner, étonner*) confound. **se ~** *v. pr.* merge. **se ~ en excuses,** apologize profusely.
confondu /kɔ̃fɔ̃dy/ *a.* (*déconcerté*) overwhelmed, confounded.
conforme /kɔ̃fɔrm/ *a.* **~ à,** in accordance with.
conformément /kɔ̃fɔrmemɑ̃/ *adv.* **~ à,** in accordance with.
conform|er /kɔ̃fɔrme/ *v.t.* adapt. **se ~er à,** conform to. **~ité** *n.f.* conformity.
conformis|te /kɔ̃fɔrmist/ *a.* &

n.m./*f.* conformist. **~me** *n.m.* conformism.

confort /kɔ̃fɔr/ *n.m.* comfort. **~able** /-tabl/ *a.* comfortable.

confrère /kɔ̃frɛr/ *n.m.* colleague.

confrérie /kɔ̃freri/ *n.f.* brotherhood.

confront|er /kɔ̃frɔ̃te/ *v.t.* confront; (*textes*) compare. **~ation** *n.f.* confrontation.

confus, ~e /kɔ̃fy, -z/ *a.* confused; (*gêné*) embarrassed.

confusion /kɔ̃fyzjɔ̃/ *n.f.* confusion; (*gêne*) embarrassment.

congé /kɔ̃ʒe/ *n.m.* holiday; (*arrêt momentané*) time off; (*mil.*) leave; (*avis de départ*) notice. **~ de maladie,** sick-leave. **jour de ~,** day off. **prendre ~ de,** take one's leave of.

congédier /kɔ̃ʒedje/ *v.t.* dismiss.

cong|eler /kɔ̃ʒle/ *v.t.* freeze. **~élateur** *n.m.* freezer.

congénère /kɔ̃ʒenɛr/ *n.m.*/*f.* fellow creature.

congénit|al (*m. pl.* **~aux**) /kɔ̃ʒenital, -o/ *a.* congenital.

congère /kɔ̃ʒɛr/ *n.f.* snow-drift.

congestion /kɔ̃ʒɛstjɔ̃/ *n.f.* congestion. **~ cérébrale,** stroke, cerebral haemorrhage. **~ner** /-jɔne/ *v.t.* congest; (*visage*) flush.

congrégation /kɔ̃gregasjɔ̃/ *n.f.* congregation.

congr|ès /kɔ̃grɛ/ *n.m.* congress. **~essiste** *n.m.*/*f.* member of a congress, delegate.

conifère /kɔnifɛr/ *n.m.* conifer.

conique /kɔnik/ *a.* conic(al).

conjectur|e /kɔ̃ʒɛktyr/ *n.f.* conjecture. **~er** *v.t.*/*i.* conjecture.

conjoint, ~e[1] /kɔ̃ʒwɛ̃, -t/ *n.m., f.* spouse.

conjoint, ~e[2] /kɔ̃ʒwɛ̃, -t/ *a.* joint. **~ement** /-tmɑ̃/ *adv.* jointly.

conjonction /kɔ̃ʒɔ̃ksjɔ̃/ *n.f.* conjunction.

conjoncture /kɔ̃ʒɔ̃ktyr/ *n.f.* circumstances; (*économique*) economic climate.

conjugaison /kɔ̃ʒygɛzɔ̃/ *n.f.* conjugation.

conjug|al (*m. pl.* **~aux**) /kɔ̃ʒygal, -o/ *a.* conjugal.

conjuguer /kɔ̃ʒyge/ *v.t.* (*gram.*) conjugate; (*efforts*) combine. **se ~** *v. pr.* (*gram.*) be conjugated.

conjur|er /kɔ̃ʒyre/ *v.t.* (*éviter*) avert; (*implorer*) entreat. **se ~er** *v. pr.* conspire. **~ation** *n.f.* conspiracy. **~é, ~ée** *n.m., f.* conspirator.

connaissance /kɔnɛsɑ̃s/ *n.f.* knowledge; (*personne*) acquaintance; (*conscience*) consciousness. **~s,** (*science*) knowledge. **faire la ~ de,** meet; (*personne connue*) get to know. **perdre ~,** lose consciousness. **sans ~,** unconscious.

connaisseur /kɔnɛsœr/ *n.m.* connoisseur.

connaître† /kɔnɛtr/ *v.t.* know; (*avoir*) have. **se ~** *v. pr.* (*se rencontrer*) meet. **faire ~,** make known. **s'y ~ à** *ou* **en,** know (all) about.

conne|cter /kɔnɛkte/ *v.t.* connect. **~xion** *n.f.* connection.

connexe /kɔnɛks/ *a.* related.

connivence /kɔnivɑ̃s/ *n.f.* connivance.

connotation /kɔnɔtasjɔ̃/ *n.f.* connotation.

connu /kɔny/ *a.* well-known.

conquér|ir /kɔ̃kerir/ *v.t.* conquer. **~ant, ~ante** *n.m., f.* conqueror.

conquête /kɔ̃kɛt/ *n.f.* conquest.

consacrer /kɔ̃sakre/ *v.t.* devote; (*relig.*) consecrate; (*sanctionner*) establish. **se ~** *v. pr.* devote o.s. (**à,** to).

consciemment /kɔ̃sjamɑ̃/ *adv.* consciously.

conscience /kɔ̃sjɑ̃s/ *n.f.* conscience; (*perception*) consciousness. **avoir/prendre ~ de,**

be/become aware of. **perdre ~,** lose consciousness.

conscienciEu|x, ~se /kɔ̃sjɑ̃sjø, -z/ *a.* conscientious.

conscient, ~e /kɔ̃sjɑ̃, -t/ *a.* conscious. **~ de,** aware *ou* conscious of.

conscription /kɔ̃skripsjɔ̃/ *n.f.* conscription.

conscrit /kɔ̃skri/ *n.m.* conscript.

consécration /kɔ̃sekrɑsjɔ̃/ *n.f.* consecration.

consécuti|f, ~ve /kɔ̃sekytif, -v/ *a.* consecutive. **~f à,** following upon. **~vement** *adv.* consecutively.

conseil /kɔ̃sɛj/ *n.m.* (piece of) advice; (*assemblée*) council, committee; (*séance*) meeting; (*personne*) consultant. **~ d'administration,** board of directors. **~ des ministres,** Cabinet. **~ municipal,** town council.

conseiller[1] /kɔ̃seje/ *v.t.* advise. **~ à qn. de,** advise s.o. to. **~ qch. à qn.,** recommend sth. to s.o.

conseill|er[2], **~ère** /kɔ̃seje, -ɛjɛr/ *n.m., f.* adviser, counsellor. **~er municipal,** town councillor.

consent|ir /kɔ̃sɑ̃tir/ *v.i.* agree (**à,** to). —*v.t.* grant. **~ement** *n.m.* consent.

conséquence /kɔ̃sekɑ̃s/ *n.f.* consequence. **en ~,** consequently; (*comme il convient*) accordingly.

conséquent, ~e /kɔ̃sekɑ̃, -t/ *a.* logical; (*important: fam.*) sizeable. **par ~,** consequently.

conserva|teur, ~trice /kɔ̃sɛrvatœr, -tris/ *a.* conservative. —*n.m., f.* (*pol.*) conservative. —*n.m.* (*de musée*) curator. **~tisme** *n.m.* conservatism.

conservatoire /kɔ̃sɛrvatwar/ *n.m.* academy.

conserve /kɔ̃sɛrv/ *n.f.* tinned *ou* canned food. **en ~,** tinned, canned.

conserv|er /kɔ̃sɛrve/ *v.t.* keep; (*en bon état*) preserve; (*culin.*) preserve. **se ~er** *v. pr.* (*culin.*) keep. **~ation** *n.f.* preservation.

considérable /kɔ̃siderabl/ *a.* considerable.

considération /kɔ̃siderɑsjɔ̃/ *n.f.* consideration; (*respect*) regard. **prendre en ~,** take into consideration.

considérer /kɔ̃sidere/ *v.t.* consider; (*respecter*) esteem. **~ comme,** consider to be.

consigne /kɔ̃siɲ/ *n.f.* (*de gare*) left luggage (office); (*Amer.*) (baggage) checkroom; (*scol.*) detention; (*somme*) deposit; (*ordres*) orders. **~ automatique,** (left-luggage) lockers; (*Amer.*) (baggage) lockers.

consigner /kɔ̃siɲe/ *v.t.* (*comm.*) charge a deposit on; (*écrire*) record; (*élève*) keep in; (*soldat*) confine.

consistan|t, ~te /kɔ̃sistɑ̃, -t/ *a.* solid; (*épais*) thick. **~ce** *n.f.* consistency; (*fig.*) solidity.

consister /kɔ̃siste/ *v.i.* **~ en/dans,** consist of/in. **~ à faire,** consist in doing.

consol|er /kɔ̃sɔle/ *v.t.* console. **se ~er** *v. pr.* be consoled (**de,** for). **~ation** *n.f.* consolation.

consolider /kɔ̃sɔlide/ *v.t.* strengthen; (*fig.*) consolidate.

consomma|teur, ~trice /kɔ̃sɔmatœr, -tris/ *n.m., f.* (*comm.*) consumer; (*dans un café*) customer.

consommé[1] /kɔ̃sɔme/ *a.* consummate.

consommé[2] /kɔ̃sɔme/ *n.m.* (*bouillon*) consommé.

consomm|er /kɔ̃sɔme/ *v.t.* consume; (*user*) use, consume; (*mariage*) consummate. —*v.i.* drink. **~ation** *n.f.* consumption; consummation; (*boisson*) drink. **de ~ation,** (*comm.*) consumer.

consonne /kɔ̃sɔn/ *n.f.* consonant.

consortium /kɔ̃sɔrsjɔm/ *n.m.* consortium.

conspir|er /kɔ̃spire/ *v.i.* conspire. **~ateur, ~atrice** *n.m., f.* conspirator. **~ation** *n.f.* conspiracy.

conspuer /kɔ̃spɥe/ *v.t.* boo.

const|ant, ~ante /kɔ̃stɑ̃, -t/ *a.* constant. **~amment** /-amɑ̃/ *adv.* constantly. **~ance** *n.f.* constancy.

constat /kɔ̃sta/ *n.m.* (official) report.

constat|er /kɔ̃state/ *v.t.* note; (*certifier*) certify. **~ation** *n.f.* observation.

constellation /kɔ̃stelɑsjɔ̃/ *n.f.* constellation.

constellé /kɔ̃stele/ *a.* **~ de,** studded with.

constern|er /kɔ̃stɛrne/ *v.t.* dismay. **~ation** *n.f.* dismay.

constip|é /kɔ̃stipe/ *a.* constipated; (*fig.*) stilted. **~ation** *n.f.* constipation.

constituer /kɔ̃stitɥe/ *v.t.* make up, constitute; (*organiser*) form; (*être*) constitute. **se ~ prisonnier,** give o.s. up.

constituti|f, ~ve /kɔ̃stitytif, -v/ *a.* constituent.

constitution /kɔ̃stitysjɔ̃/ *n.f.* formation; (*d'une équipe*) composition; (*pol., méd.*) constitution. **~nel, ~nelle** /-jɔnɛl/ *a.* constitutional.

constructeur /kɔ̃stryktœr/ *n.m.* manufacturer.

constructi|f, ~ve /kɔ̃stryktif, -v/ *a.* constructive.

constr|uire† /kɔ̃strɥir/ *v.t.* build; (*système, phrase, etc.*) construct. **~uction** *n.f.* building; (*structure*) construction.

consul /kɔ̃syl/ *n.m.* consul. **~aire** *a.* consular. **~at** *n.m.* consulate.

consult|er /kɔ̃sylte/ *v.t.* consult. —*v.i.* (*médecin*) hold surgery; (*Amer.*) hold office hours. **se ~er** *v. pr.* confer. **~ation** *n.f.* consultation; (*réception: méd.*) surgery; (*Amer.*) office.

consumer /kɔ̃syme/ *v.t.* consume. **se ~** *v. pr.* be consumed.

contact /kɔ̃takt/ *n.m.* contact; (*toucher*) touch. **mettre/couper le ~,** (*auto.*) switch on/off the ignition. **prendre ~ avec,** get in touch with. **~er** *v.t.* contact.

contag|ieux, ~ieuse /kɔ̃taʒjø, -z/ *a.* contagious. **~ion** *n.f.* contagion.

container /kɔ̃tɛnɛr/ *n.m.* container.

contamin|er /kɔ̃tamine/ *v.t.* contaminate. **~ation** *n.f.* contamination.

conte /kɔ̃t/ *n.m.* tale.

contempl|er /kɔ̃tɑ̃ple/ *v.t.* contemplate. **~ation** *n.f.* contemplation.

contemporain, ~e /kɔ̃tɑ̃pɔrɛ̃, -ɛn/ *a.* & *n.m., f.* contemporary.

contenance /kɔ̃tnɑ̃s/ *n.f.* (*contenu*) capacity; (*allure*) bearing; (*sang-froid*) composure.

contenant /kɔ̃tnɑ̃/ *n.m.* container.

contenir† /kɔ̃tnir/ *v.t.* contain; (*avoir une capacité de*) hold. **se ~** *v. pr.* contain o.s.

content, ~e /kɔ̃tɑ̃, -t/ *a.* pleased (**de,** with). **~ de faire,** pleased to do.

content|er /kɔ̃tɑ̃te/ *v.t.* satisfy. **se ~er de,** content o.s. with. **~ement** *n.m.* contentment.

contentieux /kɔ̃tɑ̃sjø/ *n.m.* matters in dispute; (*service*) legal department.

contenu /kɔ̃tny/ *n.m.* (*de contenant*) contents; (*de texte*) content.

conter /kɔ̃te/ *v.t.* tell, relate.

contestataire /kɔ̃tɛstatɛr/ *n.m./f.* protester.

conteste (sans) /(sɑ̃)kɔ̃tɛst/ *adv.* indisputably.

contest|er /kɔ̃tɛste/ *v.t.* dispute;

(*univ.*) protest against. —*v.i.* protest. **~able** *a.* debatable. **~ation** *n.f.* dispute; (*univ.*) protest.

conteu|r, ~se /kɔ̃tœr, -øz/ *n.m., f.* story-teller.

contexte /kɔ̃tɛkst/ *n.m.* context.

contigu, ~ë /kɔ̃tigy/ *a.* adjacent (**à**, to).

continent /kɔ̃tinɑ̃/ *n.m.* continent. **~al** (*m. pl.* **~aux**) /-tal, -to/ *a.* continental.

contingences /kɔ̃tɛ̃ʒɑ̃s/ *n.f. pl.* contingencies.

contingent /kɔ̃tɛ̃ʒɑ̃/ *n.m.* (*mil.*) contingent; (*comm.*) quota.

continu /kɔ̃tiny/ *a.* continuous.

continuel, ~le /kɔ̃tinɥɛl/ *a.* continual. **~lement** *adv.* continually.

contin|uer /kɔ̃tinɥe/ *v.t.* continue. —*v.i.* continue, go on. **~uer à** *ou* **de faire,** carry on *ou* go on *ou* continue doing. **~uation** *n.f.* continuation.

continuité /kɔ̃tinɥite/ *n.f.* continuity.

contorsion /kɔ̃tɔrsjɔ̃/ *n.f.* contortion.

contour /kɔ̃tur/ *n.m.* outline, contour. **~s,** (*d'une route etc.*) twists and turns, bends.

contourner /kɔ̃turne/ *v.t.* go round; (*difficulté*) get round.

contracepti|f, ~ve /kɔ̃trasɛptif, -v/ *a.* & *n.m.* contraceptive.

contraception /kɔ̃trasɛpsjɔ̃/ *n.f.* contraception.

contract|er /kɔ̃trakte/ *v.t.* (*maladie, dette*) contract; (*muscle*) tense, contract. **se ~er** *v. pr.* contract. **~é** *a.* tense. **~ion** /-ksjɔ̃/ *n.f.* contraction.

contractuel, ~le /kɔ̃traktɥɛl/ *n.m., f.* (*agent*) traffic warden.

contradiction /kɔ̃tradiksjɔ̃/ *n.f.* contradiction.

contradictoire /kɔ̃tradiktwar/ *a.* contradictory; (*débat*) open.

contraignant, ~e /kɔ̃trɛɲɑ̃, -t/ *a.* restricting.

contraindre† /kɔ̃trɛ̃dr/ *v.t.* compel.

contraint, ~e /kɔ̃trɛ̃, -t/ *a.* constrained. —*n.f.* constraint.

contraire /kɔ̃trɛr/ *a.* & *n.m.* opposite. **~ à,** contrary to. **au ~,** on the contrary. **~ment** *adv.* **~ment à,** contrary to.

contralto /kɔ̃tralto/ *n.m.* contralto.

contrar|ier /kɔ̃trarje/ *v.t.* annoy; (*action*) frustrate. **~iété** *n.f.* annoyance.

contrast|e /kɔ̃trast/ *n.m.* contrast. **~er** *v.i.* contrast.

contrat /kɔ̃tra/ *n.m.* contract.

contravention /kɔ̃travɑ̃sjɔ̃/ *n.f.* (parking-)ticket. **en ~,** in contravention (**à,** of).

contre /kɔ̃tr(ə)/ *prép.* against; (*en échange de*) for. **tout ~,** close by. **~-attaque** *n.f.*, **~-attaquer** *v.t.* counter-attack. **~-balancer** *v.t.* counterbalance. **à ~-jour** *adv.* against the (sun)light. **~-offensive** *n.f.* counter-offensive. **prendre le ~-pied,** do the opposite; (*opinion*) take the opposite view. **à ~-pied** *adv.* (*sport*) on the wrong foot. **~-plaqué** *n.m.* plywood. **~-révolution** *n.f.* counter-revolution. **~-torpilleur** *n.m.* destroyer.

contreband|e /kɔ̃trəbɑ̃d/ *n.f.* contraband. **faire la ~e de, passer en ~e,** smuggle. **~ier** *n.m.* smuggler.

contrebas (en) /(ɑ̃)kɔ̃trəbɑ/ *adv.* & *prép.* **en ~ (de),** below.

contrebasse /kɔ̃trəbɑs/ *n.f.* double-bass.

contrecarrer /kɔ̃trəkare/ *v.t.* thwart.

contrecœur (à) /(a)kɔ̃trəkœr/ *adv.* reluctantly.

contrecoup /kɔ̃trəku/ *n.m.* consequence.

contredire† /kɔ̃trədir/ *v.t.* contradict. **se ~** *v. pr.* contradict o.s.

contrée /kɔ̃tre/ *n.f.* region, land.
contrefaçon /kɔ̃trəfasɔ̃/ *n.f.* (*objet imité, action*) forgery.
contrefaire /kɔ̃trəfɛr/ *v.t.* (*falsifier*) forge; (*parodier*) mimic; (*déguiser*) disguise.
contrefait, ~e /kɔ̃trəfɛ -t/ *a.* deformed.
contreforts /kɔ̃trəfɔr/ *n.m. pl.* foothills.
contremaître /kɔ̃trəmɛtr/ *n.m.* foreman.
contrepartie /kɔ̃trəparti/ *n.f.* compensation.
contrepoids /kɔ̃trəpwa/ *n.m.* counterbalance.
contrer /kɔ̃tre/ *v.t.* counter.
contresens /kɔ̃trəsɑ̃s/ *n.m.* misinterpretation; (*absurdité*) nonsense. **à ~**, the wrong way.
contresigner /kɔ̃trəsiɲe/ *v.t.* countersign.
contretemps /kɔ̃trətɑ̃/ *n.m.* hitch. **à ~**, at the wrong time.
contrevenir /kɔ̃trəvnir/ *v.i.* **~ à**, contravene.
contribuable /kɔ̃tribɥabl/ *n.m./f.* taxpayer.
contribuer /kɔ̃tribɥe/ *v.t.* contribute (**à**, to, towards).
contribution /kɔ̃tribysjɔ̃/ *n.f.* contribution. **~s**, (*impôts*) taxes; (*administration*) tax office.
contrit, ~e /kɔ̃tri, -t/ *a.* contrite.
contrôl|e /kɔ̃trol/ *n.m.* check; (*des prix, d'un véhicule*) control; (*poinçon*) hallmark. **~e de soi-même**, self-control. **~e des changes**, exchange control. **~e des naissances** birth-control. **~er** *v.t.* check; (*surveiller, maîtriser*) control. **se ~er** *v. pr.* control o.s.
contrôleu|r, ~se /kɔ̃trolœr, -øz/ *n.m., f.* (bus) conductor *ou* conductress; (*de train*) (ticket) inspector.
contrordre /kɔ̃trɔrdr/ *n.m.* change of orders.
controvers|e /kɔ̃trɔvɛrs/ *n.f.* controversy. **~é** *a.* controversial.
contumace (par) /(par)kɔ̃tymas/ *adv.* in one's absence.
contusion /kɔ̃tyzjɔ̃/ *n.f.* bruise. **~né** /-jɔne/ *a.* bruised.
convaincre† /kɔ̃vɛ̃kr/ *v.t.* convince. **~ qn. de faire**, persuade s.o. to do.
convalescen|t, ~te /kɔ̃valesɑ̃, -t/ *a.* & *n.m.,f.* convalescent. **~ce** *n.f.* convalescence. **être en ~ce**, convalesce.
convenable /kɔ̃vnabl/ *a.* (*correct*) decent, proper; (*approprié*) suitable.
convenance /kɔ̃vnɑ̃s/ *n.f.* **à sa ~**, to one's satisfaction. **les ~s**, the proprieties.
convenir† /kɔ̃vnir/ *v.i.* be suitable. **~ à** suit. **~ de/que**, (*avouer*) admit (to)/that. **~ de**, (*s'accorder sur*) agree (up)on. **il convient de**, it is advisable to; (*selon les bienséances*) it would be right to.
convention /kɔ̃vɑ̃sjɔ̃/ *n.f.* convention. **~s**, (*convenances*) convention. **de ~**, conventional. **~nel, ~nelle** /-jɔnɛl/ *a.* conventional.
convenu /kɔ̃vny/ *a.* agreed.
converger /kɔ̃vɛrʒe/ *v.i.* converge.
convers|er /kɔ̃vɛrse/ *v.i.* converse. **~ation** *n.f.* conversation.
conver|tir /kɔ̃vɛrtir/ *v.t.* convert (**à**, to; **en**, into). **se ~tir** *v. pr.* be converted, convert. **~sion** *n.f.* conversion. **~tible** *a.* convertible.
convexe /kɔ̃vɛks/ *a.* convex.
conviction /kɔ̃viksjɔ̃/ *n.f.* conviction.
convier /kɔ̃vje/ *v.t.* invite.
convive /kɔ̃viv/ *n.m./f.* guest.
convocation /kɔ̃vɔkɑsjɔ̃/ *n.f.* summons to attend; (*d'une assemblée*) convening; (*document*) notification to attend.
convoi /kɔ̃vwa/ *n.m.* convoy;

(*train*) train. ~ (**funèbre**), funeral procession.

convoit|er /kɔ̃vwate/ *v.t.* desire, covet, envy. **~ise** *n.f.* desire, envy.

convoquer /kɔ̃vɔke/ *v.t.* (*assemblée*) convene; (*personne*) summon.

convoy|er /kɔ̃vwaje/ *v.t.* escort. **~eur** *n.m.* escort ship. **~eur de fonds,** security guard.

convulsion /kɔ̃vylsjɔ̃/ *n.f.* convulsion.

coopérati|f, ~ve /kɔɔperatif, -v/ *a.* co-operative. —*n.f.* co-operative (society).

coopér|er /kɔɔpere/ *v.i.* co-operate (**à**, in). **~ation** *n.f.* co-operation.

coopter /kɔɔpte/ *v.t.* co-opt.

coordination /kɔɔrdinɑsjɔ̃/ *n.f.* co-ordination.

coordonn|er /kɔɔrdɔne/ *v.t.* co-ordinate. **~ées** *n.f. pl.* co-ordinates; (*adresse*: *fam.*) particulars.

copain /kɔpɛ̃/ *n.m.* (*fam.*) pal.

copeau (*pl.* **~x**) /kɔpo/ *n.m.* (*lamelle de bois*) shaving.

cop|ie /kɔpi/ *n.f.* copy; (*scol.*) paper. **~ier** *v.t./i.* copy. **~ier sur,** (*scol.*) copy *ou* crib from.

copieu|x, ~se /kɔpjø, -z/ *a.* copious.

copine /kɔpin/ *n.f.* (*fam.*) pal.

copiste /kɔpist/ *n.m./f.* copyist.

copropriété /kɔprɔprijete/ *n.f.* co-ownership.

copulation /kɔpylɑsjɔ̃/ *n.f.* copulation.

coq /kɔk/ *n.m.* cock. **~-à-l'âne** *n.m. invar.* abrupt change of subject.

coque /kɔk/ *n.f.* shell; (*de bateau*) hull.

coquelicot /kɔkliko/ *n.m.* poppy.

coqueluche /kɔklyʃ/ *n.f.* whooping cough.

coquet, ~te /kɔkɛ, -t/ *a.* flirtatious; (*élégant*) pretty; (*somme*: *fam.*) tidy. **~terie** /-tri/ *n.f.* flirtatiousness.

coquetier /kɔktje/ *n.m.* egg-cup.

coquillage /kɔkijaʒ/ *n.m.* shellfish; (*coquille*) shell.

coquille /kɔkij/ *n.f.* shell; (*faute*) misprint. ~ **Saint-Jacques,** scallop.

coquin, ~e /kɔkɛ̃, -in/ *a.* naughty. —*n.m., f.* rascal.

cor /kɔr/ *n.m.* (*mus.*) horn. ~ (**au pied**), corn.

cor|ail (*pl.* **~aux**) /kɔraj, -o/ *n.m.* coral.

Coran /kɔrɑ̃/ *n.m.* Koran.

corbeau (*pl.* **~x**) /kɔrbo/ *n.m.* (*oiseau*) crow.

corbeille /kɔrbɛj/ *n.f.* basket. ~ **à papier,** waste-paper basket.

corbillard /kɔrbijar/ *n.m.* hearse.

cordage /kɔrdaʒ/ *n.m.* rope.

corde /kɔrd/ *n.f.* rope; (*d'arc, de violon, etc.*) string. ~ **à linge,** washing line. ~ **à sauter,** skipping-rope. ~ **raide,** tightrope. **~s vocales,** vocal cords.

cordée /kɔrde/ *n.f.* roped party.

cord|ial (*m. pl.* **~iaux**) /kɔrdjal, -jo/ *a.* warm, cordial. **~ialité** *n.f.* warmth.

cordon /kɔrdɔ̃/ *n.m.* string, cord. **~-bleu** (*pl.* **~s-bleus**) *n.m.* first-rate cook. ~ **de police,** police cordon.

cordonnier /kɔrdɔnje/ *n.m.* shoe mender.

Corée /kɔre/ *n.f.* Korea.

coreligionnaire /kɔrəliʒjɔnɛr/ *n.m./f.* person of the same religion.

coriace /kɔrjas/ *a.* (*aliment*) tough. —*a.* & *n.m.* tenacious and tough (person).

corne /kɔrn/ *n.f.* horn.

cornée /kɔrne/ *n.f.* cornea.

corneille /kɔrnɛj/ *n.f.* crow.

cornemuse /kɔrnəmyz/ *n.f.* bagpipes.

corner[1] /kɔrne/ *v.t.* (*page*) make

dog-eared. —*v.i.* (*auto.*) hoot; (*auto., Amer.*) honk.

corner² /kɔrnɛr/ *n.m.* (*football*) corner.

cornet /kɔrnɛ/ *n.m.* (paper) cone; (*crème glacée*) cornet, cone.

corniaud /kɔrnjo/ *n.m.* (*fam.*) nitwit.

corniche /kɔrniʃ/ *n.f.* cornice; (*route*) cliff road.

cornichon /kɔrniʃɔ̃/ *n.m.* gherkin.

corollaire /kɔrɔlɛr/ *n.m.* corollary.

corporation /kɔrpɔrɑsjɔ̃/ *n.f.* professional body.

corporel, ~le /kɔrpɔrɛl/ *a.* bodily; (*châtiment*) corporal.

corps /kɔr/ *n.m.* body; (*mil., pol.*) corps. **~ à corps,** hand to hand. **~ électoral,** electorate. **~ enseignant,** teaching profession. **faire ~ avec,** form part of.

corpulen|t, ~te /kɔrpylɑ̃, -t/ *a.* stout. **~ce** *n.f.* stoutness.

correct /kɔrɛkt/ *a.* proper, correct; (*exact*) correct. **~ement** *adv.* properly; correctly.

correc|teur, ~trice /kɔrɛktœr, -tris/ *n.m., f.* (*scol.*) examiner.

correction /kɔrɛksjɔ̃/ *n.f.* correction; (*punition*) beating.

corrélation /kɔrelɑsjɔ̃/ *n.f.* correlation.

correspondan|t, ~te /kɔrɛspɔ̃dɑ̃, -t/ *a.* corresponding. —*n.m., f.* correspondent. **~ce** *n.f.* correspondence; (*de train, d'autobus*) connection.

correspondre /kɔrɛspɔ̃dr/ *v.i.* (*s'accorder, écrire*) correspond; (*chambres*) communicate.

corrida /kɔrida/ *n.f.* bullfight.

corridor /kɔridɔr/ *n.m.* corridor.

corrig|er /kɔriʒe/ *v.t.* correct; (*devoir*) mark, correct; (*punir*) beat; (*guérir*) cure. **se ~er de,** cure o.s. of. **~é** *n.m.* (*scol.*) correct version, model answer.

corroborer /kɔrɔbɔre/ *v.t.* corroborate.

corro|der /kɔrɔde/ *v.t.* corrode. **~sion** /-ozjɔ̃/ *n.f.* corrosion.

corromp|re† /kɔrɔ̃pr/ *v.t.* corrupt; (*soudoyer*) bribe. **~u** *a.* corrupt.

corrosi|f, ~ve /kɔrozif, -v/ *a.* corrosive.

corruption /kɔrypsjɔ̃/ *n.f.* corruption.

corsage /kɔrsaʒ/ *n.m.* bodice; (*chemisier*) blouse.

corsaire /kɔrsɛr/ *n.m.* pirate.

Corse /kɔrs/ *n.f.* Corsica.

corse /kɔrs/ *a.* & *n.m./f.* Corsican.

corsé /kɔrse/ *a.* (*vin*) full-bodied; (*scabreux*) spicy.

corset /kɔrsɛ/ *n.m.* corset.

cortège /kɔrtɛʒ/ *n.m.* procession.

corvée /kɔrve/ *n.f.* chore.

cosaque /kɔzak/ *n.m.* Cossack.

cosmétique /kɔsmetik/ *n.m.* hair oil.

cosmique /kɔsmik/ *a.* cosmic.

cosmonaute /kɔsmɔnot/ *n.m./f.* cosmonaut.

cosmopolite /kɔsmɔpɔlit/ *a.* cosmopolitan.

cosmos /kɔsmɔs/ *n.m.* (*espace*) (outer) space; (*univers*) cosmos.

cosse /kɔs/ *n.f.* (*de pois*) pod.

cossu /kɔsy/ *a.* well-to-do.

costaud, ~e /kɔsto, -d/ *a.* (*fam.*) strong. —*n.m.* (*fam.*) strong man.

costum|e /kɔstym/ *n.m.* suit; (*théâtre*) costume. **~é** *a.* dressed up.

cote /kɔt/ *n.f.* (classification) mark; (*en Bourse*) quotation; (*de cheval*) odds; (*de candidat, acteur*) rating. **~ d'alerte,** danger level.

côte /kot/ *n.f.* (*littoral*) coast; (*pente*) hill; (*anat.*) rib; (*de porc*) chop. **~ à côte,** side by side. **la C~ d'Azur,** the (French) Riviera.

côté /kote/ *n.m.* side; (*direction*) way. **à ~,** nearby; (*voisin*) next-door. **à ~ de,** next to; (*comparé à*) compared to; (*cible*) wide of. **aux**

~s de, by the side of. **de ~,** aside; (*regarder*) sideways. **de ce ~,** this way. **du ~ de,** towards; (*proximité*) near; (*provenance*) from.
coteau (*pl.* **~x**) /kɔto/ *n.m.* hill.
côtelette /kotlɛt/ *n.f.* chop.
coter /kɔte/ *v.t.* (*comm.*) quote; (*apprécier, noter*) rate.
coterie /kɔtri/ *n.f.* clique.
côt|ier, ~ière /kotje, -jɛr/ *a.* coastal.
cotis|er /kɔtize/ *v.i.* pay one's contributions (**à,** to); (*à un club*) pay one's subscription. **se ~er** *v. pr.* club together. **~ation** *n.f.* contribution(s); subscription.
coton /kɔtɔ̃/ *n.m.* cotton. **~ hydrophile,** cotton wool.
côtoyer /kotwaje/ *v.t.* skirt, run along; (*fréquenter*) rub shoulders with; (*fig.*) verge on.
cotte /kɔt/ *n.f.* (*d'ouvrier*) overalls.
cou /ku/ *n.m.* neck.
couchage /kuʃaʒ/ *n.m.* sleeping arrangements.
couchant /kuʃɑ̃/ *n.m.* sunset.
couche /kuʃ/ *n.f.* layer; (*de peinture*) coat; (*de bébé*) nappy. **~s,** (*méd.*) childbirth. **~s sociales,** social strata.
coucher /kuʃe/ *n.m.* **~ (du soleil),** sunset. —*v.t.* put to bed; (*loger*) put up; (*étendre*) lay down. **~ (par écrit),** inscribe. —*v.i.* sleep. **se ~** *v. pr.* go to bed; (*s'étendre*) lie down; (*soleil*) set. **couché** *a.* in bed; (*étendu*) lying down.
couchette /kuʃɛt/ *n.f.* (*rail.*) couchette; (*naut.*) bunk.
coucou /kuku/ *n.m.* cuckoo.
coude /kud/ *n.m.* elbow; (*de rivière etc.*) bend. **~ à coude,** side by side.
cou-de-pied (*pl.* **cous-de-pied**) /kudpje/ *n.m.* instep.
coudoyer /kudwaje/ *v.t.* rub shoulders with.
coudre† /kudr/ *v.t./i.* sew.
couenne /kwan/ *n.f.* (*de jambon*) rind.
couette /kwɛt/ *n.f.* duvet, continental quilt.
couffin /kufɛ̃/ *n.m.* Moses basket.
couiner /kwine/ *v.i.* squeak.
coulant, ~e /kulɑ̃, -t/ *a.* (*indulgent*) easy-going.
coulée /kule/ *n.f.* **~ de lave,** lava flow.
couler[1] /kule/ *v.i.* flow, run; (*fromage, nez*) run; (*fuir*) leak. —*v.t.* (*sculpture, métal*) cast; (*vie*) pass, lead. **se ~** *v. pr.* (*se glisser*) slip.
couler[2] /kule/ *v.t./i.* (*bateau*) sink.
couleur /kulœr/ *n.f.* colour; (*peinture*) paint; (*cartes*) suit. **~s,** (*teint*) colour. **de ~,** (*homme, femme*) coloured. **en ~s,** (*télévision, film*) colour.
couleuvre /kulœvr/ *n.f.* (grass *ou* smooth) snake.
couliss|e /kulis/ *n.f.* (*de tiroir etc.*) runner. **~es,** (*théâtre*) wings. **à ~e,** (*porte, fenêtre*) sliding. **~er** *v.i.* slide.
couloir /kulwar/ *n.m.* corridor; (*de bus*) gangway; (*sport*) lane.
coup /ku/ *n.m.* blow; (*choc*) knock; (*sport*) stroke; (*de crayon, chance*) stroke; (*de fusil, pistolet*) shot; (*fois*) time; (*aux échecs*) move. **à ~ sûr,** definitely. **après ~,** after the event. **~ de chiffon,** wipe (with a rag). **~ de coude,** nudge. **~ de couteau,** stab. **~ d'envoi,** kick-off. **~ d'état,** (*pol.*) coup. **~ de feu,** shot. **~ de fil,** phone call. **~ de filet,** haul. **~ de frein,** sudden braking. **~ de grâce,** finishing blow. **~ de main,** helping hand. **~ d'œil,** glance. **~ de pied,** kick. **~ de poing,** punch. **~ de sang,** (*méd.*) stroke. **~ de soleil,** sunburn. **~ de sonnette,** ring (on a bell). **~ de téléphone,** telephone call. **~ de tête,** wild impulse. **~ de tonnerre,** thunderclap. **~ de vent,** gust of wind. **~ franc,** free

kick. ~ **sur coup,** in rapid succession. **d'un seul ~,** in one go. **du premier ~,** first go. **sale ~,** dirty trick. **sous le ~ de,** under the influence of. **sur le ~,** immediately.

coupable /kupabl/ *a.* guilty. —*n.m./f.* culprit.

coupe[1] /kup/ *n.f.* cup; (*de champagne*) goblet; (*à fruits*) dish.

coupe[2] /kup/ *n.f.* (*de vêtement etc.*) cut; (*dessin*) section. **~ de cheveux,** haircut.

coupé /kupe/ *n.m.* (*voiture*) coupé.

coup|er /kupe/ *v.t./i.* cut; (*arbre*) cut down; (*arrêter*) cut off; (*voyage*) break; (*appétit*) take away; (*vin*) water down. **se ~er** *v. pr.* cut o.s.; (*routes*) intersect. **~er la parole à,** cut short. **~e-papier** *n.m. invar.* paper-knife.

couperosé /kuproze/ *a.* blotchy.

couple /kupl/ *n.m.* couple.

coupler /kuple/ *v.t.* couple.

couplet /kuplɛ/ *n.m.* verse.

coupole /kupɔl/ *n.f.* dome.

coupon /kupɔ̃/ *n.m.* (*étoffe*) remnant; (*billet, titre*) coupon.

coupure /kupyr/ *n.f.* cut; (*billet de banque*) note; (*de presse*) cutting. **~ (de courant),** power cut.

cour /kur/ *n.f.* (court)yard; (*de roi*) court; (*tribunal*) court. **~ (de récréation),** playground. **~ martiale,** court martial. **faire la ~ à,** court.

courag|e /kuraʒ/ *n.m.* courage. **~eux, ~euse** *a.* courageous.

couramment /kuramɑ̃/ *adv.* frequently; (*parler*) fluently.

courant[1], **~e** /kurɑ̃, -t/ *a.* standard, ordinary; (*en cours*) current.

courant[2] /kurɑ̃/ *n.m.* current. **~ d'air,** draught. **dans le ~ de,** in the course of. **être/mettre au ~ de,** know/tell about; (*à jour*) be/bring up to date on.

courbatur|e /kurbatyr/ *n.f.* ache. **~é** *a.* aching.

courbe /kurb/ *n.f.* curve. —*a.* curved.

courber /kurbe/ *v.t./i.*, **se ~** *v. pr.* bend.

coureu|r, ~se /kurœr, -øz/ *n.m., f.* (*sport*) runner. **~r automobile,** racing driver.

courge /kurʒ/ *n.f.* marrow; (*Amer.*) squash.

courgette /kurʒɛt/ *n.f.* courgette; (*Amer.*) zucchini.

courir† /kurir/ *v.i.* run; (*se hâter*) rush; (*nouvelles etc.*) go round. —*v.t.* (*risque*) run; (*danger*) face; (*épreuve sportive*) run *ou* compete in; (*fréquenter*) do the rounds of; (*filles*) chase.

couronne /kurɔn/ *n.f.* crown; (*de fleurs*) wreath.

couronn|er /kurɔne/ *v.t.* crown. **~ement** *n.m.* coronation, crowning; (*fig.*) crowning achievement.

courrier /kurje/ *n.m.* post, mail; (*de journal*) column.

courroie /kurwa/ *n.f.* strap; (*techn.*) belt.

courroux /kuru/ *n.m.* wrath.

cours /kur/ *n.m.* (*déroulement*) course; (*leçon*) class; (*série de leçons*) course; (*prix*) price; (*cote*) rate; (*allée*) avenue. **au ~ de,** in the course of. **avoir ~,** (*monnaie*) be legal tender; (*fig.*) be current. **~ d'eau,** river, stream. **~ magistral,** (*univ.*) lecture. **en ~,** current; (*travail*) in progress. **en ~ de route,** on the way.

course /kurs/ *n.f.* run(ning); (*épreuve de vitesse*) race; (*entre rivaux: fig.*) race; (*de projectile*) flight; (*voyage*) journey; (*commission*) errand. **~s,** (*achats*) shopping; (*de chevaux*) races.

cours|ier, ~ière /kursje, -jɛr/ *n.m., f.* (*chasseur*) messenger.

court[1], **~e** /kur, -t/ *a.* short. —*adv.* short. **à ~ de,** short of. **pris de ~,** caught unawares. **~-circuit** (*pl.* **~s-circuits**) *n.m.* short circuit.

court² /kur/ *n.m.* ~ **(de tennis),** (tennis) court.
court|ier, ~ière /kurtje, -jɛr/ *n.m., f.* broker.
courtisan /kurtizɑ̃/ *n.m.* courtier.
courtisane /kurtizan/ *n.f.* courtesan.
courtiser /kurtize/ *v.t.* court.
courtois, ~e /kurtwa, -z/ *a.* courteous. **~ie** /-zi/ *n.f.* courtesy.
couscous /kuskus/ *n.m.* couscous.
cousin, ~e /kuzɛ̃, -in/ *n.m., f.* cousin. ~ **germain,** first cousin.
coussin /kusɛ̃/ *n.m.* cushion.
coût /ku/ *n.m.* cost.
couteau (*pl.* **~x**) /kuto/ *n.m.* knife. ~ **à cran d'arrêt,** flick-knife.
coutellerie /kutɛlri/ *n.f.* (*magasin*) cutlery shop.
coût|er /kute/ *v.t./i.* cost. **~e que coûte,** at all costs. **~eux, ~euse** *a.* costly.
coutum|e /kutym/ *n.f.* custom. **~ier, ~ière** *a.* customary.
coutur|e /kutyr/ *n.f.* sewing; (*métier*) dressmaking; (*points*) seam. **~ier** *n.m.* fashion designer. **~ière** *n.f.* dressmaker.
couvée /kuve/ *n.f.* brood.
couvent /kuvɑ̃/ *n.m.* convent; (*de moines*) monastery.
couver /kuve/ *v.t.* (*œufs*) hatch; (*personne*) pamper; (*maladie*) be coming down with, be sickening for. *—v.i.* (*feu*) smoulder; (*mal*) be brewing.
couvercle /kuvɛrkl/ *n.m.* lid, cover.
couvert¹, ~e /kuvɛr, -t/ *a.* covered (**de,** with); (*habillé*) covered up; (*ciel*) overcast. *—n.m.* (*abri*) cover. **à** ~, (*mil.*) under cover. **à** ~ **de,** (*fig.*) safe from.
couvert² /kuvɛr/ *n.m.* (*à table*) place-setting; (*prix*) cover charge. **~s,** (*couteaux etc.*) cutlery. **mettre le ~,** lay the table.
couverture /kuvɛrtyr/ *n.f.* cover; (*de lit*) blanket; (*toit*) roofing. ~ **chauffante,** electric blanket.
couveuse /kuvøz/ *n.f.* ~ **(artificielle),** incubator.
couvreur /kuvrœr/ *n.m.* roofer.
couvr|ir† /kuvrir/ *v.t.* cover. **se ~ir** *v. pr.* (*s'habiller*) cover up; (*se coiffer*) put one's hat on; (*ciel*) become overcast. **~e-chef** *n.m.* hat. **~e-feu** (*pl.* **~e-feux**) *n.m.* curfew. **~e-lit** *n.m.* bedspread.
cow-boy /kobɔj/ *n.m.* cowboy.
crabe /krab/ *n.m.* crab.
crachat /kraʃa/ *n.m.* spit(tle).
cracher /kraʃe/ *v.i.* spit; (*radio*) crackle. *—v.t.* spit (out).
crachin /kraʃɛ̃/ *n.m.* drizzle.
crack /krak/ *n.m.* (*fam.*) wizard, ace, prodigy.
craie /krɛ/ *n.f.* chalk.
craindre† /krɛ̃dr/ *v.t.* be afraid of, fear; (*être sensible à*) be easily damaged by.
crainte /krɛ̃t/ *n.f.* fear. **de ~ de/que,** for fear of/that.
crainti|f, ~ve /krɛ̃tif, -v/ *a.* timid.
cramoisi /kramwazi/ *a.* crimson.
crampe /krɑ̃p/ *n.f.* cramp.
crampon /krɑ̃pɔ̃/ *n.m.* (*de chaussure*) stud.
cramponner (se) /(sə)krɑ̃pɔne/ *v. pr.* **se ~ à,** cling to.
cran /krɑ̃/ *n.m.* (*entaille*) notch; (*trou*) hole; (*courage: fam.*) pluck.
crâne /krɑn/ *n.m.* skull.
crâner /krɑne/ *v.i.* (*fam.*) swank.
crapaud /krapo/ *n.m.* toad.
crapul|e /krapyl/ *n.f.* villain. **~eux, ~euse** *a.* sordid, foul.
craqu|er /krake/ *v.i.* crack, snap; (*plancher*) creak; (*couture*) split; (*fig.*) break down. *—v.t.* **~er une allumette,** strike a match. **~ement** *n.m.* crack(ing), snap(ping); creak(ing); striking.
crass|e /kras/ *n.f.* grime. **~eux, ~euse** *a.* grimy.
cratère /kratɛr/ *n.m.* crater.
cravache /kravaʃ/ *n.f.* horsewhip.

cravate /kravat/ *n.f.* tie.
crawl /krol/ *n.m.* (*nage*) crawl.
crayeu|x, ~se /krɛjø, -z/ *a.* chalky.
crayon /krɛjɔ̃/ *n.m.* pencil. **~ (de couleur)**, crayon. **~ à bille**, ball-point pen.
créanc|ier, ~ière /kreɑ̃sje, -jɛr/ *n.m., f.* creditor.
créa|teur, ~trice /kreatœr, -tris/ *a.* creative. —*n.m., f.* creator.
création /kreɑsjɔ̃/ *n.f.* creation; (*comm.*) product.
créature /kreatyr/ *n.f.* creature.
crèche /krɛʃ/ *n.f.* day nursery; (*relig.*) crib.
crédibilité /kredibilite/ *n.f.* credibility.
crédit /kredi/ *n.m.* credit; (*banque*) bank. **~s**, funds. **à ~**, on credit. **faire ~**, give credit (**à**, to). **~er** /-te/ *v.t.* credit. **~eur, ~euse** /-tœr, -tøz/ *a.* in credit; *n.m., f.* person whose account is in credit.
credo /kredo/ *n.m.* creed.
crédule /kredyl/ *a.* credulous.
créer /kree/ *v.t.* create.
crémation /kremɑsjɔ̃/ *n.f.* cremation.
crème /krɛm/ *n.f.* cream; (*dessert*) cream dessert. —*a. invar.* cream. —*n.m.* (**café**) **~**, white coffee. **~ à raser**, shaving-cream.
crémeu|x, ~se /kremø, -z/ *a.* creamy.
crém|ier, ~ière /kremje, -jɛr/ *n.m., f.* dairyman, dairywoman. **~erie** /krɛmri/ *n.f.* dairy.
créneau (*pl.* **~x**) /kreno/ *n.m.* (*trou*) gap, slot. **faire un ~**, park between two cars.
créole /kreɔl/ *n.m./f.* Creole.
crêpe[1] /krɛp/ *n.f.* (*galette*) pancake. **~rie** *n.f.* pancake shop.
crêpe[2] /krɛp/ *n.m.* (*tissu*) crêpe; (*matière*) crêpe (rubber); (*de deuil*) black band.
crépit|er /krepite/ *v.i.* crackle. **~ement** *n.m.* crackling.
crépu /krepy/ *a.* frizzy.
crépuscule /krepyskyl/ *n.m.* twilight, dusk.
crescendo /kreʃɛndo/ *adv.* & *n.m. invar.* crescendo.
cresson /kresɔ̃/ *n.m.* (water)cress.
crête /krɛt/ *n.f.* crest; (*de coq*) comb.
crétin, ~e /kretɛ̃, -in/ *n.m., f.* cretin.
creuser /krøze/ *v.t.* dig; (*évider*) hollow out; (*fig.*) go deeply into. **se ~ (la cervelle)**, (*fam.*) rack one's brains.
creuset /krøzɛ/ *n.m.* (*lieu*) melting-pot.
creu|x, ~se /krø, -z/ *a.* hollow. —*n.m.* hollow; (*de l'estomac*) pit.
crevaison /krəvɛzɔ̃/ *n.f.* puncture.
crevasse /krəvas/ *n.f.* crack; (*de glacier*) crevasse; (*de la peau*) chap.
crève-cœur /krɛvkœr/ *n.m. invar.* heart-break.
crever /krəve/ *v.t./i.* burst; (*pneu*) puncture, burst; (*exténuer*: *fam.*) exhaust; (*mourir*: *fam.*) die; (*œil*) put out.
crevette /krəvɛt/ *n.f.* **~ (grise)**, shrimp. **~ (rose)**, prawn.
cri /kri/ *n.m.* cry.
criant, ~e /krijɑ̃, -t/ *a.* glaring.
criard, ~e /krijar, -d/ *a.* (*couleur*) garish; (*voix*) bawling.
crible /kribl/ *n.m.* sieve, riddle.
criblé /krible/ *a.* **~ de**, riddled with.
cric /krik/ *n.m.* (*auto.*) jack.
crier /krije/ *v.i.* shout, cry (out); (*grincer*) creak. —*v.t.* (*ordre*) shout (out).
crim|e /krim/ *n.m.* crime; (*meurtre*) murder. **~inalité** *n.f.* crime. **~inel, ~inelle** *a.* criminal; *n.m., f.* criminal; (*assassin*) murderer.
crin /krɛ̃/ *n.m.* horsehair.
crinière /krinjɛr/ *n.f.* mane.
crique /krik/ *n.f.* creek.
criquet /krikɛ/ *n.m.* locust.

crise /kriz/ *n.f.* crisis; (*méd.*) attack; (*de colère*) fit. **~ cardiaque,** heart attack.

crisp|er /krispe/ *v.t.*, **se ~er** *v. pr.* tense; (*poings*) clench. **~ation** *n.f.* tenseness; (*spasme*) twitch. **~é** *a.* tense.

crisser /krise/ *v.i.* crunch; (*pneu*) screech.

crist|al (*pl.* **~aux**) /kristal, -o/ *n.m.* crystal.

cristallin, ~e /kristalɛ̃, -in/ *a.* (*limpide*) crystal-clear.

cristalliser /kristalize/ *v.t./i.*, **se ~** *v. pr.* crystallize.

critère /kritɛr/ *n.m.* criterion.

critérium /kriterjɔm/ *n.m.* eliminating heat.

critique /kritik/ *a.* critical. —*n.f.* criticism; (*article*) review. —*n.m.* critic. **la ~,** (*personnes*) critics.

critiquer /kritike/ *v.t.* criticize.

croc /kro/ *n.m.* (*dent*) fang; (*crochet*) hook.

croc-en-jambe (*pl.* **crocs-en-jambe**) /krɔkɑ̃ʒɑ̃b/ *n.m.* = **croche-pied.**

croche /krɔʃ/ *n.f.* quaver. **double ~,** semiquaver.

croche-pied /krɔʃpje/ *n.m.* **faire un ~ à,** trip up.

crochet /krɔʃɛ/ *n.m.* hook; (*détour*) detour; (*signe*) (square) bracket. **faire au ~,** crochet.

crochu /krɔʃy/ *a.* hooked.

crocodile /krɔkɔdil/ *n.m.* crocodile.

crocus /krɔkys/ *n.m.* crocus.

croire† /krwar/ *v.t./i.* believe (**à, en,** in); (*estimer*) think, believe (**que,** that).

croisade /krwazad/ *n.f.* crusade.

croisé /krwaze/ *a.* (*veston*) double-breasted. —*n.m.* crusader.

croisée /krwaze/ *n.f.* window. **~ des chemins,** crossroads.

crois|er[1] /krwaze/ *v.t.*, **se ~er** *v. pr.* cross; (*passant, véhicule*) pass (each other). **~ement** *n.m.* crossing; passing; (*carrefour*) crossroads.

crois|er[2] /krwaze/ *v.i.* (*bateau*) cruise. **~eur** *n.m.* cruiser. **~ière** *n.f.* cruise.

croissan|t[1], **~te** /krwasɑ̃, -t/ *a.* growing. **~ce** *n.f.* growth.

croissant[2] /krwasɑ̃/ *n.m.* crescent; (*pâtisserie*) croissant.

croître† /krwatr/ *v.i.* grow; (*lune*) wax.

croix /krwa/ *n.f.* cross. **~ gammée,** swastika. **C~-Rouge,** Red Cross.

croque-monsieur /krɔkməsjø/ *n.m. invar.* toasted ham and cheese sandwich.

croque-mort /krɔkmɔr/ *n.m.* undertaker's assistant.

croqu|er /krɔke/ *v.t./i.* crunch; (*dessiner*) sketch. **~ant, ~ante** *a.* crunchy.

croquet /krɔkɛ/ *n.m.* croquet.

croquette /krɔkɛt/ *n.f.* croquette.

croquis /krɔki/ *n.m.* sketch.

crosse /krɔs/ *n.f.* (*de fusil*) butt; (*d'évêque*) crook.

crotte /krɔt/ *n.f.* droppings.

crotté /krɔte/ *a.* muddy.

crottin /krɔtɛ̃/ *n.m.* (horse) dung.

crouler /krule/ *v.i.* collapse; (*être ruiné*) crumble.

croupe /krup/ *n.f.* rump; (*de colline*) brow. **en ~,** pillion.

croupier /krupje/ *n.m.* croupier.

croupir /krupir/ *v.i.* stagnate.

croustill|er /krustije/ *v.i.* be crusty. **~ant, ~ante** *a.* crusty; (*fig.*) spicy.

croûte /krut/ *n.f.* crust; (*de fromage*) rind; (*de plaie*) scab.

croûton /krutɔ̃/ *n.m.* (*bout de pain*) crust; (*avec potage*) *croûton.*

croyable /krwajabl/ *a.* credible.

croyan|t, ~te /krwajɑ̃, -t/ *n.m., f.* believer. **~ce** *n.f.* belief.

CRS *abrév.* (*Compagnies républicaines de sécurité*) French state security police.

cru[1] /kry/ *voir* **croire.**
cru[2] /kry/ *a.* raw; (*lumière*) harsh; (*propos*) crude. —*n.m.* vineyard; (*vin*) wine.
crû /kry/ *voir* **croître.**
cruauté /kryote/ *n.f.* cruelty.
cruche /kryʃ/ *n.f.* pitcher.
cruc|ial (*m. pl.* **~iaux**) /krysjal, -jo/ *a.* crucial.
crucif|ier /krysifje/ *v.t.* crucify. **~ixion** *n.f.* crucifixion.
crucifix /krysifi/ *n.m.* crucifix.
crudité /krydite/ *n.f.* (*de langage*) crudeness. **~s,** (*culin.*) raw vegetables *ou* fruit.
crue /kry/ *n.f.* rise in water level. **en ~,** in spate.
cruel, ~le /kryɛl/ *a.* cruel.
crûment /krymɑ̃/ *adv.* crudely.
crustacés /krystase/ *n.m. pl.* shellfish.
crypte /kript/ *n.f.* crypt.
Cuba /kyba/ *n.m.* Cuba.
cubain, ~e /kybɛ̃, -ɛn/ *a.* & *n.m., f.* Cuban.
cub|e /kyb/ *n.m.* cube. —*a.* (*mètre etc.*) cubic. **~ique** *a.* cubic.
cueill|ir† /kœjir/ *v.t.* pick, gather; (*personne*: *fam.*) pick up. **~ette** *n.f.* picking, gathering.
cuill|er, ~ère /kɥijɛr/ *n.f.* spoon. **~erée** *n.f.* spoonful.
cuir /kɥir/ *n.m.* leather. **~ chevelu,** scalp.
cuirassé /kɥirase/ *n.m.* battleship.
cuire /kɥir/ *v.t./i.* cook; (*picoter*) smart. **~ (au four),** bake. **faire ~,** cook.
cuisine /kɥizin/ *n.f.* kitchen; (*art*) cookery, cooking; (*aliments*) cooking. **faire la ~,** cook.
cuisin|er /kɥizine/ *v.t./i.* cook; (*interroger*: *fam.*) grill. **~inier, ~inière** *n.m., f.* cook; *n.f.* (*appareil*) cooker, stove.
cuisse /kɥis/ *n.f.* thigh; (*de poulet, mouton*) leg.
cuisson /kɥisɔ̃/ *n.m.* cooking.
cuit, ~e /kɥi, -t/ *a.* cooked. **bien ~,** well done *ou* cooked.
cuivr|e /kɥivr/ *n.m.* copper. **~e (jaune),** brass. **~es,** (*mus.*) brass. **~é** *a.* coppery.
cul /ky/ *n.m.* (*derrière*: *fam.*) backside, bum; (*de pot etc.*) bottom.
culbut|e /kylbyt/ *n.f.* somersault; (*chute*) tumble. **~er** *v.i.* tumble; *v.t.* knock over.
cul-de-sac (*pl.* **culs-de-sac**) /kydsak/ *n.m.* cul-de-sac.
culinaire /kylinɛr/ *a.* culinary; (*recette*) cooking.
culminer /kylmine/ *v.i.* reach the highest point.
culot[1] /kylo/ *n.m.* (*audace*: *fam.*) nerve, cheek.
culot[2] /kylo/ *n.m.* (*fond*: *techn.*) base.
culotte /kylɔt/ *n.f.* (short) trousers; (*sport*) shorts; (*de femme*) knickers; (*Amer.*) panties. **~ (de cheval),** (riding) breeches.
culpabilité /kylpabilite/ *n.f.* guilt.
culte /kylt/ *n.m.* cult, worship; (*religion*) religion; (*protestant*) service.
cultivé /kyltive/ *a.* cultured.
cultiv|er /kyltive/ *v.t.* cultivate; (*plantes*) grow. **~ateur, ~atrice** *n.m., f.* farmer.
culture /kyltyr/ *n.f.* cultivation; (*de plantes*) growing; (*agriculture*) farming; (*éducation*) culture. **~s,** (*terrains*) lands under cultivation. **~ physique,** physical training.
culturel, ~le /kyltyrɛl/ *a.* cultural.
cumuler /kymyle/ *v.t.* (*fonctions*) hold simultaneously.
cupide /kypid/ *a.* avaricious.
cur|e /kyr/ *n.f.* (course of) treatment, cure. **~able** *a.* curable.
curé /kyre/ *n.m.* (parish) priest.
cur|er /kyre/ *v.t.* clean. **~e-dent** *n.m.* toothpick. **~e-pipe** *n.m.* pipe-cleaner.

curieu|x, ~se /kyrjø, -z/ *a.* curious. —*n.m., f.* (*badaud*) onlooker. **~sement** *adv.* curiously.
curiosité /kyrjozite/ *n.f.* curiosity; (*objet*) curio; (*spectacle*) unusual sight.
cutané /kytane/ *a.* skin.
cuti-réaction /kytireaksjɔ̃/ *n.f.* skin test.
cuve /kyv/ *n.f.* tank.
cuvée /kyve/ *n.f.* (*de vin*) vintage.
cuvette /kyvɛt/ *n.f.* bowl; (*de lavabo*) (wash-)basin; (*des cabinets*) pan, bowl.
cyanure /sjanyr/ *n.m.* cyanide.
cybernétique /sibɛrnetik/ *n.f.* cybernetics.
cycl|e /sikl/ *n.m.* cycle. **~ique** *a.* cyclic(al).
cyclis|te /siklist/ *n.m./f.* cyclist. —*a.* cycle. **~me** *n.m.* cycling.
cyclomoteur /syklɔmɔtœr/ *n.m.* moped.
cyclone /syklon/ *n.m.* cyclone.
cygne /siɲ/ *n.m.* swan.
cylindr|e /silɛ̃dr/ *n.m.* cylinder. **~ique** *a.* cylindrical.
cylindrée /silɛ̃dre/ *n.f.* (*de moteur*) capacity.
cymbale /sɛ̃bal/ *n.f.* cymbal.
cyni|que /sinik/ *a.* cynical. —*n.m.* cynic. **~sme** *n.m.* cynicism.
cyprès /siprɛ/ *n.m.* cypress.
cypriote /siprijɔt/ *a.* & *n.m./f.* Cypriot.

D

d' /d/ *voir* **de.**
d'abord /dabɔr/ *adv.* first; (*au début*) at first.
dactylo /daktilo/ *n.f.* typist. **~(graphie)** *n.f.* typing. **~graphe** *n.f.* typist. **~graphier** *v.t.* type.
dada /dada/ *n.m.* hobby-horse.
dahlia /dalja/ *n.m.* dahlia.
daigner /deɲe/ *v.t.* deign.
daim /dɛ̃/ *n.m.* (fallow) deer; (*cuir*) suede.
dais /dɛ/ *n.m.* canopy.
dall|e /dal/ *n.f.* paving stone, slab. **~age** *n.m.* paving.
daltonien, ~ne /daltɔnjɛ̃, -jɛn/ *a.* colour-blind.
dame /dam/ *n.f.* lady; (*cartes, échecs*) queen. **~s,** (*jeu*) draughts; (*jeu: Amer.*) checkers.
damier /damje/ *n.m.* draughtboard; (*Amer.*) checker-board. **à ~,** chequered.
damn|er /dɑne/ *v.t.* damn. **~ation** *n.f.* damnation.
dancing /dɑ̃siŋ/ *n.m.* dance-hall.
dandiner (se) /(sə)dɑ̃dine/ *v. pr.* waddle.
Danemark /danmark/ *n.m.* Denmark.
danger /dɑ̃ʒe/ *n.m.* danger. **en ~,** in danger. **mettre en ~,** endanger.
dangereu|x, ~se /dɑ̃ʒrø, -z/ *a.* dangerous.
danois, ~e /danwa, -z/ *a.* Danish. —*n.m., f.* Dane. —*n.m.* (*lang.*) Danish.
dans /dɑ̃/ *prép.* in; (*mouvement*) into; (*à l'intérieur de*) inside, in; (*approximation*) about. **~ dix jours,** in ten days' time. **prendre/boire/***etc.* **~,** take/drink/*etc.* out of *ou* from.
dans|e /dɑ̃s/ *n.f.* dance; (*art*) dancing. **~er** *v.t./i.* dance. **~eur, ~euse** *n.m., f.* dancer.
dard /dar/ *n.m.* (*d'animal*) sting.
darder /darde/ *v.t.* shoot, cast forth.
dat|e /dat/ *n.f.* date. **~e limite,** deadline. **~er** *v.t./i.* date. **à ~er de,** as from.
datt|e /dat/ *n.f.* (*fruit*) date. **~ier** *n.m.* date-palm.
dauphin /dofɛ̃/ *n.m.* (*animal*) dolphin.
davantage /davɑ̃taʒ/ *adv.* more; (*plus longtemps*) longer. **~ de,**

more. **~ que,** more than; longer than.

de, d'* /də, d/ *prép.* (*de + le = du, de + les = des*) of; (*provenance*) from; (*moyen, manière*) with; (*agent*) by. —*article* some; (*interrogation*) any, some. **le livre ~ mon ami,** my friend's book. **un pont ~ fer,** an iron bridge. **dix mètres ~ haut,** ten metres high. **du pain,** (some) bread. **des fleurs,** (some) flowers.

dé /de/ *n.m.* (*à jouer*) dice; (*à coudre*) thimble. **~s,** (*jeu*) dice.

débâcle /debɑkl/ *n.f.* (*mil.*) rout.

déball|er /debale/ *v.t.* unpack. **~age** *n.m.* unpacking.

débandade /debɑ̃dad/ *n.f.* (headlong) flight.

débarbouiller /debarbuje/ *v.t.* wash the face of. **se ~** *v. pr.* wash one's face.

débarcadère /debarkadɛr/ *n.m.* landing-stage.

débardeur /debardœr/ *n.m.* docker.

débarqu|er /debarke/ *v.t./i.* disembark, land; (*arriver: fam.*) turn up. **~ement** *n.m.* disembarkation.

débarras /debara/ *n.m.* junk room. **bon ~!,** good riddance!

débarrasser /debarase/ *v.t.* clear (**de,** of). **~ qn. de,** take from s.o.; (*défaut, ennemi*) rid s.o. of. **se ~ de,** get rid of, rid o.s. of.

débat /deba/ *n.m.* debate.

débattre†[1] /debatr/ *v.t.* debate.

débattre†[2] **(se)** /(sə)debatr/ *v. pr.* struggle (to get free).

débauch|e /deboʃ/ *n.f.* debauchery; (*fig.*) profusion. **~er**[1] *v.t.* debauch.

débaucher[2] /deboʃe/ *v.t.* (*licencier*) lay off.

débil|e /debil/ *a.* weak. —*n.m./f.* moron. **~iter** *v.t.* debilitate.

débit /debi/ *n.m.* (rate of) flow; (*de magasin*) turnover; (*élocution*) delivery; (*de compte*) debit. **~ de tabac,** tobacconist's shop.

débi|ter /debite/ *v.t.* cut up; (*fournir*) produce; (*vendre*) sell; (*dire: péj.*) spout; (*compte*) debit. **~teur, ~trice** *n.m., f.* debtor; *a.* (*compte*) in debit.

débl|ayer /debleje/ *v.t.* clear. **~aiement** *n.m.* clearing.

débloquer /deblɔke/ *v.t.* (*prix, salaires*) free.

déboires /debwar/ *n.m. pl.* disappointments.

déboiser /debwaze/ *v.t.* clear (of trees).

déboîter /debwate/ *v.i.* (*véhicule*) pull out. —*v.t.* (*membre*) dislocate.

débonnaire /debɔnɛr/ *a.* easy-going.

débord|er /debɔrde/ *v.i.* overflow. —*v.t.* (*dépasser*) extend beyond. **~er de,** (*joie etc.*) be overflowing with. **~é** *a.* snowed under (**de,** with). **~ement** *n.m.* overflowing.

débouché /debuʃe/ *n.m.* opening; (*comm.*) outlet; (*sortie*) end, exit.

déboucher /debuʃe/ *v.t.* (*bouteille*) uncork; (*évier*) unblock. —*v.i.* emerge (**de,** from). **~ sur,** (*rue*) lead into.

débourser /deburse/ *v.t.* pay out.

déboussolé /debusɔle/ *a.* (*fam.*) disorientated, disoriented.

debout /dəbu/ *adv.* standing; (*levé, éveillé*) up. **être ~, se tenir ~,** be standing, stand. **se mettre ~,** stand up.

déboutonner /debutɔne/ *v.t.* unbutton. **se ~** *v. pr.* unbutton o.s.; (*vêtement*) come undone.

débraillé /debrɑje/ *a.* slovenly.

débrancher /debrɑ̃ʃe/ *v.t.* unplug, disconnect.

débray|er /debreje/ *v.i.* (*auto.*) declutch; (*faire grève*) stop work. **~age** /debrɛjaʒ/ *n.m.* (*pédale*) clutch; (*grève*) stoppage.

débridé /debride/ *a.* unbridled.

débris /debri/ *n.m. pl.* fragments; (*détritus*) rubbish, debris.

débrouill|er /debruje/ *v.t.* disentangle; (*problème*) sort out. **se ~er** *v. pr.* manage. **~ard, ~arde** *a.* (*fam.*) resourceful.

débroussailler /debrusaje/ *v.t.* clear (of brushwood).

débusquer /debyske/ *v.t.* drive out.

début /deby/ *n.m.* beginning. **faire ses ~s,** (*en public*) make one's début.

début|er /debyte/ *v.i.* begin; (*dans un métier etc.*) start out. **~ant, ~ante** *n.m., f.* beginner.

deçà (en) /(ɑ̃)dəsɑ/ *adv.* this side. —*prép.* **en ~ de,** this side of.

décacheter /dekaʃte/ *v.t.* open.

décade /dekad/ *n.f.* ten days; (*décennie*) decade.

décaden|t, ~te /dekadɑ̃, -t/ *a.* decadent. **~ce** *n.f.* decadence.

décalcomanie /dekalkɔmani/ *n.f.* transfer; (*Amer.*) decal.

décal|er /dekale/ *v.t.* shift. **~age** *n.m.* (*écart*) gap. **~age horaire,** time difference.

décalquer /dekalke/ *v.t.* trace.

décamper /dekɑ̃pe/ *v.i.* clear off.

décanter /dekɑ̃te/ *v.t.* allow to settle. **se ~** *v. pr.* settle.

décap|er /dekape/ *v.t.* scrape down; (*surface peinte*) strip. **~ant** *n.m.* chemical agent; (*pour peinture*) paint stripper.

décapiter /dekapite/ *v.t.* behead.

décapotable /dekapɔtabl/ *a.* convertible.

décapsul|er /dekapsyle/ *v.t.* take the cap off. **~eur** *n.m.* bottle-opener.

décéd|er /desede/ *v.i.* die. **~é** *a.* deceased.

déceler /desle/ *v.t.* detect; (*démontrer*) reveal.

décembre /desɑ̃br/ *n.m.* December.

décennie /deseni/ *n.f.* decade.

déc|ent, ~ente /desɑ̃, -t/ *a.* decent. **~emment** /-amɑ̃/ *adv.* decently. **~ence** *n.f.* decency.

décentraliser /desɑ̃tralize/ *v.t.* decentralize.

déception /desɛpsjɔ̃/ *n.f.* disappointment.

décerner /desɛrne/ *v.t.* award.

décès /desɛ/ *n.m.* death.

décevoir† /dɛsvwar/ *v.t.* disappoint.

déchaîn|er /deʃene/ *v.t.* (*violence etc.*) unleash; (*enthousiasme*) arouse a good deal of. **se ~er** *v. pr.* erupt. **~ement** /-ɛnmɑ̃/ *n.m.* (*de passions*) outburst.

déchanter /deʃɑ̃te/ *v.i.* lose one's high hopes, become disillusioned.

décharge /deʃarʒ/ *n.f.* (*salve*) volley of shots. **~ (électrique),** electrical discharge. **~ (publique),** rubbish tip.

décharg|er /deʃarʒe/ *v.t.* unload; (*arme, accusé*) discharge. **~er de,** release from. **se ~er** *v. pr.* (*batterie, pile*) go flat. **~ement** *n.m.* unloading.

décharné /deʃarne/ *a.* bony.

déchausser (se) /(sə)deʃose/ *v. pr.* take off one's shoes.

déchéance /deʃeɑ̃s/ *n.f.* decay.

déchet /deʃɛ/ *n.m.* (*reste*) scrap; (*perte*) waste. **~s,** (*ordures*) refuse.

déchiffrer /deʃifre/ *v.t.* decipher.

déchiqueter /deʃikte/ *v.t.* tear to shreds.

déchir|ant, ~ante /deʃirɑ̃, -t/ *a.* heart-breaking. **~ement** *n.m.* heart-break; (*conflit*) split.

déchir|er /deʃire/ *v.t.* tear; (*lacérer*) tear up; (*arracher*) tear off *ou* out; (*diviser*) tear apart; (*oreilles: fig.*) split. **se ~er** *v. pr.* tear. **~ure** *n.f.* tear.

déch|oir /deʃwar/ *v.i.* demean o.s. **~oir de,** (*rang*) lose, fall from. **~u** *a.* fallen.

décibel /desibɛl/ *n.m.* decibel.

décid|er /deside/ *v.t.* decide on; (*persuader*) persuade. **~er que/de,** decide that/to. —*v.i.* decide. **~er de qch.,** decide on sth. **se ~er** *v. pr.* make up one's mind (**à,** to). **~é** *a.* (*résolu*) determined; (*fixé, marqué*) decided. **~ément** *adv.* certainly.

décim|al, ~ale (*m. pl.* **~aux**) /desimal, -o/ *a.* & *n.f.* decimal.

décimer /desime/ *v.t.* decimate.

décimètre /desimɛtr/ *n.m.* decimetre.

décisi|f, ~ve /desizif, -v/ *a.* decisive.

décision /desizjɔ̃/ *n.f.* decision.

déclar|er /deklare/ *v.t.* declare; (*naissance*) register. **se ~er** *v. pr.* (*feu*) break out. **~er forfait,** (*sport*) withdraw. **~ation** *n.f.* declaration; (*commentaire politique*) statement.

déclasser /deklɑse/ *v.t.* (*coureur*) relegate; (*hôtel*) downgrade.

déclench|er /deklɑ̃ʃe/ *v.t.* (*techn.*) release, set off; (*lancer*) launch; (*provoquer*) trigger off. **se ~er** *v. pr.* (*techn.*) go off.

déclic /deklik/ *n.m.* click; (*techn.*) trigger mechanism.

déclin /deklɛ̃/ *n.m.* decline.

décliner[1] /dekline/ *v.i.* decline.

décliner[2] /dekline/ *v.t.* (*refuser*) decline; (*dire*) state.

déclivité /deklivite/ *n.f.* slope.

décocher /dekɔʃe/ *v.t.* (*coup*) fling; (*regard*) shoot.

décoder /dekɔde/ *v.t.* decode.

décoiffer /dekwafe/ *v.t.* (*ébouriffer*) disarrange the hair of. **se ~** *v. pr.* take off one's hat.

décoll|er[1] /dekɔle/ *v.i.* (*avion*) take off. **~age** *n.m.* take-off.

décoller[2] /dekɔle/ *v.t.* unstick.

décolleté /dekɔlte/ *a.* low-cut. —*n.m.* low neckline.

décolor|er /dekɔlɔre/ *v.t.* fade; (*cheveux*) bleach. **se ~er** *v. pr.* fade. **~ation** *n.f.* bleaching.

décombres /dekɔ̃br/ *n.m. pl.* rubble.

décommander /dekɔmɑ̃de/ *v.t.* cancel.

décompos|er /dekɔ̃poze/ *v.t.* break up; (*substance*) decompose; (*visage*) contort. **se ~er** *v. pr.* (*pourrir*) decompose. **~ition** *n.f.* decomposition.

décompt|e /dekɔ̃t/ *n.m.* deduction; (*détail*) breakdown. **~er** *v.t.* deduct.

déconcerter /dekɔ̃sɛrte/ *v.t.* disconcert.

déconfiture /dekɔ̃fityr/ *n.f.* collapse, ruin.

décongestionner /dekɔ̃ʒɛstjɔne/ *v.t.* relieve congestion in.

déconseill|er /dekɔ̃seje/ *v.t.* **~er qch. à qn.,** advise s.o. against sth. **~é** *a.* not advisable, inadvisable.

décontenancer /dekɔ̃tnɑ̃se/ *v.t.* disconcert.

décontracter /dekɔ̃trakte/ *v.t.*, **se ~** *v. pr.* relax.

déconvenue /dekɔ̃vny/ *n.f.* disappointment.

décor /dekɔr/ *n.m.* (*paysage, théâtre*) scenery; (*cinéma*) set; (*cadre*) setting; (*de maison*) décor.

décorati|f, ~ve /dekɔratif, -v/ *a.* decorative.

décor|er /dekɔre/ *v.t.* decorate. **~ateur, ~atrice** *n.m., f.* (interior) decorator. **~ation** *n.f.* decoration.

décortiquer /dekɔrtike/ *v.t.* shell; (*fig.*) dissect.

découdre (se) /(sə)dekudr/ *v. pr.* come unstitched.

découler /dekule/ *v.i.* **~ de,** follow from.

découp|er /dekupe/ *v.t.* cut up; (*viande*) carve; (*détacher*) cut out. **se ~er sur,** stand out against. **~age** *n.m.* (*image*) cut-out. **~ure** *n.f.* (*morceau*) piece cut out.

décourag|er /dekuraʒe/ *v.t.* discourage. **se ~er** *v. pr.* become discouraged. **~ement** *n.m.* discouragement.

découśu /dekuzy/ *a.* (*idées etc.*) disjointed.

découvert, ~e /dekuvɛr, -t/ *a.* (*tête etc.*) bare; (*terrain*) open. —*n.m.* (*de compte*) overdraft. —*n.f.* discovery. **à ~,** exposed; (*fig.*) openly. **à la ~e de,** in search of.

découvrir† /dekuvrir/ *v.t.* discover; (*enlever ce qui couvre*) uncover; (*voir*) see; (*montrer*) reveal. **se ~** *v. pr.* uncover o.s.; (*se décoiffer*) take one's hat off; (*ciel*) clear.

décrasser /dekrase/ *v.t.* clean.

décrépit, ~e /dekrepi, -t/ *a.* decrepit.

décret /dekrɛ/ *n.m.* decree. **~er** /-ete/ *v.t.* decree.

décrier /dekrije/ *v.t.* disparage.

décrire† /dekrir/ *v.t.* describe.

décroch|er /dekrɔʃe/ *v.t.* unhook; (*obtenir: fam.*) get. —*v.i.* (*abandonner: fam.*) give up. **~er (le téléphone),** pick up the phone. **~é** *a.* (*téléphone*) off the hook.

décroître /dekrwatr/ *v.i.* decrease.

décrypter /dekripte/ *v.t.* decipher.

déçu /desy/ *a.* disappointed.

déculotter (se) /(sə)dekylɔte/ *v. pr.* take one's trousers off.

décupl|e /dekypl/ *n.m.* **au ~e,** tenfold. **le ~e de,** ten times. **~er** *v.t./i.* increase tenfold.

dédaign|er /dedeɲe/ *v.t.* scorn. **~er de faire,** consider it beneath one to do. **~eux, ~euse** /dedɛɲø, -z/ *a.* scornful.

dédain /dedɛ̃/ *n.m.* scorn.

dédale /dedal/ *n.m.* maze.

dedans /dədɑ̃/ *adv.* & *n.m.* inside. **au ~ (de),** inside. **en ~,** on the inside.

dédicac|e /dedikas/ *n.f.* dedication, inscription; **~er** *v.t.* dedicate, inscribe.

dédier /dedje/ *v.t.* dedicate.

dédire (se) /(sə)dedir/ *v. pr.* go back on one's word.

dédit /dedi/ *n.m.* (*comm.*) penalty.

dédommag|er /dedɔmaʒe/ *v.t.* compensate (**de,** for). **~ement** *n.m.* compensation.

dédouaner /dedwane/ *v.t.* clear through customs.

dédoubler /deduble/ *v.t.* split into two. **~ un train,** put on a relief train.

déd|uire† /dedɥir/ *v.t.* deduct; (*conclure*) deduce. **~uction** *n.f.* deduction.

déesse /deɛs/ *n.f.* goddess.

défaillance /defajɑ̃s/ *n.f.* weakness; (*évanouissement*) black-out; (*panne*) failure.

défaill|ir /defajir/ *v.i.* faint; (*forces etc.*) fail. **~ant, ~ante** *a.* (*personne*) faint; (*candidat*) defaulting.

défaire† /defɛr/ *v.t.* undo; (*valise*) unpack; (*démonter*) take down; (*débarrasser*) rid. **se ~** *v. pr.* come undone. **se ~ de,** rid o.s. of.

défait, ~e[1] /defɛ, -t/ *a.* (*cheveux*) ruffled; (*visage*) haggard.

défaite[2] /defɛt/ *n.f.* defeat.

défaut /defo/ *n.m.* fault, defect; (*d'un verre, diamant etc.*) flaw; (*carence*) lack; (*pénurie*) shortage. **à ~ de,** for lack of. **en ~,** at fault. **faire ~,** (*argent etc.*) be lacking. **par ~,** (*jurid.*) in one's absence.

défav|eur /defavœr/ *n.f.* disfavour. **~orable** *a.* unfavourable.

défavoriser /defavɔrize/ *v.t.* put at a disadvantage.

défection /defɛksjɔ̃/ *n.f.* desertion. **faire ~,** desert.

défect|ueux, ~ueuse /defɛktɥø, -z/ *a.* faulty, defective. **~uosité** *n.f.* faultiness; (*défaut*) fault.

défendre /defɑ̃dr/ *v.t.* defend; (*interdire*) forbid. **~ à qn. de,** forbid s.o. to. **se ~** *v. pr.* defend o.s.; (*se débrouiller*) manage; (*se* *protéger*) protect o.s. **se ~ de,** (*refuser*) refrain from.

défense /defɑ̃s/ *n.f.* defence; (*d'éléphant*) tusk. **~ de fumer/** *etc.*, no smoking/*etc.*

défenseur /defɑ̃sœr/ *n.m.* defender.

défensi|f, ~ve /defɑ̃sif, -v/ *a.* & *n.f.* defensive.

déféren|t, ~te /deferɑ̃, -t/ *a.* deferential. **~ce** *n.f.* deference.

déférer /defere/ *v.t.* (*jurid.*) refer. —*v.i.* **~ à,** (*avis etc.*) defer to.

déferler /defɛrle/ *v.i.* (*vagues*) break; (*violence etc.*) erupt.

défi /defi/ *n.m.* challenge; (*refus*) defiance. **mettre au ~,** challenge.

défiance /defjɑ̃s/ *n.f.* mistrust.

déficience /defisjɑ̃s/ *n.f.* deficiency.

déficit /defisit/ *n.m.* deficit. **~aire** *a.* in deficit.

défier /defje/ *v.t.* challenge; (*braver*) defy. **se ~ de,** mistrust.

défigurer /defigyre/ *v.t.* disfigure; (*gâter*) spoil; (*texte*) deface.

défilé[1] /defile/ *n.m.* procession; (*mil.*) parade, march past; (*fig.*) (continual) stream.

défilé[2] /defile/ *n.m.* (*géog.*) gorge.

défiler /defile/ *v.i.* march (past); (*visiteurs*) stream; (*images*) flash by. **se ~** *v. pr.* (*fam.*) sneak off.

défini /defini/ *a.* definite.

définir /definir/ *v.t.* define.

définiti|f, ~ve /definitif, -v/ *a.* final; (*permanent*) definitive. **en ~ve,** in the final analysis. **~vement** *adv.* definitively, permanently.

définition /definisjɔ̃/ *n.f.* definition; (*de mots croisés*) clue.

déflagration /deflagrɑsjɔ̃/ *n.f.* explosion.

déflation /deflɑsjɔ̃/ *n.f.* deflation. **~niste** /-jɔnist/ *a.* deflationary.

défoncer /defɔ̃se/ *v.t.* (*porte etc.*) break down; (*route, terrain*) dig up; (*lit*) break the springs of.

déform|er /defɔrme/ *v.t.* put out of shape; (*membre*) deform; (*faits, pensée*) distort. **~ation** *n.f.* loss of shape; deformation; distortion.

défouler (se) /(sə)defule/ *v. pr.* let off steam.

défraîchir (se) /(sə)defreʃir/ *v. pr.* become faded.

défrayer /defreje/ *v.t.* (*payer*) pay the expenses of.

défricher /defriʃe/ *v.t.* clear (for cultivation).

défunt, ~e /defœ̃, -t/ *a.* (*mort*) late. —*n.m., f.* deceased.

dégagé /degaʒe/ *a.* clear; (*manières*) free and easy.

dégag|er /degaʒe/ *v.t.* (*exhaler*) give off; (*désencombrer*) clear; (*délivrer*) free; (*faire ressortir*) bring out. —*v.i.* (*football*) kick the ball (down the pitch *ou* field). **se ~er** *v. pr.* free o.s.; (*ciel, rue*) clear; (*odeur etc.*) emanate. **~ement** *n.m.* giving off; clearing; freeing; (*espace*) clearing; (*football*) clearance.

dégainer /degene/ *v.t./i.* draw.

dégarnir /degarnir/ *v.t.* clear, empty. **se ~** *v. pr.* clear, empty; (*crâne*) go bald.

dégâts /degɑ/ *n.m. pl.* damage.

dégel /deʒɛl/ *n.m.* thaw. **~er** /deʒle/ *v.t./i.* thaw (out). **(faire) ~er,** (*culin.*) thaw.

dégénér|er /deʒenere/ *v.i.* degenerate. **~é, ~ée** *a.* & *n.m., f.* degenerate.

dégingandé /deʒɛ̃gɑ̃de/ *a.* gangling.

dégivrer /deʒivre/ *v.t.* (*auto.*) de-ice; (*frigo*) defrost.

dégonfl|er /degɔ̃fle/ *v.t.* let down, deflate. **se ~er** *v. pr.* (*fam.*) get cold feet. **~é** *a.* (*pneu*) flat; (*lâche: fam.*) yellow.

dégorger /degɔrʒe/ *v.i.* **faire ~,** (*culin.*) soak.

dégouliner /deguline/ *v.i.* trickle.
dégourdi /degurdi/ *a.* smart.
dégourdir /degurdir/ *v.t.* (*membre, liquide*) warm up. **se ~ (les jambes)**, stretch one's legs.
dégoût /degu/ *n.m.* disgust.
dégoût|er /degute/ *v.t.* disgust. **~er qn. de qch.**, put s.o. off sth. **se ~er de**, get sick of. **~ant, ~ante** *a.* disgusting.
dégoutter /degute/ *v.i.* drip.
dégradé /degrade/ *n.m.* (*de couleurs*) gradation.
dégrader /degrade/ *v.t.* degrade; (*abîmer*) damage. **se ~** *v. pr.* (*se détériorer*) deteriorate.
dégrafer /degrafe/ *v.t.* unhook.
dégraisser /degrese/ *v.t.* (*vêtement*) remove the grease from.
degré /dəgre/ *n.m.* degree; (*d'escalier*) step.
dégrever /degrəve/ *v.t.* reduce the tax on.
dégringol|er /degrɛ̃gɔle/ *v.i.* tumble (down). —*v.t.* rush down. **~ade** *n.f.* tumble.
dégriser /degrize/ *v.t.* sober up.
dégrossir /degrɔsir/ *v.t.* (*bois*) trim; (*projet*) rough out.
déguenillé /degnije/ *a.* ragged.
déguerpir /degɛrpir/ *v.i.* clear off.
dégueulasse /degœlas/ *a.* (*argot*) disgusting, lousy.
déguis|er /degize/ *v.t.* disguise. **se ~er** *v. pr.* disguise o.s.; (*au carnaval etc.*) dress up. **~ement** *n.m.* disguise; (*de carnaval etc.*) fancy dress.
dégust|er /degyste/ *v.t.* taste, sample; (*savourer*) enjoy. **~ation** *n.f.* tasting, sampling.
déhancher (se) /(sə)deɑ̃ʃe/ *v. pr.* sway one's hips.
dehors /dəɔr/ *adv.* & *n.m.* outside. —*n.m. pl.* (*aspect de qn.*) exterior. **au ~ (de)**, outside. **en ~ de**, outside; (*hormis*) apart from. **jeter/mettre/***etc.* **~**, throw/put/ *etc.* out.
déjà /deʒa/ *adv.* already; (*avant*) before, already.
déjeuner /deʒœne/ *v.i.* (have) lunch; (*le matin*) (have) breakfast. —*n.m.* lunch. **(petit) ~**, breakfast.
déjouer /deʒwe/ *v.t.* thwart.
delà /dəla/ *adv.* & *prép.* **au ~ (de)**, **en ~ (de)**, **par ~**, beyond.
délabrer (se) /(sə)delɑbre/ *v. pr.* become dilapidated.
délacer /delase/ *v.t.* undo.
délai /delɛ/ *n.m.* time-limit; (*attente*) wait; (*sursis*) extension (of time). **sans ~**, without delay.
délaisser /delese/ *v.t.* desert.
délass|er /delɑse/ *v.t.*, **se ~er** *v. pr.* relax. **~ement** *n.m.* relaxation.
délation /delɑsjɔ̃/ *n.f.* informing.
délavé /delave/ *a.* faded.
délayer /deleje/ *v.t.* mix (with liquid); (*idée*) drag out.
délecter (se) /(sə)delɛkte/ *v. pr.* **se ~ de**, delight in.
délégation /delegɑsjɔ̃/ *n.f.* delegation.
délégu|er /delege/ *v.t.* delegate. **~é, ~ée** *n.m., f.* delegate.
délester /delɛste/ *v.t.* (*route*) relieve congestion on.
délibéré /delibere/ *a.* deliberate; (*résolu*) determined. **~ment** *adv.* deliberately.
délibér|er /delibere/ *v.i.* deliberate. **~ation** *n.f.* deliberation.
délicat, ~e /delika, -t/ *a.* delicate; (*plein de tact*) tactful; (*exigeant*) particular. **~ement** /-tmɑ̃/ *adv.* delicately; tactfully. **~esse** /-tɛs/ *n.f.* delicacy; tact. **~esses** /-tɛs/ *n.f. pl.* (kind) attentions.
délice /delis/ *n.m.* delight. **~s** *n.f. pl.* delights.
délicieu|x, ~se /delisjø, -z/ *a.* (*au goût*) delicious; (*charmant*) delightful.
délié /delje/ *a.* fine, slender; (*agile*) nimble.
délier /delje/ *v.t.* untie; (*délivrer*) free. **se ~** *v. pr.* come untied.

délimit|er /delimite/ *v.t.* determine, demarcate. **~ation** *n.f.* demarcation.

délinquan|t, ~te /delɛ̃kɑ̃, -t/ *a.* & *n.m., f.* delinquent. **~ce** *n.f.* delinquency.

délire /delir/ *n.m.* delirium; (*fig.*) frenzy.

délir|er /delire/ *v.i.* be delirious (**de,** with); (*déraisonner*) rave. **~ant, ~ante** *a.* delirious; (*frénétique*) frenzied.

délit /deli/ *n.m.* offence, crime.

délivr|er /delivre/ *v.t.* free, release; (*pays*) deliver; (*remettre*) issue. **~ance** *n.f.* release; deliverance; issue.

déloger /delɔʒe/ *v.t.* force out.

déloy|al (*m. pl.* **~aux**) /delwajal, -jo/ *a.* disloyal; (*procédé*) unfair.

delta /dɛlta/ *n.m.* delta.

déluge /delyʒ/ *n.m.* flood; (*pluie*) downpour.

déluré /delyre/ *a.* smart, sharp.

démagogue /demagɔg/ *n.m./f.* demagogue.

demain /dmɛ̃/ *adv.* tomorrow.

demande /dmɑ̃d/ *n.f.* request; (*d'emploi*) application; (*exigence*) demand. **~ en mariage,** proposal (of marriage).

demandé /dmɑ̃de/ *a.* in demand.

demander /dmɑ̃de/ *v.t.* ask for; (*chemin, heure*) ask; (*emploi*) apply for; (*nécessiter*) require. **~ que/si,** ask that/if. **~ qch. à qn.,** ask s.o. for sth. **~ à qn. de,** ask s.o. to. **~ en mariage,** propose to. **se ~ si/où/***etc.*, wonder if/where/*etc.*

démang|er /demɑ̃ʒe/ *v.t./i.* itch. **~eaison** *n.f.* itch(ing).

démanteler /demɑ̃tle/ *v.t.* break up.

démaquill|er (se) /(sə)demakije/ *v. pr.* remove one's make-up. **~ant** *n.m.* make-up remover.

démarcation /demarkɑsjɔ̃/ *n.f.* demarcation.

démarche /demarʃ/ *n.f.* walk, gait; (*procédé*) step. **faire des ~s auprès de,** make approaches to.

démarcheu|r, ~se /demarʃœr, -øz/ *n.m., f.* (door-to-door) canvasser.

démarquer /demarke/ *v.t.* (*prix*) mark down.

démarr|er /demare/ *v.i.* (*moteur*) start (up); (*partir*) move off; (*fig.*) get moving. —*v.t.* (*fam.*) get moving. **~age** *n.m.* start. **~eur** *n.m.* starter.

démasquer /demaske/ *v.t.* unmask.

démêler /demele/ *v.t.* disentangle.

démêlés /demele/ *n.m. pl.* trouble.

déménag|er /demenaʒe/ *v.i.* move (house). —*v.t.* (*meubles*) remove. **~ement** *n.m.* move; (*de meubles*) removal. **~eur** *n.m.* removal man; (*Amer.*) furniture mover.

démener (se) /(sə)demne/ *v. pr.* move about wildly; (*fig.*) exert o.s.

démen|t, ~te /demɑ̃, -t/ *a.* insane. —*n.m., f.* lunatic. **~ce** *n.f.* insanity.

démenti /demɑ̃ti/ *n.m.* denial.

démentir /demɑ̃tir/ *v.t.* refute; (*ne pas être conforme à*) belie. **~ que,** deny that.

démesuré /deməzyre/ *a.* inordinate.

démettre /demɛtr/ *v.t.* (*poignet etc.*) dislocate. **~ qn. de,** dismiss s.o. from. **se ~** *v. pr.* resign (**de,** from).

demeurant (au) /(o)dəmœrɑ̃/ *adv.* after all, for all that.

demeure /dəmœr/ *n.f.* residence. **mettre en ~ de,** order to.

demeurer /dəmœre/ *v.i.* live; (*rester*) remain.

demi, ~e /dmi/ *a.* half(-). —*n.m., f.* half. —*n.m.* (*bière*) (half-pint) glass of beer; (*football*) half-back. —*n.f.* (*à l'horloge*) half-hour. —*adv.* **à ~,** half; (*ouvrir, fermer*) half-way. **une heure et ~e,** an hour and a half; (*à l'horloge*) half past one. **une ~-journée/-livre/** *etc.*, half a day/pound/*etc.*, a half-day/-pound/*etc.* **~-cercle** *n.m.* semicircle. **~-finale** *n.f.* semi-final. **~-frère** *n.m.* stepbrother. **~-heure** *n.f.* half-hour, half an hour. **~-jour** *n.m.* half-light. **à ~-mot** *adv.* without having to express every word. **~-pension** *n.f.* half-board. **~-pensionnaire** *n.m./f.* day-boarder. **~-sel** *a. invar.* slightly salted. **~-sœur** *n.f.* stepsister. **~-tarif** *n.m.* half-fare. **~-tour** *n.m.* about turn; (*auto.*) U-turn. **faire ~-tour,** turn back.

démis, ~e /demi, -z/ *a.* dislocated.

démission /demisjɔ̃/ *n.f.* resignation. **~ner** /-jɔne/ *v.i.* resign.

démobiliser /demɔbilize/ *v.t.* demobilize.

démocrate /demɔkrat/ *n.m./f.* democrat. —*a.* democratic.

démocrat|ie /demɔkrasi/ *n.f.* democracy. **~ique** /-atik/ *a.* democratic.

démodé /demɔde/ *a.* old-fashioned.

demoiselle /dəmwazɛl/ *n.f.* young lady; (*célibataire*) spinster. **~ d'honneur,** bridesmaid.

démol|ir /demɔlir/ *v.t.* demolish. **~ition** *n.f.* demolition.

démon /demɔ̃/ *n.m.* demon.

démoniaque /demɔnjak/ *a.* fiendish.

démonstra|teur, ~trice /demɔ̃stratœr, -tris/ *n.m., f.* demonstrator. **~tion** /-ɑsjɔ̃/ *n.f.* demonstration; (*de force*) show.

démonstrati|f, ~ve /demɔ̃stratif, -v/ *a.* demonstrative.

démonter /demɔ̃te/ *v.t.* take apart, dismantle; (*installation*) take down; (*fig.*) disconcert. **se ~** *v. pr.* come apart.

démontrer /demɔ̃tre/ *v.t.* show, demonstrate.

démoraliser /demɔralize/ *v.t.* demoralize.

démuni /demyni/ *a.* impoverished. **~ de,** without.

démunir /demynir/ *v.t.* **~ de,** deprive of. **se ~ de,** part with.

démystifier /demistifje/ *v.t.* enlighten.

dénaturer /denatyre/ *v.t.* (*faits etc.*) distort.

dénégation /denegɑsjɔ̃/ *n.f.* denial.

dénicher /deniʃe/ *v.t.* (*trouver*) dig up; (*faire sortir*) flush out.

dénier /denje/ *v.t.* deny.

dénigr|er /denigre/ *v.t.* denigrate. **~ement** *n.m.* denigration.

dénivellation /denivɛlɑsjɔ̃/ *n.f.* (*pente*) slope.

dénombrer /denɔ̃bre/ *v.t.* count; (*énumérer*) enumerate.

dénomination /denɔminɑsjɔ̃/ *n.f.* designation.

dénommer /denɔme/ *v.t.* name.

dénonc|er /denɔ̃se/ *v.t.* denounce; (*scol.*) tell on. **se ~er** *v. pr.* give o.s. up. **~iateur, ~iatrice** *n.m., f.* informer; (*scol.*) tell-tale. **~iation** *n.f.* denunciation.

dénoter /denɔte/ *v.t.* denote.

dénouement /denumɑ̃/ *n.m.* outcome; (*théâtre*) dénouement.

dénouer /denwe/ *v.t.* unknot, undo. **se ~** *v.pr.* (*nœud*) come undone.

dénoyauter /denwajote/ *v.t.* stone; (*Amer.*) pit.

denrée /dɑ̃re/ *n.f.* foodstuff.

dens|e /dɑ̃s/ *a.* dense. **~ité** *n.f.* density.

dent /dɑ̃/ *n.f.* tooth; (*de roue*) cog. **faire ses ~s,** teethe. **~aire** /-tɛr/ *a.* dental.

dentelé /dɑ̃tle/ *a.* jagged.

dentelle /dɑ̃tɛl/ *n.f.* lace.

dentier /dɑ̃tje/ *n.m.* denture.

dentifrice /dɑ̃tifris/ *n.m.* toothpaste.

dentiste /dɑ̃tist/ *n.m./f.* dentist.

dentition /dɑ̃tisjɔ̃/ *n.f.* teeth.

dénud|er /denyde/ *v.t.* bare. **~é** *a.* bare.

dénué /denɥe/ *a.* **~ de,** devoid of.

dénuement /denymɑ̃/ *n.m.* destitution.

déodorant /deɔdɔrɑ̃/ *a.m.* & *n.m.* **(produit) ~,** deodorant.

dépann|er /depane/ *v.t.* repair; (*fig.*) help out. **~age** *n.m.* repair. **de ~age,** (*service etc.*) breakdown. **~euse** *n.f.* breakdown lorry; (*Amer.*) wrecker.

dépareillé /depareje/ *a.* odd, not matching.

déparer /depare/ *v.t.* mar.

départ /depar/ *n.m.* departure; (*sport*) start. **au ~,** at the outset.

départager /departaʒe/ *v.t.* settle the matter between.

département /departəmɑ̃/ *n.m.* department.

départir (se) /(sə)departir/ *v. pr.* **se ~ de,** depart from.

dépassé /depɑse/ *a.* outdated.

dépass|er /depɑse/ *v.t.* go past, pass; (*véhicule*) overtake; (*excéder*) exceed; (*rival*) surpass; (*dérouter: fam.*) be beyond. —*v.i.* stick out; (*véhicule*) overtake. **~ement** *n.m.* overtaking.

dépays|er /depeize/ *v.t.* disorientate, disorient. **~ement** *n.m.* disorientation; (*changement*) change of scenery.

dépecer /depəse/ *v.t.* carve up.

dépêch|e /depɛʃ/ *n.f.* dispatch; (*télégraphique*) telegram. **~er**[1] /-eʃe/ *v.t.* dispatch.

dépêcher[2] **(se)** /(sə)depeʃe/ *v. pr.* hurry (up).

dépeigné /depeɲe/ *a.* dishevelled.

dépeindre /depɛ̃dr/ *v.t.* depict.

dépendance /depɑ̃dɑ̃s/ *n.f.* dependence; (*bâtiment*) outbuilding.

dépendre /depɑ̃dr/ *v.t.* take down. —*v.i.* depend (**de,** on). **~ de,** (*appartenir à*) belong to.

dépens (aux) /(o)depɑ̃/ *prép.* **aux ~ de,** at the expense of.

dépens|e /depɑ̃s/ *n.f.* expense; expenditure. **~er** *v.t./i.* spend; (*énergie etc.*) expend. **se ~er** *v. pr.* exert o.s.

dépens|ier, ~ière /depɑ̃sje, -jɛr/ *a.* **être ~ier,** be a spendthrift.

dépérir /deperir/ *v.i.* wither.

dépeupler /depœple/ *v.t.* depopulate. **se ~** *v. pr.* become depopulated.

déphasé /defɑze/ *a.* (*fam.*) out of touch.

dépist|er /depiste/ *v.t.* detect; (*criminel*) track down; (*poursuivant*) throw off the scent. **~age** *n.m.* detection.

dépit /depi/ *n.m.* resentment. **en ~ de,** despite. **~é** /-te/ *a.* vexed.

déplacé /deplase/ *a.* out of place.

déplac|er /deplase/ *v.t.* move. **se ~er** *v. pr.* move; (*voyager*) travel. **~ement** *n.m.* moving; travel(ling).

déplaire /deplɛr/ *v.i.* **~ à,** (*irriter*) displease. **ça me déplaît,** I dislike that. **se ~** *v. pr.* dislike it.

déplaisant, ~e /deplɛzɑ̃, -t/ *a.* unpleasant, disagreeable.

déplaisir /deplezir/ *n.m.* displeasure.

dépliant /deplijɑ̃/ *n.m.* leaflet.

déplier /deplije/ *v.t.* unfold.

déplor|er /deplɔre/ *v.t.* (*trouver regrettable*) deplore; (*mort*) lament. **~able** *a.* deplorable.

dépl|oyer /deplwaje/ *v.t.* (*ailes, carte*) spread; (*courage*) display; (*armée*) deploy. **~oiement** *n.m.* display; deployment.

déport|er /depɔrte/ *v.t.* (*exiler*) deport; (*dévier*) carry off course. **~ation** *n.f.* deportation.

déposer /depoze/ *v.t.* put down; (*laisser*) leave; (*passager*) drop; (*argent*) deposit; (*installation*) dismantle; (*plainte*) lodge; (*armes*) lay down; (*roi*) depose. —*v.i.* (*jurid.*) testify. **se ~** *v. pr.* settle.

dépositaire /depozitɛr/ *n.m./f.* (*comm.*) agent.

déposition /depozisjɔ̃/ *n.f.* (*jurid.*) statement.

dépôt /depo/ *n.m.* (*garantie, lie*) deposit; (*entrepôt*) warehouse; (*d'autobus*) depot; (*d'ordures*) dump. **laisser en ~,** give for safe keeping.

dépotoir /depɔtwar/ *n.m.* rubbish dump.

dépouille /depuj/ *n.f.* skin, hide. **~ (mortelle),** mortal remains. **~s,** (*butin*) spoils.

dépouillé /depuje/ *a.* bare. **~ de,** bereft of.

dépouiller /depuje/ *v.t.* go through; (*votes*) count; (*écorcher*) skin. **~ de,** strip of.

dépourvu /depurvy/ *a.* **~ de,** devoid of. **prendre au ~,** catch unawares.

déprav|er /deprave/ *v.t.* deprave. **~ation** *n.f.* depravity.

dépréc|ier /depresje/ *v.t.,* **se ~ier** *v. pr.* depreciate. **~iation** *n.f.* depreciation.

déprédations /depredɑsjɔ̃/ *n.f. pl.* damage.

dépr|imer /deprime/ *v.t.* depress. **~ession** *n.f.* depression.

depuis /dəpɥi/ *prép.* since; (*durée*) for; (*à partir de*) from. —*adv.* (ever) since. **~ que,** since. **~ quand attendez-vous?,** how long have you been waiting?

députation /depytɑsjɔ̃/ *n.f.* deputation.

député, ~e /depyte/ *n.m., f.* Member of Parliament.

déraciner /derasine/ *v.t.* uproot.

déraill|er /derɑje/ *v.i.* be derailed. **faire ~er,** derail. **~ement** *n.m.* derailment. **~eur** *n.m.* (*de vélo*) gear mechanism, *dérailleur*.

déraisonnable /derɛzɔnabl/ *a.* unreasonable.

déraisonner /derɛzɔne/ *v.i.* talk nonsense.

dérang|er /derɑ̃ʒe/ *v.t.* (*gêner*) bother, disturb; (*dérégler*) upset, disrupt. **se ~er** *v. pr.* put o.s. out. **ça vous ~e si . . .?,** do you mind if . . .? **~ement** *n.m.* bother; (*désordre*) disorder, upset. **en ~ement,** out of order.

dérap|er /derape/ *v.i.* skid; (*fig.*) get out of control. **~age** *n.m.* skid.

déréglé /deregle/ *a.* (*vie*) dissolute.

dérégler /deregle/ *v.t.* put out of order. **se ~** *v. pr.* go wrong.

dérider /deride/ *v.t.* cheer up.

dérision /derizjɔ̃/ *n.f.* mockery. **par ~,** derisively.

dérisoire /derizwar/ *a.* derisory.

dérivatif /derivatif/ *n.m.* distraction.

dériv|e /deriv/ *n.f.* **aller à la ~e,** drift. **~er**[1] *v.i.* (*bateau*) drift; *v.t.* (*détourner*) divert.

dériv|er[2] /derive/ *v.i.* **~er de,** derive from. **~é** *a.* derived; *n.m.* derivative; (*techn.*) by-product.

dern|ier, ~ière /dɛrnje, -jɛr/ *a.* last; (*nouvelles, mode*) latest; (*étage*) top. —*n.m., f.* last (one). **ce ~ier,** the latter. **en ~ier,** last. **le ~ier cri,** the latest fashion.

dernièrement /dɛrnjɛrmɑ̃/ *adv.* recently.

dérobade /derɔbɑd/ *n.f.* evasion, dodge.

dérobé /derɔbe/ *a.* hidden. **à la ~e,** stealthily.

dérober /derɔbe/ *v.t.* steal; (*cacher*) hide (**à,** from). **se ~** *v. pr.* slip away. **se ~ à, (*obligation*)** shy away from; (*se cacher à*) hide from.

dérogation /derɔgɑsjɔ̃/ *n.f.* exemption.

déroul|er /derule/ *v.t.* (*fil etc.*) unwind. **se ~er** *v. pr.* unwind; (*avoir lieu*) take place; (*récit, paysage*) unfold. **~ement** *n.m.* (*d'une action*) development.

déroute /derut/ *n.f.* (*mil.*) rout.
dérouter /derute/ *v.t.* re-route; (*fig.*) disconcert.
derrière /dɛrjɛr/ *prép.* & *adv.* behind. —*n.m.* back, rear; (*postérieur*) behind. **de ~,** back, rear; (*pattes*) hind. **par ~,** (from) behind, at the back *ou* rear.
des /de/ *voir* **de.**
dès /dɛ/ *prép.* (right) from, from the time of. **~ lors,** from then on. **~ que,** as soon as.
désabusé /dezabyze/ *a.* disillusioned.
désaccord /dezakɔr/ *n.m.* disagreement. **~é** /-de/ *a.* out of tune.
désaffecté /dezafɛkte/ *a.* disused.
désaffection /dezafɛksjɔ̃/ *n.f.* alienation (**pour,** from).
désagréable /dezagreabl/ *a.* unpleasant.
désagréger (se) /(sə)dezagreʒe/ *v. pr.* disintegrate.
désagrément /dezagremɑ̃/ *n.m.* annoyance.
désaltérer /dezaltere/ *v.i.*, **se ~** *v. pr.* quench one's thirst.
désamorcer /dezamɔrse/ *v.t.* (*situation, obus*) defuse.
désappr|ouver /dezapruve/ *v.t.* disapprove of. **~obation** *n.f.* disapproval.
désarçonner /dezarsɔne/ *v.t.* disconcert, throw; (*jockey*) unseat, throw.
désarm|er /dezarme/ *v.t./i.* disarm. **~ement** *n.m.* (*pol.*) disarmament.
désarroi /dezarwa/ *n.m.* confusion.
désarticuler /dezartikyle/ *v.t.* (*déboîter*) dislocate.
désastr|e /dezastr/ *n.m.* disaster. **~eux, ~euse** *a.* disastrous.
désavantag|e /dezavɑ̃taʒ/ *n.m.* disadvantage. **~er** *v.t.* put at a disadvantage. **~eux, ~euse** *a.* disadvantageous.
désaveu (*pl.* **~x**) /dezavø/ *n.m.* repudiation.
désavouer /dezavwe/ *v.t.* repudiate.
désaxé, ~e /dezakse/ *a.* & *n.m., f.* unbalanced (person).
descendan|t, ~te /desɑ̃dɑ̃, -t/ *n.m., f.* descendant. **~ce** *n.f.* descent; (*enfants*) descendants.
descendre /desɑ̃dr/ *v.i.* (*aux. être*) go down; (*venir*) come down; (*passager*) get off *ou* out; (*nuit*) fall. **~ de,** (*être issu de*) be descended from. —*v.t.* (*aux. avoir*) (*escalier etc.*) go *ou* come down; (*objet*) take down; (*abattre*) shoot down.
descente /desɑ̃t/ *n.f.* descent; (*pente*) (downward) slope; (*raid*) raid. **~ de lit,** bedside rug.
descripti|f, ~ve /dɛskriptif, -v/ *a.* descriptive.
description /dɛskripsjɔ̃/ *n.f.* description.
désemparé /dezɑ̃pare/ *a.* distraught; (*navire*) crippled.
désemplir /dezɑ̃plir/ *v.i.* **ne pas ~,** be always crowded.
désenchanté /dezɑ̃ʃɑ̃te/ *a.* disenchanted.
désenfler /dezɑ̃fle/ *v.i.* go down.
déséquilibre /dezekilibr/ *n.m.* imbalance. **en ~,** unsteady.
déséquilibr|er /dezekilibre/ *v.t.* throw off balance. **~é, ~ée** *a.* & *n.m., f.* unbalanced (person).
désert[1], **~e** /dezɛr, -t/ *a.* deserted.
désert[2] /dezɛr/ *n.m.* desert. **~ique** /-tik/ *a.* desert.
désert|er /dezɛrte/ *v.t./i.* desert. **~eur** *n.m.* deserter. **~ion** /-ɛrsjɔ̃/ *n.f.* desertion.
désespér|er /dezɛspere/ *v.i.*, **se ~er** *v. pr.* despair. **~er de,** despair of. **~ant, ~ante** *a.* utterly disheartening. **~é** *a.* in despair; (*état, cas*) hopeless; (*effort*) desperate. **~ément** *adv.* desperately.

désespoir /dezɛspwar/ *n.m.* despair. **au ~,** in despair.

déshabill|er /dezabije/ *v.t.*, **se ~er** *v. pr.* undress, get undressed. **~é** *a.* undressed; *n.m.* négligé.

déshabituer (se) /(sə)dezabitɥe/ *v. pr.* **se ~ de,** get out of the habit of.

désherb|er /dezɛrbe/ *v.t.* weed. **~ant** *n.m.* weed-killer.

déshériter /dezerite/ *v.t.* disinherit; (*désavantager*) deprive.

déshonneur /dezɔnœr/ *n.m.* dishonour.

déshonor|er /dezɔnɔre/ *v.t.* dishonour. **~ant, ~ante** *a.* dishonourable.

déshydrater /dezidrate/ *v.t.*, **se ~** *v. pr.* dehydrate.

désignation /deziɲasjɔ̃/ *n.f.* designation.

désigner /deziɲe/ *v.t.* (*montrer*) point to *ou* out; (*élire*) appoint; (*signifier*) indicate.

désillusion /dezilyzjɔ̃/ *n.f.* disillusionment.

désinence /dezinɑ̃s/ *n.f.* (*gram.*) ending.

désinfect|er /dezɛ̃fɛkte/ *v.t.* disinfect. **~ant** *n.m.* disinfectant.

désintégrer /dezɛ̃tegre/ *v.t.*, **se ~** *v. pr.* disintegrate.

désintéressé /dezɛ̃terese/ *a.* disinterested.

désintéresser (se) /(sə)dezɛ̃terese/ *v. pr.* **se ~ de,** lose interest in.

désintoxiquer /dezɛ̃tɔksike/ *v.t.* cure of an addiction.

désinvolt|e /dezɛ̃vɔlt/ *a.* casual. **~ure** *n.f.* casualness.

désir /dezir/ *n.m.* wish, desire; (*convoitise*) desire.

désirer /dezire/ *v.t.* want; (*convoiter*) desire. **~ faire,** want *ou* wish to do.

désireu|x, ~se /dezirø, -z/ *a.* **~x de,** anxious to.

désist|er (se) /(sə)deziste/ *v. pr.* withdraw. **~ement** *n.m.* withdrawal.

désobéir /dezɔbeir/ *v.i.* **~ (à),** disobey.

désobéissan|t, ~te /dezɔbeisɑ̃, -t/ *a.* disobedient. **~ce** *n.f.* disobedience.

désobligeant, ~e /dezɔbliʒɑ̃, -t/ *a.* disagreeable, unkind.

désodorisant /dezɔdɔrizɑ̃/ *n.m.* air freshener.

désœuvr|é /dezœvre/ *a.* idle. **~ement** *n.m.* idleness.

désolé /dezɔle/ *a.* (*région*) desolate.

désol|er /dezɔle/ *v.t.* distress. **être ~é,** (*regretter*) be sorry. **~ation** *n.f.* distress.

désopilant, ~e /dezɔpilɑ̃, -t/ *a.* hilarious.

désordonné /dezɔrdɔne/ *a.* untidy; (*mouvements*) uncoordinated.

désordre /dezɔrdr/ *n.m.* disorder; (*de vêtements, cheveux*) untidiness. **mettre en ~,** make untidy.

désorganiser /dezɔrganize/ *v.t.* disorganize.

désorienter /dezɔrjɑ̃te/ *v.t.* disorientate, disorient.

désormais /dezɔrmɛ/ *adv.* from now on.

désosser /dezɔse/ *v.t.* bone.

despote /dɛspɔt/ *n.m.* despot.

desquels, desquelles /dekɛl/ *voir* **lequel.**

dessaisir (se) /(sə)desezir/ *v. pr.* **se ~ de,** relinquish, part with.

dessaler /desale/ *v.t.* (*culin.*) soak.

dessécher /deseʃe/ *v.t.*, **se ~** *v. pr.* dry out *ou* up.

dessein /desɛ̃/ *n.m.* intention. **à ~,** intentionally.

desserrer /desere/ *v.t.* loosen. **se ~** *v. pr.* come loose.

dessert /desɛr/ *n.m.* dessert.

desserte /desɛrt/ *n.f.* (*transports*) service, servicing.

desservir /desɛrvir/ *v.t./i.* clear away; (*autobus*) provide a service to, serve.

dessin /desɛ̃/ *n.m.* drawing; (*motif*)

design; (*contour*) outline. ~ **animé,** (*cinéma*) cartoon. ~ **humoristique,** cartoon.

dessin|er /desine/ *v.t./i.* draw; (*fig.*) outline. **se ~er** *v. pr.* appear, take shape. **~ateur, ~atrice** *n.m., f.* artist; (*industriel*) draughtsman. **~ateur de mode,** fashion designer.

dessoûler /desule/ *v.t./i.* sober up.

dessous /dsu/ *adv.* underneath. —*n.m.* under-side, underneath. —*n.m. pl.* underclothes. **du ~,** bottom; (*voisins*) downstairs. **en ~, par ~,** underneath. **avoir le ~,** get the worst of it. **~-de-plat** *n.m. invar.* (heat-resistant) table-mat.

dessus /dsy/ *adv.* on top (of it), on it. —*n.m.* top. **du ~,** top; (*voisins*) upstairs. **en ~,** above. **par ~,** over (it). **avoir le ~,** get the upper hand. **~-de-lit** *n.m. invar.* bedspread.

destin /dɛstɛ̃/ *n.m.* (*sort*) fate; (*avenir*) destiny.

destinataire /dɛstinatɛr/ *n.m./f.* addressee.

destination /dɛstinɑsjɔ̃/ *n.f.* destination; (*emploi*) purpose. **à ~ de,** (going) to.

destinée /dɛstine/ *n.f.* (*sort*) fate; (*avenir*) destiny.

destiner /dɛstine/ *v.t.* **~ à,** intend for; (*vouer*) destine for; (*affecter*) earmark for. **être destiné à faire,** be intended to do; (*condamné, obligé*) be destined to do. **se ~ à,** (*carrière*) intend to take up.

destit|uer /dɛstitɥe/ *v.t.* dismiss (from office). **~ution** *n.f.* dismissal.

destruc|teur, ~trice /dɛstryktœr, -tris/ *a.* destructive.

destruction /dɛstryksjɔ̃/ *n.f.* destruction.

dés|uet, ~uète /desɥɛ, -t/ *a.* outdated.

désunir /dezynir/ *v.t.* divide.

détachant /detaʃɑ̃/ *n.m.* stain-remover.

détach|é /detaʃe/ *a.* detached. **~ement** *n.m.* detachment.

détacher /detaʃe/ *v.t.* untie; (*ôter*) remove, detach; (*déléguer*) send (on assignment *ou* secondment). **se ~** *v. pr.* come off, break away; (*nœud etc.*) come undone; (*ressortir*) stand out.

détail /detaj/ *n.m.* detail; (*de compte*) breakdown; (*comm.*) retail. **au ~,** (*vendre etc.*) retail. **de ~,** (*prix etc.*) retail. **en ~,** in detail.

détaillé /detaje/ *a.* detailed.

détaill|er /detaje/ *v.t.* (*articles*) sell in small quantities, split up. **~ant, ~ante** *n.m., f.* retailer.

détaler /detale/ *v.i.* (*fam.*) make tracks, run off.

détaxer /detakse/ *v.t.* reduce the tax on.

détect|er /detɛkte/ *v.t.* detect. **~eur** *n.m.* detector. **~ion** /-ksjɔ̃/ *n.f.* detection.

détective /detɛktiv/ *n.m.* detective.

déteindre /detɛ̃dr/ *v.i.* (*couleur*) run (**sur,** on to). **~ sur,** (*fig.*) rub off on.

détend|re /detɑ̃dr/ *v.t.* slacken; (*ressort*) release; (*personne*) relax. **se ~re** *v. pr.* become slack, slacken; be released; relax. **~u** *a.* (*calme*) relaxed.

détenir† /detnir/ *v.t.* hold; (*secret, fortune*) possess.

détente /detɑ̃t/ *n.f.* relaxation; (*pol.*) détente; (*saut*) spring; (*gâchette*) trigger; (*relâchement*) release.

déten|teur, ~trice /detɑ̃tœr, -tris/ *n.m., f.* holder.

détention /detɑ̃sjɔ̃/ *n.f.* **~ préventive,** custody.

détenu, ~e /detny/ *n.m., f.* prisoner.

détergent /detɛrʒɑ̃/ *n.m.* detergent.
détérior|er /deterjɔre/ *v.t.* damage. **se ~er** *v. pr.* deteriorate. **~ation** *n.f.* damaging; deterioration.
détermin|er /detɛrmine/ *v.t.* determine. **se ~er** *v. pr.* make up one's mind (**à,** to). **~ation** *n.f.* determination. **~é** *a.* (*résolu*) determined; (*précis*) definite.
déterrer /detere/ *v.t.* dig up.
détersif /detɛrsif/ *n.m.* detergent.
détestable /detɛstabl/ *a.* foul.
détester /detɛste/ *v.t.* hate. **se ~** *v. pr.* hate each other.
déton|er /detɔne/ *v.i.* explode, detonate. **~ateur** *n.m.* detonator. **~ation** *n.f.* explosion, detonation.
détonner /detɔne/ *v.i.* clash.
détour /detur/ *n.m.* bend; (*crochet*) detour; (*fig.*) roundabout means.
détourné /deturne/ *a.* roundabout.
détourn|er /deturne/ *v.t.* divert; (*tête, yeux*) turn away; (*avion*) hijack; (*argent*) embezzle. **se ~er de,** stray from. **~ement** *n.m.* diversion; hijack(ing); embezzlement.
détrac|teur, ~trice /detraktœr, -tris/ *n.m., f.* critic.
détraquer /detrake/ *v.t.* break, put out of order; (*estomac*) upset. **se ~** *v. pr.* (*machine*) go wrong.
détrempé /detrɑ̃pe/ *a.* saturated.
détresse /detrɛs/ *n.f.* distress.
détriment /detrimɑ̃/ *n.m.* detriment.
détritus /detritys/ *n.m. pl.* rubbish.
détroit /detrwa/ *n.m.* strait.
détromper /detrɔ̃pe/ *v.t.* undeceive, enlighten.
détruire† /detrɥir/ *v.t.* destroy.
dette /dɛt/ *n.f.* debt.
deuil /dœj/ *n.m.* mourning; (*perte*) bereavement. **porter le ~,** be in mourning.
deux /dø/ *a.* & *n.m.* two. **~ fois,** twice. **tous (les) ~,** both. **~-pièces** *n.m. invar.* (*vêtement*) two-piece. **~-points** *n.m. invar.* (*gram.*) colon. **~-roues** *n.m. invar.* two-wheeled vehicle.
deuxième /døzjɛm/ *a.* & *n.m./f.* second. **~ment** *adv.* secondly.
dévaler /devale/ *v.t./i.* hurtle down.
dévaliser /devalize/ *v.t.* rob, clean out.
dévaloriser /devalɔrize/ *v.t.*, **se ~** *v. pr.* reduce in value.
déval|uer /devalɥe/ *v.t.*, **se ~uer** *v. pr.* devalue. **~uation** *n.f.* devaluation.
devancer /dəvɑ̃se/ *v.t.* be *ou* go ahead of; (*arriver*) arrive ahead of; (*prévenir*) anticipate.
devant /dvɑ̃/ *prép.* in front of; (*distance*) ahead of; (*avec mouvement*) past; (*en présence de*) before; (*face à*) in the face of. —*adv.* in front; (*à distance*) ahead. —*n.m.* front. **de ~,** front. **par ~,** at *ou* from the front, in front.
devanture /dvɑ̃tyr/ *n.f.* shop front; (*étalage*) shop-window.
dévaster /devaste/ *v.t.* devastate.
déveine /devɛn/ *n.f.* bad luck.
développ|er /devlɔpe/ *v.t.*, **se ~er** *v. pr.* develop. **~ement** *n.m.* development; (*de photos*) developing.
devenir† /dəvnir/ *v.i.* (*aux. être*) become. **qu'est-il devenu?,** what has become of him?
déverser /devɛrse/ *v.t.*, **se ~** *v. pr.* empty out, pour out.
dévêtir /devetir/ *v.t.*, **se ~** *v. pr.* undress.
déviation /devjɑsjɔ̃/ *n.f.* diversion.
dévider /devide/ *v.t.* unwind.
dévier /devje/ *v.t.* divert; (*coup*) deflect. —*v.i.* (*ballon, balle*) veer; (*personne*) deviate.

devin /dəvɛ̃/ *n.m.* fortune-teller.
deviner /dvine/ *v.t.* guess; (*prévoir*) foretell; (*apercevoir*) distinguish.
devinette /dvinɛt/ *n.f.* riddle.
devis /dvi/ *n.m.* estimate.
dévisager /devizaʒe/ *v.t.* stare at.
devise /dviz/ *n.f.* motto. **~s**, (*monnaie*) (foreign) currency.
dévisser /devise/ *v.t.* unscrew.
dévoiler /devwale/ *v.t.* reveal.
devoir[1] /dvwar/ *n.m.* duty; (*scol.*) homework; (*fait en classe*) exercise.
devoir†[2] /dvwar/ *v.t.* owe. —*v. aux.* **~ faire,** (*nécessité*) must do, have (got) to do; (*intention*) be due to do. **~ être,** (*probabilité*) must be. **vous devriez,** you should. **il aurait dû,** he should have.
dévorer /devɔre/ *v.t.* devour.
dévot, ~e /devo, -ɔt/ *a.* devout.
dévotion /devosjɔ̃/ *n.f.* (*relig.*) devotion.
dévou|er (se) /(sə)devwe/ *v. pr.* devote o.s. (**à,** to); (*se sacrifier*) sacrifice o.s. **~é** *a.* devoted. **~ement** /-vumɑ̃/ *n.m.* devotion.
dévoyé, ~e /devwaje/ *a.* & *n.m., f.* delinquent.
dextérité /dɛksterite/ *n.f.* skill.
diab|ète /djabɛt/ *n.m.* diabetes. **~étique** *a.* & *n.m./f.* diabetic.
diab|le /djɑbl/ *n.m.* devil. **~olique** *a.* diabolical.
diagnosti|c /djagnɔstik/ *n.m.* diagnosis. **~quer** *v.t.* diagnose.
diagon|al, ~ale (*m. pl.* **~aux**) /djagɔnal, -o/ *a.* & *n.f.* diagonal. **en ~ale,** diagonally.
diagramme /djagram/ *n.m.* diagram; (*graphique*) graph.
dialecte /djalɛkt/ *n.m.* dialect.
dialogu|e /djalɔg/ *n.m.* dialogue. **~er** *v.i.* (*pol.*) have a dialogue.
diamant /djamɑ̃/ *n.m.* diamond.
diamètre /djamɛtr/ *n.m.* diameter.
diapason /djapazɔ̃/ *n.m.* tuning-fork.
diaphragme /djafragm/ *n.m.* diaphragm.
diapositive /djapozitiv/ *n.f.* (colour) slide.
diarrhée /djare/ *n.f.* diarrhoea.
dictat|eur /diktatœr/ *n.m.* dictator. **~ure** *n.f.* dictatorship.
dict|er /dikte/ *v.t.* dictate. **~ée** *n.f.* dictation.
diction /diksjɔ̃/ *n.f.* diction.
dictionnaire /diksjɔnɛr/ *n.m.* dictionary.
dicton /diktɔ̃/ *n.m.* saying.
dièse /djɛz/ *n.m.* (*mus.*) sharp.
diesel /djezɛl/ *n.m.* & *a. invar.* diesel.
diète /djɛt/ *n.f.* (starvation) diet.
diététicien, ~ne /djetetisjɛ̃, -jɛn/ *n.m., f.* dietician.
diététique /djetetik/ *n.f.* dietetics. —*a.* **produit** *ou* **aliment ~,** health food.
dieu (*pl.* **~x**) /djø/ *n.m.* god. **D~,** God.
diffam|er /difame/ *v.t.* slander; (*par écrit*) libel. **~ation** *n.f.* slander; libel.
différé (en) /(ɑ̃)difere/ *adv.* (*émission*) recorded.
différemment /diferamɑ̃/ *adv.* differently.
différence /diferɑ̃s/ *n.f.* difference. **à la ~ de,** unlike.
différencier /diferɑ̃sje/ *v.t.* differentiate. **se ~ de,** (*différer de*) differ from.
différend /diferɑ̃/ *n.m.* difference (of opinion).
différent, ~e /diferɑ̃, -t/ *a.* different (**de,** from).
différentiel, ~le /diferɑ̃sjɛl/ *a.* & *n.m.* differential.
différer[1] /difere/ *v.t.* postpone.
différer[2] /difere/ *v.i.* differ.
difficile /difisil/ *a.* difficult. **~ment** *adv.* with difficulty.
difficulté /difikylte/ *n.f.* difficulty.
difform|e /difɔrm/ *a.* deformed. **~ité** *n.f.* deformity.

diffus, ~e /dify, -z/ *a.* diffuse.
diffus|er /difyze/ *v.t.* broadcast; (*lumière, chaleur*) diffuse. **~ion** *n.f.* broadcasting; diffusion.
dig|érer /diʒere/ *v.t.* digest; (*endurer: fam.*) stomach. **~este, ~estible** *adjs.* digestible. **~estion** *n.f.* digestion.
digesti|f, ~ve /diʒɛstif, -v/ *a.* digestive. —*n.m.* after-dinner liqueur.
digit|al (*m. pl.* **~aux**) /diʒital, -o/ *a.* digital.
digne /diɲ/ *a.* (*noble*) dignified; (*honnête*) worthy. **~ de,** worthy of. **~ de foi,** trustworthy.
dignitaire /diɲitɛr/ *n.m.* dignitary.
dignité /diɲite/ *n.f.* dignity.
digression /digresjɔ̃/ *n.f.* digression.
digue /dig/ *n.f.* dike.
dilapider /dilapide/ *v.t.* squander.
dilat|er /dilate/ *v.t.,* **se ~er** *v. pr.* dilate. **~ation** /-ɑsjɔ̃/ *n.f.* dilation.
dilemme /dilɛm/ *n.m.* dilemma.
dilettante /dilɛtɑ̃t/ *n.m., f.* amateur.
diligence[1] /diliʒɑ̃s/ *n.f.* (*voiture à chevaux*) stage-coach.
diligen|t, ~te /diliʒɑ̃, -t/ *a.* prompt, diligent. **~ce**[2] *n.f.* diligence.
diluer /dilɥe/ *v.t.* dilute.
dimanche /dimɑ̃ʃ/ *n.m.* Sunday.
dimension /dimɑ̃sjɔ̃/ *n.f.* (*taille*) size; (*mesure*) dimension.
dimin|uer /diminɥe/ *v.t.* reduce, decrease; (*plaisir, courage, etc.*) lessen; (*dénigrer*) lessen. —*v.i.* decrease. **~ution** *n.f.* decrease (**de,** in).
diminutif /diminytif/ *n.m.* diminutive; (*surnom*) pet name *ou* form.
dinde /dɛ̃d/ *n.f.* turkey.
dindon /dɛ̃dɔ̃/ *n.m.* turkey.
dîn|er /dine/ *n.m.* dinner. —*v.i.* have dinner. **~eur, ~euse** *n.m., f.* diner.
dingue /dɛ̃g/ *a.* (*fam.*) crazy.
dinosaure /dinozɔr/ *n.m.* dinosaur.
diocèse /djɔsɛz/ *n.m.* diocese.
diphtérie /difteri/ *n.f.* diphtheria.
diphtongue /diftɔ̃g/ *n.f.* diphthong.
diplomate /diplɔmat/ *n.m.* diplomat. —*a.* diplomatic.
diplomat|ie /diplɔmasi/ *n.f.* diplomacy. **~ique** /-atik/ *a.* diplomatic.
diplôm|e /diplom/ *n.m.* certificate, diploma; (*univ.*) degree. **~é** *a.* qualified.
dire† /dir/ *v.t.* say; (*secret, vérité, heure*) tell; (*penser*) think. **~ que,** say that. **~ à qn. que/de,** tell s.o. that/to. **se ~** *v. pr.* (*mot*) be said; (*fatigué etc.*) say that one is. **ça me/vous/***etc.* **dit de faire,** I/you/*etc.* feel like doing. **on dirait que,** it would seem that, it seems that.
direct /dirɛkt/ *a.* direct. **en ~,** (*émission*) live. **~ement** *adv.* directly.
direc|teur, ~trice /dirɛktœr, -tris/ *n.m., f.* director; (*chef de service*) manager, manageress; (*d'école*) headmaster, headmistress.
direction /dirɛksjɔ̃/ *n.f.* (*sens*) direction; (*de société etc.*) management; (*auto.*) steering. **en ~ de,** (going) to.
directive /dirɛktiv/ *n.f.* instruction.
dirigeant, ~e /diriʒɑ̃, -t/ *n.m., f.* (*pol.*) leader; (*comm.*) manager. —*a.* (*classe*) ruling.
diriger /diriʒe/ *v.t.* run, manage, direct; (*véhicule*) steer; (*orchestre*) conduct; (*braquer*) aim; (*tourner*) turn. **se ~** *v. pr.* guide o.s. **se ~ vers,** make one's way to.
dis /di/ *voir* **dire.**
discern|er /disɛrne/ *v.t.* discern. **~ement** *n.m.* discernment.
disciple /disipl/ *n.m.* disciple.
disciplin|e /disiplin/ *n.f.* disci-

pline. **~aire** *a.* disciplinary. **~er** *v.t.* discipline.

discontinu /diskɔ̃tiny/ *a.* intermittent.

discontinuer /diskɔ̃tinɥe/ *v.i.* **sans ~**, without stopping.

discordant, ~e /diskɔrdɑ̃, -t/ *a.* discordant.

discorde /diskɔrd/ *n.f.* discord.

discothèque /diskɔtɛk/ *n.f.* record library; (*club*) disco(thèque).

discourir /diskurir/ *v.i.* (*péj.*) hold forth, ramble on.

discours /diskur/ *n.m.* speech.

discréditer /diskredite/ *v.t.* discredit.

discr|et, ~ète /diskrɛ, -t/ *a.* discreet. **~ètement** *adv.* discreetly.

discrétion /diskresjɔ̃/ *n.f.* discretion. **à ~**, as much as one desires.

discrimination /diskriminɑsjɔ̃/ *n.f.* discrimination.

disculper /diskylpe/ *v.t.* exonerate.

discussion /diskysjɔ̃/ *n.f.* discussion; (*querelle*) argument.

discuté /diskyte/ *a.* controversial.

discuter /diskyte/ *v.t.* discuss; (*contester*) question. *—v.i.* (*parler*) talk; (*répliquer*) argue. **~ de**, discuss.

disette /dizɛt/ *n.f.* (food) shortage.

diseuse /dizøz/ *n.f.* **~ de bonne aventure**, fortune-teller.

disgrâce /disgrɑs/ *n.f.* disgrace.

disgracieu|x, ~se /disgrasjø, -z/ *a.* ungainly.

disjoindre /disʒwɛ̃dr/ *v.t.* take apart. **se ~** *v. pr.* come apart.

dislo|quer /dislɔke/ *v.t.* (*membre*) dislocate; (*machine etc.*) break (apart). **se ~quer** *v. pr.* (*parti, cortège*) break up; (*meuble*) come apart. **~cation** *n.f.* (*anat.*) dislocation.

dispar|aître† /disparɛtr/ *v.i.* disappear; (*mourir*) die. **faire ~aître**, get rid of. **~ition** *n.f.* disappearance; (*mort*) death. **~u, ~ue** *a.* (*soldat etc.*) missing; *n.m., f.* missing person; (*mort*) dead person.

disparate /disparat/ *a.* ill-assorted.

disparité /disparite/ *n.f.* disparity.

dispensaire /dispɑ̃sɛr/ *n.m.* clinic.

dispense /dispɑ̃s/ *n.f.* exemption.

dispenser /dispɑ̃se/ *v.t.* exempt (**de**, from). **se ~ de (faire)**, avoid (doing).

disperser /dispɛrse/ *v.t.* (*éparpiller*) scatter; (*répartir*) disperse. **se ~** *v. pr.* disperse.

disponib|le /dispɔnibl/ *a.* available. **~ilité** *n.f.* availability.

disposé /dispoze/ *a.* **bien/mal ~**, in a good/bad mood. **~ à**, prepared to. **~ envers**, disposed towards.

disposer /dispoze/ *v.t.* arrange. **~ à**, (*engager à*) incline to. *—v.i.* **~ de**, have at one's disposal. **se ~ à**, prepare to.

dispositif /dispozitif/ *n.m.* device; (*plan*) plan of action. **~ anti-parasite**, suppressor.

disposition /dispozisjɔ̃/ *n.f.* arrangement; (*humeur*) mood; (*tendance*) tendency. **~s**, (*préparatifs*) arrangements; (*aptitude*) aptitude. **à la ~ de**, at the disposal of.

disproportionné /disprɔpɔrsjɔne/ *a.* disproportionate.

dispute /dispyt/ *n.f.* quarrel.

disputer /dispyte/ *v.t.* (*match*) play; (*course*) run in; (*prix*) fight for (**à qn.**, with s.o.); (*gronder: fam.*) tell off. **se ~** *v. pr.* quarrel; (*se battre pour*) fight over; (*match*) be played.

disquaire /diskɛr/ *n.m./f.* record dealer.

disqualif|ier /diskalifje/ *v.t.* disqualify. **~ication** *n.f.* disqualification.

disque /disk/ *n.m.* (*mus.*) record; (*sport*) discus; (*cercle*) disc, disk. **~tte** /-ɛt/ *n.f.* floppy disk.
dissection /disɛksjɔ̃/ *n.f.* dissection.
dissemblable /disɑ̃blabl/ *a.* dissimilar.
disséminer /disemine/ *v.t.* scatter.
disséquer /diseke/ *v.t.* dissect.
dissertation /disɛrtɑsjɔ̃/ *n.f.* (*scol.*) essay.
disserter /disɛrte/ *v.i.* **~ sur,** comment upon.
dissiden|t, ~te /disidɑ̃, -t/ *a.* & *n.m., f.* dissident. **~ce** *n.f.* dissidence.
dissimul|er /disimyle/ *v.t.* conceal (**à,** from). **se ~er** *v. pr.* conceal o.s. **~ation** *n.f.* concealment; (*fig.*) deceit.
dissipé /disipe/ *a.* (*élève*) unruly.
dissip|er /disipe/ *v.t.* (*fumée, crainte*) dispel; (*fortune*) squander; (*personne*) lead into bad ways. **se ~er** *v. pr.* disappear. **~ation** *n.f.* squandering; (*indiscipline*) misbehaviour.
dissolu /disɔly/ *a.* dissolute.
dissolution /disɔlysjɔ̃/ *n.f.* dissolution.
dissolvant /disɔlvɑ̃/ *n.m.* solvent; (*pour ongles*) nail polish remover.
dissonant, ~e /disɔnɑ̃, -t/ *a.* discordant.
dissoudre† /disudr/ *v.t.*, **se ~** *v. pr.* dissolve.
dissua|der /disɥade/ *v.t.* dissuade (**de,** from). **~sion** /-ɥazjɔ̃/ *n.f.* dissuasion.
distance /distɑ̃s/ *n.f.* distance; (*écart*) gap. **à ~,** at *ou* from a distance.
distancer /distɑ̃se/ *v.t.* leave behind.
distant, ~e /distɑ̃, -t/ *a.* distant.
distendre /distɑ̃dr/ *v.t.*, **se ~** *v. pr.* distend.
distill|er /distile/ *v.t.* distil. **~ation** *n.f.* distillation.
distillerie /distilri/ *n.f.* distillery.
distinct, ~e /distɛ̃(kt), -ɛ̃kt/ *a.* distinct. **~ement** /-ɛ̃ktəmɑ̃/ *adv.* distinctly.
distincti|f, ~ve /distɛ̃ktif, -v/ *a.* distinctive.
distinction /distɛ̃ksjɔ̃/ *n.f.* distinction.
distingué /distɛ̃ge/ *a.* distinguished.
distinguer /distɛ̃ge/ *v.t.* distinguish.
distraction /distraksjɔ̃/ *n.f.* absent-mindedness; (*oubli*) lapse; (*passe-temps*) distraction.
distraire† /distrɛr/ *v.t.* amuse; (*rendre inattentif*) distract. **se ~** *v. pr.* amuse o.s.
distrait, ~e /distrɛ, -t/ *a.* absent-minded.
distrib|uer /distribɥe/ *v.t.* hand out, distribute; (*répartir, amener*) distribute; (*courrier*) deliver. **~uteur** *n.m.* (*auto., comm.*) distributor. **~uteur (automatique),** vending-machine. **~ution** *n.f.* distribution; (*du courrier*) delivery; (*acteurs*) cast.
district /distrikt/ *n.m.* district.
dit¹, dites /di, dit/ *voir* **dire.**
dit², ~e /di, dit/ *a.* (*décidé*) agreed; (*surnommé*) called.
divag|uer /divage/ *v.i.* rave. **~ations** *n.f. pl.* ravings.
divan /divɑ̃/ *n.m.* divan.
divergen|t, ~te /divɛrʒɑ̃, -t/ *a.* divergent. **~ce** *n.f.* divergence.
diverger /divɛrʒe/ *v.i.* diverge.
divers, ~e /divɛr, -s/ *a.* (*varié*) diverse; (*différent*) various. **~ement** /-səmɑ̃/ *adv.* variously.
diversifier /divɛrsifje/ *v.t.* diversify.
diversion /divɛrsjɔ̃/ *n.f.* diversion.
diversité /divɛrsite/ *n.f.* diversity.
divert|ir /divɛrtir/ *v.t.* amuse. **se ~ir** *v. pr.* amuse o.s. **~issement** *n.m.* amusement.

dividende /dividɑ̃d/ *n.m.* dividend.
divin, ~e /divɛ̃, -in/ *a.* divine.
divinité /divinite/ *n.f.* divinity.
divis|er /divize/ *v.t.*, **se ~er** *v. pr.* divide. **~ion** *n.f.* division.
divorc|e /divɔrs/ *n.m.* divorce. **~é ~ée** *a.* divorced; *n.m., f.* divorcee. **~er** *v.i.* **~er (d'avec),** divorce.
divulguer /divylge/ *v.t.* divulge.
dix /dis/ (/di/ *before consonant*, /diz/ *before vowel*) *a.* & *n.m.* ten. **~ième** /dizjɛm/ *a.* & *n.m./f.* tenth.
dix-huit /dizɥit/ *a.* & *n.m.* eighteen. **~ième** *a.* & *n.m./f.* eighteenth.
dix-neu|f /diznœf/ *a.* & *n.m.* nineteen. **~vième** *a.* & *n.m./f.* nineteenth.
dix-sept /disɛt/ *a.* & *n.m.* seventeen. **~ième** *a.* & *n.m./f.* seventeenth.
dizaine /dizɛn/ *n.f.* (about) ten.
docile /dɔsil/ *a.* docile.
dock /dɔk/ *n.m.* dock.
docker /dɔkɛr/ *n.m.* docker.
doct|eur /dɔktœr/ *n.m.* doctor. **~oresse** *n.f.* lady doctor.
doctorat /dɔktɔra/ *n.m.* doctorate.
doctrin|e /dɔktrin/ *n.f.* doctrine. **~aire** *a.* doctrinaire.
document /dɔkymɑ̃/ *n.m.* document. **~aire** /-tɛr/ *a.* & *n.m.* documentary.
documentaliste /dɔkymɑ̃talist/ *n.m./f.* information officer.
document|er /dɔkymɑ̃te/ *v.t.* document. **se ~er** *v. pr.* collect information. **~ation** *n.f.* information, literature. **~é** *a.* well-documented.
dodeliner /dɔdline/ *v.i.* **~ de la tête,** sway one's head, nod.
dodo /dodo/ *n.m.* **faire ~,** (*langage enfantin*) go to sleep.
dodu /dɔdy/ *a.* plump.
dogm|e /dɔgm/ *n.m.* dogma. **~atique** *a.* dogmatic.
doigt /dwa/ *n.m.* finger. **~ de pied,** toe.
doigté /dwate/ *n.m.* (*mus.*) fingering, touch; (*adresse*) tact.
doigtier /dwatje/ *n.m.* finger-stall.
dois, doit /dwa/ *voir* **devoir**[2].
doléances /dɔleɑ̃s/ *n.f. pl.* grievances.
dollar /dɔlar/ *n.m.* dollar.
domaine /dɔmɛn/ *n.m.* estate, domain; (*fig.*) domain.
dôme /dom/ *n.m.* dome.
domestique /dɔmɛstik/ *a.* domestic. —*n.m./f.* servant.
domestiquer /dɔmɛstike/ *v.t.* domesticate.
domicile /dɔmisil/ *n.m.* home. **à ~,** at home; (*livrer*) to the home.
domicilié /dɔmisilje/ *a.* resident.
domin|er /dɔmine/ *v.t./i.* dominate; (*surplomber*) tower over, dominate; (*équipe*) dictate the game (to). **~ant, ~ante** *a.* dominant; *n.f.* dominant feature. **~ation** *n.f.* domination.
domino /dɔmino/ *n.m.* domino.
dommage /dɔmaʒ/ *n.m.* (*tort*) harm. **~(s),** (*dégâts*) damage. **c'est ~,** it is a pity. **~s-intérêts** *n.m. pl.* (*jurid.*) damages.
dompt|er /dɔ̃te/ *v.t.* tame. **~eur, ~euse** *n.m., f.* tamer.
don /dɔ̃/ *n.m.* (*cadeau, aptitude*) gift.
dona|teur, ~trice /dɔnatœr, -tris/ *n.m., f.* donor.
donation /dɔnɑsjɔ̃/ *n.f.* donation.
donc /dɔ̃(k)/ *conj.* so, then; (*par conséquent*) so, therefore.
donjon /dɔ̃ʒɔ̃/ *n.m.* (*tour*) keep.
donné /dɔne/ *a.* (*fixé*) given; (*pas cher: fam.*) dirt cheap. **étant ~ que,** given that.
données /dɔne/ *n.f. pl.* (*de science*) data; (*de problème*) facts.
donner /dɔne/ *v.t.* give; (*distribuer*) give out; (*récolte etc.*) produce. —*v.i.* **~ sur,** look out on to. **~ dans,** (*piège*) fall into. **ça**

donne soif/faim, it makes one thirsty/hungry. **~ à réparer**/*etc.*, take to be repaired/*etc.* **~ lieu à,** give rise to. **se ~ à,** devote o.s. to. **se ~ du mal,** go to a lot of trouble (**pour faire,** to do).

donneu|r, ~se /dɔnœr, -øz/ *n.m., f.* (*de sang*) donor.

dont /dɔ̃/ *pron. rel.* (*chose*) whose, of which; (*personne*) whose; (*partie d'un tout*) of whom; (*chose*) of which; (*provenance*) from which; (*manière*) in which. **le père ~ la fille,** the father whose daughter. **ce ~,** what. **~ il a besoin,** which he needs. **l'enfant ~ il est fier,** the child he is proud of.

doper /dɔpe/ *v.t.* dope. **se ~** *v. pr.* take dope.

doré /dɔre/ *a.* (*couleur d'or*) golden.

dorénavant /dɔrenavɑ̃/ *adv.* henceforth.

dorer /dɔre/ *v.t.* gild; (*culin*) brown; (*peau*) tan.

dorloter /dɔrlɔte/ *v.t.* pamper.

dorm|ir† /dɔrmir/ *v.i.* sleep; (*être endormi*) be asleep. **~eur, ~euse** *n.m., f.* sleeper.

dortoir /dɔrtwar/ *n.m.* dormitory.

dorure /dɔryr/ *n.f.* gilding.

dos /do/ *n.m.* back; (*de livre*) spine. **à ~ de,** riding on. **de ~,** from behind. **~ crawlé,** backstroke.

dos|e /doz/ *n.f.* dose. **~age** *n.m.* (*mélange*) mixture. **faire le ~age de,** measure out; balance. **~er** *v.t.* measure out; (*équilibrer*) balance.

dossard /dɔsar/ *n.m.* (*sport*) number.

dossier /dɔsje/ *n.m.* (*documents*) file; (*de chaise*) back.

dot /dɔt/ *n.f.* dowry.

doter /dɔte/ *v.t.* **~ de,** equip with.

douan|e /dwan/ *n.f.* customs. **~ier, ~ière** *a.* customs; *n.m., f.* customs officer.

doubl|e /dubl/ *a.* & *adv.* double. —*n.m.* (*copie*) duplicate; (*sosie*) double. **le ~e (de),** twice as much *ou* as many (as). **~e décimètre,** ruler. **~ement**[1] *adv.* doubly.

doubl|er /duble/ *v.t./i.* double; (*dépasser*) overtake; (*vêtement*) line; (*film*) dub; (*classe*) repeat; (*cap*) round. **~ement**[2] *n.m.* doubling. **~ure** *n.f.* (*étoffe*) lining; (*acteur*) understudy.

douce /dus/ *voir* **doux.**

douceâtre /dusɑtr/ *a.* sickly sweet.

doucement /dusmɑ̃/ *adv.* gently.

douceur /dusœr/ *n.f.* (*mollesse*) softness; (*de climat*) mildness; (*de personne*) gentleness; (*joie, plaisir*) sweetness. **~s,** (*friandises*) sweet things. **en ~,** smoothly.

douch|e /duʃ/ *n.f.* shower. **~er** *v.t.* give a shower to. **se ~er** *v. pr.* have *ou* take a shower.

doué /dwe/ *a.* gifted. **~ de,** endowed with.

douille /duj/ *n.f.* (*électr.*) socket.

douillet, ~te /dujɛ, -t/ *a.* cosy, comfortable; (*personne*: *péj.*) soft.

doul|eur /dulœr/ *n.f.* pain; (*chagrin*) grief. **~oureux, ~oureuse** *a.* painful.

doute /dut/ *n.m.* doubt. **sans ~,** no doubt. **sans aucun ~,** without doubt.

douter /dute/ *v.i.* **~ de,** doubt. **se ~ de,** suspect.

douteu|x, ~se /dutø, -z/ *a.* doubtful.

douve /duv/ *n.f.* moat.

Douvres /duvr/ *n.m./f.* Dover.

doux, douce /du, dus/ *a.* (*moelleux*) soft; (*sucré*) sweet; (*clément, pas fort*) mild; (*pas brusque, bienveillant*) gentle.

douzaine /duzɛn/ *n.f.* about twelve; (*douze*) dozen. **une ~ d'œufs**/*etc.*, a dozen eggs/*etc.*

douz|e /duz/ *a.* & *n.m.* twelve. **~ième** *a.* & *n.m./f.* twelfth.

doyen, ~ne /dwajɛ̃, -jɛn/ *n.m., f.* dean; (*en âge*) most senior person.

dragée /draʒe/ *n.f.* sugared almond.
dragon /dragɔ̃/ *n.m.* dragon.
dragu|e /drag/ *n.f.* (*bateau*) dredger. **~er** *v.t.* (*rivière*) dredge; (*filles*: *fam.*) chat up, try to pick up.
drainer /drene/ *v.t.* drain.
dramatique /dramatik/ *a.* dramatic. —*n.f.* (television) drama.
dramatiser /dramatize/ *v.t.* dramatize.
dramaturge /dramatyrʒ/ *n.m.*/*f.* dramatist.
drame /dram/ *n.m.* drama.
drap /dra/ *n.m.* sheet; (*tissu*) (woollen) cloth.
drapeau (*pl.* **~x**) /drapo/ *n.m.* flag.
draper /drape/ *v.t.* drape.
draperies /drapri/ *n.f. pl.* (*tentures*) hangings.
dress|er /drese/ *v.t.* put up, erect; (*tête*) raise; (*animal*) train; (*liste*) draw up. **se ~er** *v. pr.* (*bâtiment etc.*) stand; (*personne*) draw o.s. up. **~er l'oreille,** prick up one's ears. **~age** /drɛsaʒ/ *n.m.* training. **~eur, ~euse** /drɛsœr, -øz/ *n.m.*, *f.* trainer.
dribbler /drible/ *v.t.*/*i.* (*football*) dribble.
drogue /drɔg/ *n.f.* drug. **la ~,** drugs.
drogu|er /drɔge/ *v.t.* (*malade*) drug heavily, dose up; (*victime*) drug. **se ~er** *v. pr.* take drugs. **~é, ~ée** *n.m.*, *f.* drug addict.
drogu|erie /drɔgri/ *n.f.* hardware and chemist's shop; (*Amer.*) drugstore. **~iste** *n.m.*/*f.* owner of a *droguerie*.
droit[1], **~e** /drwa, -t/ *a.* (*non courbe*) straight; (*loyal*) upright; (*angle*) right. —*adv.* straight. —*n.f.* straight line.
droit[2], **~e** /drwa, -t/ *a.* (*contraire de gauche*) right. **à ~e,** on the right; (*direction*) (to the) right. **la ~e,** the right (side); (*pol.*) the right (wing). **~ier, ~ière** /-tje, -tjɛr/ *a.* & *n.m.*, *f.* right-handed (person).
droit[3] /drwa/ *n.m.* right. **~(s),** (*taxe*) duty; (*d'inscription*) fee(s). **le ~,** (*jurid.*) law. **avoir ~ à,** be entitled to. **avoir le ~ de,** be allowed to. **~ d'auteur,** copyright. **~s d'auteur,** royalties.
drôle /drol/ *a.* funny. **~ d'air,** funny look. **~ment** *adv.* funnily; (*extrêmement*: *fam.*) dreadfully.
dromadaire /drɔmadɛr/ *n.m.* dromedary.
dru /dry/ *a.* thick. **tomber ~,** fall thick and fast.
drugstore /drœgstɔr/ *n.m.* drugstore.
du /dy/ *voir* **de.**
dû, due /dy/ *voir* **devoir**[2]. —*a.* due. —*n.m.* due; (*argent*) dues. **~ à,** due to.
duc, duchesse /dyk, dyʃɛs/ *n.m.*, *f.* duke, duchess.
duel /dɥɛl/ *n.m.* duel.
dûment /dymɑ̃/ *adv.* duly.
dune /dyn/ *n.f.* dune.
duo /dɥo/ *n.m.* (*mus.*) duet; (*fig.*) duo.
dup|e /dyp/ *n.f.* dupe. **~er** *v.t.* dupe.
duplex /dyplɛks/ *n.m.* split-level apartment; (*Amer.*) duplex; (*émission*) link-up.
duplicata /dyplikata/ *n.m. invar.* duplicate.
duplicateur /dyplikatœr/ *n.m.* duplicator.
duplicité /dyplisite/ *n.f.* duplicity.
duquel /dykɛl/ *voir* **lequel.**
dur /dyr/ *a.* hard; (*sévère*) harsh, hard; (*viande*) tough, hard; (*col, brosse*) stiff. —*adv.* hard. —*n.m.* tough guy. **~ d'oreille,** hard of hearing.
durable /dyrabl/ *a.* lasting.
durant /dyrɑ̃/ *prép.* during; (*mesure de temps*) for.
durc|ir /dyrsir/ *v.t.*/*i.*, **se ~ir**

v. pr. harden. **~issement** *n.m.* hardening.

durée /dyre/ *n.f.* length; (*période*) duration.

durement /dyrmɑ̃/ *adv.* harshly.

durer /dyre/ *v.i.* last.

dureté /dyrte/ *n.f.* hardness; (*sévérité*) harshness.

duvet /dyvɛ/ *n.m.* down; (*sac*) (down-filled) sleeping-bag.

dynami|que /dinamik/ *a.* dynamic. **~sme** *n.m.* dynamism.

dynamit|e /dinamit/ *n.f.* dynamite. **~er** *v.t.* dynamite.

dynastie /dinasti/ *n.f.* dynasty.

dysenterie /disɑ̃tri/ *n.f.* dysentery.

E

eau (*pl.* **~x**) /o/ *n.f.* water. **~ courante/dormante,** running/still water. **~ de Cologne,** eau-de-Cologne. **~ dentifrice,** mouthwash. **~ de toilette,** toilet water. **~-de-vie** (*pl.* **~x-de-vie**) *n.f.* brandy. **~ douce/salée,** fresh/salt water. **~-forte** (*pl.* **~x-fortes**) *n.f.* etching. **~ potable,** drinking water.

ébahir /ebair/ *v.t.* dumbfound.

ébats /eba/ *n.m. pl.* frolics.

ébattre (s') /(s)ebatr/ *v. pr.* frolic.

ébauch|e /eboʃ/ *n.f.* outline. **~er** *v.t.* outline. **s'~er** *v. pr.* form.

ébène /ebɛn/ *n.f.* ebony.

ébéniste /ebenist/ *n.m.* cabinet-maker.

éberlué /ebɛrlɥe/ *a.* flabbergasted.

éblou|ir /ebluir/ *v.t.* dazzle. **~issement** *n.m.* dazzle, dazzling; (*malaise*) dizzy turn.

éboueur /ebwœr/ *n.m.* dustman; (*Amer.*) garbage collector.

ébouillanter /ebujɑ̃te/ *v.t.* scald.

éboul|er (s') /(s)ebule/ *v. pr.* crumble, collapse. **~ement** *n.m.* landslide. **~is** *n.m. pl.* fallen rocks and earth.

ébouriffé /eburife/ *a.* dishevelled.

ébranler /ebrɑ̃le/ *v.t.* shake. **s'~** *v. pr.* move off.

ébrécher /ebreʃe/ *v.t.* chip.

ébriété /ebrijete/ *n.f.* intoxication.

ébrouer (s') /(s)ebrue/ *v. pr.* shake o.s.

ébruiter /ebrɥite/ *v.t.* spread about.

ébullition /ebylisjɔ̃/ *n.f.* boiling. **en ~,** boiling.

écaille /ekɑj/ *n.f.* (*de poisson*) scale; (*de peinture, roc*) flake; (*matière*) tortoiseshell.

écailler /ekɑje/ *v.t.* (*poisson*) scale. **s'~** *v. pr.* flake (off).

écarlate /ekarlat/ *a.* & *n.f.* scarlet.

écarquiller /ekarkije/ *v.t.* **~ les yeux,** open one's eyes wide.

écart /ekar/ *n.m.* gap; (*de prix etc.*) difference; (*embardée*) swerve; (*de conduite*) lapse (**de,** in). **à l'~,** out of the way. **tenir à l'~,** (*participant*) keep out of things. **à l'~ de,** away from.

écarté /ekarte/ *a.* (*lieu*) remote.

écartement /ekartəmɑ̃/ *n.m.* gap.

écarter /ekarte/ *v.t.* (*objets*) move apart; (*ouvrir*) open; (*éliminer*) dismiss. **~ qch. de,** move sth. away from. **~ qn. de,** keep s.o. away from. **s'~** *v. pr.* (*s'éloigner*) move away; (*quitter son chemin*) move aside. **s'~ de,** stray from.

ecclésiastique /eklezjastik/ *a.* ecclesiastical. —*n.m.* clergyman.

écervelé, ~e /esɛrvəle/ *a.* scatter-brained. —*n.m., f.* scatter-brain.

échafaud /eʃafo/ *n.m.* scaffold.

échafaudage /eʃafodaʒ/ *n.m.* scaffolding; (*amas*) heap.

échalote /eʃalɔt/ *n.f.* shallot.

échancr|é /eʃɑ̃kre/ *a.* (*robe*) low-cut. **~ure** *n.f.* low neckline.

échang|e /eʃɑ̃ʒ/ *n.m.* exchange. **en ~e (de),** in exchange (for). **~er** *v.t.* exchange (**contre,** for).

échangeur /eʃɑ̃ʒœr/ *n.m.* (*auto.*) interchange.
échantillon /eʃɑ̃tijɔ̃/ *n.m.* sample. **~nage** /-jɔnaʒ/ *n.m.* range of samples.
échappatoire /eʃapatwar/ *n.f.* (clever) way out.
échappée /eʃape/ *n.f.* (*sport*) break-away; (*vue*) vista.
échappement /eʃapmɑ̃/ *n.m.* exhaust.
échapper /eʃape/ *v.i.* **~ à,** escape; (*en fuyant*) escape (from). **s'~** *v. pr.* escape. **~ des mains de** *ou* **à,** slip out of the hands of. **l'~ belle,** have a narrow *ou* lucky escape.
écharde /eʃard/ *n.f.* splinter.
écharpe /eʃarp/ *n.f.* scarf; (*de maire*) sash. **en ~,** (*bras*) in a sling.
écharper /eʃarpe/ *v.t.* cut to pieces.
échasse /eʃɑs/ *n.f.* stilt.
échauffer /eʃofe/ *v.t.* heat; (*fig.*) excite. **s'~** *v. pr.* warm up.
échauffourée /eʃofure/ *n.f.* (*mil.*) skirmish; (*bagarre*) scuffle.
échéance /eʃeɑ̃s/ *n.f.* due date (for payment); (*délai*) deadline; (*obligation*) (financial) commitment.
échéant (le cas) /(ləkɑz)eʃeɑ̃/ *adv.* if the occasion arises, possibly.
échec /eʃɛk/ *n.m.* failure. **~s,** (*jeu*) chess. **~ et mat,** checkmate. **en ~,** in check.
échelle /eʃɛl/ *n.f.* ladder; (*dimension*) scale.
échelon /eʃlɔ̃/ *n.m.* rung; (*de fonctionnaire*) grade; (*niveau*) level.
échelonner /eʃlɔne/ *v.t.* spread out, space out.
échevelé /eʃəvle/ *a.* dishevelled.
échine /eʃin/ *n.f.* backbone.
échiquier /eʃikje/ *n.m.* chessboard.
écho /eko/ *n.m.* echo. **~s, (***dans la presse*) gossip.
échoppe /eʃɔp/ *n.f.* stall.
échouer[1] /eʃwe/ *v.i.* fail.
échouer[2] /eʃwe/ *v.t.* (*bateau*) ground. —*v.i.*, **s'~** *v. pr.* run aground.
éclabouss|er /eklabuse/ *v.t.* splash. **~ure** *n.f.* splash.
éclair /eklɛr/ *n.m.* (flash of) lightning; (*fig.*) flash; (*gâteau*) éclair. —*a. invar.* lightning.
éclairage /eklɛraʒ/ *n.m.* lighting; (*point de vue*) light.
éclaircie /eklɛrsi/ *n.f.* sunny interval.
éclairc|ir /eklɛrsir/ *v.t.* make lighter; (*mystère*) clear up. **s'~ir** *v. pr.* (*ciel*) clear; (*mystère*) become clearer. **~issement** *n.m.* clarification.
éclairer /eklere/ *v.t.* light (up); (*personne*) give some light to; (*fig.*) enlighten; (*situation*) throw light on. —*v.i.* give light. **s'~** *v. pr.* become clearer. **s'~ à la bougie,** use candle-light.
éclaireu|r, ~se /eklɛrœr, -øz/ *n.m., f.* (boy) scout, (girl) guide. —*n.m.* (*mil.*) scout.
éclat /ekla/ *n.m.* fragment; (*de lumière*) brightness; (*de rire*) (out)burst; (*splendeur*) brilliance.
éclatant, ~e /eklatɑ̃, -t/ *a.* brilliant.
éclat|er /eklate/ *v.i.* burst; (*exploser*) go off; (*verre*) shatter; (*guerre*) break out; (*groupe*) split up. **~er de rire,** burst out laughing. **~ement** *n.m.* bursting; (*de bombe*) explosion; (*scission*) split.
éclipse /eklips/ *n.f.* eclipse.
éclipser /eklipse/ *v.t.* eclipse. **s'~** *v. pr.* (*fam.*) slip away.
éclopé /eklɔpe/ *a.* lame.
écl|ore /eklɔr/ *v.i.* (*œuf*) hatch; (*fleur*) open. **~osion** *n.f.* hatching; opening.
écluse /eklyz/ *n.f.* (*de canal*) lock.
écœurer /ekœre/ *v.t.* sicken.
école /ekɔl/ *n.f.* school. **~**

maternelle / primaire / secondaire, nursery / primary / secondary school. **~ normale,** teachers' training college.

écol|ier, ~ière /ekɔlje, -jɛr/ *n.m., f.* schoolboy, schoolgirl.

écolog|ie /ekɔlɔʒi/ *n.f.* ecology. **~ique** *a.* ecological.

éconduire /ekɔ̃dɥir/ *v.t.* dismiss.

économe /ekɔnɔm/ *a.* thrifty. —*n.m./f.* bursar.

économ|ie /ekɔnɔmi/ *n.f.* economy. **~ies,** (*argent*) savings. **une ~ie de,** (*gain*) a saving of. **~ie politique,** economics. **~ique** *a.* (*pol.*) economic; (*bon marché*) economical. **~iser** *v.t./i.* save. **~iste** *n.m./f.* economist.

écoper /ekɔpe/ *v.t.* bail out. **~ (de),** (*fam.*) get.

écorce /ekɔrs/ *n.f.* bark; (*de fruit*) peel.

écorch|er /ekɔrʃe/ *v.t.* graze; (*animal*) skin. **s'~er** *v. pr.* graze o.s. **~ure** *n.f.* graze.

écossais, ~e /ekɔsɛ, -z/ *a.* Scottish. —*n.m., f.* Scot.

Écosse /ekɔs/ *n.f.* Scotland.

écosser /ekɔse/ *v.t.* shell.

écot /eko/ *n.m.* share.

écouler[1] /ekule/ *v.t.* dispose of, sell.

écoul|er[2] **(s')** /(s)ekule/ *v. pr.* flow (out), run (off); (*temps*) pass. **~ement** *n.m.* flow.

écourter /ekurte/ *v.t.* shorten.

écoute /ekut/ *n.f.* listening. **à l'~ (de),** listening in (to). **aux ~s,** attentive.

écout|er /ekute/ *v.t.* listen to; (*radio*) listen (in) to. —*v.i.* listen. **~eur** *n.m.* earphones; (*de téléphone*) receiver.

écran /ekrɑ̃/ *n.m.* screen.

écrasant, ~e /ekrazɑ̃, -t/ *a.* overwhelming.

écraser /ekraze/ *v.t.* crush; (*piéton*) run over. **s'~** *v. pr.* crash **(contre,** into).

écrémer /ekreme/ *v.t.* skim.

écrevisse /ekrəvis/ *n.f.* crayfish.

écrier (s') /(s)ekrije/ *v. pr.* exclaim.

écrin /ekrɛ̃/ *n.m.* case.

écrire† /ekrir/ *v.t./i.* write; (*orthographier*) spell. **s'~** *v. pr.* (*mot*) be spelt.

écrit /ekri/ *n.m.* document; (*examen*) written paper. **par ~,** in writing.

écriteau (*pl.* **~x**) /ekrito/ *n.m.* notice.

écriture /ekrityr/ *n.f.* writing. **~s,** (*comm.*) accounts. **l'É~ (sainte),** the Scriptures.

écrivain /ekrivɛ̃/ *n.m.* writer.

écrou /ekru/ *n.m.* nut.

écrouer /ekrue/ *v.t.* imprison.

écrouler (s') /(s)ekrule/ *v. pr.* collapse.

écueil /ekœj/ *n.m.* reef; (*fig.*) danger.

écuelle /ekɥɛl/ *n.f.* bowl.

éculé /ekyle/ a. (*soulier*) worn at the heel; (*fig.*) well-worn.

écume /ekym/ *n.f.* foam; (*culin.*) scum.

écum|er /ekyme/ *v.t.* skim; (*piller*) plunder. —*v.i.* foam. **~oire** *n.f.* skimmer.

écureuil /ekyrœj/ *n.m.* squirrel.

écurie /ekyri/ *n.f.* stable.

écusson /ekysɔ̃/ *n.m.* badge.

écuy|er, ~ère /ekɥije, -jɛr/ *n.m., f.* (horse) rider.

édenté /edɑ̃te/ *a.* toothless.

édifice /edifis/ *n.m.* building.

édif|ier /edifje/ *v.t.* construct; (*porter à la vertu, éclairer*) edify. **~ication** *n.f.* construction; edification.

édit /edi/ *n.m.* edict.

édi|ter /edite/ *v.t.* publish; (*annoter*) edit. **~teur, ~trice** *n.m., f.* publisher; editor.

édition /edisjɔ̃/ *n.f.* edition; (*industrie*) publishing.

éditor|ial (*pl.* **~iaux**) /editɔrjal, -jo/ *n.m.* editorial.

édredon /edrədɔ̃/ *n.m.* eiderdown.
éducati|f, ~ve /edykatif, -v/ *a.* educational.
éducation /edykɑsjɔ̃/ *n.f.* education; (*dans la famille*) upbringing; (*manières*) manners.
éduquer /edyke/ *v.t.* educate; (*à la maison*) bring up.
effac|é /efase/ *a.* (*modeste*) unassuming. **~ement** *n.m.* unassuming manner; (*suppression*) erasure.
effacer /efase/ *v.t.* (*gommer*) rub out; (*par lavage*) wash out; (*souvenir etc.*) erase. **s'~** *v. pr.* fade; (*s'écarter*) step aside.
effar|er /efare/ *v.t.* alarm. **~ement** *n.m.* alarm.
effaroucher /efaruʃe/ *v.t.* scare away.
effecti|f¹, ~ve /efɛktif, -v/ *a.* effective. **~vement** *adv.* effectively; (*en effet*) indeed.
effectif² /efɛktif/ *n.m.* size, strength. **~s,** numbers.
effectuer /efɛktɥe/ *v.t.* carry out, make.
efféminé /efemine/ *a.* effeminate.
effervescen|t, ~te /efɛrvesɑ̃, -t/ *a.* (*agité*) excited. **~ce** *n.f.* excitement.
effet /efɛ/ *n.m.* effect; (*impression*) impression. **~s,** (*habits*) clothes, things. **en ~,** indeed. **faire de l'~,** have an effect, be effective.
effeuiller /efœje/ *v.t.* remove the leaves *ou* petals from.
efficac|e /efikas/ *a.* effective; (*personne*) efficient. **~ité** *n.f.* effectiveness; efficiency.
effigie /efiʒi/ *n.f.* effigy.
effilé /efile/ *a.* slender, tapering.
effilocher (s') /(s)efilɔʃe/ *v. pr.* fray.
efflanqué /eflɑ̃ke/ *a.* emaciated.
effleurer /eflœre/ *v.t.* touch lightly; (*sujet*) touch on; (*se présenter à*) occur to.
effondr|er (s') /(s)efɔ̃dre/ *v. pr.* collapse. **~ement** *n.m.* collapse.
efforcer (s') /(s)efɔrse/ *v. pr.* try (hard) (**de,** to).
effort /efɔr/ *n.m.* effort.
effraction /efraksjɔ̃/ *n.f.* **entrer par ~,** break in.
effranger (s') /(s)efrɑ̃ʒe/ *v. pr.* fray.
effray|er /efreje/ *v.t.* frighten; (*décourager*) put off. **s'~er** *v. pr.* be frightened. **~ant, ~ante** *a.* frightening; (*fig.*) frightful.
effréné /efrene/ *a.* wild.
effriter (s') /(s)efrite/ *v. pr.* crumble.
effroi /efrwa/ *n.m.* dread.
effronté /efrɔ̃te/ *a.* impudent.
effroyable /efrwajabl/ *a.* dreadful.
effusion /efyzjɔ̃/ *n.f.* **~ de sang,** bloodshed.
égailler (s') /(s)egaje/ *v. pr.* disperse.
ég|al, ~ale (*m. pl.* **~aux**) /egal, -o/ *a.* equal; (*surface, vitesse*) even. —*n.m., f.* equal. **ça m'est/lui est ~al,** it is all the same to me/him.
également /egalmɑ̃/ *adv.* equally; (*aussi*) as well.
égaler /egale/ *v.t.* equal.
égaliser /egalize/ *v.t./i.* (*sport*) equalize; (*niveler*) level out.
égalit|é /egalite/ *n.f.* equality; (*de surface, d'humeur*) evenness. **à ~é (de points),** equal. **~aire** *a.* egalitarian.
égard /egar/ *n.m.* regard. **~s,** consideration. **à cet ~,** in this respect. **à l'~ de,** with regard to; (*envers*) towards.
égar|er /egare/ *v.t.* mislay; (*tromper*) lead astray. **s'~er** *v. pr.* get lost; (*se tromper*) go astray. **~ement** *n.m.* loss; (*affolement*) confusion.
égayer /egeje/ *v.t.* (*personne*) cheer up; (*pièce*) brighten up.
égide /eʒid/ *n.f.* aegis.
églefin /egləfɛ̃/ *n.m.* haddock.

église /egliz/ *n.f.* church.
égoïs|te /egɔist/ *a.* selfish. —*n.m./f.* egoist. **~me** *n.m.* selfishness, egoism.
égorger /egɔrʒe/ *v.t.* slit the throat of.
égosiller (s') /(s)egozije/ *v. pr.* shout one's head off.
égout /egu/ *n.m.* sewer.
égoutt|er /egute/ *v.t./i.*, **s'~er** *v. pr.* (*vaisselle*) drain. **~oir** *n.m.* draining-board; (*panier*) dish drainer.
égratign|er /egratiɲe/ *v.t.* scratch. **~ure** *n.f.* scratch.
égrener /egrəne/ *v.t.* (*raisins*) pick off; (*notes*) sound one by one.
Égypte /eʒipt/ *n.f.* Egypt.
égyptien, ~ne /eʒipsjɛ̃, -jɛn/ *a.* & *n.m., f.* Egyptian.
eh /e/ *int.* hey. **~ bien,** well.
éhonté /eɔ̃te/ *a.* shameless.
éjecter /eʒɛkte/ *v.t.* eject.
élabor|er /elabɔre/ *v.t.* elaborate. **~ation** *n.f.* elaboration.
élaguer /elage/ *v.t.* prune.
élan[1] /elɑ̃/ *n.m.* (*sport*) run-up; (*vitesse*) momentum; (*fig.*) surge.
élan[2] /elɑ̃/ *n.m.* (*animal*) moose.
élancé /elɑ̃se/ *a.* slender.
élancer (s') /(s)elɑ̃se/ *v. pr.* leap forward, dash; (*se dresser*) soar.
élarg|ir /elarʒir/ *v.t.*, **s'~ir** *v. pr.* widen. **~issement** *n.m.* widening.
élasti|que /elastik/ *a.* elastic. —*n.m.* elastic band; (*tissu*) elastic. **~cité** *n.f.* elasticity.
élec|teur, ~trice /elɛktœr, -tris/ *n.m., f.* voter, elector.
élection /elɛksjɔ̃/ *n.f.* election.
élector|al (*m. pl.* **~aux**) /elɛktɔral, -o/ *a.* (*réunion etc.*) election; (*collège*) electoral.
électorat /elɛktɔra/ *n.m.* electorate, voters.
électricien /elɛktrisjɛ̃/ *n.m.* electrician.
électricité /elɛktrisite/ *n.f.* electricity.
électrifier /elɛktrifje/ *v.t.* electrify.
électrique /elɛktrik/ *a.* electric(al).
électrocuter /elɛktrɔkyte/ *v.t.* electrocute.
électron /elɛktrɔ̃/ *n.m.* electron.
électronique /elɛktrɔnik/ *a.* electronic. —*n.f.* electronics.
électrophone /elɛktrɔfɔn/ *n.m.* record-player.
élég|ant, ~ante /elegɑ̃, -t/ *a.* elegant. **~amment** *adv.* elegantly. **~ance** *n.f.* elegance.
élément /elemɑ̃/ *n.m.* element; (*meuble*) unit. **~aire** /-ter/ *a.* elementary.
éléphant /elefɑ̃/ *n.m.* elephant.
élevage /ɛlvaʒ/ *n.m.* (stock-) breeding.
élévation /elevɑsjɔ̃/ *n.f.* raising; (*hausse*) rise; (*plan*) elevation.
élève /elɛv/ *n.m./f.* pupil.
élevé /ɛlve/ *a.* high; (*noble*) elevated. **bien ~,** well-mannered.
élever /ɛlve/ *v.t.* raise; (*enfants*) bring up, raise; (*animal*) breed. **s'~** *v. pr.* rise; (*dans le ciel*) soar up. **s'~ à,** amount to.
éleveu|r, ~se /ɛlvœr, -øz/ *n.m., f.* (stock-)breeder.
éligible /eliʒibl/ *a.* eligible.
élimé /elime/ *a.* worn thin.
élimin|er /elimine/ *v.t.* eliminate. **~ation** *n.f.* elimination. **~atoire** *a.* eliminating; *n.f.* (*sport*) heat.
élire† /elir/ *v.t.* elect.
élision /elizjɔ̃/ *n.f.* (*gram.*) elision.
élite /elit/ *n.f.* élite.
elle /ɛl/ *pron.* she; (*complément*) her; (*chose*) it. **~-même** *pron.* herself; itself.
elles /ɛl/ *pron.* they; (*complément*) them. **~-mêmes** *pron.* themselves.
ellip|se /elips/ *n.f.* ellipse. **~tique** *a.* elliptical.

élocution /elɔkysjɔ̃/ *n.f.* diction.
élog|e /elɔʒ/ *n.m.* praise. **faire l'~e de,** praise. **~ieux, ~ieuse** *a.* laudatory.
éloigné /elwaɲe/ *a.* distant. **~ de,** far away from.
éloign|er /elwaɲe/ *v.t.* take away *ou* remove (**de,** from); (*personne aimée*) estrange (**de,** from); (*danger*) ward off; (*visite*) put off. **s'~er** *v. pr.* go *ou* move away (**de,** from); (*affectivement*) become estranged (**de,** from). **~ement** *n.m.* removal; (*distance*) distance; (*oubli*) estrangement.
éloquen|t, ~te /elɔkɑ̃, -t/ *a.* eloquent. **~ce** *n.f.* eloquence.
élu, ~e /ely/ *a.* elected. —*n.m., f.* (*pol.*) elected representative.
élucider /elyside/ *v.t.* elucidate.
éluder /elyde/ *v.t.* elude.
émacié /emasje/ *a.* emaciated.
ém|ail (*pl.* **~aux**) /emaj, -o/ *n.m.* enamel.
émaillé /emaje/ *a.* enamelled. **~ de,** studded with.
émancip|er /emɑ̃sipe/ *v.t.* emancipate. **s'~er** *v. pr.* become emancipated. **~ation** *n.f.* emancipation.
éman|er /emane/ *v.i.* emanate. **~ation** *n.f.* emanation.
émarger /emarʒe/ *v.t.* initial.
emball|er /ɑ̃bale/ *v.t.* pack, wrap; (*personne*: *fam.*) enthuse. **s'~er** *v. pr.* (*moteur*) race; (*cheval*) bolt; (*personne*) get carried away. **~age** *n.m.* package, wrapping.
embarcadère /ɑ̃barkadɛr/ *n.m.* landing-stage.
embarcation /ɑ̃barkɑsjɔ̃/ *n.f.* boat.
embardée /ɑ̃barde/ *n.f.* swerve.
embargo /ɑ̃bargo/ *n.m.* embargo.
embarqu|er /ɑ̃barke/ *v.t.* embark; (*charger*) load; (*emporter*: *fam.*) cart off. —*v.i.*, **s'~er** *v. pr.* board, embark. **s'~er dans,** embark upon. **~ement** *n.m.* embarkation; loading.
embarras /ɑ̃bara/ *n.m.* obstacle; (*gêne*) embarrassment; (*difficulté*) difficulty.
embarrasser /ɑ̃barase/ *v.t.* clutter (up); (*gêner dans les mouvements*) hinder; (*fig.*) embarrass. **s'~ de,** burden o.s. with.
embauch|e /ɑ̃boʃ/ *n.f.* hiring; (*emploi*) employment. **~er** *v.t.* hire, take on.
embaumer /ɑ̃bome/ *v.t./i.* (make) smell fragrant; (*cadavre*) embalm.
embellir /ɑ̃belir/ *v.t.* brighten up; (*récit*) embellish.
embêt|er /ɑ̃bete/ *v.t.* (*fam.*) annoy. **s'~er** *v. pr.* (*fam.*) get bored. **~ant, ~ante** *a.* (*fam.*) annoying. **~ement** /ɑ̃bɛtmɑ̃/ *n.m.* (*fam.*) annoyance.
emblée (d') /(d)ɑ̃ble/ *adv.* right away.
emblème /ɑ̃blɛm/ *n.m.* emblem.
emboîter /ɑ̃bwate/ *v.t.*, **s'~** *v. pr.* fit together. **(s')~ dans,** fit into. **~ le pas à qn.,** (*imiter*) follow suit.
embonpoint /ɑ̃bɔ̃pwɛ̃/ *n.m.* stoutness.
embouchure /ɑ̃buʃyr/ *n.f.* (*de fleuve*) mouth; (*mus.*) mouthpiece.
embourber (s') /(s)ɑ̃burbe/ *v. pr.* get bogged down.
embourgeoiser (s') /(s)ɑ̃burʒwaze/ *v. pr.* become middle-class.
embouteillage /ɑ̃butɛjaʒ/ *n.m.* traffic jam.
emboutir /ɑ̃butir/ *v.t.* (*heurter*) crash into.
embranchement /ɑ̃brɑ̃ʃmɑ̃/ *n.m.* (*de routes*) junction.
embraser /ɑ̃brɑze/ *v.t.* set on fire, fire. **s'~** *v. pr.* flare up.
embrass|er /ɑ̃brase/ *v.t.* kiss; (*adopter, contenir*) embrace. **s'~er** *v. pr.* kiss. **~ades** *n.f. pl.* kissing.
embrasure /ɑ̃brɑzyr/ *n.f.* opening.
embray|er /ɑ̃breje/ *v.i.* let in the

clutch. **~age** /ɑ̃brɛjaʒ/ *n.m.* clutch.

embrigader /ɑ̃brigade/ *v.t.* enrol.

embrocher /ɑ̃brɔʃe/ *v.t.* (*viande*) spit.

embrouiller /ɑ̃bruje/ *v.t.* mix up; (*fils*) tangle. **s'~** *v. pr.* get mixed up.

embroussaillé /ɑ̃brusɑje/ *a.* (*poils, chemin*) bushy.

embryon /ɑ̃brijɔ̃/ *n.m.* embryo. **~naire** /-jɔnɛr/ *a.* embryonic.

embûches /ɑ̃byʃ/ *n.f. pl.* traps.

embuer /ɑ̃bɥe/ *v.t.* mist up.

embuscade /ɑ̃byskad/ *n.f.* ambush.

embusquer (s') /(s)ɑ̃byske/ *v. pr.* lie in ambush.

éméché /emeʃe/ *a.* tipsy.

émeraude /ɛmrod/ *n.f.* emerald.

émerger /emɛrʒe/ *v.i.* emerge; (*fig.*) stand out.

émeri /ɛmri/ *n.m.* emery.

émerveill|er /emɛrveje/ *v.t.* amaze. **s'~er de,** marvel at, be amazed at. **~ement** /-vɛjmɑ̃/ *n.m.* amazement, wonder.

émett|re† /emɛtr/ *v.t.* give out; (*message*) transmit; (*timbre, billet*) issue; (*opinion*) express. **~eur** *n.m.* transmitter.

émeut|e /emøt/ *n.f.* riot. **~ier, ~ière** *n.m., f.* rioter.

émietter /emjete/ *v.t.*, **s'~** *v. pr.* crumble.

émigrant, ~e /emigrɑ̃, -t/ *n.m., f.* emigrant.

émigré, ~e /emigre/ *n.m., f.* exile.

émigr|er /emigre/ *v.i.* emigrate. **~ation** *n.f.* emigration.

émin|ent, ~ente /eminɑ̃, -t/ *a.* eminent. **~emment** /-amɑ̃/ *adv.* eminently. **~ence** *n.f.* eminence; (*colline*) hill.

émissaire /emisɛr/ *n.m.* emissary.

émission /emisjɔ̃/ *n.f.* emission; (*de message*) transmission; (*de timbre*) issue; (*programme*) broadcast.

emmagasiner /ɑ̃magazine/ *v.t.* store.

emmanchure /ɑ̃mɑ̃ʃyr/ *n.f.* armhole.

emmêler /ɑ̃mele/ *v.t.* tangle.

emménager /ɑ̃menaʒe/ *v.i.* move in. **~ dans,** move into.

emmener /ɑ̃mne/ *v.t.* take; (*comme prisonnier*) take away.

emmerder /ɑ̃mɛrde/ *v.t.* (*argot*) bother. **s'~** *v. pr.* (*argot*) get bored.

emmitoufler /ɑ̃mitufle/ *v.t.*, **s'~** *v. pr.* wrap up (warmly).

emmurer /ɑ̃myre/ *v.t.* trap, wall in.

émoi /emwa/ *n.m.* excitement.

émoluments /emɔlymɑ̃/ *n.m.pl.* remuneration.

émonder /emɔ̃de/ *v.t.* prune.

émoti|f, ~ve /emɔtif, -v/ *a.* emotional.

émotion /emosjɔ̃/ *n.f.* emotion; (*peur*) fright. **~nel, ~nelle** /-jɔnɛl/ *a.* emotional.

émousser /emuse/ *v.t.* blunt.

émouv|oir /emuvwar/ *v.t.* move. **s'~oir** *v. pr.* be moved. **~ant, ~ante** *a.* moving.

empailler /ɑ̃pɑje/ *v.t.* stuff.

empaler /ɑ̃pale/ *v.t.* impale.

empaqueter /ɑ̃pakte/ *v.t.* package.

emparer (s') /(s)ɑ̃pare/ *v. pr.* **s'~ de,** seize.

empâter (s') /(s)ɑ̃pɑte/ *v. pr.* fill out, grow fatter.

empêchement /ɑ̃pɛʃmɑ̃/ *n.m.* hitch, difficulty.

empêcher /ɑ̃peʃe/ *v.t.* prevent. **~ de faire,** prevent *ou* stop (from) doing. **il ne peut pas s'~ de penser,** he cannot help thinking.

empeigne /ɑ̃pɛɲ/ *n.f.* upper.

empereur /ɑ̃prœr/ *n.m.* emperor.

empeser /ɑ̃pəze/ *v.t.* starch.

empester /ɑ̃pɛste/ *v.t.* make stink, stink out; (*essence etc.*) stink of. —*v.i.* stink.

empêtrer (s') /(s)ɑ̃petre/ *v. pr.* become entangled.
emphase /ɑ̃fɑz/ *n.f.* pomposity.
empiéter /ɑ̃pjete/ *v.i.* **~ sur,** encroach upon.
empiffrer (s') /(s)ɑ̃pifre/ *v. pr.* (*fam.*) gorge o.s.
empiler /ɑ̃pile/ *v.t.*, **s'~** *v. pr.* pile (up).
empire /ɑ̃pir/ *n.m.* empire; (*fig.*) control.
empirer /ɑ̃pire/ *v.i.* worsen.
empirique /ɑ̃pirik/ *a.* empirical.
emplacement /ɑ̃plasmɑ̃/ *n.m.* site.
emplâtre /ɑ̃plɑtr/ *n.m.* (*méd*) plaster.
emplette /ɑ̃plɛt/ *n.f.* purchase. **~s,** shopping.
emplir /ɑ̃plir/ *v.t.*, **s'~** *v. pr.* fill.
emploi /ɑ̃plwa/ *n.m.* use; (*travail*) job. **~ du temps,** timetable. **l'~,** (*pol.*) employment.
employ|er /ɑ̃plwaje/ *v.t.* use; (*personne*) employ. **s'~er** *v. pr.* be used. **s'~er à,** devote o.s. to. **~é, ~ée** *n.m., f.* employee. **~eur, ~euse** *n.m., f.* employer.
empocher /ɑ̃pɔʃe/ *v.t.* pocket.
empoign|er /ɑ̃pwaɲe/ *v.t.* grab. **s'~er** *v. pr.* have a row. **~ade** *n.f.* row.
empoisonn|er /ɑ̃pwazɔne/ *v.t.* poison; (*empuantir*) stink out; (*embêter: fam.*) annoy. **~ement** *n.m.* poisoning.
emport|é /ɑ̃pɔrte/ *a.* quick-tempered. **~ement** *n.m.* anger.
emporter /ɑ̃pɔrte/ *v.t.* take (away); (*entraîner*) carry away; (*prix*) carry off; (*arracher*) tear off. **~ un chapeau**/*etc.*, (*vent*) blow off a hat/*etc.* **s'~** *v. pr.* lose one's temper. **l'~,** get the upper hand (**sur,** of).
empourpré /ɑ̃purpre/ *a.* crimson.
empreint, ~e /ɑ̃prɛ̃, -t/ *a.* **~ de,** marked with. —*n.f.* mark. **~e (digitale),** fingerprint. **~e de pas,** footprint.
empress|er (s') /(s)ɑ̃prese/ *v. pr.* **s'~er auprès de,** be attentive to. **s'~er de,** hasten to. **~é** *a.* eager, attentive. **~ement** /ɑ̃prɛsmɑ̃/ *n.m.* eagerness.
emprise /ɑ̃priz/ *n.f.* influence.
emprisonn|er /ɑ̃prizɔne/ *v.t.* imprison. **~ement** *n.m.* imprisonment.
emprunt /ɑ̃prœ̃/ *n.m.* loan. **faire un ~,** take out a loan.
emprunté /ɑ̃prœ̃te/ *a.* awkward.
emprunt|er /ɑ̃prœ̃te/ *v.t.* borrow (**à,** from); (*route*) take; (*fig.*) assume. **~eur, ~euse** *n.m., f.* borrower.
empuantir /ɑ̃pɥɑ̃tir/ *v.t.* make stink, stink out.
ému /emy/ *a.* moved; (*apeuré*) nervous; (*joyeux*) excited.
émulation /emylɑsjɔ̃/ *n.f.* emulation.
émule /emyl/ *n.m./f.* imitator.
émulsion /emylsjɔ̃/ *n.f.* emulsion.
en[1] /ɑ̃/ *prép.* in; (*avec direction*) to; (*manière, état*) in, on; (*moyen de transport*) by; (*composition*) made of. **~ cadeau/médecin/***etc.*, as a present/doctor/*etc.* **~ guerre,** at war. **~ faisant,** by *ou* on *ou* while doing.
en[2] /ɑ̃/ *pron.* of it, of them; (*moyen*) with it; (*cause*) from it; (*lieu*) from there. **~ avoir/vouloir/***etc.*, have/want/*etc.* some. **ne pas ~ avoir/vouloir/***etc.*, not have/want/*etc.* any. **où ~ êtes-vous?,** where are you up to?, how far have you got?
encadr|er /ɑ̃kɑdre/ *v.t.* frame; (*entourer d'un trait*) circle; (*entourer*) surround. **~ement** *n.m.* framing; (*de porte*) frame.
encaissé /ɑ̃kese/ *a.* steep-sided.
encaiss|er /ɑ̃kese/ *v.t.* (*argent*) collect; (*chèque*) cash; (*coups: fam.*) take. **~eur** /ɑ̃kɛsœr/ *n.m.* debt-collector.
en-cas /ɑ̃kɑ/ *n.m.* (stand-by) snack.

encastrer /ãkastre/ *v.t.* embed.
encaustiqu|e /ãkɔstik/ *n.f.* wax polish. **~er** *v.t.* wax.
enceinte[1] /ãsɛ̃t/ *a.f.* pregnant.
enceinte[2] /ãsɛ̃t/ *n.f.* wall; (*espace*) enclosure.
encens /ãsã/ *n.m.* incense.
encercler /ãsɛrkle/ *v.t.* surround.
enchaîn|er /ãʃene/ *v.t.* chain (up); (*coordonner*) link (up). —*v.i.* continue. **s'~er** *v. pr.* be linked (up). **~ement** /ãʃɛnmã/ *n.m.* (*suite*) chain; (*liaison*) link(ing).
enchant|er /ãʃãte/ *v.t.* delight; (*ensorceler*) enchant. **~é** *a.* (*ravi*) delighted. **~ement** *n.m.* delight; (*magie*) enchantment.
enchâsser /ãʃɑse/ *v.t.* set.
enchère /ãʃɛr/ *n.f.* bid. **mettre** *ou* **vendre aux ~s,** sell by auction.
enchevêtrer /ãʃvetre/ *v.t.* tangle. **s'~** *v. pr.* become tangled.
enclave /ãklav/ *n.f.* enclave.
enclencher /ãklãʃe/ *v.t.* engage.
enclin, ~e /ãklɛ̃, -in/ *a.* **~ à,** inclined to.
enclore /ãklɔr/ *v.t.* enclose.
enclos /ãklo/ *n.m.* enclosure.
enclume /ãklym/ *n.f.* anvil.
encoche /ãkɔʃ/ *n.f.* notch.
encoignure /ãkɔɲyr/ *n.f.* corner.
encoller /ãkɔle/ *v.t.* paste.
encolure /ãkɔlyr/ *n.f.* neck.
encombr|er /ãkɔ̃bre/ *v.t.* clutter (up); (*gêner*) hamper. **s'~er de,** burden o.s. with. **~ant, ~ante** *a.* cumbersome. **~ement** *n.m.* congestion; (*auto.*) traffic jam; (*volume*) bulk.
encontre de (à l') /(al)ãkɔ̃trədə/ *prép.* against.
encore /ãkɔr/ *adv.* (*toujours*) still; (*de nouveau*) again; (*de plus*) more; (*aussi*) also. **~ mieux/plus grand**/*etc.*, even better/larger/*etc.* **~ une heure/un café**/*etc.*, another hour/coffee/*etc.* **pas ~,** not yet. **si ~,** if only.
encourag|er /ãkuraʒe/ *v.t.* encourage. **~ement** *n.m.* encouragement.
encourir /ãkurir/ *v.t.* incur.
encrasser /ãkrase/ *v.t.* clog up (with dirt).
encr|e /ãkr/ *n.f.* ink. **~er** *v.t.* ink.
encrier /ãkrije/ *n.m.* ink-well.
encroûter (s') /(s)ãkrute/ *v. pr.* become doggedly set in one's ways. **s'~ dans,** sink into.
encylopéd|ie /ãsiklɔpedi/ *n.f.* encyclopaedia. **~ique** *a.* encyclopaedic.
endetter /ãdete/ *v.t.*, **s'~** *v. pr.* get into debt.
endeuiller /ãdœje/ *v.t.* plunge into mourning.
endiablé /ãdjable/ *a.* wild.
endiguer /ãdige/ *v.t.* dam; (*fig.*) check.
endimanché /ãdimãʃe/ *a.* in one's Sunday best.
endive /ãdiv/ *n.f.* chicory.
endoctrin|er /ãdɔktrine/ *v.t.* indoctrinate. **~ement** *n.m.* indoctrination.
endommager /ãdɔmaʒe/ *v.t.* damage.
endorm|ir /ãdɔrmir/ *v.t.* send to sleep; (*atténuer*) allay. **s'~ir** *v. pr.* fall asleep. **~i** *a.* asleep; (*apathique*) sleepy.
endosser /ãdɔse/ *v.t.* (*vêtement*) put on; (*assumer*) assume; (*comm.*) endorse.
endroit /ãdrwa/ *n.m.* place; (*de tissu*) right side. **à l'~,** the right way round, right side out.
end|uire /ãdɥir/ *v.t.* coat. **~uit** *n.m.* coating.
endurance /ãdyrãs/ *n.f.* endurance.
endurant, ~e /ãdyrã, -t/ *a.* tough.
endurcir /ãdyrsir/ *v.t.* harden. **s'~** *v. pr.* become hard(ened).
endurer /ãdyre/ *v.t.* endure.
énerg|ie /enɛrʒi/ *n.f.* energy. **~étique** *a.* energy. **~ique** *a.* energetic.

énerver /enɛrve/ *v.t.* irritate. **s'~** *v. pr.* get worked up.
enfance /ɑ̃fɑ̃s/ *n.f.* childhood; (*début*) infancy.
enfant /ɑ̃fɑ̃/ *n.m./f.* child. **~ en bas âge,** infant. **~illage** /-tijaʒ/ *n.m.* childishness. **~in, ~ine** /-tɛ̃, -tin/ *a.* childlike; (*puéril*) childish; (*jeu, langage*) children's.
enfanter /ɑ̃fɑ̃te/ *v.t./i.* give birth (to).
enfer /ɑ̃fɛr/ *n.m.* hell.
enfermer /ɑ̃fɛrme/ *v.t.* shut up. **s'~** *v. pr.* shut o.s. up.
enferrer (s') /(s)ɑ̃fere/ *v. pr.* become entangled.
enfiévré /ɑ̃fjevre/ *a.* feverish.
enfilade /ɑ̃filad/ *n.f.* string, row.
enfiler /ɑ̃file/ *v.t.* (*aiguille*) thread; (*anneaux*) string; (*vêtement*) slip on; (*rue*) take; (*insérer*) insert.
enfin /ɑ̃fɛ̃/ *adv.* at last, finally; (*en dernier lieu*) finally; (*somme toute*) after all; (*résignation, conclusion*) well.
enflammer /ɑ̃flame/ *v.t.* set fire to; (*méd.*) inflame. **s'~** *v. pr.* catch fire.
enfl|er /ɑ̃fle/ *v.t./i.*, **s'~er** *v. pr.* swell. **~é** *a.* swollen. **~ure** *n.f.* swelling.
enfoncer /ɑ̃fɔ̃se/ *v.t.* (*épingle etc.*) push *ou* drive in; (*chapeau*) push down; (*porte*) break down; (*mettre*) thrust, put. —*v.i.*, **s'~** *v. pr.* sink (**dans,** into).
enfouir /ɑ̃fwir/ *v.t.* bury.
enfourcher /ɑ̃furʃe/ *v.t.* mount.
enfourner /ɑ̃furne/ *v.t.* put in the oven.
enfreindre /ɑ̃frɛ̃dr/ *v.t.* infringe.
enfuir† (s') /(s)ɑ̃fɥir/ *v. pr.* run off.
enfumer /ɑ̃fyme/ *v.t.* fill with smoke.
engageant, ~e /ɑ̃gaʒɑ̃, -t/ *a.* attractive.
engag|er /ɑ̃gaʒe/ *v.t.* (*lier*) bind, commit; (*embaucher*) take on; (*commencer*) start; (*introduire*) insert; (*entraîner*) involve; (*encourager*) urge; (*investir*) invest. **s'~er** *v. pr.* (*promettre*) commit o.s.; (*commencer*) start; (*soldat*) enlist; (*concurrent*) enter. **s'~er à faire,** undertake to do. **s'~er dans,** (*voie*) enter. **~ement** *n.m.* (*promesse*) promise; (*pol., comm.*) commitment; (*début*) start; (*inscription: sport*) entry.
engelure /ɑ̃ʒlyr/ *n.f.* chilblain.
engendrer /ɑ̃ʒɑ̃dre/ *v.t.* beget; (*causer*) generate.
engin /ɑ̃ʒɛ̃/ *n.m.* machine; (*outil*) instrument; (*projectile*) missile. **~ explosif,** explosive device.
englober /ɑ̃glɔbe/ *v.t.* include.
engloutir /ɑ̃glutir/ *v.t.* swallow (up). **s'~** *v. pr.* (*navire*) be engulfed.
engorger /ɑ̃gɔrʒe/ *v.t.* block.
engou|er (s') /(s)ɑ̃gwe/ *v. pr.* **s'~er de,** become infatuated with. **~ement** /-umɑ̃/ *n.m.* infatuation.
engouffrer /ɑ̃gufre/ *v.t.* devour. **s'~ dans,** rush into (with force).
engourd|ir /ɑ̃gurdir/ *v.t.* numb. **s'~ir** *v. pr.* go numb. **~i** *a.* numb.
engrais /ɑ̃grɛ/ *n.m.* manure; (*chimique*) fertilizer.
engraisser /ɑ̃grese/ *v.t.* fatten. **s'~** *v. pr.* get fat.
engrenage /ɑ̃grənaʒ/ *n.m.* gears; (*fig.*) chain (of events).
engueuler /ɑ̃gœle/ *v.t.* (*argot*) curse, swear at, hurl abuse at.
enhardir (s') /(s)ɑ̃ardir/ *v. pr.* become bolder.
énième /ɛnjɛm/ *a.* (*fam.*) umpteenth.
énigm|e /enigm/ *n.f.* riddle, enigma. **~atique** *a.* enigmatic.
enivrer /ɑ̃nivre/ *v.t.* intoxicate. **s'~** *v. pr.* get drunk.
enjamb|er /ɑ̃ʒɑ̃be/ *v.t.* step over; (*pont*) span. **~ée** *n.f.* stride.
enjeu (*pl.* **~x**) /ɑ̃ʒø/ *n.m.* stake(s).
enjôler /ɑ̃ʒole/ *v.t.* wheedle.
enjoliver /ɑ̃ʒɔlive/ *v.t.* embellish.

enjoliveur /ãʒɔlivœr/ *n.m.* hub-cap.
enjoué /ãʒwe/ *a.* cheerful.
enlacer /ãlase/ *v.t.* entwine.
enlaidir /ãledir/ *v.t.* make ugly. —*v.i.* grow ugly.
enlèvement /ãlɛvmã/ *n.m.* removal; (*rapt*) kidnapping.
enlever /ãlve/ *v.t.* (*emporter*) take (away), remove (**à**, from); (*vêtement*) take off, remove; (*tache, organe*) take out, remove; (*kidnapper*) kidnap; (*gagner*) win.
enliser (s') /(s)ãlize/ *v. pr.* get bogged down.
enneig|é /ãneʒe/ *a.* snow-covered. **~ement** /ãnɛʒmã/ *n.m.* snow conditions.
ennemi /ɛnmi/ *n.m.* & *a.* enemy. **~ de,** (*fig.*) hostile to.
ennui /ãnɥi/ *n.m.* boredom; (*tracas*) trouble, worry.
ennuyer /ãnɥije/ *v.t.* bore; (*irriter*) annoy; (*préoccuper*) worry. **s'~** *v. pr.* get bored.
ennuyeu|x, ~se /ãnɥijø, -z/ *a.* boring; (*fâcheux*) annoying.
énoncé /enɔ̃se/ *n.m.* wording, text; (*gram.*) utterance.
énoncer /enɔ̃se/ *v.t.* express, state.
enorgueillir (s') /(s)ãnɔrgœjir/ *v. pr.* **s'~ de,** pride o.s. on.
énorm|e /enɔrm/ *a.* enormous. **~ément** *adv.* enormously. **~ément de,** an enormous amount of. **~ité** *n.f.* enormous size; (*atrocité*) enormity; (*bévue*) enormous blunder.
enquérir (s') /(s)ãkerir/ *v. pr.* **s'~ de,** enquire about.
enquêt|e /ãkɛt/ *n.f.* investigation; (*jurid.*) inquiry; (*sondage*) survey. **~er** /-ete/ *v.i.* **~er (sur),** investigate. **~eur, ~euse** *n.m., f.* investigator.
enraciné /ãrasine/ *a.* deep-rooted.
enrag|er /ãraʒe/ *v.i.* be furious. **faire ~er,** annoy. **~é** *a.* furious; (*chien*) mad; (*fig.*) fanatical. **~eant, ~eante** *a.* infuriating.
enrayer /ãreje/ *v.t.* check.
enregistr|er /ãrʒistre/ *v.t.* note, record; (*mus.*) record. **(faire) ~er,** (*bagages*) register, check in. **~ement** *n.m.* recording; (*des bagages*) registration.
enrhumer (s') /(s)ãryme/ *v. pr.* catch a cold.
enrich|ir /ãriʃir/ *v.t.* enrich. **s'~ir** *v. pr.* grow rich(er). **~issement** *n.m.* enrichment.
enrober /ãrɔbe/ *v.t.* coat (**de,** with).
enrôler /ãrole/ *v.t.*, **s'~** *v. pr.* enlist, enrol.
enrou|er (s') /(s)ãrwe/ *v. pr.* become hoarse. **~é** *a.* hoarse.
enrouler /ãrule/ *v.t.*, **s'~** *v. pr.* wind. **s'~ dans une couverture,** roll o.s. up in a blanket.
ensabler /ãsable/ *v.t.*, **s'~** *v. pr.* (*port*) silt up.
ensanglanté /ãsãglãte/ *a.* blood-stained.
enseignant, ~e /ãsɛɲã, -t/ *n.m., f.* teacher. —*a.* teaching.
enseigne /ãsɛɲ/ *n.f.* sign.
enseignement /ãsɛɲmã/ *n.m.* teaching; (*instruction*) education.
enseigner /ãseɲe/ *v.t./i.* teach. **~ qch. à qn.,** teach s.o. sth.
ensemble /ãsãbl/ *adv.* together. —*n.m.* unity; (*d'objets*) set; (*mus.*) ensemble. **dans l'~,** on the whole. **d'~,** (*idée etc.*) general. **l'~ de,** (*totalité*) all of, the whole of.
ensemencer /ãsmãse/ *v.t.* sow.
enserrer /ãsere/ *v.t.* grip (tightly).
ensevelir /ãsəvlir/ *v.t.* bury.
ensoleill|é /ãsɔleje/ *a.* sunny. **~ement** /ãsɔlɛjmã/ *n.m.* (period of) sunshine.
ensommeillé /ãsɔmeje/ *a.* sleepy.
ensorceler /ãsɔrsəle/ *v.t.* bewitch.
ensuite /ãsɥit/ *adv.* next, then; (*plus tard*) later.

ensuivre (s') /(s)ɑ̃sɥivr/ *v. pr.* follow.

entaill|e /ɑ̃taj/ *n.f.* notch; (*blessure*) gash. **~er** *v.t.* notch; gash.

entamer /ɑ̃tame/ *v.t.* start; (*inciser*) cut into; (*ébranler*) shake.

entass|er /ɑ̃tase/ *v.t.*, **s'~er** *v. pr.* pile up. **(s')~er dans,** cram (together) into. **~ement** *n.m.* (*tas*) pile.

entendement /ɑ̃tɑ̃dmɑ̃/ *n.m.* understanding.

entendre /ɑ̃tɑ̃dr/ *v.t.* hear; (*comprendre*) understand; (*vouloir*) intend, mean; (*vouloir dire*) mean. **s'~** *v. pr.* (*être d'accord*) agree. **~ dire que,** hear that. **~ parler de,** hear of. **s'~ (bien),** get on (**avec,** with). **(cela) s'entend,** of course.

entendu /ɑ̃tɑ̃dy/ *a.* (*convenu*) agreed; (*sourire, air*) knowing. **bien ~,** of course. **(c'est) ~!,** all right!

entente /ɑ̃tɑ̃t/ *n.f.* understanding. **à double ~,** with a double meaning.

entériner /ɑ̃terine/ *v.t.* ratify.

enterr|er /ɑ̃tere/ *v.t.* bury. **~ement** /ɑ̃tɛrmɑ̃/ *n.m.* burial, funeral.

entêtant, ~e /ɑ̃tɛtɑ̃, -t/ *a.* heady.

en-tête /ɑ̃tɛt/ *n.m.* heading. **à ~,** headed.

entêt|é /ɑ̃tete/ *a.* stubborn. **~ement** /ɑ̃tɛtmɑ̃/ *n.m.* stubbornness.

entêter (s') /(s)ɑ̃tete/ *v. pr.* persist (**à, dans,** in).

enthousias|me /ɑ̃tuzjasm/ *n.m.* enthusiasm. **~mer** *v.t.* enthuse. **s'~mer pour,** enthuse over. **~te** *a.* enthusiastic.

enticher (s') /(s)ɑ̃tiʃe/ *v. pr.* **s'~ de,** become infatuated with.

ent|ier, ~ière /ɑ̃tje, -jɛr/ *a.* whole; (*absolu*) absolute; (*entêté*) unyielding. *—n.m.* whole. **en ~ier,** entirely. **~ièrement** *adv.* entirely.

entité /ɑ̃tite/ *n.f.* entity.

entonner /ɑ̃tɔne/ *v.t.* start singing.

entonnoir /ɑ̃tɔnwar/ *n.m.* funnel; (*trou*) crater.

entorse /ɑ̃tɔrs/ *n.f.* sprain. **~ à,** (*loi*) infringement of.

entortiller /ɑ̃tɔrtije/ *v.t.* wrap (up); (*enrouler*) wind, wrap; (*duper*) deceive.

entourage /ɑ̃turaʒ/ *n.m.* circle of family and friends; (*bordure*) surround.

entourer /ɑ̃ture/ *v.t.* surround (**de,** with); (*réconforter*) rally round. **~ de,** (*écharpe etc.*) wrap round.

entracte /ɑ̃trakt/ *n.m.* interval.

entraide /ɑ̃trɛd/ *n.f.* mutual aid.

entraider (s') /(s)ɑ̃trede/ *v. pr.* help each other.

entrailles /ɑ̃traj/ *n.f. pl.* entrails.

entrain /ɑ̃trɛ̃/ *n.m.* zest, spirit.

entraînant, ~e /ɑ̃trɛnɑ̃, -t/ *a.* rousing.

entraînement /ɑ̃trɛnmɑ̃/ *n.m.* (*sport*) training.

entraîn|er /ɑ̃trene/ *v.t.* carry away *ou* along; (*emmener, influencer*) lead; (*impliquer*) entail; (*sport*) train; (*roue*) drive. **~eur** /ɑ̃trɛnœr/ *n.m.* trainer.

entrav|e /ɑ̃trav/ *n.f.* hindrance. **~er** *v.t.* hinder.

entre /ɑ̃tr(ə)/ *prép.* between; (*parmi*) among(st). **~ autres,** among other things. **l'un d' ~ nous/vous/eux,** one of us/you/them.

entrebâillé /ɑ̃trəbɑje/ *a.* ajar.

entrechoquer (s') /(s)ɑ̃trəʃɔke/ *v. pr.* knock against each other.

entrecôte /ɑ̃trəkot/ *n.f.* rib steak.

entrecouper /ɑ̃trəkupe/ *v.t.* **~ de,** intersperse with.

entrecroiser (s') /(s)ɑ̃trəkrwaze/ *v. pr.* (*routes*) intersect.

entrée /ɑ̃tre/ *n.f.* entrance; (*accès*) admission, entry; (*billet*) ticket; (*culin.*) first course; (*de données*:

techn.) input. **~ interdite,** no entry.
entrefaites (sur ces) /(syrsez)ɑ̃trəfɛt/ *adv.* at that moment.
entrejambes /ɑ̃trəʒɑ̃b/ *n.m.* crotch.
entrelacer /ɑ̃trəlase/ *v.t.*, **s'~** *v. pr.* intertwine.
entremêler /ɑ̃trəmele/ *v.t.*, **s'~** *v. pr.* (inter)mingle.
entremets /ɑ̃trəmɛ/ *n.m.* dessert.
entre|mettre (s') /(s)ɑ̃trəmɛtr/ *v. pr.* intervene. **~mise** *n.f.* intervention. **par l'~mise de,** through.
entreposer /ɑ̃trəpoze/ *v.t.* store.
entrepôt /ɑ̃trəpo/ *n.m.* warehouse.
entreprenant, ~e /ɑ̃trəprənɑ̃, -t/ *a.* enterprising.
entreprendre† /ɑ̃trəprɑ̃dr/ *v.t.* start on; (*personne*) buttonhole. **~ de faire,** undertake to do.
entrepreneur /ɑ̃trəprənœr/ *n.m.* **~ (de bâtiments)**, (building) contractor.
entreprise /ɑ̃trəpriz/ *n.f.* undertaking; (*société*) firm.
entrer /ɑ̃tre/ *v.i.* (*aux. être*) go in, enter; (*venir*) come in, enter. **~ dans,** go *ou* come into, enter; (*club*) join. **~ en colère,** become angry. **~ en collision,** collide (**avec,** with). **faire ~,** (*personne*) show in. **laisser ~,** let in.
entresol /ɑ̃trəsɔl/ *n.m.* mezzanine.
entre-temps /ɑ̃trətɑ̃/ *adv.* meanwhile.
entretenir† /ɑ̃trətnir/ *v.t.* maintain; (*faire durer*) keep alive. **~ qn. de,** converse with s.o. about. **s'~** *v. pr.* speak (**de,** about; **avec,** to).
entretien /ɑ̃trətjɛ̃/ *n.m.* maintenance; (*discussion*) talk; (*audience*) interview.
entrevoir /ɑ̃trəvwar/ *v.t.* make out; (*brièvement*) glimpse.
entrevue /ɑ̃trəvy/ *n.f.* interview.
entrouvrir /ɑ̃truvrir/ *v.t.* half-open.
énumér|er /enymere/ *v.t.* enumerate. **~ation** *n.f.* enumeration.
envah|ir /ɑ̃vair/ *v.t.* invade, overrun; (*douleur, peur*) overcome. **~isseur** *n.m.* invader.
enveloppe /ɑ̃vlɔp/ *n.f.* envelope; (*emballage*) covering; (*techn.*) casing.
envelopper /ɑ̃vlɔpe/ *v.t.* wrap (up); (*fig.*) envelop.
envenimer /ɑ̃vnime/ *v.t.* (*plaie*) make septic; (*fig.*) embitter. **s'~** *v. pr.* turn septic; become embittered.
envergure /ɑ̃vɛrgyr/ *n.f.* wingspan; (*importance*) scope; (*qualité*) calibre.
envers /ɑ̃vɛr/ *prép.* toward(s), to. —*n.m.* (*de tissu*) wrong side. **à l'~,** upside down; (*pantalon*) back to front; (*chaussette*) inside out.
envie /ɑ̃vi/ *n.f.* desire, wish; (*jalousie*) envy. **avoir ~ de,** want, feel like. **avoir ~ de faire,** want to do, feel like doing.
envier /ɑ̃vje/ *v.t.* envy.
envieu|x, ~se /ɑ̃vjø, -z/ *a.* & *n.m.*, *f.* envious (person).
environ /ɑ̃virɔ̃/ *adv.* (round) about. **~s** *n.m. pl.* surroundings. **aux ~s de,** round about.
environnement /ɑ̃virɔnmɑ̃/ *n.m.* environment.
environn|er /ɑ̃virɔne/ *v.t.* surround. **~ant, ~ante** *a.* surrounding.
envisager /ɑ̃vizaʒe/ *v.t.* consider. **~ de faire,** consider doing.
envoi /ɑ̃vwa/ *n.m.* dispatch; (*paquet*) consignment.
envol /ɑ̃vɔl/ *n.m.* flight; (*d'avion*) take-off.
envoler (s') /(s)ɑ̃vɔle/ *v. pr.* fly away; (*avion*) take off; (*papiers*) blow away.

envoûter /ɑ̃vute/ *v.t.* bewitch.

envoyé, ~e /ɑ̃vwaje/ *n.m., f.* envoy; (*de journal*) correspondent.

envoyer† /ɑ̃vwaje/ *v.t.* send; (*lancer*) throw; (*gifle, coup*) give.

enzyme /ɑ̃zim/ *n.m.* enzyme.

épagneul, ~e /epaɲœl/ *n.m., f.* spaniel.

épais, ~se /epɛ, -s/ *a.* thick; (*corps*) thickset. **~seur** /-sœr/ *n.f.* thickness.

épaissir /epesir/ *v.t./i.*, **s'~** *v. pr.* thicken.

épanch|er (s') /(s)epɑ̃ʃe/ *v. pr.* pour out one's feelings; (*liquide*) pour out. **~ement** *n.m.* outpouring.

épanoui /epanwi/ *a.* (*joyeux*) beaming, radiant.

épan|ouir (s') /(s)epanwir/ *v. pr.* (*fleur*) open out; (*visage*) beam; (*personne*) blossom. **~ouissement** *n.m.* (*éclat*) blossoming, full bloom.

épargne /eparɲ/ *n.f.* saving; (*somme*) savings.

épargn|er /eparɲe/ *v.t./i.* save; (*ne pas tuer*) spare. **~er qch. à qn.**, spare s.o. sth. **~ant, ~ante** *n.m., f.* saver.

éparpiller /eparpije/ *v.t.* scatter; (*efforts*) dissipate. **s'~** *v. pr.* scatter.

épars, ~e /epar, -s/ *a.* scattered.

épat|er /epate/ *v.t.* (*fam.*) amaze. **~ant, ~ante** *a.* (*fam.*) amazing.

épaule /epol/ *n.f.* shoulder.

épauler /epole/ *v.t.* (*arme*) raise; (*aider*) support.

épave /epav/ *n.f.* wreck.

épée /epe/ *n.f.* sword.

épeler /ɛple/ *v.t.* spell.

éperdu /epɛrdy/ *a.* wild, frantic. **~ment** *adv.* wildly, frantically.

éperon /eprɔ̃/ *n.m.* spur. **~ner** /-ɔne/ *v.t.* spur (on).

épervier /epɛrvje/ *n.m.* sparrowhawk.

éphémère /efemɛr/ *a.* ephemeral.

éphéméride /efemerid/ *n.f.* tear-off calendar.

épi /epi/ *n.m.* (*de blé*) ear. **~ de cheveux,** tuft of hair.

épic|e /epis/ *n.f.* spice. **~é** *a.* spicy. **~er** *v.t.* spice.

épic|ier, ~ière /episje, -jɛr/ *n.m., f.* grocer. **~erie** *n.f.* grocery shop; (*produits*) groceries.

épidémie /epidemi/ *n.f.* epidemic.

épiderme /epidɛrm/ *n.m.* skin.

épier /epje/ *v.t.* spy on; (*occasion*) watch out for.

épilep|sie /epilɛpsi/ *n.f.* epilepsy. **~tique** *a.* & *n.m./f.* epileptic.

épiler /epile/ *v.t.* remove unwanted hair from; (*sourcils*) pluck.

épilogue /epilɔg/ *n.m.* epilogue; (*fig.*) outcome.

épinard /epinar/ *n.m.* (*plante*) spinach. **~s,** (*nourriture*) spinach.

épin|e /epin/ *n.f.* thorn, prickle; (*d'animal*) prickle, spine. **~eux, ~euse** *a.* thorny.

épingl|e /epɛ̃gl/ *n.f.* pin. **~e de nourrice, ~e de sûreté,** safety-pin. **~er** *v.t.* pin; (*arrêter: fam.*) nab.

épique /epik/ *a.* epic.

épisod|e /epizɔd/ *n.m.* episode. **à ~es,** serialized. **~ique** *a.* occasional.

épitaphe /epitaf/ *n.f.* epitaph.

épithète /epitɛt/ *n.f.* epithet.

épître /epitr/ *n.f.* epistle.

éploré /eplɔre/ *a.* tearful.

épluch|er /eplyʃe/ *v.t.* peel; (*examiner: fig.*) scrutinize. **~age** *n.m.* peeling; (*fig.*) scrutiny. **~ure** *n.f.* piece of peel *ou* peeling. **~ures** *n.f. pl.* peelings.

épointer /epwɛ̃te/ *v.t.* blunt.

épong|e /epɔ̃ʒ/ *n.f.* sponge. **~er** *v.t.* (*liquide*) sponge up; (*surface*) sponge (down); (*front*) mop.

épopée /epɔpe/ *n.f.* epic.

époque /epɔk/ *n.f.* time, period. **à l'~,** at the time. **d'~,** period.

épouse /epuz/ *n.f.* wife.
épouser[1] /epuze/ *v.t.* marry.
épouser[2] /epuze/ *v.t.* (*forme, idée*) assume, embrace, adopt.
épousseter /epuste/ *v.t.* dust.
époustouflant, ~e /epustuflɑ̃, -t/ *a.* (*fam.*) staggering.
épouvantable /epuvɑ̃tabl/ *a.* appalling. **~ment** /-əmɑ̃/ *adv.* appallingly.
épouvantail /epuvɑ̃taj/ *n.m.* scarecrow.
épouvant|e /epuvɑ̃t/ *n.f.* terror. **~er** *v.t* terrify.
époux /epu/ *n.m.* husband. **les ~,** the married couple.
éprendre (s') /(s)eprɑ̃dr/ *v. pr.* **s'~ de,** fall in love with.
épreuve /eprœv/ *n.f.* test; (*sport*) event; (*malheur*) ordeal; (*photo.*) print; (*d'imprimerie*) proof. **mettre à l'~,** put to the test.
éprouvé /epruve/ *a.* (well-)proven.
éprouv|er /epruve/ *v.t.* test; (*ressentir*) experience; (*affliger*) distress. **~ant, ~ante** *a.* testing.
éprouvette /epruvɛt/ *n.f.* test-tube.
épuis|er /epɥize/ *v.t.* (*fatiguer, user*) exhaust. **s'~er** *v. pr.* become exhausted. **~é** *a.* exhausted; (*livre*) out of print. **~ement** *n.m.* exhaustion.
épuisette /epɥizɛt/ *n.f.* fishing-net.
épur|er /epyre/ *v.t.* purify; (*pol.*) purge. **~ation** *n.f.* purification; (*pol.*) purge.
équat|eur /ekwatœr/ *n.m.* equator. **~orial** (*m. pl.* **~oriaux**) *a.* equatorial.
équation /ekwɑsjɔ̃/ *n.f.* equation.
équerre /ekɛr/ *n.f.* (set) square. **d'~,** square.
équilibr|e /ekilibr/ *n.m.* balance. **être** *ou* **se tenir en ~e,** (*personne*) balance; (*objet*) be balanced. **~é** *a.* well-balanced. **~er** *v.t.* balance. **s'~er** *v. pr.* (*forces etc.*) counterbalance each other.
équilibriste /ekilibrist/ *n.m./f.* tightrope walker.
équinoxe /ekinɔks/ *n.m.* equinox.
équipage /ekipaʒ/ *n.m.* crew.
équipe /ekip/ *n.f.* team. **~ de nuit/jour,** night/day shift.
équipée /ekipe/ *n.f.* escapade.
équipement /ekipmɑ̃/ *n.m.* equipment. **~s,** (*installations*) amenities, facilities.
équiper /ekipe/ *v.t.* equip (**de,** with). **s'~** *v. pr.* equip o.s.
équip|ier, ~ière /ekipje, -jɛr/ *n.m., f.* team member.
équitable /ekitabl/ *a.* fair. **~ment** /-əmɑ̃/ *adv.* fairly.
équitation /ekitɑsjɔ̃/ *n.f.* (horse-) riding.
équité /ekite/ *n.f.* equity.
équivalen|t, ~te /ekivalɑ̃, -t/ *a.* equivalent. **~ce** *n.f.* equivalence.
équivaloir /ekivalwar/ *v.i.* **~ à,** be equivalent to.
équivoque /ekivɔk/ *a.* equivocal; (*louche*) questionable. —*n.f.* ambiguity.
érable /erabl/ *n.m.* maple.
érafl|er /erafle/ *v.t.* scratch. **~ure** *n.f.* scratch.
éraillé /erɑje/ *a.* (*voix*) raucous.
ère /ɛr/ *n.f.* era.
érection /erɛksjɔ̃/ *n.f.* erection.
éreinter /erɛ̃te/ *v.t.* exhaust; (*fig.*) criticize severely.
ergoter /ɛrgɔte/ *v.i.* quibble.
ériger /eriʒe/ *v.t.* erect. **(s')~ en,** set (o.s.) up as.
ermitage /ɛrmitaʒ/ *n.m.* retreat.
ermite /ɛrmit/ *n.m.* hermit.
éroder /erɔde/ *v.t.* erode.
érosion /erozjɔ̃/ *n.f.* erosion.
éroti|que /erɔtik/ *a.* erotic. **~sme** *n.m.* eroticism.
errer /ɛre/ *v.i.* wander.
erreur /ɛrœr/ *n.f.* mistake, error. **dans l'~,** mistaken. **par ~,** by mistake.

erroné /ɛrɔne/ *a.* erroneous.

érudit, ~e /erydi, -t/ *a.* scholarly. —*n.m., f.* scholar. **~ion** /-sjɔ̃/ *n.f.* scholarship.

éruption /erypsjɔ̃/ *n.f.* eruption; (*méd.*) rash.

es /ɛ/ *voir* **être**.

escabeau (*pl.* **~x**) /ɛskabo/ *n.m.* step-ladder; (*tabouret*) stool.

escadre /ɛskadr/ *n.f.* (*naut.*) squadron.

escadrille /ɛskadrij/ *n.f.* (*aviat.*) flight, squadron.

escadron /ɛskadrɔ̃/ *n.m.* (*mil.*) squadron.

escalad|e /ɛskalad/ *n.f.* climbing; (*pol., comm.*) escalation. **~er** *v.t.* climb.

escale /ɛskal/ *n.f.* (*d'avion*) stop-over; (*port*) port of call.

escalier /ɛskalje/ *n.m.* stairs. **~ mécanique** *ou* **roulant,** escalator.

escalope /ɛskalɔp/ *n.f.* escalope.

escamotable /ɛskamɔtabl/ *a.* (*techn.*) retractable.

escamoter /ɛskamɔte/ *v.t.* make vanish; (*éviter*) dodge.

escargot /ɛskargo/ *n.m.* snail.

escarmouche /ɛskarmuʃ/ *n.f.* skirmish.

escarpé /ɛskarpe/ *a.* steep.

escarpin /ɛskarpɛ̃/ *n.m.* pump.

esclaffer (s') /(s)ɛsklafe/ *v. pr.* guffaw, burst out laughing.

esclandre /ɛsklɑ̃dr/ *n.m.* scene.

esclav|e /ɛsklav/ *n.m./f.* slave. **~age** *n.m.* slavery.

escompte /ɛskɔ̃t/ *n.m.* discount.

escompter /ɛskɔ̃te/ *v.t.* expect; (*comm.*) discount.

escort|e /ɛskɔrt/ *n.f.* escort. **~er** *v.t.* escort. **~eur** *n.m.* escort (ship).

escouade /ɛskwad/ *n.f.* squad.

escrim|e /ɛskrim/ *n.f.* fencing. **~eur, ~euse** *n.m., f.* fencer.

escrimer (s') /(s)ɛskrime/ *v. pr.* struggle.

escroc /ɛskro/ *n.m.* swindler.

escroqu|er /ɛskrɔke/ *v.t.* swindle. **~er qch. à qn.,** swindle s.o. out of sth. **~erie** *n.f.* swindle.

espace /ɛspas/ *n.m.* space. **~s verts,** gardens, parks.

espacer /ɛspase/ *v.t.* space out. **s'~** *v. pr.* become less frequent.

espadrille /ɛspadrij/ *n.f.* canvas sandal.

Espagne /ɛspaɲ/ *n.f.* Spain.

espagnol, ~e /ɛspaɲɔl/ *a.* Spanish. —*n.m., f.* Spaniard. —*n.m.* (*lang.*) Spanish.

espèce /ɛspɛs/ *n.f.* kind, sort; (*race*) species. **~s,** (*argent*) cash. **~ d'idiot/de brute/***etc.***!,** you idiot/ brute/*etc.*!

espérance /ɛsperɑ̃s/ *n.f.* hope.

espérer /ɛspere/ *v.t.* hope for. **~ faire/que,** hope to do/that. —*v.i.* hope. **~ en,** have faith in.

espiègle /ɛspjɛgl/ *a.* mischievous.

espion, ~ne /ɛspjɔ̃, -jɔn/ *n.m., f.* spy.

espionn|er /ɛspjɔne/ *v.t./i.* spy (on). **~age** *n.m.* espionage, spying.

esplanade /ɛsplanad/ *n.f.* esplanade.

espoir /ɛspwar/ *n.m.* hope.

esprit /ɛspri/ *n.m.* spirit; (*intellect*) mind; (*humour*) wit. **perdre l'~,** lose one's mind. **reprendre ses ~s,** come to.

Esquimau, ~de (*m. pl.* **~x**) /ɛskimo, -d/ *n.m., f.* Eskimo.

esquinter /ɛskɛ̃te/ *v.t.* (*fam.*) ruin.

esquiss|e /ɛskis/ *n.f.* sketch; (*fig.*) suggestion. **~er** *v.t.* sketch; (*geste etc.*) make an attempt at.

esquiv|e /ɛskiv/ *n.f.* (*sport*) dodge. **~er** *v.t.* dodge. **s'~er** *v. pr.* slip away.

essai /esɛ/ *n.m.* testing; (*épreuve*) test, trial; (*tentative*) try; (*article*) essay. **à l'~,** on trial.

essaim /esɛ̃/ *n.m.* swarm. **~er** /eseme/ *v.i.* swarm; (*fig.*) spread.

essayage /esɛjaʒ/ *n.m.* (*de vêtement*) fitting.
essayer /eseje/ *v.t./i.* try; (*vêtement*) try (on); (*voiture etc.*) try (out). **~ de faire,** try to do.
essence[1] /esɑ̃s/ *n.f.* (*carburant*) petrol; (*Amer.*) gas.
essence[2] /esɑ̃s/ *n.f.* (*nature, extrait*) essence.
essentiel, ~le /esɑ̃sjɛl/ *a.* essential. —*n.m.* **l'~,** the main thing; (*quantité*) the main part. **~lement** *adv.* essentially.
essieu (*pl.* **~x**) /esjø/ *n.m.* axle.
essor /esɔr/ *n.m.* expansion.
essor|er /esɔre/ *v.t.* (*linge*) spin-dry; (*en tordant*) wring. **~euse** *n.f.* spin-drier.
essouffler /esufle/ *v.t.* make breathless. **s'~** *v. pr.* get out of breath.
ess|uyer[1] /esɥije/ *v.t.* wipe. **s'~uyer** *v. pr.* dry *ou* wipe o.s. **~uie-glace** *n.m. invar.* windscreen wiper; (*Amer.*) windshield wiper. **~uie-mains** *n.m. invar.* hand-towel.
essuyer[2] /esɥije/ *v.t.* (*subir*) suffer.
est[1] /ɛ/ *voir* **être.**
est[2] /ɛst/ *n.m.* east. —*a. invar.* east; (*partie*) eastern; (*direction*) easterly.
estampe /ɛstɑ̃p/ *n.f.* print.
estampille /ɛstɑ̃pij/ *n.f.* stamp.
esthète /ɛstɛt/ *n.m./f.* aesthete.
esthéticienne /ɛstetisjɛn/ *n.f.* beautician.
esthétique /ɛstetik/ *a.* aesthetic.
estimable /ɛstimabl/ *a.* worthy.
estime /ɛstim/ *n.f.* esteem.
estim|er /ɛstime/ *v.t.* (*objet*) value; (*calculer*) estimate; (*respecter*) esteem; (*considérer*) consider. **~ation** *n.f.* valuation; (*calcul*) estimation.
estiv|al (*m. pl.* **~aux**) /ɛstival, -o/ *a.* summer. **~ant, ~ante** *n.m., f.* summer visitor, holiday-maker.
estomac /ɛstɔma/ *n.m.* stomach.
estomper (s') /(s)ɛstɔ̃pe/ *v. pr.* become blurred.
estrade /ɛstrad/ *n.f.* platform.
estragon /ɛstragɔ̃/ *n.m.* tarragon.
estrop|ier /ɛstrɔpje/ *v.t.* cripple; (*fig.*) mangle. **~ié, ~iée** *n.m., f.* cripple.
estuaire /ɛstɥɛr/ *n.m.* estuary.
estudiantin, ~e /ɛstydjɑ̃tɛ̃, -in/ *a.* student.
esturgeon /ɛstyrʒɔ̃/ *n.m.* sturgeon.
et /e/ *conj.* and. **~ moi/lui/***etc.***?,** what about me/him/*etc.*?
étable /etabl/ *n.f.* cow-shed.
établi /etabli/ *n.m.* work-bench.
établir /etablir/ *v.t.* establish; (*liste, facture*) draw up; (*personne, camp, record*) set up. **s'~** *v. pr.* (*personne*) establish o.s. **s'~ épicier/***etc.*, set (o.s.) up as a grocer/*etc.*
établissement /etablismɑ̃/ *n.m.* (*bâtiment, institution*) establishment.
étage /etaʒ/ *n.m.* floor, storey; (*de fusée*) stage. **à l'~,** upstairs. **au premier ~,** on the first floor.
étager (s') /(s)etaʒe/ *v. pr.* rise at different levels.
étagère /etaʒɛr/ *n.f.* shelf; (*meuble*) shelving unit.
étai /etɛ/ *n.m.* prop, buttress.
étain /etɛ̃/ *n.m.* tin; (*alliage*) pewter.
étais, était /etɛ/ *voir* **être.**
étal (*pl.* **~s**) /etal/ *n.m.* stall.
étalag|e /etalaʒ/ *n.m.* display; (*vitrine*) shop-window. **~iste** *n.m./f.* window-dresser.
étaler /etale/ *v.t.* spread; (*journal*) spread (out); (*vacances*) stagger; (*exposer*) display. **s'~** *v. pr.* (*s'étendre*) stretch out; (*tomber: fam.*) fall flat.
étalon /etalɔ̃/ *n.m.* (*cheval*) stallion; (*modèle*) standard.
étanche /etɑ̃ʃ/ *a.* watertight; (*montre*) waterproof.

étancher /etɑ̃ʃe/ *v.t.* (*soif*) quench; (*sang*) stem.
étang /etɑ̃/ *n.m.* pond.
étant /etɑ̃/ *voir* **être.**
étape /etap/ *n.f.* stage; (*lieu d'arrêt*) stopover.
état /eta/ *n.m.* state; (*liste*) statement; (*métier*) profession; (*nation*) State. **en bon/mauvais ~,** in good/bad condition. **en ~ de,** in a position to. **en ~ de marche,** in working order. **~ civil,** civil status. **~ de choses,** situation. **~-major** (*pl.* **~s-majors**) *n.m.* (*officiers*) staff. **faire ~ de,** (*citer*) mention.
étatisé /etatize/ *a.* State-controlled.
États-Unis /etazyni/ *n.m. pl.* **~ (d'Amérique),** United States (of America).
étau (*pl.* **~x**) /eto/ *n.m.* vice.
étayer /eteje/ *v.t.* prop up.
été[1] /ete/ *voir* **être.**
été[2] /ete/ *n.m.* summer.
étein|dre† /etɛ̃dr/ *v.t.* put out, extinguish; (*lumière, radio, gaz*) turn off. **s'~dre** *v. pr.* (*feu*) go out; (*mourir*) die. **~t, ~te** /etɛ̃, -t/ *a.* (*feu*) out; (*volcan*) extinct.
étendard /etɑ̃dar/ *n.m.* standard.
étendre /etɑ̃dr/ *v.t.* spread; (*journal, nappe*) spread out; (*bras, jambes*) stretch (out); (*linge*) hang out; (*agrandir*) extend. **s'~** *v. pr.* (*s'allonger*) stretch out; (*se propager*) spread; (*plaine etc.*) stretch. **s'~ sur,** (*sujet*) dwell on.
étendu, ~e /etɑ̃dy/ *a.* extensive. —*n.f.* area; (*d'eau*) stretch; (*importance*) extent.
éternel, ~le /etɛrnɛl/ *a.* eternal. **~lement** *adv.* eternally.
éterniser (s') /(s)etɛrnize/ *v. pr.* (*durer*) drag on.
éternité /etɛrnite/ *n.f.* eternity.
étern|uer /etɛrnɥe/ *v.i.* sneeze. **~uement** /-ymɑ̃/ *n.m.* sneeze.
êtes /ɛt/ *voir* **être.**
éther /etɛr/ *n.m.* ether.
Éthiopie /etjɔpi/ *n.f.* Ethiopia.
éthique /etik/ *a.* ethical. —*n.f.* ethics.
ethn|ie /ɛtni/ *n.f.* ethnic group. **~ique** *a.* ethnic.
étinceler /etɛ̃sle/ *v.i.* sparkle.
étincelle /etɛ̃sɛl/ *n.f.* spark.
étioler (s') /(s)etjɔle/ *v. pr.* wilt.
étiqueter /etikte/ *v.t.* label.
étiquette /etikɛt/ *n.f.* label; (*protocole*) etiquette.
étirer /etire/ *v.t.*, **s'~** *v. pr.* stretch.
étoffe /etɔf/ *n.f.* fabric.
étoffer /etɔfe/ *v.t.*, **s'~** *v. pr.* fill out.
étoil|e /etwal/ *n.f.* star. **à la belle ~e,** in the open. **~e de mer,** starfish. **~é** *a.* starry.
étonn|er /etɔne/ *v.t.* amaze. **s'~er** *v. pr.* be amazed (**de,** at). **~ant, ~ante** *a.* amazing. **~ement** *n.m.* amazement.
étouff|er /etufe/ *v.t./i.* suffocate; (*sentiment, révolte*) stifle; (*feu*) smother; (*bruit*) muffle. **on ~e,** it is stifling. **s'~er** *v. pr.* suffocate; (*en mangeant*) choke. **~ant, ~ante** *a.* stifling.
étourd|i, ~ie /eturdi/ *a.* unthinking, scatter-brained. —*n.m., f.* scatter-brain. **~erie** *n.f.* thoughtlessness; (*acte*) thoughtless act.
étourd|ir /eturdir/ *v.t.* stun; (*griser*) make dizzy. **~issant, ~issante** *a.* stunning. **~issement** *n.m.* (*syncope*) dizzy spell.
étourneau (*pl.* **~x**) /eturno/ *n.m.* starling.
étrange /etrɑ̃ʒ/ *a.* strange. **~ment** *adv.* strangely. **~té** *n.f.* strangeness.
étrang|er, ~ère /etrɑ̃ʒe, -ɛr/ *a.* strange, unfamiliar; (*d'un autre pays*) foreign. —*n.m., f.* foreigner; (*inconnu*) stranger. **à l'~er,** abroad. **de l'~er,** from abroad.
étrangler /etrɑ̃gle/ *v.t.* strangle; (*fureur, col*) choke. **s'~** *v. pr.* choke.

être† /ɛtr/ *v.i.* be. —*v. aux.* (*avec aller, sortir, etc.*) have. **~ donné/fait**/*etc.*, (*passif*) be given/done/*etc.* —*n.m.* (*personne, créature*) being. **~ médecin/tailleur**/*etc.*, be a doctor/a tailor/*etc.* **~ à qn.,** be s.o.'s. **c'est à faire,** it needs to be *ou* should be done. **est-ce qu'il travaille?,** is he working?, does he work? **vous travaillez, n'est-ce pas?,** you are working, aren't you?, you work, don't you? **il est deux heures**/*etc.*, it is two o'clock/*etc.* **nous sommes le six mai,** it is the sixth of May.

étrein|dre /etrɛ̃dr/ *v.t.* grasp; (*ami*) embrace. **~te** /-ɛ̃t/ *n.f.* grasp; embrace.

étrenner /etrene/ *v.t.* use for the first time.

étrennes /etrɛn/ *n.f. pl.* (*cadeau*) New Year's gift.

étrier /etrije/ *n.m.* stirrup.

étriqué /etrike/ *a.* tight; (*fig.*) narrow.

étroit, ~e /etrwa, -t/ *a.* narrow; (*vêtement*) tight; (*liens, surveillance*) close. **à l'~,** cramped. **~ement** /-tmɑ̃/ *adv.* closely. **~esse** /-tɛs/ *n.f.* narrowness.

étude /etyd/ *n.f.* study; (*bureau*) office. **(salle d')~,** (*scol.*) prep room; (*scol., Amer.*) study hall. **à l'~,** under consideration. **faire des ~s (de),** study.

étudiant, ~e /etydjɑ̃, -t/ *n.m., f.* student.

étudier /etydje/ *v.t./i.* study.

étui /etɥi/ *n.m.* (*à lunettes etc.*) case; (*de revolver*) holster.

étymologie /etimɔlɔʒi/ *n.f.* etymology.

eu, eue /y/ *voir* **avoir.**

eucalyptus /økaliptys/ *n.m.* eucalyptus.

euphémisme /øfemism/ *n.m.* euphemism.

euphorie /øfɔri/ *n.f.* euphoria.

Europe /ørɔp/ *n.f.* Europe.

européen, ~ne /ørɔpeɛ̃, -eɛn/ *a.* & *n.m., f.* European.

euthanasie /øtanazi/ *n.f.* euthanasia.

eux /ø/ *pron.* they; (*complément*) them. **~-mêmes** *pron.* themselves.

évac|uer /evakɥe/ *v.t.* evacuate. **~uation** *n.f.* evacuation.

évad|er (s') /(s)evade/ *v. pr.* escape. **~é, ~ée** *a.* escaped; *n.m., f.* escaped prisoner.

éval|uer /evalɥe/ *v.t.* assess. **~uation** *n.f.* assessment.

évang|ile /evɑ̃ʒil/ *n.m.* gospel. **l'Évangile,** the Gospel. **~élique** *a.* evangelical.

évan|ouir (s') /(s)evanwir/ *v. pr.* faint; (*disparaître*) vanish. **~ouissement** *n.m.* (*syncope*) fainting fit.

évapor|er /evapɔre/ *v.t.,* **s'~er** *v. pr.* evaporate. **~ation** *n.f.* evaporation.

évasi|f, ~ve /evazif, -v/ *a.* evasive.

évasion /evazjɔ̃/ *n.f.* escape; (*par le rêve etc.*) escapism.

évêché /eveʃe/ *n.m.* see, bishopric.

éveil /evɛj/ *n.m.* awakening. **donner l'~ à,** arouse the suspicions of. **en ~,** alert.

éveill|er /eveje/ *v.t.* awake(n); (*susciter*) arouse. **s'~er** *v. pr.* awake(n); be aroused. **~é** *a.* awake; (*intelligent*) alert.

événement /evɛnmɑ̃/ *n.m.* event.

éventail /evɑ̃taj/ *n.m.* fan; (*gamme*) range.

éventé /evɑ̃te/ *a.* (*gâté*) stale.

éventrer /evɑ̃tre/ *v.t.* (*sac etc.*) rip open.

éventualité /evɑ̃tɥalite/ *n.f.* possibility. **dans cette ~,** in that event.

éventuel, ~le /evɑ̃tɥɛl/ *a.* possible. **~lement** *adv.* possibly.

évêque /evɛk/ *n.m.* bishop.

évertuer (s') /(s)evɛrtɥe/ *v. pr.* **s'~ à,** struggle hard to.

éviction /eviksjɔ̃/ *n.f.* eviction.
évidemment /evidamɑ̃/ *adv.* obviously; (*bien sûr*) of course.
évidence /evidɑ̃s/ *n.f.* obviousness; (*fait*) obvious fact. **être en ~,** be conspicuous. **mettre en ~,** (*fait*) highlight.
évident, ~e /evidɑ̃, -t/ *a.* obvious, evident.
évider /evide/ *v.t.* hollow out.
évier /evje/ *n.m.* sink.
évincer /evɛ̃se/ *v.t.* oust.
éviter /evite/ *v.t.* avoid (**de faire,** doing). **~ à qn.,** (*dérangement etc.*) spare s.o.
évoca|teur, ~trice /evɔkatœr, -tris/ *a.* evocative.
évocation /evɔkɑsjɔ̃/ *n.f.* evocation.
évolué /evɔlɥe/ *a.* highly developed.
évol|uer /evɔlɥe/ *v.i.* develop; (*se déplacer*) manœuvre; (*Amer.*) maneuver. **~ution** *n.f.* development; (*d'une espèce*) evolution; (*déplacement*) movement.
évoquer /evɔke/ *v.t.* call to mind, evoke.
ex- /ɛks/ *préf.* ex-.
exacerber /ɛgzasɛrbe/ *v.t.* exacerbate.
exact, ~e /ɛgza(kt), -akt/ *a.* exact, accurate; (*correct*) correct; (*personne*) punctual. **~ement** /-ktəmɑ̃/ *adv.* exactly. **~itude** /-ktityd/ *n.f.* exactness; punctuality.
ex aequo /ɛgzeko/ *adv.* (*classer*) equal. **être ~,** be equally placed.
exagéré /ɛgzaʒere/ *a.* excessive.
exagér|er /ɛgzaʒere/ *v.t./i.* exaggerate; (*abuser*) go too far. **~ation** *n.f.* exaggeration.
exaltation /ɛgzaltɑsjɔ̃/ *n.f.* elation.
exalté, ~e /ɛgzalte/ *n.m., f.* fanatic.
exalter /ɛgzalte/ *v.t.* excite; (*glorifier*) exalt.
examen /ɛgzamɛ̃/ *n.m.* examination; (*scol.*) exam(ination).
examin|er /ɛgzamine/ *v.t.* examine. **~ateur, ~atrice** *n.m., f.* examiner.
exaspér|er /ɛgzaspere/ *v.t.* exasperate. **~ation** *n.f.* exasperation.
exaucer /ɛgzose/ *v.t.* grant; (*personne*) grant the wish(es) of.
excavation /ɛkskavɑsjɔ̃/ *n.f.* excavation.
excédent /ɛksedɑ̃/ *n.m.* surplus. **~ de bagages,** excess luggage. **~aire** /-tɛr/ *a.* excess, surplus.
excéder[1] /ɛksede/ *v.t.* (*dépasser*) exceed.
excéder[2] /ɛksede/ *v.t.* (*agacer*) irritate.
excellen|t, ~te /ɛksɛlɑ̃, -t/ *a.* excellent. **~ce** *n.f.* excellence.
exceller /ɛksele/ *v.i.* excel (**dans,** in).
excentri|que /ɛksɑ̃trik/ *a.* & *n.m./f.* eccentric. **~cité** *n.f.* eccentricity.
excepté /ɛksɛpte/ *a.* & *prép.* except.
excepter /ɛksɛpte/ *v.t.* except.
exception /ɛksɛpsjɔ̃/ *n.f.* exception. **à l'~ de,** except for. **d'~,** exceptional. **faire ~,** be an exception. **~nel, ~nelle** /-jɔnɛl/ *a.* exceptional. **~nellement** /-jɔnɛlmɑ̃/ *adv.* exceptionally.
excès /ɛksɛ/ *n.m.* excess. **~ de vitesse,** speeding.
excessi|f, ~ve /ɛksesif, -v/ *a.* excessive. **~vement** *adv.* excessively.
excitant /ɛksitɑ̃/ *n.m.* stimulant.
excit|er /ɛksite/ *v.t.* excite; (*encourager*) exhort (**à,** to); (*irriter: fam.*) annoy. **~ation** *n.f.* excitement.
exclam|er (s') /(s)ɛksklame/ *v. pr.* exclaim. **~ation** *n.f.* exclamation.
exclu|re† /ɛksklyr/ *v.t.* exclude; (*expulser*) expel; (*empêcher*) preclude. **~sion** *n.f.* exclusion.
exclusi|f, ~ve /ɛksklyzif, -v/ *a.* exclusive. **~vement** *adv.*

exclusively. **~vité** *n.f.* (*comm.*) exclusive rights. **en ~vité à,** (*film*) (showing) exclusively at.
excommunier /ɛkskɔmynje/ *v.t.* excommunicate.
excrément(s) /ɛkskremɑ̃/ *n.m.* (*pl.*). excrement.
excroissance /ɛkskrwasɑ̃s/ *n.f.* (out)growth, excrescence.
excursion /ɛkskyrsjɔ̃/ *n.f.* excursion; (*à pied*) hike.
excuse /ɛkskyz/ *n.f.* excuse. **~s,** apology. **faire des ~s,** apologize.
excuser /ɛkskyze/ *v.t.* excuse. **s'~** *v. pr.* apologize (**de,** for). **je m'excuse,** (*fam.*) excuse me.
exécrable /ɛgzekrabl/ *a.* abominable.
exécrer /ɛgzekre/ *v.t.* loathe.
exécut|er /ɛgzekyte/ *v.t.* carry out, execute; (*mus.*) perform; (*tuer*) execute. **~ion** /-sjɔ̃/ *n.f.* execution; (*mus.*) performance.
exécuti|f, ~ve /ɛgzekytif, -v/ *a.* & *n.m.* (*pol.*) executive.
exemplaire /ɛgzɑ̃plɛr/ *a.* exemplary. —*n.m.* copy.
exemple /ɛgzɑ̃pl/ *n.m.* example. **par ~,** for example.
exempt, ~e /ɛgzɑ̃, -t/ *a.* **~ de,** exempt from.
exempt|er /ɛgzɑ̃te/ *v.t.* exempt (**de,** from). **~ion** /-psjɔ̃/ *n.f.* exemption.
exercer /ɛgzɛrse/ *v.t.* exercise; (*influence, contrôle*) exert; (*métier*) work at; (*former*) train, exercise. **s'~ (à),** practise.
exercice /ɛgzɛrsis/ *n.m.* exercise; (*mil.*) drill; (*de métier*) practice. **en ~,** in office; (*médecin*) in practice.
exhaler /ɛgzale/ *v.t.* emit.
exhausti|f, ~ve /ɛgzostif, -v/ *a.* exhaustive.
exhiber /ɛgzibe/ *v.t.* exhibit.
exhibitionniste /ɛgzibisjɔnist/ *n.m./f.* exhibitionist.
exhorter /ɛgzɔrte/ *v.t.* exhort.
exigence /ɛgziʒɑ̃s/ *n.f.* demand.
exig|er /ɛgziʒe/ *v.t.* demand. **~eant, ~eante** *a.* demanding.
exigu, ~ë /ɛgzigy/ *a.* tiny.
exil /ɛgzil/ *n.m.* exile. **~é, ~ée** *n.m., f.* exile. **~er** *v.t.* exile. **s'~er** *v. pr.* go into exile.
existence /ɛgzistɑ̃s/ *n.f.* existence.
exist|er /ɛgziste/ *v.i.* exist. **~ant, ~ante** *a.* existing.
exode /ɛgzɔd/ *n.m.* exodus.
exonér|er /ɛgzɔnere/ *v.t.* exempt (**de,** from). **~ation** *n.f.* exemption.
exorbitant, ~e /ɛgzɔrbitɑ̃, -t/ *a.* exorbitant.
exorciser /ɛgzɔrsize/ *v.t.* exorcize.
exotique /ɛgzɔtik/ *a.* exotic.
expansi|f, ~ve /ɛkspɑ̃sif, -v/ *a.* expansive.
expansion /ɛkspɑ̃sjɔ̃/ *n.f.* expansion.
expatr|ier (s') /(s)ɛkspatrije/ *v. pr.* leave one's country. **~ié, ~iée** *n.m., f.* expatriate.
expectative /ɛkspɛktativ/ *n.f.* **dans l'~,** still waiting.
expédient, ~e /ɛkspedjɑ̃, -t/ *a.* & *n.m.* expedient.
expéd|ier /ɛkspedje/ *v.t.* send, dispatch; (*tâche*) dispatch. **~iteur, ~itrice** *n.m., f.* sender. **~ition** *n.f.* dispatch; (*voyage*) expedition.
expéditi|f, ~ve /ɛkspeditif, -v/ *a.* quick.
expérience /ɛksperjɑ̃s/ *n.f.* experience; (*scientifique*) experiment.
expérimenté /ɛksperimɑ̃te/ *a.* experienced.
expériment|er /ɛksperimɑ̃te/ *v.t.* test, experiment with. **~al** (*m. pl.* **~aux**) *a.* experimental. **~ation** *n.f.* experimentation.
expert, ~e /ɛkspɛr, -t/ *a.* expert. —*n.m.* expert; (*d'assurances*) valuer; (*Amer.*) appraiser. **~-comptable** (*pl.* **~s-comptables**) *n.m.* accountant.

expertis|e /ɛkspɛrtiz/ *n.f.* expert appraisal. **~er** *v.t.* appraise.
expier /ɛkspje/ *v.t.* atone for.
expir|er /ɛkspire/ *v.i.* breathe out; (*finir, mourir*) expire. **~ation** *n.f.* expiry.
explicati|f, ~ve /ɛksplikatif, -v/ *a.* explanatory.
explication /ɛksplikɑsjɔ̃/ *n.f.* explanation; (*fig.*) discussion; (*scol.*) commentary.
explicite /ɛksplisit/ *a.* explicit.
expliquer /ɛksplike/ *v.t.* explain. **s'~** *v. pr.* explain o.s.; (*discuter*) discuss things; (*être compréhensible*) be understandable.
exploit /ɛksplwa/ *n.m.* exploit.
exploitant /ɛksplwatɑ̃/ *n.m.* farmer.
exploit|er /ɛksplwate/ *v.t.* (*personne*) exploit; (*ferme*) run; (*champs*) work. **~ation** *n.f.* exploitation; running; working; (*affaire*) concern. **~eur, ~euse** *n.m., f.* exploiter.
explor|er /ɛksplɔre/ *v.t.* explore. **~ateur, ~atrice** *n.m., f.* explorer. **~ation** *n.f.* exploration.
explos|er /ɛksploze/ *v.i.* explode. **faire ~er,** explode; (*bâtiment*) blow up. **~ion** *n.f.* explosion.
explosi|f, ~ve /ɛksplozif, -v/ *a.* & *n.m.* explosive.
export|er /ɛkspɔrte/ *v.t.* export. **~ateur, ~atrice** *n.m., f.* exporter; *a.* exporting. **~ation** *n.f.* export.
exposant, ~e /ɛkspozɑ̃, -t/ *n.m., f.* exhibitor.
exposé /ɛkspoze/ *n.m.* talk; (*d'une action*) account.
expos|er /ɛkspoze/ *v.t.* display, show; (*expliquer*) explain; (*soumettre, mettre en danger*) expose (**à,** to); (*vie*) endanger. **~é au nord**/*etc.*, facing north/*etc.* **s'~er à,** expose o.s. to.
exposition /ɛkspozisjɔ̃/ *n.f.* display; (*salon*) exhibition. **~ à,** exposure to.
exprès¹ /ɛksprɛ/ *adv.* specially; (*délibérément*) on purpose.
expr|ès², ~esse /ɛksprɛs/ *a.* express. **~essément** *adv.* expressly.
express /ɛksprɛs/ *a.* & *n.m. invar.* **(café) ~,** espresso. **(train) ~,** fast train.
expressi|f, ~ve /ɛkspresif, -v/ *a.* expressive.
expression /ɛksprɛsjɔ̃/ *n.f.* expression.
exprimer /ɛksprime/ *v.t.* express. **s'~** *v. pr.* express o.s.
expuls|er /ɛkspylse/ *v.t.* expel; (*locataire*) evict; (*joueur*) send off. **~ion** *n.f.* expulsion; eviction.
expurger /ɛkspyrʒe/ *v.t.* expurgate.
exquis, ~e /ɛkski, -z/ *a.* exquisite.
extase /ɛkstɑz/ *n.f.* ecstasy.
extasier (s') /(s)ɛkstɑzje/ *v. pr.* **s'~ sur,** be ecstatic about.
extensible /ɛksɑ̃sibl/ *a.* expandable, extendible.
extensi|f, ~ve /ɛkstɑ̃sif, -v/ *a.* extensive.
extension /ɛkstɑ̃sjɔ̃/ *n.f.* extension; (*expansion*) expansion.
exténuer /ɛkstenɥe/ *v.t.* exhaust.
extérieur /ɛksterjœr/ *a.* outside; (*signe, gaieté*) outward; (*politique*) foreign. —*n.m.* outside, exterior; (*de personne*) exterior. **à l'~ (de),** outside. **~ement** *adv.* outwardly.
extérioriser /ɛksterjɔrize/ *v.t.* show.
extermin|er /ɛkstɛrmine/ *v.t.* exterminate. **~ation** *n.f.* extermination.
externe /ɛkstɛrn/ *a.* external. —*n.m./f.* (*scol.*) day pupil.
extincteur /ɛkstɛ̃ktœr/ *n.m.* fire extinguisher.
extinction /ɛkstɛ̃ksjɔ̃/ *n.f.* extinction. **~ de voix,** loss of voice.
extirper /ɛkstirpe/ *v.t.* eradicate.

extor|quer /ɛkstɔrke/ *v.t.* extort. **~sion** *n.f.* extortion.
extra /ɛkstra/ *a. invar.* first-rate. —*n.m. invar.* (*repas*) (special) treat.
extra- /ɛkstra/ *préf.* extra-.
extrad|er /ɛkstrade/ *v.t.* extradite. **~ition** *n.f.* extradition.
extr|aire† /ɛkstrɛr/ *v.t.* extract. **~action** *n.f.* extraction.
extrait /ɛkstrɛ/ *n.m.* extract.
extraordinaire /ɛkstraɔrdinɛr/ *a.* extraordinary.
extravagan|t, ~te /ɛkstravagɑ̃, -t/ *a.* extravagant. **~ce** *n.f.* extravagance.
extraverti, ~e /ɛkstravɛrti/ *n.m., f.* extrovert.
extrême /ɛkstrɛm/ *a.* & *n.m.* extreme. **E~-Orient** *n.m.* Far East. **~ment** *adv.* extremely.
extrémiste /ɛkstremist/ *n.m., f.* extremist.
extrémité /ɛkstremite/ *n.f.* extremity, end; (*misère*) dire straits. **~s,** (*excès*) extremes.
exubéran|t, ~te /ɛgzyberɑ̃, -t/ *a.* exuberant. **~ce** *n.f.* exuberance.
exulter /ɛgzylte/ *v.i.* exult.

F

F *abrév.* (*franc, francs*) franc, francs.
fable /fɑbl/ *n.f.* fable.
fabrique /fabrik/ *n.f.* factory.
fabri|quer /fabrike/ *v.t.* make; (*industriellement*) manufacture; (*fig.*) make up. **~cant, ~cante** *n.m., f.* manufacturer. **~cation** *n.f.* making; manufacture.
fabuleu|x, ~se /fabylø, -z/ *a.* fabulous.
façade /fasad/ *n.f.* front; (*fig.*) façade.
face /fas/ *n.f.* face; (*d'un objet*) side. **en ~ (de), d'en ~,** opposite. **en ~ de,** (*fig.*) faced with. **~ à,** facing; (*fig.*) faced with. **faire ~ à,** face.
facétie /fasesi/ *n.f.* joke.
facette /fasɛt/ *n.f.* facet.
fâch|er /fɑʃe/ *v.t.* anger. **se ~er** *v. pr.* get angry; (*se brouiller*) fall out. **~é** *a.* angry; (*désolé*) sorry.
fâcheu|x, ~se /fɑʃø, -z/ *a.* unfortunate.
facil|e /fasil/ *a.* easy; (*caractère*) easygoing. **~ement** *adv.* easily. **~ité** *n.f.* easiness; (*aisance*) ease; (*aptitude*) ability; (*possibilité*) facility.
faciliter /fasilite/ *v.t.* facilitate.
façon /fasɔ̃/ *n.f.* way; (*de vêtement*) cut. **~s,** (*chichis*) fuss. **de cette ~,** in this way. **de ~ à,** so as to. **de toute ~,** anyway.
façonner /fasɔne/ *v.t.* shape; (*faire*) make.
facteur¹ /faktœr/ *n.m.* postman.
facteur² /faktœr/ *n.m.* (*élément*) factor.
factice /faktis/ *a.* artificial.
faction /faksjɔ̃/ *n.f.* faction. **de ~,** (*mil.*) on guard.
factur|e /faktyr/ *n.f.* bill; (*comm.*) invoice. **~er** *v.t.* invoice.
facultati|f, ~ve /fakyltatif, -v/ *a.* optional.
faculté /fakylte/ *n.f.* faculty; (*possibilité*) power; (*univ.*) faculty.
fade /fad/ *a.* insipid.
fagot /fago/ *n.m.* bundle of firewood.
fagoter /fagɔte/ *v.t.* (*fam.*) rig out.
faibl|e /fɛbl/ *a.* weak; (*espoir, quantité, écart*) slight; (*revenu, intensité*) low. —*n.m.* weakling; (*penchant, défaut*) weakness. **~e d'esprit,** feeble-minded. **~esse** *n.f.* weakness. **~ir** *v.i.* weaken.
faïence /fajɑ̃s/ *n.f.* earthenware.
faille /faj/ *n.f.* (*géog.*) fault; (*fig.*) flaw.
faillir /fajir/ *v.i.* **j'ai failli acheter**/*etc.*, I almost bought/*etc.*

faillite /fajit/ *n.f.* bankruptcy; (*fig.*) collapse.
faim /fɛ̃/ *n.f.* hunger. **avoir ~,** be hungry.
fainéant, ~e /feneɑ̃, -t/ *a.* idle. —*n.m., f.* idler.
faire† /fɛr/ *v.t.* make; (*activité*) do; (*rêve, chute, etc.*) have; (*mesure*) be; (*dire*) say. —*v.i.* do; (*paraître*) look. **se ~** *v. pr.* (*petit etc.*) make o.s.; (*amis, argent*) make; (*illusions*) have; (*devenir*) become. **~ du rugby/du violon/***etc.*, play rugby/the violin/*etc.* **~ construire/punir/***etc.*, have *ou* get built/punished/*etc.* **~ pleurer/tomber/***etc.*, make cry/fall/*etc.* **se ~ tuer/***etc.*, get killed/*etc.* **il fait beau/chaud/***etc.*, it is fine/hot/*etc.* **~ l'idiot,** play the fool. **ne ~ que pleurer/***etc.*, (*faire continuellement*) do nothing but cry/*etc.* **ça ne fait rien,** it doesn't matter. **se ~ à,** get used to. **s'en ~,** worry. **ça se fait,** that is done. **~-part** *n.m. invar.* announcement.
fais, fait[1] /fɛ/ *voir* **faire.**
faisable /fəzabl/ *a.* feasible.
faisan /fəzɑ̃/ *n.m.* pheasant.
faisceau (*pl.* **~x**) /fɛso/ *n.m.* (*rayon*) beam; (*fagot*) bundle.
fait[2], **~e** /fɛ, fɛt/ *a.* done; (*fromage*) ripe; (*homme*) grown. **~ pour,** made for. **tout ~,** ready made.
fait[3] /fɛ/ *n.m.* fact; (*événement*) event. **au ~ (de),** informed (of). **de ce ~,** therefore. **du ~ de,** on account of. **~ divers,** (trivial) news item. **~ nouveau,** new development. **sur le ~,** in the act.
faîte /fɛt/ *n.m.* top; (*fig.*) peak.
faites /fɛt/ *voir* **faire.**
faitout /fɛtu/ *n.m.* stew-pot.
falaise /falɛz/ *n.f.* cliff.
falloir† /falwar/ *v.i.* **il faut qch./qn.,** we, you, *etc.* need sth./s.o. **il lui faut du pain,** he needs bread. **il faut rester,** we, you, *etc.* have to *ou* must stay. **il faut que j'y aille,** I have to *ou* must go. **il faudrait que tu partes,** you should leave. **il fallait le faire,** we, you, *etc.* should have done it. **il s'en faut de beaucoup que je sois,** I am far from being.
falsifier /falsifje/ *v.t.* falsify.
famélique /famelik/ *a.* starving.
fameu|x, ~se /famø, -z/ *a.* famous; (*excellent: fam.*) first-rate. **~sement** *adv.* (*fam.*) extremely.
famil|ial (*m. pl.* **~iaux**) /familjal, -jo/ *a.* family.
familiar|iser /familjarize/ *v.t.* familiarize (**avec,** with). **se ~iser** *v. pr.* familiarize o.s. **~isé** *a.* familiar. **~ité** *n.f.* familiarity.
famil|ier, ~ière /familje, -jɛr/ *a.* familiar; (*amical*) informal. —*n.m.* regular visitor. **~ièrement** *adv.* informally.
famille /famij/ *n.f.* family. **en ~,** with one's family.
famine /famin/ *n.f.* famine.
fan|al (*pl.* **~aux**) /fanal, -o/ *n.m.* lantern, light.
fanati|que /fanatik/ *a.* fanatical. —*n.m./f.* fanatic. **~sme** *n.m.* fanaticism.
faner (se) /(sə)fane/ *v. pr.* fade.
fanfare /fɑ̃far/ *n.f.* brass band; (*musique*) fanfare.
fanfaron, ~ne /fɑ̃farɔ̃, -ɔn/ *a.* boastful. —*n.m., f.* boaster.
fanion /fanjɔ̃/ *n.m.* pennant.
fantaisie /fɑ̃tezi/ *n.f.* imagination, fantasy; (*caprice*) whim. **(de) ~,** (*boutons etc.*) fancy.
fantaisiste /fɑ̃tezist/ *a.* unorthodox.
fantasme /fɑ̃tasm/ *n.m.* fantasy.
fantasque /fɑ̃task/ *a.* whimsical.
fantassin /fɑ̃tasɛ̃/ *n.m.* infantryman.
fantastique /fɑ̃tastik/ *a.* fantastic.
fantoche /fɑ̃tɔʃ/ *n.m.* & *a.* puppet.
fantôme /fɑ̃tom/ *n.m.* ghost. —*a.* (*péj.*) bogus.

faon /fɑ̃/ *n.m.* fawn.

farc|e[1] /fars/ *n.f.* (practical) joke; (*théâtre*) farce. **~eur, ~euse** *n.m., f.* joker.

farc|e[2] /fars/ *n.f.* (*hachis*) stuffing. **~ir** *v.t.* stuff.

fard /far/ *n.m.* make-up. **~er** /-de/ *v.t.*, **se ~er** *v. pr.* make up.

fardeau (*pl.* **~x**) /fardo/ *n.m.* burden.

farfelu, ~e /farfəly/ *a.* & *n.m., f.* eccentric.

farin|e /farin/ *n.f.* flour. **~e d'avoine,** oatmeal. **~eux, ~euse** *a.* floury.

farouche /faruʃ/ *a.* shy; (*peu sociable*) unsociable; (*violent*) fierce. **~ment** *adv.* fiercely.

fart /far(t)/ *n.m.* (ski) wax. **~er** /farte/ *v.t.* (*skis*) wax.

fascin|er /fasine/ *v.t.* fascinate. **~ation** *n.f.* fascination.

fascis|te /faʃist/ *a.* & *n.m./f.* fascist. **~me** *n.m.* fascism.

fasse /fas/ *voir* **faire.**

faste /fast/ *n.m.* splendour.

fastidieu|x, ~se /fastidjø, -z/ *a.* tedious.

fat|al (*m. pl.* **~als**) /fatal/ *a.* inevitable; (*mortel*) fatal. **~alement** *adv.* inevitably. **~alité** *n.f.* (*destin*) fate.

fataliste /fatalist/ *n.m./f.* fatalist.

fatidique /fatidik/ *a.* fateful.

fatigant, ~e /fatigɑ̃, -t/ *a.* tiring; (*ennuyeux*) tiresome.

fatigue /fatig/ *n.f.* fatigue, tiredness.

fatigu|er /fatige/ *v.t.* tire; (*yeux, moteur*) strain. *—v.i.* (*moteur*) labour. **se ~er** *v. pr.* get tired, tire (**de,** of). **~é** *a.* tired.

fatras /fatra/ *n.m.* jumble.

faubourg /fobur/ *n.m.* suburb.

fauché /foʃe/ *a.* (*fam.*) broke.

faucher /foʃe/ *v.t.* (*herbe*) mow; (*voler: fam.*) pinch. **~ qn.,** (*véhicule, tir*) mow s.o. down.

faucille /fosij/ *n.f.* sickle.

faucon /fokɔ̃/ *n.m.* falcon, hawk.

faudra, faudrait /fodra, fodrɛ/ *voir* **falloir.**

faufiler (se) /(sə)fofile/ *v. pr.* edge one's way.

faune /fon/ *n.f.* wildlife, fauna.

faussaire /fosɛr/ *n.m.* forger.

fausse /fos/ *voir* **faux**[2].

faussement /fosmɑ̃/ *adv.* falsely.

fausser /fose/ *v.t.* buckle; (*fig.*) distort. **~ compagnie à,** sneak away from.

fausseté /foste/ *n.f.* falseness.

faut /fo/ *voir* **falloir.**

faute /fot/ *n.f.* mistake; (*responsabilité*) fault; (*délit*) offence; (*péché*) sin. **en ~,** at fault. **~ de,** for want of. **~ de quoi,** failing which.

fauteuil /fotœj/ *n.m.* armchair; (*de président*) chair; (*théâtre*) seat. **~ roulant,** wheelchair.

fauti|f, ~ve /fotif, -v/ *a.* guilty; (*faux*) faulty. *—n.m., f.* guilty party.

fauve /fov/ *a.* (*couleur*) fawn. *—n.m.* wild cat.

faux[1] /fo/ *n.f.* scythe.

faux[2], **fausse** /fo, fos/ *a.* false; (*falsifié*) fake, forged; (*numéro, calcul*) wrong; (*voix*) out of tune. **c'est ~!,** that is wrong! **il est ~ de,** it is wrong to. *—adv.* (*chanter*) out of tune. *—n.m.* forgery. **fausse couche,** miscarriage. **~-filet** *n.m.* sirloin. **~-monnayeur** *n.m.* forger.

faveur /favœr/ *n.f.* favour. **de ~,** (*régime*) preferential. **en ~ de,** in favour of.

favorable /favɔrabl/ *a.* favourable.

favori, ~te /favɔri, -t/ *a.* & *n.m., f.* favourite. **~tisme** *n.m.* favouritism.

favoris /favɔri/ *n.m. pl.* sidewhiskers.

favoriser /favɔrize/ *v.t.* favour.

fébrile /febril/ *a.* feverish.

fécond, ~e /fekɔ̃, -d/ *a.* fertile. **~er** /-de/ *v.t.* fertilize. **~ité** /-dite/ *n.f.* fertility.

fécule /fekyl/ *n.f.* starch.

fédér|al (*m. pl.* **~aux**) /federal, -o/ *a.* federal.

fédération /federɑsjɔ̃/ *n.f.* federation.

fée /fe/ *n.f.* fairy.

féer|ie /fe(e)ri/ *n.f.* magical spectacle. **~ique** *a.* magical.

feindre† /fɛ̃dr/ *v.t.* feign. **~ de,** pretend to.

feinte /fɛ̃t/ *n.f.* feint.

fêler /fele/ *v.t.*, **se ~** *v. pr.* crack.

félicité /felisite/ *n.f.* bliss.

félicit|er /felisite/ *v.t.* congratulate (**de,** on). **~ations** *n.f. pl.* congratulations (**pour,** on).

félin, ~e /felɛ̃, -in/ *a.* & *n.m.* feline.

fêlure /felyr/ *n.f.* crack.

femelle /fəmɛl/ *a.* & *n.f.* female.

fémin|in, ~ine /feminɛ̃, -in/ *a.* feminine; (*sexe*) female; (*mode, équipe*) women's. —*n.m.* feminine. **~ité** *n.f.* femininity.

féministe /feminist/ *n.m./f.* feminist.

femme /fam/ *n.f.* woman; (*épouse*) wife. **~ de chambre,** chambermaid. **~ de ménage,** cleaning lady.

fémur /femyr/ *n.m.* thigh-bone.

fendiller /fɑ̃dije/ *v.t.*, **se ~** *v. pr.* crack.

fendre /fɑ̃dr/ *v.t.* (*couper*) split; (*fissurer*) crack; (*foule*) push through. **se ~** *v. pr.* crack.

fenêtre /fənɛtr/ *n.f.* window.

fenouil /fənuj/ *n.m.* fennel.

fente /fɑ̃t/ *n.f.* (*ouverture*) slit, slot; (*fissure*) crack.

féod|al (*m. pl.* **~aux**) /feɔdal, -o/ *a.* feudal.

fer /fɛr/ *n.m.* iron. **~ (à repasser),** iron. **~ à cheval,** horseshoe. **~-blanc** (*pl.* **~s-blancs**) *n.m.* tinplate. **~ de lance,** spearhead.

fera, ferait /fəra, fərɛ/ *voir* **faire.**

ferme¹ /fɛrm/ *a.* firm. —*adv.* (*travailler*) hard. **~ment** /-əmɑ̃/ *adv.* firmly.

ferme² /fɛrm/ *n.f.* farm; (*maison*) farm(house).

fermé /fɛrme/ *a.* closed; (*gaz, radio, etc.*) off.

ferment /fɛrmɑ̃/ *n.m.* ferment.

ferment|er /fɛrmɑ̃te/ *v.i.* ferment. **~ation** *n.f.* fermentation.

fermer /fɛrme/ *v.t./i.* close, shut; (*cesser d'exploiter*) close *ou* shut down; (*gaz, radio, etc.*) turn off. **se ~** *v. pr.* close, shut.

fermeté /fɛrməte/ *n.f.* firmness.

fermeture /fɛrmətyr/ *n.f.* closing; (*dispositif*) catch. **~ annuelle,** annual closure. **~ éclair,** (P.) zip(-fastener); (*Amer.*) zipper.

ferm|ier, ~ière /fɛrmje, -jɛr/ *n.m.* farmer. —*n.f.* farmer's wife. —*a.* farm.

fermoir /fɛrmwar/ *n.m.* clasp.

féroc|e /ferɔs/ *a.* ferocious. **~ité** *n.f.* ferocity.

ferraille /fɛrɑj/ *n.f.* scrap-iron.

ferré /fɛre/ *a.* (*canne*) steel-tipped. **~ en** *ou* **sur,** (*fam.*) clued up on.

ferrer /fɛre/ *v.t.* (*cheval*) shoe.

ferronnerie /fɛrɔnri/ *n.f.* ironwork.

ferroviaire /fɛrɔvjɛr/ *a.* rail(way).

ferry-boat /fɛribot/ *n.m.* ferry.

fertil|e /fɛrtil/ *a.* fertile. **~e en,** (*fig.*) rich in. **~iser** *v.t.* fertilize. **~ité** *n.f.* fertility.

ferv|ent, ~ente /fɛrvɑ̃, -t/ *a.* fervent. —*n.m., f.* enthusiast (**de,** of). **~eur** *n.f.* fervour.

fesse /fɛs/ *n.f.* buttock.

fessée /fese/ *n.f.* spanking.

festin /fɛstɛ̃/ *n.m.* feast.

festival (*pl.* **~s**) /fɛstival/ *n.m.* festival.

festivités /fɛstivite/ *n.f. pl.* festivities.

festoyer /fɛstwaje/ *v.i.* feast.

fête /fɛt/ *n.f.* holiday; (*religieuse*) feast; (*du nom*) name-day;

(*réception*) party; (*en famille*) celebration; (*foire*) fair; (*folklorique*) festival. **~ des Mères,** Mother's Day. **~ foraine,** fun-fair. **faire la ~,** make merry.

fêter /fete/ *v.t.* celebrate; (*personne*) give a celebration for.

fétiche /fetiʃ/ *n.m.* fetish; (*fig.*) mascot.

fétide /fetid/ *a.* fetid.

feu[1] (*pl.* **~x**) /fø/ *n.m.* fire; (*lumière*) light; (*de réchaud*) burner. **~x (rouges),** (traffic) lights. **à ~ doux,** on a low flame. **du ~,** (*pour cigarette*) a light. **~ d'artifice,** firework display. **~ de joie,** bonfire. **~ de position,** sidelight. **mettre le ~ à,** set fire to. **prendre ~,** catch fire.

feu[2] /fø/ *a. invar.* (*mort*) late.

feuillage /fœjaʒ/ *n.m.* foliage.

feuille /fœj/ *n.f.* leaf; (*de papier, bois, etc.*) sheet; (*formulaire*) form.

feuillet /fœjɛ/ *n.m.* leaf.

feuilleter /fœjte/ *v.t.* leaf through.

feuilleton /fœjtɔ̃/ *n.m.* (*à suivre*) serial; (*histoire complète*) series.

feuillu /fœjy/ *a.* leafy.

feutre /føtr/ *n.m.* felt; (*chapeau*) felt hat; (*crayon*) felt-tipped pen.

feutré /føtre/ *a.* (*bruit*) muffled.

fève /fɛv/ *n.f.* broad bean.

février /fevrije/ *n.m.* February.

fiable /fjabl/ *a.* reliable.

fiacre /fjakr/ *n.m.* hackney cab.

fiançailles /fjɑ̃saj/ *n.f. pl.* engagement.

fianc|er (se) /(sə)fjɑ̃se/ *v. pr.* become engaged **(avec,** to). **~é, ~ée** *a.* engaged; *n.m.* fiancé; *n.f.* fiancée.

fibre /fibr/ *n.f.* fibre. **~ de verre,** fibreglass.

ficeler /fisle/ *v.t.* tie up.

ficelle /fisɛl/ *n.f.* string.

fiche /fiʃ/ *n.f.* (index) card; (*formulaire*) form, slip; (*électr.*) plug.

ficher[1] /fiʃe/ *v.t.* (*enfoncer*) drive **(dans,** into).

ficher[2] /fiʃe/ *v.t.* (*faire: fam.*) do; (*donner: fam.*) give; (*mettre: fam.*) put. **se ~ de,** (*fam.*) make fun of. **~ le camp,** (*fam.*) clear off. **il s'en fiche,** (*fam.*) he couldn't care less.

fichier /fiʃje/ *n.m.* file.

fichu[1] /fiʃy/ *a.* (*mauvais: fam.*) rotten; (*fini: fam.*) done for.

fichu[2] /fiʃy/ *n.m.* (head)scarf.

ficti|f, ~ve /fiktif, -v/ *a.* fictitious.

fiction /fiksjɔ̃/ *n.f.* fiction.

fidèle /fidɛl/ *a.* faithful. —*n.m./f.* (*client*) regular; (*relig.*) believer. **~s,** (*à l'église*) congregation. **~ment** *adv.* faithfully.

fidélité /fidelite/ *n.f.* fidelity.

fiel /fjɛl/ *n.m.* gall.

fier[1], **fière** /fjɛr/ *a.* proud **(de,** of). **fièrement** *adv.* proudly. **~té** *n.f.* pride.

fier[2] **(se)** /(sə)fje/ *v. pr.* **se ~ à,** trust.

fièvre /fjɛvr/ *n.f.* fever.

fiévreu|x, ~se /fjevrø, -z/ *a.* feverish.

figé /fiʒe/ *a.* fixed, set; (*manières*) stiff.

figer /fiʒe/ *v.t./i.*, **se ~** *v. pr.* congeal. **~ sur place,** petrify.

fignoler /fiɲɔle/ *v.t.* refine (upon), finish off meticulously.

figu|e /fig/ *n.f.* fig. **~ier** *n.m.* fig-tree.

figurant, ~e /figyrɑ̃, -t/ *n.m., f.* (*cinéma*) extra.

figure /figyr/ *n.f.* face; (*forme, personnage*) figure; (*illustration*) picture.

figuré /figyre/ *a.* (*sens*) figurative. **au ~,** figuratively.

figurer /figyre/ *v.i.* appear. —*v.t.* represent. **se ~** *v. pr.* imagine.

fil /fil/ *n.m.* thread; (*métallique, électrique*) wire; (*de couteau*) edge; (*tissu*) linen. **au ~ de,** with the

passing of. **au ~ de l'eau,** with the current. **~ de fer,** wire.
filament /filamɑ̃/ *n.m.* filament.
filature /filatyr/ *n.f.* (textile) mill; (*surveillance*) shadowing.
file /fil/ *n.f.* line; (*voie*: *auto.*) lane. **~ (d'attente),** queue; (*Amer.*) line. **en ~ indienne,** in single file. **se mettre en ~,** line up.
filer /file/ *v.t.* spin; (*suivre*) shadow. **~ qch. à qn.,** (*fam.*) slip s.o. sth. —*v.i.* (*bas*) ladder, run; (*liquide*) run; (*aller vite*: *fam.*) speed along, fly by; (*partir*: *fam.*) dash off.
filet /filɛ/ *n.m.* net; (*d'eau*) trickle; (*de viande*) fillet. **~ (à bagages),** (luggage) rack. **~ à provisions,** string bag (*for shopping*).
fil|ial, ~iale (*m. pl.* **~iaux**) /filjal, -jo/ *a.* filial. —*n.f.* subsidiary (company).
filière /filjɛr/ *n.f.* (official) channels; (*de trafiquants*) network. **passer par** *ou* **suivre la ~,** (*employé*) work one's way up.
filigrane /filigran/ *n.m.* watermark.
filin /filɛ̃/ *n.m.* rope.
fille /fij/ *n.f.* girl; (*opposé à fils*) daughter. **~-mère** (*pl.* **~s-mères**) *n.f.* (*péj.*) unmarried mother.
fillette /fijɛt/ *n.f.* little girl.
filleul /fijœl/ *n.m.* godson. **~e** *n.f.* god-daughter.
film /film/ *n.m.* film. **~ d'épouvante/muet/parlant,** horror/silent/talking film. **~ dramatique,** drama. **~er** *v.t.* film.
filon /filɔ̃/ *n.m.* (*géol.*) seam; (*situation*) source of wealth.
fils /fis/ *n.m.* son.
filtr|e /filtr/ *n.m.* filter. **~er** *v.t./i.* filter; (*personne*) screen.
fin[1] /fɛ̃/ *n.f.* end. **à la ~,** finally. **en ~ de compte,** all things considered. **~ de semaine,** weekend. **mettre ~ à,** put an end to. **prendre ~,** come to an end.
fin[2], **fine** /fɛ̃, fin/ *a.* fine; (*tranche, couche*) thin; (*taille*) slim; (*plat*) exquisite; (*esprit, vue*) sharp. —*adv.* (*couper*) finely. **~es herbes,** herbs.
fin|al, ~ale[1] (*m. pl.* **~aux** *ou* **~als**) /final, -o/ *a.* final. —*n.f.* (*sport*) final; (*gram.*) final syllable. —*n.m.* (*pl.* **~aux** *ou* **~als**) (*mus.*) finale. **~alement** *adv.* finally; (*somme toute*) after all.
finale[2] /final/ *n.m.* (*mus.*) finale.
finaliste /finalist/ *n.m./f.* finalist.
financ|e /finɑ̃s/ *n.f.* finance. **~er** *v.t.* finance. **~ier, ~ière** *a.* financial; *n.m.* financier.
finement /finmɑ̃/ *adv.* finely; (*avec habileté*) cleverly.
finesse /finɛs/ *n.f.* fineness; (*de taille*) slimness; (*acuité*) sharpness. **~s,** (*de langue*) niceties.
fini /fini/ *a.* finished; (*espace*) finite. —*n.m.* finish.
finir /finir/ *v.t./i.* finish, end; (*arrêter*) stop; (*manger*) finish (up). **en ~ avec,** have done with. **~ par faire,** end up doing.
finition /finisjɔ̃/ *n.f.* finish.
finlandais, ~e /fɛ̃lɑ̃dɛ, -z/ *a.* Finnish. —*n.m., f.* Finn.
Finlande /fɛ̃lɑ̃d/ *n.f.* Finland.
finnois, ~e /finwa, -z/ *a.* Finnish. —*n.m.* (*lang.*) Finnish.
fiole /fjɔl/ *n.f.* phial.
firme /firm/ *n.f.* firm.
fisc /fisk/ *n.m.* tax authorities. **~al** (*m. pl.* **~aux**) *a.* tax, fiscal. **~alité** *n.f.* tax system.
fission /fisjɔ̃/ *n.f.* fission.
fissur|e /fisyr/ *n.f.* crack. **~er** *v.t.*, **se ~er** *v. pr.* crack.
fiston /fistɔ̃/ *n.m.* (*fam.*) son.
fixation /fiksɑsjɔ̃/ *n.f.* fixing; (*complexe*) fixation.
fixe /fiks/ *a.* fixed; (*stable*) steady. **à heure ~,** at a set time.

fixer /fikse/ *v.t.* fix. ~ **(du regard)**, stare at. **se** ~ *v. pr.* (*s'installer*) settle down. **être fixé,** (*personne*) have made up one's mind.
flacon /flakɔ̃/ *n.m.* bottle.
flageolet /flaʒɔlɛ/ *n.m* (*haricot*) (dwarf) kidney bean.
flagrant, ~**e** /flagrɑ̃, -t/ *a.* flagrant. **en** ~ **délit,** in the act.
flair /flɛr/ *n.m.* (sense of) smell; (*fig.*) intuition. ~**er** /flere/ *v.t.* sniff at; (*fig.*) sense.
flamand, ~**e** /flamɑ̃, -d/ *a.* Flemish. —*n.m.* (*lang.*) Flemish. —*n.m.*, *f.* Fleming.
flamant /flamɑ̃/ *n.m.* flamingo.
flambant /flɑ̃bɑ̃/ *adv.* ~ **neuf,** brand-new.
flambeau (*pl.* ~**x**) /flɑ̃bo/ *n.m.* torch.
flambée /flɑ̃be/ *n.f.* blaze; (*fig.*) explosion.
flamber /flɑ̃be/ *v.i.* blaze. —*v.t.* (*aiguille*) sterilize; (*volaille*) singe.
flamboyer /flɑ̃bwaje/ *v.i.* blaze.
flamme /flam/ *n.f.* flame; (*fig.*) ardour.
flammèche /flamɛʃ/ *n.f.* spark.
flan /flɑ̃/ *n.m.* custard-pie.
flanc /flɑ̃/ *n.m.* side; (*d'animal, d'armée*) flank.
flancher /flɑ̃ʃe/ *v.i.* (*fam.*) give in.
Flandre(s) /flɑ̃dr/ *n.f.* (*pl.*) Flanders.
flanelle /flanɛl/ *n.f.* flannel.
flân|er /flɑne/ *v.i.* stroll. ~**erie** *n.f.* stroll.
flanquer /flɑ̃ke/ *v.t.* flank; (*jeter: fam.*) chuck; (*donner: fam.*) give.
flaque /flak/ *n.f.* (*d'eau*) puddle; (*de sang*) pool.
flash (*pl.* ~**es**) /flaʃ/ *n.m.* (*photo.*) flash; (*information*) news flash.
flasque /flask/ *a.* flabby.
flatt|er /flate/ *v.t.* flatter. **se** ~**er de,** pride o.s. on. ~**erie** *n.f.* flattery. ~**eur,** ~**euse** *a.* flattering; *n.m.*, *f.* flatterer.
fléau (*pl.* ~**x**) /fleo/ *n.m.* (*désastre*) scourge; (*personne*) bane.
flèche /flɛʃ/ *n.f.* arrow; (*de clocher*) spire.
flécher /fleʃe/ *v.t.* mark *ou* sign-post (with arrows).
fléchette /fleʃɛt/ *n.f.* dart.
fléchir /fleʃir/ *v.t.* bend; (*personne*) move. —*v.i.* (*faiblir*) weaken; (*poutre*) sag, bend.
flegmatique /flɛgmatik/ *a.* phlegmatic.
flegme /flɛgm/ *n.m.* composure.
flemm|e /flɛm/ *n.f.* (*fam.*) laziness. ~**ard,** ~**arde** *a.* (*fam.*) lazy; *n.m.*, *f.* (*fam.*) lazy-bones.
flétrir /fletrir/ *v.t.*, **se** ~ *v. pr.* wither.
fleur /flœr/ *n.f.* flower; (*d'un arbre*) blossom. **à** ~ **de terre/d'eau,** just above the ground/water. **à** ~**s,** flowery. ~ **de l'âge,** prime of life.
fleur|ir /flœrir/ *v.i.* flower; (*arbre*) blossom; (*fig.*) flourish. —*v.t.* adorn with flowers. ~**i** *a.* in flower; (*fig.*) flowery.
fleuriste /flœrist/ *n.m.*/*f.* florist.
fleuve /flœv/ *n.m.* river.
flexible /flɛksibl/ *a.* flexible.
flexion /flɛksjɔ̃/ *n.f.* (*anat.*) flexing.
flic /flik/ *n.m.* (*fam.*) cop.
flirt /flœrt/ *n.m.* flirtation. ~**er** *v.i.* flirt. ~**eur,** ~**euse** *n.m.*, *f.* flirt.
flocon /flɔkɔ̃/ *n.m.* flake.
floraison /flɔrɛzɔ̃/ *n.f.* flowering.
flor|al (*m. pl.* ~**aux**) /flɔral, -o/ *a.* floral.
floralies /flɔrali/ *n.f. pl.* flower-show.
flore /flɔr/ *n.f.* flora.
florissant, ~**e** /flɔrisɑ̃, -t/ *a.* flourishing.
flot /flo/ *n.m.* flood, stream. **être à** ~, be afloat. **les** ~**s,** the waves.
flottant, ~**e** /flɔtɑ̃, -t/ *a.* (*vêtement*) loose; (*indécis*) indecisive.
flotte /flɔt/ *n.f.* fleet; (*pluie: fam.*) rain.

flottement /flɔtmɑ̃/ *n.m.* (*incertitude*) indecision.
flott|er /flɔte/ *v.i.* float; (*drapeau*) flutter; (*nuage, parfum, pensées*) drift; (*pleuvoir: fam.*) rain. **~eur** *n.m.* float.
flou /flu/ *a.* (*vague*) fuzzy.
fluct|uer /flyktɥe/ *v.i.* fluctuate. **~uation** *n.f.* fluctuation.
fluet, ~te /flyɛ, -t/ *a.* slender; (*voice*) thin.
fluid|e /flɥid/ *a.* & *n.m.* fluid. **~ité** *n.f.* fluidity.
fluor /flyɔr/ *n.m.* (*pour les dents*) fluoride.
fluorescent, ~e /flyɔresɑ̃, -t/ *a.* fluorescent.
flût|e /flyt/ *n.f.* flute; (*verre*) champagne glass. **~iste** *n.m./f.* flautist; (*Amer.*) flutist.
fluv|ial (*m. pl.* **~iaux**) /flyvjal, -jo/ *a.* river.
flux /fly/ *n.m.* flow. **~ et reflux,** ebb and flow.
fluxion /flyksjɔ̃/ *n.f.* **~ de poitrine,** pneumonia.
foc|al (*m. pl.* **~aux**) /fɔkal, -o/ *a.* focal.
fœtus /fetys/ *n.m.* foetus.
foi /fwa/ *n.f.* faith; (*promesse*) word. **être de bonne/mauvaise ~,** be acting in good/bad faith. **ma ~!,** well (indeed)!
foie /fwa/ *n.m.* liver. **~ gras,** foie gras.
foin /fwɛ̃/ *n.m.* hay.
foire /fwar/ *n.f.* fair. **faire la ~,** (*fam.*) make merry.
fois /fwa/ *n.f.* time. **une ~,** once. **deux ~,** twice. **à la ~,** at the same time. **des ~,** (*parfois*) sometimes.
foison /fwazɔ̃/ *n.f.* abundance. **à ~,** in abundance. **~ner** /-ɔne/ *v.i.* abound (**de,** in).
fol /fɔl/ *voir* **fou.**
folâtrer /fɔlɑtre/ *v.i.* frolic.
folichon, ~ne /fɔliʃɔ̃, -ɔn/ *a.* **pas ~,** (*fam.*) not much fun.
folie /fɔli/ *n.f.* madness; (*bêtise*) foolish thing, folly.
folklor|e /fɔlklɔr/ *n.m.* folklore. **~ique** *a.* folk; (*fam.*) picturesque.
folle /fɔl/ *voir* **fou.**
follement /fɔlmɑ̃/ *adv.* madly.
fomenter /fɔmɑ̃te/ *v.t.* foment.
fonc|er[1] /fɔ̃se/ *v.t./i.* darken. **~é** *a.* dark.
foncer[2] /fɔ̃se/ *v.i.* (*fam.*) dash along. **~ sur,** (*fam.*) charge at.
fonc|ier, ~ière /fɔ̃sje, -jɛr/ *a.* fundamental; (*comm.*) real estate. **~ièrement** *adv.* fundamentally.
fonction /fɔ̃ksjɔ̃/ *n.f.* function; (*emploi*) position. **~s,** (*obligations*) duties. **en ~ de,** according to. **~ publique,** civil service.
fonctionnaire /fɔ̃ksjɔnɛr/ *n.m./f.* civil servant.
fonctionnel, ~le /fɔ̃ksjɔnɛl/ *a.* functional.
fonctionn|er /fɔ̃ksjɔne/ *v.i.* work. **faire ~er,** work. **~ement** *n.m.* working.
fond /fɔ̃/ *n.m.* bottom; (*de salle, magasin, etc.*) back; (*essentiel*) basis; (*contenu*) content; (*plan*) background. **à ~,** thoroughly. **au ~,** basically. **de ~,** (*bruit*) background; (*sport*) long-distance. **de ~ en comble,** from top to bottom.
fondament|al (*m. pl.* **~aux**) /fɔ̃damɑ̃tal, -o/ *a.* fundamental.
fondation /fɔ̃dɑsjɔ̃/ *n.f.* foundation.
fond|er /fɔ̃de/ *v.t.* found; (*baser*) base (**sur,** on). **(bien) ~é,** well-founded. **~é à,** justified in. **se ~er sur,** be guided by, place one's reliance on. **~ateur, ~atrice** *n.m., f.* founder.
fonderie /fɔ̃dri/ *n.f.* foundry.
fondre /fɔ̃dr/ *v.t./i.* melt; (*dans l'eau*) dissolve; (*mélanger*) merge. **se ~** *v. pr.* merge. **faire ~,** melt; dissolve. **~ en larmes,** burst into tears. **~ sur,** swoop on.
fondrière /fɔ̃drijɛr/ *n.f.* pot-hole.

fonds /fɔ̃/ *n.m.* fund. —*n.m. pl.* (*capitaux*) funds. **~ de commerce,** business.
fondu /fɔ̃dy/ *a.* melted; (*métal*) molten.
font /fɔ̃/ *voir* **faire.**
fontaine /fɔ̃tɛn/ *n.f.* fountain; (*source*) spring.
fonte /fɔ̃t/ *n.f.* melting; (*fer*) cast iron. **~ des neiges,** thaw.
foot /fut/ *n.m.* (*fam.*) football.
football /futbol/ *n.m.* football. **~eur** *n.m.* footballer.
footing /futiŋ/ *n.m.* fast walking.
forage /fɔraʒ/ *n.m.* drilling.
forain /fɔrɛ̃/ *n.m.* fairground entertainer. **(marchand) ~,** stall-holder (*at a fair or market*).
forçat /fɔrsa/ *n.m.* convict.
force /fɔrs/ *n.f.* force; (*physique*) strength; (*hydraulique etc.*) power. **~s,** (*physiques*) strength. **à ~ de,** by sheer force of. **de ~, par la ~,** by force. **~ de dissuasion,** deterrent. **~ de frappe,** strike force, deterrent. **~ de l'âge,** prime of life. **~s de l'ordre,** police (force).
forcé /fɔrse/ *a.* forced; (*inévitable*) inevitable.
forcément /fɔrsemɑ̃/ *adv.* necessarily; (*évidemment*) obviously.
forcené, ~e /fɔrsəne/ *a.* frenzied. —*n.m., f.* maniac.
forceps /fɔrsɛps/ *n.m.* forceps.
forcer /fɔrse/ *v.t.* force (**à faire,** to do); (*voix*) strain. —*v.i.* (*exagérer*) overdo it. **se ~** *v. pr.* force o.s.
forcir /fɔrsir/ *v.i.* fill out.
forer /fɔre/ *v.t.* drill.
forest|ier, ~ière /fɔrɛstje, -jɛr/ *a.* forest.
foret /fɔrɛ/ *n.m.* drill.
forêt /fɔrɛ/ *n.f.* forest.
forfait /fɔrfɛ/ *n.m.* (*comm.*) inclusive price. **~aire** /-tɛr/ *a.* (*prix*) inclusive.
forge /fɔrʒ/ *n.f.* forge.
forger /fɔrʒe/ *v.t.* forge; (*inventer*) make up.
forgeron /fɔrʒərɔ̃/ *n.m.* blacksmith.
formaliser (se) /(sə)fɔrmalize/ *v. pr.* take offence (**de,** at).
formalité /fɔrmalite/ *n.f.* formality.
format /fɔrma/ *n.m.* format.
formation /fɔrmɑsjɔ̃/ *n.f.* formation; (*de médecin etc.*) training; (*culture*) education.
forme /fɔrm/ *n.f.* form; (*contour*) shape, form. **~s,** (*de femme*) figure. **en ~,** (*sport*) in good shape, on form. **en ~ de,** in the shape of.
formel, ~le /fɔrmɛl/ *a.* formal; (*catégorique*) positive. **~lement** *adv.* positively.
former /fɔrme/ *v.t.* form; (*instruire*) train. **se ~** *v. pr.* form.
formidable /fɔrmidabl/ *a.* fantastic.
formulaire /fɔrmylɛr/ *n.m.* form.
formul|e /fɔrmyl/ *n.f.* formula; (*expression*) expression; (*feuille*) form. **~er** *v.t.* formulate.
fort[1]**, ~e** /fɔr, -t/ *a.* strong; (*grand*) big; (*pluie*) heavy; (*bruit*) loud; (*pente*) steep; (*élève*) clever. —*adv.* (*frapper*) hard; (*parler*) loud; (*très*) very; (*beaucoup*) very much. —*n.m.* strong point. **au plus ~ de,** at the height of.
fort[2] /fɔr/ *n.m.* (*mil.*) fort.
fortement /fɔrtəmɑ̃/ *adv.* strongly; (*frapper*) hard; (*beaucoup*) greatly.
forteresse /fɔrtərɛs/ *n.f.* fortress.
fortifiant /fɔrtifjɑ̃/ *n.m.* tonic.
fortif|ier /fɔrtifje/ *v.t.* fortify. **~ication** *n.f.* fortification.
fortuit, ~e /fɔrtɥi, -t/ *a.* fortuitous.
fortune /fɔrtyn/ *n.f.* fortune. **de ~,** (*improvisé*) makeshift. **faire ~,** make one's fortune.
fortuné /fɔrtyne/ *a.* wealthy.
forum /fɔrɔm/ *n.m.* forum.

fosse /fos/ *n.f.* pit; (*tombe*) grave. **~ d'aisances,** cesspool.
fossé /fose/ *n.m.* ditch; (*fig.*) gulf.
fossette /fosɛt/ *n.f.* dimple.
fossile /fosil/ *n.m.* fossil.
fossoyeur /foswajœr/ *n.m.* grave-digger.
fou *ou* **fol*, folle** /fu, fɔl/ *a.* mad; (*course, regard*) wild; (*énorme*: *fam.*) tremendous. —*n.m.* madman; (*bouffon*) jester. —*n.f.* madwoman. **le ~ rire,** the giggles.
foudre /fudr/ *n.f.* lightning.
foudroy|er /fudrwaje/ *v.t.* strike by lightning; (*électr.*) electrocute; (*maladie etc.*) strike down; (*atterrer*) stagger. **~ant, ~ante** *a.* staggering; (*mort, maladie*) violent.
fouet /fwɛ/ *n.m.* whip; (*culin.*) whisk.
fouetter /fwete/ *v.t.* whip; (*crème etc.*) whisk.
fougère /fuʒɛr/ *n.f.* fern.
fougu|e /fug/ *n.f.* ardour. **~eux, ~euse** *a.* ardent.
fouill|e /fuj/ *n.f.* search; (*archéol.*) excavation. **~er** *v.t./i.* search; (*creuser*) dig. **~er dans,** (*tiroir*) rummage through.
fouillis /fuji/ *n.m.* jumble.
fouine /fwin/ *n.f.* beech-marten.
fouiner /fwine/ *v.i.* nose about.
foulard /fular/ *n.m.* scarf.
foule /ful/ *n.f.* crowd. **une ~ de,** (*fig.*) a mass of.
foulée /fule/ *n.f.* stride.
fouler /fule/ *v.t.* press; (*sol*) tread; (*membre*) sprain. **se ~** *v. pr.* (*fam.*) exert o.s.
foulure /fulyr/ *n.f.* sprain.
four /fur/ *n.m.* oven; (*de potier*) kiln; (*théâtre*) flop. **~ à micro-ondes,** microwave oven. **~ crématoire,** crematorium.
fourbe /furb/ *a.* deceitful.
fourbu /furby/ *a.* exhausted.
fourche /furʃ/ *n.f.* fork; (*à foin*) pitchfork.
fourchette /furʃɛt/ *n.f.* fork; (*comm.*) margin.
fourchu /furʃy/ *a.* forked.
fourgon /furgɔ̃/ *n.m.* van; (*wagon*) wagon. **~ mortuaire,** hearse.
fourgonnette /furgɔnɛt/ *n.f.* (small) van.
fourmi /furmi/ *n.f.* ant. **des ~s,** (*méd.*) pins and needles.
fourmilière /furmiljɛr/ *n.f.* ant-hill.
fourmiller /furmije/ *v.i.* swarm (**de,** with).
fournaise /furnɛz/ *n.f.* (*feu, endroit*) furnace.
fourneau (*pl.* **~x**) /furno/ *n.m.* stove.
fournée /furne/ *n.f.* batch.
fourni /furni/ *a.* (*épais*) thick.
fourn|ir /furnir/ *v.t.* supply, provide; (*client*) supply; (*effort*) put in. **~ir à qn.,** supply s.o. with. **se ~ir chez,** shop at. **~isseur** *n.m.* supplier. **~iture** *n.f.* supply.
fourrage /furaʒ/ *n.m.* fodder.
fourré[1] /fure/ *n.m.* thicket.
fourré[2] /fure/ *a.* (*vêtement*) fur-lined; (*gâteau etc.*) filled (*with jam, cream, etc.*).
fourreau (*pl.* **~x**) /furo/ *n.m.* sheath.
fourr|er /fure/ *v.t.* (*mettre*: *fam.*) stick. **~e-tout** *n.m. invar.* junk room; (*sac*) holdall.
fourreur /furœr/ *n.m.* furrier.
fourrière /furjɛr/ *n.f.* (*lieu*) pound.
fourrure /furyr/ *n.f.* fur.
fourvoyer (se) /(sə)furvwaje/ *v. pr.* go astray.
foutaise /futɛz/ *n.f.* (*argot*) rubbish.
foutre /futr/ *v.t.* (*argot*) = **ficher**[2].
foyer /fwaje/ *n.m.* home; (*âtre*) hearth; (*club*) club; (*d'étudiants*) hostel; (*théâtre*) foyer; (*photo.*) focus; (*centre*) centre.
fracas /fraka/ *n.m.* din; (*de train*) roar; (*d'objet qui tombe*) crash.
fracass|er /frakase/ *v.t.*, **se ~er**

v. pr. smash. **~ant, ~ante** *a.* (*bruyant, violent*) shattering.
fraction /fraksjɔ̃/ *n.f.* fraction. **~ner** /-jɔne/ *v.t.*, **se ~ner** *v. pr.* split (up).
fractur|e /fraktyr/ *n.f.* fracture. **~er** *v.t.* (*os*) fracture; (*porte etc.*) break open.
fragil|e /fraʒil/ *a.* fragile. **~ité** *n.f.* fragility.
fragment /fragmɑ̃/ *n.m.* bit, fragment. **~aire** /-tɛr/ *a.* fragmentary. **~er** /-te/ *v.t.* split, fragment.
frai /frɛ/ *n.m.* spawn.
fraîche /frɛʃ/ *voir* **frais**[1].
fraîchement /frɛʃmɑ̃/ *adv.* (*récemment*) freshly; (*avec froideur*) coolly.
fraîcheur /frɛʃœr/ *n.f.* coolness; (*nouveauté*) freshness.
fraîchir /freʃir/ *v.i.* freshen.
frais[1], **fraîche** /frɛ, -ʃ/ *a.* fresh; (*temps, accueil*) cool; (*peinture*) wet. —*adv.* (*récemment*) newly. —*n.m.* **mettre au ~,** put in a cool place. **~ et dispos,** fresh. **il fait ~,** it is cool.
frais[2] /frɛ/ *n.m. pl.* expenses; (*droits*) fees. **~ généraux,** (*comm.*) overheads, running expenses.
frais|e /frɛz/ *n.f.* strawberry. **~ier** *n.m.* strawberry plant.
frambois|e /frɑ̃bwaz/ *n.f.* raspberry. **~ier** *n.m.* raspberry bush.
fran|c[1], **~che** /frɑ̃, -ʃ/ *a.* frank; (*regard*) open; (*net*) clear; (*cassure*) clean; (*libre*) free; (*véritable*) downright. **~c-maçon** (*pl.* **~cs-maçons**) *n.m.* Freemason. **~c-maçonnerie** *n.f.* Freemasonry.
franc[2] /frɑ̃/ *n.m.* franc.
français, ~e /frɑ̃sɛ, -z/ *a.* French. —*n.m., f.* Frenchman, Frenchwoman. —*n.m.* (*lang.*) French.
France /frɑ̃s/ *n.f.* France.
franche /frɑ̃ʃ/ *voir* **franc**[1].
franchement /frɑ̃ʃmɑ̃/ *adv.* frankly; (*nettement*) clearly; (*tout à fait*) really.
franchir /frɑ̃ʃir/ *v.t.* (*obstacle*) get over; (*traverser*) cross; (*distance*) cover; (*limite*) exceed.
franchise /frɑ̃ʃiz/ *n.f.* frankness; (*douanière*) exemption (from duties).
franco /frɑ̃ko/ *adv.* postage paid.
franco- /frɑ̃ko/ *préf.* Franco-.
francophone /frɑ̃kɔfɔn/ *a.* French-speaking. —*n.m./f.* French speaker.
frange /frɑ̃ʒ/ *n.f.* fringe.
franquette (à la bonne) /(alabɔn)frɑ̃kɛt/ *adv.* informally.
frappant, ~e /frapɑ̃, -t/ *a.* striking.
frappe /frap/ *n.f.* (*de courrier etc.*) typing; (*de dactylo*) touch.
frapp|er /frape/ *v.t./i.* strike; (*battre*) hit, strike; (*monnaie*) mint; (*à la porte*) knock, bang. **~é de panique,** panic-stricken.
frasque /frask/ *n.f.* escapade.
fratern|el, ~elle /fratɛrnɛl/ *a.* brotherly. **~iser** *v.i.* fraternize. **~ité** *n.f.* brotherhood.
fraude /frod/ *n.f.* fraud; (*à un examen*) cheating.
fraud|er /frode/ *v.t./i.* cheat. **~eur, ~euse** *n.m., f.* cheat; (*criminel*) defrauder.
frauduleu|x, ~se /frodylø, -z/ *a.* fraudulent.
frayer /freje/ *v.t.* open up. **se ~ un passage,** force one's way (**dans,** through).
frayeur /frɛjœr/ *n.f.* fright.
fredaine /frədɛn/ *n.f.* escapade.
fredonner /frədɔne/ *v.t.* hum.
freezer /frizœr/ *n.m.* freezer.
frégate /fregat/ *n.f.* frigate.
frein /frɛ̃/ *n.m.* brake. **mettre un ~ à,** curb.
frein|er /frene/ *v.t.* slow down; (*modérer, enrayer*) curb. —*v.i.* (*auto.*) brake. **~age** /frɛnaʒ/ *n.m.* braking.

frelaté /frəlate/ *a.* adulterated.
frêle /frɛl/ *a.* frail.
frelon /frəlɔ̃/ *n.m.* hornet.
frémir /fremir/ *v.i.* shudder, shake; (*feuille, eau*) quiver.
frêne /frɛn/ *n.m.* ash.
fréné|sie /frenezi/ *n.f.* frenzy. **~tique** *a.* frenzied.
fréqu|ent, ~ente /frekɑ̃, -t/ *a.* frequent. **~emment** /-amɑ̃/ *adv.* frequently. **~ence** *n.f.* frequency.
fréquenté /frekɑ̃te/ *a.* crowded.
fréquent|er /frekɑ̃te/ *v.t.* frequent; (*école*) attend; (*personne*) see. **~ation** *n.f.* frequenting. **~ations** *n.f. pl.* acquaintances.
frère /frɛr/ *n.m.* brother.
fresque /frɛsk/ *n.f.* fresco.
fret /frɛ/ *n.m.* freight.
frétiller /fretije/ *v.i.* wriggle.
friable /frijabl/ *a.* crumbly.
friand, ~e /frijɑ̃, -d/ *a.* **~ de,** fond of.
friandise /frijɑ̃diz/ *n.f.* sweet; (*Amer.*) candy; (*gâteau*) cake.
fric /frik/ *n.m.* (*fam.*) money.
fric-frac /frikfrak/ *n.m.* (*fam.*) break-in.
friche (en) /(ɑ̃)friʃ/ *adv.* fallow. **être en ~,** lie fallow.
friction /friksjɔ̃/ *n.f.* friction; (*massage*) rub-down. **~ner** /-jɔne/ *v.t.* rub (down).
frigidaire /friʒidɛr/ *n.m.* (P.) refrigerator.
frigid|e /friʒid/ *a.* frigid. **~ité** *n.f.* frigidity.
frigo /frigo/ *n.m.* (*fam.*) fridge.
frigorif|ier /frigɔrifje/ *v.t.* refrigerate. **~ique** *a.* (*vitrine etc.*) refrigerated.
frileu|x, ~se /frilø, -z/ *a.* sensitive to cold.
frimousse /frimus/ *n.f.* (sweet) face.
fringale /frɛ̃gal/ *n.f.* (*fam.*) ravenous appetite.
fringant, ~e /frɛ̃gɑ̃, -t/ *a.* dashing.
fringues /frɛ̃g/ *n.f. pl.* (*fam.*) togs.
friper /fripe/ *v.t.*, **se ~** *v. pr.* crumple.
frip|ier, ~ière /fripje, -jɛr/ *n.m., f.* second-hand clothes dealer.
fripon, ~ne /fripɔ̃, -ɔn/ *n.m., f.* rascal. —*a.* rascally.
fripouille /fripuj/ *n.f.* rogue.
frire /frir/ *v.t./i.* fry. **faire ~,** fry.
frise /friz/ *n.f.* frieze.
fris|er[1] /frize/ *v.t./i.* (*cheveux*) curl; (*personne*) curl the hair of. **~é** *a.* curly.
friser[2] /frize/ *v.t.* (*surface*) skim.
frisquet /friskɛ/ *a.m.* (*fam.*) chilly.
frisson /frisɔ̃/ *n.m.* (*de froid*) shiver; (*de peur*) shudder. **~ner** /-ɔne/ *v.i.* shiver; shudder.
frit, ~e /fri, -t/ *a.* fried. —*n.f.* chip.
friteuse /fritøz/ *n.f.* (deep) fryer.
friture /frityr/ *n.f.* fried fish; (*huile*) (frying) oil *ou* fat.
frivol|e /frivɔl/ *a.* frivolous. **~ité** *n.f.* frivolity.
froid, ~e /frwa, -d/ *a.* & *n.m.* cold. **avoir/prendre ~,** be/catch cold. **il fait ~,** it is cold. **~ement** /-dmɑ̃/ *adv.* coldly; (*calculer*) coolly. **~eur** /-dœr/ *n.f.* coldness.
froisser /frwase/ *v.t.* crumple; (*fig.*) offend. **se ~** *v. pr.* crumple; (*fig.*) take offence.
frôler /frole/ *v.t.* brush against, skim; (*fig.*) come close to.
fromag|e /frɔmaʒ/ *n.m.* cheese. **~er, ~ère** *a.* cheese; *n.m., f.* cheese maker; (*marchand*) cheesemonger. **~erie** *n.f.* (*local*) cheese factory.
froment /frɔmɑ̃/ *n.m.* wheat.
froncer /frɔ̃se/ *v.t.* gather. **~ les sourcils,** frown.
fronde /frɔ̃d/ *n.f.* sling; (*fig.*) revolt.
front /frɔ̃/ *n.m.* forehead; (*mil., pol.*) front. **de ~,** at the same time; (*de face*) head-on; (*côte à côte*) abreast. **faire ~ à,** face up to. **~al** (*m. pl.* **~aux**) /-tal, -to/ *a.* frontal.
front|ière /frɔ̃tjɛr/ *n.f.* border,

frontier. **~alier, ~alière** *a.* border, frontier.

frott|er /frɔte/ *v.t./i.* rub; (*allumette*) strike. **~ement** *n.m.* rubbing.

frouss|e /frus/ *n.f.* (*fam.*) fear. **avoir la ~e,** (*fam.*) be scared. **~ard, ~arde** *n.m., f.* (*fam.*) coward.

fructifier /fryktifje/ *v.i.* bear fruit.

fructueu|x, ~se /fryktɥø, -z/ *a.* fruitful.

frug|al (*m. pl.* **~aux**) /frygal, -o/ *a.* frugal. **~alité** *n.f.* frugality.

fruit /frɥi/ *n.m.* fruit. **des ~s,** (some) fruit. **~s de mer,** seafood. **~é** /-te/ *a.* fruity. **~ier, ~ière** /-tje, -tjɛr/ *a.* fruit; *n.m., f.* fruiterer.

fruste /fryst/ *a.* coarse.

frustr|er /frystre/ *v.t.* frustrate. **~ation** *n.f.* frustration.

fuel /fjul/ *n.m.* fuel oil.

fugiti|f, ~ve /fyʒitif, -v/ *a.* (*passager*) fleeting. —*n.m., f.* fugitive.

fugue /fyg/ *n.f.* (*mus.*) fugue. **faire une ~,** abscond.

fuir† /fɥir/ *v.i.* flee, run away; (*temps*) fly; (*eau, robinet, etc.*) leak. —*v.t.* (*éviter*) shun.

fuite /fɥit/ *n.f.* flight; (*de liquide, d'une nouvelle*) leak. **en ~,** on the run. **mettre en ~,** put to flight. **prendre la ~,** take (to) flight.

fulgurant, ~e /fylgyrɑ̃, -t/ *a.* (*vitesse*) lightning.

fumée /fyme/ *n.f.* smoke; (*vapeur*) steam.

fum|er /fyme/ *v.t./i.* smoke; (*soupe*) steam. **~e-cigarette** *n.m. invar.* cigarette-holder. **~é** *a.* (*poisson, verre*) smoked. **~eur, ~euse** *n.m., f.* smoker.

fumet /fymɛ/ *n.m.* aroma.

fumeu|x, ~se /fymø, -z/ *a.* (*confus*) hazy.

fumier /fymje/ *n.m.* manure.

fumiste /fymist/ *n.m.* heating engineer. —*n.m./f.* (*employé: fam.*) shirker.

funambule /fynɑ̃byl/ *n.m./f.* tightrope walker.

funèbre /fynɛbr/ *a.* funeral; (*fig.*) gloomy.

funérailles /fyneraj/ *n.f. pl.* funeral.

funéraire /fynerɛr/ *a.* funeral.

funeste /fynɛst/ *a.* fatal; (*fig.*) disastrous.

funiculaire /fynikylɛr/ *n.m.* funicular.

fur /fyr/ *n.m.* **au ~ et à mesure,** as one goes along, progressively. **au ~ et à mesure que,** as.

furet /fyrɛ/ *n.m.* ferret.

fureter /fyrte/ *v.i.* nose (about).

fureur /fyrœr/ *n.f.* fury; (*passion*) passion. **avec ~,** furiously; passionately. **mettre en ~,** infuriate.

furie /fyri/ *n.f.* fury; (*femme*) shrew.

furieu|x, ~se /fyrjø, -z/ *a.* furious.

furoncle /fyrɔ̃kl/ *n.m.* boil.

furti|f, ~ve /fyrtif, -v/ *a.* furtive.

fusain /fyzɛ̃/ *n.m.* (*crayon*) charcoal; (*arbre*) spindle-tree.

fuseau (*pl.* **~x**) /fyzo/ *n.m.* ski trousers; (*pour filer*) spindle. **~ horaire,** time zone.

fusée /fyze/ *n.f.* rocket.

fuselage /fyzlaʒ/ *n.m.* fuselage.

fuser /fyze/ *v.i.* issue forth.

fusible /fyzibl/ *n.m.* fuse.

fusil /fyzi/ *n.m.* rifle, gun; (*de chasse*) shotgun. **~ mitrailleur,** machine-gun.

fusill|er /fyzije/ *v.t.* shoot. **~ade** *n.f.* shooting.

fusion /fyzjɔ̃/ *n.f.* fusion; (*comm.*) merger. **~ner** /-jɔne/ *v.t./i.* merge.

fut /fy/ *voir* **être.**

fût /fy/ *n.m.* (*tonneau*) barrel; (*d'arbre*) trunk.

futaie /fytɛ/ *n.f.* forest.

futé /fyte/ *a.* cunning.

futil|e /fytil/ *a.* futile. **~ité** *n.f.* futility.
futur /fytyr/ *a.* & *n.m.* future. **~e maman,** mother-to-be.
fuyant, ~e /fɥijɑ̃, -t/ *a.* (*front, ligne*) receding; (*personne*) evasive.
fuyard, ~e /fɥijar, -d/ *n.m., f.* runaway.

G

gabardine /gabardin/ *n.f.* gabardine.
gabarit /gabari/ *n.m.* dimension; (*patron*) template; (*fig.*) calibre.
gâcher /gɑʃe/ *v.t.* (*gâter*) spoil; (*gaspiller*) waste.
gâchette /gɑʃɛt/ *n.f.* trigger.
gâchis /gɑʃi/ *n.m.* mess; (*gaspillage*) waste.
gadoue /gadu/ *n.f.* sludge; (*neige*) slush.
gaff|e /gaf/ *n.f.* blunder. **faire ~e,** (*fam.*) be careful (**à,** of). **~er** *v.i.* blunder.
gag /gag/ *n.m.* gag.
gage /gaʒ/ *n.m.* pledge; (*de jeu*) forfeit. **~s,** (*salaire*) wages. **en ~ de,** as a token of. **mettre en ~,** pawn.
gager /gaʒe/ *v.t.* wager (**que,** that).
gageure /gaʒyr/ *n.f.* wager (against all the odds).
gagn|er /gaɲe/ *v.t.* (*match, prix, etc.*) win; (*argent, pain*) earn; (*temps, terrain*) gain; (*atteindre*) reach; (*convaincre*) win over. —*v.i.* win; (*fig.*) gain. **~er sa vie,** earn one's living. **~ant, ~ante,** *a.* winning; *n.m., f.* winner. **~e-pain** *n.m. invar.* job.
gai /ge/ *a.* cheerful; (*ivre*) merry. **~ement** *adv.* cheerfully. **~eté** *n.f.* cheerfulness. **~etés** *n.f. pl.* delights.
gaillard, ~e /gajar, -d/ *a.* hale and hearty; (*grivois*) coarse. —*n.m.* hale and hearty fellow; (*type: fam.*) fellow.
gain /gɛ̃/ *n.m.* (*salaire*) earnings; (*avantage*) gain; (*économie*) saving. **~s,** (*comm.*) profits; (*au jeu*) winnings.
gaine /gɛn/ *n.f.* (*corset*) girdle; (*étui*) sheath.
gala /gala/ *n.m.* gala.
galant, ~e /galɑ̃, -t/ *a.* courteous; (*scène, humeur*) romantic.
galaxie /galaksi/ *n.f.* galaxy.
galb|e /galb/ *n.m.* curve. **~é** *a.* shapely.
gale /gal/ *n.f.* (*de chat etc.*) mange.
galère /galɛr/ *n.f.* (*navire*) galley.
galerie /galri/ *n.f.* gallery; (*théâtre*) circle; (*de voiture*) roof-rack.
galet /galɛ/ *n.m.* pebble.
galette /galɛt/ *n.f.* flat cake.
galeu|x, ~se /galø, -z/ *a.* (*animal*) mangy.
galimatias /galimatja/ *n.m.* gibberish.
Galles /gal/ *n.f. pl.* **le pays de ~,** Wales.
gallois, ~e /galwa, -z/ *a.* Welsh. —*n.m., f.* Welshman, Welshwoman. —*n.m.* (*lang.*) Welsh.
galon /galɔ̃/ *n.m.* braid; (*mil.*) stripe.
galop /galo/ *n.m.* gallop. **aller au ~,** gallop. **~ d'essai,** trial run. **~er** /-ɔpe/ *v.i.* (*cheval*) gallop; (*personne*) run.
galopade /galɔpad/ *n.f.* wild rush.
galopin /galɔpɛ̃/ *n.m.* (*fam.*) rascal.
galvaniser /galvanize/ *v.t.* galvanize.
galvauder /galvode/ *v.t.* debase (through misuse).
gambad|e /gɑ̃bad/ *n.f.* leap. **~er** *v.i.* leap about.
gamelle /gamɛl/ *n.f.* (*de soldat*) mess bowl *ou* tin; (*d'ouvrier*) food-box.
gamin, ~e /gamɛ̃, -in/ *a.* playful. —*n.m., f.* (*fam.*) kid.

gamme /gam/ *n.f.* (*mus.*) scale; (*série*) range.

gang /gɑ̃g/ *n.m.* gang.

gangrène /gɑ̃grɛn/ *n.f.* gangrene.

gangster /gɑ̃gstɛr/ *n.m.* gangster; (*escroc*) crook.

gant /gɑ̃/ *n.m.* glove. **~ de toilette,** face-flannel, face-cloth. **~é** /gɑ̃te/ *a.* (*personne*) wearing gloves.

garag|e /garaʒ/ *n.m.* garage. **~iste** *n.m.* garage owner; (*employé*) garage mechanic.

garant, ~e /garɑ̃, -t/ *n.m., f.* guarantor. —*n.m.* guarantee. **se porter ~ de,** guarantee.

garant|ie /garɑ̃ti/ *n.f.* guarantee; (*protection*) safeguard. **~ies,** (*de police d'assurance*) cover. **~ir** *v.t.* guarantee; (*protéger*) protect (**de,** from).

garçon /garsɔ̃/ *n.m.* boy; (*célibataire*) bachelor. **~ (de café),** waiter. **~ d'honneur,** best man.

garçonnière /garsɔnjɛr/ *n.f.* bachelor flat.

garde[1] /gard/ *n.f.* guard; (*d'enfants, de bagages*) care; (*service*) guard (duty); (*infirmière*) nurse. **de ~,** on duty. **~ à vue,** (police) custody. **mettre en ~,** warn. **prendre ~,** be careful (**à,** of).

garde[2] /gard/ *n.m.* (*personne*) guard; (*de propriété, parc*) warden. **~ champêtre,** village policeman. **~ du corps,** bodyguard.

gard|er /garde/ *v.t.* (*conserver, maintenir*) keep; (*vêtement*) keep on; (*surveiller*) look after; (*défendre*) guard. **se ~er** *v. pr.* (*denrée*) keep. **~er le lit,** stay in bed. **se ~er de faire,** be careful not to do. **~e-à-vous** *int.* (*mil.*) attention. **~e-boue** *n.m. invar.* mudguard. **~e-chasse** (*pl.* **~es-chasses**) *n.m.* gamekeeper. **~e-fou** *n.m.* railing. **~e-manger** *n.m. invar.* (food) safe; (*placard*) larder. **~e-robe** *n.f.* wardrobe.

garderie /gardəri/ *n.f.* day nursery.

gardien, ~ne /gardjɛ̃, -jɛn/ *n.m., f.* (*de prison, réserve*) warden; (*d'immeuble*) caretaker; (*de musée*) attendant; (*garde*) guard. **~ de but,** goalkeeper. **~ de la paix,** policeman. **~ de nuit,** night watchman. **~ne d'enfants,** child-minder, baby-sitter.

gare[1] /gar/ *n.f.* (*rail.*) station. **~ routière,** coach station; (*Amer.*) bus station.

gare[2] /gar/ *int.* **~ à,** watch out for. **~ à toi,** watch out.

garer /gare/ *v.t.*, **se ~** *v. pr.* park. **se ~ (de),** get out of the way (of).

gargariser (se) /(sə)gargarize/ *v. pr.* gargle.

gargarisme /gargarism/ *n.m.* gargle.

gargouille /garguj/ *n.f.* (water)-spout; (*sculptée*) gargoyle.

gargouiller /garguje/ *v.i.* gurgle.

garnement /garnəmɑ̃/ *n.m.* rascal.

garn|ir /garnir/ *v.t.* fill; (*décorer*) decorate; (*couvrir*) cover; (*doubler*) line; (*culin.*) garnish. **se ~ir** *v. pr.* (*lieu*) fill. **~i** *a.* (*plat*) served with vegetables. **bien ~i,** (*rempli*) well-filled.

garnison /garnizɔ̃/ *n.f.* garrison.

garniture /garnityr/ *n.f.* (*légumes*) vegetables; (*ornement*) trimming; (*de voiture*) trim.

gars /gɑ/ *n.m.* (*fam.*) fellow.

gas-oil /gɑzɔjl/ *n.m.* diesel oil.

gaspill|er /gaspije/ *v.t.* waste. **~age** *n.m.* waste.

gastrique /gastrik/ *a.* gastric.

gastronom|e /gastrɔnɔm/ *n.m./f.* gourmet. **~ie** *n.f.* gastronomy.

gâteau (*pl.* **~x**) /gɑto/ *n.m.* cake. **~ sec,** biscuit; (*Amer.*) cookie.

gâter /gɑte/ *v.t.* spoil. **se ~** *v. pr.* (*dent, viande*) go bad; (*temps*) get worse.

gâterie /gɑtri/ *n.f.* little treat.

gâteu|x, ~se /gɑtø, -z/ *a.* senile.
gauch|e[1] /goʃ/ *a.* left. **à ~e,** on the left; (*direction*) (to the) left. **la ~e,** the left (side); (*pol.*) the left (wing). **~er, ~ère** *a.* & *n.m., f.* left-handed (person). **~iste** *a.* & *n.m./f.* (*pol.*) leftist.
gauche[2] /goʃ/ *a.* (*maladroit*) awkward. **~rie** *n.f.* awkwardness.
gauchir /goʃir/ *v.t./i.*, **se ~** *v. pr.* warp.
gaufre /gofr/ *n.f.* waffle.
gaufrette /gofrɛt/ *n.f.* wafer.
gaulois, ~e /golwa, -z/ *a.* Gallic; (*fig.*) bawdy. —*n.m., f.* Gaul.
gausser (se) /(sə)gose/ *v. pr.* **se ~ de,** deride, scoff at.
gaver /gave/ *v.t.* force-feed; (*fig.*) cram. **se ~ de,** gorge o.s. with.
gaz /gɑz/ *n.m. invar.* gas. **~ lacrymogène,** tear-gas.
gaze /gɑz/ *n.f.* gauze.
gazelle /gazɛl/ *n.f.* gazelle.
gazer /gɑze/ *v.i.* (*marcher: fam.*) be *ou* go all right.
gazette /gazɛt/ *n.f.* newspaper.
gazeu|x, ~se /gɑzø, -z/ *a.* (*boisson*) fizzy.
gazomètre /gɑzɔmɛtr/ *n.m.* gasometer.
gazon /gɑzɔ̃/ *n.m.* lawn, grass.
gazouiller /gazuje/ *v.i.* (*oiseau*) chirp; (*bébé*) babble.
geai /ʒɛ/ *n.m.* jay.
géant, ~e /ʒeɑ̃, -t/ *a.* & *n.m., f.* giant.
geindre /ʒɛ̃dr/ *v.i.* groan.
gel /ʒɛl/ *n.m.* frost; (*pâte*) gel; (*comm.*) freezing.
gélatine /ʒelatin/ *n.f.* gelatine.
gel|er /ʒəle/ *v.t./i.* freeze. **~é** *a.* frozen; (*membre abîmé*) frostbitten. **~ée** *n.f.* frost; (*culin.*) jelly. **~ée blanche,** hoar-frost.
gélule /ʒelyl/ *n.f.* (*méd.*) capsule.
gém|ir /ʒemir/ *v.i.* groan. **~issement** *n.m.* groan(ing).
gênant, ~e /ʒɛnɑ̃, -t/ *a.* embarrassing; (*irritant*) annoying.
gencive /ʒɑ̃siv/ *n.f.* gum.
gendarme /ʒɑ̃darm/ *n.m.* policeman, gendarme. **~rie** /-əri/ *n.f.* police force; (*local*) police station.
gendre /ʒɑ̃dr/ *n.m.* son-in-law.
gène /ʒɛn/ *n.m.* gene.
gêne /ʒɛn/ *n.f.* discomfort; (*confusion*) embarrassment; (*dérangement*) trouble. **dans la ~,** in financial straits.
généalogie /ʒenealɔʒi/ *n.f.* genealogy.
gên|er /ʒene/ *v.t.* bother, disturb; (*troubler*) embarrass; (*encombrer*) hamper; (*bloquer*) block. **se ~er** *v. pr.* put o.s. out. **~é** *a.* embarrassed.
génér|al (*m. pl.* **~aux**) /ʒeneral, -o/ *a.* general. —*n.m.* (*pl.* **~aux**) general. **en ~al,** in general. **~alement** *adv.* generally.
généralis|er /ʒeneralize/ *v.t./i.* generalize. **se ~er** *v. pr.* become general. **~ation** *n.f.* generalization.
généraliste /ʒeneralist/ *n.m./f.* general practitioner.
généralité /ʒeneralite/ *n.f.* majority. **~s,** general points.
génération /ʒenerɑsjɔ̃/ *n.f.* generation.
génératrice /ʒeneratris/ *n.f.* generator.
généreu|x, ~se /ʒenerø, -z/ *a.* generous. **~sement** *adv.* generously.
générique /ʒenerik/ *n.m.* (*cinéma*) credits.
générosité /ʒenerozite/ *n.f.* generosity.
genêt /ʒənɛ/ *n.m.* (*plante*) broom.
génétique /ʒenetik/ *a.* genetic. —*n.f.* genetics.
Genève /ʒənɛv/ *n.m./f.* Geneva.
gén|ial (*m. pl.* **~iaux**) /ʒenjal, -jo/ *a.* brilliant.
génie /ʒeni/ *n.m.* genius. **~ civil,** civil engineering.
génisse /ʒenis/ *n.f.* heifer.

génit|al (*m. pl.* **~aux**) /ʒenital, -o/ *a.* genital.
génocide /ʒenɔsid/ *n.m.* genocide.
genou (*pl.* **~x**) /ʒnu/ *n.m.* knee. **à ~x,** kneeling. **se mettre à ~x,** kneel.
genre /ʒɑ̃r/ *n.m.* sort, kind; (*attitude*) manner; (*gram.*) gender. **~ de vie,** life-style.
gens /ʒɑ̃/ *n.m./f. pl.* people.
genti|l, ~lle /ʒɑ̃ti, -j/ *a.* kind, nice; (*agréable*) nice; (*sage*) good. **~llesse** /-jɛs/ *n.f.* kindness. **~ment** *adv.* kindly.
géograph|ie /ʒeɔgrafi/ *n.f.* geography. **~e** *n.m./f.* geographer. **~ique** *a.* geographical.
geôl|ier, ~ière /ʒolje, -jɛr/ *n.m., f.* gaoler, jailer.
géolo|gie /ʒeɔlɔʒi/ *n.f.* geology. **~gique** *a.* geological. **~gue** *n.m./f.* geologist.
géomètre /ʒeɔmɛtr/ *n.m.* surveyor.
géométr|ie /ʒeɔmetri/ *n.f.* geometry. **~ique** *a.* geometric.
géranium /ʒeranjɔm/ *n.m.* geranium.
géran|t, ~te /ʒerɑ̃, -t/ *n.m., f.* manager, manageress. **~t d'immeuble,** landlord's agent. **~ce** *n.f.* management.
gerbe /ʒɛrb/ *n.f.* (*de fleurs, d'eau*) spray; (*de blé*) sheaf.
ger|cer /ʒɛrse/ *v.t./i.,* **se ~cer** *v. pr.* chap. **~çure** *n.f.* chap.
gérer /ʒere/ *v.t.* manage.
germanique /ʒɛrmanik/ *a.* Germanic.
germ|e /ʒɛrm/ *n.m.* germ. **~er** *v.i.* germinate.
gésir /ʒezir/ *v.i.* be lying.
gestation /ʒɛstɑsjɔ̃/ *n.f.* gestation.
geste /ʒɛst/ *n.m.* gesture.
gesticul|er /ʒɛstikyle/ *v.i.* gesticulate. **~ation** *n.f.* gesticulation.
gestion /ʒɛstjɔ̃/ *n.f.* management.
geyser /ʒɛzɛr/ *n.m.* geyser.
ghetto /gɛto/ *n.m.* ghetto.
gibecière /ʒibsjɛr/ *n.f.* shoulder-bag.
gibet /ʒibɛ/ *n.m.* gallows.
gibier /ʒibje/ *n.m.* (*animaux*) game.
giboulée /ʒibule/ *n.f.* shower.
gicl|er /ʒikle/ *v.i.* squirt. **faire ~er,** squirt. **~ée** *n.f.* squirt.
gifl|e /ʒifl/ *n.f.* slap (in the face). **~er** *v.t.* slap.
gigantesque /ʒigɑ̃tɛsk/ *a.* gigantic.
gigot /ʒigo/ *n.m.* leg (of mutton).
gigoter /ʒigɔte/ *v.i.* (*fam.*) wriggle.
gilet /ʒilɛ/ *n.m.* waistcoat; (*cardigan*) cardigan. **~ (de corps),** vest. **~ de sauvetage,** life-jacket.
gin /dʒin/ *n.m.* gin.
gingembre /ʒɛ̃ʒɑ̃br/ *n.m.* ginger.
girafe /ʒiraf/ *n.f.* giraffe.
giroflée /ʒirɔfle/ *n.f.* wallflower.
girouette /ʒirwɛt/ *n.f.* weather-cock, weather-vane.
gisement /ʒizmɑ̃/ *n.m.* deposit.
gitan, ~e /ʒitɑ̃, -an/ *n.m., f.* gypsy.
gîte /ʒit/ *n.m.* (*maison*) home; (*abri*) shelter.
givr|e /ʒivr/ *n.m.* (hoar-)frost. **~er** *v.t.,* **se ~er** *v. pr.* frost (up).
glace /glas/ *n.f.* ice; (*crème*) ice-cream; (*vitre*) window; (*miroir*) mirror; (*verre*) glass.
glac|er /glase/ *v.t.* freeze; (*gâteau, boisson*) ice; (*papier*) glaze; (*pétrifier*) chill. **se ~er** *v. pr.* freeze. **~é** *a.* (*vent, accueil*) icy.
glac|ial (*m. pl.* **~iaux**) /glasjal, -jo/ *a.* icy.
glacier /glasje/ *n.m.* (*géog.*) glacier; (*vendeur*) ice-cream man.
glacière /glasjɛr/ *n.f.* icebox.
glaçon /glasɔ̃/ *n.m.* block of ice; (*pour boisson*) ice-cube; (*sur le toit*) icicle.
glaïeul /glajœl/ *n.m.* gladiolus.
glaise /glɛz/ *n.f.* clay.
gland /glɑ̃/ *n.m.* acorn; (*ornement*) tassel.
glande /glɑ̃d/ *n.f.* gland.
glaner /glane/ *v.t.* glean.

glapir /glapir/ *v.i.* yelp.
glas /glɑ/ *n.m.* knell.
glissant, ~e /glisɑ̃, -t/ *a.* slippery.
gliss|er /glise/ *v.i.* slide; (*sur l'eau*) glide; (*déraper*) slip; (*véhicule*) skid. —*v.t.*, **se ~er** *v. pr.* slip (**dans,** into). **~ade** *n.f.* sliding; (*endroit*) slide. **~ement** *n.m.* sliding; gliding; (*fig.*) shift. **~ement de terrain,** landslide.
glissière /glisjɛr/ *n.f.* groove. **à ~,** (*porte, système*) sliding.
glob|al (*m. pl.* **~aux**) /glɔbal, -o/ *a.* (*entier, général*) overall. **~alement** *adv.* as a whole.
globe /glɔb/ *n.m.* globe. **~ oculaire,** eyeball. **~ terrestre,** globe.
globule /glɔbyl/ *n.m.* (*du sang*) corpuscle.
gloire /glwar/ *n.f.* glory.
glorieu|x, ~se /glɔrjø, -z/ *a.* glorious. **~sement** *adv.* gloriously.
glorifier /glɔrifje/ *v.t.* glorify.
glossaire /glɔsɛr/ *n.m.* glossary.
glouss|er /gluse/ *v.i.* chuckle; (*poule*) cluck. **~ement** *n.m.* chuckle; cluck.
glouton, ~ne /glutɔ̃, -ɔn/ *a.* gluttonous. —*n.m., f.* glutton.
gluant, ~e /glyɑ̃, -t/ *a.* sticky.
glucose /glykoz/ *n.m.* glucose.
glycérine /gliserin/ *n.f.* glycerine.
glycine /glisin/ *n.f.* wistaria.
gnome /gnom/ *n.m.* gnome.
goal /gol/ *n.m.* goalkeeper.
gobelet /gɔblɛ/ *n.m.* tumbler, mug.
gober /gɔbe/ *v.t.* swallow (whole).
godasse /gɔdas/ *n.f.* (*fam.*) shoe.
godet /gɔdɛ/ *n.m.* (small) pot.
goéland /gɔelɑ̃/ *n.m.* (sea)gull.
goélette /gɔelɛt/ *n.f.* schooner.
gogo /gɔgo/ *n.m.* (*fam.*) sucker.
gogo (à) /(a)gɔgo/ *adv.* (*fam.*) galore, in abundance.
goguenard, ~e /gɔgnar, -d/ *a.* mocking.
goguette (en) /(ɑ̃)gɔgɛt/ *adv.* (*fam.*) having a binge *ou* spree.
goinfr|e /gwɛ̃fr/ *n.m.* (*glouton*: *fam.*) pig. **se ~er** *v. pr.* (*fam.*) stuff o.s. like a pig (**de,** with).
golf /gɔlf/ *n.m.* golf.
golfe /gɔlf/ *n.m.* gulf.
gomm|e /gɔm/ *n.f.* rubber; (*Amer.*) eraser; (*résine*) gum. **~er** *v.t.* rub out.
gond /gɔ̃/ *n.m.* hinge.
gondol|e /gɔ̃dɔl/ *n.f.* gondola. **~ier** *n.m.* gondolier.
gondoler (se) /(sə)gɔ̃dɔle/ *v. pr.* warp; (*rire*: *fam.*) split one's sides.
gonfl|er /gɔ̃fle/ *v.t./i.* swell; (*ballon, pneu*) pump up, blow up; (*exagérer*) inflate. **se ~er** *v. pr.* swell. **~é** *a.* swollen; (*courageux*: *fam.*) plucky. **~ement** *n.m.* swelling. **~eur** *n.m.* air pump.
gong /gɔ̃g/ *n.m.* gong.
gorge /gɔrʒ/ *n.f.* throat; (*poitrine*) breast; (*vallée*) gorge.
gorgée /gɔrʒe/ *n.f.* sip, gulp.
gorg|er /gɔrʒe/ *v.t.* fill (**de,** with). **se ~er** *v. pr.* gorge o.s. (**de,** with). **~é de,** full of.
gorille /gɔrij/ *n.m.* gorilla; (*garde*: *fam.*) bodyguard.
gosier /gozje/ *n.m.* throat.
gosse /gɔs/ *n.m./f.* (*fam.*) kid.
gothique /gɔtik/ *a.* Gothic.
goudron /gudrɔ̃/ *n.m.* tar. **~ner** /-ɔne/ *v.t.* tar.
gouffre /gufr/ *n.m.* gulf, abyss.
goujat /guʒa/ *n.m.* lout, boor.
goulot /gulo/ *n.m.* neck.
goulu, ~e /guly/ *a.* gluttonous. —*n.m., f.* glutton.
gourde /gurd/ *n.f.* (*à eau*) flask; (*idiot*: *fam.*) chump.
gourdin /gurdɛ̃/ *n.m.* club, cudgel.
gourer (se) /(sə)gure/ *v. pr.* (*fam.*) make a mistake.
gourmand, ~e /gurmɑ̃, -d/ *a.* greedy. —*n.m., f.* glutton. **~ise** /-diz/ *n.f.* greed; (*mets*) delicacy.
gourmet /gurmɛ/ *n.m.* gourmet.

gourmette /gurmɛt/ *n.f.* chain bracelet.
gousse /gus/ *n.f.* **~ d'ail,** clove of garlic.
goût /gu/ *n.m.* taste.
goûter /gute/ *v.t.* taste; (*apprécier*) enjoy. *—v.i.* have tea. *—n.m.* tea, snack. **~ à** *ou* **de,** taste.
goutt|e /gut/ *n.f.* drop; (*méd.*) gout. **~er** *v.i.* drip.
gouttelette /gutlɛt/ *n.f.* droplet.
gouttière /gutjɛr/ *n.f.* gutter.
gouvernail /guvɛrnaj/ *n.m.* rudder; (*barre*) helm.
gouvernante /guvɛrnɑ̃t/ *n.f.* governess.
gouvernement /guvɛrnəmɑ̃/ *n.m.* government. **~al** (*m. pl.* **~aux**) /-tal, -to/ *a.* government.
gouvern|er /guvɛrne/ *v.t./i.* govern. **~eur** *n.m.* governor.
grâce /grɑs/ *n.f.* (*charme*) grace; (*faveur*) favour; (*relig.*) grace. **~ à,** thanks to.
gracier /grasje/ *v.t.* pardon.
gracieu|x, ~se /grasjø, -z/ *a.* graceful; (*gratuit*) free. **~sement** *adv.* gracefully; free (of charge).
gracile /grasil/ *a.* slender.
gradation /gradɑsjɔ̃/ *n.f.* gradation.
grade /grad/ *n.m.* rank.
gradé /grade/ *n.m.* non-commissioned officer.
gradin /gradɛ̃/ *n.m.* tier, step. **en ~s,** terraced.
graduel, ~le /gradɥɛl/ *a.* gradual.
grad|uer /gradɥe/ *v.t.* (*règle etc.*) graduate. **~uation** *n.f.* graduation.
graffiti /grafiti/ *n.m. pl.* graffiti.
grain /grɛ̃/ *n.m.* grain; (*de café*) bean; (*de chapelet*) bead. **~ de beauté,** mole; (*sur le visage*) beauty spot. **~ de raisin,** grape.
graine /grɛn/ *n.f.* seed.
graissage /grɛsaʒ/ *n.m.* lubrication.
graiss|e /grɛs/ *n.f.* fat; (*lubrifiant*) grease. **~er** *v.t.* grease. **~eux, ~euse** *a.* greasy.
gramm|aire /gramɛr/ *n.f.* grammar. **~atical** (*m. pl.* **~aticaux**) *a.* grammatical.
gramme /gram/ *n.m.* gram.
grand, ~e /grɑ̃, -d/ *a.* big, large; (*haut*) tall; (*mérite, distance, ami*) great; (*bruit*) loud; (*plus âgé*) big. *—adv.* (*ouvrir*) wide. *—n.m., f.* (*adulte*) grown-up; (*enfant*) older child. **au ~ air,** in the open air. **au ~ jour,** in broad daylight; (*fig.*) in the open. **de ~e envergure,** large-scale. **en ~e partie,** largely. **~e banlieue,** outer suburbs. **G~e-Bretagne** *n.f.* Great Britain. **pas ~-chose,** not much. **~e école,** university. **~ ensemble,** housing estate. **~es lignes,** (*rail.*) main lines. **~ magasin,** department store. **~-mère** (*pl.* **~s-mères**) *n.f.* grandmother. **~s-parents** *n.m. pl.* grandparents. **~-père** (*pl.* **~s-pères**) *n.m.* grandfather. **~e personne,** grown-up. **~ public,** general public. **~-rue** *n.f.* high street. **~e surface,** hypermarket. **~es vacances,** summer holidays.
grandement /grɑ̃dmɑ̃/ *adv.* greatly.
grandeur /grɑ̃dœr/ *n.f.* greatness; (*dimension*) size.
grandiose /grɑ̃djoz/ *a.* grandiose.
grandir /grɑ̃dir/ *v.i.* grow; (*bruit*) grow louder. *—v.t.* magnify; (*personne*) make taller.
grange /grɑ̃ʒ/ *n.f.* barn.
granit /granit/ *n.m.* granite.
granulé /granyle/ *n.m.* granule.
graphique /grafik/ *a.* graphic. *—n.m.* graph.
grappe /grap/ *n.f.* cluster. **~ de raisin,** bunch of grapes.
gras, ~se /grɑ, -s/ *a.* fat; (*aliment*) fatty; (*surface*) greasy; (*épais*) thick; (*caractères*) bold. *—n.m.*

(*culin.*) fat. **faire la ~se matinée,** sleep late. **~sement payé,** highly paid.
gratification /gratifikɑsjɔ̃/ *n.f.* bonus.
gratifier /gratifje/ *v.t.* favour, reward (**de,** with).
gratin /gratɛ̃/ *n.m.* baked dish with cheese topping; (*élite*: *fam.*) upper crust.
gratis /gratis/ *adv.* free.
gratitude /gratityd/ *n.f.* gratitude.
gratt|er /grate/ *v.t./i.* scratch; (*avec un outil*) scrape. **se ~er** *v. pr.* scratch o.s. **ça me ~e,** (*fam.*) it itches. **~e-ciel** *n.m. invar.* sky-scraper. **~oir** *n.m.* scraper.
gratuit, ~e /gratɥi, -t/ *a.* free; (*acte*) gratuitous. **~ement** /-tmɑ̃/ *adv.* free (of charge).
gravats /gravɑ/ *n.m. pl.* rubble.
grave /grav/ *a.* serious; (*solennel*) grave; (*voix*) deep; (*accent*) grave. **~ment** *adv.* seriously; gravely.
grav|er /grave/ *v.t.* engrave; (*sur bois*) carve. **~eur** *n.m.* engraver.
gravier /gravje/ *n.m.* gravel; (*morceau*) bit of gravel.
gravillon /gravijɔ̃/ *n.m.* gravel; (*morceau*) bit of gravel. **~s,** gravel.
gravir /gravir/ *v.t.* climb.
gravitation /gravitɑsjɔ̃/ *n.f.* gravitation.
gravité /gravite/ *n.f.* gravity.
graviter /gravite/ *v.i.* revolve.
gravure /gravyr/ *n.f.* engraving; (*de tableau, photo*) print, plate.
gré /gre/ *n.m.* (*volonté*) will; (*goût*) taste. **à son ~,** (*agir*) as one likes. **de bon ~,** willingly.
grec, ~que /grɛk/ *a.* & *n.m., f.* Greek. —*n.m.* (*lang.*) Greek.
Grèce /grɛs/ *n.f.* Greece.
greff|e /grɛf/ *n.f.* graft; (*d'organe*) transplant. **~er** /grefe/ *v.t.* graft; transplant.
greffier /grefje/ *n.m.* clerk of the court.
grégaire /gregɛr/ *a.* gregarious.
grêle[1] /grɛl/ *a.* (*maigre*) spindly; (*voix*) shrill.
grêl|e[2] /grɛl/ *n.f.* hail. **~er** /grele/ *v.i.* hail. **~on** *n.m.* hailstone.
grelot /grəlo/ *n.m.* (little) bell.
grelotter /grəlɔte/ *v.i.* shiver.
grenade[1] /grənad/ *n.f.* (*fruit*) pomegranate.
grenade[2] /grənad/ *n.f.* (*explosif*) grenade.
grenat /grəna/ *a. invar.* dark red.
grenier /grənje/ *n.m.* attic; (*pour grain*) loft.
grenouille /grənuj/ *n.f.* frog.
grésiller /grezije/ *v.i.* sizzle; (*radio*) crackle.
grève[1] /grɛv/ *n.f.* strike. **se mettre en ~,** go on strike. **~ du zèle,** work-to-rule; (*Amer.*) rule-book slow-down. **~ perlée,** go-slow; (*Amer.*) slow-down strike. **~ sauvage,** wildcat strike.
grève[2] /grɛv/ *n.f.* (*rivage*) shore.
gréviste /grevist/ *n.m./f.* striker.
gribouill|er /gribuje/ *v.t./i.* scribble. **~is** /-ji/ *n.m.* scribble.
grief /grijɛf/ *n.m.* grievance.
grièvement /grijɛvmɑ̃/ *adv.* seriously.
griff|e /grif/ *n.f.* claw; (*de couturier*) label. **~er** *v.t.* scratch, claw.
griffonner /grifɔne/ *v.t./i.* scrawl.
grignoter /griɲɔte/ *v.t./i.* nibble.
gril /gril/ *n.m.* grill, grid(iron).
grillade /grijad/ *n.f.* (*viande*) grill.
grillage /grijaʒ/ *n.m.* wire netting.
grille /grij/ *n.f.* railings; (*portail*) (metal) gate; (*de fenêtre*) bars; (*de cheminée*) grate; (*fig.*) grid.
grill|er /grije/ *v.t./i.* burn; (*ampoule*) blow; (*feu rouge*) go through. **(faire) ~er,** (*pain*) toast; (*viande*) grill; (*café*) roast. **~e-pain** *n.m. invar.* toaster.
grillon /grijɔ̃/ *n.m.* cricket.
grimace /grimas/ *n.f.* (funny) face; (*de douleur, dégoût*) grimace.

grimer /grime/ *v.t.*, **se ~** *v. pr.* make up.

grimper /grɛ̃pe/ *v.t./i.* climb.

grinc|er /grɛ̃se/ *v.i.* creak. **~er des dents,** grind one's teeth. **~ement** *n.m.* creak(ing).

grincheu|x, ~se /grɛ̃ʃø, -z/ *a.* grumpy.

gripp|e /grip/ *n.f.* influenza, flu. **être ~é,** have (the) flu; (*mécanisme*) be seized up *ou* jammed.

gris, ~e /gri, -z/ *a.* grey; (*saoul*) tipsy.

grisaille /grizɑj/ *n.f.* greyness, gloom.

griser /grize/ *v.t.* intoxicate.

grisonner /grizɔne/ *v.i.* go grey.

grive /griv/ *n.f.* (*oiseau*) thrush.

grivois, ~e /grivwa, -z/ *a.* bawdy.

grog /grɔg/ *n.m.* grog.

grogn|er /grɔɲe/ *v.i.* growl; (*cochon*) grunt. **~ement** *n.m.* growl; grunt.

grognon, ~ne /grɔɲɔ̃, -ɔn/ *a.* grumpy.

groin /grwɛ̃/ *n.m.* snout.

grommeler /grɔmle/ *v.t./i.* mutter.

grond|er /grɔ̃de/ *v.i.* rumble; (*chien*) growl; (*conflit etc.*) be brewing. —*v.t.* scold. **~ement** *n.m.* rumbling; growling.

groom /grum/ *n.m.* page(-boy).

gros, ~se /gro, -s/ *a.* big, large; (*gras*) fat; (*important*) great; (*épais*) thick; (*lourd*) heavy. —*adv.* (*beaucoup*) a lot. —*n.m., f.* fat man, fat woman. —*n.m.* **le ~ de,** the bulk of. **de ~,** (*comm.*) wholesale. **en ~,** roughly; (*comm.*) wholesale. **~ bonnet,** (*fam.*) bigwig. **~ lot,** jackpot. **~ mot,** rude word. **~ titre,** headline.

groseille /grozɛj/ *n.f.* (red *ou* white) currant. **~ à maquereau,** gooseberry.

grosse /gros/ *voir* **gros.**

grossesse /grosɛs/ *n.f.* pregnancy.

grosseur /grosœr/ *n.f.* (*volume*) size; (*enflure*) lump.

gross|ier, ~ière /grosje, -jɛr/ *a.* coarse, rough; (*imitation, instrument*) crude; (*vulgaire*) coarse; (*insolent*) rude; (*erreur*) gross. **~ièrement** *adv.* (*sommairement*) roughly; (*vulgairement*) coarsely. **~ièreté** *n.f.* coarseness; crudeness; rudeness; (*mot*) rude word.

grossir /grosir/ *v.t./i.* swell; (*personne*) put on weight; (*au microscope*) magnify; (*augmenter*) grow; (*exagérer*) magnify.

grossiste /grosist/ *n.m./f.* wholesaler.

grosso modo /grosomɔdo/ *adv.* roughly.

grotesque /grɔtɛsk/ *a.* grotesque; (*ridicule*) ludicrous.

grotte /grɔt/ *n.f.* cave, grotto.

grouill|er /gruje/ *v.i.* be swarming (**de,** with). **~ant, ~ante** *a.* swarming.

groupe /grup/ *n.m.* group. **~ électrogène,** generating set. **~ scolaire,** school block.

group|er /grupe/ *v.t.*, **se ~er** *v. pr.* group (together). **~ement** *n.m.* grouping.

grue /gry/ *n.f.* (*machine, oiseau*) crane.

grumeau (*pl.* **~x**) /grymo/ *n.m.* lump (*in gravy, soup, etc.*).

gruyère /gryjɛr/ *n.m.* gruyère (cheese).

gué /ge/ *n.m.* ford. **passer** *ou* **traverser à ~,** ford.

guenille /gənij/ *n.f.* rag.

guenon /gənɔ̃/ *n.f.* female monkey.

guépard /gepar/ *n.m.* cheetah.

guêp|e /gɛp/ *n.f.* wasp. **~ier** /gepje/ *n.m.* wasp's nest; (*fig.*) trap.

guère /gɛr/ *adv.* **(ne) ~,** hardly. **il n'y a ~ de pain,** there is hardly any bread.

guéridon /geridɔ̃/ *n.m.* pedestal table.

guérill|a /gerija/ *n.f.* guerrilla

warfare. **~ero** /-jero/ *n.m.* guerrilla.

guér|ir /gerir/ *v.t.* (*personne, maladie, mal*) cure (**de,** of); (*plaie, membre*) heal. —*v.i.* get better. **~ir de,** recover from. **~ison** *n.f.* curing; healing; (*de personne*) recovery. **~isseur, ~isseuse** *n.m., f.* healer.

guérite /gerit/ *n.f.* (*mil.*) sentry-box.

guerre /gɛr/ *n.f.* war. **en ~,** at war. **faire la ~,** wage war (**à,** against). **~ civile,** civil war. **~ d'usure,** war of attrition.

guerr|ier, ~ière /gɛrje, -jɛr/ *a.* warlike. —*n.m., f.* warrior.

guet /gɛ/ *n.m.* watch. **faire le ~,** be on the watch. **~-apens** /gɛtapɑ̃/ *n.m. invar.* ambush.

guetter /gete/ *v.t.* watch; (*attendre*) watch out for.

guetteur /gɛtœr/ *n.m.* look-out.

gueule /gœl/ *n.f.* mouth; (*figure: fam.*) face.

gueuler /gœle/ *v.i.* (*fam.*) bawl.

gueuleton /gœltɔ̃/ *n.m.* (*repas: fam.*) blow-out, slap-up meal.

gui /gi/ *n.m.* mistletoe.

guichet /giʃɛ/ *n.m.* window, counter; (*de gare*) ticket-office (window); (*de théâtre*) box-office (window).

guide /gid/ *n.m.* guide. —*n.f.* (*fille scout*) girl guide. **~s** *n.f. pl.* (*rênes*) reins.

guider /gide/ *v.t.* guide.

guidon /gidɔ̃/ *n.m.* handlebars.

guignol /giɲɔl/ *n.m.* puppet; (*personne*) clown; (*spectacle*) puppet-show.

guillemets /gijmɛ/ *n.m. pl.* quotation marks, inverted commas.

guilleret, ~te /gijrɛ, -t/ *a.* sprightly, jaunty.

guillotin|e /gijɔtin/ *n.f.* guillotine. **~er** *v.t.* guillotine.

guimauve /gimov/ *n.f.* marshmallow.

guindé /gɛ̃de/ *a.* stilted.

guirlande /girlɑ̃d/ *n.f.* garland.

guise /giz/ *n.f.* **à sa ~,** as one pleases. **en ~ de,** by way of.

guitar|e /gitar/ *n.f.* guitar. **~iste** *n.m./f.* guitarist.

guttur|al (*m. pl.* **~aux**) /gytyral, -o/ *a.* guttural.

gym /ʒim/ *n.f.* gym.

gymnas|e /ʒimnɑz/ *n.m.* gym(nasium). **~te** /-ast/ *n.m./f.* gymnast. **~tique** /-astik/ *n.f.* gymnastics.

gynécolo|gie /ʒinekɔlɔʒi/ *n.f.* gynaecology. **~gique** *a.* gynaecological. **~gue** *n.m./f.* gynaecologist.

H

habile /abil/ *a.* skilful, clever. **~té** *n.f.* skill.

habill|er /abije/ *v.t.* dress (**de,** in); (*équiper*) clothe; (*recouvrir*) cover (**de,** with). **s'~er** *v. pr.* dress (o.s.), get dressed; (*se déguiser*) dress up. **~é** *a.* (*costume*) dressy. **~ement** *n.m.* clothing.

habit /abi/ *n.m.* dress, outfit; (*de cérémonie*) tails. **~s,** clothes.

habitable /abitabl/ *a.* (in)habitable.

habitant, ~e /abitɑ̃, -t/ *n.m., f.* (*de maison*) occupant; (*de pays*) inhabitant.

habitat /abita/ *n.m.* housing conditions; (*d'animal*) habitat.

habitation /abitɑsjɔ̃/ *n.f.* living; (*logement*) house.

habit|er /abite/ *v.i.* live. —*v.t.* live in; (*planète, zone*) inhabit. **~é** *a.* (*terre*) inhabited.

habitude /abityd/ *n.f.* habit. **avoir l'~ de faire,** be used to doing. **d'~,** usually.

habitué, ~e /abitɥe/ *n.m., f.* regular visitor; (*client*) regular.

habituel, ~le /abitɥɛl/ *a.* usual. **~lement** *adv.* usually.
habituer /abitɥe/ *v.t.* **~ à,** accustom to. **s'~ à,** get used to.
hache /'aʃ/ *n.f.* axe.
haché /'aʃe/ *a.* (*phrases*) jerky.
hacher /'aʃe/ *v.t.* mince; (*au couteau*) chop; (*fig.*) cut to pieces.
hachette /'aʃɛt/ *n.f.* hatchet.
hachis /'aʃi/ *n.m.* minced meat; (*Amer.*) ground meat.
hachisch /'aʃiʃ/ *n.m.* hashish.
hachoir /'aʃwar/ *n.m.* (*appareil*) mincer; (*couteau*) chopper.
hagard, ~e /'agar, -d/ *a.* wild (-looking).
haie /'ɛ/ *n.f.* hedge; (*rangée*) row; (*de coureur*) hurdle.
haillon /'ɑjɔ̃/ *n.m.* rag.
hain|e /'ɛn/ *n.f.* hatred. **~eux, ~euse** *a.* full of hatred.
haïr /'air/ *v.t.* hate.
hâl|e /'ɑl/ *n.m.* (sun-)tan. **~é** *a.* (sun-)tanned.
haleine /alɛn/ *n.f.* breath.
hal|er /'ale/ *v.t.* tow. **~age** *n.m.* towing.
haleter /'alte/ *v.i.* pant.
hall /'ol/ *n.m.* hall; (*de gare*) concourse.
halle /'al/ *n.f.* (covered) market. **~s,** (main) food market.
hallucination /alysinɑsjɔ̃/ *n.f.* hallucination.
halo /'alo/ *n.m.* halo.
halte /'alt/ *n.f.* stop; (*repos*) break; (*escale*) stopping place. —*int.* stop; (*mil.*) halt. **faire ~,** stop.
halt|ère /altɛr/ *n.m.* dumb-bell. **~érophilie** *n.f.* weight-lifting.
hamac /'amak/ *n.m.* hammock.
hameau (*pl.* **~x**) /'amo/ *n.m.* hamlet.
hameçon /amsɔ̃/ *n.m.* (fish-)hook.
hanche /'ɑ̃ʃ/ *n.f.* hip.
hand-ball /'ɑ̃dbal/ *n.m.* handball.
handicap /'ɑ̃dikap/ *n.m.* handicap. **~é, ~ée** *a.* & *n.m., f.* handicapped (person). **~er** *v.t.* handicap.
hangar /'ɑ̃gar/ *n.m.* shed; (*pour avions*) hangar.
hanneton /'antɔ̃/ *n.m.* May-bug.
hanter /'ɑ̃te/ *v.t.* haunt.
hantise /'ɑ̃tiz/ *n.f.* obsession (**de,** with).
happer /'ape/ *v.t.* snatch, catch.
haras /'arɑ/ *n.m.* stud-farm.
harasser /'arase/ *v.t.* exhaust.
harceler /'arsəle/ *v.t.* harass.
hardi /'ardi/ *a.* bold. **~esse** /-djɛs/ *n.f.* boldness. **~ment** *adv.* boldly.
hareng /'arɑ̃/ *n.m.* herring.
hargn|e /'arɲ/ *n.f.* (aggressive) bad temper. **~eux, ~euse** *a.* bad-tempered.
haricot /'ariko/ *n.m.* bean. **~ vert,** French *ou* string bean; (*Amer.*) green bean.
harmonica /armɔnika/ *n.m.* harmonica.
harmon|ie /armɔni/ *n.f.* harmony. **~ieux, ~ieuse** *a.* harmonious.
harmoniser /armɔnize/ *v.t.*, **s'~** *v. pr.* harmonize.
harnacher /'arnaʃe/ *v.t.* harness.
harnais /'arnɛ/ *n.m.* harness.
harp|e /'arp/ *n.f.* harp. **~iste** *n.m./f.* harpist.
harpon /'arpɔ̃/ *n.m.* harpoon. **~ner** /-ɔne/ *v.t.* harpoon; (*arrêter: fam.*) detain.
hasard /'azar/ *n.m.* chance; (*coïncidence*) coincidence. **~s,** (*risques*) hazards. **au ~,** (*choisir etc.*) at random; (*flâner*) aimlessly. **~eux, ~euse** /-dø, -z/ *a.* risky.
hasarder /'azarde/ *v.t.* risk; (*remarque*) venture. **se ~ dans,** risk going into. **se ~ à faire,** risk doing.
haschisch /'aʃiʃ/ *n.m.* hashish.
hâte /'ɑt/ *n.f.* haste. **à la ~, en ~,** hurriedly. **avoir ~ de,** be eager to.
hâter /'ɑte/ *v.t.* hasten. **se ~** *v. pr.* hurry (**de,** to).
hâti|f, ~ve /'ɑtif, -v/ *a.* hasty; (*précoce*) early.

hauss|e /'os/ *n.f.* rise (**de,** in). **en ~e,** rising. **~er** *v.t.* raise; (*épaules*) shrug. **se ~er** *v. pr.* stand up, raise o.s. up.

haut, ~e /'o, 'ot/ *a.* high; (*de taille*) tall. —*adv.* high; (*parler*) loud(ly); (*lire*) aloud. —*n.m.* top. **à ~e voix,** aloud. **des ~s et des bas,** ups and downs. **en ~,** (*regarder, jeter*) up; (*dans une maison*) upstairs. **en ~ (de),** at the top (of). **~ en couleur,** colourful. **plus ~,** further up, higher up; (*dans un texte*) above. **~-de-forme** (*pl.* **~s-de-forme**) *n.m.* top hat. **~-fourneau** (*pl.* **~s-fourneaux**) *n.m.* blast-furnace. **~-le-cœur** *n.m. invar.* nausea. **~-parleur** *n.m.* loudspeaker.

hautain, ~e /'otɛ̃, -ɛn/ *a.* haughty.

hautbois /'obwɑ/ *n.m.* oboe.

hautement /'otmɑ̃/ *adv.* highly.

hauteur /'otœr/ *n.f.* height; (*colline*) hill; (*arrogance*) haughtiness. **à la ~,** (*fam.*) up to it. **à la ~ de,** level with; (*tâche, situation*) equal to.

hâve /'ɑv/ *a.* gaunt.

havre /'ɑvr/ *n.m.* haven.

Haye (La) /(la)'ɛ/ *n.f.* The Hague.

hayon /'ɛjɔ̃/ *n.m.* (*auto.*) rear opening, tail-gate.

hebdomadaire /ɛbdɔmadɛr/ *a.* & *n.m.* weekly.

héberg|er /ebɛrʒe/ *v.t.* accommodate. **~ement** *n.m.* accommodation.

hébéter /ebete/ *v.t.* stupefy.

hébraïque /ebraik/ *a.* Hebrew.

hébreu (*pl.* **~x**) /ebrø/ *a.m.* Hebrew. —*n.m.* (*lang.*) Hebrew.

hécatombe /ekatɔ̃b/ *n.f.* slaughter.

hectare /ɛktar/ *n.m.* hectare (*= 10,000 square metres*).

hégémonie /eʒemɔni/ *n.f.* hegemony.

hein /'ɛ̃/ *int.* (*fam.*) eh.

hélas /'elɑs/ *int.* alas. —*adv.* sadly.

héler /'ele/ *v.t.* hail.

hélice /elis/ *n.f.* propeller.

hélicoptère /elikɔptɛr/ *n.m.* helicopter.

héliport /elipɔr/ *n.m.* heliport.

helvétique /ɛlvetik/ *a.* Swiss.

hémisphère /emisfɛr/ *n.m.* hemisphere.

hémorragie /emɔraʒi/ *n.f.* haemorrhage.

hémorroïde /emɔrɔid/ *n.f.* pile.

henn|ir /'enir/ *v.i.* neigh. **~issement** *n.m.* neigh.

hep /'ɛp/ *int.* hey.

herbage /ɛrbaʒ/ *n.m.* pasture.

herb|e /ɛrb/ *n.f.* grass; (*méd., culin.*) herb. **en ~e,** green; (*fig.*) budding. **~eux, ~euse** *a.* grassy.

herbicide /ɛrbisid/ *n.m.* weed-killer.

hérédit|é /eredite/ *n.f.* heredity. **~aire** *a.* hereditary.

héré|sie /erezi/ *n.f.* heresy. **~tique** *a.* heretical; *n.m./f.* heretic.

hériss|er /'erise/ *v.t.*, **se ~er** *v. pr.* bristle. **~er qn.**, ruffle s.o. **~é** *a.* bristling (**de,** with).

hérisson /'erisɔ̃/ *n.m.* hedgehog.

héritage /eritaʒ/ *n.m.* inheritance; (*spirituel etc.*) heritage.

hérit|er /erite/ *v.t./i.* inherit (**de,** from). **~er de qch.**, inherit sth. **~ier, ~ière** *n.m., f.* heir, heiress.

hermétique /ɛrmetik/ *a.* airtight; (*fig.*) unfathomable. **~ment** *adv.* hermetically.

hermine /ɛrmin/ *n.f.* ermine.

hernie /'ɛrni/ *n.f.* hernia.

héroïne[1] /erɔin/ *n.f.* (*femme*) heroine.

héroïne[2] /erɔin/ *n.f.* (*drogue*) heroin.

héroï|que /erɔik/ *a.* heroic. **~sme** *n.m.* heroism.

héron /'erɔ̃/ *n.m.* heron.

héros /'ero/ *n.m.* hero.

hésit|er /ezite/ *v.i.* hesitate (**à,** to). **en ~ant,** hesitantly. **~ant,**

~ante *a.* hesitant. **~ation** *n.f.* hesitation.

hétéroclite /eterɔklit/ *a.* heterogeneous.

hétérogène /eterɔʒɛn/ *a.* heterogeneous.

hêtre /'ɛtr/ *n.m.* beech.

heure /œr/ *n.f.* time; (*mesure de durée*) hour; (*scol.*) period. **quelle ~ est-il?**, what time is it? **il est dix**/*etc.* **~s,** it is ten/*etc.* o'clock. **à l'~,** (*venir, être*) on time. **d'~ en heure,** hourly. **~ avancée,** late hour. **~ d'affluence, ~ de pointe,** rush-hour. **~ indue,** ungodly hour. **~s creuses,** off-peak periods. **~s supplémentaires,** overtime.

heureusement /œrøzmɑ̃/ *adv.* fortunately.

heureu|x, ~se /œrø, -z/ *a.* happy; (*chanceux*) lucky, fortunate.

heurt /'œr/ *n.m.* collision; (*conflit*) clash.

heurter /'œrte/ *v.t.* (*cogner*) hit; (*mur etc.*) bump into, hit; (*choquer*) offend. **se ~ à,** bump into, hit; (*fig.*) come up against.

hexagone /ɛgzagɔn/ *n.m.* hexagon.

hiberner /ibɛrne/ *v.i.* hibernate.

hibou (*pl.* **~x**) /'ibu/ *n.m.* owl.

hideu|x, ~se /'idø, -z/ *a.* hideous.

hier /jɛr/ *adv.* yesterday. **~ soir,** last night, yesterday evening.

hiérarch|ie /'jerarʃi/ *n.f.* hierarchy. **~ique** *a.* hierarchical.

hi-fi /'ifi/ *a. invar.* & *n.f.* (*fam.*) hi-fi.

hilare /ilar/ *a.* merry.

hilarité /ilarite/ *n.f.* laughter.

hindou, ~e /ɛ̃du/ *a.* & *n.m., f.* Hindu.

hippi|que /ipik/ *a.* horse, equestrian. **~sme** *n.m.* horse-riding.

hippodrome /ipɔdrom/ *n.m.* racecourse.

hippopotame /ipɔpɔtam/ *n.m.* hippopotamus.

hirondelle /irɔ̃dɛl/ *n.f.* swallow.

hirsute /irsyt/ *a.* shaggy.

hispanique /ispanik/ *a.* Spanish, Hispanic.

hisser /'ise/ *v.t.* hoist, haul. **se ~** *v. pr.* raise o.s.

histoire /istwar/ *n.f.* (*récit, mensonge*) story; (*étude*) history; (*affaire*) business. **~(s),** (*chichis*) fuss. **~s,** (*ennuis*) trouble.

historien, ~ne /istɔrjɛ̃, -jɛn/ *n.m., f.* historian.

historique /istɔrik/ *a.* historical.

hiver /ivɛr/ *n.m.* winter. **~nal** (*m. pl.* **~naux**) *a.* winter; (*glacial*) wintry. **~ner** *v.i.* winter.

H.L.M. /'aʃɛlɛm/ *n.m./f.* (= *habitation à loyer modéré*) block of council flats; (*Amer.*) (government-sponsored) low-cost apartment building.

hocher /'ɔʃe/ *v.t.* **~ la tête,** (*pour dire oui*) nod; (*pour dire non*) shake one's head.

hochet /'ɔʃɛ/ *n.m.* rattle.

hockey /'ɔkɛ/ *n.m.* hockey. **~ sur glace,** ice hockey.

hold-up /'ɔldœp/ *n.m. invar.* (*attaque*) hold-up.

hollandais, ~e /'ɔlɑ̃dɛ, -z/ *a.* Dutch. —*n.m., f.* Dutchman, Dutchwoman. —*n.m.* (*lang.*) Dutch.

Hollande /'ɔlɑ̃d/ *n.f.* Holland.

homard /'ɔmar/ *n.m.* lobster.

homicide /ɔmisid/ *n.m.* homicide. **~ involontaire,** manslaughter.

hommage /ɔmaʒ/ *n.m.* tribute, homage. **~s,** (*salutations*) respects. **en ~ de,** as a token of.

homme /ɔm/ *n.m.* man; (*espèce*) man(kind). **~ d'affaires,** businessman. **~ de la rue,** man in the street. **~ d'État,** statesman. **~ de paille,** stooge. **~-grenouille** (*pl.* **~s-grenouilles**) *n.m.* frogman. **~ politique,** politician.

homog|ène /ɔmɔʒɛn/ *a.* homogeneous. **~énéité** *n.f.* homogeneity.

homologue /ɔmɔlɔg/ *n.m./f.* counterpart.
homologuer /ɔmɔlɔge/ *v.t.* recognize (officially), validate.
homonyme /ɔmɔnim/ *n.m.* (*personne*) namesake.
homosex|uel, ~uelle /ɔmɔsɛksɥɛl/ *a.* & *n.m., f.* homosexual. **~ualité** *n.f.* homosexuality.
Hongrie /'ɔ̃gri/ *n.f.* Hungary.
hongrois, ~e /'ɔ̃grwa, -z/ *a.* & *n.m., f.* Hungarian.
honnête /ɔnɛt/ *a.* honest; (*satisfaisant*) fair. **~ment** *adv.* honestly; fairly. **~té** *n.f.* honesty.
honneur /ɔnœr/ *n.m.* honour; (*mérite*) credit. **d'~,** (*invité, place*) of honour; (*membre*) honorary. **en ~,** in favour. **en quel ~?,** (*fam.*) why? **faire ~ à,** (*équipe, famille*) bring credit to.
honorable /ɔnɔrabl/ *a.* honourable; (*convenable*) respectable. **~ment** /-əmɑ̃/ *adv.* honourably; respectably.
honoraire /ɔnɔrɛr/ *a.* honorary. **~s** *n.m. pl.* fees.
honorer /ɔnɔre/ *v.t.* honour; (*faire honneur à*) do credit to. **s'~ de,** pride o.s. on.
honorifique /ɔnɔrifik/ *a.* honorary.
hont|e /'ɔ̃t/ *n.f.* shame. **avoir ~e,** be ashamed (**de,** of). **faire ~e à,** make ashamed. **~eux, ~euse** *a.* (*personne*) ashamed (**de,** of); (*action*) shameful. **~eusement** *adv.* shamefully.
hôpit|al (*pl.* **~aux**) /ɔpital, -o/ *n.m.* hospital.
hoquet /'ɔkɛ/ *n.m.* hiccup. **le ~,** (the) hiccups. **~er** /'ɔkte/ *v.i.* hiccup.
horaire /ɔrɛr/ *a.* hourly. —*n.m.* timetable.
horizon /ɔrizɔ̃/ *n.m.* horizon; (*perspective*) view.
horizont|al (*m. pl.* **~aux**) /ɔrizɔ̃tal, -o/ *a.* horizontal. **~alement** *adv.* horizontally.
horloge /ɔrlɔʒ/ *n.f.* clock. **~rie** *n.f.* (*magasin*) watchmaker's shop.
horlog|er, ~ère /ɔrlɔʒe, -ɛr/ *n.m., f.* watchmaker.
hormis /'ɔrmi/ *prép.* save.
hormone /ɔrmɔn/ *n.f.* hormone.
horoscope /ɔrɔskɔp/ *n.m.* horoscope.
horreur /ɔrœr/ *n.f.* horror. **avoir ~ de,** detest.
horrible /ɔribl/ *a.* horrible. **~ment** /-əmɑ̃/ *adv.* horribly.
horrifier /ɔrifje/ *v.t.* horrify.
hors /'ɔr/ *prép.* **~ de,** out of; (*à l'extérieur de*) outside. **~-bord** *n.m. invar.* speedboat. **~ d'atteinte,** out of reach. **~ d'haleine,** out of breath. **~-d'œuvre** *n.m invar.* hors-d'œuvre. **~ de prix,** exorbitant. **~ de soi,** beside o.s. **~-jeu** *a. invar.* offside. **~-la-loi** *n.m. invar.* outlaw. **~ pair,** outstanding. **~-taxe** *a. invar.* duty-free.
hortensia /ɔrtɑ̃sja/ *n.m.* hydrangea.
horticulture /ɔrtikyltyr/ *n.f.* horticulture.
hospice /ɔspis/ *n.m.* home.
hospital|ier, ~ière[1] /ɔspitalje, -jɛr/ *a.* hospitable. **~ité** *n.f.* hospitality.
hospital|ier, ~ière[2] /ɔspitalje, -jɛr/ *a.* (*méd.*) hospital. **~iser** *v.t.* take to hospital.
hostie /ɔsti/ *n.f.* (*relig.*) host.
hostil|e /ɔstil/ *a.* hostile. **~ité** *n.f.* hostility.
hôte /ot/ *n.m.* (*maître*) host; (*invité*) guest.
hôtel /otɛl/ *n.m.* hotel. **~ (particulier),** (private) mansion. **~ de ville,** town hall. **~ier, ~ière** /otəlje, -jɛr/ *a.* hotel; *n.m., f.* hotelier. **~lerie** *n.f.* hotel business; (*auberge*) country hotel.

hôtesse /otɛs/ *n.f.* hostess. **~ de l'air,** air hostess.
hotte /'ɔt/ *n.f.* basket; (*de cuisinière*) hood.
houblon /'ublɔ̃/ *n.m.* **le ~,** hops.
houill|e /'uj/ *n.f.* coal. **~e blanche,** hydroelectric power. **~er, ~ère** *a.* coal; *n.f.* coal-mine.
houl|e /'ul/ *n.f.* (*de mer*) swell. **~eux, ~euse** *a.* stormy.
houppette /'upɛt/ *n.f.* powder-puff.
hourra /'ura/ *n.m.* & *int.* hurrah.
housse /'us/ *n.f.* dust-cover.
houx /'u/ *n.m.* holly.
hublot /'yblo/ *n.m.* porthole.
huche /'yʃ/ *n.f.* **~ à pain,** bread-bin.
huer /'ɥe/ *v.t.* boo. **huées** *n.f. pl.* boos.
huil|e /ɥil/ *n.f.* oil; (*personne: fam.*) bigwig. **~er** *v.t.* oil. **~eux, ~euse** *a.* oily.
huissier /ɥisje/ *n.m.* (*appariteur*) usher; (*jurid.*) bailiff.
huit /'ɥi(t)/ *a.* eight. —*n.m.* eight. **~ jours,** a week. **~aine** /'ɥitɛn/ *n.f.* about eight; (*semaine*) week. **~ième** /'ɥitjɛm/ *a.* & *n.m./f.* eighth.
huître /ɥitr/ *n.f.* oyster.
humain, ~e /ymɛ̃, ymɛn/ *a.* human; (*compatissant*) humane. **~ement** /ymɛnmɑ̃/ *adv.* humanly; humanely.
humanitaire /ymanitɛr/ *a.* humanitarian.
humanité /ymanite/ *n.f.* humanity.
humble /œ̃bl/ *a.* humble.
humecter /ymɛkte/ *v.t.* moisten.
humer /'yme/ *v.t.* smell.
humeur /ymœr/ *n.f.* mood, humour; (*tempérament*) temper. **de bonne/mauvaise ~,** in a good/bad mood.
humid|e /ymid/ *a.* damp; (*chaleur, climat*) humid; (*lèvres, yeux*) moist. **~ité** *n.f.* humidity.
humil|ier /ymilje/ *v.t.* humiliate. **~iation** *n.f.* humiliation.
humilité /ymilite/ *n.f.* humility.
humorist|e /ymɔrist/ *n.m./f.* humorist. **~ique** *a.* humorous.
humour /ymur/ *n.m.* humour; (*sens*) sense of humour.
huppé /'ype/ *a.* (*fam.*) high-class.
hurl|er /'yrle/ *v.t./i.* howl. **~ement** *n.m.* howl(ing).
hurluberlu /yrlybɛrly/ *n.m.* scatter-brain.
hutte /'yt/ *n.f.* hut.
hybride /ibrid/ *a.* & *n.m.* hybrid.
hydrate /idrat/ *n.m.* **~ de carbone,** carbohydrate.
hydraulique /idrolik/ *a.* hydraulic.
hydravion /idravjɔ̃/ *n.m.* seaplane.
hydro-électrique /idrɔelɛktrik/ *a.* hydroelectric.
hydrogène /idrɔʒɛn/ *n.m.* hydrogen.
hyène /jɛn/ *n.f.* hyena.
hyg|iène /iʒjɛn/ *n.f.* hygiene. **~iénique** *a.* /iʒjenik/ hygienic.
hymne /imn/ *n.m.* hymn. **~ national,** national anthem.
hyper- /ipɛr/ *préf.* hyper-.
hypermarché /ipɛrmarʃe/ *n.m.* (*supermarché*) hypermarket.
hypertension /ipɛrtɑ̃sjɔ̃/ *n.f.* high blood-pressure.
hypno|se /ipnoz/ *n.f.* hypnosis. **~tique** /-ɔtik/ *a.* hypnotic. **~tisme** /-ɔtism/ *n.m.* hypnotism.
hypnotis|er /ipnɔtize/ *v.t.* hypnotize. **~eur** *n.m.* hypnotist.
hypocris|ie /ipɔkrizi/ *n.f.* hypocrisy.
hypocrite /ipɔkrit/ *a.* hypocritical. —*n.m./f.* hypocrite.
hypoth|èque /ipɔtɛk/ *n.f.* mortgage. **~équer** *v.t.* mortgage.
hypoth|èse /ipɔtɛz/ *n.f.* hypothesis. **~étique** *a.* hypothetical.
hystér|ie /isteri/ *n.f.* hysteria. **~ique** *a.* hysterical.

I

iceberg /isbɛrg/ *n.m.* iceberg.

ici /isi/ *adv.* (*espace*) here; (*temps*) now. **d'~ demain,** by tomorrow. **d'~ là,** in the meantime. **d'~ peu,** shortly. **~ même,** in this very place.

icône /ikon/ *n.f.* icon.

idé|al (*m. pl.* **~aux**) /ideal, -o/ *a.* ideal. —*n.m.* (*pl.* **~aux**) ideal. **~aliser** *v.t.* idealize.

idéalis|te /idealist/ *a.* idealistic. —*n.m./f.* idealist. **~me** *n.m.* idealism.

idée /ide/ *n.f.* idea; (*esprit*) mind. **~ fixe,** obsession. **~ reçue,** conventional opinion.

identif|ier /idɑ̃tifje/ *v.t.*, **s'~ier** *v. pr.* identify (**à,** with). **~ication** *n.f.* identification.

identique /idɑ̃tik/ *a.* identical.

identité /idɑ̃tite/ *n.f.* identity.

idéolog|ie /ideɔlɔʒi/ *n.f.* ideology. **~ique** *a.* ideological.

idiom|e /idjom/ *n.m.* idiom. **~atique** /idjɔmatik/ *a.* idiomatic.

idiot, ~e /idjo, idjɔt/ *a.* idiotic. —*n.m., f.* idiot. **~ie** /idjɔsi/ *n.f.* idiocy; (*acte, parole*) idiotic thing.

idiotisme /idjɔtism/ *n.m.* idiom.

idolâtrer /idɔlatre/ *v.t.* idolize.

idole /idɔl/ *n.f.* idol.

idyllique /idilik/ *a.* idyllic.

if /if/ *n.m.* (*arbre*) yew.

igloo /iglu/ *n.m.* igloo.

ignare /iɲar/ *a.* ignorant. —*n.m./f.* ignoramus.

ignoble /iɲɔbl/ *a.* vile.

ignoran|t, ~te /iɲɔrɑ̃, -t/ *a.* ignorant. —*n.m., f.* ignoramus. **~ce** *n.f.* ignorance.

ignorer /iɲɔre/ *v.t.* not know; (*personne*) ignore.

il /il/ *pron.* he; (*chose*) it. **~ est vrai**/*etc.* **que,** it is true/*etc.* that. **~ neige**/**pleut**/*etc.*, it is snowing/raining/*etc.* **~ y a,** there is; (*pluriel*) there are; (*temps*) ago; (*durée*) for.

île /il/ *n.f.* island. **~ déserte,** desert island. **~s anglo-normandes,** Channel Islands. **~s Britanniques,** British Isles.

illég|al (*m. pl.* **~aux**) /ilegal, -o/ *a.* illegal. **~alité** *n.f.* illegality.

illégitim|e /ileʒitim/ *a.* illegitimate. **~ité** *n.f.* illegitimacy.

illettré, ~e /iletre/ *a.* & *n.m., f.* illiterate.

illicite /ilisit/ *a.* illicit.

illimité /ilimite/ *a.* unlimited.

illisible /ilizibl/ *a.* illegible; (*livre*) unreadable.

illogique /ilɔʒik/ *a.* illogical.

illumin|er /ilymine/ *v.t.*, **s'~er** *v. pr.* light up. **~ation** *n.f.* illumination. **~é** *a.* (*monument*) floodlit.

illusion /ilyzjɔ̃/ *n.f.* illusion. **se faire des ~s,** delude o.s. **~ner** /-jɔne/ *v.t.* delude. **~niste** /-jɔnist/ *n.m./f.* conjuror.

illusoire /ilyzwar/ *a.* illusory.

illustre /ilystr/ *a.* illustrious.

illustr|er /ilystre/ *v.t.* illustrate. **s'~er** *v. pr.* become famous. **~ation** *n.f.* illustration. **~é** *a.* illustrated; *n.m.* illustrated magazine.

îlot /ilo/ *n.m.* island; (*de maisons*) block.

ils /il/ *pron.* they.

imag|e /imaʒ/ *n.f.* picture; (*métaphore*) image; (*reflet*) reflection. **~é** *a.* full of imagery.

imaginaire /imaʒinɛr/ *a.* imaginary.

imaginati|f, ~ve /imaʒinatif, -v/ *a.* imaginative.

imagin|er /imaʒine/ *v.t.* imagine; (*inventer*) think up. **s'~er** *v. pr.* imagine (**que,** that). **~ation** *n.f.* imagination.

imbattable /ɛ̃batabl/ *a.* unbeatable.

imbécil|e /ɛ̃besil/ *a.* idiotic.

—*n.m.*/*f.* idiot. **~lité** *n.f.* idiocy; (*action*) idiotic thing.
imbiber /ɛ̃bibe/ *v.t.* soak (**de,** with). **s'~** *v. pr.* become soaked.
imbriqué /ɛ̃brike/ *a.* (*lié*) linked.
imbu /ɛ̃by/ *a.* **~ de,** full of.
imbuvable /ɛ̃byvabl/ *a.* undrinkable; (*personne*: *fam.*) insufferable.
imit|er /imite/ *v.t.* imitate; (*personnage*) impersonate; (*faire comme*) do the same as; (*document*) copy. **~ateur, ~atrice** *n.m., f.* imitator; impersonator. **~ation** *n.f.* imitation; impersonation.
immaculé /imakyle/ *a.* spotless.
immangeable /ɛ̃mɑ̃ʒabl/ *a.* inedible.
immatricul|er /imatrikyle/ *v.t.* register. **(se) faire ~er,** register. **~ation** *n.f.* registration.
immédiat, ~e /imedja, -t/ *a.* immediate. —*n.m.* **dans l'~,** for the moment. **~ement** /-tmɑ̃/ *adv.* immediately.
immens|e /imɑ̃s/ *a.* immense. **~ément** *adv.* immensely. **~ité** *n.f.* immensity.
immer|ger /imɛrʒe/ *v.t.* immerse. **s'~ger** *v. pr.* submerge. **~sion** *n.f.* immersion.
immeuble /imœbl/ *n.m.* block of flats, building. **~ (de bureaux),** (office) building *ou* block.
immigr|er /imigre/ *v.i.* immigrate. **~ant, ~ante** *a.* & *n.m., f.* immigrant. **~ation** *n.f.* immigration. **~é, ~ée** *a.* & *n.m., f.* immigrant.
imminen|t, ~te /iminɑ̃, -t/ *a.* imminent. **~ce** *n.f.* imminence.
immiscer (s') /(s)imise/ *v. pr.* interfere (**dans,** in).
immobil|e /imɔbil/ *a.* still, motionless. **~ité** *n.f.* stillness; (*inaction*) immobility.
immobil|ier, ~ière /imɔbilje, -jɛr/ *a.* property. **agence ~ière,** estate agent's office; (*Amer.*) real estate office. **agent ~ier,** estate agent; (*Amer.*) real estate agent.
immobilis|er /imɔbilize/ *v.t.* immobilize; (*stopper*) stop. **s'~er** *v. pr.* stop. **~ation** *n.f.* immobilization.
immodéré /imɔdere/ *a.* immoderate.
immoler /imɔle/ *v.t.* sacrifice.
immonde /imɔ̃d/ *a.* filthy.
immondices /imɔ̃dis/ *n.f. pl.* refuse.
immor|al (*m. pl.* **~aux**) /imɔral, -o/ *a.* immoral. **~alité** *n.f.* immorality.
immortaliser /imɔrtalize/ *v.t.* immortalize.
immort|el, ~elle /imɔrtɛl/ *a.* immortal. **~alité** *n.f.* immortality.
immuable /imɥabl/ *a.* unchanging.
immunis|er /imynize/ *v.t.* immunize. **~é contre,** (*à l'abri de*) immune to.
immunité /imynite/ *n.f.* immunity.
impact /ɛ̃pakt/ *n.m.* impact.
impair[1] /ɛ̃pɛr/ *a.* (*numéro*) odd.
impair[2] /ɛ̃pɛr/ *n.m.* blunder.
impardonnable /ɛ̃pardɔnabl/ *a.* unforgivable.
imparfait, ~e /ɛ̃parfɛ, -t/ *a.* & *n.m.* imperfect.
impart|ial (*m. pl.* **~iaux**) /ɛ̃parsjal, -jo/ *a.* impartial. **~ialité** *n.f.* impartiality.
impasse /ɛ̃pɑs/ *n.f.* (*rue*) dead end; (*situation*) deadlock.
impassible /ɛ̃pasibl/ *a.* impassive.
impat|ient, ~iente /ɛ̃pasjɑ̃, -t/ *a.* impatient. **~iemment** /-jamɑ̃/ *adv.* impatiently. **~ience** *n.f.* impatience.
impatienter /ɛ̃pasjɑ̃te/ *v.t.* annoy. **s'~** *v. pr.* lose patience (**contre,** with).

impayable /ɛ̃pɛjabl/ *a.* (killingly) funny, hilarious.
impayé /ɛ̃peje/ *a.* unpaid.
impeccable /ɛ̃pekabl/ *a.* impeccable.
impénétrable /ɛ̃penetrabl/ *a.* impenetrable.
impénitent, ~e /ɛ̃penitɑ̃, -t/ *a.* unrepentant.
impensable /ɛ̃pɑ̃sabl/ *a.* unthinkable.
impérati|f, ~ve /ɛ̃peratif, -v/ *a.* imperative. —*n.m.* requirement; (*gram.*) imperative.
impératrice /ɛ̃peratris/ *n.f.* empress.
imperceptible /ɛ̃pɛrsɛptibl/ *a.* imperceptible.
imperfection /ɛ̃pɛrfɛksjɔ̃/ *n.f.* imperfection.
impér|ial (*m. pl.* **~iaux**) /ɛ̃perjal, -jo/ *a.* imperial. **~ialisme** *n.m.* imperialism.
impériale /ɛ̃perjal/ *n.f.* upper deck.
impérieu|x, ~se /ɛ̃perjø, -z/ *a.* imperious; (*pressant*) pressing.
impérissable /ɛ̃perisabl/ *a.* undying.
imperméable /ɛ̃pɛrmeabl/ *a.* impervious (**à,** to); (*manteau, tissu*) waterproof. —*n.m.* raincoat.
impersonnel, ~le /ɛ̃pɛrsɔnɛl/ *a.* impersonal.
impertinen|t, ~te /ɛ̃pɛrtinɑ̃, -t/ *a.* impertinent. **~ce** *n.f.* impertinence.
imperturbable /ɛ̃pɛrtyrbabl/ *a.* unshakeable.
impét|ueux, ~ueuse /ɛ̃petɥø, -z/ *a.* impetuous. **~uosité** *n.f.* impetuosity.
impie /ɛ̃pi/ *a.* ungodly.
impitoyable /ɛ̃pitwajabl/ *a.* merciless.
implacable /ɛ̃plakabl/ *a.* implacable.
implant|er /ɛ̃plɑ̃te/ *v.t.* establish. **s'~er** *v. pr.* become established. **~ation** *n.f.* establishment.
implication /ɛ̃plikɑsjɔ̃/ *n.f.* implication.
implicite /ɛ̃plisit/ *a.* implicit.
impliquer /ɛ̃plike/ *v.t.* imply (**que,** that). **~ dans,** implicate in.
implorer /ɛ̃plɔre/ *v.t.* implore.
impoli /ɛ̃pɔli/ *a.* impolite. **~tesse** *n.f.* impoliteness; (*remarque*) impolite remark.
impondérable /ɛ̃pɔ̃derabl/ *a.* & *n.m.* imponderable.
impopulaire /ɛ̃pɔpylɛr/ *a.* unpopular.
importance /ɛ̃pɔrtɑ̃s/ *n.f.* importance; (*taille*) size; (*ampleur*) extent.
important, ~e /ɛ̃pɔrtɑ̃, -t/ *a.* important; (*en quantité*) considerable, sizeable, big. —*n.m.* **l'~,** the important thing.
import|er[1] /ɛ̃pɔrte/ *v.t.* (*comm.*) import. **~ateur, ~atrice** *n.m., f.* importer; *a.* importing. **~ation** *n.f.* import.
import|er[2] /ɛ̃pɔrte/ *v.i.* matter, be important (**à,** to). **il ~e que,** it is important that. **n'~e, peu ~e,** it does not matter. **n'~e comment,** anyhow. **n'~e où,** anywhere. **n'~e qui,** anybody. **n'~e quoi,** anything.
importun, ~e /ɛ̃pɔrtœ̃, -yn/ *a.* troublesome. —*n.m., f.* nuisance. **~er** /-yne/ *v.t.* trouble.
imposant, ~e /ɛ̃pozɑ̃, -t/ *a.* imposing.
imposer /ɛ̃poze/ *v.t.* impose (**à,** on); (*taxer*) tax. **s'~** *v. pr.* (*action*) be essential; (*se faire reconnaître*) stand out.
impossibilité /ɛ̃pɔsibilite/ *n.f.* impossibility. **dans l'~ de,** unable to.
impossible /ɛ̃pɔsibl/ *a.* & *n.m.* impossible.
impost|eur /ɛ̃pɔstœr/ *n.m.* impostor. **~ure** *n.f.* imposture.

impôt /ɛ̃po/ *n.m.* tax. **~s,** (*contributions*) tax(ation), taxes. **~ sur le revenu,** income tax.
impotent, ~e /ɛ̃pɔtɑ̃, -t/ *a.* crippled. —*n.m., f.* cripple.
impraticable /ɛ̃pratikabl/ *a.* (*route*) impassable.
imprécis, ~e /ɛ̃presi, -z/ *a.* imprecise. **~ion** /-izjɔ̃/ *n.f.* imprecision.
imprégner /ɛ̃preɲe/ *v.t.* fill (**de,** with); (*imbiber*) impregnate (**de,** with). **s'~ de,** become filled with; (*s'imbiber*) become impregnated with.
imprenable /ɛ̃prənabl/ *a.* impregnable.
impresario /ɛ̃presarjo/ *n.m.* manager.
impression /ɛ̃presjɔ̃/ *n.f.* impression; (*de livre*) printing.
impressionn|er /ɛ̃presjɔne/ *v.t.* impress. **~able** *a.* impressionable. **~ant, ~ante** *a.* impressive.
imprévisible /ɛ̃previzibl/ *a.* unpredictable.
imprévoyance /ɛ̃prevwajɑ̃s/ *n.f.* lack of foresight.
imprévu /ɛ̃prevy/ *a.* unexpected. —*n.m.* unexpected incident.
imprim|er /ɛ̃prime/ *v.t.* print; (*marquer*) imprint; (*transmettre*) impart. **~ante** *n.f.* (*d'un ordinateur*) printer. **~é** *a.* printed; *n.m.* (*formulaire*) printed form. **~erie** *n.f.* (*art*) printing; (*lieu*) printing works. **~eur** *n.m.* printer.
improbable /ɛ̃prɔbabl/ *a.* unlikely, improbable.
impromptu /ɛ̃prɔ̃pty/ *a.* & *adv.* impromptu.
impropr|e /ɛ̃prɔpr/ *a.* incorrect. **~e à,** unfit for. **~iété** *n.f.* incorrectness; (*erreur*) error.
improvis|er /ɛ̃prɔvize/ *v.t./i.* improvise. **~ation** *n.f.* improvisation.
improviste (à l') /(al)ɛ̃prɔvist/ *adv.* unexpectedly.
imprud|ent, ~ente /ɛ̃prydɑ̃, -t/ *a.* careless. **il est ~ent de,** it is unwise to. **~emment** /-amɑ̃/ *adv.* carelessly. **~ence** *n.f.* carelessness; (*acte*) careless action.
impuden|t, ~te /ɛ̃pydɑ̃, -t/ *a.* impudent. **~ce** *n.f.* impudence.
impuissan|t, ~te /ɛ̃pɥisɑ̃, -t/ *a.* helpless; (*méd.*) impotent. **~t à,** powerless to. **~ce** *n.f.* helplessness; (*méd.*) impotence.
impulsi|f, ~ve /ɛ̃pylsif, -v/ *a.* impulsive.
impulsion /ɛ̃pylsjɔ̃/ *n.f.* (*poussée, influence*) impetus; (*instinct, mouvement*) impulse.
impunément /ɛ̃pynemɑ̃/ *adv.* with impunity.
impuni /ɛ̃pyni/ *a.* unpunished.
impur /ɛ̃pyr/ *a.* impure. **~eté** *n.f.* impurity.
imputer /ɛ̃pyte/ *v.t.* **~ à,** impute to.
inabordable /inabɔrdabl/ *a.* (*prix*) prohibitive.
inacceptable /inaksɛptabl/ *a.* unacceptable; (*scandaleux*) outrageous.
inaccessible /inaksesibl/ *a.* inaccessible.
inaccoutumé /inakutyme/ *a.* unaccustomed.
inachevé /inaʃve/ *a.* unfinished.
inacti|f, ~ve /inaktif, -v/ *a.* inactive.
inaction /inaksjɔ̃/ *n.f.* inactivity.
inadapté, ~e /inadapte/ *n.m., f.* (*psych.*) maladjusted person.
inadmissible /inadmisibl/ *a.* unacceptable.
inaltérable /inalterabl/ *a.* stable, that does not deteriorate; (*sentiment*) unfailing.
inanimé /inanime/ *a.* (*évanoui*) unconscious; (*mort*) lifeless; (*matière*) inanimate.
inaperçu /inapɛrsy/ *a.* unnoticed.
inappréciable /inapresjabl/ *a.* invaluable.

inapte /inapt/ *a.* unsuited (**à,** to). **~ à faire,** incapable of doing.
inarticulé /inartikyle/ *a.* inarticulate.
inattendu /inatɑ̃dy/ *a.* unexpected.
inattenti|f, ~ve /inatɑ̃tif, -v/ *a.* inattentive (**à,** to).
inattention /inatɑ̃sjɔ̃/ *n.f.* inattention.
inaugur|er /inɔgyre/ *v.t.* inaugurate. **~ation** *n.f.* inauguration.
inaugur|al (*m. pl.* **~aux**) /inɔgyral, -o/ *a.* inaugural.
incalculable /ɛ̃kalkylabl/ *a.* incalculable.
incapable /ɛ̃kapabl/ *a.* incapable (**de qch.,** of sth.). **~ de faire,** unable to do, incapable of doing. —*n.m./f.* incompetent.
incapacité /ɛ̃kapasite/ *n.f.* incapacity. **dans l'~ de,** unable to.
incarcérer /ɛ̃karsere/ *v.t.* incarcerate.
incarn|er /ɛ̃karne/ *v.t.* embody. **~ation** *n.f.* embodiment, incarnation.
incartade /ɛ̃kartad/ *n.f.* indiscretion, misdeed, prank.
incassable /ɛ̃kɑsabl/ *a.* unbreakable.
incendiaire /ɛ̃sɑ̃djɛr/ *a.* incendiary. —*n.m./f.* arsonist.
incend|ie /ɛ̃sɑ̃di/ *n.m.* fire. **~ie criminel,** arson. **~ier** *v.t.* set fire to.
incert|ain, ~aine /ɛ̃sɛrtɛ̃, -ɛn/ *a.* uncertain; (*contour*) vague. **~itude** *n.f.* uncertainty.
incessamment /ɛ̃sɛsamɑ̃/ *adv.* immediately.
incessant, ~e /ɛ̃sɛsɑ̃, -t/ *a.* incessant.
incest|e /ɛ̃sɛst/ *n.m.* incest. **~ueux, ~ueuse** *a.* incestuous.
inchangé /ɛ̃ʃɑ̃ʒe/ *a.* unchanged.
incidence /ɛ̃sidɑ̃s/ *n.f.* effect.
incident /ɛ̃sidɑ̃/ *n.m.* incident. **~ technique,** technical hitch.
incinér|er /ɛ̃sinere/ *v.t.* incinerate; (*mort*) cremate. **~ateur** *n.m.* incinerator.
incis|er /ɛ̃size/ *v.t.* (*abcès etc.*) lance. **~ion** *n.f.* lancing; (*entaille*) incision.
incisi|f, ~ve /ɛ̃sizif, -v/ *a.* incisive.
incit|er /ɛ̃site/ *v.t.* incite (**à,** to). **~ation** *n.f.* incitement.
inclinaison /ɛ̃klinɛzɔ̃/ *n.f.* incline; (*de la tête*) tilt.
inclination[1] /ɛ̃klinɑsjɔ̃/ *n.f.* (*penchant*) inclination.
inclin|er /ɛ̃kline/ *v.t.* tilt, lean; (*courber*) bend; (*inciter*) encourage (**à,** to). —*v.i.* **~er à,** be inclined to. **s'~er** *v. pr.* (*se courber*) bow down; (*céder*) give in; (*chemin*) slope. **~er la tête,** (*approuver*) nod; (*révérence*) bow. **~ation[2]** *n.f.* (*de la tête*) nod; (*du buste*) bow.
incl|ure /ɛ̃klyr/ *v.t.* include; (*enfermer*) enclose. **jusqu'au lundi ~us,** up to and including Monday. **~usion** *n.f.* inclusion.
incognito /ɛ̃kɔɲito/ *adv.* incognito.
incohéren|t, ~te /ɛ̃kɔerɑ̃, -t/ *a.* incoherent. **~ce** *n.f.* incoherence.
incolore /ɛ̃kɔlɔr/ *a.* colourless; (*crème, verre*) clear.
incomber /ɛ̃kɔ̃be/ *v.i.* **il vous/***etc.* **incombe de,** it is your/*etc.* responsibility to.
incommode /ɛ̃kɔmɔd/ *a.* awkward.
incommoder /ɛ̃kɔmɔde/ *v.t.* inconvenience.
incomparable /ɛ̃kɔ̃parabl/ *a.* incomparable.
incompatib|le /ɛ̃kɔ̃patibl/ *a.* incompatible. **~ilité** *n.f.* incompatibility.
incompéten|t, ~te /ɛ̃kɔ̃petɑ̃, -t/ *a.* incompetent. **~ce** *n.f.* incompetence.
incompl|et, ~ète /ɛ̃kɔ̃plɛ, -t/ *a.* incomplete.

incompréhensible /ɛ̃kɔ̃preɑ̃sibl/ *a.* incomprehensible.
incompréhens|if, ~ive /ɛ̃kɔ̃preɑ̃sif, -v/ *a.* lacking in understanding. **~ion** *n.f.* lack of understanding.
incompris, ~e /ɛ̃kɔ̃pri, -z/ *a.* misunderstood.
inconcevable /ɛ̃kɔ̃svabl/ *a.* inconceivable.
inconciliable /ɛ̃kɔ̃siljabl/ *a.* irreconcilable.
inconditionnel, ~le /ɛ̃kɔ̃disjɔnɛl/ *a.* unconditional.
inconfort /ɛ̃kɔ̃fɔr/ *n.m.* discomfort. **~able** /-tabl/ *a.* uncomfortable.
incongru /ɛ̃kɔ̃gry/ *a.* unseemly.
inconnu, ~e /ɛ̃kɔny/ *a.* unknown (**à**, to). —*n.m., f* stranger. —*n.m.* **l'~**, the unknown. —*n.f.* unknown (quantity).
inconsc|ient, ~iente /ɛ̃kɔ̃sjɑ̃, -t/ *a.* unconscious (**de**, of); (*fou*) mad. —*n.m.* (*psych.*) subconscious. **~iemment** /-jamɑ̃/ *adv.* unconsciously. **~ience** *n.f.* unconsciousness; (*folie*) madness.
inconsidéré /ɛ̃kɔ̃sidere/ *a.* thoughtless.
inconsolable /ɛ̃kɔ̃sɔlabl/ *a.* inconsolable.
inconstan|t, ~te /ɛ̃kɔ̃stɑ̃, -t/ *a.* fickle. **~ce** *n.f.* fickleness.
incontest|able /ɛ̃kɔ̃tɛstabl/ *a.* indisputable. **~é** *a.* undisputed.
incontinen|t, ~te /ɛ̃kɔ̃tinɑ̃, -t/ *a.* incontinent. **~ce** *n.f.* incontinence.
incontrôlable /ɛ̃kɔ̃trolabl/ *a.* unverifiable.
inconvenan|t, ~te /ɛ̃kɔ̃vnɑ̃, -t/ *a.* improper. **~ce** *n.f.* impropriety.
inconvénient /ɛ̃kɔ̃venjɑ̃/ *n.m.* disadvantage; (*risque*) risk; (*objection*) objection.
incorpor|er /ɛ̃kɔrpɔre/ *v.t.* incorporate; (*mil.*) enlist. **~ation** *n.f.* incorporation; (*mil.*) enlistment.
incorrect /ɛ̃kɔrɛkt/ *a.* (*faux*) incorrect; (*malséant*) improper; (*impoli*) impolite.
incorrigible /ɛ̃kɔriʒibl/ *a.* incorrigible.
incrédul|e /ɛ̃kredyl/ *a.* incredulous. **~ité** *n.f.* incredulity.
incriminer /ɛ̃krimine/ *v.t.* incriminate.
incroyable /ɛ̃krwajabl/ *a.* incredible.
incroyant, ~e /ɛ̃krwajɑ̃, -t/ *n.m., f.* non-believer.
incrust|er /ɛ̃kryste/ *v.t.* (*décorer*) inlay (**de**, with). **s'~er dans,** become embedded in. **~ation** *n.f.* inlay.
inculp|er /ɛ̃kylpe/ *v.t.* charge (**de**, with). **~ation** *n.f.* charge. **~é, ~ée** *n.m., f.* accused.
inculquer /ɛ̃kylke/ *v.t.* instil (**à**, into).
inculte /ɛ̃kylt/ *a.* uncultivated; (*cheveux*) unkempt; (*personne*) uneducated.
incurable /ɛ̃kyrabl/ *a.* incurable.
incursion /ɛ̃kyrsjɔ̃/ *n.f.* incursion.
incurver /ɛ̃kyrve/ *v.t.*, **s'~** *v. pr.* curve.
Inde /ɛ̃d/ *n.f.* India.
indécen|t, ~te /ɛ̃desɑ̃, -t/ *a.* indecent. **~ce** *n.f.* indecency.
indéchiffrable /ɛ̃deʃifrabl/ *a.* indecipherable.
indécis, ~e /ɛ̃desi, -z/ *a.* indecisive; (*qui n'a pas encore pris de décision*) undecided. **~ion** /-izjɔ̃/ *n.f.* indecision.
indéfini /ɛ̃defini/ *a.* indefinite; (*vague*) undefined. **~ment** *adv.* indefinitely. **~ssable** *a.* indefinable.
indélébile /ɛ̃delebil/ *a.* indelible.
indélicat, ~e /ɛ̃delika, -t/ *a.* (*malhonnête*) unscrupulous.
indemne /ɛ̃dɛmn/ *a.* unharmed.

indemniser /ɛ̃dɛmnize/ *v.t.* indemnify, compensate.

indemnité /ɛ̃dɛmnite/ *n.f.* indemnity; (*allocation*) allowance.

indéniable /ɛ̃denjabl/ *a.* undeniable.

indépend|ant, ~ante /ɛ̃depɑ̃dɑ̃, -t/ *a.* independent. **~amment** *adv.* independently. **~amment de,** apart from. **~ance** *n.f.* independence.

indescriptible /ɛ̃dɛskriptibl/ *a.* indescribable.

indésirable /ɛ̃dezirabl/ *a.* & *n.m./f.* undesirable.

indestructible /ɛ̃dɛstryktibl/ *a.* indestructible.

indétermination /ɛ̃detɛrminɑsjɔ̃/ *n.f.* indecision.

indéterminé /ɛ̃detɛrmine/ *a.* unspecified.

index /ɛ̃dɛks/ *n.m.* forefinger; (*liste*) index. **~er** *v.t.* index.

indica|teur, ~trice /ɛ̃dikatœr, -tris/ *n.m., f.* (police) informer. —*n.m.* (*livre*) guide; (*techn.*) indicator.

indicati|f, ~ve /ɛ̃dikatif, -v/ *a.* indicative (**de,** of). —*n.m.* (*radio*) signature tune; (*téléphonique*) dialling code; (*gram.*) indicative.

indication /ɛ̃dikɑsjɔ̃/ *n.f.* indication; (*renseignement*) information; (*directive*) instruction.

indice /ɛ̃dis/ *n.m.* sign; (*dans une enquête*) clue; (*des prix*) index; (*d'octane, de salaire*) rating.

indien, ~ne /ɛ̃djɛ̃, -jɛn/ *a.* & *n.m., f.* Indian.

indifféremment /ɛ̃diferamɑ̃/ *adv.* equally.

indifféren|t, ~te /ɛ̃diferɑ̃, -t/ *a.* indifferent (**à,** to). **ça m'est ~t,** it makes no difference to me. **~ce** *n.f.* indifference.

indigène /ɛ̃diʒɛn/ *a.* & *n.m./f.* native.

indigen|t, ~te /ɛ̃diʒɑ̃, -t/ *a.* poor. **~ce** *n.f.* poverty.

indigest|e /ɛ̃diʒɛst/ *a.* indigestible. **~ion** *n.f.* indigestion.

indignation /ɛ̃diɲɑsjɔ̃/ *n.f.* indignation.

indign|e /ɛ̃diɲ/ *a.* unworthy (**de,** of); (*acte*) vile. **~ité** *n.f.* unworthiness; (*acte*) vile act.

indigner /ɛ̃diɲe/ *v.t.* make indignant. **s'~** *v. pr.* become indignant (**de,** at).

indiqu|er /ɛ̃dike/ *v.t.* show, indicate; (*renseigner sur*) point out, tell; (*déterminer*) give, state, appoint. **~er du doigt,** point to *ou* out *ou* at. **~é** *a.* (*heure*) appointed; (*opportun*) appropriate; (*conseillé*) recommended.

indirect /ɛ̃dirɛkt/ *a.* indirect.

indiscipliné /ɛ̃disipline/ *a.* unruly.

indiscr|et, ~ète /ɛ̃diskrɛ, -t/ *a.* indiscreet; (*curieux*) inquisitive. **~étion** *n.f.* indiscretion; inquisitiveness.

indiscutable /ɛ̃diskytabl/ *a.* unquestionable.

indispensable /ɛ̃dispɑ̃sabl/ *a.* indispensable. **il est ~ que,** it is essential that.

indispos|er /ɛ̃dispoze/ *v.t.* make unwell. **~er (contre soi),** (*mécontenter*) antagonize. **~é** *a.* unwell. **~ition** *n.f.* indisposition.

indistinct, ~e /ɛ̃distɛ̃(kt), -ɛ̃kt/ *a.* indistinct. **~ement** /-ɛ̃ktəmɑ̃/ *adv.* indistinctly; (*également*) without distinction.

individ|u /ɛ̃dividy/ *n.m.* individual. **~ualiser** *v.t.* individualize. **~ualiste** *n.m./f.* individualist.

individuel, ~le /ɛ̃dividɥɛl/ *a.* individual; (*propriété, opinion*) personal. **~lement** *adv.* individually.

indivisible /ɛ̃divizibl/ *a.* indivisible.

Indochine /ɛ̃dɔʃin/ *n.f.* Indo-China.

indolen|t, ~te /ɛ̃dɔlɑ̃, -t/ *a.* indolent. **~ce** *n.f.* indolence.
indolore /ɛ̃dɔlɔr/ *a.* painless.
Indonésie /ɛ̃dɔnezi/ *n.f.* Indonesia.
indonésien, ~ne /ɛ̃dɔnezjɛ̃, -jɛn/ *a.* & *n.m., f.* Indonesian.
induire /ɛ̃dɥir/ *v.t.* infer (**de,** from). **~ en erreur,** mislead.
indulgen|t, ~te /ɛ̃dylʒɑ̃, -t/ *a.* indulgent; (*clément*) lenient. **~ce** *n.f.* indulgence; leniency.
industr|ie /ɛ̃dystri/ *n.f.* industry. **~ialisé** *a.* industrialized.
industriel, ~le /ɛ̃dystrijɛl/ *a.* industrial. —*n.m.* industrialist. **~lement** *adv.* industrially.
inébranlable /inebrɑ̃labl/ *a.* unshakeable.
inédit, ~e /inedi, -t/ *a.* unpublished; (*fig.*) original.
ineffable /inefabl/ *a.* sublime.
inefficace /inefikas/ *a.* ineffective.
inég|al (*m. pl.* **~aux**) /inegal, -o/ *a.* unequal; (*irrégulier*) uneven. **~alé** *a.* unequalled. **~alité** *n.f.* (*injustice*) inequality; (*irrégularité*) unevenness; (*différence*) difference (**de,** between).
inéluctable /inelyktabl/ *a.* inescapable.
inept|e /inɛpt/ *a.* inept, absurd. **~ie** /inɛpsi/ *n.f.* ineptitude.
inépuisable /inepɥizabl/ *a.* inexhaustible.
inert|e /inɛrt/ *a.* inert; (*mort*) lifeless. **~ie** /inɛrsi/ *n.f.* inertia.
inespéré /inɛspere/ *a.* unhoped for.
inestimable /inɛstimabl/ *a.* priceless.
inévitable /inevitabl/ *a.* inevitable.
inexact, ~e /inɛgza(kt), -akt/ *a.* (*imprécis*) inaccurate; (*incorrect*) incorrect.
inexcusable /inɛkskyzabl/ *a.* unforgivable.
inexistant, ~e /inɛgzistɑ̃, -t/ *a.* non-existent.
inexorable /inɛgzɔrabl/ *a.* inexorable.
inexpérience /inɛksperjɑ̃s/ *n.f.* inexperience.
inexpli|cable /inɛksplikabl/ *a.* inexplicable. **~qué** *a.* unexplained.
inextricable /inɛkstrikabl/ *a.* inextricable.
infaillible /ɛ̃fajibl/ *a.* infallible.
infâme /ɛ̃fɑm/ *a.* vile.
infamie /ɛ̃fami/ *n.f.* infamy; (*action*) vile action.
infanterie /ɛ̃fɑ̃tri/ *n.f.* infantry.
infantile /ɛ̃fɑ̃til/ *a.* infantile.
infarctus /ɛ̃farktys/ *n.m.* coronary (thrombosis).
infatigable /ɛ̃fatigabl/ *a.* tireless.
infect /ɛ̃fɛkt/ *a.* revolting.
infect|er /ɛ̃fɛkte/ *v.t.* infect. **s'~er** *v. pr.* become infected. **~ion** /-ksjɔ̃/ *n.f.* infection; (*odeur*) stench.
infectieu|x, ~se /ɛ̃fɛksjø, -z/ *a.* infectious.
inférieur, ~e /ɛ̃ferjœr/ *a.* (*plus bas*) lower; (*moins bon*) inferior (**à,** to). —*n.m., f.* inferior. **~ à,** (*plus petit que*) smaller than.
infériorité /ɛ̃ferjɔrite/ *n.f.* inferiority.
infern|al (*m. pl.* **~aux**) /ɛ̃fɛrnal, -o/ *a.* infernal.
infester /ɛ̃fɛste/ *v.t.* infest.
infid|èle /ɛ̃fidɛl/ *a.* unfaithful. **~élité** *n.f.* unfaithfulness; (*acte*) infidelity.
infiltr|er (s') /(s)ɛ̃filtre/ *v. pr.* **s'~er (dans),** (*personnes, idées, etc.*) infiltrate; (*liquide*) percolate. **~ation** *n.f.* infiltration.
infime /ɛ̃fim/ *a.* tiny.
infini /ɛ̃fini/ *a.* infinite. —*n.m.* infinity. **à l'~,** endlessly. **~ment** *adv.* infinitely.
infinité /ɛ̃finite/ *n.f.* **une ~ de,** an infinite amount of.
infinitif /ɛ̃finitif/ *n.m.* infinitive.
infirm|e /ɛ̃firm/ *a.* & *n.m./f.* dis-

abled (person). **~ité** *n.f.* disability.
infirmer /ɛ̃firme/ *v.t.* invalidate.
infirm|erie /ɛ̃firməri/ *n.f.* sickbay, infirmary. **~ier** *n.m.* (male) nurse. **~ière** *n.f.* nurse.
inflammable /ɛ̃flamabl/ *a.* (in)flammable.
inflammation /ɛ̃flamɑsjɔ̃/ *n.f.* inflammation.
inflation /ɛ̃flɑsjɔ̃/ *n.f.* inflation.
inflexible /ɛ̃flɛksibl/ *a.* inflexible.
inflexion /ɛ̃flɛksjɔ̃/ *n.f.* inflexion.
infliger /ɛ̃fliʒe/ *v.t.* inflict; (*sanction*) impose.
influen|ce /ɛ̃flyɑ̃s/ *n.f.* influence. **~çable** *a.* easily influenced. **~cer** *v.t.* influence.
influent, ~e /ɛ̃flyɑ̃, -t/ *a.* influential.
influer /ɛ̃flye/ *v.i.* **~ sur,** influence.
informa|teur, ~trice /ɛ̃fɔrmatœr, -tris/ *n.m., f.* informant.
informaticien, ~ne /ɛ̃fɔrmatisjɛ̃, -jɛn/ *n.m., f.* computer scientist.
information /ɛ̃fɔrmɑsjɔ̃/ *n.f.* information; (*jurid.*) inquiry. **une ~,** (some) information; (*nouvelle*) (some) news. **les ~s,** the news.
informati|que /ɛ̃fɔrmatik/ *n.f.* computer science; (*techniques*) data processing. **~ser** *v.t.* computerize.
informe /ɛ̃fɔrm/ *a.* shapeless.
informer /ɛ̃fɔrme/ *v.t.* inform (**de,** about, of). **s'~** *v. pr.* enquire (**de,** about).
infortun|e /ɛ̃fɔrtyn/ *n.f.* misfortune. **~é, ~ée** *a.* wretched; *n.m., f.* wretch.
infraction /ɛ̃fraksjɔ̃/ *n.f.* offence. **~ à,** breach of.
infranchissable /ɛ̃frɑ̃ʃisabl/ *a.* impassable; (*fig.*) insuperable.
infrarouge /ɛ̃fraruʒ/ *a.* infra-red.
infructueu|x, ~se /ɛ̃fryktɥø, -z/ *a.* fruitless.
infus|er /ɛ̃fyze/ *v.t./i.* infuse, brew. **~ion** *n.f.* herb-tea, infusion.
ingénier (s') /(s)ɛ̃ʒenje/ *v. pr.* **s'~ à,** strive to.
ingénieur /ɛ̃ʒenjœr/ *n.m.* engineer.
ingén|ieux, ~ieuse /ɛ̃ʒenjø, -z/ *a.* ingenious. **~iosité** *n.f.* ingenuity.
ingénu /ɛ̃ʒeny/ *a.* naïve.
ingér|er (s') /(s)ɛ̃ʒere/ *v. pr.* **s'~er dans,** interfere in. **~ence** *n.f.* interference.
ingrat, ~e /ɛ̃gra, -t/ *a.* ungrateful; (*pénible*) thankless; (*disgracieux*) unattractive. **~itude** /-tityd/ *n.f.* ingratitude.
ingrédient /ɛ̃gredjɑ̃/ *n.m.* ingredient.
inguérissable /ɛ̃gerisabl/ *a.* incurable.
ingurgiter /ɛ̃gyrʒite/ *v.t.* swallow.
inhabité /inabite/ *a.* uninhabited.
inhabituel, ~le /inabitɥɛl/ *a.* unusual.
inhalation /inalɑsjɔ̃/ *n.f.* inhaling.
inhérent, ~e /inerɑ̃, -t/ *a.* inherent (**à,** in).
inhibition /inibisjɔ̃/ *n.f.* inhibition.
inhospital|ier, ~ière /inɔspitalje, -jɛr/ *a.* inhospitable.
inhumain, ~e /inymɛ̃, -ɛn/ *a.* inhuman.
inhum|er /inyme/ *v.t.* bury. **~ation** *n.f.* burial.
inimaginable /inimaʒinabl/ *a.* unimaginable.
inimitié /inimitje/ *n.f.* enmity.
ininterrompu /inɛ̃tɛrɔ̃py/ *a.* continuous, uninterrupted.
iniqu|e /inik/ *a.* iniquitous. **~ité** *n.f.* iniquity.
init|ial (*m. pl.* **~iaux**) /inisjal, -jo/ *a.* initial. **~ialement** *adv.* initially.
initiale /inisjal/ *n.f.* initial.
initiative /inisjativ/ *n.f.* initiative.
init|ier /inisje/ *v.t.* initiate. **s'~ier**

v. pr. become initiated (**à**, into). **~iateur, ~iatrice** *n.m., f.* initiator. **~iation** *n.f.* initiation.
inject|er /ɛ̃ʒɛkte/ *v.t.* inject. **~é de sang,** bloodshot. **~ion** /-ksjɔ̃/ *n.f.* injection.
injur|e /ɛ̃ʒyr/ *n.f.* insult. **~ier** *v.t.* insult. **~ieux, ~ieuse** *a.* insulting.
injust|e /ɛ̃ʒyst/ *a.* unjust, unfair. **~ice** *n.f.* injustice.
inlassable /ɛ̃lɑsabl/ *a.* tireless.
inné /ine/ *a.* innate.
innocen|t, ~te /inɔsɑ̃, -t/ *a.* & *n.m., f.* innocent. **~ce** *n.f.* innocence.
innocenter /inɔsɑ̃te/ *v.t.* (*disculper*) clear, prove innocent.
innombrable /inɔ̃brabl/ *a.* countless.
innov|er /inɔve/ *v.i.* innovate. **~ateur, ~atrice** *n.m., f.* innovator. **~ation** *n.f.* innovation.
inoccupé /inɔkype/ *a.* unoccupied.
inoculer /inɔkyle/ *v.t.* **~ qch. à qn.,** infect s.o. with sth.
inodore /inɔdɔr/ *a.* odourless.
inoffensi|f, ~ve /inɔfɑ̃sif, -v/ *a.* harmless.
inond|er /inɔ̃de/ *v.t.* flood; (*mouiller*) soak; (*envahir*) inundate (**de,** with). **~é de soleil,** bathed in sunlight. **~ation** *n.f.* flood; (*action*) flooding.
inopérant, ~e /inɔperɑ̃, -t/ *a.* inoperative.
inopportun, ~e /inɔpɔrtœ̃, -yn/ *a.* inopportune.
inoubliable /inublijabl/ *a.* unforgettable.
inouï /inwi/ *a.* incredible.
inoxydable /inɔksidabl/ *a.* (*couteau*) stainless-steel. **acier ~,** stainless steel.
inqualifiable /ɛ̃kalifjabl/ *a.* unspeakable.
inqu|iet, ~iète /ɛ̃kjɛ, ɛ̃kjɛt/ *a.* worried. —*n.m., f.* worrier.
inquiét|er /ɛ̃kjete/ *v.t.* worry. **s'~er** worry (**de,** about). **~ant, ~ante** *a.* worrying.
inquiétude /ɛ̃kjetyd/ *n.f.* anxiety, worry.
inquisition /ɛ̃kizisjɔ̃/ *n.f.* inquisition.
insalubre /ɛ̃salybr/ *a.* unhealthy.
insanité /ɛ̃sanite/ *n.f.* insanity.
insatiable /ɛ̃sasjabl/ *a.* insatiable.
inscription /ɛ̃skripsjɔ̃/ *n.f.* inscription; (*immatriculation*) enrolment.
inscrire† /ɛ̃skrir/ *v.t.* write (down); (*graver, tracer*) inscribe; (*personne*) enrol; (*sur une liste*) put down. **s'~** *v. pr.* put one's name down. **s'~ à,** (*école*) enrol at; (*club, parti*) join; (*examen*) enter for. **s'~ dans le cadre de,** come within the framework of.
insecte /ɛ̃sɛkt/ *n.m.* insect.
insecticide /ɛ̃sɛktisid/ *n.m.* insecticide.
insécurité /ɛ̃sekyrite/ *n.f.* insecurity.
insensé /ɛ̃sɑ̃se/ *a.* senseless.
insensib|le /ɛ̃sɑ̃sibl/ *a.* insensitive (**à,** to); (*graduel*) imperceptible. **~ilité** *n.f.* insensitivity.
inséparable /ɛ̃separabl/ *a.* inseparable.
insérer /ɛ̃sere/ *v.t.* insert. **s'~ dans,** be part of.
insidieu|x, ~se /ɛ̃sidjø, -z/ *a.* insidious.
insigne /ɛ̃siɲ/ *n.m.* badge. **~(s),** (*d'une fonction*) insignia.
insignifian|t, ~te /ɛ̃siɲifjɑ̃, -t/ *a.* insignificant. **~ce** *n.f.* insignificance.
insinuation /ɛ̃sinɥɑsjɔ̃/ *n.f.* insinuation.
insinuer /ɛ̃sinɥe/ *v.t.* insinuate. **s'~ dans,** penetrate.
insipide /ɛ̃sipid/ *a.* insipid.
insistan|t, ~te /ɛ̃sistɑ̃, -t/ *a.* insistent. **~ce** *n.f.* insistence.
insister /ɛ̃siste/ *v.i.* insist (**pour faire,** on doing). **~ sur,** stress.

insociable /ɛ̃sɔsjabl/ *a.* unsociable.
insolation /ɛ̃sɔlɑsjɔ̃/ *n.f.* (*méd.*) sunstroke.
insolen|t, ~te /ɛ̃sɔlɑ̃, -t/ *a.* insolent. **~ce** *n.f.* insolence.
insolite /ɛ̃sɔlit/ *a.* unusual.
insoluble /ɛ̃sɔlybl/ *a.* insoluble.
insolvable /ɛ̃sɔlvabl/ *a.* insolvent.
insomnie /ɛ̃sɔmni/ *n.f.* insomnia.
insonoriser /ɛ̃sɔnɔrize/ *v.t.* soundproof.
insoucian|t, ~te /ɛ̃susjɑ̃, -t/ *a.* carefree. **~ce** *n.f.* unconcern.
insoumission /ɛ̃sumisjɔ̃/ *n.f.* rebelliousness.
insoutenable /ɛ̃sutnabl/ *a.* unbearable; (*argument*) untenable.
inspec|ter /ɛ̃spɛkte/ *v.t.* inspect. **~teur, ~trice** *n.m., f.* inspector. **~tion** /-ksjɔ̃/ *n.f.* inspection.
inspir|er /ɛ̃spire/ *v.t.* inspire. —*v.i.* breathe in. **~er à qn.,** inspire s.o. with. **s'~er de,** be inspired by. **~ation** *n.f.* inspiration; (*respiration*) breath.
instab|le /ɛ̃stabl/ *a.* unstable; (*meuble, équilibre*) unsteady. **~ilité** *n.f.* instability; unsteadiness.
install|er /ɛ̃stale/ *v.t.* install; (*gaz, meuble*) put in; (*étagère*) put up; (*équiper*) fit out. **s'~er** *v. pr.* settle (down); (*emménager*) settle in. **s'~er comme,** set o.s. up as. **~ation** *n.f.* installation; (*de local*) fitting out; (*de locataire*) settling in. **~ations** *n.f. pl.* (*appareils*) fittings.
instance /ɛ̃stɑ̃s/ *n.f.* authority; (*prière*) entreaty. **avec ~,** with insistence. **en ~ de,** in the course of, on the point of.
instant /ɛ̃stɑ̃/ *n.m.* moment, instant. **à l'~,** this instant.
instantané /ɛ̃stɑ̃tane/ *a.* instantaneous; (*café*) instant. —*n.m.* snapshot.
instaur|er /ɛ̃stɔre/ *v.t.* institute. **~ation** *n.f.* institution.
instiga|teur, ~trice /ɛ̃stigatœr, -tris/ *n.m., f.* instigator. **~tion** /-ɑsjɔ̃/ *n.f.* instigation.
instinct /ɛ̃stɛ̃/ *n.m.* instinct. **d'~,** instinctively.
instincti|f, ~ve /ɛ̃stɛ̃ktif, -v/ *a.* instinctive. **~vement** *adv.* instinctively.
instituer /ɛ̃stitɥe/ *v.t.* establish.
institut /ɛ̃stity/ *n.m.* institute. **~ de beauté,** beauty parlour. **~ universitaire de technologie,** polytechnic, technical college.
institu|teur, ~trice /ɛ̃stitytœr, -tris/ *n.m., f.* primary-school teacher.
institution /ɛ̃stitysjɔ̃/ *n.f.* institution; (*école*) private school.
instructi|f, ~ve /ɛ̃stryktif, -v/ *a.* instructive.
instruction /ɛ̃stryksjɔ̃/ *n.f.* education; (*document*) directive. **~s,** (*ordres, mode d'emploi*) instructions.
instruire† /ɛ̃strɥir/ *v.t.* teach, educate. **~ de,** inform of. **s'~** *v. pr.* educate o.s. **s'~ de,** enquire about.
instruit, ~e /ɛ̃strɥi, -t/ *a.* educated.
instrument /ɛ̃strymɑ̃/ *n.m.* instrument; (*outil*) implement.
insu /ɛ̃sy/ *n.m.* **à l'~ de,** without the knowledge of.
insubordination /ɛ̃sybɔrdinɑsjɔ̃/ *n.f.* insubordination.
insuffisan|t, ~te /ɛ̃syfizɑ̃, -t/ *a.* inadequate; (*en nombre*) insufficient. **~ce** *n.f.* inadequacy.
insulaire /ɛ̃sylɛr/ *a.* island. —*n.m./f.* islander.
insuline /ɛ̃sylin/ *n.f.* insulin.
insult|e /ɛ̃sylt/ *n.f.* insult. **~er** *v.t.* insult.
insupportable /ɛ̃sypɔrtabl/ *a.* unbearable.
insurg|er (s') /(s)ɛ̃syrʒe/ *v. pr.*

rebel. **~é, ~ée** *a.* & *n.m., f.* rebel.
insurmontable /ɛ̃syrmɔ̃tabl/ *a.* insurmountable.
insurrection /ɛ̃syrɛksjɔ̃/ *n.f.* insurrection.
intact /ɛ̃takt/ *a.* intact.
intangible /ɛ̃tɑ̃ʒibl/ *a.* intangible.
intarissable /ɛ̃tarisabl/ *a.* inexhaustible.
intégr|al (*m. pl.* **~aux**) /ɛ̃tegral, -o/ *a.* complete; (*édition*) unabridged. **~alement** *adv.* in full. **~alité** *n.f.* whole. **dans son ~alité,** in full.
intègre /ɛ̃tɛgr/ *a.* upright.
intégr|er /ɛ̃tegre/ *v.t.*, **s'~er** *v. pr.* integrate. **~ation** *n.f.* integration.
intégrité /ɛ̃tegrite/ *n.f.* integrity.
intellect /ɛ̃telɛkt/ *n.m.* intellect. **~uel, ~uelle** *a.* & *n.m, f.* intellectual.
intelligence /ɛ̃teliʒɑ̃s/ *n.f.* intelligence; (*compréhension*) understanding; (*complicité*) complicity.
intellig|ent, ~ente /ɛ̃teliʒɑ̃, -t/ *a.* intelligent. **~emment** /-amɑ̃/ *adv.* intelligently.
intelligible /ɛ̃teliʒibl/ *a.* intelligible.
intempérance /ɛ̃tɑ̃perɑ̃s/ *n.f.* intemperance.
intempéries /ɛ̃tɑ̃peri/ *n.f. pl.* severe weather.
intempesti|f, ~ve /ɛ̃tɑ̃pɛstif, -v/ *a.* untimely.
intenable /ɛ̃tnabl/ *a.* unbearable; (*position*) untenable.
intendan|t, ~te /ɛ̃tɑ̃dɑ̃, -t/ *n.m.* (*mil.*) quartermaster. *—n.m., f.* (*scol.*) bursar. **~ce** *n.f.* (*scol.*) bursar's office.
intens|e /ɛ̃tɑ̃s/ *a.* intense; (*circulation*) heavy. **~ément** *adv.* intensely. **~ifier** *v.t.*, **s'~ifier** *v. pr.* intensify. **~ité** *n.f.* intensity.
intensi|f, ~ve /ɛ̃tɑ̃sif, -v/ *a.* intensive.
intenter /ɛ̃tɑ̃te/ *v.t.* **~ un procès** *ou* **une action,** institute proceedings (**à, contre,** against).
intention /ɛ̃tɑ̃sjɔ̃/ *n.f.* intention (**de faire,** of doing). **à l'~ de qn.,** for s.o. **~né** /-jɔne/ *a.* **bien/mal ~né,** well-/ill-intentioned.
intentionnel, ~le /ɛ̃tɑ̃sjɔnɛl/ *a.* intentional.
inter- /ɛ̃tɛr/ *préf.* inter-.
interaction /ɛ̃tɛraksjɔ̃/ *n.f.* interaction.
intercaler /ɛ̃tɛrkale/ *v.t.* insert.
intercéder /ɛ̃tɛrsede/ *v.i.* intercede.
intercept|er /ɛ̃tɛrsɛpte/ *v.t.* intercept. **~ion** /-psjɔ̃/ *n.f.* interception.
interchangeable /ɛ̃tɛrʃɑ̃ʒabl/ *a.* interchangeable.
interdiction /ɛ̃tɛrdiksjɔ̃/ *n.f.* ban. **~ de fumer,** no smoking.
interdire† /ɛ̃tɛrdir/ *v.t.* forbid; (*officiellement*) ban, prohibit. **~ à qn. de faire,** forbid s.o. to do; (*empêcher*) prevent s.o. from doing.
interdit, ~e /ɛ̃tɛrdi, -t/ *a.* (*étonné*) nonplussed.
intéressant, ~e /ɛ̃terɛsɑ̃, -t/ *a.* interesting; (*avantageux*) attractive.
intéressé, ~e /ɛ̃terese/ *a.* (*en cause*) concerned; (*égoïste*) selfish. *—n.m., f.* person concerned.
intéresser /ɛ̃terese/ *v.t.* interest; (*concerner*) concern. **s'~ à,** be interested in.
intérêt /ɛ̃terɛ/ *n.m.* interest; (*égoïsme*) self-interest. **~(s),** (*comm.*) interest. **vous avez ~ à,** it is in your interest to.
interférence /ɛ̃tɛrferɑ̃s/ *n.f.* interference.
intérieur, ~e /ɛ̃terjœr/ *a.* inner, inside; (*vol, politique*) domestic; (*vie, calme*) inner. *—n.m.* interior; (*de boîte, tiroir*) inside. **à l'~ (de),** inside; (*fig.*) within. **~ement** *adv.* inwardly.

intérim /ɛ̃terim/ *n.m.* interim. **assurer l'~,** deputize (**de**, for). **par ~,** acting. **~aire** *a.* temporary, interim.

interjection /ɛ̃tɛrʒɛksjɔ̃/ *n.f.* interjection.

interlocu|teur, ~trice /ɛ̃tɛrlɔkytœr, -tris/ *n.m., f.* **son ~teur,** the person one is speaking to.

interloquer /ɛ̃tɛrlɔke/ *v.t.* take aback.

intermède /ɛ̃tɛrmɛd/ *n.m.* interlude.

intermédiaire /ɛ̃tɛrmedjɛr/ *a.* intermediate. —*n.m./f.* intermediary.

interminable /ɛ̃tɛrminabl/ *a.* endless.

intermittent, ~e /ɛ̃tɛrmitɑ̃, -t/ *a.* intermittent.

internat /ɛ̃tɛrna/ *n.m.* boarding-school.

internation|al (*m. pl.* **~aux**) /ɛ̃tɛrnasjɔnal, -o/ *a.* international.

interne /ɛ̃tɛrn/ *a.* internal. —*n.m./f.* (*scol.*) boarder.

intern|er /ɛ̃tɛrne/ *v.t.* (*pol.*) intern; (*méd.*) confine. **~ement** *n.m.* (*pol.*) internment.

interpell|er /ɛ̃tɛrpele/ *v.t.* shout to; (*apostropher*) shout at; (*interroger*) question. **~ation** *n.f.* (*pol.*) questioning.

interphone /ɛ̃tɛrfɔn/ *n.m.* intercom.

interposer (s') /(s)ɛ̃tɛrpoze/ *v. pr.* intervene.

interpr|ète /ɛ̃tɛrprɛt/ *n.m./f.* interpreter; (*artiste*) performer. **~étariat** *n.m.* interpreting.

interprét|er /ɛ̃tɛrprete/ *v.t.* interpret; (*jouer*) play; (*chanter*) sing. **~ation** *n.f.* interpretation; (*d'artiste*) performance.

interrogati|f, ~ve /ɛ̃tɛrɔgatif, -v/ *a.* & *n.m.* interrogative.

interrogatoire /ɛ̃terɔgatwar/ *n.m.* interrogation.

interro|ger /ɛ̃terɔʒe/ *v.t.* question; (*élève*) test. **~gateur, ~gatrice** *a.* questioning. **~gation** *n.f.* question; (*action*) questioning; (*épreuve*) test.

interr|ompre† /ɛ̃terɔ̃pr/ *v.t.* break off, interrupt; (*personne*) interrupt. **s'~ompre** *v. pr.* break off. **~upteur** *n.m.* switch. **~uption** *n.f.* interruption; (*arrêt*) break.

intersection /ɛ̃tɛrsɛksjɔ̃/ *n.f.* intersection.

interstice /ɛ̃tɛrstis/ *n.m.* crack.

interurbain /ɛ̃tɛryrbɛ̃/ *n.m.* long-distance telephone service.

intervalle /ɛ̃tɛrval/ *n.m.* space; (*temps*) interval. **dans l'~,** in the meantime.

interven|ir† /ɛ̃tɛrvənir/ *v.i.* intervene; (*survenir*) occur; (*méd.*) operate. **~tion** /-vɑ̃sjɔ̃/ *n.f.* intervention; (*méd.*) operation.

intervertir /ɛ̃tɛrvɛrtir/ *v.t.* invert.

interview /ɛ̃tɛrvju/ *n.f.* interview. **~er** /-ve/ *v.t.* interview.

intestin /ɛ̃tɛstɛ̃/ *n.m.* intestine.

intim|e /ɛ̃tim/ *a.* intimate; (*fête, vie*) private; (*dîner*) quiet. —*n.m./f.* intimate friend. **~ement** *adv.* intimately. **~ité** *n.f.* intimacy; (*vie privée*) privacy.

intimid|er /ɛ̃timide/ *v.t.* intimidate. **~ation** *n.f.* intimidation.

intituler /ɛ̃tityle/ *v.t.* entitle. **s'~** *v. pr.* be entitled.

intolérable /ɛ̃tɔlerabl/ *a.* intolerable.

intoléran|t, ~te /ɛ̃tɔlerɑ̃, -t/ *a.* intolerant. **~ce** *n.f.* intolerance.

intonation /ɛ̃tɔnɑsjɔ̃/ *n.f.* intonation.

intoxiqué, ~e /ɛ̃tɔksike/ *n.m., f.* (*par la drogue, le tabac, etc.*) addict.

intoxi|quer /ɛ̃tɔksike/ *v.t.* poison; (*pol.*) brainwash. **~cation** *n.f.* poisoning; (*pol.*) brainwashing.

intraduisible /ɛ̃tradɥizibl/ *a.* untranslatable.

intraitable /ɛ̃trɛtabl/ *a.* inflexible.

intransigean|t, ~te /ɛ̃trɑ̃siʒɑ̃, -t/ *a.* intransigent. **~ce** *n.f.* intransigence.

intransiti|f, ~ve /ɛ̃trɑ̃zitif, -v/ *a.* intransitive.

intraveineu|x, ~se /ɛ̃travɛnø, -z/ *a.* intravenous.

intrépide /ɛ̃trepid/ *a.* fearless.

intrigu|e /ɛ̃trig/ *n.f.* intrigue; (*théâtre*) plot. **~er** *v.t./i.* intrigue.

intrinsèque /ɛ̃trɛ̃sɛk/ *a.* intrinsic.

introduction /ɛ̃trɔdyksjɔ̃/ *n.f.* introduction.

introduire† /ɛ̃trɔdɥir/ *v.t.* introduce, bring in; (*insérer*) put in, insert. **~ qn.,** show s.o. in. **s'~ dans,** get into, enter.

introspecti|f, ~ve /ɛ̃trɔspɛktif, -v/ *a.* introspective.

introuvable /ɛ̃truvabl/ *a.* that cannot be found.

introverti, ~e /ɛ̃trɔvɛrti/ *n.m., f.* introvert. —*a.* introverted.

intrus, ~e /ɛ̃try, -z/ *n.m., f.* intruder. **~ion** /-zjɔ̃/ *n.f.* intrusion.

intuiti|f, ~ve /ɛ̃tɥitif, -v/ *a.* intuitive.

intuition /ɛ̃tɥisjɔ̃/ *n.f.* intuition.

inusable /inyzabl/ *a.* hard-wearing.

inusité /inyzite/ *a.* uncommon.

inutil|e /inytil/ *a.* useless; (*vain*) needless. **~ement** *adv.* needlessly. **~ité** *n.f.* uselessness.

inutilisable /inytilizabl/ *a.* unusable.

invalid|e /ɛ̃valid/ *a.* & *n.m.|f.* disabled (person). **~ité** *n.f.* disablement.

invariable /ɛ̃varjabl/ *a.* invariable.

invasion /ɛ̃vɑzjɔ̃/ *n.f.* invasion.

invectiv|e /ɛ̃vɛktiv/ *n.f.* invective. **~er** *v.t.* abuse.

invend|able /ɛ̃vɑ̃dabl/ *a.* unsaleable. **~u** *a.* unsold.

inventaire /ɛ̃vɑ̃tɛr/ *n.m.* inventory; (*recensement*) survey. **faire l'~ de,** take stock of.

invent|er /ɛ̃vɑ̃te/ *v.t.* invent. **~eur** *n.m.* inventor. **~ion** /ɛ̃vɑ̃sjɔ̃/ *n.f.* invention.

inventi|f, ~ve /ɛ̃vɑ̃tif, -v/ *a.* inventive.

inverse /ɛ̃vɛrs/ *a.* opposite; (*ordre*) reverse. —*n.m.* reverse. **~ment** /-əmɑ̃/ *adv.* conversely.

invers|er /ɛ̃vɛrse/ *v.t.* reverse, invert. **~ion** *n.f.* inversion.

investigation /ɛ̃vɛstigɑsjɔ̃/ *n.f.* investigation.

invest|ir /ɛ̃vɛstir/ *v.t.* invest. **~issement** *n.m.* (*comm.*) investment.

investiture /ɛ̃vɛstityr/ *n.f.* nomination.

invétéré /ɛ̃vetere/ *a.* inveterate.

invincible /ɛ̃vɛ̃sibl/ *a.* invincible.

invisible /ɛ̃vizibl/ *a.* invisible.

invit|er /ɛ̃vite/ *v.t.* invite (**à,** to). **~ation** *n.f.* invitation. **~é, ~ée** *n.m., f.* guest.

invivable /ɛ̃vivabl/ *a.* unbearable.

involontaire /ɛ̃vɔlɔ̃tɛr/ *a.* involuntary.

invoquer /ɛ̃vɔke/ *v.t.* call upon, invoke; (*alléguer*) plead.

invraisembl|able /ɛ̃vrɛsɑ̃blabl/ *a.* improbable; (*incroyable*) incredible. **~ance** *n.f.* improbability.

invulnérable /ɛ̃vylnerabl/ *a.* invulnerable.

iode /jɔd/ *n.m.* iodine.

ira, irait /ira, irɛ/ *voir* **aller**[1].

Irak /irak/ *n.m.* Iraq. **~ien, ~ienne** *a.* & *n.m., f.* Iraqi.

Iran /irɑ̃/ *n.m.* Iran. **~ien, ~ienne** /iranjɛ̃, -jɛn/ *a.* & *n.m., f.* Iranian.

irascible /irasibl/ *a.* irascible.

iris /iris/ *n.m.* iris.

irlandais, ~e /irlɑ̃dɛ, -z/ *a.* Irish. —*n.m., f.* Irishman, Irishwoman.

Irlande /irlɑ̃d/ *n.f.* Ireland.

iron|ie /irɔni/ *n.f.* irony. **~ique** *a.* ironic(al).
irraisonné /irɛzɔne/ *a.* irrational.
irréalisable /irealizabl/ *a.* (*projet*) unworkable.
irrécupérable /irekyperabl/ *a.* irretrievable, beyond recall.
irréel, ~le /ireɛl/ *a.* unreal.
irréfléchi /irefleʃi/ *a.* thoughtless.
irréfutable /irefytabl/ *a.* irrefutable.
irrégul|ier, ~ière /iregylje, -jɛr/ *a.* irregular. **~arité** *n.f.* irregularity.
irrémédiable /iremedjabl/ *a.* irreparable.
irremplaçable /irɑ̃plasabl/ *a.* irreplaceable.
irréparable /ireparabl/ *a.* beyond repair.
irréprochable /ireprɔʃabl/ *a.* flawless.
irrésistible /irezistibl/ *a.* irresistible; (*drôle*) hilarious.
irrésolu /irezɔly/ *a.* indecisive.
irrespirable /irɛspirabl/ *a.* stifling.
irresponsable /irɛspɔ̃sabl/ *a.* irresponsible.
irréversible /ireversibl/ *a.* irreversible.
irrévocable /irevɔkabl/ *a.* irrevocable.
irrigation /irigɑsjɔ̃/ *n.f.* irrigation.
irriguer /irige/ *v.t.* irrigate.
irrit|er /irite/ *v.t.* irritate. **s'~er de,** be annoyed at. **~able** *a.* irritable. **~ation** *n.f.* irritation.
irruption /irypsjɔ̃/ *n.f.* **faire ~ dans,** burst into.
Islam /islam/ *n.m.* Islam.
islamique /islamik/ *a.* Islamic.
islandais, ~e /islɑ̃dɛ, -z/ *a.* Icelandic. —*n.m., f.* Icelander. —*n.m.* (*lang.*) Icelandic.
Islande /islɑ̃d/ *n.f.* Iceland.
isolé /izɔle/ *a.* isolated. **~ment** *adv.* in isolation.
isol|er /izɔle/ *v.t.* isolate; (*électr.*) insulate. **s'~er** *v. pr.* isolate o.s. **~ant** *n.m.* insulating material. **~ation** *n.f.* insulation. **~ement** *n.m.* isolation.
isoloir /izɔlwar/ *n.m.* polling booth.
Isorel /izɔrɛl/ *n.m.* (P.) hardboard.
isotope /izɔtɔp/ *n.m.* isotope.
Israël /israɛl/ *n.m.* Israel.
israélien, ~ne /israeljɛ̃, -jɛn/ *a.* & *n.m., f.* Israeli.
israélite /israelit/ *a.* Jewish. —*n.m./f.* Jew, Jewess.
issu /isy/ *a.* **être ~ de,** come from.
issue /isy/ *n.f.* exit; (***résultat***) outcome; (*fig.*) solution. **à l'~ de,** at the conclusion of. **rue** *ou* **voie sans ~,** dead end.
isthme /ism/ *n.m.* isthmus.
Italie /itali/ *n.f.* Italy.
italien, ~ne /italjɛ̃, -jɛn/ *a.* & *n.m., f.* Italian. —*n.m.* (*lang.*) Italian.
italique /italik/ *n.m.* italics.
itinéraire /itinerɛr/ *n.m.* itinerary, route.
itinérant, ~e /itinerɑ̃, -t/ *a.* itinerant.
ivoire /ivwar/ *n.m.* ivory.
ivr|e /ivr/ *a.* drunk. **~esse** *n.f.* drunkenness. **~ogne** *n.m.* drunk(ard).

J

j' /ʒ/ *voir* **je.**
jacasser /ʒakase/ *v.i.* chatter.
jachère (en) /(ɑ̃)ʒaʃɛr/ *adv.* fallow.
jacinthe /ʒasɛ̃t/ *n.f.* hyacinth.
jade /ʒad/ *n.m.* jade.
jadis /ʒadis/ *adv.* long ago.
jaillir /ʒajir/ *v.i.* (*liquide*) spurt (out); (*lumière*) stream out; (*apparaître, fuser*) burst forth.
jais /ʒɛ/ *n.m.* **(noir) de ~,** jet-black.
jalon /ʒalɔ̃/ *n.m.* (*piquet*) marker. **~ner** /-ɔne/ *v.t.* mark (out).

jalou|x, ~se /ʒalu, -z/ *a.* jealous. **~ser** *v.t.* be jealous of. **~sie** *n.f.* jealousy; (*store*) (venetian) blind.
jamais /ʒamɛ/ *adv.* ever. **(ne) ~,** never. **il ne boit ~,** he never drinks. **à ~,** for ever. **si ~,** if ever.
jambe /ʒɑ̃b/ *n.f.* leg.
jambon /ʒɑ̃bɔ̃/ *n.m.* ham. **~neau** (*pl.* **~neaux**) /-ɔno/ *n.m.* knuckle of ham.
jante /ʒɑ̃t/ *n.f.* rim.
janvier /ʒɑ̃vje/ *n.m.* January.
Japon /ʒapɔ̃/ *n.m.* Japan.
japonais, ~e /japɔnɛ, -z/ *a.* & *n.m., f.* Japanese. —*n.m.* (*lang.*) Japanese.
japper /ʒape/ *v.i.* yelp.
jaquette /ʒakɛt/ *n.f.* (*de livre, femme*) jacket; (*d'homme*) morning coat.
jardin /ʒardɛ̃/ *n.m.* garden. **~ d'enfants,** nursery (school). **~ public,** public park.
jardin|er /ʒardine/ *v.i.* garden. **~age** *n.m.* gardening. **~ier, ~ière** *n.m., f.* gardener; *n.f.* (*meuble*) plant-stand. **~ière de légumes,** mixed vegetables.
jargon /ʒargɔ̃/ *n.m.* jargon.
jarret /ʒarɛ/ *n.m.* back of the knee.
jarretelle /ʒartɛl/ *n.f.* suspender; (*Amer.*) garter.
jarretière /ʒartjɛr/ *n.f.* garter.
jaser /ʒaze/ *v.i.* jabber.
jasmin /ʒasmɛ̃/ *n.m.* jasmine.
jatte /ʒat/ *n.f.* bowl.
jaug|e /ʒoʒ/ *n.f.* capacity; (*de navire*) tonnage; (*compteur*) gauge. **~er** *v.t.* gauge.
jaun|e /ʒon/ *a.* & *n.m.* yellow. **~e d'œuf,** (egg) yolk. **~ir** *v.t./i.* turn yellow.
jaunisse /ʒonis/ *n.f.* jaundice.
javelot /ʒavlo/ *n.m.* javelin.
jazz /dʒɑz/ *n.m.* jazz.
je, j'* /ʒə, ʒ/ *pron.* I.
jean /dʒin/ *n.m.* jeans.
jeep /(d)ʒip/ *n.f.* jeep.
jerrycan /(d)ʒerikan/ *n.m.* jerrycan.
jersey /ʒɛrzɛ/ *n.m.* jersey.
Jersey /ʒɛrzɛ/ *n.f.* Jersey.
Jésus /ʒezy/ *n.m.* Jesus.
jet[1] /ʒɛ/ *n.m.* throw; (*de liquide, vapeur*) jet; (*de lumière*) flash. **~ d'eau,** fountain.
jet[2] /dʒɛt/ *n.m.* (*avion*) jet.
jetée /ʒte/ *n.f.* pier.
jeter /ʒte/ *v.t.* throw; (*au rebut*) throw away; (*regard, ancre, lumière*) cast; (*cri*) utter; (*bases*) lay. **~ un coup d'œil,** have *ou* take a look (**à,** at). **se ~ contre,** (*heurter*) bash into. **se ~ dans,** (*fleuve*) flow into. **se ~ sur,** (*se ruer sur*) rush at.
jeton /ʒtɔ̃/ *n.m.* token; (*pour compter*) counter.
jeu (*pl.* **~x**) /ʒø/ *n.m.* game; (*amusement*) play; (*au casino etc.*) gambling; (*théâtre*) acting; (*série*) set; (*de lumière, ressort*) play. **en ~,** (*honneur*) at stake; (*forces*) at work. **~ de cartes,** (*paquet*) pack of cards. **~ d'échecs,** (*boîte*) chess set. **~ de mots,** pun. **~ télévisé,** television quiz.
jeudi /ʒødi/ *n.m.* Thursday.
jeun (à) /(a)ʒœ̃/ *adv.* without food.
jeune /ʒœn/ *a.* young; (*cadet*) younger. —*n.m./f.* young person. **~ fille,** girl. **~s mariés,** newlyweds. **les ~s,** young people.
jeûn|e /ʒøn/ *n.m.* fast. **~er** *v.i.* fast.
jeunesse /ʒœnɛs/ *n.f.* youth; (*apparence*) youthfulness. **la ~,** (*jeunes*) the young.
joaill|ier, ~ière /ʒɔɑje, -jɛr/ *n.m., f.* jeweller. **~erie** *n.f.* jewellery; (*magasin*) jeweller's shop.
jockey /ʒɔkɛ/ *n.m.* jockey.
joie /ʒwa/ *n.f.* joy.
joindre† /ʒwɛ̃dr/ *v.t.* join; (*mains, pieds*) put together; (*efforts*) combine; (*dans une enveloppe*) enclose. **se ~ à,** join.
joint, ~e /ʒwɛ̃, -t/ *a.* (*efforts*) joint;

(*pieds*) together. —*n.m.* joint; (*ligne*) join; (*de robinet*) washer. **~ure** /-tyr/ *n.f.* joint; (*ligne*) join.
joker /ʒɔkɛr/ *n.m.* (*carte*) joker.
joli /ʒɔli/ *a.* pretty, nice; (*somme, profit*) nice. **c'est bien ~ mais,** that is all very well but. **~ment** *adv.* prettily; (*très: fam.*) awfully.
jonc /ʒɔ̃/ *n.m.* (bul)rush.
joncher /ʒɔ̃ʃe/ *v.t.* litter (**de,** with).
jonction /ʒɔ̃ksjɔ̃/ *n.f.* junction.
jongl|er /ʒɔ̃gle/ *v.i.* juggle. **~eur, ~euse** *n.m., f.* juggler.
jonquille /ʒɔ̃kij/ *n.f.* daffodil.
Jordanie /ʒɔrdani/ *n.f.* Jordan.
joue /ʒu/ *n.f.* cheek.
jouer /ʒwe/ *v.t./i.* play; (*théâtre*) act; (*au casino etc.*) gamble; (*fonctionner*) work; (*film, pièce*) put on; (*cheval*) back; (*être important*) count. **~ à** *ou* **de,** play. **~ la comédie,** put on an act. **se ~ de,** make light of.
jouet /ʒwɛ/ *n.m.* toy; (*personne: fig.*) plaything; (*victime*) victim.
joueu|r, ~se /ʒwœr, -øz/ *n.m., f.* player; (*parieur*) gambler.
joufflu /ʒufly/ *a.* chubby-cheeked; (*visage*) chubby.
joug /ʒu/ *n.m.* yoke.
jouir /ʒwir/ *v.i.* **~ de,** enjoy.
jouissance /ʒwisɑ̃s/ *n.f.* pleasure; (*usage*) use.
joujou (*pl.* **~x**) /ʒuʒu/ *n.m.* (*fam.*) toy.
jour /ʒur/ *n.m.* day; (*opposé à nuit*) day(time); (*lumière*) daylight; (*aspect*) light; (*ouverture*) gap. **de nos ~s,** nowadays. **du ~ au lendemain,** overnight. **il fait ~,** it is (day)light. **~ chômé** *ou* **férié,** public holiday. **~ de fête,** holiday. **~ ouvrable, ~ de travail,** working day. **mettre à ~,** update. **mettre au ~,** uncover.
journ|al (*pl.* **~aux**) /ʒurnal, -o/ *n.m.* (news)paper; (*spécialisé*) journal; (*intime*) diary; (*radio*) news. **~al de bord,** log-book.
journal|ier, ~ière /ʒurnalje, -jɛr/ *a.* daily.
journalis|te /ʒurnalist/ *n.m./f.* journalist. **~me** *n.m.* journalism.
journée /ʒurne/ *n.f.* day.
journellement /ʒurnɛlmɑ̃/ *adv.* daily.
jov|ial (*m. pl.* **~iaux**) /ʒɔvjal, -jo/ *a.* jovial.
joyau (*pl.* **~x**) /ʒwajo/ *n.m.* gem.
joyeu|x, ~se /ʒwajø, -z/ *a.* merry, joyful. **~x anniversaire,** happy birthday. **~sement** *adv.* merrily.
jubilé /ʒybile/ *n.m.* jubilee.
jubil|er /ʒybile/ *v.i.* be jubilant. **~ation** *n.f.* jubilation.
jucher /ʒyʃe/ *v.t.,* **se ~** *v. pr.* perch.
judaï|que /ʒydaik/ *a.* Jewish. **~sme** *n.m.* Judaism.
judas /ʒyda/ *n.m.* peep-hole.
judiciaire /ʒydisjɛr/ *a.* judicial.
judicieu|x, ~se /ʒydisjø, -z/ *a.* judicious.
judo /ʒydo/ *n.m.* judo.
juge /ʒyʒ/ *n.m.* judge; (*arbitre*) referee. **~ de paix,** Justice of the Peace. **~ de touche,** linesman.
jugé (au) /(o)ʒyʒe/ *adv.* by guesswork.
jugement /ʒyʒmɑ̃/ *n.m.* judgement; (*criminel*) sentence.
jugeote /ʒyʒɔt/ *n.f.* (*fam.*) gumption, common sense.
juger /ʒyʒe/ *v.t./i.* judge; (*estimer*) consider (**que,** that). **~ de,** judge.
juguler /ʒygyle/ *v.t.* stifle, check.
jui|f, ~ve /ʒɥif, -v/ *a.* Jewish. —*n.m., f.* Jew, Jewess.
juillet /ʒɥijɛ/ *n.m.* July.
juin /ʒɥɛ̃/ *n.m.* June.
jum|eau, ~elle (*m. pl.* **~eaux**) /ʒymo, -ɛl/ *a.* & *n.m., f.* twin. **~elage** *n.m.* twinning. **~eler** *v.t.* (*villes*) twin.
jumelles /ʒymɛl/ *n.f. pl.* binoculars.
jument /ʒymɑ̃/ *n.f.* mare.

jungle /ʒœ̃gl/ *n.f.* jungle.
junte /ʒœ̃t/ *n.f.* junta.
jupe /ʒyp/ *n.f.* skirt.
junior /ʒynjɔr/ *n.m./f.* & *a.* junior.
jupon /ʒypɔ̃/ *n.m.* slip, petticoat.
juré, ~e /ʒyre/ *n.m., f.* juror. —*a.* sworn.
jurer /ʒyre/ *v.t.* swear (**que,** that). —*v.i.* (*pester*) swear; (*contraster*) clash (**avec,** with). **~ de qch./de faire,** swear to sth./to do.
juridiction /ʒyridiksjɔ̃/ *n.f.* jurisdiction; (*tribunal*) court of law.
juridique /ʒyridik/ *a.* legal.
juriste /ʒyrist/ *n.m./f.* legal expert.
juron /ʒyrɔ̃/ *n.m.* swear-word.
jury /ʒyri/ *n.m.* jury.
jus /ʒy/ *n.m.* juice; (*de viande*) gravy; (*café: fam.*) coffee.
jusque /ʒysk(ə)/ *prép.* **jusqu'à,** (up) to, as far as; (*temps*) until, till; (*limite*) up to; (*y compris*) even. **jusqu'à ce que,** until. **jusqu'en,** until. **jusqu'où?,** how far? **~ dans, ~ sur,** as far as.
juste /ʒyst/ *a.* fair, just; (*légitime*) just; (*correct, exact*) right; (*vrai*) true; (*vêtement*) tight; (*quantité*) on the short side. —*adv.* rightly, correctly; (*chanter*) in tune; (*seulement, exactement*) just. (**un peu**) **~,** (*calculer, mesurer*) a bit fine *ou* close. **au ~,** exactly. **c'était ~,** (*presque raté*) it was a close thing.
justement /ʒystəmɑ̃/ *adv.* just; (*avec justice ou justesse*) justly.
justesse /ʒystɛs/ *n.f.* accuracy. **de ~,** just, narrowly.
justice /ʒystis/ *n.f.* justice; (*autorités*) law; (*tribunal*) court.
justif|ier /ʒystifje/ *v.t.* justify. —*v.i.* **~ier de,** prove. **se ~ier** *v. pr.* justify o.s. **~iable** *a.* justifiable. **~ication** *n.f.* justification.
juteu|x, ~se /ʒytø, -z/ *a.* juicy.
juvénile /ʒyvenil/ *a.* youthful.
juxtaposer /ʒykstapoze/ *v.t.* juxtapose.

K

kaki /kaki/ *a. invar.* & *n.m.* khaki.
kaléidoscope /kaleidɔskɔp/ *n.m.* kaleidoscope.
kangourou /kɑ̃guru/ *n.m.* kangaroo.
karaté /karate/ *n.m.* karate.
kart /kart/ *n.m.* go-cart.
kascher /kaʃɛr/ *a. invar.* kosher.
képi /kepi/ *n.m.* kepi.
kermesse /kɛrmɛs/ *n.f.* fair; (*de charité*) fête.
kérosène /kerozɛn/ *n.m.* kerosene, aviation fuel.
kibboutz /kibuts/ *n.m.* kibbutz.
kidnapp|er /kidnape/ *v.t.* kidnap. **~eur, ~euse** *n.m., f.* kidnapper.
kilo /kilo/ *n.m.* kilo.
kilogramme /kilɔgram/ *n.m.* kilogram.
kilohertz /kilɔɛrts/ *n.m.* kilohertz.
kilom|ètre /kilɔmɛtr/ *n.m.* kilometre. **~étrage** *n.m.* (*approx.*) mileage.
kilowatt /kilɔwat/ *n.m.* kilowatt.
kinésithérapie /kineziterapi/ *n.f.* physiotherapy.
kiosque /kjɔsk/ *n.m.* kiosk. **~ à musique,** bandstand.
klaxon /klaksɔn/ *n.m.* (P.) (*auto.*) horn. **~ner** /-e/ *v.i.* sound one's horn.
knock-out /nɔkawt/ *n.m.* knock-out.
kyste /kist/ *n.m.* cyst.

L

l', la /l, la/ *voir* **le.**
-là /la/ *adv.* (*après un nom précédé de ce, cette, etc.*) **cet homme-là,** that man. **ces maisons-là,** those houses.
là /la/ *adv.* there; (*ici*) here; (*chez soi*) in; (*temps*) then. **c'est ~ que,**

this is where. **~ où,** where. **~-bas** *adv.* over there. **~-dedans** *adv.* inside, in there. **~-dessous** *adv.* underneath, under there. **~-dessus** *adv.* on there. **~-haut** *adv.* up there; (*à l'étage*) upstairs.

label /labɛl/ *n.m.* (*comm.*) seal.

labeur /labœr/ *n.m.* toil.

labo /labo/ *n.m.* (*fam.*) lab.

laboratoire /labɔratwar/ *n.m.* laboratory.

laborieu|x, ~se /labɔrjø, -z/ *a.* laborious; (*personne*) industrious. **classes/masses ~ses,** working classes/masses.

labour /labur/ *n.m.* ploughing; (*Amer.*) plowing. **~er** *v.t./i.* plough; (*Amer.*) plow. **être ~é,** (*déchiré*) be furrowed. **~eur** *n.m.* ploughman; (*Amer.*) plowman.

labyrinthe /labirɛ̃t/ *n.m.* maze.

lac /lak/ *n.m.* lake.

lacer /lase/ *v.t.* lace up.

lacérer /lasere/ *v.t.* tear (up).

lacet /lasɛ/ *n.m.* (shoe-)lace; (*de route*) sharp bend, zigzag.

lâche /lɑʃ/ *a.* cowardly; (*détendu*) loose. *—n.m./f.* coward. **~ment** *adv.* in a cowardly way.

lâcher /lɑʃe/ *v.t.* let go of; (*abandonner*) give up; (*laisser*) leave; (*libérer*) release; (*parole*) utter; (*desserrer*) loosen. *—v.i.* give way. **~ prise,** let go.

lâcheté /lɑʃte/ *n.f.* cowardice.

laconique /lakɔnik/ *a.* laconic.

lacté /lakte/ *a.* milk.

lacune /lakyn/ *n.f.* gap.

ladite /ladit/ *voir* **ledit.**

lagune /lagyn/ *n.f.* lagoon.

laïc /laik/ *n.m.* layman.

laid, ~e /lɛ, lɛd/ *a.* ugly; (*action*) vile. **~eur** /lɛdœr/ *n.f.* ugliness.

lain|e /lɛn/ *n.f.* wool. **de ~e,** woollen. **~age** *n.m.* woollen garment.

laïque /laik/ *a.* secular; (*habit, personne*) lay. *—n.m./f.* layman, laywoman.

laisse /lɛs/ *n.f.* lead, leash.

laisser /lese/ *v.t.* leave. **~ qn. faire,** let s.o. do. **~ qch. à qn.,** let s.o. have sth., leave s.o. sth. **~ tomber,** drop. **se ~ aller,** let o.s. go. **~-aller** *n.m. invar.* carelessness. **laissez-passer** *n.m. invar.* pass.

lait /lɛ/ *n.m.* milk. **frère/sœur de ~,** foster-brother/-sister. **~age** /lɛtaʒ/ *n.m.* milk product. **~eux, ~euse** /lɛtø, -z/ *a.* milky.

lait|ier, ~ière /letje, lɛtjɛr/ *a.* dairy. *—n.m., f.* dairyman, dairywoman. *—n.m.* (*livreur*) milkman. **~erie** /lɛtri/ *n.f.* dairy.

laiton /lɛtɔ̃/ *n.m.* brass.

laitue /lety/ *n.f.* lettuce.

lama /lama/ *n.m.* llama.

lambeau (*pl.* **~x**) /lɑ̃bo/ *n.m.* shred. **en ~x,** in shreds.

lambin, ~e /lɑ̃bɛ̃, -in/ *a.* (*fam.*) sluggish. *—n.m., f.* (*fam.*) dawdler.

lambris /lɑ̃bri/ *n.m.* panelling.

lame /lam/ *n.f.* blade; (*lamelle*) strip; (*vague*) wave. **~ de fond,** ground swell.

lamelle /lamɛl/ *n.f.* (thin) strip.

lamentable /lamɑ̃tabl/ *a.* deplorable.

lament|er (se) /(sə)lamɑ̃te/ *v. pr.* moan. **~ation(s)** *n.f.* (*pl.*) moaning.

laminé /lamine/ *a.* laminated.

lampadaire /lɑ̃padɛr/ *n.m.* standard lamp; (*de rue*) street lamp.

lampe /lɑ̃p/ *n.f.* lamp; (*de radio*) valve; (*Amer.*) vacuum tube. **~ (de poche),** torch; (*Amer.*) flashlight. **~ de chevet,** bedside lamp.

lampion /lɑ̃pjɔ̃/ *n.m.* (Chinese) lantern.

lance /lɑ̃s/ *n.f.* spear; (*de tournoi*) lance; (*tuyau*) hose; (*bout de tuyau*) nozzle.

lanc|er /lɑ̃se/ *v.t.* throw; (*avec force*) hurl; (*navire, idée, personne*) launch; (*émettre*) give out;

(*regard*) cast; (*moteur*) start. **se ~er** *v. pr.* (*sport*) gain momentum; (*se précipiter*) rush. **se ~er dans,** launch into. —*n.m.* throw; (*action*) throwing. **~ement** *n.m.* throwing; (*de navire*) launching. **~e-missiles** *n.m. invar.* missile launcher. **~e-pierres** *n.m. invar.* catapult.
lancinant, ~e /lɑ̃sinɑ̃, -t/ *a.* haunting; (*douleur*) throbbing.
landau /lɑ̃do/ *n.m.* pram; (*Amer.*) baby carriage.
lande /lɑ̃d/ *n.f.* heath, moor.
langage /lɑ̃gaʒ/ *n.m.* language.
lang|e /lɑ̃ʒ/ *n.f.* baby's blanket. **~er** *v.t.* (*bébé*) change.
langoureu|x, ~se /lɑ̃gurø, -z/ *a.* languid.
langoust|e /lɑ̃gust/ *n.f.* (spiny) lobster. **~ine** *n.f.* (Norway) lobster.
langue /lɑ̃g/ *n.f.* tongue; (*idiome*) language. **de ~ anglaise/française,** English-/French-speaking. **~ maternelle,** mother tongue.
languette /lɑ̃gɛt/ *n.f.* tongue.
langueur /lɑ̃gœr/ *n.f.* languor.
langu|ir /lɑ̃gir/ *v.i.* languish. **~issant, ~issante** *a.* languid.
lanière /lanjɛr/ *n.f.* strap.
lanterne /lɑ̃tɛrn/ *n.f.* lantern; (*électrique*) lamp; (*de voiture*) sidelight.
laper /lape/ *v.t./i.* lap.
lapider /lapide/ *v.t.* stone.
lapin /lapɛ̃/ *n.m.* rabbit.
laps /laps/ *n.m.* **~ de temps,** lapse of time.
lapsus /lapsys/ *n.m.* slip (of the tongue).
laquais /lakɛ/ *n.m.* lackey.
laqu|e /lak/ *n.f.* lacquer. **~er** *v.t.* lacquer.
laquelle /lakɛl/ *voir* **lequel.**
larcin /larsɛ̃/ *n.m.* theft.
lard /lar/ *n.m.* (pig's) fat; (*viande*) bacon.
large /larʒ/ *a.* wide, broad; (*grand*) large; (*non borné*) broad; (*généreux*) generous. —*adv.* (*mesurer*) broadly; (*voir*) big. —*n.m.* **de ~,** (*mesure*) wide. **le ~,** (*mer*) the open sea. **au ~ de,** (*en face de*: *naut.*) off. **~ d'esprit,** broad-minded. **~ment** /-əmɑ̃/ *adv.* widely; (*ouvrir*) wide; (*amplement*) amply; (*généreusement*) generously; (*au moins*) easily.
largesse /larʒɛs/ *n.f.* generosity.
largeur /larʒœr/ *n.f.* width, breadth; (*fig.*) breadth.
larguer /large/ *v.t.* drop. **~ les amarres,** cast off.
larme /larm/ *n.f.* tear; (*goutte*: *fam.*) drop.
larmoyant, ~e /larmwajɑ̃, -t/ *a.* tearful.
larron /larɔ̃/ *n.m.* thief.
larve /larv/ *n.f.* larva.
larvé /larve/ *a.* latent.
laryngite /larɛ̃ʒit/ *n.f.* laryngitis.
larynx /larɛ̃ks/ *n.m.* larynx.
las, ~se /lɑ, lɑs/ *a.* weary.
lascar /laskar/ *n.m.* (*fam.*) fellow.
lasci|f, ~ve /lasif, -v/ *a.* lascivious.
laser /lazɛr/ *n.m.* laser.
lasse /lɑs/ *voir* **las.**
lasser /lɑse/ *v.t.* weary. **se ~** *v. pr.* weary (**de,** of).
lassitude /lɑsityd/ *n.f.* weariness.
lasso /laso/ *n.m.* lasso.
latent, ~e /latɑ̃, -t/ *a.* latent.
latér|al (*m. pl.* **~aux**) /lateral, -o/ *a.* lateral.
latin, ~e /latɛ̃, -in/ *a.* & *n.m., f.* Latin. —*n.m.* (*lang.*) Latin.
latitude /latityd/ *n.f.* latitude.
latrines /latrin/ *n.f. pl.* latrine(s).
latte /lat/ *n.f.* lath; (*de plancher*) board.
lauréat, ~e /lɔrea, -t/ *a.* prize-winning. —*n.m., f.* prize-winner.
laurier /lɔrje/ *n.m.* laurel; (*culin.*) bay-leaves.
lavable /lavabl/ *a.* washable.

lavabo /lavabo/ *n.m.* wash-basin. **~s,** toilet(s).
lavage /lavaʒ/ *n.m.* washing. **~ de cerveau,** brainwashing.
lavande /lavɑ̃d/ *n.f.* lavender.
lave /lav/ *n.f.* lava.
lav|er /lave/ *v.t.* wash; (*injure etc.*) avenge. **se ~er** *v. pr.* wash (o.s.) **(se) ~er de,** clear (o.s.) of. **~e-glace** *n.m.* windscreen washer. **~eur de carreaux,** window-cleaner. **~e-vaisselle** *n.m. invar.* dishwasher.
laverie /lavri/ *n.f.* **~ (automatique),** launderette; (*Amer.*) laundromat.
lavette /lavɛt/ *n.f.* dishcloth.
lavoir /lavwar/ *n.m.* wash-house.
laxati|f, ~ve /laksatif, -v/ *a.* & *n.m.* laxative.
laxisme /laksism/ *n.m.* laxity.
layette /lɛjɛt/ *n.f.* baby clothes.
le *ou* **l'*, la** *ou* **l'*** (*pl.* **les**) /lə, l, la, le/ *article* the; (*mesure*) a, per. —*pron.* (*homme*) him; (*femme*) her; (*chose, animal*) it. **les** *pron.* them. **aimer ~ thé/la France,** like tea/France. **~ matin,** in the morning. **il sort ~ mardi,** he goes out on Tuesdays. **levez ~ bras,** raise your arm. **je ~ connais,** I know him. **je ~ sais,** I know (it).
lécher /leʃe/ *v.t.* lick.
lèche-vitrines /lɛʃvitrin/ *n.m.* **faire du ~,** (*fam.*) go window-shopping.
leçon /ləsɔ̃/ *n.f.* lesson. **faire la ~ à,** lecture.
lec|teur, ~trice /lɛktœr, -tris/ *n.m., f.* reader; (*univ.*) foreign language assistant.
lecture /lɛktyr/ *n.f.* reading.
ledit, ladite (*pl.* **lesdit(e)s**) /lədi, ladit, ledi(t)/ *a.* the aforesaid.
lég|al (*m. pl.* **~aux**) /legal, -o/ *a.* legal. **~alement** *adv.* legally. **~aliser** *v.t.* legalize. **~alité** *n.f.* legality; (*loi*) law.
légation /legɑsjɔ̃/ *n.f.* legation.
légend|e /leʒɑ̃d/ *n.f.* (*histoire, inscription*) legend. **~aire** *a.* legendary.
lég|er, ~ère /leʒe, -ɛr/ *a.* light; (*bruit, faute, maladie*) slight; (*café, argument*) weak; (*imprudent*) thoughtless; (*frivole*) fickle. **à la ~ère,** thoughtlessly. **~èrement** /-ɛrmɑ̃/ *adv.* lightly; (*agir*) thoughtlessly; (*un peu*) slightly. **~èreté** /-ɛrte/ *n.f.* lightness; thoughtlessness.
légion /leʒjɔ̃/ *n.f.* legion. **~naire** /-jɔnɛr/ *n.m.* (*mil.*) legionnaire.
législati|f, ~ve /leʒislatif, -v/ *a.* legislative.
législation /leʒislɑsjɔ̃/ *n.f.* legislation.
legislature /leʒislatyr/ *n.f.* term of office.
légitim|e /leʒitim/ *a.* legitimate. **en état de ~e défense,** acting in self-defence. **~ité** *n.f.* legitimacy.
legs /lɛg/ *n.m.* legacy.
léguer /lege/ *v.t.* bequeath.
légume /legym/ *n.m.* vegetable.
lendemain /lɑ̃dmɛ̃/ *n.m.* **le ~,** the next day, the day after; (*fig.*) the future. **le ~ de,** the day after. **le ~ matin/soir,** the next morning/evening.
lent, ~e /lɑ̃, lɑ̃t/ *a.* slow. **~ement** /lɑ̃tmɑ̃/ *adv.* slowly. **~eur** /lɑ̃tœr/ *n.f.* slowness.
lentille[1] /lɑ̃tij/ *n.f.* (*plante*) lentil.
lentille[2] /lɑ̃tij/ *n.f.* (*verre*) lens.
léopard /leɔpar/ *n.m.* leopard.
lèpre /lɛpr/ *n.f.* leprosy.
lépreu|x, ~se /leprø, -z/ *a.* leprous. —*n.m., f.* leper.
lequel, laquelle (*pl.* **lesquel(le)s**) /ləkɛl, lakɛl, lekɛl/ *pron.* (*à* + *lequel* = *auquel*, *à* + *lesquel(le)s* = *auxquel(le)s*; *de* + *lequel* = *duquel*, *de* + *lesquel(le)s* = *desquel(le)s*) which; (*interrogatif*) which (one); (*personne*) who; (*complément indirect*) whom.

les /le/ *voir* **le.**
lesbienne /lɛsbjɛn/ *n.f.* lesbian.
léser /leze/ *v.t.* wrong.
lésiner /lezine/ *v.i.* be stingy (**sur,** with).
lésion /lezjɔ̃/ *n.f.* lesion.
lesquels, lesquelles /lekɛl/ *voir* **lequel.**
lessiv|e /lesiv/ *n.f.* washing-powder; (*linge, action*) washing. **~er** *v.t.* wash.
lest /lɛst/ *n.m.* ballast. **~er** *v.t.* ballast.
leste /lɛst/ *a.* nimble; (*grivois*) coarse.
létharg|ie /letarʒi/ *n.f.* lethargy. **~ique** *a.* lethargic.
lettre /lɛtr/ *n.f.* letter. **à la ~,** literally. **en toutes ~s,** in full. **~ exprès,** express letter. **les ~s,** (*univ.*) (the) arts.
lettré /letre/ *a.* well-read.
leucémie /løsemi/ *n.f.* leukaemia.
leur /lœr/ *a.* (*f. invar.*) their. *—pron.* (to) them. **le ~, la ~, les ~s,** theirs.
leurr|e /lœr/ *n.m.* illusion; *duperie*) deception. **~er** *v.t.* delude.
levé /ləve/ *a.* (*debout*) up.
levée /ləve/ *n.f.* lifting; (*de courrier*) collection; (*de troupes, d'impôts*) levying.
lever /ləve/ *v.t.* lift (up), raise; (*interdiction*) lift; (*séance*) close; (*armée, impôts*) levy. *—v.i.* (*pâte*) rise. **se ~** *v. pr.* get up; (*soleil, rideau*) rise; (*jour*) break. *—n.m.* **~ du jour,** daybreak. **~ du rideau,** (*théâtre*) curtain (up). **~ du soleil,** sunrise.
levier /ləvje/ *n.m.* lever; (*pour soulever*) crowbar.
lèvre /lɛvr/ *n.f.* lip.
lévrier /levrije/ *n.m.* greyhound.
levure /ləvyr/ *n.f.* yeast.
lexicographie /lɛksikɔgrafi/ *n.f.* lexicography.
lexique /lɛksik/ *n.m.* vocabulary; (*glossaire*) lexicon.
lézard /lezar/ *n.m.* lizard.
lézard|e /lezard/ *n.f.* crack. **se ~er** *v. pr.* crack.
liaison /ljɛzɔ̃/ *n.f.* connection; (*transport*) link; (*contact*) contact; (*gram., mil.*) liaison; (*amoureuse*) affair.
liane /ljan/ *n.f.* jungle vine.
liasse /ljas/ *n.f.* bundle.
Liban /libɑ̃/ *n.m.* Lebanon.
libanais, ~e /libanɛ, -z/ *a.* & *n.m., f.* Lebanese.
libeller /libele/ *v.t.* write, draw up.
libellule /libelyl/ *n.f.* dragonfly.
libér|al (*m. pl.* **~aux**) /liberal, -o/ *a.* liberal. **~alement** *adv.* liberally. **~alisme** *n.m.* liberalism. **~alité** *n.f.* liberality.
libér|er /libere/ *v.t.* (*personne*) free, release; (*pays*) liberate, free. **se ~er** *v. pr.* free o.s. **~ateur, ~atrice** *a.* liberating; *n.m., f.* liberator. **~ation** *n.f.* release; (*de pays*) liberation.
liberté /libɛrte/ *n.f.* freedom, liberty; (*loisir*) free time. **en ~ provisoire,** on bail. **être/mettre en ~,** be/set free.
libertin, ~e /libɛrtɛ̃, -in/ *a.* & *n.m., f.* libertine.
librair|e /librɛr/ *n.m./f.* bookseller. **~ie** /-eri/ *n.f.* bookshop.
libre /libr/ *a.* free; (*place, pièce*) vacant, free; (*passage*) clear; (*école*) private (*usually religious*). **~ de qch./de faire,** free from sth./to do. **~-échange** *n.m.* free trade. **~ment** /-əmɑ̃/ *adv.* freely. **~-service** (*pl.* **~s-services**) *n.m.* self-service.
Libye /libi/ *n.f.* Libya.
libyen, ~ne /libjɛ̃, -jɛn/ *a.* & *n.m., f.* Libyan.
licence /lisɑ̃s/ *n.f.* licence; (*univ.*) degree.
licencié, ~e /lisɑ̃sje/ *n.m., f.* **~ ès lettres/sciences,** Bachelor of Arts/Science.
licenc|ier /lisɑ̃sje/ *v.t.* lay off,

dismiss. **~iement** *n.m.* dismissal.
licencieu|x, ~se /lisɑ̃sjø, -z/ *a.* licentious, lascivious.
lichen /likɛn/ *n.m.* lichen.
licite /lisit/ *a.* lawful.
licorne /likɔrn/ *n.f.* unicorn.
lie /li/ *n.f.* dregs.
liège /ljɛʒ/ *n.m.* cork.
lien /ljɛ̃/ *n.m.* (*rapport*) link; (*attache*) bond, tie; (*corde*) rope.
lier /lje/ *v.t.* tie (up), bind; (*relier*) link; (*engager, unir*) bind. **~ conversation,** strike up a conversation. **se ~ avec,** make friends with. **très lié avec,** very friendly with.
lierre /ljɛr/ *n.m.* ivy.
lieu (*pl.* **~x**) /ljø/ *n.m.* place. **~x,** (*locaux*) premises; (*d'un accident*) scene. **au ~ de,** instead of. **en premier ~,** firstly. **en dernier ~,** lastly. **~ commun,** commonplace.
lieutenant /ljøtnɑ̃/ *n.m.* lieutenant.
lièvre /ljɛvr/ *n.m.* hare.
ligament /ligamɑ̃/ *n.m.* ligament.
ligne /liɲ/ *n.f.* line; (*trajet*) route; (*formes*) lines; (*de femme*) figure. **en ~,** (*joueurs etc.*) lined up; (*personne au téléphone*) connected.
lignée /liɲe/ *n.f.* ancestry, line.
ligoter /ligɔte/ *v.t.* tie up.
ligu|e /lig/ *n.f.* league. **se ~er** *v. pr.* form a league (**contre,** against).
lilas /lilɑ/ *n.m.* & *a. invar.* lilac.
limace /limas/ *n.f.* slug.
limande /limɑ̃d/ *n.f.* (*poisson*) dab.
lim|e /lim/ *n.f.* file. **~er** *v.t.* file.
limier /limje/ *n.m.* bloodhound; (*policier*) sleuth.
limitation /limitɑsjɔ̃/ *n.f.* limitation. **~ de vitesse,** speed limit.
limit|e /limit/ *n.f.* limit; (*de jardin, champ*) boundary. —*a.* (*vitesse, âge*) maximum; (*cas*) extreme. **~er** *v.t.* limit; (*délimiter*) form the border of.
limoger /limɔʒe/ *v.t.* dismiss.
limonade /limɔnad/ *n.f.* lemonade.
limpid|e /lɛ̃pid/ *a.* limpid, clear. **~ité** *n.f.* clearness.
lin /lɛ̃/ *n.m.* flax.
linceul /lɛ̃sœl/ *n.m.* shroud.
linéaire /lineɛr/ *a.* linear.
linge /lɛ̃ʒ/ *n.m.* linen; (*lessive*) washing; (*torchon*) cloth. **~ (de corps),** underwear. **~rie** *n.f.* underwear.
lingot /lɛ̃go/ *n.m.* ingot.
linguiste /lɛ̃gɥist/ *n.m./f.* linguist.
linguistique /lɛ̃gɥistik/ *a.* linguistic. —*n.f.* linguistics.
lino /lino/ *n.m.* lino.
linoléum /linɔleɔm/ *n.m.* linoleum.
lion, ~ne /ljɔ̃, ljɔn/ *n.m., f.* lion, lioness.
liquéfier /likefje/ *v.t.*, **se ~** *v. pr.* liquefy.
liqueur /likœr/ *n.f.* liqueur.
liquide /likid/ *a.* & *n.m.* liquid. **(argent) ~,** ready money.
liquid|er /likide/ *v.t.* liquidate; (*vendre*) sell. **~ation** *n.f.* liquidation; (*vente*) (clearance) sale.
lire[1]† /lir/ *v.t./i.* read.
lire[2] /lir/ *n.f.* lira.
lis[1] /li/ *voir* **lire**[1].
lis[2] /lis/ *n.m.* (*fleur*) lily.
lisible /lizibl/ *a.* legible; (*roman etc.*) readable.
lisière /lizjɛr/ *n.f.* edge.
liss|e /lis/ *a.* smooth. **~er** *v.t.* smooth.
liste /list/ *n.f.* list.
lit[1] /li/ *voir* **lire**[1].
lit[2] /li/ *n.m.* (*de personne, fleuve*) bed. **~ de camp,** camp-bed. **~ d'enfant,** cot. **~ d'une personne,** single bed.
litanie /litani/ *n.f.* litany.
literie /litri/ *n.f.* bedding.
litière /litjɛr/ *n.f.* (*paille*) litter.
litige /litiʒ/ *n.m.* dispute.
litre /litr/ *n.m.* litre.

littéraire /literɛr/ *a.* literary.
littér|al (*m. pl.* **~aux**) /literal, -o/ *a.* literal. **~alement** *adv.* literally.
littérature /literatyr/ *n.f.* literature.
littor|al (*pl.* **~aux**) /litɔral, -o/ *n.m.* coast.
liturg|ie /lityrʒi/ *n.f.* liturgy. **~ique** *a.* liturgical.
livide /livid/ *a.* (*blême*) pallid; (*bleu*) livid.
livraison /livrɛzɔ̃/ *n.f.* delivery.
livre[1] /livr/ *n.m.* book. **~ de bord,** log-book. **~ de poche,** paperback.
livre[2] /livr/ *n.f.* (*monnaie, poids*) pound.
livrée /livre/ *n.f.* livery.
livr|er /livre/ *v.t.* deliver; (*abandonner*) give over (**à,** to); (*secret*) give away. **~é à soi-même,** left to o.s. **se ~er à,** give o.s. over to; (*actes, boisson*) indulge in; (*se confier à*) confide in; (*effectuer*) carry out.
livret /livrɛ/ *n.m.* book; (*mus.*) libretto. **~ scolaire,** school report (book).
livreu|r, ~se /livrœr, -øz/ *n.m., f.* delivery boy *ou* girl.
lobe /lɔb/ *n.m.* lobe.
loc|al[1] (*m. pl.* **~aux**) /lɔkal, -o/ *a.* local. **~alement** *adv.* locally.
loc|al[2] (*pl.* **~aux**) /lɔkal, -o/ *n.m.* premises. **~aux,** premises.
localisé /lɔkalize/ *a.* localized.
localité /lɔkalite/ *n.f.* locality.
locataire /lɔkatɛr/ *n.m./f.* tenant; (*de chambre, d'hôtel*) lodger.
location /lɔkɑsjɔ̃/ *n.f.* (*de maison*) renting; (*de voiture*) hiring, renting; (*de place*) booking, reservation; (*par propriétaire*) renting out; hiring out. **en ~,** (*voiture*) on hire, rented.
lock-out /lɔkawt/ *n.m. invar.* lock-out.
locomotion /lɔkɔmosjɔ̃/ *n.f.* locomotion.
locomotive /lɔkɔmɔtiv/ *n.f.* engine, locomotive.
locution /lɔkysjɔ̃/ *n.f.* phrase.
logarithme /lɔgaritm/ *n.m.* logarithm.
loge /lɔʒ/ *n.f.* (*de concierge*) lodge; (*d'acteur*) dressing-room; (*de spectateur*) box.
logement /lɔʒmɑ̃/ *n.m.* accommodation; (*appartement*) flat; (*habitat*) housing.
log|er /lɔʒe/ *v.t.* accommodate. —*v.i.*, **se ~er** *v. pr.* live. **(trouver à) se ~er,** find accommodation. **être ~é,** live. **se ~er dans,** (*balle*) lodge itself in.
logeu|r, ~se /lɔʒœr, -øz/ *n.m., f.* landlord, landlady.
logiciel /lɔʒisjɛl/ *n.m.* software.
logique /lɔʒik/ *a.* logical. —*n.f.* logic. **~ment** *adv.* logically.
logis /lɔʒi/ *n.m.* dwelling.
logistique /lɔʒistik/ *n.f.* logistics.
loi /lwa/ *n.f.* law.
loin /lwɛ̃/ *adv.* far (away). **au ~,** far away. **de ~,** from far away; (*de beaucoup*) by far. **~ de là,** far from it. **plus ~,** further.
lointain, ~e /lwɛ̃tɛ̃, -ɛn/ *a.* distant. —*n.m.* distance.
loir /lwar/ *n.m.* dormouse.
loisir /lwazir/ *n.m.* (spare) time. **~s,** spare time; (*distractions*) spare time activities.
londonien, ~ne /lɔ̃dɔnjɛ̃, -jɛn/ *a.* London. —*n.m., f.* Londoner.
Londres /lɔ̃dr/ *n.m./f.* London.
long, ~ue /lɔ̃, lɔ̃g/ *a.* long. —*n.m.* **de ~,** (*mesure*) long. **à la ~ue,** in the end. **à ~ terme,** long-term. **de ~ en large,** back and forth. **~ à faire,** a long time doing. **(tout) le ~ de,** (all) along.
longer /lɔ̃ʒe/ *v.t.* go along; (*limiter*) border.
longévité /lɔ̃ʒevite/ *n.f.* longevity.
longitude /lɔ̃ʒityd/ *n.f.* longitude.
longtemps /lɔ̃tɑ̃/ *adv.* a long time.

avant ~, before long. **trop ~,** too long.
longue /lɔ̃g/ *voir* **long.**
longuement /lɔ̃gmɑ̃/ *adv.* at length.
longueur /lɔ̃gœr/ *n.f.* length. **~s,** (*de texte etc.*) over-long parts. **à ~ de journée,** all day long. **~ d'onde,** wavelength.
lopin /lɔpɛ̃/ *n.m.* **~ de terre,** patch of land.
loquace /lɔkas/ *a.* talkative.
loque /lɔk/ *n.f.* **~s,** rags. **~ (humaine),** (human) wreck.
loquet /lɔkɛ/ *n.m.* latch.
lorgner /lɔrɲe/ *v.t.* eye.
lorgnon /lɔrɲɔ̃/ *n.m.* eyeglasses.
lors de /lɔrdə/ *prép.* at the time of.
lorsque /lɔrsk(ə)/ *conj.* when.
losange /lɔzɑ̃ʒ/ *n.m.* diamond.
lot /lo/ *n.m.* prize; (*portion, destin*) lot.
loterie /lɔtri/ *n.f.* lottery.
lotion /losjɔ̃/ *n.f.* lotion.
lotissement /lɔtismɑ̃/ *n.m.* building plot.
louable /lwabl/ *a.* praiseworthy.
louange /lwɑ̃ʒ/ *n.f.* praise.
louche[1] /luʃ/ *a.* shady, dubious.
louche[2] /luʃ/ *n.f.* ladle.
loucher /luʃe/ *v.i.* squint.
louer[1] /lwe/ *v.t.* (*maison*) rent; (*voiture*) hire, rent; (*place*) book, reserve; (*propriétaire*) rent out; hire out.
louer[2] /lwe/ *v.t.* (*approuver*) praise (**de,** for). **se ~ de,** congratulate o.s. on.
loufoque /lufɔk/ *a.* (*fam.*) crazy.
loup /lu/ *n.m.* wolf.
loupe /lup/ *n.f.* magnifying glass.
louper /lupe/ *v.t.* (*manquer: fam.*) miss; (*bâcler: fam.*) mess up.
lourd, ~e /lur, -d/ *a.* heavy; (*chaleur*) close; (*faute*) gross. **~ement** /-dəmɑ̃/ *adv.* heavily. **~eur** /-dœr/ *n.f.* heaviness.
lourdaud, ~e /lurdo, -d/ *a.* loutish. —*n.m., f.* lout, oaf.
loutre /lutr/ *n.f.* otter.
louve /luv/ *n.f.* she-wolf.
louveteau (*pl.* **~x**) /luvto/ *n.m.* (*scout*) Cub (Scout).
loy|al (*m. pl.* **~aux**) /lwajal, -o/ *a.* loyal; (*honnête*) fair. **~alement** *adv.* loyally; fairly. **~auté** *n.f.* loyalty; fairness.
loyer /lwaje/ *n.m.* rent.
lu /ly/ *voir* **lire**[1].
lubie /lybi/ *n.f.* whim.
lubrif|ier /lybrifje/ *v.t.* lubricate. **~iant** *n.m.* lubricant.
lubrique /lybrik/ *a.* lewd.
lucarne /lykarn/ *n.f.* skylight.
lucid|e /lysid/ *a.* lucid. **~ité** *n.f.* lucidity.
lucrati|f, ~ve /lykratif, -v/ *a.* lucrative. **à but non ~f,** non-profit-making.
lueur /lɥœr/ *n.f.* (faint) light, glimmer; (*fig.*) glimmer, gleam.
luge /lyʒ/ *n.f.* toboggan.
lugubre /lygybr/ *a.* gloomy.
lui /lɥi/ *pron.* him; (*sujet*) he; (*chose*) it; (*objet indirect*) (to) him; (*femme*) (to) her; (*chose*) (to) it. **~-même** *pron.* himself; itself.
luire† /lɥir/ *v.i.* shine; (*reflet humide*) glisten; (*reflet chaud, faible*) glow.
lumbago /lɔ̃bago/ *n.m.* lumbago.
lumière /lymjɛr/ *n.f.* light. **~s,** (*connaissances*) knowledge. **faire (toute) la ~ sur,** clear up.
luminaire /lyminɛr/ *n.m.* lamp.
lumineu|x, ~se /lyminø, -z/ *a.* luminous; (*éclairé*) illuminated; (*source, rayon*) (of) light; (*vif*) bright.
lunaire /lynɛr/ *a.* lunar.
lunatique /lynatik/ *a.* temperamental.
lunch /lœntʃ/ *n.m.* buffet lunch.
lundi /lœ̃di/ *n.m.* Monday.
lune /lyn/ *n.f.* moon. **~ de miel,** honeymoon.
lunette /lynɛt/ *n.f.* **~s,** glasses; (*de protection*) goggles. **~ arrière,**

(*auto.*) rear window. **~ d'approche,** telescope. **~s de soleil,** sun-glasses.
luron /lyrɔ̃/ *n.m.* **gai** *ou* **joyeux ~,** (*fam.*) quite a lad.
lustre /lystr/ *n.m.* (*éclat*) lustre; (*objet*) chandelier.
lustré /lystre/ *a.* shiny.
luth /lyt/ *n.m.* lute.
lutin /lytɛ̃/ *n.m.* goblin.
lutrin /lytrɛ̃/ *n.m.* lectern.
lutt|e /lyt/ *n.f.* fight, struggle; (*sport*) wrestling. **~er** *v.i.* fight, struggle; (*sport*) wrestle. **~eur, ~euse** *n.m., f.* fighter; (*sport*) wrestler.
luxe /lyks/ *n.m.* luxury. **de ~,** luxury; (*produit*) de luxe.
Luxembourg /lyksɑ̃bur/ *n.m.* Luxemburg.
lux|er /lykse/ *v.t.* dislocate. **~ation** *n.f.* dislocation.
luxueu|x, ~se /lyksɥø, -z/ *a.* luxurious.
luxure /lyksyr/ *n.f.* lust.
luxuriant, ~e /lyksyrjɑ̃, -t/ *a.* luxuriant.
luzerne /lyzɛrn/ *n.f.* (*plante*) lucerne, alfalfa.
lycée /lise/ *n.m.* (secondary) school. **~n, ~nne** /-ɛ̃, -ɛn/ *n.m., f.* pupil (at secondary school).
lynch|er /lɛ̃ʃe/ *v.t.* lynch. **~age** *n.m.* lynching.
lynx /lɛ̃ks/ *n.m.* lynx.
lyre /lir/ *n.f.* lyre.
lyri|que /lirik/ *a.* (*poésie*) lyric; (*passionné*) lyrical. **artiste/ théâtre ~que,** opera singer/-house. **~sme** *n.m.* lyricism.
lys /lis/ *n.m.* lily.

M

m' /m/ *voir* **me.**
ma /ma/ *voir* **mon.**
macabre /makabr/ *a.* gruesome, macabre.
macadam /makadam/ *n.m.* (*goudronné*) Tarmac (P.).
macaron /makarɔ̃/ *n.m.* (*gâteau*) macaroon; (*insigne*) badge.
macaronis /makarɔni/ *n.m. pl.* macaroni.
macédoine /masedwan/ *n.f.* mixed vegetables. **~ de fruits,** fruit salad.
macérer /masere/ *v.t./i.* soak; (*dans du vinaigre*) pickle.
Mach /mak/ *n.m.* (**nombre de**) **~,** Mach (number).
mâchefer /mɑʃfɛr/ *n.m.* clinker.
mâcher /mɑʃe/ *v.t.* chew. **ne pas ~ ses mots,** not mince one's words.
machiavélique /makjavelik/ *a.* machiavellian.
machin /maʃɛ̃/ *n.m.* (*chose: fam.*) thing; (*personne: fam.*) what's-his-name.
machin|al (*m. pl.* **~aux**) /maʃinal, -o/ *a.* automatic. **~alement** *adv.* automatically.
machinations /maʃinɑsjɔ̃/ *n.f. pl.* machinations.
machine /maʃin/ *n.f.* machine; (*d'un train, navire*) engine. **~ à écrire,** typewriter. **~ à laver/ coudre,** washing-/sewing-machine. **~ à sous,** fruit machine; (*Amer.*) slot-machine. **~-outil** (*pl.* **~s-outils**) *n.f.* machine tool. **~rie** *n.f.* machinery.
machiner /maʃine/ *v.t.* plot.
machiniste /maʃinist/ *n.m.* (*théâtre*) stage-hand; (*conducteur*) driver.
macho /ma(t)ʃo/ *n.m.* (*fam.*) macho.
mâchoire /mɑʃwar/ *n.f.* jaw.
maçon /masɔ̃/ *n.m.* builder; (*poseur de briques*) bricklayer. **~nerie** /-ɔnri/ *n.f.* brickwork; (*pierres*) stonework, masonry.

maçonnique /masɔnik/ *a.* Masonic.
macrobiotique /makrɔbjɔtik/ *a.* macrobiotic.
maculer /makyle/ *v.t.* stain.
Madagascar /madagaskar/ *n.f.* Madagascar.
madame (*pl.* **mesdames**) /madam, medam/ *n.f.* madam. **M~** *ou* **Mme Dupont,** Mrs Dupont. **bonsoir, mesdames,** good evening, ladies.
madeleine /madlɛn/ *n.f.* madeleine (*small shell-shaped sponge-cake*).
mademoiselle (*pl.* **mesdemoiselles**) /madmwazɛl, medmwazɛl/ *n.f.* miss. **M~** *ou* **Mlle Dupont,** Miss Dupont. **bonsoir, mesdemoiselles,** good evening, ladies.
madère /madɛr/ *n.m.* (*vin*) Madeira.
madone /madɔn/ *n.f.* madonna.
madré /madre/ *a.* wily.
madrig|al (*pl.* **~aux**) /madrigal, -o/ *n.m.* madrigal.
maestro /maɛstro/ *n.m.* maestro.
maf(f)ia /mafja/ *n.f.* Mafia.
magasin /magazɛ̃/ *n.m.* shop, store; (*entrepôt*) warehouse; (*d'une arme etc.*) magazine.
magazine /magazin/ *n.m.* magazine; (*émission*) programme.
magicien, ~ne /maʒisjɛ̃, -jɛn/ *n.m., f.* magician.
magie /maʒi/ *n.f.* magic.
magique /maʒik/ *a.* magic; (*mystérieux*) magical.
magistr|al (*m. pl.* **~aux**) /maʒistral, -o/ *a.* masterly; (*grand: hum.*) colossal. **~alement** *adv.* in a masterly fashion.
magistrat /maʒistra/ *n.m.* magistrate.
magistrature /maʒistratyr/ *n.f.* judiciary.
magnanim|e /maɲanim/ *a.* magnanimous. **~ité** *n.f.* magnanimity.
magnat /magna/ *n.m.* tycoon, magnate.
magner (se) /(sə)maɲe/ *v. pr.* (*argot*) hurry.
magnésie /maɲezi/ *n.f.* magnesia.
magnéti|que /maɲetik/ *a.* magnetic. **~ser** *v.t.* magnetize. **~sme** *n.m.* magnetism.
magnétophone /maɲetɔfɔn/ *n.m.* tape recorder. **~ à cassettes,** cassette recorder.
magnétoscope /maɲetɔskɔp/ *n.m.* video-recorder.
magnifi|que /maɲifik/ *a.* magnificent. **~cence** *n.f.* magnificence.
magnolia /maɲɔlja/ *n.m.* magnolia.
magot /mago/ *n.m.* (*fam.*) hoard (of money).
mahométan, ~e /maɔmetɑ̃, -an/ *a.* & *n.m., f.* Muhammedan.
mai /mɛ/ *n.m.* May.
maigr|e /mɛgr/ *a.* thin; (*viande, joue*) lean; (*yaourt*) low-fat; (*fig.*) poor, meagre. **faire ~e,** abstain from meat. **~ement** *adv.* poorly. **~eur** *n.f.* thinness; leanness; (*fig.*) meagreness.
maigrir /megrir/ *v.i.* get thin(ner); (*en suivant un régime*) slim. —*v.t.* make thin(ner).
maille /mɑj/ *n.f.* stitch; (*de filet*) mesh. **~ filée,** ladder, run.
maillet /majɛ/ *n.m.* mallet.
maillon /mɑjɔ̃/ *n.m.* link.
maillot /majo/ *n.m.* (*de danseur*) tights; (*tricot*) jersey; (*de bébé*) swaddling-clothes. **~ (de corps),** vest. **~ de bain,** swim-suit; (*d'homme*) (swimming) trunks.
main /mɛ̃/ *n.f.* hand. **avoir la ~ heureuse,** be lucky. **donner la ~ à qn.,** hold s.o.'s hand. **en ~s propres,** in person. **~ courante,** handrail. **~-d'œuvre** (*pl.* **~s-d'œuvre**) *n.f.* labour; (*ensemble d'ouvriers*) labour force. **~-forte** *n.f. invar.* assistance.

sous la ~, handy. **vol/attaque à ~ armée,** armed robbery/attack.

maint, ~e /mɛ̃, mɛ̃t/ *a.* many a. **~s,** many.

maintenant /mɛ̃tnɑ̃/ *adv.* now; (*de nos jours*) nowadays.

maintenir† /mɛ̃tnir/ *v.t.* keep, maintain; (*soutenir*) hold up; (*affirmer*) maintain. **se ~** *v. pr.* (*continuer*) persist; (*rester*) remain.

maintien /mɛ̃tjɛ̃/ *n.m.* (*attitude*) bearing; (*conservation*) maintenance.

maire /mɛr/ *n.m.* mayor.

mairie /meri/ *n.f.* town hall; (*administration*) town council.

mais /mɛ/ *conj.* but. **~ oui, ~ si,** of course. **~ non,** definitely not.

maïs /mais/ *n.m.* maize; (*Amer.*) corn.

maison /mɛzɔ̃/ *n.f.* house; (*foyer*) home; (*immeuble*) building. **~ (de commerce),** firm. *—a. invar.* (*culin.*) home-made. **à la ~,** at home. **rentrer** *ou* **aller à la ~,** go home. **~ des jeunes,** youth centre. **~ de repos, ~ de convalescence,** convalescent home. **~ de retraite,** old people's home.

maisonnée /mɛzɔne/ *n.f.* household.

maisonnette /mɛzɔnɛt/ *n.f.* small house, cottage.

maître /mɛtr/ *n.m.* master. **~ (d'école),** schoolmaster. **~ de,** in control of. **se rendre ~ de,** gain control of; (*incendie*) bring under control. **~ assistant/de conférences,** junior/senior lecturer. **~ chanteur,** blackmailer. **~ d'hôtel,** head waiter; (*domestique*) butler. **~ nageur,** swimming instructor.

maîtresse /mɛtrɛs/ *n.f.* mistress. **~ (d'école),** schoolmistress. *—a.f.* (*idée, poutre, qualité*) main. **~ de,** in control of.

maîtris|e /metriz/ *n.f.* mastery; (*univ.*) master's degree. **~e (de soi),** self-control. **~er** *v.t.* master; (*incendie*) control; (*personne*) subdue. **se ~er** *v. pr.* control o.s.

majesté /maʒɛste/ *n.f.* majesty.

majestueu|x, ~se /maʒɛstɥø, -z/ *a.* majestic. **~sement** *adv.* majestically.

majeur /maʒœr/ *a.* major; (*jurid.*) of age. *—n.m.* middle finger. **en ~e partie,** mostly. **la ~e partie de,** most of.

major|er /maʒɔre/ *v.t.* increase. **~ation** *n.f.* increase (**de**, in).

majorit|é /maʒɔrite/ *n.f.* majority. **en ~é,** chiefly. **~aire** *a.* majority. **être ~aire,** be in the majority.

Majorque /maʒɔrk/ *n.f.* Majorca.

majuscule /maʒyskyl/ *a.* capital. *—n.f.* capital letter.

mal[1] /mal/ *adv.* badly; (*incorrectement*) wrong(ly). **~ (à l'aise),** uncomfortable. **aller ~,** (*malade*) be bad. **c'est ~ de,** it is wrong *ou* bad to. **entendre/comprendre ~,** not hear/understand properly. **~ famé,** of ill repute. **~ fichu,** (*personne*: *fam.*) feeling lousy.

mal[2] (*pl.* **maux**) /mal, mo/ *n.m.* evil; (*douleur*) pain, ache; (*maladie*) disease; (*effort*) trouble; (*dommage*) harm; (*malheur*) misfortune. **avoir ~ à la tête/aux dents/à la gorge,** have a headache/a toothache/a sore throat. **avoir le ~ de mer/du pays,** be seasick/homesick. **faire du ~ à,** hurt, harm.

malade /malad/ *a.* sick, ill; (*bras, gorge*) bad; (*plante*) diseased. *—n.m./f.* sick person; (*d'un médecin*) patient.

maladie /maladi/ *n.f.* illness, disease; (*fig.*) mania.

maladi|f, ~ve /maladif, -v/ *a.* sickly; (*peur*) morbid.

maladresse /maladrɛs/ *n.f.* clumsiness; (*erreur*) blunder.
maladroit, ~e /maladrwa, -t/ *a.* & *n.m., f.* clumsy (person).
malais, ~e[1] /malɛ, -z/ *a.* & *n.m., f.* Malay.
malaise[2] /malɛz/ *n.m.* feeling of faintness *ou* dizziness; (*fig.*) uneasiness, malaise.
malaisé /maleze/ *a.* difficult.
Malaysia /malɛzja/ *n.f.* Malaysia.
malaria /malarja/ *n.f.* malaria.
malaxer /malakse/ *v.t.* (*pétrir*) knead; (*mêler*) mix.
malchanc|e /malʃɑ̃s/ *n.f.* misfortune. **~eux, ~euse** *a.* unlucky.
mâle /mɑl/ *a.* male; (*viril*) manly. —*n.m.* male.
malédiction /malediksjɔ̃/ *n.f.* curse.
maléfice /malefis/ *n.m.* evil spell.
maléfique /malefik/ *a.* evil.
malencontreu|x, ~se /malɑ̃kɔ̃trø, -z/ *a.* unfortunate.
mal-en-point /malɑ̃pwɛ̃/ *a. invar.* in a bad way.
malentendu /malɑ̃tɑ̃dy/ *n.m.* misunderstanding.
malfaçon /malfasɔ̃/ *n.f.* fault.
malfaisant, ~e /malfəzɑ̃, -t/ *a.* harmful.
malfaiteur /malfɛtœr/ *n.m.* criminal.
malformation /malfɔrmɑsjɔ̃/ *n.f.* malformation.
malgache /malgaʃ/ *a.* & *n.m./f.* Malagasy.
malgré /malgre/ *prép.* in spite of, despite. **~ tout,** after all.
malhabile /malabil/ *a.* clumsy.
malheur /malœr/ *n.m.* misfortune; (*accident*) accident.
malheureu|x, ~se /malœrø, -z/ *a.* unhappy; (*regrettable*) unfortunate; (*sans succès*) unlucky; (*insignifiant*) wretched. —*n.m., f.* (poor) wretch. **~sement** *adv.* unfortunately.
malhonnête /malɔnɛt/ *a.* dishonest; (*impoli*) rude. **~té** *n.f.* dishonesty; rudeness; (*action*) dishonest action.
malic|e /malis/ *n.f.* mischievousness; (*méchanceté*) malice. **~ieux, ~ieuse** *a.* mischievous.
mal|in, ~igne /malɛ̃, -iɲ/ *a.* clever, smart; (*méchant*) malicious; (*tumeur*) malignant; (*difficile: fam.*) difficult. **~ignité** *n.f.* malignancy.
malingre /malɛ̃gr/ *a.* puny.
malintentionné /malɛ̃tɑ̃sjɔne/ *a.* malicious.
malle /mal/ *n.f.* (*valise*) trunk; (*auto.*) boot; (*auto., Amer.*) trunk.
malléable /maleabl/ *a.* malleable.
mallette /malɛt/ *n.f.* (small) suitcase.
malmener /malməne/ *v.t.* manhandle, handle roughly.
malodorant, ~e /malɔdɔrɑ̃, -t/ *a.* smelly, foul-smelling.
malotru /malɔtry/ *n.m.* boor.
malpoli /malpɔli/ *a.* impolite.
malpropre /malprɔpr/ *a.* dirty. **~té** /-əte/ *n.f.* dirtiness.
malsain, ~e /malsɛ̃, -ɛn/ *a.* unhealthy.
malt /malt/ *n.m.* malt.
maltais, ~e /maltɛ, -z/ *a.* & *n.m., f.* Maltese.
Malte /malt/ *n.f.* Malta.
maltraiter /maltrete/ *v.t.* ill-treat.
malveillan|t, ~te /malvɛjɑ̃, -t/ *a.* malevolent. **~ce** *n.f.* malevolence.
maman /mamɑ̃/ *n.f.* mum(my), mother.
mamelle /mamɛl/ *n.f.* teat; (*de femme*) breast.
mamelon /mamlɔ̃/ *n.m.* (*colline*) hillock.
mamie /mami/ *n.f.* (*fam.*) granny.
mammifère /mamifɛr/ *n.m.* mammal.
mammouth /mamut/ *n.m.* mammoth.

manche[1] /mɑ̃ʃ/ *n.f.* sleeve; (*sport, pol.*) round. **la M~,** the Channel.
manche[2] /mɑ̃ʃ/ *n.m.* (*d'un instrument*) handle. **~ à balai,** broomstick.
manchette /mɑ̃ʃɛt/ *n.f.* cuff; (*de journal*) headline.
manchot[1], **~e** /mɑ̃ʃo, -ɔt/ *a.* & *n.m., f.* one-armed (person); (*sans bras*) armless (person).
manchot[2] /mɑ̃ʃo/ *n.m.* (*oiseau*) penguin.
mandarin /mɑ̃darɛ̃/ *n.m.* (*fonctionnaire*) mandarin.
mandarine /mɑ̃darin/ *n.f.* tangerine, mandarin (orange).
mandat /mɑ̃da/ *n.m.* (*postal*) money order; (*pol.*) mandate; (*procuration*) proxy; (*de police*) warrant. **~aire** /-tɛr/ *n.m.* (*représentant*) representative. **~er** /-te/ *v.t.* (*pol.*) delegate.
manège /manɛʒ/ *n.m.* riding-school; (*à la foire*) merry-go-round; (*manœuvre*) wiles, ploy.
manette /manɛt/ *n.f.* lever.
mangeable /mɑ̃ʒabl/ *a.* edible.
mangeaille /mɑ̃ʒaj/ *n.f.* (*fam.*) (bad) food.
mangeoire /mɑ̃ʒwar/ *n.f.* trough.
mang|er /mɑ̃ʒe/ *v.t./i.* eat; (*fortune*) go through; (*essence, gaz*) consume, go through. —*n.m.* food. **donner à ~er à,** feed. **~eur, ~euse** *n.m., f.* eater.
mangue /mɑ̃g/ *n.f.* mango.
maniable /manjabl/ *a.* easy to handle.
maniaque /manjak/ *a.* fussy. —*n.m./f.* fuss-pot; (*fou*) maniac. **un ~ de,** a maniac for.
manie /mani/ *n.f.* habit; (*obsession*) mania.
man|ier /manje/ *v.t.* handle. **~iement** *n.m.* handling.
manière /manjɛr/ *n.f.* way, manner. **~s,** (*politesse*) manners; (*chichis*) fuss. **de cette ~,** in this way. **de ~ à,** so as to. **de toute ~,** anyway, in any case.
maniéré /manjere/ *a.* affected.
manif /manif/ *n.f.* (*fam.*) demo.
manifestant, ~e /manifɛstɑ̃, -t/ *n.m., f.* demonstrator.
manifeste /manifɛst/ *a.* obvious. —*n.m.* manifesto.
manifest|er[1] /manifɛste/ *v.t.* show, manifest. **se ~er** *v. pr.* (*sentiment*) show itself; (*apparaître*) appear. **~ation**[1] *n.f.* expression, demonstration, manifestation; (*de maladie*) appearance.
manifest|er[2] /manifɛste/ *v.i.* (*pol.*) demonstrate. **~ation**[2] *n.f.* (*pol.*) demonstration; (*événement*) event.
maniganc|e /manigɑ̃s/ *n.f.* little plot. **~er** *v.t.* plot.
manipul|er /manipyle/ *v.t.* handle; (*péj.*) manipulate. **~ation** *n.f.* handling; (*péj.*) manipulation.
manivelle /manivɛl/ *n.f.* crank.
manne /man/ *n.f.* (*aubaine*) godsend.
mannequin /mankɛ̃/ *n.m.* (*personne*) model; (*statue*) dummy.
manœuvr|e[1] /manœvr/ *n.f.* manœuvre. **~er** *v.t./i.* manœuvre; (*machine*) operate.
manœuvre[2] /manœvr/ *n.m.* (*ouvrier*) labourer.
manoir /manwar/ *n.m.* manor.
manque /mɑ̃k/ *n.m.* lack (**de,** of); (*vide*) gap. **~s,** (*défauts*) faults. **~ à gagner,** loss of profit.
manqué /mɑ̃ke/ *a.* (*écrivain etc.*) failed.
manquement /mɑ̃kmɑ̃/ *n.m.* **~ à,** breach of.
manquer /mɑ̃ke/ *v.t.* miss; (*gâcher*) spoil; (*examen*) fail. —*v.i.* be short *ou* lacking; (*absent*) be absent; (*en moins, disparu*) be missing; (*échouer*) fail. **~ à,** (*devoir*) fail in. **~ de,** be short of, lack. **il/ça lui manque,** he misses

him/it. **~ (de) faire,** (*faillir*) nearly do. **ne pas ~ de,** not fail to.
mansarde /mɑ̃sard/ *n.f.* attic.
manteau (*pl.* **~x**) /mɑ̃to/ *n.m.* coat.
manucur|e /manykyr/ *n.m./f.* manicurist. **~er** *v.t.* manicure.
manuel, ~le /manɥɛl/ *a.* manual. —*n.m.* (*livre*) manual. **~lement** *adv.* manually.
manufactur|e /manyfaktyr/ *n.f.* factory. **~er** *v.t.* manufacture.
manuscrit, ~e /manyskri, -t/ *a.* handwritten. —*n.m.* manuscript.
manutention /manytɑ̃sjɔ̃/ *n.f.* handling.
mappemonde /mapmɔ̃d/ *n.f.* world map; (*sphère*) globe.
maquereau (*pl.* **~x**) /makro/ *n.m.* (*poisson*) mackerel.
maquette /makɛt/ *n.f.* (scale) model.
maquill|er /makije/ *v.t.* make up; (*truquer*) fake. **se ~er** *v. pr.* make (o.s.) up. **~age** *n.m.* make-up.
maquis /maki/ *n.m.* (*paysage*) scrub; (*mil.*) Maquis, underground.
maraîch|er, ~ère /mareʃe, -ɛʃɛr/ *n.m., f.* market gardener; (*Amer.*) truck farmer.
marais /marɛ/ *n.m.* marsh.
marasme /marasm/ *n.m.* slump.
marathon /maratɔ̃/ *n.m.* marathon.
marbre /marbr/ *n.m.* marble.
marc /mar/ *n.m.* (*eau-de-vie*) marc. **~ de café,** coffee-grounds.
marchand, ~e /marʃɑ̃, -d/ *n.m., f.* trader; (*de charbon, vins*) merchant. —*a.* (*valeur*) market. **~ de couleurs,** ironmonger; (*Amer.*) hardware merchant. **~ de journaux,** newsagent. **~ de légumes,** greengrocer. **~ de poissons,** fishmonger.
marchand|er /marʃɑ̃de/ *v.t.* haggle over. —*v.i.* haggle. **~age** *n.m.* haggling.
marchandise /marʃɑ̃diz/ *n.f.* goods.
marche /marʃ/ *n.f.* (*démarche, trajet*) walk; (*rythme*) pace; (*mil., mus.*) march; (*d'escalier*) step; (*sport*) walking; (*de machine*) working; (*de véhicule*) running; (*de maladie*) course. **en ~,** (*train etc.*) moving. **faire ~ arrière,** (*véhicule*) reverse. **mettre en ~,** start (up). **se mettre en ~,** start moving.
marché /marʃe/ *n.m.* market; (*contrat*) deal. **faire son ~,** do one's shopping. **~ aux puces,** flea market. **M~ commun,** Common Market. **~ noir,** black market.
marchepied /marʃəpje/ *n.m.* (*de train, camion*) step.
march|er /marʃe/ *v.i.* walk; (*aller*) go; (*fonctionner*) work, run; (*prospérer*) go well; (*consentir: fam.*) agree. **~er (au pas),** (*mil.*) march. **faire ~er qn.,** pull s.o.'s leg. **~eur, ~euse** *n.m., f.* walker.
mardi /mardi/ *n.m.* Tuesday. **M~ gras,** Shrove Tuesday.
mare /mar/ *n.f.* (*étang*) pond; (*flaque*) pool.
marécag|e /marekaʒ/ *n.m.* marsh. **~eux, ~euse** *a.* marshy.
maréch|al (*pl.* **~aux**) /mareʃal, -o/ *n.m.* marshal. **~al-ferrant** (*pl.* **~aux-ferrants**) blacksmith.
marée /mare/ *n.f.* tide; (*poissons*) fresh fish. **~ noire,** oil-slick.
marelle /marɛl/ *n.f.* hopscotch.
margarine /margarin/ *n.f.* margarine.
marge /marʒ/ *n.f.* margin. **en ~ de,** (*à l'écart de*) on the fringe(s) of.
margin|al, ~ale (*m. pl.* **~aux**) /marʒinal, -o/ *a.* marginal. —*n.m., f.* drop-out.
marguerite /margərit/ *n.f.* daisy.
mari /mari/ *n.m.* husband.

mariage /marjaʒ/ *n.m.* marriage; (*cérémonie*) wedding.

marié, ~e /marje/ *a.* married. —*n.m.* (bride)groom. —*n.f.* bride. **les ~s,** the bride and groom.

marier /marje/ *v.t.* marry. **se ~** *v. pr.* get married, marry. **se ~ avec,** marry, get married to.

marin, ~e /marɛ̃, -in/ *a.* sea. —*n.m.* sailor. —*n.f.* navy. **~e marchande,** merchant navy.

mariner /marine/ *v.t./i.* marinate.

marionnette /marjɔnɛt/ *n.f.* puppet; (*à fils*) marionette.

maritalement /maritalmɑ̃/ *adv.* as husband and wife.

maritime /maritim/ *a.* maritime, coastal; (*droit, agent*) shipping.

marmaille /marmaj/ *n.f.* (*enfants*: *fam.*) brats.

marmelade /marməlad/ *n.f.* stewed fruit.

marmite /marmit/ *n.f.* (cooking-) pot.

marmonner /marmɔne/ *v.t./i.* mumble.

marmot /marmo/ *n.m.* (*fam.*) kid.

marmotter /marmɔte/ *v.t./i.* mumble.

Maroc /marɔk/ *n.m.* Morocco.

marocain, ~e /marɔkɛ̃, -ɛn/ *a.* & *n.m., f.* Moroccan.

maroquinerie /marɔkinri/ *n.f.* (*magasin*) leather goods shop.

marotte /marɔt/ *n.f.* fad, craze.

marquant, ~e /markɑ̃, -t/ *a.* outstanding.

marque /mark/ *n.f.* mark; (*de produits*) brand, make; (*score*) score. **de ~,** (*comm.*) brand-name; (*fig.*) important. **~ de fabrique,** trade mark. **~ déposée,** registered trade mark.

marqué /marke/ *a.* marked.

marquer /marke/ *v.t.* mark; (*indiquer*) show; (*écrire*) note down; (*point, but*) score; (*joueur*) mark; (*animal*) brand. —*v.i.* (*trace*) leave a mark; (*événement*) stand out.

marquis, ~e[1] /marki, -z/ *n.m., f.* marquis, marchioness.

marquise[2] /markiz/ *n.f.* (*auvent*) glass awning.

marraine /marɛn/ *n.f.* godmother.

marrant, ~e /marɑ̃, -t/ *a.* (*fam.*) funny.

marre /mar/ *adv.* **en avoir ~,** (*fam.*) be fed up (**de,** with).

marrer (se) /(sə)mare/ *v. pr.* (*fam.*) laugh, have a (good) laugh.

marron /marɔ̃/ *n.m.* chestnut; (*couleur*) brown; (*coup*: *fam.*) thump. —*a.* *invar.* brown. **~ d'Inde,** horse-chestnut.

mars /mars/ *n.m.* March.

marsouin /marswɛ̃/ *n.m.* porpoise.

marteau (*pl.* **~x**) /marto/ *n.m.* hammer. **~ (de porte),** (door) knocker. **~ piqueur** *ou* **pneumatique,** pneumatic drill.

marteler /martəle/ *v.t.* hammer.

mart|ial (*m. pl.* **~iaux**) /marsjal, -jo/ *a.* martial.

martien, ~ne /marsjɛ̃, -jɛn/ *a.* & *n.m., f.* Martian.

martyr, ~e[1] /martir/ *n.m., f.* martyr. —*a.* martyred. **~iser** *v.t.* martyr; (*fig.*) batter.

martyre[2] /martir/ *n.m.* (*souffrance*) martyrdom.

marxis|te /marksist/ *a.* & *n.m./f.* Marxist. **~me** *n.m.* Marxism.

mascarade /maskarad/ *n.f.* masquerade.

mascotte /maskɔt/ *n.f.* mascot.

masculin, ~e /maskylɛ̃, -in/ *a.* masculine; (*sexe*) male; (*mode, équipe*) men's. —*n.m.* masculine. **~ité** /-inite/ *n.f.* masculinity.

masochis|te /mazɔʃist/ *n.m./f.* masochist. **~me** *n.m.* masochism.

masqu|e /mask/ *n.m.* mask. **~er** *v.t.* mask (**à,** from); (*lumière*) block (off).

massacr|e /masakr/ *n.m.* massacre. **~er** *v.t.* massacre; (*abîmer*: *fam.*) spoil.
massage /masaʒ/ *n.m.* massage.
masse /mas/ *n.f.* (*volume*) mass; (*gros morceau*) lump, mass; (*outil*) sledge-hammer. **en ~,** (*vendre*) in bulk; (*venir*) in force; (*production*) mass. **la ~,** (*foule*) the masses. **une ~ de,** (*fam.*) masses of.
masser[1] /mase/ *v.t.*, **se ~** *v. pr.* (*gens, foule*) mass.
mass|er[2] /mase/ *v.t.* (*pétrir*) massage. **~eur, ~euse** *n.m., f.* masseur, masseuse.
massi|f, ~ve /masif, -v/ *a.* massive; (*or, argent*) solid. —*n.m.* (*de fleurs*) clump; (*géog.*) massif. **~vement** *adv.* (*en masse*) in large numbers.
massue /masy/ *n.f.* club, bludgeon.
mastic /mastik/ *n.m.* putty.
mastiquer /mastike/ *v.t.* (*mâcher*) chew.
masturb|er (se) /(sə)mastyrbe/ *v. pr.* masturbate. **~ation** *n.f.* masturbation.
masure /mazyr/ *n.f.* hovel.
mat /mat/ *a.* (*couleur*) matt; (*bruit*) dull. **être ~,** (*aux échecs*) be checkmate.
mât /mɑ/ *n.m.* mast; (*pylône*) pole.
match /matʃ/ *n.m.* match; (*Amer.*) game. **(faire) ~ nul,** tie, draw. **~ retour,** return match.
matelas /matla/ *n.m.* mattress.
matelasser /matlase/ *v.t.* pad; (*tissu*) quilt.
matelot /matlo/ *n.m.* sailor.
mater /mate/ *v.t.* (*personne*) subdue; (*réprimer*) stifle.
matérialiser (se) /(sə)materjalize/ *v. pr.* materialize.
matérialiste /materjalist/ *a.* materialistic. —*n.m./f.* materialist.
matériaux /materjo/ *n.m. pl.* materials.
matériel, ~le /materjɛl/ *a.* material. —*n.m.* equipment, materials; (*d'un ordinateur*) hardware.
maternel, ~le /matɛrnɛl/ *a.* motherly, maternal; (*rapport de parenté*) maternal. —*n.f.* nursery school.
maternité /matɛrnite/ *n.f.* maternity hospital; (*état de mère*) motherhood.
mathémati|que /matematik/ *a.* mathematical. —*n.f. pl.* mathematics. **~cien, ~cienne** *n.m., f.* mathematician.
maths /mat/ *n.f. pl.* (*fam.*) maths.
matière /matjɛr/ *n.f.* matter; (*produit*) material; (*sujet*) subject. **en ~ de,** as regards. **~ plastique,** plastic. **~s grasses,** fat.
matin /matɛ̃/ *n.m.* morning.
matin|al (*m. pl.* **~aux**) /matinal, -o/ *a.* morning; (*de bonne heure*) early.
matinée /matine/ *n.f.* morning; (*spectacle*) matinée.
matou /matu/ *n.m.* tom-cat.
matraqu|e /matrak/ *n.f.* (*de police*) truncheon; (*Amer.*) billy (club); (*de malfaiteur*) cosh, club. **~er** *v.t.* club, beat; (*message*) plug.
matrice /matris/ *n.f.* womb; (*techn.*) matrix.
matrimon|ial (*m. pl.* **~iaux**) /matrimɔnjal, -jo/ *a.* matrimonial.
maturité /matyrite/ *n.f.* maturity.
maudire† /modir/ *v.t.* curse.
maudit, ~e /modi, -t/ *a.* (*fam.*) damned.
maugréer /mogree/ *v.i.* grumble.
mausolée /mozɔle/ *n.m.* mausoleum.
maussade /mosad/ *a.* gloomy.
mauvais, ~e /mɔvɛ, -z/ *a.* bad; (*erroné*) wrong; (*malveillant*) evil; (*désagréable*) nasty, bad; (*mer*) rough. —*n.m.* **le ~,** the bad. **il fait ~,** the weather is bad. **~e herbe,** weed. **~e langue,** gossip. **~e**

passe, tight spot. **~ traitements,** ill-treatment.
mauve /mov/ *a.* & *n.m.* mauve.
mauviette /movjɛt/ *n.f.* weakling.
maux /mo/ *voir* **mal**[2].
maxim|al (*m. pl.* **~aux**) /maksimal, -o/ *a.* maximum.
maxime /maksim/ *n.f.* maxim.
maximum /maksimɔm/ *a.* & *n.m.* maximum. **au ~,** as much as possible; (*tout au plus*) at most.
mayonnaise /majɔnɛz/ *n.f.* mayonnaise.
mazout /mazut/ *n.m.* heating oil.
me, m'* /mə, m/ *pron.* me; (*indirect*) (to) me; (*réfléchi*) myself.
méandre /meɑ̃dr/ *n.m.* meander.
mec /mek/ *n.m.* (*fam.*) bloke, guy.
mécanicien /mekanisjɛ̃/ *n.m.* mechanic; (*rail.*) train driver.
mécani|que /mekanik/ *a.* mechanical; (*jouet*) clockwork. —*n.f.* mechanics; (*mécanisme*) mechanism. **~ser** *v.t.* mechanize.
mécanisme /mekanism/ *n.m.* mechanism.
méch|ant, ~ante /meʃɑ̃, -t/ *a.* (*cruel*) wicked; (*désagréable*) nasty; (*enfant*) naughty; (*chien*) vicious; (*sensationnel*: *fam.*) terrific. —*n.m., f.* (*enfant*) naughty child. **~amment** *adv.* wickedly. **~anceté** *n.f.* wickedness; (*action*) wicked action.
mèche /mɛʃ/ *n.f.* (*de cheveux*) lock; (*de bougie*) wick; (*d'explosif*) fuse.
méconnaissable /mekɔnɛsabl/ *a.* unrecognizable.
méconn|aître /mekɔnɛtr/ *v.t.* be ignorant of; (*mésestimer*) underestimate. **~aissance** *n.f.* ignorance. **~u** *a.* unrecognized.
mécontent, ~e /mekɔ̃tɑ̃, -t/ *a.* dissatisfied (**de,** with); (*irrité*) annoyed (**de,** at, with). **~ement** /-tmɑ̃/ *n.m.* dissatisfaction; annoyance. **~er** /-te/ *v.t.* dissatisfy; (*irriter*) annoy.
médaill|e /medaj/ *n.f.* medal; (*insigne*) badge; (*bijou*) medallion. **~é, ~ée** *n.m., f.* medal holder.
médaillon /medajɔ̃/ *n.m.* medallion; (*bijou*) locket.
médecin /mɛdsɛ̃/ *n.m.* doctor.
médecine /mɛdsin/ *n.f.* medicine.
média|teur, ~trice /medjatœr, -tris/ *n.m., f.* mediator.
médiation /medjɑsjɔ̃/ *n.f.* mediation.
médic|al (*m. pl.* **~aux**) /medikal, -o/ *a.* medical.
médicament /medikamɑ̃/ *n.m.* medicine.
médicin|al (*m. pl.* **~aux**) /medisinal, -o/ *a.* medicinal.
médico-lég|al (*m. pl.* **~aux**) /medikɔlegal, -o/ *a.* forensic.
médiév|al (*m. pl.* **~aux**) /medjeval, -o/ *a.* medieval.
médiocr|e /medjɔkr/ *a.* mediocre, poor. **~ement** *adv.* (*peu*) not very; (*mal*) in a mediocre way. **~ité** *n.f.* mediocrity.
médire /medir/ *v.i.* **~ de,** speak ill of.
médisance /medizɑ̃s/ *n.f.* **~(s),** malicious gossip.
méditati|f, ~ve /meditatif, -v/ *a.* (*pensif*) thoughtful.
médit|er /medite/ *v.t./i.* meditate. **~er de,** plan to. **~ation** *n.f.* meditation.
Méditerranée /meditɛrane/ *n.f.* **la ~,** the Mediterranean.
méditerranéen, ~ne /meditɛraneɛ̃, -ɛn/ *a.* Mediterranean.
médium /medjɔm/ *n.m.* (*personne*) medium.
méduse /medyz/ *n.f.* jellyfish.
meeting /mitiŋ/ *n.m.* meeting.
méfait /mefɛ/ *n.m.* misdeed. **les ~s de,** (*conséquences*) the ravages of.
méfian|t, ~te /mefjɑ̃, -t/ *a.* distrustful. **~ce** *n.f.* distrust.
méfier (se) /(sə)mefje/ *v. pr.* be

wary *ou* careful. **se ~ de,** distrust, be wary of.

mégarde (par) /(par)megard/ *adv.* by accident, accidentally.

mégère /meʒɛr/ *n.f.* (*femme*) shrew.

mégot /mego/ *n.m.* (*fam.*) cigarette-end.

meilleur, ~e /mɛjœr/ *a.* & *adv.* better (**que,** than). **le ~ livre**/*etc.*, the best book/*etc.* **mon ~ ami**/*etc.*, my best friend/*etc.* —*n.m., f.* best (one). **~ marché,** cheaper.

mélancol|ie /melɑ̃kɔli/ *n.f.* melancholy. **~ique** *a.* melancholy.

mélang|e /melɑ̃ʒ/ *n.m.* mixture, blend. **~er** *v.t.*, **se ~er** *v. pr.* mix, blend; (*embrouiller*) mix up.

mélasse /melas/ *n.f.* treacle; (*Amer.*) molasses.

mêlée /mele/ *n.f.* scuffle; (*rugby*) scrum.

mêler /mele/ *v.t.* mix (**à,** with); (*qualités*) combine; (*embrouiller*) mix up. **~ à,** (*impliquer dans*) involve in. **se ~** *v. pr.* mix; combine. **se ~ à,** (*se joindre à*) join. **se ~ de,** meddle in.

mélod|ie /melɔdi/ *n.f.* melody. **~ieux, ~ieuse** *a.* melodious. **~ique** *a.* melodic.

mélodram|e /melɔdram/ *n.m.* melodrama. **~atique** *a.* melodramatic.

mélomane /melɔman/ *n.m./f.* music lover.

melon /mlɔ̃/ *n.m.* melon. **(chapeau) ~,** bowler (hat).

membrane /mɑ̃bran/ *n.f.* membrane.

membre[1] /mɑ̃br/ *n.m.* limb.

membre[2] /mɑ̃br/ *n.m.* (*adhérent*) member.

même /mɛm/ *a.* same. **ce livre**/*etc.* **~,** this very book/*etc.* **la bonté**/*etc.* **~,** kindness/*etc.* itself. —*pron.* same (one). —*adv.* even. **à ~,** (*sur*) directly on. **à ~ de,** in a position to. **de ~,** (*aussi*) too; (*de la même façon*) likewise. **de ~ que,** just as. **en ~ temps,** at the same time.

mémé /meme/ *n.f.* (*fam.*) granny.

mémoire /memwar/ *n.f.* memory. —*n.m.* (*requête*) memorandum; (*univ.*) dissertation. **~s,** (*souvenirs écrits*) memoirs. **à la ~ de,** to the memory of. **de ~,** from memory.

mémorable /memɔrabl/ *a.* memorable.

mémorandum /memɔrɑ̃dɔm/ *n.m.* memorandum.

mémor|ial (*pl.* **~iaux**) /memɔrjal, -jo/ *n.m.* memorial.

menac|e /mənas/ *n.f.* threat. **~er** *v.t.* threaten (**de faire,** to do).

ménage /menaʒ/ *n.m.* (married) couple; (*travail*) housework. **se mettre en ~,** set up house.

ménagement /menaʒmɑ̃/ *n.m.* care and consideration.

ménag|er[1], **~ère** /menaʒe, -ɛr/ *a.* household, domestic. —*n.f.* housewife.

ménager[2] /menaʒe/ *v.t.* treat with tact; (*utiliser*) be sparing in the use of; (*organiser*) prepare (carefully).

ménagerie /menaʒri/ *n.f.* menagerie.

mendiant, ~e /mɑ̃djɑ̃, -t/ *n.m., f.* beggar.

mendicité /mɑ̃disite/ *n.f.* begging.

mendier /mɑ̃dje/ *v.t.* beg for. —*v.i.* beg.

menées /məne/ *n.f. pl.* schemings.

mener /məne/ *v.t.* lead; (*entreprise, pays*) run. —*v.i.* lead. **~ à,** (*accompagner à*) take to. **~ à bien,** see through.

meneur /mənœr/ *n.m.* (*chef*) (ring)leader. **~ de jeu,** compère; (*Amer.*) master of ceremonies.

méningite /menɛ̃ʒit/ *n.f.* meningitis.

ménopause /menɔpoz/ *n.f.* menopause.
menotte /mənɔt/ *n.f.* (*fam.*) hand. **~s,** handcuffs.
mensong|e /mɑ̃sɔ̃ʒ/ *n.m.* lie; (*action*) lying. **~er, ~ère** *a.* untrue.
menstruation /mɑ̃stryɑsjɔ̃/ *n.f.* menstruation.
mensualité /mɑ̃sɥalite/ *n.f.* monthly payment.
mensuel, ~le /mɑ̃sɥɛl/ *a.* & *n.m.* monthly. **~lement** *adv.* monthly.
mensurations /mɑ̃syrɑsjɔ̃/ *n.f. pl.* measurements.
ment|al (*m. pl.* **~aux**) /mɑ̃tal, -o/ *a.* mental.
mentalité /mɑ̃talite/ *n.f.* mentality.
menteu|r, ~se /mɑ̃tœr, -z/ *n.m., f.* liar. —*a.* untruthful.
menthe /mɑ̃t/ *n.f.* mint.
mention /mɑ̃sjɔ̃/ *n.f.* mention; (*annotation*) note; (*scol.*) grade. **~ bien,** (*scol.*) distinction. **~ner** /-jɔne/ *v.t.* mention.
mentir† /mɑ̃tir/ *v.i.* lie.
menton /mɑ̃tɔ̃/ *n.m.* chin.
menu[1] /məny/ *n.m.* (*carte*) menu; (*repas*) meal.
menu[2] /məny/ *a.* (*petit*) tiny; (*fin*) fine; (*insignifiant*) minor. —*adv.* (*couper*) fine.
menuis|ier /mənɥizje/ *n.m.* carpenter, joiner. **~erie** *n.f.* carpentry, joinery.
méprendre (se) /(sə)meprɑ̃dr/ *v. pr.* **se ~ sur,** be mistaken about.
mépris /mepri/ *n.m.* contempt, scorn (**de,** for). **au ~ de,** in defiance of.
méprisable /meprizabl/ *a.* despicable.
méprise /mepriz/ *n.f.* mistake.
mépris|er /meprize/ *v.t.* scorn, despise. **~ant, ~ante** *a.* scornful.
mer /mɛr/ *n.f.* sea; (*marée*) tide. **en haute ~,** on the open sea.
mercenaire /mɛrsənɛr/ *n.m.* & *a.* mercenary.
merc|ier, ~ière /mɛrsje, -jɛr/ *n.m., f.* haberdasher; (*Amer.*) notions merchant. **~erie** *n.f.* haberdashery; (*Amer.*) notions store.
merci /mɛrsi/ *int.* thank you, thanks (**de, pour,** for). —*n.f.* mercy. **~ beaucoup, ~ bien,** thank you very much.
mercredi /mɛrkrədi/ *n.m.* Wednesday. **~ des Cendres,** Ash Wednesday.
mercure /mɛrkyr/ *n.m.* mercury.
merde /mɛrd/ *int.* (*fam.*) oh hell.
mère /mɛr/ *n.f.* mother. **~ de famille,** mother.
méridien /meridjɛ̃/ *n.m.* meridian.
méridion|al, ~ale (*m. pl.* **~aux**) /meridjɔnal, -o/ *a.* southern. —*n.m., f.* southerner.
meringue /mərɛ̃g/ *n.f.* meringue.
mérite /merit/ *n.m.* merit.
mérit|er /merite/ *v.t.* deserve. **~ant, ~ante** *a.* deserving.
méritoire /meritwar/ *a.* commendable.
merlan /mɛrlɑ̃/ *n.m.* whiting.
merle /mɛrl/ *n.m.* blackbird.
merveille /mɛrvɛj/ *n.f.* wonder, marvel. **à ~,** wonderfully.
merveilleu|x, ~se /mɛrvɛjø, -z/ *a.* wonderful, marvellous. **~sement** *adv.* wonderfully.
mes /me/ *voir* **mon.**
mésange /mezɑ̃ʒ/ *n.f.* tit(mouse).
mésaventure /mezavɑ̃tyr/ *n.f.* misadventure.
mesdames /medam/ *voir* **madame.**
mesdemoiselles /medmwazɛl/ *voir* **mademoiselle.**
mésentente /mezɑ̃tɑ̃t/ *n.f.* disagreement.
mesquin, ~e /mɛskɛ̃, -in/ *a.* mean. **~erie** /-inri/ *n.f.* meanness.
mess /mɛs/ *n.m.* (*mil.*) mess.

messag|e /mesaʒ/ *n.m.* message. **~er, ~ère** *n.m., f.* messenger.
messe /mɛs/ *n.f.* (*relig.*) mass.
Messie /mesi/ *n.m.* Messiah.
messieurs /mesjø/ *voir* **monsieur.**
mesure /məzyr/ *n.f.* measurement; (*quantité, étalon*) measure; (*disposition*) measure, step; (*cadence*) time; (*modération*) moderation. **à ~ que,** as. **dans la ~ où,** in so far as. **dans une certaine ~,** to some extent. **en ~ de,** in a position to.
mesuré /məzyre/ *a.* measured; (*personne*) moderate.
mesurer /məzyre/ *v.t.* measure; (*juger*) assess; (*argent, temps*) ration. **~ à** *ou* **sur,** match to. **se ~ avec,** pit o.s. against.
met /mɛ/ *voir* **mettre.**
métabolisme /metabɔlism/ *n.m.* metabolism.
mét|al (*pl.* **~aux**) /metal, -o/ *n.m.* metal. **~allique** *a.* (*objet*) metal; (*éclat etc.*) metallic.
métallurg|ie /metalyrʒi/ *n.f.* (*industrie*) steel *ou* metal industry. **~iste** *n.m.* steel *ou* metal worker.
métamorphos|e /metamɔrfoz/ *n.f.* metamorphosis. **~er** *v.t.*, **se ~er** *v. pr.* transform.
métaphor|e /metafɔr/ *n.f.* metaphor. **~ique** *a.* metaphorical.
météo /meteo/ *n.f.* (*bulletin*) weather forecast.
météore /meteɔr/ *n.m.* meteor.
météorolog|ie /meteɔrɔlɔʒi/ *n.f.* meteorology; (*service*) weather bureau. **~ique** *a.* weather; (*études etc.*) meteorological.
méthod|e /metɔd/ *n.f.* method; (*ouvrage*) course, manual. **~ique** *a.* methodical.
méticuleu|x, ~se /metikylø, -z/ *a.* meticulous.
métier /metje/ *n.m.* job; (*manuel*) trade; (*intellectuel*) profession; (*expérience*) skill. **~ (à tisser),** loom.
métis, ~se /metis/ *a.* & *n.m., f.* half-caste.
métrage /metraʒ/ *n.m.* length. **court ~,** short film. **long ~,** full-length film.
mètre /mɛtr/ *n.m.* metre; (*règle*) rule. **~ à ruban,** tape-measure.
métreur /metrœr/ *n.m.* quantity surveyor.
métrique /metrik/ *a.* metric.
métro /metro/ *n.m.* underground; (*à Paris*) Métro.
métropol|e /metrɔpɔl/ *n.f.* metropolis; (*pays*) mother country. **~itain, ~itaine** *a.* metropolitan.
mets[1] /mɛ/ *n.m.* dish.
mets[2] /mɛ/ *voir* **mettre.**
mettable /mɛtabl/ *a.* wearable.
metteur /mɛtœr/ *n.m.* **~ en scène,** (*théâtre*) producer; (*cinéma*) director.
mettre† /mɛtr/ *v.t.* put; (*vêtement*) put on; (*radio, gaz, etc.*) put *ou* switch on; (*table*) lay; (*pendule*) set; (*temps*) take; (*installer*) put in; (*supposer*) suppose. **se ~** *v. pr.* put o.s.; (*objet*) go; (*porter*) wear. **~ bas,** give birth. **~ qn. en boîte,** pull s.o.'s leg. **~ en cause** *ou* **en question,** question. **~ en colère,** make angry. **~ en valeur,** highlight; (*un bien*) exploit. **se ~ à,** (*entrer dans*) get *ou* go into. **se ~ à faire,** start doing. **se ~ à l'aise,** make o.s. comfortable. **se ~ à table,** sit down at the table. **se ~ au travail,** set to work. **(se) ~ en ligne,** line up.
meuble /mœbl/ *n.m.* piece of furniture. **~s,** furniture.
meubler /mœble/ *v.t.* furnish; (*fig.*) fill. **se ~** *v. pr.* buy furniture.
meugl|er /møgle/ *v.i.* moo. **~ement(s)** *n.m.* (*pl.*) mooing.
meule /møl/ *n.f.* (*de foin*) haystack; (*à moudre*) millstone.

meun|ier, ~ière /mønje -jɛr/ *n.m.,f.* miller.
meurs, meurt /mœr/ *voir* **mourir.**
meurtr|e /mœrtr/ *n.m.* murder. **~ier, ~ière** *a.* deadly; *n.m.* murderer; *n.f.* murderess.
meurtr|ir /mœrtrir/ *v.t.* bruise. **~issure** *n.f.* bruise.
meute /møt/ *n.f.* (*troupe*) pack.
mexicain, ~e /mɛksikɛ̃, -ɛn/ *a.* & *n.m.,f.* Mexican.
Mexique /mɛksik/ *n.m.* Mexico.
mi- /mi/ *préf.* mid-, half-. **à ~-chemin,** half-way. **à ~-côte,** half-way up the hill. **la ~-juin/** *etc.*, mid-June/*etc.*
miaou /mjau/ *n.m.* mew.
miaul|er /mjole/ *v.i.* mew. **~ement** *n.m.* mew.
miche /miʃ/ *n.f.* round loaf.
micro /mikro/ *n.m.* microphone, mike.
micro- /mikro/ *préf.* micro-
microbe /mikrɔb/ *n.m.* germ.
microfilm /mikrɔfilm/ *n.m.* microfilm.
micro-onde /mikrɔɔ̃d/ *n.f.* microwave.
microphone /mikrɔfɔn/ *n.m.* microphone.
microplaquette /mikrɔplakɛt/ *n.f.* (micro)chip.
microscop|e /mikrɔskɔp/ *n.m.* microscope. **~ique** *a.* microscopic.
microsillon /mikrɔsijɔ̃/ *n.m.* long-playing record.
midi /midi/ *n.m.* twelve o'clock, midday, noon; (*déjeuner*) lunchtime; (*sud*) south. **le M~,** the South of France.
mie /mi/ *n.f.* soft part (of the loaf).
miel /mjɛl/ *n.m.* honey.
mielleu|x, ~se /mjɛlø, -z/ *a.* unctuous.
mien, ~ne /mjɛ̃, mjɛn/ *pron.* **le ~, la ~ne, les ~(ne)s,** mine.
miette /mjɛt/ *n.f.* crumb; (*fig.*) scrap. **en ~s,** in pieces.
mieux /mjø/ *adv.* & *a. invar.* better (**que,** than). **le** *ou* **la** *ou* **les ~,** (the) best. —*n.m.* best; (*progrès*) improvement. **faire de son ~,** do one's best. **faire ~ de,** be better off to. **le ~ serait de,** the best thing would be to.
mièvre /mjɛvr/ *a.* genteel and insipid.
mignon, ~ne /miɲɔ̃, -ɔn/ *a.* pretty.
migraine /migrɛn/ *n.f.* headache.
migration /migrasjɔ̃/ *n.f.* migration.
mijoter /miʒɔte/ *v.t./i.* simmer; (*tramer: fam.*) cook up.
mil /mil/ *n.m.* a thousand.
milic|e /milis/ *n.f.* militia. **~ien** *n.m.* militiaman.
milieu (*pl.* **~x**) /miljø/ *n.m.* middle; (*environnement*) environment; (*groupe*) circle; (*mesure*) medium; (*voie*) middle way; (*criminel*) underworld. **au ~ de,** in the middle of.
militaire /militɛr/ *a.* military. —*n.m.* soldier.
milit|er /milite/ *v.i.* be a militant. **~er pour,** militate in favour of. **~ant, ~ante** *n.m.,f.* militant.
mille[1] /mil/ *a.* & *n.m. invar.* a thousand. **deux ~,** two thousand.
mille[2] /mil/ *n.m.* **~ (marin),** (nautical) mile.
millénaire /milenɛr/ *n.m.* millennium.
mille-pattes /milpat/ *n.m. invar.* centipede.
millésime /milezim/ *n.m.* year.
millet /mijɛ/ *n.m* millet.
milliard /miljar/ *n.m.* thousand million, billion. **~aire** /-dɛr/ *n.m./f.* multimillionaire.
millier /milje/ *n.m.* thousand. **un ~ (de),** about a thousand.
millimètre /milimɛtr/ *n.m.* millimetre.
million /miljɔ̃/ *n.m.* million. **deux**

~s (de), two million. **~naire** /-jɔnɛr/ *n.m./f.* millionaire.

mim|e /mim/ *n.m./f.* (*personne*) mime. —*n.m.* (*art*) mime. **~er** *v.t.* mime; (*singer*) mimic.

mimique /mimik/ *n.f.* (expressive) gestures.

mimosa /mimoza/ *n.m.* mimosa.

minable /minabl/ *a.* shabby.

minaret /minarɛ/ *n.m.* minaret.

minauder /minode/ *v.i.* simper.

minc|e /mɛ̃s/ *a.* thin; (*svelte, insignifiant*) slim. —*int.* dash (it). **~eur** *n.f.* thinness; slimness.

mine[1] /min/ *n.f.* expression; (*allure*) appearance. **avoir bonne ~,** look well. **faire ~ de,** make as if to.

mine[2] /min/ *n.f.* (*exploitation, explosif*) mine; (*de crayon*) lead. **~ de charbon,** coal-mine.

miner /mine/ *v.t.* (*saper*) undermine; (*garnir d'explosifs*) mine.

minerai /minrɛ/ *n.m.* ore.

minér|al (*m. pl.* **~aux**) /mineral, -o/ *a.* mineral. —*n.m.* (*pl.* **~aux**) mineral.

minet, ~te /minɛ, -t/ *n.m., f.* (*chat: fam.*) puss(y).

mineur[1], **~e** /minœr/ *a.* minor; (*jurid.*) under age. —*n.m., f.* (*jurid.*) minor.

mineur[2] /minœr/ *n.m.* (*ouvrier*) miner.

mini- /mini/ *préf.* mini-.

miniature /minjatyr/ *n.f.* & *a.* miniature.

minibus /minibys/ *n.m.* minibus.

min|ier, ~ière /minje, -jɛr/ *a.* mining.

minim|al (*m. pl.* **~aux**) /minimal, -o/ *a.* mimimum.

minime /minim/ *a.* minor. —*n.m./f.* (*sport*) junior.

minimiser /minimize/ *v.t.* minimize.

minimum /minimɔm/ *a.* & *n.m.* minimum. **au ~,** (*pour le moins*) at the very least.

minist|ère /ministɛr/ *n.m.* ministry; (*gouvernement*) government. **~ère de l'Intérieur,** Home Office; (*Amer.*) Department of the Interior. **~ériel, ~érielle** *a.* ministerial, government.

ministre /ministr/ *n.m.* minister. **~ de l'Intérieur,** Home Secretary; (*Amer.*) Secretary of the Interior.

minorer /minɔre/ *v.t.* reduce.

minorit|é /minɔrite/ *n.f.* minority. **~aire** *a.* minority. **être ~aire,** be in the minority.

Minorque /minɔrk/ *n.f.* Minorca.

minuit /minɥi/ *n.m.* midnight.

minuscule /minyskyl/ *a.* minute. —*n.f.* **(lettre) ~,** small letter.

minut|e /minyt/ *n.f.* minute. **~er** *v.t.* time (to the minute).

minuterie /minytri/ *n.f.* time-switch.

minutie /minysi/ *n.f.* meticulousness.

minutieu|x, ~se /minysjø, -z/ *a.* meticulous. **~sement** *adv.* meticulously.

mioche /mjɔʃ/ *n.m., f.* (*fam.*) youngster, kid.

mirabelle /mirabɛl/ *n.f.* (mirabelle) plum.

miracle /mirɑkl/ *n.m.* miracle.

miraculeu|x, ~se /mirakylø, -z/ *a.* miraculous. **~sement** *adv.* miraculously.

mirage /miraʒ/ *n.m.* mirage.

mirobolant, ~e /mirɔbɔlɑ̃, -t/ *a.* (*fam.*) marvellous.

miroir /mirwar/ *n.m.* mirror.

miroiter /mirwate/ *v.i.* gleam, shimmer.

mis, ~e[1] /mi, miz/ *voir* **mettre.** —*a.* **bien ~,** well-dressed.

mise[2] /miz/ *n.f.* putting; (*argent*) stake; (*tenue*) attire. **~ à feu,** blast-off. **~ au point,** adjustment; (*fig.*) clarification. **~ de fonds,** capital outlay. **~ en garde,** warning. **~ en scène,**

(*théâtre*) production; (*cinéma*) direction.

miser /mize/ *v.t.* (*argent*) bet, stake (**sur,** on). **~ sur,** (*compter sur*: *fam.*) bank on.

misérable /mizerabl/ *a.* miserable, wretched; (*indigent*) poverty-stricken; (*minable*) seedy. —*n.m.*/*f.* wretch.

mis|ère /mizɛr/ *n.f.* (grinding) poverty; (*malheur*) misery. **~éreux, ~éreuse** *n.m.*, *f.* pauper.

miséricorde /mizerikɔrd/ *n.f.* mercy.

missel /misɛl/ *n.m.* missal.

missile /misil/ *n.m.* missile.

mission /misjɔ̃/ *n.m.* mission. **~naire** /-jɔnɛr/ *n.m.*/*f.* missionary.

missive /misiv/ *n.f.* missive.

mistral /mistral/ *n.m. invar.* (*vent*) mistral.

mitaine /mitɛn/ *n.f.* mitten.

mit|e /mit/ *n.f.* (clothes-)moth. **~é** *a.* moth-eaten.

mi-temps /mitɑ̃/ *n.f. invar.* (*repos*: *sport*) half-time; (*période*: *sport*) half. **à ~,** part time.

miteu|x, ~se /mitø, -z/ *a.* shabby.

mitigé /mitiʒe/ *a.* (*modéré*) lukewarm; (*mélangé*: *fam.*) mixed.

mitraill|e /mitrɑj/ *n.f.* gunfire. **~er** *v.t.* machine-gun.

mitraill|ette /mitrɑjɛt/ *n.f.* sub-machine-gun. **~euse** *n.f.* machine-gun.

mi-voix (à) /(a)mivwa/ *adv.* in an undertone.

mixeur /miksœr/ *n.m.* liquidizer, blender.

mixte /mikst/ *a.* mixed; (*usage*) dual; (*tribunal*) joint; (*école*) coeducational.

mixture /mikstyr/ *n.f.* (*péj.*) mixture.

mobile[1] /mɔbil/ *a.* mobile; (*pièce*) moving; (*fête*) movable; (*feuillet*) loose. —*n.m.* (*art*) mobile.

mobile[2] /mɔbil/ *n.m.* (*raison*) motive.

mobilier /mɔbilje/ *n.m.* furniture.

mobilis|er /mɔbilize/ *v.t.* mobilize. **~ation** *n.f.* mobilization.

mobilité /mɔbilite/ *n.f.* mobility.

mobylette /mɔbilɛt/ *n.f.* (P.) moped.

mocassin /mɔkasɛ̃/ *n.m.* moccasin.

moche /mɔʃ/ *a.* (*laid*: *fam.*) ugly; (*mauvais*: *fam.*) lousy.

modalité /mɔdalite/ *n.f.* mode.

mode[1] /mɔd/ *n.f.* fashion; (*coutume*) custom. **à la ~,** fashionable.

mode[2] /mɔd/ *n.m.* method, mode; (*genre*) way. **~ d'emploi,** directions (for use).

modèle /mɔdɛl/ *n.m.* & *a.* model. **~ réduit,** (small-scale) model.

modeler /mɔdle/ *v.t.* model (**sur,** on). **se ~ sur,** model o.s. on.

modéré, ~e /mɔdere/ *a.* & *n.m.*, *f.* moderate. **~ment** *adv.* moderately.

modér|er /mɔdere/ *v.t.* moderate. **se ~er** *v. pr.* restrain o.s. **~ateur, ~atrice** *a.* moderating. **~ation** *n.f.* moderation.

modern|e /mɔdɛrn/ *a.* modern. —*n.m.* modern style. **~iser** *v.t.* modernize.

modest|e /mɔdɛst/ *a.* modest. **~ement** *adv.* modestly. **~ie** *n.f.* modesty.

modicité /mɔdisite/ *n.f.* lowness.

modif|ier /mɔdifje/ *v.t.* modify. **se ~ier** *v. pr.* alter. **~ication** *n.f.* modification.

modique /mɔdik/ *a.* low.

modiste /mɔdist/ *n.f.* milliner.

module /mɔdyl/ *n.m.* module.

modul|er /mɔdyle/ *v.t.*/*i.* modulate. **~ation** *n.f.* modulation.

moelle /mwal/ *n.f.* marrow. **~ épinière,** spinal cord.

moelleu|x, ~se /mwalø, -z/ *a.* soft; (*onctueux*) smooth.

mœurs /mœr(s)/ *n.f. pl.* (*morale*) morals; (*habitudes*) customs; (*manières*) ways.
moi /mwa/ *pron.* me; (*indirect*) (to) me; (*sujet*) I. —*n.m.* self. **~-même** *pron.* myself.
moignon /mwaɲɔ̃/ *n.m.* stump.
moindre /mwɛ̃dr/ *a.* (*moins grand*) less(er). **le** *ou* **la ~, les ~s,** the slightest, the least.
moine /mwan/ *n.m.* monk.
moineau (*pl.* **~x**) /mwano/ *n.m.* sparrow.
moins /mwɛ̃/ *adv.* less (**que,** than). —*prép.* (*soustraction*) minus. **~ de,** (*quantité*) less, not so much (**que,** as); (*objets, personnes*) fewer, not so many (**que,** as). **~ de dix francs/d'une livre**/*etc.*, less than ten francs/one pound/*etc.* **le** *ou* **la** *ou* **les ~,** the least. **le ~ grand/ haut,** the smallest/lowest. **au ~, du ~,** at least. **de ~,** less. **en ~,** less; (*manquant*) missing. **une heure ~ dix,** ten to one. **à ~ que,** unless.
mois /mwa/ *n.m.* month.
mois|i /mwazi/ *a.* mouldy. —*n.m.* mould. **de ~i,** (*odeur, goût*) musty. **~ir** *v.i.* go mouldy. **~issure** *n.f.* mould.
moisson /mwasɔ̃/ *n.f.* harvest.
moissonn|er /mwasɔne/ *v.t.* harvest, reap. **~eur, ~euse** *n.m., f.* harvester. **~euse-batteuse** (*pl.* **~euses-batteuses**) *n.f.* combine harvester.
moit|e /mwat/ *a.* sticky, clammy. **~eur** *n.f.* stickiness.
moitié /mwatje/ *n.f.* half; (*milieu*) half-way mark. **à ~,** half-way. **à ~ vide/fermé**/*etc.*, half empty/closed/*etc.* **à ~ prix,** at half-price. **la ~ de,** half (of).
moka /mɔka/ *n.m.* (*gâteau*) coffee cream cake.
mol /mɔl/ *voir* **mou.**
molaire /mɔlɛr/ *n.f.* molar.
molécule /mɔlekyl/ *n.f.* molecule.
molester /mɔlɛste/ *v.t.* manhandle, rough up.
molle /mɔl/ *voir* **mou.**
moll|ement /mɔlmɑ̃/ *adv.* softly; (*faiblement*) feebly. **~esse** *n.f.* softness; (*faiblesse, indolence*) feebleness.
mollet /mɔlɛ/ *n.m.* (*de jambe*) calf.
molletonné /mɔltɔne/ *a.* (fleece-) lined.
mollir /mɔlir/ *v.i.* soften; (*céder*) yield.
mollusque /mɔlysk/ *n.m.* mollusc.
môme /mom/ *n.m./f.* (*fam.*) kid.
moment /mɔmɑ̃/ *n.m.* moment; (*période*) time. **(petit) ~,** short while. **au ~ où,** when. **du ~ où** *ou* **que,** seeing that. **en ce ~,** at the moment.
momentané /mɔmɑ̃tane/ *a.* momentary. **~ment** *adv.* momentarily; (*en ce moment*) at present.
momie /mɔmi/ *n.f.* mummy.
mon, ma *ou* **mon*** (*pl.* **mes**) /mɔ̃, ma, mɔ̃n, me/ *a.* my.
Monaco /mɔnako/ *n.f.* Monaco.
monarchie /mɔnarʃi/ *n.f.* monarchy.
monarque /mɔnark/ *n.m.* monarque.
monastère /mɔnastɛr/ *n.m.* monastery.
monceau (*pl.* **~x**) /mɔ̃so/ *n.m.* heap, pile.
mondain, **~e** /mɔ̃dɛ̃, -ɛn/ *a.* society, social.
monde /mɔ̃d/ *n.m.* world. **du ~,** (a lot of) people; (*quelqu'un*) somebody. **le (grand) ~,** (high) society.
mond|ial (*m. pl.* **~iaux**) /mɔ̃djal, -jo/ *a.* world; (*influence*) worldwide. **~ialement** *adv.* the world over.
monégasque /mɔnegask/ *a.* & *n.m./f.* Monegasque.
monétaire /mɔnetɛr/ *a.* monetary.
mongolien, ~ne /mɔ̃gɔljɛ̃, -jɛn/ *n.m., f.* & *a.* (*méd.*) mongol.

moni|teur, ~trice /mɔnitœr, -tris/ *n.m., f.* instructor, instructress; (*de colonie de vacances*) assistant, minder; (*Amer.*) (camp) counselor.

monnaie /mɔnɛ/ *n.f.* currency; (*pièce*) coin; (*appoint*) change. **faire la ~ de,** get change for. **faire à qn. la ~ de,** give s.o. change for. **menue** *ou* **petite ~,** small change.

monnayer /mɔneje/ *v.t.* convert into cash.

mono /mɔno/ *a. invar.* mono.

monocle /mɔnɔkl/ *n.m.* monocle.

monocorde /mɔnɔkɔrd/ *a.* monotonous.

monogramme /mɔnɔgram/ *n.m.* monogram.

monologue /mɔnɔlɔg/ *n.m.* monologue.

monopol|e /mɔnɔpɔl/ *n.m.* monopoly. **~iser** *v.t.* monopolize.

monosyllabe /mɔnɔsilab/ *n.m.* monosyllable.

monoton|e /mɔnɔtɔn/ *a.* monotonous. **~ie** *n.f.* monotony.

monseigneur /mɔ̃sɛɲœr/ *n.m.* Your *ou* His Grace.

monsieur (*pl.* **messieurs**) /məsjø, mesjø/ *n.m.* gentleman. **M~** *ou* **M. Dupont,** Mr Dupont. **Messieurs** *ou* **MM. Dupont,** Messrs Dupont. **oui ~,** yes; (*avec déférence*) yes, sir.

monstre /mɔ̃str/ *n.m.* monster. —*a.* (*fam.*) colossal.

monstr|ueux, ~ueuse /mɔ̃stryø, -z/ *a.* monstrous. **~uosité** *n.f.* monstrosity.

mont /mɔ̃/ *n.m.* mount.

montage /mɔ̃taʒ/ *n.m.* (*assemblage*) assembly; (*cinéma*) editing.

montagn|e /mɔ̃taɲ/ *n.f.* mountain; (*région*) mountains. **~es russes,** roller-coaster. **~ard, ~arde** *n.m., f.* mountain dweller. **~eux, ~euse** *a.* mountainous.

montant[1], **~e** /mɔ̃tɑ̃, -t/ *a.* rising; (*robe*) high-necked.

montant[2] /mɔ̃tɑ̃/ *n.m.* amount; (*pièce de bois*) upright.

mont-de-piété (*pl.* **monts-de-piété**) /mɔ̃dpjete/ *n.m.* pawnshop.

monte-charge /mɔ̃tʃarʒ/ *n.m. invar.* service lift; (*Amer.*) dumb waiter.

montée /mɔ̃te/ *n.f.* ascent, climb; (*de prix*) rise; (*côte*) hill.

monter /mɔ̃te/ *v.i.* (*aux. être*) go *ou* come up; (*grimper*) climb; (*prix, mer*) rise. **~ à,** (*cheval*) mount. **~ dans,** (*train*) get on to; (*voiture*) get into. **~ sur,** (*colline*) climb up; (*trône*) ascend. —*v.t.* (*aux. avoir*) go *ou* come up; (*objet*) take *ou* bring up; (*cheval, garde*) mount; (*société*) set up. **~ à cheval,** (*sport*) ride. **~ en flèche,** soar. **~ en graine,** go to seed.

monteu|r, ~se /mɔ̃tœr, -øz/ *n.m., f.* (*techn.*) fitter; (*cinéma*) editor.

monticule /mɔ̃tikyl/ *n.m.* mound.

montre /mɔ̃tr/ *n.f.* watch. **~-bracelet** (*pl.* **~s-bracelets**) *n.f.* wrist-watch. **faire ~ de,** show.

montrer /mɔ̃tre/ *v.t.* show (**à,** to). **se ~** *v. pr.* show o.s.; (*être*) be; (*s'avérer*) prove to be. **~ du doigt,** point to.

monture /mɔ̃tyr/ *n.f.* (*cheval*) mount; (*de lunettes*) frame; (*de bijou*) setting.

monument /mɔnymɑ̃/ *n.m.* monument. **~ aux morts,** war memorial. **~al** (*m. pl.* **~aux**) /-tal, -to/ *a.* monumental.

moqu|er (se) /(sə)mɔke/ *v. pr.* **se ~er de,** make fun of. **je m'en ~e,** (*fam.*) I couldn't care less. **~erie** *n.f.* mockery. **~eur, ~euse** *a.* mocking.

moquette /mɔkɛt/ *n.f.* fitted carpet; (*Amer.*) wall-to-wall carpeting.

mor|al, ~ale (*m. pl.* **~aux**) /mɔral, -o/ *a.* moral. —*n.m.* (*pl.*

~aux) morale. —*n.f.* moral code; (*mœurs*) morals; (*de fable*) moral. **faire la ~ale à,** lecture. **~alement** *adv.* morally. **~alité** *n.f.* morality; (*de fable*) moral.

moralisa|teur, ~trice /mɔralizatœr, -tris/ *a.* moralizing.

morbide /mɔrbid/ *a.* morbid.

morceau (*pl.* **~x**) /mɔrso/ *n.m.* piece, bit; (*de sucre*) lump; (*de viande*) cut; (*passage*) passage.

morceler /mɔrsəle/ *v.t.* fragment.

mordant, ~e /mɔrdɑ̃, -t/ *a.* scathing; (*froid*) biting. —*n.m.* (*énergie*) vigour, punch.

mordiller /mɔrdije/ *v.t.* nibble.

mord|re /mɔrdr/ *v.t./i.* bite. **~re sur,** overlap into. **~u, ~ue** *n.m., f.* (*fam.*) fan; *a.* bitten. **~u de,** (*fam.*) crazy about.

morfondre (se) /(sə)mɔrfɔ̃dr/ *v. pr.* mope, wait anxiously.

morgue[1] /mɔrg/ *n.f.* morgue, mortuary.

morgue[2] /mɔrg/ *n.f.* (*attitude*) haughtiness.

moribond, ~e /mɔribɔ̃, -d/ *a.* dying.

morne /mɔrn/ *a.* dull.

morose /mɔroz/ *a.* morose.

morphine /mɔrfin/ *n.f.* morphine.

mors /mɔr/ *n.m.* (*de cheval*) bit.

morse[1] /mɔrs/ *n.m.* walrus.

morse[2] /mɔrs/ *n.m.* (*code*) Morse code.

morsure /mɔrsyr/ *n.f.* bite.

mort[1] /mɔr/ *n.f.* death.

mort[2], **~e** /mɔr, -t/ *a.* dead. —*n.m., f.* dead man, dead woman. **les ~s,** the dead. **~ de fatigue,** dead tired. **~-né** *a.* stillborn.

mortadelle /mɔrtadɛl/ *n.f.* mortadella.

mortalité /mɔrtalite/ *n.f.* death rate.

mortel, ~le /mɔrtɛl/ *a.* mortal; (*accident*) fatal; (*poison, silence*) deadly. —*n.m., f.* mortal. **~lement** *adv.* mortally.

mortier /mɔrtje/ *n.m.* mortar.

mortifier /mɔrtifje/ *v.t.* mortify.

mortuaire /mɔrtɥɛr/ *a.* (*cérémonie*) funeral; (*avis*) death.

morue /mɔry/ *n.f.* cod.

mosaïque /mɔzaik/ *n.f.* mosaic.

Moscou /mɔsku/ *n.m./f.* Moscow.

mosquée /mɔske/ *n.f.* mosque.

mot /mo/ *n.m.* word; (*lettre, message*) line, note. **~ d'ordre,** watchword. **~ de passe,** password. **~s croisés,** crossword (puzzle).

motard /mɔtar/ *n.m.* (*fam.*) police motorcyclist.

motel /mɔtɛl/ *n.m.* motel.

moteur[1] /mɔtœr/ *n.m.* engine, motor.

mo|teur[2], **~trice** /mɔtœr, -tris/ *a.* (*nerf*) motor; (*force*) driving.

motif /mɔtif/ *n.m.* reason; (*jurid.*) motive; (*dessin*) pattern.

motion /mosjɔ̃/ *n.f.* motion.

motiv|er /mɔtive/ *v.t.* motivate; (*justifier*) justify. **~ation** *n.f.* motivation.

moto /mɔto/ *n.f.* motor cycle. **~cycliste** *n.m./f.* motorcyclist.

motoriser /mɔtɔrize/ *v.t.* motorize.

motrice /mɔtris/ *voir* **moteur**[2].

motte /mɔt/ *n.f.* lump; (*de terre*) clod. **~ de gazon,** turf.

mou *ou* **mol*, molle** /mu, mɔl/ *a.* soft; (*faible, indolent*) feeble. —*n.m.* **du ~,** slack. **avoir du ~,** be slack.

mouchard, ~e /muʃar, -d/ *n.m., f.* informer; (*scol.*) sneak. **~er** /-de/ *v.t.* (*fam.*) inform on.

mouche /muʃ/ *n.f.* fly.

moucher (se) /(sə)muʃe/ *v. pr.* blow one's nose.

moucheron /muʃrɔ̃/ *n.m.* midge.

moucheté /muʃte/ *a.* speckled.

mouchoir /muʃwar/ *n.m.* handkerchief; (*en papier*) tissue.

moudre /mudr/ *v.t.* grind.

moue /mu/ *n.f.* long face. **faire la ~,** pull a long face.
mouette /mwɛt/ *n.f.* (sea)gull.
moufle /mufl/ *n.f.* (*gant*) mitten.
mouill|er /muje/ *v.t.* wet, make wet. **se ~er** *v. pr.* get (o.s.) wet. **~er (l'ancre),** anchor. **~é** *a.* wet.
moulage /mulaʒ/ *n.m.* cast.
moul|e[1] /mul/ *n.m.* mould. **~er** *v.t.* mould; (*statue*) cast.
moule[2] /mul/ *n.f.* (*coquillage*) mussel.
moulin /mulɛ̃/ *n.m.* mill; (*moteur*: *fam.*) engine. **~ à vent,** windmill.
moulinet /mulinɛ/ *n.m.* (*de canne à pêche*) reel.
moulu /muly/ *a.* ground; (*fatigué*: *fam.*) dead beat.
moulure /mulyr/ *n.f.* moulding.
mourant, ~e /murɑ̃, -t/ *a.* dying. —*n.m., f.* dying person.
mourir† /murir/ *v.i.* (*aux. être*) die. **~ d'envie de,** be dying to. **~ de faim,** be starving. **~ d'ennui,** be dead bored.
mousquetaire /muskətɛr/ *n.m.* musketeer.
mousse[1] /mus/ *n.f.* moss; (*écume*) froth, foam; (*de savon*) lather; (*dessert*) mousse.
mousse[2] /mus/ *n.m.* ship's boy.
mousseline /muslin/ *n.f.* muslin.
mousser /muse/ *v.i.* froth, foam; (*savon*) lather.
mousseu|x, ~se /musø, -z/ *a.* frothy. —*n.m.* sparkling wine.
mousson /musɔ̃/ *n.f.* monsoon.
moustach|e /mustaʃ/ *n.f.* moustache. **~es,** (*d'animal*) whiskers. **~u** *a.* wearing a moustache.
moustiquaire /mustikɛr/ *n.f.* mosquito-net.
moustique /mustik/ *n.m.* mosquito.
moutarde /mutard/ *n.f.* mustard.
mouton /mutɔ̃/ *n.m.* sheep; (*peau*) sheepskin; (*viande*) mutton.
mouvant, ~e /muvɑ̃, -t/ *a.* changing; (*terrain*) shifting.
mouvement /muvmɑ̃/ *n.m.* movement; (*agitation*) bustle; (*en gymnastique*) exercise; (*impulsion*) impulse; (*de colère*) outburst; (*tendance*) tendency. **en ~,** in motion.
mouvementé /muvmɑ̃te/ *a.* eventful.
mouvoir† /muvwar/ *v.t.* drive; (*membre*) move. **se ~** *v. pr.* move.
moyen[1]**, ~ne** /mwajɛ̃, -jɛn/ *a.* average; (*médiocre*) poor. —*n.f.* average; (*scol.*) pass-mark. **de taille ~ne,** medium-sized. **~ âge,** Middle Ages. **~ne d'âge,** average age. **M~-Orient** *n.m.* Middle East. **~nement** /-jɛnmɑ̃/ *adv.* moderately.
moyen[2] /mwajɛ̃/ *n.m.* means, way. **~s,** means; (*dons*) abilities. **au ~ de,** by means of. **il n'y a pas ~ de,** it is not possible to.
moyennant /mwajɛnɑ̃/ *prép.* (*pour*) for; (*grâce à*) with.
moyeu (*pl.* **~x**) /mwajø/ *n.m.* hub.
mû, mue[1] /my/ *a.* driven (**par,** by).
mue[2] /my/ *n.f.* moulting; (*de voix*) breaking of the voice.
muer /mɥe/ *v.i.* moult; (*voix*) break. **se ~ en,** change into.
muet, ~te /mɥɛ, -t/ *a.* (*personne*) dumb; (*fig.*) speechless (**de,** with); (*silencieux*) silent. —*n.m., f.* dumb person.
mufle /myfl/ *n.m.* nose, muzzle; (*personne*: *fam.*) boor, lout.
mugir /myʒir/ *v.i.* (*vache*) moo; (*bœuf*) bellow; (*fig.*) howl.
muguet /mygɛ/ *n.m.* lily of the valley.
mule /myl/ *n.f.* (she-)mule; (*pantoufle*) mule.
mulet /mylɛ/ *n.m.* (he-)mule.
multi- /mylti/ *préf.* multi-.
multicolore /myltikɔlɔr/ *a.* multicoloured.
multination|al, ~ale (*m. pl.*

~aux) /myltinasjɔnal, -o/ *a.* & *n.f.* multinational.
multiple /myltipl/ *a.* & *n.m.* multiple.
multiplicité /myltiplisite/ *n.f.* multiplicity, abundance.
multipl|ier /myltiplije/ *v.t.*, **se ~ier** *v. pr.* multiply. **~ication** *n.f.* multiplication.
multitude /myltityd/ *n.f.* multitude, mass.
municip|al (*m. pl.* **~aux** /mynisipal, -o/ *a.* municipal; (*conseil*) town. **~alité** *n.f.* (*ville*) municipality; (*conseil*) town council.
munir /mynir/ *v.t.* **~ de,** provide with. **se ~ de,** provide o.s. with.
munitions /mynisjɔ̃/ *n.f. pl.* ammunition.
mur /myr/ *n.m.* wall. **~ du son,** sound barrier.
mûr /myr/ *a.* ripe; (*personne*) mature.
muraille /myrɑj/ *n.f.* (high) wall.
mur|al (*m. pl.* **~aux**) /myral, -o/ *a.* wall; (*tableau*) mural.
mûre /myr/ *n.f.* blackberry.
muret /myrɛ/ *n.m.* low wall.
mûrir /myrir/ *v.t./i.* ripen; (*personne, projet*) mature.
murmur|e /myrmyr/ *n.m.* murmur. **~er** *v.t./i.* murmur.
musc /mysk/ *n.m.* musk.
muscade /myskad/ *n.f.* nutmeg.
muscl|e /myskl/ *n.m.* muscle. **~é** *a.* muscular, brawny.
muscul|aire /myskylɛr/ *a.* muscular. **~ature** *n.f.* muscles.
museau (*pl.* **~x**) /myzo/ *n.m.* muzzle; (*de porc*) snout.
musée /myze/ *n.m.* museum; (*de peinture*) art gallery.
museler /myzle/ *v.t.* muzzle.
muselière /myzəljɛr/ *n.f.* muzzle.
musette /myzɛt/ *n.f.* haversack.
muséum /myzeɔm/ *n.m.* (natural history) museum.
music|al (*m. pl.* **~aux**) /myzikal, -o/ *a.* musical.
music-hall /myzikol/ *n.m.* variety theatre.
musicien, ~ne /myzisjɛ̃, -jɛn/ *a.* musical. —*n.m., f.* musician.
musique /myzik/ *n.f.* music; (*orchestre*) band.
musulman, ~e /myzylmɑ̃, -an/ *a.* & *n.m., f.* Muslim.
mutation /mytɑsjɔ̃/ *n.f.* change; (*biologique*) mutation.
muter /myte/ *v.t.* transfer.
mutil|er /mytile/ *v.t.* mutilate. **~ation** *n.f.* mutilation. **~é, ~ée** *a.* & *n.m., f.* disabled (person).
mutin, ~e /mytɛ̃, -in/ *a.* saucy. —*n.m., f.* rebel.
mutin|er (se) /(sə)mytine/ *v. pr.* mutiny. **~é** *a.* mutinous. **~erie** *n.f.* mutiny.
mutisme /mytism/ *n.m.* silence.
mutuel, ~le /mytɥɛl/ *a.* mutual. —*n.f.* Friendly Society; (*Amer.*) benefit society. **~lement** *adv.* mutually; (*l'un l'autre*) each other.
myop|e /mjɔp/ *a.* short-sighted. **~ie** *n.f.* short-sightedness.
myosotis /mjozɔtis/ *n.m.* forget-me-not.
myriade /mirjad/ *n.f.* myriad.
myrtille /mirtij/ *n.f.* bilberry; (*Amer.*) blueberry.
mystère /mistɛr/ *n.m.* mystery.
mystérieu|x, ~se /misterjø, -z/ *a.* mysterious.
mystif|ier /mistifje/ *v.t.* deceive, hoax. **~ication** *n.f.* hoax.
mysti|que /mistik/ *a.* mystic(al). —*n.m./f.* mystic. —*n.f.* (*puissance*) mystique. **~cisme** *n.m.* mysticism.
myth|e /mit/ *n.m.* myth. **~ique** *a.* mythical.
mytholog|ie /mitɔlɔʒi/ *n.f.* mythology. **~ique** *a.* mythological.
mythomane /mitɔman/ *n.m./f.* compulsive liar (and fantasizer).

N

n' /n/ *voir* **ne.**

nacr|e /nakr/ *n.f.* mother-of-pearl. **~é** *a.* pearly.

nage /naʒ/ *n.f.* swimming; (*manière*) (swimming) stroke. **à la ~,** by swimming. **traverser à la ~,** swim across. **en ~,** sweating.

nageoire /naʒwar/ *n.f.* fin.

nag|er /naʒe/ *v.t./i.* swim. **~eur, ~euse** *n.m.,f.* swimmer.

naguère /nagɛr/ *adv.* not long ago.

naï|f, ~ve /naif, -v/ *a.* naïve. *—n.m.,f.* innocent.

nain, ~e /nɛ̃, nɛn/ *n.m., f.* & *a.* dwarf.

naissance /nɛsɑ̃s/ *n.f.* birth; (*de rivière*) source. **donner ~ à,** give birth to.

naître† /nɛtr/ *v.i.* be born; (*résulter*) arise (**de,** from). **faire ~,** (*susciter*) give rise to.

naïveté /naivte/ *n.f.* naïvety.

nana /nana/ *n.f.* (*fam.*) girl.

nanti /nɑ̃ti/ *a.* affluent.

nantir /nɑ̃tir/ *v.t.* **~ de,** provide with.

naphtaline /naftalin/ *n.f.* moth-balls.

nappe /nap/ *n.f.* table-cloth; (*d'eau*) sheet; (*de brouillard, gaz*) layer.

napperon /naprɔ̃/ *n.m.* (cloth) table-mat. **~ (individuel),** place-mat.

narcotique /narkɔtik/ *a.* & *n.m.* narcotic.

narguer /narge/ *v.t.* mock.

narine /narin/ *n.f.* nostril.

narquois, ~e /narkwa, -z/ *a.* derisive.

narr|er /nare/ *v.t.* narrate. **~ateur, ~atrice** *n.m., f.* narrator. **~ation** *n.f.* narrative; (*action*) narration; (*scol.*) composition.

nas|al (*m. pl.* **~aux**) /nazal, -o/ *a.* nasal.

naseau (*pl.* **~x**) /nazo/ *n.m.* nostril.

nasiller /nazije/ *v.i.* have a nasal twang.

nat|al (*m. pl.* **~als**) /natal/ *a.* native.

natalité /natalite/ *n.f.* birth rate.

natation /natɑsjɔ̃/ *n.f.* swimming.

nati|f, ~ve /natif, -v/ *a.* native.

nation /nɑsjɔ̃/ *n.f.* nation.

nation|al, ~ale (*m. pl.* **~aux**) /nasjɔnal, -o/ *a.* national. *—n.f.* trunk-road; (*Amer.*) highway. **~aliser** *v.t.* nationalize. **~alisme** *n.m.* nationalism.

nationalité /nasjɔnalite/ *n.f.* nationality.

Nativité /nativite/ *n.f.* **la ~,** the Nativity.

natte /nat/ *n.f.* (*de cheveux*) plait; (*tapis de paille*) mat.

naturaliser /natyralize/ *v.t.* naturalize.

nature /natyr/ *n.f.* nature. *—a. invar.* (*eau, omelette, etc.*) plain. **de ~ à,** likely to. **en ~,** in kind. **~ morte,** still life.

naturel, ~le /natyrɛl/ *a.* natural. *—n.m.* nature; (*simplicité*) naturalness. **~lement** *adv.* naturally.

naufrag|e /nofraʒ/ *n.m.* (ship)-wreck. **faire ~e,** be shipwrecked; (*bateau*) be wrecked. **~é, ~ée** *a.* & *n.m.,f.* shipwrecked (person).

nauséabond, ~e /nozeabɔ̃, -d/ *a.* nauseating.

nausée /noze/ *n.f.* nausea.

nautique /notik/ *a.* nautical; (*sports*) aquatic.

naval (*m. pl.* **~s**) /naval/ *a.* naval.

navet /navɛ/ *n.m.* turnip; (*film, tableau*) dud.

navette /navɛt/ *n.f.* shuttle (service). **faire la ~,** shuttle back and forth.

navigable /navigabl/ *a.* navigable.

navig|uer /navige/ *v.i.* sail; (*avion*) fly; (*piloter*) navigate. **~ateur**

n.m. seafarer; (*d'avion*) navigator. **~ation** *n.f.* navigation; (*trafic*) shipping.
navire /navir/ *n.m.* ship.
navré /navre/ *a.* sorry (**de**, to).
navrer /navre/ *v.t.* upset.
ne, n'* /nə, n/ *adv.* **~ pas,** not. **~ jamais,** never. **~ plus,** (*temps*) no longer, not any more. **~ que,** only. **je crains qu'il ne parte,** (*sans valeur négative*) I am afraid he will leave.
né, née /ne/ *voir* **naître.** —*a.* & *n.m., f.* born. **il est ~,** he was born. **premier-/dernier-~,** first-/last-born.
néanmoins /neɑ̃mwɛ̃/ *adv.* nevertheless.
néant /neɑ̃/ *n.m.* nothingness; (*aucun*) none.
nébuleu|x, ~se /nebylø, -z/ *a.* nebulous.
nécessaire /nesesɛr/ *a.* necessary. —*n.m.* (*sac*) bag; (*trousse*) kit. **le ~,** (*l'indispensable*) the necessities. **faire le ~,** do what is necessary. **~ment** *adv.* necessarily.
nécessité /nesesite/ *n.f.* necessity.
nécessiter /nesesite/ *v.t.* necessitate.
nécrologie /nekrɔlɔʒi/ *n.f.* obituary.
néerlandais, ~e /neɛrlɑ̃dɛ, -z/ *a.* Dutch. —*n.m., f.* Dutchman, Dutchwoman. —*n.m.* (*lang.*) Dutch.
nef /nɛf/ *n.f.* nave.
néfaste /nefast/ *a.* harmful (**à**, to); (*funeste*) ill-fated.
négati|f, ~ve /negatif, -v/ *a.* & *n.m., f.* negative.
négation /negɑsjɔ̃/ *n.f.* negation.
négligé /negliʒe/ *a.* (*tenue, travail*) slovenly. —*n.m.* (*tenue*) négligé.
négligeable /negliʒabl/ *a.* negligible, insignificant.
négligen|t, ~te /negliʒɑ̃, -t/ *a.* careless, negligent. **~ce** *n.f.* carelessness, negligence; (*erreur*) omission.
négliger /negliʒe/ *v.t.* neglect; (*ne pas tenir compte de*) disregard. **se ~** *v. pr.* neglect o.s.
négoc|e /negɔs/ *n.m.* business. **~iant, ~iante** *n.m., f.* merchant.
négoc|ier /negɔsje/ *v.t./i.* negotiate. **~iable** *a.* negotiable. **~iateur, ~iatrice** *n.m., f.* negotiator. **~iation** *n.f.* negotiation.
nègre[1] /nɛgr/ *a.* (*musique etc.*) Negro.
nègre[2] /nɛgr/ *n.m.* (*écrivain*) ghost writer.
neig|e /nɛʒ/ *n.f.* snow. **~eux, ~euse** *a.* snowy.
neiger /neʒe/ *v.i.* snow.
nénuphar /nenyfar/ *n.m.* waterlily.
néologisme /neɔlɔʒism/ *n.m.* neologism.
néon /neɔ̃/ *n.m.* neon.
néo-zélandais, ~e /neɔzelɑ̃dɛ, -z/ *a.* New Zealand. —*n.m., f.* New Zealander.
nerf /nɛr/ *n.m.* nerve; (*vigueur: fam.*) stamina.
nerv|eux, ~euse /nɛrvø, -z/ *a.* nervous; (*irritable*) nervy; (*centre, cellule*) nerve-; (*voiture*) responsive. **~eusement** *adv.* nervously. **~osité** *n.f.* nervousness; (*irritabilité*) touchiness.
nervure /nɛrvyr/ *n.f.* (*bot.*) vein.
net, ~te /nɛt/ *a.* (*clair, distinct*) clear; (*propre*) clean; (*soigné*) neat; (*prix, poids*) net. —*adv.* (*s'arrêter*) dead; (*refuser*) flatly; (*parler*) plainly; (*se casser*) clean. **~tement** *adv.* clearly; (*certainement*) definitely.
netteté /nɛtte/ *n.f.* clearness.
nettoy|er /nɛtwaje/ *v.t.* clean. **~age** *n.m.* cleaning. **~age à sec,** dry-cleaning.
neuf[1] /nœf/ (/nœv/ *before heures, ans*) *a.* & *n.m.* nine.

neu|f[2], **~ve** /nœf, -v/ *a.* & *n.m.* new. **à ~f,** (*refaire*) like new. **du ~f,** (*fait nouveau*) some new development.
neutr|e /nøtr/ *a.* neutral; (*gram.*) neuter. —*n.m.* (*gram.*) neuter. **~alité** *n.f.* neutrality.
neutron /nøtrɔ̃/ *n.m.* neutron.
neuve /nœv/ *voir* **neuf**[2].
neuvième /nœvjɛm/ *a.* & *n.m./f.* ninth.
neveu (*pl.* **~x**) /nəvø/ *n.m.* nephew.
névros|e /nevroz/ *n.f.* neurosis. **~é, ~ée** *a.* & *n.m., f.* neurotic.
nez /ne/ *n.m.* nose. **~ à nez,** face to face. **~ épaté,** flat nose.
ni /ni/ *conj.* neither, nor. **~ grand ni petit,** neither big nor small. **~ l'un ni l'autre ne fument,** neither (one nor the other) smokes.
niais, ~e /njɛ, -z/ *a.* silly. —*n.m., f.* simpleton. **~erie** /-zri/ *n.f.* silliness.
niche /niʃ/ *n.f.* (*de chien*) kennel; (*cavité*) niche; (*farce*) trick.
nichée /niʃe/ *n.f.* brood.
nicher /niʃe/ *v.i.* nest. **se ~** *v. pr.* nest; (*se cacher: fam.*) hide.
nickel /nikɛl/ *n.m.* nickel.
nicotine /nikɔtin/ *n.f.* nicotine.
nid /ni/ *n.m.* nest. **~ de poule,** pot-hole.
nièce /njɛs/ *n.f.* niece.
nier /nje/ *v.t.* deny.
nigaud, ~e /nigo, -d/ *a.* silly. —*n.m., f.* silly idiot.
nippon, ~e /nipɔ̃, -ɔn/ *a.* & *n.m., f.* Japanese.
niveau (*pl.* **~x**) /nivo/ *n.m.* level; (*compétence*) standard. **au ~,** up to standard. **~ à bulle,** spirit-level. **~ de vie,** standard of living.
nivel|er /nivle/ *v.t.* level. **~lement** /-ɛlmɑ̃/ *n.m.* levelling.
noble /nɔbl/ *a.* noble. —*n.m./f.* nobleman, noblewoman.
noblesse /nɔblɛs/ *n.f.* nobility.
noce /nɔs/ *n.f.* wedding; (*personnes*) wedding guests. **~s,** wedding. **faire la ~,** (*fam.*) make merry.
noci|f, ~ve /nɔsif, -v/ *a.* harmful.
noctambule /nɔktɑ̃byl/ *n.m./f.* night-owl, late-night reveller.
nocturne /nɔktyrn/ *a.* nocturnal.
Noël /nɔɛl/ *n.m.* Christmas.
nœud[1] /nø/ *n.m.* knot; (*ornemental*) bow. **~s,** (*fig.*) ties. **~ coulant,** noose. **~ papillon,** bow-tie.
nœud[2] /nø/ *n.m.* (*naut.*) knot.
noir, ~e /nwar/ *a.* black; (*obscur, sombre*) dark; (*triste*) gloomy. —*n.m.* black; (*obscurité*) dark. —*n.m., f.* (*personne*) Black. —*n.f.* (*mus.*) crotchet. **~ceur** *n.f.* blackness; (*indignité*) vileness.
noircir /nwarsir/ *v.t./i.*, **se ~** *v. pr.* blacken.
nois|ette /nwazɛt/ *n.f.* hazel-nut. **~etier** *n.m.* hazel.
noix /nwa/ *n.f.* nut; (*du noyer*) walnut; (*de beurre*) knob.
nom /nɔ̃/ *n.m.* name; (*gram.*) noun. **au ~ de,** on behalf of. **~ de famille,** surname. **~ de jeune fille,** maiden name. **~ propre,** proper noun.
nomade /nɔmad/ *a.* nomadic. —*n.m./f.* nomad.
nombre /nɔ̃br/ *n.m.* number. **au ~ de,** (*parmi*) among; (*l'un de*) one of. **en (grand) ~,** in large numbers.
nombreu|x, ~se /nɔ̃brø, -z/ *a.* numerous; (*important*) large.
nombril /nɔ̃bri/ *n.m.* navel.
nomin|al (*m. pl.* **~aux**) /nɔminal, -o/ *a.* nominal.
nomination /nɔminɑsjɔ̃/ *n.f.* appointment.
nommément /nɔmemɑ̃/ *adv.* by name.
nommer /nɔme/ *v.t.* name; (*élire*) appoint. **se ~** *v. pr.* (*s'appeler*) be called.

non /nɔ̃/ *adv.* no; (*pas*) not. —*n.m. invar.* no. **~ (pas) que,** not that. **il vient, ~?,** he is coming, isn't he? **moi ~ plus,** neither am, do, can, *etc.* I.
non- /nɔ̃/ *préf.* non-.
nonante /nɔnɑ̃t/ *a.* & *n.m.* ninety.
nonchalance /nɔ̃ʃalɑ̃s/ *n.f.* nonchalance.
non-sens /nɔ̃sɑ̃s/ *n.m.* absurdity.
nord /nɔr/ *n.m.* north. —*a. invar.* north; (*partie*) northern; (*direction*) northerly. **~-africain, ~-africaine** *a.* & *n.m., f.* North African. **~-est** *n.m* north-east. **~-ouest** *n.m.* north-west.
nordique /nɔrdik/ *a.* & *n.m./f.* Scandinavian.
norm|al, ~ale (*m. pl.* **~aux**) /nɔrmal, -o/ *a.* normal. —*n.f.* normality; (*norme*) norm; (*moyenne*) average. **~alement** *adv.* normally.
normand, ~e /nɔrmɑ̃, -d/ *a.* & *n.m., f.* Norman.
Normandie /nɔrmɑ̃di/ *n.f.* Normandy.
norme /nɔrm/ *n.f.* norm; (*de production*) standard.
Norvège /nɔrvɛʒ/ *n.f.* Norway.
norvégien, ~ne /nɔrveʒjɛ̃, -jɛn/ *a.* & *n.m., f.* Norwegian.
nos /no/ *voir* **notre.**
nostalg|ie /nɔstalʒi/ *n.f.* nostalgia. **~ique** *a.* nostalgic.
notable /nɔtabl/ *a.* & *n.m.* notable.
notaire /nɔtɛr/ *n.m.* notary.
notamment /nɔtamɑ̃/ *adv.* notably.
notation /nɔtasjɔ̃/ *n.f.* notation; (*remarque*) remark.
note /nɔt/ *n.f.* (*remarque*) note; (*chiffrée*) mark; (*facture*) bill; (*mus.*) note. **~ (de service),** memorandum. **prendre ~ de,** take note of.
not|er /nɔte/ *v.t.* note, notice; (*écrire*) note (down); (*devoir*) mark. **bien/mal ~é,** (*employé etc.*) highly/poorly rated.
notice /nɔtis/ *n.f.* note; (*mode d'emploi*) directions.
notif|ier /nɔtifje/ *v.t.* notify. **~ication** *n.f.* notification.
notion /nosjɔ̃/ *n.f.* notion.
notoire /nɔtwar/ *a.* well-known; (*criminel*) notorious.
notre (*pl.* **nos**) /nɔtr, no/ *a.* our.
nôtre /notr/ *pron.* **le** *ou* **la ~, les ~s,** ours.
nouer /nwe/ *v.t.* tie, knot; (*relations*) strike up.
noueu|x, ~se /nwø, -z/ *a.* gnarled.
nougat /nuga/ *n.m.* nougat.
nouille /nuj/ *n.f.* (*idiot: fam.*) idiot.
nouilles /nuj/ *n.f. pl.* noodles.
nounours /nunurs/ *n.m.* teddy bear.
nourri /nuri/ *a.* intense.
nourrice /nuris/ *n.f.* child-minder; (*qui allaite*) wet-nurse.
nourr|ir /nurir/ *v.t.* feed; (*faire vivre*) feed, provide for; (*sentiment: fig.*) nourish. —*v.i.* be nourishing. **se ~ir** *v. pr.* eat. **se ~ir de,** feed on. **~issant, ~issante** *a.* nourishing.
nourrisson /nurisɔ̃/ *n.m.* infant.
nourriture /nurityr/ *n.f.* food; (*régime*) diet.
nous /nu/ *pron.* we; (*complément*) us; (*indirect*) (to) us; (*réfléchi*) ourselves; (*l'un l'autre*) each other. **~-mêmes** *pron.* ourselves.
nouveau *ou* **nouvel*, nouvelle**[1] (*m. pl.* **~x**) /nuvo, nuvɛl/ *a.* & *n.m.* new. —*n.m., f.* (*élève*) new boy, new girl. **de ~, à ~,** again. **du ~,** (*fait nouveau*) some new development. **nouvel an,** new year. **~x mariés,** newly-weds. **~-né, ~-née** *a.* new-born; *n.m., f.* new-born baby. **~ venu, nouvelle venue,** newcomer. **Nouvelle Zélande,** New Zealand.
nouveauté /nuvote/ *n.f.* novelty; (*chose*) new thing.

nouvelle[2] /nuvɛl/ *n.f.* (piece of) news; (*récit*) short story. **~s,** news.
nouvellement /nuvɛlmɑ̃/ *adv.* newly, recently.
novembre /nɔvɑ̃br/ *n.m.* November.
novice /nɔvis/ *a.* inexperienced. —*n.m./f.* novice.
noyade /nwajad/ *n.f.* drowning.
noyau (*pl.* **~x**) /nwajo/ *n.m.* (*de fruit*) stone; (*de cellule*) nucleus; (*groupe*) group; (*centre: fig.*) core.
noy|er[1] /nwaje/ *v.t.* drown; (*inonder*) flood. **se ~er** *v. pr.* drown; (*volontairement*) drown o.s. **~é, ~ée** *n.m., f.* drowning person; (*mort*) drowned person.
noyer[2] /nwaje/ *n.m.* (*arbre*) walnut-tree.
nu /ny/ *a.* naked; (*mains, mur, fil*) bare. —*n.m.* nude. **(se) mettre à ~,** strip. **~-pieds** *adv.* barefoot; *n.m.pl.* beach shoes. **~-tête** *adv.* bareheaded.
nuag|e /nɥaʒ/ *n.m.* cloud. **~eux, ~euse** *a.* cloudy.
nuance /nɥɑ̃s/ *n.f.* shade; (*de sens*) nuance; (*différence*) difference.
nuancer /nɥɑ̃se/ *v.t.* (*opinion*) qualify.
nucléaire /nykleɛr/ *a.* nuclear.
nudis|te /nydist/ *n.m./f.* nudist. **~me** *n.m.* nudism.
nudité /nydite/ *n.f.* (*de personne*) nudity; (*de chambre etc.*) bareness.
nuée /nɥe/ *n.f.* (*foule*) host.
nuire† /nɥir/ *v.i.* **~ à,** harm.
nuisible /nɥizibl/ *a.* harmful.
nuit /nɥi/ *n.f.* night. **cette ~,** tonight; (*hier*) last night. **il fait ~,** it is dark. **~ blanche,** sleepless night. **la ~, de ~,** at night.
nul, ~le /nyl/ *a.* (*aucun*) no; (*zéro*) nil; (*qui ne vaut rien*) useless; (*non valable*) null. —*pron.* no one. **~ autre,** no one else. **~le part,** nowhere. **~lement** *adv.* not at all. **~lité** *n.f.* uselessness; (*personne*) useless person.
numéraire /nymerɛr/ *n.m.* cash.
numér|al (*pl.* **~aux**) /nymeral, -o/ *n.m.* numeral.
numérique /nymerik/ *a.* numerical; (*montre, horloge*) digital.
numéro /nymero/ *n.m.* number; (*de journal*) issue; (*spectacle*) act. **~ter** /-ɔte/ *v.t.* number.
nupt|ial (*m. pl.* **~iaux**) /nypsjal, -jo/ *a.* wedding.
nuque /nyk/ *n.f.* nape (of the neck).
nurse /nœrs/ *n.f.* (children's) nurse.
nutriti|f, ~ve /nytritif, -v/ *a.* nutritious; (*valeur*) nutritional.
nutrition /nytrisjɔ̃/ *n.f.* nutrition.
nylon /nilɔ̃/ *n.m.* nylon.
nymphe /nɛ̃f/ *n.f.* nymph.

O

oasis /ɔazis/ *n.f.* oasis.
obéir /ɔbeir/ *v.i.* obey. **~ à,** obey. **être obéi,** be obeyed.
obéissan|t, ~te /ɔbeisɑ̃, -t/ *a.* obedient. **~ce** *n.f.* obedience.
obèse /ɔbɛz/ *a.* obese.
obésité /ɔbezite/ *n.f.* obesity.
object|er /ɔbʒɛkte/ *v.t.* put forward (as an excuse). **~er que,** object that. **~ion** /-ksjɔ̃/ *n.f.* objection.
objecti|f, ~ve /ɔbʒɛktif, -v/ *a.* objective. —*n.m.* objective. **~vement** *adv.* objectively. **~vité** *n.f.* objectivity.
objet /ɔbʒɛ/ *n.m.* object; (*sujet*) subject. **être** *ou* **faire l'~ de,** be the subject of; (*recevoir*) receive. **~s de toilette,** toilet requisites. **~s trouvés,** lost property; (*Amer.*) lost and found.
obligation /ɔbligɑsjɔ̃/ *n.f.* obligation; (*comm.*) bond.
obligatoire /ɔbligatwar/ *a.* com-

pulsory. **~ment** *adv.* of necessity; (*fam.*) inevitably.

obligean|t, ~te /ɔbliʒɑ̃, -t/ *a.* obliging, kind. **~ce** *n.f.* kindness.

oblig|er /ɔbliʒe/ *v.t.* compel, oblige (**à faire,** to do); (*aider*) oblige. **être ~é de,** have to. **~é à qn.,** obliged to s.o. (**de,** for).

oblique /ɔblik/ *a.* oblique. **en ~,** at an angle.

obliquer /ɔblike/ *v.i.* turn off.

oblitérer /ɔblitere/ *v.t.* (*timbre*) cancel.

oblong, ~ue /ɔblɔ̃, -g/ *a.* oblong.

obsc|ène /ɔpsɛn/ *a.* obscene. **~énité** *n.f.* obscenity.

obscur /ɔpskyr/ *a.* dark; (*confus, humble*) obscure.

obscurcir /ɔpskyrsir/ *v.t.* darken; (*fig.*) obscure. **s'~** *v. pr.* (*ciel etc.*) darken.

obscurité /ɔpskyrite/ *n.f.* dark(ness); (*passage, situation*) obscurity.

obséd|er /ɔpsede/ *v.t.* obsess. **~ant, ~ante** *a.* obsessive. **~é, ~ée** *n.m., f.* maniac.

obsèques /ɔpsɛk/ *n.f. pl.* funeral.

observation /ɔpsɛrvɑsjɔ̃/ *n.f.* observation; (*reproche*) criticism; (*obéissance*) observance.

observatoire /ɔpsɛrvatwar/ *n.m.* observatory; (*mil.*) observation post.

observ|er /ɔpsɛrve/ *v.t.* observe; (*surveiller*) watch, observe. **faire ~er qch.,** point sth. out (**à,** to). **~ateur, ~atrice** *a.* observant; *n.m., f.* observer.

obsession /ɔpsesjɔ̃/ *n.f.* obsession.

obstacle /ɔpstakl/ *n.m.* obstacle. **faire ~ à,** stand in the way of.

obstétrique /ɔpstetrik/ *n.f.* obstetrics.

obstin|é /ɔpstine/ *a.* obstinate. **~ation** *n.f.* obstinacy.

obstiner (s') /(s)ɔpstine/ *v. pr.* persist (**à,** in).

obstruction /ɔpstryksjɔ̃/ *n.f.* obstruction. **faire de l'~,** obstruct.

obstruer /ɔpstrye/ *v.t.* obstruct.

obten|ir† /ɔptənir/ *v.t.* get, obtain. **~tion** /-ɑ̃sjɔ̃/ *n.f.* obtaining.

obturateur /ɔptyratœr/ *n.m.* (*photo.*) shutter.

obtus, ~e /ɔpty, -z/ *a.* obtuse.

obus /ɔby/ *n.m.* shell.

occasion /ɔkazjɔ̃/ *n.f.* opportunity (**de faire,** of doing); (*circonstance*) occasion; (*achat*) bargain; (*article non neuf*) second-hand buy. **à l'~,** sometimes. **d'~,** second-hand. **~nel, ~nelle** /-jɔnɛl/ *a.* occasional.

occasionner /ɔkazjɔne/ *v.t.* cause.

occident /ɔksidɑ̃/ *n.m.* west. **~al, ~ale** (*m. pl.* **~aux**) /-tal, -to/ *a.* western. —*n.m., f.* westerner.

occulte /ɔkylt/ *a.* occult.

occupant, ~e /ɔkypɑ̃, -t/ *n.m., f.* occupant. —*n.m.* (*mil.*) forces of occupation.

occupation /ɔkypɑsjɔ̃/ *n.f.* occupation.

occupé /ɔkype/ *a.* busy; (*place, pays*) occupied; (*téléphone*) engaged; (*Amer.*) busy.

occuper /ɔkype/ *v.t.* occupy; (*ouvrier*) employ; (*poste*) hold. **s'~** *v. pr.* (*s'affairer*) keep busy (**à faire,** doing). **s'~ de,** (*personne, problème*) take care of; (*bureau, firme*) be in charge of.

occurrence (en l') /(ɑ̃l)ɔkyrɑ̃s/ *adv.* in this case.

océan /ɔseɑ̃/ *n.m.* ocean.

ocre /ɔkr/ *a. invar.* ochre.

octane /ɔktan/ *n.m.* octane.

octave /ɔktav/ *n.f.* (*mus.*) octave.

octobre /ɔktɔbr/ *n.m.* October.

octogone /ɔktɔgɔn/ *n.m.* octagon.

octroyer /ɔktrwaje/ *v.t.* grant.

oculaire /ɔkylɛr/ *a.* ocular.

oculiste /ɔkylist/ *n.m./f.* eye-specialist.

ode /ɔd/ *n.f.* ode.

odeur /ɔdœr/ *n.f.* smell.

odieu|x, ~se /ɔdjø, -z/ *a.* odious.
odorant, ~e /ɔdɔrɑ̃, -t/ *a.* sweet-smelling.
odorat /ɔdɔra/ *n.m.* (sense of) smell.
œcuménique /ekymenik/ *a.* ecumenical.
œil (*pl.* **yeux**) /œj, jø/ *n.m.* eye. **à l'~,** (*fam.*) free. **à mes yeux,** in my view. **faire de l'~ à,** make eyes at. **faire les gros yeux à,** scowl at. **fermer l'~,** shut one's eyes. **~ poché,** black eye. **yeux bridés,** slit eyes.
œillade /œjad/ *n.f.* wink.
œillères /œjɛr/ *n.f. pl.* blinkers.
œillet /œjɛ/ *n.m.* (*plante*) carnation; (*trou*) eyelet.
œuf (*pl.* **~s**) /œf, ø/ *n.m.* egg. **~ à la coque/dur/sur le plat,** boiled/hard-boiled/fried egg.
œuvre /œvr/ *n.f.* (*ouvrage, travail*) work. **~ (de bienfaisance),** charity. **être à l'~,** be at work. **mettre en ~,** (*moyens*) implement.
œuvrer /œvre/ *v.i.* work.
offense /ɔfɑ̃s/ *n.f.* insult; (*péché*) offence.
offens|er /ɔfɑ̃se/ *v.t.* offend. **s'~er de,** take offence at. **~ant, ~ante** *a.* offensive.
offensi|f, ~ve /ɔfɑ̃sif, -v/ *a.* & *n.f.* offensive.
offert, ~e /ɔfɛr, -t/ *voir* **offrir.**
office /ɔfis/ *n.m.* office; (*relig.*) service; (*de cuisine*) pantry. **d'~,** automatically.
officiel, ~le /ɔfisjɛl/ *a.* & *n.m., f.* official. **~lement** *adv.* officially.
officier[1] /ɔfisje/ *n.m.* officer.
officier[2] /ɔfisje/ *v.i.* (*relig.*) officiate.
officieu|x, ~se /ɔfisjø, -z/ *a.* unofficial. **~sement** *adv.* unofficially.
offrande /ɔfrɑ̃d/ *n.f.* offering.
offrant /ɔfrɑ̃/ *n.m.* **au plus ~,** to the highest bidder.
offre /ɔfr/ *n.f.* offer; (*aux enchères*) bid. **l'~ et la demande,** supply and demand. **~s d'emploi,** (*dans un journal*) jobs advertised, situations vacant.
offrir† /ɔfrir/ *v.t.* offer **(de faire,** to do); (*cadeau*) give; (*acheter*) buy. **s'~** *v. pr.* offer o.s. **(comme,** as); (*spectacle*) present itself; (*s'acheter*) treat o.s. to. **~ à boire à,** offer a drink to.
offusquer /ɔfyske/ *v.t.* offend.
ogive /ɔʒiv/ *n.f.* (*atomique etc.*) warhead.
ogre /ɔgr/ *n.m.* ogre.
oh /o/ *int.* oh.
oie /wa/ *n.f.* goose.
oignon /ɔɲɔ̃/ *n.m.* (*légume*) onion; (*de tulipe etc.*) bulb.
oiseau (*pl.* **~x**) /wazo/ *n.m.* bird.
oisi|f, ~ve /wazif, -v/ *a.* idle. **~veté** *n.f.* idleness.
oléoduc /ɔleɔdyk/ *n.m.* oil pipeline.
oliv|e /ɔliv/ *n.f.* & *a. invar.* olive. **~ier** *n.m.* olive-tree.
olympique /ɔlɛ̃pik/ *a.* Olympic.
ombrag|e /ɔ̃braʒ/ *n.m.* shade. **prendre ~e de,** take offence at. **~é** *a.* shady. **~eux, ~euse** *a.* easily offended.
ombre /ɔ̃br/ *n.f.* (*pénombre*) shade; (*contour*) shadow; (*soupçon: fig.*) hint, shadow. **dans l'~,** (*secret*) in the dark. **faire de l'~ à qn.,** be in s.o.'s light.
ombrelle /ɔ̃brɛl/ *n.f.* parasol.
omelette /ɔmlɛt/ *n.f.* omelette.
omettre† /ɔmɛtr/ *v.t.* omit.
omission /ɔmisjɔ̃/ *n.f.* omission.
omnibus /ɔmnibys/ *n.m.* slow train.
omoplate /ɔmɔplat/ *n.f.* shoulder-blade.
on /ɔ̃/ *pron.* we, you, one; (*les gens*) people, they; (*quelqu'un*) someone. **~ dit,** people say, they say, it is said **(que,** that).
once /ɔ̃s/ *n.f.* ounce.

oncle /ɔ̃kl/ *n.m.* uncle.
onctueu|x, ~se /ɔ̃ktɥø, -z/ *a.* smooth.
onde /ɔ̃d/ *n.f.* wave. **~s courtes/longues,** short/long wave. **sur les ~s,** on the radio.
ondée /ɔ̃de/ *n.f.* shower.
on-dit /ɔ̃di/ *n.m. invar.* rumour.
ondul|er /ɔ̃dyle/ *v.i.* undulate; (*cheveux*) be wavy. **~ation** *n.f.* wave, undulation. **~é** *a.* (*chevelure*) wavy.
onéreu|x, ~se /ɔnerø, -z/ *a.* costly.
ongl|e /ɔ̃gl/ *n.m.* (finger-)nail. **avoir l' ~ée,** have frozen fingertips.
ont /ɔ̃/ *voir* **avoir.**
ONU *abrév.* (*Organisation des nations unies*) UN.
onyx /ɔniks/ *n.m.* onyx.
onz|e /ɔ̃z/ *a.* & *n.m.* eleven. **~ième** *a.* & *n.m./f.* eleventh.
opale /ɔpal/ *n.f.* opal.
opa|que /ɔpak/ *a.* opaque. **~cité** *n.f.* opaqueness.
opéra /ɔpera/ *n.m.* opera; (*édifice*) opera-house. **~-comique** (*pl.* **~s-comiques**) *n.m.* light opera.
opérateur /ɔperatœr/ *n.m.* (*caméraman*) cameraman.
opération /ɔperɑsjɔ̃/ *n.f.* operation; (*comm.*) deal.
opérationnel, ~le /ɔperasjɔnɛl/ *a.* operational.
opératoire /ɔperatwar/ *a.* (*méd.*) surgical.
opérer /ɔpere/ *v.t.* (*personne*) operate on; (*kyste etc.*) remove; (*exécuter*) carry out, make. *—v.i.* (*méd.*) operate; (*faire effet*) work. **s'~** *v. pr.* (*se produire*) occur.
opérette /ɔperɛt/ *n.f.* operetta.
opiner /ɔpine/ *v.i.* nod.
opiniâtre /ɔpinjɑtr/ *a.* obstinate.
opinion /ɔpinjɔ̃/ *n.f.* opinion.
opium /ɔpjɔm/ *n.m.* opium.
opportun, ~e /ɔpɔrtœ̃, -yn/ *a.* opportune. **~ité** /-ynite/ *n.f.* opportuneness.
opposant, ~e /ɔpozɑ̃, -t/ *n.m., f.* opponent.
opposé /ɔpoze/ *a.* (*sens, angle, etc.*) opposite; (*factions*) opposing; (*intérêts*) conflicting. *—n.m.* opposite. **à l'~,** (*opinion etc.*) contrary (**de,** to). **être ~ à,** be opposed to.
opposer /ɔpoze/ *v.t.* (*objets*) place opposite each other; (*personnes*) oppose; (*contraster*) contrast; (*résistance, argument*) put up. **s'~** *v. pr.* (*personnes*) confront each other; (*styles*) contrast. **s'~ à,** oppose.
opposition /ɔpozisjɔ̃/ *n.f.* opposition. **faire ~ à,** oppose.
oppress|er /ɔprese/ *v.t.* oppress. **~ant, ~ante** *a.* oppressive. **~eur** *n.m.* oppressor. **~ion** *n.f.* oppression.
opprimer /ɔprime/ *v.t.* oppress.
opter /ɔpte/ *v.i.* **~ pour,** opt for.
opticien, ~ne /ɔptisjɛ̃, -jɛn/ *n.m., f.* optician.
optimis|te /ɔptimist/ *n.m./f.* optimist. *—a.* optimistic. **~me** *n.m.* optimism.
optimum /ɔptimɔm/ *a.* & *n.m.* optimum.
option /ɔpsjɔ̃/ *n.f.* option.
optique /ɔptik/ *a.* (*verre*) optical. *—n.f.* (*perspective*) perspective.
opulen|t, ~te /ɔpylɑ̃, -t/ *a.* opulent. **~ce** *n.f.* opulence.
or[1] /ɔr/ *n.m.* gold. **d'~,** golden. **en ~,** gold; (*occasion*) golden.
or[2] /ɔr/ *conj.* now, well.
oracle /ɔrɑkl/ *n.m.* oracle.
orag|e /ɔraʒ/ *n.m.* (thunder)storm. **~eux, ~euse** *a.* stormy.
oraison /ɔrɛzɔ̃/ *n.f.* prayer.
or|al (*m. pl.* **~aux**) /ɔral, -o/ *a.* oral. *—n.m.* (*pl.* **~aux**) oral.
orang|e /ɔrɑ̃ʒ/ *n.f.* & *a. invar.* orange. **~é** *a.* orange-coloured. **~er** *n.m.* orange(-tree).
orangeade /ɔrɑ̃ʒad/ *n.f.* orangeade.

orateur /ɔratœr/ *n.m.* speaker.

oratorio /ɔratɔrjo/ *n.m.* oratorio.

orbite /ɔrbit/ *n.f.* orbit; (*d'œil*) socket.

orchestr|e /ɔrkɛstr/ *n.m.* orchestra; (*de jazz*) band; (*parterre*) stalls. **~er** *v.t.* orchestrate.

orchidée /ɔrkide/ *n.f.* orchid.

ordinaire /ɔrdinɛr/ *a.* ordinary; (*habituel*) usual; (*qualité*) standard. *—n.m.* **l'~,** the ordinary; (*nourriture*) the standard fare. **d'~, à l'~,** usually. **~ment** *adv.* usually.

ordinateur /ɔrdinatœr/ *n.m.* computer.

ordination /ɔrdinɑsjɔ̃/ *n.f.* (*relig.*) ordination.

ordonnance /ɔrdɔnɑ̃s/ *n.f.* (*ordre, décret*) order; (*de médecin*) prescription; (*soldat*) orderly.

ordonné /ɔrdɔne/ *a.* orderly.

ordonner /ɔrdɔne/ *v.t.* order (**à qn. de,** s.o. to); (*agencer*) arrange; (*méd.*) prescribe; (*prêtre*) ordain.

ordre /ɔrdr/ *n.m.* order; (*propreté*) tidiness. **aux ~s de qn.,** at s.o.'s disposal. **avoir de l'~,** be tidy. **de premier ~,** first-rate. **l'~ du jour,** (*programme*) agenda. **mettre en ~,** tidy (up).

ordure /ɔrdyr/ *n.f.* filth. **~s,** (*détritus*) rubbish; (*Amer.*) garbage.

oreille /ɔrɛj/ *n.f.* ear.

oreiller /ɔreje/ *n.m.* pillow.

oreillons /ɔrɛjɔ̃/ *n.m. pl.* mumps.

orfèvr|e /ɔrfɛvr/ *n.m.* goldsmith, silversmith. **~erie** *n.f.* goldsmith's *ou* silversmith's trade.

organe /ɔrgan/ *n.m.* organ; (*porte-parole*) mouthpiece.

organigramme /ɔrganigram/ *n.m.* flow chart.

organique /ɔrganik/ *a.* organic.

organisation /ɔrganizɑsjɔ̃/ *n.f.* organization.

organis|er /ɔrganize/ *v.t.* organize. **s'~er** *v. pr.* organize o.s. **~ateur, ~atrice** *n.m., f.* organizer.

organisme /ɔrganism/ *n.m.* body, organism.

organiste /ɔrganist/ *n.m./f.* organist.

orgasme /ɔrgasm/ *n.m.* orgasm.

orge /ɔrʒ/ *n.f.* barley.

orgelet /ɔrʒəlɛ/ *n.m.* (*furoncle*) sty.

orgie /ɔrʒi/ *n.f.* orgy.

orgue /ɔrg/ *n.m.* organ. **~s** *n.f. pl.* organ. **~ de Barbarie,** barrel-organ.

orgueil /ɔrgœj/ *n.m.* pride.

orgueilleu|x, ~se /ɔrgœjø, -z/ *a.* proud.

Orient /ɔrjɑ̃/ *n.m.* **l'~,** the Orient.

orientable /ɔrjɑ̃tabl/ *a.* adjustable.

orient|al, ~ale (*m. pl.* **~aux**) /ɔrjɑ̃tal, -o/ *a.* eastern; (*de l'Orient*) oriental. *—n.m., f.* Oriental.

orientation /ɔrjɑ̃tɑsjɔ̃/ *n.f.* direction; (*d'une politique*) course; (*de maison*) aspect. **~ professionnelle,** careers advisory service.

orienté /ɔrjɑ̃te/ *a.* (*partial*) slanted, tendentious.

orienter /ɔrjɑ̃te/ *v.t.* position; (*personne*) direct. **s'~** *v. pr.* (*se repérer*) find one's bearings. **s'~ vers,** turn towards.

orifice /ɔrifis/ *n.m.* orifice.

originaire /ɔriʒinɛr/ *a.* **être ~ de,** be a native of.

origin|al, ~ale (*m. pl.* **~aux**) /ɔriʒinal, -o/ *a.* original; (*curieux*) eccentric. *—n.m.* original. *—n.m., f.* eccentric. **~alité** *n.f.* originality; eccentricity.

origine /ɔriʒin/ *n.f.* origin. **à l'~,** originally. **d'~,** (*pièce, pneu*) original.

originel, ~le /ɔriʒinɛl/ *a.* original.

orme /ɔrm/ *n.m.* elm.

ornement /ɔrnəmɑ̃/ *n.m.* ornament. **~al** (*m. pl.* **~aux**) /-tal, -to/ *a.* ornamental.

orner /ɔrne/ *v.t.* decorate.

ornière /ɔrnjɛr/ *n.f.* rut.
ornithologie /ɔrnitɔlɔʒi/ *n.f.* ornithology.
orphelin, ~e /ɔrfəlɛ̃, -in/ *n.m., f.* orphan. —*a.* orphaned. **~at** /-ina/ *n.m.* orphanage.
orteil /ɔrtɛj/ *n.m.* toe.
orthodox|e /ɔrtɔdɔks/ *a.* orthodox. **~ie** *n.f.* orthodoxy.
orthograph|e /ɔrtɔgraf/ *n.f.* spelling. **~ier** *v.t.* spell.
orthopédique /ɔrtɔpedik/ *a.* orthopaedic.
ortie /ɔrti/ *n.f.* nettle.
os (*pl.* **os**) /ɔs, o/ *n.m.* bone.
OS *abrév. voir* **ouvrier spécialisé.**
oscill|er /ɔsile/ *v.i.* sway; (*techn.*) oscillate; (*hésiter*) waver, fluctuate. **~ation** *n.f.* (*techn.*) oscillation; (*variation*) fluctuation.
oseille /ozɛj/ *n.f.* (*plante*) sorrel.
os|er /oze/ *v.t./i.* dare. **~é** *a.* daring.
osier /ozje/ *n.m.* wicker.
ossature /ɔsatyr/ *n.f.* frame.
ossements /ɔsmɑ̃/ *n.m. pl.* bones.
osseu|x, ~se /ɔsø, -z/ *a.* bony; (*tissu*) bone.
ostensible /ɔstɑ̃sibl/ *a.* conspicuous, obvious.
ostentation /ɔstɑ̃tɑsjɔ̃/ *n.f.* ostentation.
otage /ɔtaʒ/ *n.m.* hostage.
otarie /ɔtari/ *n.f.* sea-lion.
ôter /ote/ *v.t.* remove (**à qn.,** from s.o.); (*déduire*) take away.
otite /ɔtit/ *n.f.* ear infection.
ou /u/ *conj.* or. **~ bien,** or else. **~ vous ou moi,** either you or me.
où /u/ *adv.* & *pron.* where; (*dans lequel*) in which; (*sur lequel*) on which; (*auquel*) at which. **d'~,** from which; (*pour cette raison*) hence. **d'~?,** from where? **par ~,** through which. **par ~?,** which way? **~ qu'il soit,** wherever he may be. **le jour ~,** the day when.
ouate /wat/ *n.f.* cotton wool; (*Amer.*) absorbent cotton.
oubli /ubli/ *n.m.* forgetfulness; (*trou de mémoire*) lapse of memory; (*négligence*) oversight. **l'~,** (*tomber dans, sauver de*) oblivion.
oublier /ublije/ *v.t.* forget. **s'~** *v. pr.* forget o.s.; (*chose*) be forgotten.
oublieu|x, ~se /ublijø, -z/ *a.* forgetful (**de,** of).
ouest /wɛst/ *n.m.* west. —*a. invar.* west; (*partie*) western; (*direction*) westerly.
ouf /uf/ *int.* phew.
oui /wi/ *adv.* yes.
ouï-dire (par) /(par)widir/ *adv.* by hearsay.
ouïe /wi/ *n.f.* hearing.
ouïes /wi/ *n.f. pl.* gills.
ouille /uj/ *int.* ouch.
ouïr /wir/ *v.t.* hear.
ouragan /uragɑ̃/ *n.m.* hurricane.
ourler /urle/ *v.t.* hem.
ourlet /urlɛ/ *n.m.* hem.
ours /urs/ *n.m.* bear. **~ blanc,** polar bear. **~ en peluche,** teddy bear.
ouste /ust/ *int.* (*fam.*) scram.
outil /uti/ *n.m.* tool.
outillage /utijaʒ/ *n.m.* tools; (*d'une usine*) equipment.
outiller /utije/ *v.t.* equip.
outrage /utraʒ/ *n.m* (grave) insult.
outrag|er /utraʒe/ *v.t.* offend. **~eant, ~eante** *a.* offensive.
outranc|e /utrɑ̃s/ *n.f.* excess. **à ~e,** to excess; (*guerre*) all-out. **~ier, ~ière** *a.* excessive.
outre /utr/ *prép.* besides. **en ~,** besides. **~-mer** *adv.* overseas. **~ mesure,** excessively.
outrepasser /utrəpɑse/ *v.t.* exceed.
outrer /utre/ *v.t.* exaggerate; (*indigner*) incense.
outsider /awtsajdœr/ *n.m.* outsider.
ouvert, ~e /uvɛr, -t/ *voir* **ouvrir.** —*a.* open; (*gaz, radio, etc.*) on. **~ement** /-təmɑ̃/ *adv.* openly.

ouverture /uvɛrtyr/ *n.f.* opening; (*mus.*) overture. **~s,** (*offres*) overtures. **~ d'esprit,** open-mindedness.
ouvrag|e /uvraʒ/ *n.m.* (*travail, livre*) work; (*couture*) needlework. **~é** *a.* finely worked.
ouvreuse /uvrøz/ *n.f.* usherette.
ouvr|ier, ~ière /uvrije, -jɛr/ *n.m., f.* worker. —*a.* working-class; (*conflit*) industrial; (*syndicat*) workers'. **~ier qualifié/spécialisé,** skilled/unskilled worker.
ouvr|ir† /uvrir/ *v.t.* open (up); (*gaz, radio, etc.*) turn *ou* switch on. —*v.i.* open (up). **s'~ir** *v. pr.* open (up). **s'~ir à qn.,** open one's heart to s.o. **~e-boîte(s)** *n.m.* tin-opener. **~e-bouteille(s)** *n.m.* bottle-opener.
ovaire /ɔvɛr/ *n.m.* ovary.
ovale /ɔval/ *a.* & *n.m.* oval.
ovation /ɔvɑsjɔ̃/ *n.f.* ovation.
oxygène /ɔksiʒɛn/ *n.m.* oxygen.
oxygéner (s') /(s)ɔksiʒene/ *v. pr.* (*fam.*) get some fresh air.

P

pachyderme /paʃidɛrm/ *n.m.* elephant.
pacifier /pasifje/ *v.t.* pacify.
pacifique /pasifik/ *a.* peaceful; (*personne*) peaceable; (*géog.*) Pacific. —*n.m.* **P~,** Pacific (Ocean).
pacifiste /pasifist/ *n.m./f.* pacifist.
pacotille /pakɔtij/ *n.f.* trash.
pacte /pakt/ *n.m.* pact.
pactiser /paktize/ *v.i.* **~ avec,** be in league *ou* agreement with.
paddock /padɔk/ *n.m.* paddock.
pag|aie /pagɛ/ *n.f.* paddle. **~ayer** *v.i.* paddle.
pagaille /pagaj/ *n.f.* mess, shambles.
page /paʒ/ *n.f.* page. **être à la ~,** be up to date.
pagode /pagɔd/ *n.f.* pagoda.
paie /pɛ/ *n.f.* pay.
paiement /pɛmɑ̃/ *n.m.* payment.
païen, ~ne /pajɛ̃, -jɛn/ *a.* & *n.m., f.* pagan.
paillasse /pajas/ *n.f.* straw mattress; (*d'un évier*) draining-board.
paillasson /pajasɔ̃/ *n.m.* doormat.
paille /pɑj/ *n.f.* straw; (*défaut*) flaw.
paillette /pajɛt/ *n.f.* (*sur robe*) sequin; (*de savon*) flake. **~s d'or,** gold-dust.
pain /pɛ̃/ *n.m.* bread; (*unité*) loaf (of bread); (*de savon etc.*) bar. **~ d'épice,** gingerbread. **~ grillé,** toast.
pair[1] /pɛr/ *a.* (*nombre*) even.
pair[2] /pɛr/ *n.m.* (*personne*) peer. **au ~,** (*jeune fille etc.*) au pair. **de ~,** together (**avec,** with).
paire /pɛr/ *n.f.* pair.
paisible /pezibl/ *a.* peaceful.
paître /pɛtr/ *v.i.* (*brouter*) graze.
paix /pɛ/ *n.f.* peace; (*papier*) peace treaty.
Pakistan /pakistɑ̃/ *n.m.* Pakistan.
pakistanais, ~e /pakistanɛ, -z/ *a.* & *n.m., f.* Pakistani.
palace /palas/ *n.m.* luxury hotel.
palais[1] /palɛ/ *n.m.* palace. **P~ de Justice,** Law Courts. **~ des sports,** sports stadium.
palais[2] /palɛ/ *n.m.* (*anat.*) palate.
palan /palɑ̃/ *n.m.* hoist.
pâle /pɑl/ *a.* pale.
Palestine /palɛstin/ *n.f.* Palestine.
palestinien, ~ne /palɛstinjɛ̃, -jɛn/ *a.* & *n.m., f.* Palestinian.
palet /palɛ/ *n.m.* (*hockey*) puck.
paletot /palto/ *n.m.* thick jacket.
palette /palɛt/ *n.f.* palette.
pâleur /pɑlœr/ *n.f.* paleness.
palier /palje/ *n.m.* (*d'escalier*) landing; (*étape*) stage; (*de route*) level stretch.

pâlir /pɑlir/ *v.t./i.* (turn) pale.
palissade /palisad/ *n.f.* fence.
pallier /palje/ *v.i.* ~ **à,** alleviate.
palmarès /palmarɛs/ *n.m.* list of prize-winners.
palm|e /palm/ *n.f.* palm leaf; (*symbole*) palm; (*de nageur*) flipper. **~ier** *n.m.* palm(-tree).
palmé /palme/ *a.* (*patte*) webbed.
pâlot, ~te /pɑlo, -ɔt/ *a.* pale.
palourde /palurd/ *n.f.* clam.
palper /palpe/ *v.t.* feel.
palpit|er /palpite/ *v.i.* (*battre*) pound, palpitate; (*frémir*) quiver. **~ations** *n.f. pl.* palpitations.
paludisme /palydism/ *n.m.* malaria.
pâmer (se) /(sə)pɑme/ *v. pr.* swoon.
pamphlet /pɑ̃flɛ/ *n.m.* satirical pamphlet.
pamplemousse /pɑ̃pləmus/ *n.m.* grapefruit.
pan[1] /pɑ̃/ *n.m.* piece; (*de chemise*) tail.
pan[2] /pɑ̃/ *int.* bang.
panacée /panase/ *n.f.* panacea.
panache /panaʃ/ *n.m.* plume; (*bravoure*) gallantry; (*allure*) panache.
panaché /panaʃe/ *a.* (*bariolé, mélangé*) motley. —*n.m.* shandy. **bière ~e, demi ~,** shandy.
pancarte /pɑ̃kart/ *n.f.* sign; (*de manifestant*) placard.
pancréas /pɑ̃kreɑs/ *n.m.* pancreas.
pané /pane/ *a.* breaded.
panier /panje/ *n.m.* basket. **~ à provisions,** shopping basket. **~ à salade,** (*fam.*) police van.
paniqu|e /panik/ *n.f.* panic. **~er** *v.i.*, **se ~er** *v. pr.* panic.
panne /pan/ *n.f.* breakdown. **être en ~,** have broken down. **être en ~ sèche,** have run out of petrol *ou* gas (*Amer.*). **~ de courant,** power failure.
panneau (*pl.* **~x**) /pano/ *n.m.* sign; (*publicitaire*) hoarding; (*de porte etc.*) panel. **~ (d'affichage),** notice-board. **~ (de signalisation),** road sign.
panoplie /panɔpli/ *n.f.* (*jouet*) outfit; (*gamme*) range.
panoram|a /panɔrama/ *n.m.* panorama. **~ique** *a.* panoramic.
panse /pɑ̃s/ *n.f.* paunch.
pans|er /pɑ̃se/ *v.t.* (*plaie*) dress; (*personne*) dress the wound(s) of; (*cheval*) groom. **~ement** *n.m.* dressing. **~ement adhésif,** sticking-plaster.
pantalon /pɑ̃talɔ̃/ *n.m.* (pair of) trousers. **~s,** trousers.
panthère /pɑ̃tɛr/ *n.f.* panther.
pantin /pɑ̃tɛ̃/ *n.m.* puppet.
pantomime /pɑ̃tɔmim/ *n.f.* mime; (*spectacle*) mime show.
pantoufle /pɑ̃tufl/ *n.f.* slipper.
paon /pɑ̃/ *n.m.* peacock.
papa /papa/ *n.m.* dad(dy).
papauté /papote/ *n.f.* papacy.
pape /pap/ *n.m.* pope.
paperass|e /papras/ *n.f.* **~e(s),** (*péj.*) papers. **~erie** *n.f.* (*péj.*) papers; (*tracasserie*) red tape.
papet|ier, ~ière /paptje, -jɛr/ *n.m., f.* stationer. **~erie** /papetri/ *n.f.* (*magasin*) stationer's shop.
papier /papje/ *n.m.* paper; (*formulaire*) form. **~ à lettres,** writing-paper. **~ aluminium,** tin foil. **~ buvard,** blotting-paper. **~ calque,** tracing-paper. **~ carbone,** carbon paper. **~ collant,** sticky tape. **~ de verre,** sandpaper. **~ hygiénique,** toilet-paper. **~ journal,** newspaper. **~ mâché,** papier mâché. **~ peint,** wallpaper.
papillon /papijɔ̃/ *n.m.* butterfly; (*contravention*) parking-ticket. **~ (de nuit),** moth.
papot|er /papɔte/ *v.i.* prattle. **~age** *n.m.* prattle.
paprika /paprika/ *n.m.* paprika.
Pâque /pɑk/ *n.f.* Passover.

paquebot /pakbo/ *n.m.* liner.
pâquerette /pɑkrɛt/ *n.f.* daisy.
Pâques /pɑk/ *n.f. pl.* & *n.m.* Easter.
paquet /pakɛ/ *n.m.* packet; (*de cartes*) pack; (*colis*) parcel. **un ~ de,** (*tas*) a mass of.
par /par/ *prép.* by; (*à travers*) through; (*motif*) out of, from; (*provenance*) from. **commencer/finir ~ qch.,** begin/end with sth. **commencer/finir ~ faire,** begin by/end up (by) doing. **~ an/mois/** *etc.*, a *ou* per year/month/*etc.* **~ avion,** (*lettre*) (by) airmail. **~-ci, par-là,** here and there. **~ contre,** on the other hand. **~ hasard,** by chance. **~ ici/là,** this/that way. **par inadvertance,** inadvertently. **~ intermittence,** intermittently. **~ l'intermédiaire de,** through. **~ malheur** *ou* **malchance,** unfortunately. **~ miracle,** miraculously. **~ moments,** at times. **~ opposition à,** as opposed to.
parabole /parabɔl/ *n.f.* (*relig.*) parable.
parachever /paraʃve/ *v.t.* perfect.
parachut|e /paraʃyt/ *n.m.* parachute. **~er** *v.t.* parachute. **~iste** *n.m./f.* parachutist; (*mil.*) paratrooper.
parad|e /parad/ *n.f.* parade; (*sport*) parry; (*réplique*) reply. **~er** *v.i.* show off.
paradis /paradi/ *n.m.* paradise.
paradox|e /paradɔks/ *n.m.* paradox. **~al** (*m. pl.* **~aux**) *a.* paradoxical.
paraffine /parafin/ *n.f.* paraffin wax.
parages /paraʒ/ *n.m. pl.* area, vicinity.
paragraphe /paragraf/ *n.m.* paragraph.
paraître† /parɛtr/ *v.i.* appear; (*sembler*) seem, appear; (*ouvrage*) be published, come out. **faire ~,** (*ouvrage*) bring out.
parallèle /paralɛl/ *a.* parallel; (*illégal*) unofficial. —*n.m.* parallel. —*n.f.* parallel (line). **~ment** *adv.* parallel (**à,** to).
paraly|ser /paralize/ *v.t.* paralyse. **~sie** *n.f.* paralysis. **~tique** *a.* & *n.m./f.* paralytic.
paramètre /paramɛtr/ *n.m.* parameter.
paranoïa /paranɔja/ *n.f.* paranoia.
parapet /parapɛ/ *n.m.* parapet.
paraphe /paraf/ *n.m.* signature.
paraphrase /parafraz/ *n.f.* paraphrase.
parapluie /paraplɥi/ *n.m.* umbrella.
parasite /parazit/ *n.m.* parasite. **~s,** (*radio*) interference. —*a.* parasitic.
parasol /parasɔl/ *n.m.* sunshade.
paratonnerre /paratɔnɛr/ *n.m.* lightning-conductor *ou* -rod.
paravent /paravɑ̃/ *n.m.* screen.
parc /park/ *n.m.* park; (*de bétail*) pen; (*de bébé*) play-pen; (*entrepôt*) depot. **~ de stationnement,** car-park.
parcelle /parsɛl/ *n.f.* fragment; (*de terre*) plot.
parce que /parsk(ə)/ *conj.* because.
parchemin /parʃəmɛ̃/ *n.m.* parchment.
parcimon|ie /parsimɔni/ *n.f.* **avec ~ie,** parsimoniously. **~ieux, ~ieuse** *a.* parsimonious.
parcmètre /parkmɛtr/ *n.m.* parking-meter.
parcourir† /parkurir/ *v.t.* travel *ou* go through; (*distance*) travel; (*des yeux*) glance at *ou* over.
parcours /parkur/ *n.m.* route; (*voyage*) journey.
par-delà /pardəla/ *prép.* & *adv.* beyond.
par-derrière /pardɛrjɛr/ *prép.* & *adv.* behind, at the back *ou* rear (of).
par-dessous /pardsu/ *prép.* & *adv.* under(neath).

pardessus /pardəsy/ *n.m.* overcoat.
par-dessus /pardsy/ *prép.* & *adv.* over. **~ bord,** overboard. **~ le marché,** into the bargain. **~ tout,** above all.
par-devant /pardvɑ̃/ *adv.* at *ou* from the front, in front.
pardon /pardɔ̃/ *n.m.* forgiveness. **(je vous demande) ~!,** (I am) sorry!; (*pour demander qch.*) excuse me!
pardonn|er /pardɔne/ *v.t.* forgive. **~er qch. à qn.,** forgive s.o. for sth. **~able** *a.* forgivable.
paré /pare/ *a.* ready.
pare-balles /parbal/ *a. invar.* bullet-proof.
pare-brise /parbriz/ *n.m. invar.* windscreen; (*Amer.*) windshield.
pare-chocs /parʃɔk/ *n.m. invar.* bumper.
pareil, ~le /parɛj/ *a.* similar **(à,** to); (*tel*) such (a). *—n.m., f.* equal. *—adv.* (*fam.*) the same. **c'est ~,** it is the same. **vos ~s,** (*péj.*) those of your type, those like you. **~lement** *adv.* the same.
parement /parmɑ̃/ *n.m.* facing.
parent, ~e /parɑ̃, -t/ *a.* related **(de,** to). *—n.m., f.* relative, relation. **~s** (*père et mère*) *n.m. pl.* parents.
parenté /parɑ̃te/ *n.f.* relationship.
parenthèse /parɑ̃tɛz/ *n.f.* bracket, parenthesis; (*fig.*) digression.
parer[1] /pare/ *v.t.* (*coup*) parry. *—v.i.* **~ à,** deal with.
parer[2] /pare/ *v.t.* (*orner*) adorn.
paress|e /parɛs/ *n.f.* laziness. **~er** /-ese/ *v.i.* laze (about). **~eux, ~euse** *a.* lazy; *n.m., f.* lazybones.
parfaire /parfɛr/ *v.t.* perfect.
parfait, ~e /parfɛ, -t/ *a.* perfect. **~ement** /-tmɑ̃/ *adv.* perfectly; (*bien sûr*) certainly.
parfois /parfwa/ *adv.* sometimes.
parfum /parfœ̃/ *n.m.* scent; (*substance*) perfume, scent; (*goût*) flavour.
parfum|er /parfyme/ *v.t.* perfume; (*gâteau*) flavour. **se ~er** *v. pr.* put on one's perfume. **~é** *a.* fragrant; (*savon*) scented. **~erie** *n.f.* (*produits*) perfumes; (*boutique*) perfume shop.
pari /pari/ *n.m.* bet.
par|ier /parje/ *v.t.* bet. **~ieur, ~ieuse** *n.m., f.* punter, better.
Paris /pari/ *n.m./f.* Paris.
parisien, ~ne /parizjɛ̃, -jɛn/ *a.* Paris, Parisian. *—n.m., f.* Parisian.
parit|é /parite/ *n.f.* parity. **~aire** *a.* (*commission*) joint.
parjur|e /parʒyr/ *n.m.* perjury. *—n.m./f.* perjurer. **se ~er** *v. pr.* perjure o.s.
parking /parkiŋ/ *n.m.* car-park; (*Amer.*) parking-lot; (*stationnement*) parking.
parlement /parləmɑ̃/ *n.m.* parliament. **~aire** /-tɛr/ *a.* parliamentary; *n.m./f.* Member of Parliament; (*fig.*) negotiator. **~er** /-te/ *v.i.* negotiate.
parl|er /parle/ *v.i.* talk, speak **(à,** to). *—v.t.* (*langue*) speak; (*politique, affaires, etc.*) talk. **se ~er** *v. pr.* (*langue*) be spoken. *—n.m.* speech; (*dialecte*) dialect. **~ant, ~ante** *a.* (*film*) talking; (*fig.*) eloquent. **~eur, ~euse** *n.m., f.* talker.
parmi /parmi/ *prép.* among(st).
parod|ie /parɔdi/ *n.f.* parody. **~ier** *v.t.* parody.
paroi /parwa/ *n.f.* wall; (*cloison*) partition (wall).
paroiss|e /parwas/ *n.f.* parish. **~ial** (*m. pl.* **~iaux)** *a.* parish. **~ien, ~ienne** *n.m., f.* parishioner.
parole /parɔl/ *n.f.* (*mot, promesse*) word; (*langage*) speech. **demander la ~,** ask to speak. **prendre la ~,** (begin to) speak.
paroxysme /parɔksism/ *n.m.* height, highest point.

parquer /parke/ *v.t.*, **se ~** *v. pr.* (*auto.*) park.

parquet /parkɛ/ *n.m.* floor; (*jurid.*) public prosecutor's department.

parrain /parɛ̃/ *n.m.* godfather; (*fig.*) sponsor. **~er** /-ene/ *v.t.* sponsor.

pars, part[1] /par/ *voir* **partir.**

parsemer /parsəme/ *v.t.* strew (**de,** with).

part[2] /par/ *n.f.* share, part. **à ~,** (*de côté*) aside; (*séparément*) apart; (*excepté*) apart from. **d'autre ~,** on the other hand; (*de plus*) moreover. **de la ~ de,** from. **de toutes ~s,** from all sides. **d'une ~,** on the one hand. **faire ~ à qn.,** inform s.o. (**de,** of). **prendre ~ à,** take part in; (*joie, douleur*) share.

partag|e /partaʒ/ *n.m.* dividing; sharing out; (*part*) share. **~er** *v.t.* divide; (*distribuer*) share out; (*avoir en commun*) share. **se ~er qch.,** share sth.

partance (en) /(ɑ̃)partɑ̃s/ *adv.* about to depart.

partant /partɑ̃/ *n.m.* (*sport*) starter.

partenaire /partənɛr/ *n.m./f.* partner.

parterre /partɛr/ *n.m.* flower-bed; (*théâtre*) stalls.

parti /parti/ *n.m.* (*pol.*) party; (*en mariage*) match; (*décision*) decision. **~ pris,** prejudice. **prendre ~ pour,** side with.

part|ial (*m. pl.* **~iaux**) /parsjal, -jo/ *a.* biased. **~ialité** *n.f.* bias.

participe /partisip/ *n.m.* (*gram.*) participle.

particip|er /partisipe/ *v.i.* **~er à,** take part in, participate in; (*profits, frais*) share; (*spectacle*) appear in. **~ant, ~ante** *n.m., f.* participant (**à,** in); (*à un concours*) entrant. **~ation** *n.f.* participation; sharing; (*d'un artiste*) appearance.

particularité /partikylarite/ *n.f.* particularity.

particule /partikyl/ *n.f.* particle.

particul|ier, ~ière /partikylje, -jɛr/ *a.* (*spécifique*) particular; (*bizarre*) peculiar; (*privé*) private. —*n.m.* private individual. **en ~ier,** in particular; (*en privé*) in private. **~ier à,** peculiar to. **~ièrement** *adv.* particularly.

partie /parti/ *n.f.* part; (*cartes, sport*) game; (*jurid.*) party; (*sortie*) outing, party. **en ~,** partly. **faire ~ de,** be part of; (*adhérer à*) belong to. **~ intégrante,** integral part.

partiel, ~le /parsjɛl/ *a.* partial. —*n.m.* (*univ.*) class examination. **~lement** *adv.* partially, partly.

partir† /partir/ *v.i.* (*aux. être*) go; (*quitter un lieu*) leave, go; (*tache*) come out; (*bouton*) come off; (*coup de feu*) go off; (*commencer*) start. **à ~ de,** from.

partisan, ~e /partizɑ̃, -an/ *n.m., f.* supporter. —*n.m.* (*mil.*) partisan. **être ~ de,** be in favour of.

partition /partisjɔ̃/ *n.f.* (*mus.*) score.

partout /partu/ *adv.* everywhere. **~ où,** wherever.

paru /pary/ *voir* **paraître.**

parure /paryr/ *n.f.* adornment; (*bijoux*) (set of) jewels, jewellery.

parution /parysjɔ̃/ *n.f.* publication.

parvenir† /parvənir/ *v.i.* (*aux. être*) **~ à,** reach; (*résultat*) achieve. **~ à faire,** manage to do.

parvenu, ~e /parvəny/ *n.m., f.* upstart.

parvis /parvi/ *n.m.* (*place*) square.

pas[1] /pɑ/ *adv.* not. **(ne) ~,** not. **je ne sais ~,** I do not know. **~ de sucre/livres/***etc.*, no sugar/books/*etc.* **~ du tout,** not at all. **~ encore,** not yet. **~ mal,** not bad; (*beaucoup*) quite a lot (**de,** of). **~ vrai?,** (*fam.*) isn't that so?

pas[2] /pa/ *n.m.* step; (*bruit*) footstep; (*trace*) footprint; (*vitesse*) pace; (*de vis*) thread. **à deux ~ (de),** close by. **au ~,** at a walking pace; (*véhicule*) very slowly. **au ~ (cadencé),** in step. **~ de la porte,** doorstep.

passable /pasabl/ *a.* tolerable. **~ment** /-əmɑ̃/ *adv.* (*pas trop mal*) tolerably; (*beaucoup*) quite a bit.

passage /pasaʒ/ *n.m.* passing, passage; (*traversée*) crossing; (*arrivée*) arrival; (*visite*) visit; (*chemin*) way, passage; (*d'une œuvre*) passage. **de ~,** (*voyageur*) visiting. **~ à niveau,** level crossing. **~ clouté,** pedestrian crossing. **~ interdit,** (*panneau*) no thoroughfare. **~ souterrain,** subway; (*Amer.*) underpass.

passag|er, ~ère /pasaʒe, -ɛr/ *a.* temporary. *—n.m., f.* passenger. **~er clandestin,** stowaway.

passant, ~e /pasɑ̃, -t/ *a.* (*rue*) busy. *—n.m., f.* passer-by. *—n.m.* (*anneau*) loop.

passe /pas/ *n.f.* pass. **bonne/mauvaise ~,** good/bad patch. **en ~ de,** on the road to. **~-montagne** *n.m.* Balaclava. **~-partout** *n.m. invar.* master-key; *a. invar.* for all occasions. **~-temps** *n.m. invar.* pastime.

passé /pase/ *a.* (*révolu*) past; (*dernier*) last; (*fini*) over; (*fané*) faded. *—prép.* after. *—n.m.* past. **~ de mode,** out of fashion.

passeport /paspɔr/ *n.m.* passport.

passer /pase/ *v.i.* (*aux. être ou avoir*) pass; (*aller*) go; (*venir*) come; (*temps*) pass (by), go by; (*film*) be shown; (*couleur*) fade. *—v.t.* (*aux. avoir*) pass, cross; (*donner*) pass, hand; (*mettre*) put; (*oublier*) overlook; (*enfiler*) slip on; (*dépasser*) go beyond; (*temps*) spend, pass; (*film*) show; (*examen*) take; (*commande*) place; (*soupe*) strain. **se ~** *v. pr.* happen, take place. **laisser ~,** let through; (*occasion*) miss. **~ à tabac,** (*fam.*) beat up. **~ devant,** (*édifice*) go past. **~ en fraude,** smuggle. **~ outre,** take no notice (**à,** of). **~ pour,** (*riche etc.*) be taken to be. **~ sur,** (*détail*) pass over. **~ un coup de fil à qn.,** give s.o. a ring. **se ~ de,** go *ou* do without.

passerelle /pasrɛl/ *n.f.* footbridge; (*pour accéder à un avion, à un navire*) gangway.

passible /pasibl/ *a.* **~ de,** liable to.

passi|f, ~ve /pasif, -v/ *a.* passive. *—n.m.* (*comm.*) liabilities. **~vité** *n.f.* passiveness.

passion /pasjɔ̃/ *n.f.* passion.

passionn|er /pasjɔne/ *v.t.* fascinate. **se ~er pour,** have a passion for. **~é** *a.* passionate. **être ~é de,** have a passion for. **~ément** *adv.* passionately.

passoire /paswar/ *n.f.* (*à thé*) strainer; (*à légumes*) colander.

pastel /pastɛl/ *n.m.* & *a. invar.* pastel.

pastèque /pastɛk/ *n.f.* water-melon.

pasteur /pastœr/ *n.m.* (*relig.*) minister.

pasteuriser /pastœrize/ *v.t.* pasteurize.

pastiche /pastiʃ/ *n.m.* pastiche.

pastille /pastij/ *n.f.* (*bonbon*) pastille, lozenge.

pastis /pastis/ *n.m.* aniseed liqueur.

pastor|al (*m. pl.* **~aux**) /pastɔral, -o/ *a.* pastoral.

patate /patat/ *n.f.* (*fam.*) potato.

patauger /patoʒe/ *v.i.* splash about.

pâte /pɑt/ *n.f.* paste; (*farine*) dough; (*à tarte*) pastry; (*à frire*) batter. **~s (alimentaires),** pasta. **~ à modeler,** Plasticine (P.). **~ dentifrice,** toothpaste.

pâté /pɑte/ *n.m.* (*culin.*) pâté; (*d'encre*) ink-blot. **~ de maisons,**

block of houses. **~ en croûte,** meat pie.

pâtée /pate/ *n.f.* feed, mash.

patelin /patlɛ̃/ *n.m.* (*fam.*) village.

patent, ~e[1] /patɑ̃, -t/ *a.* patent.

patent|e[2] /patɑ̃t/ *n.f.* trade licence. **~é** *a.* licensed.

patère /patɛr/ *n.f.* (coat) peg.

patern|el, ~elle /patɛrnɛl/ *a.* paternal. **~ité** *n.f.* paternity.

pâteu|x, ~se /pɑtø, -z/ *a.* pasty; (*langue*) coated.

pathétique /patetik/ *a.* moving. —*n.m.* pathos.

patholog|ie /patɔlɔʒi/ *n.f.* pathology. **~ique** *a.* pathological.

pat|ient, ~iente /pasjɑ̃, -t/ *a.* & *n.m., f.* patient. **~iemment** /-jamɑ̃/ *adv.* patiently. **~ience** *n.f.* patience.

patienter /pasjɑ̃te/ *v.i.* wait.

patin /patɛ̃/ *n.m.* skate. **~ à roulettes,** roller-skate.

patin|er /patine/ *v.i.* skate; (*voiture*) spin. **~age** *n.m.* skating. **~eur, ~euse** *n.m., f.* skater.

patinette /patinɛt/ *n.f.* scooter.

patinoire /patinwar/ *n.f.* skating-rink.

pâtir /pɑtir/ *v.i.* suffer (**de,** from).

pâtiss|ier, ~ière /pɑtisje, -jɛr/ *n.m., f.* pastry-cook, cake shop owner. **~erie** *n.f.* cake shop; (*gâteau*) pastry; (*art*) cake making.

patois /patwa/ *n.m.* patois.

patraque /patrak/ *a.* (*fam.*) peaky, out of sorts.

patrie /patri/ *n.f.* homeland.

patrimoine /patrimwan/ *n.m.* heritage.

patriot|e /patrijɔt/ *a.* patriotic. —*n.m./f.* patriot. **~ique** *a.* patriotic. **~isme** *n.m.* patriotism.

patron[1], **~ne** /patrɔ̃, -ɔn/ *n.m., f.* employer, boss; (*propriétaire*) owner, boss; (*saint*) patron saint. **~al** (*m. pl.* **~aux**) /-ɔnal, -o/ *a.* employers'. **~at** /-ɔna/ *n.m.* employers.

patron[2] /patrɔ̃/ *n.m.* (*couture*) pattern.

patronage /patrɔnaʒ/ *n.m.* patronage; (*foyer*) youth club.

patronner /patrɔne/ *v.t.* support.

patrouill|e /patruj/ *n.f.* patrol. **~er** *v.i.* patrol.

patte /pat/ *n.f.* leg; (*pied*) foot; (*de chat*) paw; (*main*: *fam.*) hand; (*de poche, d'enveloppe*) flap. **~s,** (*favoris*) sideburns.

pâturage /pɑtyraʒ/ *n.m.* pasture.

pâture /pɑtyr/ *n.f.* food.

paume /pom/ *n.f.* (*de main*) palm.

paumé, ~e /pome/ *n.m., f.* (*fam.*) wretch, loser.

paumer /pome/ *v.t.* (*fam.*) lose.

paupière /popjɛr/ *n.f.* eyelid.

pause /poz/ *n.f.* pause; (*halte*) break.

pauvre /povr/ *a.* poor. —*n.m./f.* poor man, poor woman. **~ment** /-əmɑ̃/ *adv.* poorly. **~té** /-əte/ *n.f.* poverty.

pavaner (se) /(sə)pavane/ *v. pr.* strut.

pav|er /pave/ *v.t.* pave; (*chaussée*) cobble. **~é** *n.m.* paving-stone; cobble(-stone).

pavillon[1] /pavijɔ̃/ *n.m.* house; (*de gardien*) lodge.

pavillon[2] /pavijɔ̃/ *n.m.* (*drapeau*) flag.

pavoiser /pavwaze/ *v.t.* deck with flags. —*v.i.* put out the flags.

pavot /pavo/ *n.m.* poppy.

payant, ~e /pɛjɑ̃, -t/ *a.* (*billet*) for which a charge is made; (*spectateur*) (fee-)paying; (*rentable*) profitable.

payer /peje/ *v.t./i.* pay; (*service, travail, etc.*) pay for; (*acheter*) buy (**à,** for). **se ~** *v. pr.* (*s'acheter*) buy o.s. **faire ~ à qn.,** (*cent francs etc.*) charge s.o. (**pour,** for). **se ~ la tête de,** make fun of.

pays /pei/ *n.m.* country; (*région*)

region; (*village*) village. **du ~,** local. **les P~-Bas,** the Netherlands. **le ~ de Galles,** Wales.

paysage /peizaʒ/ *n.m.* landscape.

paysan, ~ne /peizɑ̃, -an/ *n.m., f.* farmer, country person; (*péj.*) peasant. —*a.* (*agricole*) farming; (*rural*) country.

PCV (en) /(ɑ̃)peseve/ *adv.* **appeler** *ou* **téléphoner en ~,** reverse the charges; (*Amer.*) call collect.

PDG *abrév. voir* **président directeur général.**

péage /peaʒ/ *n.m.* toll; (*lieu*) tollgate.

peau (*pl.* **~x**) /po/ *n.f.* skin; (*cuir*) hide. **~ de chamois,** chamois (-leather). **~ de mouton,** sheepskin. **P~-Rouge** (*pl.* **P~x-Rouges**) *n.m./f.* Red Indian.

pêche[1] /pɛʃ/ *n.f.* peach.

pêche[2] /pɛʃ/ *n.f.* (*activité*) fishing; (*poissons*) catch. **~ à la ligne,** angling.

péché /peʃe/ *n.m.* sin.

péch|er /peʃe/ *v.i.* sin. **~er par timidité**/*etc.*, be too timid/*etc.* **~eur, ~eresse** *n.m., f.* sinner.

pêch|er /peʃe/ *v.t.* (*poisson*) catch; (*dénicher: fam.*) dig up. —*v.i.* fish. **~eur** *n.m.* fisherman; (*à la ligne*) angler.

pécule /pekyl/ *n.m.* (*économies*) savings.

pécuniaire /pekynjɛr/ *a.* financial.

pédago|gie /pedagɔʒi/ *n.f.* education. **~gique** *a.* educational. **~gue** *n.m./f.* teacher.

pédal|e /pedal/ *n.f.* pedal. **~er** *v.i.* pedal.

pédalo /pedalo/ *n.m.* pedal boat.

pédant, ~e /pedɑ̃, -t/ *a.* pedantic.

pédéraste /pederast/ *n.m.* homosexual.

pédiatre /pedjatr/ *n.m./f.* paediatrician.

pédicure /pedikyr/ *n.m./f.* chiropodist.

pedigree /pedigri/ *n.m.* pedigree.

pègre /pɛgr/ *n.f.* underworld.

peign|e /pɛɲ/ *n.m.* comb. **~er** /peɲe/ *v.t.* comb; (*personne*) comb the hair of. **se ~er** *v. pr.* comb one's hair.

peignoir /pɛɲwar/ *n.m.* dressing-gown.

peindre† /pɛ̃dr/ *v.t.* paint.

peine /pɛn/ *n.f.* sadness, sorrow; (*effort, difficulté*) trouble; (*punition*) punishment; (*jurid.*) sentence. **avoir de la ~,** feel sad. **ce n'est pas la ~ de faire,** it is not worth (while) doing.

peine (à) /(a)pɛn/ *adv.* hardly.

peiner /pene/ *v.i.* struggle. —*v.t.* sadden.

peintre /pɛ̃tr/ *n.m.* painter. **~ en bâtiment,** house painter.

peinture /pɛ̃tyr/ *n.f.* painting; (*matière*) paint. **~ à l'huile,** oil-painting.

péjorati|f, ~ve /peʒɔratif, -v/ *a.* pejorative.

pelage /pəlaʒ/ *n.m.* coat, fur.

pêle-mêle /pɛlmɛl/ *adv.* in confusion.

peler /pəle/ *v.t./i.* peel.

pèlerin /pɛlrɛ̃/ *n.m.* pilgrim. **~age** /-inaʒ/ *n.m.* pilgrimage.

pèlerine /pɛlrin/ *n.f.* cape.

pélican /pelikɑ̃/ *n.m.* pelican.

pelle /pɛl/ *n.f.* shovel; (*d'enfant*) spade. **~tée** *n.f.* shovelful.

pellicule /pelikyl/ *n.f.* film. **~s,** (*méd.*) dandruff.

pelote /pəlɔt/ *n.f.* ball; (*d'épingles*) pincushion.

peloton /plɔtɔ̃/ *n.m.* troop, squad; (*sport*) pack. **~ d'exécution,** firing-squad.

pelotonner (se) /(sə)plɔtɔne/ *v. pr.* curl up.

pelouse /pluz/ *n.f.* lawn.

peluche /plyʃ/ *n.f.* (*tissu*) plush. **en ~,** (*lapin, chien*) fluffy, furry.

pelure /plyr/ *n.f.* peeling.

pén|al (*m. pl.* **~aux**) /penal, -o/

a. penal. **~aliser** *v.t.* penalize. **~alité** *n.f.* penalty.
penalt|y (*pl.* **~ies**) /penalti/ *n.m.* penalty (kick).
penaud, ~e /pəno, -d/ *a.* sheepish.
penchant /pɑ̃ʃɑ̃/ *n.m.* inclination; (*goût*) liking (**pour,** for).
pench|er /pɑ̃ʃe/ *v.t.* tilt. —*v.i.* lean (over), tilt. **se ~er** *v. pr.* lean (forward). **~er pour,** favour. **se ~er sur,** (*problème etc.*) examine.
pendaison /pɑ̃dɛzɔ̃/ *n.f.* hanging.
pendant[1] /pɑ̃dɑ̃/ *prép.* (*au cours de*) during; (*durée*) for. **~ que,** while.
pendant[2], **~e** /pɑ̃dɑ̃, -t/ *a.* hanging; (*question etc.*) pending. —*n.m.* (*contrepartie*) matching piece (**de,** to). **~ d'oreille,** drop earring.
pendentif /pɑ̃dɑ̃tif/ *n.m.* pendant.
penderie /pɑ̃dri/ *n.f.* wardrobe.
pend|re /pɑ̃dr/ *v.t./i.* hang. **se ~re** *v. pr.* hang (**à,** from); (*se tuer*) hang o.s. **~re la crémaillère,** have a house-warming. **~u, ~ue** *a.* hanging (**à,** from); *n.m., f.* hanged man, hanged woman.
pendul|e /pɑ̃dyl/ *n.f.* clock. —*n.m.* pendulum. **~ette** *n.f.* (travelling) clock.
pénétr|er /penetre/ *v.i.* **~er (dans),** enter. —*v.t.* penetrate. **se ~er de,** become convinced of. **~ant, ~ante** *a.* penetrating.
pénible /penibl/ *a.* difficult; (*douloureux*) painful; (*fatigant*) tiresome. **~ment** /-əmɑ̃/ *adv.* with difficulty; (*cruellement*) painfully.
péniche /peniʃ/ *n.f.* barge.
pénicilline /penisilin/ *n.f.* penicillin.
péninsule /penɛ̃syl/ *n.f.* peninsula.
pénis /penis/ *n.m.* penis.
pénitence /penitɑ̃s/ *n.f.* (*peine*) penance; (*regret*) penitence; (*fig.*) punishment. **faire ~,** repent.
péniten|cier /penitɑ̃sje/ *n.m.* penitentiary. **~tiaire** /-sjɛr/ *a.* prison.
pénombre /penɔ̃br/ *n.f.* half-light.
pensée[1] /pɑ̃se/ *n.f.* thought.
pensée[2] /pɑ̃se/ *n.f.* (*fleur*) pansy.
pens|er /pɑ̃se/ *v.t./i.* think. **~er à,** (*réfléchir à*) think about; (*se souvenir de, prévoir*) think of. **~er faire,** think of doing. **~eur** *n.m.* thinker.
pensi|f, ~ve /pɑ̃sif, -v/ *a.* pensive.
pension /pɑ̃sjɔ̃/ *n.f.* (*scol.*) boarding-school; (*repas, somme*) board; (*allocation*) pension. **~ (de famille),** guest-house. **~ alimentaire,** (*jurid.*) alimony. **~naire** /-jɔnɛr/ *n.m./f.* boarder; (*d'hôtel*) guest. **~nat** /-jɔna/ *n.m.* boarding-school.
pente /pɑ̃t/ *n.f.* slope. **en ~,** sloping.
Pentecôte /pɑ̃tkot/ *n.f.* Whitsun.
pénurie /penyri/ *n.f.* shortage.
pépé /pepe/ *n.m.* (*fam.*) grandad.
pépier /pepje/ *v.i.* chirp.
pépin /pepɛ̃/ *n.m.* (*graine*) pip; (*ennui*: *fam.*) hitch; (*parapluie*: *fam.*) brolly.
pépinière /pepinjɛr/ *n.f.* (tree) nursery.
perçant, ~e /pɛrsɑ̃, -t/ *a.* (*froid*) piercing; (*yeux*) keen.
percée /pɛrse/ *n.f.* opening; (*attaque*) breakthrough.
perce-neige /pɛrsənɛʒ/ *n.m./f. invar.* snowdrop.
percepteur /pɛrsɛptœr/ *n.m.* tax-collector.
perceptible /pɛrsɛptibl/ *a.* perceptible.
perception /pɛrsɛpsjɔ̃/ *n.f.* perception; (*d'impôts*) collection.
percer /pɛrse/ *v.t.* pierce; (*avec perceuse*) drill; (*mystère*) penetrate; (*dent*) cut. —*v.i.* break through.
perceuse /pɛrsøz/ *n.f.* drill.

percevoir† /pɛrsəvwar/ *v.t.* perceive; (*impôt*) collect.
perche /pɛrʃ/ *n.f.* (*bâton*) pole.
perch|er /pɛrʃe/ *v.t.*, **se ~er** *v. pr.* perch. **~oir** *n.m.* perch.
percussion /pɛrkysjɔ̃/ *n.f.* percussion.
percuter /pɛrkyte/ *v.t.* strike; (*véhicule*) crash into.
perd|re /pɛrdr/ *v.t./i.* lose; (*gaspiller*) waste; (*ruiner*) ruin. **se ~re** *v. pr.* get lost; (*rester inutilisé*) go to waste. **~ant, ~ante** *a.* losing; *n.m., f.* loser. **~u** *a.* (*endroit*) isolated; (*moments*) spare; (*malade*) finished.
perdreau (*pl.* **~x**) /pɛrdro/ *n.m.* (young) partridge.
perdrix /pɛrdri/ *n.f.* partridge.
père /pɛr/ *n.m.* father.
péremptoire /perɑ̃ptwar/ *a.* peremptory.
perfection /pɛrfɛksjɔ̃/ *n.f.* perfection.
perfectionn|er /pɛrfɛksjɔne/ *v.t.* improve. **se ~er en anglais**/*etc.*, improve one's English/*etc.* **~é** *a.* sophisticated. **~ement** *n.m.* improvement.
perfectionniste /pɛrfɛksjɔnist/ *n.m./f.* perfectionist.
perfid|e /pɛrfid/ *a.* perfidious, treacherous. **~ie** *n.f.* perfidy.
perfor|er /pɛrfɔre/ *v.t.* perforate; (*billet, bande*) punch. **~ateur** *n.m.* (*appareil*) punch. **~ation** *n.f.* perforation; (*trou*) hole.
performan|ce /pɛrfɔrmɑ̃s/ *n.f.* performance. **~t, ~te** *a.* high-performance, successful.
péricliter /periklite/ *v.i.* decline, be in rapid decline.
péril /peril/ *n.m.* peril.
périlleu|x, ~se /perijø, -z/ *a.* perilous.
périmé /perime/ *a.* expired; (*désuet*) outdated.
périmètre /perimɛtr/ *n.m.* perimeter.
périod|e /perjɔd/ *n.f.* period. **~ique** *a.* periodic(al); *n.m.* (*journal*) periodical.
péripétie /peripesi/ *n.f.* (unexpected) event, adventure.
périphér|ie /periferi/ *n.f.* periphery; (*banlieue*) outskirts. **~ique** *a.* peripheral; *n.m.* (**boulevard**) **~**, ring road.
périple /peripl/ *n.m.* journey.
pér|ir /perir/ *v.i.* perish, die. **~issable** *a.* perishable.
périscope /periskɔp/ *n.m.* periscope.
perle /pɛrl/ *n.f.* (*bijou*) pearl; (*boule*) bead.
permanence /pɛrmanɑ̃s/ *n.f.* permanence; (*bureau*) duty office; (*scol.*) study room. **de ~**, on duty. **en ~**, permanently.
permanent, ~e /pɛrmanɑ̃, -t/ *a.* permanent; (*spectacle*) continuous; (*comité*) standing. —*n.f.* (*coiffure*) perm.
perméable /pɛrmeabl/ *a.* permeable; (*personne*) susceptible (**à**, to).
permettre† /pɛrmɛtr/ *v.t.* allow, permit. **~ à qn. de,** allow *ou* permit s.o. to. **se ~ de,** take the liberty to.
permis, ~e /permi, -z/ *a.* allowed. —*n.m.* licence, permit. **~ de conduire,** driving-licence.
permission /pɛrmisjɔ̃/ *n.f.* permission; (*mil.*) leave.
permut|er /pɛrmyte/ *v.t.* change round. **~ation** *n.f.* permutation.
pernicieu|x, ~se /pɛrnisjø, -z/ *a.* pernicious.
Pérou /peru/ *n.m.* Peru.
perpendiculaire /pɛrpɑ̃dikylɛr/ *a.* & *n.f.* perpendicular.
perpétrer /pɛrpetre/ *v.t.* perpetrate.
perpétuel, ~le /pɛrpetɥɛl/ *a.* perpetual.
perpétuer /pɛrpetɥe/ *v.t.* perpetuate.

perpétuité (à) /(a)pɛrpetɥite/ *adv.* for life.

perplex|e /pɛrplɛks/ *a.* perplexed. **~ité** *n.f.* perplexity.

perquisition /pɛrkizisjɔ̃/ *n.f.* (police) search. **~ner** /-jɔne/ *v.t./i.* search.

perron /pɛrɔ̃/ *n.m.* (front) steps.

perroquet /pɛrɔkɛ/ *n.m.* parrot.

perruche /peryʃ/ *n.f.* budgerigar.

perruque /peryk/ *n.f.* wig.

persan, ~e /pɛrsɑ̃, -an/ *a.* & *n.m.* (*lang.*) Persian.

persécut|er /pɛrsekyte/ *v.t.* persecute. **~ion** /-ysjɔ̃/ *n.f.* persecution.

persévér|er /pɛrsevere/ *v.i.* persevere. **~ance** *n.f.* perseverance.

persienne /pɛrsjɛn/ *n.f.* (outside) shutter.

persil /pɛrsi/ *n.m.* parsley.

persistan|t, ~te /pɛrsistɑ̃, -t/ *a.* persistent; (*feuillage*) evergreen. **~ce** *n.f.* persistence.

persister /pɛrsiste/ *v.i.* persist **(à faire,** in doing).

personnage /pɛrsɔnaʒ/ *n.m.* character; (*important*) personality.

personnalité /pɛrsɔnalite/ *n.f.* personality.

personne /pɛrsɔn/ *n.f.* person. **~s,** people. —*pron.* (*quelqu'un*) anybody. **(ne) ~,** nobody.

personnel, ~le /pɛrsɔnɛl/ *a.* personal; (*égoïste*) selfish. —*n.m.* staff. **~lement** *adv.* personally.

personnifier /pɛrsɔnifje/ *v.t.* personify.

perspective /pɛrspɛktiv/ *n.f.* (*art*) perspective; (*vue*) view; (*possibilité*) prospect; (*point de vue*) viewpoint, perspective.

perspicac|e /pɛrspikas/ *a.* shrewd. **~ité** *n.f.* shrewdness.

persua|der /pɛrsɥade/ *v.t.* persuade **(de faire,** to do). **~sion** /-ɥazjɔ̃/ *n.f.* persuasion.

persuasi|f, ~ve /pɛrsɥazif, -v/ *a.* persuasive.

perte /pɛrt/ *n.f.* loss; (*ruine*) ruin. **à ~ de vue,** as far as the eye can see. **~ de,** (*temps, argent*) waste of.

pertinen|t, ~te /pɛrtinɑ̃, -t/ *a.* pertinent; (*esprit*) judicious. **~ce** *n.f.* pertinence.

perturb|er /pɛrtyrbe/ *v.t.* disrupt; (*personne*) perturb. **~ateur, ~atrice** *a.* disruptive; *n.m., f.* disruptive element. **~ation** *n.f.* disruption.

pervenche /pɛrvɑ̃ʃ/ *n.f.* periwinkle.

pervers, ~e /pɛrvɛr, -s/ *a.* perverse; (*dépravé*) perverted. **~ion** /-sjɔ̃/ *n.f.* perversion.

pervert|ir /pɛrvɛrtir/ *v.t.* pervert. **~i, ~ie** *n.m., f.* pervert.

pes|ant, ~ante /pəzɑ̃, -t/ *a.* heavy. **~amment** *adv.* heavily. **~anteur** *n.f.* heaviness. **la ~anteur,** (*force*) gravity.

pèse-personne /pɛzpɛrsɔn/ *n.m.* (bathroom) scales.

pes|er /pəze/ *v.t./i.* weigh. **~er sur,** bear upon. **~ée** *n.f.* weighing; (*effort*) pressure.

peseta /pezeta/ *n.f.* peseta.

pessimis|te /pesimist/ *a.* pessimistic. —*n.m.* pessimist. **~me** *n.m.* pessimism.

peste /pɛst/ *n.f.* plague; (*personne*) pest.

pester /pɛste/ *v.i.* **~ (contre),** curse.

pestilentiel, ~le /pɛstilɑ̃sjɛl/ *a.* fetid, stinking.

pétale /petal/ *n.m.* petal.

pétanque /petɑ̃k/ *n.f.* bowls.

pétarader /petarade/ *v.i.* backfire.

pétard /petar/ *n.m.* banger.

péter /pete/ *v.i.* (*fam.*) go bang; (*casser: fam.*) snap.

pétill|er /petije/ *v.i.* (*feu*) crackle; (*eau, yeux*) sparkle. **~ant, ~ante** *a.* (*gazeux*) fizzy.

petit, ~e /pti, -t/ *a.* small; (*avec nuance affective*) little; (*jeune*) young, small; (*faible*) slight; (*mesquin*) petty. —*n.m., f.* little child; (*scol.*) junior. **~s,** (*de chat*) kittens; (*de chien*) pups. **en ~,** in miniature. **~ ami,** boy-friend. **~e amie,** girl-friend. **~ à petit,** little by little. **~es annonces,** small ads. **~e cuiller,** teaspoon. **~ déjeuner,** breakfast. **~-enfant** (*pl.* **~s-enfants**) *n.m.* grandchild. **~e-fille** (*pl.* **~es-filles**) *n.f.* granddaughter. **~-fils** (*pl.* **~s-fils**) *n.m.* grandson. **~ pain,** roll. **~-pois** (*pl.* **~s-pois**) *n.m.* garden pea. **~e vérole,** smallpox.

petitesse /ptitɛs/ *n.f.* smallness; (*péj.*) meanness.

pétition /petisjɔ̃/ *n.f.* petition.

pétrifier /petrifje/ *v.t.* petrify.

pétrin /petrɛ̃/ *n.m.* (*situation: fam.*) fix.

pétrir /petrir/ *v.t.* knead.

pétrol|e /petrɔl/ *n.m.* (*brut*) oil; (*pour lampe etc.*) paraffin. **~ier, ~ière** *a.* oil; *n.m.* (*navire*) oil-tanker.

pétulant, ~e /petylɑ̃, -t/ *a.* exuberant, full of high spirits.

peu /pø/ *adv.* **~ (de),** (*quantité*) little, not much; (*nombre*) few, not many. **~ intéressant**/*etc.*, not very interesting/*etc.* —*pron.* few. —*n.m.* little. **un ~ (de),** a little. **à ~ près,** more or less. **de ~,** only just. **~ à peu,** gradually. **~ après/avant,** shortly after/before. **~ de chose,** not much. **~ nombreux,** few. **~ souvent,** seldom.

peuplade /pœplad/ *n.f.* tribe.

peuple /pœpl/ *n.m.* people.

peupler /pœple/ *v.t.* populate.

peuplier /pøplije/ *n.m.* poplar.

peur /pœr/ *n.f.* fear. **avoir ~,** be afraid (**de,** of). **de ~ de,** for fear of. **faire ~ à,** frighten. **~eux, ~euse** *a.* fearful, timid.

peut /pø/ *voir* **pouvoir**[1].

peut-être /pøtɛtr/ *adv.* perhaps, maybe. **~ que,** perhaps, maybe.

peux /pø/ *voir* **pouvoir**[1].

phallique /falik/ *a.* phallic.

phantasme /fɑ̃tasm/ *n.m.* fantasy.

phare /far/ *n.m.* (*tour*) lighthouse; (*de véhicule*) headlight.

pharmaceutique /farmasøtik/ *a.* pharmaceutical.

pharmac|ie /farmasi/ *n.f.* (*magasin*) chemist's (shop); (*Amer.*) pharmacy; (*science*) pharmacy. **~ien, ~ienne** *n.m., f.* chemist, pharmacist.

pharyngite /farɛ̃ʒit/ *n.f.* pharyngitis.

phase /fɑz/ *n.f.* phase.

phénomène /fenɔmɛn/ *n.m.* phenomenon; (*original: fam.*) eccentric.

philanthrop|e /filɑ̃trɔp/ *n.m./f.* philanthropist. **~ique** *a.* philanthropic.

philatél|ie /filateli/ *n.f.* philately. **~iste** *n.m./f.* philatelist.

philharmonique /filarmɔnik/ *a.* philharmonic.

Philippines /filipin/ *n.f. pl.* **les ~,** the Philippines.

philosoph|e /filɔzɔf/ *n.m./f.* philosopher. —*a.* philosophical. **~ie** *n.f.* philosophy. **~ique** *a.* philosophical.

phobie /fɔbi/ *n.f.* phobia.

phonétique /fɔnetik/ *a.* phonetic.

phonographe /fɔnɔgraf/ *n.m.* gramophone; (*Amer.*) phonograph.

phoque /fɔk/ *n.m.* (*animal*) seal.

phosphate /fɔsfat/ *n.m.* phosphate.

phosphore /fɔsfɔr/ *n.m.* phosphorus.

photo /fɔto/ *n.f.* photo; (*art*) photography.

photocop|ie /fɔtɔkɔpi/ *n.f.* photocopy. **~ier** *v.t.* photocopy.

photogénique /fɔtɔʒenik/ *a.* photogenic.

photograph|e /fɔtɔgraf/ *n.m./f.* photographer. **~ie** *n.f.* photograph; (*art*) photography. **~ier** *v.t.* photograph. **~ique** *a.* photographic.
phrase /frɑz/ *n.f.* sentence.
physicien, ~ne /fizisjɛ̃, -jɛn/ *n.m., f.* physicist.
physiologie /fizjɔlɔʒi/ *n.f.* physiology.
physionomie /fizjɔnɔmi/ *n.f.* face.
physique[1] /fizik/ *a.* physical. —*n.m.* physique. **au ~,** physically. **~ment** *adv.* physically.
physique[2] /fizik/ *n.f.* physics.
piailler /pjɑje/ *v.i.* squeal, squawk.
pian|o /pjano/ *n.m.* piano. **~iste** *n.m./f.* pianist.
pic /pik/ *n.m.* (*outil*) pickaxe; (*sommet*) peak; (*oiseau*) woodpecker. **à ~,** (*verticalement*) sheer; (*couler*) straight to the bottom.
pichenette /piʃnɛt/ *n.f.* flick.
pichet /piʃɛ/ *n.m.* pitcher.
pickpocket /pikpɔkɛt/ *n.m.* pickpocket.
pick-up /pikœp/ *n.m. invar.* record-player.
picorer /pikɔre/ *v.t./i.* peck.
picot|er /pikɔte/ *v.t.* prick; (*yeux*) make smart. **~ement** *n.m.* pricking; smarting.
pie /pi/ *n.f.* magpie.
pièce /pjɛs/ *n.f.* piece; (*chambre*) room; (*pour raccommoder*) patch; (*écrit*) document. **~ (de monnaie),** coin. **~ (de théâtre),** play. **dix francs**/*etc.* **(la) ~,** ten francs/*etc.* each. **~ de rechange,** spare part. **~ détachée,** part. **~ d'identité,** identity paper.
pied /pje/ *n.m.* foot; (*de meuble*) leg; (*de lampe*) base; (*de salade*) plant. **à ~,** on foot. **au ~ de la lettre,** literally. **avoir ~,** have a footing. **comme un ~,** (*fam.*) terribly. **mettre sur ~,** set up. **~ bot,** club-foot. **un ~ d'égalité,** an equal footing. **~-noir** (*pl.* **~s-noirs**) *n.m.* Algerian Frenchman.
piédest|al (*pl.* **~aux**) /pjedɛstal, -o/ *n.m.* pedestal.
piège /pjɛʒ/ *n.m.* trap.
piég|er /pjeʒe/ *v.t.* trap; (*avec explosifs*) booby-trap. **lettre/voiture ~ée,** letter-/car-bomb.
pierr|e /pjɛr/ *n.f.* stone. **~e d'achoppement,** stumbling-block. **~e de touche,** touchstone. **~e tombale,** tombstone. **~eux, ~euse** *a.* stony.
piété /pjete/ *n.f.* piety.
piétiner /pjetine/ *v.i.* stamp one's feet; (*ne pas avancer*: *fig.*) mark time. —*v.t.* trample (on).
piéton /pjetɔ̃/ *n.m.* pedestrian. **~nier, ~nière** /-ɔnje, -jɛr/ *a.* pedestrian.
piètre /pjɛtr/ *a.* wretched.
pieu (*pl.* **~x**) /pjø/ *n.m.* post, stake.
pieuvre /pjœvr/ *n.f.* octopus.
pieu|x, ~se /pjø, -z/ *a.* pious.
pif /pif/ *n.m.* (*fam.*) nose.
pigeon /piʒɔ̃/ *n.m.* pigeon.
piger /piʒe/ *v.t./i.* (*fam.*) understand.
pigment /pigmɑ̃/ *n.m.* pigment.
pignon /piɲɔ̃/ *n.m.* (*de maison*) gable.
pile /pil/ *n.f.* (*tas, pilier*) pile; (*électr.*) battery; (*atomique*) pile. —*adv.* (*s'arrêter*: *fam.*) dead. **à dix heures ~,** (*fam.*) at ten on the dot. **~ ou face?,** heads or tails?
piler /pile/ *v.t.* pound.
pilier /pilje/ *n.m.* pillar.
pill|er /pije/ *v.t.* loot. **~age** *n.m.* looting. **~ard, ~arde** *n.m., f.* looter.
pilonner /pilɔne/ *v.t.* pound.
pilori /pilɔri/ *n.m.* pillory.
pilot|e /pilɔt/ *n.m.* pilot; (*auto.*) driver. —*a.* pilot. **~er** *v.t.* (*aviat., naut.*) pilot; (*auto.*) drive; (*fig.*) guide.
pilule /pilyl/ *n.f.* pill.
piment /pimɑ̃/ *n.m.* pepper,

pimento; (*fig.*) spice. **~é** /-te/ *a.* spicy.

pimpant, ~e /pɛ̃pɑ̃, -t/ *a.* spruce.

pin /pɛ̃/ *n.m.* pine.

pinard /pinar/ *n.m.* (*vin*: *fam.*) plonk, cheap wine.

pince /pɛ̃s/ *n.f.* (*outil*) pliers; (*levier*) crowbar; (*de crabe*) pincer; (*à sucre*) tongs. **~ (à épiler)**, tweezers. **~ (à linge)**, (clothes-) peg.

pinceau (*pl.* **~x**) /pɛ̃so/ *n.m.* paint-brush.

pinc|er /pɛ̃se/ *v.t.* pinch; (*arrêter*: *fam.*) pinch. **se ~er le doigt**, catch one's finger. **~é** *a.* (*ton, air*) stiff. **~ée** *n.f.* pinch (**de**, of).

pincettes /pɛ̃sɛt/ *n.f. pl.* (fire) tongs.

pinède /pinɛd/ *n.f.* pine forest.

pingouin /pɛ̃gwɛ̃/ *n.m.* penguin; (*au sens strict*) auk.

ping-pong /piŋpɔ̃g/ *n.m.* table tennis, ping-pong.

pingre /pɛ̃gr/ *a.* miserly.

pinson /pɛ̃sɔ̃/ *n.m.* chaffinch.

pintade /pɛ̃tad/ *n.f.* guinea-fowl.

pioch|e /pjɔʃ/ *n.f.* pick(axe). **~er** *v.t./i.* dig; (*étudier*: *fam.*) study hard, slog away (at).

pion /pjɔ̃/ *n.m.* (*de jeu*) piece; (*échecs*) pawn; (*scol.*, *péj.*) supervisor.

pionnier /pjɔnje/ *n.m.* pioneer.

pipe /pip/ *n.f.* pipe. **fumer la ~**, smoke a pipe.

pipe-line /piplin/ *n.m.* pipeline.

piquant, ~e /pikɑ̃, -t/ *a.* (*barbe etc.*) prickly; (*goût*) pungent; (*détail etc.*) spicy. —*n.m.* prickle; (*de hérisson*) spine, prickle; (*fig.*) piquancy.

pique[1] /pik/ *n.f.* (*arme*) pike.

pique[2] /pik/ *n.m.* (*cartes*) spades.

piqué /pike/ *a.* (*couvre-lit*) quilted; (*vin*) sour; (*visage*) pitted.

pique-niqu|e /piknik/ *n.m.* picnic. **~er** *v.i.* picnic.

piquer /pike/ *v.t.* prick; (*langue*) burn, sting; (*abeille etc.*) sting; (*serpent etc.*) bite; (*enfoncer*) stick; (*coudre*) (machine-)stitch; (*curiosité*) excite; (*crise*) have; (*voler*: *fam.*) pinch. —*v.i.* (*avion*) dive; (*goût*) be hot. **~ une tête**, plunge headlong. **se ~ de**, pride o.s. on.

piquet /pikɛ/ *n.m.* stake; (*de tente*) peg. **au ~**, (*scol.*) in the corner. **~ de grève**, (strike) picket.

piqueter /pikte/ *v.t.* dot.

piqûre /pikyr/ *n.f.* prick; (*d'abeille etc.*) sting; (*de serpent etc.*) bite; (*point*) stitch; (*méd.*) injection, shot, jab; (*trou*) hole.

pirate /pirat/ *n.m.* pirate. **~ de l'air**, hijacker. **~rie** *n.f.* piracy.

pire /pir/ *a.* worse (**que**, than). **le ~ livre**/*etc.*, the worst book/*etc.* —*n.m.* **le ~**, the worst (thing). **au ~**, at worst.

pirogue /pirɔg/ *n.f.* canoe, dug-out.

pirouette /pirwɛt/ *n.f.* pirouette.

pis[1] /pi/ *n.m* (*de vache*) udder.

pis[2] /pi/ *a. invar.* & *adv.* worse. —*n.m.* **le ~**, the worst.

pis-aller /pizale/ *n.m. invar.* stop-gap, temporary expedient.

piscine /pisin/ *n.f.* swimming-pool.

pissenlit /pisɑ̃li/ *n.m.* dandelion.

pistache /pistaʃ/ *n.f.* pistachio.

piste /pist/ *n.f.* track; (*de personne, d'animal*) track, trail; (*aviat.*) runway; (*de cirque*) ring; (*de patinage*) rink; (*de danse*) floor; (*sport*) race-track. **~ cyclable**, cycle-track; (*Amer.*) bicycle path.

pistolet /pistɔlɛ/ *n.m.* gun, pistol; (*de peintre*) spray-gun.

piston /pistɔ̃/ *n.m.* (*techn.*) piston.

pistonner /pistɔne/ *v.t.* (*fam.*) recommend, pull strings for.

piteu|x, ~se /pitø, -z/ *a.* pitiful.

pitié /pitje/ *n.f.* pity. **il me fait ~, j'ai ~ de lui**, I pity him.

piton /pitɔ̃/ *n.m.* (*à crochet*) hook; (*sommet pointu*) peak.

pitoyable /pitwajabl/ *a.* pitiful.

pitre /pitr/ *n.m.* clown.

pittoresque /pitɔrɛsk/ *a.* picturesque.

pivot /pivo/ *n.m.* pivot. **~er** /-ɔte/ *v.i.* revolve; (*personne*) swing round.

pizza /pidza/ *n.f.* pizza.

placage /plakaʒ/ *n.m.* (*en bois*) veneer; (*sur un mur*) facing.

placard /plakar/ *n.m.* cupboard; (*affiche*) poster. **~er** /-de/ *v.t.* (*affiche*) post up; (*mur*) cover with posters.

place /plas/ *n.f.* place; (*espace libre*) room, space; (*siège*) seat, place; (*prix d'un trajet*) fare; (*esplanade*) square; (*emploi*) position; (*de parking*) space. **à la ~ de,** instead of. **en ~, à sa ~,** in its place. **faire ~ à,** give way to.

plac|er /plase/ *v.t.* place; (*invité, spectateur*) seat; (*argent*) invest. **se ~er** *v. pr.* (*personne*) take up a position; (*troisième etc.: sport*) come (in). **~é** *a.* (*sport*) placed. **bien ~é pour,** in a position to. **~ement** *n.m.* (*d'argent*) investment.

placide /plasid/ *a.* placid.

plafond /plafɔ̃/ *n.m.* ceiling.

plage /plaʒ/ *n.f.* beach; (*station*) (seaside) resort; (*aire*) area.

plaid /plɛd/ *n.m.* travelling-rug.

plaider /plede/ *v.t./i.* plead.

plaid|oirie /plɛdwari/ *n.f.* (defence) speech. **~oyer** *n.m.* plea.

plaie /plɛ/ *n.f.* wound; (*personne: fam.*) nuisance.

plaignant, ~e /plɛɲɑ̃, -t/ *n.m., f.* plaintiff.

plaindre† /plɛ̃dr/ *v.t.* pity. **se ~** *v. pr.* complain (**de,** about). **se ~ de,** (*souffrir de*) complain of.

plaine /plɛn/ *n.f.* plain.

plaint|e /plɛ̃t/ *n.f.* complaint; (*gémissement*) groan. **~if, ~ive** *a.* plaintive.

plaire† /plɛr/ *v.i.* **~ à,** please. **ça lui plaît,** he likes it. **elle lui plaît,** he likes her, she pleases him. **se ~** *v. pr.* (*à Londres etc.*) like *ou* enjoy it. **se ~ à faire,** like *ou* enjoy doing.

plaisance /plɛzɑ̃s/ *n.f.* **la (navigation de) ~,** yachting.

plaisant, ~e /plɛzɑ̃, -t/ *a.* pleasant; (*drôle*) amusing.

plaisant|er /plɛzɑ̃te/ *v.i.* joke. **~erie** *n.f.* joke. **~in** *n.m.* joker.

plaisir /plezir/ *n.m.* pleasure. **faire ~ à,** please.

plan¹ /plɑ̃/ *n.m.* plan; (*de ville*) map; (*surface, niveau*) plane. **~ d'eau,** expanse of water. **premier ~,** foreground. **dernier ~,** background.

plan², ~e /plɑ̃, plan/ *a.* flat.

planche /plɑ̃ʃ/ *n.f.* board, plank; (*gravure*) plate; (*de potager*) bed. **~ à repasser,** ironing-board.

plancher /plɑ̃ʃe/ *n.m.* floor.

plan|er /plane/ *v.i.* glide. **~er sur,** (*mystère, danger*) hang over. **~eur** *n.m.* (*avion*) glider.

planète /planɛt/ *n.f.* planet.

planif|ier /planifje/ *v.t.* plan. **~ication** *n.f.* planning.

planqu|e /plɑ̃k/ *n.f.* (*fam.*) hideout; (*emploi: fam.*) cushy job. **~er** *v.t.,* **se ~er** *v. pr.* hide.

plant /plɑ̃/ *n.m.* seedling; (*de légumes*) bed.

plante /plɑ̃t/ *n.f.* plant. **~ des pieds,** sole (of the foot).

plant|er /plɑ̃te/ *v.t.* (*plante etc.*) plant; (*enfoncer*) drive in; (*installer*) put up; (*mettre*) put. **rester ~é,** stand still, remain standing. **~ation** *n.f.* planting; (*de tabac etc.*) plantation.

planton /plɑ̃tɔ̃/ *n.m.* (*mil.*) orderly.

plantureu|x, ~se /plɑ̃tyrø, -z/ *a.* abundant.

plaque /plak/ *n.f.* plate; (*de marbre*) slab; (*insigne*) badge; (*commémorative*) plaque. **~ chauffante,** hotplate. **~ minéralogique,** number-plate.

plaqu|er /plake/ *v.t.* (*bois*) veneer;

(*bijou*) plate; (*cheveux*) plaster; (*aplatir*) flatten; (*rugby*) tackle; (*abandonner*: *fam.*) ditch. **~age** *n.m.* (*rugby*) tackle.

plasma /plasma/ *n.m.* plasma.

plastic /plastik/ *n.m.* plastic explosive.

plastique /plastik/ *a.* & *n.m.* plastic. **en ~,** plastic.

plastiquer /plastike/ *v.t.* blow up.

plastron /plastrɔ̃/ *n.m.* shirt-front.

plat[1], **~e** /pla, -t/ *a.* flat. —*n.m.* (*de main*) flat. **à ~** *adv.* (*poser*) flat; *a.* (*batterie, pneu*) flat. **à ~ ventre,** flat on one's face.

plat[2] /pla/ *n.m.* (*culin.*) dish; (*partie de repas*) course.

platane /platan/ *n.m.* plane(-tree).

plateau (*pl.* **~x**) /plato/ *n.m.* tray; (*d'électrophone*) turntable, deck; (*de balance*) pan; (*géog.*) plateau. **~ de fromages,** cheeseboard.

plate-bande (*pl.* **plates-bandes**) /platbɑ̃d/ *n.f.* flower-bed.

plate-forme (*pl.* **plates-formes**) /platfɔrm/ *n.f.* platform.

platine[1] /platin/ *n.m.* platinum.

platine[2] /platin/ *n.f.* (*de tourne-disque*) turntable.

platitude /platityd/ *n.f.* platitude.

platonique /platɔnik/ *a.* platonic.

plâtr|e /plɑtr/ *n.m.* plaster; (*méd.*) (plaster) cast. **~er** *v.t.* plaster; (*membre*) put in plaster.

plausible /plozibl/ *a.* plausible.

plébiscite /plebisit/ *n.m.* plebiscite.

plein, ~e /plɛ̃, plɛn/ *a.* full (**de,** of); (*total*) complete. —*n.m.* **faire le ~ (d'essence),** fill up (the tank). **à ~,** to the full. **à ~ temps,** full-time. **en ~ air,** in the open air. **en ~ milieu/visage,** right in the middle/the face. **en ~e nuit**/*etc.*, in the middle of the night/*etc.* **~ les mains,** all over one's hands.

pleinement /plɛnmɑ̃/ *adv.* fully.

pléthore /pletɔr/ *n.f.* overabundance, plethora.

pleurer /plœre/ *v.i.* cry, weep (**sur,** over); (*yeux*) water. —*v.t.* mourn.

pleurésie /plœrezi/ *n.f.* pleurisy.

pleurnicher /plœrniʃe/ *v.i.* (*fam.*) snivel.

pleurs (en) /(ɑ̃)plœr/ *adv.* in tears.

pleuvoir† /pløvwar/ *v.i.* rain; (*fig.*) rain *ou* shower down. **il pleut,** it is raining. **il pleut à verse** *ou* **à torrents,** it is pouring.

pli /pli/ *n.m.* fold; (*de jupe*) pleat; (*de pantalon*) crease; (*enveloppe*) cover; (*habitude*) habit. **(faux) ~,** crease.

pliant, ~e /plijɑ̃, -t/ *a.* folding; (*parapluie*) telescopic. —*n.m.* folding stool, camp-stool.

plier /plije/ *v.t.* fold; (*courber*) bend; (*personne*) submit (**à,** to). —*v.i.* bend; (*personne*) submit. **se ~** *v. pr.* fold. **se ~ à,** submit to.

plinthe /plɛ̃t/ *n.f.* skirting-board; (*Amer.*) baseboard.

plisser /plise/ *v.t.* crease; (*yeux*) screw up; (*jupe*) pleat.

plomb /plɔ̃/ *n.m.* lead; (*fusible*) fuse. **~s,** (*de chasse*) lead shot. **de** *ou* **en ~,** lead. **de ~,** (*ciel*) leaden.

plomb|er /plɔ̃be/ *v.t.* (*dent*) fill. **~age** *n.m.* filling.

plomb|ier /plɔ̃bje/ *n.m.* plumber. **~erie** *n.f.* plumbing.

plongeant, ~e /plɔ̃ʒɑ̃, -t/ *a.* plunging.

plongeoir /plɔ̃ʒwar/ *n.m.* diving-board.

plongeon /plɔ̃ʒɔ̃/ *n.m.* dive.

plong|er /plɔ̃ʒe/ *v.i.* dive; (*route*) plunge. —*v.t.* plunge. **se ~er** *v. pr.* plunge (**dans,** into). **~é dans,** (*lecture*) immersed in. **~ée** *n.f.* diving. **en ~ée,** (*sous-marin*) submerged. **~eur, ~euse** *n.m., f.* diver; (*employé*) dishwasher.

plouf /pluf/ *n.m.* & *int.* splash.

ployer /plwaje/ *v.t./i.* bend.

plu /ply/ *voir* **plaire, pleuvoir.**

pluie /plɥi/ *n.f.* rain; (*averse*)

shower. **~battante/diluvienne,** driving/torrential rain.
plumage /plymaʒ/ *n.m.* plumage.
plume /plym/ *n.f.* feather; (*stylo*) pen; (*pointe*) nib.
plumeau (*pl.* **~x**) /plymo/ *n.m.* feather duster.
plumer /plyme/ *v.t.* pluck.
plumet /plymɛ/ *n.m.* plume.
plumier /plymje/ *n.m.* pencil box.
plupart /plypar/ *n.f.* most. **la ~ des,** (*gens, cas, etc.*) most. **la ~ du temps,** most of the time.
pluriel, ~le /plyrjɛl/ *a.* & *n.m.* plural. **au ~,** (*nom*) plural.
plus[1] /ply/ *adv. de négation.* **(ne) ~,** (*temps*) no longer, not any more. **(ne) ~ de,** (*quantité*) no more. **je n'y vais ~,** I do not go there any longer *ou* any more. **(il n'y a) ~ de pain,** (there is) no more bread.
plus[2] /ply/ (/plyz/ *before vowel,* /plys/ *in final position*) *adv.* more **(que,** than). **~ âgé/tard**/*etc.*, older/later/*etc.* **~ beau**/*etc.*, more beautiful/*etc.* **le ~,** the most. **le ~ beau**/*etc.*, the most beautiful; (*de deux*) the more beautiful. **le ~ de,** (*gens etc.*) most. **~ de,** (*pain etc.*) more; (*dix jours etc.*) more than. **il est ~ de huit heures**/*etc.* it is after eight/*etc.* o'clock. **de ~,** more **(que,** than); (*en outre*) moreover. **(âgés) de ~ de** (*huit ans etc.*) over, more than. **de ~ en plus,** more and more. **en ~,** extra. **en ~ de,** in addition to. **~ ou moins,** more or less.
plus[3] /plys/ *conj.* plus.
plusieurs /plyzjœr/ *a.* & *pron.* several.
plus-value /plyvaly/ *n.f.* (*bénéfice*) profit.
plutôt /plyto/ *adv.* rather **(que,** than).
pluvieu|x, ~se /plyvjø, -z/ *a.* rainy.
pneu (*pl.* **~s**) /pnø/ *n.m.* tyre; (*lettre*) express letter. **~matique** *a.* (*gonflable*) inflatable; *n.m.* tyre; (*lettre*) express letter.
pneumonie /pnømɔni/ *n.f.* pneumonia.
poche /pɔʃ/ *n.f.* pocket; (*sac*) bag. **~s,** (*sous les yeux*) bags.
pocher /pɔʃe/ *v.t.* (*œuf*) poach.
pochette /pɔʃɛt/ *n.f.* pack(et), envelope; (*sac*) bag, pouch; (*d'allumettes*) book; (*de disque*) sleeve; (*mouchoir*) pocket handkerchief.
podium /pɔdjɔm/ *n.m.* rostrum.
poêle[1] /pwal/ *n.f.* **~ (à frire),** frying-pan.
poêle[2] /pwal/ *n.m.* stove.
poème /pɔɛm/ *n.m.* poem.
poésie /pɔezi/ *n.f.* poetry; (*poème*) poem.
poète /pɔɛt/ *n.m.* poet.
poétique /pɔetik/ *a.* poetic.
poids /pwa/ *n.m.* weight. **~ coq/lourd/plume,** bantamweight/heavyweight/featherweight. **~ lourd,** (*camion*) lorry, juggernaut; (*Amer.*) truck.
poignant, ~e /pwaɲɑ̃, -t/ *a.* poignant.
poignard /pwaɲar/ *n.m.* dagger. **~er** /-de/ *v.t.* stab.
poigne /pwaɲ/ *n.f.* grip.
poignée /pwaɲe/ *n.f.* handle; (*quantité*) handful. **~ de main,** handshake.
poignet /pwaɲɛ/ *n.m.* wrist; (*de chemise*) cuff.
poil /pwal/ *n.m.* hair; (*pelage*) fur; (*de brosse*) bristle. **~s,** (*de tapis*) pile. **à ~,** (*fam.*) naked. **~u** *a.* hairy.
poinçon /pwɛ̃sɔ̃/ *n.m.* awl; (*marque*) hallmark. **~ner** /-ɔne/ *v.t.* (*billet*) punch. **~neuse** /-ɔnøz/ *n.f.* punch.
poing /pwɛ̃/ *n.m.* fist.
point[1] /pwɛ̃/ *n.m.* point; (*note*: *scol.*) mark; (*tache*) spot, dot; (*de couture*) stitch. **~ (final),** full

stop, period. **à ~,** (*culin.*) medium; (*arriver*) at the right time. **faire le ~,** take stock. **mettre au ~,** (*photo*) focus; (*technique*) perfect; (*fig.*) clear up. **~ culminant,** peak. **~ de repère,** landmark. **~ de suture,** (*méd.*) stitch. **~ de vue,** point of view. **~ d'interrogation/d'exclamation,** question/exclamation mark. **~ du jour,** daybreak. **~ mort,** (*auto.*) neutral. **~ virgule,** semicolon. **sur le ~ de,** about to.

point[2] /pwɛ̃/ *adv.* **(ne) ~,** not.

pointe /pwɛ̃t/ *n.f.* point, tip; (*clou*) tack; (*de grille*) spike; (*fig.*) touch **(de,** of). **de ~,** (*industrie*) highly advanced. **en ~,** pointed. **sur la ~ des pieds,** on tiptoe.

pointer[1] /pwɛ̃te/ *v.t.* (*cocher*) tick off. —*v.i.* (*employé*) clock in *ou* out. **se ~** *v. pr.* (*fam.*) turn up.

pointer[2] /pwɛ̃te/ *v.t.* (*diriger*) point, aim.

pointillé /pwɛ̃tije/ *n.m.* dotted line. —*a.* dotted.

pointilleu|x, ~se /pwɛ̃tijø, -z/ *a.* fastidious, particular.

pointu /pwɛ̃ty/ *a.* pointed; (*aiguisé*) sharp.

pointure /pwɛ̃tyr/ *n.f.* size.

poire /pwar/ *n.f.* pear.

poireau (*pl.* **~x**) /pwaro/ *n.m.* leek.

poirier /pwarje/ *n.m.* pear-tree.

pois /pwa/ *n.m.* pea; (*dessin*) dot.

poison /pwazɔ̃/ *n.m.* poison.

poisseu|x, ~se /pwasø, -z/ *a.* sticky.

poisson /pwasɔ̃/ *n.m.* fish. **~ rouge,** goldfish.

poissonn|ier, ~ière /pwasɔnje, -jɛr/ *n.m., f.* fishmonger. **~erie** *n.f.* fish shop.

poitrail /pwatraj/ *n.m.* breast.

poitrine /pwatrin/ *n.f.* chest; (*seins*) bosom; (*culin.*) breast.

poivr|e /pwavr/ *n.m.* pepper. **~é** *a.* peppery. **~ière** *n.f.* pepper-pot.

poivron /pwavrɔ̃/ *n.m.* pepper, capsicum.

poivrot, ~e /pwavro, -ɔt/ *n.m., f.* (*fam.*) drunkard.

poker /pɔkɛr/ *n.m.* poker.

polaire /pɔlɛr/ *a.* polar.

polariser /pɔlarize/ *v.t.* polarize.

pôle /pol/ *n.m.* pole.

polémique /pɔlemik/ *n.f.* argument. —*a.* controversial.

poli /pɔli/ *a.* (*personne*) polite. **~ment** *adv.* politely.

polic|e[1] /pɔlis/ *n.f.* police; (*discipline*) (law and) order. **~ier, ~ière** *a.* police; (*roman*) detective; *n.m.* policeman.

police[2] /pɔlis/ *n.f.* (*d'assurance*) policy.

polio(myélite) /pɔljɔ(mjelit)/ *n.f.* polio(myelitis).

polir /pɔlir/ *v.t.* polish.

polisson, ~ne /pɔlisɔ̃, -ɔn/ *a.* naughty. —*n.m., f.* rascal.

politesse /pɔlitɛs/ *n.f.* politeness; (*parole*) polite remark.

politicien, ~ne /pɔlitisjɛ̃, -jɛn/ *n.m., f.* (*péj.*) politician.

politi|que /pɔlitik/ *a.* political. —*n.f.* politics; (*ligne de conduite*) policy. **~ser** *v.t.* politicize.

pollen /pɔlɛn/ *n.m.* pollen.

poll|uer /pɔlɥe/ *v.t.* pollute. **~ution** *n.f.* pollution.

polo /pɔlo/ *n.m.* polo; (*vêtement*) sports shirt, tennis shirt.

Pologne /pɔlɔɲ/ *n.f.* Poland.

polonais, ~e /pɔlɔnɛ, -z/ *a.* Polish. —*n.m., f.* Pole. —*n.m.* (*lang.*) Polish.

poltron, ~ne /pɔltrɔ̃, -ɔn/ *a.* cowardly. —*n.m., f.* coward.

polycopier /pɔlikɔpje/ *v.t.* duplicate, stencil.

polygamie /pɔligami/ *n.f.* polygamy.

polyglotte /pɔliglɔt/ *n.m./f.* polyglot.

polyvalent, ~e /pɔlivalɑ̃, -t/ *a.* varied; (*personne*) versatile.

pommade /pɔmad/ *n.f.* ointment.

pomme /pɔm/ *n.f.* apple; (*d'arrosoir*) rose. **~ d'Adam,** Adam's apple. **~ de terre,** potato. **~s frites,** chips; (*Amer.*) French fries.

pommeau (*pl.* **~x**) /pɔmo/ *n.m.* (*de canne*) knob.

pommette /pɔmɛt/ *n.f.* cheekbone.

pommier /pɔmje/ *n.m.* apple-tree.

pompe /pɔ̃p/ *n.f.* pump; (*splendeur*) pomp. **~ à incendie,** fire-engine. **~s funèbres,** undertaker's.

pomper /pɔ̃pe/ *v.t./i.* pump; (*épuiser: fam.*) tire out.

pompeu|x, ~se /pɔ̃pø, -z/ *a.* pompous.

pompier /pɔ̃pje/ *n.m.* fireman.

pompiste /pɔ̃pist/ *n.m./f.* petrol pump attendant; (*Amer.*) gas station attendant.

pompon /pɔ̃pɔ̃/ *n.m.* pompon.

pomponner /pɔ̃pɔne/ *v.t.* deck out.

poncer /pɔ̃se/ *v.t.* rub down.

ponctuation /pɔ̃ktɥasjɔ̃/ *n.f.* punctuation.

ponct|uel, ~uelle /pɔ̃ktɥɛl/ *a.* punctual. **~ualité** *n.f.* punctuality.

ponctuer /pɔ̃ktɥe/ *v.t.* punctuate.

pondéré /pɔ̃dere/ *a.* level-headed.

pondre /pɔ̃dr/ *v.t./i.* lay.

poney /pɔnɛ/ *n.m.* pony.

pont /pɔ̃/ *n.m.* bridge; (*de navire*) deck; (*de graissage*) ramp. **faire le ~,** take the extra day(s) off (*between holidays*). **~ aérien,** airlift. **~-levis** (*pl.* **~s-levis**) *n.m.* drawbridge.

ponte /pɔ̃t/ *n.f.* laying (of eggs).

pontife /pɔ̃tif/ *n.m.* **(souverain) ~,** pope.

pontific|al (*m. pl.* **~aux**) /pɔ̃tifikal, -o/ *a.* papal.

pop /pɔp/ *n.m.* & *a. invar.* (*mus.*) pop.

popote /pɔpɔt/ *n.f.* (*fam.*) cooking.

populace /pɔpylas/ *n.f.* rabble.

popul|aire /pɔpylɛr/ *a.* popular; (*expression*) colloquial; (*quartier, origine*) working-class. **~arité** *n.f.* popularity.

population /pɔpylɑsjɔ̃/ *n.f.* population.

populeu|x, ~se /pɔpylø, -z/ *a.* populous.

porc /pɔr/ *n.m.* pig; (*viande*) pork.

porcelaine /pɔrsəlɛn/ *n.f.* china, porcelain.

porc-épic (*pl.* **porcs-épics**) /pɔrkepik/ *n.m.* porcupine.

porche /pɔrʃ/ *n.m.* porch.

porcherie /pɔrʃəri/ *n.f.* pigsty.

por|e /pɔr/ *n.m.* pore. **~eux, ~euse** *a.* porous.

pornograph|ie /pɔrnɔgrafi/ *n.f.* pornography. **~ique** *a.* pornographic.

port[1] /pɔr/ *n.m.* port, harbour. **à bon ~,** safely. **~ maritime,** seaport.

port[2] /pɔr/ *n.m.* (*transport*) carriage; (*d'armes*) carrying; (*de barbe*) wearing.

portail /pɔrtaj/ *n.m.* portal.

portant, ~e /pɔrtɑ̃, -t/ *a.* **bien/mal ~,** in good/bad health.

portati|f, ~ve /pɔrtatif, -v/ *a.* portable.

porte /pɔrt/ *n.f.* door; (*passage*) doorway; (*de jardin, d'embarquement*) gate. **mettre à la ~,** throw out. **~ d'entrée,** front door. **~-fenêtre** (*pl.* **~s-fenêtres**) *n.f.* French window.

porté /pɔrte/ *a.* **~ à,** inclined to. **~ sur,** fond of.

portée /pɔrte/ *n.f.* (*d'une arme*) range; (*de voûte*) span; (*d'animaux*) litter; (*impact*) significance; (*mus.*) stave. **à ~ de,** within reach of.

portefeuille /pɔrtəfœj/ *n.m.* wallet; (*de ministre*) portfolio.

portemanteau (*pl.* **~x**) /pɔrtmɑ̃to/ *n.m.* coat *ou* hat stand.

port|er /pɔrte/ *v.t.* carry; (*vêtement, bague*) wear; (*fruits, responsabilité, nom*) bear; (*coup*) strike; (*amener*) bring; (*inscrire*) enter. —*v.i.* (*bruit*) carry; (*coup*) hit home. **~er sur,** rest on; (*concerner*) bear on. **se ~er bien,** be *ou* feel well. **se ~er candidat,** stand as a candidate. **~er aux nues,** praise to the skies. **~e-avions** *n.m. invar.* aircraft-carrier. **~e-bagages** *n.m. invar.* luggage rack. **~e-bonheur** *n.m. invar.* (*objet*) charm. **~e-clefs** *n.m. invar.* key-ring. **~e-documents** *n.m. invar.* attaché case, document wallet. **~e-monnaie** *n.m. invar.* purse. **~e-parole** *n.m. invar.* spokesman. **~e-voix** *n.m. invar.* megaphone.

porteu|r, ~se /pɔrtœr, -øz/ *n.m., f.* (*de nouvelles*) bearer; (*méd.*) carrier. —*n.m.* (*rail.*) porter.

portier /pɔrtje/ *n.m.* door-man.

portière /pɔrtjɛr/ *n.f.* door.

portillon /pɔrtijɔ̃/ *n.m.* gate.

portion /pɔrsjɔ̃/ *n.f.* portion.

portique /pɔrtik/ *n.m.* portico; (*sport*) crossbar.

porto /pɔrto/ *n.m.* port (wine).

portrait /pɔrtrɛ/ *n.m.* portrait. **~-robot** (*pl.* **~s-robots**) *n.m.* identikit, photofit.

portuaire /pɔrtɥɛr/ *a.* port.

portugais, ~e /pɔrtygɛ, -z/ *a.* & *n.m., f.* Portuguese. —*n.m.* (*lang.*) Portuguese.

Portugal /pɔrtygal/ *n.m.* Portugal.

pose /poz/ *n.f.* installation; (*attitude*) pose; (*photo.*) exposure.

posé /poze/ *a.* calm.

poser /poze/ *v.t.* put (down); (*installer*) install, put in; (*mine, fondations*) lay; (*question*) ask; (*problème*) pose. —*v.i.* (*modèle*) pose. **se ~** *v. pr.* (*avion, oiseau*) land; (*regard*) alight; (*se présenter*) arise. **~ sa candidature,** apply (**à,** for).

positi|f, ~ve /pozitif, -v/ *a.* positive.

position /pozisjɔ̃/ *n.f.* position.

poss|éder /pɔsede/ *v.t.* possess; (*propriété*) own, possess. **~esseur** *n.m.* possessor; owner.

possessi|f, ~ve /pɔsesif, -v/ *a.* possessive.

possession /pɔsesjɔ̃/ *n.f.* possession. **prendre ~ de,** take possession of.

possibilité /pɔsibilite/ *n.f.* possibility.

possible /pɔsibl/ *a.* possible. —*n.m.* **le ~,** what is possible. **faire son ~,** do one's utmost. **le plus tard**/*etc.* **~,** as late/*etc.* as possible. **pas ~,** impossible.

post- /pɔst/ *préf.* post-.

post|al (*m. pl.* **~aux**) /pɔstal, -o/ *a.* postal.

poste[1] /pɔst/ *n.f.* (*service*) post; (*bureau*) post office. **~ aérienne,** airmail. **mettre à la ~,** post. **Postes et Télécommunications,** Post Office. **P~s, Télégraphes, Téléphones,** Post Office.

poste[2] /pɔst/ *n.m.* (*lieu, emploi*) post; (*de radio, télévision*) set; (*téléphone*) extension (number). **~ d'essence,** petrol *ou* gas (*Amer.*) station. **~ de pilotage,** cockpit. **~ de police,** police station.

poster[1] /pɔste/ *v.t.* (*lettre, personne*) post.

poster[2] /pɔstɛr/ *n.m.* poster.

postérieur /pɔsterjœr/ *a.* later; (*partie*) back. **~ à,** after. —*n.m.* (*fam.*) posterior.

postérité /pɔsterite/ *n.f.* posterity.

posthume /pɔstym/ *a.* posthumous.

postiche /pɔstiʃ/ *a.* false.

post|ier, ~ière /pɔstje, -jɛr/ *n.m., f.* postal worker.

post-scriptum /pɔstskriptɔm/ *n.m. invar.* postscript.

postul|er /pɔstyle/ *v.t.* apply for; (*principe*) postulate. **~ant, ~ante** *n.m., f.* applicant.
posture /pɔstyr/ *n.f.* posture.
pot /po/ *n.m.* pot; (*en carton*) carton; (*en verre*) jar; (*chance: fam.*) luck; (*boisson: fam.*) drink. **~-au-feu** /pɔtofø/ *n.m. invar.* (*plat*) beef stew. **~ de chambre,** chamber-pot. **~ d'échappement,** exhaust-pipe. **~-de-vin** (*pl.* **~s-de-vin**) *n.m.* bribe.
potable /pɔtabl/ *a.* drinkable.
potage /pɔtaʒ/ *n.m.* soup.
potag|er, ~ère /pɔtaʒe, -ɛr/ *a.* vegetable. —*n.m.* vegetable garden.
pote /pɔt/ *n.m.* (*fam.*) chum.
poteau (*pl.* **~x**) /pɔto/ *n.m.* post; (*télégraphique*) pole. **~ indicateur,** signpost.
potelé /pɔtle/ *a.* plump.
potence /pɔtɑ̃s/ *n.f.* gallows.
potentiel, ~le /pɔtɑ̃sjɛl/ *a.* & *n.m.* potential.
pot|erie /pɔtri/ *n.f.* pottery; (*objet*) piece of pottery. **~ier** *n.m.* potter.
potins /pɔtɛ̃/ *n.m. pl.* gossip.
potion /posjɔ̃/ *n.f.* potion.
potiron /pɔtirɔ̃/ *n.m.* pumpkin.
pou (*pl.* **~x**) /pu/ *n.m.* louse.
poubelle /pubɛl/ *n.f.* dustbin; (*Amer.*) garbage can.
pouce /pus/ *n.m.* thumb; (*de pied*) big toe; (*mesure*) inch.
poudr|e /pudr/ *n.f.* powder. **~e (à canon),** gunpowder. **en ~e,** (*lait*) powdered; (*chocolat*) drinking. **~er** *v.t.* powder. **~eux, ~euse** *a.* powdery.
poudrier /pudrije/ *n.m.* (powder) compact.
poudrière /pudrijɛr/ *n.f.* (*région*) powder-keg.
pouf /puf/ *n.m.* pouffe.
pouffer /pufe/ *v.i.* guffaw.
pouilleu|x, ~se /pujø, -z/ *a.* filthy.
poulailler /pulɑje/ *n.m.* (hen-) coop.
poulain /pulɛ̃/ *n.m.* foal.
poule /pul/ *n.f.* hen; (*culin.*) fowl; (*femme: fam.*) tart; (*rugby*) group.
poulet /pulɛ/ *n.m.* chicken.
pouliche /puliʃ/ *n.f.* filly.
poulie /puli/ *n.f.* pulley.
pouls /pu/ *n.m.* pulse.
poumon /pumɔ̃/ *n.m.* lung.
poupe /pup/ *n.f.* stern.
poupée /pupe/ *n.f.* doll.
poupon /pupɔ̃/ *n.m.* baby. **~nière** /-ɔnjɛr/ *n.f.* crèche, day nursery.
pour /pur/ *prép.* for; (*envers*) to; (*à la place de*) on behalf of; (*comme*) as. **~ cela,** for that reason. **~ cent,** per cent. **~ de bon,** for good. **~ faire,** (in order) to do. **~ que,** so that. **~ moi,** as for me. **~ petit**/*etc.* **qu'il soit,** however small/*etc.* he may be. **trop poli**/*etc.* **~,** too polite/*etc.* to. **le ~ et le contre,** the pros and cons.
pourboire /purbwar/ *n.m.* tip.
pourcentage /pursɑ̃taʒ/ *n.m.* percentage.
pourchasser /purʃase/ *v.t.* pursue.
pourparlers /purparle/ *n.m. pl.* talks.
pourpre /purpr/ *a.* & *n.m.* crimson; (*violet*) purple.
pourquoi /purkwa/ *conj.* & *adv.* why. —*n.m. invar.* reason.
pourra, pourrait /pura, purɛ/ *voir* **pouvoir**[1].
pourr|ir /purir/ *v.t./i.* rot. **~i** *a.* rotten. **~iture** *n.f.* rot.
poursuite /pursɥit/ *n.f.* pursuit (**de,** of). **~s,** (*jurid.*) legal action.
poursuiv|re† /pursɥivr/ *v.t.* pursue; (*continuer*) continue (with). **~re (en justice),** (*au criminel*) prosecute; (*au civil*) sue. —*v.i.,* **se ~re** *v. pr.* continue. **~ant, ~ante** *n.m., f.* pursuer.
pourtant /purtɑ̃/ *adv.* yet.
pourtour /purtur/ *n.m.* perimeter.
pourv|oir† /purvwar/ *v.t.* **~oir**

de, provide with. —*v.i.* **~oir à,** provide for. **~u de,** supplied with. **~oyeur, ~oyeuse** *n.m., f.* supplier.

pourvu que /purvyk(ə)/ *conj.* (*condition*) provided (that); (*souhait*) let us hope (that).

pousse /pus/ *n.f.* growth; (*bourgeon*) shoot.

poussé /puse/ *a.* (*études*) advanced.

poussée /puse/ *n.f.* pressure; (*coup*) push; (*de prix*) upsurge; (*méd.*) outbreak.

pousser /puse/ *v.t.* push; (*du coude*) nudge; (*cri*) let out; (*soupir*) heave; (*continuer*) continue; (*exhorter*) urge (**à,** to); (*forcer*) drive (**à,** to); (*amener*) bring (**à,** to). —*v.i.* push; (*grandir*) grow. **se ~** *v. pr.* move over *ou* up.

poussette /pusɛt/ *n.f.* push-chair; (*Amer.*) (baby) stroller.

pouss|ière /pusjɛr/ *n.f.* dust. **~iéreux, ~iéreuse** *a.* dusty.

poussi|f, ~ve /pusif, -v/ *a.* short-winded, wheezing.

poussin /pusɛ̃/ *n.m.* chick.

poutre /putr/ *n.f.* beam; (*en métal*) girder.

pouvoir[1]† /puvwar/ *v. aux.* (*possibilité*) can, be able; (*permission, éventualité*) may, can. **il peut/pouvait/pourrait venir,** he can/could/might come. **je n'ai pas pu,** I could not. **j'ai pu faire,** (*réussi à*) I managed to do. **je n'en peux plus,** I am exhausted. **il se peut que,** it may be that.

pouvoir[2] /puvwar/ *n.m.* power; (*gouvernement*) government. **au ~,** in power. **~s publics,** authorities.

prairie /preri/ *n.f.* meadow.

praline /pralin/ *n.f.* sugared almond.

praticable /pratikabl/ *a.* practicable.

praticien, ~ne /pratisjɛ̃, -jɛn/ *n.m., f.* practitioner.

pratiquant, ~e /pratikɑ̃, -t/ *a.* practising. —*n.m., f.* churchgoer.

pratique /pratik/ *a.* practical. —*n.f.* practice; (*expérience*) experience. **la ~ du golf/du cheval,** golfing/riding. **~ment** *adv.* in practice; (*presque*) practically.

pratiquer /pratike/ *v.t./i.* practise; (*sport*) play; (*faire*) make.

pré /pre/ *n.m.* meadow.

pré- /pre/ *préf.* pre-.

préalable /prealabl/ *a.* preliminary, prior. —*n.m.* precondition. **au ~,** first.

préambule /preɑ̃byl/ *n.m.* preamble.

préau (*pl.* **~x**) /preo/ *n.m.* (*scol.*) covered playground.

préavis /preavi/ *n.m.* (advance) notice.

précaire /prekɛr/ *a.* precarious.

précaution /prekosjɔ̃/ *n.f.* (*mesure*) precaution; (*prudence*) caution.

précéd|ent, ~ente /presedɑ̃, -t/ *a.* previous. —*n.m.* precedent. **~emment** /-amɑ̃/ *adv.* previously.

précéder /presede/ *v.t./i.* precede.

précepte /presɛpt/ *n.m.* precept.

précep|teur, ~trice /presɛptœr, -tris/ *n.m., f.* tutor.

prêcher /preʃe/ *v.t./i.* preach.

précieu|x, ~se /presjø, -z/ *a.* precious.

précipice /presipis/ *n.m.* abyss, chasm.

précipit|é /presipite/ *a.* hasty. **~amment** *adv.* hastily. **~ation** *n.f.* haste.

précipiter /presipite/ *v.t.* throw, precipitate; (*hâter*) hasten. **se ~** *v. pr.* rush (**sur,** at, on to); (*se jeter*) throw o.s; (*s'accélérer*) speed up.

précis, ~e /presi, -z/ *a.* precise; (*mécanisme*) accurate. —*n.m.* summary. **dix heures**/*etc.* **~es,**

ten o'clock/*etc*. sharp. **~ément** /-zemɑ̃/ *adv*. precisely.

préciser /presize/ *v.t./i*. specify. **se ~** *v. pr*. become clear(er).

précision /presizjɔ̃/ *n.f*. precision; (*détail*) detail.

précoc|e /prekɔs/ *a*. early; (*enfant*) precocious. **~ité** *n.f*. earliness; precociousness

préconçu /prekɔ̃sy/ *a*. preconceived.

préconiser /prekɔnize/ *v.t*. advocate.

précurseur /prekyrsœr/ *n.m*. forerunner.

prédécesseur /predesesœr/ *n.m*. predecessor.

prédicateur /predikatœr/ *n.m*. preacher.

prédilection /predilɛksjɔ̃/ *n.f*. preference.

préd|ire† /predir/ *v.t*. predict. **~iction** *n.f*. prediction.

prédisposer /predispoze/ *v.t*. predispose.

prédominant, ~e /predɔminɑ̃, -t/ *a*. predominant.

prédominer /predɔmine/ *v.i*. predominate.

préfabriqué /prefabrike/ *a*. prefabricated.

préface /prefas/ *n.f*. preface.

préfecture /prefɛktyr/ *n.f*. prefecture. **~ de police,** police headquarters.

préférence /preferɑ̃s/ *n.f*. preference. **de ~,** preferably. **de ~ à,** in preference to.

préférentiel, ~le /preferɑ̃sjɛl/ *a*. preferential.

préfér|er /prefere/ *v.t*. prefer (**à,** to). **~er faire,** prefer to do. **~able** *a*. preferable. **~é, ~ée** *a*. & *n.m., f*. favourite.

préfet /prefɛ/ *n.m*. prefect. **~ de police,** prefect *ou* chief of police.

préfixe /prefiks/ *n.m*. prefix.

préhistorique /preistɔrik/ *a*. prehistoric.

préjudic|e /preʒydis/ *n.m*. harm, prejudice. **porter ~e à,** harm. **~iable** *a*. harmful.

préjugé /preʒyʒe/ *n.m*. prejudice.

préjuger /preʒyʒe/ *v.i*. **~ de,** prejudge.

prélasser (se) /(sə)prelɑse/ *v. pr*. loll (about).

prél|ever /prelve/ *v.t*. deduct; (*sang*) take. **~èvement** *n.m*. deduction. **~èvement de sang,** blood sample.

préliminaire /preliminɛr/ *a*. & *n.m*. preliminary.

prélude /prelyd/ *n.m*. prelude.

prématuré /prematyre/ *a*. premature. —*n.m*. premature baby.

prémédit|er /premedite/ *v.t*. premeditate. **~ation** *n.f*. premeditation.

prem|ier, ~ière /prəmje, -jɛr/ *a*. first; (*rang*) front, first; (*enfance*) early; (*nécessité, souci*) prime; (*qualité*) top, prime; (*état*) original. —*n.m., f*. first (one). —*n.m*. (*date*) first; (*étage*) first floor. —*n.f*. (*rail*.) first class; (*exploit jamais vu*) first; (*cinéma, théâtre*) première. **de ~ier ordre,** first-rate. **en ~ier,** first. **~ier jet,** first draft. **~ier ministre,** Prime Minister.

premièrement /prəmjɛrmɑ̃/ *adv*. firstly.

prémisse /premis/ *n.f*. premiss.

prémonition /premɔnisjɔ̃/ *n.f*. premonition.

prémunir /premynir/ *v.t*. protect.

prenant, ~e /prənɑ̃, -t/ *a*. (*activité*) engrossing.

prénatal (*m. pl.* **~s**) /prenatal/ *a*. antenatal; (*Amer*.) prenatal.

prendre† /prɑ̃dr/ *v.t*. take; (*attraper*) catch, get; (*acheter*) get; (*repas*) have; (*engager, adopter*) take on; (*poids, voix*) put on; (*chercher*) pick up; (*panique, colère*) take hold of. —*v.i*. (*liquide*) set; (*feu*) catch; (*vaccin*) take; (*aller*) go. **se ~ en glace,** freeze over. **se ~ pour,** think one is. **s'en ~ à,** attack; (*rendre responsable*) blame. **s'y ~,** set about (it).

preneu|r, ~se /prənœr, -øz/ *n.m., f.* buyer.

prénom /prenɔ̃/ *n.m.* first name. **~mer** /-ɔme/ *v.t.* call. **se ~mer** *v. pr.* be called.

préoccup|er /preɔkype/ *v.t.* worry; (*absorber*) preoccupy. **se ~er de,** be worried about; be preoccupied about. **~ation** *n.f.* worry; (*idée fixe*) preoccupation.

préparatifs /preparatif/ *n.m. pl.* preparations.

préparatoire /preparatwar/ *a.* preparatory.

prépar|er /prepare/ *v.t.* prepare; (*repas, café*) make. **se ~er** *v. pr.* prepare o.s.; (*être proche*) be brewing. **~er à qn.,** (*surprise*) have (got) in store for s.o. **~ation** *n.f.* preparation.

prépondéran|t, ~te /prepɔ̃derɑ̃, -t/ *a.* dominant. **~ce** *n.f.* dominance.

prépos|er /prepoze/ *v.t.* put in charge (**à,** of). **~é, ~ée** *n.m., f.* employee; (*des postes*) postman, postwoman.

préposition /prepozisjɔ̃/ *n.f.* preposition.

préretraite /prerətrɛt/ *n.f.* early retirement.

prérogative /prerɔgativ/ *n.f.* prerogative.

près /prɛ/ *adv.* near, close. **~ de,** near (to), close to; (*presque*) nearly. **à cela ~,** apart from that. **de ~,** closely.

présag|e /prezaʒ/ *n.m.* foreboding, omen. **~er** *v.t.* forebode.

presbyte /prɛsbit/ *a.* long-sighted, far-sighted.

presbytère /prɛsbitɛr/ *n.m.* presbytery.

prescr|ire† /prɛskrir/ *v.t.* prescribe. **~iption** *n.f.* prescription.

préséance /preseɑ̃s/ *n.f.* precedence.

présence /prezɑ̃s/ *n.f.* presence; (*scol.*) attendance.

présent, ~e /prezɑ̃, -t/ *a.* present. —*n.m.* (*temps, cadeau*) present. **à ~,** now.

présent|er /prezɑ̃te/ *v.t.* present; (*personne*) introduce (**à,** to); (*montrer*) show. **se ~er** *v. pr.* introduce o.s. (**à,** to); (*aller*) go; (*apparaître*) appear; (*candidat*) come forward; (*occasion etc.*) arise. **se ~er à,** (*examen*) sit for; (*élection*) stand for. **se ~er bien,** look good. **~able** *a.* presentable. **~ateur, ~atrice** *n.m., f.* presenter. **~ation** *n.f.* presentation; introduction.

préserv|er /prezɛrve/ *v.t.* protect. **~ation** *n.f.* protection, preservation.

présiden|t, ~te /prezidɑ̃, -t/ *n.m., f.* president; (*de firme, comité*) chairman, chairwoman. **~t directeur général,** managing director. **~ce** *n.f.* presidency; chairmanship.

présidentiel, ~le /prezidɑ̃sjɛl/ *a.* presidential.

présider /prezide/ *v.t.* preside over. —*v.i.* preside.

présomption /prezɔ̃psjɔ̃/ *n.f.* presumption.

présomptueu|x, ~se /prezɔ̃ptɥø, -z/ *a.* presumptuous.

presque /prɛsk(ə)/ *adv.* almost, nearly. **~ jamais,** hardly ever. **~ rien,** hardly anything.

presqu'île /prɛskil/ *n.f.* peninsula.

pressant, ~e /prɛsɑ̃, -t/ *a.* pressing, urgent; (*personne*) pressing.

presse /prɛs/ *n.f.* (*journaux, appareil*) press.

pressent|ir /presɑ̃tir/ *v.t.* sense. **~iment** *n.m.* presentiment.

press|er /prese/ *v.t.* squeeze, press; (*appuyer sur, harceler*) press; (*hâter*) hasten; (*inciter*) urge (**de,**

to). —*v.i.* (*temps*) press; (*affaire*) be pressing. **se ~er** *v. pr.* (*se hâter*) hurry; (*se grouper*) crowd. **~é** *a.* in a hurry; (*air*) hurried. **citron ~é,** lemon juice. **orange ~ée,** orange juice. **~e-papiers** *n.m. invar.* paperweight.

pressing /presiŋ/ *n.m.* steam pressing; (*magasin*) dry-cleaner's.

pression /prɛsjɔ̃/ *n.f.* pressure. —*n.m.*/*f.* (*bouton*) press-stud; (*Amer.*) snap.

pressoir /prɛswar/ *n.m.* press.

pressuriser /presyrize/ *v.t.* pressurize.

prestance /prɛstɑ̃s/ *n.f.* (imposing) presence.

prestation /prɛstɑsjɔ̃/ *n.f.* allowance; (*d'artiste etc.*) performance.

prestidigita|teur, ~trice /prɛstidiʒitatœr, -tris/ *n.m.*, *f.* conjuror. **~tion** /-ɑsjɔ̃/ *n.f.* conjuring.

prestig|e /prɛstiʒ/ *n.m.* prestige. **~ieux, ~ieuse** *a.* prestigious.

présumer /prezyme/ *v.t.* presume.

prêt[1], **~e** /prɛ, -t/ *a.* ready (**à qch.,** for sth., **à faire,** to do). **~-à-porter** /prɛtapɔrte/ *n.m. invar.* ready-to-wear clothes.

prêt[2] /prɛ/ *n.m.* loan.

prétendant /pretɑ̃dɑ̃/ *n.m.* (*amoureux*) suitor.

prétend|re /pretɑ̃dr/ *v.t.* claim (**que,** that); (*vouloir*) intend. **~re qn. riche**/*etc.*, claim that s.o. is rich/*etc.* **~u** *a.* so-called. **~ument** *adv.* supposedly, allegedly.

prétent|ieux, ~ieuse /pretɑ̃sjø, -z/ *a.* pretentious. **~ion** *n.f.* pretentiousness; (*exigence*) claim.

prêt|er /prete/ *v.t.* lend (**à,** to); (*attribuer*) attribute. —*v.i.* **~er à,** be open to. **~er attention,** pay attention. **~er serment,** take an oath. **~eur, ~euse** /prɛtœr, -øz/ *n.m.*, *f.* (money-)lender. **~eur sur gages,** pawnbroker.

prétext|e /pretɛkst/ *n.m.* pretext, excuse. **~er** *v.t.* plead.

prêtre /prɛtr/ *n.m.* priest.

prêtrise /pretriz/ *n.f.* priesthood.

preuve /prœv/ *n.f.* proof. **faire ~ de,** show.

prévaloir /prevalwar/ *v.i.* prevail.

prévenan|t, ~te /prɛvnɑ̃, -t/ *a.* thoughtful. **~ce(s)** *n.f.* (*pl.*) thoughtfulness.

prévenir† /prɛvnir/ *v.t.* (*menacer*) warn; (*informer*) tell; (*éviter, anticiper*) forestall.

préventi|f, ~ve /prevɑ̃tif, -v/ *a.* preventive.

prévention /prevɑ̃sjɔ̃/ *n.f.* prevention; (*préjugé*) prejudice. **~ routière,** road safety.

prévenu, ~e /prɛvny/ *n.m.*, *f.* defendant.

prév|oir† /prevwar/ *v.t.* foresee; (*temps*) forecast; (*organiser*) plan (for), provide for; (*envisager*) allow (for). **~u pour,** (*jouet etc.*) designed for. **~isible** *a.* foreseeable. **~ision** *n.f.* prediction; (*météorologique*) forecast.

prévoyan|t, ~te /prevwajɑ̃, -t/ *a.* showing foresight. **~ce** *n.f.* foresight.

prier /prije/ *v.i.* pray. —*v.t.* pray to; (*implorer*) beg (**de,** to); (*demander à*) ask (**de,** to). **je vous en prie,** please; (*il n'y a pas de quoi*) don't mention it.

prière /prijɛr/ *n.f.* prayer; (*demande*) request. **~ de,** (*vous êtes prié de*) will you please.

primaire /primɛr/ *a.* primary.

primauté /primote/ *n.f.* primacy.

prime /prim/ *n.f.* free gift; (*d'employé*) bonus; (*subvention*) subsidy; (*d'assurance*) premium.

primé /prime/ *a.* prize-winning.

primer /prime/ *v.t.*/*i.* excel.

primeurs /primœr/ *n.f. pl.* early fruit and vegetables.

primevère /primvɛr/ *n.f.* primrose.

primiti|f, ~ve /primitif, -v/ *a.*

primitive; (*originel*) original. —*n.m., f.* primitive.

primord|ial (*m. pl.* **~iaux**) /primɔrdjal, -jo/ *a.* essential.

princ|e /prɛ̃s/ *n.m.* prince. **~esse** *n.f.* princess. **~ier, ~ière** *a.* princely.

princip|al (*m. pl.* **~aux**) /prɛ̃sipal, -o/ *a.* main, principal. —*n.m.* (*pl.* **~aux**) headmaster; (*chose*) main thing. **~alement** *adv.* mainly.

principauté /prɛ̃sipote/ *n.f.* principality.

principe /prɛ̃sip/ *n.m.* principle. **en ~,** theoretically; (*d'habitude*) as a rule.

printan|ier, ~ière /prɛ̃tanje, -jɛr/ *a.* spring(-like).

printemps /prɛ̃tɑ̃/ *n.m.* spring.

priorit|é /prijɔrite/ *n.f.* priority; (*auto.*) right of way. **~aire** *a.* priority. **être ~aire,** have priority.

pris, ~e[1] /pri, -z/ *voir* **prendre.** —*a.* (*place*) taken; (*crème*) set; (*personne, journée*) busy; (*gorge*) infected. **~ de,** (*peur, fièvre, etc.*) stricken with. **~ de panique,** panic-stricken.

prise[2] /priz/ *n.f.* hold, grip; (*animal etc. attrapé*) catch; (*mil.*) capture. **~ (de courant),** (*mâle*) plug; (*femelle*) socket. **aux ~s avec,** at grips with. **~ de conscience,** awareness. **~ de contact,** first contact, initial meeting. **~ de position,** stand. **~ de sang,** blood test. **~ de vues,** filming

priser /prize/ *v.t.* (*estimer*) prize.

prisme /prism/ *n.m.* prism.

prison /prizɔ̃/ *n.f.* prison, gaol, jail; (*réclusion*) imprisonment. **~nier, ~nière** /-ɔnje, -jɛr/ *n.m., f.* prisoner.

privé /prive/ *a.* private. —*n.m.* (*comm.*) private sector. **en ~, dans le ~,** in private.

priv|er /prive/ *v.t.* **~er de,** deprive of. **se ~er de,** go without. **~ation** *n.f.* deprivation; (*sacrifice*) hardship.

privil|ège /privilɛʒ/ *n.m.* privilege. **~égié, ~égiée** *a.* & *n.m., f.* privileged (person).

prix /pri/ *n.m.* price; (*récompense*) prize. **à tout ~,** at all costs. **au ~ de,** (*fig.*) at the expense of. **~ coûtant, ~ de revient,** cost price. **~ fixe,** set price; (*repas*) set meal.

pro- /pro/ *préf.* pro-.

probab|le /prɔbabl/ *a.* probable, likely. **~ilité** *n.f.* probability. **~lement** *adv.* probably.

probant, ~e /prɔbɑ̃, -t/ *a.* convincing, conclusive.

probité /prɔbite/ *n.f.* integrity.

problème /prɔblɛm/ *n.m.* problem.

procéd|er /prɔsede/ *v.i.* proceed. **~er à,** carry out. **~é** *n.m.* process; (*conduite*) behaviour.

procédure /prɔsedyr/ *n.f.* procedure.

procès /prɔsɛ/ *n.m.* (*criminel*) trial; (*civil*) lawsuit, proceedings. **~-verbal** (*pl.* **~-verbaux**) *n.m.* report; (*contravention*) ticket.

procession /prɔsesjɔ̃/ *n.f.* procession.

processus /prɔsesys/ *n.m.* process.

prochain, ~e /prɔʃɛ̃, -ɛn/ *a.* (*suivant*) next; (*proche*) imminent; (*avenir*) near. —*n.m.* fellow. **~ement** /-ɛnmɑ̃/ *adv.* soon.

proche /prɔʃ/ *a.* near, close; (*avoisinant*) neighbouring; (*parent, ami*) close. **~ de,** close *ou* near to. **être ~,** (*imminent*) be approaching. **~s** *n.m. pl.* close relations. **P~-Orient** *n.m.* Near East.

proclam|er /prɔklame/ *v.t.* declare, proclaim. **~ation** *n.f.* declaration, proclamation.

procréation /prɔkreɑsjɔ̃/ *n.f.* procreation.

procuration /prɔkyrɑsjɔ̃/ *n.f.* proxy.

procurer /prɔkyre/ *v.t.* bring (**à,** to). **se ~** *v. pr.* obtain.

procureur /prɔkyrœr/ *n.m.* public prosecutor.

prodig|e /prɔdiʒ/ *n.m.* marvel; (*personne*) prodigy. **~ieux, ~ieuse** *a.* tremendous, prodigious.

prodigu|e /prɔdig/ *a.* wasteful. **~er** *v.t.* **~er à,** lavish on.

producti|f, ~ve /prɔdyktif, -v/ *a.* productive. **~vité** *n.f.* productivity.

prod|uire† /prɔdɥir/ *v.t.* produce. **se ~uire** *v.pr.* (*survenir*) happen. **~ucteur, ~uctrice** *a.* producing; *n.m., f.* producer. **~uction** *n.f.* production; (*produit*) product.

produit /prɔdɥi/ *n.m.* product. **~s,** (*de la terre*) produce. **~ chimique,** chemical. **~s alimentaires,** foodstuffs.

proéminent, ~e /prɔeminɑ̃, -t/ *a.* prominent.

prof /prɔf/ *n.m.* (*fam.*) teacher.

profane /prɔfan/ *a.* secular. —*n.m.*/*f.* lay person.

profaner /prɔfane/ *v.t.* desecrate.

proférer /prɔfere/ *v.t.* utter.

professer[1] /prɔfese/ *v.t.* (*déclarer*) profess.

professer[2] /prɔfese/ *v.t.*/*i.* (*enseigner*) teach.

professeur /prɔfɛsœr/ *n.m.* teacher; (*univ.*) lecturer; (*avec chaire*) professor.

profession /prɔfɛsjɔ̃/ *n.f.* occupation; (*intellectuelle*) profession. **~nel, ~nelle** /-jɔnɛl/ *a.* professional; (*école*) vocational; *n.m., f.* professional.

professorat /prɔfɛsɔra/ *n.m.* teaching.

profil /prɔfil/ *n.m.* profile.

profiler (se) /(sə)prɔfile/ *v. pr.* be outlined.

profit /prɔfi/ *n.m.* profit. **au ~ de,** in aid of. **~able** /-tabl/ *a.* profitable.

profiter /prɔfite/ *v.i.* **~ à,** benefit. **~ de,** take advantage of.

profond, ~e /prɔfɔ̃, -d/ *a.* deep; (*sentiment, intérêt*) profound; (*causes*) underlying. **au plus ~ de,** in the depths of. **~ément** /-demɑ̃/ *adv.* deeply; (*différent, triste*) profoundly; (*dormir*) soundly. **~eur** /-dœr/ *n.f.* depth.

profusion /prɔfyzjɔ̃/ *n.f.* profusion.

progéniture /prɔʒenityr/ *n.f.* offspring.

programmation /prɔgramɑsjɔ̃/ *n.f.* programming.

programm|e /prɔgram/ *n.m.* programme; (*matières: scol.*) syllabus; (*informatique*) program. **~e (d'études),** curriculum. **~er** *v.t.* (*ordinateur*) program; (*émission*) bill. **~eur, ~euse** *n.m., f.* computer programmer.

progrès /prɔgrɛ/ *n.m.* & *n.m.pl.* progress.

progress|er /prɔgrese/ *v.i.* progress. **~ion** /-ɛsjɔ̃/ *n.f.* progression.

progressi|f, ~ve /prɔgresif, -v/ *a.* progressive. **~vement** *adv.* progressively.

progressiste /prɔgresist/ *a.* progressive.

prohib|er /prɔibe/ *v.t.* prohibit. **~ition** *n.f.* prohibition.

prohibiti|f, ~ve /prɔibitif, -v/ *a.* prohibitive.

proie /prwa/ *n.f.* prey. **en ~ à,** tormented by.

projecteur /prɔʒɛktœr/ *n.m.* floodlight; (*mil.*) searchlight; (*cinéma*) projector.

projectile /prɔʒɛktil/ *n.m.* missile.

projection /prɔʒɛksjɔ̃/ *n.f.* projection; (*séance*) show.

projet /prɔʒɛ/ *n.m.* plan; (*ébauche*) draft. **~ de loi,** bill.

projeter /prɔʒte/ *v.t.* plan (**de,** to);

(*film*) project, show; (*jeter*) hurl, project.

prolét|aire /prɔletɛr/ *n.m./f.* proletarian. **~ariat** *n.m.* proletariat. **~arien, ~arienne** *a.* proletarian.

proliférer|er /prɔlifere/ *v.i.* proliferate. **~ation** *n.f.* proliferation.

prolifique /prɔlifik/ *a.* prolific.

prologue /prɔlɔg/ *n.m.* prologue.

prolongation /prɔlɔ̃gɑsjɔ̃/ *n.f.* extension. **~s,** (*football*) extra time.

prolong|er /prɔlɔ̃ʒe/ *v.t.* prolong. **se ~er** *v. pr.* continue, extend. **~é** *a.* prolonged. **~ement** *n.m.* extension.

promenade /prɔmnad/ *n.f.* walk; (*à bicyclette, à cheval*) ride; (*en auto*) drive, ride. **faire une ~,** go for a walk.

promen|er /prɔmne/ *v.t.* take for a walk. **~er sur qch.,** (*main, regard*) run over sth. **se ~er** *v. pr.* walk. **(aller) se ~er,** go for a walk. **~eur, ~euse** *n.m., f.* walker.

promesse /prɔmɛs/ *n.f.* promise.

promett|re† /prɔmɛtr/ *v.t./i.* promise. **~re (beaucoup),** be promising. **se ~re de,** resolve to. **~eur, ~euse** *a.* promising.

promontoire /prɔmɔ̃twar/ *n.m.* headland.

promoteur /prɔmɔtœr/ *n.m.* (*immobilier*) property developer.

prom|ouvoir /prɔmuvwar/ *v.t.* promote. **être ~u,** be promoted. **~otion** *n.f.* promotion; (*univ.*) year; (*comm.*) special offer.

prompt, ~e /prɔ̃, -t/ *a.* swift.

prôner /prone/ *v.t.* extol; (*préconiser*) preach, advocate.

pronom /prɔnɔ̃/ *n.m.* pronoun. **~inal** (*m. pl.* **~inaux**) /-ɔminal, -o/ *a.* pronominal.

prononc|er /prɔnɔ̃se/ *v.t.* pronounce; (*discours*) make. **se ~er** *v. pr.* (*mot*) be pronounced; (*personne*) make a decision **(pour,** in favour of). **~é** *a.* pronounced. **~iation** *n.f.* pronunciation.

pronosti|c /prɔnɔstik/ *n.m.* forecast. **~quer** *v.t.* forecast.

propagande /prɔpagɑ̃d/ *n.f.* propaganda.

propag|er /prɔpaʒe/ *v.t.*, **se ~er** *v. pr.* spread. **~ation** /-gɑsjɔ̃/ *n.f.* spread(ing).

proph|ète /prɔfɛt/ *n.m.* prophet. **~étie** /-esi/ *n.f.* prophecy. **~étique** *a.* prophetic. **~étiser** *v.t./i.* prophesy.

propice /prɔpis/ *a.* favourable.

proportion /prɔpɔrsjɔ̃/ *n.f.* proportion; (*en mathématiques*) ratio. **~né** /-jɔne/ *a.* proportionate **(à,** to). **~nel, ~nelle** /-jɔnɛl/ *a.* proportional. **~ner** /-jɔne/ *v.t.* proportion.

propos /prɔpo/ *n.m.* intention; (*sujet*) subject. —*n.m. pl.* (*paroles*) remarks. **à ~,** at the right time; (*dans un dialogue*) by the way. **à ~ de,** about.

propos|er /prɔpoze/ *v.t.* propose; (*offrir*) offer. **se ~er** *v. pr.* volunteer **(pour,** to); (*but*) set o.s. **se ~er de faire,** propose to do. **~ition** *n.f.* proposal; (*affirmation*) proposition; (*gram.*) clause.

propre[1] /prɔpr/ *a.* clean; (*soigné*) neat; (*honnête*) decent. **~ment**[1] /-əmɑ̃/ *adv.* cleanly; neatly; decently.

propre[2] /prɔpr/ *a.* (*à soi*) own; (*sens*) literal. **~ à,** (*qui convient*) suited to; (*spécifique*) peculiar to. **~ment**[2] /-əmɑ̃/ *adv.* strictly. **le bureau**/*etc.* **~ment dit,** the office/*etc.* itself.

propreté /prɔprəte/ *n.f.* cleanliness; (*netteté*) neatness.

propriétaire /prɔprijetɛr/ *n.m./f.* owner; (*comm.*) proprietor; (*qui loue*) landlord, landlady.

propriété /prɔprijete/ *n.f.* property; (*d'un terme*) propriety.
propuls|er /prɔpylse/ *v.t.* propel. **~ion** *n.f.* propulsion.
prosaïque /prozaik/ *a.* prosaic.
proscr|ire /prɔskrir/ *v.t.* proscribe. **~it, ~ite** *a.* proscribed; *n.m., f.* (*exilé*) exile.
prose /proz/ *n.f.* prose.
prospec|ter /prɔspɛkte/ *v.t.* prospect. **~teur, ~trice** *n.m., f.* prospector. **~tion** /-ksjɔ̃/ *n.f.* prospecting.
prospectus /prɔspɛktys/ *n.m.* leaflet.
prosp|ère /prɔspɛr/ *a.* flourishing, thriving. **~érer** *v.i.* thrive, prosper. **~érité** *n.f.* prosperity.
prostern|er (se) /(sə)prɔstɛrne/ *v. pr.* bow down. **~é** *a.* prostrate.
prostit|uée /prɔstitɥe/ *n.f.* prostitute. **~ution** *n.f.* prostitution.
prostré /prɔstre/ *a.* prostrate.
protagoniste /prɔtagɔnist/ *n.m.* protagonist.
protec|teur, ~trice /prɔtɛktœr, -tris/ *n.m., f.* protector. —*a.* protective.
protection /prɔtɛksjɔ̃/ *n.f.* protection; (*fig.*) patronage.
protég|er /prɔteʒe/ *v.t.* protect; (*fig.*) patronize. **se ~er** *v. pr.* protect o.s. **~é** *n.m.* protégé. **~ée** *n.f.* protégée.
protéine /prɔtein/ *n.f.* protein.
protestant, ~e /prɔtɛstɑ̃, -t/ *a.* & *n.m., f.* Protestant.
protest|er /prɔtɛste/ *v.t./i.* protest. **~ation** *n.f.* protest.
protocole /prɔtɔkɔl/ *n.m.* protocol.
prototype /prɔtɔtip/ *n.m.* prototype.
protubéran|t, ~te /prɔtyberɑ̃, -t/ *a.* bulging. **~ce,** *n.f.* protuberance.
proue /pru/ *n.f.* bow, prow.
prouesse /pruɛs/ *n.f.* feat, exploit.
prouver /pruve/ *v.t.* prove.
provenance /prɔvnɑ̃s/ *n.f.* origin. **en ~ de,** from.
provenç|al, ~ale (*m. pl.* **~aux**) /prɔvɑ̃sal, -o/ *a.* & *n.m., f.* Provençal.
Provence /prɔvɑ̃s/ *n.f.* Provence.
provenir† /prɔvnir/ *v.i.* **~ de,** come from.
proverb|e /prɔvɛrb/ *n.m.* proverb. **~ial** (*m. pl.* **~iaux**) *a.* proverbial.
providence /prɔvidɑ̃s/ *n.f.* providence.
provinc|e /prɔvɛ̃s/ *n.f.* province. **de ~e,** provincial. **la ~e,** the provinces. **~ial, ~iale** (*m. pl.* **~iaux**) *a.* & *n.m., f.* provincial.
proviseur /prɔvizœr/ *n.m.* headmaster.
provision /prɔvizjɔ̃/ *n.f.* supply, store; (*acompte*) deposit. **~s,** (*achats*) shopping; (*vivres*) provisions.
provisoire /prɔvizwar/ *a.* temporary. **~ment** *adv.* temporarily.
provo|quer /prɔvɔke/ *v.t.* cause; (*exciter*) arouse; (*défier*) provoke. **~cant, ~cante** *a.* provocative. **~cation** *n.f.* provocation.
proximité /prɔksimite/ *n.f.* proximity. **à ~ de,** close to.
prude /pryd/ *a.* prudish. —*n.f.* prude.
prud|ent, ~ente /prydɑ̃, -t/ *a.* cautious; (*sage*) wise. **soyez ~ent,** be careful. **~emment** /-amɑ̃/ *adv.* cautiously; wisely. **~ence** *n.f.* caution; wisdom.
prune /pryn/ *n.f.* plum.
pruneau (*pl.* **~x**) /pryno/ *n.m.* prune.
prunelle[1] /prynɛl/ *n.f.* (*pupille*) pupil.
prunelle[2] /prynɛl/ *n.f.* (*fruit*) sloe.
psaume /psom/ *n.m.* psalm.
pseudo- /psødɔ/ *préf.* pseudo-.
pseudonyme /psødɔnim/ *n.m.* pseudonym.
psychanalys|e /psikanaliz/ *n.f.*

psychoanalysis. **~er** *v.t.* psychoanalyse. **~te** /-st/ *n.m./f.* psychoanalyst.

psychiatr|e /psikjatr/ *n.m./f.* psychiatrist. **~ie** *n.f.* psychiatry. **~ique** *a.* psychiatric.

psychique /psiʃik/ *a.* mental, psychological.

psycholo|gie /psikɔlɔʒi/ *n.f.* psychology. **~gique** *a.* psychological. **~gue** *n.m./f.* psychologist.

PTT *abrév.* (*Postes, Télégraphes, Téléphones*) Post Office.

pu /py/ *voir* **pouvoir**[1].

puant, ~e /pɥɑ̃, -t/ *a.* stinking. **~eur** /-tœr/ *n.f.* stink.

puberté /pybɛrte/ *n.f.* puberty.

publi|c, ~que /pyblik/ *a.* public. —*n.m.* public; (*assistance*) audience. **en ~c,** in public.

publicit|é /pyblisite/ *n.f.* publicity, advertising; (*annonce*) advertisement; (*intérêt général*) publicity. **~aire** *a.* publicity.

publ|ier /pyblije/ *v.t.* publish. **~ication** *n.f.* publication.

publiquement /pyblikmɑ̃/ *adv.* publicly.

puce[1] /pys/ *n.f.* flea.

puce[2] /pys/ *n.f.* (*électronique*) chip.

pud|eur /pydœr/ *n.f.* modesty. **~ique** *a.* modest.

pudibond, ~e /pydibɔ̃, -d/ *a.* prudish.

puer /pɥe/ *v.i.* stink. —*v.t.* stink of.

puéricultrice /pɥerikyltris/ *n.f.* children's nurse.

puéril /pɥeril/ *a.* puerile.

puis /pɥi/ *adv.* then.

puiser /pɥize/ *v.t.* draw **(qch. dans,** sth. from). —*v.i.* **~ dans qch.,** dip into sth.

puisque /pɥisk(ə)/ *conj.* since, as.

puissance /pɥisɑ̃s/ *n.f.* power. **en ~** *a.* potential; *adv.* potentially.

puiss|ant, ~ante /pɥisɑ̃, -t/ *a.* powerful. **~amment** *adv.* powerfully.

puits /pɥi/ *n.m.* well; (*de mine*) shaft.

pull(-over) /pyl(ɔvɛr)/ *n.m.* pullover.

pulpe /pylp/ *n.f.* pulp.

pulsation /pylsɑsjɔ̃/ *n.f.* (heart)-beat.

pulvéris|er /pylverize/ *v.t.* pulverize; (*liquide*) spray. **~ateur** *n.m.* spray.

punaise /pynɛz/ *n.f.* (*insecte*) bug; (*clou*) drawing-pin; (*Amer.*) thumbtack.

pun|ir /pynir/ *v.t.* punish. **~ition** *n.f.* punishment.

pupille[1] /pypij/ *n.f.* (*de l'œil*) pupil.

pupille[2] /pypij/ *n.m./f.* (*enfant*) ward.

pupitre /pypitr/ *n.m.* (*scol.*) desk. **~ à musique,** music stand.

pur /pyr/ *a.* pure; (*whisky*) neat. **~ement** *adv.* purely. **~eté** *n.f.* purity. **~-sang** *n.m. invar.* (*cheval*) thoroughbred.

purée /pyre/ *n.f.* purée; (*de pommes de terre*) mashed potatoes.

purgatoire /pyrgatwar/ *n.m.* purgatory.

purg|e /pyrʒ/ *n.f.* purge. **~er** *v.t.* (*pol., méd.*) purge; (*peine: jurid.*) serve.

purif|ier /pyrifje/ *v.t.* purify. **~ication** *n.f.* purification.

purin /pyrɛ̃/ *n.m.* (liquid) manure.

puritain, ~e /pyritɛ̃, -ɛn/ *n.m., f.* puritan. —*a.* puritanical.

pus /py/ *n.m.* pus.

pustule /pystyl/ *n.f.* pimple.

putain /pytɛ̃/ *n.f.* (*fam.*) whore.

putréfier (se) /(sə)pytrefje/ *v. pr.* putrefy.

puzzle /pœzl/ *n.m.* jigsaw (puzzle).

P-V *abrév.* (*procès-verbal*) ticket, traffic fine.

pygmée /pigme/ *n.m.* pygmy.

pyjama /piʒama/ *n.m.* pyjamas. **un ~,** a pair of pyjamas.

pylône /pilon/ *n.m.* pylon.

pyramide /piramid/ *n.f.* pyramid.

Pyrénées /pirene/ *n.f.pl.* **les ~,** the Pyrenees.
pyromane /pirɔman/ *n.m./f.* arsonist.

Q

QI *abrév.* (*quotient intellectuel*) IQ.
qu' /k/ *voir* **que.**
quadrill|er /kadrije/ *v.t.* (*zone*) comb, control. **~age** *n.m.* (*mil.*) control. **~é** *a.* (*papier*) squared.
quadrupède /kadrypɛd/ *n.m.* quadruped.
quadrupl|e /kadrypl/ *a.* & *n.m.* quadruple. **~er** *v.t./i.* quadruple. **~és, ~ées** *n.m., f. pl.* quadruplets.
quai /ke/ *n.m.* (*de gare*) platform; (*de port*) quay; (*de rivière*) embankment.
qualificatif /kalifikatif/ *n.m.* (*épithète*) term.
qualif|ier /kalifje/ *v.t.* qualify; (*décrire*) describe (**de,** as). **se ~ier** *v. pr.* qualify (**pour,** for). **~ication** *n.f.* qualification; description. **~ié** *a.* qualified; (*main-d'œuvre*) skilled.
qualit|é /kalite/ *n.f.* quality; (*titre*) occupation. **en ~é de,** in one's capacity as. **~atif, ~ative** *a.* qualitative.
quand /kɑ̃/ *conj.* & *adv.* when. **~ même,** all the same. **~ (bien) même,** even if.
quant (à) /kɑ̃t(a)/ *prép.* as for.
quantit|é /kɑ̃tite/ *n.f.* quantity. **une ~é de,** a lot of. **~atif, ~ative** *a.* quantitative.
quarantaine /karɑ̃tɛn/ *n.f.* (*méd.*) quarantine. **une ~ (de),** about forty.
quarant|e /karɑ̃t/ *a.* & *n.m.* forty. **~ième** *a.* & *n.m./f.* fortieth.
quart /kar/ *n.m.* quarter; (*naut.*) watch. **~ (de litre),** quarter litre. **~ de finale,** quarter-final. **~ d'heure,** quarter of an hour.
quartier /kartje/ *n.m.* neighbourhood, district; (*de lune, bœuf*) quarter; (*de fruit*) segment. **~s,** (*mil.*) quarters. **de ~, du ~,** local. **~ général,** headquarters.
quartz /kwarts/ *n.m.* quartz.
quasi- /kazi/ *préf.* quasi-.
quasiment /kazimɑ̃/ *adv.* almost.
quatorz|e /katɔrz/ *a.* & *n.m.* fourteen. **~ième** *a.* & *n.m./f.* fourteenth.
quatre /katr(ə)/ *a.* & *n.m.* four. **~-vingt(s)** *a.* & *n.m.* eighty. **~-vingt-dix** *a.* & *n.m.* ninety.
quatrième /katrijɛm/ *a.* & *n.m./f.* fourth. **~ment** *adv.* fourthly.
quatuor /kwatɥɔr/ *n.m.* quartet.
que, qu'* /kə, k/ *conj.* that; (*comparaison*) than. **qu'il vienne,** let him come. **qu'il vienne ou non,** whether he comes or not. **ne faire ~ demander**/*etc.*, only ask/*etc.* —*adv.* **(ce) ~ tu es bête, qu'est-ce ~ tu es bête,** how silly you are. **~ de,** what a lot of. —*pron. rel.* (*personne*) that, whom; (*chose*) that, which; (*temps, moment*) when; (*interrogatif*) what. **un jour**/*etc.* **~,** one day/*etc.* when. **~ faites-vous?, qu'est-ce ~ vous faites?,** what are you doing?
Québec /kebɛk/ *n.m.* Quebec.
quel, ~le /kɛl/ *a.* what; (*interrogatif*) which, what; (*qui*) who. —*pron.* which. **~ dommage,** what a pity. **~ qu'il soit,** (*chose*) whatever *ou* whichever it may be; (*personne*) whoever he may be.
quelconque /kɛlkɔ̃k/ *a.* any, some; (*banal*) ordinary; (*médiocre*) poor.
quelque /kɛlkə/ *a.* some. **~s,** a few, some. —*adv.* (*environ*) some. **et ~,** (*fam.*) and a bit. **~ chose,** something; (*interrogation*) anything. **~ part,** somewhere. **~ peu,** somewhat.

quelquefois /kɛlkəfwa/ *adv.* sometimes.
quelques|-uns, ~-unes /kɛlkəzœ̃, -yn/ *pron.* some, a few.
quelqu'un /kɛlkœ̃/ *pron.* someone, somebody; (*interrogation*) anyone, anybody.
quémander /kemɑ̃de/ *v.t.* beg for.
qu'en-dira-t-on /kɑ̃diratɔ̃/ *n.m. invar.* gossip.
querell|e /kərɛl/ *n.f.* quarrel. **~eur, ~euse** *a.* quarrelsome.
quereller (se) /(sə)kərele/ *v. pr.* quarrel.
question /kɛstjɔ̃/ *n.f.* question; (*affaire*) matter, question. **en ~,** in question; (*en jeu*) at stake. **il est ~ de,** (*cela concerne*) it is about; (*on parle de*) there is talk of. **il n'en est pas ~,** it is out of the question. **~ner** /-jɔne/ *v.t.* question.
questionnaire /kɛstjɔnɛr/ *n.m.* questionnaire.
quêt|e /kɛt/ *n.f.* (*relig.*) collection. **en ~e de,** in search of. **~er** /kete/ *v.i.* collect money; *v.t.* seek.
queue /kø/ *n.f.* tail; (*de poêle*) handle; (*de fruit*) stalk; (*de fleur*) stem; (*file*) queue; (*file*: *Amer.*) line; (*de train*) rear. **faire la ~,** queue (up); (*Amer.*) line up. **~ de cheval,** pony-tail.
qui /ki/ *pron. rel.* (*personne*) who; (*chose*) which, that; (*interrogatif*) who; (*après prép.*) whom; (*quiconque*) whoever. **à ~ est ce stylo**/*etc.*?, whose pen/*etc.* is this? **qu'est-ce ~?,** what? **~ est-ce qui?,** who? **~ que ce soit,** anyone.
quiche /kiʃ/ *n.f.* quiche.
quiconque /kikɔ̃k/ *pron.* whoever; (*n'importe qui*) anyone.
quiétude /kjetyd/ *n.f.* quiet.
quille[1] /kij/ *n.f.* (*de bateau*) keel.
quille[2] /kij/ *n.f.* (*jouet*) skittle.
quincaill|ier, ~ière /kɛ̃kɑje, -jɛr/ *n.m., f.* hardware dealer. **~erie** *n.f.* hardware; (*magasin*) hardware shop.
quinine /kinin/ *n.f.* quinine.
quinquenn|al (*m.pl.* **~aux**) /kɛ̃kenal, -o/ *a.* five-year.
quint|al (*pl.* **~aux**) /kɛ̃tal, -o/ *n.m.* quintal (= *100 kg.*).
quintette /kɛ̃tɛt/ *n.m.* quintet.
quintupl|e /kɛ̃typl/ *a.* fivefold. —*n.m.* quintuple. **~er** *v.t./i.* increase fivefold. **~és, ~ées,** *n.m., f. pl.* quintuplets.
quinzaine /kɛ̃zɛn/ *n.f.* **une ~ (de),** about fifteen.
quinz|e /kɛ̃z/ *a.* & *n.m.* fifteen. **~e jours,** two weeks. **~ième** *a.* & *n.m./f.* fifteenth.
quiproquo /kiprɔko/ *n.m.* misunderstanding.
quittance /kitɑ̃s/ *n.f.* receipt.
quitte /kit/ *a.* quits (**envers,** with). **~ à faire,** even if it means doing.
quitter /kite/ *v.t.* leave; (*vêtement*) take off. **se ~** *v. pr.* part.
quoi /kwa/ *pron.* what; (*après prép.*) which. **de ~ vivre/manger**/*etc.*, (*assez*) enough to live on/to eat/*etc.* **de ~ écrire,** sth. to write with, what is necessary to write with. **~ que,** whatever. **~ que ce soit,** anything.
quoique /kwak(ə)/ *conj.* (al)though.
quolibet /kɔlibɛ/ *n.m.* gibe.
quorum /k(w)ɔrɔm/ *n.m.* quorum.
quota /k(w)ɔta/ *n.m.* quota.
quote-part (*pl.* **quotes-parts**) /kɔtpar/ *n.f.* share.
quotidien, ~ne /kɔtidjɛ̃, -jɛn/ *a.* daily; (*banal*) everyday. —*n.m.* daily (paper). **~nement** /-jɛnmɑ̃/ *adv.* daily.
quotient /kɔsjɑ̃/ *n.m.* quotient.

R

rabâcher /rabɑʃe/ *v.t.* keep repeating.
rabais /rabɛ/ *n.m.* (price) reduction.
rabaisser /rabese/ *v.t.* (*déprécier*) belittle; (*réduire*) reduce.
rabat /raba/ *n.m.* flap. **~-joie** *n.m. invar.* killjoy.
rabattre /rabatr/ *v.t.* pull *ou* put down; (*diminuer*) reduce; (*déduire*) take off. **se ~** *v. pr.* (*se refermer*) close; (*véhicule*) cut in, turn sharply. **se ~ sur,** fall back on.
rabbin /rabɛ̃/ *n.m.* rabbi.
rabibocher /rabibɔʃe/ *v.t.* (*fam.*) reconcile.
rabiot /rabjo/ *n.m.* (*fam.*) extra.
râblé /rɑble/ *a.* stocky, sturdy.
rabot /rabo/ *n.m.* plane. **~er** /-ɔte/ *v.t.* plane.
raboteu|x, ~se /rabɔtø, -z/ *a.* uneven.
rabougri /rabugri/ *a.* stunted.
rabrouer /rabrue/ *v.t.* snub.
racaille /rakɑj/ *n.f.* rabble.
raccommoder /rakɔmɔde/ *v.t.* mend; (*personnes*: *fam.*) reconcile.
raccompagner /rakɔ̃paɲe/ *v.t.* see *ou* take back (home).
raccord /rakɔr/ *n.m.* link; (*de papier peint*) join. **~ (de peinture),** touch-up.
raccord|er /rakɔrde/ *v.t.* connect, join. **~ement** *n.m.* connection.
raccourci /rakursi/ *n.m.* short cut. **en ~,** in brief.
raccourcir /rakursir/ *v.t.* shorten. —*v.i.* get shorter.
raccrocher /rakrɔʃe/ *v.t.* hang back up; (*personne*) grab hold of; (*relier*) connect. **~ (le récepteur),** hang up. **se ~ à,** cling to; (*se relier à*) be connected to *ou* with.
raccroc (par) /(par)rakro/ *adv.* by a stroke of luck, by a fluke.
rac|e /ras/ *n.f.* race; (*animale*) breed. **de ~e,** pure-bred. **~ial** (*m. pl.* **~iaux**) *a.* racial.
rachat /raʃa/ *n.m.* buying (back); (*de pécheur*) redemption.
racheter /raʃte/ *v.t.* buy (back); (*davantage*) buy more; (*nouvel objet*) buy another; (*pécheur*) redeem; (*défaut*) make up for. **se ~** *v. pr.* make amends.
racine /rasin/ *n.f.* root.
racis|te /rasist/ *a.* & *n.m./f.* racist. **~me** *n.m.* racism.
raclée /rɑkle/ *n.f.* (*fam.*) thrashing.
racler /rɑkle/ *v.t.* scrape. **se ~ la gorge,** clear one's throat.
racol|er /rakɔle/ *v.t.* solicit. **~age** *n.m.* soliciting.
racontars /rakɔ̃tar/ *n.m. pl.* (*fam.*) gossip, stories.
raconter /rakɔ̃te/ *v.t.* (*histoire*) tell, relate; (*vacances etc.*) tell about. **~ à qn. que,** tell s.o. that, say to s.o. that.
racorni /rakɔrni/ *a.* hard(ened).
radar /radar/ *n.m.* radar.
rade /rad/ *n.f.* harbour. **en ~,** (*personne*: *fam.*) stranded, behind.
radeau (*pl.* **~x**) /rado/ *n.m.* raft.
radiateur /radjatœr/ *n.m.* radiator; (*électrique*) heater.
radiation /radjɑsjɔ̃/ *n.f.* (*énergie*) radiation.
radic|al (*m. pl.* **~aux**) /radikal, -o/ *a.* radical. —*n.m.* (*pl.* **~aux**) radical.
radier /radje/ *v.t.* cross off.
radieu|x, ~se /radjø, -z/ *a.* radiant.
radin, ~e /radɛ̃, -in/ *a.* (*fam.*) stingy.
radio /radjo/ *n.f.* radio; (*radiographie*) X-ray.
radioacti|f, ~ve /radjɔaktif, -v/ *a.* radioactive. **~vité** *n.f.* radioactivity.

radiodiffus|er /radjɔdifyze/ *v.t.* broadcast. **~ion** *n.f.* broadcasting.
radiograph|ie /radjɔgrafi/ *n.f.* (*photographie*) X-ray. **~ier** *v.t.* X-ray. **~ique** *a.* X-ray.
radiologue /radjɔlɔg/ *n.m./f.* radiographer.
radiophonique /radjɔfɔnik/ *a.* radio.
radis /radi/ *n.m.* radish.
radoter /radɔte/ *v.i.* (*fam.*) talk drivel.
radouc|ir (se) /(sə)radusir/ *v. pr.* calm down; (*temps*) become milder. **~issement** *n.m.* (*du temps*) milder weather.
rafale /rafal/ *n.f.* (*de vent*) gust; (*tir*) burst of gunfire.
raffermir /rafɛrmir/ *v.t.* strengthen. **se ~** *v. pr.* become stronger.
raffin|é /rafine/ *a.* refined. **~ement** *n.m.* refinement.
raffin|er /rafine/ *v.t.* refine. **~age** *n.m.* refining. **~erie** *n.f.* refinery.
raffoler /rafɔle/ *v.i.* **~ de,** be extremely fond of.
raffut /rafy/ *n.m.* (*fam.*) din.
rafiot /rafjo/ *n.m.* (*fam.*) boat.
rafistoler /rafistɔle/ *v.t.* (*fam.*) patch up.
rafle /rɑfl/ *n.f.* (police) raid.
rafler /rɑfle/ *v.t.* grab, swipe.
rafraîch|ir /rafreʃir/ *v.t.* cool (down); (*raviver*) brighten up; (*personne, mémoire*) refresh. **se ~ir** *v. pr.* (*se laver*) freshen up; (*boire*) refresh o.s.; (*temps*) get cooler. **~issant, ~issante** *a.* refreshing.
rafraîchissement /rafreʃismɑ̃/ *n.m.* (*boisson*) cold drink. **~s,** (*fruits etc.*) refreshments.
ragaillardir /ragajardir/ *v.t.* (*fam.*) buck up.
rag|e /raʒ/ *n.f.* rage; (*maladie*) rabies. **faire ~e,** rage. **~e de dents,** raging toothache. **~er** *v.i.* rage. **~eur, ~euse** *a.* ill-tempered.
ragot(s) /rago/ *n.m.* (*pl.*) (*fam.*) gossip.
ragoût /ragu/ *n.m.* stew.
raid /rɛd/ *n.m.* (*mil.*) raid; (*sport*) rally.
raid|e /rɛd/ *a.* stiff; (*côte*) steep; (*corde*) tight; (*cheveux*) straight. —*adv.* (*en pente*) steeply. **~eur** *n.f.* stiffness; steepness.
raidir /redir/ *v.t.*, **se ~** *v. pr.* stiffen; (*position*) harden; (*corde*) tighten.
raie[1] /rɛ/ *n.f.* line; (*bande*) strip; (*de cheveux*) parting.
raie[2] /rɛ/ *n.f.* (*poisson*) skate.
raifort /rɛfɔr/ *n.m.* horse-radish.
rail /rɑj/ *n.m.* (*barre*) rail. **le ~,** (*transport*) rail.
raill|er /rɑje/ *v.t.* mock (at). **~erie** *n.f.* mocking remark. **~eur, ~euse** *a.* mocking.
rainure /renyr/ *n.f.* groove.
raisin /rɛzɛ̃/ *n.m.* **~(s),** grapes. **~ sec,** raisin.
raison /rɛzɔ̃/ *n.f.* reason. **à ~ de,** at the rate of. **avec ~,** rightly. **avoir ~,** be right (**de faire,** to do). **avoir ~ de qn.,** get the better of s.o. **donner ~ à,** prove right. **en ~ de,** (*cause*) because of.
raisonnable /rɛzɔnabl/ *a.* reasonable, sensible.
raisonn|er /rɛzɔne/ *v.i.* reason. —*v.t.* (*personne*) reason with. **~ement** *n.m.* reasoning; (*propositions*) argument.
rajeunir /raʒœnir/ *v.t.* make (look) younger; (*moderniser*) modernize; (*méd.*) rejuvenate. —*v.i.* look younger.
rajout /raʒu/ *n.m.* addition. **~er** /-te/ *v.t.* add.
rajust|er /raʒyste/ *v.t.* straighten; (*salaires*) (re)adjust. **~ement** *n.m.* (re)adjustment.
râl|e /rɑl/ *n.m.* (*de blessé*) groan.

~er *v.i.* groan; (*protester*: *fam.*) moan.

ralent|ir /ralɑ̃tir/ *v.t./i.*, **se ~ir** *v. pr.* slow down. **~i** *a.* slow; *n.m.* (*cinéma*) slow motion. **être** *ou* **tourner au ~i,** tick over, idle.

rall|ier /ralje/ *v.t.* rally; (*rejoindre*) rejoin. **se ~ier** *v. pr.* rally. **se ~ier à,** (*avis*) come over to. **~iement** *n.m.* rallying.

rallonge /ralɔ̃ʒ/ *n.f.* (*de table*) extension. **~ de,** (*supplément de*) extra.

rallonger /ralɔ̃ʒe/ *v.t.* lengthen.

rallumer /ralyme/ *v.t.* light (up) again; (*lampe*) switch on again; (*ranimer*: *fig.*) revive.

rallye /rali/ *n.m.* rally.

ramassé /ramɑse/ *a.* squat; (*concis*) concise.

ramass|er /ramɑse/ *v.t.* pick up; (*récolter*) gather; (*recueillir*) collect. **se ~er** *v. pr.* draw o.s. together, curl up. **~age** *n.m.* (*cueillette*) gathering. **~age scolaire,** school bus service.

rambarde /rɑ̃bard/ *n.f.* guard-rail.

rame /ram/ *n.f.* (*aviron*) oar; (*train*) train; (*perche*) stake.

rameau (*pl.* **~x**) /ramo/ *n.m.* branch.

ramener /ramne/ *v.t.* bring back. **~ à,** (*réduire à*) reduce to. **se ~** *v. pr.* (*fam.*) turn up. **se ~ à,** (*problème*) come down to.

ram|er /rame/ *v.i.* row. **~eur, ~euse** *n.m., f.* rower.

ramif|ier (se) /(sə)ramifje/ *v. pr.* ramify. **~ication** *n.f.* ramification.

ramollir /ramɔlir/ *v.t.*, **se ~** *v. pr.* soften.

ramon|er /ramɔne/ *v.t.* sweep. **~eur** *n.m.* (chimney-)sweep.

rampe /rɑ̃p/ *n.f.* banisters; (*pente*) ramp. **~ de lancement,** launching pad.

ramper /rɑ̃pe/ *v.i.* crawl.

rancart /rɑ̃kar/ *n.m.* **mettre** *ou* **jeter au ~,** (*fam.*) scrap.

ranc|e /rɑ̃s/ *a.* rancid. **~ir** *v.i.* go *ou* turn rancid.

rancœur /rɑ̃kœr/ *n.f.* resentment.

rançon /rɑ̃sɔ̃/ *n.f.* ransom. **~ner** /-ɔne/ *v.t.* hold to ransom.

rancun|e /rɑ̃kyn/ *n.f.* grudge. **~ier, ~ière** *a.* vindictive.

randonnée /rɑ̃dɔne/ *n.f.* walk; (*en auto, vélo*) ride.

rang /rɑ̃/ *n.m.* row; (*hiérarchie, condition*) rank. **se mettre en ~s,** line up.

rangée /rɑ̃ʒe/ *n.f.* row.

rang|er /rɑ̃ʒe/ *v.t.* put away; (*chambre etc.*) tidy (up); (*disposer*) place; (*véhicule*) park. **se ~er** *v. pr.* (*véhicule*) park; (*s'écarter*) stand aside; (*s'assagir*) settle down. **se ~er à,** (*avis*) accept. **~ement** *n.m.* (*de chambre*) tidying (up); (*espace*) storage space.

ranimer /ranime/ *v.t.*, **se ~** *v. pr.* revive.

rapace[1] /rapas/ *n.m.* bird of prey.

rapace[2] /rapas/ *a.* grasping.

rapatr|ier /rapatrije/ *v.t.* repatriate. **~iement** *n.m.* repatriation.

râp|e /rɑp/ *n.f.* (*culin.*) grater; (*lime*) rasp. **~er** *v.t.* grate; (*bois*) rasp.

râpé /rɑpe/ *a.* threadbare.

rapetisser /raptise/ *v.t.* make smaller. —*v.i.* get smaller.

râpeu|x, ~se /rɑpø, -z/ *a.* rough.

rapid|e /rapid/ *a.* fast, rapid. —*n.m.* express (train). **~ement** *adv.* fast, rapidly. **~ité** *n.f.* speed.

rapiécer /rapjese/ *v.t.* patch.

rappel /rapɛl/ *n.m.* recall; (*deuxième avis*) reminder; (*de salaire*) back pay.

rappeler /raple/ *v.t.* call back; (*diplomate, réserviste*) recall; (*évoquer*) remind, recall. **~ qch. à**

qn., (*redire*) remind s.o. of sth. **se ~** *v. pr.* remember, recall.
rapport /rapɔr/ *n.m.* connection; (*compte rendu*) report; (*profit*) yield. **~s,** (*relations*) relations. **en ~ avec,** (*accord*) in keeping with. **mettre/se mettre en ~ avec,** put/get in touch with. **par ~ à,** in relation to.
rapport|er /rapɔrte/ *v.t.* bring back; (*profit*) bring in; (*dire, répéter*) report. —*v.i.* (*comm.*) bring in a good return; (*mouchard*: *fam.*) tell tales. **se ~er à,** relate to. **s'en ~er à,** rely on. **~eur, ~euse** *n.m., f.* (*mouchard*) tell-tale; *n.m.* (*instrument*) protractor.
rapproch|er /raprɔʃe/ *v.t.* bring closer (**de,** to); (*réconcilier*) bring together; (*comparer*) compare. **se ~er** *v. pr.* get *ou* come closer (**de,** to); (*personnes, pays*) come together; (*s'apparenter*) be close (**de,** to). **~é** *a.* close. **~ement** *n.m.* reconciliation; (*rapport*) connection; (*comparaison*) parallel.
rapt /rapt/ *n.m.* abduction.
raquette /rakɛt/ *n.f.* (*de tennis*) racket; (*de ping-pong*) bat.
rare /rar/ *a.* rare; (*insuffisant*) scarce. **~ment** *adv.* rarely, seldom. **~té** *n.f.* rarity; scarcity; (*objet*) rarity.
raréfié /rarefje/ *a.* rarefied.
raréfier (se) /(sə)rarefje/ *v. pr.* (*nourriture etc.*) become scarce.
ras, ~e /rɑ, rɑz/ *a.* (*herbe, poil*) short. **à ~ de,** very close to. **en avoir ~ le bol,** (*fam.*) be really fed up. **~e campagne,** open country.
ras|er /rɑze/ *v.t.* shave; (*cheveux, barbe*) shave off; (*frôler*) skim; (*abattre*) raze; (*ennuyer*: *fam.*) bore. **se ~er** *v. pr.* shave. **~age** *n.m.* shaving. **~eur, ~euse** *n.m., f.* (*fam.*) bore.
rasoir /rɑzwar/ *n.m.* razor.
rassas|ier /rasazje/ *v.t.* satisfy. **être ~ié de,** have had enough of.
rassembl|er /rasɑ̃ble/ *v.t.* gather; (*courage*) muster. **se ~er** *v. pr.* gather. **~ement** *n.m.* gathering.
rasseoir (se) /(sə)raswar/ *v. pr.* sit down again.
rass|is, ~ise *ou* **~ie** /rasi, -z/ *a.* (*pain*) stale.
rassurer /rasyre/ *v.t.* reassure.
rat /ra/ *n.m.* rat.
ratatiner (se) /(sə)ratatine/ *v. pr.* shrivel up.
rate /rat/ *n.f.* spleen.
râteau (*pl.* **~x**) /rɑto/ *n.m.* rake.
râtelier /rɑtəlje/ *n.m.* (*de bétail*) (stable-)rack; (*support*) rack.
rat|er /rate/ *v.t./i.* miss; (*gâcher*) spoil; (*échouer*) fail. **~é, ~ée** *n.m., f.* (*personne*) failure. **avoir des ~és,** (*auto.*) backfire.
ratif|ier /ratifje/ *v.t.* ratify. **~ication** *n.f.* ratification.
ration /rɑsjɔ̃/ *n.f.* ration.
rationaliser /rasjɔnalize/ *v.t.* rationalize.
rationnel, ~le /rasjɔnɛl/ *a.* rational.
rationn|er /rasjɔne/ *v.t.* ration. **~ement** *n.m.* rationing.
ratisser /ratise/ *v.t.* rake; (*fouiller*) comb.
rattacher /rataʃe/ *v.t.* tie up again; (*relier*) link; (*incorporer*) join.
rattrapage /ratrapaʒ/ *n.m.* **~ scolaire,** remedial classes.
rattraper /ratrape/ *v.t.* catch; (*rejoindre*) catch up with; (*retard, erreur*) make up for. **se ~** *v. pr.* catch up; (*se dédommager*) make up for it. **se ~ à,** catch hold of.
ratur|e /ratyr/ *n.f.* deletion. **~er** *v.t.* delete.
rauque /rok/ *a.* raucous, harsh.
ravager /ravaʒe/ *v.t.* devastate, ravage.
ravages /ravaʒ/ *n.m. pl.* **faire des ~,** wreak havoc.
raval|er /ravale/ *v.t.* (*façade etc.*)

clean; (*humilier*) lower. **~ement** *n.m.* cleaning.
ravauder /ravode/ *v.t.* mend.
ravi /ravi/ *a.* delighted (**que,** that).
ravier /ravje/ *n.m.* hors-d'œuvre dish.
ravigoter /ravigɔte/ *v.t.* (*fam.*) buck up.
ravin /ravɛ̃/ *n.m.* ravine.
ravioli /ravjɔli/ *n.m. pl.* ravioli.
ravir /ravir/ *v.t.* delight. **~ à qn.,** (*enlever*) rob s.o. of.
raviser (se) /(sə)ravize/ *v. pr.* change one's mind.
ravissant, ~e /ravisɑ̃, -t/ *a.* beautiful.
ravisseu|r, ~se /ravisœr, -øz/ *n.m., f.* kidnapper.
ravitaill|er /ravitɑje/ *v.t.* provide with supplies; (*avion*) refuel. **se ~er** *v. pr.* stock up. **~ement** *n.m.* provision of supplies (**de,** to); refuelling; (*denrées*) supplies.
raviver /ravive/ *v.t.* revive.
rayé /reje/ *a.* striped.
rayer /reje/ *v.t.* scratch; (*biffer*) cross out.
rayon /rɛjɔ̃/ *n.m.* ray; (*planche*) shelf; (*de magasin*) department; (*de roue*) spoke; (*de cercle*) radius. **~ d'action,** range. **~ de miel,** honeycomb. **~ X,** X-ray.
rayonn|er /rɛjɔne/ *v.i.* radiate; (*de joie*) beam; (*se déplacer*) tour around (*from a central point*). **~ement** *n.m.* (*éclat*) radiance; (*influence*) influence; (*radiations*) radiation.
rayure /rejyr/ *n.f.* scratch; (*dessin*) stripe. **à ~s,** striped.
raz-de-marée /rɑdmare/ *n.m. invar.* tidal wave. **~ électoral,** landslide.
re- /rə/ *préf.* re-.
ré- /re/ *préf.* re-.
réacteur /reaktœr/ *n.m.* jet engine; (*nucléaire*) reactor.
réaction /reaksjɔ̃/ *n.f.* reaction. **~ en chaîne,** chain reaction. **~naire** /-jɔnɛr/ *a.* & *n.m./f.* reactionary.
réadapter /readapte/ *v.t.,* **se ~** *v. pr.* readjust.
réaffirmer /reafirme/ *v.t.* reaffirm.
réagir /reaʒir/ *v.i.* react.
réalis|er /realize/ *v.t.* carry out; (*effort, bénéfice, achat*) make; (*rêve*) fulfil; (*film*) produce, direct; (*capital*) realize; (*se rendre compte de*: *fam.*) realize. **se ~er** *v. pr.* materialize. **~ateur, ~atrice** *n.m., f.* (*cinéma*) director; (*TV*) producer. **~ation** *n.f.* realization; (*œuvre*) achievement.
réalis|te /realist/ *a.* realistic. —*n.m./f.* realist. **~me** *n.m.* realism.
réalité /realite/ *n.f.* reality.
réanim|er /reanime/ *v.t.* resuscitate. **~ation** *n.f.* resuscitation.
réapparaître /reaparɛtr/ *v.i.* reappear.
réarm|er (se) /(sə)rearme/ *v. pr.* rearm. **~ement** *n.m.* rearmament.
rébarbati|f, ~ve /rebarbatif, -v/ *a.* forbidding, off-putting.
rebâtir /rəbɑtir/ *v.t.* rebuild.
rebattu /rəbaty/ *a.* hackneyed.
rebelle /rəbɛl/ *a.* rebellious; (*soldat*) rebel. —*n.m./f.* rebel.
rebeller (se) /(sə)rəbele/ *v. pr.* rebel, hit back defiantly.
rébellion /rebeljɔ̃/ *n.f.* rebellion.
rebiffer (se) /(sə)rəbife/ *v. pr.* (*fam.*) rebel.
rebond /rəbɔ̃/ *n.m.* bounce; (*par ricochet*) rebound. **~ir** /-dir/ *v.i.* bounce; rebound.
rebondi /rəbɔ̃di/ *a.* chubby.
rebondissement /rəbɔ̃dismɑ̃/ *n.m.* (new) development.
rebord /rəbɔr/ *n.m.* edge. **~ de la fenêtre,** window-ledge.
rebours (à) /(a)rəbur/ *adv.* the wrong way.

rebrousser /rəbruse/ *v.t.* **~ chemin,** turn back.

rebuffade /rəbyfad/ *n.f.* rebuff.

rébus /rebys/ *n.m.* rebus.

rebut /rəby/ *n.m.* **mettre** *ou* **jeter au ~,** scrap.

rebut|er /rəbyte/ *v.t.* put off. **~ant, ~ante** *a.* off-putting.

récalcitrant, ~e /rekalsitrɑ̃, -t/ *a.* stubborn.

recal|er /rəkale/ *v.t.* (*fam.*) fail. **être ~é,** fail.

récapitul|er /rekapityle/ *v.t./i.* recapitulate. **~ation** *n.f.* recapitulation.

recel /rəsɛl/ *n.m.* receiving. **~er** /rəs(ə)le/ *v.t.* (*objet volé*) receive; (*cacher*) conceal.

récemment /resamɑ̃/ *adv.* recently.

recens|er /rəsɑ̃se/ *v.t.* (*population*) take a census of; (*objets*) list. **~ement** *n.m.* census; list.

récent, ~e /resɑ̃, -t/ *a.* recent.

récépissé /resepise/ *n.m.* receipt.

récepteur /resɛptœr/ *n.m.* receiver.

récepti|f, ~ve /resɛptif, -v/ *a.* receptive.

réception /resɛpsjɔ̃/ *n.f.* reception. **~ de,** (*lettre etc.*) receipt of. **~niste** /-jɔnist/ *n.m./f.* receptionist.

récession /resesjɔ̃/ *n.f.* recession.

recette /rəsɛt/ *n.f.* (*culin.*) recipe; (*argent*) takings. **~s,** (*comm.*) receipts.

receveu|r, ~se /rəsvœr, -øz/ *n.m., f.* (*d'autobus*) (bus-)conductor, (bus-)conductress; (*des impôts*) tax collector.

recevoir† /rəsvwar/ *v.t.* receive; (*obtenir*) get, receive. **être reçu (à),** pass. —*v.i.* (*médecin*) receive patients. **se ~** *v. pr.* (*tomber*) land.

rechange (de) /(də)rəʃɑ̃ʒ/ *a.* (*roue, vêtements, etc.*) spare; (*politique etc.*) alternative.

réchapper /reʃape/ *v.i.* **~ de** *ou* **à,** come through, survive.

recharg|e /rəʃarʒ/ *n.f.* (*de stylo*) refill. **~er** *v.t.* refill; (*batterie*) recharge.

réchaud /reʃo/ *n.m.* stove.

réchauff|er /reʃofe/ *v.t.* warm up. **se ~er** *v. pr.* warm o.s. up; (*temps*) get warmer. **~ement** *n.m.* (*de température*) rise (**de,** in).

rêche /rɛʃ/ *a.* harsh.

recherche /rəʃɛrʃ/ *n.f.* search (**de,** for); (*raffinement*) elegance. **~(s),** (*univ.*) research. **~s,** (*enquête*) investigations.

recherch|er /rəʃɛrʃe/ *v.t.* search for. **~é** *a.* in great demand; (*élégant*) elegant. **~é pour meurtre,** wanted for murder.

rechigner /rəʃiɲe/ *v.i.* **~ à,** balk at.

rechut|e /rəʃyt/ *n.f.* (*méd.*) relapse. **~er** *v.i.* relapse.

récidiv|e /residiv/ *n.f.* second offence. **~er** *v.i.* commit a second offence.

récif /resif/ *n.m.* reef.

récipient /resipjɑ̃/ *n.m.* container.

réciproque /resiprɔk/ *a.* mutual, reciprocal. **~ment** *adv.* each other; (*inversement*) conversely.

récit /resi/ *n.m.* (*compte rendu*) account, story; (*histoire*) story.

récital (*pl.* **~s**) /resital/ *n.m.* recital.

récit|er /resite/ *v.t.* recite. **~ation** *n.f.* recitation.

réclame /reklam/ *n.f.* advertising; (*annonce*) advertisement.

réclam|er /reklame/ *v.t.* call for, demand; (*revendiquer*) claim. —*v.i.* complain. **~ation** *n.f.* complaint.

reclus, ~e /rəkly, -z/ *n.m., f.* recluse. —*a.* cloistered.

réclusion /reklyzjɔ̃/ *n.f.* imprisonment.

recoin /rəkwɛ̃/ *n.m.* nook.

récolt|e /rekɔlt/ *n.f.* (*action*) harvest; (*produits*) crop, harvest;

(*fig.*) crop. **~er** *v.t.* harvest, gather; (*fig.*) collect.

recommand|er /rəkɔmɑ̃de/ *v.t.* recommend; (*lettre*) register. **~ation** *n.f.* recommendation.

recommencer /rəkɔmɑ̃se/ *v.t./i.* (*reprendre*) begin *ou* start again; (*refaire*) repeat.

récompens|e /rekɔ̃pɑ̃s/ *n.f.* reward; (*prix*) award. **~er** *v.t.* reward (**de,** for).

réconcil|ier /rekɔ̃silje/ *v.t.* reconcile. **se ~ier** *v. pr.* become reconciled. **~iation** *n.f.* reconciliation.

reconduire† /rəkɔ̃dɥir/ *v.t.* see home; (*à la porte*) show out; (*renouveler*) renew.

réconfort /rekɔ̃fɔr/ *n.m.* comfort. **~er** /-te/ *v.t.* comfort.

reconnaissable /rəkɔnɛsabl/ *a.* recognizable.

reconnaissan|t, ~te /rəkɔnɛsɑ̃, -t/ *a.* grateful (**de,** for). **~ce** *n.f.* gratitude; (*fait de reconnaître*) recognition; (*mil.*) reconnaissance.

reconnaître† /rəkɔnɛtr/ *v.t.* recognize; (*admettre*) admit (**que,** that); (*mil.*) reconnoitre. **se ~** *v. pr.* (*s'orienter*) find one's bearings.

reconstituant /rəkɔ̃stitɥɑ̃/ *n.m.* tonic.

reconstituer /rəkɔ̃stitɥe/ *v.t.* reconstitute; (*crime*) reconstruct.

reconstr|uire† /rəkɔ̃strɥir/ *v.t.* rebuild. **~uction** *n.f.* rebuilding.

reconversion /rəkɔ̃vɛrsjɔ̃/ *n.f.* (*de main-d'œuvre*) redeployment.

record /rəkɔr/ *n.m.* & *a. invar.* record.

recouper /rəkupe/ *v.t.* confirm. **se ~** *v. pr.* check, tally, match up.

recourbé /rəkurbe/ *a.* curved; (*nez*) hooked.

recourir /rəkurir/ *v.i.* **~ à,** resort to.

recours /rəkur/ *n.m.* resort. **avoir ~ à,** have recourse to, resort to.

recouvrer /rəkuvre/ *v.t.* recover.

recouvrir† /rəkuvrir/ *v.t.* cover.

récréation /rekreɑsjɔ̃/ *n.f.* recreation; (*scol.*) playtime.

récrier (se) /(sə)rekrije/ *v. pr.* cry out.

récrimination /rekriminɑsjɔ̃/ *n.f.* recrimination.

recroqueviller (se) /(sə)rəkrɔkvije/ *v. pr.* curl up.

recrudescence /rəkrydesɑ̃s/ *n.f.* new outbreak.

recrue /rəkry/ *n.f.* recruit.

recrut|er /rəkryte/ *v.t.* recruit. **~ement** *n.m.* recruitment.

rectang|le /rɛktɑ̃gl/ *n.m.* rectangle. **~ulaire** *a.* rectangular.

rectif|ier /rɛktifje/ *v.t.* correct, rectify. **~ication** *n.f.* correction.

recto /rɛkto/ *n.m.* front of the page.

reçu /rəsy/ *voir* **recevoir.** *—n.m.* receipt. *—a.* accepted; (*candidat*) successful.

recueil /rəkœj/ *n.m.* collection.

recueill|ir† /rəkœjir/ *v.t.* collect; (*prendre chez soi*) take in. **se ~ir** *v. pr.* meditate. **~ement** *n.m.* meditation. **~i** *a.* meditative.

recul /rəkyl/ *n.m.* retreat; (*éloignement*) distance; (*déclin*) decline. (**mouvement de**) **~,** backward movement. **~ade** *n.f.* retreat.

reculé /rəkyle/ *a.* remote.

reculer /rəkyle/ *v.t./i.* move back; (*véhicule*) reverse; (*armée*) retreat; (*diminuer*) decline; (*différer*) postpone. **~ devant,** (*fig.*) shrink from.

reculons (à) /(a)rəkylɔ̃/ *adv.* backwards.

récupér|er /rekypere/ *v.t./i.* recover; (*vieux objets*) salvage. **~ation** *n.f.* recovery; salvage.

récurer /rekyre/ *v.t.* scour.

récuser /rekyze/ *v.t.* challenge. **se ~** *v. pr.* state that one is not qualified to judge.

recycl|er /rəsikle/ *v.t.* (*personne*) retrain; (*chose*) recycle. **se ~er**

v. pr. retrain. **~age** *n.m.* retraining; recycling.

rédac|teur, ~trice /redaktœr, -tris/ *n.m., f.* writer, editor. **le ~teur en chef,** the editor (in chief).

rédaction /redaksjõ/ *n.f.* writing; (*scol.*) composition; (*personnel*) editorial staff.

reddition /redisjõ/ *n.f.* surrender.

redevance /rədvɑ̃s/ *n.f.* (*de télévision*) licence fee.

rédiger /rediʒe/ *v.t.* write; (*contrat*) draw up.

redire† /rədir/ *v.t.* repeat. **avoir** *ou* **trouver à ~ à,** find fault with.

redondant, ~e /rədõdɑ̃, -t/ *a.* superfluous.

redonner /rədɔne/ *v.t.* give back; (*davantage*) give more.

redoubl|er /rəduble/ *v.t./i.* increase; (*classe: scol.*) repeat. **~er de prudence**/*etc.*, be more careful/*etc.* **~ement** *n.m.* (*accroissement*) increase (**de,** in).

redout|er /rədute/ *v.t.* dread. **~able** *a.* formidable.

redoux /rədu/ *n.m.* milder weather.

redress|er /rədrese/ *v.t.* straighten (out *ou* up); (*situation*) right, redress. **se ~er** *v. pr.* (*personne*) straighten (o.s) up; (*se remettre debout*) stand up; (*pays, économie*) recover. **~ement** /rədrɛsmɑ̃/ *n.m.* (*relèvement*) recovery.

réduction /redyksjõ/ *n.f.* reduction.

réduire† /redɥir/ *v.t.* reduce (**à,** to). **se ~ à,** (*revenir à*) come down to.

réduit[1], **~e** /redɥi, -t/ *a.* (*objet*) small-scale; (*limité*) limited.

réduit[2] /redɥi/ *n.m.* recess.

réédu|quer /reedyke/ *v.t.* (*personne*) rehabilitate; (*membre*) re-educate. **~cation** *n.f.* rehabilitation; re-education.

réel, ~le /reɛl/ *a.* real. —*n.m.* reality. **~lement** *adv.* really.

réexpédier /reɛkspedje/ *v.t.* forward; (*retourner*) send back.

refaire† /rəfɛr/ *v.t.* do again; (*erreur, voyage*) make again; (*réparer*) do up, redo.

réfection /refɛksjõ/ *n.f.* repair.

réfectoire /refɛktwar/ *n.m.* refectory.

référence /referɑ̃s/ *n.f.* reference.

référendum /referɛ̃dɔm/ *n.m.* referendum.

référer /refere/ *v.i.* **en ~ à,** refer the matter to. **se ~ à,** refer to.

refermer /rəfɛrme/ *v.t.,* **se ~,** *v. pr.* close (again).

refiler /rəfile/ *v.t.* (*fam.*) palm off (**à,** on).

réfléch|ir /refleʃir/ *v.i.* think (**à,** about). —*v.t.* reflect. **se ~ir** *v. pr.* be reflected. **~i** *a.* (*personne*) thoughtful; (*verbe*) reflexive.

refl|et /rəflɛ/ *n.m.* reflection; (*lumière*) light. **~éter** /-ete/ *v.t.* reflect. **se ~éter** *v. pr.* be reflected.

réflexe /reflɛks/ *a.* & *n.m.* reflex.

réflexion /reflɛksjõ/ *n.f.* reflection; (*pensée*) thought, reflection. **à la ~,** on second thoughts.

refluer /rəflye/ *v.i.* flow back; (*foule*) retreat.

reflux /rəfly/ *n.m.* (*de marée*) ebb.

refondre /rəfõdr/ *v.t.* recast.

réform|e /refɔrm/ *n.f.* reform. **~ateur, ~atrice** *n.m., f.* reformer. **~er** *v.t.* reform; (*soldat*) invalid (out of the army). **se ~er** *v. pr.* mend one's ways.

refoul|er /rəfule/ *v.t.* force back; (*désir*) repress. **~é** *a.* repressed. **~ement** *n.m.* repression.

réfractaire /refraktɛr/ *a.* **être ~ à,** resist.

refrain /rəfrɛ̃/ *n.m.* chorus.

refréner /rəfrene/ *v.t.* curb, check.

réfrigér|er /refriʒere/ *v.t.* refrigerate. **~ateur** *n.m.* refrigerator.

refroid|ir /rəfrwadir/ *v.t./i.* cool (down). **se ~ir** *v. pr.* (*personne, temps*) get cold; (*ardeur*) cool (off). **~issement** *n.m.* cooling; (*rhume*) chill.
refuge /rəfyʒ/ *n.m.* refuge; (*chalet*) mountain hut.
réfug|ier (se) /(sə)refyʒje/ *v. pr.* take refuge. **~ié, ~iée** *n.m., f.* refugee.
refus /rəfy/ *n.m.* refusal. **~er** /-ze/ *v.t.* refuse (**de,** to); (*recaler*) fail. **se ~er à,** (*évidence etc.*) reject.
réfuter /refyte/ *v.t.* refute.
regagner /rəgɑɲe/ *v.t.* regain; (*revenir à*) get back to.
regain /rəgɛ̃/ *n.m.* **~ de,** renewal of.
régal (*pl.* **~s**) /regal/ *n.m.* treat. **~er** *v.t.* treat (**de,** to). **se ~er** *v. pr.* treat o.s. (**de,** to).
regard /rəgar/ *n.m.* (*expression, coup d'œil*) look; (*fixe*) stare; (*vue, œil*) eye. **au ~ de,** in regard to. **en ~ de,** compared with.
regardant, ~e /rəgardɑ̃, -t/ *a.* careful (with money).
regarder /rəgarde/ *v.t.* look at; (*observer*) watch; (*considérer*) consider; (*concerner*) concern. **~ (fixement),** stare at. *—v.i.* look. **~ à,** (*qualité etc.*) pay attention to. **~ vers,** (*maison*) face. **se ~** *v. pr.* (*personnes*) look at each other.
régates /regat/ *n.f. pl.* regatta.
régénérer /reʒenere/ *v.t.* regenerate.
régen|t, ~te /reʒɑ̃, -t/ *n.m., f.* regent. **~ce** *n.f.* regency.
régenter /reʒɑ̃te/ *v.t.* rule.
régie /reʒi/ *n.f.* (*entreprise*) public corporation.
regimber /rəʒɛ̃be/ *v.i.* balk.
régime /reʒim/ *n.m.* system; (*pol.*) regime; (*méd.*) diet; (*de moteur*) speed; (*de bananes*) bunch.
régiment /reʒimɑ̃/ *n.m.* regiment.
région /reʒjɔ̃/ *n.f.* region. **~al** (*m. pl.* **~aux**) /-jɔnal, -o/ *a.* regional.
régir /reʒir/ *v.t.* govern.
régisseur /reʒisœr/ *n.m.* (*théâtre*) stage-manager.
registre /rəgistr/ *n.m.* register.
réglage /reglaʒ/ *n.m.* adjustment.
règle /rɛgl/ *n.f.* rule; (*instrument*) ruler. **~s,** (*de femme*) period. **en ~,** in order. **~ à calculer,** slide-rule.
réglé /regle/ *a.* (*vie*) ordered.
règlement /rɛgləmɑ̃/ *n.m.* regulation; (*règles*) regulations; (*solution, paiement*) settlement. **~aire** /-tɛr/ *a.* (*uniforme*) regulation.
réglement|er /rɛgləmɑ̃te/ *v.t.* regulate. **~ation** *n.f.* regulation.
régler /regle/ *v.t.* settle; (*machine*) adjust; (*personne*) settle up with; (*papier*) rule. *—v.i.* (*payer*) settle (up). **~ son compte à,** settle a score with.
réglisse /reglis/ *n.f.* liquorice.
règne /rɛɲ/ *n.m.* reign; (*végétal, animal, minéral*) kingdom.
régner /reɲe/ *v.i.* reign.
regorger /rəgɔrʒe/ *v.i.* **~ de,** be overflowing with.
regret /rəgrɛ/ *n.m.* regret. **à ~,** with regret.
regrett|er /rəgrete/ *v.t.* regret; (*personne*) miss. **~able** *a.* regrettable.
regrouper /rəgrupe/ *v.t.,* **se ~** *v. pr.* gather (together).
régulariser /regylarize/ *v.t.* regularize.
régulation /regylɑsjɔ̃/ *n.f.* regulation.
régul|ier, ~ière /regylje, -jɛr/ *a.* regular; (*qualité, vitesse*) steady, even; (*ligne, paysage*) even; (*légal*) legal; (*honnête*) honest. **~arité** *n.f.* regularity; steadiness; evenness. **~ièrement** *adv.* regularly; (*d'ordinaire*) normally.
réhabilit|er /reabilite/ *n.f.* rehabilitate. **~ation** *n.f.* rehabilitation.

rehausser /rəose/ *v.t.* raise; (*faire valoir*) enhance.
rein /rɛ̃/ *n.m.* kidney. **~s,** (*dos*) small of the back.
reine /rɛn/ *n.f.* queen. **~-claude** *n.f.* greengage.
réinsertion /reɛ̃sɛrsjɔ̃/ *n.f.* reintegration, rehabilitation.
réitérer /reitere/ *v.t.* repeat.
rejaillir /rəʒajir/ *v.i.* **~ sur,** rebound on.
rejet /rəʒɛ/ *n.m.* rejection.
rejeter /rəʒte/ *v.t.* throw back; (*refuser*) reject; (*vomir*) bring up; (*déverser*) discharge. **~ une faute**/*etc.* **sur qn.,** shift the blame for a mistake/*etc.* on to s.o.
rejeton(s) /rəʒtɔ̃/ *n.m.* (*pl.*) (*fam.*) offspring.
rejoindre† /rəʒwɛ̃dr/ *v.t.* go back to, rejoin; (*rattraper*) catch up with; (*rencontrer*) join, meet. **se ~** *v. pr.* (*personnes*) meet; (*routes*) join, meet.
réjoui /reʒwi/ *a.* joyful.
réjou|ir /reʒwir/ *v.t.* delight. **se ~ir** *v. pr.* be delighted (**de qch.,** at sth.). **~issances** *n.f. pl.* festivities. **~issant, ~issante** *a.* cheering.
relâche /rəlɑʃ/ *n.m.* (*repos*) respite. **faire ~,** (*théâtre*) close.
relâché /rəlɑʃe/ *a.* lax.
relâch|er /rəlɑʃe/ *v.t.* slacken; (*personne*) release; (*discipline*) relax. **se ~er** *v. pr.* slacken. **~ement** *n.m.* slackening.
relais /rəlɛ/ *n.m.* relay. **~ (routier),** roadside café.
relanc|e /rəlɑ̃s/ *n.f.* boost. **~er** *v.t.* boost, revive; (*renvoyer*) throw back.
relati|f, ~ve /rəlatif, -v/ *a.* relative.
relation /rəlɑsjɔ̃/ *n.f.* relation(ship); (*ami*) acquaintance; (*récit*) account. **~s,** relations. **en ~ avec qn.,** in touch with s.o.
relativement /rəlativmɑ̃/ *adv.* relatively. **~ à,** in relation to.
relativité /rəlativite/ *n.f.* relativity.
relax|er (se) /(sə)rəlakse/ *v. pr.* relax. **~ation** *n.f.* relaxation.
relayer /rəleje/ *v.t.* relieve; (*émission*) relay. **se ~** *v. pr.* take over from one another.
reléguer /rəlege/ *v.t.* relegate.
relent /rəlɑ̃/ *n.m.* stench.
relève /rəlɛv/ *n.f.* relief. **prendre** *ou* **assurer la ~,** take over (**de,** from).
relevé /rəlve/ *n.m.* list; (*de compte*) statement; (*de compteur*) reading.
relèvement /rəlɛvmɑ̃/ *n.m.* recovery.
relever /rəlve/ *v.t.* pick up; (*personne tombée*) help up; (*remonter*) raise; (*col*) turn up; (*manches*) roll up; (*sauce*) season; (*goût*) bring out; (*compteur*) read; (*défi*) accept; (*relayer*) relieve; (*remarquer, noter*) note; (*rebâtir*) rebuild. **~ qn. de,** relieve s.o. of. —*v.i.* **~ de,** (*dépendre de*) be the concern of; (*méd.*) recover from. **se ~** *v. pr.* (*personne*) get up (again); (*pays, économie*) recover.
relief /rəljɛf/ *n.m.* relief. **mettre en ~,** highlight.
relier /rəlje/ *v.t.* link (**à,** to); (*ensemble*) link together; (*livre*) bind.
religieu|x, ~se /rəliʒjø, -z/ *a.* religious. —*n.m.* monk. —*n.f.* nun.
religion /rəliʒjɔ̃/ *n.f.* religion.
reliquat /rəlika/ *n.m.* residue.
relique /rəlik/ *n.f.* relic.
reliure /rəljyr/ *n.f.* binding.
reluire /rəlɥir/ *v.i.* shine. **faire ~,** shine.
reluisant, ~e /rəlɥizɑ̃, -t/ *a.* shiny. **peu** *ou* **pas ~,** not brilliant.
reman|ier /rəmanje/ *v.t.* revise; (*ministère*) reshuffle. **~iement** *n.m.* revision; reshuffle.

remarier (se) /(sə)rəmarje/ *v. pr.* remarry.

remarquable /rəmarkabl/ *a.* remarkable.

remarque /rəmark/ *n.f.* remark.

remarquer /rəmarke/ *v.t.* notice; (*dire*) say. **faire ~,** point out (**à,** to). **se faire ~,** attract attention.

remblai /rɑ̃blɛ/ *n.m.* embankment.

rembourrer /rɑ̃bure/ *v.t.* pad.

rembours|er /rɑ̃burse/ *v.t.* repay; (*billet, frais*) refund. **~ement** *n.m.* repayment; refund.

remède /rəmɛd/ *n.m.* remedy; (*médicament*) medicine.

remédier /rəmedje/ *v.i.* **~ à,** remedy.

remémorer (se) /(sə)rəmemɔre/ *v. pr.* recall.

remerc|ier /rəmɛrsje/ *v.t.* thank (**de,** for); (*licencier*) dismiss. **~iements** *n.m. pl.* thanks.

remettre† /rəmɛtr/ *v.t.* put back; (*vêtement*) put back on; (*donner*) hand (over); (*devoir, démission*) hand in; (*restituer*) give back; (*différer*) put off; (*ajouter*) add; (*se rappeler*) remember; (*peine*) remit. **se ~** *v. pr.* (*guérir*) recover. **se ~ à,** go back to. **se ~ à faire,** start doing again. **s'en ~ à,** leave it to. **~ en cause** *ou* **en question,** call into question.

remise[1] /rəmiz/ *n.f.* (*abri*) shed.

remise[2] /rəmiz/ *n.f.* (*rabais*) discount; (*livraison*) delivery; (*ajournement*) postponement. **~ en cause** *ou* **en question,** calling into question.

remiser /rəmize/ *v.t.* put away.

rémission /remisjɔ̃/ *n.f.* remission.

remontant /rəmɔ̃tɑ̃/ *n.m.* tonic.

remontée /rəmɔ̃te/ *n.f.* ascent; (*d'eau, de prix*) rise. **~ mécanique,** ski-lift.

remont|er /rəmɔ̃te/ *v.i.* go *ou* come (back) up; (*prix, niveau*) rise (again); (*revenir*) go back. —*v.t.* (*rue etc.*) go *ou* come (back) up; (*relever*) raise; (*montre*) wind up; (*objet démonté*) put together again; (*personne*) buck up. **~e-pente** *n.m.* ski-lift.

remontoir /rəmɔ̃twar/ *n.m.* winder.

remontrer /rəmɔ̃tre/ *v.t.* show again.

remords /rəmɔr/ *n.m.* remorse. **avoir un** *ou* **des ~,** feel remorse.

remorqu|e /rəmɔrk/ *n.f.* (*véhicule*) trailer. **en ~e,** on tow. **~er** *v.t.* tow.

remorqueur /rəmɔrkœr/ *n.m.* tug.

remous /rəmu/ *n.m.* eddy; (*de bateau*) backwash; (*fig.*) turmoil.

rempart /rɑ̃par/ *n.m.* rampart.

remplaçant, ~e /rɑ̃plasɑ̃, -t/ *n.m., f.* replacement; (*joueur*) reserve.

remplac|er /rɑ̃plase/ *v.t.* replace. **~ement** *n.m.* replacement.

rempli /rɑ̃pli/ *a.* full (**de,** of).

rempl|ir /rɑ̃plir/ *v.t.* fill (up); (*formulaire*) fill (in *ou* out); (*tâche, condition*) fulfil. **se ~ir** *v. pr.* fill (up). **~issage** *n.m.* filling; (*de texte*) padding.

remporter /rɑ̃pɔrte/ *v.t.* take back; (*victoire*) win.

remuant, ~e /rəmɥɑ̃, -t/ *a.* restless.

remue-ménage /rəmymenaʒ/ *n.m. invar.* commotion, bustle.

remuer /rəmɥe/ *v.t./i.* move; (*thé, café*) stir; (*gigoter*) fidget; (*dent*) be loose. **se ~** *v. pr.* move.

rémunér|er /remynere/ *v.t.* pay. **~ation** *n.f.* payment.

renâcler /rənɑkle/ *v.i.* snort. **~ à,** balk at, jib at.

ren|aître /rənɛtr/ *v.i.* be reborn; (*sentiment*) be revived. **~aissance** *n.f.* rebirth.

renard /rənar/ *n.m.* fox.

renchérir /rɑ̃ʃerir/ *v.i.* become dearer. **~ sur,** go one better than.

rencontr|e /rɑ̃kɔ̃tr/ *n.f.* meeting;

(*de routes*) junction; (*mil.*) encounter; (*match*) match; (*Amer.*) game. **~er** *v.t.* meet; (*heurter*) strike; (*trouver*) find. **se ~er** *v. pr.* meet.

rendement /rɑ̃dmɑ̃/ *n.m.* yield; (*travail*) output.

rendez-vous /rɑ̃devu/ *n.m.* appointment; (*d'amoureux*) date; (*lieu*) meeting-place.

rendormir (se) /(sə)rɑ̃dɔrmir/ *v. pr.* go back to sleep.

rendre /rɑ̃dr/ *v.t.* give back, return; (*donner en retour*) return; (*son, monnaie*) give; (*hommage*) pay; (*justice*) dispense; (*jugement*) pronounce; (*expression*) render. **~ heureux/possible**/*etc.*, make happy/possible/*etc.* —*v.i.* (*terres*) yield; (*vomir*) vomit. **se ~** *v. pr.* (*capituler*) surrender; (*aller*) go (**à**, to); (*ridicule, utile, etc.*) make o.s. **~ compte de**, report on. **~ des comptes à**, be accountable to. **~ justice à qn.**, do s.o. justice. **~ service (à)**, help. **~ visite à**, visit. **se ~ compte de**, realize.

rendu /rɑ̃dy/ *a.* (*fatigué*) exhausted. **être ~**, (*arrivé*) have arrived.

rêne /rɛn/ *n.f.* rein.

renégat, ~e /rənega, -t/ *n.m., f.* renegade.

renfermé /rɑ̃fɛrme/ *n.m.* stale smell. **sentir le ~**, smell stale.

renferm|er /rɑ̃fɛrme/ *v.t.* contain. **se ~er (en soi-même)**, withdraw (into o.s.).

renfl|é /rɑ̃fle/ *a.* bulging. **~ement** *n.m.* bulge.

renflouer /rɑ̃flue/ *v.t.* refloat.

renfoncement /rɑ̃fɔ̃smɑ̃/ *n.m.* recess.

renforcer /rɑ̃fɔrse/ *v.t.* reinforce.

renfort /rɑ̃fɔr/ *n.m.* reinforcement. **de ~**, (*armée, personnel*) back-up.

renfrogn|er (se) /(sə)rɑ̃frɔɲe/ *v. pr.* scowl. **~é** *a.* surly, sullen.

rengaine /rɑ̃gɛn/ *n.f.* old song.

renier /rənje/ *v.t.* (*personne, pays*) disown, deny; (*foi*) renounce.

renifler /rənifle/ *v.t./i.* sniff.

renne /rɛn/ *n.m.* reindeer.

renom /rənɔ̃/ *n.m.* renown; (*réputation*) reputation. **~mé** /-ɔme/ *a.* famous. **~mée** /-ɔme/ *n.f.* fame; reputation.

renonc|er /rənɔ̃se/ *v.i.* **~er à**, (*habitude, ami, etc.*) give up, renounce. **~er à faire**, give up (all thought of) doing. **~ement** *n.m.*, **~iation** *n.f.* renunciation.

renouer /rənwe/ *v.t.* tie up (again); (*reprendre*) renew. —*v.i.* **~ avec**, start up again with.

renouveau (*pl.* **~x**) /rənuvo/ *n.m.* revival.

renouvel|er /rənuvle/ *v.t.* renew; (*réitérer*) repeat. **se ~er** *v. pr.* be renewed; be repeated. **~lement** /-vɛlmɑ̃/ *n.m.* renewal.

rénov|er /renɔve/ *v.t.* (*édifice*) renovate; (*institution*) reform. **~ation** *n.f.* renovation; reform.

renseignement /rɑ̃sɛɲmɑ̃/ *n.m.* **~(s)**, information.

renseigner /rɑ̃seɲe/ *v.t.* inform, give information to. **se ~** *v. pr.* enquire, make enquiries, find out.

rentab|le /rɑ̃tabl/ *a.* profitable. **~ilité** *n.f.* profitability.

rent|e /rɑ̃t/ *n.f.* (private) income; (*pension*) pension, annuity. **~ier, ~ière** *n.m., f.* person of private means.

rentrée /rɑ̃tre/ *n.f.* return; (*d'un acteur*) come-back; (*parlementaire*) reopening; (*scol.*) start of the new year.

rentrer /rɑ̃tre/ (*aux. être*) *v.i.* go *ou* come back home, return home; (*entrer*) go *ou* come in; (*entrer à nouveau*) go *ou* come back in; (*revenu*) come in; (*élèves*) go back. **~ dans**, (*heurter*) smash into. —*v.t.* (*aux. avoir*) bring in; (*griffes*) draw in; (*vêtement*) tuck in.

renverse (à la) /(ala)rɑ̃vɛrs/ *adv.* backwards.

renvers|er /rɑ̃vɛrse/ *v.t.* knock over *ou* down; (*piéton*) knock down; (*liquide*) upset, spill; (*mettre à l'envers*) turn upside down; (*gouvernement*) overturn; (*inverser*) reverse; (*étonner: fam.*) astound. **se ~er** *v. pr.* (*véhicule*) overturn; (*verre, vase*) fall over. **~ement** *n.m.* (*pol.*) overthrow.

renv|oi /rɑ̃vwa/ *n.m.* return; dismissal; expulsion; postponement; reference; (*rot*) belch. **~oyer**† *v.t.* send back, return; (*employé*) dismiss; (*élève*) expel; (*ajourner*) postpone; (*référer*) refer; (*réfléchir*) reflect.

réorganiser /reɔrganize/ *v.t.* reorganize.

réouverture /reuvɛrtyr/ *n.f.* reopening.

repaire /rəpɛr/ *n.m.* den.

répandre /repɑ̃dr/ *v.t.* (*liquide*) spill; (*étendre, diffuser*) spread; (*lumière, sang*) shed; (*odeur*) give off. **se ~** *v. pr.* spread; (*liquide*) spill. **se ~ en,** (*injures etc.*) pour forth, launch forth into.

répandu /repɑ̃dy/ *a.* (*courant*) widespread.

répar|er /repare/ *v.t.* repair, mend; (*faute*) make amends for; (*remédier à*) put right. **~ateur** *n.m.* repairer. **~ation** *n.f.* repair; (*compensation*) compensation.

repartie /rəparti/ *n.f.* retort.

repartir† /rəpartir/ *v.i.* start (up) again; (*voyageur*) set off again; (*s'en retourner*) go back.

répart|ir /repartir/ *v.t.* distribute; (*partager*) share out; (*étaler*) spread. **~ition** *n.f.* distribution.

repas /rəpɑ/ *n.m.* meal.

repass|er /rəpɑse/ *v.i.* come *ou* go back. —*v.t.* (*linge*) iron; (*leçon*) go over; (*couteau*) sharpen. **~age** *n.m.* ironing.

repêcher /rəpeʃe/ *v.t.* fish out; (*candidat*) allow to pass.

repentir /rəpɑ̃tir/ *n.m.* repentance. **se ~** *v. pr.* (*relig.*) repent (**de,** of). **se ~ de,** (*regretter*) regret.

répercu|ter /repɛrkyte/ *v.t.* (*bruit*) echo. **se ~ter** *v. pr.* echo. **se ~ter sur,** have repercussions on. **~ssion** *n.f.* repercussion.

repère /rəpɛr/ *n.m.* mark; (*jalon*) marker; (*fig.*) landmark.

repérer /rəpere/ *v.t.* locate, spot. **se ~** *v. pr.* find one's bearings.

répert|oire /repɛrtwar/ *n.m.* index; (*artistique*) repertoire. **~orier** *v.t.* index.

répéter /repete/ *v.t.* repeat. —*v.t./i.* (*théâtre*) rehearse. **se ~** *v. pr.* be repeated; (*personne*) repeat o.s.

répétition /repetisjɔ̃/ *n.f.* repetition; (*théâtre*) rehearsal.

repiquer /rəpike/ *v.t.* (*plante*) plant out; (*photo, texte*) touch up.

répit /repi/ *n.m.* rest, respite.

replacer /rəplase/ *v.t.* replace.

repl|i /rəpli/ *n.m.* fold; (*retrait*) withdrawal. **~ier** *v.t.* fold (up); (*ailes, jambes*) tuck in. **se ~ier** *v. pr.* withdraw (**sur soi-même,** into o.s.).

répliqu|e /replik/ *n.f.* reply; (*riposte*) retort; (*discussion*) objection; (*théâtre*) line(s); (*copie*) replica. **~er** *v.t./i.* reply; (*riposter*) retort; (*objecter*) answer back.

répondant, ~e /repɔ̃dɑ̃, -t/ *n.m., f.* guarantor. **avoir du ~,** have money behind one.

répondre /repɔ̃dr/ *v.t.* (*remarque etc.*) reply with. **~ que,** answer *ou* reply that. —*v.i.* answer, reply; (*être insolent*) answer back; (*réagir*) respond (**à,** to). **~ à,** answer. **~ de,** answer for.

réponse /repɔ̃s/ *n.f.* answer, reply; (*fig.*) response.

report /rəpɔr/ *n.m.* (*transcription*) transfer; (*renvoi*) postponement.

reportage /rəpɔrtaʒ/ *n.m.* report; (*en direct*) commentary.

reporter[1] /rəpɔrte/ *v.t.* take back; (*ajourner*) put off; (*transcrire*) transfer. **se ~ à,** refer to.

reporter[2] /rəpɔrtɛr/ *n.m.* reporter.

repos /rəpo/ *n.m.* rest; (*paix*) peace; (*tranquillité*) peace and quiet; (*moral*) peace of mind.

repos|er /rəpoze/ *v.t.* put down again; (*délasser*) rest. —*v.i.* rest (**sur,** on). **se ~er** *v. pr.* rest. **se ~er sur,** rely on. **~ant, ~ante** *a.* restful.

repoussant, ~e /rəpusɑ̃, -t/ *a.* repulsive.

repousser /rəpuse/ *v.t.* push back; (*écarter*) push away; (*dégoûter*) repel; (*décliner*) reject; (*ajourner*) put back. —*v.i.* grow again.

répréhensible /repreɑ̃sibl/ *a.* blameworthy.

reprendre† /rəprɑ̃dr/ *v.t.* take back; (*retrouver*) regain; (*souffle*) get back; (*évadé*) recapture; (*recommencer*) resume; (*redire*) repeat; (*modifier*) alter; (*blâmer*) reprimand. **~ du pain**/*etc.*, take some more bread/*etc.* —*v.i.* (*recommencer*) resume; (*affaires*) pick up. **se ~** *v. pr.* (*se ressaisir*) pull o.s. together; (*se corriger*) correct o.s.

représailles /rəprezɑj/ *n.f. pl.* reprisals.

représentati|f, ~ve /rəprezɑ̃tatif, -v/ *a.* representative.

représent|er /rəprezɑ̃te/ *v.t.* represent; (*théâtre*) perform. **se ~er** *v. pr.* (*s'imaginer*) imagine. **~ant, ~ante** *n.m., f.* representative. **~ation** *n.f.* representation; (*théâtre*) performance.

réprimand|e /reprimɑ̃d/ *n.f.* reprimand. **~er** *v.t.* reprimand.

répr|imer /reprime/ *v.t.* repress. **~ession** *n.f.* repression.

repris /rəpri/ *n.m.* **~ de justice,** ex-convict.

reprise /rəpriz/ *n.f.* resumption; (*théâtre*) revival; (*télévision*) repeat; (*de tissu*) darn, mend; (*essor*) recovery; (*comm.*) part-exchange, trade-in. **à plusieurs ~s,** on several occasions.

repriser /rəprize/ *v.t.* darn, mend.

réprobation /reprɔbɑsjɔ̃/ *n.f.* condemnation.

reproch|e /rəprɔʃ/ *n.m.* reproach, blame. **~er** *v.t.* **~er qch. à qn.,** reproach *ou* blame s.o. for sth.

reprod|uire† /rəprɔdɥir/ *v.t.* reproduce. **se ~uire** *v. pr.* reproduce; (*arriver*) recur. **~ucteur, ~uctrice** *a.* reproductive. **~uction** *n.f.* reproduction.

réprouver /repruve/ *v.t.* condemn.

reptile /rɛptil/ *n.m.* reptile.

repu /rəpy/ *a.* satiated.

républi|que /repyblik/ *n.f.* republic. **~que populaire,** people's republic. **~cain, ~caine** *a.* & *n.m., f.* republican.

répudier /repydje/ *v.t.* repudiate.

répugnance /repyɲɑ̃s/ *n.f.* repugnance; (*hésitation*) reluctance.

répugn|er /repyɲe/ *v.i.* **~er à,** be repugnant to. **~er à faire,** be reluctant to do. **~ant, ~ante** *a.* repulsive.

répulsion /repylsjɔ̃/ *n.f.* repulsion.

réputation /repytɑsjɔ̃/ *n.f.* reputation.

réputé /repyte/ *a.* renowned. **~ pour être,** reputed to be.

requérir /rəkerir/ *v.t.* require, demand.

requête /rəkɛt/ *n.f.* request; (*jurid.*) petition.

requiem /rekɥijɛm/ *n.m. invar.* requiem.

requin /rəkɛ̃/ *n.m.* shark.

requis, ~e /rəki, -z/ *a.* required.

réquisition /rekizisjɔ̃/ *n.f.* requisition. **~ner** /-jɔne/ *v.t.* requisition.

rescapé, ~e /rɛskape/ *n.m., f.* survivor. —*a.* surviving.
rescousse /rɛskus/ *n.f.* **à la ~,** to the rescue.
réseau (*pl.* **~x**) /rezo/ *n.m.* network.
réservation /rezɛrvɑsjɔ̃/ *n.f.* reservation.
réserve /rezɛrv/ *n.f.* reserve; (*restriction*) reservation, reserve; (*indienne*) reservation; (*entrepôt*) store-room. **en ~,** in reserve. **les ~s,** (*mil.*) the reserves.
réserv|er /rezɛrve/ *v.t.* reserve; (*place*) book, reserve. **se ~er le droit de,** reserve the right to. **~é** *a.* (*personne, place*) reserved.
réserviste /rezɛrvist/ *n.m.* reservist.
réservoir /rezɛrvwar/ *n.m.* tank; (*lac*) reservoir.
résidence /rezidɑ̃s/ *n.f.* residence.
résident, ~e /rezidɑ̃, -t/ *n.m., f.* resident foreigner. **~iel, ~ielle** /-sjɛl/ *a.* residential.
résider /rezide/ *v.i.* reside.
résidu /rezidy/ *n.m.* residue.
résign|er (se) /(sə)reziɲe/ *v. pr.* resign o.s. **~ation** *n.f.* resignation.
résilier /rezilje/ *v.t.* terminate.
résille /rezij/ *n.f.* (hair-)net.
résine /rezin/ *n.f.* resin.
résistance /rezistɑ̃s/ *n.f.* resistance; (*fil électrique*) element.
résistant, ~e /rezistɑ̃, -t/ *a.* tough.
résister /reziste/ *v.i.* resist. **~ à,** resist; (*examen, chaleur*) stand up to.
résolu /rezɔly/ *voir* **résoudre.** —*a.* resolute. **~ à,** resolved to. **~ment** *adv.* resolutely.
résolution /rezɔlysjɔ̃/ *n.f.* resolution.
résonance /rezɔnɑ̃s/ *n.f.* resonance.
résonner /rezɔne/ *v.i.* resound.
résor|ber /rezɔrbe/ *v.t.* reduce. **se ~ber** *v. pr.* be reduced. **~ption** *n.f.* reduction.
résoudre† /rezudr/ *v.t.* solve; (*décider*) decide on. **~ de, se ~ à,** resolve to.
respect /rɛspɛ/ *n.m.* respect.
respectab|le /rɛspɛktabl/ *a.* respectable. **~ilité** *n.f.* respectability.
respecter /rɛspɛkte/ *v.t.* respect. **faire ~,** (*loi, décision*) enforce.
respecti|f, ~ve /rɛspɛktif, -v/ *a.* respective. **~vement** *adv.* respectively.
respectueu|x, ~se /rɛspɛktɥø, -z/ *a.* respectful.
respir|er /rɛspire/ *v.i.* breathe; (*se reposer*) get one's breath. —*v.t.* breathe; (*exprimer*) radiate. **~ation** *n.f.* breathing; (*haleine*) breath. **~atoire** *a.* breathing.
resplend|ir /rɛsplɑ̃dir/ *v.i.* shine. **~issant, ~issante** *a.* radiant.
responsabilité /rɛspɔ̃sabilite/ *n.f.* responsibility; (*légale*) liability.
responsable /rɛspɔ̃sabl/ *a.* responsible (**de,** for). **~ de,** (*chargé de*) in charge of. —*n.m./f.* person in charge; (*coupable*) person responsible.
resquiller /rɛskije/ *v.i.* get in without paying; (*dans la queue*) jump the queue.
ressaisir (se) /(sə)rəsezir/ *v. pr.* pull o.s. together.
ressasser /rəsase/ *v.t.* (*rabâcher, ruminer*) keep going over.
ressembl|er /rəsɑ̃ble/ *v.i.* **~er à,** resemble, look like. **se ~er** *v. pr.* look alike. **~ance** *n.f.* resemblance. **~ant, ~ante** *a.* (*photo etc.*) true to life; (*pareil*) alike.
ressemeler /rəsəmle/ *v.t.* sole.
ressentiment /rəsɑ̃timɑ̃/ *n.m.* resentment.
ressentir /rəsɑ̃tir/ *v.t.* feel. **se ~ de,** feel the effects of.
resserre /rəsɛr/ *n.f.* shed.

resserrer /rəsere/ *v.t.* tighten; (*contracter*) contract. **se ~** *v. pr.* tighten; contract; (*route etc.*) narrow.
resservir /rəsɛrvir/ *v.i.* come in useful (again).
ressort /rəsɔr/ *n.m.* (*objet*) spring; (*fig.*) energy. **du ~ de,** within the jurisdiction *ou* scope of. **en dernier ~,** in the last resort.
ressortir† /rəsɔrtir/ *v.i.* go *ou* come back out; (*se voir*) stand out. **faire ~,** bring out. **~ de,** (*résulter*) result *ou* emerge from.
ressortissant, ~e /rəsɔrtisɑ̃, -t/ *n.m., f.* national.
ressource /rəsurs/ *n.f.* resource. **~s,** resources.
ressusciter /resysite/ *v.i.* come back to life.
restant, ~e /rɛstɑ̃, -t/ *a.* remaining. —*n.m.* remainder.
restaur|ant /rɛstɔrɑ̃/ *n.m.* restaurant. **~ateur, ~atrice** *n.m., f.* restaurant owner.
restaur|er /rɛstɔre/ *v.t.* restore. **se ~er** *v. pr.* eat. **~ation** *n.f.* restoration; (*hôtellerie*) catering.
reste /rɛst/ *n.m.* rest; (*d'une soustraction*) remainder. **~s,** remains (**de,** of); (*nourriture*) leftovers. **un ~ de pain**/*etc.*, some left-over bread/*etc.* **au ~, du ~,** moreover, besides.
rest|er /rɛste/ *v.i.* (*aux. être*) stay, remain; (*subsister*) be left, remain. **il ~e du pain**/*etc.*, there is some bread/*etc.* left (over). **il me ~e du pain,** I have some bread left (over). **il me ~e à,** it remains for me to. **en ~er à,** go no further than. **en ~er là,** stop there.
restit|uer /rɛstitɥe/ *v.t.* (*rendre*) return, restore; (*son*) reproduce. **~ution** *n.f.* return.
restreindre† /rɛstrɛ̃dr/ *v.t.* restrict. **se ~** *v. pr.* (*dans les dépenses*) cut down.
restricti|f, ~ve /rɛstriktif, -v/ *a.* restrictive.
restriction /rɛstriksjɔ̃/ *n.f.* restriction; (*réticence*) reservation.
résultat /rezylta/ *n.m.* result.
résulter /rezylte/ *v.i.* **~ de,** result from.
résum|er /rezyme/ *v.t.*, **se ~er** *v. pr.* summarize. **~é** *n.m.* summary. **en ~é,** in short.
résurrection /rezyrɛksjɔ̃/ *n.f.* resurrection; (*renouveau*) revival.
rétabl|ir /retablir/ *v.t.* restore; (*personne*) restore to health. **se ~ir** *v. pr.* be restored; (*guérir*) recover. **~issement** *n.m.* restoring; (*méd.*) recovery.
retaper /rətape/ *v.t.* (*maison etc.*) do up. **se ~** *v. pr.* (*guérir*) get back on one's feet.
retard /rətar/ *n.m.* lateness; (*sur un programme*) delay; (*infériorité*) backwardness. **avoir du ~,** be late; (*montre*) be slow. **en ~,** late; (*retardé*) backward. **en ~ sur,** behind. **rattraper** *ou* **combler son ~,** catch up.
retardataire /rətardatɛr/ *n.m./f.* late comer. —*a.* (*arrivant*) late.
retardé /rətarde/ *a.* backward.
retardement (à) /(a)rətardəmɑ̃/ *a.* (*bombe etc.*) delayed-action.
retarder /rətarde/ *v.t.* delay; (*sur un programme*) set back; (*montre*) put back. —*v.i.* (*montre*) be slow.
retenir† /rətnir/ *v.t.* hold back; (*haleine, attention, prisonnier*) hold; (*eau, chaleur*) retain, hold; (*garder*) keep; (*retarder*) detain; (*réserver*) book; (*se rappeler*) remember; (*déduire*) deduct; (*accepter*) accept. **se ~** *v. pr.* (*se contenir*) restrain o.s. **se ~ à,** hold on to. **se ~ de,** stop o.s. from.
rétention /retɑ̃sjɔ̃/ *n.f.* retention.
retent|ir /rətɑ̃tir/ *v.i.* ring out (**de,** with). **~issant, ~issante** *a.* resounding. **~issement** *n.m.* (*effet, répercussion*) effect.

retenue /rətny/ *n.f.* restraint; (*somme*) deduction; (*scol.*) detention.
réticen|t, ~te /retisɑ̃, -t/ *a.* (*hésitant*) reluctant; (*réservé*) reticent. **~ce** *n.f.* reluctance; reticence.
rétif, ~ve /retif, -v/ *a.* restive, recalcitrant.
rétine /retin/ *n.f.* retina.
retiré /rətire/ *a.* secluded.
retirer /rətire/ *v.t.* (*sortir*) take out; (*ôter*) take off; (*argent*, *candidature*) withdraw; (*avantage*) derive. **~ à qn.,** take away from s.o. **se ~** *v. pr.* withdraw, retire.
retombées /rətɔ̃be/ *n.f. pl.* fall-out.
retomber /rətɔ̃be/ *v.i.* fall; (*à nouveau*) fall again. **~ dans,** (*erreur etc.*) fall back into.
rétorquer /retɔrke/ *v.t.* retort.
rétorsion /retɔrsjɔ̃/ *n.f.* retaliation.
retouch|e /rətuʃ/ *n.f.* touch-up; alteration. **~er** *v.t.* touch up; (*vêtement*) alter.
retour /rətur/ *n.m.* return. **être de ~,** be back (**de,** from). **~ en arrière,** flashback.
retourner /rəturne/ *v.t.* (*aux. avoir*) turn over; (*vêtement*) turn inside out; (*lettre*, *compliment*) return; (*émouvoir*: *fam.*) upset. —*v.i.* (*aux. être*) go back, return. **se ~** *v. pr.* turn round; (*dans son lit*) twist and turn. **s'en ~,** go back. **se ~ contre,** turn against.
retracer /rətrase/ *v.t.* retrace.
rétracter /retrakte/ *v.t.*, **se ~** *v. pr.* retract.
retrait /rətrɛ/ *n.m.* withdrawal; (*des eaux*) ebb, receding. **être (situé) en ~,** be set back.
retraite /rətrɛt/ *n.f.* retirement; (*pension*) (retirement) pension; (*fuite*, *refuge*) retreat. **en ~,** retired. **mettre à la ~,** pension off. **prendre sa ~,** retire.
retraité, ~e /rətrete/ *a.* retired. —*n.m.*, *f.* (old-age) pensioner, senior citizen.
retrancher /rətrɑ̃ʃe/ *v.t.* remove; (*soustraire*) deduct. **se ~** *v. pr.* (*mil.*) entrench o.s.
retransm|ettre /rətrɑ̃smɛtr/ *v.t.* broadcast. **~ission** *n.f.* broadcast.
rétrécir /retresir/ *v.t.* narrow; (*vêtement*) take in. —*v.i.*, **se ~** *v. pr.* (*tissu*) shrink; (*rue*) narrow.
rétrib|uer /retribɥe/ *v.t.* pay. **~ution** *n.f.* payment.
rétrograd|e /retrɔgrad/ *a.* retrograde. **~er** *v.i.* (*reculer*) fall back, recede; *v.t.* demote.
rétrospectivement /retrɔspɛktivmɑ̃/ *adv.* in retrospect.
retrousser /rətruse/ *v.t.* pull up.
retrouvailles /rətruvɑj/ *n.f. pl.* reunion.
retrouver /rətruve/ *v.t.* find (again); (*rejoindre*) meet (again); (*forces*, *calme*) regain; (*se rappeler*) remember. **se ~** *v. pr.* find o.s. (back); (*se réunir*) meet (again). **s'y ~,** (*s'orienter*) find one's way.
rétroviseur /retrɔvizœr/ *n.m.* (*auto.*) (rear-view) mirror.
réunion /reynjɔ̃/ *n.f.* meeting; (*d'objets*) collection.
réunir /reynir/ *v.t.* gather, collect; (*rapprocher*) bring together; (*convoquer*) call together; (*raccorder*) join; (*qualités*) combine. **se ~** *v. pr.* meet.
réussi /reysi/ *a.* successful.
réussir /reysir/ *v.i.* succeed, be successful (**à faire,** in doing). **~ à qn.,** work well for s.o.; (*climat etc.*) agree with s.o. —*v.t.* make a success of.
réussite /reysit/ *n.f.* success.
revaloriser /rəvalɔrize/ *v.t.* revalue.
revanche /rəvɑ̃ʃ/ *n.f.* revenge; (*sport*) return *ou* revenge match. **en ~,** on the other hand.

rêvasser /rɛvase/ *v.i.* day-dream.
rêve /rɛv/ *n.m.* dream. **faire un ~,** have a dream.
revêche /rəvɛʃ/ *a.* ill-tempered.
réveil /revɛj/ *n.m.* awakening; (*pendule*) alarm-clock.
réveill|er /reveje/ *v.t.*, **se ~er** *v. pr.* wake (up); (*fig.*) awaken. **~é** *a.* awake. **~e-matin** *n.m. invar.* alarm-clock.
réveillon /revɛjɔ̃/ *n.m.* midnight meal (on Christmas Eve *ou* New Year's Eve). **~ner** /-jɔne/ *v.i.* celebrate the *réveillon.*
révél|er /revele/ *v.t.* reveal. **se ~er** *v. pr.* be revealed. **se ~er facile/***etc.*, prove easy/*etc.* **~ateur, ~atrice** *a.* revealing. **~ation** *n.f.* revelation.
revenant /rəvnɑ̃/ *n.m.* ghost.
revendi|quer /rəvɑ̃dike/ *v.t.* claim. **~catif, ~cative** *a.* (*mouvement etc.*) in support of one's claims. **~cation** *n.f.* claim; (*action*) claiming.
revend|re /rəvɑ̃dr/ *v.t.* sell (again). **~eur, ~euse** *n.m., f.* dealer.
revenir† /rəvnir/ *v.i.* (*aux. être*) come back, return (**à**, to). **~ à,** (*activité*) go back to; (*se résumer à*) come down to; (*échoir à*) fall to; (*coûter*) cost. **~ à soi,** come to. **~ de,** (*maladie, surprise*) get over. **~ sur ses pas,** retrace one's steps.
revente /rəvɑ̃t/ *n.f.* resale.
revenu /rəvny/ *n.m.* income; (*d'un état*) revenue.
rêver /reve/ *v.t./i.* dream.
réverbération /revɛrberɑsjɔ̃/ *n.f.* reflection, reverberation.
réverbère /revɛrbɛr/ *n.m.* street lamp.
révérenc|e /reverɑ̃s/ *n.f.* reverence; (*salut d'homme*) bow; (*salut de femme*) curtsy. **~ieux, ~ieuse** *a.* reverent.
révérend, ~e /reverɑ̃, -d/ *a.* & *n.m.* reverend.
rêverie /rɛvri/ *n.f.* day-dream; (*activité*) day-dreaming.
revers /rəvɛr/ *n.m.* reverse; (*de main*) back; (*d'étoffe*) wrong side; (*de veste*) lapel; (*tennis*) backhand; (*fig.*) set-back.
réversible /revɛrsibl/ *a.* reversible.
revêt|ir /rəvetir/ *v.t.* cover; (*habit*) put on; (*prendre, avoir*) assume. **~ement** /-vɛtmɑ̃/ *n.m.* covering; (*de route*) surface.
rêveu|r, ~se /rɛvœr, -øz/ *a.* dreamy. —*n.m., f.* dreamer.
revigorer /rəvigɔre/ *v.t.* revive.
revirement /rəvirmɑ̃/ *n.m.* sudden change.
révis|er /revize/ *v.t.* revise; (*véhicule*) overhaul. **~ion** *n.f.* revision; overhaul.
revivre† /rəvivr/ *v.i.* live again. —*v.t.* relive. **faire ~,** revive.
révocation /revɔkɑsjɔ̃/ *n.f.* repeal; (*d'un fonctionnaire*) dismissal.
revoir† /rəvwar/ *v.t.* see (again); (*réviser*) revise. **au ~,** goodbye.
révolte /revɔlt/ *n.f.* revolt.
révolt|er /revɔlte/ *v.t.*, **se ~er** *v. pr.* revolt. **~ant, ~ante** *a.* revolting. **~é, ~ée** *n.m., f.* rebel.
révolu /revɔly/ *a.* past.
révolution /revɔlysjɔ̃/ *n.f.* revolution. **~naire** /-jɔnɛr/ *a.* & *n.m./f.* revolutionary. **~ner** /-jɔne/ *v.t.* revolutionize.
revolver /revɔlvɛr/ *n.m.* revolver, gun.
révoquer /revɔke/ *v.t.* repeal; (*fonctionnaire*) dismiss.
revue /rəvy/ *n.f.* (*examen, défilé*) review; (*magazine*) magazine; (*spectacle*) variety show.
rez-de-chaussée /redʃose/ *n.m. invar.* ground floor; (*Amer.*) first floor.
RF *abrév.* (*République Française*) French Republic.
rhabiller (se) /(sə)rabije/ *v. pr.* get dressed (again), dress (again).

rhapsodie /rapsɔdi/ *n.f.* rhapsody.
rhétorique /retɔrik/ *n.f.* rhetoric. —*a.* rhetorical.
rhinocéros /rinɔserɔs/ *n.m.* rhinoceros.
rhubarbe /rybarb/ *n.f.* rhubarb.
rhum /rɔm/ *n.m.* rum.
rhumatis|me /rymatism/ *n.m.* rheumatism. **~ant, ~ante** /-zɑ̃, -t/ *a.* rheumatic.
rhume /rym/ *n.m.* cold. **~ des foins,** hay fever.
ri /ri/ *voir* **rire.**
riant, ~e /rjɑ̃, -t/ *a.* cheerful.
ricaner /rikane/ *v.i.* snigger, giggle.
riche /riʃ/ *a.* rich **(en,** in). —*n.m./f.* rich person. **~ment** *adv.* richly.
richesse /riʃɛs/ *n.f.* wealth; (*de sol, décor*) richness. **~s,** wealth.
ricoch|er /rikɔʃe/ *v.i.* rebound, ricochet. **~et** *n.m.* rebound, ricochet.
rictus /riktys/ *n.m.* grin, grimace.
rid|e /rid/ *n.f.* wrinkle; (*sur l'eau*) ripple. **~er** *v.t.* wrinkle; (*eau*) ripple.
rideau (*pl.* **~x**) /rido/ *n.m.* curtain; (*métallique*) shutter; (*fig.*) screen. **~ de fer,** (*pol.*) Iron Curtain.
ridicul|e /ridikyl/ *a.* ridiculous. —*n.m.* absurdity. **le ~e,** ridicule. **~iser** *v.t.* ridicule.
rien /rjɛ̃/ *pron.* **(ne) ~,** nothing. —*n.m.* trifle. **de ~!,** (*fam.*) don't mention it! **~ d'autre/de plus,** nothing else/more. **~ du tout,** nothing at all. **~ que,** just, only.
rieu|r, ~se /rjœr, rjøz/ *a.* merry.
rigid|e /riʒid/ *a.* rigid; (*muscle*) stiff. **~ité** *n.f.* rigidity; stiffness.
rigole /rigɔl/ *n.f.* channel.
rigol|er /rigɔle/ *v.i.* laugh; (*s'amuser*) have some fun; (*plaisanter*) joke. **~ade** *n.f.* fun.
rigolo, ~te /rigɔlo, -ɔt/ *a.* (*fam.*) funny. —*n.m., f.* (*fam.*) joker.
rigoureu|x, ~se /rigurø, -z/ *a.* rigorous; (*hiver*) harsh. **~sement** *adv.* rigorously.
rigueur /rigœr/ *n.f.* rigour. **à la ~,** at a pinch. **être de ~,** be the rule.
rim|e /rim/ *n.f.* rhyme. **~er** *v.i.* rhyme **(avec,** with). **cela ne ~e à rien,** it makes no sense.
rin|cer /rɛ̃se/ *v.t.* rinse. **~çage** *n.m.* rinse; (*action*) rinsing.
ring /riŋ/ *n.m.* boxing ring.
ripost|e /ripɔst/ *n.f.* retort; (*mil.*) reprisal. **~er** *v.i.* retaliate; *v.t.* retort **(que,** that). **~er à,** (*attaque*) counter; (*insulte etc.*) reply to.
rire† /rir/ *v.i.* laugh **(de,** at); (*plaisanter*) joke; (*s'amuser*) have fun. —*n.m.* laugh. **~s, le ~,** laughter.
risée /rize/ *n.f.* **la ~ de,** the laughing-stock of.
risible /rizibl/ *a.* laughable.
risqu|e /risk/ *n.m.* risk. **~é** *a.* risky; (*osé*) daring. **~er** *v.t.* risk. **~er de faire,** stand a good chance of doing. **se ~er à/dans,** venture to/into.
rissoler /risɔle/ *v.t./i.* brown.
ristourne /risturn/ *n.f.* discount.
rite /rit/ *n.m.* rite.
rituel, ~le /ritɥɛl/ *a.* & *n.m.* ritual.
rivage /rivaʒ/ *n.m.* shore.
riv|al, ~ale (*m. pl.* **~aux)** /rival, -o/ *n.m., f.* rival. —*a.* rival. **~aliser** *v.i.* compete **(avec,** with). **~alité** *n.f.* rivalry.
rive /riv/ *n.f.* (*de fleuve*) bank; (*de lac*) shore.
riv|er /rive/ *v.t.* rivet. **~et** *n.m.* rivet.
riverain, ~e /rivrɛ̃, -ɛn/ *a.* riverside. —*n.m., f.* riverside resident; (*d'une rue*) resident.
rivière /rivjɛr/ *n.f.* river.
rixe /riks/ *n.f.* brawl.
riz /ri/ *n.m.* rice. **~ière** /rizjɛr/ *n.f.* paddy(-field), rice field.
robe /rɔb/ *n.f.* (*de femme*) dress; (*de

juge) robe; (*de cheval*) coat. **~ de chambre,** dressing-gown.
robinet /rɔbinɛ/ *n.m.* tap; (*Amer.*) faucet.
robot /rɔbo/ *n.m.* robot.
robuste /rɔbyst/ *a.* robust. **~sse** /-ɛs/ *n.f.* robustness.
roc /rɔk/ *n.m.* rock.
rocaill|e /rɔkɑj/ *n.f.* rocky ground; (*de jardin*) rockery. **~eux, ~euse** *a.* (*terrain*) rocky.
roch|e /rɔʃ/ *n.f.* rock. **~eux, ~euse** *a.* rocky.
rocher /rɔʃe/ *n.m.* rock.
rock /rɔk/ *n.m.* (*mus.*) rock.
rod|er /rɔde/ *v.t.* (*auto.*) run in; (*auto., Amer.*) break in. **~age** *n.m.* running in; breaking in.
rôd|er /rode/ *v.i.* roam; (*suspect*) prowl. **~eur, ~euse** *n.m., f.* prowler.
rogne /rɔɲ/ *n.f.* (*fam.*) anger.
rogner /rɔɲe/ *v.t.* trim; (*réduire*) cut.
rognon /rɔɲɔ̃/ *n.m.* (*culin.*) kidney.
rognures /rɔɲyr/ *n.f. pl.* scraps.
roi /rwa/ *n.m.* king. **les Rois mages,** the Magi.
roitelet /rwatlɛ/ *n.m.* wren.
rôle /rol/ *n.m.* role, part.
romain, ~e /rɔmɛ̃, -ɛn/ *a.* & *n.m., f.* Roman. —*n.f.* (*laitue*) cos.
roman /rɔmɑ̃/ *n.m.* novel; (*fig.*) story; (*genre*) fiction.
romance /rɔmɑ̃s/ *n.f.* sentimental ballad.
romanc|ier, ~ière /rɔmɑ̃sje, -jɛr/ *n.m., f.* novelist.
romanesque /rɔmanɛsk/ *a.* romantic; (*incroyable*) incredible.
romanichel, ~le /rɔmaniʃɛl/ *n.m., f.* gypsy.
romanti|que /rɔmɑ̃tik/ *a.* & *n.m./f.* romantic. **~sme** *n.m.* romanticism.
rompre† /rɔ̃pr/ *v.t./i.* break; (*relations*) break off; (*fiancés*) break it off. **se ~** *v. pr.* break.
rompu /rɔ̃py/ *a.* (*exténué*) exhausted.
ronces /rɔ̃s/ *n.f. pl.* brambles.
ronchonner /rɔ̃ʃɔne/ *v.i.* (*fam.*) grumble.
rond, ~e[1] /rɔ̃, rɔ̃d/ *a.* round; (*gras*) plump; (*ivre: fam.*) tight. —*n.m.* (*cercle*) ring; (*tranche*) slice. **~ement** /rɔ̃dmɑ̃/ *adv.* briskly; (*franchement*) straight. **~eur** /rɔ̃dœr/ *n.f.* roundness; (*franchise*) frankness; (*embonpoint*) plumpness. **~-point** (*pl.* **~s-points**) *n.m.* roundabout; (*Amer.*) traffic circle.
ronde[2] /rɔ̃d/ *n.f.* round(s); (*de policier*) beat; (*mus.*) semibreve.
rondelet, ~te /rɔ̃dlɛ, -t/ *a.* chubby.
rondelle /rɔ̃dɛl/ *n.f.* (*techn.*) washer; (*tranche*) slice.
rondin /rɔ̃dɛ̃/ *n.m.* log.
ronfl|er /rɔ̃fle/ *v.i.* snore; (*moteur*) hum. **~ement(s)** *n.m.* (*pl.*) snoring; humming.
rong|er /rɔ̃ʒe/ *v.t.* gnaw (at); (*vers, acide*) eat into; (*personne: fig.*) consume. **se ~er les ongles,** bite one's nails. **~eur** *n.m.* rodent.
ronronn|er /rɔ̃rɔne/ *v.i.* purr. **~ement** *n.m.* purr(ing).
roquette /rɔkɛt/ *n.f.* rocket.
rosaire /rozɛr/ *n.m.* rosary.
rosbif /rɔsbif/ *n.m.* roast beef.
rose /roz/ *n.f.* rose. —*a.* pink; (*situation, teint*) rosy. —*n.m.* pink.
rosé /roze/ *a.* pinkish; (*vin*) *rosé.* —*n.m. rosé.*
roseau (*pl.* **~x**) /rozo/ *n.m.* reed.
rosée /roze/ *n.f.* dew.
roseraie /rozrɛ/ *n.f.* rose garden.
rosette /rozɛt/ *n.f.* rosette.
rosier /rozje/ *n.m.* rose-bush.
rosse /rɔs/ *a.* (*fam.*) nasty.
rosser /rɔse/ *v.t.* thrash.
rossignol /rɔsiɲɔl/ *n.m.* nightingale.
rot /ro/ *n.m.* (*fam.*) burp.
rotati|f, ~ve /rɔtatif, -v/ *a.* rotary.
rotation /rɔtɑsjɔ̃/ *n.f.* rotation.

roter /rɔte/ *v.i.* (*fam.*) burp.
rotin /rɔtɛ̃/ *n.m.* (rattan) cane.
rôt|ir /rotir/ *v.t./i.*, **se ~ir** *v. pr.* roast. **~i** *n.m.* roasting meat; (*cuit*) roast. **~i de porc,** roast pork.
rôtisserie /rotisri/ *n.f.* grill-room.
rôtissoire /rotiswar/ *n.f.* (roasting) spit.
rotule /rɔtyl/ *n.f.* kneecap.
rouage /rwaʒ/ *n.m.* (*techn.*) (working) part. **~s,** (*d'une organisation*: *fig.*) wheels.
roucouler /rukule/ *v.i.* coo.
roue /ru/ *n.f.* wheel. **~ (dentée),** cog(-wheel).
roué /rwe/ *a.* wily, calculating.
rouer /rwe/ *v.t.* **~ de coups,** thrash.
rouet /rwɛ/ *n.m.* spinning-wheel.
rouge /ruʒ/ *a.* red; (*fer*) red-hot. —*n.m.* red; (*vin*) red wine; (*fard*) rouge. **~ (à lèvres),** lipstick. —*n.m./f.* (*pol.*) red. **~-gorge** (*pl.* **~s-gorges**) *n.m.* robin.
rougeole /ruʒɔl/ *n.f.* measles.
rougeoyer /ruʒwaje/ *v.i.* glow (red).
rougeur /ruʒœr/ *n.f.* redness; (*tache*) red blotch; (*gêne, honte*) red face.
rougir /ruʒir/ *v.t./i.* turn red; (*de honte*) blush.
rouill|e /ruj/ *n.f.* rust. **~é** *a.* rusty. **~er** *v.i.*, **se ~er** *v. pr.* get rusty, rust.
roulant, ~e /rulɑ̃, -t/ *a.* (*meuble*) on wheels; (*escalier*) moving.
rouleau (*pl.* **~x**) /rulo/ *n.m.* roll; (*outil, vague*) roller. **~ à pâtisserie,** rolling-pin. **~ compresseur,** steamroller.
roulement /rulmɑ̃/ *n.m.* rotation; (*bruit*) rumble; (*d'yeux, de tambour*) roll. **~ à billes,** ball-bearing.
rouler /rule/ *v.t./i.* roll; (*ficelle, manches*) roll up; (*duper*: *fam.*) cheat; (*véhicule, train*) go, travel; (*conducteur*) drive. **se ~** *v. pr.* roll (over).
roulette /rulɛt/ *n.f.* (*de meuble*) castor; (*de dentiste*) drill; (*jeu*) roulette.
roulis /ruli/ *n.m.* rolling.
roulotte /rulɔt/ *n.f.* caravan.
roumain, ~e /rumɛ̃, -ɛn/ *a.* & *n.m.*, *f.* Romanian.
Roumanie /rumani/ *n.f.* Romania.
roupiller /rupije/ *v.i.* (*fam.*) sleep.
rouquin, ~e /rukɛ̃, -in/ *a.* (*fam.*) red-haired. —*n.m.*, *f.* (*fam.*) redhead.
rouspéter /ruspete/ *v.i.* (*fam.*) grumble, moan, complain.
rousse /rus/ *voir* **roux.**
roussir /rusir/ *v.t.* scorch. —*v.i.* turn brown.
route /rut/ *n.f.* road; (*naut.*, *aviat.*) route; (*direction*) way; (*voyage*) journey; (*chemin*: *fig.*) path. **en ~,** on the way. **en ~!,** let's go! **mettre en ~,** start. **~ nationale,** trunk road, main road. **se mettre en ~,** set out.
rout|ier, ~ière /rutje, -jɛr/ *a.* road. —*n.m.* long-distance lorry driver *ou* truck driver (*Amer.*); (*restaurant*) roadside café.
routine /rutin/ *n.f.* routine.
rou|x, ~sse /ru, rus/ *a.* red, reddish-brown; (*personne*) red-haired. —*n.m.*, *f.* redhead.
roy|al (*m. pl.* **~aux**) /rwajal, -jo/ *a.* royal; (*total*: *fam.*) thorough. **~alement** *adv.* royally.
royaume /rwajom/ *n.m.* kingdom. **R~-Uni** *n.m.* United Kingdom.
royauté /rwajote/ *n.f.* royalty.
ruade /ryad, rɥad/ *n.f.* kick.
ruban /rybɑ̃/ *n.m.* ribbon; (*de magnétophone*) tape; (*de chapeau*) band. **~ adhésif,** sticky tape.
rubéole /rybeɔl/ *n.f.* German measles.
rubis /rybi/ *n.m.* ruby; (*de montre*) jewel.

rubrique /rybrik/ *n.f.* heading; (*article*) column.
ruche /ryʃ/ *n.f.* beehive.
rude /ryd/ *a.* rough; (*pénible*) tough; (*grossier*) crude; (*fameux: fam.*) tremendous. **~ment** *adv.* (*frapper etc.*) hard; (*traiter*) harshly; (*très: fam.*) awfully.
rudiment|s /rydimɑ̃/ *n.m. pl.* rudiments. **~aire** /-tɛr/ *a.* rudimentary.
rudoyer /rydwaje/ *v.t.* treat harshly.
rue /ry/ *n.f.* street.
ruée /rɥe/ *n.f.* rush.
ruelle /rɥɛl/ *n.f.* alley.
ruer /rɥe/ *v.i.* (*cheval*) kick. **se ~ dans/vers,** rush into/towards. **se ~ sur,** pounce on.
rugby /rygbi/ *n.m.* Rugby.
rugby|man (*pl.* **~men**) /rygbiman, -mɛn/ *n.m.* Rugby player.
rug|ir /ryʒir/ *v.i.* roar. **~issement** *n.m.* roar.
rugueu|x, ~se /rygø, -z/ *a.* rough.
ruin|e /rɥin/ *n.f.* ruin. **~er** *v.t.* ruin.
ruineu|x, ~se /rɥinø, -z/ *a.* ruinous.
ruisseau (*pl.* **~x**) /rɥiso/ *n.m.* stream; (*rigole*) gutter.
ruisseler /rɥisle/ *v.i.* stream.
rumeur /rymœr/ *n.f.* (*nouvelle*) rumour; (*son*) murmur, hum; (*protestation*) rumblings.
ruminer /rymine/ *v.t./i.* (*méditer*) meditate.
rupture /ryptyr/ *n.f.* break; (*action*) breaking; (*de contrat*) breach; (*de pourparlers*) breakdown.
rur|al (*m. pl.* **~aux**) /ryral, -o/ *a.* rural.
rus|e /ryz/ *n.f.* cunning; (*perfidie*) trickery. **une ~e,** a trick, a ruse. **~é** *a.* cunning.
russe /rys/ *a.* & *n.m./f.* Russian. —*n.m.* (*lang.*) Russian.
Russie /rysi/ *n.f.* Russia.
rustique /rystik/ *a.* rustic.
rustre /rystr/ *n.m.* lout, boor.
rutilant, ~e /rytilɑ̃, -t/ *a.* sparkling, gleaming.
rythm|e /ritm/ *n.m.* rhythm; (*vitesse*) rate; (*de la vie*) pace. **~é, ~ique** *adjs.* rhythmical.

S

s' /s/ *voir* **se.**
sa /sa/ *voir* **son**[1].
SA *abrév.* (*société anonyme*) PLC.
sabbat /saba/ *n.m.* sabbath.
sabl|e /sɑbl/ *n.m.* sand. **~es mouvants,** quicksands. **~er** *v.t.* sand. **~eux, ~euse, ~onneux, ~onneuse** *adjs.* sandy.
sablier /sɑblije/ *n.m.* (*culin.*) egg-timer.
saborder /sabɔrde/ *v.t.* (*navire*) scuttle.
sabot /sabo/ *n.m.* (*de cheval etc.*) hoof; (*chaussure*) clog; (*de frein*) shoe.
sabot|er /sabɔte/ *v.t.* sabotage; (*bâcler*) botch. **~age** *n.m.* sabotage; (*acte*) act of sabotage. **~eur, ~euse** *n.m., f.* saboteur.
sabre /sɑbr/ *n.m.* sabre.
sac /sak/ *n.m.* bag; (*grand, en toile*) sack. **mettre à ~,** (*maison*) ransack; (*ville*) sack. **~ à dos,** rucksack. **~ à main,** handbag. **~ de couchage,** sleeping-bag.
saccad|e /sakad/ *n.f.* jerk. **~é** *a.* jerky.
saccager /sakaʒe/ *v.t.* (*ville, pays*) sack; (*maison*) ransack; (*bouleverser*) wreck.
saccharine /sakarin/ *n.f.* saccharin.
sacerdoce /sasɛrdɔs/ *n.m.* priesthood; (*fig.*) vocation.
sachet /saʃɛ/ *n.m.* (small) bag; (*de shampooing etc.*) sachet. **~ de thé,** tea-bag.

sacoche /sakɔʃ/ *n.f.* bag; (*d'élève*) satchel; (*de moto*) saddle-bag.
sacquer /sake/ *v.t.* (*renvoyer: fam.*) sack.
sacr|e /sakr/ *n.m.* (*de roi*) coronation; (*d'évêque*) consecration. **~er** *v.t.* crown; consecrate.
sacré /sakre/ *a.* sacred; (*maudit: fam.*) damned.
sacrement /sakrəmɑ̃/ *n.m.* sacrament.
sacrifice /sakrifis/ *n.m.* sacrifice.
sacrifier /sakrifje/ *v.t.* sacrifice. **se ~** *v. pr.* sacrifice o.s.
sacrilège /sakrilɛʒ/ *n.m.* sacrilege. —*a.* sacrilegious.
sacristain /sakristɛ̃/ *n.m.* sexton.
sacristie /sakristi/ *n.f.* vestry.
sacro-saint, ~e /sakrɔsɛ̃, -t/ *a.* sacrosanct.
sadi|que /sadik/ *a.* sadistic. —*n.m./f.* sadist. **~sme** *n.m.* sadism.
safari /safari/ *n.m.* safari.
sagace /sagas/ *a.* shrewd.
sage /saʒ/ *a.* wise; (*docile*) good; (*modeste*) sober. —*n.m.* wise man. **~-femme** (*pl.* **~s-femmes**) *n.f.* midwife. **~ment** *adv.* wisely; (*docilement*) quietly. **~sse** /-ɛs/ *n.f.* wisdom; (*docilité*) good behaviour.
saignant, ~e /sɛɲɑ̃, -t/ *a.* (*culin.*) rare.
saign|er /seɲe/ *v.t./i.* bleed. **~ée** *n.f.* bleeding; (*perte: fig.*) heavy sacrifice. **~ement** *n.m.* bleeding. **~ement de nez,** nosebleed.
saill|ie /saji/ *n.f.* projection. **faire ~ie,** project. **~ant, ~ante** *a.* projecting; (*remarquable*) salient.
sain, ~e /sɛ̃, sɛn/ *a.* healthy; (*moralement*) sane. **~ et sauf,** safe and sound. **~ement** /sɛnmɑ̃/ *adv.* healthily; (*juger*) sanely.
saindoux /sɛ̃du/ *n.m.* lard.
saint, ~e /sɛ̃, sɛ̃t/ *a.* holy; (*bon, juste*) saintly. —*n.m., f.* saint. **S~-Esprit** *n.m.* Holy Spirit. **S~-Siège** *n.m.* Holy See. **S~-Sylvestre** *n.f.* New Year's Eve. **Sainte Vierge,** Blessed Virgin.
sainteté /sɛ̃tte/ *n.f.* holiness; (*de mariage, lieu*) sanctity.
sais /sɛ/ *voir* **savoir.**
saisie /sezi/ *n.f.* (*jurid.*) seizure.
sais|ir /sezir/ *v.t.* grab (hold of), seize; (*occasion, biens*) seize; (*comprendre*) grasp; (*frapper*) strike. **~i de,** (*peur*) stricken by, overcome by. **se ~ir de,** seize. **~issant, ~issante** *a.* (*spectacle*) gripping.
saison /sɛzɔ̃/ *n.f.* season. **~nier, ~nière** /-ɔnje, -jɛr/ *a.* seasonal.
sait /sɛ/ *voir* **savoir.**
salad|e /salad/ *n.f.* salad; (*laitue*) lettuce; (*désordre: fam.*) mess. **~ier** *n.m.* salad bowl.
salaire /salɛr/ *n.m.* wages, salary.
salaisons /salɛzɔ̃/ *n.f. pl.* salt meat *ou* fish.
salami /salami/ *n.m.* salami.
salarié, ~e /salarje/ *a.* wage-earning. —*n.m., f.* wage-earner.
salaud /salo/ *n.m.* (*argot*) bastard.
sale /sal/ *a.* dirty, filthy; (*mauvais*) nasty.
sal|er /sale/ *v.t.* salt. **~é** *a.* (*goût*) salty; (*plat*) salted; (*viande, poisson*) salt; (*grivois: fam.*) spicy; (*excessif: fam.*) steep.
saleté /salte/ *n.f.* dirtiness; (*crasse*) dirt; (*action*) dirty trick; (*obscénité*) obscenity. **~(s),** (*camelote*) rubbish. **~s,** (*détritus*) mess.
salière /saljɛr/ *n.f.* salt-cellar.
salin, ~e /salɛ̃, -in/ *a.* saline.
sal|ir /salir/ *v.t.* (make) dirty; (*réputation*) tarnish. **se ~ir** *v. pr.* get dirty. **~issant, ~issante** *a.* dirty; (*étoffe*) easily dirtied.
salive /saliv/ *n.f.* saliva.
salle /sal/ *n.f.* room; (*grande, publique*) hall; (*d'hôpital*) ward; (*théâtre, cinéma*) auditorium. **~ à manger,** dining-room. **~**

d'attente, waiting-room. **~ de bains,** bathroom. **~ de séjour,** living-room.

salon /salɔ̃/ *n.m.* lounge; (*de coiffure, beauté*) salon; (*exposition*) show. **~ de thé,** tea-room.

salope /salɔp/ *n.f.* (*argot*) bitch.

saloperie /salɔpri/ *n.f.* (*action: fam.*) dirty trick; (*camelote: fam.*) rubbish.

salopette /salɔpɛt/ *n.f.* dungarees; (*d'ouvrier*) overalls.

saltimbanque /saltɛ̃bɑ̃k/ *n.m./f.* (street *ou* fairground) acrobat.

salubre /salybr/ *a.* healthy.

saluer /salɥe/ *v.t.* greet; (*en partant*) take one's leave of; (*de la tête*) nod to; (*de la main*) wave to; (*mil.*) salute.

salut /saly/ *n.m.* greeting; (*de la tête*) nod; (*de la main*) wave; (*mil.*) salute; (*sauvegarde, rachat*) salvation. —*int.* (*bonjour: fam.*) hallo; (*au revoir: fam.*) bye-bye.

salutaire /salytɛr/ *a.* salutary.

salutation /salytɑsjɔ̃/ *n.f.* greeting.

salve /salv/ *n.f.* salvo.

samedi /samdi/ *n.m.* Saturday.

sanatorium /sanatɔrjɔm/ *n.m.* sanatorium.

sanctifier /sɑ̃ktifje/ *v.t.* sanctify.

sanction /sɑ̃ksjɔ̃/ *n.f.* sanction. **~ner** /-jɔne/ *v.t.* sanction; (*punir*) punish.

sanctuaire /sɑ̃ktɥɛr/ *n.m.* sanctuary.

sandale /sɑ̃dal/ *n.f.* sandal.

sandwich /sɑ̃dwitʃ/ *n.m.* sandwich.

sang /sɑ̃/ *n.m.* blood. **~-froid** *n.m. invar.* calm, self-control.

sanglant, ~e /sɑ̃glɑ̃, -t/ *a.* bloody.

sangl|e /sɑ̃gl/ *n.f.* strap. **~er** *v.t.* strap.

sanglier /sɑ̃glije/ *n.m.* wild boar.

sanglot /sɑ̃glo/ *n.m.* sob. **~er** /-ɔte/ *v.i.* sob.

sangsue /sɑ̃sy/ *n.f.* leech.

sanguin, ~e /sɑ̃gɛ̃, -in/ *a.* (*groupe etc.*) blood; (*caractère*) fiery.

sanguinaire /sɑ̃ginɛr/ *a.* bloodthirsty.

sanitaire /sanitɛr/ *a.* health; (*conditions*) sanitary; (*appareils, installations*) bathroom, sanitary.

sans /sɑ̃/ *prép.* without. **~ que vous le sachiez,** without your knowing. **~-abri** /sɑ̃zabri/ *n.m./f. invar.* homeless person. **~ ça, ~ quoi,** otherwise. **~ arrêt,** nonstop. **~ encombre/faute/ tarder,** without incident/fail/ delay. **~ fin/goût/limite,** endless/tasteless/limitless. **~-gêne** *a.invar.* inconsiderate, thoughtless; *n.m. invar.* thoughtlessness. **~ importance / pareil / précédent / travail,** unimportant / unparalleled / unprecedented / unemployed. **~ plus,** but no more than that, but nothing more.

santé /sɑ̃te/ *n.f.* health.

saoul, ~e /su, sul/ *voir* **soûl.**

saper /sape/ *v.t.* undermine.

sapeur /sapœr/ *n.m.* (*mil.*) sapper. **~-pompier** (*pl.* **~s-pompiers**) *n.m.* fireman.

saphir /safir/ *n.m.* sapphire.

sapin /sapɛ̃/ *n.m.* fir(-tree). **~ de Noël,** Christmas tree.

sarbacane /sarbakan/ *n.f.* (*jouet*) pea-shooter.

sarcas|me /sarkasm/ *n.m.* sarcasm. **~tique** *a.* sarcastic.

sarcler /sarkle/ *v.t.* weed.

sardine /sardin/ *n.f.* sardine.

sardonique /sardɔnik/ *a.* sardonic.

sarment /sarmɑ̃/ *n.m.* vine shoot.

sas /sɑ(s)/ *n.m.* (*naut., aviat.*) airlock.

satané /satane/ *a.* (*fam.*) blasted.

satanique /satanik/ *a.* satanic.

satellite /satelit/ *n.m.* satellite.

satin /satɛ̃/ *n.m.* satin.

satir|e /satir/ *n.f.* satire. **~ique** *a.* satirical.

satisfaction /satisfaksjɔ̃/ *n.f.* satisfaction.

satis|faire† /satisfɛr/ *v.t.* satisfy. *—v.i.* **~faire à,** satisfy. **~faisant, ~faisante** *a.* (*acceptable*) satisfactory. **~fait, ~faite** *a.* satisfied (**de,** with).

satur|er /satyre/ *v.t.* saturate. **~ation** *n.f.* saturation.

sauc|e /sos/ *n.f.* sauce; (*jus de viande*) gravy. **~e tartare,** tartar sauce. **~ière** *n.f.* sauce-boat.

saucisse /sosis/ *n.f.* sausage.

saucisson /sosisɔ̃/ *n.m.* (cold) sausage.

sauf¹ /sof/ *prép.* except. **~ erreur/imprévu,** barring error/ the unforeseen.

sau|f², ~ve /sof, sov/ *a.* safe, unharmed. **~f-conduit** *n.m.* safe conduct.

sauge /soʒ/ *n.f.* (*culin.*) sage.

saugrenu /sogrəny/ *a.* preposterous, ludicrous.

saule /sol/ *n.m.* willow. **~ pleureur,** weeping willow.

saumâtre /somɑtr/ *a.* briny.

saumon /somɔ̃/ *n.m.* salmon. *—a. invar.* salmon-pink.

saumure /somyr/ *n.f.* brine.

sauna /sona/ *n.m.* sauna.

saupoudrer /sopudre/ *v.t.* sprinkle.

saut /so/ *n.m.* jump, leap. **faire un ~ chez,** pop round to. **le ~,** (*sport*) jumping. **~ en hauteur/ longueur,** high/long jump. **~ périlleux,** somersault.

sauté /sote/ *a.* & *n.m.* (*culin.*) sauté.

saut|er /sote/ *v.i.* jump, leap; (*exploser*) blow up; (*fusible*) blow; (*se détacher*) come off. *—v.t.* jump (over); (*page, classe*) skip. **faire ~er,** (*détruire*) blow up; (*fusible*) blow; (*casser*) break; (*renvoyer*: *fam.*) kick out. **~er à la corde,** skip. **~er aux yeux,** be obvious. **~e-mouton** *n.m.* leap-frog.

sauterelle /sotrɛl/ *n.f.* grasshopper.

sautiller /sotije/ *v.i.* hop.

sautoir /sotwar/ *n.m.* (*sport*) jumping area.

sauvage /sovaʒ/ *a.* wild; (*primitif, cruel*) savage; (*farouche*) unsociable; (*illégal*) unauthorized. *—n.m./f.* unsociable person; (*brute*) savage. **~rie** *n.f.* savagery.

sauve /sov/ *voir* **sauf²**.

sauvegard|e /sovgard/ *n.f.* safeguard. **~er** *v.t.* safeguard.

sauv|er /sove/ *v.t.* save; (*d'un danger*) rescue, save; (*matériel*) salvage. **se ~er** *v. pr.* (*fuir*) run away; (*partir*: *fam.*) go (away). **~e-qui-peut** *n.m. invar.* stampede. **~etage** *n.m.* rescue; salvage. **~eteur** *n.m.* rescuer. **~eur** *n.m.* saviour.

sauvette (à la) /(ala)sovɛt/ *adv.* hastily; (*vendre*) illicitly.

savamment /savamɑ̃/ *adv.* learnedly; (*avec habileté*) skilfully.

savan|t, ~e /savɑ̃, -t/ *a.* learned; (*habile*) skilful. *—n.m.* scientist.

saveur /savœr/ *n.f.* flavour.

savoir† /savwar/ *v.t.* know; (*pouvoir*) be able to; (*apprendre*) hear. *—n.m.* learning. **à ~,** namely. **faire ~ à qn. que,** inform s.o. that. **je ne saurais pas,** I could not, I cannot. **(pas) que je sache,** (not) as far as I know.

savon /savɔ̃/ *n.m.* soap; (*réprimande*: *fam.*) dressing down. **~ner** /-ɔne/ *v.t.* soap. **~nette** /-ɔnɛt/ *n.f.* bar of soap. **~neux, ~neuse** /-ɔnø, -z/ *a.* soapy.

savour|er /savure/ *v.t.* savour. **~eux, ~euse** *a.* tasty; (*fig.*) spicy.

saxophone /saksɔfɔn/ *n.m.* saxophone.

scabreu|x, ~se /skabrø, -z/ *a.* risky; (*indécent*) obscene.

scalpel /skalpɛl/ *n.m.* scalpel.
scalper /skalpe/ *v.t.* scalp.
scandal|e /skɑ̃dal/ *n.m.* scandal; (*tapage*) uproar; (*en public*) noisy scene. **faire ~e,** shock people. **~eux, ~euse** *a.* scandalous. **~iser** *v.t.* scandalize, shock.
scander /skɑ̃de/ *v.t.* (*vers*) scan; (*slogan*) chant.
scandinave /skɑ̃dinav/ *a.* & *n.m./f.* Scandinavian.
Scandinavie /skɑ̃dinavi/ *n.f.* Scandinavia.
scaphandr|e /skafɑ̃dr/ *n.m.* diving-suit; (*aviat.*) spacesuit. **~e autonome,** aqualung. **~ier** *n.m.* diver.
scarabée /skarabe/ *n.m.* beetle.
scarlatine /skarlatin/ *n.f.* scarlet fever.
scarole /skarɔl/ *n.f.* endive.
sceau (*pl.* **~x**) /so/ *n.m.* seal.
scélérat /selera/ *n.m.* scoundrel.
scell|er /sele/ *v.t.* seal; (*fixer*) cement. **~és** *n.m. pl.* seals.
scénario /senarjo/ *n.m.* scenario.
scène /sɛn/ *n.f.* scene; (*estrade, art dramatique*) stage. **mettre en ~,** (*pièce*) stage.
scepti|que /sɛptik/ *a.* sceptical. —*n.m./f.* sceptic. **~cisme** *n.m.* scepticism.
sceptre /sɛptr/ *n.m.* sceptre.
schéma /ʃema/ *n.m.* diagram. **~tique** *a.* diagrammatic; (*sommaire*) sketchy.
schisme /ʃism/ *n.m.* schism.
schizophrène /skizɔfrɛn/ *a.* & *n.m./f.* schizophrenic.
scie /si/ *n.f.* saw.
sciemment /sjamɑ̃/ *adv.* knowingly.
scien|ce /sjɑ̃s/ *n.f.* science; (*savoir*) knowledge. **~ce-fiction** *n.f.* science fiction. **~tifique** *a.* scientific; *n.m./f.* scientist.
scier /sje/ *v.t.* saw.
scinder /sɛ̃de/ *v.t.*, **se ~** *v. pr.* split.
scintill|er /sɛ̃tije/ *v.i.* glitter; (*étoile*) twinkle. **~ement** *n.m.* glittering; twinkling.
scission /sisjɔ̃/ *n.f.* split.
sciure /sjyr/ *n.f.* sawdust.
sclérose /skleroz/ *n.f.* sclerosis.
scol|aire /skɔlɛr/ *a.* school. **~arisation** *n.f.*, **~arité** *n.f.* schooling. **~arisé** *a.* provided with schooling.
scorbut /skɔrbyt/ *n.m.* scurvy.
score /skɔr/ *n.m.* score.
scories /skɔri/ *n.f. pl.* slag.
scorpion /skɔrpjɔ̃/ *n.m.* scorpion.
scotch[1] /skɔtʃ/ *n.m.* (*boisson*) Scotch (whisky).
scotch[2] /skɔtʃ/ *n.m.* (P.) Sellotape (P.); (*Amer.*) Scotch (tape) (P.).
scout, ~e /skut/ *n.m.* & *a.* scout.
script /skript/ *n.m.* (*écriture*) printing.
scrupul|e /skrypyl/ *n.m.* scruple. **~eusement** *adv.* scrupulously. **~eux, ~euse** *a.* scrupulous.
scruter /skryte/ *v.t.* examine, scrutinize.
scrutin /skrytɛ̃/ *n.m.* (*vote*) ballot; (*opération électorale*) poll.
sculpt|er /skylte/ *v.t.* sculpture, carve. **~eur** *n.m.* sculptor. **~ure** *n.f.* sculpture.
se, s'* /sə, s/ *pron.* himself; (*femelle*) herself; (*indéfini*) oneself; (*non humain*) itself; (*pl.*) themselves; (*réciproque*) each other, one another. **~ parler,** (*indirect*) speak to o.s. **~ faire,** (*passif*) be done. **~ laver les mains,** (*possessif*) wash one's hands.
séance /seɑ̃s/ *n.f.* session; (*cinéma, théâtre*) show. **~ de pose,** sitting. **~ tenante,** forthwith.
séant, ~e /seɑ̃, -t/ *a.* seemly.
seau (*pl.* **~x**) /so/ *n.m.* bucket, pail.
sec, sèche /sɛk, sɛʃ/ *a.* dry; (*fruits*) dried; (*coup, bruit*) sharp; (*cœur*) hard; (*whisky*) neat; (*Amer.*) straight. —*adv.* (*frapper, pleuvoir*) hard. —*n.m.* **à ~,** (*sans eau*) dry. **au ~,** in a dry place.

sécateur /sekatœr/ *n.m.* (pruning) shears.

sécession /sesesjɔ̃/ *n.f.* secession. **faire ~,** secede.

sèche /sɛʃ/ *voir* **sec. ~ment** *adv.* drily.

sèche-cheveux /sɛʃʃəvø/ *n.m. invar.* hair-drier.

sécher /seʃe/ *v.t./i.* dry; (*cours*: *fam.*) skip; (*ignorer*: *argot*) be stumped. **se ~** *v. pr.* dry o.s.

sécheresse /sɛʃrɛs/ *n.f.* dryness; (*temps sec*) drought.

séchoir /seʃwar/ *n.m.* drier.

second, ~e[1] /sgɔ̃, -d/ *a.* & *n.m., f.* second. —*n.m.* (*adjoint*) second in command; (*étage*) second floor. —*n.f.* (*transport*) second class.

secondaire /sgɔ̃dɛr/ *a.* secondary.

seconde[2] /sgɔ̃d/ *n.f.* (*instant*) second.

seconder /sgɔ̃de/ *v.t.* assist.

secouer /skwe/ *v.t.* shake; (*poussière, torpeur*) shake off. **se ~,** (*fam.*) shake o.s. out of it.

secour|ir /skurir/ *v.t.* assist, help. **~able** *a.* helpful. **~iste** *n.m./f.* first-aid worker.

secours /skur/ *n.m.* assistance, help; (*mil.*) relief. —*n.m. pl.* (*méd.*) first aid; (*mil.*) relief. **au ~!,** help! **de ~,** emergency; (*équipe, opération*) rescue.

secousse /skus/ *n.f.* jolt, jerk; (*morale*) shock; (*séisme*) tremor.

secr|et, ~ète /səkrɛ, -t/ *a.* secret. —*n.m.* secret; (*discrétion*) secrecy. **en ~et,** in secret, secretly.

secrétaire /skretɛr/ *n.m./f.* secretary. —*n.m.* (*meuble*) writing-desk. **~ d'État,** junior minister.

secrétariat /skretarja/ *n.m.* secretarial work; (*bureau*) secretary's office; (*d'un organisme*) secretariat.

sécrét|er /sekrete/ *v.t.* secrete. **~ion** /-sjɔ̃/ *n.f.* secretion.

sect|e /sɛkt/ *n.f.* sect. **~aire** *a.* sectarian.

secteur /sɛktœr/ *n.m.* area; (*mil., comm.*) sector; (*circuit*: *électr.*) mains.

section /sɛksjɔ̃/ *n.f.* section; (*transports publics*) fare stage; (*mil.*) platoon. **~ner** /-jɔne/ *v.t.* sever.

séculaire /sekylɛr/ *a.* age-old.

sécul|ier, ~ière /sekylje, -jɛr/ *a.* secular.

sécuriser /sekyrize/ *v.t.* reassure.

sécurité /sekyrite/ *n.f.* security; (*absence de danger*) safety. **en ~,** safe, secure. **S~ sociale,** social services, social security services.

sédatif /sedatif/ *n.m.* sedative.

sédentaire /sedɑ̃tɛr/ *a.* sedentary.

sédiment /sedimɑ̃/ *n.m.* sediment.

séditieu|x, ~se /sedisjø, -z/ *a.* seditious.

sédition /sedisjɔ̃/ *n.f.* sedition.

séd|uire† /sedɥir/ *v.t.* charm; (*plaire à*) appeal to; (*abuser de*) seduce. **~ucteur, ~uctrice** *a.* seductive; *n.m., f.* seducer. **~uction** *n.f.* seduction; (*charme*) charm. **~uisant, ~uisante** *a.* attractive.

segment /sɛgmɑ̃/ *n.m.* segment.

ségrégation /segregɑsjɔ̃/ *n.f.* segregation.

seigle /sɛgl/ *n.m.* rye.

seigneur /sɛɲœr/ *n.m.* lord. **le S~,** the Lord.

sein /sɛ̃/ *n.m.* breast; (*fig.*) bosom. **au ~ de,** in the midst of.

Seine /sɛn/ *n.f.* Seine.

séisme /seism/ *n.m.* earthquake.

seiz|e /sɛz/ *a.* & *n.m.* sixteen. **~ième** *a.* & *n.m./f.* sixteenth.

séjour /seʒur/ *n.m.* stay; (*pièce*) living-room. **~ner** *v.i.* stay.

sel /sɛl/ *n.m.* salt; (*piquant*) spice.

sélect /selɛkt/ *a.* select.

sélecti|f, ~ve /selɛktif, -v/ *a.* selective.

sélection /selɛksjɔ̃/ *n.f.* selection. **~ner** /-jɔne/ *v.t.* select.

self(-service) /sɛlf(sɛrvis)/ *n.m.* self-service.
selle /sɛl/ *n.f.* saddle.
seller /sele/ *v.t.* saddle.
sellette /sɛlɛt/ *n.f.* **sur la ~,** under examination.
selon /slɔ̃/ *prép.* according to (**que,** whether).
semailles /smɑj/ *n.f. pl.* sowing; (*époque*) seed-time.
semaine /smɛn/ *n.f.* week. **en ~,** in the week.
sémantique /semɑ̃tik/ *a.* semantic. —*n.f.* semantics.
sémaphore /semafɔr/ *n.m.* (*appareil*) semaphore.
semblable /sɑ̃blabl/ *a.* similar (**à,** to). **de ~s propos**/*etc.*, (*tels*) such remarks/*etc.* —*n.m.* fellow (creature).
semblant /sɑ̃blɑ̃/ *n.m.* **faire ~ de,** pretend to. **un ~ de,** a semblance of.
sembl|er /sɑ̃ble/ *v.i.* seem (**à,** to; **que,** that). **il me ~e que,** it seems to me that.
semelle /smɛl/ *n.f.* sole.
semence /smɑ̃s/ *n.f.* seed; (*clou*) tack. **~s,** (*graines*) seed.
sem|er /sme/ *v.t.* sow; (*jeter, parsemer*) strew; (*répandre*) spread; (*personne*: *fam.*) lose. **~eur, ~euse** *n.m., f.* sower.
semestr|e /smɛstr/ *n.m.* half-year; (*univ.*) semester. **~iel, ~ielle** *a.* half-yearly.
semi- /səmi/ *préf.* semi-.
séminaire /seminɛr/ *n.m.* (*relig.*) seminary; (*univ.*) seminar.
semi-remorque /səmirəmɔrk/ *n.m.* articulated lorry; (*Amer.*) semi(-trailer).
semis /smi/ *n.m.* (*terrain*) seed-bed; (*plant*) seedling.
sémit|e /semit/ *a.* Semitic. —*n.m./f.* Semite. **~ique** *a.* Semitic.
semonce /səmɔ̃s/ *n.f.* reprimand. **coup de ~,** warning shot.
semoule /smul/ *n.f.* semolina.
sénat /sena/ *n.m.* senate. **~eur** /-tœr/ *n.m.* senator.
sénil|e /senil/ *a.* senile. **~ité** *n.f.* senility.
sens /sɑ̃s/ *n.m.* sense; (*signification*) meaning, sense; (*direction*) direction. **à mon ~,** to my mind. **à ~ unique,** (*rue etc.*) one-way. **ça n'a pas de ~,** that does not make sense. **~ commun,** common sense. **~ giratoire,** roundabout; (*Amer.*) rotary. **~ interdit,** no entry; (*rue*) one-way street.
sensation /sɑ̃sɑsjɔ̃/ *n.f.* feeling, sensation. **faire ~,** create a sensation. **~nel, ~nelle** /-jɔnɛl/ *a.* sensational.
sensé /sɑ̃se/ *a.* sensible.
sensibiliser /sɑ̃sibilize/ *v.t.* **~ à,** make sensitive to.
sensib|le /sɑ̃sibl/ *a.* sensitive (**à,** to); (*appréciable*) noticeable. **~ilité** *n.f.* sensitivity. **~lement** *adv.* noticeably; (*à peu près*) more or less.
sensoriel, ~le /sɑ̃sɔrjɛl/ *a.* sensory.
sens|uel, ~uelle /sɑ̃sɥɛl/ *a.* sensuous; (*sexuel*) sensual. **~ualité** *n.f.* sensuousness; sensuality.
sentence /sɑ̃tɑ̃s/ *n.f.* (*jurid.*) sentence; (*adage*) maxim.
senteur /sɑ̃tœr/ *n.f.* scent.
sentier /sɑ̃tje/ *n.m.* path.
sentiment /sɑ̃timɑ̃/ *n.m.* feeling. **avoir le ~ de,** be aware of.
sentiment|al (*m. pl.* **~aux**) /sɑ̃timɑ̃tal, -o/ *a.* sentimental. **~alité** *n.f.* sentimentality.
sentinelle /sɑ̃tinɛl/ *n.f.* sentry.
sentir† /sɑ̃tir/ *v.t.* feel; (*odeur*) smell; (*goût*) taste; (*pressentir*) sense; (*supporter*: *fam.*) bear. **~ la lavande**/*etc.*, smell of lavender/*etc.* —*v.i.* smell. **se ~ fier**/**mieux**/*etc.*, feel proud/better/*etc.*
séparé /separe/ *a.* separate. **~ment** *adv.* separately.

sépar|er /separe/ *v.t.* separate; (*en deux*) split. **se ~er** *v. pr.* separate, part (**de**, from); (*se détacher*) split. **se ~er de,** (*se défaire de*) part with. **~ation** *n.f.* separation.
sept /sɛt/ *a.* & *n.m.* seven.
septante /sɛptɑ̃t/ *a.* & *n.m.* (*en Belgique, Suisse*) seventy.
septembre /sɛptɑ̃br/ *n.m.* September.
septentrion|al (*m. pl.* **~aux**) /sɛptɑ̃trijɔnal, -o/ *a.* northern.
septième /sɛtjɛm/ *a.* & *n.m./f.* seventh.
sépulcre /sepylkr/ *n.m.* (*relig.*) sepulchre.
sépulture /sepyltyr/ *n.f.* burial; (*lieu*) burial place.
séquelles /sekɛl/ *n.f. pl.* (*de guerre*) aftermath.
séquence /sekɑ̃s/ *n.f.* sequence.
séquestrer /sekɛstre/ *v.t.* confine (illegally), lock away.
sera, serait /sra, srɛ/ *voir* **être.**
serein, ~e /sərɛ̃, -ɛn/ *a.* serene.
sérénade /serenad/ *n.f.* serenade.
sérénité /serenite/ *n.f.* serenity.
sergent /sɛrʒɑ̃/ *n.m.* sergeant.
série /seri/ *n.f.* series; (*d'objets*) set. **de ~,** (*véhicule etc.*) standard. **fabrication** *ou* **production en ~,** mass production.
sérieu|x, ~se /serjø, -z/ *a.* serious; (*digne de foi*) reliable; (*authentique*) genuine; (*chances, raison*) good. —*n.m.* seriousness. **garder/perdre son ~x,** keep/be unable to keep a straight face. **prendre au ~x,** take seriously. **~sement** *adv.* seriously.
serin /srɛ̃/ *n.m.* canary.
seringue /srɛ̃g/ *n.f.* syringe.
serment /sɛrmɑ̃/ *n.m.* oath; (*promesse*) pledge.
sermon /sɛrmɔ̃/ *n.m.* sermon. **~ner** /-ɔne/ *v.t.* (*fam.*) lecture.
serpe /sɛrp/ *n.f.* bill(hook).
serpent /sɛrpɑ̃/ *n.m.* snake. **~ à sonnettes,** rattlesnake.
serpenter /sɛrpɑ̃te/ *v.i.* meander.
serpentin /sɛrpɑ̃tɛ̃/ *n.m.* streamer.
serpillière /sɛrpijɛr/ *n.f.* floorcloth.
serre[1] /sɛr/ *n.f.* (*local*) greenhouse.
serre[2] /sɛr/ *n.f.* (*griffe*) claw.
serré /sere/ *a.* (*habit, nœud, programme*) tight; (*personnes*) packed, crowded; (*lutte, mailles*) close; (*cœur*) heavy.
serrer /sere/ *v.t.* (*saisir*) grip; (*presser*) squeeze; (*vis, corde, ceinture*) tighten; (*poing*) clench; (*pieds*) pinch; (*rangs*) close; (*embrasser*) hug; (*rapprocher*) squeeze up. **~ qn.,** (*vêtement*) be tight on s.o. —*v.i.* **~ à droite,** keep over to the right. **se ~** *v. pr.* (*se rapprocher*) squeeze (up) (**contre,** against). **~ de près,** follow closely. **~ la main à,** shake hands with.
serrur|e /seryr/ *n.f.* lock. **~ier** *n.m.* locksmith.
sertir /sɛrtir/ *v.t.* (*bijou*) set.
sérum /serɔm/ *n.m.* serum.
servante /sɛrvɑ̃t/ *n.f.* (maid)servant.
serveu|r, ~se /sɛrvœr, -øz/ *n.m., f.* waiter, waitress; (*au bar*) barman, barmaid.
serviable /sɛrvjabl/ *a.* helpful.
service /sɛrvis/ *n.m.* service; (*fonction, temps de travail*) duty; (*pourboire*) service (charge). **être de ~,** be on duty. **rendre un ~/ mauvais ~ à qn.,** do s.o. a favour/disservice. **~ d'ordre,** (*policiers*) police.
serviette /sɛrvjɛt/ *n.f.* (*de toilette*) towel; (*sac*) briefcase. **~ (de table),** serviette; (*Amer.*) napkin.
servile /sɛrvil/ *a.* servile.
servir† /sɛrvir/ *v.t./i.* serve; (*être utile*) be of use, serve. **~ qn. (à table),** wait on s.o. **ça sert à,** (*outil, récipient, etc.*) it is used for. **ça me sert à/de,** I use it for/as. **~ de,** serve as, be used as. **~ à qn.**

de guide/*etc.*, act as a guide/*etc.* for s.o. **se ~** *v. pr.* (*à table*) help o.s. (**de,** to). **se ~ de,** use.
serviteur /sɛrvitœr/ *n.m.* servant.
servitude /sɛrvityd/ *n.f.* servitude.
ses /se/ *voir* **son**¹.
session /sesjɔ̃/ *n.f.* session.
seuil /sœj/ *n.m.* doorstep; (*entrée*) doorway; (*fig.*) threshold.
seul, ~e /sœl/ *a.* alone, on one's own; (*unique*) only. **un ~ travail**/*etc.*, only one job/*etc.* **pas un ~ ami**/*etc.*, not a single friend/*etc.* —*n.m., f.* **le ~, la ~e,** the only one. **un ~, une ~e,** only one. **pas un ~,** not (a single) one.
seulement /sœlmɑ̃/ *adv.* only.
sève /sɛv/ *n.f.* sap.
sév|ère /sevɛr/ *a.* severe. **~èrement** *adv.* severely. **~érité** /-erite/ *n.f.* severity.
sévices /sevis/ *n.m. pl.* cruelty.
sévir /sevir/ *v.i.* (*fléau*) rage. **~ contre,** punish.
sevrer /səvre/ *v.t.* wean.
sexe /sɛks/ *n.m.* sex; (*organes*) sex organs.
sex|uel, ~uelle /sɛksɥɛl/ *a.* sexual. **~ualité** *n.f.* sexuality.
seyant, ~e /sɛjɑ̃, -t/ *a.* becoming.
shampooing /ʃɑ̃pwɛ̃/ *n.m.* shampoo.
shérif /ʃerif/ *n.m.* sheriff.
short /ʃɔrt/ *n.m.* (pair of) shorts.
si¹ (**s'** *before il, ils*) /si, s/ *conj.* if; (*interrogation indirecte*) if, whether. **~ on partait?,** (*suggestion*) what about going? **s'il vous** *ou* **te plaît,** please. **~ oui,** if so. **~ seulement,** if only.
si² /si/ *adv.* (*tellement*) so; (*oui*) yes. **un ~ bon repas,** such a good meal. **pas ~ riche que,** not as rich as. **~ habile qu'il soit,** however skilful he may be. **~ bien que,** with the result that.
siamois, ~e /sjamwa, -z/ *a.* Siamese.
Sicile /sisil/ *n.f.* Sicily.
sida /sida/ *n.m.* (*méd.*) AIDS.
sidérer /sidere/ *v.t.* (*fam.*) stagger.
sidérurgie /sideryrʒi/ *n.f.* iron and steel industry.
siècle /sjɛkl/ *n.m.* century; (*époque*) age.
siège /sjɛʒ/ *n.m.* seat; (*mil.*) siege. **~ éjectable,** ejector seat. **~ social,** head office, headquarters.
siéger /sjeʒe/ *v.i.* (*assemblée*) sit.
sien, ~ne /sjɛ̃, sjɛn/ *pron.* **le ~, la ~ne, les ~(ne)s,** his; (*femme*) hers; (*chose*) its. **les ~s,** (*famille*) one's family.
sieste /sjɛst/ *n.f.* siesta.
siffl|er /sifle/ *v.i.* whistle; (*avec un sifflet*) blow one's whistle; (*serpent, gaz*) hiss. —*v.t.* (*air*) whistle; (*chien*) whistle to *ou* for; (*acteur*) hiss; (*signaler*) blow one's whistle for. **~ement** *n.m.* whistling. **un ~ement,** a whistle.
sifflet /siflɛ/ *n.m.* whistle. **~s,** (*huées*) boos.
siffloter /siflɔte/ *v.t./i.* whistle.
sigle /sigl/ *n.m.* abbreviation, acronym.
sign|al (*pl.* **~aux**) /siɲal, -o/ *n.m.* signal. **~aux lumineux,** (*auto.*) traffic signals.
signal|er /siɲale/ *v.t.* indicate; (*par une sonnerie, un écriteau*) signal; (*dénoncer, mentionner*) report; (*faire remarquer*) point out. **se ~er par,** distinguish o.s. by. **~ement** *n.m.* description.
signalisation /siɲalizɑsjɔ̃/ *n.f.* signalling, signposting; (*signaux*) signals.
signataire /siɲatɛr/ *n.m./f.* signatory.
signature /siɲatyr/ *n.f.* signature; (*action*) signing.
signe /siɲ/ *n.m.* sign; (*de ponctuation*) mark. **faire ~ à,** beckon (**de,** to); (*contacter*) contact. **faire ~ que non,** shake one's head. **faire ~ que oui,** nod.

signer /siɲe/ *v.t.* sign. **se ~** *v. pr.* (*relig.*) cross o.s.

significati|f, ~ve /siɲifikatif, -v/ *a.* significant.

signification /siɲifikɑsjɔ̃/ *n.f.* meaning.

signifier /siɲifje/ *v.t.* mean, signify; (*faire connaître*) make known (**à**, to).

silenc|e /silɑ̃s/ *n.m.* silence; (*mus.*) rest. **garder le ~e,** keep silent. **~ieux, ~ieuse** *a.* silent; *n.m.* (*auto.*) silencer; (*auto., Amer.*) muffler.

silex /silɛks/ *n.m.* flint.

silhouette /silwɛt/ *n.f.* outline, silhouette.

silicium /silisjɔm/ *n.m.* silicon.

sillage /sijaʒ/ *n.m.* (*trace d'eau*) wake.

sillon /sijɔ̃/ *n.m.* furrow; (*de disque*) groove.

sillonner /sijɔne/ *v.t.* criss-cross.

silo /silo/ *n.m.* silo.

simagrées /simagre/ *n.f. pl.* fuss, pretence.

simil|aire /similɛr/ *a.* similar. **~itude** *n.f.* similarity.

simple /sɛ̃pl/ *a.* simple; (*non double*) single. —*n.m.* (*tennis*) singles. **~ d'esprit** *n.m./f.* simpleton. **~ particulier,** ordinary individual. **~ soldat,** private. **~ment** /-əmɑ̃/ *adv.* simply.

simplicité /sɛ̃plisite/ *n.f.* simplicity; (*naïveté*) simpleness.

simplif|ier /sɛ̃plifje/ *v.t.* simplify. **~ication** *n.f.* simplification.

simulacre /simylakr/ *n.m.* pretence, sham.

simul|er /simyle/ *v.t.* simulate. **~ation** *n.f.* simulation.

simultané /simyltane/ *a.* simultaneous. **~ment** *adv.* simultaneously.

sinc|ère /sɛ̃sɛr/ *a.* sincere. **~èrement** *adv.* sincerely. **~érité** *n.f.* sincerity.

singe /sɛ̃ʒ/ *n.m.* monkey, ape.

singer /sɛ̃ʒe/ *v.t.* mimic, ape.

singeries /sɛ̃ʒri/ *n.f. pl.* antics.

singulariser (se) /(sə)sɛ̃gylarize/ *v. pr.* make o.s. conspicuous.

singul|ier, ~ière /sɛ̃gylje, -jɛr/ *a.* peculiar, remarkable; (*gram.*) singular. —*n.m.* (*gram.*) singular. **~arité** *n.f.* peculiarity. **~ièrement** *adv.* peculiarly; (*beaucoup*) remarkably.

sinistre[1] /sinistr/ *a.* sinister.

sinistr|e[2] /sinistr/ *n.m.* disaster; (*incendie*) blaze; (*dommages*) damage. **~é** *a.* disaster-stricken; *n.m., f.* disaster victim.

sinon /sinɔ̃/ *conj.* (*autrement*) otherwise; (*sauf*) except (**que,** that); (*si ce n'est*) if not.

sinueu|x, ~se /sinɥø, -z/ *a.* winding; (*fig.*) tortuous.

sinus /sinys/ *n.m.* (*anat.*) sinus.

sionisme /sjɔnism/ *n.m.* Zionism.

siphon /sifɔ̃/ *n.m.* siphon.

sirène[1] /sirɛn/ *n.f.* (*appareil*) siren.

sirène[2] /sirɛn/ *n.f.* (*femme*) mermaid.

sirop /siro/ *n.m.* syrup; (*boisson*) cordial.

siroter /sirɔte/ *v.t.* sip.

sirupeu|x, ~se /sirypø, -z/ *a.* syrupy.

sis, ~e /si, siz/ *a.* situated.

site /sit/ *n.m.* setting; (*pittoresque*) beauty spot; (*emplacement*) site; (*monument etc.*) place of interest.

sitôt /sito/ *adv.* **~ entré**/*etc.*, immediately after coming in/*etc.* **~ que,** as soon as. **pas de ~,** not for a while.

situation /sitɥɑsjɔ̃/ *n.f.* situation, position. **~ de famille,** marital status.

situ|er /sitɥe/ *v.t.* situate, locate. **se ~er** *v. pr.* (*se trouver*) be situated. **~é** *a.* situated.

six /sis/ (/si/ *before consonant*, /siz/ *before vowel*) *a.* & *n.m.* six. **~ième** /sizjɛm/ *a.* & *n.m./f.* sixth.

sketch (*pl.* **~es**) /skɛtʃ/ *n.m.* (*théâtre*) sketch.

ski /ski/ *n.m.* (*patin*) ski; (*sport*) skiing. **faire du ~,** ski.

sk|ier /skje/ *v.i.* ski. **~ieur, ~ieuse** *n.m., f.* skier.

slalom /slalɔm/ *n.m.* slalom.

slave /slav/ *a.* Slav; (*lang.*) Slavonic. —*n.m./f.* Slav.

slip /slip/ *n.m.* (*d'homme*) (under)-pants; (*de femme*) knickers; (*Amer.*) panties. **~ de bain,** (swimming) trunks; (*du bikini*) briefs.

slogan /slɔgɑ̃/ *n.m.* slogan.

smoking /smɔkiŋ/ *n.m.* evening *ou* dinner suit, dinner-jacket.

snack(-bar) /snak(bar)/ *n.m.* snack-bar.

snob /snɔb/ *n.m./f.* snob. —*a.* snobbish. **~isme** *n.m.* snobbery.

sobr|e /sɔbr/ *a.* sober. **~iété** *n.f.* sobriety.

sobriquet /sɔbrikɛ/ *n.m.* nick-name.

sociable /sɔsjabl/ *a.* sociable.

soc|ial (*m. pl.* **~iaux**) /sɔsjal, -jo/ *a.* social.

socialis|te /sɔsjalist/ *n.m./f.* socialist. **~me** *n.m.* socialism.

sociétaire /sɔsjetɛr/ *n.m./f.* (society) member.

société /sɔsjete/ *n.f.* society; (*compagnie, firme*) company.

sociolo|gie /sɔsjɔlɔʒi/ *n.f.* sociology. **~gique** *a.* sociological. **~gue** *n.m./f.* sociologist.

socle /sɔkl/ *n.m.* (*de colonne, statue*) plinth; (*de lampe*) base.

socquette /sɔkɛt/ *n.f.* ankle sock.

soda /sɔda/ *n.m.* (fizzy) drink.

sodium /sɔdjɔm/ *n.m.* sodium.

sœur /sœr/ *n.f.* sister.

sofa /sɔfa/ *n.m.* sofa.

soi /swa/ *pron.* oneself. **en ~,** in itself. **~-disant** *a. invar.* so-called, self-styled; *adv.* supposedly.

soie /swa/ *n.f.* silk.

soif /swaf/ *n.f.* thirst. **avoir ~,** be thirsty.

soigné /swaɲe/ *a.* tidy, neat.

soigner /swaɲe/ *v.t.* look after, take care of; (*tenue, style*) take care over; (*maladie*) treat. **se ~** *v. pr.* look after o.s.

soigneu|x, ~se /swaɲø, -z/ *a.* careful (**de,** about); (*ordonné*) tidy. **~sement** *adv.* carefully.

soi-même /swamɛm/ *pron.* oneself.

soin /swɛ̃/ *n.m.* care; (*ordre*) tidiness. **~s,** care; (*méd.*) treatment. **avoir** *ou* **prendre ~ de qn./de faire,** take care of s.o./to do.

soir /swar/ *n.m.* evening.

soirée /sware/ *n.f.* evening; (*réception*) party. **~ dansante,** dance.

soit /swa/ *voir* **être.** —*conj.* (*à savoir*) that is to say. **~ . . . soit,** either . . . or.

soixantaine /swasɑ̃tɛn/ *n.f.* **une ~ (de),** about sixty.

soixant|e /swasɑ̃t/ *a.* & *n.m.* sixty. **~e-dix** *a.* & *n.m.* seventy. **~e-dixième** *a.* & *n.m./f.* seventieth. **~ième** *a.* & *n.m./f.* sixtieth.

soja /sɔʒa/ *n.m.* (*graines*) soya beans; (*plante*) soya.

sol /sɔl/ *n.m.* ground; (*de maison*) floor; (*terrain agricole*) soil.

solaire /sɔlɛr/ *a.* solar; (*rayons, lumière*) sun's; (*huile, filtre*) sun.

soldat /sɔlda/ *n.m.* soldier.

solde[1] /sɔld/ *n.f.* (*salaire*) pay.

solde[2] /sɔld/ *n.m.* (*comm.*) balance. **~s,** (*articles*) sale goods. **en ~,** (*acheter etc.*) at sale price. **les ~s,** the sales.

solder /sɔlde/ *v.t.* sell off at sale price; (*compte*) settle. **se ~ par,** (*aboutir à*) end in.

sole /sɔl/ *n.f.* (*poisson*) sole.

soleil /sɔlɛj/ *n.m.* sun; (*chaleur*) sunshine; (*fleur*) sunflower. **il fait du ~,** it is sunny.

solennel, ~le /sɔlanɛl/ *a.* solemn.

solennité /sɔlanite/ *n.f.* solemnity.
solex /sɔlɛks/ *n.m.* (P.) moped.
solfège /sɔlfɛʒ/ *n.m.* elementary musical theory.
solid|aire /sɔlidɛr/ *a.* (*mécanismes*) interdependent; (*personnes*) who show solidarity. **~arité** *n.f.* solidarity.
solidariser (se) /(sə)sɔlidarize/ *v. pr.* show solidarity (**avec,** with).
solid|e /sɔlid/ *a.* solid. —*n.m.* (*corps*) solid. **~ement** *adv.* solidly. **~ité** *n.f.* solidity.
solidifier /sɔlidifje/ *v.t.*, **se ~** *v. pr.* solidify.
soliste /sɔlist/ *n.m./f.* soloist.
solitaire /sɔlitɛr/ *a.* solitary. —*n.m./f.* (*ermite*) hermit; (*personne insociable*) loner.
solitude /sɔlityd/ *n.f.* solitude.
solive /sɔliv/ *n.f.* joist.
sollicit|er /sɔlisite/ *v.t.* request; (*attirer, pousser*) prompt; (*tenter*) tempt. **~ation** *n.f.* earnest request.
sollicitude /sɔlisityd/ *n.f.* concern.
solo /sɔlo/ *n.m.* & *a. invar.* (*mus.*) solo.
solstice /sɔlstis/ *n.m.* solstice.
soluble /sɔlybl/ *a.* soluble.
solution /sɔlysjɔ̃/ *n.f.* solution.
solvable /sɔlvabl/ *a.* solvent.
solvant /sɔlvɑ̃/ *n.m.* solvent.
sombre /sɔ̃br/ *a.* dark; (*triste*) sombre.
sombrer /sɔ̃bre/ *v.i.* sink (**dans,** into).
sommaire /sɔmɛr/ *a.* summary; (*tenue, repas*) scant. —*n.m.* summary.
sommation /sɔmɑsjɔ̃/ *n.f.* (*mil.*) warning; (*jurid.*) summons.
somme[1] /sɔm/ *n.f.* sum. **en ~, ~ toute,** in short. **faire la ~ de,** add (up), total (up).
somme[2] /sɔm/ *n.m.* (*sommeil*) nap.
sommeil /sɔmɛj/ *n.m.* sleep; (*besoin de dormir*) drowsiness. **avoir ~,** be *ou* feel sleepy. **~ler** /-meje/ *v.i.* doze; (*fig.*) lie dormant.
sommelier /sɔməlje/ *n.m* wine waiter.
sommer /sɔme/ *v.t.* summon.
sommes /sɔm/ *voir* **être.**
sommet /sɔmɛ/ *n.m.* top; (*de montagne, gloire*) summit; (*de triangle*) apex.
sommier /sɔmje/ *n.m.* bed springs.
somnambule /sɔmnɑ̃byl/ *n.m.* sleep-walker.
somnifère /sɔmnifɛr/ *n.m.* sleeping-pill.
somnolen|t, ~te /sɔmnɔlɑ̃, -t/ *a.* drowsy. **~ce** *n.f.* drowsiness.
somnoler /sɔmnɔle/ *v.i.* doze.
somptu|eux, ~euse /sɔ̃ptɥø, -z/ *a.* sumptuous. **~osité** *n.f.* sumptuousness.
son[1], **sa** *ou* **son*** (*pl.* **ses**) /sɔ̃, sa, sɔ̃n, se/ *a.* his; (*femme*) her; (*chose*) its; (*indéfini*) one's.
son[2] /sɔ̃/ *n.m.* (*bruit*) sound.
son[3] /sɔ̃/ *n.m.* (*de blé*) bran.
sonate /sɔnat/ *n.f.* sonata.
sonde /sɔ̃d/ *n.f.* (*pour les forages*) drill; (*méd.*) probe.
sond|er /sɔ̃de/ *v.t.* sound; (*terrain*) drill; (*personne*) sound out. **~age** *n.m.* sounding; drilling. **~age (d'opinion),** (opinion) poll.
song|e /sɔ̃ʒ/ *n.m.* dream. **~er** *v.i.* dream; *v.t.* **~er que,** think that. **~er à,** think about. **~eur, ~euse** *a.* pensive.
sonnantes /sɔnɑ̃t/ *a.f. pl.* **à six**/*etc.* **heures ~,** on the stroke of six/*etc.*
sonné /sɔne/ *a.* (*fam.*) crazy.
sonner /sɔne/ *v.t./i.* ring; (*clairon, glas*) sound; (*heure*) strike; (*domestique*) ring for. **midi sonné,** well past noon. **~ de,** (*clairon etc.*) sound, blow.
sonnerie /sɔnri/ *n.f.* ringing; (*de clairon*) sound; (*mécanisme*) bell.
sonnet /sɔnɛ/ *n.m.* sonnet.
sonnette /sɔnɛt/ *n.f.* bell.

sonor|e /sɔnɔr/ *a.* resonant; (*onde, effets, etc.*) sound. **~ité** *n.f.* resonance; (*d'un instrument*) tone.
sonoris|er /sɔnɔrize/ *v.t.* (*salle*) wire for sound. **~ation** *n.f.* (*matériel*) sound equipment.
sont /sɔ̃/ *voir* **être.**
sophistiqué /sɔfistike/ *a.* sophisticated.
soporifique /sɔpɔrifik/ *a.* soporific.
sorbet /sɔrbɛ/ *n.m.* water-ice.
sorcellerie /sɔrsɛlri/ *n.f.* witchcraft.
sorc|ier /sɔrsje/ *n.m.* sorcerer. **~ière** *n.f.* witch.
sordide /sɔrdid/ *a.* sordid; (*lieu*) squalid.
sort /sɔr/ *n.m.* (*destin, hasard*) fate; (*condition*) lot; (*maléfice*) spell.
sortant, ~e /sɔrtɑ̃, -t/ *a.* (*président etc.*) outgoing.
sorte /sɔrt/ *n.f.* sort, kind. **de ~ que,** so that. **en quelque ~,** in a way. **faire en ~ que,** see to it that.
sortie /sɔrti/ *n.f.* departure, exit; (*porte*) exit; (*promenade*) outing; (*invective*) outburst; (*parution*) appearance; (*de disque, gaz*) release; (*d'un ordinateur*) output. **~s,** (*argent*) outgoings.
sortilège /sɔrtilɛʒ/ *n.m.* (magic) spell.
sortir† /sɔrtir/ *v.i.* (*aux. être*) go out, leave; (*venir*) come out; (*aller au spectacle etc.*) go out; (*livre, film*) come out; (*plante*) come up. **~ de,** (*pièce*) leave; (*milieu social*) come from; (*limites*) go beyond. *—v.t.* (*aux. avoir*) take out; (*livre, modèle*) bring out; (*dire: fam.*) come out with. **~ d'affaire, (s')en ~,** get out of an awkward situation. **~ du commun** *ou* **de l'ordinaire,** be out of the ordinary.
sosie /sɔzi/ *n.m.* double.
sot, ~te /so, sɔt/ *a.* foolish.
sottise /sɔtiz/ *n.f.* foolishness; (*action, remarque*) foolish thing.
sou /su/ *n.m.* **~s,** money. **pas un ~,** not a penny. **sans le ~,** without a penny.
soubresaut /subrəso/ *n.m.* (sudden) start.
souche /suʃ/ *n.f.* (*d'arbre*) stump; (*de famille, vigne*) stock; (*de carnet*) counterfoil.
souci[1] /susi/ *n.m.* (*inquiétude*) worry; (*préoccupation*) concern. **se faire du ~,** worry.
souci[2] /susi/ *n.m.* (*plante*) marigold.
soucier (se) /(sə)susje/ *v. pr.* **se ~ de,** be concerned about.
soucieu|x, ~se /susjø, -z/ *a.* concerned (**de,** about).
soucoupe /sukup/ *n.f.* saucer.
soudain, ~e /sudɛ̃, -ɛn/ *a.* sudden. *—adv.* suddenly. **~ement** /-ɛnmɑ̃/ *adv.* suddenly. **~eté** /-ɛnte/ *n.f.* suddenness.
soude /sud/ *n.f.* soda.
soud|er /sude/ *v.t.* solder, weld. **se ~er** *v. pr.* (*os*) knit (together). **~ure** *n.f.* soldering, welding; (*substance*) solder.
soudoyer /sudwaje/ *v.t.* bribe.
souffle /sufl/ *n.m.* blow, puff; (*haleine*) breath; (*respiration*) breathing; (*explosion*) blast; (*vent*) breath of air.
soufflé /sufle/ *n.m.* (*culin.*) soufflé.
souffl|er /sufle/ *v.i.* blow; (*haleter*) puff. *—v.t.* (*bougie*) blow out; (*poussière, fumée*) blow; (*par explosion*) destroy; (*chuchoter*) whisper. **~er son rôle à,** prompt. **~eur, ~euse** *n.m., f.* (*théâtre*) prompter.
soufflet /suflɛ/ *n.m.* (*instrument*) bellows.
souffrance /sufrɑ̃s/ *n.f.* suffering. **en ~,** (*affaire*) pending.
souffr|ir† /sufrir/ *v.i.* suffer (**de,** from). *—v.t.* (*endurer*) suffer; (*admettre*) admit of. **il ne peut**

pas le ~ir, he cannot stand *ou* bear him. **~ant, ~ante** *a.* unwell.

soufre /sufr/ *n.m.* sulphur.

souhait /swɛ/ *n.m.* wish. **nos ~s de,** (*vœux*) good wishes for.

souhait|er /swete/ *v.t.* (*bonheur etc.*) wish for. **~er qch. à qn.,** wish s.o. sth. **~er que/faire,** hope that/to do. **~able** /swɛtabl/ *a.* desirable.

souiller /suje/ *v.t.* soil.

soûl, ~e /su, sul/ *a.* drunk. —*n.m.* **tout son ~,** as much as one can.

soulag|er /sulaʒe/ *v.t.* relieve. **~ement** *n.m.* relief.

soûler /sule/ *v.t.* make drunk. **se ~** *v. pr.* get drunk.

soulèvement /sulɛvmɑ̃/ *n.m.* uprising.

soulever /sulve/ *v.t.* lift, raise; (*exciter*) stir; (*question, poussière*) raise. **se ~** *v. pr.* lift *ou* raise o.s. up; (*se révolter*) rise up.

soulier /sulje/ *n.m.* shoe.

souligner /suliɲe/ *v.t.* underline; (*taille, yeux*) emphasize.

soum|ettre† /sumɛtr/ *v.t.* (*dompter, assujettir*) subject (**à,** to); (*présenter*) submit (**à,** to). **se ~ettre** *v. pr.* submit (**à,** to). **~is, ~ise** *a.* submissive. **~ission** *n.f.* submission.

soupape /supap/ *n.f.* valve.

soupçon /supsɔ̃/ *n.m.* suspicion. **un ~ de,** (*fig.*) a touch of. **~ner** /-ɔne/ *v.t.* suspect. **~neux, ~neuse** /-ɔnø, -z/ *a.* suspicious.

soupe /sup/ *n.f.* soup.

souper /supe/ *n.m.* supper. —*v.i.* have supper.

soupeser /supəze/ *v.t.* judge the weight of; (*fig.*) weigh up.

soupière /supjɛr/ *n.f.* (soup) tureen.

soupir /supir/ *n.m.* sigh. **~er** *v.i.* sigh.

soupir|ail (*pl.* **~aux**) /supiraj, -o/ *n.m.* small basement window.

soupirant /supirɑ̃/ *n.m.* suitor.

souple /supl/ *a.* supple; (*règlement, caractère*) flexible. **~sse** /-ɛs/ *n.f.* suppleness; flexibility.

source /surs/ *n.f.* source; (*eau*) spring. **~ thermale,** hot springs.

sourcil /sursi/ *n.m.* eyebrow.

sourciller /sursije/ *v.i.* bat an eyelid.

sourd, ~e /sur, -d/ *a.* deaf; (*bruit, douleur*) dull; (*caché*) secret, hidden. —*n.m., f.* deaf person. **faire la ~e oreille,** turn a deaf ear. **~-muet** (*pl.* **~s-muets**), **~e-muette** (*pl.* **~es-muettes**) *a.* deaf and dumb; *n.m., f.* deaf mute.

sourdine /surdin/ *n.f.* (*mus.*) mute. **en ~,** quietly.

souricière /surisjɛr/ *n.f.* mousetrap; (*fig.*) trap.

sourire /surir/ *n.m.* smile. —*v.i.* smile (**à,** at). **~ à,** (*fortune*) smile on.

souris /suri/ *n.f.* mouse.

sournois, ~e /surnwa, -z/ *a.* sly, underhand. **~ement** /-zmɑ̃/ *adv.* slyly.

sous /su/ *prép.* under, beneath. **~ la main,** handy. **~ la pluie,** in the rain. **~ peu,** shortly. **~ terre,** underground.

sous- /su/ *préf.* (*subordination*) sub-; (*insuffisance*) under-.

sous-bois /subwa/ *n.m. invar.* undergrowth.

souscr|ire /suskrir/ *v.i.* **~ire à,** subscribe to. **~iption** *n.f.* subscription.

sous-entend|re /suzɑ̃tɑ̃dr/ *v.t.* imply. **~u** *n.m.* insinuation.

sous-estimer /suzɛstime/ *v.t.* underestimate.

sous-jacent, ~e /suʒasɑ̃, -t/ *a.* underlying.

sous-marin, ~e /sumarɛ̃, -in/ *a.* underwater. —*n.m.* submarine.

sous-officier /suzɔfisje/ *n.m.* non-commissioned officer.

sous-préfecture /suprefɛktyr/ *n.f.* sub-prefecture.
sous-produit /suprɔdɥi/ *n.m.* by-product.
soussigné, ~e /susiɲe/ *a.* & *n.m., f.* undersigned.
sous-sol /susɔl/ *n.m.* (*cave*) basement.
sous-titr|e /sutitr/ *n.m.* subtitle. **~er** *v.t.* subtitle.
soustr|aire† /sustrɛr/ *v.t.* remove; (*déduire*) subtract. **se ~aire à,** escape from. **~action** *n.f.* (*déduction*) subtraction.
sous-traiter /sutrete/ *v.t.* subcontract.
sous-verre /suvɛr/ *n.m. invar.* picture frame, glass mount.
sous-vêtement /suvɛtmɑ̃/ *n.m.* undergarment. **~s,** underwear.
soutane /sutan/ *n.f.* cassock.
soute /sut/ *n.f.* (*de bateau*) hold. **~ à charbon,** coal-bunker.
soutenir† /sutnir/ *v.t.* support; (*fortifier, faire durer*) sustain; (*résister à*) withstand. **~ que,** maintain that. **se ~** *v. pr.* (*se tenir debout*) support o.s.
soutenu /sutny/ *a.* (*constant*) sustained; (*style*) lofty.
souterrain, ~e /sutɛrɛ̃, -ɛn/ *a.* underground. —*n.m.* underground passage, subway.
soutien /sutjɛ̃/ *n.m.* support. **~-gorge** (*pl.* **~s-gorge**) *n.m.* bra.
soutirer /sutire/ *v.t.* **~ à qn.,** extract from s.o.
souvenir[1] /suvnir/ *n.m.* memory, recollection; (*objet*) memento; (*cadeau*) souvenir.
souvenir[2]**† (se)** /(sə)suvnir/ *v. pr.* **se ~ de,** remember. **se ~ que,** remember that.
souvent /suvɑ̃/ *adv.* often.
souverain, ~e /suvrɛ̃, -ɛn/ *a.* sovereign; (*extrême: péj.*) supreme. —*n.m., f.* sovereign. **~ pontife,** pope. **~eté** /-ɛnte/ *n.f.* sovereignty.
soviétique /sɔvjetik/ *a.* Soviet. —*n.m./f.* Soviet citizen.
soyeu|x, ~se /swajø, -z/ *a.* silky.
spacieu|x, ~se /spasjø, -z/ *a.* spacious.
spaghetti /spageti/ *n.m. pl.* spaghetti.
sparadrap /sparadra/ *n.m.* sticking-plaster; (*Amer.*) adhesive tape *ou* bandage.
spasm|e /spasm/ *n.m.* spasm. **~odique** *a.* spasmodic.
spat|ial (*m. pl.* **~iaux**) /spasjal, -jo/ *a.* space.
spatule /spatyl/ *n.f.* spatula.
speaker, ~ine /spikœr, -rin/ *n.m., f.* announcer.
spéc|ial (*m. pl.* **~iaux**) /spesjal, -jo/ *a.* special; (*singulier*) peculiar. **~ialement** *adv.* especially; (*exprès*) specially.
spécialis|er (se) /(sə)spesjalize/ *v. pr.* specialize (**dans,** in). **~ation** *n.f.* specialization.
spécialiste /spesjalist/ *n.m./f.* specialist.
spécialité /spesjalite/ *n.f.* speciality; (*Amer.*) specialty.
spécif|ier /spesifje/ *v.t.* specify. **~ication** *n.f.* specification.
spécifique /spesifik/ *a.* specific.
spécimen /spesimɛn/ *n.m.* specimen.
spectacle /spɛktakl/ *n.m.* sight, spectacle; (*représentation*) show.
spectaculaire /spɛktakylɛr/ *a.* spectacular.
specta|teur, ~trice /spɛktatœr, -tris/ *n.m., f.* onlooker; (*sport*) spectator. **les ~teurs,** (*théâtre*) the audience.
spectre /spɛktr/ *n.m.* (*revenant*) spectre; (*images*) spectrum.
spécul|er /spekyle/ *v.i.* speculate. **~ateur, ~atrice** *n.m., f.* speculator. **~ation** *n.f.* speculation.
spéléologie /speleɔlɔʒi/ *n.f.* cave exploration, pot-holing; (*Amer.*) spelunking

sperme /spɛrm/ *n.m.* sperm.
sph|ère /sfɛr/ *n.f.* sphere. **~érique** *a.* spherical.
sphinx /sfɛ̃ks/ *n.m.* sphinx.
spirale /spiral/ *n.f.* spiral.
spirite /spirit/ *n.m./f.* spiritualist.
spirituel, ~le /spiritɥɛl/ *a.* spiritual; (*amusant*) witty.
spiritueux /spiritɥø/ *n.m.* (*alcool*) spirit.
splend|ide /splɑ̃did/ *a.* splendid. **~eur** *n.f.* splendour.
spongieu|x, ~se /spɔ̃ʒjø, -z/ *a.* spongy.
spontané /spɔ̃tane/ *a.* spontaneous. **~ité** *n.f.* spontaneity. **~ment** *adv.* spontaneously.
sporadique /spɔradik/ *a.* sporadic.
sport /spɔr/ *n.m.* sport. —*a. invar.* (*vêtements*) casual. **veste/voiture de ~,** sports jacket/car.
sporti|f, ~ve /spɔrtif, -v/ *a.* sporting; (*résultats*) sports. —*n.m.* sportsman. —*n.f.* sportswoman.
spot /spɔt/ *n.m.* spotlight.
sprint /sprint/ *n.m.* sprint. **~er** *v.i.* sprint; *n.m.* /-œr/ sprinter.
square /skwar/ *n.m.* (public) garden.
squelett|e /skəlɛt/ *n.m.* skeleton. **~ique** /-etik/ *a.* skeletal.
stabiliser /stabilize/ *v.t.* stabilize.
stab|le /stabl/ *a.* stable. **~ilité** *n.f.* stability.
stade[1] /stad/ *n.m.* (*sport*) stadium.
stade[2] /stad/ *n.m.* (*phase*) stage.
stag|e /staʒ/ *n.m.* training period. **~iaire** *a.* & *n.m./f.* trainee.
stagn|er /stagne/ *v.i.* stagnate. **~ant, ~ante** *a.* stagnant. **~ation** *n.f.* stagnation.
stand /stɑ̃d/ *n.m.* stand, stall. **~ de tir,** (shooting-)range.
standard[1] /stɑ̃dar/ *n.m.* switchboard. **~iste** /-dist/ *n.m./f.* switchboard operator.
standard[2] /stɑ̃dar/ *a. invar.* standard. **~iser** /-dize/ *v.t.* standardize.
standing /stɑ̃diŋ/ *n.m.* status, standing. **de ~,** (*hôtel etc.*) luxury.
star /star/ *n.f.* (*actrice*) star.
starter /startɛr/ *n.m.* (*auto.*) choke.
station /stasjɔ̃/ *n.f.* station; (*halte*) stop. **~ balnéaire,** seaside resort. **~ debout,** standing position. **~ de taxis,** taxi rank; (*Amer.*) taxi stand. **~-service** (*pl.* **~s-service**) *n.f.* service station. **~ thermale,** spa.
stationnaire /stasjɔnɛr/ *a.* stationary.
stationn|er /stasjɔne/ *v.i.* park. **~ement** *n.m.* parking.
statique /statik/ *a.* static.
statistique /statistik/ *n.f.* statistic; (*science*) statistics. —*a.* statistical.
statue /staty/ *n.f.* statue.
statuer /statɥe/ *v.i.* **~ sur,** rule on.
statu quo /statykwo/ *n.m.* status quo.
stature /statyr/ *n.f.* stature.
statut /staty/ *n.m.* status. **~s,** (*règles*) statutes. **~aire** /-tɛr/ *a.* statutory.
steak /stɛk/ *n.m.* steak.
stencil /stɛnsil/ *n.m.* stencil.
sténo /steno/ *n.f.* (*personne*) stenographer; (*sténographie*) shorthand.
sténodactylo /stenɔdaktilo/ *n.f.* shorthand typist; (*Amer.*) stenographer.
sténographie /stenɔgrafi/ *n.f.* shorthand.
stéréo /stereo/ *n.f.* & *a. invar.* stereo. **~phonique** /-eɔfɔnik/ *a.* stereophonic.
stéréotyp|e /stereɔtip/ *n.m.* stereotype. **~é** *a.* stereotyped.
stéril|e /steril/ *a.* sterile. **~ité** *n.f.* sterility.
stérilis|er /sterilize/ *v.t.* sterilize. **~ation** *n.f.* sterilization.

stéthoscope /stetɔskɔp/ *n.m.* stethoscope.
stigmat|e /stigmat/ *n.m.* mark, stigma. **~iser** *v.t.* stigmatize.
stimul|er /stimyle/ *v.t.* stimulate. **~ant** *n.m.* stimulus; (*médicament*) stimulant. **~ation** *n.f.* stimulation.
stipul|er /stipyle/ *v.t.* stipulate. **~ation** *n.f.* stipulation.
stock /stɔk/ *n.m.* stock. **~er** *v.t.* stock. **~iste** *n.m.* stockist; (*Amer.*) dealer.
stoïque /stɔik/ *a.* stoical. —*n.m./f.* stoic.
stop /stɔp/ *int.* stop. —*n.m.* stop sign; (*feu arrière*) brake light. **faire du ~,** (*fam.*) hitch-hike.
stopper /stɔpe/ *v.t./i.* stop; (*vêtement*) mend, reweave.
store /stɔr/ *n.m.* blind; (*Amer.*) shade; (*de magasin*) awning.
strabisme /strabism/ *n.m.* squint.
strapontin /strapɔ̃tɛ̃/ *n.m.* folding seat, jump seat.
stratagème /stratazɛm/ *n.m.* stratagem.
stratég|ie /strateʒi/ *n.f.* strategy. **~ique** *a.* strategic.
strict /strikt/ *a.* strict; (*tenue, vérité*) plain. **~ement** *adv.* strictly.
strident, ~e /stridɑ̃, -t/ *a.* shrill.
str|ie /stri/ *n.f.* streak. **~ier** *v.t.* streak.
strip-tease /striptiz/ *n.m.* strip-tease.
strophe /strɔf/ *n.f.* stanza.
structur|e /stryktyr/ *n.f.* structure. **~al** (*m. pl.* **~aux**) *a.* structural. **~er** *v.t.* structure.
studieu|x, ~se /stydjø, -z/ *a.* studious; (*période*) devoted to study.
studio /stydjo/ *n.m.* (*d'artiste, de télévision, etc.*) studio; (*logement*) studio flat, bed-sitter.
stupéf|ait, ~aite /stypefɛ, -t/ *a.* amazed. **~action** *n.f.* amazement.
stupéf|ier /stypefje/ *v.t.* amaze. **~iant, ~iante** *a.* amazing; *n.m.* drug, narcotic.
stupeur /stypœr/ *n.f.* amazement; (*méd.*) stupor.
stupid|e /stypid/ *a.* stupid. **~ité** *n.f.* stupidity.
styl|e /stil/ *n.m.* style. **~isé** *a.* stylized.
stylé /stile/ *a.* well-trained.
stylo /stilo/ *n.m.* pen. **~ à bille,** ball-point pen. **~ à encre,** fountain-pen.
su /sy/ *voir* **savoir.**
suave /sɥav/ *a.* sweet.
subalterne /sybaltɛrn/ *a.* & *n.m./f.* subordinate.
subconscient, ~e /sypkɔ̃sjɑ̃, -t/ *a.* & *n.m.* subconscious.
subdiviser /sybdivize/ *v.t.* subdivide.
subir /sybir/ *v.t.* suffer; (*traitement, expériences*) undergo.
subit, ~e /sybi, -t/ *a.* sudden. **~ement** /-tmɑ̃/ *adv.* suddenly.
subjecti|f, ~ve /sybʒɛktif, -v/ *a.* subjective. **~vité** *n.f.* subjectivity.
subjonctif /sybʒɔ̃ktif/ *a.* & *n.m.* subjunctive.
subjuguer /sybʒyge/ *v.t.* (*charmer*) captivate.
sublime /syblim/ *a.* sublime.
sublimer /syblime/ *v.t.* sublimate.
submer|ger /sybmɛrʒe/ *v.t.* submerge; (*fig.*) overwhelm. **~sion** *n.f.* submersion.
subordonné, ~e /sybɔrdɔne/ *a.* & *n.m., f.* subordinate.
subord|onner /sybɔrdɔne/ *v.t.* subordinate (**à,** to). **~ination** *n.f.* subordination.
subreptice /sybrɛptis/ *a.* surreptitious.
subside /sybzid/ *n.m.* grant.
subsidiaire /sypsidjɛr/ *a.* subsidiary.
subsist|er /sybziste/ *v.i.* subsist;

(*durer, persister*) exist. **~ance** *n.f.* subsistence.

substance /sypstɑ̃s/ *n.f.* substance.

substantiel, ~le /sypstɑ̃sjɛl/ *a.* substantial.

substantif /sypstɑ̃tif/ *n.m.* noun.

substit|uer /sypstitɥe/ *v.t.* substitute (**à,** for). **se ~uer à,** (*remplacer*) substitute for; (*évincer*) take over from. **~ution** *n.f.* substitution.

subterfuge /syptɛrfyʒ/ *n.m.* subterfuge.

subtil /syptil/ *a.* subtle. **~ité** *n.f.* subtlety.

subtiliser /syptilize/ *v.t.* steal.

subvenir /sybvənir/ *v.i.* **~ à,** provide for.

subvention /sybvɑ̃sjɔ̃/ *n.f.* subsidy. **~ner** /-jɔne/ *v.t.* subsidize.

subversi|f, ~ve /sybvɛrsif, -v/ *a.* subversive.

subversion /sybvɛrsjɔ̃/ *n.f.* subversion.

suc /syk/ *n.m.* juice.

succédané /syksedane/ *n.m.* substitute (**de,** for).

succéder /syksede/ *v.i.* **~ à,** succeed. **se ~** *v. pr.* succeed one another.

succès /syksɛ/ *n.m.* success. **à ~,** (*film, livre, etc.*) successful. **avoir du ~,** be a success.

successeur /syksesœr/ *n.m.* successor.

successi|f, ~ve /syksesif, -v/ *a.* successive. **~vement** *adv.* successively.

succession /syksesjɔ̃/ *n.f.* succession.

succinct, ~e /syksɛ̃, -t/ *a.* succinct.

succion /syksjɔ̃/ *n.f.* suction.

succomber /sykɔ̃be/ *v.i.* die. **~ à,** succumb to.

succulent, ~e /sykylɑ̃, -t/ *a.* succulent.

succursale /sykyrsal/ *n.f.* (*comm.*) branch.

sucer /syse/ *v.t.* suck.

sucette /sysɛt/ *n.f.* (*bonbon*) lollipop; (*tétine*) dummy; (*Amer.*) pacifier.

sucr|e /sykr/ *n.m.* sugar. **~e d'orge,** barley sugar. **~e en poudre,** castor sugar; (*Amer.*) finely ground sugar. **~ier, ~ière** *a.* sugar; *n.m.* (*récipient*) sugar-bowl.

sucr|er /sykre/ *v.t.* sugar, sweeten. **~é** *a.* sweet; (*additionné de sucre*) sweetened.

sucreries /sykrəri/ *n.f. pl.* sweets.

sud /syd/ *n.m.* south. —*a. invar.* south; (*partie*) southern; (*direction*) southerly. **~-africain, ~-africaine** *a.* & *n.m., f.* South African. **~-est** *n.m.* south-east. **~-ouest** *n.m.* south-west.

Suède /sɥɛd/ *n.f.* Sweden.

suédois, ~e /sɥedwa, -z/ *a.* Swedish. —*n.m., f.* Swede. —*n.m.* (*lang.*) Swedish.

suer /sɥe/ *v.t./i.* sweat.

sueur /sɥœr/ *n.f.* sweat. **en ~,** sweating.

suff|ire† /syfir/ *v.i.* be enough (**à qn.,** for s.o.). **il ~it de faire,** one only has to do. **il ~it d'une goutte pour,** a drop is enough to. **~ire à,** (*besoin*) satisfy. **se ~ire à soi-même,** be self-sufficient.

suffis|ant, ~ante /syfizɑ̃, -t/ *a.* sufficient; (*vaniteux*) conceited. **~amment** *adv.* sufficiently. **~amment de,** sufficient. **~ance** *n.f.* (*vanité*) conceit.

suffixe /syfiks/ *n.m.* suffix.

suffo|quer /syfɔke/ *v.t./i.* choke, suffocate. **~cation** *n.f.* (*asphyxie*) feeling of suffocation.

suffrage /syfraʒ/ *n.m.* (*voix: pol.*) vote; (*modalité*) suffrage.

sugg|érer /sygʒere/ *v.t.* suggest. **~estion** /-ʒɛstjɔ̃/ *n.f.* suggestion.

suggesti|f, ~ve /sygʒɛstif, -v/ *a.* suggestive.

suicid|e /sɥisid/ *n.m.* suicide. **~aire** *a.* suicidal.
suicid|er (se) /(sə)sɥiside/ *v. pr.* commit suicide. **~é, ~ée** *n.m., f.* suicide.
suie /sɥi/ *n.f.* soot.
suint|er /sɥɛ̃te/ *v.i.* ooze. **~ement** *n.m.* oozing.
suis /sɥi/ *voir* **être, suivre.**
Suisse /sɥis/ *n.f.* Switzerland.
suisse /sɥis/ *a.* & *n.m.* Swiss. **~sse** /-ɛs/ *n.f.* Swiss (woman).
suite /sɥit/ *n.f.* continuation, rest; (*d'un film*) sequel; (*série*) series; (*appartement, escorte*) suite; (*résultat*) consequence; (*cohérence*) order. **~s,** (*de maladie*) after-effects. **à la ~, de ~,** (*successivement*) in succession. **à la ~ de,** (*derrière*) behind. **à la ~ de, par ~ de,** as a result of. **faire ~ (à),** follow. **par la ~,** afterwards.
suivant[1], **~e** /sɥivɑ̃, -t/ *a.* following, next. —*n.m., f.* following *ou* next person.
suivant[2] /sɥivɑ̃/ *prép.* (*selon*) according to.
suivi /sɥivi/ *a.* steady, sustained; (*cohérent*) consistent. **peu/très ~,** (*cours*) poorly-/well-attended.
suivre† /sɥivr/ *v.t./i.* follow; (*comprendre*) keep up (with), follow. **se ~** *v. pr.* follow each other. **faire ~,** (*courrier etc.*) forward.
sujet[1], **~te** /syʒɛ, -t/ *a.* **~ à,** liable *ou* subject to. —*n.m., f.* (*gouverné*) subject.
sujet[2] /syʒɛ/ *n.m.* (*matière, individu*) subject; (*motif*) cause; (*gram.*) subject. **au ~ de,** about.
sujétion /syʒesjɔ̃/ *n.f.* (*obligation*) constraint; (*esclavage*) subjection.
sulfurique /sylfyrik/ *a.* sulphuric.
sultan /syltɑ̃/ *n.m.* sultan.
summum /sɔmɔm/ *n.m.* height.
superbe /sypɛrb/ *a.* superb.
supercarburant /sypɛrkarbyrɑ̃/ *n.m.* high-octane petrol; (*Amer.*) high-octane gasoline.
supercherie /sypɛrʃəri/ *n.f.* trickery.
superficie /sypɛrfisi/ *n.f.* area.
superficiel, ~le /sypɛrfisjɛl/ *a.* superficial.
superflu /sypɛrfly/ *a.* superfluous. —*n.m.* (*excédent*) surplus.
supérieur, ~e /syperjœr/ *a.* (*plus haut*) upper; (*quantité, nombre*) greater (**à,** than); (*études, principe*) higher (**à,** than); (*meilleur, hautain*) superior (**à,** to). —*n.m., f.* superior.
supériorité /syperjɔrite/ *n.f.* superiority.
superlati|f, ~ve /sypɛrlatif, -v/ *a.* & *n.m.* superlative.
supermarché /sypɛrmarʃe/ *n.m.* supermarket.
superposer /sypɛrpoze/ *v.t.* superimpose.
superpuissance /sypɛrpɥisɑ̃s/ *n.f.* superpower.
supersonique /sypɛrsɔnik/ *a.* supersonic.
superstit|ion /sypɛrstisjɔ̃/ *n.f.* superstition. **~ieux, ~ieuse** *a.* superstitious.
superviser /sypɛrvize/ *v.t.* supervise.
supplanter /syplɑ̃te/ *v.t.* supplant.
suppléan|t, ~te /sypleɑ̃, -t/ *n.m., f.* (temporary) replacement. —*a.* temporary. **~ce** *n.f.* (*fonction*) temporary appointment.
suppléer /syplee/ *v.t.* (*remplacer*) replace; (*ajouter*) supply. —*v.i.* **~ à,** (*compenser*) make up for.
supplément /syplemɑ̃/ *n.m.* (*argent*) extra charge; (*de livre*) supplement. **en ~,** extra. **un ~ de,** (*travail etc.*) extra. **~aire** /-tɛr/ *a.* extra, additional.
supplic|e /syplis/ *n.m.* torture. **~ier** *v.t.* torture.
supplier /syplije/ *v.t.* beg, beseech (**de,** to).
support /sypɔr/ *n.m.* support; (*publicitaire: fig.*) medium.

support|er[1] /syporte/ *v.t.* (*endurer*) bear; (*subir*) suffer; (*soutenir*) support; (*résister à*) withstand. **~able** *a.* bearable.
supporter[2] /syportɛr/ *n.m.* (*sport*) supporter.
suppos|er /sypoze/ *v.t.* suppose; (*impliquer*) imply. **à ~er que,** supposing that. **~ition** *n.f.* supposition.
suppr|imer /syprime/ *v.t.* get rid of, remove; (*annuler*) cancel; (*mot*) delete. **~imer à qn.,** (*enlever*) take away from s.o. **~ession** *n.f.* removal; cancellation; deletion.
suprématie /sypremasi/ *n.f.* supremacy.
suprême /syprɛm/ *a.* supreme.
sur /syr/ *prép.* on, upon; (*par-dessus*) over; (*au sujet de*) about, on; (*proportion*) out of; (*mesure*) by. **aller/tourner**/*etc.* **~,** go/turn/*etc.* towards. **mettre/jeter**/*etc.* **~,** put/throw/*etc.* on to. **~-le-champ** *adv.* immediately. **~ le qui-vive,** on the alert. **~ mesure,** made to measure. **~ place,** on the spot.
sur- /syr/ *préf.* over-.
sûr /syr/ *a.* certain, sure; (*sans danger*) safe; (*digne de confiance*) reliable; (*main*) steady; (*jugement*) sound.
surabondance /syrabɔ̃dɑ̃s/ *n.f.* superabundance.
suranné /syrane/ *a.* outmoded.
surcharg|e /syrʃarʒ/ *n.f.* overloading; (*poids*) extra load. **~er** *v.t.* overload; (*texte*) alter.
surchauffer /syrʃofe/ *v.t.* overheat.
surchoix /syrʃwa/ *a. invar.* of finest quality.
surclasser /syrklɑse/ *v.t.* outclass.
surcroît /syrkrwa/ *n.m.* increase (**de,** in), additional amount (**de,** of). **de ~,** in addition.
surdité /syrdite/ *n.f.* deafness.
sureau (*pl.* **~x**) /syro/ *n.m.* (*arbre*) elder.
surélever /syrɛlve/ *v.t.* raise.
sûrement /syrmɑ̃/ *adv.* certainly; (*sans danger*) safely.
surench|ère /syrɑ̃ʃɛr/ *n.f.* higher bid. **~érir** *v.i.* bid higher (**sur,** than).
surestimer /syrɛstime/ *v.t.* overestimate.
sûreté /syrte/ *n.f.* safety; (*garantie*) surety; (*d'un geste*) steadiness. **être en ~,** be safe. **S~ (nationale),** *division of French Ministère de l'Intérieur in charge of police.*
surexcité /syrɛksite/ *a.* very excited.
surf /syrf/ *n.m.* surf-riding.
surface /syrfas/ *n.f.* surface. **faire ~,** (*sous-marin etc.*) surface.
surfait, ~e /syrfɛ, -t/ *a.* overrated.
surgelé /syrʒəle/ *a.* (deep-)frozen.
surgir /syrʒir/ *v.i.* appear (suddenly).
surhomme /syrɔm/ *n.m.* superman.
surhumain, ~e /syrymɛ̃, -ɛn/ *a.* superhuman.
surlendemain /syrlɑ̃dmɛ̃/ *n.m.* **le ~,** two days later. **le ~ de,** two days after.
surmen|er /syrməne/ *v.t.,* **se ~er** *v. pr.* overwork. **~age** *n.m.* overworking; (*méd.*) overwork.
surmonter /syrmɔ̃te/ *v.t.* (*vaincre*) overcome, surmount; (*être au-dessus de*) surmount, top.
surnager /syrnaʒe/ *v.i.* float.
surnaturel, ~le /syrnatyrɛl/ *a.* supernatural.
surnom /syrnɔ̃/ *n.m.* nickname. **~mer** /-ɔme/ *v.t.* nickname.
surnombre (en) /(ɑ̃)syrnɔ̃br/ *adv.* too many. **il est en ~,** he is one too many.
surpasser /syrpɑse/ *v.t.* surpass.
surpeuplé /syrpœple/ *a.* overpopulated.

surplomb /syrplɔ̃/ *n.m.* overhang. **en ~,** overhanging. **~er** /-be/ *v.t./i.* overhang.
surplus /syrply/ *n.m.* surplus.
surpr|endre† /syrprɑ̃dr/ *v.t.* (*étonner*) surprise; (*prendre au dépourvu*) catch, surprise; (*entendre*) overhear; (*découvrir*) discover. **~enant, ~enante** *a.* surprising. **~is, ~ise** *a.* surprised (**de,** at).
surprise /syrpriz/ *n.f.* surprise. **~-partie** (*pl.* **~s-parties**) *n.f.* party.
surréalisme /syrrealism/ *n.m.* surrealism.
sursaut /syrso/ *n.m.* start, jump. **en ~,** with a start. **~ de,** (*regain*) burst of. **~er** /-te/ *v.i.* start, jump.
sursis /syrsi/ *n.m.* reprieve; (*mil.*) deferment. **deux ans (de prison) avec ~,** a two-year suspended sentence.
surtaxe /syrtaks/ *n.f.* surcharge.
surtout /syrtu/ *adv.* especially, mainly; (*avant tout*) above all. **~ pas,** certainly not.
surveillant, ~e /syrvɛjɑ̃, -t/ *n.m., f.* (*de prison*) warder; (*au lycée*) supervisor (in charge of discipline).
surveill|er /syrveje/ *v.t.* watch; (*travaux, élèves*) supervise. **~ance** *n.f.* watch; supervision; (*de la police*) surveillance.
survenir /syrvənir/ *v.i.* occur, come about; (*personne*) turn up.
survêtement /syrvɛtmɑ̃/ *n.m.* (*sport*) track suit.
survie /syrvi/ *n.f.* survival.
survivance /syrvivɑ̃s/ *n.f.* survival.
surviv|re† /syrvivr/ *v.i.* survive. **~re à,** (*conflit etc.*) survive; (*personne*) outlive. **~ant, ~ante** *a.* surviving; *n.m., f.* survivor.
survol /syrvɔl/ *n.m.* **le ~ de,** flying over. **~er** *v.t.* fly over; (*livre*) skim through.
survolté /syrvɔlte/ *a.* (*surexcité*) worked up.
susceptib|le /sysɛptibl/ *a.* touchy. **~le de faire,** (*possibilité*) liable to do; (*capacité*) able to do. **~ilité** *n.f.* susceptibility.
susciter /sysite/ *v.t.* (*éveiller*) arouse; (*occasionner*) create.
suspect, ~e /syspɛ(kt), -ɛkt/ *a.* suspect, suspicious. **~ de,** suspected of. *—n.m., f.* suspect. **~er** /-ɛkte/ *v.t.* suspect.
suspend|re /syspɑ̃dr/ *v.t.* (*arrêter, différer, destituer*) suspend; (*accrocher*) hang (up). **se ~re à,** hang from. **~u à,** hanging from.
suspens (en) /(ɑ̃)syspɑ̃/ *adv.* (*affaire*) in abeyance; (*dans l'indécision*) in suspense.
suspense /syspɑ̃s/ *n.m.* suspense.
suspension /syspɑ̃sjɔ̃/ *n.f.* suspension; (*lustre*) chandelier.
suspicion /syspisjɔ̃/ *n.f.* suspicion.
susurrer /sysyre/ *v.t./i.* murmur.
sutur|e /sytyr/ *n.f.* (*méd.*) stitching. **~er** *v.t.* stitch (up).
svelte /svɛlt/ *a.* slender.
S.V.P. *abrév. voir* **s'il vous plaît.**
syllabe /silab/ *n.f.* syllable.
symbol|e /sɛ̃bɔl/ *n.m.* symbol. **~ique** *a.* symbolic(al). **~iser** *v.t.* symbolize.
symétr|ie /simetri/ *n.f.* symmetry. **~ique** *a.* symmetrical.
sympath|ie /sɛ̃pati/ *n.f.* (*goût*) liking; (*affinité*) affinity; (*condoléances*) sympathy. **~ique** *a.* nice, pleasant.
sympathis|er /sɛ̃patize/ *v.i.* get on well (**avec,** with). **~ant, ~ante** *n.m., f.* sympathizer.
symphon|ie /sɛ̃fɔni/ *n.f.* symphony. **~ique** *a.* symphonic; (*orchestre*) symphony.
symposium /sɛ̃pozjɔm/ *n.m.* symposium.
sympt|ôme /sɛ̃ptom/ *n.m.* symptom. **~omatique** /-ɔmatik/ *a.* symptomatic.

synagogue /sinagɔg/ *n.f.* synagogue.
synchroniser /sɛ̃krɔnize/ *v.t.* synchronize.
syncope /sɛ̃kɔp/ *n.f.* (*méd.*) black-out.
syncoper /sɛ̃kɔpe/ *v.t.* syncopate.
syndic|at /sɛ̃dika/ *n.m.* (trade) union. **~at d'initiative,** tourist office. **~al** (*m. pl.* **~aux**) *a.* (trade-)union. **~aliste** *n.m./f.* trade-unionist; *a.* (trade-)union.
syndiqué, ~e /sɛ̃dike/ *n.m., f.* (trade-)union member.
syndrome /sɛ̃drom/ *n.m.* syndrome.
synonyme /sinɔnim/ *a.* synonymous. —*n.m.* synonym.
syntaxe /sɛ̃taks/ *n.f.* syntax.
synthèse /sɛ̃tɛz/ *n.f.* synthesis.
synthétique /sɛ̃tetik/ *a.* synthetic.
syphilis /sifilis/ *n.f.* syphilis.
Syrie /siri/ *n.f.* Syria.
syrien, ~ne /sirjɛ̃, -jɛn/ *a.* & *n.m., f.* Syrian.
systématique /sistematik/ *a.* systematic. **~ment** *adv.* systematically.
système /sistɛm/ *n.m.* system.

T

t' /t/ *voir* **te.**
ta /ta/ *voir* **ton**[1].
tabac /taba/ *n.m.* tobacco; (*magasin*) tobacconist's shop. —*a. invar.* buff. **~ à priser,** snuff.
tabasser /tabase/ *v.t.* (*fam.*) beat up.
tabernacle /tabɛrnakl/ *n.m.* tabernacle.
table /tabl/ *n.f.* table. **à ~!**, come and eat! **faire ~ rase,** make a clean sweep **(de,** of). **~ de nuit,** bedside table. **~ des matières,** table of contents. **~ roulante,** (tea-)trolley; (*Amer.*) (serving) cart.
tableau (*pl.* **~x**) /tablo/ *n.m.* picture; (*peinture*) painting; (*panneau*) board; (*graphique*) chart; (*liste*) list. **~ (noir),** blackboard. **~ d'affichage,** notice-board. **~ de bord,** dashboard.
tabler /table/ *v.i.* **~ sur,** count on.
tablette /tablɛt/ *n.f.* shelf. **~ de chocolat,** bar of chocolate.
tablier /tablije/ *n.m.* apron; (*de pont*) platform; (*de magasin*) shutter.
tabou /tabu/ *n.m.* & *a.* taboo.
tabouret /taburɛ/ *n.m.* stool.
tabulateur /tabylatœr/ *n.m.* tabulator.
tac /tak/ *n.m.* **du ~ au tac,** tit for tat.
tache /taʃ/ *n.f.* mark, spot; (*salissure*) stain. **faire ~ d'huile,** spread. **~ de rousseur,** freckle.
tâche /tɑʃ/ *n.f.* task, job.
tacher /taʃe/ *v.t.* stain. **se ~** *v. pr.* (*personne*) get stains on one's clothes.
tâcher /tɑʃe/ *v.i.* **~ de faire,** try to do.
tacheté /taʃte/ *a.* spotted.
tacite /tasit/ *a.* tacit.
taciturne /tasityrn/ *a.* taciturn.
tact /takt/ *n.m.* tact.
tactile /taktil/ *a.* tactile.
tactique /taktik/ *a.* tactical. —*n.f.* tactics. **une ~,** a tactic.
taie /tɛ/ *n.f.* **~ d'oreiller,** pillow-case.
taillader /tɑjade/ *v.t.* gash, slash.
taille[1] /tɑj/ *n.f.* (*ceinture*) waist; (*hauteur*) height; (*grandeur*) size. **de ~,** sizeable.
taill|e[2] /tɑj/ *n.f.* cutting; pruning; (*forme*) cut. **~er** *v.t.* cut; (*arbre*) prune; (*crayon*) sharpen; (*vêtement*) cut out. **se ~er** *v. pr.* (*argot*) clear off. **~e-crayon(s)** *n.m. invar.* pencil-sharpener.

tailleur /tajœr/ *n.m.* tailor; (*costume*) lady's suit.
taillis /taji/ *n.m.* copse.
taire† /tɛr/ *v.t.* say nothing about. **se ~** *v. pr.* be silent *ou* quiet; (*devenir silencieux*) fall silent. **faire ~,** silence.
talc /talk/ *n.m.* talcum powder.
talent /talɑ̃/ *n.m.* talent. **~ueux, ~ueuse** /-tɥø, -z/ *a.* talented.
taloche /talɔʃ/ *n.f.* (*fam.*) slap (in the face).
talon /talɔ̃/ *n.m.* heel; (*de chèque*) stub.
talonner /talɔne/ *v.t.* follow hard on the heels of.
talus /taly/ *n.m.* embankment.
tambour /tɑ̃bur/ *n.m.* drum; (*personne*) drummer; (*porte*) revolving door.
tambourin /tɑ̃burɛ̃/ *n.m.* tambourine.
tambouriner /tɑ̃burine/ *v.t./i.* drum (**sur,** on).
tamis /tami/ *n.m.* sieve. **~er** /-ze/ *v.t.* sieve.
Tamise /tamiz/ *n.f.* Thames.
tamisé /tamize/ *a.* (*lumière*) subdued.
tampon /tɑ̃pɔ̃/ *n.m.* (*pour boucher*) plug; (*ouate*) wad, pad; (*timbre*) stamp; (*de train*) buffer. **~ hygiénique,** tampon.
tamponner /tɑ̃pɔne/ *v.t.* crash into; (*timbrer*) stamp; (*plaie*) dab; (*mur*) plug. **se ~** *v. pr.* (*véhicules*) crash into each other.
tandem /tɑ̃dɛm/ *n.m.* (*bicyclette*) tandem; (*personnes*: *fig.*) duo.
tandis que /tɑ̃dik(ə)/ *conj.* while.
tangage /tɑ̃gaʒ/ *n.m.* pitching.
tangente /tɑ̃ʒɑ̃t/ *n.f.* tangent.
tangible /tɑ̃ʒibl/ *a.* tangible.
tango /tɑ̃go/ *n.m.* tango.
tanguer /tɑ̃ge/ *v.i.* pitch.
tanière /tanjɛr/ *n.f.* den.
tank /tɑ̃k/ *n.m.* tank.
tann|er /tane/ *v.t.* tan. **~é** *a.* (*visage*) tanned, weather-beaten.
tant /tɑ̃/ *adv.* (*travailler, manger, etc.*) so much. **~ (de),** (*quantité*) so much; (*nombre*) so many. **~ que,** as long as; (*autant que*) as much as. **en ~ que,** (*comme*) as. **~ mieux!,** fine!, all the better! **~ pis!,** too bad!, it can't be helped.
tante /tɑ̃t/ *n.f.* aunt.
tantôt /tɑ̃to/ *adv.* sometimes; (*cet après-midi*) this afternoon.
tapag|e /tapaʒ/ *n.m.* din. **~eur, ~euse** *a.* rowdy; (*tape-à-l'œil*) flashy.
tapant, ~e /tapɑ̃, -t/ *a.* (*précis*) sharp.
tape /tap/ *n.f.* slap. **~-à-l'œil** *a. invar.* flashy, tawdry.
taper /tape/ *v.t.* bang; (*enfant*) slap; (*emprunter*: *fam.*) touch for money. **~ (à la machine),** type. —*v.i.* (*cogner*) bang; (*soleil*) beat down. **~ dans,** (*puiser dans*) dig into. **~ sur,** thump; (*critiquer*: *fam.*) knock. **se ~** *v. pr.* (*repas*: *fam.*) put away; (*corvée*: *fam.*) do.
tapioca /tapjɔka/ *n.m.* tapioca.
tap|ir (se) /(sə)tapir/ *v. pr.* crouch. **~i** *a.* crouching.
tapis /tapi/ *n.m.* carpet; (*petit*) rug; (*pour meuble*) cloth. **~-brosse** *n.m.* doormat. **~ de sol,** groundsheet. **~ roulant,** (*pour objets*) conveyor belt.
tapiss|er /tapise/ *v.t.* (wall)paper; (*fig.*) cover (**de,** with). **~erie** *n.f.* tapestry; (*papier peint*) wallpaper. **~ier, ~ière** *n.m., f.* (*décorateur*) interior decorator; (*qui recouvre un siège*) upholsterer.
tapoter /tapɔte/ *v.t.* tap, pat.
taquin, ~e /takɛ̃, -in/ *a.* fond of teasing. —*n.m., f.* tease(r). **~er** /-ine/ *v.t.* tease. **~erie(s)** /-inri/ *n.f.* (*pl.*) teasing.
tarabiscoté /tarabiskɔte/ *a.* over-elaborate.
tard /tar/ *adv.* late. **au plus ~,** at the latest. **plus ~,** later.
tarder /tarde/ *v.i.* (*être lent à venir*)

be a long time coming. **~ (à faire),** take a long time (doing), delay (doing). **il me tarde de,** I long to.

tardi|f, ~ve /tardif, -v/ *a.* late; (*regrets*) belated.

tare /tar/ *n.f.* (*défaut*) defect.

taré /tare/ *a.* (*méd.*) degenerate.

targette /tarʒɛt/ *n.f.* bolt.

targuer (se) /(sə)targe/ *v. pr.* **se ~ de,** boast about.

tarif /tarif/ *n.m.* tariff; (*de train, taxi*) fare. **~s postaux,** postage *ou* postal rates. **~aire** *a.* tariff.

tarir /tarir/ *v.t./i.*, **se ~** *v. pr.* dry up.

tarte /tart/ *n.f.* tart; (*Amer.*) (open) pie. *—a. invar.* (*sot: fam.*) stupid; (*laid: fam.*) ugly.

tartin|e /tartin/ *n.f.* slice of bread (and butter). **~er** *v.t.* spread.

tartre /tartr/ *n.m.* (*bouilloire*) fur, calcium deposit; (*dents*) tartar.

tas /tɑ/ *n.m.* pile, heap. **un** *ou* **des ~ de,** (*fam.*) lots of.

tasse /tɑs/ *n.f.* cup. **~ à thé,** teacup.

tasser /tɑse/ *v.t.* pack, squeeze; (*terre*) pack (down). **se ~** *v. pr.* (*terrain*) sink; (*se serrer*) squeeze up.

tâter /tɑte/ *v.t.* feel: (*fig.*) sound out. *—v.i.* **~ de,** try out.

tatillon, ~ne /tatijɔ̃, -jɔn/ *a.* finicky.

tâtonn|er /tɑtɔne/ *v.i.* grope about. **~ements** *n.m. pl.* (*essais*) trial and error.

tâtons (à) /(a)tɑtɔ̃/ *adv.* **avancer** *ou* **marcher à ~,** grope one's way along.

tatou|er /tatwe/ *v.t.* tattoo. **~age** *n.m.* (*dessin*) tattoo.

taudis /todi/ *n.m.* hovel.

taule /tol/ *n.f.* (*fam.*) prison.

taup|e /top/ *n.f.* mole. **~inière** *n.f.* molehill.

taureau (*pl.* **~x**) /tɔro/ *n.m.* bull.

taux /to/ *n.m.* rate.

taverne /tavɛrn/ *n.f.* tavern.

tax|e /taks/ *n.f.* tax. **~e sur la valeur ajoutée,** value added tax. **~er** *v.t.* tax; (*produit*) fix the price of. **~er qn. de,** accuse s.o. of.

taxi /taksi/ *n.m.* taxi(-cab); (*personne: fam.*) taxi-driver.

taxiphone /taksifɔn/ *n.m.* pay phone.

Tchécoslovaquie /tʃekɔslɔvaki/ *n.f.* Czechoslovakia.

tchèque /tʃɛk/ *a.* & *n.m./f.* Czech.

te, t'* /tə, t/ *pron.* you; (*indirect*) (to) you; (*réfléchi*) yourself.

technicien, ~ne /tɛknisjɛ̃, -jɛn/ *n.m., f.* technician.

technique /tɛknik/ *a.* technical. *—n.f.* technique. **~ment** *adv.* technically.

technolog|ie /tɛknɔlɔʒi/ *n.f.* technology. **~ique** *a.* technological.

teck /tɛk/ *n.m.* teak.

teindre† /tɛ̃dr/ *v.t.* dye. **se ~** *v. pr.* (*personne*) dye one's hair.

teint /tɛ̃/ *n.m.* complexion.

teint|e /tɛ̃t/ *n.f.* shade, tint. **une ~e de,** (*fig.*) a tinge of. **~er** *v.t.* (*papier, verre, etc.*) tint; (*bois*) stain.

teintur|e /tɛ̃tyr/ *n.f.* dyeing; (*produit*) dye. **~erie** *n.f.* (*boutique*) dry-cleaner's (and dyer's). **~ier, ~ière** *n.m., f.* dry-cleaner (and dyer).

tel, ~le /tɛl/ *a.* such. **un ~ livre/** *etc.*, such a book/*etc.* **un ~ chagrin/***etc.*, such sorrow/*etc.* **~ que,** such as, like; (*ainsi que*) (just) as. **~ ou tel,** such-and-such. **~ quel,** (just) as it is.

télé /tele/ *n.f.* (*fam.*) TV.

télécommander /telekɔmɑ̃de/ *v.t.* operate by remote control.

télécommunications /telekɔmynikɑsjɔ̃/ *n.f. pl.* telecommunications.

télégramme /telegram/ *n.m.* telegram.

télégraph|e /telegraf/ *n.m.* telegraph. **~ier** *v.t./i.* **~ier (à),** cable. **~ique** *a.* telegraphic; (*fil, poteau*) telegraph.

téléguid|er /telegide/ *v.t.* control by radio. **~é** *a.* radio-controlled.

télématique /telematik/ *n.f.* computer communications.

télépathie /telepati/ *n.f.* telepathy.

téléphérique /teleferik/ *n.m.* cable-car.

téléphon|e /telefɔn/ *n.m.* (tele)-phone. **~e rouge,** (*pol.*) hot line. **~er** *v.t./i.* **~er (à),** (tele)phone. **~ique** *a.* (tele)phone. **~iste** *n.m./f.* operator.

télescop|e /telɛskɔp/ *n.m.* telescope. **~ique** *a.* telescopic.

télescoper /telɛskɔpe/ *v.t.* smash into. **se ~** *v. pr.* (*véhicules*) smash into each other.

télésiège /telesjɛʒ/ *n.m.* chair-lift.

téléski /teleski/ *n.m.* ski tow.

téléspecta|teur, ~trice /telespɛktatœr, -tris/ *n.m., f.* (television) viewer.

télévis|er /televize/ *v.t.* televise. **~eur** *n.m.* television set.

télévision /televizjɔ̃/ *n.f.* television.

télex /telɛks/ *n.m.* telex.

telle /tɛl/ *voir* **tel.**

tellement /tɛlmɑ̃/ *adv.* (*tant*) so much; (*si*) so. **~ de,** (*quantité*) so much; (*nombre*) so many.

témér|aire /temerɛr/ *a.* rash. **~ité** *n.f.* rashness.

témoignage /temwaɲaʒ/ *n.m.* testimony, evidence; (*récit*) account. **~ de,** (*sentiment*) token of.

témoigner /temwaɲe/ *v.i.* testify **(de,** to). *—v.t.* show. **~ que,** testify that.

témoin /temwɛ̃/ *n.m.* witness; (*sport*) baton. **être ~ de,** witness. **~ oculaire,** eyewitness.

tempe /tɑ̃p/ *n.f.* (*anat.*) temple.

tempérament /tɑ̃peramɑ̃/ *n.m.* temperament; (*physique*) constitution. **à ~,** (*acheter*) on hire-purchase; (*Amer.*) on the installment plan.

tempérance /tɑ̃perɑ̃s/ *n.f.* temperance.

température /tɑ̃peratyr/ *n.f.* temperature.

tempér|er /tɑ̃pere/ *v.t.* temper. **~é** *a.* (*climat*) temperate.

tempête /tɑ̃pɛt/ *n.f.* storm. **~ de neige,** snowstorm.

tempêter /tɑ̃pete/ *v.i.* (*crier*) rage.

temple /tɑ̃pl/ *n.m.* temple; (*protestant*) church.

temporaire /tɑ̃pɔrɛr/ *a.* temporary. **~ment** *adv.* temporarily.

temporel, ~le /tɑ̃pɔrɛl/ *a.* temporal.

temporiser /tɑ̃pɔrize/ *v.i.* play for time.

temps[1] /tɑ̃/ *n.m.* time; (*gram.*) tense; (*étape*) stage. **à ~ partiel/plein,** part-/full-time. **ces derniers ~,** lately. **dans le ~,** at one time. **dans quelque ~,** in a while. **de ~ en temps,** from time to time. **~ d'arrêt,** pause.

temps[2] /tɑ̃/ *n.m.* (*atmosphère*) weather. **~ de chien,** filthy weather.

tenace /tənas/ *a.* stubborn.

ténacité /tenasite/ *n.f.* stubbornness.

tenaille(s) /tənɑj/ *n.f.* (*pl.*) pincers.

tenanc|ier, ~ière /tənɑ̃sje, -jɛr/ *n.m., f.* keeper **(de,** of).

tenant /tənɑ̃/ *n.m.* (*partisan*) supporter; (*d'un titre*) holder.

tendance /tɑ̃dɑ̃s/ *n.f.* tendency; (*opinions*) leanings; (*évolution*) trend. **avoir ~ à,** have a tendency to, tend to.

tendon /tɑ̃dɔ̃/ *n.m.* tendon.

tendre[1] /tɑ̃dr/ *v.t.* stretch; (*piège*) set; (*bras*) stretch out; (*main*) hold out; (*cou*) crane; (*tapisserie*) hang. **~ à qn.,** hold out to s.o. *—v.i.* **~ à,** tend to. **~ l'oreille,** prick up one's ears.

tendre[2] /tɑ̃dr/ *a.* tender; (*couleur,*

bois) soft. **~ment** /-əmɑ̃/ *adv.* tenderly. **~sse** /-ɛs/ *n.f.* tenderness. **~té** /-əte/ *n.f.* (*de viande*) tenderness.

tendu /tɑ̃dy/ *a.* (*corde*) tight; (*personne, situation*) tense; (*main*) outstretched.

tén|èbres /tenɛbr/ *n.f. pl.* darkness. **~ébreux, ~ébreuse** *a.* dark.

teneur /tənœr/ *n.f.* content.

tenir† /tənir/ *v.t.* hold; (*pari, promesse, hôtel*) keep; (*place*) take up; (*propos*) utter; (*rôle*) play. **~ de,** (*avoir reçu de*) have got from. **~ pour,** regard as. **~ propre/chaud/***etc.*, keep clean/warm/*etc.* —*v.i.* hold. **~ à,** be attached to. **~ à faire,** be anxious to do. **~ dans,** fit into. **~ de qn.,** take after s.o. **se ~** *v. pr.* (*rester*) remain; (*debout*) stand; (*avoir lieu*) be held. **se ~ à,** hold on to. **se ~ bien,** behave o.s. **s'en ~ à,** (*se limiter à*) confine o.s. to. **~ bon,** stand firm. **~ compte de,** take into account. **~ le coup,** hold out. **~ tête à,** stand up to. **tiens!,** (*surprise*) hey!

tennis /tenis/ *n.m.* tennis; (*terrain*) tennis-court. —*n.m. pl.* (*chaussures*) sneakers. **~ de table,** table tennis.

ténor /tenɔr/ *n.m.* tenor.

tension /tɑ̃sjɔ̃/ *n.f.* tension. **avoir de la ~,** have high blood-pressure.

tentacule /tɑ̃takyl/ *n.m.* tentacle.

tentative /tɑ̃tativ/ *n.f.* attempt.

tente /tɑ̃t/ *n.f.* tent.

tenter[1] /tɑ̃te/ *v.t.* try (**de faire,** to do).

tent|er[2] /tɑ̃te/ *v.t.* (*allécher*) tempt. **~é de,** tempted to. **~ation** *n.f.* temptation.

tenture /tɑ̃tyr/ *n.f.* (wall) hanging; (*collectif*) drapery.

tenu /təny/ *voir* **tenir.** —*a.* **bien ~,** well-kept. **~ de,** obliged to.

ténu /teny/ *a.* (*fil etc.*) fine; (*cause, nuance*) tenuous.

tenue /təny/ *n.f.* (*habillement*) dress; (*de sport*) clothes; (*de maison*) upkeep; (*conduite*) (good) behaviour; (*maintien*) posture. **~ de soirée,** evening dress.

ter /tɛr/ *a. invar.* (*numéro*) B, b.

térébenthine /terebɑ̃tin/ *n.f.* turpentine.

tergiverser /tɛrʒivɛrse/ *v.i.* procrastinate.

terme /tɛrm/ *n.m.* (*mot*) term; (*date limite*) time-limit; (*fin*) end; (*date de loyer*) term. **à long/court ~,** long-/short-term. **en bons ~s,** on good terms (**avec,** with).

termin|al, ~ale (*m. pl.* **~aux**) /tɛrminal, -o/ *a.* terminal. (**classe**) **~ale,** sixth form; (*Amer.*) twelfth grade. —*n.m.* (*pl.* **~aux**) terminal.

termin|er /tɛrmine/ *v.t./i.* finish; (*soirée, débat*) end, finish. **se ~er** *v. pr.* end (**par,** with). **~aison** *n.f.* (*gram.*) ending.

terminologie /tɛrminɔlɔʒi/ *n.f.* terminology.

terminus /tɛrminys/ *n.m.* terminus.

terne /tɛrn/ *a.* dull, drab.

ternir /tɛrnir/ *v.t./i.,* **se ~** *v. pr.* tarnish.

terrain /tɛrɛ̃/ *n.m.* ground; (*parcelle*) piece of land; (*à bâtir*) plot. **~ d'aviation,** airfield. **~ de camping,** campsite. **~ de golf,** golf-course. **~ de jeu,** playground. **~ vague,** waste ground; (*Amer.*) vacant lot.

terrasse /tɛras/ *n.f.* terrace; (*de café*) pavement area.

terrassement /tɛrasmɑ̃/ *n.m.* excavation.

terrasser /tɛrase/ *v.t.* floor, overwhelm.

terrassier /tɛrasje/ *n.m.* navvy, labourer, ditch-digger.

terre /tɛr/ *n.f.* (*planète, matière*)

earth; (*étendue, pays*) land; (*sol*) ground; (*domaine*) estate. **à ~,** (*naut.*) ashore. **par ~,** (*tomber, jeter*) to the ground; (*s'asseoir, poser*) on the ground. **~ (cuite),** (baked) clay. **~-à-terre** *a. invar.* matter-of-fact, down-to-earth. **~-plein** *n.m.* (*auto.*) earth platform, central reservation.

terreau /tɛro/ *n.m. invar.* compost.

terrer (se) /(sə)tɛre/ *v. pr.* hide o.s., dig o.s. in.

terrestre /tɛrɛstr/ *a.* land; (*de notre planète*) earth's; (*fig.*) earthly.

terreur /tɛrœr/ *n.f.* terror.

terreu|x, ~se /tɛrø, -z/ *a.* earthy; (*sale*) grubby.

terrible /tɛribl/ *a.* terrible; (*formidable*: *fam.*) terrific.

terrien, ~ne /tɛrjɛ̃, -jɛn/ *n.m., f.* earth-dweller.

terrier /tɛrje/ *n.m.* (*trou de lapin etc.*) burrow; (*chien*) terrier.

terrifier /tɛrifje/ *v.t.* terrify.

terrine /tɛrin/ *n.f.* (*culin.*) terrine.

territ|oire /tɛritwar/ *n.m.* territory. **~orial** (*m. pl.* **~oriaux**) *a.* territorial.

terroir /tɛrwar/ *n.m.* (*sol*) soil; (*région*) region. **du ~,** rural.

terroriser /tɛrɔrize/ *v.t.* terrorize.

terroris|te /tɛrɔrist/ *n.m./f.* terrorist. **~me** *n.m.* terrorism.

tertre /tɛrtr/ *n.m.* mound.

tes /te/ *voir* **ton**[1].

tesson /tesɔ̃/ *n.m.* **~ de bouteille,** piece of broken bottle.

test /tɛst/ *n.m.* test. **~er** *v.t.* test.

testament /tɛstamɑ̃/ *n.m.* (*jurid.*) will; (*politique, artistique*) testament. **Ancien/Nouveau T~,** Old/New Testament.

testicule /tɛstikyl/ *n.m.* testicle.

tétanos /tetanos/ *n.m.* tetanus.

têtard /tɛtar/ *n.m.* tadpole.

tête /tɛt/ *n.f.* head; (*figure*) face; (*cheveux*) hair; (*cerveau*) brain. **à la ~ de,** at the head of. **à ~ reposée,** in a leisurely moment. **de ~,** (*calculer*) in one's head. **en ~,** (*sport*) in the lead. **faire la ~,** sulk. **faire une ~,** (*football*) head the ball. **~-à-queue** *n.m. invar.* (*auto.*) spin. **~-à-tête** *n.m. invar.* tête-à-tête. **en ~-à-tête,** in private.

tétée /tete/ *n.f.* feed.

téter /tete/ *v.t./i.* suck.

tétine /tetin/ *n.f.* (*mamelle*) teat; (*sucette*) dummy; (*Amer.*) pacifier.

têtu /tety/ *a.* stubborn.

texte /tɛkst/ *n.m.* text; (*de leçon*) subject; (*morceau choisi*) passage.

textile /tɛkstil/ *n.m.* & *a.* textile.

textuel, ~le /tɛkstɥɛl/ *a.* literal.

texture /tɛkstyr/ *n.f.* texture.

thaïlandais, ~e /tailɑ̃dɛ, -z/ *a.* & *n.m., f.* Thai.

Thaïlande /tailɑ̃d/ *n.f.* Thailand.

thé /te/ *n.m.* tea.

théâtr|al (*m. pl.* **~aux**) /teɑtral, -o/ *a.* theatrical.

théâtre /teɑtr/ *n.m.* theatre; (*jeu forcé*) play-acting; (*d'un crime*) scene. **faire du ~,** act.

théière /tejɛr/ *n.f.* teapot.

thème /tɛm/ *n.m.* theme; (*traduction*: *scol.*) prose, translation (*into the foreign language*).

théolog|ie /teɔlɔʒi/ *n.f.* theology. **~ien** *n.m.* theologian. **~ique** *a.* theological.

théorème /teɔrɛm/ *n.m.* theorem.

théor|ie /teɔri/ *n.f.* theory. **~icien, ~icienne** *n.m., f.* theorist. **~ique** *a.* theoretical.

thérap|ie /terapi/ *n.f.* therapy. **~eutique** *a.* therapeutic.

thermique /tɛrmik/ *a.* thermal.

thermomètre /tɛrmɔmɛtr/ *n.m.* thermometer.

thermonucléaire /tɛrmɔnykleɛr/ *a.* thermonuclear.

thermos /tɛrmos/ *n.m./f.* (P.) Thermos (P.) (flask).

thermostat /tɛrmɔsta/ *n.m.* thermostat.

thésauriser /tezɔrize/ *v.t./i.* hoard.
thèse /tɛz/ *n.f.* thesis.
thon /tɔ̃/ *n.m.* (*poisson*) tuna.
thrombose /trɔ̃boz/ *n.f.* thrombosis.
thym /tɛ̃/ *n.m.* thyme.
thyroïde /tirɔid/ *n.f.* thyroid.
tibia /tibja/ *n.m.* shin-bone.
tic /tik/ *n.m.* (*contraction*) twitch; (*manie*) mannerism.
ticket /tikɛ/ *n.m.* ticket.
tic-tac /tiktak/ *n.m. invar.* (*de pendule*) tick(ing).
tiède /tjɛd/ *a.* lukewarm; (*atmosphère*) mild. **tiédeur** /tjedœr/ *n.f.* lukewarmness; mildness.
tiédir /tjedir/ *v.t./i.* **(faire) ~,** warm slightly.
tien, ~ne /tjɛ̃, tjɛn/ *pron.* **le ~, la ~ne, les ~(ne)s,** yours.
tiens, tient /tjɛ̃/ *voir* **tenir.**
tiercé /tjɛrse/ *n.m.* place-betting.
tier|s, ~ce /tjɛr, -s/ *a.* third. —*n.m.* (*fraction*) third; (*personne*) third party. **T~s-Monde** *n.m.* Third World.
tige /tiʒ/ *n.f.* (*bot.*) stem, stalk; (*en métal*) shaft.
tignasse /tiɲas/ *n.f.* mop of hair.
tigre /tigr/ *n.m.* tiger. **~sse** /-ɛs/ *n.f.* tigress.
tigré /tigre/ *a.* spotted; (*rayé*) striped.
tilleul /tijœl/ *n.m.* lime(-tree), linden(-tree); (*infusion*) lime tea.
timbale /tɛ̃bal/ *n.f.* (*gobelet*) (metal) tumbler.
timbr|e /tɛ̃br/ *n.m.* stamp; (*sonnette*) bell; (*de voix*) tone. **~e-poste** (*pl.* **~es-poste)** *n.m.* postage stamp. **~er** *v.t.* stamp.
timbré /tɛ̃bre/ *a.* (*fam.*) crazy.
timid|e /timid/ *a.* timid. **~ité** *n.f.* timidity.
timoré /timɔre/ *a.* timorous.
tintamarre /tɛ̃tamar/ *n.m.* din.
tint|er /tɛ̃te/ *v.i.* ring; (*clefs*) jingle. **~ement** *n.m.* ringing; jingling.
tique /tik/ *n.f.* (*insecte*) tick.
tir /tir/ *n.m.* (*sport*) shooting; (*action de tirer*) firing; (*feu, rafale*) fire. **~ à l'arc,** archery. **~ forain,** shooting-gallery.
tirade /tirad/ *n.f.* soliloquy.
tirage /tiraʒ/ *n.m.* (*de photo*) printing; (*de journal*) circulation; (*de livre*) edition; (*de loterie*) draw; (*de cheminée*) draught.
tiraill|er /tirɑje/ *v.t.* pull (away) at; (*harceler*) plague. **~é entre,** (*possibilités etc.*) torn between. **~ement** *n.m.* (*douleur*) gnawing pain; (*conflit*) conflict.
tiré /tire/ *a.* (*traits*) drawn.
tire-bouchon /tirbuʃɔ̃/ *n.m.* corkscrew.
tirelire /tirlir/ *n.f.* money-box; (*Amer.*) coin-bank.
tirer /tire/ *v.t.* pull; (*navire*) tow, tug; (*langue*) stick out; (*conclusion, trait, rideaux*) draw; (*coup de feu*) fire; (*gibier*) shoot; (*photo*) print. **~ de,** (*sortir*) take *ou* get out of; (*extraire*) extract from; (*plaisir, nom*) derive from. —*v.i.* shoot, fire **(sur,** at). **~ sur,** (*couleur*) verge on; (*corde*) pull at. **se ~** *v. pr.* (*fam.*) clear off. **se ~ de,** get out of. **s'en ~,** (*en réchapper: fam.*) pull through; (*réussir: fam.*) cope. **~ à sa fin,** be drawing to a close. **~ au clair,** clarify. **~ au sort,** draw lots (for). **~ parti de,** take advantage of. **~ profit de,** profit from.
tiret /tirɛ/ *n.m.* dash.
tireur /tirœr/ *n.m.* gunman. **~ d'élite,** marksman. **~ isolé,** sniper.
tiroir /tirwar/ *n.m.* drawer. **~-caisse** (*pl.* **~s-caisses)** *n.m.* till.
tisane /tizan/ *n.f.* herb-tea.
tison /tizɔ̃/ *n.m.* ember.
tisonnier /tizɔnje/ *n.m.* poker.
tiss|er /tise/ *v.t.* weave. **~age** *n.m.* weaving. **~erand** /tisrɑ̃/ *n.m.* weaver.

tissu /tisy/ *n.m.* fabric, material; (*biologique*) tissue. **un ~ de,** (*fig.*) a web of. **~-éponge** (*pl.* **~s-éponge**) *n.m.* towelling.
titre /titr/ *n.m.* title; (*diplôme*) qualification; (*comm.*) bond. **~s,** (*droits*) claims. **(gros) ~s,** headlines. **à ce ~,** (*pour cette qualité*) as such. **à ~ d'exemple,** as an example. **à juste ~,** rightly. **à ~ privé,** in a private capacity. **~ de propriété,** title-deed.
titré /titre/ *a.* titled.
titrer /titre/ *v.t.* (*journal*) give as a headline.
tituber /titybe/ *v.i.* stagger.
titul|aire /tityler/ *a.* **être ~aire,** have tenure. **être ~aire de,** hold. —*n.m.*/*f.* (*de permis etc.*) holder. **~ariser** *v.t.* give tenure to.
toast /tost/ *n.m.* piece of toast; (*allocution*) toast.
toboggan /tɔbɔgɑ̃/ *n.m.* (*traîneau*) toboggan; (*glissière*) slide; (*auto.*) flyover; (*auto., Amer.*) overpass.
toc /tɔk/ *int.* **~ toc!,** knock knock!
tocsin /tɔksɛ̃/ *n.m.* alarm (bell).
toge /tɔʒ/ *n.f.* (*de juge etc.*) gown.
tohu-bohu /tɔybɔy/ *n.m.* hubbub.
toi /twa/ *pron.* you; (*réfléchi*) yourself. **lève-~,** stand up.
toile /twal/ *n.f.* cloth; (*sac, tableau*) canvas; (*coton*) cotton. **~ d'araignée,** cobweb. **~ de fond,** backdrop, backcloth.
toilette /twalɛt/ *n.f.* washing; (*habillement*) clothes, dress. **~s,** (*cabinets*) toilet(s). **de ~,** (*articles, savon, etc.*) toilet. **faire sa ~,** wash (and get ready).
toi-même /twamɛm/ *pron.* yourself.
toiser /twaze/ *v.t.* **~ qn.,** look s.o. up and down.
toison /twazɔ̃/ *n.f.* (*laine*) fleece.
toit /twa/ *n.m.* roof. **~ ouvrant,** (*auto.*) sun-roof.
toiture /twatyr/ *n.f.* roof.
tôle /tol/ *n.f.* (*plaque*) iron sheet. **~ ondulée,** corrugated iron.
tolérable /tɔlerabl/ *a.* tolerable.
toléran|t, ~te /tɔlerɑ̃, -t/ *a.* tolerant. **~ce** *n.f.* tolerance; (*importations: comm.*) allowance.
tolérer /tɔlere/ *v.t.* tolerate; (*importations: comm.*) allow.
tollé /tɔle/ *n.m.* hue and cry.
tomate /tɔmat/ *n.f.* tomato.
tombe /tɔ̃b/ *n.f.* grave; (*avec monument*) tomb.
tombeau (*pl.* **~x**) /tɔ̃bo/ *n.m.* tomb.
tombée /tɔ̃be/ *n.f.* **~ de la nuit,** nightfall.
tomber /tɔ̃be/ *v.i.* (*aux. être*) fall; (*fièvre, vent*) drop; (*enthousiasme*) die down. **faire ~,** knock over; (*gouvernement*) bring down. **~ à l'eau,** (*projet*) fall through. **~ bien** *ou* **à point,** come at the right time. **~ en panne,** break down. **~ en syncope,** faint. **~ sur,** (*trouver*) run across.
tombola /tɔ̃bɔla/ *n.f.* tombola; (*Amer.*) lottery.
tome /tɔm/ *n.m.* volume.
ton[1], **ta** *ou* **ton*** (*pl.* **tes**) /tɔ̃, ta, tɔ̃n, te/ *a.* your.
ton[2] /tɔ̃/ *n.m.* tone; (*gamme: mus.*) key; (*hauteur de la voix*) pitch. **de bon ~,** in good taste.
tonalité /tɔnalite/ *n.f.* tone; (*téléphone*) dialling tone; (*téléphone: Amer.*) dial tone.
tond|re /tɔ̃dr/ *v.t.* (*herbe*) mow; (*mouton*) shear; (*cheveux*) clip. **~euse** *n.f.* shears; clippers. **~euse (à gazon),** (lawn-)mower.
tonifier /tɔnifje/ *v.t.* tone up.
tonique /tɔnik/ *a.* & *n.m.* tonic.
tonne /tɔn/ *n.f.* ton(ne).
tonneau (*pl.* **~x**) /tɔno/ *n.m.* (*récipient*) barrel; (*naut.*) ton; (*culbute*) somersault.
tonnelle /tɔnɛl/ *n.f.* bower.
tonner /tɔne/ *v.i.* thunder.
tonnerre /tɔnɛr/ *n.m.* thunder.

tonte /tɔ̃t/ *n.f.* (*de gazon*) mowing; (*de moutons*) shearing.
tonton /tɔ̃tɔ̃/ *n.m.* (*fam.*) uncle.
tonus /tɔnys/ *n.m.* energy.
top /tɔp/ *n.m.* (*signal pour marquer un instant précis*) stroke.
topo /tɔpo/ *n.m.* (*fam.*) talk, oral report.
toquade /tɔkad/ *n.f.* craze; (*pour une personne*) infatuation.
toque /tɔk/ *n.f.* (fur) hat; (*de jockey*) cap.
toqué /tɔke/ *a.* (*fam.*) crazy.
torche /tɔrʃ/ *n.f.* torch.
torcher /tɔrʃe/ *v.t.* (*fam.*) wipe.
torchon /tɔrʃɔ̃/ *n.m.* cloth, duster; (*pour la vaisselle*) tea-towel; (*Amer.*) dish-towel.
tordre /tɔrdr/ *v.t.* twist; (*linge*) wring. **se ~** *v. pr.* twist, bend; (*de douleur*) writhe. **se ~ (de rire),** split one's sides.
tordu /tɔrdy/ *a.* twisted, bent; (*esprit*) warped.
tornade /tɔrnad/ *n.f.* tornado.
torpeur /tɔrpœr/ *n.f.* lethargy.
torpill|e /tɔrpij/ *n.f.* torpedo. **~er** *v.t.* torpedo.
torrent /tɔrɑ̃/ *n.m.* torrent. **~iel, ~ielle** /-sjɛl/ *a.* torrential.
torride /tɔrid/ *a.* torrid.
torsade /tɔrsad/ *n.f.* twist.
torse /tɔrs/ *n.m.* chest; (*sculpture*) torso.
tort /tɔr/ *n.m.* wrong. **à ~,** wrongly. **avoir ~,** be wrong (**de faire,** to do). **donner ~ à,** prove wrong. **faire (du) ~ à,** harm.
torticolis /tɔrtikɔli/ *n.m.* stiff neck.
tortiller /tɔrtije/ *v.t.* twist, twirl. **se ~** *v. pr.* wriggle, wiggle.
tortionnaire /tɔrsjɔnɛr/ *n.m.* torturer.
tortue /tɔrty/ *n.f.* tortoise; (*de mer*) turtle.
tortueu|x, ~se /tɔrtɥø, -z/ *a.* tortuous.
tortur|e(s) /tɔrtyr/ *n.f.* (*pl.*) torture. **~er** *v.t.* torture.
tôt /to/ *adv.* early. **plus ~,** earlier. **au plus ~,** at the earliest. **le plus ~ possible,** as soon as possible. **~ ou tard,** sooner or later.
tot|al (*m. pl.* **~aux**) /tɔtal, -o/ *a.* total. —*n.m.* (*pl.* **~aux**) total. —*adv.* (*fam.*) to conclude, in short. **au ~al,** all in all. **~alement** *adv.* totally. **~aliser** *v.t.* total.
totalitaire /tɔtalitɛr/ *a.* totalitarian.
totalité /tɔtalite/ *n.f.* entirety. **la ~ de,** all of.
toubib /tubib/ *n.m.* (*fam.*) doctor.
touchant, ~e /tuʃɑ̃, -t/ *a.* (*émouvant*) touching.
touche /tuʃ/ *n.f.* (*de piano*) key; (*de peintre*) touch. **(ligne de) ~,** touch-line. **une ~ de,** a touch of.
toucher[1] /tuʃe/ *v.t.* touch; (*émouvoir*) move, touch; (*contacter*) get in touch with; (*cible*) hit; (*argent*) draw; (*chèque*) cash; (*concerner*) affect. —*v.i.* **~ à,** touch; (*question*) touch on; (*fin, but*) approach. **se ~** *v. pr.* (*lignes*) touch.
toucher[2] /tuʃe/ *n.m.* (*sens*) touch.
touffe /tuf/ *n.f.* (*de poils, d'herbe*) tuft; (*de plantes*) clump.
touffu /tufy/ *a.* thick, bushy; (*fig.*) complex.
toujours /tuʒur/ *adv.* always; (*encore*) still; (*en tout cas*) anyhow. **pour ~,** for ever.
toupet /tupɛ/ *n.m.* (*culot: fam.*) cheek, nerve.
toupie /tupi/ *n.f.* (*jouet*) top.
tour[1] /tur/ *n.f.* tower; (*immeuble*) tower block; (*échecs*) rook.
tour[2] /tur/ *n.m.* (*mouvement, succession, tournure*) turn; (*excursion*) trip; (*à pied*) walk; (*en auto*) drive; (*artifice*) trick; (*circonférence*) circumference; (*techn.*) lathe. **~ (de piste),** lap. **à ~ de rôle,** in turn. **à mon**/*etc.* **~,** when it is my/*etc.* turn. **c'est mon**/*etc.* **~**

de, it is my/*etc.* turn to. **faire le ~ de,** go round; (*question*) survey. **~ d'horizon,** survey. **~ de passe-passe,** sleight of hand. **~ de taille,** waist measurement.

tourbe /turb/ *n.f.* peat.

tourbillon /turbijɔ̃/ *n.m.* whirlwind; (*d'eau*) whirlpool; (*fig.*) whirl, swirl. **~ner** /-jɔne/ *v.i.* whirl, swirl.

tourelle /turɛl/ *n.f.* turret.

tourisme /turism/ *n.m.* tourism. **faire du ~,** do some sightseeing.

tourist|e /turist/ *n.m.*/*f.* tourist. **~ique** *a.* tourist; (*route*) scenic.

tourment /turmɑ̃/ *n.m.* torment. **~er** /-te/ *v.t.* torment. **se ~er** *v. pr.* worry.

tournage /turnaʒ/ *n.m.* (*cinéma*) shooting.

tournant[1], **~e** /turnɑ̃, -t/ *a.* (*qui pivote*) revolving.

tournant[2] /turnɑ̃/ *n.m.* bend; (*fig.*) turning-point.

tourne-disque /turnədisk/ *n.m.* record-player.

tournée /turne/ *n.f.* (*voyage, consommations*) round; (*théâtre*) tour. **faire la ~,** make the rounds (**de,** of).

tourner /turne/ *v.t.* turn; (*film*) shoot, make. *—v.i.* turn; (*toupie, tête*) spin; (*moteur, usine*) run. **se ~** *v. pr.* turn. **~ au froid,** turn cold. **~ autour de,** go round; (*personne, maison*) hang around; (*terre*) revolve round; (*question*) centre on. **~ de l'œil,** (*fam.*) faint. **~ en dérision,** mock. **~ en ridicule,** ridicule. **~ mal,** turn out badly.

tournesol /turnəsɔl/ *n.m.* sunflower.

tournevis /turnəvis/ *n.m.* screwdriver.

tourniquet /turnikɛ/ *n.m.* (*barrière*) turnstile.

tournoi /turnwa/ *n.m.* tournament.

tournoyer /turnwaje/ *v.i.* whirl.

tournure /turnyr/ *n.f.* turn; (*locution*) turn of phrase.

tourterelle /turtərɛl/ *n.f.* turtledove.

Toussaint /tusɛ̃/ *n.f.* **la ~,** All Saints' Day.

tousser /tuse/ *v.i.* cough.

tout[1], **~e** (*pl.* **tous, toutes**) /tu, tut/ *a.* all; (*n'importe quel*) any; (*tout à fait*) entirely. **~ le pays/***etc.*, the whole country/*etc.*, all the country/*etc.* **~e la nuit/journée,** the whole night/day. **tous les jours/mois/***etc.*, every day/month/*etc.* *—pron.* everything, all. **tous** /tus/, **toutes,** all. **prendre ~,** take everything, take it all. **~ ce que,** all that. **~ le monde,** everyone. **tous les deux, toutes les deux,** both of them. *—adv.* (*très*) very; (*tout à fait*) quite. **~ au bout/début/***etc.*, right at the end/beginning/*etc.* **~ en chantant/marchant/***etc.*, while singing/walking/*etc.* **~ à coup,** all of a sudden. **~ à fait,** quite, completely. **~ à l'heure,** in a moment; (*passé*) a moment ago. **~ au** *ou* **le long de,** throughout. **~ au plus/moins,** at most/least. **~ de même,** all the same. **~ de suite,** straight away. **~ entier,** whole. **~ le contraire,** quite the opposite. **~ neuf,** brand-new. **~ nu,** stark naked. **~ près,** nearby. **~-puissant, ~e-puissante** *a.* omnipotent. **~ seul,** alone.

tout[2] /tu/ *n.m.* (*ensemble*) whole. **en ~,** in all.

tout-à-l'égout /tutalegu/ *n.m.* main drainage.

toutefois /tutfwa/ *adv.* however.

toux /tu/ *n.f.* cough.

toxicomane /tɔksikɔman/ *n.m.*/*f.* drug addict.

toxine /tɔksin/ *n.f.* toxin.

toxique /tɔksik/ *a.* toxic.

trac /trak/ *n.m.* **le ~,** nerves; (*théâtre*) stage fright.

tracas /traka/ *n.m.* worry. **~ser** /-se/ *v.t.*, **se ~ser** *v. pr.* worry.

trace /tras/ *n.f.* trace, mark; (*d'animal, de pneu*) tracks; (*vestige*) trace. **sur la ~ de,** on the track of. **~s de pas,** footprints.

tracé /trase/ *n.m.* (*ligne*) line; (*plan*) layout.

tracer /trase/ *v.t.* draw, trace; (*écrire*) write; (*route*) mark out.

trachée(-artère) /traʃe(artɛr)/ *n.f.* windpipe.

tract /trakt/ *n.m.* leaflet.

tractations /traktɑsjɔ̃/ *n.f. pl.* dealings.

tracteur /traktœr/ *n.m.* tractor.

traction /traksjɔ̃/ *n.f.* (*sport*) press-up, push-up.

tradition /tradisjɔ̃/ *n.f.* tradition. **~nel, ~nelle** /-jɔnɛl/ *a.* traditional.

trad|uire† /tradɥir/ *v.t.* translate; (*sentiment*) express. **~uire en justice,** take to court. **~ucteur, ~uctrice** *n.m., f.* translator. **~uction** *n.f.* translation.

trafic /trafik/ *n.m.* (*commerce, circulation*) traffic.

trafiqu|er /trafike/ *v.i.* traffic. *—v.t.* (*fam.*) doctor. **~ant, ~ante** *n.m., f.* trafficker; (*d'armes, de drogues*) dealer.

tragédie /traʒedi/ *n.f.* tragedy.

tragique /traʒik/ *a.* tragic. **~ment** *adv.* tragically.

trah|ir /trair/ *v.t.* betray. **~ison** *n.f.* betrayal; (*crime*) treason.

train /trɛ̃/ *n.m.* (*rail.*) train; (*allure*) pace; (*ensemble*) set. **en ~,** (*en forme*) in shape. **en ~ de faire,** (busy) doing. **mettre en ~,** start up. **~ d'atterrissage,** undercarriage. **~ de vie,** lifestyle.

traînard, ~e /trɛnar, -d/ *n.m., f.* slowcoach; (*Amer.*) slowpoke; (*en marchant*) straggler.

traîne /trɛn/ *n.f.* (*de robe*) train. **à la ~,** lagging behind; (*en remorque*) in tow.

traîneau (*pl.* **~x**) /trɛno/ *n.m.* sledge.

traînée /trene/ *n.f.* (*trace*) trail; (*bande*) streak; (*femme: péj.*) prostitute.

traîner /trene/ *v.t.* drag (along); (*véhicule*) pull. *—v.i.* (*pendre*) trail; (*rester en arrière*) trail behind; (*flâner*) hang about; (*papiers, affaires*) lie around. **~ (en longueur),** drag on. **se ~** *v. pr.* (*par terre*) crawl. **(faire) ~ en longueur,** drag out. **~ ses mots** *ou* **sa voix,** drawl.

train-train /trɛ̃trɛ̃/ *n.m.* routine.

traire† /trɛr/ *v.t.* milk.

trait /trɛ/ *n.m.* line; (*en dessinant*) stroke; (*caractéristique*) feature, trait; (*acte*) act. **~s,** (*du visage*) features. **avoir ~ à,** relate to. **d'un ~,** (*boire*) in one gulp. **~ d'union,** hyphen; (*fig.*) link.

traite /trɛt/ *n.f.* (*de vache*) milking; (*comm.*) draft. **d'une seule ~,** in one go, at a stretch.

traité /trete/ *n.m.* (*pacte*) treaty; (*ouvrage*) treatise.

traitement /trɛtmɑ̃/ *n.m.* treatment; (*salaire*) salary. **~ de données,** data processing. **~ de texte,** word processing.

traiter /trete/ *v.t.* treat; (*affaire*) deal with; (*données, produit*) process. **~ qn. de lâche**/*etc.*, call s.o. a coward/*etc.* *—v.i.* deal **(avec,** with). **~ de,** (*sujet*) deal with.

traiteur /trɛtœr/ *n.m.* caterer.

traître, ~sse /trɛtr, -ɛs/ *a.* treacherous. *—n.m./f.* traitor.

trajectoire /traʒɛktwar/ *n.f.* path.

trajet /traʒɛ/ *n.m.* distance; (*voyage*) journey; (*itinéraire*) route.

trame /tram/ *n.f.* (*de récit etc.*) framework.

tramer /trame/ *v.t.* plot; (*complot*) hatch.
tramway /tramwɛ/ *n.m.* tram; (*Amer.*) streetcar.
tranchant, ~e /trɑ̃ʃɑ̃, -t/ *a.* sharp. —*n.m.* cutting edge.
tranche /trɑ̃ʃ/ *n.f.* (*rondelle*) slice; (*bord*) edge; (*partie*) portion.
tranchée /trɑ̃ʃe/ *n.f.* trench.
tranch|er[1] /trɑ̃ʃe/ *v.t.* cut; (*question*) decide. —*v.i.* (*décider*) decide. **~é** *a.* (*net*) clear-cut.
trancher[2] /trɑ̃ʃe/ *v.i.* (*contraster*) contrast (**sur,** with).
tranquill|e /trɑ̃kil/ *a.* quiet; (*esprit*) at rest; (*conscience*) clear. **être/laisser ~e,** be/leave in peace. **~ement** *adv.* quietly. **~ité** *n.f.* (peace and) quiet; (*d'esprit*) peace of mind.
tranquillisant /trɑ̃kilizɑ̃/ *n.m.* tranquillizer.
tranquilliser /trɑ̃kilize/ *v.t.* reassure.
transaction /trɑ̃zaksjɔ̃/ *n.f.* transaction.
transatlantique /trɑ̃zatlɑ̃tik/ *n.m.* transatlantic liner; (*chaise*) deck-chair.
transborder /trɑ̃sbɔrde/ *v.t.* transfer, transship.
transcend|er /trɑ̃sɑ̃de/ *v.t.* transcend. **~ant, ~ante** *a.* transcendent.
transcr|ire /trɑ̃skrir/ *v.t.* transcribe. **~iption** *n.f.* transcription; (*copie*) transcript.
transe /trɑ̃s/ *n.f.* **en ~,** in a trance; (*fig.*) very excited. **dans les ~s,** in sheer agony (**de,** over).
transférer /trɑ̃sfere/ *v.t.* transfer.
transfert /trɑ̃sfɛr/ *n.m.* transfer.
transform|er /trɑ̃sfɔrme/ *v.t.* change; (*radicalement*) transform; (*vêtement*) alter. **se ~er** *v. pr.* change; be transformed. **(se) ~er en,** turn into. **~ateur** *n.m.* transformer. **~ation** *n.f.* change; transformation.
transfuge /trɑ̃sfyʒ/ *n.m.* renegade.
transfusion /trɑ̃sfyzjɔ̃/ *n.f.* transfusion.
transgresser /trɑ̃sgrese/ *v.t.* disobey.
transiger /trɑ̃siʒe/ *v.i.* compromise.
transir /trɑ̃zir/ *v.t.* numb.
transistor /trɑ̃zistɔr/ *n.m.* (*dispositif, poste de radio*) transistor.
transit /trɑ̃zit/ *n.m.* transit. **~er** *v.t./i.* pass in transit.
transiti|f, ~ve /trɑ̃zitif, -v/ *a.* transitive.
transi|tion /trɑ̃zisjɔ̃/ *n.f.* transition. **~toire** *a.* (*provisoire*) transitional; (*fugitif*) fleeting.
translucide /trɑ̃slysid/ *a.* translucent.
transm|ettre† /trɑ̃smɛtr/ *v.t.* pass on; (*techn.*) transmit; (*radio*) broadcast. **~ission** *n.f.* transmission; (*radio*) broadcasting.
transparaître /trɑ̃sparɛtr/ *v.i.* show (through).
transparen|t, ~te /trɑ̃sparɑ̃, -t/ *a.* transparent. **~ce** *n.f.* transparency.
transpercer /trɑ̃spɛrse/ *v.t.* pierce.
transpir|er /trɑ̃spire/ *v.i.* perspire. **~ation** *n.f.* perspiration.
transplant|er /trɑ̃splɑ̃te/ *v.t.* transplant. **~ation** *n.f.* transplantation; (*greffe*) transplant.
transport /trɑ̃spɔr/ *n.m.* transport(ation); (*sentiment*) rapture. **les ~s,** transport. **les ~s en commun,** public transport.
transport|er /trɑ̃spɔrte/ *v.t.* transport; (*à la main*) carry. **se ~er** *v. pr.* take o.s. (**à,** to). **~eur** *n.m.* haulier; (*Amer.*) trucker.
transposer /trɑ̃spoze/ *v.t.* transpose.
transvaser /trɑ̃svaze/ *v.t.* decant.
transvers|al (*m. pl.* **~aux**) /trɑ̃svɛrsal, -o/ *a.* cross, transverse.

trap|èze /trapɛz/ *n.m.* (*sport*) trapeze. **~éziste** /-ezist/ *n.m.*/*f.* trapeze artist.
trappe /trap/ *n.f.* trapdoor.
trappeur /trapœr/ *n.m.* trapper.
trapu /trapy/ *a.* stocky.
traquenard /traknar/ *n.m.* trap.
traquer /trake/ *v.t.* track down.
traumatis|me /tromatism/ *n.m.* trauma. **~ant, ~ante** /-zɑ̃, -t/ *a.* traumatic.
trav|ail (*pl.* **~aux**) /travaj, -o/ *n.m.* work; (*emploi, poste*) job; (*façonnage*) working. **~aux,** work. **en ~ail,** (*femme*) in labour. **~ail à la chaîne,** production-line work. **~ail à la pièce** *ou* **à la tâche,** piece-work. **~ail noir,** (*fam.*) moonlighting. **~aux forcés,** hard labour. **~aux ménagers,** housework.
travaill|er /travaje/ *v.i.* work; (*se déformer*) warp. **~er à,** (*livre etc.*) work on. —*v.t.* (*façonner*) work; (*étudier*) work at *ou* on; (*tourmenter*) worry. **~eur, ~euse** *n.m., f.* worker; *a.* hard-working.
travailliste /travajist/ *a.* Labour. —*n.m.*/*f.* Labour party member.
travée /trave/ *n.f.* (*rangée*) row.
travers /travɛr/ *n.m.* (*défaut*) failing. **à ~,** through. **au ~ (de),** through. **de ~,** (*chapeau, nez*) crooked; (*mal*) badly, the wrong way; (*regarder*) askance. **en ~ (de),** across.
traverse /travɛrs/ *n.f.* (*rail.*) sleeper; (*rail., Amer.*) tie.
traversée /travɛrse/ *n.f.* crossing.
traverser /travɛrse/ *v.t.* cross; (*transpercer*) go (right) through; (*période, forêt*) go *ou* pass through.
traversin /travɛrsɛ̃/ *n.m.* bolster.
travestir /travɛstir/ *v.t.* disguise; (*vérité*) misrepresent.
trébucher /trebyʃe/ *v.i.* stumble, trip (over). **faire ~,** trip (up).
trèfle /trɛfl/ *n.m.* (*plante*) clover; (*cartes*) clubs.
treillage /trɛjaʒ/ *n.m.* trellis.
treillis[1] /treji/ *n.m.* trellis; (*en métal*) wire mesh.
treillis[2] /treji/ *n.m.* (*tenue militaire*) combat uniform.
treiz|e /trɛz/ *a.* & *n.m.* thirteen. **~ième** *a.* & *n.m.*/*f.* thirteenth.
tréma /trema/ *n.m.* (*gram.*) diaeresis.
trembl|er /trɑ̃ble/ *v.i.* shake, tremble; (*lumière, voix*) quiver. **~ement** *n.m.* shaking; (*frisson*) shiver. **~ement de terre,** earthquake.
trembloter /trɑ̃blɔte/ *v.i.* quiver.
trémousser (se) /(sə)tremuse/ *v. pr.* wriggle, wiggle.
trempe /trɑ̃p/ *n.f.* (*caractère*) calibre.
tremper /trɑ̃pe/ *v.t.*/*i.* soak; (*plonger*) dip; (*acier*) temper. **se ~** *v. pr.* (*se baigner*) have a dip.
tremplin /trɑ̃plɛ̃/ *n.m.* spring-board.
trentaine /trɑ̃tɛn/ *n.f.* **une ~ (de),** about thirty.
trent|e /trɑ̃t/ *a.* & *n.m.* thirty. **~ième** *a.* & *n.m.*/*f.* thirtieth.
trépider /trepide/ *v.i.* vibrate.
trépied /trepje/ *n.m.* tripod.
trépigner /trepiɲe/ *v.i.* stamp one's feet.
très /trɛ/ (/trɛz/ *before vowel*) *adv.* very. **~ aimé/estimé,** much liked/esteemed.
trésor /trezɔr/ *n.m.* treasure; (*ressources: comm.*) finances. **le T~,** the revenue department.
trésorerie /trezɔrri/ *n.f.* (*bureaux*) accounts department; (*du Trésor*) revenue office; (*argent*) finances; (*gestion*) accounts.
trésor|ier, ~ière /trezɔrje, -jɛr/ *n.m., f.* treasurer.
tressaill|ir /tresajir/ *v.i.* shake, quiver; (*sursauter*) start. **~ement** *n.m.* quiver; start.

tressauter /tresote/ *v.i.* (*sursauter*) start.
tresse /trɛs/ *n.f.* braid, plait.
tresser /trese/ *v.t.* braid, plait.
tréteau (*pl.* **~x**) /treto/ *n.m.* trestle. **~x,** (*théâtre*) stage.
treuil /trœj/ *n.m.* winch.
trêve /trɛv/ *n.f.* truce; (*fig.*) respite.
tri /tri/ *n.m.* (*classement*) sorting; (*sélection*) selection. **faire le ~ de,** sort; select. **~age** /-jaʒ/ *n.m.* sorting.
triang|le /trijɑ̃gl/ *n.m.* triangle. **~ulaire** *a.* triangular.
trib|al (*m. pl.* **~aux**) /tribal, -o/ *a.* tribal.
tribord /tribɔr/ *n.m.* starboard.
tribu /triby/ *n.f.* tribe.
tribulations /tribylɑsjɔ̃/ *n.f. pl.* tribulations.
tribun|al (*m. pl.* **~aux**) /tribynal, -o/ *n.m.* court. **~al d'instance,** magistrates' court.
tribune /tribyn/ *n.f.* (public) gallery; (*dans un stade*) grandstand; (*d'orateur*) rostrum; (*débat*) forum.
tribut /triby/ *n.m.* tribute.
tributaire /tribytɛr/ *a.* **~ de,** dependent on.
trich|er /triʃe/ *v.i.* cheat. **~erie** *n.f.* cheating. **une ~erie,** piece of trickery. **~eur, ~euse** *n.m., f.* cheat.
tricolore /trikɔlɔr/ *a.* red, white and blue; (*français*: *fig.*) French.
tricot /triko/ *n.m.* knitting; (*pull*) sweater. **en ~,** knitted. **~ de corps,** vest; (*Amer.*) undershirt. **~er** /-ɔte/ *v.t./i.* knit.
trictrac /triktrak/ *n.m.* backgammon.
tricycle /trisikl/ *n.m.* tricycle.
trier /trije/ *v.t.* (*classer*) sort; (*choisir*) select.
trilogie /trilɔʒi/ *n.f.* trilogy.
trimbaler /trɛ̃bale/ *v.t.,* **se ~** *v. pr.* (*fam.*) trail around.
trimer /trime/ *v.i.* (*fam.*) slave.
trimestr|e /trimɛstr/ *n.m.* quarter; (*scol.*) term. **~iel, ~ielle** *a.* quarterly; (*bulletin*) end-of-term.
tringle /trɛ̃gl/ *n.f.* rod.
Trinité /trinite/ *n.f.* **la ~,** (*dogme*) the Trinity; (*fête*) Trinity.
trinquer /trɛ̃ke/ *v.i.* clink glasses.
trio /trijo/ *n.m.* trio.
triomph|e /trijɔ̃f/ *n.m.* triumph. **~al** (*m. pl.* **~aux**) *a.* triumphant.
triomph|er /trijɔ̃fe/ *v.i.* triumph **(de,** over); (*jubiler*) be triumphant. **~ant, ~ante** *a.* triumphant.
trip|es /trip/ *n.f. pl.* (*mets*) tripe; (*entrailles*: *fam.*) guts. **~ier, ~ière** *n.m., f.* tripe butcher.
triple /tripl/ *a.* triple, treble. —*n.m.* **le ~,** three times as much **(de,** as). **~ment** /-əmɑ̃/ *adv.* trebly.
tripl|er /triple/ *v.t./i.* triple, treble. **~és, ~ées** *n.m., f. pl.* triplets.
tripot /tripo/ *n.m.* gambling den.
tripoter /tripɔte/ *v.t.* (*fam.*) fiddle with. —*v.i.* (*fam.*) fiddle about.
trique /trik/ *n.f.* cudgel.
triste /trist/ *a.* sad; (*rue, temps, couleur*) gloomy; (*lamentable*) wretched, dreadful. **~ment** /-əmɑ̃/ *adv.* sadly. **~sse** /-ɛs/ *n.f.* sadness; gloominess.
triturer /trityre/ *v.t.* (*pâte*) knead.
triv|ial (*m. pl.* **~iaux**) /trivjal, -jo/ *a.* coarse. **~ialité** *n.f.* coarseness.
troc /trɔk/ *n.m.* exchange.
troène /trɔɛn/ *n.m.* (*bot.*) privet.
trognon /trɔɲɔ̃/ *n.m.* (*de pomme*) core.
trois /trwɑ/ *a.* & *n.m.* three. **~ième** /-zjɛm/ *a.* & *n.m./f.* third. **~ièmement** /-zjɛmmɑ̃/ *adv.* thirdly.
trolleybus /trɔlɛbys/ *n.m.* trolleybus.
trombe /trɔ̃b/ *n.f.* **~ d'eau,** downpour.
trombone /trɔ̃bɔn/ *n.m.* (*mus.*) trombone; (*agrafe*) paper-clip.

trompe /trɔ̃p/ *n.f.* (*d'éléphant*) trunk; (*mus.*) horn.
tromp|er /trɔ̃pe/ *v.t.* deceive, mislead; (*déjouer*) elude. **se ~er** *v. pr.* be mistaken. **se ~er de route/train**/*etc.*, take the wrong road/train/*etc.* **~erie** *n.f.* deception. **~eur, ~euse** *a.* (*personne*) deceitful; (*chose*) deceptive.
trompette /trɔ̃pɛt/ *n.f.* trumpet.
tronc /trɔ̃/ *n.m.* trunk; (*boîte*) collection box.
tronçon /trɔ̃sɔ̃/ *n.m.* section. **~ner** /-ɔne/ *v.t.* cut into sections.
trôn|e /tron/ *n.m.* throne. **~er** *v.i.* occupy the place of honour.
tronquer /trɔ̃ke/ *v.t.* truncate.
trop /tro/ *adv.* (*grand, loin, etc.*) too; (*boire, marcher, etc.*) too much. **~ (de),** (*quantité*) too much; (*nombre*) too many. **de ~, en ~,** too much; too many. **de ~,** (*intrus*) in the way. **~-plein** *n.m.* excess; (*dispositif*) overflow.
trophée /trɔfe/ *n.m.* trophy.
tropic|al (*m. pl.* **~aux**) /trɔpikal, -o/ *a.* tropical.
tropique /trɔpik/ *n.m.* tropic. **~s,** tropics.
troquer /trɔke/ *v.t.* exchange.
trot /tro/ *n.m.* trot. **aller au ~,** trot. **au ~,** (*fam.*) on the double.
trotter /trɔte/ *v.i.* trot.
trotteuse /trɔtøz/ *n.f.* (*aiguille de montre*) second hand.
trottiner /trɔtine/ *v.i.* patter along.
trottinette /trɔtinɛt/ *n.f.* (*jouet*) scooter.
trottoir /trɔtwar/ *n.m.* pavement; (*Amer.*) sidewalk. **~ roulant,** moving walkway.
trou /tru/ *n.m.* hole; (*moment*) gap; (*lieu: péj.*) dump. **~ (de mémoire),** lapse (of memory). **~ de la serrure,** keyhole.
trouble /trubl/ *a.* (*eau, image*) unclear; (*louche*) shady. —*n.m.* agitation. **~s,** (*pol.*) disturbances; (*méd.*) trouble.
troubl|er /truble/ *v.t.* disturb; (*eau*) make cloudy; (*inquiéter*) trouble. **se ~er** *v. pr.* (*personne*) become flustered. **~-fête** *n.m./f. invar.* killjoy.
trouée /true/ *n.f.* gap, open space; (*mil.*) breach (**dans,** in).
trouer /true/ *v.t.* make a hole *ou* holes in.
trouille /truj/ *n.f.* **avoir la ~,** (*fam.*) be scared.
troupe /trup/ *n.f.* troop; (*d'acteurs*) troupe. **~s,** (*mil.*) troops.
troupeau (*pl.* **~x**) /trupo/ *n.m.* herd; (*de moutons*) flock.
trousse /trus/ *n.f.* case, bag; (*de réparations*) kit. **aux ~s de,** on the tail of.
trousseau (*pl.* **~x**) /truso/ *n.m.* (*de clefs*) bunch; (*de mariée*) trousseau.
trouvaille /truvɑj/ *n.f.* find.
trouver /truve/ *v.t.* find; (*penser*) think. **aller/venir ~,** (*rendre visite à*) go/come and see. **se ~** *v. pr.* find o.s.; (*être*) be; (*se sentir*) feel. **il se trouve que,** it happens that. **se ~ mal,** faint.
truand /tryɑ̃/ *n.m.* gangster.
truc /tryk/ *n.m.* (*moyen*) way; (*artifice*) trick; (*chose: fam.*) thing. **~age** *n.m.* = **truquage.**
truchement /tryʃmɑ̃/ *n.m.* **par le ~ de,** through.
truculent, ~e /trykylɑ̃, -t/ *a.* colourful.
truelle /tryɛl/ *n.f.* trowel.
truffe /tryf/ *n.f.* (*champignon*) truffle; (*nez*) nose.
truffer /tryfe/ *v.t.* (*fam.*) fill, pack (**de,** with).
truie /trɥi/ *n.f.* (*animal*) sow.
truite /trɥit/ *n.f.* trout.
truqu|er /tryke/ *v.t.* fix, rig; (*photo, texte*) fake. **~age** *n.m.* fixing; faking; (*cinéma*) special effect.
trust /trœst/ *n.m* (*comm.*) trust.
tsar /tsar/ *n.m.* tsar, czar.
tsigane /tsigan/ *a.* & *n.m./f.* (Hungarian) gypsy.

tu[1] /ty/ *pron.* (*parent, ami, enfant, etc.*) you.
tu[2] /ty/ *voir* **taire.**
tuba /tyba/ *n.m.* (*mus.*) tuba; (*sport*) snorkel.
tube /tyb/ *n.m.* tube.
tubercul|eux, ~euse /tybɛrkylø, -z/ *a.* **être ~eux,** have tuberculosis. **~ose** *n.f.* tuberculosis.
tubulaire /tybylɛr/ *a.* tubular.
tubulure /tybylyr/ *n.f.* tubing.
tu|er /tɥe/ *v.t.* kill; (*d'une balle*) shoot, kill; (*épuiser*) exhaust. **se ~er** *v. pr.* kill o.s.; (*accident*) be killed. **~é, ~ée** *n.m., f.* person killed. **~eur, ~euse** *n.m., f.* killer.
tuerie /tyri/ *n.f.* slaughter.
tue-tête (à) /(a)tytɛt/ *adv.* at the top of one's voice.
tuile /tɥil/ *n.f.* tile; (*malchance: fam.*) (stroke of) bad luck.
tulipe /tylip/ *n.f.* tulip.
tuméfié /tymefje/ *a.* swollen.
tumeur /tymœr/ *n.f.* tumour.
tumult|e /tymylt/ *n.m.* commotion; (*désordre*) turmoil. **~ueux, ~ueuse** *a.* turbulent.
tunique /tynik/ *n.f.* tunic.
Tunisie /tynizi/ *n.f.* Tunisia.
tunisien, ~ne /tynizjɛ̃, -jɛn/ *a.* & *n.m., f.* Tunisian.
tunnel /tynɛl/ *n.m.* tunnel.
turban /tyrbɑ̃/ *n.m.* turban.
turbine /tyrbin/ *n.f.* turbine.
turbulen|t, ~te /tyrbylɑ̃, -t/ *a.* boisterous, turbulent. **~ce** *n.f.* turbulence.
tur|c, ~que /tyrk/ *a.* Turkish. —*n.m., f.* Turk. —*n.m.* (*lang.*) Turkish.
turf /tyrf/ *n.m.* **le ~,** the turf. **~iste** *n.m./f.* racegoer.
Turquie /tyrki/ *n.f.* Turkey.
turquoise /tyrkwaz/ *a. invar.* turquoise.
tutelle /tytɛl/ *n.f.* (*jurid.*) guardianship; (*fig.*) protection.
tu|teur, ~trice /tytœr, -tris/ *n.m., f.* (*jurid.*) guardian. —*n.m.* (*bâton*) stake.
tut|oyer /tytwaje/ *v.t.* address familiarly (using *tu*). **~oiement** *n.m.* use of (familiar) *tu*.
tuyau (*pl.* **~x**) /tɥijo/ *n.m.* pipe; (*conseil: fam.*) tip. **~ d'arrosage,** hose-pipe. **~ter** *v.t.* (*fam.*) give a tip to. **~terie** *n.f.* piping.
TVA *abrév.* (*taxe sur la valeur ajoutée*) VAT.
tympan /tɛ̃pɑ̃/ *n.m.* ear-drum.
type /tip/ *n.m.* (*modèle*) type; (*traits*) features; (*individu: fam.*) bloke, guy. —*a. invar.* typical. **le ~ même de,** a classic example of.
typhoïde /tifɔid/ *n.f.* typhoid (fever).
typhon /tifɔ̃/ *n.m.* typhoon.
typhus /tifys/ *n.m.* typhus.
typique /tipik/ *a.* typical. **~ment** *adv.* typically.
tyran /tirɑ̃/ *n.m.* tyrant.
tyrann|ie /tirani/ *n.f.* tyranny. **~ique** *a.* tyrannical. **~iser** *v.t.* oppress, tyrannize.

U

ulcère /ylsɛr/ *n.m.* ulcer.
ulcérer /ylsere/ *v.t.* (*vexer*) embitter, gall.
ultérieur /ylterjœr/ *a.*, **~ement** *adv.* later.
ultimatum /yltimatɔm/ *n.m.* ultimatum.
ultime /yltim/ *a.* final.
ultra- /yltra/ *préf.* ultra-.
un, une /œ̃, yn/ *a.* one; (*indéfini*) a, an. **~ enfant,** /œ̃nɑ̃fɑ̃/ a child. —*pron.* & *n.m., f.* one. **l'~,** one. **les ~s,** some. **l'~ et l'autre,** both. **l'~ l'autre, les ~s les autres,** each other. **l'~ ou l'autre,** either. **la ~e,** (*de journal*) front page. **~ autre,** another.
unanim|e /ynanim/ *a.* unanimous.

~ité *n.f.* unanimity. **à l'~ité,** unanimously.

uni /yni/ *a.* united; (*couple*) close; (*surface*) smooth; (*sans dessins*) plain.

unième /ynjɛm/ *a.* -first. **vingt et ~,** twenty-first. **cent ~,** one hundred and first.

unif|ier /ynifje/ *v.t.* unify. **~ication** *n.f.* unification.

uniform|e /ynifɔrm/ *n.m.* uniform. —*a.* uniform. **~ément** *adv.* uniformly. **~iser** *v.t.* standardize. **~ité** *n.f.* uniformity.

unilatér|al (*m. pl.* **~aux**) /ynilateral, -o/ *a.* unilateral.

union /ynjɔ̃/ *n.f.* union. **l'U~ soviétique,** the Soviet Union.

unique /ynik/ *a.* (*seul*) only; (*prix, voie*) one; (*incomparable*) unique. **~ment** *adv.* only, solely.

unir /ynir/ *v.t.*, **s'~** *v. pr.* unite, join.

unisson (à l') /(al)ynisɔ̃/ *adv.* in unison.

unité /ynite/ *n.f.* unit; (*harmonie*) unity.

univers /ynivɛr/ *n.m.* universe.

universel, ~le /ynivɛrsɛl/ *a.* universal.

universit|é /ynivɛrsite/ *n.f.* university. **~aire** *a.* university; *n.m./f.* academic.

uranium /yranjɔm/ *n.m.* uranium.

urbain, ~e /yrbɛ̃, -ɛn/ *a.* urban.

urbanisme /yrbanism/ *n.m.* town planning; (*Amer.*) city planning.

urgence /yrʒɑ̃s/ *n.f.* (*cas*) emergency; (*de situation, tâche, etc.*) urgency. **d'~** *a.* emergency; *adv.* urgently.

urgent, ~e /yrʒɑ̃, -t/ *a.* urgent.

urin|e /yrin/ *n.f.* urine. **~er** *v.i.* urinate.

urinoir /yrinwar/ *n.m.* urinal.

urne /yrn/ *n.f.* (*électorale*) ballot-box; (*vase*) urn. **aller aux ~s,** go to the polls.

URSS *abrév.* (*Union des Républiques Socialistes Soviétiques*) USSR.

usage /yzaʒ/ *n.m.* use; (*coutume*) custom; (*de langage*) usage. **à l'~ de,** for. **d'~,** (*habituel*) customary. **faire ~ de,** make use of.

usagé /yzaʒe/ *a.* worn.

usager /yzaʒe/ *n.m.* user.

usé /yze/ *a.* worn (out); (*banal*) trite.

user /yze/ *v.t.* wear (out); (*consommer*) use (up). —*v.i.* **~ de,** use. **s'~** *v. pr.* (*tissu etc.*) wear (out).

usine /yzin/ *n.f.* factory; (*de métallurgie*) works.

usité /yzite/ *a.* common.

ustensile /ystɑ̃sil/ *n.m.* utensil.

usuel, ~le /yzɥɛl/ *a.* ordinary, everyday.

usure /yzyr/ *n.f.* (*détérioration*) wear (and tear).

usurper /yzyrpe/ *v.t.* usurp.

utérus /yterys/ *n.m.* womb, uterus.

utile /ytil/ *a.* useful. **~ment** *adv.* usefully.

utilis|er /ytilize/ *v.t.* use. **~able** *a.* usable. **~ation** *n.f.* use.

utilitaire /ytilitɛr/ *a.* utilitarian.

utilité /ytilite/ *n.f.* use(fulness).

utop|ie /ytɔpi/ *n.f.* Utopia; (*idée*) Utopian idea. **~ique** *a.* Utopian.

V

va /va/ *voir* **aller**[1].

vacanc|e /vakɑ̃s/ *n.f.* (*poste*) vacancy. **~es,** holiday(s); (*Amer.*) vacation. **en ~es,** on holiday. **~ier, ~ière** *n.m., f.* holiday-maker; (*Amer.*) vacationer.

vacant, ~e /vakɑ̃, -t/ *a.* vacant.

vacarme /vakarm/ *n.m.* uproar.

vaccin /vaksɛ̃/ *n.m.* vaccine; (*inoculation*) vaccination.

vaccin|er /vaksine/ *v.t.* vaccinate. **~ation** *n.f.* vaccination.

vache /vaʃ/ *n.f.* cow. —*a.* (*méchant*: *fam.*) nasty. **~ment** *adv.* (*très*: *fam.*) damned; (*pleuvoir, manger, etc.*: *fam.*) a hell of a lot. **~r** /-e/ *n.m.* cowherd. **~rie** *n.f.* (*fam.*) nastiness; (*chose*: *fam.*) nasty thing.

vacill|er /vasije/ *v.i.* sway, wobble; (*lumière*) flicker; (*fig.*) falter. **~ant, ~ante** *a.* (*mémoire, démarche*) shaky.

vadrouiller /vadruje/ *v.i.* (*fam.*) wander about.

va-et-vient /vaevjɛ̃/ *n.m. invar.* to and fro motion; (*de personnes*) comings and goings.

vagabond, ~e /vagabɔ̃, -d/ *n.m., f.* vagrant, vagabond. **~er** /-de/ *v.i.* wander.

vagin /vaʒɛ̃/ *n.m.* vagina.

vagir /vaʒir/ *v.i.* cry.

vague[1] /vag/ *a.* vague. —*n.m.* vagueness. **il est resté dans le ~,** he was vague about it. **~ment** *adv.* vaguely.

vague[2] /vag/ *n.f.* wave. **~ de fond,** ground swell. **~ de froid,** cold spell.

vaill|ant, ~ante /vajɑ̃, -t/ *a.* brave; (*vigoureux*) healthy. **~amment** /-amɑ̃/ *adv.* bravely. **~ance** *n.f.* bravery.

vaille /vaj/ *voir* **valoir.**

vain, ~e /vɛ̃, vɛn/ *a.* vain. **en ~,** in vain. **~ement** /vɛnmɑ̃/ *adv.* vainly.

vain|cre† /vɛ̃kr/ *v.t.* defeat; (*surmonter*) overcome. **~cu, ~cue** *n.m., f.* (*sport*) loser. **~queur** *n.m.* victor; (*sport*) winner.

vais /vɛ/ *voir* **aller**[1]**.**

vaisseau (*pl.* **~x**) /vɛso/ *n.m.* ship; (*veine*) vessel. **~ spatial,** spaceship.

vaisselle /vɛsɛl/ *n.f.* crockery; (*à laver*) dishes. **faire la ~,** do the washing-up, wash the dishes.

val (*pl.* **~s** *ou* **vaux**) /val, vo/ *n.m.* valley.

valable /valabl/ *a.* valid; (*de qualité*) worthwhile.

valet /valɛ/ *n.m.* (*cartes*) jack. **~ (de chambre),** manservant. **~ de ferme,** farm-hand.

valeur /valœr/ *n.f.* value; (*mérite*) worth, value. **~s,** (*comm.*) stocks and shares. **avoir de la ~,** be valuable.

valid|e /valid/ *a.* (*personne*) fit; (*billet*) valid. **~er** *v.t.* validate. **~ité** *n.f.* validity.

valise /valiz/ *n.f.* (suit)case. **faire ses ~s,** pack (one's bags).

vallée /vale/ *n.f.* valley.

vallon /valɔ̃/ *n.m.* (small) valley. **~né** /-ɔne/ *a.* undulating.

valoir† /valwar/ *v.i.* be worth; (*s'appliquer*) apply. **~ qch.,** be worth sth.; (*être aussi bon que*) be as good as sth. —*v.t.* **~ qch. à qn.,** bring s.o. sth. **se ~** *v. pr.* (*être équivalents*) be as good as each other. **faire ~,** put forward to advantage; (*droit*) assert. **~ la peine, ~ le coup,** be worth it. **ça ne vaut rien,** it is no good. **~ mieux faire,** be better to do.

valoriser /valɔrize/ *v.t.* increase the worth of.

vals|e /vals/ *n.f.* waltz. **~er** *v.i.* waltz.

valve /valv/ *n.f.* valve.

vampire /vɑ̃pir/ *n.m.* vampire.

vandal|e /vɑ̃dal/ *n.m./f.* vandal. **~isme** *n.m.* vandalism.

vanille /vanij/ *n.f.* vanilla.

vanit|é /vanite/ *n.f.* vanity. **~eux, ~euse** *a.* vain, conceited.

vanne /van/ *n.f.* (*d'écluse*) sluice(-gate).

vant|ail (*pl.* **~aux**) /vɑ̃taj, -o/ *n.m.* door, flap.

vantard, ~e /vɑ̃tar, -d/ *a.* boastful; *n.m., f.* boaster. **~ise** /-diz/ *n.f.* boastfulness; (*acte*) boast.

vanter /vɑ̃te/ *v.t.* praise. **se ~** *v. pr.* boast (**de**, about).

va-nu-pieds /vanypje/ *n.m./f. invar.* vagabond, beggar.

vapeur[1] /vapœr/ *n.f.* (*eau*) steam; (*brume, émanation*) vapour.

vapeur[2] /vapœr/ *n.m.* (*bateau*) steamer.

vaporeu|x, ~se /vapɔrø, -z/ *a.* hazy; (*léger*) filmy, flimsy.

vaporis|er /vapɔrize/ *v.t.* spray. **~ateur** *n.m.* spray.

vaquer /vake/ *v.i.* **~ à,** attend to.

varappe /varap/ *n.f.* rock climbing.

vareuse /varøz/ *n.f.* (*d'uniforme*) tunic.

variable /varjabl/ *a.* variable; (*temps*) changeable.

variante /varjɑ̃t/ *n.f.* variant.

varicelle /varisɛl/ *n.f.* chicken-pox.

varices /varis/ *n.f. pl.* varicose veins.

var|ier /varje/ *v.t./i.* vary. **~iation** *n.f.* variation. **~ié** *a.* (*non monotone, étendu*) varied; (*divers*) various.

variété /varjete/ *n.f.* variety. **~s,** (*spectacle*) variety.

variole /varjɔl/ *n.f.* smallpox.

vase[1] /vɑz/ *n.m.* vase.

vase[2] /vɑz/ *n.f.* (*boue*) silt, mud.

vaseu|x, ~se /vɑzø, -z/ *a.* (*confus: fam.*) woolly, hazy.

vasistas /vazistɑs/ *n.m.* fan-light, hinged panel (*in door or window*).

vaste /vast/ *a.* vast, huge.

vaudeville /vodvil/ *n.m.* vaude-ville, light comedy.

vau-l'eau (à) /(a)volo/ *adv.* on the road to ruin.

vaurien, ~ne /vorjɛ̃, -jɛn/ *n.m., f.* good-for-nothing.

vautour /votur/ *n.m.* vulture.

vautrer (se) /(sə)votre/ *v. pr.* sprawl. **se ~ dans,** (*vice, boue*) wallow in.

va-vite (à la) /(ala)vavit/ *adv.* (*fam.*) in a hurry.

veau (*pl.* **~x**) /vo/ *n.m.* calf; (*viande*) veal.

vécu /veky/ *voir* **vivre.** *—a.* (*réel*) true, real.

vedette[1] /vədɛt/ *n.f.* (*artiste*) star. **en ~,** (*objet*) in a prominent position; (*personne*) in the limelight.

vedette[2] /vədɛt/ *n.f.* (*bateau*) launch.

végét|al (*m. pl.* **~aux**) /veʒetal, -o/ *a.* plant. *—n.m.* (*pl.* **~aux**) plant.

végétarien, ~ne /veʒetarjɛ̃, -jɛn/ *n.m., f.* vegetarian.

végétation /veʒetɑsjɔ̃/ *n.f.* vegetation. **~s,** (*méd.*) adenoids.

végéter /veʒete/ *v.i.* vegetate.

véhémen|t, ~te /veemɑ̃, -t/ *a.* vehement. **~ce** *n.f.* vehemence.

véhicul|e /veikyl/ *n.m.* vehicle. **~er** *v.t.* convey.

veille[1] /vɛj/ *n.f.* **la ~ (de),** the day before. **la ~ de Noël,** Christmas Eve. **à la ~ de,** on the eve of.

veille[2] /vɛj/ *n.f.* (*état*) wakefulness.

veillée /veje/ *n.f.* evening (gathering); (*mortuaire*) vigil, wake.

veiller /veje/ *v.i.* stay up *ou* awake. **~ à,** attend to. **~ sur,** watch over. *—v.t.* (*malade*) watch over.

veilleur /vɛjœr/ *n.m.* **~ de nuit,** night-watchman.

veilleuse /vɛjøz/ *n.f.* night-light; (*de véhicule*) sidelight; (*de réchaud*) pilot-light.

veinard, ~e /vɛnar, -d/ *n.m., f.* (*fam.*) lucky devil.

veine[1] /vɛn/ *n.f.* (*anat.*) vein; (*nervure, filon*) vein.

veine[2] /vɛn/ *n.f.* (*chance: fam.*) luck. **avoir de la ~,** (*fam.*) be lucky.

vélo /velo/ *n.m.* bicycle, bike; (*activité*) cycling.

vélodrome /velɔdrɔm/ *n.m.* velo-drome, cycle-racing track.

vélomoteur /velɔmɔtœr/ *n.m.* moped.

velours /vlur/ *n.m.* velvet. **~ côtelé, ~ à côtes,** corduroy.

velouté /vəlute/ *a.* smooth. —*n.m.* smoothness.

velu /vəly/ *a.* hairy.

venaison /vənɛzɔ̃/ *n.f.* venison.

vendang|e(s) /vɑ̃dɑ̃ʒ/ *n.f.* (*pl.*) grape harvest. **~er** *v.i.* pick the grapes. **~eur, ~euse** *n.m., f.* grape-picker.

vendetta /vɑ̃deta/ *n.f.* vendetta.

vendeu|r, ~se /vɑ̃dœr, -øz/ *n.m., f.* shop assistant; (*marchand*) salesman, saleswoman; (*jurid.*) vendor, seller.

vendre /vɑ̃dr/ *v.t.*, **se ~** *v. pr.* sell. **à ~,** for sale.

vendredi /vɑ̃drədi/ *n.m.* Friday. **V~ saint,** Good Friday.

vénéneu|x, ~se /venenø, -z/ *a.* poisonous.

vénérable /venerabl/ *a.* venerable.

vénérer /venere/ *v.t.* revere.

vénérien, ~ne /venerjɛ̃, -jɛn/ *a.* venereal.

vengeance /vɑ̃ʒɑ̃s/ *n.f.* revenge, vengeance.

veng|er /vɑ̃ʒe/ *v.t.* avenge. **se ~er** *v. pr.* take (one's) revenge (**de,** for). **~eur, ~eresse** *a.* vengeful; *n.m., f.* avenger.

ven|in /vənɛ̃/ *n.m.* venom. **~imeux, ~imeuse** *a.* poisonous, venomous.

venir† /vənir/ *v.i.* (*aux. être*) come (**de,** from). **~ faire,** come to do. **venez faire,** come and do. **il vient/venait d'arriver,** he has/had just arrived. **en ~ à,** (*question, conclusion, etc.*) come to. **en ~ aux mains,** come to blows. **faire ~,** send for. **il m'est venu à l'esprit** *ou* **à l'idée que,** it occurred to me that.

vent /vɑ̃/ *n.m.* wind. **être dans le ~,** (*fam.*) be with it. **il fait du ~,** it is windy.

vente /vɑ̃t/ *n.f.* sale. **~ (aux enchères),** auction. **en ~,** on *ou* for sale. **~ de charité,** (charity) bazaar.

ventil|er /vɑ̃tile/ *v.t.* ventilate. **~ateur** *n.m.* fan, ventilator. **~ation** *n.f.* ventilation.

ventouse /vɑ̃tuz/ *n.f.* (*dispositif*) suction pad; (*pour déboucher l'évier etc.*) plunger.

ventre /vɑ̃tr/ *n.m.* belly, stomach; (*utérus*) womb. **avoir/prendre du ~,** have/develop a paunch.

ventriloque /vɑ̃trilɔk/ *n.m./f.* ventriloquist.

ventru /vɑ̃try/ *a.* pot-bellied.

venu /vəny/ *voir* **venir.** —*a.* **bien ~,** (*à propos*) timely. **mal ~,** untimely. **être mal ~ de faire,** have no grounds for doing.

venue /vəny/ *n.f.* coming.

vêpres /vɛpr/ *n.f. pl.* vespers.

ver /vɛr/ *n.m.* worm; (*des fruits, de la viande*) maggot.

véranda /verɑ̃da/ *n.f.* veranda.

verb|e /vɛrb/ *n.m.* (*gram.*) verb. **~al** (*m. pl.* **~aux**) *a.* verbal.

verbeu|x, ~se /vɛrbø, -z/ *a.* verbose.

verdâtre /vɛrdɑtr/ *a.* greenish.

verdict /vɛrdikt/ *n.m.* verdict.

verdir /vɛrdir/ *v.i.* turn green.

verdoyant, ~e /vɛrdwajɑ̃, -t/ *a.* green, verdant.

verdure /vɛrdyr/ *n.f.* greenery.

véreu|x, ~se /verø, -z/ *a.* maggoty, wormy; (*malhonnête: fig.*) shady.

verger /vɛrʒe/ *n.m.* orchard.

vergla|s /vɛrgla/ *n.m.* (black) ice; (*Amer.*) sleet. **~cé** *a.* icy.

vergogne (sans) /(sɑ̃)vɛrgɔɲ/ *a.* shameless. —*adv.* shamelessly.

véridique /veridik/ *a.* truthful.

vérif|ier /verifje/ *v.t.* check, verify; (*compte*) audit; (*confirmer*) confirm. **~ication** *n.f.* check(ing), verification.

véritable /veritabl/ *a.* true, real; (*authentique*) real. **~ment** /-əmɑ̃/ *adv.* really.

vérité /verite/ *n.f.* truth; (*de tableau, roman*) trueness to life. **en ~,** in fact.
vermeil, ~le /vɛrmɛj/ *a.* bright red, vermilion.
vermicelle(s) /vɛrmisɛl/ *n.m.* (*pl.*) vermicelli.
vermine /vɛrmin/ *n.f.* vermin.
vermoulu /vɛrmuly/ *a.* worm-eaten.
vermouth /vɛrmut/ *n.m.* (*apéritif*) vermouth.
verni /vɛrni/ *a.* (*fam.*) lucky.
vernir /vɛrnir/ *v.t.* varnish.
vernis /vɛrni/ *n.m.* varnish; (*de poterie*) glaze. **~ à ongles,** nail polish *ou* varnish.
vernisser /vɛrnise/ *v.t.* glaze.
verra, verrait /vɛra, vɛrɛ/ *voir* **voir.**
verre /vɛr/ *n.m.* glass. **prendre** *ou* **boire un ~,** have a drink. **~ de contact,** contact lens. **~ dépoli/grossissant,** frosted/magnifying glass. **~rie** *n.f.* (*objets*) glassware.
verrière /vɛrjɛr/ *n.f.* (*toit*) glass roof; (*paroi*) glass wall.
verrou /vɛru/ *n.m.* bolt. **sous les ~s,** behind bars.
verrouiller /vɛruje/ *v.t.* bolt.
verrue /vɛry/ *n.f.* wart.
vers[1] /vɛr/ *prép.* towards; (*temps*) about.
vers[2] /vɛr/ *n.m.* (*ligne*) line. **les ~,** (*poésie*) verse.
versant /vɛrsɑ̃/ *n.m.* slope, side.
versatile /vɛrsatil/ *a.* fickle.
verse (à) /(a)vɛrs/ *adv.* in torrents.
versé /vɛrse/ *a.* **~ dans,** versed in.
vers|er /vɛrse/ *v.t./i.* pour; (*larmes, sang*) shed; (*basculer*) overturn; (*payer*) pay. **~ement** *n.m.* payment.
verset /vɛrsɛ/ *n.m.* (*relig.*) verse.
version /vɛrsjɔ̃/ *n.f.* version; (*traduction*) translation.
verso /vɛrso/ *n.m.* back (of the page).
vert, ~e /vɛr, -t/ *a.* green; (*vieillard*) sprightly. —*n.m.* green.
vertèbre /vɛrtɛbr/ *n.f.* vertebra.
vertement /vɛrtəmɑ̃/ *adv.* sharply.
vertic|al, ~ale (*m. pl.* **~aux**) /vɛrtikal, -o/ *a.* & *n.f.* vertical. **à la ~ale, ~alement** *adv.* vertically.
vertig|e /vɛrtiʒ/ *n.m.* dizziness. **~es,** dizzy spells. **avoir le** *ou* **un ~e,** feel dizzy. **~ineux, ~ineuse** *a.* dizzy; (*très grand*) staggering.
vertu /vɛrty/ *n.f.* virtue. **en ~ de,** by virtue of. **~eux, ~euse** /-tɥø, -z/ *a.* virtuous.
verve /vɛrv/ *n.f.* spirit, wit.
vessie /vesi/ *n.f.* bladder.
veste /vɛst/ *n.f.* jacket.
vestiaire /vɛstjɛr/ *n.m.* cloakroom; (*sport*) changing-room.
vestibule /vɛstibyl/ *n.m.* hall.
vestige /vɛstiʒ/ *n.m.* (*objet*) relic; (*trace*) vestige.
veston /vɛstɔ̃/ *n.m.* jacket.
vêtement /vɛtmɑ̃/ *n.m.* article of clothing. **~s,** clothes.
vétéran /veterɑ̃/ *n.m.* veteran.
vétérinaire /veterinɛr/ *n.m./f.* veterinary surgeon, (*Amer.*) veterinarian. —*a.* veterinary.
vétille /vetij/ *n.f.* trifle.
vêt|ir /vetir/ *v.t.*, **se ~ir** *v. pr.* dress. **~u** *a.* dressed (**de,** in).
veto /veto/ *n.m. invar.* veto.
vétuste /vetyst/ *a.* dilapidated.
veu|f, ~ve /vœf, -v/ *a.* widowed. —*n.m.* widower. —*n.f.* widow.
veuille /vœj/ *voir* **vouloir.**
veule /vøl/ *a.* feeble.
veut, veux /vø/ *voir* **vouloir.**
vexation /vɛksɑsjɔ̃/ *n.f.* humiliation.
vex|er /vɛkse/ *v.t.* upset, hurt. **se ~er** *v. pr.* be upset, be hurt. **~ant, ~ante** *a.* upsetting.
via /vja/ *prép.* via.
viable /vjabl/ *a.* viable.
viaduc /vjadyk/ *n.m.* viaduct.

viande /vjɑ̃d/ *n.f.* meat.

vibr|er /vibre/ *v.i.* vibrate; (*être ému*) thrill. **~ant, ~ante** *a.* (*émouvant*) vibrant. **~ation** *n.f.* vibration.

vicaire /vikɛr/ *n.m.* curate.

vice /vis/ *n.m.* (*moral*) vice; (*défectuosité*) defect.

vice- /vis/ *préf.* vice-.

vice versa /vis(e)vɛrsa/ *adv.* vice versa.

vicier /visje/ *v.t.* taint.

vicieu|x, ~se /visjø, -z/ *a.* depraved. —*n.m., f.* pervert.

vicin|al (*pl.* **~aux**) /visinal, -o/ *a.m.* **chemin ~al,** by-road, minor road.

vicomte /vikɔ̃t/ *n.m.* viscount.

victime /viktim/ *n.f.* victim; (*d'un accident*) casualty.

vict|oire /viktwar/ *n.f.* victory; (*sport*) win. **~orieux, ~orieuse** *a.* victorious; (*équipe*) winning.

victuailles /viktɥɑj/ *n.f. pl.* provisions.

vidang|e /vidɑ̃ʒ/ *n.f.* emptying; (*auto.*) oil change; (*dispositif*) waste pipe. **~er** *v.t.* empty.

vide /vid/ *a.* empty. —*n.m.* emptiness, void; (*trou, manque*) gap; (*espace sans air*) vacuum. **à ~,** empty.

vidéo /video/ *a. invar.* video.

vider /vide/ *v.t.* empty; (*poisson*) gut; (*lieu*) vacate; (*expulser: fam.*) throw out. **se ~** *v. pr.* empty.

vie /vi/ *n.f.* life; (*durée*) lifetime. **à ~, pour la ~,** for life. **donner la ~ à,** give birth to. **en ~,** alive. **~ chère,** high cost of living.

vieil /vjɛj/ *voir* **vieux.**

vieillard /vjɛjar/ *n.m.* old man.

vieille /vjɛj/ *voir* **vieux.**

vieillesse /vjɛjɛs/ *n.f.* old age.

vieill|ir /vjejir/ *v.i.* grow old, age; (*mot, idée*) become old-fashioned. —*v.t.* age. **~issement** *n.m.* ageing.

viens, vient /vjɛ̃/ *voir* **venir.**

vierge /vjɛrʒ/ *n.f.* virgin. —*a.* virgin; (*feuille, film*) blank.

vieux *ou* **vieil*, vieille** (*m. pl.* **vieux**) /vjø, vjɛj/ *a.* old. —*n.m.* old man. —*n.f.* old woman. **les ~,** old people. **mon ~,** (*fam.*) old man *ou* boy. **ma vieille,** (*fam.*) old girl, dear. **vieille fille,** (*péj.*) spinster. **~ garçon,** bachelor. **~ jeu** *a. invar.* old-fashioned.

vif, vive /vif, viv/ *a.* lively; (*émotion, vent*) keen; (*froid*) biting; (*lumière*) bright; (*douleur, parole*) sharp; (*souvenir, style, teint*) vivid; (*succès, impatience*) great. **brûler/enterrer ~,** burn/bury alive.

vigie /viʒi/ *n.f.* look-out.

vigilan|t, ~te /viʒilɑ̃, -t/ *a.* vigilant. **~ce** *n.f.* vigilance.

vigne /viɲ/ *n.f.* (*plante*) vine; (*vignoble*) vineyard.

vigneron, ~ne /viɲrɔ̃, -ɔn/ *n.m., f.* wine-grower.

vignette /viɲɛt/ *n.f.* (*étiquette*) label; (*auto.*) road tax sticker.

vignoble /viɲɔbl/ *n.m.* vineyard.

vigoureu|x, ~se /vigurø, -z/ *a.* vigorous, sturdy.

vigueur /vigœr/ *n.f.* vigour. **être/entrer en ~,** (*loi*) be/come into force. **en ~,** (*terme*) in use.

vil /vil/ *a.* vile, base.

vilain, ~e /vilɛ̃, -ɛn/ *a.* (*mauvais*) nasty; (*laid*) ugly.

villa /villa/ *n.f.* (detached) house.

village /vilaʒ/ *n.m.* village.

villageois, ~e /vilaʒwa, -z/ *a.* village. —*n.m., f.* villager.

ville /vil/ *n.f.* town; (*importante*) city. **~ d'eaux,** spa.

vin /vɛ̃/ *n.m.* wine. **~ d'honneur,** reception. **~ ordinaire,** table wine.

vinaigre /vinɛgr/ *n.m.* vinegar.

vinaigrette /vinɛgrɛt/ *n.f.* oil and vinegar dressing, vinaigrette.

vindicati|f, ~ve /vɛ̃dikatif, -v/ *a.* vindictive.

vingt /vɛ̃/ (/vɛ̃t/ *before vowel and in numbers 22-29*) *a.* & *n.m.* twenty. **~ième** *a.* & *n.m./f.* twentieth.

vingtaine /vɛ̃tɛn/ *n.f.* **une ~ (de),** about twenty.

vinicole /vinikɔl/ *a.* wine(-growing).

vinyle /vinil/ *n.m.* vinyl.

viol /vjɔl/ *n.m.* (*de femme*) rape; (*de lieu, loi*) violation.

violacé /vjɔlase/ *a.* purplish.

viol|ent, ~ente /vjɔlɑ̃, -t/ *a.* violent. **~emment** /-amɑ̃/ *adv.* violently. **~ence** *n.f.* violence; (*acte*) act of violence.

violenter /vjɔlɑ̃te/ *v.t.* rape.

viol|er /vjɔle/ *v.t.* rape; (*lieu, loi*) violate. **~ation** *n.f.* violation.

violet, ~te /vjɔlɛ, -t/ *a.* & *n.m.* purple. —*n.f.* violet.

violon /vjɔlɔ̃/ *n.m.* violin. **~iste** /-ɔnist/ *n.m./f.* violinist.

violoncell|e /vjɔlɔ̃sɛl/ *n.m.* cello. **~iste** /-elist/ *n.m./f.* cellist.

vipère /vipɛr/ *n.f.* viper, adder.

virage /viraʒ/ *n.m.* bend; (*de véhicule*) turn; (*changement d'attitude: fig.*) change of course.

virée /vire/ *n.f.* (*fam.*) trip, outing.

vir|er /vire/ *v.i.* turn; (*avion*) bank. **~er au rouge**/*etc.*, turn red/*etc.* —*v.t.* (*argent*) transfer; (*expulser: fam.*) throw out. **~ement** *n.m.* (*comm.*) (credit) transfer.

virevolter /virvɔlte/ *v.i.* spin round, swing round.

virginité /virʒinite/ *n.f.* virginity.

virgule /virgyl/ *n.f.* comma; (*dans un nombre*) (decimal) point.

viril /viril/ *a.* manly, virile. **~ité** *n.f.* manliness, virility.

virtuel, ~le /virtɥɛl/ *a.* virtual. **~lement** *adv.* virtually.

virtuos|e /virtɥoz/ *n.m./f.* virtuoso. **~ité** *n.f.* virtuosity.

virulen|t, ~te /virylɑ̃, -t/ *a.* virulent. **~ce** *n.f.* virulence.

virus /virys/ *n.m.* virus.

vis[1] /vi/ *voir* **vivre, voir.**

vis[2] /vis/ *n.f.* screw.

visa /viza/ *n.m.* visa.

visage /vizaʒ/ *n.m.* face.

vis-à-vis /vizavi/ *adv.* face to face, opposite. **~ de,** opposite; (*à l'égard de*) with respect to. —*n.m. invar.* (*personne*) person opposite.

viscères /visɛr/ *n.m. pl.* intestines.

visée /vize/ *n.f.* aim.

viser /vize/ *v.t.* aim at; (*concerner*) be aimed at; (*timbrer*) stamp. —*v.i.* aim. **~ à,** aim at; (*mesure, propos*) be aimed at.

visib|le /vizibl/ *a.* visible. **~ilité** *n.f.* visibility. **~lement** *adv.* visibly.

visière /vizjɛr/ *n.f.* (*de casquette*) peak; (*de casque*) visor.

vision /vizjɔ̃/ *n.f.* vision.

visionnaire /vizjɔnɛr/ *a.* & *n.m./f.* visionary.

visionn|er /vizjɔne/ *v.t.* view. **~euse** *n.f.* (*appareil*) viewer.

visite /vizit/ *n.f.* visit; (*examen*) examination; (*personne*) visitor. **de ~,** (*heure, carte*) visiting. **~ guidée,** guided tour.

visit|er /vizite/ *v.t.* visit; (*examiner*) examine. **~eur, ~euse** *n.m., f.* visitor.

vison /vizɔ̃/ *n.m.* mink.

visqueu|x, ~se /viskø, -z/ *a.* viscous.

visser /vise/ *v.t.* screw (on).

visuel, ~le /vizɥɛl/ *a.* visual.

vit /vi/ *voir* **vivre, voir.**

vit|al (*m. pl.* **~aux**) /vital, -o/ *a.* vital. **~alité** *n.f.* vitality.

vitamine /vitamin/ *n.f.* vitamin.

vite /vit/ *adv.* fast, quickly; (*tôt*) soon. **~!,** quick!

vitesse /vitɛs/ *n.f.* speed; (*régime: auto.*) gear. **à toute ~,** at top speed. **en ~,** in a hurry, quickly.

vitic|ole /vitikɔl/ *a.* wine. **~ulteur** *n.m.* wine-grower. **~ulture** *n.f.* wine-growing.

vitrage /vitraʒ/ *n.m.* (*vitres*) windows.

vitr|ail (*pl.* **~aux**) /vitraj, -o/ *n.m.* stained-glass window.

vitr|e /vitr/ *n.f.* (window) pane; (*de véhicule*) window. **~é** *a.* glass, glazed. **~er** *v.t.* glaze.

vitrine /vitrin/ *n.f.* (shop) window; (*meuble*) display cabinet.

vivable /vivabl/ *a.* (*personne*) easy to live with; (*maison*) liveable.

vivace /vivas/ *a.* (*plante, sentiment*) perennial.

vivacité /vivasite/ *n.f.* liveliness; (*agilité*) quickness; (*d'émotion, de l'air*) keenness; (*de souvenir, style, teint*) vividness.

vivant, ~e /vivɑ̃, -t/ *a.* (*doué de vie, en usage*) living; (*en vie*) alive, living; (*actif, vif*) lively. —*n.m.* **de son ~,** in one's lifetime. **les ~s,** the living.

vivats /viva/ *n.m. pl.* cheers.

vive[1] /viv/ *voir* **vif.**

vive[2] /viv/ *int.* **~ le roi/président**/*etc.*!, long live the king/president/*etc.*! **~(nt) les vacances!,** hurrah for the holidays!

vivement /vivmɑ̃/ *adv.* (*vite, sèchement*) sharply; (*avec éclat*) vividly; (*beaucoup*) greatly. **~ la fin!,** roll on the end, I'll be glad when it's the end!

viveur /vivœr/ *n.m.* pleasure-seeker.

vivier /vivje/ *n.m.* fish-pond.

vivifier /vivifje/ *v.t.* invigorate.

vivisection /vivisɛksjɔ̃/ *n.f.* vivisection.

vivoter /vivɔte/ *v.i.* plod on, get by.

vivre† /vivr/ *v.i.* live. **~ de,** (*nourriture*) live on. —*v.t.* (*vie*) live; (*période, aventure*) live through. **~s** *n.m. pl.* supplies. **faire ~,** (*famille etc.*) support. **~ encore,** be still alive.

vlan /vlɑ̃/ *int.* bang.

vocabulaire /vɔkabylɛr/ *n.m.* vocabulary.

voc|al (*m. pl.* **~aux**) /vɔkal, -o/ *a.* vocal.

vocalise /vɔkaliz/ *n.f.* voice exercise.

vocation /vɔkɑsjɔ̃/ *n.f.* vocation.

vodka /vɔdka/ *n.f.* vodka.

vœu (*pl.* **~x**) /vø/ *n.m.* (*souhait*) wish; (*promesse*) vow.

vogue /vɔg/ *n.f.* fashion, vogue.

voguer /vɔge/ *v.i.* sail.

voici /vwasi/ *prép.* here is, this is; (*au pluriel*) here are, these are. **me ~,** here I am. **~ un an,** (*temps passé*) a year ago. **~ un an que,** it is a year since.

voie /vwa/ *n.f.* (*route*) road; (*chemin*) way; (*moyen*) means, way; (*partie de route*) lane; (*rails*) track; (*quai*) platform. **en ~ de,** in the process of. **en ~ de développement,** (*pays*) developing. **par la ~ des airs,** by air. **~ de dégagement,** slip-road. **~ ferrée,** railway; (*Amer.*) railroad. **~ lactée,** Milky Way. **~ navigable,** waterway. **~ publique,** public highway. **~ sans issue,** cul-de-sac, dead end.

voilà /vwala/ *prép.* there is, that is; (*au pluriel*) there are, those are; (*voici*) here is; here are. **le ~,** there he is. **~!,** right!; (*en offrant qch.*) there you are! **~ un an,** (*temps passé*) a year ago. **~ un an que,** it is a year since.

voilage /vwalaʒ/ *n.m.* net curtain.

voile[1] /vwal/ *n.f.* (*de bateau*) sail; (*sport*) sailing.

voile[2] /vwal/ *n.m.* veil; (*tissu léger et fin*) net.

voil|er[1] /vwale/ *v.t.* veil. **se ~er** *v. pr.* (*devenir flou*) become hazy. **~é** *a.* (*terme, femme*) veiled; (*flou*) hazy.

voiler[2] /vwale/ *v.t.*, **se ~** *v. pr.* (*roue etc.*) buckle.

voilier /vwalje/ *n.m.* sailing-ship.

voilure /vwalyr/ *n.f.* sails.

voir† /vwar/ *v.t./i.* see. **se ~** *v. pr.* (*être visible*) show; (*se produire*) be seen; (*se trouver*) find o.s.; (*se*

vouer /vwe/ *v.t.* dedicate (**à,** to); (*promettre*) vow. **~ à l'échec,** doom to failure.

vouloir† /vulwar/ *v.t.* want (**faire,** to do). **ça ne veut pas bouger/** *etc.*, it will not move/*etc.* **je voudrais/voudrais bien venir/** *etc.*, I should *ou* would like/really like to come/*etc.* **je veux bien venir/***etc.*, I am happy to come/ *etc.* **voulez-vous attendre/***etc.***?**, will you wait/*etc.*? **veuillez attendre/***etc.*, kindly wait/*etc.* **~ absolument faire,** insist on doing. **comme** *ou* **si vous voulez,** if you like *ou* wish. **en ~ à qn.,** have a grudge against s.o.; (*être en colère contre*) be annoyed with s.o. **ne pas ~ de qch./qn.,** not want sth./s.o. **~ dire,** mean. **~ du bien à,** wish well.

voulu /vuly/ *a.* (*délibéré*) intentional; (*requis*) required.

vous /vu/ *pron.* (*sujet, complément*) you; (*indirect*) (to) you; (*réfléchi*) yourself; (*pl.*) yourselves; (*l'un l'autre*) each other. **~-même** *pron.* yourself. **~-mêmes** *pron.* yourselves.

voûte /vut/ *n.f.* (*plafond*) vault; (*porche*) archway.

voûté /vute/ *a.* bent, stooped.

vouv|oyer /vuvwaje/ *v.t.* address politely (using *vous*). **~oiement** *n.m.* use of (polite) *vous*.

voyage /vwajaʒ/ *n.m.* journey, trip; (*par mer*) voyage. **~(s),** (*action*) travelling. **de ~,** (*compagnon etc.*) travelling. **~ organisé,** (package) tour.

voyag|er /vwajaʒe/ *v.i.* travel. **~eur, ~euse** *n.m., f.* traveller.

voyant[1], **~e** /vwajɑ̃, -t/ *a.* gaudy. —*n.f.* (*femme*) clairvoyant.

voyant[2] /vwajɑ̃/ *n.m.* (*signal*) (warning) light.

voyelle /vwajɛl/ *n.f.* vowel.

voyou /vwaju/ *n.m.* hooligan.

vrac (en) /(ɑ̃)vrak/ *adv.* in disorder; (*sans emballage, au poids*) loose, in bulk.

vrai /vrɛ/ *a.* true; (*réel*) real. —*n.m.* truth. **à ~ dire,** to tell the truth.

vraiment /vrɛmɑ̃/ *adv.* really.

vraisembl|able /vrɛsɑ̃blabl/ *a.* likely. **~ablement** *adv.* very likely. **~ance** *n.f.* likelihood, plausibility.

vrille /vrij/ *n.f.* (*aviat.*) spin.

vromb|ir /vrɔ̃bir/ *v.i.* hum. **~issement** *n.m.* humming.

vu /vy/ *voir* **voir.** —*a.* **bien/mal ~,** well/not well thought of. —*prép.* in view of. **~ que,** seeing that.

vue /vy/ *n.f.* (*spectacle*) sight; (*sens*) (eye)sight; (*panorama, idée*) view. **avoir en ~,** have in mind. **à ~,** (*tirer, payable*) at sight. **de ~,** by sight. **perdre de ~,** lose sight of. **en ~,** (*proche*) in sight; (*célèbre*) in the public eye. **en ~ de faire,** with a view to doing.

vulg|aire /vylgɛr/ *a.* (*grossier*) vulgar; (*ordinaire*) common. **~arité** *n.f.* vulgarity.

vulgariser /vylgarize/ *v.t.* popularize.

vulnérab|le /vylnerabl/ *a.* vulnerable. **~ilité** *n.f.* vulnerability.

W

wagon /vagɔ̃/ *n.m.* (*de voyageurs*) carriage; (*Amer.*) car; (*de marchandises*) wagon; (*Amer.*) freight car. **~-lit** (*pl.* **~s-lits**) *n.m.* sleeping-car, sleeper. **~-restaurant** (*pl.* **~s-restaurants**) *n.m.* dining-car.

wallon, ~ne /walɔ̃, -ɔn/ *a.* & *n.m., f.* Walloon.

waters /watɛr/ *n.m. pl.* toilet.

watt /wat/ *n.m.* watt.

w.-c. /(dublə)vese/ *n.m. pl.* toilet.

week-end /wikɛnd/ *n.m.* weekend.

western /wɛstɛrn/ *n.m.* western.
whisk|y (*pl.* **~ies**) /wiski/ *n.m.* whisky.

X

xénophob|e /ksenɔfɔb/ *a.* xenophobic. —*n.m.*/*f.* xenophobe. **~ie** *n.f.* xenophobia.
xérès /gzerɛs/ *n.m.* sherry.
xylophone /ksilɔfɔn/ *n.m.* xylophone.

Y

y /i/ *adv.* & *pron.* there; (*dessus*) on it; (*pl.*) on them; (*dedans*) in it; (*pl.*) in them. **s'~ habituer,** (*à cela*) get used to it. **s'~ attendre,** expect it. **~ penser,** think of it. **il ~ entra,** (*dans cela*) he entered it. **j'~ courus,** (*vers cela*) I ran to it. **ça ~ est,** that is it. **~ être pour qch.,** have sth. to do with it.
yacht /jɔt/ *n.m.* yacht.
yaourt /jaur(t)/ *n.m.* yoghurt.
yeux /jø/ *voir* **œil.**
yiddish /(j)idiʃ/ *n.m.* Yiddish.
yoga /jɔga/ *n.m.* yoga.
yougoslave /jugɔslav/ *a.* & *n.m.*/*f.* Yugoslav.
Yougoslavie /jugɔslavi/ *n.f.* Yugoslavia.
yo-yo /jojo/ *n.m. invar.* (P.) yo-yo (P.).

Z

zèbre /zɛbr/ *n.m.* zebra.
zébré /zebre/ *a.* striped.
zèle /zɛl/ *n.m.* zeal.
zélé /zele/ *a.* zealous.
zénith /zenit/ *n.m.* zenith.
zéro /zero/ *n.m.* nought, zero; (*température*) zero; (*dans un numéro*) 0; (*football*) nil; (*football: Amer.*) zero; (*personne*) nonentity. **(re)partir de ~,** start from scratch.
zeste /zɛst/ *n.m.* peel.
zézayer /zezeje/ *v.i.* lisp.
zigzag /zigzag/ *n.m.* zigzag. **en ~,** zigzag. **~uer** /-e/ *v.i.* zigzag.
zinc /zɛ̃g/ *n.m.* (*métal*) zinc; (*comptoir: fam.*) bar.
zodiaque /zɔdjak/ *n.m.* zodiac.
zona /zona/ *n.m.* (*méd.*) shingles.
zone /zon/ *n.f.* zone, area; (*faubourgs*) shanty town. **~ bleue,** restricted parking zone.
zoo /zo(o)/ *n.m.* zoo.
zoolog|ie /zɔɔlɔʒi/ *n.f.* zoology. **~ique** *a.* zoological. **~iste** *n.m.*/*f.* zoologist.
zoom /zum/ *n.m.* zoom lens.
zut /zyt/ *int.* blast (it), (oh) hell.

ANGLAIS-FRANÇAIS
ENGLISH-FRENCH

A

a /eɪ, *unstressed* ə/ *a.* (*before vowel* **an** /æn, ən/) un(e). **ten pence ~ kilo,** dix pence le kilo. **once ~ year,** une fois par an.

aback /ə'bæk/ *adv.* **taken ~,** déconcerté, interdit.

abandon /ə'bændən/ *v.t.* abandonner. —*n.* désinvolture *f.* **~ed** *a.* (*behaviour*) débauché. **~ment** *n.* abandon *m.*

abase /ə'beɪs/ *v.t.* humilier.

abashed /ə'bæʃt/ *a.* confus.

abate /ə'beɪt/ *v.i.* se calmer. —*v.t.* diminuer. **~ment** *n.* diminution *f.*

abattoir /'æbətwɑː(r)/ *n.* abattoir *m.*

abbey /'æbɪ/ *n.* abbaye *f.*

abb|ot /'æbət/ *n.* abbé *m.* **~ess** *n.* abbesse *f.*

abbreviat|e /ə'briːvɪeɪt/ *v.t.* abréger. **~ion** /-'eɪʃn/ *n.* abréviation *f.*

abdicat|e /'æbdɪkeɪt/ *v.t./i.* abdiquer. **~ion** /-'keɪʃn/ *n.* abdication *f.*

abdom|en /'æbdəmən/ *n.* abdomen *m.* **~inal** /-'dɒmɪnl/ *a.* abdominal.

abduct /æb'dʌkt/ *v.t.* enlever. **~ion** /-kʃn/ *n.* rapt *m.* **~or** *n.* ravisseu|r, -se *m., f.*

aberration /æbə'reɪʃn/ *n.* aberration *f.*

abet /ə'bet/ *v.t.* (*p.t.* **abetted**) (*jurid.*) encourager.

abeyance /ə'beɪəns/ *n.* **in ~,** (*matter*) en suspens; (*custom*) en désuétude.

abhor /əb'hɔː(r)/ *v.t.* (*p.t.* **abhorred**) exécrer. **~rence** /-'hɒrəns/ *n.* horreur *f.* **~rent** /-'hɒrənt/ *a.* exécrable.

abide /ə'baɪd/ *v.t.* (*p.t.* **abided**) supporter. —*v.i.* (*old use*; *p.t.* **abode**) demeurer. **~ by,** rester fidèle à.

abiding /ə'baɪdɪŋ/ *a.* éternel.

ability /ə'bɪlətɪ/ *n.* aptitude *f.* (**to do,** à faire); (*talent*) talent *m.*

abject /'æbdʒekt/ *a.* abject.

ablaze /ə'bleɪz/ *a.* en feu. **~ with,** (*anger etc.*: *fig.*) enflammé de.

abl|e /'eɪbl/ *a.* (**-er, -est**) capable (**to,** de). **be ~e,** pouvoir; (*know how to*) savoir. **~y** *adv.* habilement.

ablutions /ə'bluːʃnz/ *n. pl.* ablutions *f. pl.*

abnormal /æb'nɔːml/ *a.* anormal. **~ity** /-'mælətɪ/ *n.* anomalie *f.* **~ly** *adv.* (*unusually*) exceptionnellement.

aboard /ə'bɔːd/ *adv.* à bord. —*prep.* à bord de.

abode /ə'bəʊd/ *see* **abide.** —*n.* (*old use*) demeure *f.*

aboli|sh /ə'bɒlɪʃ/ *v.t.* supprimer, abolir. **~tion** /æbə'lɪʃn/ *n.* suppression *f.*, abolition *f.*

abominable /ə'bɒmɪnəbl/ *a.* abominable.

abominat|e /ə'bɒmɪneɪt/ *v.t.* exécrer. **~ion** /-'neɪʃn/ *n.* abomination *f.*
aboriginal /æbə'rɪdʒənl/ *a.* & *n.* aborigène (*m.*).
aborigines /æbə'rɪdʒəniːz/ *n. pl.* aborigènes *m. pl.*
abort /ə'bɔːt/ *v.t.* faire avorter. —*v.i.* avorter. **~ive** *a.* (*attempt etc.*) manqué.
abortion /ə'bɔːʃn/ *n.* avortement *m.* **have an ~,** se faire avorter. **~ist** *n.* avorteu|r, -se *m.*, *f.*
abound /ə'baʊnd/ *v.i.* abonder (**in,** en).
about /ə'baʊt/ *adv.* (*approximately*) environ; (*here and there*) çà et là; (*all round*) partout, autour; (*nearby*) dans les parages; (*of rumour*) en circulation. —*prep.* au sujet de; (*round*) autour de; (*somewhere in*) dans. **~-face, ~-turn** *ns.* (*fig.*) volte-face *f. invar.* **~ here,** par ici. **be ~ to,** être sur le point de. **how** *or* **what ~ leaving,** si on partait. **talk ~,** parler de.
above /ə'bʌv/ *adv.* au-dessus; (*on page*) ci-dessus. —*prep.* au-dessus de. **he is not ~ lying,** il n'est pas incapable de mentir. **~ all,** pardessus tout. **~-board** *a.* honnête.
abrasion /ə'breɪʒn/ *n.* frottement *m.*; (*injury*) écorchure *f.*
abrasive /ə'breɪsɪv/ *a.* abrasif; (*irritating*: *fig.*) agaçant. —*n.* abrasif *m.*
abreast /ə'brest/ *adv.* de front. **keep ~ of,** se tenir au courant de.
abridge /ə'brɪdʒ/ *v.t.* abréger. **~ment** *n.* abrégement *m.*, réduction *f.*; (*abridged text*) abrégé *m.*
abroad /ə'brɔːd/ *adv.* à l'étranger; (*far and wide*) de tous côtés.
abrupt /ə'brʌpt/ *a.* (*sudden, curt*) brusque; (*steep*) abrupt. **~ly** *adv.* (*suddenly*) brusquement; (*curtly, rudely*) avec brusquerie. **~ness** *n.* brusquerie *f.*
abscess /'æbses/ *n.* abcès *m.*
abscond /əb'skɒnd/ *v.i.* s'enfuir.
absen|t[1] /'æbsənt/ *a.* absent; (*look etc.*) distrait. **~ce** *n.* absence *f.*; (*lack*) manque *m.* **in the ~ce of,** à défaut de. **~tly** *adv.* distraitement. **~t-minded** *a.* distrait. **~t-mindedness** *n.* distraction *f.*
absent[2] /əb'sent/ *v. pr.* **~ o.s.,** s'absenter.
absentee /æbsən'tiː/ *n.* absent(e) *m.* (*f.*). **~ism** *n.* absentéisme *m.*
absinthe /'æbsɪnθ/ *n.* absinthe *f.*
absolute /'æbsəluːt/ *a.* absolu; (*coward etc.*: *fam.*) véritable. **~ly** *adv.* absolument.
absolution /æbsə'luːʃn/ *n.* absolution *f.*
absolve /əb'zɒlv/ *v.t.* (*from sin*) absoudre (**from,** de); (*from vow etc.*) délier (**from, de**).
absor|b /əb'sɔːb/ *v.t.* absorber. **~ption** *n.* absorption *f.*
absorbent /əb'sɔːbənt/ *a.* absorbant. **~ cotton,** (*Amer.*) coton hydrophile *m.*
abst|ain /əb'steɪn/ *v.i.* s'abstenir (**from,** de). **~ention** /-'stenʃn/ *n.* abstention *f.*; (*from drink*) abstinence *f.*
abstemious /əb'stiːmɪəs/ *a.* sobre.
abstinen|ce /'æbstɪnəns/ *n.* abstinence *f.* **~t** *a.* sobre.
abstract[1] /'æbstrækt/ *a.* abstrait. —*n.* (*quality*) abstrait *m.*; (*summary*) résumé *m.*
abstract[2] /əb'strækt/ *v.t.* retirer, extraire. **~ion** /-kʃn/ *n.* extraction *f.*; (*idea*) abstraction *f.*
abstruse /əb'struːs/ *a.* obscur.
absurd /əb'sɜːd/ *a.* absurde. **~ity** *n.* absurdité *f.*
abundan|t /ə'bʌndənt/ *a.* abondant. **~ce** *n.* abondance *f.* **~tly** *adv.* (*entirely*) tout à fait.
abuse[1] /ə'bjuːz/ *v.t.* (*misuse*) abuser de; (*ill-treat*) maltraiter; (*insult*) injurier.

abus|e² /əˈbjuːs/ *n.* (*misuse*) abus *m.* (**of**, de); (*insults*) injures *f. pl.* **~ive** *a.* injurieux.
abut /əˈbʌt/ *v.i.* (*p.t.* **abutted**) être contigu (**on**, à).
abysmal /əˈbɪzməl/ *a.* (*great*) profond; (*bad*: *fam.*) exécrable.
abyss /əˈbɪs/ *n.* abîme *m.*
academic /ækəˈdemɪk/ *a.* universitaire; (*scholarly*) intellectuel; (*pej.*) théorique. —*n.* universitaire *m./f.* **~ally** /-lɪ/ *adv.* intellectuellement.
academ|y /əˈkædəmɪ/ *n.* (*school*) école *f.* **A~y**, (*society*) Académie *f.* **~ician** /-ˈmɪʃn/ *n.* académicien(ne) *m.* (*f.*).
accede /əkˈsiːd/ *v.i.* **~ to**, (*request, post, throne*) accéder à.
accelerat|e /əkˈseləreɪt/ *v.t.* accélérer. —*v.i.* (*speed up*) s'accélérer; (*auto.*) accélérer. **~ion** /-ˈreɪʃn/ *n.* accélération *f.*
accelerator /əkˈseləreɪtə(r)/ *n.* (*auto.*) accélérateur *m.*
accent¹ /ˈæksənt/ *n.* accent *m.*
accent² /ækˈsent/ *v.t.* accentuer.
accentuat|e /əkˈsentʃʊeɪt/ *v.t.* accentuer. **~ion** /-ˈeɪʃn/ *n.* accentuation *f.*
accept /əkˈsept/ *v.t.* accepter. **~able** *a.* acceptable. **~ance** *n.* acceptation *f.*; (*approval, favour*) approbation *f.*
access /ˈækses/ *n.* accès *m.* (**to sth.**, à qch.; **to s.o.**, auprès de qn.). **~ible** /əkˈsesəbl/ *a.* accessible.
accession /ækˈseʃn/ *n.* accession *f.*; (*thing added*) nouvelle acquisition *f.*
accessory /əkˈsesərɪ/ *a.* accessoire. —*n.* accessoire *m.*; (*person*: *jurid.*) complice *m./f.*
accident /ˈæksɪdənt/ *n.* accident *m.*; (*chance*) hasard *m.* **~al** /-ˈdentl/ *a.* accidentel, fortuit. **~ally** /-ˈdentəlɪ/ *adv.* involontairement.
acclaim /əˈkleɪm/ *v.t.* acclamer. —*n.* acclamation(s) *f.* (*pl.*).
acclimat|e /ˈæklɪmeɪt/ *v.t./i.* (*Amer.*) (s')acclimater. **~ion** /-ˈmeɪʃn/ *n.* (*Amer.*) acclimatation *f.*
acclimatiz|e /əˈklaɪmətaɪz/ *v.t./i.* (s')acclimater. **~ation** /-ˈzeɪʃn/ *n.* acclimatation *f.*
accolade /ˈækəleɪd/ *n.* (*of knight*) accolade *f.*; (*praise*) louange *f.*
accommodat|e /əˈkɒmədeɪt/ *v.t.* loger, avoir de la place pour; (*adapt*) adapter; (*supply*) fournir; (*oblige*) obliger. **~ing** *a.* obligeant. **~ion** /-ˈdeɪʃn/ *n.* (*living-premises*) logement *m.*; (*rented rooms*) chambres *f. pl.*
accompan|y /əˈkʌmpənɪ/ *v.t.* accompagner. **~iment** *n.* accompagnement *m.* **~ist** *n.* accompagna|teur, -trice *m.*, *f.*
accomplice /əˈkʌmplɪs/ *n.* complice *m./f.*
accomplish /əˈkʌmplɪʃ/ *v.t.* (*perform*) accomplir; (*achieve*) réaliser. **~ed** *a.* accompli. **~ment** *n.* accomplissement *m.* **~ments** *n.pl.* (*abilities*) talents *m.pl.*
accord /əˈkɔːd/ *v.i.* concorder. —*v.t.* accorder. —*n.* accord *m.* **of one's own ~**, de sa propre initiative. **~ance** *n.* **in ~ance with**, conformément à.
according /əˈkɔːdɪŋ/ *adv.* **~ to**, selon, suivant. **~ly** *adv.* en conséquence.
accordion /əˈkɔːdɪən/ *n.* accordéon *m.*
accost /əˈkɒst/ *v.t.* aborder.
account /əˈkaʊnt/ *n.* (*comm.*) compte *m.*; (*description*) compte rendu *m.*; (*importance*) importance *f.* —*v.t.* considérer. **~ for**, rendre compte de, expliquer. **on ~ of**, à cause de. **on no ~**, en aucun cas. **take into ~**, tenir compte de. **~able** *a.* responsable

(**for**, de). **~ability** /-əˈbɪlətɪ/ *n.* responsabilité *f.*

accountan|t /əˈkaʊntənt/ *n.* comptable *m./f.*, expert-comptable *m.* **~cy** *n.* comptabilité *f.*

accoutrements /əˈkuːtrəmənts/ *n. pl.* équipement *m.*

accredited /əˈkredɪtɪd/ *a.* accrédité.

accrue /əˈkruː/ *v.i.* s'accumuler. **~ to**, (*come to*) revenir à.

accumulat|e /əˈkjuːmjʊleɪt/ *v.t./i.* (s')accumuler. **~ion** /-ˈleɪʃn/ *n.* accumulation *f.*

accumulator /əˈkjuːmjʊleɪtə(r)/ *n.* (*battery*) accumulateur *m.*

accura|te /ˈækjərət/ *a.* exact, précis. **~cy** *n.* exactitude *f.*, précision *f.* **~tely** *adv.* exactement, avec précision.

accus|e /əˈkjuːz/ *v.t.* accuser. **the ~ed**, l'accusé(e) *m.*(*f.*). **~ation** /ækjuːˈzeɪʃn/ *n.* accusation *f.*

accustom /əˈkʌstəm/ *v.t.* accoutumer. **~ed** *a.* accoutumé. **become ~ed to**, s'accoutumer à.

ace /eɪs/ *n.* (*card, person*) as *m.*

ache /eɪk/ *n.* douleur *f.*, mal *m.* —*v.i.* faire mal. **my leg ~s**, ma jambe me fait mal, j'ai mal à la jambe.

achieve /əˈtʃiːv/ *v.t.* réaliser, accomplir; (*success*) obtenir. **~ment** *n.* réalisation *f.* (**of**, de); (*feat*) exploit *m.*, réussite *f.*

acid /ˈæsɪd/ *a.* & *n.* acide (*m.*). **~ity** /əˈsɪdətɪ/ *n.* acidité *f.*

acknowledge /əkˈnɒlɪdʒ/ *v.t.* reconnaître. **~ (receipt of)**, accuser réception de. **~ment** *n.* reconnaissance *f.*; accusé de réception *m.*

acme /ˈækmɪ/ *n.* sommet *m.*

acne /ˈæknɪ/ *n.* acné *f.*

acorn /ˈeɪkɔːn/ *n.* (*bot.*) gland *m.*

acoustic /əˈkuːstɪk/ *a.* acoustique. **~s** *n. pl.* acoustique *f.*

acquaint /əˈkweɪnt/ *v.t.* **~ s.o. with sth.**, mettre qn. au courant de qch. **be ~ed with**, (*person*) connaître; (*fact*) savoir. **~ance** *n.* (*knowledge, person*) connaissance *f.*

acquiesce /ækwɪˈes/ *v.i.* consentir. **~nce** *n.* consentement *m.*

acqui|re /əˈkwaɪə(r)/ *v.t.* acquérir; (*habit*) prendre. **~sition** /ækwɪˈzɪʃn/ *n.* acquisition *f.* **~sitive** /əˈkwɪzətɪv/ *a.* avide, âpre au gain.

acquit /əˈkwɪt/ *v.t.* (*p.t.* **acquitted**) acquitter. **~ o.s. well**, bien s'en tirer. **~tal** *n.* acquittement *m.*

acre /ˈeɪkə(r)/ *n.* (*approx.*) demi-hectare *m.* **~age** *n.* superficie *f.*

acrid /ˈækrɪd/ *a.* âcre.

acrimon|ious /ækrɪˈməʊnɪəs/ *a.* acerbe, acrimonieux. **~y** /ˈækrɪmənɪ/ *n.* acrimonie *f.*

acrobat /ˈækrəbæt/ *n.* acrobate *m./f.* **~ic** /-ˈbætɪk/ *a.* acrobatique. **~ics** /-ˈbætɪks/ *n. pl.* acrobatie *f.*

acronym /ˈækrənɪm/ *n.* sigle *m.*

across /əˈkrɒs/ *adv.* & *prep.* (*side to side*) d'un côté à l'autre (de); (*on other side*) de l'autre côté (de); (*crosswise*) en travers (de), à travers. **go** *or* **walk ~**, traverser.

act /ækt/ *n.* (*deed, theatre*) acte *m.*; (*in variety show*) numéro *m.*; (*decree*) loi *f.* —*v.i.* agir; (*theatre*) jouer; (*function*) marcher; (*pretend*) jouer la comédie. —*v.t.* (*part, role*) jouer. **~ as**, servir de. **~ing** *a.* (*temporary*) intérimaire; *n.* (*theatre*) jeu *m.*

action /ˈækʃn/ *n.* action *f.*; (*mil.*) combat *m.* **out of ~**, hors de service. **take ~**, agir.

activate /ˈæktɪveɪt/ *v.t.* (*machine*) actionner.

activ|e /ˈæktɪv/ *a.* actif; (*interest*) vif; (*volcano*) en activité. **~ity** /-ˈtɪvətɪ/ *n.* activité *f.*

ac|tor /ˈaektə(r)/ *n.* acteur *m.* **~tress** *n.* actrice *f.*

actual /ˈæktʃʊəl/ *a.* réel; (*example*) concret. **the ~ pen which**, le

stylo même que. **~ity** /-'æləti/ *n.* réalité *f.* **~ly** *adv.* (*in fact*) en réalité, réellement.
actuary /'æktʃʊəri/ *n.* actuaire *m./f.*
acumen /'ækjʊmen, *Amer.* ə'kjuːmən/ *n.* perspicacité *f.*
acupunctur|e /'ækjʊpʌŋktʃə(r)/ *n.* acupuncture *f.* **~ist** *n.* acupuncteur *m.*
acute /ə'kjuːt/ *a.* aigu; (*mind*) pénétrant; (*emotion*) intense, vif; (*shortage*) grave. **~ly** *adv.* vivement. **~ness** *n.* intensité *f.*
ad /æd/ *n.* (*fam.*) annonce *f.*
AD *abbr.* après J.-C.
adamant /'ædəmənt/ *a.* inflexible.
Adam's apple /'ædəmz'æpl/ *n.* pomme d'Adam *f.*
adapt /ə'dæpt/ *v.t./i.* (s')adapter. **~ation** /-'teɪʃn/ *n.* adaptation *f.* **~or** *n.* (*electr.*) adaptateur *m.*
adaptab|le /ə'dæptəbl/ *a.* souple. **~ility** /-'bɪləti/ *n.* souplesse *f.*
add /æd/ *v.t./i.* ajouter. **~ (up)**, (*total*) additionner. **~ up to,** (*total*) s'élever à. **~ing machine,** machine à calculer *f.*
adder /'ædə(r)/ *n.* vipère *f.*
addict /'ædɪkt/ *n.* intoxiqué(e) *m.* (*f.*); (*fig.*) fanatique *m./f.*
addict|ed /ə'dɪktɪd/ *a.* **~ed to,** (*drink*) adonné à. **be ~ed to,** (*fig.*) être un fanatique de. **~ion** /-kʃn/ *n.* (*med.*) dépendance *f.*; (*fig.*) manie *f.* **~ive** *a.* (*drug etc.*) qui crée une dépendance.
addition /ə'dɪʃn/ *n.* addition *f.* **in ~,** en outre. **~al** /-ʃənl/ *a.* supplémentaire.
additive /'ædɪtɪv/ *n.* additif *m.*
address /ə'dres/ *n.* adresse *f.*; (*speech*) allocution *f.* —*v.t.* adresser; (*speak to*) s'adresser à. **~ee** /ædre'siː/ *n.* destinataire *m./f.*
adenoids /'ædɪnɔɪdz/ *n. pl.* végétations (adénoïdes) *f. pl.*
adept /'ædept, *Amer.* ə'dept/ *a.* & *n.* expert (**at,** en) (*m.*).
adequa|te /'ædɪkwət/ *a.* suffisant; (*satisfactory*) satisfaisant. **~cy** *n.* quantité suffisante *f.*; (*of person*) compétence *f.* **~tely** *adv.* suffisamment.
adhere /əd'hɪə(r)/ *v.i.* adhérer (**to,** à). **~ to,** (*fig.*) respecter. **~nce** /-rəns/ *n.* adhésion *f.*
adhesion /əd'hiːʒn/ *n.* (*grip*) adhérence *f.*; (*support*: *fig.*) adhésion *f.*
adhesive /əd'hiːsɪv/ *a.* & *n.* adhésif (*m.*).
ad infinitum /ædɪnfɪ'naɪtəm/ *adv.* à l'infini.
adjacent /ə'dʒeɪsnt/ *a.* contigu (**to,** à).
adjective /'ædʒɪktɪv/ *n.* adjectif *m.*
adjoin /ə'dʒɔɪn/ *v.t.* être contigu à.
adjourn /ə'dʒɜːn/ *v.t.* ajourner. —*v.t./i.* **~ (the meeting),** suspendre la séance. **~ to,** (*go*) se retirer à.
adjudicate /ə'dʒuːdɪkeɪt/ *v.t./i.* juger.
adjust /ə'dʒʌst/ *v.t.* (*machine*) régler; (*prices*) (r)ajuster; (*arrange*) rajuster, arranger. —*v.t./i.* **~ (o.s.) to,** s'adapter à. **~able** *a.* réglable. **~ment** *n.* (*techn.*) réglage *m.*; (*of person*) adaptation *f.*
ad lib /æd'lɪb/ *v.i.* (*p.t.* **ad libbed**) (*fam.*) improviser.
administer /ad'mɪnɪstə(r)/ *v.t.* administrer.
administration /ədmɪnɪ'streɪʃn/ *n.* administration *f.*
administrator /əd'mɪnɪstreɪtə(r)/ *n.* administra|teur, -trice *m., f.*
administrative /əd'mɪnɪstrətɪv/ *a.* administratif.
admirable /'ædmərəbl/ *a.* admirable.
admiral /'ædmərəl/ *n.* amiral *m.*
admir|e /əd'maɪə(r)/ *v.t.* admirer. **~ation** /ædmə'reɪʃn/ *n.* admiration *f.* **~er** *n.* admira|teur, -trice *m., f.*

admissible /əd'mɪsəbl/ *a.* admissible.
admission /əd'mɪʃn/ *n.* admission *f.*; (*to museum, theatre, etc.*) entrée *f.*; (*confession*) aveu *m.*
admit /əd'mɪt/ *v.t.* (*p.t.* **admitted**) laisser entrer; (*acknowledge*) reconnaître, admettre. **~ to,** avouer. **~tance** *n.* entrée *f.* **~tedly** *adv.* il est vrai (que).
admonish /əd'mɒnɪʃ/ *v.t.* réprimander.
ado /ə'duː/ *n.* (*fuss*) cérémonies *f. pl.*; (*excitement*) agitation *f.*
adolescen|t /ædə'lesnt/ *n.* & *a.* adolescent(e) (*m.* (*f.*)). **~ce** *n.* adolescence *f.*
adopt /ə'dɒpt/ *v.t.* adopter. **~ed** *a.* (*child*) adoptif. **~ion** /-pʃn/ *n.* adoption *f.*
adoptive /ə'dɒptɪv/ *a.* adoptif.
ador|e /ə'dɔː(r)/ *v.t.* adorer. **~able** *a.* adorable. **~ation** /ædə'reɪʃn/ *n.* adoration *f.*
adorn /ə'dɔːn/ *v.t.* orner. **~ment** *n.* ornement *m.*
adrift /ə'drɪft/ *a.* & *adv.* à la dérive.
adroit /ə'drɔɪt/ *a.* adroit.
adulation /ædjʊ'leɪʃn/ *n.* adulation *f.*
adult /'ædʌlt/ *a.* & *n.* adulte (*m.*/*f.*). **~hood** *n.* condition d'adulte *f.*
adulterate /ə'dʌltəreɪt/ *v.t.* falsifier, frelater, altérer.
adulter|y /ə'dʌltərɪ/ *n.* adultère *m.* **~er, ~ess** *ns.* épou/x, -se adultère *m., f.* **~ous** *a.* adultère.
advance /əd'vɑːns/ *v.t.* avancer. —*v.i.* (s')avancer; (*progress*) avancer. —*n.* avance *f.* —*a.* (*payment*) anticipé. **in ~,** à l'avance. **~d** *a.* avancé; (*studies*) supérieur. **~ment** *n.* avancement *m.*
advantage /əd'vɑːntɪdʒ/ *n.* avantage *m.* **take ~ of,** profiter de; (*person*) exploiter. **~ous** /ædvən'teɪdʒəs/ *a.* avantageux.
advent /'ædvənt/ *n.* arrivée *f.*
Advent /'ædvənt/ *n.* Avent *m.*
adventur|e /əd'ventʃə(r)/ *n.* aventure *f.* **~er** *n.* explora|teur, -trice *m.*, *f.*; (*pej.*) aventur|ier, -ière *m.*, *f.* **~ous** *a.* aventureux.
adverb /'ædvɜːb/ *n.* adverbe *m.*
adversary /'ædvəsərɪ/ *n.* adversaire *m.*/*f.*
advers|e /'ædvɜːs/ *a.* défavorable. **~ity** /əd'vɜːsətɪ/ *n.* adversité *f.*
advert /'ædvɜːt/ *n.* (*fam.*) annonce *f.* **~isement** /əd'vɜːtɪsmənt/ *n.* publicité *f.*; (*in paper etc.*) annonce *f.*
advertise /'ædvətaɪz/ *v.t.*/*i.* faire de la publicité (pour); (*sell*) mettre une annonce (pour vendre). **~ for,** (*seek*) chercher (par voie d'annonce). **~r** /-ə(r)/ *n.* annonceur *m.*
advice /əd'vaɪs/ *n.* conseil(s) *m.* (*pl.*); (*comm.*) avis *m.*
advis|e /əd'vaɪz/ *v.t.* conseiller; (*inform*) aviser. **~e against,** déconseiller. **~able** *a.* conseillé, prudent (**to,** de). **~er** *n.* conseill|er, -ère *m.*, *f.* **~ory** *a.* consultatif.
advocate[1] /'ædvəkət/ *n.* (*jurid.*) avocat *m.*
advocate[2] /'ædvəkeɪt/ *v.t.* recommander.
aegis /'iːdʒɪs/ *n.* égide *f.*
aeon /'iːən/ *n.* éternité *f.*
aerial /'eərɪəl/ *a.* aérien. —*n.* antenne *f.*
aerobatics /eərə'bætɪks/ *n. pl.* acrobatie aérienne *f.*
aerodrome /'eərədrəʊm/ *n.* aérodrome *m.*
aerodynamic /eərəʊdaɪ'næmɪk/ *a.* aérodynamique.
aeroplane /'eərəpleɪn/ *n.* avion *m.*
aerosol /'eərəsɒl/ *n.* atomiseur *m.*
aesthetic /iːs'θetɪk, *Amer.* es'θetɪk/ *a.* esthétique.
afar /ə'fɑː(r)/ *adv.* **from ~,** de loin.
affable /'æfəbl/ *a.* affable.
affair /ə'feə(r)/ *n.* (*matter*) affaire *f.*; (*romance*) liaison *f.*

affect /ə'fekt/ *v.t.* affecter. **~ation** /æfek'teɪʃn/ *n.* affectation *f.* **~ed** *a.* affecté.
affection /ə'fekʃn/ *n.* affection *f.*
affectionate /ə'fekʃənət/ *a.* affectueux.
affiliat|e /ə'fɪlɪeɪt/ *v.t.* affilier. **~ed company,** filiale *f.* **~ion** /-'eɪʃn/ *n.* affiliation *f.*
affinity /ə'fɪnətɪ/ *n.* affinité *f.*
affirm /ə'fɜːm/ *v.t.* affirmer. **~ation** /æfə'meɪʃn/ *n.* affirmation *f.*
affirmative /ə'fɜːmətɪv/ *a.* affirmatif. —*n.* affirmative *f.*
affix /ə'fɪks/ *v.t.* apposer.
afflict /ə'flɪkt/ *v.t.* affliger. **~ion** /-kʃn/ *n.* affliction *f.*, détresse *f.*
affluen|t /'æflʊənt/ *a.* riche. **~ce** *n.* richesse *f.*
afford /ə'fɔːd/ *v.t.* avoir les moyens d'acheter; (*provide*) fournir. **~ to do,** avoir les moyens de faire; (*be able*) se permettre de faire. **can you ~ the time?,** avez-vous le temps?
affray /ə'freɪ/ *n.* rixe *f.*
affront /ə'frʌnt/ *n.* affront *m.* —*v.t.* insulter.
afield /ə'fiːld/ *adv.* **far ~,** loin.
afloat /ə'fləʊt/ *adv.* à flot.
afoot /ə'fʊt/ *adv.* **sth. is ~,** il se trame *or* se prépare qch.
aforesaid /ə'fɔːsed/ *a.* susdit.
afraid /ə'freɪd/ *a.* **be ~,** avoir peur (**of, to,** de; **that,** que); (*be sorry*) regretter. **I am ~ that,** (*regret to say*) je regrette de dire que.
afresh /ə'freʃ/ *adv.* de nouveau.
Africa /'æfrɪkə/ *n.* Afrique *f.* **~n** *a.* & *n.* africain(e) (*m.* (*f.*)).
after /'ɑːftə(r)/ *adv.* & *prep.* après. —*conj.* après que. **~ doing,** après avoir fait. **~-effect** *n.* suite *f.* **~ the manner of,** d'après. **be ~,** (*seek*) chercher.
aftermath /'ɑːftəmɑːθ/ *n.* suites *f. pl.*
afternoon /ɑːftə'nuːn/ *n.* après-midi *m.*/*f. invar.*
afters /'ɑːftəz/ *n. pl.* (*fam.*) dessert *m.*
aftershave /'ɑːftəʃeɪv/ *n.* lotion après-rasage *f.*
afterthought /'ɑːftəθɔːt/ *n.* réflexion après coup *f.*
afterwards /'ɑːftəwədz/ *adv.* après, par la suite.
again /ə'gen/ *adv.* de nouveau, encore une fois; (*besides*) en outre.
against /ə'genst/ *prep.* contre. **~ the law,** illégal.
age /eɪdʒ/ *n.* âge *m.* —*v.t.*/*i.* (*pres. p.* **ageing**) vieillir. **~s,** (*fam.*) une éternité. **of ~,** (*jurid.*) majeur. **ten years of ~,** âgé de dix ans. **~less** *a.* toujours jeune.
aged[1] /eɪdʒd/ *a.* **~ six,** âgé de six ans.
aged[2] /'eɪdʒɪd/ *a.* âgé, vieux.
agen|cy /'eɪdʒənsɪ/ *n.* agence *f.*; (*means*) entremise *f.* **~t** *n.* agent *m.*
agenda /ə'dʒendə/ *n.* ordre du jour *m.*
agglomeration /əglɒmə'reɪʃn/ *n.* agglomération *f.*
aggravat|e /'ægrəveɪt/ *v.t.* (*make worse*) aggraver; (*annoy*: *fam.*) exaspérer. **~ion** /-'veɪʃn/ *n.* aggravation *f.*; exaspération *f.*; (*trouble*: *fam.*) ennuis *m. pl.*
aggregate /'ægrɪgət/ *a.* & *n.* total (*m.*).
aggress|ive /ə'gresɪv/ *a.* agressif. **~ion** /-ʃn/ *n.* agression *f.* **~iveness** *n.* agressivité *f.* **~or** *n.* agresseur *m.*
aggrieved /ə'griːvd/ *a.* peiné.
aghast /ə'gɑːst/ *a.* horrifié..
agil|e /'ædʒaɪl, *Amer.* 'ædʒl/ *a.* agile. **~ity** /ə'dʒɪlətɪ/ *n.* agilité *f.*
agitat|e /'ædʒɪteɪt/ *v.t.* agiter. **~ion** /-'teɪʃn/ *n.* agitation *f.* **~or** *n.* agita|teur, -trice *m.*, *f.*
agnostic /æg'nɒstɪk/ *a.* & *n.* agnostique (*m.*/*f.*).
ago /ə'gəʊ/ *adv.* il y a. **a month ~,**

il y a un mois. **long ~,** il y a longtemps.

agog /ə'gɒg/ *a.* impatient, en émoi.

agon|y /'ægənɪ/ *n.* grande souffrance *f.*; (*mental*) angoisse *f.* **~ize** *v.i.* souffrir. **~ized** *a.* angoissé. **~izing** *a.* angoissant.

agree /ə'griː/ *v.t./i.* être *or* se mettre d'accord; (*of figures*) concorder. **~ that,** reconnaître que. **~ to do,** accepter de faire. **~ to sth.,** accepter qch. **~ with,** (*of food etc.*) convenir à. **~d** *a.* (*time, place*) convenu. **be ~d,** être d'accord.

agreeable /ə'griːəbl/ *a.* agréable. **be ~,** (*willing*) être d'accord.

agreement /ə'griːmənt/ *n.* accord *m.* **in ~,** d'accord.

agricultur|e /'ægrɪkʌltʃə(r)/ *n.* agriculture *f.* **~al** /-'kʌltʃərəl/ *a.* agricole.

aground /ə'graʊnd/ *adv.* **run ~,** (*of ship*) (s')échouer.

ahead /ə'hed/ *adv.* (*in front*) en avant, devant; (*in advance*) à l'avance. **~ of s.o.,** devant qn.; en avance sur qn. **~ of time,** en avance.

aid /eɪd/ *v.t.* aider. *—n.* aide *f.* **in ~ of,** au profit de.

aide /eɪd/ *n.* (*Amer.*) aide *m./f.*

AIDS /eɪdz/ *n.* (*med.*) sida *m.*

ail /eɪl/ *v.t.* **what ~s you?,** qu'avez-vous? **~ing** *a.* souffrant. **~ment** *n.* maladie *f.*

aim /eɪm/ *v.t.* diriger; (*gun*) braquer (**at,** sur). *—v.i.* viser. *—n.* but *m.* **~ at,** viser. **~ to,** avoir l'intention de. **take ~,** viser. **~less** *a.*, **~lessly** *adv.* sans but.

air /eə(r)/ *n.* air *m.* *—v.t.* aérer; (*views*) exposer librement. *—a.* (*base etc.*) aérien. **~-conditioned** *a.* climatisé. **~-conditioning** *n.* climatisation *f.* **~ force/hostess,** armée/hôtesse de l'air *f.* **~mail,** poste aérienne *f.* **by ~mail,** par avion. **~ raid,** attaque aérienne *f.* **by ~,** par avion. **in the ~,** (*rumour*) répandu; (*plan*) incertain. **on the ~,** sur l'antenne.

airborne /'eəbɔːn/ *a.* en (cours de) vol; (*troops*) aéroporté.

aircraft /'eəkrɑːft/ *n.* *invar.* avion *m.* **~-carrier** *n.* porte-avions *m. invar.*

airfield /'eəfiːld/ *n.* terrain d'aviation *m.*

airgun /'eəgʌn/ *n.* carabine à air comprimé *f.*

airlift /'eəlɪft/ *n.* pont aérien *m.*

airline /'eəlaɪn/ *n.* ligne aérienne *f.* **~r** /-ə(r)/ *n.* avion de ligne *m.*

airlock /'eəlɒk/ *n.* (*in pipe*) bulle d'air *f.*; (*chamber*: *techn.*) sas *m.*

airman /'eəmən/ *n.* (*pl.* **-men**) aviateur *m.*

airplane /'eəpleɪn/ *n.* (*Amer.*) avion *m.*

airport /'eəpɔːt/ *n.* aéroport *m.*

airsickness /'eəsɪknɪs/ *n.* mal de l'air *m.*

airtight /'eətaɪt/ *a.* hermétique.

airways /'eəweɪz/ *n. pl.* compagnie d'aviation *f.*

airworthy /'eəwɜːðɪ/ *a.* en état de navigation.

airy /'eərɪ/ *a.* (**-ier, -iest**) bien aéré; (*manner*) désinvolte.

aisle /aɪl/ *n.* (*of church*) nef latérale *f.*; (*gangway*) couloir *m.*

ajar /ə'dʒɑː(r)/ *adv.* & *a.* entr'ouvert.

akin /ə'kɪn/ *a.* **~ to,** apparenté à.

alabaster /'æləbɑːstə(r)/ *n.* albâtre *m.*

à la carte /ɑːlɑː'kɑːt/ *adv.* & *a.* (*culin.*) à la carte.

alacrity /ə'lækrətɪ/ *n.* empressement *m.*

alarm /ə'lɑːm/ *n.* alarme *f.*; (*clock*) réveil *m.* *—v.t.* alarmer. **~-clock** *n.* réveil *m.*, réveille-matin *m. invar.* **~ist** *n.* alarmiste *m./f.*

alas /ə'læs/ *int.* hélas.

albatross /'ælbətrɒs/ *n.* albatros *m.*

albino /æl'biːnəʊ, *Amer.* æl'baɪnəʊ/ *n.* (*pl.* **-os**) albinos *m./f.*
album /'ælbəm/ *n.* album *m.*
alchem|y /'ælkɪmɪ/ *n.* alchimie *f.* **~ist** *n.* alchimiste *m.*
alcohol /'ælkəhɒl/ *n.* alcool *m.* **~ic** /-'hɒlɪk/ *a.* alcoolique; (*drink*) alcoolisé; *n.* alcoolique *m./f.* **~ism** *n.* alcoolisme *m.*
alcove /'ælkəʊv/ *n.* alcôve *f.*
ale /eɪl/ *n.* bière *f.*
alert /ə'lɜːt/ *a.* (*lively*) vif; (*watchful*) vigilant. —*n.* alerte *f.* —*v.t.* alerter. **on the ~,** sur le qui-vive. **~ness** *n.* vivacité *f.*; vigilance *f.*
algebra /'ældʒɪbrə/ *n.* algèbre *f.* **~ic** /-'breɪɪk/ *a.* algébrique.
Algeria /æl'dʒɪərɪə/ *n.* Algérie *f.* **~n** *a.* & *n.* algérien(ne) (*m.* (*f.*)).
alias /'eɪlɪəs/ *n.* (*pl.* **-ases**) faux nom *m.* —*adv.* alias.
alibi /'ælɪbaɪ/ *n.* (*pl.* **-is**) alibi *m.*
alien /'eɪlɪən/ *n.* & *a.* étrang|er, -ère (*m.*, *f.*).
alienat|e /'eɪlɪəneɪt/ *v.t.* aliéner. **~e one's friends**/*etc.*, s'aliéner ses amis/*etc.* **~ion** /-'neɪʃn/ *n.* aliénation *f.*
alight[1] /ə'laɪt/ *v.i.* (*person*) descendre; (*bird*) se poser.
alight[2] /ə'laɪt/ *a.* en feu, allumé.
align /ə'laɪn/ *v.t.* aligner. **~ment** *n.* alignement *m.*
alike /ə'laɪk/ *a.* semblable. —*adv.* de la même façon. **look** *or* **be ~,** se ressembler.
alimony /'ælɪmənɪ, *Amer.* -məʊnɪ/ *n.* pension alimentaire *f.*
alive /ə'laɪv/ *a.* vivant. **~ to,** sensible à, sensibilisé à. **~ with,** grouillant de.
alkali /'ælkəlaɪ/ *n.* (*pl.* **-is**) alcali *m.*
all /ɔːl/ *a.* tout(e), tous, toutes. —*pron.* tous, toutes; (*everything*) tout. —*adv.* tout. **~ (the) men,** tous les hommes. **~ of it,** (le) tout. **~ but,** presque. **~-clear** *n.* fin d'alerte *f.* **~ in,** (*exhausted*) épuisé. **~ out,** à fond. **~-out** *a.* (*effort*) maximum. **~ over,** partout (sur *or* dans); (*finished*) fini. **~ right,** bien; (*consenting*) bon! **~ round,** dans tous les domaines; (*for all*) pour tous. **~-round** *a.* général. **~ there,** (*alert*) éveillé. **~ the same,** tout de même.
allay /ə'leɪ/ *v.t.* calmer.
allegation /ælɪ'geɪʃn/ *n.* allégation *f.*
allege /ə'ledʒ/ *v.t.* prétendre. **~dly** /-ɪdlɪ/ *adv.* d'après ce qu'on dit.
allegiance /ə'liːdʒəns/ *n.* fidélité *f.*
allegor|y /'ælɪgərɪ, *Amer.* -gɔːrɪ/ *n.* allégorie *f.* **~ical** /-'gɒrɪkl/ *a.* allégorique.
alleluia /ælɪ'luːjə/ *int.* & *n.* alléluia (*m.*).
allerg|y /'ælədʒɪ/ *n.* allergie *f.* **~ic** /ə'lɜːdʒɪk/ *a.* allergique.
alleviate /ə'liːvɪeɪt/ *v.t.* alléger.
alley /'ælɪ/ *n.* (*street*) ruelle *f.*; (*in park*) allée *f.*
alliance /ə'laɪəns/ *n.* alliance *f.*
allied /'ælaɪd/ *a.* allié.
alligator /'ælɪgeɪtə(r)/ *n.* alligator *m.*
allocat|e /'æləkeɪt/ *v.t.* (*assign*) attribuer; (*share out*) distribuer. **~ion** /-'keɪʃn/ *n.* allocation *f.*
allot /ə'lɒt/ *v.t.* (*p.t.* **allotted**) attribuer. **~ment** *n.* attribution *f.*; (*share*) partage *m.*; (*land*) parcelle de terre *f.* (*louée pour la culture*).
allow /ə'laʊ/ *v.t.* permettre; (*grant*) accorder; (*reckon on*) prévoir; (*agree*) reconnaître. **~ s.o. to,** permettre à qn. de. **~ for,** tenir compte de.
allowance /ə'laʊəns/ *n.* allocation *f.*, indemnité *f.* **make ~s for,** être indulgent envers; (*take into account*) tenir compte de.
alloy /'ælɔɪ/ *n.* alliage *m.*
allude /ə'luːd/ *v.i.* **~ to,** faire allusion à.
allure /ə'lʊə(r)/ *v.t.* attirer.

allusion /ə'luːʒn/ *n.* allusion *f.*
ally[1] /'ælaɪ/ *n.* allié(e) *m.* (*f.*).
ally[2] /ə'laɪ/ *v.t.* allier. **~ o.s. with,** s'allier à *or* avec.
almanac /'ɔːlmənæk/ *n.* almanach *m.*
almighty /ɔːl'maɪtɪ/ *a.* tout-puissant; (*very great: fam.*) sacré, formidable. *—n.* **the A~,** le Tout-Puissant.
almond /'ɑːmənd/ *n.* amande *f.*
almost /'ɔːlməʊst/ *adv.* presque.
alms /ɑːmz/ *n.* aumône *f.*
alone /ə'ləʊn/ *a.* & *adv.* seul.
along /ə'lɒŋ/ *prep.* le long de. *—adv.* **come ~,** venir. **go** *or* **walk ~,** passer. **all ~,** (*time*) tout le temps, depuis le début. **~ with,** avec.
alongside /əlɒŋ'saɪd/ *adv.* (*naut.*) bord à bord. **come ~,** accoster. *—prep.* le long de.
aloof /ə'luːf/ *adv.* à l'écart. *—a.* distant. **~ness** *n.* réserve *f.*
aloud /ə'laʊd/ *adv.* à haute voix.
alphabet /'ælfəbet/ *n.* alphabet *m.* **~ical** /-'betɪkl/ *a.* alphabétique.
alpine /'ælpaɪn/ *a.* (*landscape*) alpestre; (*climate*) alpin.
Alpine /'ælpaɪn/ *a.* des Alpes.
Alps /ælps/ *n. pl.* **the ~,** les Alpes *f. pl.*
already /ɔːl'redɪ/ *adv.* déjà.
Alsatian /æl'seɪʃn/ *n.* (*dog*) berger allemand *m.*
also /'ɔːlsəʊ/ *adv.* aussi.
altar /'ɔːltə(r)/ *n.* autel *m.*
alter /'ɔːltə(r)/ *v.t./i.* changer. **~ation** /-'reɪʃn/ *n.* changement *m.*; (*to garment*) retouche *f.*
alternate[1] /ɔːl'tɜːnət/ *a.* alterné, alternatif. **~ days**/*etc.*, (*first one then the other*) tous les deux jours/*etc.* **~ly** *adv.* tour à tour.
alternate[2] /'ɔːltəneɪt/ *v.i.* alterner. *—v.t.* faire alterner.
alternative /ɔːl'tɜːnətɪv/ *a.* autre; (*policy*) de rechange. *—n.* alternative *f.*, choix *m.* **~ly** *adv.* comme alternative. **or ~ly,** ou alors.
although /ɔːl'ðəʊ/ *conj.* bien que.
altitude /'æltɪtjuːd/ *n.* altitude *f.*
altogether /ɔːltə'geðə(r)/ *adv.* (*completely*) tout à fait; (*on the whole*) à tout prendre.
altruist /'æltruːɪst/ *n.* altruiste *m./f.* **~ic** /-'ɪstɪk/ *a.* altruiste.
aluminium /æljʊ'mɪnɪəm/ (*Amer.* **aluminum** /ə'luːmɪnəm/) *n.* aluminium *m.*
always /'ɔːlweɪz/ *adv.* toujours.
am /æm/ *see* **be.**
a.m. /eɪ'em/ *adv.* du matin.
amalgamate /ə'mælgəmeɪt/ *v.t./i.* (s')amalgamer; (*comm.*) fusionner.
amass /ə'mæs/ *v.t.* amasser.
amateur /'æmətə(r)/ *n.* amateur *m.* *—a.* (*musician etc.*) amateur *invar.* **~ish** *a.* (*pej.*) d'amateur. **~ishly** *adv.* en amateur.
amaz|e /ə'meɪz/ *v.t.* stupéfier. **~ed** *a.* stupéfait. **~ement** *n.* stupéfaction *f.* **~ingly** *adv.* étonnament.
ambassador /æm'bæsədə(r)/ *n.* ambassadeur *m.*
amber /'æmbə(r)/ *n.* ambre *m.*; (*auto.*) feu orange *m.*
ambidextrous /æmbɪ'dekstrəs/ *a.* ambidextre.
ambigu|ous /æm'bɪgjʊəs/ *a.* ambigu. **~ity** /-'gjuːətɪ/ *n.* ambiguïté *f.*
ambit /'æmbɪt/ *n.* limites *f. pl.*
ambiti|on /æm'bɪʃn/ *n.* ambition *f.* **~ous** *a.* ambitieux.
ambivalent /æm'bɪvələnt/ *a.* ambigu, ambivalent.
amble /'æmbl/ *v.i.* marcher sans se presser, s'avancer lentement.
ambulance /'æmbjʊləns/ *n.* ambulance *f.*
ambush /'æmbʊʃ/ *n.* embuscade *f.* *—v.t.* tendre une embuscade à.
amen /ɑː'men/ *int.* amen.
amenable /ə'miːnəbl/ *a.* obligeant. **~ to,** (*responsive*) sensible à.

amend /ə'mend/ *v.t.* modifier, corriger. **~ment** *n.* (*to rule*) amendement *m.*

amends /ə'mends/ *n. pl.* **make ~,** réparer son erreur.

amenities /ə'mi:nətɪz/ *n. pl.* (*pleasant features*) attraits *m. pl.*; (*facilities*) aménagements *m. pl.*

America /ə'merɪkə/ *n.* Amérique *f.* **~n** *a.* & *n.* américain(e) (*m.* (*f.*)). **~nism** *n.* américanisme *m.* **~nize** *v.t.* américaniser.

amiable /'eɪmɪəbl/ *a.* aimable.

amicable /'æmɪkəbl/ *a.* amical.

amid(st) /ə'mɪd(st)/ *prep.* au milieu de.

amiss /ə'mɪs/ *a.* & *adv.* mal. **sth. ~,** qch. qui ne va pas.

ammonia /ə'məʊnɪə/ *n.* (*gas*) ammoniac *m.*; (*water*) ammoniaque *f.*

ammunition /æmjʊ'nɪʃn/ *n.* munitions *f. pl.*

amnesia /æm'ni:zɪə/ *n.* amnésie *f.*

amnesty /'æmnəstɪ/ *n.* amnistie *f.*

amok /ə'mɒk/ *adv.* **run ~,** devenir fou furieux; (*crowd*) se déchaîner.

among(st) /ə'mʌŋ(st)/ *prep.* parmi, entre. **~ the crowd,** (*in the middle of*) parmi la foule. **~ the English**/*etc.*, (*race, group*) chez les Anglais/*etc.* **~ ourselves**/*etc.*, entre nous/*etc.*

amoral /eɪ'mɒrəl/ *a.* amoral.

amorous /'æmərəs/ *a.* amoureux.

amorphous /ə'mɔ:fəs/ *a.* amorphe.

amount /ə'maʊnt/ *n.* quantité *f.*; (*total*) montant *m.*; (*sum of money*) somme *f.* —*v.i.* **~ to,** (*add up to*) s'élever à; (*be equivalent to*) revenir à.

amp /æmp/ *n.* (*fam.*) ampère *m.*

ampere /'æmpeə(r)/ *n.* ampère *m.*

amphibi|an /æm'fɪbɪən/ *n.* amphibie *m.* **~ous** *a.* amphibie.

amphitheatre /'æmfɪθɪətə(r)/ *n.* amphithéâtre *m.*

ampl|e /'æmpl/ *a.* (**-er, -est**) (*enough*) (bien) assez de; (*large, roomy*) ample. **~y** *adv.* amplement.

amplif|y /'æmplɪfaɪ/ *v.t.* amplifier. **~ier** *n.* amplificateur *m.*

amputat|e /'æmpjʊteɪt/ *v.t.* amputer. **~ion** /-'teɪʃn/ *n.* amputation *f.*

amuck /ə'mʌk/ *see* **amok.**

amuse /ə'mju:z/ *v.t.* amuser. **~ment** *n.* amusement *m.*, divertissement *m.* **~ arcade,** salle de jeux *f.*

an /æn, *unstressed* ən/ *see* **a.**

anachronism /ə'nækrənɪzəm/ *n.* anachronisme *m.*

anaem|ia /ə'ni:mɪə/ *n.* anémie *f.* **~ic** *a.* anémique.

anaesthetic /ænɪs'θetɪk/ *n.* anesthésique *m.* **give an ~,** faire une anesthésie (**to,** à).

anagram /'ænəgræm/ *n.* anagramme *f.*

analogy /ə'nælədʒɪ/ *n.* analogie *f.*

analys|e (*Amer.* **analyze**) /'ænəlaɪz/ *v.t.* analyser. **~t** /-ɪst/ *n.* analyste *m.*/*f.*

analysis /ə'næləsɪs/ *n.* (*pl.* **-yses** /-əsi:z/) analyse *f.*

analytic(al) /ænə'lɪtɪk(l)/ *a.* analytique.

anarch|y /'ænəkɪ/ *n.* anarchie *f.* **~ist** *n.* anarchiste *m.*/*f.*

anathema /ə'næθəmə/ *n.* **that is ~ to me,** j'ai cela en abomination.

anatom|y /ə'nætəmɪ/ *n.* anatomie *f.* **~ical** /ænə'tɒmɪkl/ *a.* anatomique.

ancest|or /'ænsestə(r)/ *n.* ancêtre *m.* **~ral** /-'sestrəl/ *a.* ancestral.

ancestry /'ænsestrɪ/ *n.* ascendance *f.*

anchor /'æŋkə(r)/ *n.* ancre *f.* —*v.t.* mettre à l'ancre. —*v.i.* jeter l'ancre.

anchovy /'æntʃəvɪ/ *n.* anchois *m.*

ancient /'eɪnʃənt/ *a.* ancien.

ancillary /æn'sɪlərɪ/ *a.* auxiliaire.

and /ænd, *unstressed* ən(d)/ *conj.*

et. **go ~ see him,** allez le voir. **richer ~ richer,** de plus en plus riche.

anecdote /'ænɪkdəʊt/ *n.* anecdote *f.*

anew /ə'nju:/ *adv.* de *or* à nouveau.

angel /'eɪndʒl/ *n.* ange *m.* **~ic** /æn'dʒelɪk/ *a.* angélique.

anger /'æŋgə(r)/ *n.* colère *f.* —*v.t.* mettre en colère, fâcher.

angle[1] /'æŋgl/ *n.* angle *m.*

angle[2] /'æŋgl/ *v.i.* pêcher (à la ligne). **~ for,** (*fig.*) quêter. **~r** /-ə(r)/ *n.* pêcheu|r, -se *m.*, *f.*

Anglican /'æŋglɪkən/ *a.* & *n.* anglican(e) (*m.* (*f.*)).

Anglo- /'æŋgləʊ/ *pref.* anglo-.

Anglo-Saxon /'æŋgləʊ'sæksn/ *a.* & *n.* anglo-saxon(ne) (*m.* (*f.*)).

angr|y /'æŋgrɪ/ *a.* **(-ier, -iest)** fâché, en colère. **get ~y,** se fâcher, se mettre en colère (**with,** contre). **~ily** *adv.* en colère.

anguish /'æŋgwɪʃ/ *n.* angoisse *f.*

angular /'æŋgjʊlə(r)/ *a.* (*features*) anguleux.

animal /'ænɪml/ *n.* & *a.* animal (*m.*).

animate[1] /'ænɪmət/ *a.* animé.

animat|e[2] /'ænɪmeɪt/ *v.t.* animer. **~ion** /-'meɪʃn/ *n.* animation *f.*

animosity /ænɪ'mɒsətɪ/ *n.* animosité *f.*

aniseed /'ænɪsi:d/ *n.* anis *m.*

ankle /'æŋkl/ *n.* cheville *f.* **~ sock,** socquette *f.*

annals /'ænlz/ *n. pl.* annales *f. pl.*

annex /ə'neks/ *v.t.* annexer. **~ation** /ænek'seɪʃn/ *n.* annexion *f.*

annexe /'æneks/ *n.* annexe *f.*

annihilate /ə'naɪəleɪt/ *v.t.* anéantir.

anniversary /ænɪ'vɜ:sərɪ/ *n.* anniversaire *m.*

annotat|e /'ænəteɪt/ *v.t.* annoter. **~ion** /-'teɪʃn/ *n.* annotation *f.*

announce /ə'naʊns/ *v.t.* annoncer. **~ment** *n.* annonce *f.* **~r** /-ə(r)/ *n.* (*radio, TV*) speaker(ine) *m.* (*f.*).

annoy /ə'nɔɪ/ *v.t.* agacer, ennuyer. **~ance** *n.* contrariété *f.* **~ed** *a.* fâché (**with,** contre). **get ~ed,** se fâcher. **~ing** *a.* ennuyeux.

annual /'ænjʊəl/ *a.* annuel. —*n.* publication annuelle *f.* **~ly** *adv.* annuellement.

annuity /ə'nju:ətɪ/ *n.* rente (viagère) *f.*

annul /ə'nʌl/ *v.t.* (*p.t.* **annulled**) annuler. **~ment** *n.* annulation *f.*

anoint /ə'nɔɪnt/ *v.t.* oindre.

anomal|y /ə'nɒməlɪ/ *n.* anomalie *f.* **~ous** *a.* anormal.

anon /ə'nɒn/ *adv.* (*old use*) bientôt.

anonym|ous /ə'nɒnɪməs/ *a.* anonyme. **~ity** /ænə'nɪmətɪ/ *n.* anonymat *m.*

anorak /'ænəræk/ *n.* anorak *m.*

another /ə'nʌðə(r)/ *a.* & *pron.* un(e) autre. **~ coffee,** (*one more*) encore un café. **~ ten minutes,** encore dix minutes.

answer /'ɑ:nsə(r)/ *n.* réponse *f.*; (*solution*) solution *f.* —*v.t.* répondre à; (*prayer*) exaucer. —*v.i.* répondre. **~ the door,** ouvrir la porte. **~ back,** répondre. **~ for,** répondre de. **~able** *a.* responsable (**for,** de; **to,** devant).

ant /ænt/ *n.* fourmi *f.*

antagonis|m /æn'tægənɪzəm/ *n.* antagonisme *m.* **~tic** /-'nɪstɪk/ *a.* antagoniste.

antagonize /æn'tægənaɪz/ *v.t.* provoquer l'hostilité de.

Antarctic /æn'tɑ:ktɪk/ *a.* & *n.* antarctique (*m.*).

ante- /'æntɪ/ *pref.* anti-, anté-.

antecedent /æntɪ'si:dnt/ *n.* antécédent *m.*

antelope /'æntɪləʊp/ *n.* antilope *f.*

antenatal /'æntɪneɪtl/ *a.* prénatal.

antenna /æn'tenə/ *n.* (*pl.* **-ae** /-i:/) (*of insect*) antenne *f.*; (*pl.* **-as**; *aerial*: *Amer.*) antenne *f.*

anthem /'ænθəm/ *n.* (*relig.*) motet *m.*; (*of country*) hymne national *m.*
anthill /'ænthɪl/ *n.* fourmilière *f.*
anthology /æn'θɒlədʒɪ/ *n.* anthologie *f.*
anthropolog|y /ænθrə'pɒlədʒɪ/ *n.* anthropologie *f.* **~ist** *n.* anthropologue *m./f.*
anti- /'æntɪ/ *pref.* anti-. **~-aircraft** *a.* antiaérien.
antibiotic /æntɪbaɪ'ɒtɪk/ *n.* antibiotique *m.*
antibody /'æntɪbɒdɪ/ *n.* anticorps *m.*
antic /'æntɪk/ *n.* bouffonnerie *f.*
anticipat|e /æn'tɪsɪpeɪt/ *v.t.* (*foresee, expect*) prévoir, s'attendre à; (*forestall*) devancer. **~ion** /-'peɪʃn/ *n.* attente *f.* **in ~ion of,** en prévision *or* attente de.
anticlimax /æntɪ'klaɪmæks/ *n.* (*let-down*) déception *f.*; (*event*) événement de moindre importance *m.* **it was an ~,** ça n'a pas répondu à l'attente.
anticlockwise /æntɪ'klɒkwaɪz/ *adv.* & *a.* dans le sens inverse des aiguilles d'une montre.
anticyclone /æntɪ'saɪkləʊn/ *n.* anticyclone *m.*
antidote /'æntɪdəʊt/ *n.* antidote *m.*
antifreeze /'æntɪfriːz/ *n.* antigel *m.*
antipathy /æn'tɪpəθɪ/ *n.* antipathie *f.*
antiquarian /æntɪ'kweərɪən/ *a.* (*bookseller*) spécialisé dans le livre ancien.
antiquated /'æntɪkweɪtɪd/ *a.* vieillot, suranné.
antique /æn'tiːk/ *a.* (*old*) ancien; (*from antiquity*) antique. *—n.* objet ancien *m.*, antiquité *f.* **~ dealer,** antiquaire *m./f.* **~ shop,** magasin d'antiquités *m.*
antiquity /æn'tɪkwətɪ/ *n.* antiquité *f.*
anti-Semiti|c /æntɪsɪ'mɪtɪk/ *a.* antisémite. **~sm** /-'semɪtɪzəm/ *n.* antisémitisme *m.*
antiseptic /æntɪ'septɪk/ *a.* & *n.* antiseptique (*m.*).
antisocial /æntɪ'səʊʃl/ *a.* asocial, antisocial; (*unsociable*) insociable.
antithesis /æn'tɪθəsɪs/ *n.* (*pl.* **-eses** /-əsiːz/) antithèse *f.*
antlers /'æntləz/ *n. pl.* bois *m. pl.*
anus /'eɪnəs/ *n.* anus *m.*
anvil /'ænvɪl/ *n.* enclume *f.*
anxiety /æŋ'zaɪətɪ/ *n.* (*worry*) anxiété *f.*; (*eagerness*) impatience *f.*
anxious /'æŋkʃəs/ *a.* (*troubled*) anxieux; (*eager*) impatient (**to,** de). **~ly** *adv.* anxieusement; impatiemment.
any /'enɪ/ *a.* (*some*) du, de l', de la, des; (*after negative*) de, d'; (*every*) tout; (*no matter which*) n'importe quel. **at ~ moment,** à tout moment. **have you ~ water?,** avez-vous de l'eau? *—pron.* (*no matter which one*) n'importe lequel; (*someone*) quelqu'un; (*any amount of it or them*) en. **I do not have ~,** je n'en ai pas. *—adv.* (*a little*) un peu. **not ~,** nullement.
anybody /'enɪbɒdɪ/ *pron.* n'importe qui; (*somebody*) quelqu'un; (*after negative*) personne. **he did not see ~,** il n'a vu personne.
anyhow /'enɪhaʊ/ *adv.* de toute façon; (*badly*) n'importe comment.
anyone /'enɪwʌn/ *pron.* = **anybody.**
anything /'enɪθɪŋ/ *pron.* n'importe quoi; (*something*) quelque chose; (*after negative*) rien. **he did not see ~,** il n'a rien vu. **~ but,** (*cheap etc.*) nullement. **~ you do,** tout ce que tu fais.
anyway /'enɪweɪ/ *adv.* de toute façon.
anywhere /'enɪweə(r)/ *adv.* n'importe où; (*somewhere*) quelque part; (*after negative*)

nulle part. **he does not go ~,** il ne va nulle part. **~ you go,** partout où tu vas, où que tu ailles. **~ else,** partout ailleurs.

apace /ə'peɪs/ *adv.* rapidement.

apart /ə'pɑːt/ *adv.* (*on or to one side*) à part; (*separated*) séparé; (*into pieces*) en pièces. **~ from,** à part, excepté. **ten metres ~,** (*distant*) à dix mètres l'un de l'autre. **come ~,** se séparer; (*machine*) se démonter. **keep ~,** séparer. **take ~,** démonter.

apartment /ə'pɑːtmənt/ *n.* (*Amer.*) appartement *m.* **~s,** logement *m.*

apath|y /'æpəθɪ/ *n.* apathie *f.* **~etic** /-'θetɪk/ *a.* apathique.

ape /eɪp/ *n.* singe *m.* —*v.t.* singer.

aperitif /ə'perətɪf/ *n.* apéritif *m.*

aperture /'æpətʃə(r)/ *n.* ouverture *f.*

apex /'eɪpeks/ *n.* sommet *m.*

aphrodisiac /æfrə'dɪzɪæk/ *a.* & *n.* aphrodisiaque (*m.*).

apiece /ə'piːs/ *adv.* chacun.

aplomb /ə'plɒm/ *n.* sang-froid *m.*

Apocalypse /ə'pɒkəlɪps/ *n.* Apocalypse *f.* **apocalyptic** /-'lɪptɪk/ *a.* apocalyptique.

apologetic /əpɒlə'dʒetɪk/ *a.* (*tone etc.*) d'excuse. **be ~,** s'excuser. **~ally** /-lɪ/ *adv.* en s'excusant.

apologize /ə'pɒlədʒaɪz/ *v.i.* s'excuser (**for,** de; **to,** auprès de).

apology /ə'pɒlədʒɪ/ *n.* excuses *f. pl.*; (*defence of belief*) apologie *f.*

apople|xy /'æpəpleksɪ/ *n.* apoplexie *f.* **~ctic** /-'plektɪk/ *a.* apoplectique.

Apostle /ə'pɒsl/ *n.* apôtre *m.*

apostrophe /ə'pɒstrəfɪ/ *n.* apostrophe *f.*

appal /ə'pɔːl/ *v.t.* (*p.t.* **appalled**) épouvanter. **~ling** *a.* épouvantable.

apparatus /æpə'reɪtəs/ *n.* (*machine & anat.*) appareil *m.*

apparel /ə'pærəl/ *n.* habillement *m.*

apparent /ə'pærənt/ *a.* apparent. **~ly** *adv.* apparemment.

apparition /æpə'rɪʃn/ *n.* apparition *f.*

appeal /ə'piːl/ *n.* appel *m.*; (*attractiveness*) attrait *m.*, charme *m.* —*v.i.* (*jurid.*) faire appel. **~ to s.o.,** (*beg*) faire appel à qn.; (*attract*) plaire à qn. **~ to s.o. for sth.,** demander qch. à qn. **~ing** *a.* (*attractive*) attirant.

appear /ə'pɪə(r)/ *v.i.* apparaître; (*arrive*) se présenter; (*seem, be published*) paraître; (*theatre*) jouer. **~ance** *n.* apparition *f.*; (*aspect*) apparence *f.*

appease /ə'piːz/ *v.t.* apaiser.

append /ə'pend/ *v.t.* joindre.

appendage /ə'pendɪdʒ/ *n.* appendice *m.*

appendicitis /əpendɪ'saɪtɪs/ *n.* appendicite *f.*

appendix /ə'pendɪks/ *n.* (*pl.* **-ices** /-ɪsiːz/) appendice *m.*

appertain /æpə'teɪn/ *v.i.* **~ to,** se rapporter à.

appetite /'æpɪtaɪt/ *n.* appétit *m.*

appetizer /'æpɪtaɪzə(r)/ *n.* (*snack*) amuse-gueule *m. invar.*; (*drink*) apéritif *m.*

appetizing /'æpɪtaɪzɪŋ/ *a.* appétissant.

applau|d /ə'plɔːd/ *v.t./i.* applaudir; (*decision*) applaudir à. **~se** *n.* applaudissements *m. pl.*

apple /'æpl/ *n.* pomme *f.* **~-tree** *n.* pommier *m.*

appliance /ə'plaɪəns/ *n.* appareil *m.*

applicable /'æplɪkəbl/ *a.* applicable.

applicant /'æplɪkənt/ *n.* candidat(e) *m.* (*f.*) (**for,** à).

application /æplɪ'keɪʃn/ *n.* application *f.*; (*request, form*) demande *f.*; (*for job*) candidature *f.*

apply /ə'plaɪ/ *v.t.* appliquer. —*v.i.* **~ to,** (*refer*) s'appliquer à; (*ask*) s'adresser à. **~ for,** (*job, grant*) demander. **~ o.s. to,** s'appliquer à. **applied** *a.* appliqué.

appoint /ə'pɔɪnt/ *v.t.* (*to post*) nommer; (*fix*) désigner. **well-~ed** *a.* bien équipé. **~ment** *n.* nomination *f.*; (*meeting*) rendez-vous *m. invar.*; (*job*) poste *m.*

apportion /ə'pɔːʃn/ *v.t.* répartir.

apprais|e /ə'preɪz/ *v.t.* évaluer. **~al** *n.* évaluation *f.*

appreciable /ə'priːʃəbl/ *a.* appréciable.

appreciat|e /ə'priːʃɪeɪt/ *v.t.* (*like*) apprécier; (*understand*) comprendre; (*be grateful for*) être reconnaissant de. *—v.i.* prendre de la valeur. **~ion** /-'eɪʃn/ *n.* appréciation *f.*; (*gratitude*) reconnaissance *f.*; (*rise*) augmentation *f.* **~ive** /ə'priːʃɪətɪv/ *a.* reconnaissant.

apprehen|d /æprɪ'hend/ *v.t.* (*arrest, fear*) appréhender; (*understand*) comprendre. **~sion** *n.* appréhension *f.*

apprehensive /æprɪ'hensɪv/ *a.* inquiet. **be ~ of,** craindre.

apprentice /ə'prentɪs/ *n.* apprenti *m.* *—v.t.* mettre en apprentissage. **~ship** *n.* apprentissage *m.*

approach /ə'prəʊtʃ/ *v.t.* (s')approcher de; (*accost*) aborder. *—v.i.* (s')approcher. *—n.* approche *f.* **an ~ to,** (*problem*) une façon d'aborder; (*person*) une démarche auprès de. **~able** *a.* accessible; (*person*) abordable.

appropriate[1] /ə'prəʊprɪət/ *a.* approprié, propre. **~ly** *adv.* à propos.

appropriate[2] /ə'prəʊprɪeɪt/ *v.t.* s'approprier.

approval /ə'pruːvl/ *n.* approbation *f.* **on ~,** à *or* sous condition.

approv|e /ə'pruːv/ *v.t./i.* approuver. **~e of,** approuver. **~ingly** *adv.* d'un air *or* d'un ton approbateur.

approximate[1] /ə'prɒksɪmət/ *a.* approximatif. **~ly** *adv.* approximativement.

approximat|e[2] /ə'prɒksɪmeɪt/ *v.t.* se rapprocher de. **~ion** /-'meɪʃn/ *n.* approximation *f.*

apricot /'eɪprɪkɒt/ *n.* abricot *m.*

April /'eɪprəl/ *n.* avril *m.* **make an ~ fool of,** faire un poisson d'avril à.

apron /'eɪprən/ *n.* tablier *m.*

apse /æps/ *n.* (*of church*) abside *f.*

apt /æpt/ *a.* (*suitable*) approprié; (*pupil*) doué. **be ~ to,** avoir tendance à. **~ly** *adv.* à propos.

aptitude /'æptɪtjuːd/ *n.* aptitude *f.*

aqualung /'ækwəlʌŋ/ *n.* scaphandre autonome *m.*

aquarium /ə'kweərɪəm/ *n.* (*pl.* **-ums**) aquarium *m.*

aquatic /ə'kwætɪk/ *a.* aquatique; (*sport*) nautique.

aqueduct /'ækwɪdʌkt/ *n.* aqueduc *m.*

aquiline /'ækwɪlaɪn/ *a.* aquilin.

Arab /'ærəb/ *n.* & *a.* arabe (*m./f.*). **~ic** *a.* & *n.* (*lang.*) arabe (*m.*). **~ic numerals,** chiffres arabes *m. pl.*

Arabian /ə'reɪbɪən/ *a.* arabe.

arable /'ærəbl/ *a.* arable.

arbiter /'ɑːbɪtə(r)/ *n.* arbitre *m.*

arbitrary /'ɑːbɪtrərɪ/ *a.* arbitraire.

arbitrat|e /'ɑːbɪtreɪt/ *v.i.* arbitrer. **~ion** /-'treɪʃn/ *n.* arbitrage *m.* **~or** *n.* arbitre *m.*

arc /ɑːk/ *n.* arc *m.*

arcade /ɑː'keɪd/ *n.* (*shops*) galerie *f.*; (*arches*) arcades *f. pl.*

arcane /ɑː'keɪn/ *a.* mystérieux.

arch[1] /ɑːtʃ/ *n.* arche *f.*; (*in church etc.*) arc *m.*; (*of foot*) voûte plantaire *f.* *—v.t./i.* (s')arquer.

arch[2] /ɑːtʃ/ *a.* (*playful*) malicieux.

arch- /ɑːtʃ/ *pref.* (*hypocrite etc.*) grand, achevé.

archaeolog|y /ɑːkɪ'ɒlədʒɪ/ *n.* archéologie *f.* **~ical** /-ə'lɒdʒɪkl/ *a.* archéologique. **~ist** *n.* archéologue *m./f.*

archaic /ɑːˈkeɪɪk/ *a.* archaïque.
archbishop /ɑːtʃˈbɪʃəp/ *n.* archevêque *m.*
arch-enemy /ɑːtʃˈenəmɪ/ *n.* ennemi numéro un *m.*
archer /ˈɑːtʃə(r)/ *n.* archer *m.* **~y** *n.* tir à l'arc *m.*
archetype /ˈɑːkɪtaɪp/ *n.* archétype *m.*, modèle *m.*
archipelago /ɑːkɪˈpeləgəʊ/ *n.* (*pl.* **-os**) archipel *m.*
architect /ˈɑːkɪtekt/ *n.* architecte *m.*
architectur|e /ˈɑːkɪtektʃə(r)/ *n.* architecture *f.* **~al** /-ˈtektʃərəl/ *a.* architectural.
archiv|es /ˈɑːkaɪvz/ *n. pl.* archives *f. pl.* **~ist** /-ɪvɪst/ *n.* archiviste *m./f.*
archway /ˈɑːtʃweɪ/ *n.* voûte *f.*
Arctic /ˈɑːktɪk/ *a.* & *n.* arctique (*m.*). **arctic** *a.* glacial.
ardent /ˈɑːdnt/ *a.* ardent. **~ly** *adv.* ardemment.
ardour /ˈɑːdə(r)/ *n.* ardeur *f.*
arduous /ˈɑːdjʊəs/ *a.* ardu.
are /ɑː(r)/ *see* **be.**
area /ˈeərɪə/ *n.* (*surface*) superficie *f.*; (*region*) région *f.*; (*district*) quartier *m.*; (*fig.*) domaine *m.*
arena /əˈriːnə/ *n.* arène *f.*
aren't /ɑːnt/ = **are not.**
Argentin|a /ɑːdʒənˈtiːnə/ *n.* Argentine *f.* **~e** /ˈɑːdʒəntaɪn/, **~ian** /-ˈtɪnɪən/ *a.* & *n.* argentin(e) (*m.* (*f.*)).
argu|e /ˈɑːgjuː/ *v.i.* (*quarrel*) se disputer; (*reason*) argumenter. —*v.t.* (*debate*) discuter. **~e that,** alléguer que. **~able** /-ʊəbl/ *a.* discutable.
argument /ˈɑːgjʊmənt/ *n.* dispute *f.*; (*reasoning*) argument *m.* **~ative** /-ˈmentətɪv/ *a.* raisonneur, contrariant.
arid /ˈærɪd/ *a.* aride.
arise /əˈraɪz/ *v.i.* (*p.t.* **arose,** *p.p.* **arisen**) se présenter; (*old use*) se lever. **~ from,** résulter de.
aristocracy /ærɪˈstɒkrəsɪ/ *n.* aristocratie *f.*
aristocrat /ˈærɪstəkræt, *Amer.* əˈrɪstəkræt/ *n.* aristocrate *m./f.* **~ic** /-ˈkrætɪk/ *a.* aristocratique.
arithmetic /əˈrɪθmətɪk/ *n.* arithmétique *f.*
ark /ɑːk/ *n.* (*relig.*) arche *f.*
arm[1] /ɑːm/ *n.* bras *m.* **~ in arm,** bras dessus bras dessous. **~-band** *n.* brassard *m.*
arm[2] /ɑːm/ *v.t.* armer. **~ed robbery,** vol à main armée *m.*
armament /ˈɑːməmənt/ *n.* armement *m.*
armchair /ˈɑːmtʃeə(r)/ *n.* fauteuil *m.*
armful /ˈɑːmfʊl/ *n.* brassée *f.*
armistice /ˈɑːmɪstɪs/ *n.* armistice *m.*
armlet /ˈɑːmlɪt/ *n.* brassard *m.*
armour /ˈɑːmə(r)/ *n.* armure *f.*; (*on tanks etc.*) blindage *m.* **~-clad, ~ed** *adjs.* blindé.
armoury /ˈɑːmərɪ/ *n.* arsenal *m.*
armpit /ˈɑːmpɪt/ *n.* aisselle *f.*
arms /ɑːmz/ *n. pl.* (*weapons*) armes *f. pl.*
army /ˈɑːmɪ/ *n.* armée *f.*
aroma /əˈrəʊmə/ *n.* arôme *m.* **~tic** /ærəˈmætɪk/ *a.* aromatique.
arose /əˈrəʊz/ *see* **arise.**
around /əˈraʊnd/ *adv.* (tout) autour; (*here and there*) çà et là. —*prep.* autour de. **~ here,** par ici.
arouse /əˈraʊz/ *v.t.* (*awaken, cause*) éveiller; (*excite*) exciter.
arpeggio /ɑːˈpedʒɪəʊ/ *n.* (*pl.* **-os**) arpège *m.*
arrange /əˈreɪndʒ/ *v.t.* arranger; (*time, date*) fixer. **~ to,** s'arranger pour. **~ment** *n.* arrangement *m.* **make ~ments,** prendre des dispositions.
array /əˈreɪ/ *v.t.* (*mil.*) déployer; (*dress*) vêtir. —*n.* **an ~ of,** (*display*) un étalage impressionnant de.
arrears /əˈrɪəz/ *n. pl.* arriéré *m.*

in ~, (*rent*) arriéré. **he is in ~,** il a des paiements en retard.
arrest /ə'rest/ *v.t.* arrêter; (*attention*) retenir. —*n.* arrestation *f.* **under ~,** en état d'arrestation.
arrival /ə'raɪvl/ *n.* arrivée *f.* **new ~,** arrivant(e) *m.* (*f.*).
arrive /ə'raɪv/ *v.i.* arriver.
arrogan|t /'ærəgənt/ *a.* arrogant. **~ce** *n.* arrogance *f.* **~tly** *adv.* avec arrogance.
arrow /'ærəʊ/ *n.* flèche *f.*
arsenal /'ɑːsənl/ *n.* arsenal *m.*
arsenic /'ɑːsnɪk/ *n.* arsenic *m.*
arson /'ɑːsn/ *n.* incendie criminel *m.* **~ist** *n.* incendiaire *m.*/*f.*
art[1] /ɑːt/ *n.* art *m.*; (*fine arts*) beaux-arts *m. pl.* **~s,** (*univ.*) lettres *f. pl.* **~ gallery,** (*public*) musée (d'art) *m.*; (*private*) galerie (d'art) *f.* **~ school,** école des beaux-arts *f.*
art[2] /ɑːt/ (*old use, with* **thou**) = **are.**
artefact /'ɑːtɪfækt/ *n.* objet fabriqué *m.*
arter|y /'ɑːtərɪ/ *n.* artère *f.* **~ial** /-'tɪərɪəl/ *a.* artériel. **~ial road,** route principale *f.*
artful /'ɑːtfl/ *a.* astucieux, rusé. **~ness** *n.* astuce *f.*
arthriti|s /ɑː'θraɪtɪs/ *n.* arthrite *f.* **~c** /-ɪtɪk/ *a.* arthritique.
artichoke /'ɑːtɪtʃəʊk/ *n.* artichaut *m.*
article /'ɑːtɪkl/ *n.* article *m.* **~ of clothing,** vêtement *m.* **~d** *a.* (*jurid.*) en stage.
articulate[1] /ɑː'tɪkjʊlət/ *a.* (*person*) capable de s'exprimer clairement; (*speech*) distinct.
articulat|e[2] /ɑː'tɪkjʊleɪt/ *v.t.*/*i.* articuler. **~ed lorry,** semi-remorque *m.* **~ion** /-'leɪʃn/ *n.* articulation *f.*
artifice /'ɑːtɪfɪs/ *n.* artifice *m.*
artificial /ɑːtɪ'fɪʃl/ *a.* artificiel. **~ity** /-ʃɪ'ælətɪ/ *n.* manque de naturel *m.*
artillery /ɑː'tɪlərɪ/ *n.* artillerie *f.*
artisan /ɑːtɪ'zæn/ *n.* artisan *m.*
artist /'ɑːtɪst/ *n.* artiste *m.*/*f.* **~ic** /-'tɪstɪk/ *a.* artistique. **~ry** *n.* art *m.*
artiste /ɑː'tiːst/ *n.* (*entertainer*) artiste *m.*/*f.*
artless /'ɑːtlɪs/ *a.* ingénu, naïf.
arty /'ɑːtɪ/ *a.* (*fam., péj.*) qui est du genre artiste.
as /æz, *unstressed* əz/ *adv.* & *conj.* comme; (*while*) pendant que. **~ you get older,** en vieillissant. **~ a gift,** en cadeau. **~ tall as,** aussi grand que. **~ for, ~ to,** quant à. **~ much, ~ many,** autant (**as,** que). **~ soon as,** aussitôt que. **~ well,** aussi (**as,** bien que).
asbestos /æz'bestɒs/ *n.* amiante *f.*
ascend /ə'send/ *v.t.* gravir; (*throne*) monter sur. —*v.i.* monter. **~ant** *n.* **in the ~ant,** qui monte.
ascent /ə'sent/ *n.* (*climbing*) ascension *f.*; (*slope*) côte *f.*
ascertain /æsə'teɪn/ *v.t.* s'assurer de. **~ that,** s'assurer que.
ascetic /ə'setɪk/ *a.* ascétique. —*n.* ascète *m.*/*f.*
ascribe /ə'skraɪb/ *v.t.* attribuer.
ash[1] /æʃ/ *n.* **~(-tree),** frêne *m.*
ash[2] /æʃ/ *n.* cendre *f.* **A~ Wednesday,** Mercredi des Cendres *m.* **~en** *a.* cendreux.
ashamed /ə'ʃeɪmd/ *a.* **be ~,** avoir honte, être honteux (**of,** de).
ashore /ə'ʃɔː(r)/ *adv.* à terre.
ashtray /'æʃtreɪ/ *n.* cendrier *m.*
Asia /'eɪʃə, *Amer.* 'eɪʒə/ *n.* Asie *f.* **~n** *a.* & *n.* asiatique (*m.*/*f.*). **~tic** /-ɪ'ætɪk/ *a.* asiatique.
aside /ə'saɪd/ *adv.* de côté. —*n.* aparté *m.* **~ from,** (*Amer.*) à part.
asinine /'æsɪnaɪn/ *a.* stupide.
ask /ɑːsk/ *v.t.*/*i.* demander; (*a question*) poser; (*invite*) inviter. **~ s.o. sth.,** demander qch. à qn. **~ about,** (*thing*) se renseigner sur; (*person*) demander des nouvelles de. **~ for,** demander.

askance /ə'skæns/ *adv.* **look ~ at,** regarder avec méfiance.

askew /ə'skju:/ *adv.* & *a.* de travers.

asleep /ə'sli:p/ *a.* endormi; (*numb*) engourdi. —*adv.* **fall ~,** s'endormir.

asp /æsp/ *n.* (*snake*) aspic *m.*

asparagus /ə'spærəgəs/ *n.* (*plant*) asperge *f.*; (*culin.*) asperges *f. pl.*

aspect /'æspekt/ *n.* aspect *m.*; (*direction*) orientation *f.*

aspersions /ə'spɜ:ʃnz/ *n. pl.* **cast ~ on,** calomnier.

asphalt /'æsfælt, *Amer.* 'æsfɔ:lt/ *n.* asphalte *m.* —*v.t.* asphalter.

asphyxia /æs'fɪksɪə/ *n.* asphyxie *f.*

asphyxiat|e /əs'fɪksɪeɪt/ *v.t./i.* (s')asphyxier. **~ion** /-'eɪʃn/ *n.* asphyxie *f.*

aspir|e /əs'paɪə(r)/ *v.i.* **~e to,** aspirer à. **~ation** /æspə'reɪʃn/ *n.* aspiration *f.*

aspirin /'æsprɪn/ *n.* aspirine *f.*

ass /æs/ *n.* âne *m.*; (*person: fam.*) idiot(e) *m.* (*f.*).

assail /ə'seɪl/ *v.t.* assaillir. **~ant** *n.* agresseur *m.*

assassin /ə'sæsɪn/ *n.* assassin *m.*

assassinat|e /ə'sæsɪneɪt/ *v.t.* assassiner. **~ion** /-'neɪʃn/ *n.* assassinat *m.*

assault /ə'sɔ:lt/ *n.* (*mil.*) assaut *m.*; (*jurid.*) agression *f.* —*v.t.* (*person: jurid.*) agresser.

assembl|e /ə'sembl/ *v.t.* (*things*) assembler; (*people*) rassembler. —*v.i.* s'assembler, se rassembler. **~age** *n.* assemblage *m.*

assembly /ə'semblɪ/ *n.* assemblée *f.* **~ line,** chaîne de montage *f.*

assent /ə'sent/ *n.* assentiment *m.* —*v.i.* consentir.

assert /ə'sɜ:t/ *v.t.* affirmer; (*one's rights*) revendiquer. **~ion** /-ʃn/ *n.* affirmation *f.* **~ive** *a.* affirmatif, péremptoire.

assess /ə'ses/ *v.t.* évaluer; (*payment*) déterminer le montant de. **~ment** *n.* évaluation *f.* **~or** *n.* (*valuer*) expert *m.*

asset /'æset/ *n.* (*advantage*) atout *m.* **~s,** (*comm.*) actif *m.*

assiduous /ə'sɪdjʊəs/ *a.* assidu.

assign /ə'saɪn/ *v.t.* (*allot*) assigner. **~ s.o. to,** (*appoint*) affecter qn. à.

assignment /ə'saɪnmənt/ *n.* (*task*) mission *f.*, tâche *f.*

assimilat|e /ə'sɪməleɪt/ *v.t./i.* (s')assimiler. **~ion** /-'leɪʃn/ *n.* assimilation *f.*

assist /ə'sɪst/ *v.t./i.* aider. **~ance** *n.* aide *f.*

assistant /ə'sɪstənt/ *n.* aide *m./f.*; (*in shop*) vendeu|r, -se *m.*, *f.* —*a.* (*manager etc.*) adjoint.

associat|e[1] /ə'səʊʃɪeɪt/ *v.t.* associer. —*v.i.* **~e with,** fréquenter. **~ion** /-'eɪʃn/ *n.* association *f.* **A~ion football,** football *m.*

associate[2] /ə'səʊʃɪət/ *n.* & *a.* associé(e) (*m.* (*f.*)).

assort|ed /ə'sɔ:tɪd/ *a.* divers; (*foods*) assortis. **~ment** *n.* assortiment *m.* **an ~ment of guests/***etc.*, des invités/*etc.* divers.

assume /ə'sju:m/ *v.t.* supposer, présumer; (*power, attitude*) prendre; (*role, burden*) assumer.

assumption /ə'sʌmpʃn/ *n.* (*sth. supposed*) supposition *f.*

assurance /ə'ʃʊərəns/ *n.* assurance *f.*

assure /ə'ʃʊə(r)/ *v.t.* assurer. **~d** *a.* assuré. **~dly** /-rɪdlɪ/ *adv.* assurément.

asterisk /'æstərɪsk/ *n.* astérisque *m.*

astern /ə'stɜ:n/ *adv.* à l'arrière.

asthma /'æsmə/ *n.* asthme *m.* **~tic** /-'mætɪk/ *a.* & *n.* asthmatique (*m./f.*).

astonish /ə'stɒnɪʃ/ *v.t.* étonner. **~ingly** *adv.* étonnamment. **~ment** *n.* étonnement *m.*

astound /ə'staʊnd/ *v.t.* stupéfier.

astray /ə'streɪ/ *adv.* & *a.* **go ~,** s'égarer. **lead ~,** égarer.

astride /əˈstraɪd/ *adv.* & *prep.* à califourchon (sur).
astringent /əˈstrɪndʒənt/ *a.* astringent; (*severe*: *fig.*) austère. —*n.* astringent *m.*
astrolog|y /əˈstrɒlədʒɪ/ *n.* astrologie *f.* **~er** *n.* astrologue *m.*
astronaut /ˈæstrənɔːt/ *n.* astronaute *m.*/*f.*
astronom|y /əˈstrɒnəmɪ/ *n.* astronomie *f.* **~er** *n.* astronome *m.* **~ical** /æstrəˈnɒmɪkl/ *a.* astronomique.
astute /əˈstjuːt/ *a.* astucieux. **~ness** *n.* astuce *f.*
asunder /əˈsʌndə(r)/ *adv.* en morceaux; (*in two*) en deux.
asylum /əˈsaɪləm/ *n.* asile *m.*
at /æt, *unstressed* ət/ *prep.* à. **~ the doctor's**/*etc.*, chez le médecin/*etc.* **surprised ~**, (*cause*) étonné de. **angry ~**, fâché contre. **not ~ all**, pas du tout. **no wind**/*etc.* **~ all**, (*of any kind*) pas le moindre vent/*etc.* **~ night**, la nuit. **~ once**, tout de suite; (*simultaneously*) à la fois. **~ sea**, en mer. **~ times**, parfois.
ate /et/ *see* **eat.**
atheis|t /ˈeɪθɪɪst/ *n.* athée *m.*/*f.* **~m** /-zəm/ *n.* athéisme *m.*
athlet|e /ˈæθliːt/ *n.* athlète *m.*/*f.* **~ic** /-ˈletɪk/ *a.* athlétique. **~ics** /-ˈletɪks/ *n. pl.* athlétisme *m.*
Atlantic /ətˈlæntɪk/ *a.* atlantique. —*n.* **~ (Ocean)**, Atlantique *m.*
atlas /ˈætləs/ *n.* atlas *m.*
atmospher|e /ˈætməsfɪə(r)/ *n.* atmosphère *f.* **~ic** /-ˈferɪk/ *a.* atmosphérique.
atmospherics /ætməsˈferɪks/ *n. pl.* parasites *m. pl.*
atom /ˈætəm/ *n.* atome *m.* **~ic** /əˈtɒmɪk/ *a.* atomique. **~(ic) bomb,** bombe atomique *f.*
atomize /ˈætəmaɪz/ *v.t.* atomiser. **~r** /-ə(r)/ *n.* atomiseur *m.*
atone /əˈtəʊn/ *v.i.* **~ for,** expier. **~ment** *n.* expiation *f.*
atrocious /əˈtrəʊʃəs/ *a.* atroce.
atrocity /əˈtrɒsətɪ/ *n.* atrocité *f.*
atrophy /ˈætrəfɪ/ *n.* atrophie *f.* —*v.t.*/*i.* (s')atrophier.
attach /əˈtætʃ/ *v.t.*/*i.* (s')attacher; (*letter*) joindre (**to,** à). **~ed** *a.* **be ~ed to,** (*like*) être attaché à. **the ~ed letter,** la lettre ci-jointe. **~ment** *n.* (*accessory*) accessoire *m.*; (*affection*) attachement *m.*
attaché /əˈtæʃeɪ/ *n.* (*pol.*) attaché(e) *m.* (*f.*). **~ case,** mallette *f.*
attack /əˈtæk/ *n.* attaque *f.* —*v.t.*/*i.* attaquer. **~er** *n.* aggresseur *m.*, attaquant(e) *m.* (*f.*).
attain /əˈteɪn/ *v.t.* atteindre (à); (*gain*) acquérir. **~able** *a.* accessible. **~ment** *n.* acquisition *f.* (**of,** de). **~ments,** réussites *f. pl.*
attempt /əˈtempt/ *v.t.* tenter. —*n.* tentative *f.* **an ~ on s.o.'s life,** un attentat contre qn.
attend /əˈtend/ *v.t.* assister à; (*class*) suivre; (*school, church*) aller à; (*escort*) accompagner. —*v.i.* assister. **~ (to),** (*look after*) s'occuper de. **~ance** *n.* présence *f.*; (*people*) assistance *f.*
attendant /əˈtendənt/ *n.* employé(e) *m.* (*f.*); (*servant*) serviteur *m.*
attention /əˈtenʃn/ *n.* attention *f.*; **~!**, (*mil.*) garde-à-vous! **pay ~,** faire *or* prêter attention (**to,** à).
attentive /əˈtentɪv/ *a.* attentif; (*considerate*) attentionné. **~ly** *adv.* attentivement. **~ness** *n.* attention *f.*
attenuate /əˈtenjʊeɪt/ *v.t.* atténuer.
attest /əˈtest/ *v.t.*/*i.* **~ (to),** attester. **~ation** /æteˈsteɪʃn/ *n.* attestation *f.*
attic /ˈætɪk/ *n.* grenier *m.*
attire /əˈtaɪə(r)/ *n.* vêtements *m. pl.* —*v.t.* vêtir.
attitude /ˈætɪtjuːd/ *n.* attitude *f.*
attorney /əˈtɜːnɪ/ *n.* mandataire *m.*; (*Amer.*) avocat *m.*

attract /ə'trækt/ *v.t.* attirer. **~ion** /-kʃn/ *n.* attraction *f.*; (*charm*) attrait *m.*

attractive /ə'træktɪv/ *a.* attrayant, séduisant. **~ly** *adv.* agréablement. **~ness** *n.* attrait *m.*, beauté *f.*

attribute[1] /ə'trɪbjuːt/ *v.t.* **~ to**, attribuer à.

attribute[2] /'ætrɪbjuːt/ *n.* attribut *m.*

attrition /ə'trɪʃn/ *n.* **war of ~**, guerre d'usure *f.*

aubergine /'əʊbəʒiːn/ *n.* aubergine *f.*

auburn /'ɔːbən/ *a.* châtain roux *invar.*

auction /'ɔːkʃn/ *n.* vente aux enchères *f.* —*v.t.* vendre aux enchères. **~eer** /-ə'nɪə(r)/ *n.* commissaire-priseur *m.*

audaci|ous /ɔː'deɪʃəs/ *a.* audacieux. **~ty** /-æsətɪ/ *n.* audace *f.*

audible /'ɔːdəbl/ *a.* audible.

audience /'ɔːdɪəns/ *n.* auditoire *m.*; (*theatre, radio*) public *m.*; (*interview*) audience *f.*

audio typist /'ɔːdɪəʊ'taɪpɪst/ *n.* audiotypiste *m./f.*

audio-visual /ɔːdɪəʊ'vɪʒʊəl/ *a.* audio-visuel.

audit /'ɔːdɪt/ *n.* vérification des comptes *f.* —*v.t.* vérifier.

audition /ɔː'dɪʃn/ *n.* audition *f.* —*v.t./i.* auditionner.

auditor /'ɔːdɪtə(r)/ *n.* commissaire aux comptes *m.*

auditorium /ɔːdɪ'tɔːrɪəm/ *n.* (*of theatre etc.*) salle *f.*

augment /ɔːg'ment/ *v.t.* augmenter.

augur /'ɔːgə(r)/ *v.i.* **~ well/ill**, être de bon/mauvais augure.

august /ɔː'gʌst/ *a.* auguste.

August /'ɔːgəst/ *n.* août *m.*

aunt /ɑːnt/ *n.* tante *f.*

au pair /əʊ'peə(r)/ *n.* jeune fille au pair *f.*

aura /'ɔːrə/ *n.* atmosphère *f.*

auspices /'ɔːspɪsɪz/ *n. pl.* auspices *m. pl.*, égide *f.*

auspicious /ɔː'spɪʃəs/ *a.* favorable.

auster|e /ɔː'stɪə(r)/ *a.* austère. **~ity** /-erətɪ/ *n.* austérité *f.*

Australia /ɒ'streɪlɪə/ *n.* Australie *f.* **~n** *a.* & *n.* australien(ne) (*m.* (*f.*)).

Austria /'ɒstrɪə/ *n.* Autriche *f.* **~n** *a.* & *n.* autrichien(ne) (*m.* (*f.*)).

authentic /ɔː'θentɪk/ *a.* authentique. **~ity** /-ən'tɪsətɪ/ *n.* authenticité *f.*

authenticate /ɔː'θentɪkeɪt/ *v.t.* authentifier.

author /'ɔːθə(r)/ *n.* auteur *m.* **~ess** *n.* femme auteur *f.* **~ship** *n.* (*origin*) paternité *f.*

authoritarian /ɔːθɒrɪ'teərɪən/ *a.* autoritaire.

authorit|y /ɔː'θɒrətɪ/ *n.* autorité *f.*; (*permission*) autorisation *f.* **~ative** /-ɪtətɪv/ *a.* (*trusted*) autorisé; (*manner*) autoritaire.

authoriz|e /'ɔːθəraɪz/ *v.t.* autoriser. **~ation** /-'zeɪʃn/ *n.* autorisation *f.*

autistic /ɔː'tɪstɪk/ *a.* autistique.

autobiography /ɔːtəbaɪ'ɒgrəfɪ/ *n.* autobiographie *f.*

autocracy /ɔː'tɒkrəsɪ/ *n.* autocratie *f.*

autocrat /'ɔːtəkræt/ *n.* autocrate *m.* **~ic** /-'krætɪk/ *a.* autocratique.

autograph /'ɔːtəgrɑːf/ *n.* autographe *m.* —*v.t.* signer, dédicacer.

automat|e /'ɔːtəmeɪt/ *v.t.* automatiser. **~ion** /-'meɪʃn/ *n.* automatisation *f.*

automatic /ɔːtə'mætɪk/ *a.* automatique. **~ally** /-klɪ/ *adv.* automatiquement.

automaton /ɔː'tɒmətən/ *n.* (*pl.* **-s** *or collectively* **-ta**) automate *m.*

automobile /'ɔːtəməbiːl/ *n.* (*Amer.*) auto(mobile) *f.*

autonom|y /ɔː'tɒnəmɪ/ *n.* autonomie *f.* **~ous** *a.* autonome.

autopsy /'ɔːtɒpsɪ/ *n.* autopsie *f.*

autumn /ˈɔːtəm/ *n.* automne *m.* **~al** /-ˈtʌmnəl/ *a.* automnal.

auxiliary /ɔːgˈzɪlɪərɪ/ *a.* & *n.* auxiliaire (*m.*/*f.*). **~** **(verb)**, auxiliaire *m.*

avail /əˈveɪl/ *v.t.* **~ o.s. of,** profiter de. *—n.* **of no ~,** inutile. **to no ~,** sans résultat.

availab|le /əˈveɪləbl/ *a.* disponible. **~ility** /-ˈbɪlətɪ/ *n.* disponibilité *f.*

avalanche /ˈævəlɑːnʃ/ *n.* avalanche *f.*

avaric|e /ˈævərɪs/ *n.* avarice *f.* **~ious** /-ˈrɪʃəs/ *a.* avare.

avenge /əˈvendʒ/ *v.t.* venger. **~ o.s.,** se venger **(on,** de).

avenue /ˈævənjuː/ *n.* avenue *f.*; (*line of approach*: *fig.*) voie *f.*

average /ˈævərɪdʒ/ *n.* moyenne *f.* *—a.* moyen. *—v.t.*/*i.* faire la moyenne de; (*produce, do*) faire en moyenne. **on ~,** en moyenne.

avers|e /əˈvɜːs/ *a.* **be ~e to,** répugner à. **~ion** /-ʃn/ *n.* aversion *f.*

avert /əˈvɜːt/ *v.t.* (*turn away*) détourner; (*ward off*) éviter.

aviary /ˈeɪvɪərɪ/ *n.* volière *f.*

aviation /eɪvɪˈeɪʃn/ *n.* aviation *f.*

aviator /ˈeɪvɪeɪtə(r)/ *n.* (*old use*) avia|teur, -trice *m.*, *f.*

avid /ˈævɪd/ *a.* avide.

avocado /ævəˈkɑːdəʊ/ *n.* (*pl.* **-os**) avocat *m.*

avoid /əˈvɔɪd/ *v.t.* éviter. **~able** *a.* évitable. **~ance** *n.* **the ~ance of s.o./sth. is . . .,** éviter qn./qch., c'est . . .

avuncular /əˈvʌŋkjʊlə(r)/ *a.* avunculaire.

await /əˈweɪt/ *v.t.* attendre.

awake /əˈweɪk/ *v.t.*/*i.* (*p.t.* **awoke,** *p.p.* **awoken)** (s')éveiller. *—a.* **be ~,** ne pas dormir, être (r)éveillé.

awaken /əˈweɪkən/ *v.t.*/*i.* (s')éveiller.

award /əˈwɔːd/ *v.t.* attribuer. *—n.* récompense *f.*, prix *m.*; (*scholarship*) bourse *f.*

aware /əˈweə(r)/ *a.* averti. **~ of,** conscient de. **become ~ of,** prendre conscience de. **~ness** *n.* conscience *f.*

awash /əˈwɒʃ/ *a.* inondé **(with,** de).

away /əˈweɪ/ *adv.* (*far*) (au) loin; (*absent*) absent, parti; (*persistently*) sans arrêt; (*entirely*) complètement. **six kilometres ~,** à six kilomètres (de distance). *—a.* & *n.* **~ (match),** match à l'extérieur *m.*

awe /ɔː/ *n.* crainte (révérencielle) *f.* **~-inspiring, ~some** *adjs.* terrifiant; (*sight*) imposant. **~struck** *a.* terrifié.

awful /ˈɔːfl/ *a.* affreux. **~ly** /ˈɔːflɪ/ *adv.* (*badly*) affreusement; (*very*: *fam.*) rudement.

awhile /əˈwaɪl/ *adv.* quelque temps.

awkward /ˈɔːkwəd/ *a.* difficile; (*inconvenient*) inopportun; (*clumsy*) maladroit; (*embarrassing*) gênant; (*embarrassed*) gêné. **~ly** *adv.* maladroitement; avec gêne. **~ness** *n.* maladresse *f.*; (*discomfort*) gêne *f.*

awning /ˈɔːnɪŋ/ *n.* auvent *m.*; (*of shop*) store *m.*

awoke, awoken /əˈwəʊk, əˈwəʊkən/ *see* **awake.**

awry /əˈraɪ/ *adv.* **go ~,** mal tourner. **sth. is ~,** qch. ne va pas.

axe /æks/ *n.* hache *f.* *—v.t.* (*pres. p.* **axing)** réduire; (*eliminate*) supprimer; (*employee*) renvoyer.

axiom /ˈæksɪəm/ *n.* axiome *m.*

axis /ˈæksɪs/ *n.* (*pl.* **axes** /-siːz/) axe *m.*

axle /ˈæksl/ *n.* essieu *m.*

ay(e) /aɪ/ *adv.* & *n.* oui (*m. invar.*).

B

BA *abbr. see* **Bachelor of Arts.**

babble /ˈbæbl/ *v.i.* babiller;

(*stream*) gazouiller. —*n*. babillage *m*.

baboon /bəˈbuːn/ *n*. babouin *m*.

baby /ˈbeɪbɪ/ *n*. bébé *m*. **~ carriage,** (*Amer*.) voiture d'enfant *f*. **~-sit** *v.i.* garder les enfants. **~-sitter** *n*. baby-sitter *m./f.*

babyish /ˈbeɪbɪɪʃ/ *a*. enfantin.

bachelor /ˈbætʃələ(r)/ *n*. célibataire *m*. **B~ of Arts/Science,** licencié(e) ès lettres/sciences *m*. (*f*.).

back /bæk/ *n*. (*of person, hand, page, etc*.) dos *m*.; (*of house*) derrière *m*.; (*of vehicle*) arrière *m*.; (*of room*) fond *m*.; (*of chair*) dossier *m*.; (*football*) arrière *m*. —*a*. de derrière, arrière *invar*.; (*taxes*) arriéré. —*adv*. en arrière; (*returned*) de retour, rentré. —*v.t.* (*support*) appuyer; (*bet on*) miser sur; (*vehicle*) faire reculer. —*v.i.* (*of person, vehicle*) reculer. **at the ~ of beyond,** au diable. **in ~ of,** (*Amer*.) derrière. **~-bencher** *n*. (*pol*.) membre sans portefeuille *m*. **~ down,** abandonner, se dégonfler. **~ number,** vieux numéro *m*. **~ out,** se dégager, se dégonfler. **~ up,** (*support*) appuyer. **~-up** *n*. appui *m*.; (*Amer., fam*.) embouteillage *m*.; *a*. de réserve.

backache /ˈbækeɪk/ *n*. mal de reins *m*., mal aux reins *m*.

backbiting /ˈbækbaɪtɪŋ/ *n*. médisance *f*.

backbone /ˈbækbəʊn/ *n*. colonne vertébrale *f*.

backchat /ˈbæktʃæt/ *n*. réplique (impertinente) *f*.

backdate /bækˈdeɪt/ *v.t.* antidater.

backer /ˈbækə(r)/ *n*. partisan *m*.; (*comm*.) bailleur de fonds *m*.

backfire /bækˈfaɪə(r)/ *v.i.* (*auto*.) pétarader; (*fig*.) mal tourner.

backgammon /bækˈgæmən/ *n*. trictrac *m*.

background /ˈbækgraʊnd/ *n*. fond *m*., arrière-plan *m*.; (*context*) contexte *m*.; (*environment*) milieu *m*.; (*experience*) formation *f*. —*a*. (*music, noise*) de fond.

backhand /ˈbækhænd/ *n*. revers *m*. **~ed** *a*. équivoque. **~ed stroke,** revers *m*. **~er** *n*. revers *m*.; (*bribe*: *sl*.) pot de vin *m*.

backing /ˈbækɪŋ/ *n*. appui *m*.

backlash /ˈbæklæʃ/ *n*. choc en retour *m*., répercussions *f. pl.*

backlog /ˈbæklɒg/ *n*. accumulation (de travail) *f*.

backside /ˈbæksaɪd/ *n*. (*buttocks*: *fam*.) derrière *m*.

backstage /bækˈsteɪdʒ/ *a*. & *adv*. dans les coulisses.

backstroke /ˈbækstrəʊk/ *n*. dos crawlé *m*.

backtrack /ˈbæktræk/ *v.i.* rebrousser chemin; (*change one's opinion*) faire marche arrière.

backward /ˈbækwəd/ *a*. (*step etc*.) en arrière; (*retarded*) arriéré.

backwards /ˈbækwədz/ *adv*. en arrière; (*walk*) à reculons; (*read*) à l'envers; (*fall*) à la renverse. **go ~ and forwards,** aller et venir.

backwater /ˈbækwɔːtə(r)/ *n*. (*pej*.) trou perdu *m*.

bacon /ˈbeɪkən/ *n*. lard *m*.; (*in rashers*) bacon *m*.

bacteria /bækˈtɪərɪə/ *n. pl.* bactéries *f. pl.* **~l** *a*. bactérien.

bad /bæd/ *a*. (**worse, worst**) mauvais; (*wicked*) méchant; (*ill*) malade; (*accident*) grave; (*food*) gâté. **feel ~,** se sentir mal. **~ language,** gros mots *m. pl.* **~-mannered** *a*. mal élevé. **~-tempered** *a*. grincheux. **~ly** *adv*. mal; (*hurt*) grièvement. **want ~ly,** avoir grande envie de.

badge /bædʒ/ *n*. insigne *m*.; (*of identity*) plaque *f*.

badger /ˈbædʒə(r)/ *n*. blaireau *m*. —*v.t.* harceler.

badminton /ˈbædmɪntən/ *n*. badminton *m*.

baffle /ˈbæfl/ *v.t.* déconcerter.

bag /bæg/ *n.* sac *m.* **~s,** (*luggage*) bagages *m. pl.*; (*under eyes*) poches *f. pl.* —*v.t.* (*p.t.* **bagged**) mettre en sac; (*take*: *fam.*) s'adjuger. **~s of,** (*fam.*) beaucoup de.

baggage /ˈbægɪdʒ/ *n.* bagages *m. pl.*

baggy /ˈbægɪ/ *a.* (*trousers etc.*) qui fait des poches.

bagpipes /ˈbægpaɪps/ *n. pl.* cornemuse *f.*

Bahamas /bəˈhɑːməz/ *n. pl.* **the ~,** les Bahamas *f. pl.*

bail[1] /beɪl/ *n.* caution *f.* **on ~,** sous caution. —*v.t.* mettre en liberté (provisoire) sous caution. **~ out,** (*fig.*) sortir d'affaire.

bail[2] /beɪl/ *n.* (*cricket*) bâtonnet *m.*

bail[3] /beɪl/ *v.t.* (*naut.*) écoper.

bailiff /ˈbeɪlɪf/ *n.* huissier *m.*

bait /beɪt/ *n.* appât *m.* —*v.t.* appâter; (*fig.*) tourmenter.

bak|e /beɪk/ *v.t.* (faire) cuire (au four). —*v.i.* cuire (au four); (*person*) faire du pain *or* des gâteaux. **~er** *n.* boulang|er, -ère *m.*, *f.* **~ing** *n.* cuisson *f.* **~ing-powder** *n.* levure *f.*

bakery /ˈbeɪkərɪ/ *n.* boulangerie *f.*

Balaclava /bæləˈklɑːvə/ *n.* **~ (helmet),** passe-montagne *m.*

balance /ˈbæləns/ *n.* équilibre *m.*; (*scales*) balance *f.*; (*outstanding sum*: *comm.*) solde *m.*; (*of payments, of trade*) balance *f.*; (*remainder*) reste *m.* —*v.t.* tenir en équilibre; (*weigh up & comm.*) balancer; (*budget*) équilibrer. —*v.i.* être en équilibre. **~d** *a.* équilibré.

balcony /ˈbælkənɪ/ *n.* balcon *m.*

bald /bɔːld/ *a.* (**-er, -est**) chauve; (*tyre*) lisse; (*fig.*) simple. **~ing** *a.* **be ~ing,** perdre ses cheveux. **~ly** *adv.* (*speak*) crûment. **~ness** *n.* calvitie *f.*

balderdash /ˈbɔːldədæʃ/ *n.* balivernes *f. pl.*

bale[1] /beɪl/ *n.* (*of cotton*) balle *f.*; (*of straw*) botte *f.*

bale[2] /beɪl/ *v.i.* **~ out,** sauter en parachute.

baleful /ˈbeɪlfʊl/ *a.* sinistre.

balk /bɔːk/ *v.t.* contrecarrer. —*v.i.* **~ at,** reculer devant.

ball[1] /bɔːl/ *n.* (*golf, tennis, etc.*) balle *f.*; (*football*) ballon *m.*; (*croquet, billiards, etc.*) boule *f.*; (*of wool*) pelote *f.*; (*sphere*) boule *f.* **~-bearing** *n.* roulement à billes *m.* **~-cock** *n.* robinet à flotteur *m.* **~-point** *n.* stylo à bille *m.*

ball[2] /bɔːl/ *n.* (*dance*) bal *m.*

ballad /ˈbæləd/ *n.* ballade *f.*

ballast /ˈbæləst/ *n.* lest *m.*

ballerina /bæləˈriːnə/ *n.* ballerine *f.*

ballet /ˈbæleɪ/ *n.* ballet *m.*

ballistic /bəˈlɪstɪk/ *a.* **~ missile,** engin balistique *m.*

balloon /bəˈluːn/ *n.* ballon *m.*

ballot /ˈbælət/ *n.* scrutin *m.* **~-(paper),** bulletin de vote *m.* **~-box** *n.* urne *f.* —*v.i.* (*p.t.* **balloted**) (*pol.*) voter. —*v.t.* (*members*) consulter par voie de scrutin.

ballroom /ˈbɔːlrʊm/ *n.* salle de bal *f.*

ballyhoo /bælɪˈhuː/ *n.* (*publicity*) battage *m.*; (*uproar*) tapage *m.*

balm /bɑːm/ *n.* baume *m.* **~y** *a.* (*fragrant*) embaumé; (*mild*) doux; (*crazy*: *sl.*) dingue.

baloney /bəˈləʊnɪ/ *n.* (*sl.*) idioties *f. pl.*, calembredaines *f. pl.*

balustrade /bæləˈstreɪd/ *n.* balustrade *f.*

bamboo /bæmˈbuː/ *n.* bambou *m.*

bamboozle /bæmˈbuːzl/ *v.t.* (*cheat*: *sl.*) entortiller; (*confuse*: *sl.*) embrouiller.

ban /bæn/ *v.t.* (*p.t.* **banned**) interdire. **~ from,** exclure de. —*n.* interdiction *f.*

banal /bəˈnɑːl, *Amer.* ˈbeɪnl/ *a.* banal. **~ity** /-ælətɪ/ *n.* banalité *f.*

banana /bəˈnɑːnə/ *n.* banane *f.*

band /bænd/ *n.* (*strip, group of people*) bande *f.*; (*mus.*) orchestre *m.*; (*mil.*) fanfare *f.* —*v.i.* ~ **together,** se liguer.

bandage /'bændɪdʒ/ *n.* pansement *m.* —*v.t.* bander, panser.

bandit /'bændɪt/ *n.* bandit *m.*

bandstand /'bændstænd/ *n.* kiosque à musique *m.*

bandwagon /'bændwægən/ *n.* **climb on the ~,** prendre le train en marche.

bandy[1] /'bændɪ/ *v.t.* ~ **about,** (*rumours, ideas, etc.*) faire circuler.

bandy[2] /'bændɪ/ *a.* (**-ier, -iest**) bancal.

bane /beɪn/ *n.* fléau *m.* **~ful** *a.* funeste.

bang /bæŋ/ *n.* (*blow, noise*) coup (violent) *m.*; (*explosion*) détonation *f.*; (*of door*) claquement *m.* —*v.t./i.* frapper; (*door*) claquer. —*int.* vlan. —*adv.* (*fam.*) exactement. ~ **in the middle,** en plein milieu.

banger /'bæŋə(r)/ *n.* (*firework*) pétard *m.*; (*culin., sl.*) saucisse *f.* (**old**) **~,** (*car: sl.*) guimbarde *f.*

bangle /'bæŋgl/ *n.* bracelet *m.*

banish /'bænɪʃ/ *v.t.* bannir.

banisters /'bænɪstəz/ *n. pl.* rampe (d'escalier) *f.*

banjo /'bændʒəʊ/ (*pl.* **-os**) banjo *m.*

bank[1] /bæŋk/ *n.* (*of river*) rive *f.*; (*of earth*) talus *m.*; (*of sand*) banc *m.* —*v.t.* (*earth*) amonceler; (*fire*) couvrir. —*v.i.* (*aviat.*) virer.

bank[2] /bæŋk/ *n.* banque *f.* —*v.t.* mettre en banque. —*v.i.* ~ **with,** avoir un compte à. ~ **account,** compte en banque *m.* ~ **holiday,** jour férié *m.* ~ **on,** compter sur.

bank|ing /'bæŋkɪŋ/ *n.* opérations bancaires *f. pl.*; (*as career*) la banque. **~er** *n.* banquier *m.*

banknote /'bæŋknəʊt/ *n.* billet de banque *m.*

bankrupt /'bæŋkrʌpt/ *a.* **be ~,** être en faillite. **go ~,** faire faillite. —*n.* failli(e) *m.* (*f.*). —*v.t.* mettre en faillite. **~cy** *n.* faillite *f.*

banner /'bænə(r)/ *n.* bannière *f.*

banns /bænz/ *n. pl.* bans *m. pl.*

banquet /'bæŋkwɪt/ *n.* banquet *m.*

bantamweight /'bæntəmweɪt/ *n.* poids coq *m.*

banter /'bæntə(r)/ *n.* plaisanterie *f.* —*v.i.* plaisanter.

bap /bæp/ *n.* petit pain *m.*

baptism /'bæptɪzəm/ *n.* baptême *m.*

Baptist /'bæptɪst/ *n.* baptiste *m./f.*

baptize /bæp'taɪz/ *v.t.* baptiser.

bar /bɑː(r)/ *n.* (*of metal*) barre *f.*; (*on window & jurid.*) barreau *m.*; (*of chocolate*) tablette *f.*; (*pub*) bar *m.*; (*counter*) comptoir *m.*, bar *m.*; (*division: mus.*) mesure *f.*; (*fig.*) obstacle *m.* —*v.t.* (*p.t.* **barred**) (*obstruct*) barrer; (*prohibit*) interdire; (*exclude*) exclure. —*prep.* sauf. ~ **of soap,** savonnette *f.*

Barbados /bɑː'beɪdɒs/ *n.* Barbade *f.*

barbarian /bɑː'beərɪən/ *n.* barbare *m./f.*

barbari|c /bɑː'bærɪk/ *a.* barbare. **~ty** /-ətɪ/ *n.* barbarie *f.*

barbarous /'bɑːbərəs/ *a.* barbare.

barbecue /'bɑːbɪkjuː/ *n.* barbecue *m.* —*v.t.* griller, rôtir (au barbecue).

barbed /bɑːbd/ *a.* ~ **wire,** fil de fer barbelé *m.*

barber /'bɑːbə(r)/ *n.* coiffeur *m.* (*pour hommes*).

barbiturate /bɑː'bɪtjʊrət/ *n.* barbiturique *m.*

bare /beə(r)/ *a.* (**-er, -est**) (*not covered or adorned*) nu; (*cupboard*) vide; (*mere*) simple. —*v.t.* mettre à nu.

bareback /'beə(r)bæk/ *adv.* à cru.

barefaced /'beə(r)feɪst/ *a.* éhonté.

bareheaded /'beə(r)hedɪd/ *a.* nu-tête *invar.*

barely /'beə(r)lɪ/ *adv.* à peine.

bargain /ˈbɑːɡɪn/ *n.* (*deal*) marché *m.*; (*cheap thing*) occasion *f.* —*v.i.* négocier; (*haggle*) marchander. **~ for,** (*expect*) s'attendre à.

barge /bɑːdʒ/ *n.* chaland *m.* —*v.i.* **~ in,** interrompre; (*into room*) faire irruption.

baritone /ˈbærɪtəʊn/ *n.* baryton *m.*

bark[1] /bɑːk/ *n.* (*of tree*) écorce *f.*

bark[2] /bɑːk/ *n.* (*of dog*) aboiement *m.* —*v.i.* aboyer.

barley /ˈbɑːlɪ/ *n.* orge *f.* **~ sugar,** sucre d'orge *m.* **~-water** *n.* orgeat *m.*

barmaid /ˈbɑːmeɪd/ *n.* serveuse *f.*

barman /ˈbɑːmən/ *n.* (*pl.* **-men**) barman *m.*

barmy /ˈbɑːmɪ/ *a.* (*sl.*) dingue.

barn /bɑːn/ *n.* grange *f.*

barometer /bəˈrɒmɪtə(r)/ *n.* baromètre *m.*

baron /ˈbærən/ *n.* baron *m.* **~ess** *n.* baronne *f.*

baroque /bəˈrɒk, *Amer.* bəˈrəʊk/ *a.* & *n.* baroque (*m.*).

barracks /ˈbærəks/ *n.pl.* caserne *f.*

barrage /ˈbærɑːʒ, *Amer.* bəˈrɑːʒ/ *n.* (*barrier*) barrage *m.*; (*mil.*) tir de barrage *m.*

barrel /ˈbærəl/ *n.* tonneau *m.*; (*of oil*) baril *m.*; (*of gun*) canon *m.* **~-organ** *n.* orgue de Barbarie *m.*

barren /ˈbærən/ *a.* stérile.

barricade /bærɪˈkeɪd/ *n.* barricade *f.* —*v.t.* barricader.

barrier /ˈbærɪə(r)/ *n.* barrière *f.*

barring /ˈbɑːrɪŋ/ *prep.* sauf.

barrister /ˈbærɪstə(r)/ *n.* avocat *m.*

barrow /ˈbærəʊ/ *n.* charrette à bras *f.*; (*wheelbarrow*) brouette *f.*

barter /ˈbɑːtə(r)/ *n.* troc *m.*, échange *m.* —*v.t.* troquer, échanger.

base /beɪs/ *n.* base *f.* —*v.t.* baser (**on,** sur; **in,** à). —*a.* bas, ignoble. **~less** *a.* sans fondement.

baseball /ˈbeɪsbɔːl/ *n.* base-ball *m.*

baseboard /ˈbeɪsbɔːd/ *n.* (*Amer.*) plinthe *f.*

basement /ˈbeɪsmənt/ *n.* sous-sol *m.*

bash /bæʃ/ *v.t.* cogner. —*n.* coup (violent) *m.* **have a ~ at,** (*sl.*) s'essayer à. **~ed in,** enfoncé. **~ing** *n.* (*thrashing*) raclée *f.*

bashful /ˈbæʃfl/ *a.* timide.

basic /ˈbeɪsɪk/ *a.* fondamental, élémentaire. **~ally** /-klɪ/ *adv.* au fond.

basilica /bəˈzɪlɪkə/ *n.* basilique *f.*

basin /ˈbeɪsn/ *n.* (*for liquids*) cuvette *f.*; (*for food*) bol *m.*; (*for washing*) lavabo *m.*; (*of river*) bassin *m.*

basis /ˈbeɪsɪs/ *n.* (*pl.* **bases** /-siːz/) base *f.*

bask /bɑːsk/ *v.i.* se chauffer.

basket /ˈbɑːskɪt/ *n.* corbeille *f.*; (*with handle*) panier *m.*

basketball /ˈbɑːskɪtbɔːl/ *n.* basket(-ball) *m.*

Basque /bɑːsk/ *a.* & *n.* basque (*m.*/*f.*).

bass[1] /beɪs/ *a.* (*mus.*) bas, grave. —*n.* (*pl.* **basses**) basse *f.*

bass[2] /bæs/ *n. invar.* (*freshwater fish*) perche *f.*; (*sea*) bar *m.*

bassoon /bəˈsuːn/ *n.* basson *m.*

bastard /ˈbɑːstəd/ *n.* bâtard(e) *m.* (*f.*).; (*sl.*) sal|aud, -ope *m.*, *f.*

baste[1] /beɪst/ *v.t.* (*sew*) bâtir.

baste[2] /beɪst/ *v.t.* (*culin.*) arroser.

bastion /ˈbæstɪən/ *n.* bastion *m.*

bat[1] /bæt/ *n.* (*cricket etc.*) batte *f.*; (*table tennis*) raquette *f.* —*v.t.* (*p.t.* **batted**) (*ball*) frapper. **not ~ an eyelid,** ne pas sourciller.

bat[2] /bæt/ *n.* (*animal*) chauve-souris *f.*

batch /bætʃ/ *n.* (*of people*) fournée *f.*; (*of papers*) paquet *m.*; (*of goods*) lot *m.*

bated /ˈbeɪtɪd/ *a.* **with ~ breath,** en retenant son souffle.

bath /bɑːθ/ *n.* (*pl.* **-s** /bɑːðz/) bain *m.*; (*tub*) baignoire *f.* **the ~s,** (*washing*) les bains (publics); (*swimming*) la piscine. —*v.t.*

donner un bain à. *—v.i.* prendre un bain.

bathe /beɪð/ *v.t.* baigner. *—v.i.* se baigner; (*Amer.*) prendre un bain. *—n.* bain (de mer) *m.* **~r** /-ə(r)/ *n.* baigneu|r, -se *m., f.*

bathing /ˈbeɪðɪŋ/ *n.* baignade *f.* **~-costume** *n.* maillot de bain *m.*

bathrobe /ˈbæθrəʊb/ *m.* (*Amer.*) robe de chambre *f.*

bathroom /ˈbɑːθrʊm/ *n.* salle de bains *f.*

baton /ˈbætən/ *n.* (*mus., mil.*) bâton *m.*

battalion /bəˈtæljən/ *n.* bataillon *m.*

batter /ˈbætə(r)/ *v.t.* (*strike*) battre; (*ill-treat*) maltraiter. *—n.* (*culin.*) pâte (à frire) *f.* **~ed** *a.* (*pan, car*) cabossé; (*face*) meurtri. **~ing** *n.* **take a ~ing,** subir des coups.

battery /ˈbætərɪ/ *n.* (*mil., auto.*) batterie *f.*; (*of torch, radio*) pile *f.*

battle /ˈbætl/ *n.* bataille *f.*; (*fig.*) lutte *f.* *—v.i.* se battre.

battleaxe /ˈbætəlæks/ *n.* (*woman: fam.*) harpie *f.*

battlefield /ˈbætlfiːld/ *n.* champ de bataille *m.*

battlements /ˈbætlmənts/ *n. pl.* (*crenellations*) créneaux *m. pl.*; (*wall*) remparts *m. pl.*

battleship /ˈbætlʃɪp/ *n.* cuirassé *m.*

baulk /bɔːk/ *v.t./i.* = **balk.**

bawd|y /ˈbɔːdɪ/ *a.* (**-ier, -iest**) paillard. **~iness** *n.* paillardise *f.*

bawl /bɔːl/ *v.t./i.* brailler.

bay[1] /beɪ/ *n.* (*bot.*) laurier *m.*

bay[2] /beɪ/ *n.* (*geog., archit.*) baie *f.*; (*area*) aire *f.* **~ window,** fenêtre en saillie *f.*

bay[3] /beɪ/ *n.* (*bark*) aboiement *m.* *—v.i.* aboyer. **at ~,** aux abois. **keep** *or* **hold at ~,** tenir à distance.

bayonet /ˈbeɪənɪt/ *n.* baïonnette *f.*

bazaar /bəˈzɑː(r)/ *n.* (*shop, market*) bazar *m.*; (*sale*) vente *f.*

bazooka /bəˈzuːkə/ *n.* bazooka *m.*

BC *abbr.* (*before Christ*) avant J.-C.

be /biː/ *v.i.* (*present tense* **am, are, is;** *p.t.* **was, were;** *p.p.* **been**) être. **~ hot/right**/*etc.*, avoir chaud/raison/*etc.* **he is 30,** (*age*) il a 30 ans. **it is fine/cold**/*etc.*, (*weather*) il fait beau/froid/*etc.* **how are you?,** (*health*) comment allez-vous? **he is to come,** (*must*) il doit venir. **how much is it?,** (*cost*) ça fait *or* c'est combien? **~ reading/walking**/*etc.*, (*aux.*) lire/marcher/*etc.* **have been to,** avoir été à, être allé à.

beach /biːtʃ/ *n.* plage *f.*

beachcomber /ˈbiːtʃkəʊmə(r)/ *n.* ramasseu|r, -se d'épaves *m., f.*

beacon /ˈbiːkən/ *n.* (*lighthouse*) phare *m.*; (*marker*) balise *f.*

bead /biːd/ *n.* perle *f.*

beak /biːk/ *n.* bec *m.*

beaker /ˈbiːkə(r)/ *n.* gobelet *m.*

beam /biːm/ *n.* (*timber*) poutre *f.*; (*of light*) rayon *m.*; (*of torch*) faisceau *m.* *—v.i.* (*radiate*) rayonner. *—v.t.* (*broadcast*) diffuser. **~ing** *a.* radieux.

bean /biːn/ *n.* haricot *m.*; (*of coffee*) grain *m.*

beano /ˈbiːnəʊ/ *n.* (*pl.* **-os**) (*sl.*) fête *f.*

bear[1] /beə(r)/ *n.* ours *m.*

bear[2] /beə(r)/ *v.t.* (*p.t.* **bore,** *p.p.* **borne**) (*carry, show, feel*) porter; (*endure, sustain*) supporter; (*child*) mettre au monde. *—v.i.* **~ left**/*etc.*, (*go*) prendre à gauche/*etc.* **~ in mind,** tenir compte de. **~ on,** se rapporter à. **~ out,** corroborer. **~ up!,** courage! **~able** *a.* supportable. **~er** *n.* porteu|r, -se *m., f.*

beard /bɪəd/ *n.* barbe *f.* **~ed** *a.* barbu.

bearing /ˈbeərɪŋ/ *n.* (*behaviour*) maintien *m.*; (*relevance*) rapport *m.* **get one's ~s,** s'orienter.

beast /biːst/ *n.* bête *f.*; (*person*) brute *f.*
beastly /ˈbiːstlɪ/ *a.* (**-ier, -iest**) (*fam.*) détestable.
beat /biːt/ *v.t./i.* (*p.t.* **beat,** *p.p.* **beaten**) battre. —*n.* (*of drum, heart*) battement *m.*; (*mus.*) mesure *f.*; (*of policeman*) ronde *f.* **~ a retreat,** battre en retraite. **~ up,** tabasser. **it ~s me,** (*fam.*) ça me dépasse. **~er** *n.* batteur *m.* **~ing** *n.* raclée *f.*
beautician /bjuːˈtɪʃn/ *n.* esthéticien(ne) *m.* (*f.*).
beautiful /ˈbjuːtɪfl/ *a.* beau. **~ly** /-flɪ/ *adv.* merveilleusement.
beautify /ˈbjuːtɪfaɪ/ *v.t.* embellir.
beauty /ˈbjuːtɪ/ *n.* beauté *f.* **~ parlour,** institut de beauté *m.* **~ spot,** grain de beauté *m.*; (*fig.*) site pittoresque *m.*
beaver /ˈbiːvə(r)/ *n.* castor *m.*
became /bɪˈkeɪm/ *see* **become.**
because /bɪˈkɒz/ *conj.* parce que. **~ of,** à cause de.
beck /bek/ *n.* **at the ~ and call of,** aux ordres de.
beckon /ˈbekən/ *v.t./i.* **~ (to),** faire signe à.
become /bɪˈkʌm/ *v.t./i.* (*p.t.* **became,** *p.p.* **become**) devenir; (*befit*) convenir à. **what has ~ of her?,** qu'est-elle devenue?
becoming /bɪˈkʌmɪŋ/ *a.* (*seemly*) bienséant; (*clothes*) seyant.
bed /bed/ *n.* lit *m.*; (*layer*) couche *f.*; (*of sea*) fond *m.*; (*of flowers*) parterre *m.* **go to ~,** (aller) se coucher. —*v.i.* (*p.t.* **bedded**). **~ down,** se coucher. **~ding** *n.* literie *f.*
bedbug /ˈbedbʌg/ *n.* punaise *f.*
bedclothes /ˈbedkləʊðz/ *n. pl.* couvertures *f. pl.* et draps *m. pl.*
bedevil /bɪˈdevl/ *v.t.* (*p.t.* **bedevilled**) (*confuse*) embrouiller; (*plague*) tourmenter.
bedlam /ˈbedləm/ *n.* chahut *m.*
bedpost /ˈbedpəʊst/ *n.* colonne de lit *f.*
bedraggled /bɪˈdrægld/ *a.* (*untidy*) débraillé.
bedridden /ˈbedrɪdn/ *a.* cloué au lit.
bedroom /ˈbedrʊm/ *n.* chambre à coucher *f.*
bedside /ˈbedsaɪd/ *n.* chevet *m.* **~ book,** livre de chevet *m.*
bedsit, bedsitter /bedˈsɪt, -ə(r)/ *ns.* (*fam.*) = **bed-sitting-room.**
bed-sitting-room /bedˈsɪtɪŋrʊm/ *n.* chambre meublée *f.*, studio *m.*
bedspread /ˈbedspred/ *n.* dessus-de-lit *m. invar.*
bedtime /ˈbedtaɪm/ *n.* heure du coucher *f.*
bee /biː/ *n.* abeille *f.* **make a ~-line for,** aller tout droit vers.
beech /biːtʃ/ *n.* hêtre *m.*
beef /biːf/ *n.* bœuf *m.* —*v.i.* (*grumble*: *sl.*) rouspéter.
beefburger /ˈbiːfbɜːgə(r)/ *n.* hamburger *m.*
beefeater /ˈbiːfiːtə(r)/ *n.* hallebardier *m.*
beefy /ˈbiːfɪ/ *a.* (**-ier, -iest**) musclé.
beehive /ˈbiːhaɪv/ *n.* ruche *f.*
been /biːn/ *see* **be.**
beer /bɪə(r)/ *n.* bière *f.* **~y** *a.* (*person, room*) qui sent la bière.
beet /biːt/ *n.* (*plant*) betterave *f.*
beetle /ˈbiːtl/ *n.* scarabée *m.*
beetroot /ˈbiːtruːt/ *n. invar.* (*culin.*) betterave *f.*
befall /bɪˈfɔːl/ *v.t.* (*p.t.* **befell,** *p.p.* **befallen**) arriver à.
befit /bɪˈfɪt/ *v.t.* (*p.t.* **befitted**) convenir à, seoir à.
before /bɪˈfɔː(r)/ *prep.* (*time*) avant; (*place*) devant. —*adv.* avant; (*already*) déjà. —*conj.* **~ leaving,** avant de partir. **~ he leaves,** avant qu'il (ne) parte.
beforehand /bɪˈfɔːhænd/ *adv.* à l'avance, avant.
befriend /bɪˈfrend/ *v.t.* offrir son amitié à, aider.

beg /beg/ *v.t.* (*p.t.* **begged**) (*entreat*) supplier (**to do,** de faire). **~ (for),** (*money, food*) mendier; (*request*) solliciter, demander. *—v.i.* **~ (for alms),** mendier. **it is going ~ging,** personne n'en veut.

began /bɪ'gæn/ *see* **begin.**

beget /bɪ'get/ *v.t.* (*p.t.* **begot,** *p.p.* **begotten,** *pres. p.* **begetting**) engendrer.

beggar /'begə(r)/ *n.* mendiant(e) *m.* (*f.*).; (*sl.*) individu *m.*

begin /bɪ'gɪn/ *v.t./i.* (*p.t.* **began,** *p.p.* **begun,** *pres. p.* **beginning**) commencer (**to do,** à faire). **~ner** *n.* débutant(e) *m.* (*f.*). **~ning** *n.* commencement *m.*, début *m.*

begrudge /bɪ'grʌdʒ/ *v.t.* (*envy*) envier; (*give unwillingly*) donner à contrecœur. **~ doing,** faire à contrecœur.

beguile /bɪ'gaɪl/ *v.t.* tromper.

begun /bɪ'gʌn/ *see* **begin.**

behalf /bɪ'hɑːf/ *n.* **on ~ of,** pour; (*as representative*) au nom de, pour (le compte de).

behave /bɪ'heɪv/ *v.i.* se conduire. **~ (o.s.),** se conduire bien.

behaviour /bɪ'heɪvjə(r)/ *n.* conduite *f.*, comportement *m.*

behead /bɪ'hed/ *v.t.* décapiter.

behind /bɪ'haɪnd/ *prep.* derrière; (*in time*) en retard sur. *—adv.* derrière; (*late*) en retard. *—n.* (*buttocks*) derrière *m.*

behold /bɪ'həʊld/ *v.t.* (*p.t.* **beheld**) (*old use*) voir.

beholden /bɪ'həʊldən/ *a.* redevable (**to,** à; **for,** de).

beige /beɪʒ/ *a.* & *n.* beige (*m.*).

being /'biːɪŋ/ *n.* (*person*) être *m.* **bring into ~,** créer. **come into ~,** prendre naissance.

belated /bɪ'leɪtɪd/ *a.* tardif.

belch /beltʃ/ *v.i.* faire un renvoi. *—v.t.* **~ out,** (*smoke*) vomir. *—n.* renvoi *m.*

belfry /'belfrɪ/ *n.* beffroi *m.*

Belgi|um /'beldʒəm/ *n.* Belgique *f.* **~an** *a.* & *n.* belge (*m./f.*).

belie /bɪ'laɪ/ *v.t.* démentir.

belief /bɪ'liːf/ *n.* croyance *f.*; (*trust*) confiance *f.*; (*faith*: *relig.*) foi *f.*

believ|e /bɪ'liːv/ *v.t./i.* croire. **~e in,** croire à; (*deity*) croire en. **~able** *a.* croyable. **~er** *n.* croyant(e) *m.* (*f.*).

belittle /bɪ'lɪtl/ *v.t.* déprécier.

bell /bel/ *n.* cloche *f.*; (*small*) clochette *f.*; (*on door*) sonnette *f.*; (*of phone*) sonnerie *f.*

belligerent /bɪ'lɪdʒərənt/ *a.* & *n.* belligérant(e) (*m.* (*f.*)).

bellow /'beləʊ/ *v.t./i.* beugler.

bellows /'beləʊz/ *n. pl.* soufflet *m.*

belly /'belɪ/ *n.* ventre *m.* **~-ache** *n.* mal au ventre *m.*

bellyful /'belɪfʊl/ *n.* **have a ~,** en avoir plein le dos.

belong /bɪ'lɒŋ/ *v.i.* **~ to,** appartenir à; (*club*) être membre de.

belongings /bɪ'lɒŋɪŋz/ *n. pl.* affaires *f. pl.*

beloved /bɪ'lʌvɪd/ *a.* & *n.* bien-aimé(e) (*m.* (*f.*)).

below /bɪ'ləʊ/ *prep.* au-dessous de; (*fig.*) indigne de. *—adv.* en dessous; (*on page*) ci-dessous.

belt /belt/ *n.* ceinture *f.*; (*techn.*) courroie *f.*; (*fig.*) région *f.* *—v.t.* (*hit*: *sl.*) rosser. *—v.i.* (*rush*: *sl.*) filer à toute allure.

bemused /bɪ'mjuːzd/ *a.* (*confused*) stupéfié; (*thoughtful*) pensif.

bench /bentʃ/ *n.* banc *m.*; (*working-table*) établi *m.* **the ~,** (*jurid.*) la magistrature (assise).

bend /bend/ *v.t./i.* (*p.t.* **bent**) (se) courber; (*arm, leg*) plier. *—n.* courbe *f.*; (*in road*) virage *m.*; (*of arm, knee*) pli *m.* **~ down** *or* **over,** se pencher.

beneath /bɪ'niːθ/ *prep.* sous, au-dessous de; (*fig.*) indigne de. *—adv.* (au-)dessous.

benediction /benɪ'dɪkʃn/ *n.* bénédiction *f.*

benefactor /ˈbenɪfæktə(r)/ *n.* bienfai|teur, -trice *m., f.*
beneficial /benɪˈfɪʃl/ *a.* avantageux, favorable.
benefit /ˈbenɪfɪt/ *n.* avantage *m.*; (*allowance*) allocation *f.* —*v.t.* (*p.t.* **benefited,** *pres. p.* **benefiting**) (*be useful to*) profiter à; (*do good to*) faire du bien à. **~ from,** tirer profit de.
benevolen|t /bɪˈnevələnt/ *a.* bienveillant. **~ce** *n.* bienveillance *f.*
benign /bɪˈnaɪn/ *a.* (*kindly*) bienveillant; (*med.*) bénin.
bent /bent/ *see* **bend.** —*n.* (*talent*) aptitude *f.*; (*inclination*) penchant *m.* —*a.* tordu; (*sl.*) corrompu. **~ on doing,** décidé à faire.
bequeath /bɪˈkwiːð/ *v.t.* léguer.
bequest /bɪˈkwest/ *n.* legs *m.*
bereave|d /bɪˈriːvd/ *a.* **the ~d wife**/*etc.*, la femme/*etc.* du disparu. **~ment** *n.* deuil *m.*
bereft /bɪˈreft/ *a.* **~ of,** dénué de.
beret /ˈbereɪ/ *n.* béret *m.*
Bermuda /bəˈmjuːdə/ *n.* Bermudes *f. pl.*
berry /ˈberɪ/ *n.* baie *f.*
berserk /bəˈsɜːk/ *a.* **go ~,** devenir fou furieux.
berth /bɜːθ/ *n.* (*in train, ship*) couchette *f.*; (*anchorage*) mouillage *m.* —*v.i.* mouiller. **give a wide ~ to,** éviter.
beseech /bɪˈsiːtʃ/ *v.t.* (*p.t.* **besought**) implorer, supplier.
beset /bɪˈset/ *v.t.* (*p.t.* **beset,** *pres. p.* **besetting**) (*attack*) assaillir; (*surround*) entourer.
beside /bɪˈsaɪd/ *prep.* à côté de. **~ o.s.,** hors de soi. **~ the point,** sans rapport.
besides /bɪˈsaɪdz/ *prep.* en plus de; (*except*) excepté. —*adv.* en plus.
besiege /bɪˈsiːdʒ/ *v.t.* assiéger.
best /best/ *a.* meilleur. **the ~ book**/*etc.*, le meilleur livre/*etc.* —*adv.* **(the) ~,** (*sing etc.*) le mieux. —*n.* **the ~ (one),** le meilleur, la meilleure. **~ man,** garçon d'honneur *m.* **the ~ part of,** la plus grande partie de. **the ~ thing is to . . .,** le mieux est de . . . **do one's ~,** faire de son mieux. **make the ~ of,** s'accommoder de.
bestow /bɪˈstəʊ/ *v.t.* accorder.
best-seller /bestˈselə(r)/ *n.* best-seller *m.*, succès de librairie *m.*
bet /bet/ *n.* pari *m.* —*v.t./i.* (*p.t.* **bet** *or* **betted,** *pres. p.* **betting**) parier.
betray /bɪˈtreɪ/ *v.t.* trahir. **~al** *n.* trahison *f.*
betrothed /bɪˈtrəʊðd/ *n.* fiancé(e) *m.* (*f.*).
better /ˈbetə(r)/ *a.* meilleur. —*adv.* mieux. —*v.t.* (*improve*) améliorer; (*do better than*) surpasser. —*n.* **one's ~s,** ses supérieurs *m. pl.* **I had ~ go,** je ferais mieux de partir. **the ~ part of,** la plus grande partie de. **get ~,** s'améliorer; (*recover*) se remettre. **get the ~ of,** l'emporter sur.
betting-shop /ˈbetɪŋʃɒp/ *n.* bureau de P.M.U. *m.*
between /bɪˈtwiːn/ *prep.* entre. —*adv.* **in ~,** au milieu.
beverage /ˈbevərɪdʒ/ *n.* boisson *f.*
bevy /ˈbevɪ/ *n.* essaim *m.*
beware /bɪˈweə(r)/ *v.i.* prendre garde (**of,** à).
bewilder /bɪˈwɪldə(r)/ *v.t.* désorienter, embarrasser. **~ment** *n.* désorientation *f.*
bewitch /bɪˈwɪtʃ/ *v.t.* enchanter.
beyond /bɪˈjɒnd/ *prep.* au-delà de; (*doubt, reach*) hors de; (*besides*) excepté. —*adv.* au-delà. **it is ~ me,** ça me dépasse.
bias /ˈbaɪəs/ *n.* (*inclination*) penchant *m.*; (*prejudice*) préjugé *m.* —*v.t.* (*p.t.* **biased**) influencer. **~ed** *a.* partial.
bib /bɪb/ *n.* bavoir *m.*
Bible /ˈbaɪbl/ *n.* Bible *f.*
biblical /ˈbɪblɪkl/ *a.* biblique.

bibliography /bɪblɪ'ɒgrəfɪ/ *n.* bibliographie *f.*
bicarbonate /baɪ'kɑːbənət/ *n.* bicarbonate *m.*
biceps /'baɪseps/ *n.* biceps *m.*
bicker /'bɪkə(r)/ *v.i.* se chamailler.
bicycle /'baɪsɪkl/ *n.* bicyclette *f.* —*v.i.* faire de la bicyclette.
bid[1] /bɪd/ *n.* (*at auction*) offre *f.*, enchère *f.*; (*attempt*) tentative *f.* —*v.t./i.* (*p.t.* & *p.p.* **bid,** *pres. p.* **bidding**) (*offer*) faire une offre *or* une enchère (de). **the highest ~der,** le plus offrant.
bid[2] /bɪd/ *v.t.* (*p.t.* **bade** /bæd/, *p.p.* **bidden** *or* **bid,** *pres. p.* **bidding**) ordonner; (*say*) dire. **~ding** *n.* ordre *m.*
bide /baɪd/ *v.t.* **~ one's time,** attendre le bon moment.
biennial /baɪ'enɪəl/ *a.* biennal.
bifocals /baɪ'fəʊklz/ *n. pl.* lunettes bifocales *f. pl.*
big /bɪg/ *a.* (**bigger, biggest**) grand; (*in bulk*) gros; (*generous*: *sl.*) généreux. —*adv.* (*fam.*) en grand; (*earn*: *fam.*) gros. **~-headed** *a.* prétentieux. **think ~,** (*fam.*) voir grand.
bigam|y /'bɪgəmɪ/ *n.* bigamie *f.* **~ist** *n.* bigame *m./f.* **~ous** *a.* bigame.
bigot /'bɪgət/ *n.* fanatique *m./f.* **~ed** *a.* fanatique. **~ry** *n.* fanatisme *m.*
bigwig /'bɪgwɪg/ *n.* (*fam.*) gros bonnet *m.*, ponte *m.*
bike /baɪk/ *n.* (*fam.*) vélo *m.*
bikini /bɪ'kiːnɪ/ *n.* (*pl.* **-is**) bikini *m.*
bilberry /'bɪlbərɪ/ *n.* myrtille *f.*
bile /baɪl/ *n.* bile *f.*
bilingual /baɪ'lɪŋgwəl/ *a.* bilingue.
bilious /'bɪlɪəs/ *a.* bilieux.
bill[1] /bɪl/ *n.* (*invoice*) facture *f.*; (*in hotel, for gas, etc.*) note *f.*; (*in restaurant*) addition *f.*; (*of sale*) acte *m.*; (*pol.*) projet de loi *m.*; (*banknote*: *Amer.*) billet de banque *m.* —*v.t.* (*person*: *comm.*) envoyer la facture à; (*theatre*) mettre à l'affiche.
bill[2] /bɪl/ *n.* (*of bird*) bec *m.*
billboard /'bɪlbɔːd/ *n.* panneau d'affichage *m.*
billet /'bɪlɪt/ *n.* cantonnement *m.* —*v.t.* (*p.t.* **billeted**) cantonner (**on,** chez).
billiards /'bɪljədz/ *n.* billard *m.*
billion /'bɪljən/ *n.* billion *m.*; (*Amer.*) milliard *m.*
billy-goat /'bɪlɪgəʊt/ *n.* bouc *m.*
bin /bɪn/ *n.* (*for rubbish, litter*) boîte (à ordures) *f.*; (*for bread*) huche *f.*, coffre *m.*
bind /baɪnd/ *v.t.* (*p.t.* **bound**) lier; (*book*) relier; (*jurid.*) obliger. —*n.* (*bore*: *sl.*) plaie *f.* **be ~ing on,** être obligatoire pour.
binding /'baɪndɪŋ/ *n.* reliure *f.*
binge /bɪndʒ/ *n.* **go on a ~,** (*spree*: *sl.*) faire la bringue.
bingo /'bɪŋgəʊ/ *n.* loto *m.*
binoculars /bɪ'nɒkjʊləz/ *n. pl.* jumelles *f. pl.*
biochemistry /baɪəʊ'kemɪstrɪ/ *n.* biochimie *f.*
biograph|y /baɪ'ɒgrəfɪ/ *n.* biographie *f.* **~er** *n.* biographe *m./f.*
biolog|y /baɪ'ɒlədʒɪ/ *n.* biologie *f.* **~ical** /-ə'lɒdʒɪkl/ *a.* biologique. **~ist** *n.* biologiste *m./f.*
biped /'baɪped/ *n.* bipède *m.*
birch /bɜːtʃ/ *n.* (*tree*) bouleau *m.*; (*whip*) verge *f.*, fouet *m.*
bird /bɜːd/ *n.* oiseau *m.*; (*fam.*) individu *m.*; (*girl*: *sl.*) poule *f.*
Biro /'baɪərəʊ/ *n.* (*pl.* **-os**) (P.) stylo à bille *m.*, Bic *m.* (P.).
birth /bɜːθ/ *n.* naissance *f.* **~ certificate,** acte de naissance *m.* **~-control** *n.* contrôle des naissances *m.* **~-rate** *n.* natalité *f.*
birthday /'bɜːθdeɪ/ *n.* anniversaire *m.*
birthmark /'bɜːθmɑːk/ *n.* tache de vin *f.*, envie *f.*
birthright /'bɜːθraɪt/ *n.* patrimoine *m.*

biscuit /ˈbɪskɪt/ *n.* biscuit *m.*; (*Amer.*) petit pain (au lait) *m.*
bisect /baɪˈsekt/ *v.t.* couper en deux.
bishop /ˈbɪʃəp/ *n.* évêque *m.*
bit[1] /bɪt/ *n.* morceau *m.*; (*of horse*) mors *m.*; (*of tool*) mèche *f.* **a ~,** (*a little*) un peu.
bit[2] /bɪt/ *see* **bite.**
bitch /bɪtʃ/ *n.* chienne *f.*; (*woman*: *fam.*) garce *f.* —*v.i.* (*grumble*: *fam.*) râler. **~y** *a.* (*fam.*) vache.
bite /baɪt/ *v.t./i.* (*p.t.* **bit,** *p.p.* **bitten**) mordre. —*n.* morsure *f.*; (*mouthful*) bouchée *f.* **~ one's nails,** se ronger les ongles. **have a ~,** manger un morceau.
biting /ˈbaɪtɪŋ/ *a.* mordant.
bitter /ˈbɪtə(r)/ *a.* amer; (*weather*) glacial, âpre. —*n.* bière anglaise *f.* **~ly** *adv.* amèrement. **it is ~ly cold,** il fait un temps glacial. **~ness** *n.* amertume *f.*
bitty /ˈbɪtɪ/ *a.* décousu.
bizarre /bɪˈzɑː(r)/ *a.* bizarre.
blab /blæb/ *v.i.* (*p.t.* **blabbed**) jaser.
black /blæk/ *a.* (**-er, -est**) noir. —*n.* (*colour*) noir *m.* **B~,** (*person*) Noir(e) *m.* (*f.*). —*v.t.* noircir; (*goods*) boycotter. **~ and blue,** couvert de bleus. **~ eye,** œil poché *m.* **~ list,** liste noire *f.* **~ market,** marché noir *m.* **~ sheep,** brebis galeuse *f.* **~ spot,** point noir *m.*
blackberry /ˈblækbərɪ/ *n.* mûre *f.*
blackbird /ˈblækbɜːd/ *n.* merle *m.*
blackboard /ˈblækbɔːd/ *n.* tableau noir *m.*
blackcurrant /ˈblækkʌrənt/ *n.* cassis *m.*
blacken /ˈblækən/ *v.t./i.* noircir.
blackguard /ˈblægɑːd, *Amer.* ˈblægəd/ / *n.* canaille *f.*
blackleg /ˈblækleg/ *n.* jaune *m.*
blacklist /ˈblæklɪst/ *v.t.* mettre sur la liste noire *or* à l'index.
blackmail /ˈblækmeɪl/ *n.* chantage *m.* —*v.t.* faire chanter. **~er** *n.* maître-chanteur *m.*
blackout /ˈblækaʊt/ *n.* panne d'électricité *f.*; (*med.*) syncope *f.*
blacksmith /ˈblæksmɪθ/ *n.* forgeron *m.*
bladder /ˈblædə(r)/ *n.* vessie *f.*
blade /bleɪd/ *n.* (*of knife etc.*) lame *f.*; (*of propeller, oar*) pale *f.* **~ of grass,** brin d'herbe *m.*
blame /bleɪm/ *v.t.* accuser. —*n.* faute *f.* **~ s.o. for sth.,** reprocher qch. à qn. **he is to ~,** il est responsable (**for,** de). **~less** *a.* irréprochable.
bland /blænd/ *a.* (**-er, -est**) (*gentle*) doux; (*insipid*) fade.
blank /blæŋk/ *a.* blanc; (*look*) vide; (*cheque*) en blanc. —*n.* blanc *m.* **~ (cartridge),** cartouche à blanc *f.*
blanket /ˈblæŋkɪt/ *n.* couverture *f.*; (*layer*: *fig.*) couche *f.* —*v.t.* (*p.t.* **blanketed**) recouvrir.
blare /bleə(r)/ *v.t./i.* beugler. —*n.* vacarme *m.*, beuglement *m.*
blarney /ˈblɑːnɪ/ *n.* boniment *m.*
blasé /ˈblɑːzeɪ/ *a.* blasé.
blaspheme /blæsˈfiːm/ *v.t./i.* blasphémer.
blasphem|y /ˈblæsfəmɪ/ *n.* blasphème *m.* **~ous** *a.* blasphématoire; (*person*) blasphémateur.
blast /blɑːst/ *n.* explosion *f.*; (*wave of air*) souffle *m.*; (*of wind*) rafale *f.*; (*noise from siren etc.*) coup *m.* —*v.t.* (*blow up*) faire sauter. **~ed** *a.* (*fam.*) maudit, fichu. **~-furnace** *n.* haut fourneau *m.* **~ off,** être mis à feu. **~-off** *n.* mise à feu *f.*
blatant /ˈbleɪtnt/ *a.* (*obvious*) flagrant; (*shameless*) éhonté.
blaze[1] /bleɪz/ *n.* flamme *f.*; (*conflagration*) incendie *m.*; (*fig.*) éclat *m.* —*v.i.* (*fire*) flamber; (*sky, eyes, etc.*) flamboyer.
blaze[2] /bleɪz/ *v.t.* **~ a trail,** montrer *or* marquer la voie.
blazer /ˈbleɪzə(r)/ *n.* blazer *m.*

bleach /bliːtʃ/ *n.* décolorant *m.*; (*for domestic use*) eau de Javel *f.* —*v.t./i.* blanchir; (*hair*) décolorer.

bleak /bliːk/ *a.* (**-er, -est**) morne.

bleary /ˈblɪərɪ/ *a.* (*eyes*) voilé.

bleat /bliːt/ *n.* bêlement *m.* —*v.i.* bêler.

bleed /bliːd/ *v.t./i.* (*p.t.* **bled**) saigner.

bleep /bliːp/ *n.* bip *m.* **~er** *n.* bip *m.*

blemish /ˈblemɪʃ/ *n.* tare *f.*, défaut *m.*; (*on reputation*) tache *f.* —*v.t.* entacher.

blend /blend/ *v.t./i.* (se) mélanger. —*n.* mélange *m.*

bless /bles/ *v.t.* bénir. **be ~ed with,** avoir le bonheur de posséder. **~ing** *n.* bénédiction *f.*; (*benefit*) avantage *m.*; (*stroke of luck*) chance *f.*

blessed /ˈblesɪd/ *a.* (*holy*) saint; (*damned: fam.*) sacré.

blew /bluː/ *see* **blow**[1].

blight /blaɪt/ *n.* (*disease: bot.*) rouille *f.*; (*fig.*) fléau *m.*

blighter /ˈblaɪtə(r)/ *n.* (*sl.*) type *m.*

blind /blaɪnd/ *a.* aveugle. —*v.t.* aveugler. —*n.* (*on window*) store *m.*; (*deception*) feinte *f.* **be ~ to,** ne pas voir. **~ alley,** impasse *f.* **~ man,** aveugle *m.* **~ers** *n. pl.* (*Amer.*) œillères *f. pl.* **~ly** *adv.* aveuglément. **~ness** *n.* cécité *f.*

blindfold /ˈblaɪndfəʊld/ *a.* & *adv.* les yeux bandés. —*n.* bandeau *m.* —*v.t.* bander les yeux à.

blink /blɪŋk/ *v.i.* cligner des yeux; (*of light*) clignoter.

blinkers /ˈblɪŋkəz/ *n. pl.* œillères *f. pl.*

bliss /blɪs/ *n.* félicité *f.* **~ful** *a.* bienheureux. **~fully** *adv.* joyeusement, merveilleusement.

blister /ˈblɪstə(r)/ *n.* ampoule *f.* —*v.i.* se couvrir d'ampoules.

blithe /blaɪð/ *a.* joyeux.

blitz /blɪts/ *n.* (*aviat.*) raid éclair *m.* —*v.t.* bombarder.

blizzard /ˈblɪzəd/ *n.* tempête de neige *f.*

bloated /ˈbləʊtɪd/ *a.* gonflé.

bloater /ˈbləʊtə(r)/ *n.* hareng saur *m.*

blob /blɒb/ *n.* (*drop*) (grosse) goutte *f.*; (*stain*) tache *f.*

bloc /blɒk/ *n.* bloc *m.*

block /blɒk/ *n.* bloc *m.*; (*buildings*) pâté de maisons *m.*; (*in pipe*) obstruction *f.* **~ (of flats),** immeuble *m.* —*v.t.* bloquer. **~ letters,** majuscules *f. pl.* **~age** *n.* obstruction *f.*

blockade /blɒˈkeɪd/ *n.* blocus *m.* —*v.t.* bloquer.

blockhead /ˈblɒkhed/ *n.* imbécile *m./f.*

bloke /bləʊk/ *n.* (*fam.*) type *m.*

blond /blɒnd/ *a.* & *n.* blond (*m.*).

blonde /blɒnd/ *a.* & *n.* blonde (*f.*).

blood /blʌd/ *n.* sang *m.* —*a.* (*donor, bath, etc.*) de sang; (*bank, poisoning, etc.*) du sang; (*group, vessel*) sanguin. **~-curdling** *a.* à tourner le sang. **~less** *a.* (*fig.*) pacifique. **~-pressure** *n.* tension artérielle *f.*

bloodhound /ˈblʌdhaʊnd/ *n.* limier *m.*

bloodshed /ˈblʌdʃed/ *n.* effusion de sang *f.*

bloodshot /ˈblʌdʃɒt/ *a.* injecté de sang.

bloodstream /ˈblʌdstriːm/ *n.* sang *m.*

bloodthirsty /ˈblʌdθɜːstɪ/ *a.* sanguinaire.

bloody /ˈblʌdɪ/ *a.* (**-ier, -iest**) sanglant; (*sl.*) sacré. —*adv.* (*sl.*) vachement. **~-minded** *a.* (*fam.*) hargneux, obstiné.

bloom /bluːm/ *n.* fleur *f.* —*v.i.* fleurir; (*fig.*) s'épanouir.

bloomer /ˈbluːmə(r)/ *n.* (*sl.*) gaffe *f.*

blossom /ˈblɒsəm/ *n.* fleur(s) *f.* (*pl.*). —*v.i.* fleurir; (*person: fig.*) s'épanouir.

blot /blɒt/ *n.* tache *f.* —*v.t.* (*p.t.* **blotted**) tacher; (*dry*) sécher. **~ out,** effacer. **~ter, ~ting-paper** *ns.* buvard *m.*
blotch /blɒtʃ/ *n.* tache *f.* **~y** *a.* couvert de taches.
blouse /blaʊz/ *n.* chemisier *m.*
blow[1] /bləʊ/ *v.t./i.* (*p.t.* **blew,** *p.p.* **blown**) souffler; (*fuse*) (faire) sauter; (*squander*: *sl.*) perdre. **~ one's nose,** se moucher. **~ a whistle,** siffler. **~ away** *or* **off,** emporter. **~-dry** *v.t.* sécher. **~ out,** (*candle*) souffler. **~-out** *n.* (*of tyre*) éclatement *m.* **~ over,** passer. **~ up,** (faire) sauter; (*tyre*) gonfler.
blow[2] /bləʊ/ *n.* coup *m.*
blowlamp /ˈbləʊlæmp/ *n.* chalumeau *m.*
blown /bləʊn/ *see* **blow**[1].
blowtorch /ˈbləʊtɔːtʃ/ *n.* (*Amer.*) chalumeau *m.*
blowy /ˈbləʊɪ/ *a.* **it is ~,** il y a du vent.
blowzy /ˈblaʊzɪ/ *a.* débraillé.
blubber /ˈblʌbə(r)/ *n.* graisse de baleine *f.*
bludgeon /ˈblʌdʒən/ *n.* gourdin *m.* —*v.t.* matraquer.
blue /bluː/ *a.* (**-er, -est**) bleu. —*n.* bleu *m.* **come out of the ~,** être inattendu. **have the ~s,** avoir le cafard.
bluebell /ˈbluːbel/ *n.* jacinthe des bois *f.*
bluebottle /ˈbluːbɒtl/ *n.* mouche à viande *f.*
blueprint /ˈbluːprɪnt/ *n.* plan *m.*
bluff[1] /blʌf/ *v.t./i.* bluffer. —*n.* bluff *m.*
bluff[2] /blʌf/ *a.* (*person*) brusque.
blunder /ˈblʌndə(r)/ *v.i.* faire une gaffe; (*move*) avancer à tâtons. —*n.* gaffe *f.*
blunt /blʌnt/ *a.* (*knife*) émoussé; (*person*) brusque. —*v.t.* émousser. **~ly** *adv.* carrément. **~ness** *n.* brusquerie *f.*
blur /blɜː(r)/ *n.* tache floue *f.* —*v.t.* (*p.t.* **blurred**) rendre flou.
blurb /blɜːb/ *n.* résumé publicitaire *m.*
blurt /blɜːt/ *v.t.* **~ out,** lâcher, dire.
blush /blʌʃ/ *v.i.* rougir. —*n.* rougeur *f.*
bluster /ˈblʌstə(r)/ *v.i.* (*wind*) faire rage; (*swagger*) fanfaronner. **~y** *a.* à bourrasques.
boar /bɔː(r)/ *n.* sanglier *m.*
board /bɔːd/ *n.* planche *f.*; (*for notices*) tableau *m.*; (*food*) pension *f.*; (*committee*) conseil *m.* —*v.t./i.* monter à bord (de). **on ~,** à bord. **~ up,** boucher. **~ with,** être en pension chez. **~er** *n.* pensionnaire *m./f.* **~ing-house** *n.* pension (de famille) *f.* **~ing-school** *n.* pensionnat *m.*, pension *f.*
boast /bəʊst/ *v.i.* se vanter. —*v.t.* s'enorgueillir de. —*n.* vantardise *f.* **~er** *n.* vantard(e) *m.* (*f.*). **~ful** *a.* vantard. **~fully** *adv.* en se vantant.
boat /bəʊt/ *n.* bateau *m.*; (*small*) canot *m.* **in the same ~,** logé à la même enseigne. **~ing** *n.* canotage *m.*
boatswain /ˈbəʊsn/ *n.* maître d'équipage *m.*
bob[1] /bɒb/ *v.i.* (*p.t.* **bobbed**). **~ up and down,** monter et descendre.
bob[2] /bɒb/ *n. invar.* (*sl.*) shilling *m.*
bobbin /ˈbɒbɪn/ *n.* bobine *f.*
bobby /ˈbɒbɪ/ *n.* (*fam.*) flic *m.*
bobsleigh /ˈbɒbsleɪ/ *n.* bob(sleigh) *m.*
bode /bəʊd/ *v.i.* **~ well/ill,** être de bon/mauvais augure.
bodice /ˈbɒdɪs/ *n.* corsage *m.*
bodily /ˈbɒdɪlɪ/ *a.* physique, corporel. —*adv.* physiquement; (*in person*) en personne.
body /ˈbɒdɪ/ *n.* corps *m.*; (*mass*) masse *f.*; (*organization*) organisme *m.* **~(work),** (*auto.*) carrosserie *f.* **the main ~ of,** le gros de.

bodyguard /'bɒdɪgɑːd/ *n.* garde du corps *m.*

boffin /'bɒfɪn/ *n.* (*sl.*) chercheu/r, -se (scientifique) *m., f.*

bog /bɒg/ *n.* marécage *m.* —*v.t.* (*p.t.* **bogged**). **get ~ged down,** s'embourber.

boggle /'bɒgl/ *v.i.* **the mind ~s,** on est stupéfait.

bogus /'bəʊgəs/ *a.* faux.

bogy /'bəʊgɪ/ *n.* (*annoyance*) embêtement *m.* **~(man),** croque-mitaine *m.*

boil[1] /bɔɪl/ *n.* furoncle *m.*

boil[2] /bɔɪl/ *v.t./i.* (faire) bouillir. **~ down to,** se ramener à. **~ over,** déborder. **~ing hot,** bouillant. **~ed** *a.* (*egg*) à la coque; (*potatoes*) à l'eau.

boiler /'bɔɪlə(r)/ *n.* chaudière *f.* **~ suit,** bleu (de travail) *m.*

boisterous /'bɔɪstərəs/ *a.* tapageur.

bold /bəʊld/ *a.* (**-er, -est**) hardi. **~ness** *n.* hardiesse *f.*

Bolivia /bə'lɪvɪə/ *n.* Bolivie *f.* **~n** *a.* & *n.* bolivien(ne) (*m.* (*f.*)).

bollard /'bɒləd/ *n.* (*on road*) borne *f.*

bolster /'bəʊlstə(r)/ *n.* traversin *m.* —*v.t.* soutenir.

bolt /bəʊlt/ *n.* verrou *m.*; (*for nut*) boulon *m.*; (*lightning*) éclair *m.* —*v.t.* (*door etc.*) verrouiller; (*food*) engouffrer. —*v.i.* se sauver. **~ upright,** tout droit.

bomb /bɒm/ *n.* bombe *f.* —*v.t.* bombarder. **~er** *n.* (*aircraft*) bombardier *m.*; (*person*) plastiqueur *m.*

bombard /bɒm'bɑːd/ *v.t.* bombarder.

bombastic /bɒm'bæstɪk/ *a.* grandiloquent.

bombshell /'bɒmʃel/ *n.* **be a ~,** tomber comme une bombe.

bona fide /bəʊnə'faɪdɪ/ *a.* de bonne foi.

bonanza /bə'nænzə/ *n.* aubaine *f.*

bond /bɒnd/ *n.* (*agreement*) engagement *m.*; (*link*) lien *m.*; (*comm.*) obligation *f.*, bon *m.* **in ~,** (entreposé) en douane.

bondage /'bɒndɪdʒ/ *n.* esclavage *m.*

bone /bəʊn/ *n.* os *m.*; (*of fish*) arête *f.* —*v.t.* désosser. **~-dry** *a.* tout à fait sec. **~ idle,** paresseux comme une couleuvre.

bonfire /'bɒnfaɪə(r)/ *n.* feu *m.*; (*for celebration*) feu de joie *m.*

bonnet /'bɒnɪt/ *n.* (*hat*) bonnet *m.*; (*of vehicle*) capot *m.*

bonus /'bəʊnəs/ *n.* prime *f.*

bony /'bəʊnɪ/ *a.* (**-ier, -iest**) (*thin*) osseux; (*meat*) plein d'os; (*fish*) plein d'arêtes.

boo /buː/ *int.* hou. —*v.t./i.* huer. —*n.* huée *f.*

boob /buːb/ *n.* (*blunder*: *sl.*) gaffe *f.* —*v.i.* (*sl.*) gaffer.

booby /'buːbɪ/ *n.* nigaud(e) *m.* (*f.*) **~ trap,** engin piégé *m.* **~-trap** *v.t.* (*p.t.* **-trapped**) piéger.

book /bʊk/ *n.* livre *m.*; (*of tickets etc.*) carnet *m.* **~s,** (*comm.*) comptes *m. pl.* —*v.t.* (*reserve*) retenir; (*write down*) inscrire. —*v.i.* retenir des places. **~able** *a.* qu'on peut retenir. (**fully**) **~ed,** complet. **~ing office,** guichet *m.*

bookcase /'bʊkkeɪs/ *n.* bibliothèque *f.*

bookkeeping /'bʊkkiːpɪŋ/ *n.* comptabilité *f.*

booklet /'bʊklɪt/ *n.* brochure *f.*

bookmaker /'bʊkmeɪkə(r)/ *n.* bookmaker *m.*

bookseller /'bʊkselə(r)/ *n.* libraire *m./f.*

bookshop /'bʊkʃɒp/ *n.* librairie *f.*

bookstall /'bʊkstɔːl/ *n.* kiosque (à journaux) *m.*

boom /buːm/ *v.i.* (*gun, wind, etc.*) gronder; (*trade*) prospérer. —*n.* grondement *m.*; (*comm.*) boom *m.*, prospérité *f.*

boon /buːn/ *n.* (*benefit*) aubaine *f.*

boor /bʊə(r)/ *n.* rustre *m.* **~ish** *a.* rustre.

boost /buːst/ *v.t.* développer, stimuler; (*morale*) remonter; (*price*) augmenter; (*publicize*) faire de la réclame pour. —*n.* **give a ~ to,** = **boost.**

boot /buːt/ *n.* botte *f.*, chaussure (montante) *f.*; (*of vehicle*) coffre *m.* **get the ~,** (*sl.*) être mis à la porte.

booth /buːð/ *n.* (*for telephone*) cabine *f.*; (*at fair*) baraque *f.*

booty /ˈbuːtɪ/ *n.* butin *m.*

booze /buːz/ *v.i.* (*fam.*) boire (beaucoup). —*n.* (*fam.*) alcool *m.*; (*spree*) beuverie *f.*

border /ˈbɔːdə(r)/ *n.* (*edge*) bord *m.*; (*frontier*) frontière *f.*; (*in garden*) bordure *f.* —*v.i.* **~ on,** (*be next to, come close to*) être voisin de, avoisiner.

borderline /ˈbɔːdəlaɪn/ *n.* ligne de démarcation *f.* **~ case,** cas limite *m.*

bore[1] /bɔː(r)/ *see* **bear**[2].

bore[2] /bɔː(r)/ *v.t./i.* (*techn.*) forer.

bore[3] /bɔː(r)/ *v.t.* ennuyer. —*n.* raseu|r, -se *m.*, *f.*; (*thing*) ennui *m.* **be ~d,** s'ennuyer. **~dom** *n.* ennui *m.* **boring** *a.* ennuyeux.

born /bɔːn/ *a.* né. **be ~,** naître.

borne /bɔːn/ *see* **bear**[2].

borough /ˈbʌrə/ *n.* municipalité *f.*

borrow /ˈbɒrəʊ/ *v.t.* emprunter (**from,** à). **~ing** *n.* emprunt *m.*

Borstal /ˈbɔːstl/ *n.* maison d'éducation surveillée *f.*

bosom /ˈbʊzəm/ *n.* sein *m.* **~ friend,** ami(e) intime *m.* (*f.*).

boss /bɒs/ *n.* (*fam.*) patron(ne) *m.* (*f.*) —*v.t.* **~ (about),** (*fam.*) donner des ordres à, régenter.

bossy /ˈbɒsɪ/ *a.* autoritaire.

botan|y /ˈbɒtənɪ/ *n.* botanique *f.* **~ical** /bəˈtænɪkl/ *a.* botanique. **~ist** *n.* botaniste *m.*/*f.*

botch /bɒtʃ/ *v.t.* bâcler, saboter.

both /bəʊθ/ *a.* les deux. —*pron.* tous *or* toutes (les) deux, l'un(e) et l'autre. —*adv.* à la fois.

bother /ˈbɒðə(r)/ *v.t.* (*annoy, worry*) ennuyer; (*disturb*) déranger. —*v.i.* se déranger. —*n.* ennui *m.*; (*effort*) peine *f.* **~ about,** (*deal with*) s'occuper de; (*worry about*) s'inquiéter de. **~ doing** *or* **to do,** prendre la peine de faire.

bottle /ˈbɒtl/ *n.* bouteille *f.*; (*for baby*) biberon *m.* —*v.t.* mettre en bouteille(s). **~-opener** *n.* ouvre-bouteille(s) *m.* **~ up,** étouffer.

bottleneck /ˈbɒtlnek/ *n.* (*traffic jam*) bouchon *m.*

bottom /ˈbɒtəm/ *n.* fond *m.*; (*of hill, page, etc.*) bas *m.*; (*buttocks*) derrière *m.* —*a.* inférieur, du bas. **~less** *a.* insondable.

bough /baʊ/ *n.* rameau *m.*

bought /bɔːt/ *see* **buy.**

boulder /ˈbəʊldə(r)/ *n.* rocher *m.*

boulevard /ˈbuːləvɑːd/ *n.* boulevard *m.*

bounce /baʊns/ *v.i.* rebondir; (*person*) faire des bonds, bondir; (*cheque*: *sl.*) être refusé. —*v.t.* faire rebondir. —*n.* rebond *m.*

bouncing /ˈbaʊnsɪŋ/ *a.* robuste.

bound[1] /baʊnd/ *v.i.* (*leap*) bondir. —*n.* bond *m.*

bound[2] /baʊnd/ *see* **bind.** —*a.* **be ~ for,** être en route pour, aller vers. **~ to,** (*obliged*) obligé de; (*certain*) sûr de.

boundary /ˈbaʊndrɪ/ *n.* limite *f.*

bound|s /baʊndz/ *n. pl.* limites *f. pl.* **out of ~s,** interdit. **~ed by,** limité par. **~less** *a.* sans bornes.

bountiful /ˈbaʊntɪfl/ *a.* généreux.

bouquet /bʊˈkeɪ/ *n.* bouquet *m.*

bout /baʊt/ *n.* période *f.*; (*med.*) accès *m.*; (*boxing*) combat *m.*

boutique /buːˈtiːk/ *n.* boutique (de mode) *f.*

bow[1] /bəʊ/ *n.* (*weapon*) arc *m.*; (*mus.*) archet *m.*; (*knot*) nœud *m.*

~-legged *a.* aux jambes arquées. **~-tie** *n.* nœud papillon *m.*

bow[2] /baʊ/ *n.* (*with head*) salut *m.*; (*with body*) révérence *f.* —*v.t.*/*i.* (s')incliner.

bow[3] /baʊ/ *n.* (*naut.*) proue *f.*

bowels /ˈbaʊəlz/ *n. pl.* intestins *m. pl.*; (*fig.*) entrailles *f. pl.*

bowl[1] /bəʊl/ *n.* cuvette *f.*; (*for food*) bol *m.*

bowl[2] /bəʊl/ *n.* (*ball*) boule *f.* —*v.t.*/*i.* (*cricket*) lancer. **~ over,** bouleverser. **~ing** *n.* jeu de boules *m.* **~ing-alley** *n.* bowling *m.*

bowler[1] /ˈbəʊlə(r)/ *n.* (*cricket*) lanceur *m.*

bowler[2] /ˈbəʊlə(r)/ *n.* **~ (hat),** (chapeau) melon *m.*

box[1] /bɒks/ *n.* boîte *f.*; (*theatre*) loge *f.* —*v.t.* mettre en boîte. **~ in,** enfermer. **~-office** *n.* bureau de location *m.*

box[2] /bɒks/ *v.t.*/*i.* (*sport*) boxer. **~ s.o.'s ears,** gifler qn. **~ing** *n.* boxe *f.* **Boxing Day,** le lendemain de Noël.

boy /bɔɪ/ *n.* garçon *m.* **~-friend** *n.* (petit) ami *m.* **~hood** *n.* enfance *f.* **~ish** *a.* enfantin, de garçon.

boycott /ˈbɔɪkɒt/ *v.t.* boycotter. —*n.* boycottage *m.*

bra /brɑː/ *n.* soutien-gorge *m.*

brace /breɪs/ *n.* (*fastener*) attache *f.*; (*dental*) appareil *m.* **~s,** (*for trousers*) bretelles *f. pl.* —*v.t.* soutenir. **~ o.s.,** rassembler ses forces.

bracelet /ˈbreɪslɪt/ *n.* bracelet *m.*

bracing /ˈbreɪsɪŋ/ *a.* vivifiant.

bracken /ˈbrækən/ *n.* fougère *f.*

bracket /ˈbrækɪt/ *n.* (*for shelf etc.*) tasseau *m.*, support *m.*; (*group*) tranche *f.* **(round) ~,** (*printing sign*) parenthèse *f.* **(square) ~,** crochet *m.* —*v.t.* (*p.t.* **bracketed**) mettre entre parenthèses *or* crochets.

brag /bræg/ *v.i.* (*p.t.* **bragged**) se vanter.

braid /breɪd/ *n.* (*trimming*) galon *m.*; (*of hair*) tresse *f.*

Braille /breɪl/ *n.* braille *m.*

brain /breɪn/ *n.* cerveau *m.* **~s,** (*fig.*) intelligence *f.* —*v.t.* assommer. **~-child** *n.* invention personnelle *f.* **~-drain** *n.* exode des cerveaux *m.* **~less** *a.* stupide.

brainwash /ˈbreɪnwɒʃ/ *v.t.* faire un lavage de cerveau à.

brainwave /ˈbreɪnweɪv/ *n.* idée géniale *f.*, trouvaille *f.*

brainy /ˈbreɪnɪ/ *a.* **(-ier, -iest)** intelligent.

braise /breɪz/ *v.t.* braiser.

brake /breɪk/ *n.* (*auto.* & *fig.*) frein *m.* —*v.t.*/*i.* freiner.

bramble /ˈbræmbl/ *n.* ronce *f.*

bran /bræn/ *n.* (*husks*) son *m.*

branch /brɑːntʃ/ *n.* branche *f.*; (*of road*) embranchement *m.*; (*comm.*) succursale *f.* —*v.i.* **~ (off),** bifurquer.

brand /brænd/ *n.* marque *f.* —*v.t.* **~ s.o. as,** donner à qn. la réputation de. **~-new** *a.* tout neuf.

brandish /ˈbrændɪʃ/ *v.t.* brandir.

brandy /ˈbrændɪ/ *n.* cognac *m.*

brash /bræʃ/ *a.* effronté.

brass /brɑːs/ *n.* cuivre *m.* **get down to ~ tacks,** en venir aux choses sérieuses. **top ~,** (*sl.*) gros bonnets *m. pl.*

brassière /ˈbræsɪə(r), *Amer.* brəˈzɪər/ *n.* soutien-gorge *m.*

brat /bræt/ *n.* (*child*: *pej.*) môme *m.*/*f.*; (*ill-behaved*) garnement *m.*

bravado /brəˈvɑːdəʊ/ *n.* bravade *f.*

brave /breɪv/ *a.* **(-er, -est)** courageux, brave. —*n.* (*Red Indian*) brave *m.* —*v.t.* braver. **~ry** /-ərɪ/ *n.* courage *m.*

bravo /ˈbrɑːvəʊ/ *int.* bravo.

brawl /brɔːl/ *n.* bagarre *f.* —*v.i.* se bagarrer.

brawn /brɔːn/ *n.* muscles *m. pl.* **~y** *a.* musclé.

bray /breɪ/ *n.* braiment *m.* —*v.i.* braire.
brazen /ˈbreɪzn/ *a.* effronté.
brazier /ˈbreɪzɪə(r)/ *n.* brasero *m.*
Brazil /brəˈzɪl/ *n.* Brésil *m.* **~ian** *a.* & *n.* brésilien(ne) (*m.* (*f.*)).
breach /briːtʃ/ *n.* violation *f.*; (*of contract*) rupture *f.*; (*gap*) brèche *f.* —*v.t.* ouvrir une brèche dans.
bread /bred/ *n.* pain *m.* **~ and butter,** tartine *f.* **~-winner** *n.* soutien de famille *m.*
breadcrumbs /ˈbredkrʌmz/ *n. pl.* (*culin.*) chapelure *f.*
breadline /ˈbredlaɪn/ *n.* **on the ~,** dans l'indigence.
breadth /bretθ/ *n.* largeur *f.*
break /breɪk/ *v.t.* (*p.t.* **broke,** *p.p.* **broken**) casser; (*smash into pieces*) briser; (*vow, silence, rank, etc.*) rompre; (*law*) violer; (*a record*) battre; (*news*) révéler; (*journey*) interrompre; (*heart, strike, ice*) briser. —*v.i.* (se) casser; se briser. —*n.* cassure *f.*, rupture *f.*; (*in relationship, continuity*) rupture *f.*; (*interval*) interruption *f.*; (*for coffee*) pause *f.*; (*luck: fam.*) chance *f.* **~ down** *v.i.* (*collapse*) s'effondrer; (*fail*) échouer; (*machine*) tomber en panne; *v.t.* (*door*) enfoncer; (*analyse*) analyser. **~-in** *n.* cambriolage *m.* **~ off,** (se) détacher; (*suspend*) rompre. **~ out,** (*fire, war, etc.*) éclater. **~ up,** (*end*) (faire) cesser; (*marriage*) (se) briser; (*crowd*) (se) disperser; (*schools*) entrer en vacances. **~able** *a.* cassable. **~age** *n.* casse *f.*
breakdown /ˈbreɪkdaʊn/ *n.* (*techn.*) panne *f.*; (*med.*) dépression *f.*; (*of figures*) analyse *f.* —*a.* (*auto.*) de dépannage.
breaker /ˈbreɪkə(r)/ *n.* (*wave*) brisant *m.*
breakfast /ˈbrekfəst/ *n.* petit déjeuner *m.*
breakthrough /ˈbreɪkθruː/ *n.* percée *f.*
breakwater /ˈbreɪkwɔːtə(r)/ *n.* brise-lames *m. invar.*
breast /brest/ *n.* sein *m.*; (*chest*) poitrine *f.* **~-stroke** *n.* brasse *f.*
breath /breθ/ *n.* souffle *m.*, haleine *f.* **out of ~,** essoufflé. **under one's ~,** tout bas.
breathalyser /ˈbreθəlaɪzə(r)/ *n.* alcootest *m.*
breath|e /briːð/ *v.t./i.* respirer. **~ing** *n.* respiration *f.*
breather /ˈbriːðə(r)/ *n.* moment de repos *m.*
breathtaking /ˈbreθteɪkɪŋ/ *a.* à vous couper le souffle.
bred /bred/ *see* **breed.**
breeches /ˈbrɪtʃɪz/ *n. pl.* culotte *f.*
breed /briːd/ *v.t.* (*p.t.* **bred**) élever; (*give rise to*) engendrer. —*v.i.* se reproduire. —*n.* race *f.* **~er** *n.* éleveur *m.* **~ing** *n.* élevage *m.*; (*fig.*) éducation *f.*
breez|e /briːz/ *n.* brise *f.* **~y** *a.* (*weather*) frais; (*cheerful*) jovial; (*casual*) désinvolte.
Breton /ˈbretn/ *a.* & *n.* breton(ne) (*m.* (*f.*)).
brevity /ˈbrevətɪ/ *n.* brièveté *f.*
brew /bruː/ *v.t.* (*beer*) brasser; (*tea*) faire infuser. —*v.i.* fermenter; infuser; (*fig.*) se préparer. —*n.* décoction *f.* **~er** *n.* brasseur *m.* **~ery** *n.* brasserie *f.*
bribe /braɪb/ *n.* pot-de-vin *m.* —*v.t.* soudoyer, acheter. **~ry** /-ərɪ/ *n.* corruption *f.*
brick /brɪk/ *n.* brique *f.* —*v.t.* **~ up,** murer.
bricklayer /ˈbrɪkleɪə(r)/ *n.* maçon *m.*
bridal /ˈbraɪdl/ *a.* nuptial.
bride /braɪd/ *n.* mariée *f.*
bridegroom /ˈbraɪdgrʊm/ *n.* marié *m.*
bridesmaid /ˈbraɪdzmeɪd/ *n.* demoiselle d'honneur *f.*

bridge[1] /brɪdʒ/ *n.* pont *m.*; (*of nose*) arête *f.* —*v.t.* ~ **a gap,** combler une lacune.

bridge[2] /brɪdʒ/ *n.* (*cards*) bridge *m.*

bridle /'braɪdl/ *n.* bride *f.* —*v.t.* brider. **~-path** *n.* allée cavalière *f.*

brief[1] /briːf/ *a.* (**-er, -est**) bref. **~ly** *adv.* brièvement. **~ness** *n.* brièveté *f.*

brief[2] /briːf/ *n.* instructions *f. pl.*; (*jurid.*) dossier *m.* —*v.t.* donner des instructions à.

briefcase /'briːfkeɪs/ *n.* serviette *f.*

briefs /briːfs/ *n. pl.* slip *m.*

brigad|e /brɪ'geɪd/ *n.* brigade *f.* **~ier** /-ə'dɪə(r)/ *n.* général de brigade *m.*

bright /braɪt/ *a.* (**-er, -est**) brillant, vif; (*day, room*) clair; (*cheerful*) gai; (*clever*) intelligent. **~ly** *adv.* brillamment. **~ness** *n.* éclat *m.*

brighten /'braɪtn/ *v.t.* égayer. —*v.i.* (*weather*) s'éclaircir; (*of face*) s'éclairer.

brillian|t /'brɪljənt/ *a.* brillant; (*light*) éclatant. **~ce** *n.* éclat *m.*

brim /brɪm/ *n.* bord *m.* —*v.i.* (*p.t.* **brimmed**). ~ **over,** déborder.

brine /braɪn/ *n.* saumure *f.*

bring /brɪŋ/ *v.t.* (*p.t.* **brought**) (*thing*) apporter; (*person, vehicle*) amener. ~ **about,** provoquer. ~ **back,** rapporter; ramener. ~ **down,** faire tomber; (*shoot down, knock down*) abattre. ~ **off,** réussir. ~ **out,** (*take out*) sortir; (*show*) faire ressortir; (*book*) publier. ~ **round** *or* **to,** ranimer. ~ **to bear,** (*pressure etc.*) exercer. ~ **up,** élever; (*med.*) vomir; (*question*) soulever.

brink /brɪŋk/ *n.* bord *m.*

brisk /brɪsk/ *a.* (**-er, -est**) vif. **~ness** *n.* vivacité *f.*

bristl|e /'brɪsl/ *n.* poil *m.* —*v.i.* se hérisser. **~ing with,** hérissé de.

Britain /'brɪtn/ *n.* Grande-Bretagne *f.*

British /'brɪtɪʃ/ *a.* britannique. **the ~,** les Britanniques *m. pl.*

Briton /'brɪtn/ *n.* Britannique *m./f.*

Brittany /'brɪtənɪ/ *n.* Bretagne *f.*

brittle /'brɪtl/ *a.* fragile.

broach /brəʊtʃ/ *v.t.* entamer.

broad /brɔːd/ *a.* (**-er, -est**) large; (*daylight, outline*) grand. **~ bean,** fève *f.* **~-minded** *a.* large d'esprit. **~ly** *adv.* en gros.

broadcast /'brɔːdkɑːst/ *v.t./i.* (*p.t.* **broadcast**) diffuser; (*person*) parler à la télévision *or* à la radio. —*n.* émission *f.*

broaden /'brɔːdn/ *v.t./i.* (s')élargir.

broccoli /'brɒkəlɪ/ *n. invar.* brocoli *m.*

brochure /'brəʊʃə(r)/ *n.* brochure *f.*

broke /brəʊk/ *see* **break.** —*a.* (*penniless: sl.*) fauché.

broken /'brəʊkən/ *see* **break.** —*a.* ~ **English,** mauvais anglais *m.* **~-hearted** *a.* au cœur brisé.

broker /'brəʊkə(r)/ *n.* courtier *m.*

brolly /'brɒlɪ/ *n.* (*fam.*) pépin *m.*

bronchitis /brɒŋ'kaɪtɪs/ *n.* bronchite *f.*

bronze /brɒnz/ *n.* bronze *m.* —*v.t./i.* (se) bronzer.

brooch /brəʊtʃ/ *n.* broche *f.*

brood /bruːd/ *n.* nichée *f.*, couvée *f.* —*v.i.* couver; (*fig.*) méditer tristement. **~y** *a.* mélancolique.

brook[1] /brʊk/ *n.* ruisseau *m.*

brook[2] /brʊk/ *v.t.* souffrir.

broom /bruːm/ *n.* balai *m.*

broomstick /'bruːmstɪk/ *n.* manche à balai *m.*

broth /brɒθ/ *n.* bouillon *m.*

brothel /'brɒθl/ *n.* maison close *f.*

brother /'brʌðə(r)/ *n.* frère *m.* **~hood** *n.* fraternité *f.* **~-in-law** *n.* (*pl.* **~s-in-law**) beau-frère *m.* **~ly** *a.* fraternel.

brought /brɔːt/ *see* **bring.**

brow /braʊ/ *n.* front *m.*; (*of hill*) sommet *m.*

browbeat /ˈbraʊbiːt/ *v.t.* (*p.t.* **-beat,** *p.p.* **-beaten**) intimider.
brown /braʊn/ *a.* (**-er, -est**) brun. —*n.* brun *m.* —*v.t./i.* brunir; (*culin.*) (faire) dorer. **be ~ed off,** (*sl.*) en avoir ras le bol.
Brownie /ˈbraʊnɪ/ *n.* jeannette *f.*
browse /braʊz/ *v.i.* feuilleter; (*animal*) brouter.
bruise /bruːz/ *n.* bleu *m.* —*v.t.* (*hurt*) faire un bleu à; (*fruit*) abîmer. **~d** *a.* couvert de bleus.
brunch /brʌntʃ/ *n.* petit déjeuner copieux *m.* (*pris comme déjeuner*).
brunette /bruːˈnet/ *n.* brunette *f.*
brunt /brʌnt/ *n.* **the ~ of,** le plus fort de.
brush /brʌʃ/ *n.* brosse *f.*; (*skirmish*) accrochage *m.*; (*bushes*) broussailles *f. pl.* —*v.t.* brosser. **~ against,** effleurer. **~ aside,** écarter. **~ off,** (*reject*: *fam.*) envoyer promener. **~ up (on),** se remettre à.
Brussels /ˈbrʌslz/ *n.* Bruxelles *m./f.* **~ sprouts,** choux de Bruxelles *m. pl.*
brutal /ˈbruːtl/ *a.* brutal. **~ity** /-ˈtælətɪ/ *n.* brutalité *f.*
brute /bruːt/ *n.* brute *f.* **by ~ force,** par la force.
B.Sc. *abbr. see* **Bachelor of Science.**
bubble /ˈbʌbl/ *n.* bulle *f.* —*v.i.* bouillonner. **~ over,** déborder.
buck[1] /bʌk/ *n.* mâle *m.* —*v.i.* ruer. **~ up,** (*sl.*) prendre courage; (*hurry*: *sl.*) se grouiller.
buck[2] /bʌk/ *n.* (*Amer., sl.*) dollar *m.*
buck[3] /bʌk/ *n.* **pass the ~ to,** renvoyer la balle à, rejeter la responsabilité sur.
bucket /ˈbʌkɪt/ *n.* seau *m.*
buckle /ˈbʌkl/ *n.* boucle *f.* —*v.t./i.* (*fasten*) (se) boucler; (*bend*) voiler. **~ down to,** s'atteler à.
bud /bʌd/ *n.* bourgeon *m.* —*v.i.* (*p.t.* **budded**) bourgeonner.
Buddhis|t /ˈbʊdɪst/ *a.* & *n.* bouddhiste (*m./f.*) **~m** /-ɪzəm/ *n.* bouddhisme *m.*
budding /ˈbʌdɪŋ/ *a.* (*talent etc.*) naissant; (*film star etc.*) en herbe.
buddy /ˈbʌdɪ/ *n.* (*fam.*) copain *m.*
budge /bʌdʒ/ *v.t./i.* (faire) bouger.
budgerigar /ˈbʌdʒərɪgɑː(r)/ *n.* perruche *f.*
budget /ˈbʌdʒɪt/ *n.* budget *m.* —*v.i.* (*p.t.* **budgeted**). **~ for,** prévoir (dans son budget).
buff /bʌf/ *n.* (*colour*) chamois *m.*; (*Amer., fam.*) fanatique *m./f.* **in the ~,** tout nu.
buffalo /ˈbʌfələʊ/ *n.* (*pl.* **-oes** *or* **-o**) buffle *m.*; (*Amer.*) bison *m.*
buffer /ˈbʌfə(r)/ *n.* tampon *m.* **~ zone,** zone tampon *f.*
buffet[1] /ˈbʊfeɪ/ *n.* (*meal, counter*) buffet *m.*
buffet[2] /ˈbʌfɪt/ *n.* (*blow*) soufflet *m.* —*v.t.* (*p.t.* **buffeted**) souffleter.
buffoon /bəˈfuːn/ *n.* bouffon *m.*
bug /bʌg/ *n.* (*insect*) punaise *f.*; (*any small insect*) bestiole *f.*; (*germ*: *sl.*) microbe *m.*; (*device*: *sl.*) micro *m.*; (*defect*: *sl.*) défaut *m.* —*v.t.* (*p.t.* **bugged**) mettre des micros dans; (*Amer., sl.*) embêter.
bugle /ˈbjuːgl/ *n.* clairon *m.*
build /bɪld/ *v.t./i.* (*p.t.* **built**) bâtir, construire. —*n.* carrure *f.* **~ up,** (*increase*) augmenter, monter; (*accumulate*) (s')accumuler. **~-up** *n.* accumulation *f.*; (*fig.*) publicité *f.* **~er** *n.* entrepreneur *m.*; (*workman*) ouvrier *m.*
building /ˈbɪldɪŋ/ *n.* bâtiment *m.*; (*dwelling*) immeuble *m.* **~ society,** caisse d'épargne-logement *f.*
built /bɪlt/ *see* **build. ~-in** *a.* encastré. **~-up area,** agglomération *f.*, zone urbanisée *f.*
bulb /bʌlb/ *n.* oignon *m.*; (*electr.*) ampoule *f.* **~ous** *a.* bulbeux.
Bulgaria /bʌlˈgeərɪə/ *n.* Bulgarie *f.* **~n** *a.* & *n.* bulgare (*m./f.*).
bulg|e /bʌldʒ/ *n.* renflement *m.*; (*in*

numbers) augmentation temporaire *f.* —*v.i.* se renfler, être renflé. **be ~ing with,** être gonflé *or* bourré de.

bulk /bʌlk/ *n.* grosseur *f.* **in ~,** en gros; (*loose*) en vrac. **the ~ of,** la majeure partie de. **~y** *a.* gros.

bull /bʊl/ *n.* taureau *m.* **~'s-eye** *n.* centre (de la cible) *m.*

bulldog /ˈbʊldɒg/ *n.* bouledogue *m.*

bulldoze /ˈbʊldəʊz/ *v.t.* raser au bulldozer. **~r** /-ə(r)/ *n.* bulldozer *m.*

bullet /ˈbʊlɪt/ *n.* balle *f.* **~-proof** *a.* pare-balles *invar.*; (*vehicle*) blindé.

bulletin /ˈbʊlətɪn/ *n.* bulletin *m.*

bullfight /ˈbʊlfaɪt/ *n.* corrida *f.*

bullion /ˈbʊljən/ *n.* or *or* argent en lingots *m.*

bullring /ˈbʊlrɪŋ/ *n.* arène *f.*

bully /ˈbʊlɪ/ *n.* brute *f.*; tyran *m.* —*v.t.* (*treat badly*) brutaliser; (*persecute*) tyranniser; (*coerce*) forcer (**into,** à).

bum[1] /bʌm/ *n.* (*sl.*) derrière *m.*

bum[2] /bʌm/ *n.* (*Amer.*, *sl.*) vagabond(e) *m.* (*f.*).

bumble-bee /ˈbʌmblbiː/ *n.* bourdon *m.*

bump /bʌmp/ *n.* choc *m.*; (*swelling*) bosse *f.* —*v.t.*/*i.* cogner, heurter. **~ along,** cahoter. **~ into,** (*hit*) rentrer dans; (*meet*) tomber sur. **~y** *a.* cahoteux.

bumper /ˈbʌmpə(r)/ *n.* pare-chocs *m. invar.* —*a.* exceptionnel.

bumpkin /ˈbʌmpkɪn/ *n.* rustre *m.*

bumptious /ˈbʌmpʃəs/ *a.* prétentieux.

bun /bʌn/ *n.* (*cake*) petit pain au lait *m.*; (*hair*) chignon *m.*

bunch /bʌntʃ/ *n.* (*of flowers*) bouquet *m.*; (*of keys*) trousseau *m.*; (*of people*) groupe *m.*: (*of bananas*) régime *m.* **~ of grapes,** grappe de raisin *f.*

bundle /ˈbʌndl/ *n.* paquet *m.* —*v.t.* mettre en paquet; (*push*) pousser.

bung /bʌŋ/ *n.* bonde *f.* —*v.t.* boucher; (*throw*: *sl.*) flanquer.

bungalow /ˈbʌŋgələʊ/ *n.* bungalow *m.*

bungle /ˈbʌŋgl/ *v.t.* gâcher.

bunion /ˈbʌnjən/ *n.* (*med.*) oignon *m.*

bunk[1] /bʌŋk/ *n.* couchette *f.* **~-beds** *n. pl.* lits superposés *m. pl.*

bunk[2] /bʌŋk/ *n.* (*bunkum*: *sl.*) foutaise(s) *f.* (*pl.*).

bunker /ˈbʌŋkə(r)/ *n.* (*mil.*) bunker *m.*

bunkum /ˈbʌŋkəm/ *n.* balivernes *f. pl.*, foutaise(s) *f.* (*pl.*).

bunny /ˈbʌnɪ/ *n.* (*children's use*) (Jeannot) lapin *m.*

buoy /bɔɪ/ *n.* bouée *f.* —*v.t.* **~ up,** (*hearten*) soutenir, encourager.

buoyan|t /ˈbɔɪənt/ *a.* (*cheerful*) gai. **~cy** *n.* gaieté *f.*

burden /ˈbɜːdn/ *n.* fardeau *m.* —*v.t.* accabler. **~some** *a.* lourd.

bureau /ˈbjʊərəʊ/ *n.* (*pl.* **-eaux** /-əʊz/) bureau *m.*

bureaucracy /bjʊəˈrɒkrəsɪ/ *n.* bureaucratie *f.*

bureaucrat /ˈbjʊərəkræt/ *n.* bureaucrate *m.*/*f.* **~ic** /-ˈkrætɪk/ *a.* bureaucratique.

burglar /ˈbɜːglə(r)/ *n.* cambrioleur *m.* **~ize** *v.t.* (*Amer.*) cambrioler. **~y** *n.* cambriolage *m.*

burgle /ˈbɜːgl/ *v.t.* cambrioler.

Burgundy /ˈbɜːgəndɪ/ *n.* (*wine*) bourgogne *m.*

burial /ˈberɪəl/ *n.* enterrement *m.*

burlesque /bɜːˈlesk/ *n.* (*imitation*) parodie *f.*

burly /ˈbɜːlɪ/ *a.* (**-ier, -iest**) costaud, solidement charpenté.

Burm|a /ˈbɜːmə/ *n.* Birmanie *f.* **~ese** /-ˈmiːz/ *a.* & *n.* birman(e) (*m.* (*f.*)).

burn /bɜːn/ *v.t.*/*i.* (*p.t.* **burned** *or* **burnt**) brûler. —*n.* brûlure *f.* **~ down** *or* **be burned down,** être réduit en cendres. **~er** *n.* brûleur *m.* **~ing** *a.* (*fig.*) brûlant.

burnish /ˈbɜːnɪʃ/ *v.t.* polir.
burnt /bɜːnt/ *see* **burn.**
burp /bɜːp/ *n.* (*fam.*) rot *m.* —*v.i.* (*fam.*) roter.
burrow /ˈbʌrəʊ/ *n.* terrier *m.* —*v.t.* creuser.
bursar /ˈbɜːsə(r)/ *n.* économe *m.*/*f.*
bursary /ˈbɜːsərɪ/ *n.* bourse *f.*
burst /bɜːst/ *v.t.*/*i.* (*p.t.* **burst**) crever, (faire) éclater. —*n.* explosion *f.*; (*of laughter*) éclat *m.*; (*surge*) élan *m.* **~ into tears,** fondre en larmes. **~ out laughing,** éclater de rire.
bury /ˈberɪ/ *v.t.* (*person etc.*) enterrer; (*hide, cover*) enfouir; (*engross, thrust*) plonger.
bus /bʌs/ *n.* (*pl.* **buses**) (auto)bus *m.* —*v.i.* (*p.t.* **bussed**) prendre l'autobus. **~-stop** *n.* arrêt d'autobus *m.*
bush /bʊʃ/ *n.* buisson *m.*; (*land*) brousse *f.* **~y** *a.* broussailleux.
business /ˈbɪznɪs/ *n.* (*task, concern*) affaire *f.*; (*commerce*) affaires *f. pl.*; (*line of work*) métier *m.*; (*shop*) commerce *m.* **he has no ~ to,** il n'a pas le droit de. **that's none of your ~!,** ça ne vous regarde pas! **~ man,** homme d'affaires *m.*
businesslike /ˈbɪznɪslaɪk/ *a.* sérieux.
busker /ˈbʌskə(r)/ *n.* musicien(ne) des rues *m.* (*f.*).
bust[1] /bʌst/ *n.* buste *m.*; (*bosom*) poitrine *f.*
bust[2] /bʌst/ *v.t.*/*i.* (*p.t.* **busted** *or* **bust**) (*burst*: *sl.*) crever; (*break*: *sl.*) (se) casser. —*a.* (*broken, finished*: *sl.*) fichu. **~-up** *n.* (*sl.*) engueulade *f.* **go ~,** (*sl.*) faire faillite.
bustl|e /ˈbʌsl/ *v.i.* s'affairer. —*n.* affairement *m.*, remue-ménage *m.* **~ing** *a.* (*place*) bruyant, animé.
bus|y /ˈbɪzɪ/ *a.* (**-ier, -iest**) occupé; (*street*) animé; (*day*) chargé. —*v.t.* **~y o.s. with,** s'occuper à. **~ily** *adv.* activement.
busybody /ˈbɪzɪbɒdɪ/ *n.* **be a ~,** faire la mouche du coche.
but /bʌt, *unstressed* bət/ *conj.* mais. —*prep.* sauf. —*adv.* (*only*) seulement. **~ for,** sans. **nobody ~,** personne d'autre que.
butane /ˈbjuːteɪn/ *n.* butane *m.*
butcher /ˈbʊtʃə(r)/ *n.* boucher *m.* —*v.t.* massacrer. **~y** *n.* boucherie *f.*, massacre *m.*
butler /ˈbʌtlə(r)/ *n.* maître d'hôtel *m.*
butt /bʌt/ *n.* (*of gun*) crosse *f.*; (*of cigarette*) mégot *m.*; (*target*) cible *f.* —*v.i.* **~ in,** interrompre.
butter /ˈbʌtə(r)/ *n.* beurre *m.* —*v.t.* beurrer. **~-bean** *n.* haricot blanc *m.* **~-fingers** *n.* maladroit(e) *m.* (*f.*).
buttercup /ˈbʌtəkʌp/ *n.* bouton-d'or *m.*
butterfly /ˈbʌtəflaɪ/ *n.* papillon *m.*
buttock /ˈbʌtək/ *n.* fesse *f.*
button /ˈbʌtn/ *n.* bouton *m.* —*v.t.*/*i.* **~ (up),** (se) boutonner.
buttonhole /ˈbʌtnhəʊl/ *n.* boutonnière *f.* —*v.t.* accrocher.
buttress /ˈbʌtrɪs/ *n.* contrefort *m.* —*v.t.* soutenir.
buxom /ˈbʌksəm/ *a.* bien en chair.
buy /baɪ/ *v.t.* (*p.t.* **bought**) acheter (**from,** à); (*believe*: *sl.*) croire, avaler. —*n.* achat *m.* **~er** *n.* acheteu|r, -se *m.*, *f.*
buzz /bʌz/ *n.* bourdonnement *m.* —*v.i.* bourdonner. **~ off,** (*sl.*) fiche(r) le camp. **~er** *n.* sonnerie *f.*
by /baɪ/ *prep.* par, de; (*near*) à côté de; (*before*) avant; (*means*) en, à, par. **~ bike,** à vélo. **~ car,** en auto. **~ day,** de jour. **~ the kilo,** au kilo. **~ running**/*etc.*, en courant/*etc.* **~ sea,** par mer. —*adv.* (*near*) tout près. **~ and large,** dans l'ensemble. **~-election** *n.* élection partielle *f.* **~-law** *n.* arrêté *m.*; (*of club etc.*) statut *m.* **~ o.s.,** tout seul.

~-product *n.* sous-produit *m.* **~-road** *n.* chemin de traverse *m.*
bye(-bye) /baɪ('baɪ)/ *int.* (*fam.*) au revoir, salut.
bygone /'baɪgɒn/ *a.* passé.
bypass /'baɪpɑːs/ *n.* route qui contourne *f.* —*v.t.* contourner.
bystander /'baɪstændə(r)/ *n.* specta|teur, -trice *m., f.*
byword /'baɪwɜːd/ *n.* **be a ~ for,** être connu pour.

C

cab /kæb/ *n.* taxi *m.*; (*of lorry, train*) cabine *f.*
cabaret /'kæbəreɪ/ *n.* spectacle (de cabaret) *m.*
cabbage /'kæbɪdʒ/ *n.* chou *m.*
cabin /'kæbɪn/ *n.* (*hut*) cabane *f.*; (*in ship, aircraft*) cabine *f.*
cabinet /'kæbɪnɪt/ *n.* (petite) armoire *f.*, meuble de rangement *m.*; (*for filing*) classeur *m.* **C~,** (*pol.*) cabinet *m.* **~-maker** *n.* ébéniste *m.*
cable /'keɪbl/ *n.* câble *m.* —*v.t.* câbler. **~-car** *n.* téléphérique *m.* **~ railway,** funiculaire *m.*
caboose /kə'buːs/ *n.* (*rail., Amer.*) fourgon *m.*
cache /kæʃ/ *n.* (*place*) cachette *f.* **a ~ of arms,** des armes cachées.
cackle /'kækl/ *n.* caquet *m.* —*v.i.* caqueter.
cactus /'kæktəs/ *n.* (*pl.* **-ti** /-taɪ/ *or* **-tuses**) cactus *m.*
cad /kæd/ *n.* malotru *m.* **~dish** *a.* grossier.
caddie /'kædɪ/ *n.* (*golf*) caddie *m.*
caddy /'kædɪ/ *n.* boîte à thé *f.*
cadence /'keɪdns/ *n.* cadence *f.*
cadet /kə'det/ *n.* élève officier *m.*
cadge /kædʒ/ *v.t.* se fairer payer, écornifler. —*v.i.* quémander. **~ money from,** taper. **~r** /-ə(r)/ *n.* écornifleu|r, -se *m., f.*
Caesarean /sɪ'zeərɪən/ *a.* **~ (section),** césarienne *f.*
café /'kæfeɪ/ *n.* café(-restaurant) *m.*
cafeteria /kæfɪ'tɪərɪə/ *n.* cafétéria *f.*
caffeine /'kæfiːn/ *n.* caféine *f.*
cage /keɪdʒ/ *n.* cage *f.* —*v.t.* mettre en cage.
cagey /'keɪdʒɪ/ *a.* (*secretive: fam.*) peu communicatif.
Cairo /'kaɪərəʊ/ *n.* le Caire *m.*
cajole /kə'dʒəʊl/ *v.t.* cajoler.
cake /keɪk/ *n.* gâteau *m.* **~d** *a.* durci. **~d with,** raidi par.
calamit|y /kə'læmətɪ/ *n.* calamité *f.* **~ous** *a.* désastreux.
calcium /'kælsɪəm/ *n.* calcium *m.*
calculat|e /'kælkjʊleɪt/ *v.t./i.* calculer; (*Amer.*) supposer. **~ed** *a.* (*action*) délibéré. **~ing** *a.* calculateur. **~ion** /-'leɪʃn/ *n.* calcul *m.* **~or** *n.* calculatrice *f.*
calculus /'kælkjʊləs/ *n.* (*pl.* **-li** /-laɪ/ *or* **-luses**) calcul *m.*
calendar /'kælɪndə(r)/ *n.* calendrier *m.*
calf[1] /kɑːf/ *n.* (*pl.* **calves**) (*young cow or bull*) veau *m.*
calf[2] /kɑːf/ *n.* (*pl.* **calves**) (*of leg*) mollet *m.*
calibre /'kælɪbə(r)/ *n.* calibre *m.*
calico /'kælɪkəʊ/ *n.* calicot *m.*
call /kɔːl/ *v.t./i.* appeler. **~ (in *or* round),** (*visit*) passer. —*n.* appel *m.*; (*of bird*) cri *m.*; visite *f.* **be ~ed,** (*named*) s'appeler. **be on ~,** être de garde. **~ back,** rappeler; (*visit*) repasser. **~-box** *n.* cabine téléphonique *f.* **~ for,** (*require*) demander; (*fetch*) passer prendre. **~-girl** *n.* call-girl *f.* **~ off,** annuler. **~ out (to),** appeler. **~ on,** (*visit*) passer chez; (*appeal to*) faire appel à. **~ up,** appeler (au téléphone); (*mil.*) mobiliser, appeler. **~er** *n.* visiteu|r, -se *m., f.* **~ing** *n.* vocation *f.*
callous /'kæləs/ *a.*, **~ly** *adv.*

sans pitié. **~ness** *n.* manque de pitié *m.*

callow /ˈkæləʊ/ *a.* (**-er, -est**) inexpérimenté.

calm /kɑːm/ *a.* (**-er, -est**) calme. —*n.* calme *m.* —*v.t./i.* **~ (down)**, (se) calmer. **~ness** *n.* calme *m.*

calorie /ˈkælərɪ/ *n.* calorie *f.*

camber /ˈkæmbə(r)/ *n.* (*of road*) bombement *m.*

came /keɪm/ *see* **come.**

camel /ˈkæml/ *n.* chameau *m.*

cameo /ˈkæmɪəʊ/ *n.* (*pl.* **-os**) camée *m.*

camera /ˈkæmərə/ *n.* appareil (-photo) *m.*; (*for moving pictures*) caméra *f.* **~man** *n.* (*pl.* **-men**) caméraman *m.*

camouflage /ˈkæməflɑːʒ/ *n.* camouflage *m.* —*v.t.* camoufler.

camp[1] /kæmp/ *n.* camp *m.* —*v.i.* camper. **~-bed** *n.* lit de camp *m.* **~er** *n.* campeu|r, -se *m., f.* **~ing** *n.* camping *m.*

camp[2] /kæmp/ *a.* (*mannered*) affecté; (*vulgar*) de mauvais goût.

campaign /kæmˈpeɪn/ *n.* campagne *f.* —*v.i.* faire campagne.

campsite /ˈkæmpsaɪt/ *n.* (*for holiday-makers*) camping *m.*

campus /ˈkæmpəs/ *n.* (*pl.* **-puses**) campus *m.*

can[1] /kæn/ *n.* bidon *m.*; (*sealed container for food*) boîte *f.* —*v.t.* (*p.t.* **canned**) mettre en boîte. **~ it!**, (*Amer., sl.*) ferme-la! **~ned music,** musique de fond enregistrée *f.* **~-opener** *n.* ouvre-boîte(s) *m.*

can[2] /kæn, *unstressed* kən/ *v. aux.* (*be able to*) pouvoir; (*know how to*) savoir.

Canad|a /ˈkænədə/ *n.* Canada *m.* **~ian** /kəˈneɪdɪən/ *a.* & *n.* canadien(ne) (*m.* (*f.*)).

canal /kəˈnæl/ *n.* canal *m.*

canary /kəˈneərɪ/ *n.* canari *m.*

cancel /ˈkænsl/ *v.t./i.* (*p.t.* **cancelled**) (*call off, revoke*) annuler; (*cross out*) barrer; (*a stamp*) oblitérer. **~ out,** (se) neutraliser. **~lation** /-əˈleɪʃn/ *n.* annulation *f.*; oblitération *f.*

cancer /ˈkænsə(r)/ *n.* cancer *m.* **~ous** *a.* cancéreux.

candid /ˈkændɪd/ *a.* franc. **~ness** *n.* franchise *f.*

candida|te /ˈkændɪdeɪt/ *n.* candidat(e) *m.* (*f.*). **~cy** /-əsɪ/ *n.* candidature *f.*

candle /ˈkændl/ *n.* bougie *f.*, chandelle *f.*; (*in church*) cierge *m.*

candlestick /ˈkændlstɪk/ *n.* bougeoir *m.*, chandelier *m.*

candour /ˈkændə(r)/ *n.* franchise *f.*

candy /ˈkændɪ/ *n.* (*Amer.*) bonbon(s) *m.* (*pl.*) **~-floss** *n.* barbe à papa *f.*

cane /keɪn/ *n.* canne *f.*; (*for baskets*) rotin *m.*; (*for punishment: schol.*) baguette *f.*, bâton *m.* —*v.t.* donner des coups de baguette *or* de bâton à, fustiger.

canine /ˈkeɪnaɪn/ *a.* canin.

canister /ˈkænɪstə(r)/ *n.* boîte *f.*

cannabis /ˈkænəbɪs/ *n.* cannabis *m.*

cannibal /ˈkænɪbl/ *n.* cannibale *m./f.* **~ism** *n.* cannibalisme *m.*

cannon /ˈkænən/ *n.* (*pl.* **~** *or* **~s**) canon *m.* **~-ball** *n.* boulet de canon *m.*

cannot /ˈkænət/ = **can not.**

canny /ˈkænɪ/ *a.* rusé, madré.

canoe /kəˈnuː/ *n.* (*sport*) canoë *m.*, kayak *m.* —*v.i.* faire du canoë *or* du kayak. **~ist** *n.* canoéiste *m./f.*

canon /ˈkænən/ *n.* (*clergyman*) chanoine *m.*; (*rule*) canon *m.*

canonize /ˈkænənaɪz/ *v.t.* canoniser.

canopy /ˈkænəpɪ/ *n.* dais *m.*; (*over doorway*) marquise *f.*

cant /kænt/ *n.* jargon *m.*

can't /kɑːnt/ = **can not.**

cantankerous /kænˈtæŋkərəs/ *a.* acariâtre, grincheux.

canteen /kæn'tiːn/ *n.* (*restaurant*) cantine *f.*; (*flask*) bidon *m.*
canter /'kæntə(r)/ *n.* petit galop *m.* —*v.i.* aller au petit galop.
canvas /'kænvəs/ *n.* toile *f.*
canvass /'kænvəs/ *v.t./i.* (*comm.*, *pol.*) solliciter des commandes *or* des voix (de). **~ing** *n.* (*comm.*) démarchage *m.*; (*pol.*) démarchage électoral *m.*
canyon /'kænjən/ *n.* cañon *m.*
cap /kæp/ *n.* (*hat*) casquette *f.*; (*of bottle, tube*) bouchon *m.*, (*of beer or milk bottle*) capsule *f.*; (*of pen*) capuchon *m.*; (*for toy gun*) amorce *f.* —*v.t.* (*p.t.* **capped**) (*bottle*) capsuler; (*outdo*) surpasser. **~ped with,** coiffé de.
capab|le /'keɪpəbl/ *a.* (*person*) capable (**of,** de), compétent. **be ~le of,** (*of situation, text, etc.*) être susceptible de. **~ility** /-'bɪlətɪ/ *n.* capacité *f.* **~ly** *adv.* avec compétence.
capacity /kə'pæsətɪ/ *n.* capacité *f.* **in one's ~ as,** en sa qualité de.
cape[1] /keɪp/ *n.* (*cloak*) cape *f.*
cape[2] /keɪp/ *n.* (*geog.*) cap *m.*
caper[1] /'keɪpə(r)/ *v.i.* gambader. —*n.* (*prank*) farce *f.*; (*activity: sl.*) affaire *f.*
caper[2] /'keɪpə(r)/ *n.* (*culin.*) câpre *f.*
capital /'kæpɪtl/ *a.* capital. —*n.* (*town*) capitale *f.*; (*money*) capital *m.* **~ (letter),** majuscule *f.*
capitalis|t /'kæpɪtəlɪst/ *a.* & *n.* capitaliste (*m.*/*f.*). **~m** /-zəm/ *n.* capitalisme *m.*
capitalize /'kæpɪtəlaɪz/ *v.i.* **~ on,** tirer profit de.
capitulat|e /kə'pɪtʃʊleɪt/ *v.i.* capituler. **~ion** /-'leɪʃn/ *n.* capitulation *f.*
capricious /kə'prɪʃəs/ *a.* capricieux.
capsize /kæp'saɪz/ *v.t./i.* (faire) chavirer.
capsule /'kæpsjuːl/ *n.* capsule *f.*
captain /'kæptɪn/ *n.* capitaine *m.* —*v.t.* commander, être le capitaine de.
caption /'kæpʃn/ *n.* (*for illustration*) légende *f.*; (*heading*) soustitre *m.*
captivate /'kæptɪveɪt/ *v.t.* captiver.
captiv|e /'kæptɪv/ *a.* & *n.* capti|f, -ve (*m.*, *f.*). **~ity** /-'tɪvətɪ/ *n.* captivité *f.*
capture /'kæptʃə(r)/ *v.t.* (*person, animal*) prendre, capturer; (*attention*) retenir. —*n.* capture *f.*
car /kɑː(r)/ *n.* voiture *f.*, auto *f.* **~-park** *n.* parking *m.* **~-wash** *n.* station de lavage *f.*, lave-auto *m.*
carafe /kə'ræf/ *n.* carafe *f.*
caramel /'kærəmel/ *n.* caramel *m.*
carat /'kærət/ *n.* carat *m.*
caravan /'kærəvæn/ *n.* caravane *f.*
carbohydrate /kɑːbəʊ'haɪdreɪt/ *n.* hydrate de carbone *m.*
carbon /'kɑːbən/ *n.* carbone *m.* **~ copy, ~ paper,** carbone *m.*
carburettor /kɑːbjʊ'retə(r)/ *n.* carburateur *m.*
carcass /'kɑːkəs/ *n.* carcasse *f.*
card /kɑːd/ *n.* carte *f.* **~-index** *n.* fichier *m.*
cardboard /'kɑːdbɔːd/ *n.* carton *m.*
cardiac /'kɑːdɪæk/ *a.* cardiaque.
cardigan /'kɑːdɪgən/ *n.* cardigan *m.*
cardinal /'kɑːdɪnl/ *a.* cardinal. —*n.* (*relig.*) cardinal *m.*
care /keə(r)/ *n.* (*attention*) soin *m.*, attention *f.*; (*worry*) souci *m.*; (*protection*) garde *f.* —*v.i.* **~ about,** s'intéresser à. **~ for,** s'occuper de; (*invalid*) soigner. **~ to** *or* **for,** aimer, vouloir. **I don't ~,** ça m'est égal. **take ~ of,** s'occuper de.
career /kə'rɪə(r)/ *n.* carrière *f.* —*v.i.* aller à toute vitesse.
carefree /'keəfriː/ *a.* insouciant.
careful /'keəfl/ *a.* soigneux; (*cautious*) prudent. **~!,** attention! **~ly** *adv.* avec soin.

careless /ˈkeəlɪs/ *a.* négligent; (*work*) peu soigné. **~ about,** peu soucieux de. **~ly** *adv.* négligemment. **~ness** *n.* négligence *f.*

caress /kəˈres/ *n.* caresse *f.* —*v.t.* caresser.

caretaker /ˈkeəteɪkə(r)/ *n.* gardien(ne) *m.* (*f.*).

cargo /ˈkɑːgəʊ/ *n.* (*pl.* **-oes**) cargaison *f.* **~ boat,** cargo *m.*

Caribbean /kærɪˈbiːən/ *a.* caraïbe. —*n.* **the ~,** les Antilles *f. pl.*

caricature /ˈkærɪkətjʊə(r)/ *n.* caricature *f.* —*v.t.* caricaturer.

caring /ˈkeərɪŋ/ *a.* (*mother, son, etc.*) aimant. —*n.* affection *f.*

carnage /ˈkɑːnɪdʒ/ *n.* carnage *m.*

carnal /ˈkɑːnl/ *a.* charnel.

carnation /kɑːˈneɪʃn/ *n.* œillet *m.*

carnival /ˈkɑːnɪvl/ *n.* carnaval *m.*

carol /ˈkærəl/ *n.* chant (de Noël) *m.*

carouse /kəˈraʊz/ *v.i.* faire la fête.

carp[1] /kɑːp/ *n. invar.* carpe *f.*

carp[2] /kɑːp/ *v.i.* **~ (at),** critiquer.

carpent|er /ˈkɑːpɪntə(r)/ *n.* charpentier *m.*; (*for light woodwork, furniture*) menuisier *m.* **~ry** *n.* charpenterie *f.*; menuiserie *f.*

carpet /ˈkɑːpɪt/ *n.* tapis *m.* —*v.t.* (*p.t.* **carpeted**) recouvrir d'un tapis. **~-sweeper** *n.* balai mécanique *m.* **on the ~,** (*fam.*) sur la sellette.

carriage /ˈkærɪdʒ/ *n.* (*rail. & horse-drawn*) voiture *f.*; (*of goods*) transport *m.*; (*cost*) port *m.*

carriageway /ˈkærɪdʒweɪ/ *n.* chaussée *f.*

carrier /ˈkærɪə(r)/ *n.* transporteur *m.*; (*med.*) porteu|r, -se *m., f.* **~ (bag),** sac en plastique *m.*

carrot /ˈkærət/ *n.* carotte *f.*

carry /ˈkærɪ/ *v.t./i.* porter; (*goods*) transporter; (*involve*) comporter. **be carried away,** s'emballer. **~-cot** *n.* porte-bébé *m.* **~ off,** enlever; (*prize*) remporter. **~ on,** continuer; (*behave*: *fam.*) se conduire (mal). **~ out,** (*an order, plan*) exécuter; (*duty*) accomplir; (*task*) effectuer.

cart /kɑːt/ *n.* charrette *f.* —*v.t.* transporter; (*heavy object*: *sl.*) trimballer.

cartilage /ˈkɑːtɪlɪdʒ/ *n.* cartilage *m.*

carton /ˈkɑːtn/ *n.* (*box*) carton *m.*; (*of yoghurt, cream*) pot *m.*; (*of cigarettes*) cartouche *f.*

cartoon /kɑːˈtuːn/ *n.* dessin (humoristique) *m.*; (*cinema*) dessin animé *m.* **~ist** *n.* dessina|teur, -trice *m., f.*

cartridge /ˈkɑːtrɪdʒ/ *n.* cartouche *f.*

carve /kɑːv/ *v.t.* tailler; (*meat*) découper.

cascade /kæsˈkeɪd/ *n.* cascade *f.* —*v.i.* tomber en cascade.

case[1] /keɪs/ *n.* cas *m.*; (*jurid.*) affaire *f.*; (*phil.*) arguments *m. pl.* **in ~ he comes,** au cas où il viendrait. **in ~ of,** en cas de.

case[2] /keɪs/ *n.* (*crate*) caisse *f.*; (*for camera, cigarettes, spectacles, etc.*) étui *m.*; (*suitcase*) valise *f.*

cash /kæʃ/ *n.* argent *m.* —*a.* (*price etc.*) (au) comptant. —*v.t.* encaisser. **~ a cheque,** (*person*) encaisser un chèque; (*bank*) payer un chèque. **pay ~/in ~,** payer comptant/en espèces. **~ desk,** caisse *f.* **~ in (on),** profiter (de).

cashew /ˈkæʃuː/ *n.* noix de cajou *f.*

cashier /kæˈʃɪə(r)/ *n.* caiss|ier, -ière *m., f.*

cashmere /kæʃˈmɪə(r)/ *n.* cachemire *m.*

casino /kəˈsiːnəʊ/ *n.* (*pl.* **-os**) casino *m.*

cask /kɑːsk/ *n.* tonneau *m.*

casket /ˈkɑːskɪt/ *n.* (*box*) coffret *m.*; (*coffin*: *Amer.*) cercueil *m.*

casserole /ˈkæsərəʊl/ *n.* (*utensil*) cocotte *f.*; (*stew*) daube *f.*

cassette /kəˈset/ *n.* cassette *f.*

cast /kɑːst/ *v.t.* (*p.t.* **cast**) (*throw*)

jeter; (*glance, look*) jeter; (*shadow*) projeter; (*vote*) donner; (*metal*) couler. ~ (**off**), (*shed*) se dépouiller de.—*n.* (*theatre*) distribution *f.*; (*of dice*) coup *m.*; (*mould*) moule *m.*; (*med.*) plâtre *m.* ~ **iron,** fonte *f.* ~**-iron** *a.* de fonte; (*fig.*) solide. ~**-offs** *n. pl.* vieux vêtements *m. pl.*

castanets /kæstə'nets/ *n. pl.* castagnettes *f. pl.*

castaway /'kɑːstəweɪ/ *n.* naufragé(e) *m.* (*f.*).

caste /kɑːst/ *n.* caste *f.*

castle /'kɑːsl/ *n.* château *m.*; (*chess*) tour *f.*

castor /'kɑːstə(r)/ *n.* (*wheel*) roulette *f.* ~ **sugar,** sucre en poudre *m.*

castrat|e /kæ'streɪt/ *v.t.* châtrer. ~**ion** /-ʃn/ *n.* castration *f.*

casual /'kæʒʊəl/ *a.* (*remark*) fait au hasard; (*meeting*) fortuit; (*attitude*) désinvolte; (*work*) temporaire; (*clothes*) sport *invar.* ~**ly** *adv.* par hasard; (*carelessly*) avec désinvolture.

casualty /'kæʒʊəltɪ/ *n.* (*dead*) mort(e) *m.* (*f.*).; (*injured*) blessé(e) *m.* (*f.*); (*accident victim*) accidenté(e) *m.* (*f.*).

cat /kæt/ *n.* chat *m.* **C~'s-eyes** *n. pl.* (P.) cataphotes *m. pl.* (P.).

cataclysm /'kætəklɪzəm/ *n.* cataclysme *m.*

catalogue /'kætəlɒg/ *n.* catalogue *m.* —*v.t.* cataloguer.

catalyst /'kætəlɪst/ *n.* catalyseur *m.*

catapult /'kætəpʌlt/ *n.* lance-pierres *m. invar.* —*v.t.* catapulter.

cataract /'kætərækt/ *n.* (*waterfall* & *med.*) cataracte *f.*

catarrh /kə'tɑː(r)/ *n.* rhume *m.*, catarrhe *m.*

catastroph|e /kə'tæstrəfɪ/ *n.* catastrophe *f.* ~**ic** /kætə'strɒfɪk/ *a.* catastrophique.

catch /kætʃ/ *v.t.* (*p.t.* **caught**) attraper; (*grab*) prendre, saisir; (*catch unawares*) surprendre; (*jam, trap*) prendre; (*understand*) saisir. —*v.i.* prendre; (*get stuck*) se prendre (**in,** dans). —*n.* capture *f.*, prise *f.*; (*on door*) loquet *m.*; (*fig.*) piège *m.* ~ **fire,** prendre feu. ~ **on,** (*fam.*) prendre, devenir populaire. ~**-phrase** *n.* slogan *m.* ~ **sight of,** apercevoir. ~ **up,** se rattraper. ~ **up (with),** rattraper.

catching /'kætʃɪŋ/ *a.* contagieux.

catchment /'kætʃmənt/ *n.* ~ **area,** circonscription (administrative) *f.*

catchy /'kætʃɪ/ *a.* facile à retenir.

catechism /'kætɪkɪzəm/ *n.* catéchisme *m.*

categorical /kætɪ'gɒrɪkl/ *a.* catégorique.

category /'kætɪgərɪ/ *n.* catégorie *f.*

cater /'keɪtə(r)/ *v.i.* s'occuper de la nourriture. ~ **for,** (*pander to*) satisfaire; (*of magazine etc.*) s'adresser à. ~**er** *n.* traiteur *m.*

caterpillar /'kætəpɪlə(r)/ *n.* chenille *f.*

cathedral /kə'θiːdrəl/ *n.* cathédrale *f.*

catholic /'kæθəlɪk/ *a.* universel. **C~** *a.* & *n.* catholique (*m.*/*f.*). ~**ism** /kə'θɒlɪsɪzəm/ *n.* catholicisme *m.*

cattle /'kætl/ *n. pl.* bétail *m.*

catty /'kætɪ/ *a.* méchant.

caucus /'kɔːkəs/ *n.* comité électoral *m.*

caught /kɔːt/ *see* **catch.**

cauldron /'kɔːldrən/ *n.* chaudron *m.*

cauliflower /'kɒlɪflaʊə(r)/ *n.* chou-fleur *m.*

cause /kɔːz/ *n.* cause *f.*; (*reason*) raison *f.*, motif *m.* —*v.t.* causer. ~ **sth. to grow/move/***etc.*, faire pousser/bouger/*etc.* qch.

causeway /'kɔːzweɪ/ *n.* chaussée *f.*

caustic /'kɔːstɪk/ *a.* & *n.* caustique (*m.*).

cauti|on /ˈkɔːʃn/ *n.* prudence *f.*; (*warning*) avertissement *m.* —*v.t.* avertir. **~ous** *a.* prudent. **~ously** *adv.* prudemment.
cavalier /kævəˈlɪə(r)/ *a.* cavalier.
cavalry /ˈkævəlrɪ/ *n.* cavalerie *f.*
cave /keɪv/ *n.* caverne *f.*, grotte *f.* —*v.i.* **~ in,** s'effondrer.
caveman /ˈkeɪvmæn/ *n.* (*pl.* **-men**) homme des cavernes *m.*
cavern /ˈkævən/ *n.* caverne *f.*
caviare, *Amer.* **caviar** /ˈkævɪɑː(r)/ *n.* caviar *m.*
caving /ˈkeɪvɪŋ/ *n.* spéléologie *f.*
cavity /ˈkævətɪ/ *n.* cavité *f.*
cavort /kəˈvɔːt/ *v.i.* gambader.
cease /siːs/ *v.t./i.* cesser. **~-fire** *n.* cessez-le-feu *m. invar.* **without ~,** sans cesse. **~less** *a.* incessant.
cedar /ˈsiːdə(r)/ *n.* cèdre *m.*
cede /siːd/ *v.t.* céder.
cedilla /sɪˈdɪlə/ *n.* cédille *f.*
ceiling /ˈsiːlɪŋ/ *n.* plafond *m.*
celebrat|e /ˈselɪbreɪt/ *v.t.* (*perform, glorify*) célébrer; (*event*) fêter, célébrer. —*v.i.* **we shall ~e,** on va fêter ça. **~ion** /-ˈbreɪʃn/ *n.* fête *f.*
celebrated /ˈselɪbreɪtɪd/ *a.* célèbre.
celebrity /sɪˈlebrətɪ/ *n.* célébrité *f.*
celery /ˈselərɪ/ *n.* céleri *m.*
celiba|te /ˈselɪbət/ *a.* **be ~te,** vivre dans le célibat. **~cy** *n.* célibat *m.*
cell /sel/ *n.* cellule *f.*; (*electr.*) élément *m.*
cellar /ˈselə(r)/ *n.* cave *f.*
cell|o /ˈtʃeləʊ/ *n.* (*pl.* **-os**) violoncelle *m.* **~ist** *n.* violoncelliste *m./f.*
Cellophane /ˈseləfeɪn/ *n.* (P.) cellophane *f.* (P.).
Celt /kelt/ *n.* Celte *m./f.* **~ic** *a.* celtique, celte.
cement /sɪˈment/ *n.* ciment *m.* —*v.t.* cimenter. **~-mixer** *n.* bétonnière *f.*
cemetery /ˈsemətrɪ/ *n.* cimetière *m.*
cenotaph /ˈsenətɑːf/ *n.* cénotaphe *m.*
censor /ˈsensə(r)/ *n.* censeur *m.* —*v.t.* censurer. **~ship** *n.* censure *f.*
censure /ˈsenʃə(r)/ *n.* blâme *m.* —*v.t.* blâmer.
census /ˈsensəs/ *n.* recensement *m.*
cent /sent/ *n.* (*coin*) cent *m.*
centenary /senˈtiːnərɪ, *Amer.* ˈsentənerɪ/ *n.* centenaire *m.*
centigrade /ˈsentɪgreɪd/ *a.* centigrade.
centilitre /ˈsentɪliːtə(r)/ *n.* centilitre *m.*
centimetre /ˈsentɪmiːtə(r)/ *n.* centimètre *m.*
centipede /ˈsentɪpiːd/ *n.* millepattes *m. invar.*
central /ˈsentrəl/ *a.* central. **~ heating,** chauffage central *m.* **~ize** *v.t.* centraliser. **~ly** *adv.* (*situated*) au centre.
centre /ˈsentə(r)/ *n.* centre *m.* —*v.t.* (*p.t.* **centred**) centrer. —*v.i.* **~ on,** tourner autour de. **~-forward** *n.* avant-centre *m.*
centrifugal /senˈtrɪfjʊgl/ *a.* centrifuge.
century /ˈsentʃərɪ/ *n.* siècle *m.*
ceramic /sɪˈræmɪk/ *a.* (*art*) céramique; (*object*) en céramique.
cereal /ˈsɪərɪəl *n.* céréale *f.*
cerebral /ˈserɪbrəl, *Amer.* səˈriːbrəl/ *a.* cérébral.
ceremonial /serɪˈməʊnɪəl/ *a.* de cérémonie. —*n.* cérémonial *m.*
ceremon|y /ˈserɪmənɪ/ *n.* cérémonie *f.* **~ious** /-ˈməʊnɪəs/ *a.* solennel.
certain /ˈsɜːtn/ *a.* certain. **for ~,** avec certitude. **make ~ of,** s'assurer de. **~ly** *adv.* certainement. **~ty** *n.* certitude *f.*
certificate /səˈtɪfɪkət/ *n.* certificat *m.*
certify /ˈsɜːtɪfaɪ/ *v.t.* certifier.
cessation /seˈseɪʃn/ *n.* cessation *f.*
cesspit, cesspool /ˈsespɪt, ˈsespuːl/ *ns.* fosse d'aisances *f.*
chafe /tʃeɪf/ *v.t.* frotter (contre).

chaff /tʃɑːf/ *v.t.* taquiner.
chaffinch /'tʃæfɪntʃ/ *n.* pinson *m.*
chagrin /'ʃægrɪn/ *n.* vif dépit *m.*
chain /tʃeɪn/ *n.* chaîne *f.* —*v.t.* enchaîner. ~ **reaction,** réaction en chaîne *f.* ~**-smoke** *v.i.* fumer de manière ininterrompue. ~ **store,** magasin à succursales multiples *m.*
chair /tʃeə(r)/ *n.* chaise *f.*; (*armchair*) fauteuil *m.*; (*univ.*) chaire *f.* —*v.t.* (*preside over*) présider.
chairman /'tʃeəmən/ *n.* (*pl.* **-men**) président(e) *m.* (*f.*).
chalet /'ʃæleɪ/ *n.* chalet *m.*
chalk /tʃɔːk/ *n.* craie *f.* ~**y** *a.* crayeux.
challeng|e /'tʃælɪndʒ/ *n.* défi *m.*; (*task*) gageure *f.* —*v.t.* (*summon*) défier (**to do,** de faire); (*question truth of*) contester. ~**er** *n.* (*sport*) challenger *m.* ~**ing** *a.* stimulant.
chamber /'tʃeɪmbə(r)/ *n.* (*old use*) chambre *f.* ~ **music,** musique de chambre *f.* ~**-pot** *n.* pot de chambre *m.*
chambermaid /'tʃeɪmbəmeɪd/ *n.* femme de chambre *f.*
chamois /'ʃæmɪ/ *n.* ~**(-leather),** peau de chamois *f.*
champagne /ʃæm'peɪn/ *n.* champagne *m.*
champion /'tʃæmpɪən/ *n.* champion(ne) *m.* (*f.*). —*v.t.* défendre. ~**ship** *n.* championnat *m.*
chance /tʃɑːns/ *n.* (*luck*) hasard *m.*; (*opportunity*) occasion *f.*; (*likelihood*) chances *f. pl.*; (*risk*) risque *m.* —*a.* fortuit. —*v.t.* ~ **doing,** prendre le risque de faire. ~ **it,** risquer le coup.
chancellor /'tʃɑːnsələ(r)/ *n.* chancelier *m.* **C~ of the Exchequer,** Chancelier de l'Échiquier.
chancy /'tʃɑːnsɪ/ *a.* risqué.
chandelier /ʃændə'lɪə(r)/ *n.* lustre *m.*
change /tʃeɪndʒ/ *v.t.* (*alter*) changer; (*exchange*) échanger (**for,** contre); (*money*) changer. ~ **trains/one's dress/***etc.*, (*by substitution*) changer de train/de robe/*etc.* —*v.i* changer; (*change clothes*) se changer. —*n.* changement *m.*; (*money*) monnaie *f.* **a ~ of clothes,** des vêtements de rechange. ~ **one's mind,** changer d'avis. ~ **over,** passer (**to,** à). ~**-over** *n.* passage *m.* ~**able** *a.* changeant; (*weather*) variable.
channel /'tʃænl/ *n.* chenal *m.*; (*TV*) chaîne *f.*, canal *m.*; (*medium, agency*) canal *m.*; (*groove*) rainure *f.* —*v.t.* (*p.t.* **channelled**) (*direct*) canaliser. **the (English) C~,** la Manche. **the C~ Islands,** les îles anglo-normandes *f. pl.*
chant /tʃɑːnt/ *n.* (*relig.*) psalmodie *f.*; (*of demonstrators*) chant (scandé) *m.* —*v.t./i.* psalmodier; scander (des slogans).
chao|s /'keɪɒs/ *n.* chaos *m.* ~**tic** /-'ɒtɪk/ *a.* chaotique.
chap[1] /tʃæp/ *n.* (*man: fam.*) type *m.*
chap[2] /tʃæp/ *n.* gerçure *f.* —*v.t./i.* (*p.t.* **chapped**) (se) gercer.
chapel /'tʃæpl/ *n.* chapelle *f.*; (*Nonconformist*) église (nonconformiste) *f.*
chaperon /'ʃæpərəʊn/ *n.* chaperon *m.* —*v.t.* chaperonner.
chaplain /'tʃæplɪn/ *n.* aumônier *m.*
chapter /'tʃæptə(r)/ *n.* chapitre *m.*
char[1] /tʃɑː(r)/ *n.* (*fam.*) femme de ménage *f.*
char[2] /tʃɑː(r)/ *v.t.* (*p.t.* **charred**) carboniser.
character /'kærəktə(r)/ *n.* caractère *m.*; (*in novel, play*) personnage *m.* **of good ~,** de bonne réputation. ~**ize** *v.t.* caractériser.
characteristic /kærəktə'rɪstɪk/ *a.* & *n.* caractéristique (*f.*). ~**ally** *adv.* typiquement.
charade /ʃə'rɑːd/ *n.* charade *f.*
charcoal /'tʃɑːkəʊl/ *n.* charbon (de bois) *m.*
charge /tʃɑːdʒ/ *n.* prix *m.*; (*mil.*)

charge *f.*; (*jurid.*) inculpation *f.*, accusation *f.*; (*task, custody*) charge *f.* **~s,** frais *m. pl.* —*v.t.* faire payer; (*ask*) demander (**for,** pour); (*enemy, gun*) charger; (*jurid.*) inculper, accuser. —*v.i.* foncer, se précipiter. **in ~ of,** responsable de. **take ~ of,** prendre en charge, se charger de. **~able to,** (*comm.*) aux frais de.

chariot /ˈtʃærɪət/ *n.* char *m.*

charisma /kəˈrɪzmə/ *n.* magnétisme *m.*

charit|y /ˈtʃærətɪ/ *n.* charité *f.*; (*society*) fondation charitable *f.* **~able** *a.* charitable.

charlatan /ˈʃɑːlətən/ *n.* charlatan *m.*

charm /tʃɑːm/ *n.* charme *m.*; (*trinket*) amulette *f.* —*v.t.* charmer. **~ing** *a.* charmant.

chart /tʃɑːt/ *n.* (*naut.*) carte (marine) *f.*; (*table*) tableau *m.*, graphique *m.* —*v.t.* (*route*) porter sur la carte.

charter /ˈtʃɑːtə(r)/ *n.* charte *f.* **~ (flight),** charter *m.* —*v.t.* affréter. **~ed accountant,** expert-comptable *m.*

charwoman /ˈtʃɑːwʊmən/ *n.* (*pl.* **-women**) femme de ménage *f.*

chase /tʃeɪs/ *v.t.* poursuivre. —*v.i.* courir (**after,** après). —*n.* chasse *f.* **~ away** *or* **off,** chasser.

chasm /ˈkæzəm/ *n.* abîme *m.*

chassis /ˈʃæsɪ/ *n.* châssis *m.*

chaste /tʃeɪst/ *a.* chaste.

chastise /tʃæˈstaɪz/ *v.t.* châtier.

chastity /ˈtʃæstətɪ/ *n.* chasteté *f.*

chat /tʃæt/ *n.* causette *f.* —*v.i.* (*p.t.* **chatted**) bavarder. **have a ~,** bavarder. **~ty** *a.* bavard.

chatter /ˈtʃætə(r)/ *n.* bavardage *m.* —*v.i.* bavarder. **his teeth are ~ing,** il claque des dents.

chatterbox /ˈtʃætəbɒks/ *n.* bavard(e) *m.* (*f.*).

chauffeur /ˈʃəʊfə(r)/ *n.* chauffeur (de particulier) *m.*

chauvinis|t /ˈʃəʊvɪnɪst/ *n.* chauvin(e) *m.* (*f.*). **male ~t,** (*pej.*) phallocrate *m.* **~m** /-zəm/ *n.* chauvinisme *m.*

cheap /tʃiːp/ *a.* (**-er, -est**) bon marché *invar.*; (*fare, rate*) réduit; (*worthless*) sans valeur. **~er,** meilleur marché. *invar.* **~(ly)** *adv.* à bon marché. **~ness** *n.* bas prix *m.*

cheapen /ˈtʃiːpən/ *v.t.* déprécier.

cheat /ˈtʃiːt/ *v.i.* tricher; (*by fraud*) frauder. —*v.t.* (*defraud*) frauder; (*deceive*) tromper. —*n.* escroc *m.*

check[1] /tʃek/ *v.t./i.* vérifier; (*tickets*) contrôler; (*stop*) enrayer, arrêter; (*restrain*) contenir; (*rebuke*) réprimander; (*tick off*: *Amer.*) cocher. —*n.* vérification *f.*; contrôle *m.*; (*curb*) frein *m.*; (*chess*) échec *m.*; (*bill*: *Amer.*) addition *f.*; (*cheque*: *Amer.*) chèque *m.* **~ in,** signer le registre; (*at airport*) passer à l'enregistrement. **~ out,** régler sa note. **~-up** *n.* examen médical *m.*

check[2] /tʃek/ *n.* (*pattern*) carreaux *m. pl.* **~ed** *a.* à carreaux.

checkmate /ˈtʃekmeɪt/ *n.* échec et mat *m.*

checkroom /ˈtʃekrʊm/ *n.* (*Amer.*) vestiaire *m.*

cheek /tʃiːk/ *n.* joue *f.*; (*impudence*) culot *m.* **~y** *a.* effronté.

cheer /tʃɪə(r)/ *n.* gaieté *f.* **~s,** acclamations *f. pl.* —*int.* à votre santé. —*v.t.* acclamer, applaudir. **~ (up),** (*gladden*) remonter le moral à. **~ up,** prendre courage. **~ful** *a.* gai. **~fulness** *n.* gaieté *f.*

cheerio /tʃɪərɪˈəʊ/ *int.* (*fam.*) salut.

cheerless /ˈtʃɪəlɪs/ *a.* morne.

cheese /tʃiːz/ *n.* fromage *m.*

cheetah /ˈtʃiːtə/ *n.* guépard *m.*

chef /ʃef/ *n.* (*cook*) chef *m.*

chemical /ˈkemɪkl/ *a.* chimique. —*n.* produit chimique *m.*

chemist /ˈkemɪst/ *n.* pharmacien(ne) *m.* (*f.*).; (*scientist*)

chimiste *m./f.* **~'s shop,** pharmacie *f.* **~ry** *n.* chimie *f.*
cheque /tʃek/ *n.* chèque *m.* **~-book** *n.* chéquier *m.*
chequered /'tʃekəd/ *a.* (*pattern*) à carreaux; (*fig.*) mouvementé.
cherish /'tʃerɪʃ/ *v.t.* chérir; (*hope*) nourrir, caresser.
cherry /'tʃerɪ/ *n.* cerise *f.*
chess /tʃes/ *n.* échecs *m. pl.* **~-board** *n.* échiquier *m.*
chest /tʃest/ *n.* (*anat.*) poitrine *f.*; (*box*) coffre *m.* **~ of drawers,** commode *f.*
chestnut /'tʃesnʌt/ *n.* châtaigne *f.*; (*edible*) marron *m.*, châtaigne *f.*
chew /tʃuː/ *v.t.* mâcher. **~ing-gum** *n.* chewing-gum *m.*
chic /ʃiːk/ *a.* chic *invar.*
chick /tʃɪk/ *n.* poussin *m.*
chicken /'tʃɪkɪn/ *n.* poulet *m.* —*a.* (*sl.*) froussard. —*v.i.* **~ out,** (*sl.*) se dégonfler. **~-pox** *n.* varicelle *f.*
chicory /'tʃɪkərɪ/ *n.* (*for salad*) endive *f.*; (*in coffee*) chicorée *f.*
chief /tʃiːf/ *n.* chef *m.* —*a.* principal. **~ly** *adv.* principalement.
chilblain /'tʃɪlbleɪn/ *n.* engelure *f.*
child /tʃaɪld/ *n.* (*pl.* **children** /'tʃɪldrən/) enfant *m./f.* **~hood** *n.* enfance *f.* **~ish** *a.* enfantin. **~less** *a.* sans enfants. **~like** *a.* innocent, candide.
childbirth /'tʃaɪldbɜːθ/ *n.* accouchement *m.*
Chile /'tʃɪlɪ/ *n.* Chili *m.* **~an** *a.* & *n.* chilien(ne) (*m.* (*f.*)).
chill /tʃɪl/ *n.* froid *m.*; (*med.*) refroidissement *m.* —*a.* froid. —*v.t.* (*person*) donner froid à; (*wine*) rafraîchir; (*food*) mettre au frais. **~y** *a.* froid; (*sensitive to cold*) frileux. **be** *or* **feel ~y,** avoir froid.
chilli /'tʃɪlɪ/ *n.* (*pl.* **-ies**) piment *m.*
chime /tʃaɪm/ *n.* carillon *m.* —*v.t./i.* carillonner.
chimney /'tʃɪmnɪ/ *n.* cheminée *f.* **~-sweep** *n.* ramoneur *m.*
chimpanzee /tʃɪmpæn'ziː/ *n.* chimpanzé *m.*
chin /tʃɪn/ *n.* menton *m.*
china /'tʃaɪnə/ *n.* porcelaine *f.*
Chin|a /'tʃaɪnə/ *n.* Chine *f.* **~ese** /-'niːz/ *a.* & *n.* chinois(e) (*m.* (*f.*)).
chink[1] /tʃɪŋk/ *n.* (*slit*) fente *f.*
chink[2] /tʃɪŋk/ *n.* tintement *m.* —*v.t./i.* (faire) tinter.
chip /tʃɪp/ *n.* (*on plate etc.*) ébréchure *f.*; (*piece*) éclat *m.*; (*culin.*) frite *f.*; (*microchip*) microplaquette *f.*, puce *f.* —*v.t./i.* (*p.t.* **chipped**) (s')ébrécher. **~ in,** (*fam.*) dire son mot; (*with money: fam.*) contribuer. **(potato) ~s,** (*Amer.*) chips *m. pl.*
chipboard /'tʃɪpbɔːd/ *n.* aggloméré *m.*
chiropodist /kɪ'rɒpədɪst/ *n.* pédicure *m./f.*
chirp /tʃɜːp/ *n.* pépiement *m.* —*v.i.* pépier.
chirpy /'tʃɜːpɪ/ *a.* gai.
chisel /'tʃɪzl/ *n.* ciseau *m.* —*v.t.* (*p.t.* **chiselled**) ciseler.
chit /tʃɪt/ *n.* note *f.*, mot *m.*
chit-chat /'tʃɪttʃæt/ *n.* bavardage *m.*
chivalr|y /'ʃɪvlrɪ/ *n.* galanterie *f.* **~ous** *a.* chevaleresque.
chives /tʃaɪvz/ *n. pl.* ciboulette *f.*
chlorine /'klɔːriːn/ *n.* chlore *m.*
choc-ice /'tʃɒkaɪs/ *n.* esquimau *m.*
chock /tʃɒk/ *n.* cale *f.* **~-a-block, ~-full** *adjs.* archiplein.
chocolate /'tʃɒklət/ *n.* chocolat *m.*
choice /tʃɔɪs/ *n.* choix *m.* —*a.* de choix.
choir /'kwaɪə(r)/ *n.* chœur *m.*
choirboy /'kwaɪəbɔɪ/ *n.* jeune choriste *m.*
choke /tʃəʊk/ *v.t./i.* (s')étrangler. —*n.* starter *m.* **~ (up),** boucher.
cholera /'kɒlərə/ *n.* choléra *m.*
cholesterol /kə'lestərɒl/ *n.* cholestérol *m.*

choose /tʃuːz/ *v.t./i.* (*p.t.* **chose**, *p.p.* **chosen**) choisir. **~ to do,** décider de faire.
choosy /ˈtʃuːzɪ/ *a.* (*fam.*) exigeant.
chop /tʃɒp/ *v.t./i.* (*p.t.* **chopped**) (*wood*) couper (à la hache); (*food*) hacher. *—n.* (*meat*) côtelette *f.* **~ down,** abattre. **~per** *n.* hachoir *m.*; (*sl.*) hélicoptère *m.*
choppy /ˈtʃɒpɪ/ *a.* (*sea*) agité.
chopstick /ˈtʃɒpstɪk/ *n.* baguette *f.*
choral /ˈkɔːrəl/ *a.* choral.
chord /kɔːd/ *n.* (*mus.*) accord *m.*
chore /tʃɔː(r)/ *n.* travail (routinier) *m.*; (*unpleasant task*) corvée *f.*
choreographer /kɒrɪˈɒgrəfə(r)/ *n.* chorégraphe *m./f.*
chortle /ˈtʃɔːtl/ *n.* gloussement *m. —v.i.* glousser.
chorus /ˈkɔːrəs/ *n.* chœur *m.*; (*of song*) refrain *m.*
chose, chosen /tʃəʊz, ˈtʃəʊzn/ *see* **choose.**
Christ /kraɪst/ *n.* le Christ *m.*
christen /ˈkrɪsn/ *v.t.* baptiser. **~ing** *n.* baptême *m.*
Christian /ˈkrɪstʃən/ *a.* & *n.* chrétien(ne) (*m.* (*f.*)). **~ name,** prénom *m.* **~ity** /-stɪˈænətɪ/ *n.* christianisme *m.*
Christmas /ˈkrɪsməs/ *n.* Noël *m.* *—a.* (*card, tree, etc.*) de Noël. **~-box** *n.* étrennes *f. pl.* **~ Day/Eve,** le jour/la veille de Noël.
chrome /krəʊm/ *n.* chrome *m.*
chromium /ˈkrəʊmɪəm/ *n.* chrome *m.*
chromosome /ˈkrəʊməsəʊm/ *n.* chromosome *m.*
chronic /ˈkrɒnɪk/ *a.* (*situation, disease*) chronique; (*bad*: *fam.*) affreux.
chronicle /ˈkrɒnɪkl/ *n.* chronique *f.*
chronolog|y /krəˈnɒlədʒɪ/ *n.* chronologie *f.* **~ical** /krɒnəˈlɒdʒɪkl/ *a.* chronologique.
chrysanthemum /krɪˈsænθəməm/ *n.* chrysanthème *m.*
chubby /ˈtʃʌbɪ/ *a.* (**-ier, -iest**) dodu, potelé.
chuck /tʃʌk/ *v.t.* (*fam.*) lancer. **~ away** *or* **out,** (*fam.*) balancer.
chuckle /ˈtʃʌkl/ *n.* gloussement *m. —v.i.* glousser, rire.
chuffed /tʃʌft/ *a.* (*sl.*) bien content.
chum /tʃʌm/ *n.* cop|ain, -ine *m., f.* **~my** *a.* amical. **~my with,** copain avec.
chunk /tʃʌŋk/ *n.* (gros) morceau *m.*
chunky /ˈtʃʌŋkɪ/ *a.* trapu.
church /ˈtʃɜːtʃ/ *n.* église *f.*
churchyard /ˈtʃɜːtʃjɑːd/ *n.* cimetière *m.*
churlish /ˈtʃɜːlɪʃ/ *a.* grossier.
churn /ˈtʃɜːn/ *n.* baratte *f.*; (*milk-can*) bidon *m. —v.t.* baratter. **~ out,** produire (en série).
chute /ʃuːt/ *n.* glissière *f.*; (*for rubbish*) vide-ordures *m. invar.*
chutney /ˈtʃʌtnɪ/ *n.* condiment (de fruits) *m.*
cider /ˈsaɪdə(r)/ *n.* cidre *m.*
cigar /sɪˈgɑː(r)/ *n.* cigare *m.*
cigarette /sɪgəˈret/ *n.* cigarette *f.* **~-holder** *n.* fume-cigarette *m. invar.*
cinder /ˈsɪndə(r)/ *n.* cendre *f.*
cine-camera /ˈsɪnɪkæmərə/ *n.* caméra *f.*
cinema /ˈsɪnəmə/ *n.* cinéma *m.*
cinnamon /ˈsɪnəmən/ *n.* cannelle *f.*
cipher /ˈsaɪfə(r)/ *n.* (*numeral, code*) chiffre *m.*; (*person*) nullité *f.*
circle /ˈsɜːkl/ *n.* cercle *m.*; (*theatre*) balcon *m. —v.t.* (*go round*) faire le tour de; (*word, error, etc.*) entourer d'un cercle. *—v.i.* décrire des cercles.
circuit /ˈsɜːkɪt/ *n.* circuit *m.*
circuitous /sɜːˈkjuːɪtəs/ *a.* indirect.
circular /ˈsɜːkjʊlə(r)/ *a.* & *n.* circulaire (*f.*).
circulat|e /ˈsɜːkjʊleɪt/ *v.t./i.* (faire) circuler. **~ion** /-ˈleɪʃn/ *n.* circulation *f.*; (*of newspaper*) tirage *m.*

circumcis|e /ˈsɜːkəmsaɪz/ *v.t.* circoncire. **~ion** /-ˈsɪʒn/ *n.* circoncision *f.*
circumference /sɜːˈkʌmfərəns/ *n.* circonférence *f.*
circumflex /ˈsɜːkəmfleks/ *n.* circonflexe *m.*
circumspect /ˈsɜːkəmspekt/ *a.* circonspect.
circumstance /ˈsɜːkəmstəns/ *n.* circonstance *f.* **~s,** (*financial*) situation financière *f.*
circus /ˈsɜːkəs/ *n.* cirque *m.*
cistern /ˈsɪstən/ *n.* réservoir *m.*
citadel /ˈsɪtədel/ *n.* citadelle *f.*
cit|e /saɪt/ *v.t.* citer. **~ation** /-ˈteɪʃn/ *n.* citation *f.*
citizen /ˈsɪtɪzn/ *n.* citoyen(ne) *m.* (*f.*); (*of town*) habitant(e) *m.* (*f.*). **~ship** *n.* citoyenneté *f.*
citrus /ˈsɪtrəs/ *a.* **~ fruit(s),** agrumes *m. pl.*
city /ˈsɪtɪ/ *n.* (grande) ville *f.* **the C~,** la Cité de Londres.
civic /ˈsɪvɪk/ *a.* civique. **~ centre,** centre administratif *m.* **~s** *n. pl.* instruction civique *f.*
civil /ˈsɪvl/ *a.* civil; (*rights*) civique; (*defence*) passif. **C~ Servant,** fonctionnaire *m./f.* **C~ Service,** fonction publique *f.* **~ war,** guerre civile *f.* **~ity** /sɪˈvɪlətɪ/ *n.* civilité *f.*
civilian /sɪˈvɪlɪən/ *a.* & *n.* civil(e) (*m.* (*f.*)).
civiliz|e /ˈsɪvəlaɪz/ *v.t.* civiliser. **~ation** /-ˈzeɪʃn/ *n.* civilisation *f.*
civvies /ˈsɪvɪz/ *n. pl.* **in ~,** (*sl.*) en civil.
clad /klæd/ *see* **clothe.**
claim /kleɪm/ *v.t.* revendiquer, réclamer; (*assert*) prétendre. *—n.* revendication *f.*, prétention *f.*; (*assertion*) affirmation *f.*; (*right*) droit *m.*
claimant /ˈkleɪmənt/ *n.* (*of social benefits*) demandeur *m.*
clairvoyant /kleəˈvɔɪənt/ *n.* voyant(e) *m.* (*f.*).
clam /klæm/ *n.* palourde *f.*
clamber /ˈklæmbə(r)/ *v.i.* grimper.
clammy /ˈklæmɪ/ *a.* (**-ier, -iest**) moite.
clamour /ˈklæmə(r)/ *n.* clameur *f.*, cris *m. pl.* *—v.i.* **~ for,** demander à grands cris.
clamp /klæmp/ *n.* agrafe *f.*; (*large*) crampon *m.*; (*for carpentry*) serre-joint(s) *m.* *—v.t.* serrer. **~ down on,** sévir contre.
clan /klæn/ *n.* clan *m.*
clandestine /klænˈdestɪn/ *a.* clandestin.
clang /klæŋ/ *n.* son métallique *m.*
clanger /ˈklæŋə(r)/ *n.* (*sl.*) bévue *f.*
clap /klæp/ *v.t./i.* (*p.t.* **clapped**) applaudir; (*put forcibly*) mettre. *—n.* applaudissement *m.*; (*of thunder*) coup *m.* **~ one's hands,** battre des mains.
claptrap /ˈklæptræp/ *n.* baratin *m.*
claret /ˈklærət/ *n.* bordeaux rouge *m.*
clarif|y /ˈklærɪfaɪ/ *v.t./i.* (se) clarifier. **~ication** /-ɪˈkeɪʃn/ *n.* clarification *f.*
clarinet /klærɪˈnet/ *n.* clarinette *f.*
clarity /ˈklærətɪ/ *n.* clarté *f.*
clash /klæʃ/ *n.* choc *m.*; (*fig.*) conflit *m.* *—v.i.* (*metal objects*) s'entrechoquer; (*fig.*) se heurter.
clasp /klɑːsp/ *n.* (*fastener*) fermoir *m.*, agrafe *f.* *—v.t.* serrer.
class /klɑːs/ *n.* classe *f.* *—v.t.* classer.
classic /ˈklæsɪk/ *a.* & *n.* classique (*m.*). **~s,** (*univ.*) les humanités *f. pl.* **~al** *a.* classique.
classif|y /ˈklæsɪfaɪ/ *v.t.* classifier. **~ication** /-ɪˈkeɪʃn/ *n.* classification *f.* **~ied** *a.* (*information etc.*) secret. **~ied advertisement,** petite annonce *f.*
classroom /ˈklɑːsrʊm/ *n.* salle de classe *f.*
classy /ˈklɑːsɪ/ *a.* (*sl.*) chic *invar.*
clatter /ˈklætə(r)/ *n.* cliquetis *m.* *—v.i.* cliqueter.

clause /klɔːz/ *n.* clause *f.*; (*gram.*) proposition *f.*
claustrophob|ia /klɔːstrəˈfəʊbɪə/ *n.* claustrophobie *f.* **~ic** *a.* & *n.* claustrophobe (*m.*/*f.*).
claw /klɔː/ *n.* (*of animal, small bird*) griffe *f.*; (*of bird of prey*) serre *f.*; (*of lobster*) pince *f.* —*v.t.* griffer.
clay /kleɪ/ *n.* argile *f.*
clean /kliːn/ *a.* (**-er, -est**) propre; (*shape, stroke, etc.*) net. —*adv.* complètement. —*v.t.* nettoyer. —*v.i.* **~ up,** faire le nettoyage. **~-shaven** *a.* glabre. **~er** *n.* femme de ménage *f.*; (*of clothes*) teinturl|ier, -ière *m.*, *f.* **~ly** *adv.* proprement; (*sharply*) nettement.
cleanliness /ˈklenlɪnɪs/ *n.* propreté *f.*
cleans|e /klenz/ *v.t.* nettoyer; (*fig.*) purifier. **~ing cream,** crème démaquillante *f.*
clear /klɪə(r)/ *a.* (**-er, -est**) clair; (*glass*) transparent; (*profit*) net; (*road*) dégagé. —*adv.* complètement. —*v.t.* (*free*) dégager (**of,** de); (*table*) débarrasser; (*jump over*) franchir; (*debt*) liquider; (*jurid.*) disculper. **~ (away** *or* **off),** (*remove*) enlever. —*v.i.* (*fog*) se dissiper. **~ of,** (*away from*) à l'écart de. **~ off** *or* **out,** (*sl.*) décamper. **~ out,** (*clean*) nettoyer. **~ up,** (*tidy*) ranger; (*mystery*) éclaircir; (*of weather*) s'éclaircir. **~ly** *adv.* clairement.
clearance /ˈklɪərəns/ *n.* (*permission*) autorisation *f.*; (*space*) dégagement *m.* **~ sale,** soldes *m. pl.*
clearing /ˈklɪərɪŋ/ *n.* clairière *f.*
clearway /ˈklɪəweɪ/ *n.* route à stationnement interdit *f.*
cleavage /ˈkliːvɪdʒ/ *n.* clivage *m.*; (*fig.*) naissance des seins *f.*
clef /klef/ *n.* (*mus.*) clé *f.*
cleft /kleft/ *n.* fissure *f.*
clemen|t /ˈklemənt/ *a.* clément. **~cy** *n.* clémence *f.*
clench /klentʃ/ *v.t.* serrer.
clergy /ˈklɜːdʒɪ/ *n.* clergé *m.* **~man** *n.* (*pl.* **-men**) ecclésiastique *m.*
cleric /ˈklerɪk/ *n.* clerc *m.* **~al** *a.* (*relig.*) clérical; (*of clerks*) de bureau, d'employé.
clerk /klɑːk, *Amer.* klɜːk/ *n.* employé(e) de bureau *m.* (*f.*).
clever /ˈklevə(r)/ *a.* (**-er, -est**) intelligent; (*skilful*) habile. **~ly** *adv.* intelligemment; habilement. **~ness** *n.* intelligence *f.*
cliché /ˈkliːʃeɪ/ *n.* cliché *m.*
click /klɪk/ *n.* déclic *m.* —*v.i.* faire un déclic; (*people*: *sl.*) s'entendre, se plaire.
client /ˈklaɪənt/ *n.* client(e) *m.* (*f.*).
clientele /kliːənˈtel/ *n.* clientèle *f.*
cliff /klɪf/ *n.* falaise *f.*
climat|e /ˈklaɪmɪt/ *n.* climat *m.* **~ic** /-ˈmætɪk/ *a.* climatique.
climax /ˈklaɪmæks/ *n.* point culminant *m.*; (*sexual*) orgasme *m.*
climb /klaɪm/ *v.t.* (*stairs*) monter, grimper; (*tree, ladder*) monter *or* grimper à; (*mountain*) faire l'ascension de. —*v.i.* monter, grimper. —*n.* montée *f.* **~ down,** (*fig.*) en rabattre. **~er** *n.* (*sport*) alpiniste *m.*/*f.*
clinch /klɪntʃ/ *v.t.* (*a deal*) conclure.
cling /klɪŋ/ *v.i.* (*p.t.* **clung**) se cramponner (**to,** à); (*stick*) coller.
clinic /ˈklɪnɪk/ *n.* centre médical *m.*; (*private*) clinique *f.*
clinical /ˈklɪnɪkl/ *a.* clinique.
clink /klɪŋk/ *n.* tintement *m.* —*v.t.*/*i.* (faire) tinter.
clinker /ˈklɪŋkə(r)/ *n.* mâchefer *m.*
clip[1] /klɪp/ *n.* (*for paper*) trombone *m.*; (*for hair*) barrette *f.*; (*for tube*) collier *m.* —*v.t.* (*p.t.* **clipped**) attacher (**to,** à).
clip[2] /klɪp/ *v.t.* (*p.t.* **clipped**) (*cut*) couper. —*n.* coupe *f.*; (*of film*)

extrait *m.*; (*blow*: *fam.*) taloche *f.* **~ping** *n.* coupure *f.*
clippers /ˈklɪpəz/ *n. pl.* tondeuse *f.*; (*for nails*) pince à ongles *f.*
clique /kliːk/ *n.* clique *f.*
cloak /kləʊk/ *n.* (grande) cape *f.*, manteau ample *m.*
cloakroom /ˈkləʊkrʊm/ *n.* vestiaire *m.*; (*toilet*) toilettes *f. pl.*
clobber /ˈklɒbə(r)/ *n.* (*sl.*) affaires *f. pl.* —*v.t.* (*hit*: *sl.*) rosser.
clock /klɒk/ *n.* pendule *f.*; (*large*) horloge *f.* —*v.i.* **~ in** *or* **out,** pointer. **~ up,** (*miles etc.*: *fam.*) faire. **~-tower** *n.* clocher *m.*
clockwise /ˈklɒkwaɪz/ *a.* & *adv.* dans le sens des aiguilles d'une montre.
clockwork /ˈklɒkwɜːk/ *n.* mécanisme *m.* —*a.* mécanique.
clod /klɒd/ *n.* (*of earth*) motte *f.*; (*person*: *fam.*) lourdaud(e) *m.* (*f.*).
clog /klɒg/ *n.* sabot *m.* —*v.t.*/*i.* (*p.t.* **clogged**) (se) boucher.
cloister /ˈklɔɪstə(r)/ *n.* cloître *m.*
close[1] /kləʊs/ *a.* (**-er, -est**) (*near*) proche (**to,** de); (*link, collaboration*) étroit; (*friend*) intime; (*order, match*) serré; (*weather*) lourd. **~ together,** (*crowded*) serrés. —*adv.* (tout) près. —*n.* (*street*) impasse *f.* **~ by, ~ at hand,** tout près. **~-up** *n.* gros plan *m.* **have a ~ shave,** l'échapper belle. **~ly** *adv.* (*follow*) de près. **~ness** *n.* proximité *f.*
close[2] /kləʊz/ *v.t.* fermer. —*v.i.* se fermer; (*of shop etc.*) fermer; (*end*) (se) terminer. —*n.* fin *f.* **~d shop,** organisation qui exclut les travailleurs non syndiqués *f.*
closet /ˈklɒzɪt/ *n.* (*Amer.*) placard *m.*
closure /ˈkləʊʒə(r)/ *n.* fermeture *f.*
clot /klɒt/ *n.* (*of blood*) caillot *m.*; (*in sauce*) grumeau *m.*; (*sl.*) imbécile *m.*/*f.* —*v.t.*/*i.* (*p.t.* **clotted**) (se) coaguler.
cloth /klɒθ/ *n.* tissu *m.*; (*duster*) linge *m.*; (*table-cloth*) nappe *f.*
cloth|e /kləʊð/ *v.t.* (*p.t.* **clothed** *or* **clad**) vêtir. **~ing** *n.* vêtements *m. pl.*
clothes /kləʊðz/ *n. pl.* vêtements *m. pl.*, habits *m. pl.*
cloud /klaʊd/ *n.* nuage *m.* —*v.i.* se couvrir (de nuages); (*become gloomy*) s'assombrir. **~y** *a.* (*sky*) couvert; (*liquid*) trouble.
cloudburst /ˈklaʊdbɜːst/ *n.* trombe d'eau *f.*
clout /klaʊt/ *n.* (*blow*) coup de poing *m.*; (*power*: *fam.*) pouvoir effectif *m.* —*v.t.* frapper.
clove /kləʊv/ *n.* clou de girofle *m.* **~ of garlic,** gousse d'ail *f.*
clover /ˈkləʊvə(r)/ *n.* trèfle *m.*
clown /klaʊn/ *n.* clown *m.* —*v.i.* faire le clown.
cloy /klɔɪ/ *v.t.* écœurer.
club /klʌb/ *n.* (*group*) club *m.*; (*weapon*) massue *f.* **~s,** (*cards*) trèfle *m.* —*v.t.*/*i.* (*p.t.* **clubbed**) matraquer. **~ together,** (*share costs*) se cotiser.
cluck /klʌk/ *v.i.* glousser.
clue /kluː/ *n.* indice *m.*; (*in crossword*) définition *f.* **he does not have a ~, he is ~less,** (*fam.*) il n'en a pas la moindre idée.
clump /klʌmp/ *n.* massif *m.*
clums|y /ˈklʌmzɪ/ *a.* (**-ier, -iest**) maladroit; (*tool*) peu commode. **~iness** *n.* maladresse *f.*
clung /klʌŋ/ *see* **cling.**
cluster /ˈklʌstə(r)/ *n.* (petit) groupe *m.* —*v.i.* se grouper.
clutch /klʌtʃ/ *v.t.* (*hold*) serrer fort; (*grasp*) saisir. —*v.i.* **~ at,** (*try to grasp*) essayer de saisir. —*n.* étreinte *f.*; (*auto.*) embrayage *m.*
clutter /ˈklʌtə(r)/ *n.* désordre *m.*, fouillis *m.* —*v.t.* encombrer.
coach /kəʊtʃ/ *n.* autocar *m.*; (*of train*) wagon *m.*; (*horse-drawn*) carrosse *m.*; (*sport*) entraîneu|r, -se *m.*, *f.* —*v.t.* donner des leçons

(particulières) à; (*sport*) entraîner.
coagulate /kəʊ'ægjʊleɪt/ *v.t./i.* (se) coaguler.
coal /kəʊl/ *n.* charbon *m.*
coalfield /'kəʊlfiːld/ *n.* bassin houiller *m.*
coalition /kəʊə'lɪʃn/ *n.* coalition *f.*
coarse /kɔːs/ *a.* (**-er, -est**) grossier. **~ness** *n.* caractère grossier *m.*
coast /kəʊst/ *n.* côte *f.* —*v.i.* (*car, bicycle*) descendre en roue libre. **~al** *a.* côtier.
coaster /'kəʊstə(r)/ *n.* (*ship*) caboteur *m.*; (*mat*) dessous de verre *m.*
coastguard /'kəʊstgɑːd/ *n.* garde-côte *m.*
coastline /'kəʊstlaɪn/ *n.* littoral *m.*
coat /kəʊt/ *n.* manteau *m.*; (*of animal*) pelage *m.*; (*of paint*) couche *f.* —*v.t.* enduire, couvrir; (*with chocolate*) enrober (**with,** de). **~ of arms,** armoiries *f. pl.* **~ing** *n.* couche *f.*
coax /kəʊks/ *v.t.* amadouer.
cob /kɒb/ *n.* (*of corn*) épi *m.*
cobble[1] /'kɒbl/ *n.* pavé *m.* **~-stone** *n.* pavé *m.*
cobble[2] /'kɒbl/ *v.t.* rapetasser.
cobbler /'kɒblə(r)/ *n.* (*old use*) cordonnier *m.*
cobweb /'kɒbweb/ *n.* toile d'araignée *f.*
cocaine /kəʊ'keɪn/ *n.* cocaïne *f.*
cock /kɒk/ *n.* (oiseau) mâle *m.*; (*rooster*) coq *m.* —*v.t.* (*gun*) armer; (*ears*) dresser. **~-and-bull story,** histoire à dormir debout *f.* **~-eyed** *a.* (*askew: sl.*) de travers.
cockerel /'kɒkərəl/ *n.* jeune coq *m.*
cockle /'kɒkl/ *n.* (*culin.*) coque *f.*
cockney /'kɒknɪ/ *n.* Cockney *m./f.*
cockpit /'kɒkpɪt/ *n.* poste de pilotage *m.*
cockroach /'kɒkrəʊtʃ/ *n.* cafard *m.*
cocksure /kɒk'ʃʊə(r)/ *a.* sûr de soi.
cocktail /'kɒkteɪl/ *n.* cocktail *m.* **fruit ~,** macédoine (de fruits) *f.*
cocky /'kɒkɪ/ *a.* (**-ier, -iest**) trop sûr de soi, arrogant.
cocoa /'kəʊkəʊ/ *n.* cacao *m.*
coconut /'kəʊkənʌt/ *n.* noix de coco *f.*
cocoon /kə'kuːn/ *n.* cocon *m.*
COD *abbr.* (*cash on delivery*) paiement à la livraison *m.*
cod /kɒd/ *n. invar.* morue *f.* **~-liver oil,** huile de foie de morue *f.*
coddle /'kɒdl/ *v.t.* dorloter.
code /kəʊd/ *n.* code *m.* —*v.t.* coder.
codify /'kəʊdɪfaɪ/ *v.t.* codifier.
coeducational /kəʊedʒʊ'keɪʃənl/ *a.* (*school, teaching*) mixte.
coerc|e /kəʊ'ɜːs/ *v.t.* contraindre. **~ion** /-ʃn/ *n.* contrainte *f.*
coexist /kəʊɪg'zɪst/ *v.i.* coexister. **~ence** *n.* coexistence *f.*
coffee /'kɒfɪ/ *n.* café *m.* **~ bar,** café *m.*, cafétéria *f.* **~-pot** *n.* cafetière *f.* **~-table** *n.* table basse *f.*
coffer /'kɒfə(r)/ *n.* coffre *m.*
coffin /'kɒfɪn/ *n.* cercueil *m.*
cog /kɒg/ *n.* dent *f.*; (*fig.*) rouage *m.*
cogent /'kəʊdʒənt/ *a.* convaincant; (*relevant*) pertinent.
cognac /'kɒnjæk/ *n.* cognac *m.*
cohabit /kəʊ'hæbɪt/ *v.i.* vivre en concubinage.
coherent /kəʊ'hɪərənt/ *a.* cohérent.
coil /kɔɪl/ *v.t./i.* (s')enrouler. —*n.* rouleau *m.*; (*one ring*) spire *f.*
coin /kɔɪn/ *n.* pièce (de monnaie) *f.* —*v.t.* (*word*) inventer. **~age** *n.* monnaie *f.*; (*fig.*) invention *f.*
coincide /kəʊɪn'saɪd/ *v.i.* coïncider.
coinciden|ce /kəʊ'ɪnsɪdəns/ *n.* coïncidence *f.* **~tal** /-'dentl/ *a.* dû à une coïncidence.
coke /kəʊk/ *n.* coke *m.*
colander /'kʌləndə(r)/ *n.* passoire *f.*
cold /kəʊld/ *a.* (**-er, -est**) froid. **be** *or* **feel ~,** avoir froid. **it is ~,** il fait froid. —*n.* froid *m.*; (*med.*) rhume *m.* **~-blooded** *a.* sans

pitié. ~ **cream,** crème de beauté *f.* ~ **feet,** la frousse. **~-shoulder** *v.t.* snober. **~ness** *n.* froideur *f.*

coleslaw /ˈkəʊlslɔː/ *n.* salade de chou cru *f.*

colic /ˈkɒlɪk/ *n.* coliques *f. pl.*

collaborat|e /kəˈlæbəreɪt/ *v.i.* collaborer. **~ion** /-ˈreɪʃn/ *n.* collaboration *f.* **~or** *n.* collabora|teur, -trice *m., f.*

collage /ˈkɒlɑːʒ/ *n.* collage *m.*

collapse /kəˈlæps/ *v.i.* s'effondrer; (*med.*) avoir un malaise. —*n.* effondrement *m.*

collapsible /kəˈlæpsəbl/ *a.* pliant.

collar /ˈkɒlə(r)/ *n.* col *m.*; (*of dog*) collier *m.* —*v.t.* (*appropriate: sl.*) piquer. **~-bone** *n.* clavicule *f.*

colleague /ˈkɒliːg/ *n.* collègue *m./f.*

collect /kəˈlekt/ *v.t.* rassembler; (*pick up*) ramasser; (*call for*) passer prendre; (*money, rent*) encaisser; (*taxes*) percevoir; (*as hobby*) collectionner. —*v.i.* se rassembler; (*dust*) s'amasser. —*adv.* **call ~,** (*Amer.*) téléphoner en PCV. **~ion** /-kʃn/ *n.* collection *f.*; (*in church*) quête *f.*; (*of mail*) levée *f.* **~or** *n.* (*as hobby*) collectionneu|r, -se *m., f.*

collective /kəˈlektɪv/ *a.* collectif.

college /ˈkɒlɪdʒ/ *n.* (*for higher education*) institut *m.*, école *f.*; (*within university*) collège *m.* **be in ~,** être en faculté.

collide /kəˈlaɪd/ *v.i.* entrer en collision (**with,** avec).

colliery /ˈkɒlɪərɪ/ *n.* houillère *f.*

collision /kəˈlɪʒn/ *n.* collision *f.*

colloquial /kəˈləʊkwɪəl/ *a.* familier. **~ism** *n.* expression familière *f.*

collusion /kəˈluːʒn/ *n.* collusion *f.*

colon /ˈkəʊlən/ *n.* (*gram.*) deux-points *m. invar.*; (*anat.*) côlon *m.*

colonel /ˈkɜːnl/ *n.* colonel *m.*

colonize /ˈkɒlənaɪz/ *v.t.* coloniser.

colon|y /ˈkɒlənɪ/ *n.* colonie *f.* **~ial** /kəˈləʊnɪəl/ *a.* & *n.* colonial(e) (*m.* (*f.*)).

colossal /kəˈlɒsl/ *a.* colossal.

colour /ˈkʌlə(r)/ *n.* couleur *f.* —*a.* (*photo etc.*) en couleur; (*TV set*) couleur *invar.* —*v.t.* colorer; (*with crayon*) colorier. **~-blind** *a.* daltonien. **~ful** *a.* coloré.

coloured /ˈkʌləd/ *a.* (*person, pencil*) de couleur. —*n.* personne de couleur *f.*

colt /kəʊlt/ *n.* poulain *m.*

column /ˈkɒləm/ *n.* colonne *f.*

columnist /ˈkɒləmnɪst/ *n.* journaliste chroniqueur *m.*

coma /ˈkəʊmə/ *n.* coma *m.*

comb /kəʊm/ *n.* peigne *m.* —*v.t.* peigner; (*search*) ratisser. ~ **one's hair,** se peigner.

combat /ˈkɒmbæt/ *n.* combat *m.* —*v.t.* (*p.t.* **combated**) combattre. **~ant** /-ətənt/ *n.* combattant(e) *m.* (*f.*).

combination /kɒmbɪˈneɪʃn/ *n.* combinaison *f.*

combine[1] /kəmˈbaɪn/ *v.t./i.* (se) combiner, (s')unir.

combine[2] /ˈkɒmbaɪn/ *n.* (*comm.*) trust *m.*, cartel *m.* ~ **harvester,** moissonneuse-batteuse *f.*

combustion /kəmˈbʌstʃən/ *n.* combustion *f.*

come /kʌm/ *v.i.* (*p.t.* **came,** *p.p.* **come**) venir; (*occur*) arriver. ~ **about,** arriver. ~ **across,** rencontrer *or* trouver par hasard. ~ **away** *or* **off,** se détacher, partir. ~ **back,** revenir. **~-back** *n.* rentrée *f.*; (*retort*) réplique *f.* ~ **by,** obtenir. ~ **down,** descendre; (*price*) baisser. **~-down** *n.* humiliation *f.* ~ **in,** entrer. ~ **in for,** recevoir. ~ **into,** (*money*) hériter de. ~ **off,** (*succeed*) réussir; (*fare*) s'en tirer. ~ **out,** sortir. ~ **round** *or* **to,** revenir à soi. ~ **through,** s'en tirer (indemne de). ~ **to,** (*amount*) revenir à. ~ **up,** monter; (*fig.*)

se présenter. **~-uppance** *n.* (*fam.*) punition (méritée) *f.* **~ up with,** (*find*) trouver; (*produce*) produire.

comedian /kə'mi:dɪən/ *n.* comique *m.*

comedy /'kɒmədɪ/ *n.* comédie *f.*

comely /'kʌmlɪ/ *a.* (**-ier, -iest**) (*old use*) avenant, beau.

comet /'kɒmɪt/ *n.* comète *f.*

comfort /'kʌmfət/ *n.* confort *m.*; (*consolation*) réconfort *m.* —*v.t.* consoler. **one's ~s,** ses aises. **~able** *a.* (*chair, car, etc.*) confortable; (*person*) à l'aise, bien; (*wealthy*) aisé.

comforter /'kʌmfətə(r)/ *n.* (*baby's dummy*) sucette *f.*; (*quilt: Amer.*) édredon *m.*

comfy /'kʌmfɪ/ *a.* (*fam.*) = **comfortable.**

comic /'kɒmɪk/ *a.* comique. —*n.* (*person*) comique *m.*; (*periodical*) comic *m.* **~ strip,** bande dessinée *f.* **~al** *a.* comique.

coming /'kʌmɪŋ/ *n.* arrivée *f.* —*a.* à venir. **~s and goings,** allées et venues *f. pl.*

comma /'kɒmə/ *n.* virgule *f.*

command /kə'mɑ:nd/ *n.* (*authority*) commandement *m.*; (*order*) ordre *m.*; (*mastery*) maîtrise *f.* —*v.t.* commander (**s.o. to,** à qn. de); (*be able to use*) disposer de; (*require*) nécessiter; (*respect*) inspirer. **~er** *n.* commandant *m.* **~ing** *a.* imposant.

commandeer /kɒmən'dɪə(r)/ *v.t.* réquisitionner.

commandment /kə'mɑ:ndmənt/ *n.* commandement *m.*

commando /kə'mɑ:ndəʊ/ *n.* (*pl.* **-os**) commando *m.*

commemorat|e /kə'meməreɪt/ *v.t.* commémorer. **~ion** /-'reɪʃn/ *n.* commémoration *f.* **~ive** /-ətɪv/ *a.* commémoratif.

commence /kə'mens/ *v.t./i.* commencer. **~ment** *n.* commencement *m.*; (*univ., Amer.*) cérémonie de distribution des diplômes *f.*

commend /kə'mend/ *v.t.* (*praise*) louer; (*entrust*) confier. **~able** *a.* louable. **~ation** /kɒmen'deɪʃn/ *n.* éloge *m.*

commensurate /kə'menʃərət/ *a.* proportionné.

comment /'kɒment/ *n.* commentaire *m.* —*v.i.* faire des commentaires. **~ on,** commenter.

commentary /'kɒməntrɪ/ *n.* commentaire *m.*; (*radio, TV*) reportage *m.*

commentat|e /'kɒmənteɪt/ *v.i.* faire un reportage. **~or** *n.* commenta|teur, -trice *m., f.*

commerce /'kɒmɜ:s/ *n.* commerce *m.*

commercial /kə'mɜ:ʃl/ *a.* commercial; (*traveller*) de commerce. **~ize** *v.t.* commercialiser.

commiserat|e /kə'mɪzəreɪt/ *v.i.* **~e with,** s'apitoyer sur le sort de. **~ion** /-'reɪʃn/ *n.* commisération *f.*

commission /kə'mɪʃn/ *n.* commission *f.*; (*order for work*) commande *f.* —*v.t.* (*order*) commander; (*mil.*) nommer officier. **~ to do,** charger de faire. **out of ~,** hors service. **~er** *n.* préfet (de police) *m.*

commissionaire /kəmɪʃə'neə(r)/ *n.* commissionnaire *m.*

commit /kə'mɪt/ *v.t.* (*p.t.* **committed**) commettre; (*entrust*) confier. **~ o.s.,** s'engager. **~ to memory,** apprendre par cœur. **~ment** *n.* engagement *m.*

committee /kə'mɪtɪ/ *n.* comité *m.*

commodity /kə'mɒdətɪ/ *n.* produit *m.*, article *m.*

common /'kɒmən/ *a.* (**-er, -est**) (*shared by all*) commun; (*usual*) courant, commun; (*vulgar*) vulgaire, commun. —*n.* terrain communal *m.* **~ law,** droit coutumier *m.* **C~ Market,** Marché Commun *m.* **~-room** *n.* (*schol.*)

salle commune *f.* **~ sense,** bon sens *m.* **House of C~s,** Chambre des Communes *f.* **in ~,** en commun. **~ly** *adv.* communément.

commoner /'kɒmənə(r)/ *n.* roturlier, -ière *m., f.*

commonplace /'kɒmənpleɪs/ *a.* banal. —*n.* banalité *f.*

Commonwealth /'kɒmənwelθ/ *n.* **the ~,** le Commonwealth *m.*

commotion /kə'məʊʃn/ *n.* agitation *f.*, remue-ménage *m. invar.*

communal /'kɒmjʊnl/ *a.* (*shared*) commun; (*life*) collectif.

commune /'kɒmjuːn/ *n.* (*group*) communauté *f.*

communicat|e /kə'mjuːnɪkeɪt/ *v.t./i.* communiquer. **~ion** /-'keɪʃn/ *n.* communication *f.* **~ive** /-ətɪv/ *a.* communicatif.

communion /kə'mjuːnɪən/ *n.* communion *f.*

communiqué /kə'mjuːnɪkeɪ/ *n.* communiqué *m.*

Communis|t /'kɒmjʊnɪst/ *n.* communiste *m./f.* **~m** /-zəm/ *n.* communisme *m.*

community /kə'mjuːnətɪ/ *n.* communauté *f.*

commute /kə'mjuːt/ *v.i.* faire la navette. —*v.t.* (*jurid.*) commuer. **~r** /-ə(r)/ *n.* banlieusard(e) *m.* (*f.*).

compact[1] /kəm'pækt/ *a.* compact.

compact[2] /'kɒmpækt/ *n.* (*lady's case*) poudrier *m.*

companion /kəm'pænjən/ *n.* comp|agnon, -agne *m., f.* **~ship** *n.* camaraderie *f.*

company /'kʌmpənɪ/ *n.* (*companionship, firm*) compagnie *f.*; (*guests*) invité(e)s *m.* (*f.*) *pl.*

comparable /'kɒmpərəbl/ *a.* comparable.

compar|e /kəm'peə(r)/ *v.t.* comparer (**with, to,** à). **~ed with** *or* **to,** en comparaison de. —*v.i.* être comparable. **~ative** /-'pærətɪv/ *a.* (*study, form*) comparatif; (*comfort etc.*) relatif. **~atively** /-'pærətɪvlɪ/ *adv.* relativement.

comparison /kəm'pærɪsn/ *n.* comparaison *f.*

compartment /kəm'pɑːtmənt/ *n.* compartiment *m.*

compass /'kʌmpəs/ *n.* (*for direction*) boussole *f.*; (*scope*) portée *f.* **~(es),** (*for drawing*) compas *m.*

compassion /kəm'pæʃn/ *n.* compassion *f.* **~ate** *a.* compatissant.

compatib|le /kəm'pætəbl/ *a.* compatible. **~ility** /-'bɪlətɪ/ *n.* compatibilité *f.*

compatriot /kəm'pætrɪət/ *n.* compatriote *m./f.*

compel /kəm'pel/ *v.t.* (*p.t.* **compelled**) contraindre. **~ling** *a.* irrésistible.

compendium /kəm'pendɪəm/ *n.* abrégé *m.*, résumé *m.*

compensat|e /'kɒmpənseɪt/ *v.t./i.* (*financially*) dédommager (**for,** de). **~e for sth.,** compenser qch. **~ion** /-'seɪʃn/ *n.* compensation *f.*; (*financial*) dédommagement *m.*

compère /'kɒmpeə(r)/ *n.* animalteur, -trice *m., f.* —*v.t.* animer.

compete /kəm'piːt/ *v.i.* concourir. **~ with,** rivaliser avec.

competen|t /'kɒmpɪtənt/ *a.* compétent. **~ce** *n.* compétence *f.*

competition /kɒmpə'tɪʃn/ *n.* (*contest*) concours *m.*; (*sport*) compétition *f.*; (*comm.*) concurrence *f.*

competitive /kəm'petətɪv/ *a.* (*prices*) concurrentiel, compétitif. **~ examination,** concours *m.*

competitor /kəm'petɪtə(r)/ *n.* concurrent(e) *m.* (*f.*).

compile /kəm'paɪl/ *v.t.* (*list*) dresser; (*book*) rédiger. **~r** /-ə(r)/ *n.* rédacteur, -trice *m., f.*

complacen|t /kəm'pleɪsnt/ *a.* content de soi. **~cy** *n.* contentement de soi *m.*

complain /kəm'pleɪn/ *v.i.* se plaindre (**about, of,** de).

complaint /kəm'pleɪnt/ *n.* plainte

f.; (*in shop etc.*) réclamation *f.*; (*illness*) maladie *f.*
complement /ˈkɒmplɪmənt/ *n.* complément *m.* —*v.t.* compléter. **~ary** /-ˈmentrɪ/ *a.* complémentaire.
complet|e /kəmˈpliːt/ *a.* complet; (*finished*) achevé; (*downright*) parfait. —*v.t.* achever; (*a form*) remplir. **~ely** *adv.* complètement. **~ion** /-ʃn/ *n.* achèvement *m.*
complex /ˈkɒmpleks/ *a.* complexe. —*n.* (*psych., archit.*) complexe *m.* **~ity** /kəmˈpleksətɪ/ *n.* complexité *f.*
complexion /kəmˈplekʃn/ *n.* (*of face*) teint *m.*; (*fig.*) caractère *m.*
compliance /kəmˈplaɪəns/ *n.* (*agreement*) conformité *f.*
complicat|e /ˈkɒmplɪkeɪt/ *v.t.* compliquer. **~ed** *a.* compliqué. **~ion** /-ˈkeɪʃn/ *n.* complication *f.*
complicity /kəmˈplɪsətɪ/ *n.* complicité *f.*
compliment /ˈkɒmplɪmənt/ *n.* compliment *m.* —*v.t.* /ˈkɒmplɪment/ complimenter.
complimentary /kɒmplɪˈmentrɪ/ *a.* (cffert) à titre gracieux; (*praising*) flatteur.
comply /kəmˈplaɪ/ *v.i.* **~ with**, se conformer à, obéir à.
component /kəmˈpəʊnənt/ *n.* (*of machine etc.*) pièce *f.*; (*chemical substance*) composant *m.*; (*element: fig.*) composante *f.* —*a.* constituant.
compose /kəmˈpəʊz/ *v.t.* composer. **~ o.s.**, se calmer. **~d** *a.* calme. **~r** /-ə(r)/ *n.* (*mus.*) compositeur *m.*
composition /kɒmpəˈzɪʃn/ *n.* composition *f.*
compost /ˈkɒmpɒst, *Amer.* ˈkɒmpəʊst/ *n.* compost *m.*
composure /kəmˈpəʊʒə(r)/ *n.* calme *m.*
compound[1] /ˈkɒmpaʊnd/ *n.* (*substance, word*) composé *m.*; (*enclosure*) enclos *m.* —*a.* composé.
compound[2] /kəmˈpaʊnd/ *v.t.* (*problem etc.*) aggraver.
comprehen|d /kɒmprɪˈhend/ *v.t.* comprendre. **~sion** *n.* compréhension *f.*
comprehensive /kɒmprɪˈhensɪv/ *a.* étendu, complet; (*insurance*) tous-risques *invar.* **~ school,** collège d'enseignement secondaire *m.*
compress /kəmˈpres/ *v.t.* comprimer. **~ion** /-ʃn/ *n.* compression *f.*
comprise /kəmˈpraɪz/ *v.t.* comprendre, inclure.
compromise /ˈkɒmprəmaɪz/ *n.* compromis *m.* —*v.t.* compromettre. —*v.i.* transiger.
compulsion /kəmˈpʌlʃn/ *n.* contrainte *f.*
compulsive /kəmˈpʌlsɪv/ *a.* (*psych.*) compulsif; (*liar, smoker*) invétéré.
compulsory /kəmˈpʌlsərɪ/ *a.* obligatoire.
compunction /kəmˈpʌŋkʃn/ *n.* scrupule *m.*
computer /kəmˈpjuːtə(r)/ *n.* ordinateur *m.* **~ science,** informatique *f.* **~ize** *v.t.* informatiser.
comrade /ˈkɒmr(e)ɪd/ *n.* camarade *m./f.* **~ship** *n.* camaraderie *f.*
con[1] /kɒn/ *v.t.* (*p.t.* **conned**) (*sl.*) escroquer. —*n.* (*sl.*) escroquerie *f.* **~ man,** (*sl.*) escroc *m.*
con[2] /kɒn/ *see* **pro.**
concave /ˈkɒŋkeɪv/ *a.* concave.
conceal /kənˈsiːl/ *v.t.* dissimuler. **~ment** *n.* dissimulation *f.*
concede /kənˈsiːd/ *v.t.* concéder. —*v.i.* céder.
conceit /kənˈsiːt/ *n.* suffisance *f.* **~ed** *a.* suffisant.
conceivabl|e /kənˈsiːvəbl/ *a.* concevable. **~y** *adv.* **this may ~y be done,** il est concevable que cela puisse se faire.

conceive /kən'siːv/ *v.t./i.* concevoir. **~ of,** concevoir.
concentrat|e /'kɒnsntreɪt/ *v.t./i.* (se) concentrer. **~ion** /-'treɪʃn/ *n.* concentration *f.*
concept /'kɒnsept/ *n.* concept *m.* **~ual** /kən'septʃʊəl/ *a.* notionnel.
conception /kən'sepʃn/ *n.* conception *f.*
concern /kən'sɜːn/ *n.* (*interest, business*) affaire *f.*; (*worry*) inquiétude *f.*; (*firm: comm.*) entreprise *f.*, affaire *f.* —*v.t.* concerner. **~ o.s. with, be ~ed with,** s'occuper de. **~ing** *prep.* en ce qui concerne.
concerned /kən'sɜːnd/ *a.* inquiet.
concert /'kɒnsət/ *n.* concert *m.* **in ~,** ensemble.
concerted /kən'sɜːtɪd/ *a.* concerté.
concertina /kɒnsə'tiːnə/ *n.* concertina *m.*
concerto /kən'tʃeətəʊ/ *n.* (*pl.* **-os**) concerto *m.*
concession /kən'seʃn/ *n.* concession *f.*
conciliate /kən'sɪlɪeɪt/ *v.t.* (*soothe*) apaiser; (*win over*) se concilier (l'amitié de).
concise /kən'saɪs/ *a.* concis. **~ly** *adv.* avec concision. **~ness** *n.* concision *f.*
conclu|de /kən'kluːd/ *v.t.* conclure. —*v.i.* se terminer. **~ding** *a.* final. **~sion** *n.* conclusion *f.*
conclusive /kən'kluːsɪv/ *a.* concluant. **~ly** *adv.* de manière concluante.
concoct /kən'kɒkt/ *v.t.* confectionner; (*invent: fig.*) fabriquer. **~ion** /-kʃn/ *n.* mélange *m.*
concourse /'kɒŋkɔːs/ *n.* (*rail.*) hall *m.*
concrete /'kɒŋkriːt/ *n.* béton *m.* —*a.* concret. —*v.t.* bétonner.
concur /kən'kɜː(r)/ *v.i.* (*p.t.* **concurred**) être d'accord.
concurrently /kən'kʌrəntlɪ/ *adv.* simultanément.
concussion /kən'kʌʃn/ *n.* commotion (cérébrale) *f.*
condemn /kən'dem/ *v.t.* condamner. **~ation** /kɒndem'neɪʃn/ *n.* condamnation *f.*
condens|e /kən'dens/ *v.t./i.* (se) condenser. **~ation** /kɒnden'seɪʃn/ *n.* condensation *f.*; (*mist*) buée *f.*
condescend /kɒndɪ'send/ *v.i.* condescendre.
condiment /'kɒndɪmənt/ *n.* condiment *m.*
condition /kən'dɪʃn/ *n.* condition *f.* —*v.t.* conditionner. **on ~ that,** à condition que. **~al** *a.* conditionnel. **be ~al upon,** dépendre de.
condolences /kən'dəʊlənsɪz/ *n. pl.* condoléances *f. pl.*
condom /'kɒndəm/ *n.* préservatif *m.*
condominium /kɒndə'mɪnɪəm/ *n.* (*Amer.*) copropriété *f.*
condone /kən'dəʊn/ *v.t.* pardonner, fermer les yeux sur.
conducive /kən'djuːsɪv/ *a.* **~ to,** favorable à.
conduct[1] /kən'dʌkt/ *v.t.* conduire; (*orchestra*) diriger.
conduct[2] /'kɒndʌkt/ *n.* conduite *f.*
conduct|or /kən'dʌktə(r)/ *n.* chef d'orchestre *m.*; (*of bus*) receveur *m.* **~ress** *n.* receveuse *f.*
cone /kəʊn/ *n.* cône *m.*; (*of ice-cream*) cornet *m.*
confectioner /kən'fekʃənə(r)/ *n.* confiseu|r, -se *m., f.* **~y** *n.* confiserie *f.*
confederate /kən'fedərət/ *n.* (*accomplice*) complice *m./f.*
confederation /kənfedə'reɪʃn/ *n.* confédération *f.*
confer /kən'fɜː(r)/ *v.t./i.* (*p.t.* **conferred**) conférer.
conference /'kɒnfərəns/ *n.* conférence *f.*
confess /kən'fes/ *v.t./i.* avouer; (*relig.*) (se) confesser. **~ion** /-ʃn/ *n.* confession *f.*

confessional /kən'feʃənl/ *n.* confessionnal *m.*

confetti /kən'fetɪ/ *n.* confettis *m. pl.*

confide /kən'faɪd/ *v.t.* confier. —*v.i.* ~ **in,** se confier à.

confiden|t /'kɒnfɪdənt/ *a.* sûr. **~ce** *n.* (*trust*) confiance *f.*; (*boldness*) confiance en soi *f.*; (*secret*) confidence *f.* **~ce trick,** escroquerie *f.* **in ~ce,** en confidence.

confidential /kɒnfɪ'denʃl/ *a.* confidentiel.

confine /kən'faɪn/ *v.t.* enfermer; (*limit*) limiter. **~ment** *n.* détention *f.*; (*med.*) couches *f. pl.*

confines /'kɒnfaɪnz/ *n. pl.* confins *m. pl.*

confirm /kən'fɜːm/ *v.t.* confirmer. **~ation** /kɒnfə'meɪʃn/ *n.* confirmation *f.* **~ed** *a.* (*bachelor*) endurci.

confiscat|e /'kɒnfɪskeɪt/ *v.t.* confisquer. **~ion** /-'keɪʃn/ *n.* confiscation *f.*

conflagration /kɒnflə'greɪʃn/ *n.* incendie *m.*

conflict[1] /'kɒnflɪkt/ *n.* conflit *m.*

conflict[2] /kən'flɪkt/ *v.i.* être en contradiction. **~ing** *a.* contradictoire.

conform /kən'fɔːm/ *v.t./i.* (se) conformer. **~ist** *n.* conformiste *m./f.*

confound /kən'faʊnd/ *v.t.* confondre. **~ed** *a.* (*fam.*) sacré.

confront /kən'frʌnt/ *v.t.* se trouver en face de; (*danger*) affronter. **~ with,** confronter avec. **~ation** /kɒnfrʌn'teɪʃn/ *n.* confrontation *f.*

confus|e /kən'fjuːz/ *v.t.* embrouiller; (*mistake, confound*) confondre. **become ~ed,** s'embrouiller. **I am ~ed,** je m'y perds. **~ing** *a.* déroutant. **~ion** /-ʒn/ *n.* confusion *f.*

congeal /kən'dʒiːl/ *v.t./i.* (se) figer.

congenial /kən'dʒiːmɪəl/ *a.* sympathique.

congenital /kən'dʒenɪtl/ *a.* congénital.

congest|ed /kən'dʒestɪd/ *a.* encombré; (*med.*) congestionné. **~ion** /-stʃən/ *n.* (*traffic*) encombrement(s) *m.* (*pl.*); (*med.*) congestion *f.*

congratulat|e /kən'grætjʊleɪt/ *v.t.* féliciter (**on,** de). **~ions** /-'leɪʃnz/ *n. pl.* félicitations *f. pl.*

congregat|e /'kɒŋgrɪgeɪt/ *v.i.* se rassembler. **~ion** /-'geɪʃn/ *n.* assemblée *f.*

congress /'kɒŋgres/ *n.* congrès *m.* **C~,** (*Amer.*) Congrès *m.*

conic(al) /'kɒnɪk(l)/ *a.* conique.

conifer /'kɒnɪfə(r)/ *n.* conifère *m.*

conjecture /kən'dʒektʃə(r)/ *n.* conjecture *f.* —*v.t./i.* conjecturer.

conjugal /'kɒndʒʊgl/ *a.* conjugal.

conjugat|e /'kɒndʒʊgeɪt/ *v.t.* conjuguer. **~ion** /-'geɪʃn/ *n.* conjugaison *f.*

conjunction /kən'dʒʌŋkʃn/ *n.* conjonction *f.* **in ~ with,** conjointement avec.

conjur|e /'kʌndʒə(r)/ *v.i.* faire des tours de passe-passe. —*v.t.* **~e up,** faire apparaître. **~or** *n.* prestidigita|teur, -trice *m., f.*

conk /kɒŋk/ *v.i.* **~ out,** (*sl.*) tomber en panne.

conker /'kɒŋkə(r)/ *n.* (*horse-chestnut fruit: fam.*) marron *m.*

connect /kə'nekt/ *v.t./i.* (se) relier; (*install, wire up to mains*) brancher. **~ with,** (*of train*) assurer la correspondance avec. **~ed** *a.* lié. **be ~ed with,** avoir rapport à; (*deal with*) avoir des rapports avec.

connection /kə'nekʃn/ *n.* rapport *m.*; (*rail.*) correspondance *f.*; (*phone call*) communication *f.*; (*electr.*) contact *m.*; (*joining piece*) raccord *m.* **~s,** (*comm.*) relations *f. pl.*

conniv|e /kə'naɪv/ *v.i.* **~e at,** se

faire le complice de. **~ance** *n.* connivence *f.*
connoisseur /kɒnəˈsɜː(r)/ *n.* connaisseur *m.*
connot|e /kəˈnəʊt/ *v.t.* impliquer. **~ation** /kɒnəˈteɪʃn/ *n.* connotation *f.*
conquer /ˈkɒŋkə(r)/ *v.t.* vaincre; (*country*) conquérir. **~or** *n.* conquérant *m.*
conquest /ˈkɒŋkwest/ *n.* conquête *f.*
conscience /ˈkɒnʃəns/ *n.* conscience *f.*
conscientious /kɒnʃɪˈenʃəs/ *a.* consciencieux.
conscious /ˈkɒnʃəs/ *a.* conscient; (*deliberate*) voulu. **~ly** *adv.* consciemment. **~ness** *n.* conscience *f.*; (*med.*) connaissance *f.*
conscript[1] /kənˈskrɪpt/ *v.t.* recruter par conscription. **~ion** /-pʃn/ *n.* conscription *f.*
conscript[2] /ˈkɒnskrɪpt/ *n.* conscrit *m.*
consecrate /ˈkɒnsɪkreɪt/ *v.t.* consacrer.
consecutive /kənˈsekjʊtɪv/ *a.* consécutif. **~ly** *adv.* consécutivement.
consensus /kənˈsensəs/ *n.* consensus *m.*
consent /kənˈsent/ *v.i.* consentir. —*n.* consentement *m.*
consequence /ˈkɒnsɪkwəns/ *n.* conséquence *f.*
consequent /ˈkɒnsɪkwənt/ *a.* résultant. **~ly** *adv.* par conséquent.
conservation /kɒnsəˈveɪʃn/ *n.* préservation *f.*
conservationist /kɒnsəˈveɪʃənɪst/ *n.* partisan(e) de la défense de l'environnement *m.* (*f.*).
conservative /kənˈsɜːvətɪv/ *a.* conservateur; (*estimate*) modeste. **C~** *a.* & *n.* conserva|teur, -trice (*m.* (*f.*)).
conservatory /kənˈsɜːvətrɪ/ *n.* (*greenhouse*) serre *f.*
conserve /kənˈsɜːv/ *v.t.* conserver.
consider /kənˈsɪdə(r)/ *v.t.* considérer; (*allow for*) tenir compte de. **~ation** /-ˈreɪʃn/ *n.* considération *f.*; (*respect*) égard(s) *m.* (*pl.*). **~ing** *prep.* compte tenu de.
considerabl|e /kənˈsɪdərəbl/ *a.* considérable; (*much*) beaucoup de. **~ly** *adv.* beaucoup, considérablement.
considerate /kənˈsɪdərət/ *a.* prévenant, attentionné.
consign /kənˈsaɪn/ *v.t.* (*entrust*) confier; (*send*) expédier. **~ment** *n.* envoi *m.*
consist /kənˈsɪst/ *v.i.* consister (**of,** en; **in doing,** à faire).
consisten|t /kənˈsɪstənt/ *a.* cohérent. **~t with,** conforme à. **~cy** *n.* (*of liquids*) consistance *f.*; (*fig.*) cohérence *f.* **~tly** *adv.* régulièrement.
consol|e /kənˈsəʊl/ *v.t.* consoler. **~ation** /kɒnsəˈleɪʃn/ *n.* consolation *f.*
consolidat|e /kənˈsɒlɪdeɪt/ *v.t./i.* (se) consolider. **~ion** /-ˈdeɪʃn/ *n.* consolidation *f.*
consonant /ˈkɒnsənənt/ *n.* consonne *f.*
consort[1] /ˈkɒnsɔːt/ *n.* époux *m.*, épouse *f.*
consort[2] /kənˈsɔːt/ *v.i.* **~ with,** fréquenter.
consortium /kənˈsɔːtɪəm/ *n.* (*pl.* **-tia**) consortium *m.*
conspicuous /kənˈspɪkjʊəs/ *a.* (*easily seen*) en évidence; (*showy*) voyant; (*noteworthy*) remarquable.
conspiracy /kənˈspɪrəsɪ/ *n.* conspiration *f.*
conspire /kənˈspaɪə(r)/ *v.i.* (*person*) comploter (**to do,** de faire), conspirer; (*events*) conspirer (**to do,** à faire).
constable /ˈkʌnstəbl/ *n.* agent de police *m.*, gendarme *m.*

constant /ˈkɒnstənt/ *a.* incessant; (*unchanging*) constant; (*friend*) fidèle. **~ly** *adv.* constamment.

constellation /kɒnstəˈleɪʃn/ *n.* constellation *f.*

consternation /kɒnstəˈneɪʃn/ *n.* consternation *f.*

constipat|e /ˈkɒnstɪpeɪt/ *v.t.* constiper. **~ion** /-ˈpeɪʃn/ *n.* constipation *f.*

constituency /kənˈstɪtjʊənsɪ/ *n.* circonscription électorale *f.*

constituent /kənˈstɪtjʊənt/ *a.* constitutif. —*n.* élément constitutif *m.*; (*pol.*) élec|teur, -trice *m., f.*

constitut|e /ˈkɒnstɪtjuːt/ *v.t.* constituer. **~ion** /-ˈtjuːʃn/ *n.* constitution *f.* **~ional** /-ˈtjuːʃənl/ *a.* constitutionnel; *n.* promenade *f.*

constrain /kənˈstreɪn/ *v.t.* contraindre.

constraint /kənˈstreɪnt/ *n.* contrainte *f.*

constrict /kənˈstrɪkt/ *v.t.* resserrer; (*movement*) gêner. **~ion** /-kʃn/ *n.* resserrement *m.*

construct /kənˈstrʌkt/ *v.t.* construire. **~ion** /-kʃn/ *n.* construction *f.*

constructive /kənˈstrʌktɪv/ *a.* constructif.

construe /kənˈstruː/ *v.t.* interpréter.

consul /ˈkɒnsl/ *n.* consul *m.* **~ar** /-jʊlə(r)/ *a.* consulaire.

consulate /ˈkɒnsjʊlət/ *n.* consulat *m.*

consult /kənˈsʌlt/ *v.t.* consulter. —*v.i.* **~ with,** conférer avec. **~ation** /kɒnslˈteɪʃn/ *n.* consultation *f.*

consultant /kənˈsʌltənt/ *n.* conseill|er, -ère *m., f.*; (*med.*) spécialiste *m./f.*

consume /kənˈsjuːm/ *v.t.* consommer; (*destroy*) consumer. **~r** /-ə(r)/ *n.* consomma|teur, -trice *m., f.* —*a.* (*society*) de consommation.

consumerism /kənˈsjuːmərɪzəm/ *n.* protection des consommateurs *f.*

consummate /ˈkɒnsəmeɪt/ *v.t.* consommer.

consumption /kənˈsʌmpʃn/ *n.* consommation *f.*; (*med.*) phtisie *f.*

contact /ˈkɒntækt/ *n.* contact *m.*; (*person*) relation *f.* —*v.t.* contacter. **~ lenses,** verres de contact *m. pl.*

contagious /kənˈteɪdʒəs/ *a.* contagieux.

contain /kənˈteɪn/ *v.t.* contenir. **~ o.s.,** se contenir. **~er** *n.* récipient *m.*; (*for transport*) container *m.*

contaminat|e /kənˈtæmɪneɪt/ *v.t.* contaminer. **~ion** /-ˈneɪʃn/ *n.* contamination *f.*

contemplat|e /ˈkɒntempleɪt/ *v.t.* (*gaze at*) contempler; (*think about*) envisager. **~ion** /-ˈpleɪʃn/ *n.* contemplation *f.*

contemporary /kənˈtemprərɪ/ *a.* & *n.* contemporain(e) (*m.* (*f.*)).

contempt /kənˈtempt/ *n.* mépris *m.* **~ible** *a.* méprisable. **~uous** /-tʃʊəs/ *a.* méprisant.

contend /kənˈtend/ *v.t.* soutenir. —*v.i.* **~ with,** (*compete*) rivaliser avec; (*face*) faire face à. **~er** *n.* adversaire *m./f.*

content[1] /kənˈtent/ *a.* satisfait. —*v.t.* contenter. **~ed** *a.* satisfait. **~ment** *n.* contentement *m.*

content[2] /ˈkɒntent/ *n.* contenu *m.* **~s,** contenu *m.*

contention /kənˈtenʃn/ *n.* dispute *f.*; (*claim*) affirmation *f.*

contest[1] /ˈkɒntest/ *n.* (*competition*) concours *m.*; (*fight*) combat *m.*

contest[2] /kənˈtest/ *v.t.* contester; (*compete for or in*) disputer. **~ant** *n.* concurrent(e) *m.* (*f.*).

context /ˈkɒntekst/ *n.* contexte *m.*

continent /ˈkɒntɪnənt/ *n.* continent *m.* **the C~,** l'Europe (continentale) *f.* **~al** /-'nentl/ *a.* continental; européen.

contingen|t /kən'tɪndʒənt/ *a.* **be ~t upon,** dépendre de. —*n.* (*mil.*) contingent *m.* **~cy** *n.* éventualité *f.* **~cy plan,** plan d'urgence *m.*

continual /kən'tɪnjʊəl/ *a.* continuel. **~ly** *adv.* continuellement.

continu|e /kən'tɪnjuː/ *v.t./i.* continuer; (*resume*) reprendre. **~ance** *n.* continuation *f.* **~ation** /-ʊ'eɪʃn/ *n.* continuation *f.*; (*after interruption*) reprise *f.*; (*new episode*) suite *f.* **~ed** *a.* continu.

continuity /kɒntɪ'njuːətɪ/ *n.* continuité *f.*

continuous /kən'tɪnjʊəs/ *a.* continu. **~ly** *adv.* sans interruption, continûment.

contort /kən'tɔːt/ *v.t.* tordre. **~ o.s.,** se contorsionner. **~ion** /-ʃn/ *n.* torsion *f.*; contorsion *f.* **~ionist** /-ʃənɪst/ *n.* contorsionniste *m./f.*

contour /'kɒntʊə(r)/ *n.* contour *m.*

contraband /'kɒntrəbænd/ *n.* contrebande *f.*

contraception /kɒntrə'sepʃn/ *n.* contraception *f.*

contraceptive /kɒntrə'septɪv/ *a.* & *n.* contraceptif (*m.*).

contract[1] /'kɒntrækt/ *n.* contrat *m.*

contract[2] /kən'trækt/ *v.t./i.* (se) contracter. **~ion** /-kʃn/ *n.* contraction *f.*

contractor /kən'træktə(r)/ *n.* entrepreneur *m.*

contradict /kɒntrə'dɪkt/ *v.t.* contredire. **~ion** /-kʃn/ *n.* contradiction *f.* **~ory** *a.* contradictoire.

contralto /kən'træltəʊ/ *n.* (*pl.* **-os**) contralto *m.*

contraption /kən'træpʃn/ *n.* (*fam.*) engin *m.*, truc *m.*

contrary[1] /'kɒntrərɪ/ *a.* contraire (**to,** à). —*n.* contraire *m.* —*adv.* **~ to,** contrairement à. **on the ~,** au contraire.

contrary[2] /kən'treərɪ/ *a.* entêté.

contrast[1] /'kɒntrɑːst/ *n.* contraste *m.*

contrast[2] /kən'trɑːst/ *v.t./i.* contraster. **~ing** *a.* contrasté.

contraven|e /kɒntrə'viːn/ *v.t.* enfreindre. **~tion** /-'venʃn/ *n.* infraction *f.*

contribut|e /kən'trɪbjuːt/ *v.t.* donner. —*v.i.* **~ to,** contribuer à; (*take part*) participer à; (*newspaper*) collaborer à. **~ion** /kɒntrɪ'bjuːʃn/ *n.* contribution *f.* **~or** *n.* collabora|teur, -trice *m., f.*

contrivance /kən'traɪvəns/ *n.* (*device*) appareil *m.*, truc *m.*

contrive /kən'traɪv/ *v.t.* imaginer. **~ to do,** trouver moyen de faire.

control /kən'trəʊl/ *v.t.* (*p.t.* **controlled**) (*a firm etc.*) diriger; (*check*) contrôler; (*restrain*) maîtriser. —*n.* contrôle *m.*; (*mastery*) maîtrise *f.* **~s,** commandes *f. pl.*; (*knobs*) boutons *m. pl.* **have under ~,** (*event*) avoir en main. **in ~ of,** maître de.

controversial /kɒntrə'vɜːʃl/ *a.* discutable, discuté.

controversy /'kɒntrəvɜːsɪ/ *n.* controverse *f.*

conurbation /kɒnɜː'beɪʃn/ *n.* agglomération *f.*, conurbation *f.*

convalesce /kɒnvə'les/ *v.i.* être en convalescence. **~nce** *n.* convalescence *f.* **~nt** *a.* & *n.* convalescent(e) (*m.* (*f.*)). **~nt home,** maison de convalescence *f.*

convector /kən'vektə(r)/ *n.* radiateur à convection *m.*

convene /kən'viːn/ *v.t.* convoquer. —*v.i.* se réunir.

convenience /kən'viːnɪəns/ *n.* commodité *f.* **~s,** toilettes *f. pl.* **all modern ~s,** tout le confort moderne. **at your ~,** quand cela vous conviendra, à votre convenance.

convenient /kən'viːnɪənt/ *a.* commode, pratique; (*time*) bien choisi. **be ~ for,** convenir à. **~ly**

adv. (*arrive*) à propos. **~ly situated,** bien situé.
convent /'kɒnvənt/ *n.* couvent *m.*
convention /kən'venʃn/ *n.* (*assembly, agreement*) convention *f.*; (*custom*) usage *m.* **~al** *a.* conventionnel.
converge /kən'vɜːdʒ/ *v.i.* converger.
conversant /kən'vɜːsnt/ *a.* **be ~ with,** connaître; (*fact*) savoir; (*machinery*) s'y connaître en.
conversation /kɒnvə'seɪʃn/ *n.* conversation *f.* **~al** *a.* (*tone etc.*) de la conversation. **~alist** *n.* causeu|r, -se *m., f.*
converse[1] /kən'vɜːs/ *v.i.* s'entretenir, converser (**with,** avec).
converse[2] /'kɒnvɜːs/ *a.* & *n.* inverse (*m.*). **~ly** *adv.* inversement.
conver|t[1] /kən'vɜːt/ *v.t.* convertir; (*house*) aménager. **~sion** /-ʃn/ *n.* conversion *f.* **~tible** *a.* convertible. —*n.* (*car*) décapotable *f.*
convert[2] /'kɒnvɜːt/ *n.* converti(e) *m.* (*f.*).
convex /'kɒnveks/ *a.* convexe.
convey /kən'veɪ/ *v.t.* (*wishes, order*) transmettre; (*goods, people*) transporter; (*idea, feeling*) communiquer. **~ance** *n.* transport *m.* **~or belt,** tapis roulant *m.*
convict[1] /kən'vɪkt/ *v.t.* déclarer coupable. **~ion** /-kʃn/ *n.* condamnation *f.*; (*opinion*) conviction *f.*
convict[2] /'kɒnvɪkt/ *n.* forçat *m.*
convinc|e /kən'vɪns/ *v.t.* convaincre. **~ing** *a.* convaincant.
convivial /kən'vɪvɪəl/ *a.* joyeux.
convoke /kən'vəʊk/ *v.t.* convoquer.
convoluted /'kɒnvəluːtɪd/ *a.* (*argument etc.*) compliqué.
convoy /'kɒnvɔɪ/ *n.* convoi *m.*
convuls|e /kən'vʌls/ *v.t.* convulser; (*fig.*) bouleverser. **be ~ed with laughter,** se tordre de rire. **~ion** /-ʃn/ *n.* convulsion *f.*
coo /kuː/ *v.i.* roucouler.
cook /kʊk/ *v.t./i.* (faire) cuire; (*of person*) faire la cuisine. —*n.* cuisin|ier, -ière *m., f.* **~ up,** (*fam.*) fabriquer.
cooker /'kʊkə(r)/ *n.* (*stove*) cuisinière *f.*; (*apple*) pomme à cuire *f.*
cookery /'kʊkərɪ/ *n.* cuisine *f.*
cookie /'kʊkɪ/ *n.* (*Amer.*) biscuit *m.*
cool /kuːl/ *a.* (**-er, -est**) frais; (*calm*) calme; (*unfriendly*) froid. —*n.* fraîcheur *f.*; (*calmness*: *sl.*) sang-froid *m.* —*v.t./i.* rafraîchir. **in the ~,** au frais. **~er** *n.* (*for food*) glacière *f.* **~ly** *adv.* calmement; froidement. **~ness** *n.* fraîcheur *f.*; froideur *f.*
coop /kuːp/ *n.* poulailler *m.* —*v.t.* **~ up,** enfermer.
co-operat|e /kəʊ'ɒpəreɪt/ *v.i.* coopérer. **~ion** /-'reɪʃn/ *n.* coopération *f.*
co-operative /kəʊ'ɒpərətɪv/ *a.* coopératif. —*n.* coopérative *f.*
co-opt /kəʊ'ɒpt/ *v.t.* coopter.
co-ordinat|e /kəʊ'ɔːdɪneɪt/ *v.t.* coordonner. **~ion** /-'neɪʃn/ *n.* coordination *f.*
cop /kɒp/ *v.t.* (*p.t.* **copped**) (*sl.*) piquer. —*n.* (*policeman*: *sl.*) flic *m.*
cope /kəʊp/ *v.i.* (*fam.*) se débrouiller. **~ with,** s'occuper de.
copious /'kəʊpɪəs/ *a.* copieux.
copper[1] /'kɒpə(r)/ *n.* cuivre *m.*; (*coin*) sou *m.* —*a.* de cuivre.
copper[2] /'kɒpə(r)/ *n.* (*sl.*) flic *m.*
coppice, copse /'kɒpɪs, kɒps/ *ns.* taillis *m.*
copulat|e /'kɒpjʊleɪt/ *v.i.* s'accoupler. **~ion** /-'leɪʃn/ *n.* copulation *f.*
copy /'kɒpɪ/ *n.* copie *f.*; (*of book, newspaper*) exemplaire *m.*; (*print*: *photo.*) épreuve *f.* —*v.t./i.* copier.
copyright /'kɒpɪraɪt/ *n.* droit d'auteur *m.*, copyright *m.*
coral /'kɒrəl/ *n.* corail *m.*
cord /kɔːd/ *n.* (petite) corde *f.*; (*of curtain, pyjamas, etc.*) cordon *m.*;

(*electr.*) cordon électrique *m.*; (*fabric*) velours côtelé *m.*
cordial /ˈkɔːdɪəl/ *a.* cordial. *—n.* (*fruit-flavoured drink*) sirop *m.*
cordon /ˈkɔːdn/ *n.* cordon *m.* *—v.t.* **~ off,** mettre un cordon autour de.
corduroy /ˈkɔːdərɔɪ/ *n.* velours côtelé *m.*, velours à côtes *m.*
core /kɔː(r)/ *n.* (*of apple*) trognon *m.*; (*of problem*) cœur *m.*; (*techn.*) noyau *m.* *—v.t.* vider.
cork /kɔːk/ *n.* liège *m.*; (*for bottle*) bouchon *m.* *—v.t.* boucher.
corkscrew /ˈkɔːkskruː/ *n.* tire-bouchon *m.*
corn[1] /kɔːn/ *n.* blé *m.*; (*maize*: *Amer.*) maïs *m.*; (*seed*) grain *m.*
corn[2] /kɔːn/ *n.* (*hard skin*) cor *m.*
cornea /ˈkɔːnɪə/ *n.* cornée *f.*
corned /kɔːnd/ *a.* **~ beef,** corned-beef *m.*
corner /ˈkɔːnə(r)/ *n.* coin *m.*; (*bend in road*) virage *m.*; (*football*) corner *m.* *—v.t.* coincer, acculer; (*market*) accaparer. *—v.i.* prendre un virage. **~-stone** *n.* pierre angulaire *f.*
cornet /ˈkɔːnɪt/ *n.* cornet *m.*
cornflakes /ˈkɔːnfleɪks/ *n. pl.* céréales *f. pl.* (*flocons de maïs*).
cornflour /ˈkɔːnflaʊə(r)/ *n.* farine de maïs *f.*
cornice /ˈkɔːnɪs/ *n.* corniche *f.*
cornucopia /kɔːnjʊˈkəʊpɪə/ *n.* corne d'abondance *f.*
Corn|wall /ˈkɔːnwəl/ *n.* Cornouailles *f.* **~ish** *a.* de Cornouailles.
corny /ˈkɔːnɪ/ *a.* (**-ier, -iest**) (*trite*: *fam.*) rebattu; (*mawkish*: *fam.*) à l'eau de rose.
corollary /kəˈrɒlərɪ, *Amer.* ˈkɒrəlerɪ/ *n.* corollaire *m.*
coronary /ˈkɒrənərɪ/ *n.* infarctus *m.*
coronation /kɒrəˈneɪʃn/ *n.* couronnement *m.*
coroner /ˈkɒrənə(r)/ *n.* coroner *m.*
corporal[1] /ˈkɔːpərəl/ *n.* caporal *m.*
corporal[2] /ˈkɔːpərəl/ *a.* **~ punishment,** châtiment corporel *m.*
corporate /ˈkɔːpərət/ *a.* en commun; (*body*) constitué.
corporation /kɔːpəˈreɪʃn/ *n.* (*comm.*) société *f.*; (*of town*) municipalité *f.*; (*abdomen*: *fam.*) bedaine *f.*
corps /kɔː(r)/ *n.* (*pl.* **corps** /kɔːz/) corps *m.*
corpse /kɔːps/ *n.* cadavre *m.*
corpulent /ˈkɔːpjʊlənt/ *a.* corpulent.
corpuscle /ˈkɔːpʌsl/ *n.* globule *m.*
corral /kəˈrɑːl/ *n.* (*Amer.*) corral *m.*
correct /kəˈrekt/ *a.* (*right*) exact, juste, correct; (*proper*) correct. **you are ~,** vous avez raison. *—v.t.* corriger. **~ion** /-kʃn/ *n.* correction *f.*
correlat|e /ˈkɒrəleɪt/ *v.t./i.* (faire) correspondre. **~ion** /-ˈleɪʃn/ *n.* corrélation *f.*
correspond /kɒrɪˈspɒnd/ *v.i.* correspondre. **~ence** *n.* correspondance *f.* **~ent** *n.* correspondant(e) *m.* (*f.*).
corridor /ˈkɒrɪdɔː(r)/ *n.* couloir *m.*
corroborate /kəˈrɒbəreɪt/ *v.t.* corroborer.
corro|de /kəˈrəʊd/ *v.t./i.* (se) corroder. **~sion** *n.* corrosion *f.*
corrosive /kəˈrəʊsɪv/ *a.* corrosif.
corrugated /ˈkɒrəgeɪtɪd/ *a.* ondulé. **~ iron,** tôle ondulée *f.*
corrupt /kəˈrʌpt/ *a.* corrompu. *—v.t.* corrompre. **~ion** /-pʃn/ *n.* corruption *f.*
corset /ˈkɔːsɪt/ *n.* (*boned*) corset *m.*; (*elasticated*) gaine *f.*
Corsica /ˈkɔːsɪkə/ *n.* Corse *f.*
cos /kɒs/ *n.* laitue romaine *f.*
cosh /kɒʃ/ *n.* matraque *f.* *—v.t.* matraquer.
cosmetic /kɒzˈmetɪk/ *n.* produit de beauté *m.* *—a.* cosmétique; (*fig.*, *pej.*) superficiel.
cosmic /ˈkɒzmɪk/ *a.* cosmique.

cosmonaut /ˈkɒzmənɔːt/ *n.* cosmonaute *m.*/*f.*
cosmopolitan /kɒzməˈpɒlɪt(ə)n/ *a.* & *n.* cosmopolite (*m.*/*f.*).
cosmos /ˈkɒzmɒs/ *n.* cosmos *m.*
Cossack /ˈkɒsæk/ *n.* cosaque *m.*
cosset /ˈkɒsɪt/ *v.t.* (*p.t.* **cosseted**) dorloter.
cost /kɒst/ *v.t.* (*p.t.* **cost**) coûter; (*p.t.* **costed**) établir le prix de. —*n.* coût *m.* **~s,** (*jurid.*) dépens *m. pl.* **at all ~s,** à tout prix. **to one's ~,** à ses dépens.
co-star /ˈkəʊstɑː(r)/ *n.* partenaire *m.*/*f.*
costly /ˈkɒstlɪ/ *a.* (**-ier, -iest**) coûteux; (*valuable*) précieux.
costume /ˈkɒstjuːm/ *n.* costume *m.*
cos|y /ˈkəʊzɪ/ *a.* (**-ier, -iest**) confortable, intime. —*n.* couvre-théière *m.* **~iness** *n.* confort *m.*
cot /kɒt/ *n.* lit d'enfant *m.*; (*camp-bed*: *Amer.*) lit de camp *m.*
cottage /ˈkɒtɪdʒ/ *n.* petite maison de campagne *f.*; (*thatched*) chaumière *f.* **~ cheese,** fromage blanc (maigre) *m.* **~ industry,** activité artisanale *f.* **~ pie,** hachis Parmentier *m.*.
cotton /ˈkɒtn/ *n.* coton *m.* —*v.i.* **~ on,** (*sl.*) piger. **~ candy,** (*Amer.*) barbe à papa *f.* **~ wool,** coton hydrophile *m.*
couch /kaʊtʃ/ *n.* divan *m.* —*v.t.* (*express*) formuler.
couchette /kuːˈʃet/ *n.* couchette *f.*
cough /kɒf/ *v.i.* tousser. —*n.* toux *f.* **~ up,** (*sl.*) cracher, payer.
could /kʊd, *unstressed* kəd/ *p.t. of* **can²**.
couldn't /ˈkʊdnt/ = **could not.**
council /ˈkaʊnsl/ *n.* conseil *m.* **~ house,** maison construite par la municipalité *f.*, (*approx.*) H.L.M. *m.*/*f.*
councillor /ˈkaʊnsələ(r)/ *n.* conseill|er, -ère municipal(e) *m.*, *f.*
counsel /ˈkaʊnsl/ *n.* conseil *m.* —*n.* *invar.* (*jurid.*) avocat(e) *m.* (*f.*). **~lor** *n.* conseill|er, -ère *m.*, *f.*
count¹ /kaʊnt/ *v.t.*/*i.* compter. —*n.* compte *m.* **~ on,** compter sur.
count² /kaʊnt/ *n.* (*nobleman*) comte *m.*
countdown /ˈkaʊntdaʊn/ *n.* compte à rebours *m.*
countenance /ˈkaʊntɪnəns/ *n.* mine *f.* —*v.t.* admettre, approuver.
counter¹ /ˈkaʊntə(r)/ *n.* comptoir *m.*; (*in bank etc.*) guichet *m.*; (*token*) jeton *m.*
counter² /ˈkaʊntə(r)/ *adv.* **~ to,** à l'encontre de. —*a.* opposé. —*v.t.* opposer; (*blow*) parer. —*v.i.* riposter.
counter- /ˈkaʊntə(r)/ *pref.* contre-.
counteract /kaʊntərˈækt/ *v.t.* neutraliser.
counter-attack /ˈkaʊntərətæk/ *n.* contre-attaque *f.* —*v.t.*/*i.* contre-attaquer.
counterbalance /ˈkaʊntəbæləns/ *n.* contrepoids *m.* —*v.t.* contre-balancer.
counter-clockwise /kaʊntəˈklɒkwaɪz/ *a.* & *adv.* (*Amer.*) dans le sens inverse des aiguilles d'une montre.
counterfeit /ˈkaʊntəfɪt/ *a.* & *n.* faux (*m.*). —*v.t.* contrefaire.
counterfoil /ˈkaʊntəfɔɪl/ *n.* souche *f.*
counterpart /ˈkaʊntəpɑːt/ *n.* équivalent *m.*; (*person*) homologue *m.*/*f.*
counter-productive /kaʊntəprəˈdʌktɪv/ *a.* (*measure*) qui produit l'effet contraire.
countersign /ˈkaʊntəsaɪn/ *v.t.* contresigner.
countess /ˈkaʊntɪs/ *n.* comtesse *f.*
countless /ˈkaʊntlɪs/ *a.* innombrable.
countrified /ˈkʌntrɪfaɪd/ *a.* rustique.
country /ˈkʌntrɪ/ *n.* (*land, region*) pays *m.*; (*homeland*) patrie *f.*;

(*countryside*) campagne *f.* ~ **dance,** danse folklorique *f.*
countryman /ˈkʌntrɪmən/ *n.* (*pl.* **-men**) campagnard *m.*; (*fellow citizen*) compatriote *m.*
countryside /ˈkʌntrɪsaɪd/ *n.* campagne *f.*
county /ˈkaʊntɪ/ *n.* comté *m.*
coup /kuː/ *n.* (*pol.*) coup d'état *m.*
coupé /ˈkuːpeɪ/ *n.* (*car*) coupé *m.*
couple /ˈkʌpl/ *n.* (*people, animals*) couple *m.* —*v.t./i.* (s')accoupler. **a ~ (of),** (*two or three*) deux ou trois.
coupon /ˈkuːpɒn/ *n.* coupon *m.*
courage /ˈkʌrɪdʒ/ *n.* courage *m.* **~ous** /kəˈreɪdʒəs/ *a.* courageux.
courgette /kʊəˈʒet/ *n.* courgette *f.*
courier /ˈkʊrɪə(r)/ *n.* messag|er, -ère *m.*, *f.*; (*for tourists*) guide *m.*
course /kɔːs/ *n.* cours *m.*; (*series*) série *f.*; (*culin.*) plat *m.*; (*for golf*) terrain *m.*; (*fig.*) voie *f.* **in due ~,** en temps utile. **of ~,** bien sûr.
court /kɔːt/ *n.* cour *f.*; (*tennis*) court *m.* —*v.t.* faire la cour à; (*danger*) rechercher. **~ martial,** (*pl.* **courts martial**) conseil de guerre *m.* **~-martial** *v.t.* (*p.t.* **-martialled**) faire passer en conseil de guerre.
courteous /ˈkɜːtɪəs/ *a.* courtois.
courtesan /kɔːtɪˈzæn, *Amer.* ˈkɔːtɪzn/ *n.* (*old use*) courtisane *f.*
courtesy /ˈkɜːtəsɪ/ *n.* courtoisie *f.* **by ~ of,** avec la permission de.
courtier /ˈkɔːtɪə(r)/ *n.* (*old use*) courtisan *m.*
courtyard /ˈkɔːtjɑːd/ *n.* cour *f.*
cousin /ˈkʌzn/ *n.* cousin(e) *m.* (*f.*). **first ~,** cousin(e) germain(e) *m.* (*f.*).
cove /kəʊv/ *n.* anse *f.*, crique *f.*
covenant /ˈkʌvənənt/ *n.* convention *f.*
Coventry /ˈkɒvntrɪ/ *n.* **send to ~,** mettre en quarantaine.
cover /ˈkʌvə(r)/ *v.t.* couvrir. —*n.* (*for bed, book, etc.*) couverture *f.*; (*lid*) couvercle *m.*; (*for furniture*) housse *f.*; (*shelter*) abri *m.* **~ charge,** couvert *m.* **~ up,** cacher. **~-up** *n.* tentative pour cacher la vérité *f.* **take ~,** se mettre à l'abri. **~ing** *n.* enveloppe *f.* **~ing letter,** lettre *f.* (*jointe à un document*).
coverage /ˈkʌvərɪdʒ/ *n.* reportage *m.*
covet /ˈkʌvɪt/ *v.t.* convoiter.
cow /kaʊ/ *n.* vache *f.*
coward /ˈkaʊəd/ *n.* lâche *m.*/*f.* **~ly** *a.* lâche.
cowardice /ˈkaʊədɪs/ *n.* lâcheté *f.*
cowboy /ˈkaʊbɔɪ/ *n.* cow-boy *m.*
cower /ˈkaʊə(r)/ *v.i.* se recroqueviller (sous l'effet de la peur).
cowshed /ˈkaʊʃed/ *n.* étable *f.*
cox /kɒks/ *n.* barreur *m.* —*v.t.* barrer.
coxswain /ˈkɒksn/ *n.* barreur *m.*
coy /kɔɪ/ *a.* (**-er, -est**) (faussement) timide, qui fait le *or* la timide.
cozy /ˈkəʊzɪ/ *Amer.* = **cosy.**
crab /kræb/ *n.* crabe *m.* —*v.i.* (*p.t.* **crabbed**) rouspéter. **~-apple** *n.* pomme sauvage *f.*
crack /kræk/ *n.* fente *f.*; (*in glass*) fêlure *f.*; (*noise*) craquement *m.*; (*joke: sl.*) plaisanterie *f.* —*a.* (*fam.*) d'élite. —*v.t./i.* (*break partially*) (se) fêler; (*split*) (se) fendre; (*nut*) casser; (*joke*) raconter; (*problem*) résoudre. **~ down on,** (*fam.*) sévir contre. **~ up,** (*fam.*) craquer. **get ~ing,** (*fam.*) s'y mettre.
cracked /krækt/ *a.* (*sl.*) cinglé.
cracker /ˈkrækə(r)/ *n.* pétard *m.*; (*culin.*) biscuit (salé) *m.*
crackers /ˈkrækəz/ *a.* (*sl.*) cinglé.
crackle /ˈkrækl/ *v.i.* crépiter. —*n.* crépitement *m.*
crackpot /ˈkrækpɒt/ *n.* (*sl.*) cinglé(e) *m.* (*f.*).
cradle /ˈkreɪdl/ *n.* berceau *m.* —*v.t.* bercer.
craft[1] /krɑːft/ *n.* métier artisanal *m.*; (*technique*) art *m.*; (*cunning*) ruse *f.*

craft² /krɑːft/ *n. invar.* (*boat*) bateau *m.*
craftsman /ˈkrɑːftsmən/ *n.* (*pl.* **-men**) artisan *m.* **~ship** *n.* art *m.*
crafty /ˈkrɑːftɪ/ *a.* (**-ier, -iest**) rusé.
crag /kræg/ *n.* rocher à pic *m.* **~gy** *a.* à pic; (*face*) rude.
cram /kræm/ *v.t./i.* (*p.t.* **crammed**). **~ (for an exam),** bachoter. **~ into,** (*pack*) (s')entasser dans. **~ with,** (*fill*) bourrer de.
cramp /kræmp/ *n.* crampe *f.*
cramped /kræmpt/ *a.* à l'étroit.
cranberry /ˈkrænbərɪ/ *n.* canneberge *f.*
crane /kreɪn/ *n.* grue *f.* —*v.t.* (*neck*) tendre.
crank¹ /kræŋk/ *n.* (*techn.*) manivelle *f.*
crank² /kræŋk/ *n.* excentrique *m./f.* **~y** *a.* excentrique.
cranny /ˈkrænɪ/ *n.* fissure *f.*
craps /kræps/ *n.* **shoot ~,** (*Amer.*) jouer aux dés.
crash /kræʃ/ *n.* accident *m.*; (*noise*) fracas *m.*; (*of thunder*) coup *m.*; (*of firm*) faillite *f.* —*v.t./i.* avoir un accident (avec); (*of plane*) s'écraser; (*two vehicles*) se percuter. —*a.* (*course*) intensif. **~-helmet** *n.* casque (anti-choc) *m.* **~ into,** rentrer dans. **~-land** *v.i.* atterrir en catastrophe.
crass /kræs/ *a.* grossier.
crate /kreɪt/ *n.* cageot *m.*
crater /ˈkreɪtə(r)/ *n.* cratère *m.*
cravat /krəˈvæt/ *n.* foulard *m.*
crav|e /kreɪv/ *v.t./i.* **~ (for),** désirer ardemment. **~ing** *n.* envie irrésistible *f.*
crawl /krɔːl/ *v.i.* ramper; (*vehicle*) se traîner. —*n.* (*pace*) pas *m.*; (*swimming*) crawl *m.* **be ~ing with,** grouiller de.
crayfish /ˈkreɪfɪʃ/ *n. invar.* écrevisse *f.*
crayon /ˈkreɪən/ *n.* crayon *m.*
craze /kreɪz/ *n.* engouement *m.*
crazed /kreɪzd/ *a.* affolé.
craz|y /ˈkreɪzɪ/ *a.* (**-ier, -iest**) fou. **~y about,** (*person*) fou de; (*thing*) fana *or* fou de. **~iness** *n.* folie *f.* **~y paving,** dallage irrégulier *m.*
creak /kriːk/ *n.* grincement *m.* —*v.i.* grincer. **~y** *a.* grinçant.
cream /kriːm/ *n.* crème *f.* —*a.* crème *invar.* —*v.t.* écrémer. **~ cheese,** fromage frais *m.* **~y** *a.* crémeux.
crease /kriːs/ *n.* pli *m.* —*v.t./i.* (se) froisser.
creat|e /kriːˈeɪt/ *v.t.* créer. **~ion** /-ʃn/ *n.* création *f.* **~ive** *a.* créateur. **~or** *n.* créa|teur, -trice *m., f.*
creature /ˈkriːtʃə(r)/ *n.* créature *f.*
crèche /kreʃ/ *n.* crèche *f.*
credence /ˈkriːdns/ *n.* foi *f.*
credentials /krɪˈdenʃlz/ *n. pl.* (*identity*) pièces d'identité *f. pl.*; (*competence*) références *f. pl.*
credib|le /ˈkredəbl/ *a.* (*excuse etc.*) croyable, plausible. **~ility** /-ˈbɪlətɪ/ *n.* crédibilité *f.*
credit /ˈkredɪt/ *n.* crédit *m.*; (*honour*) honneur *m.* **in ~,** créditeur. **~s,** (*cinema*) générique *m.* —*a.* (*balance*) créditeur. —*v.t.* (*p.t.* **credited**) croire; (*comm.*) créditer. **~ card,** carte de crédit *f.* **~ s.o. with,** attribuer à qn. **~or** *n.* créanc|ier, -ière *m., f.*
creditable /ˈkredɪtəbl/ *a.* méritoire, honorable.
credulous /ˈkredjʊləs/ *a.* crédule.
creed /kriːd/ *n.* credo *m.*
creek /kriːk/ *n.* crique *f.* **up the ~,** (*sl.*) dans le pétrin.
creep /kriːp/ *v.i.* (*p.t.* **crept**) ramper; (*fig.*) se glisser. —*n.* (*person: sl.*) pauvre type *m.* **give s.o. the ~s,** faire frissonner qn. **~y** *a.* qui fait frissonner.
cremat|e /krɪˈmeɪt/ *v.t.* incinérer. **~ion** /-ʃn/ *n.* incinération *f.*
crematorium /kreməˈtɔːrɪəm/ *n.* (*pl.* **-ia**) crématorium *m.*

Creole /ˈkriːəʊl/ *n.* créole *m./f.*
crêpe /kreɪp/ *n.* crêpe *m.* **~ paper,** papier crêpon *m.*
crept /krept/ *see* **creep.**
crescendo /krɪˈʃendəʊ/ *n.* (*pl.* **-os**) crescendo *m.*
crescent /ˈkresnt/ *n.* croissant *m.*; (*fig.*) rue en demi-lune *f.*
cress /kres/ *n.* cresson *m.*
crest /krest/ *n.* crête *f.*; (*coat of arms*) armoiries *f. pl.*
Crete /kriːt/ *n.* Crète *f.*
cretin /ˈkretɪn, *Amer.* ˈkriːtn/ *n.* crétin(e) *m.* (*f.*). **~ous** *a.* crétin.
crevasse /krɪˈvæs/ *n.* crevasse *f.*
crevice /ˈkrevɪs/ *n.* fente *f.*
crew /kruː/ *n.* équipage *m.*; (*gang*) équipe *f.* **~ cut,** coupe en brosse *f.*
crib[1] /krɪb/ *n.* lit d'enfant *m.*
crib[2] /krɪb/ *v.t./i.* (*p.t.* **cribbed**) copier. —*n.* (*schol.*, *fam.*) traduction *f.*, aide-mémoire *m. invar.*
crick /krɪk/ *n.* (*in neck*) torticolis *m.*
cricket[1] /ˈkrɪkɪt/ *n.* (*sport*) cricket *m.* **~er** *n.* joueur de cricket *m.*
cricket[2] /ˈkrɪkɪt/ *n.* (*insect*) grillon *m.*
crime /kraɪm/ *n.* crime *m.*; (*minor*) délit *m.*; (*acts*) criminalité *f.*
criminal /ˈkrɪmɪnl/ *a.* & *n.* criminel(le) (*m.* (*f.*)).
crimp /krɪmp/ *v.t.* (*hair*) friser.
crimson /ˈkrɪmzn/ *a.* & *n.* cramoisi (*m.*).
cring|e /krɪndʒ/ *v.i.* reculer; (*fig.*) s'humilier. **~ing** *a.* servile.
crinkle /ˈkrɪŋkl/ *v.t./i.* (se) froisser. —*n.* pli *m.*
cripple /ˈkrɪpl/ *n.* infirme *m./f.* —*v.t.* estropier; (*fig.*) paralyser.
crisis /ˈkraɪsɪs/ *n.* (*pl.* **crises** /-siːz/) crise *f.*
crisp /krɪsp/ *a.* (**-er, -est**) (*culin.*) croquant; (*air*, *reply*) vif. **~s** *n. pl.* chips *m. pl.*
criss-cross /ˈkrɪskrɒs/ *a.* entrecroisé. —*v.t./i.* (s')entrecroiser.
criterion /kraɪˈtɪərɪən/ *n.* (*pl.* **-ia**) critère *m.*
critic /ˈkrɪtɪk/ *n.* critique *m.* **~al** *a.* critique. **~ally** *adv.* d'une manière critique; (*ill*) gravement.
criticism /ˈkrɪtɪsɪzəm/ *n.* critique *f.*
criticize /ˈkrɪtɪsaɪz/ *v.t./i.* critiquer.
croak /krəʊk/ *n.* coassement *m.* —*v.i.* coasser.
crochet /ˈkrəʊʃeɪ/ *n.* crochet *m.* —*v.t.* faire au crochet.
crock /krɒk/ *n.* (*person*: *fam.*) croulant *m.*; (*car*: *fam.*) guimbarde *f.*
crockery /ˈkrɒkərɪ/ *n.* vaisselle *f.*
crocodile /ˈkrɒkədaɪl/ *n.* crocodile *m.*
crocus /ˈkrəʊkəs/ *n.* (*pl.* **-uses**) crocus *m.*
crony /ˈkrəʊnɪ/ *n.* cop|ain, -ine *m.*, *f.*
crook /krʊk/ *n.* (*criminal*: *fam.*) escroc *m.*; (*stick*) houlette *f.*
crooked /ˈkrʊkɪd/ *a.* tordu; (*winding*) tortueux; (*askew*) de travers; (*dishonest*: *fig.*) malhonnête. **~ly** *adv.* de travers.
croon /kruːn/ *v.t./i.* chantonner.
crop /krɒp/ *n.* récolte *f.*; (*fig.*) quantité *f.* —*v.t.* (*p.t.* **cropped**) couper. —*v.i.* **~ up,** se présenter.
cropper /ˈkrɒpə(r)/ *n.* **come a ~,** (*sl.*) ramasser une bûche.
croquet /ˈkrəʊkeɪ/ *n.* croquet *m.*
croquette /krəʊˈket/ *n.* croquette *f.*
cross /krɒs/ *n.* croix *f.*; (*hybrid*) hybride *m.* —*v.t./i.* traverser; (*legs*, *animals*) croiser; (*cheque*) barrer; (*paths*) se croiser. —*a.* en colère, fâché (**with,** contre). **~ off** *or* **out,** rayer. **~ s.o.'s mind,** venir à l'esprit de qn. **talk at ~ purposes,** parler sans se comprendre. **~ly** *adv.* avec colère.
crossbar /ˈkrɒsbɑː(r)/ *n.* barre transversale *f.*
cross-examine /krɒsɪgˈzæmɪn/

v.t. faire subir un examen contradictoire à.

cross-eyed /'krɒsaɪd/ *a.* **be ~,** loucher.

crossfire /'krɒsfaɪə(r)/ *n.* feux croisés *m. pl.*

crossing /'krɒsɪŋ/ *n.* (*by boat*) traversée *f.*; (*on road*) passage clouté *m.*

cross-reference /krɒs'refrəns/ *n.* renvoi *m.*

crossroads /'krɒsrəʊdz/ *n.* carrefour *m.*

cross-section /krɒs'sekʃn/ *n.* coupe transversale *f.*; (*sample*: *fig.*) échantillon *m.*

crosswise /'krɒswaɪz/ *adv.* en travers.

crossword /'krɒswɜːd/ *n.* mots croisés *m. pl.*

crotch /krɒtʃ/ *n.* (*of garment*) entre-jambes *m. invar.*

crotchet /'krɒtʃɪt/ *n.* (*mus.*) noire *f.*

crotchety /'krɒtʃɪtɪ/ *a.* grincheux.

crouch /kraʊtʃ/ *v.i.* s'accroupir.

crow /krəʊ/ *n.* corbeau *m.* —*v.i.* (*of cock*) (*p.t.* **crew**) chanter; (*fig.*) jubiler. **as the ~ flies,** à vol d'oiseau.

crowbar /'krəʊbɑː(r)/ *n.* levier *m.*

crowd /kraʊd/ *n.* foule *f.* —*v.i.* affluer. —*v.t.* remplir. **~ into,** (s')entasser dans. **~ed** *a.* plein.

crown /kraʊn/ *n.* couronne *f.*; (*top part*) sommet *m.* —*v.t.* couronner. **C~ Court,** Cour d'assises *f.* **C~ prince,** prince héritier *m.*

crucial /'kruːʃl/ *a.* crucial.

crucifix /'kruːsɪfɪks/ *n.* crucifix *m.*

crucif|y /'kruːsɪfaɪ/ *v.t.* crucifier. **~ixion** /-'fɪkʃn/ *n.* crucifixion *f.*

crude /kruːd/ *a.* (**-er, -est**) (*raw*) brut; (*rough, vulgar*) grossier.

cruel /krʊəl/ *a.* (**crueller, cruellest**) cruel. **~ty** *n.* cruauté *f.*

cruet /'kruːɪt/ *n.* huilier *m.*

cruis|e /kruːz/ *n.* croisière *f.* —*v.i.* (*ship*) croiser; (*tourists*) faire une croisière; (*vehicle*) rouler. **~er** *n.* croiseur *m.* **~ing speed,** vitesse de croisière *f.*

crumb /krʌm/ *n.* miette *f.*

crumble /'krʌmbl/ *v.t./i.* (s')effriter; (*bread*) (s')émietter; (*collapse*) s'écrouler.

crummy /'krʌmɪ/ *a.* (**-ier, -iest**) (*sl.*) moche, minable.

crumpet /'krʌmpɪt/ *n.* (*culin.*) petite crêpe (grillée) *f.*

crumple /'krʌmpl/ *v.t./i.* (se) froisser.

crunch /krʌntʃ/ *v.t.* croquer. —*n.* (*event*) moment critique *m.*

crusade /kruː'seɪd/ *n.* croisade *f.* **~r** /-ə(r)/ *n.* (*knight*) croisé *m.*; (*fig.*) militant(e) *m.* (*f.*).

crush /krʌʃ/ *v.t.* écraser; (*clothes*) froisser. —*n.* (*crowd*) presse *f.* **a ~ on,** (*sl.*) le béguin pour. **orange ~,** orange pressée *f.*

crust /krʌst/ *n.* croûte *f.* **~y** *a.* croustillant.

crutch /krʌtʃ/ *n.* béquille *f.*; (*crotch*) entre-jambes *m. invar.*

crux /krʌks/ *n.* **the ~ of,** (*problem etc.*) le nœud de.

cry /kraɪ/ *n.* cri *m.* —*v.i.* (*weep*) pleurer; (*call out*) crier. **~-baby** *n.* pleurnicheu|r, -se *m., f.* **~ off,** abandonner.

crying /'kraɪɪŋ/ *a.* (*evil etc.*) flagrant. **a ~ shame,** une vraie honte.

crypt /krɪpt/ *n.* crypte *f.*

cryptic /'krɪptɪk/ *a.* énigmatique.

crystal /'krɪstl/ *n.* cristal *m.* **~lize** *v.t./i.* (se) cristalliser.

cub /kʌb/ *n.* petit *m.* **C~ (Scout),** louveteau *m.*

Cuba /'kjuːbə/ *n.* Cuba *m.* **~n** *a.* & *n.* cubain(e) (*m.* (*f.*)).

cubby-hole /'kʌbɪhəʊl/ *n.* cagibi *m.*

cub|e /kjuːb/ *n.* cube *m.* **~ic** *a.* cubique; (*metre etc.*) cube.

cubicle /'kjuːbɪkl/ *n.* (*in room, hospital, etc.*) box *m.*; (*at swimming-pool*) cabine *f.*

cuckoo /'kuku:/ *n.* coucou *m.*
cucumber /'kju:kʌmbə(r)/ *n.* concombre *m.*
cuddl|e /'kʌdl/ *v.t.* serrer dans ses bras. —*v.i.* **(kiss and) ~e,** s'embrasser. —*n.* caresse *f.* **~y** *a.* câlin, caressant.
cudgel /'kʌdʒl/ *n.* gourdin *m.*
cue[1] /kju:/ *n.* signal *m.*; (*theatre*) réplique *f.*
cue[2] /kju:/ *n.* (*billiards*) queue *f.*
cuff /kʌf/ *n.* manchette *f.* —*v.t.* gifler. **~-link** *n.* bouton de manchette *m.* **off the ~,** impromptu.
cul-de-sac /'kʌldəsæk/ *n.* (*pl.* **culs-de-sac**) impasse *f.*
culinary /'kʌlɪnərɪ/ *a.* culinaire.
cull /kʌl/ *v.t.* (*select*) choisir; (*kill*) abattre sélectivement.
culminat|e /'kʌlmɪneɪt/ *v.i.* **~e in,** se terminer par. **~ion** /-'neɪʃn/ *n.* point culminant *m.*
culprit /'kʌlprɪt/ *n.* coupable *m.*/*f.*
cult /kʌlt/ *n.* culte *m.*
cultivat|e /'kʌltɪveɪt/ *v.t.* cultiver. **~ion** /-'veɪʃn/ *n.* culture *f.*
cultural /'kʌltʃərəl/ *a.* culturel.
culture /'kʌltʃə(r)/ *n.* culture *f.* **~d** *a.* cultivé.
cumbersome /'kʌmbəsəm/ *a.* encombrant.
cumulative /'kju:mjʊlətɪv/ *a.* cumulatif.
cunning /'kʌnɪŋ/ *a.* rusé. —*n.* astuce *f.*, ruse *f.*
cup /kʌp/ *n.* tasse *f.*; (*prize*) coupe *f.* **C~ Final,** finale de la coupe *f.* **~-tie** *n.* match de coupe *m.*
cupboard /'kʌbəd/ *n.* placard *m.*, armoire *f.*
cupful /'kʌpfʊl/ *n.* tasse *f.*
Cupid /'kju:pɪd/ *n.* Cupidon *m.*
curable /'kjʊərəbl/ *a.* guérissable.
curate /'kjʊərət/ *n.* vicaire *m.*
curator /kjʊə'reɪtə(r)/ *n.* (*of museum*) conservateur *m.*
curb[1] /kɜ:b/ *n.* (*restraint*) frein *m.* —*v.t.* (*desires etc.*) refréner; (*price increase etc.*) freiner.
curb[2] /kɜ:b/ *n.* (*kerb*: *Amer.*) bord du trottoir *m.*
curdle /'kɜ:dl/ *v.t.*/*i.* (se) cailler.
curds /kɜ:dz/ *n. pl.* lait caillé *m.*
cure[1] /kjʊə(r)/ *v.t.* guérir; (*fig.*) éliminer. —*n.* (*recovery*) guérison *f.*; (*remedy*) remède *m.*
cure[2] /kjʊə(r)/ *v.t.* (*culin.*) fumer, saler.
curfew /'kɜ:fju:/ *n.* couvre-feu *m.*
curio /'kjʊərɪəʊ/ *n.* (*pl.* **-os**) curiosité *f.*, bibelot *m.*
curi|ous /'kjʊərɪəs/ *a.* curieux. **~osity** /-'ɒsətɪ/ *n.* curiosité *f.*
curl /kɜ:l/ *v.t.*/*i.* (*hair*) boucler. —*n.* boucle *f.* **~ up,** se pelotonner; (*shrivel*) se racornir.
curler /'kɜ:lə(r)/ *n.* bigoudi *m.*
curly /'kɜ:lɪ/ *a.* (**-ier, -iest**) bouclé.
currant /'kʌrənt/ *n.* raisin de Corinthe *m.*; (*berry*) groseille *f.*
currency /'kʌrənsɪ/ *n.* (*money*) monnaie *f.*; (*acceptance*) cours *m.*
current /'kʌrənt/ *a.* (*common*) courant; (*topical*) actuel; (*year etc.*) en cours. —*n.* courant *m.* **~ events,** actualité *f.* **~ly** *adv.* actuellement.
curriculum /kə'rɪkjʊləm/ *n.* (*pl.* **-la**) programme scolaire *m.*
curry[1] /'kʌrɪ/ *n.* curry *m.*, cari *m.*
curry[2] /'kʌrɪ/ *v.t.* **~ favour with,** chercher les bonnes grâces de.
curse /kɜ:s/ *n.* malédiction *f.*; (*oath*) juron *m.* —*v.t.* maudire. —*v.i.* (*swear*) jurer.
cursory /'kɜ:sərɪ/ *a.* (trop) rapide.
curt /kɜ:t/ *a.* brusque.
curtail /kɜ:'teɪl/ *v.t.* écourter, raccourcir; (*expenses etc.*) réduire.
curtain /'kɜ:tn/ *n.* rideau *m.*
curtsy /'kɜ:tsɪ/ *n.* révérence *f.* —*v.i.* faire une révérence.
curve /kɜ:v/ *n.* courbe *f.* —*v.t.*/*i.* (se) courber; (*of road*) tourner.
cushion /'kʊʃn/ *n.* coussin *m.* —*v.t.* (*a blow*) amortir; (*fig.*) protéger.
cushy /'kʊʃɪ/ *a.* (**-ier, -iest**) (*job etc.*: *fam.*) pépère.

custard /ˈkʌstəd/ *n.* crème anglaise *f.*; (*set*) crème renversée *f.*
custodian /kʌˈstəʊdɪən/ *n.* gardien(ne) *m.* (*f.*).
custody /ˈkʌstədɪ/ *n.* garde *f.*; (*jurid.*) détention préventive *f.*
custom /ˈkʌstəm/ *n.* coutume *f.*; (*patronage: comm.*) clientèle *f.* **~ary** *a.* d'usage.
customer /ˈkʌstəmə(r)/ *n.* client(e) *m.* (*f.*).
customs /ˈkʌstəmz/ *n. pl.* douane *f.* —*a.* douanier. **~ officer,** douanier *m.*
cut /kʌt/ *v.t./i.* (*p.t.* **cut,** *pres. p.* **cutting**) couper; (*hedge, jewel*) tailler; (*prices etc.*) réduire. —*n.* coupure *f.*; (*of clothes*) coupe *f.*; (*piece*) morceau *m.*; réduction *f.* **~ back** *or* **down (on),** réduire. **~-back** *n.* réduction *f.* **~ in,** (*auto.*) se rabattre. **~ off,** couper; (*fig.*) isoler. **~ out,** découper; (*leave out*) supprimer. **~-price** *a.* à prix réduit. **~ short,** (*visit*) écourter. **~ up,** couper; (*carve*) découper. **~ up about,** démoralisé par.
cute /kjuːt/ *a.* (**-er, -est**) (*fam.*) astucieux; (*Amer.*) mignon.
cuticle /ˈkjuːtɪkl/ *n.* petites peaux *f. pl.* (*de l'ongle*).
cutlery /ˈkʌtlərɪ/ *n.* couverts *m. pl.*
cutlet /ˈkʌtlɪt/ *n.* côtelette *f.*
cutting /ˈkʌtɪŋ/ *a.* cinglant. —*n.* (*from newspaper*) coupure *f.*; (*plant*) bouture *f.* **~ edge,** tranchant *m.*
cyanide /ˈsaɪənaɪd/ *n.* cyanure *m.*
cybernetics /saɪbəˈnetɪks/ *n.* cybernétique *f.*
cycl|e /ˈsaɪkl/ *n.* cycle *m.*; (*bicycle*) vélo *m.* —*v.i.* aller à vélo. **~ing** *n.* cyclisme *m.* **~ist** *n.* cycliste *m.*/*f.*
cyclic(al) /ˈsaɪklɪk(l)/ *a.* cyclique.
cyclone /ˈsaɪkləʊn/ *n.* cyclone *m.*
cylind|er /ˈsɪlɪndə(r)/ *n.* cylindre *m.* **~rical** /-ˈlɪndrɪkl/ *a.* cylindrique.
cymbal /ˈsɪmbl/ *n.* cymbale *f.*
cynic /ˈsɪnɪk/ *n.* cynique *m.*/*f.* **~al** *a.* cynique. **~ism** /-sɪzəm/ *n.* cynisme *m.*
cypress /ˈsaɪprəs/ *n.* cyprès *m.*
Cypr|us /ˈsaɪprəs/ *n.* Chypre *f.* **~iot** /ˈsɪprɪət/ *a.* & *n.* cypriote (*m.*/*f.*).
cyst /sɪst/ *n.* kyste *m.*
czar /zɑː(r)/ *n.* tsar *m.*
Czech /tʃek/ *a.* & *n.* tchèque (*m.*/*f.*).
Czechoslovak /tʃekəˈsləʊvæk/ *a.* & *n.* tchécoslovaque (*m.*/*f.*). **~ia** /-sləˈvækɪə/ *n.* Tchécoslovaquie *f.*

D

dab /dæb/ *v.t.* (*p.t.* **dabbed**) tamponner. —*n.* **a ~ of,** un petit coup de. **~ sth. on,** appliquer qch. à petits coups sur.
dabble /ˈdæbl/ *v.i.* **~ in,** se mêler un peu de. **~r** /-ə(r)/ *n.* amateur *m.*
dad /dæd/ *n.* (*fam.*) papa *m.* **~dy** *n.* (*children's use*) papa *m.*
daffodil /ˈdæfədɪl/ *n.* jonquille *f.*
daft /dɑːft/ *a.* (**-er, -est**) idiot.
dagger /ˈdægə(r)/ *n.* poignard *m.*
dahlia /ˈdeɪlɪə/ *n.* dahlia *m.*
daily /ˈdeɪlɪ/ *a.* quotidien. —*adv.* tous les jours. —*n.* (*newspaper*) quotidien *m.*; (*charwoman: fam.*) femme de ménage *f.*
dainty /ˈdeɪntɪ/ *a.* (**-ier, -iest**) délicat.
dairy /ˈdeərɪ/ *n.* (*on farm*) laiterie *f.*; (*shop*) crémerie *f.* —*a.* laitier.
daisy /ˈdeɪzɪ/ *n.* pâquerette *f.*
dale /deɪl/ *n.* vallée *f.*
dally /ˈdælɪ/ *v.i.* lanterner.
dam /dæm/ *n.* barrage *m.* —*v.t.* (*p.t.* **dammed**) endiguer.
damag|e /ˈdæmɪdʒ/ *n.* dégâts *m. pl.*, dommages *m. pl.*; (*harm: fig.*) préjudice *m.* **~es,** (*jurid.*) dommages et intérêts *m. pl.* —*v.t.* abîmer; (*fig.*) nuire à. **~ing** *a.* nuisible.

dame /deɪm/ *n.* (*old use*) dame *f.*; (*Amer., sl.*) fille *f.*
damn /dæm/ *v.t.* (*relig.*) damner; (*swear at*) maudire; (*condemn*: *fig.*) condamner. —*int.* zut, merde. —*n.* **not care a ~,** s'en moquer éperdument. —*a.* sacré. —*adv.* rudement. **~ation** /-ˈneɪʃn/ *n.* damnation *f.*
damp /dæmp/ *n.* humidité *f.* —*a.* (**-er, -est**) humide. —*v.t.* humecter; (*fig.*) refroidir. **~en** *v.t.* = **damp. ~ness** *n.* humidité *f.*
damsel /ˈdæmzl/ *n.* demoiselle *f.*
dance /dɑːns/ *v.t./i.* danser. —*n.* danse *f.*; (*gathering*) bal *m.* **~ hall,** dancing *m.*, salle de danse *f.* **~r** /-ə(r)/ *n.* danseu|r, -se *m., f.*
dandelion /ˈdændɪlaɪən/ *n.* pissenlit *m.*
dandruff /ˈdændrʌf/ *n.* pellicules *f. pl.*
dandy /ˈdændɪ/ *n.* dandy *m.*
Dane /deɪn/ *n.* Danois(e) *m.* (*f.*).
danger /ˈdeɪndʒə(r)/ *n.* danger *m.*; (*risk*) risque *m.* **be in ~ of,** risquer de. **~ous** *a.* dangereux.
dangle /ˈdæŋgl/ *v.t./i.* (se) balancer, (laisser) pendre.
Danish /ˈdeɪnɪʃ/ *a.* danois. —*n.* (*lang.*) danois *m.*
dank /dæŋk/ *a.* (**-er, -est**) humide et froid.
dapper /ˈdæpə(r)/ *a.* élégant.
dare /deə(r)/ *v.t.* **~ (to) do,** oser faire. **~ s.o. to do,** défier qn. de faire. —*n.* défi *m.* **I ~ say,** je suppose (**that,** que).
daredevil /ˈdeədevl/ *n.* casse-cou *m. invar.*
daring /ˈdeərɪŋ/ *a.* audacieux.
dark /dɑːk/ *a.* (**-er, -est**) obscur, sombre, noir; (*colour*) foncé, sombre; (*skin*) brun, foncé; (*gloomy*) sombre. —*n.* noir *m.*; (*nightfall*) tombée de la nuit *f.* **~ horse,** individu aux talents inconnus *m.* **~-room** *n.* chambre noire *f.* **in the ~,** (*fig.*) dans l'ignorance (**about,** de). **~ness** *n.* obscurité *f.*
darken /ˈdɑːkən/ *v.t./i.* (s')assombrir.
darling /ˈdɑːlɪŋ/ *a.* & *n.* chéri(e) (*m.* (*f.*)).
darn /dɑːn/ *v.t.* repriser.
dart /dɑːt/ *n.* fléchette *f.* **~s,** (*game*) fléchettes *f. pl.* —*v.i.* s'élancer.
dartboard /ˈdɑːtbɔːd/ *n.* cible *f.*
dash /dæʃ/ *v.i.* se précipiter. —*v.t.* jeter (avec violence); (*hopes*) briser. —*n.* ruée *f.*; (*stroke*) tiret *m.* **a ~ of,** un peu de. **~ off,** (*leave*) partir en vitesse.
dashboard ˈdæʃbɔːd/ *n.* tableau de bord *m.*
dashing /ˈdæʃɪŋ/ *a.* fringant.
data /ˈdeɪtə/ *n. pl.* données *f. pl.* **~ processing,** informatique *f.*
date[1] /deɪt/ *n.* date *f.*; (*meeting*: *fam.*) rendez-vous *m.* —*v.t./i.* dater; (*go out with*: *fam.*) sortir avec. **to ~,** à ce jour. **~d** /-ɪd/ *a.* démodé.
date[2] /deɪt/ *n.* (*fruit*) datte *f.*
daub /dɔːb/ *v.t.* barbouiller.
daughter /ˈdɔːtə(r)/ *n.* fille *f.* **~-in-law** *n.* (*pl.* **~s-in-law**) belle-fille *f.*
daunt /dɔːnt/ *v.t.* décourager.
dauntless /ˈdɔːntlɪs/ *a.* intrépide.
dawdle /ˈdɔːdl/ *v.i.* lambiner. **~r** /-ə(r)/ *n.* lambin(e) *m.* (*f.*).
dawn /dɔːn/ *n.* aube *f.* —*v.i.* poindre; (*fig.*) naître.
day /deɪ/ *n.* jour *m.*; (*whole day*) journée *f.*; (*period*) époque *f.* **~-break** *n.* point du jour *m.* **~-dream** *n.* rêverie *f.*; *v.i.* rêvasser. **the ~ before,** la veille. **the following** *or* **next ~,** le lendemain.
daylight /ˈdeɪlaɪt/ *n.* jour *m.*
daytime /ˈdeɪtaɪm/ *n.* jour *m.*, journée *f.*
daze /deɪz/ *v.t.* étourdir; (*with drugs*) hébéter. —*n.* **in a ~,** étourdi; hébété.

dazzle /ˈdæzl/ *v.t.* éblouir.
deacon /ˈdiːkən/ *n.* diacre *m.*
dead /ded/ *a.* mort; (*numb*) engourdi. —*adv.* complètement. —*n.* **in the ~ of,** au cœur de. **the ~,** les morts. **~ beat,** éreinté. **~ end,** impasse *f.* **~-pan** *a.* impassible. **in ~ centre,** au beau milieu. **stop ~,** s'arrêter pile. **the race was a ~ heat,** ils ont été classés ex aequo.
deaden /ˈdedn/ *v.t.* (*sound, blow*) amortir; (*pain*) calmer.
deadline /ˈdedlaɪn/ *n.* date limite *f.*
deadlock /ˈdedlɒk/ *n.* impasse *f.*
deadly /ˈdedlɪ/ *a.* (**-ier, -iest**) mortel; (*weapon*) meurtrier.
deaf /def/ *a.* (**-er, -est**) sourd. **~-aid** *n.* appareil acoustique *m.* **~ness** *n.* surdité *f.*
deafen /ˈdefn/ *v.t.* assourdir.
deal /diːl/ *v.t.* (*p.t.* **dealt**) donner; (*a blow*) porter. —*v.i.* (*trade*) commercer. —*n.* affaire *f.*; (*cards*) donne *f.* **a great** *or* **good ~,** beaucoup (**of,** de). **~ in,** faire le commerce de. **~ with,** (*handle, manage*) s'occuper de; (*be about*) traiter de. **~er** *n.* marchand(e) *m.* (*f.*).; (*agent*) concessionnaire *m./f.*
dealings /ˈdiːlɪŋz/ *n. pl.* relations *f. pl.*
dean /diːn/ *n.* doyen *m.*
dear /dɪə(r)/ *a.* (**-er, -est**) cher. —*n.* (**my**) **~,** mon cher, ma chère; (*darling*) (mon) chéri, (ma) chérie. —*adv.* cher. —*int.* **oh ~!,** oh mon Dieu! **~ly** *adv.* tendrement; (*pay*) cher.
dearth /dɜːθ/ *n.* pénurie *f.*
death /deθ/ *n.* mort *f.* **~ certificate,** acte de décès *m.* **~ duty,** droits de succession *m. pl.* **~ penalty,** peine de mort *f.* **it is a ~-trap,** (*place, vehicle*) il y a danger de mort. **~ly** *a.* de mort, mortel.
debar /dɪˈbɑː(r)/ *v.t.* (*p.t.* **debarred**) exclure.
debase /dɪˈbeɪs/ *v.t.* avilir.
debat|e /dɪˈbeɪt/ *n.* discussion *f.* —*v.t.* discuter. **~e whether,** se demander si. **~able** *a.* discutable.
debauch /dɪˈbɔːtʃ/ *v.t.* débaucher. **~ery** *n.* débauche *f.*
debilitate /dɪˈbɪlɪteɪt/ *v.t.* débiliter.
debility /dɪˈbɪlətɪ/ *n.* débilité *f.*
debit /ˈdebɪt/ *n.* débit *m.* **in ~,** débiteur. —*a.* (*balance*) débiteur. —*v.t.* (*p.t.* **debited**) débiter.
debris /ˈdeɪbriː/ *n.* débris *m. pl.*
debt /det/ *n.* dette *f.* **in ~,** endetté. **~or** *n.* débi|teur, -trice *m., f.*
debunk /diːˈbʌŋk/ *v.t.* (*fam.*) démythifier.
decade /ˈdekeɪd/ *n.* décennie *f.*
decaden|t /ˈdekədənt/ *a.* décadent. **~ce** *n.* décadence *f.*
decanter /dɪˈkæntə(r)/ *n.* carafe *f.*
decapitate /dɪˈkæpɪteɪt/ *v.t.* décapiter.
decay /dɪˈkeɪ/ *v.i.* se gâter, pourrir; (*fig.*) décliner. —*n.* pourriture *f.*; (*of tooth*) carie *f.*; (*fig.*) déclin *m.*
deceased /dɪˈsiːst/ *a.* décédé. —*n.* défunt(e) *m.* (*f.*).
deceit /dɪˈsiːt/ *n.* tromperie *f.* **~ful** *a.* trompeur. **~fully** *adv.* d'une manière trompeuse.
deceive /dɪˈsiːv/ *v.t.* tromper.
December /dɪˈsembə(r)/ *n.* décembre *m.*
decen|t /ˈdiːsnt/ *a.* décent, convenable; (*good*: *fam.*) (assez) bon; (*kind*: *fam.*) gentil. **~cy** *n.* décence *f.* **~tly** *adv.* décemment.
decentralize /diːˈsentrəlaɪz/ *v.t.* décentraliser.
decept|ive /dɪˈseptɪv/ *a.* trompeur. **~ion** /-pʃn/ *n.* tromperie *f.*
decibel /ˈdesɪbel/ *n.* décibel *m.*
decide /dɪˈsaɪd/ *v.t./i.* décider. **~ on,** se décider pour. **~ to do,** décider de faire. **~d** /-ɪd/ *a.* (*firm*) résolu; (*clear*) net. **~dly** /-ɪdlɪ/ *adv.* résolument; nettement.
decimal /ˈdesɪml/ *a.* décimal. —*n.* décimale *f.* **~ point,** virgule *f.*

decimate /ˈdesɪmeɪt/ *v.t.* décimer.
decipher /dɪˈsaɪfə(r)/ *v.t.* déchiffrer.
decision /dɪˈsɪʒn/ *n.* décision *f.*
decisive /dɪˈsaɪsɪv/ *a.* (*conclusive*) décisif; (*firm*) décidé. **~ly** *adv.* d'une façon décidée.
deck[1] /dek/ *n.* pont *m.*; (*of cards*: *Amer.*) jeu *m.* **~-chair** *n.* chaise longue *f.* **top ~,** (*of bus*) impériale *f.*
deck[2] /dek/ *v.t.* (*adorn*) orner.
declar|e /dɪˈkleə(r)/ *v.t.* déclarer. **~ation** /dekləˈreɪʃn/ *n.* déclaration *f.*
decline /dɪˈklaɪn/ *v.t./i.* refuser (poliment); (*deteriorate*) décliner; (*fall*) baisser. —*n.* déclin *m.*; baisse *f.*
decode /diːˈkəʊd/ *v.t.* décoder.
decompos|e /diːkəmˈpəʊz/ *v.t./i.* (se) décomposer. **~ition** /-ɒmpəˈzɪʃn/ *n.* décomposition *f.*
décor /ˈdeɪkɔː(r)/ *n.* décor *m.*
decorat|e /ˈdekəreɪt/ *v.t.* décorer; (*room*) tapisser. **~ion** /-ˈreɪʃn/ *n.* décoration *f.* **~ive** /-ətɪv/ *a.* décoratif.
decorator /ˈdekəreɪtə(r)/ *n.* peintre en bâtiment *m.* **(interior) ~,** décora|teur, -trice d'appartements *m.*, *f.*
decorum /dɪˈkɔːrəm/ *n.* décorum *m.*
decoy[1] /ˈdiːkɔɪ/ *n.* (*bird*) appeau *m.*; (*trap*) piège *m.*, leurre *m.*
decoy[2] /dɪˈkɔɪ/ *v.t.* attirer, appâter.
decrease /dɪˈkriːs/ *v.t./i.* diminuer. —*n.* /ˈdiːkriːs/ diminution *f.*
decree /dɪˈkriː/ *n.* (*pol.*, *relig.*) décret *m.*; (*jurid.*) jugement *m.* —*v.t.* (*p.t.* **decreed**) décréter.
decrepit /dɪˈkrepɪt/ *a.* (*building*) délabré; (*person*) décrépit.
decry /dɪˈkraɪ/ *v.t.* dénigrer.
dedicat|e /ˈdedɪkeɪt/ *v.t.* dédier. **~e o.s. to,** se consacrer à. **~ed** *a.* dévoué. **~ion** /-ˈkeɪʃn/ *n.* dévouement *m.*; (*in book*) dédicace *f.*
deduce /dɪˈdjuːs/ *v.t.* déduire.
deduct /dɪˈdʌkt/ *v.t.* déduire. **~ion** /-kʃn/ *n.* déduction *f.*
deed /diːd/ *n.* acte *m.*
deem /diːm/ *v.t.* juger.
deep /diːp/ *a.* (**-er, -est**) profond. —*adv.* profondément. **~ in thought,** absorbé dans ses pensées. **~ into the night,** tard dans la nuit. **~-freeze** *n.* congélateur *m.*; *v.t.* surgeler. **~ly** *adv.* profondément.
deepen /ˈdiːpən/ *v.t.* approfondir. —*v.i.* devenir plus profond; (*mystery*, *night*) s'épaissir.
deer /dɪə(r)/ *n. invar.* cerf *m.*
deface /dɪˈfeɪs/ *v.t.* dégrader.
defamation /defəˈmeɪʃn/ *n.* diffamation *f.*
default /dɪˈfɔːlt/ *v.i.* (*jurid*) faire défaut. —*n.* **by ~,** (*jurid.*) par défaut. **win by ~,** gagner par forfait.
defeat /dɪˈfiːt/ *v.t.* vaincre; (*thwart*) faire échouer. —*n.* défaite *f.*; (*of plan etc.*) échec *m.*
defect[1] /ˈdiːfekt/ *n.* défaut *m.* **~ive** /dɪˈfektɪv/ *a.* défectueux.
defect[2] /dɪˈfekt/ *v.i.* faire défection. **~ to,** passer à. **~or** *n.* transfuge *m.*/*f.*
defence /dɪˈfens/ *n.* défense *f.* **~less** *a.* sans défense.
defend /dɪˈfend/ *v.t.* défendre. **~ant** *n.* (*jurid.*) accusé(e) *m.* (*f.*).
defensive /dɪˈfensɪv/ *a.* défensif. —*n.* défensive *f.*
defer /dɪˈfɜː(r)/ *v.t.* (*p.t.* **deferred**) (*postpone*) différer, remettre.
deferen|ce /ˈdefərəns/ *n.* déférence *f.* **~tial** /-ˈrenʃl/ *a.* déférent.
defian|ce /dɪˈfaɪəns/ *n.* défi *m.* **in ~ce of,** au mépris de. **~t** *a.* de défi. **~tly** *adv.* d'un air de défi.
deficien|t /dɪˈfɪʃnt/ *a.* insuffisant. **be ~t in,** manquer de. **~cy** *n.* insuffisance *f.*; (*fault*) défaut *m.*
deficit /ˈdefɪsɪt/ *n.* déficit *m.*
defile /dɪˈfaɪl/ *v.t.* souiller.

define /dɪˈfaɪn/ *v.t.* définir.
definite /ˈdefɪnɪt/ *a.* précis; (*obvious*) net; (*firm*) catégorique; (*certain*) certain. **~ly** *adv.* certainement; (*clearly*) nettement.
definition /defɪˈnɪʃn/ *n.* définition *f.*
definitive /dɪˈfɪnətɪv/ *a.* définitif.
deflat|e /dɪˈfleɪt/ *v.t.* dégonfler. **~ion** /-ʃn/ *n.* dégonflement *m.*; (*comm.*) déflation *f.*
deflect /dɪˈflekt/ *v.t./i.* (faire) dévier.
deform /dɪˈfɔːm/ *v.t.* déformer. **~ed** *a.* difforme. **~ity** *n.* difformité *f.*
defraud /dɪˈfrɔːd/ *v.t.* (*state, customs*) frauder. **~ s.o. of sth.,** escroquer qch. à qn.
defray /dɪˈfreɪ/ *v.t.* payer.
defrost /diːˈfrɒst/ *v.t.* dégivrer.
deft /deft/ *a.* **(-er, -est)** adroit. **~ness** *n.* adresse *f.*
defunct /dɪˈfʌŋkt/ *a.* défunt.
defuse /diːˈfjuːz/ *v.t.* désamorcer.
defy /dɪˈfaɪ/ *v.t.* défier; (*attempts*) résister à.
degenerate[1] /dɪˈdʒenəreɪt/ *v.i.* dégénérer (**into,** en).
degenerate[2] /dɪˈdʒenərət/ *a.* & *n.* dégénéré(e) (*m.* (*f.*)).
degrad|e /dɪˈgreɪd/ *v.t.* dégrader. **~ation** /degrəˈdeɪʃn/ *n.* dégradation *f.*; (*state*) déchéance *f.*
degree /dɪˈgriː/ *n.* degré *m.*; (*univ.*) diplôme universitaire *m.*; (*Bachelor's degree*) licence *f.* **higher ~,** (*univ.*) maîtrise *f.*, doctorat *m.* **to such a ~ that,** à tel point que.
dehydrate /diːˈhaɪdreɪt/ *v.t./i.* (se) déshydrater.
de-ice /diːˈaɪs/ *v.t.* dégivrer.
deign /deɪn/ *v.t.* **~ to do,** daigner faire.
deity /ˈdiːɪtɪ/ *n.* divinité *f.*
deject|ed /dɪˈdʒektɪd/ *a.* abattu. **~ion** /-kʃn/ *n.* abattement *m.*
delay /dɪˈleɪ/ *v.t.* retarder. *—v.i.* tarder. *—n.* (*lateness, time overdue*) retard *m.*; (*waiting*) délai *m.*
delectable /dɪˈlektəbl/ *a.* délectable, très agréable.
delegate[1] /ˈdelɪgət/ *n.* délégué(e) *m.* (*f.*).
delegat|e[2] /ˈdelɪgeɪt/ *v.t.* déléguer. **~ion** /-ˈgeɪʃn/ *n.* délégation *f.*
delet|e /dɪˈliːt/ *v.t.* rayer. **~ion** /-ʃn/ *n.* rature *f.*
deliberate[1] /dɪˈlɪbərət/ *a.* délibéré; (*steps, manner*) mesuré. **~ly** *adv.* exprès, délibérément.
deliberat|e[2] /dɪˈlɪbəreɪt/ *v.i.* délibérer. *—v.t.* considérer. **~ion** /-ˈreɪʃn/ *n.* délibération *f.*
delica|te /ˈdelɪkət/ *a.* délicat. **~cy** *n.* délicatesse *f.*; (*food*) mets délicat *or* raffiné *m.*
delicatessen /delɪkəˈtesn/ *n.* épicerie fine *f.*, charcuterie *f.*
delicious /dɪˈlɪʃəs/ *a.* délicieux.
delight /dɪˈlaɪt/ *n.* grand plaisir *m.*, joie *f.*, délice *m.* (*f. in pl.*); (*thing*) délice *m.* (*f. in pl.*). *—v.t.* réjouir. *—v.i.* **~ in,** prendre plaisir à. **~ed** *a.* ravi. **~ful** *a.* charmant, très agréable.
delinquen|t /dɪˈlɪŋkwənt/ *a.* & *n.* délinquant(e) (*m.* (*f.*)). **~cy** *n.* délinquance *f.*
deliri|ous /dɪˈlɪrɪəs/ *a.* **be ~ous,** délirer. **~um** *n.* délire *m.*
deliver /dɪˈlɪvə(r)/ *v.t.* (*message*) remettre; (*goods*) livrer; (*letters*) distribuer; (*free*) délivrer; (*utter*) prononcer; (*med.*) accoucher; (*a blow*) porter. **~ance** *n.* délivrance *f.* **~y** *n.* livraison *f.*; distribution *f.*; accouchement *m.*
delta /ˈdeltə/ *n.* delta *m.*
delu|de /dɪˈluːd/ *v.t.* tromper. **~de o.s.,** se faire des illusions. **~sion** /-ʒn/ *n.* illusion *f.*
deluge /ˈdeljuːdʒ/ *n.* déluge *m.* *—v.t.* inonder (**with,** de).
de luxe /dəˈlʌks/ *a.* de luxe.
delve /delv/ *v.i.* fouiller.

demagogue /ˈdeməgɒg/ *n.* démagogue *m./f.*
demand /dɪˈmɑːnd/ *v.t.* exiger. —*n.* exigence *f.*; (*claim*) revendication *f.*; (*comm.*) demande *f.* **in ~,** recherché. **~ing** *a.* exigeant.
demarcation /diːmɑːˈkeɪʃn/ *n.* démarcation *f.*
demean /dɪˈmiːn/ *v.t.* **~ o.s.,** s'abaisser, s'avilir.
demeanour /dɪˈmiːnə(r)/ *n.* comportement *m.*
demented /dɪˈmentɪd/ *a.* dément.
demerara /deməˈreərə/ *n.* (*brown sugar*) cassonade *f.*
demise /dɪˈmaɪz/ *n.* décès *m.*
demo /ˈdeməʊ/ *n.* (*pl.* **-os**) (*demonstration: fam.*) manif *f.*
demobilize /diːˈməʊbəlaɪz/ *v.t.* démobiliser.
democracy /dɪˈmɒkrəsɪ/ *n.* démocratie *f.*
democrat /ˈdeməkræt/ *n.* démocrate *m./f.* **~ic** /-ˈkrætɪk/ *a.* démocratique.
demoli|sh /dɪˈmɒlɪʃ/ *v.t.* démolir. **~tion** /deməˈlɪʃn/ *n.* démolition *f.*
demon /ˈdiːmən/ *n.* démon *m.*
demonstrat|e /ˈdemənstreɪt/ *v.t.* démontrer. —*v.i.* (*pol.*) manifester. **~ion** /-ˈstreɪʃn/ *n.* démonstration *f.*; (*pol.*) manifestation *f.* **~or** *n.* manifestant(e) *m.* (*f.*).
demonstrative /dɪˈmɒnstrətɪv/ *a.* démonstratif.
demoralize /dɪˈmɒrəlaɪz/ *v.t.* démoraliser.
demote /dɪˈməʊt/ *v.t.* rétrograder.
demure /dɪˈmjʊə(r)/ *a.* modeste.
den /den/ *n.* antre *m.*
denial /dɪˈnaɪəl/ *n.* dénégation *f.*; (*statement*) démenti *m.*
denigrate /ˈdenɪgreɪt/ *v.t.* dénigrer.
denim /ˈdenɪm/ *n.* toile de coton *f.* **~s,** (*jeans*) blue-jeans *m. pl.*
Denmark /ˈdenmɑːk/ *n.* Danemark *m.*
denomination /dɪnɒmɪˈneɪʃn/ *n.* (*relig.*) confession *f.*; (*money*) valeur *f.*
denote /dɪˈnəʊt/ *v.t.* dénoter.
denounce /dɪˈnaʊns/ *v.t.* dénoncer.
dens|e /dens/ *a.* (**-er, -est**) dense; (*person*) obtus. **~ely** *adv.* (*packed etc.*) très. **~ity** *n.* densité *f.*
dent /dent/ *n.* bosse *f.* —*v.t.* cabosser. **there is a ~ in the car door,** la portière est cabossée.
dental /ˈdentl/ *a.* dentaire; (*surgeon*) dentiste.
dentist /ˈdentɪst/ *n.* dentiste *m./f.* **~ry** *n.* art dentaire *m.*
denture /ˈdentʃə(r)/ *n.* dentier *m.*
denude /dɪˈnjuːd/ *v.t.* dénuder.
denunciation /dɪnʌnsɪˈeɪʃn/ *n.* dénonciation *f.*
deny /dɪˈnaɪ/ *v.t.* nier (**that,** que); (*rumour*) démentir; (*disown*) renier; (*refuse*) refuser.
deodorant /diːˈəʊdərənt/ *n.* & *a.* déodorant (*m.*).
depart /dɪˈpɑːt/ *v.i.* partir. **~ from,** (*deviate*) s'écarter de.
department /dɪˈpɑːtmənt/ *n.* département *m.*; (*in shop*) rayon *m.*; (*in office*) service *m.* **~ store,** grand magasin *m.*
departure /dɪˈpɑːtʃə(r)/ *n.* départ *m.* **a ~ from,** (*custom, diet, etc.*) une entorse à.
depend /dɪˈpend/ *v.i.* dépendre (**on,** de). **~ on,** (*rely on*) compter sur. **~able** *a.* sûr. **~ence** *n.* dépendance *f.* **~ent** *a.* dépendant. **be ~ent on,** dépendre de.
dependant /dɪˈpendənt/ *n.* personne à charge *f.*
depict /dɪˈpɪkt/ *v.t.* (*describe*) dépeindre; (*in picture*) représenter.
deplete /dɪˈpliːt/ *v.t.* (*reduce*) réduire; (*use up*) épuiser.
deplor|e /dɪˈplɔː(r)/ *v.t.* déplorer. **~able** *a.* déplorable.
deploy /dɪˈplɔɪ/ *v.t.* déployer.
depopulate /diːˈpɒpjʊleɪt/ *v.t.* dépeupler.

deport /dɪˈpɔːt/ *v.t.* expulser. **~ation** /diːpɔːˈteɪʃn/ *n.* expulsion *f.*

depose /dɪˈpəʊz/ *v.t.* déposer.

deposit /dɪˈpɒzɪt/ *v.t.* (*p.t.* **deposited**) déposer. —*n.* dépôt *m.*; (*of payment*) acompte *m.*; (*against damage*) caution *f.*; (*on bottle etc.*) consigne *f.* **~or** *n.* (*comm.*) déposant(e) *m.* (*f.*), épargnant(e) *m.* (*f.*).

depot /ˈdepəʊ, *Amer.* ˈdiːpəʊ/ *n.* dépôt *m.*; (*Amer.*) gare (routière) *f.*

deprav|e /dɪˈpreɪv/ *v.t.* dépraver. **~ity** /-ˈprævətɪ/ *n.* dépravation *f.*

deprecate /ˈdeprəkeɪt/ *v.t.* désapprouver.

depreciat|e /dɪˈpriːʃɪeɪt/ *v.t./i.* (se) déprécier. **~ion** /-ˈeɪʃn/ *n.* dépréciation *f.*

depress /dɪˈpres/ *v.t.* (*sadden*) déprimer; (*push down*) appuyer sur. **become ~ed**, se décourager. **~ion** /-ʃn/ *n.* dépression *f.*

deprivation /deprɪˈveɪʃn/ *n.* privation *f.*

deprive /dɪˈpraɪv/ *v.t.* **~ of,** priver de. **~d** *a.* (*child etc.*) déshérité.

depth /depθ/ *n.* profondeur *f.* **be out of one's ~**, perdre pied; (*fig.*) être perdu. **in the ~s of,** au plus profond de.

deputation /depjʊˈteɪʃn/ *n.* députation *f.*

deputize /ˈdepjʊtaɪz/ *v.i.* assurer l'intérim (**for,** de). —*v.t.* (*Amer.*) déléguer, nommer.

deputy /ˈdepjʊtɪ/ *n.* suppléant(e) *m.* (*f.*). —*a.* adjoint. **~ chairman,** vice-président *m.*

derail /dɪˈreɪl/ *v.t.* faire dérailler. **be ~ed,** dérailler. **~ment** *n.* déraillement *m.*

deranged /dɪˈreɪndʒd/ *a.* (*mind*) dérangé.

derelict /ˈderəlɪkt/ *a.* abandonné.

deri|de /dɪˈraɪd/ *v.t.* railler. **~sion** /-ˈrɪʒn/ *n.* dérision *f.* **~sive** *a.* (*laughter, person*) railleur.

derisory /dɪˈraɪsərɪ/ *a.* (*scoffing*) railleur; (*offer etc.*) dérisoire.

derivative /dɪˈrɪvətɪv/ *a.* & *n.* dérivé (*m.*).

deriv|e /dɪˈraɪv/ *v.t.* **~e from,** tirer de. —*v.i.* **~e from,** dériver de. **~ation** /derɪˈveɪʃn/ *n.* dérivation *f.*

derogatory /dɪˈrɒgətrɪ/ *a.* (*word*) péjoratif; (*remark*) désobligeant.

derv /dɜːv/ *n.* gas-oil *m.*, gazole *m.*

descend /dɪˈsend/ *v.t./i.* descendre. **be ~ed from,** descendre de. **~ant** *n.* descendant(e) *m.* (*f.*).

descent /dɪˈsent/ *n.* descente *f.*; (*lineage*) origine *f.*

descri|be /dɪˈskraɪb/ *v.t.* décrire. **~ption** /-ˈskrɪpʃn/ *n.* description *f.* **~ptive** /-ˈskrɪptɪv/ *a.* descriptif.

desecrat|e /ˈdesɪkreɪt/ *v.t.* profaner. **~ion** /-ˈkreɪʃn/ *n.* profanation *f.*

desert[1] /ˈdezət/ *n.* désert *m.* —*a.* désertique. **~ island,** île déserte *f.*

desert[2] /dɪˈzɜːt/ *v.t./i.* déserter. **~ed** *a.* désert. **~er** *n.* déserteur *m.* **~ion** /-ʃn/ *n.* désertion *f.*

deserts /dɪˈzɜːts/ *n. pl.* **one's ~,** ce qu'on mérite.

deserv|e /dɪˈzɜːv/ *v.t.* mériter. **~edly** /-ɪdlɪ/ *adv.* à juste titre. **~ing** *a.* (*person*) méritant; (*action*) méritoire.

design /dɪˈzaɪn/ *n.* (*sketch*) dessin *m.*, plan *m.*; (*construction*) conception *f.*; (*pattern*) motif *m.*; (*style of dress*) modèle *m.*, (*aim*) dessein *m.* —*v.t.* (*sketch*) dessiner; (*devise, intend*) concevoir. **~er** *n.* dessina|teur, -trice *m.*, *f.*

designat|e /ˈdezɪgneɪt/ *v.t.* désigner. **~ion** /-ˈneɪʃn/ *n.* désignation *f.*

desir|e /dɪˈzaɪə(r)/ *n.* désir *m.* —*v.t.* désirer. **~able** *a.* désirable. **~ability** /-əˈbɪlətɪ/ *n.* attrait *m.*

desk /desk/ *n.* bureau *m.*; (*of pupil*) pupitre *m.*; (*in hotel*) réception *f.*; (*in bank*) caisse *f.*

desolat|e /'desələt/ *a.* (*place*) désolé; (*bleak*: *fig.*) morne. **~ion** /-'leɪʃn/ *n.* désolation *f.*

despair /dɪ'speə(r)/ *n.* désespoir *m.* —*v.i.* désespérer (**of,** de).

desperate /'despərət/ *a.* désespéré; (*criminal*) prêt à tout. **be ~ for,** avoir une envie folle de. **~ly** *adv.* désespérément.

desperation /despə'reɪʃn/ *n.* désespoir *m.*

despicable /dɪ'spɪkəbl/ *a.* méprisable, infâme.

despise /dɪ'spaɪz/ *v.t.* mépriser.

despite /dɪ'spaɪt/ *prep.* malgré.

desponden|t /dɪ'spɒndənt/ *a.* découragé. **~cy** *n.* découragement *m.*

despot /'despɒt/ *n.* despote *m.*

dessert /dɪ'zɜːt/ *n.* dessert *m.* **~-spoon** *n.* cuiller à dessert *f.*

destination /destɪ'neɪʃn/ *n.* destination *f.*

destine /'destɪn/ *v.t.* destiner.

destiny /'destɪnɪ/ *n.* destin *m.*

destitute /'destɪtjuːt/ *a.* indigent. **~ of,** dénué de.

destr|oy /dɪ'strɔɪ/ *v.t.* détruire; (*animal*) abattre. **~uction** *n.* destruction *f.* **~uctive** *a.* destructeur.

destroyer /dɪ'strɔɪə(r)/ *n.* (*warship*) contre-torpilleur *m.*

detach /dɪ'tætʃ/ *v.t.* détacher. **~able** *a.* détachable. **~ed** *a.* détaché. **~ed house,** maison individuelle *f.*

detachment /dɪ'tætʃmənt/ *n.* détachement *m.*

detail /'diːteɪl/ *n.* détail *m.* —*v.t.* exposer en détail; (*troops*) détacher. **~ed** *a.* détaillé.

detain /dɪ'teɪn/ *v.t.* retenir; (*in prison*) détenir. **~ee** /diːteɪ'niː/ *n.* détenu(e) *m.* (*f.*).

detect /dɪ'tekt/ *v.t.* découvrir; (*perceive*) distinguer; (*mine*) détecter. **~ion** /-kʃn/ *n.* découverte *f.*; détection *f.* **~or** *n.* détecteur *m.*

detective /dɪ'tektɪv/ *n.* policier *m.*; (*private*) détective *m.*

detention /dɪ'tenʃn/ *n.* détention *f.*; (*schol.*) retenue *f.*

deter /dɪ'tɜː(r)/ *v.t.* (*p.t.* **deterred**) dissuader (**from,** de).

detergent /dɪ'tɜːdʒənt/ *a.* & *n.* détergent (*m.*).

deteriorat|e /dɪ'tɪərɪəreɪt/ *v.i.* se détériorer. **~ion** /-'reɪʃn/ *n.* détérioration *f.*

determin|e /dɪ'tɜːmɪn/ *v.t.* déterminer. **~e to do,** décider de faire. **~ation** /-'neɪʃn/ *n.* détermination *f.* **~ed** *a.* déterminé. **~ed to do,** décidé à faire.

deterrent /dɪ'terənt, *Amer.* dɪ'tɜːrənt/ *n.* force de dissuasion *f.*

detest /dɪ'test/ *v.t.* détester. **~able** *a.* détestable.

detonat|e /'detəneɪt/ *v.t./i.* (faire) détoner. **~ion** /-'neɪʃn/ *n.* détonation *f.* **~or** *n.* détonateur *m.*

detour /'diːtʊə(r)/ *n.* détour *m.*

detract /dɪ'trækt/ *v.i.* **~ from,** (*lessen*) diminuer.

detriment /'detrɪmənt/ *n.* détriment *m.* **~al** /-'mentl/ *a.* préjudiciable (**to,** à).

devalu|e /diː'væljuː/ *v.t.* dévaluer. **~ation** /-jʊ'eɪʃn/ *n.* dévaluation *f.*

devastat|e /'devəsteɪt/ *v.t.* dévaster; (*overwhelm*: *fig.*) accabler. **~ing** *a.* accablant.

develop /dɪ'veləp/ *v.t./i.* (*p.t.* **developed**) (se) développer; (*contract*) contracter; (*build on, transform*) exploiter, aménager; (*appear*) se manifester. **~ into,** devenir. **~ing country,** pays en voie de développement *m.* **~ment** *n.* développement *m.* (**new**) **~ment,** fait nouveau *m.*

deviant /'diːvɪənt/ *a.* anormal. —*n.* (*psych.*) déviant *m.*

deviat|e /'diːvɪeɪt/ *v.i.* dévier. **~e from,** (*norm*) s'écarter de. **~ion** /-'eɪʃn/ *n.* déviation *f.*

device /dɪ'vaɪs/ *n.* appareil *m.*; (*scheme*) procédé *m.*
devil /'devl/ *n.* diable *m.* **~ish** *a.* diabolique.
devious /'diːvɪəs/ *a.* tortueux. **he is ~,** il a l'esprit tortueux.
devise /dɪ'vaɪz/ *v.t.* inventer; (*plan, means*) combiner, imaginer.
devoid /dɪ'vɔɪd/ *a.* **~ of,** dénué de.
devolution /diːvə'luːʃn/ *n.* décentralisation *f.*; (*of authority, power*) délégation *f.* **(to,** à).
devot|e /dɪ'vəʊt/ *v.t.* consacrer. **~ed** *a.* dévoué. **~edly** *adv.* avec dévouement. **~ion** /-ʃn/ *n.* dévouement *m.*; (*relig.*) dévotion *f.* **~ions,** (*relig.*) dévotions *f. pl.*
devotee /devə'tiː/ *n.* **~ of,** passionné(e) de *m.* (*f.*).
devour /dɪ'vaʊə(r)/ *v.t.* dévorer.
devout /dɪ'vaʊt/ *a.* (*person*) dévot; (*prayer*) fervent.
dew /djuː/ *n.* rosée *f.*
dexterity /dek'sterətɪ/ *n.* dextérité *f.*
diabet|es /daɪə'biːtiːz/ *n.* diabète *m.* **~ic** /-'betɪk/ *a.* & *n.* diabétique (*m.*/*f.*).
diabolical /daɪə'bɒlɪkl/ *a.* diabolique; (*bad: fam.*) atroce.
diagnose /'daɪəgnəʊz/ *v.t.* diagnostiquer.
diagnosis /daɪəg'nəʊsɪs/ *n.* (*pl.* **-oses**) /-siːz/) diagnostic *m.*
diagonal /daɪ'ægənl/ *a.* diagonal. —*n.* diagonale *f.* **~ly** *adv.* en diagonale.
diagram /'daɪəgræm/ *n.* schéma *m.*
dial /'daɪəl/ *n.* cadran *m.* —*v.t.* (*p.t.* **dialled**) (*number*) faire; (*person*) appeler. **~ling tone,** (*Amer.*) **~ tone,** tonalité *f.*
dialect /'daɪəlekt/ *n.* dialecte *m.*
dialogue /'daɪəlɒg/ *n.* dialogue *m.*
diameter /daɪ'æmɪtə(r)/ *n.* diamètre *m.*
diamond /'daɪəmənd/ *n.* diamant *m.*; (*shape*) losange *m.*; (*baseball*) terrain *m.* **~s,** (*cards*) carreau *m.*
diaper /'daɪəpə(r)/ *n.* (*baby's nappy: Amer.*) couche *f.*
diaphragm /'daɪəfræm/ *n.* diaphragme *m.*
diarrhoea /daɪə'rɪə/ *n.* diarrhée *f.*
diary /'daɪərɪ/ *n.* (*for appointments etc.*) agenda *m.*; (*for private thoughts*) journal intime *m.*
dice /daɪs/ *n. invar.* dé *m.* —*v.t.* (*food*) couper en dés.
dicey /'daɪsɪ/ *a.* (*fam.*) risqué.
dictat|e /dɪk'teɪt/ *v.t./i.* dicter. **~ion** /-ʃn/ *n.* dictée *f.*
dictates /'dɪkteɪts/ *n. pl.* préceptes *m. pl.*
dictator /dɪk'teɪtə(r)/ *n.* dictateur *m.* **~ship** *n.* dictature *f.*
dictatorial /dɪktə'tɔːrɪəl/ *a.* dictatorial.
diction /'dɪkʃn/ *n.* diction *f.*
dictionary /'dɪkʃənrɪ/ *n.* dictionnaire *m.*
did /dɪd/ *see* **do.**
diddle /'dɪdl/ *v.t.* (*sl.*) escroquer.
didn't /'dɪdnt/ = **did not.**
die[1] /daɪ/ *v.i.* (*pres. p.* **dying**) mourir. **~ down,** diminuer. **~ out,** disparaître. **be dying to,** mourir d'envie de.
die[2] /daɪ/ *n.* (*metal mould*) matrice *f.*, étampe *f.*
die-hard /'daɪhɑːd/ *n.* réactionnaire *m.*/*f.*
diesel /'diːzl/ *n.* diesel *m.* **~ engine,** moteur diesel *m.*
diet /'daɪət/ *n.* (*habitual food*) alimentation *f.*; (*restricted*) régime *m.* —*v.i.* suivre un régime.
diet|etic /daɪə'tetɪk/ *a.* diététique. **~ician** *n.* diététicien(ne) *m.* (*f.*).
differ /'dɪfə(r)/ *v.i.* différer; (*disagree*) ne pas être d'accord.
differen|t /'dɪfrənt/ *a.* différent. **~ce** *n.* différence *f.*; (*disagreement*) différend *m.* **~tly** *adv.* différemment **(from,** de).
differential /dɪfə'renʃl/ *a.* & *n.* différentiel (*m.*).
differentiate /dɪfə'renʃɪeɪt/ *v.t.*

différencier. —*v.i.* faire la différence (**between,** entre).

difficult /ˈdɪfɪkəlt/ *a.* difficile. **~y** *n.* difficulté *f.*

diffiden|t /ˈdɪfɪdənt/ *a.* qui manque d'assurance. **~ce** *n.* manque d'assurance *m.*

diffuse[1] /dɪˈfjuːs/ *a.* diffus.

diffus|e[2] /dɪˈfjuːz/ *v.t.* diffuser. **~ion** /-ʒn/ *n.* diffusion *f.*

dig /dɪg/ *v.t./i.* (*p.t.* **dug,** *pres. p.* **digging**) creuser; (*thrust*) enfoncer. —*n.* (*poke*) coup de coude *m.*; (*remark*) coup de patte *m.*; (*archaeol.*) fouilles *f. pl.* **~s,** (*lodgings*:*fam.*) chambre meublée *f.* **~ up,** déterrer.

digest[1] /dɪˈdʒest/ *v.t./i.* digérer. **~ible** *a.* digestible. **~ion** /-stʃən/ *n.* digestion *f.*

digest[2] /ˈdaɪdʒest/ *n.* sommaire *m.*

digestive /dɪˈdʒestɪv/ *a.* digestif.

digger /ˈdɪgə(r)/ *n.* (*techn.*) pelleteuse *f.*

digit /ˈdɪdʒɪt/ *n.* chiffre *m.*

digital /ˈdɪdʒɪtl/ *a.* (*clock*) numérique, à affichage numérique.

dignif|y /ˈdɪgnɪfaɪ/ *v.t.* donner de la dignité à. **~ied** *a.* digne.

dignitary /ˈdɪgnɪtərɪ/ *n.* dignitaire *m.*

dignity /ˈdɪgnɪtɪ/ *n.* dignité *f.*

digress /daɪˈgres/ *v.i.* faire une digression **~ from,** s'écarter de. **~ion** /-ʃn/ *n.* digression *f.*

dike /daɪk/ *n.* digue *f.*

dilapidated /dɪˈlæpɪdeɪtɪd/ *a.* délabré.

dilat|e /daɪˈleɪt/ *v.t./i.* (se) dilater. **~ion** /-ʃn/ *n.* dilatation *f.*

dilatory /ˈdɪlətərɪ/ *a.* dilatoire.

dilemma /dɪˈlemə/ *n.* dilemme *m.*

dilettante /dɪlɪˈtæntɪ/ *n.* dilettante *m./f.*

diligen|t /ˈdɪlɪdʒənt/ *a.* assidu. **~ce** *n.* assiduité *f.*

dilly-dally /ˈdɪlɪdælɪ/ *v.i.* (*fam.*) lanterner.

dilute /daɪˈljuːt/ *v.t.* diluer.

dim /dɪm/ *a.* (**dimmer, dimmest**) (*weak*) faible; (*dark*) sombre; (*indistinct*) vague; (*fam.*) stupide. —*v.t./i.* (*p.t.* **dimmed**) (*light*) (s')atténuer. **~ly** *adv.* (*shine*) faiblement; (*remember*) vaguement. **~ness** *n.* faiblesse *f.*; (*of room etc.*) obscurité *f.*

dime /daɪm/ *n.* (*in USA, Canada*) pièce de dix cents *f.*

dimension /daɪˈmenʃn/ *n.* dimension *f.*

diminish /dɪˈmɪnɪʃ/ *v.t./i.* diminuer.

diminutive /dɪˈmɪnjʊtɪv/ *a.* minuscule. —*n.* diminutif *m.*

dimple /ˈdɪmpl/ *n.* fossette *f.*

din /dɪn/ *n.* vacarme *m.*

dine /daɪn/ *v.i.* dîner. **~r** /-ə(r)/ *n.* dîneu|r, -se *m., f.*; (*rail.*) wagon-restaurant *m.*; (*Amer.*) restaurant à service rapide *m.*

dinghy /ˈdɪŋgɪ/ *n.* canot *m.*; (*inflatable*) canot pneumatique *m.*

ding|y /ˈdɪndʒɪ/ *a.* (**-ier, -iest**) miteux, minable. **~iness** *n.* aspect miteux *or* minable *m.*

dining-room /ˈdaɪnɪŋrʊm/ *n.* salle à manger *f.*

dinner /ˈdɪnə(r)/ *n.* (*evening meal*) dîner *m.*; (*lunch*) déjeuner *m.* **~-jacket** *n.* smoking *m.*

dinosaur /ˈdaɪnəsɔː(r)/ *n.* dinosaure *m.*

dint /dɪnt/ *n.* **by ~ of,** à force de.

diocese /ˈdaɪəsɪs/ *n.* diocèse *m.*

dip /dɪp/ *v.t./i.* (*p.t.* **dipped**) plonger. —*n.* (*slope*) déclivité *f.*; (*in sea*) bain rapide *m.* **~ into,** (*book*) feuilleter; (*savings*) puiser dans. **~ one's headlights,** se mettre en code.

diphtheria /dɪfˈθɪərɪə/ *n.* diphtérie *f.*

diphthong /ˈdɪfθɒŋ/ *n.* diphtongue *f.*

diploma /dɪˈpləʊmə/ *n.* diplôme *m.*

diplomacy /dɪˈpləʊməsɪ/ *n.* diplomatie *f.*

diplomat /ˈdɪpləmæt/ *n.* diplomate *m.*/*f.* **~ic** /-ˈmætɪk/ *a.* (*pol.*) diplomatique; (*person*: *fig.*) diplomate.

dire /daɪə(r)/ *a.* (**-er, -est**) affreux; (*need, poverty*) extrême.

direct /dɪˈrekt/ *a.* direct. —*adv.* directement. —*v.t.* diriger; (*letter, remark*) adresser; (*a play*) mettre en scène. **~ s.o. to,** indiquer à qn. le chemin de. **~ness** *n.* franchise *f.*

direction /dɪˈrekʃn/ *n.* direction *f.*; (*theatre*) mise en scène *f.* **~s,** indications *f. pl.* **~s for use,** mode d'emploi *m.*

directly /dɪˈrektlɪ/ *adv.* directement; (*at once*) tout de suite. —*conj.* (*fam.*) dès que.

director /dɪˈrektə(r)/ *n.* direc|teur, -trice *m., f.*; (*theatre*) metteur en scène *m.*

directory /dɪˈrektərɪ/ *n.* (*phone book*) annuaire *m.*

dirt /dɜːt/ *n.* saleté *f.* **~ cheap,** (*sl.*) très bon marché *invar.* **~-track** *n.* (*sport*) cendrée *f.*

dirty /ˈdɜːtɪ/ *a.* (**-ier, -iest**) sale; (*word*) grossier. —*v.t.*/*i.* (se) salir.

disability /dɪsəˈbɪlətɪ/ *n.* infirmité *f.*

disable /dɪsˈeɪbl/ *v.t.* rendre infirme. **~d** *a.* infirme.

disadvantage /dɪsədˈvɑːntɪdʒ/ *n.* désavantage *m.* **~d** *a.* déshérité.

disagree /dɪsəˈgriː/ *v.i.* ne pas être d'accord (**with,** avec). **~ with s.o.,** (*food, climate*) ne pas convenir à qn. **~ment** *n.* désaccord *m.*; (*quarrel*) différend *m.*

disagreeable /dɪsəˈgriːəbl/ *a.* désagréable.

disappear /dɪsəˈpɪə(r)/ *v.i.* disparaître. **~ance** *n.* disparition *f.*

disappoint /dɪsəˈpɔɪnt/ *v.t.* décevoir. **~ment** *n.* déception *f.*

disapprov|e /dɪsəˈpruːv/ *v.i.* **~e (of),** désapprouver. **~al** *n.* désapprobation *f.*

disarm /dɪsˈɑːm/ *v.t.*/*i.* désarmer. **~ament** *n.* désarmement *m.*

disarray /dɪsəˈreɪ/ *n.* désordre *m.*

disast|er /dɪˈzɑːstə(r)/ *n.* désastre *m.* **~rous** *a.* désastreux.

disband /dɪsˈbænd/ *v.t.*/*i.* (se) disperser.

disbelief /dɪsbɪˈliːf/ *n.* incrédulité *f.*

disc /dɪsk/ *n.* disque *m.* **~ jockey,** disc-jockey *m.*, animateur *m.*

discard /dɪˈskɑːd/ *v.t.* se débarrasser de; (*beliefs etc.*) abandonner.

discern /dɪˈsɜːn/ *v.t.* discerner. **~ible** *a.* perceptible. **~ing** *a.* perspicace.

discharge[1] /dɪsˈtʃɑːdʒ/ *v.t.* (*unload*) décharger; (*liquid*) déverser; (*duty*) remplir; (*dismiss*) renvoyer; (*prisoner*) libérer. —*v.i.* (*of pus*) s'écouler.

discharge[2] /ˈdɪstʃɑːdʒ/ *n.* (*of pus*) écoulement *m.*; (*dismissal*) renvoi *m.*

disciple /dɪˈsaɪpl/ *n.* disciple *m.*

disciplinarian /dɪsəplɪˈneərɪən/ *n.* personne qui sait régner la discipline *f.*

disciplin|e /ˈdɪsɪplɪn/ *n.* discipline *f.* —*v.t.* discipliner; (*punish*) punir. **~ary** *a.* disciplinaire.

disclaim /dɪsˈkleɪm/ *v.t.* désavouer. **~er** *n.* démenti *m.*

disclos|e /dɪsˈkləʊz/ *v.t.* révéler. **~ure** /-ʒə(r)/ *n.* révélation *f.*

disco /ˈdɪskəʊ/ *n.* (*pl.* **-os**) (*club*: *fam.*) discothèque *f.*, disco *m.*

discol|our /dɪsˈkʌlə(r)/ *v.t.*/*i.* (se) décolorer. **~oration** /-ˈreɪʃn/ *n.* décoloration *f.*

discomfort /dɪsˈkʌmfət/ *n.* gêne *f.*

disconcert /dɪskənˈsɜːt/ *v.t.* déconcerter.

disconnect /dɪskəˈnekt/ *v.t.* détacher; (*unplug*) débrancher; (*cut off*) couper.

discontent /dɪskənˈtent/ *n.* mécontentement *m.* **~ed** *a.* mécontent.

discontinue /dɪskənˈtɪnjuː/ *v.t.* interrompre, cesser.

discord /ˈdɪskɔːd/ *n.* discorde *f.*; (*mus.*) dissonance *f.* **~ant** /-ˈskɔːdənt/ *a.* discordant.
discothèque /ˈdɪskətek/ *n.* discothèque *f.*
discount[1] /ˈdɪskaʊnt/ *n.* rabais *m.*
discount[2] /dɪsˈkaʊnt/ *v.t.* ne pas tenir compte de.
discourage /dɪˈskʌrɪdʒ/ *v.t* décourager.
discourse /ˈdɪskɔːs/ *n.* discours *m.*
discourteous /dɪsˈkɜːtɪəs/ *a.* impoli, peu courtois.
discover /dɪˈskʌvə(r)/ *v.t.* découvrir. **~y** *n.* découverte *f.*
discredit /dɪsˈkredɪt/ *v.t.* (*p.t.* **discredited**) discréditer. —*n.* discrédit *m.*
discreet /dɪˈskriːt/ *a.* discret. **~ly** *adv.* discrètement.
discrepancy /dɪˈskrepənsɪ/ *n.* contradiction *f.*, incohérence *f.*
discretion /dɪˈskreʃn/ *n.* discrétion *f.*
discriminat|e /dɪˈskrɪmɪneɪt/ *v.t./i.* distinguer. **~e against,** établir une discrimination contre. **~ing** *a.* (*person*) qui a du discernement. **~ion** /-ˈneɪʃn/ *n.* discernement *m.*; (*bias*) discrimination *f.*
discus /ˈdɪskəs/ *n.* disque *m.*
discuss /dɪˈskʌs/ *v.t.* (*talk about*) discuter de; (*argue about, examine critically*) discuter. **~ion** /-ʃn/ *n.* discussion *f.*
disdain /dɪsˈdeɪn/ *n.* dédain *m.* **~ful** *a.* dédaigneux.
disease /dɪˈziːz/ *n.* maladie *f.* **~d** *a.* malade.
disembark /dɪsɪmˈbɑːk/ *v.t./i.* débarquer.
disembodied /dɪsɪmˈbɒdɪd/ *a.* désincarné.
disenchant /dɪsɪnˈtʃɑːnt/ *v.t.* désenchanter. **~ment** *n.* désenchantement *m.*
disengage /dɪsɪnˈgeɪdʒ/ *v.t.* dégager. **~ment** *n.* dégagement *m.*
disentangle /dɪsɪnˈtæŋgl/ *v.t.* démêler.
disfavour /dɪsˈfeɪvə(r)/ *n.* défaveur *f.*
disfigure /dɪsˈfɪgə(r)/ *v.t.* défigurer.
disgrace /dɪsˈgreɪs/ *n.* (*shame*) honte *f.*; (*disfavour*) disgrâce *f.* —*v.t.* déshonorer. **~d** *a.* (*in disfavour*) disgracié. **~ful** *a.* honteux.
disgruntled /dɪsˈgrʌntld/ *a.* mécontent.
disguise /dɪsˈgaɪz/ *v.t.* déguiser. —*n.* déguisement *m.* **in ~,** déguisé.
disgust /dɪsˈgʌst/ *n.* dégoût *m.* —*v.t.* dégoûter. **~ing** *a.* dégoûtant.
dish /dɪʃ/ *n.* plat *m.* —*v.t.* **~ out,** (*fam.*) distribuer. **~ up,** servir. **the ~es,** (*crockery*) la vaisselle.
dishcloth /ˈdɪʃklɒθ/ *n.* lavette *f.*; (*for drying*) torchon *m.*
dishearten /dɪsˈhɑːtn/ *v.t.* décourager.
dishevelled /dɪˈʃevld/ *a.* échevelé.
dishonest /dɪsˈɒnɪst/ *a.* malhonnête. **~y** *n.* malhonnêteté *f.*
dishonour /dɪsˈɒnə(r)/ *n.* déshonneur *m.* —*v.t.* déshonorer. **~able** *a.* déshonorant. **~ably** *adv.* avec déshonneur.
dishwasher /ˈdɪʃwɒʃə(r)/ *n.* lave-vaisselle *m. invar.*
disillusion /dɪsɪˈluːʒn/ *v.t.* désillusionner. **~ment** *n.* désillusion *f.*
disincentive /dɪsɪnˈsentɪv/ *n.* **be a ~ to,** décourager.
disinclined /dɪsɪnˈklaɪnd/ *a.* **~ to,** peu disposé à.
disinfect /dɪsɪnˈfekt/ *v.t.* désinfecter. **~ant** *n.* désinfectant *m.*
disinherit /dɪsɪnˈherɪt/ *v.t.* déshériter.
disintegrate /dɪsˈɪntɪgreɪt/ *v.t./i.* (se) désintégrer.
disinterested /dɪsˈɪntrəstɪd/ *a.* désintéressé.

disjointed /dɪs'dʒɔɪntɪd/ *a.* (*talk*) décousu.
disk /dɪsk/ *n.* = **disc.**
dislike /dɪs'laɪk/ *n.* aversion *f.* —*v.t.* ne pas aimer.
dislocat|e /'dɪsləkeɪt/ *v.t.* (*limb*) disloquer. **~ion** /-'keɪʃn/ *n.* dislocation *f.*
dislodge /dɪs'lɒdʒ/ *v.t.* (*move*) déplacer; (*drive out*) déloger.
disloyal /dɪs'lɔɪəl/ *a.* déloyal. **~ty** *n.* déloyauté *f.*
dismal /'dɪzməl/ *a.* morne, triste.
dismantle /dɪs'mæntl/ *v.t.* démonter, défaire.
dismay /dɪs'meɪ/ *n.* consternation *f.* —*v.t.* consterner.
dismiss /dɪs'mɪs/ *v.t.* renvoyer; (*from mind*) écarter. **~al** *n.* renvoi *m.*
dismount /dɪs'maʊnt/ *v.i.* descendre, mettre pied à terre.
disobedien|t /dɪsə'biːdɪənt/ *a.* désobéissant. **~ce** *n.* désobéissance *f.*
disobey /dɪsə'beɪ/ *v.t.* désobéir à. —*v.i.* désobéir.
disorder /dɪs'ɔːdə(r)/ *n.* désordre *m.*; (*ailment*) trouble(s) *m.* (*pl.*). **~ly** *a.* désordonné.
disorganize /dɪs'ɔːgənaɪz/ *v.t.* désorganiser.
disorientate /dɪs'ɔːrɪənteɪt/ *v.t.* désorienter.
disown /dɪs'əʊn/ *v.t.* renier.
disparaging /dɪ'spærɪdʒɪŋ/ *a.* désobligeant. **~ly** *adv.* de façon désobligeante.
disparity /dɪ'spærətɪ/ *n.* disparité *f.*, écart *m.*
dispassionate /dɪ'spæʃənət/ *a.* impartial; (*unemotional*) calme.
dispatch /dɪ'spætʃ/ *v.t.* (*send, complete*) expédier; (*troops*) envoyer. —*n.* expédition *f.*; envoi *m.*; (*report*) dépêche *f.* **~-rider** *n.* estafette *f.*
dispel /dɪ'spel/ *v.t.* (*p.t.* **dispelled**) dissiper.
dispensary /dɪ'spensərɪ/ *n.* pharmacie *f.*, officine *f.*
dispense /dɪ'spens/ *v.t.* distribuer; (*medicine*) préparer. —*v.i.* **~ with,** se passer de. **~r** /-ə(r)/ *n.* (*container*) distributeur *m.*
dispers|e /dɪ'spɜːs/ *v.t./i.* (se) disperser. **~al** *n.* dispersion *f.*
dispirited /dɪ'spɪrɪtɪd/ *a.* découragé, abattu.
displace /dɪs'pleɪs/ *v.t.* déplacer.
display /dɪ'spleɪ/ *v.t.* montrer, exposer; (*feelings*) manifester. —*n.* exposition *f.*; manifestation *f.*; (*comm.*) étalage *m.*; (*of computer*) visuel *m.*
displeas|e /dɪs'pliːz/ *v.t.* déplaire à. **~ed with,** mécontent de. **~ure** /-'pleʒə(r)/ *n.* mécontentement *m.*
disposable /dɪ'spəʊzəbl/ *a.* à jeter.
dispos|e /dɪ'spəʊz/ *v.t.* disposer. —*v.i.* **~e of,** se débarrasser de. **well ~ed to,** bien disposé envers. **~al** *n.* (*of waste*) évacuation *f.* **at s.o.'s ~al,** à la disposition de qn.
disposition /dɪspə'zɪʃn/ *n.* disposition *f.*; (*character*) naturel *m.*
disproportionate /dɪsprə'pɔːʃənət/ *a.* disproportionné.
disprove /dɪs'pruːv/ *v.t.* réfuter.
dispute /dɪ'spjuːt/ *v.t.* contester. —*n.* discussion *f.*; (*pol.*) conflit *m.* **in ~,** contesté.
disqualif|y /dɪs'kwɒlɪfaɪ/ *v.t.* rendre inapte; (*sport*) disqualifier. **~y from driving,** retirer le permis à. **~ication** /-ɪ'keɪʃn/ *n.* disqualification *f.*
disquiet /dɪs'kwaɪət/ *n.* inquiétude *f.* **~ing** *a.* inquiétant.
disregard /dɪsrɪ'gɑːd/ *v.t.* ne pas tenir compte de. —*n.* indifférence *f.* (**for,** à).
disrepair /dɪsrɪ'peə(r)/ *n.* mauvais état *m.*, délabrement *m.*
disreputable /dɪs'repjʊtəbl/ *a.* peu recommendable.
disrepute /dɪsrɪ'pjuːt/ *n.* discrédit *m.*

disrespect /dɪsrɪ'spekt/ *n.* manque de respect *m.* **~ful** *a.* irrespectueux.

disrupt /dɪs'rʌpt/ *v.t.* (*disturb, break up*) perturber; (*plans*) déranger. **~ion** /-pʃn/ *n.* perturbation *f.* **~ive** *a.* perturbateur.

dissatisf|ied /dɪs'sætɪsfaɪd/ *a.* mécontent. **~action** /dɪsætɪs'fækʃn/ *n.* mécontentement *m.*

dissect /dɪ'sekt/ *v.t.* disséquer. **~ion** /-kʃn/ *n.* dissection *f.*

disseminate /dɪ'semɪneɪt/ *v.t.* disséminer.

dissent /dɪ'sent/ *v.i.* différer (**from,** de). —*n.* dissentiment *m.*

dissertation /dɪsə'teɪʃn/ *n.* (*univ.*) mémoire *m.*

disservice /dɪs'sɜːvɪs/ *n.* mauvais service *m.*

dissident /'dɪsɪdənt/ *a.* & *n.* dissident(e) (*m.* (*f.*)).

dissimilar /dɪ'sɪmɪlə(r)/ *a.* dissemblable, différent.

dissipate /'dɪsɪpeɪt/ *v.t./i.* se dissiper; (*efforts*) gaspiller. **~d** /-ɪd/ *a.* (*person*) débauché.

dissociate /dɪ'səʊʃɪeɪt/ *v.t.* dissocier. **~ o.s. from,** se désolidariser de.

dissolute /'dɪsəluːt/ *a.* dissolu.

dissolution /dɪsə'luːʃn/ *n.* dissolution *f.*

dissolve /dɪ'zɒlv/ *v.t./i.* (se) dissoudre.

dissuade /dɪ'sweɪd/ *v.t.* dissuader.

distance /'dɪstəns/ *n.* distance *f.* **from a ~,** de loin. **in the ~,** au loin.

distant /'dɪstənt/ *a.* éloigné, lointain; (*relative*) éloigné; (*aloof*) distant.

distaste /dɪs'teɪst/ *n.* dégoût *m.* **~ful** *a.* désagréable.

distemper /dɪ'stempə(r)/ *n.* (*paint*) badigeon *m.*; (*animal disease*) maladie *f.* —*v.t.* badigeonner.

distend /dɪ'stend/ *v.t./i.* (se) distendre.

distil /dɪ'stɪl/ *v.t.* (*p.t.* **distilled**) distiller. **~lation** /-'leɪʃn/ *n.* distillation *f.*

distillery /dɪ'stɪlərɪ/ *n.* distillerie *f.*

distinct /dɪ'stɪŋkt/ *a.* distinct; (*marked*) net. **~ion** /-kʃn/ *n.* distinction *f.*; (*in exam*) mention très bien *f.* **~ive** *a.* distinctif. **~ly** *adv.* (*see*) distinctement; (*forbid*) expressément; (*markedly*) nettement.

distinguish /dɪ'stɪŋgwɪʃ/ *v.t./i.* distinguer. **~ed** *a.* distingué.

distort /dɪ'stɔːt/ *v.t.* déformer. **~ion** /-ʃn/ *n.* distorsion *f.*; (*of facts*) déformation *f.*

distract /dɪ'strækt/ *v.t.* distraire. **~ed** *a.* (*distraught*) éperdu. **~ing** *a.* gênant. **~ion** /-kʃn/ *n.* (*lack of attention, entertainment*) distraction *f.*

distraught /dɪ'strɔːt/ *a.* éperdu.

distress /dɪ'stres/ *n.* douleur *f.*; (*poverty, danger*) détresse *f.* —*v.t.* peiner. **~ing** *a.* pénible.

distribut|e /dɪ'strɪbjuːt/ *v.t.* distribuer. **~ion** /-'bjuːʃn/ *n.* distribution *f.* **~or** *n.* distributeur *m.*

district /'dɪstrɪkt/ *n.* région *f.*; (*of town*) quartier *m.*

distrust /dɪs'trʌst/ *n.* méfiance *f.* —*v.t.* se méfier de.

disturb /dɪ'stɜːb/ *v.t.* déranger; (*alarm, worry*) troubler. **~ance** *n.* dérangement *m.* (**of,** de); (*noise*) tapage *m.* **~ances** *n. pl.* (*pol.*) troubles *m. pl.* **~ed** *a.* troublé. **~ing** *a.* troublant.

disused /dɪs'juːzd/ *a.* désaffecté.

ditch /dɪtʃ/ *n.* fossé *m.* —*v.t.* (*sl.*) abandonner.

dither /'dɪðə(r)/ *v.i.* hésiter.

ditto /'dɪtəʊ/ *adv.* idem.

divan /dɪ'væn/ *n.* divan *m.*

div|e /daɪv/ *v.i.* plonger; (*rush*) se précipiter. —*n.* plongeon *m.*; (*of plane*) piqué *m.*; (*place: sl.*) bouge *m.* **~er** *n.* plongeu|r, -se *m., f.*

~ing-board *n.* plongeoir *m.* **~ing-suit** *n.* scaphandre *m.*
diverge /daɪˈvɜːdʒ/ *v.i.* diverger.
divergent /daɪˈvɜːdʒənt/ *a.* divergent.
diverse /daɪˈvɜːs/ *a.* divers.
diversify /daɪˈvɜːsɪfaɪ/ *v.t.* diversifier.
diversity /daɪˈvɜːsətɪ/ *n.* diversité *f.*
diver|t /daɪˈvɜːt/ *v.t.* détourner; (*traffic*) dévier. **~sion** /-ʃn/ *n.* détournement *m.*; (*distraction*) diversion *f.*; (*of traffic*) déviation *f.*
divest /daɪˈvest/ *v.t.* **~ of,** (*strip of*) priver de, déposséder de.
divide /dɪˈvaɪd/ *v.t./i.* (se) diviser.
dividend /ˈdɪvɪdend/ *n.* dividende *m.*
divine /dɪˈvaɪn/ *a.* divin.
divinity /dɪˈvɪnətɪ/ *n.* divinité *f.*
division /dɪˈvɪʒn/ *n.* division *f.*
divorce /dɪˈvɔːs/ *n.* divorce *m.* (**from,** d'avec). *—v.t./i.* divorcer (d'avec). **~d** *a.* divorcé.
divorcee /dɪvɔːˈsiː, *Amer.* dɪvɔːˈseɪ/ *n.* divorcé(e) *m.* (*f.*).
divulge /daɪˈvʌldʒ/ *v.t.* divulguer.
DIY *abbr.* **do-it-yourself.**
dizz|y /ˈdɪzɪ/ *a.* (**-ier, -iest**) vertigineux. **be** *or* **feel ~y,** avoir le vertige. **~iness** *n.* vertige *m.*
do /duː/ *v.t./i.* (*3 sing. present tense* **does**; *p.t.* **did**; *p.p.*, **done**) faire; (*progress, be suitable*) aller; (*be enough*) suffire; (*swindle*: *sl.*) avoir. **well done!,** bravo! **well done,** (*culin.*) bien cuit. **done for,** (*fam.*) fichu. *—v. aux.* **~ you see?,** voyez-vous? **I ~ not smoke,** je ne fume pas. **don't you?, doesn't he?,** *etc.*, n'est-ce pas? *—n.* (*pl.* **dos** *or* **do's**) soirée *f.*, fête *f.* **~ away with,** supprimer. **~ in,** (*sl.*) tuer. **~-it-yourself** *n.* bricolage *m.*; *a.* (*shop, book*) de bricolage. **~ out,** (*clean*) nettoyer. **~ up,** (*fasten*) fermer; (*house*) refaire. **~ with,** (*want, need*) aimer bien avoir. **~ without,** se passer de.
docile /ˈdəʊsaɪl/ *a.* docile.
dock[1] /dɒk/ *n.* dock *m.* *—v.t./i.* (se) mettre à quai. **~er** *n.* docker *m.*
dock[2] /dɒk/ *n.* (*jurid.*) banc des accusés *m.*
dock[3] /dɒk/ *v.t.* (*money*) retrancher.
dockyard /ˈdɒkjɑːd/ *n.* chantier naval *m.*
doctor /ˈdɒktə(r)/ *n.* médecin *m.*, docteur *m.*; (*univ.*) docteur *m.* *—v.t.* (*cat*) châtrer; (*fig.*) altérer.
doctorate /ˈdɒktərət/ *n.* doctorat *m.*
doctrine /ˈdɒktrɪn/ *n.* doctrine *f.*
document /ˈdɒkjʊmənt/ *n.* document *m.* **~ary** /-ˈmentrɪ/ *a.* & *n.* documentaire (*m.*).
doddering /ˈdɒdərɪŋ/ *a.* gâteux.
dodge /dɒdʒ/ *v.t.* esquiver. *—v.i.* faire un saut de côté. *—n.* (*fam.*) truc *m.*
dodgems /ˈdɒdʒəmz/ *n. pl.* autos tamponneuses *f. pl.*
dodgy /ˈdɒdʒɪ/ *a.* (**-ier, -iest**) (*fam.*) épineux, délicat.
doe /dəʊ/ *n.* (*deer*) biche *f.*
does /dʌz/ *see* **do.**
doesn't /ˈdʌznt/ = **does not.**
dog /dɒg/ *n.* chien *m.* *—v.t.* (*p.t.* **dogged**) poursuivre. **~-collar** *n.* (*fam.*) (faux) col d'ecclésiastique *m.* **~-eared** *a.* écorné.
dogged /ˈdɒgɪd/ *a.* obstiné.
dogma /ˈdɒgmə/ *n.* dogme *m.* **~tic** /-ˈmætɪk/ *a.* dogmatique.
dogsbody /ˈdɒgzbɒdɪ/ *n.* factotum *m.*, bonne à tout faire *f.*
doily /ˈdɔɪlɪ/ *n.* napperon *m.*
doings /ˈduːɪŋz/ *n. pl.* (*fam.*) activités *f. pl.*, occupations *f. pl.*
doldrums /ˈdɒldrəmz/ *n. pl.* **be in the ~,** (*person*) avoir le cafard.
dole /dəʊl/ *v.t.* **~ out,** distribuer. *—n.* (*fam.*) indemnité de chômage *f.* **on the ~,** (*fam.*) au chômage.
doleful /ˈdəʊlfl/ *a.* triste, morne.

doll /dɒl/ *n.* poupée *f.* —*v.t.* **~ up,** (*fam.*) bichonner.

dollar /ˈdɒlə(r)/ *n.* dollar *m.*

dollop /ˈdɒləp/ *n.* (*of food etc.*: *fam.*) gros morceau *m.*

dolphin /ˈdɒlfɪn/ *n.* dauphin *m.*

domain /dəˈmeɪn/ *n.* domaine *m.*

dome /dəʊm/ *n.* dôme *m.*

domestic /dəˈmestɪk/ *a.* familial; (*trade, flights, etc.*) intérieur; (*animal*) domestique. **~ science,** arts ménagers *m. pl.* **~ated** *a.* (*animal*) domestiqué.

domesticity /dɒmeˈstɪsətɪ/ *n.* vie de famille *f.*

dominant /ˈdɒmɪnənt/ *a.* dominant.

dominat|e /ˈdɒmɪneɪt/ *v.t./i.* dominer. **~ion** /-ˈneɪʃn/ *n.* domination *f.*

domineer /dɒmɪˈnɪə(r)/ *v.i.* être dominateur *or* autoritaire.

dominion /dəˈmɪnjən/ *n.* (*British pol.*) dominion *m.*

domino /ˈdɒmɪnəʊ/ *n.* (*pl.* **-oes**) domino *m.* **~es,** (*game*) dominos *m. pl.*

don[1] /dɒn/ *v.t.* (*p.t.* **donned**) revêtir, endosser.

don[2] /dɒn/ *n.* professeur d'université *m.*

donat|e /dəʊˈneɪt/ *v.t.* faire don de. **~ion** /-ʃn/ *n.* don *m.*

done /dʌn/ *see* **do.**

donkey /ˈdɒŋkɪ/ *n.* âne *m.* **~-work** *n.* travail pénible et ingrat *m.*

donor /ˈdəʊnə(r)/ *n.* dona|teur, -trice *m., f.*; (*of blood*) donneu|r, -se *m., f.*

don't /dəʊnt/ = **do not.**

doodle /ˈduːdl/ *v.i.* griffonner.

doom /duːm/ *n.* (*ruin*) ruine *f.*; (*fate*) destin *m.* —*v.t.* **be ~ed to,** être destiné *or* condamné à. **~ed (to failure),** voué à l'échec.

door /dɔː(r)/ *n.* porte *f.*; (*of vehicle*) portière *f.*, porte *f.*

doorman /ˈdɔːmən/ *n.* (*pl.* **-men**) portier *m.*

doormat /ˈdɔːmæt/ *n.* paillasson *m.*

doorstep /ˈdɔːstep/ *n.* pas de (la) porte *m.*, seuil *m.*

doorway /ˈdɔːweɪ/ *n.* porte *f.*

dope /dəʊp/ *n.* (*fam.*) drogue *f.*; (*idiot*: *sl.*) imbécile *m./f.* —*v.t.* doper. **~y** *a.* (*foolish*: *sl.*) imbécile.

dormant /ˈdɔːmənt/ *a.* en sommeil.

dormitory /ˈdɔːmɪtrɪ, *Amer.* ˈdɔːmɪtɔːrɪ/ *n.* dortoir *m.*; (*univ., Amer.*) résidence *f.*

dormouse /ˈdɔːmaʊs/ *n.* (*pl.* **-mice**) loir *m.*

dos|e /dəʊs/ *n.* dose *f.* **~age** *n.* dose *f.*; (*on label*) posologie *f.*

doss /dɒs/ *v.i.* (*sl.*) roupiller. **~-house** *n.* asile de nuit *m.*

dot /dɒt/ *n.* point *m.* **on the ~,** (*fam.*) à l'heure pile.

dote /dəʊt/ *v.i.* **~ on,** être gaga de.

dotted /ˈdɒtɪd/ *a.* (*fabric*) à pois. **~ line,** ligne en pointillés *f.* **~ with,** parsemé de.

dotty /ˈdɒtɪ/ *a.* (**-ier, -iest**) (*fam.*) cinglé, dingue.

double /ˈdʌbl/ *a.* double; (*room, bed*) pour deux personnes. —*adv.* deux fois. —*n.* double *m.* **~s,** (*tennis*) double *m.* —*v.t./i.* doubler; (*fold*) plier en deux. **at or *on* the ~,** au pas de course. **~-bass** *n.* (*mus.*) contrebasse *f.* **~-breasted** *a.* croisé. **~ chin,** double menton *m.* **~-cross** *v.t.* tromper. **~-dealing** *n.* double jeu *m.* **~-decker** *n.* autobus à impériale *m.* **~ Dutch,** baragouin *m.* **doubly** *adv.* doublement.

doubt /daʊt/ *n.* doute *m.* —*v.t.* douter de. **~ if *or* that,** douter que. **~ful** *a.*, incertain, douteux; (*person*) qui a des doutes. **~less** *adv.* sans doute.

dough /dəʊ/ *n.* pâte *f.*; (*money*: *sl.*) fric *m.*

doughnut /ˈdəʊnʌt/ *n.* beignet *m.*

douse /daʊs/ *v.t.* arroser; (*lumière*) éteindre.

dove /dʌv/ *n.* colombe *f.*

Dover /ˈdəʊvə(r)/ *n.* Douvres *m./f.*

dowdy /ˈdaʊdɪ/ *a.* (**-ier, -iest**) (*clothes*) sans chic, monotone.

down[1] /daʊn/ *n.* (*fluff*) duvet *m.*

down[2] /daʊn/ *adv.* en bas; (*of sun*) couché; (*lower*) plus bas; *—prep.* en bas de; (*along*) le long de. *—v.t.* (*knock down, shoot down*) abattre; (*drink*) vider. **come** *or* **go ~,** descendre. **~-and-out** *n.* clochard(e) *m.* (*f.*) **~-hearted** *a.* découragé. **~ payment,** acompte *m.* **~-to-earth** *a.* terre-à-terre *invar.* **~ under,** aux antipodes. **~ with,** à bas.

downcast /ˈdaʊnkɑːst/ *a.* démoralisé.

downfall /ˈdaʊnfɔːl/ *n.* chute *f.*

downgrade /daʊnˈgreɪd/ *v.t.* déclasser.

downhill /daʊnˈhɪl/ *adv.* **go ~,** descendre.

downpour /ˈdaʊnpɔː(r)/ *n.* grosse averse *f.*

downright /ˈdaʊnraɪt/ *a.* (*utter*) véritable; (*honest*) franc. *—adv.* carrément.

downs /daʊnz/ *n. pl.* région de collines *f.*

downstairs /daʊnˈsteəz/ *adv.* en bas. *—a.* d'en bas.

downstream /ˈdaʊnstriːm/ *adv.* en aval.

downtown /ˈdaʊntaʊn/ *a.* (*Amer.*) du centre de la ville. **~ Boston**/*etc.*, le centre de Boston/*etc.*

downtrodden /ˈdaʊntrɒdn/ *a.* opprimé.

downward /ˈdaʊnwəd/ *a.* & *adv.*, **~s** *adv.* vers le bas.

dowry /ˈdaʊərɪ/ *n.* dot *f.*

doze /dəʊz/ *v.i.* sommeiller. **~ off,** s'assoupir. *—n.* somme *m.*

dozen /ˈdʌzn/ *n.* douzaine *f.* **~s of,** (*fam.*) des dizaines de.

Dr *abbr.* (*Doctor*) Docteur.

drab /dræb/ *a.* terne.

draft[1] /drɑːft/ *n.* (*outline*) brouillon *m.*; (*comm.*) traite *f.* *—v.t.* faire le brouillon de; (*draw up*) rédiger. **the ~,** (*mil., Amer.*) la conscription.

draft[2] /drɑːft/ *n.* (*Amer.*) = **draught.**

drag /dræg/ *v.t./i.* (*p.t.* **dragged**) traîner; (*river*) draguer; (*pull away*) arracher. *—n.* (*task: fam.*) corvée *f.*; (*person: fam.*) raseu|r, -se *m., f.*; (*clothes: sl.*) travesti *m.*

dragon /ˈdrægən/ *n.* dragon *m.*

dragon-fly /ˈdrægənflaɪ/ *n.* libellule *f.*

drain /dreɪn/ *v.t.* (*land*) drainer; (*vegetables*) égoutter; (*tank, glass*) vider; (*use up*) épuiser. **~ (off),** (*liquid*) faire écouler. *—v.i.* **~ (off),** (*of liquid*) s'écouler. *—n.* (*sewer*) égout *m.* **~(-pipe),** tuyau d'écoulement *m.* **be a ~ on,** pomper. **~ing-board** *n.* égouttoir *m.*

drama /ˈdrɑːmə/ *n.* art dramatique *m.*, théâtre *m.*; (*play, event*) drame *m.* **~tic** /drəˈmætɪk/ *a.* dramatique. **~tist** /ˈdræmətɪst/ *n.* dramaturge *m.* **~tize** /ˈdræmətaɪz/ *v.t.* adapter pour la scène; (*fig.*) dramatiser.

drank /dræŋk/ *see* **drink.**

drape /dreɪp/ *v.t.* draper. **~s** *n. pl.* (*Amer.*) rideaux *m. pl.*

drastic /ˈdræstɪk/ *a.* sévère.

draught /drɑːft/ *n.* courant d'air *m.* **~s,** (*game*) dames *f. pl.* **~ beer,** bière (à la) pression *f.* **~y** *a.* plein de courants d'air.

draughtsman /ˈdrɑːftsmən/ *n.* (*pl.* **-men**) dessina|teur, -trice industriel(le) *m., f.*

draw /drɔː/ *v.t.* (*p.t.* **drew,** *p.p.* **drawn**) (*pull*) tirer; (*attract*) attirer; (*pass*) passer; (*picture*) dessiner; (*line*) tracer. *—v.i.* dessiner; (*sport*) faire match nul; (*come, move*) venir. *—n.* (*sport*) match nul *m.*; (*in lottery*) tirage au sort *m.* **~ back,** (*recoil*) reculer.

~ in, (*days*) diminuer. **~ near,** (s')approcher (**to,** de). **~ out,** (*money*) retirer. **~ up** *v.i.* (*stop*) s'arrêter; *v.t.* (*document*) dresser; (*chair*) approcher.
drawback /'drɔːbæk/ *n.* inconvénient *m.*
drawbridge /'drɔːbrɪdʒ/ *n.* pont-levis *m.*
drawer /drɔː(r)/ *n.* tiroir *m.*
drawers /drɔːz/ *n. pl.* culotte *f.*
drawing /'drɔːɪŋ/ *n.* dessin *m.* **~-pin** *n.* punaise *f.* **~-room** *n.* salon *m.*
drawl /drɔːl/ *n.* voix traînante *f.*
drawn /drɔːn/ *see* **draw.** —*a.* (*features*) tiré; (*match*) nul.
dread /dred/ *n.* terreur *f.*, crainte *f.* —*v.t.* redouter.
dreadful /'dredfl/ *a.* épouvantable, affreux. **~ly** *adv.* terriblement.
dream /driːm/ *n.* rêve *m.* —*v.t./i.* (*p.t.* **dreamed** *or* **dreamt**) rêver. —*a.* (*ideal*) de ses rêves. **~ up,** imaginer. **~er** *n.* rêveu|r, -se *m.*, *f.* **~y** *a.* rêveur.
drear|y /'drɪərɪ/ *a.* (**-ier, -iest**) triste; (*boring*) monotone. **~iness** *n.* tristesse *f.*; monotonie *f.*
dredge /dredʒ/ *n.* drague *f.* —*v.t./i.* draguer. **~r** /-ə(r)/ *n.* dragueur *m.*
dregs /dregz/ *n. pl.* lie *f.*
drench /drentʃ/ *v.t.* tremper.
dress /dres/ *n.* robe *f.*; (*clothing*) tenue *f.* —*v.t./i.* (s')habiller; (*food*) assaisonner; (*wound*) panser. **~ circle,** premier balcon *m.* **~ up as,** se déguiser en. **get ~ed,** s'habiller.
dresser /'dresə(r)/ *n.* buffet *m.*
dressing /'dresɪŋ/ *n.* (*sauce*) assaisonnement *m.*; (*bandage*) pansement *m.* **~-gown** *n.* robe de chambre *f.* **~-room** *n.* (*sport*) vestiaire *m.*; (*theatre*) loge *f.* **~-table** *n.* coiffeuse *f.*
dressmak|er /'dresmeɪkə(r)/ *n.* couturière *f.* **~ing** *n.* couture *f.*
dressy /'dresɪ/ *a.* (**-ier, -iest**) chic *invar.*
drew /druː/ *see* **draw.**
dribble /'drɪbl/ *v.i.* couler goutte à goutte; (*person*) baver; (*football*) dribbler.
dribs and drabs /drɪbzn'dræbz/ *n. pl.* petites quantités *f. pl.*
dried /draɪd/ *a.* (*fruit etc.*) sec.
drier /'draɪə(r)/ *n.* séchoir *m.*
drift /drɪft/ *v.i.* aller à la dérive; (*pile up*) s'amonceler. —*n.* dérive *f.*; amoncellement *m.*; (*of events*) tournure *f.*; (*meaning*) sens *m.* **~ towards,** glisser vers. **~er** *n.* personne sans but dans la vie *f.*
driftwood /'drɪftwʊd/ *n.* bois flotté *m.*
drill /drɪl/ *n.* (*tool*) perceuse *f.*; (*training*) exercice *m.*; (*procedure*: *fam.*) marche à suivre *f.* (**pneumatic**) **~,** marteau pneumatique *m.* —*v.t.* percer; (*train*) entraîner. —*v.i.* être à l'exercice.
drily /'draɪlɪ/ *adv.* sèchement.
drink /drɪŋk/ *v.t./i.* (*p.t.* **drank,** *p.p.* **drunk**) boire. —*n.* (*liquid*) boisson *f.*; (*glass of alcohol*) verre *m.* **a ~ of water,** un verre d'eau. **~able** *a.* (*not unhealthy*) potable; (*palatable*) buvable. **~er** *n.* buveu|r, -se *m.*, *f.* **~ing water,** eau potable *f.*
drip /drɪp/ *v.i.* (*p.t.* **dripped**) (dé)goutter; (*washing*) s'égoutter. —*n.* goutte *f.*; (*person*: *sl.*) lavette *f.* **~-dry** *v.t.* laisser égoutter; *a.* sans repassage.
dripping /'drɪpɪŋ/ *n.* (*Amer.* **~s**) graisse de rôti *f.*
drive /draɪv/ *v.t.* (*p.t.* **drove,** *p.p.* **driven**) chasser, pousser; (*vehicle*) conduire; (*machine*) actionner. —*v.i.* conduire. —*n.* promenade en voiture *f.*; (*private road*) allée *f.*; (*fig.*) énergie *f.*; (*psych.*) instinct *m.*; (*pol.*) campagne *f.* **~ at,** en venir à. **~ away,**

(*of car*) partir. **~ in,** (*force in*) enfoncer. **~ mad,** rendre fou.
drivel /ˈdrɪvl/ *n.* radotage *m.*
driver /ˈdraɪvə(r)/ *n.* conduc|teur, -trice *m., f.*, chauffeur *m.*
driving /ˈdraɪvɪŋ/ *n.* conduite *f.* **~ licence,** permis de conduire *m.* **~ rain,** pluie battante *f.* **~ school,** auto-école *f.*
drizzle /ˈdrɪzl/ *n.* bruine *f.* —*v.i.* bruiner.
dromedary /ˈdrɒmədərɪ, (*Amer.*) ˈdrɒmədern/ *n.* dromadaire *m.*
drone /drəʊn/ *n.* (*noise*) bourdonnement *m.*; (*bee*) faux bourdon *m.* —*v.i.* bourdonner; (*fig.*) parler d'une voix monotone.
drool /druːl/ *v.i.* baver.
droop /druːp/ *v.i.* pencher, tomber.
drop /drɒp/ *n.* goutte *f.*; (*fall, lowering*) chute *f.* —*v.t./i.* (*p.t.* **dropped**) (laisser) tomber; (*decrease, lower*) baisser. **~ (off),** (*person from car*) déposer. **~ a line,** écrire un mot (**to,** à). **~ in,** passer (**on,** chez). **~ off,** (*doze*) s'assoupir. **~ out,** se retirer (**of,** de); (*of student*) abandonner. **~-out** *n.* marginal(e) *m.* (*f.*), raté(e) *m.* (*f.*).
droppings /ˈdrɒpɪŋz/ *n. pl.* crottes *f. pl.*
dross /drɒs/ *n.* déchets *m. pl.*
drought /draʊt/ *n.* sécheresse *f.*
drove /drəʊv/ *see* **drive.**
droves /drəʊvz/ *n. pl.* foule(s) *f.*(*pl.*).
drown /draʊn/ *v.t./i.* (se) noyer.
drowsy /ˈdraʊzɪ/ *a.* somnolent. **be** *or* **feel ~,** avoir envie de dormir.
drudge /drʌdʒ/ *n.* esclave du travail *m.* **~ry** /-ərɪ/ *n.* travail pénible et ingrat *m.*
drug /drʌg/ *n.* drogue *f.*; (*med.*) médicament *m.* —*v.t.* (*p.t.* **drugged**) droguer. **~ addict,** drogué(e) *m.* (*f.*).
drugstore /ˈdrʌgstɔː(r)/ *n.* (*Amer.*) drugstore *m.*
drum /drʌm/ *n.* tambour *m.*; (*for oil*) bidon *m.* —*v.i.* (*p.t.* **drummed**) tambouriner. —*v.t.* **~ into s.o.,** répéter sans cesse à qn. **~ up,** (*support*) susciter; (*business*) créer. **~mer** *n.* tambour *m.*
drumstick /ˈdrʌmstɪk/ *n.* baguette de tambour *f.*; (*of chicken*) pilon *m.*
drunk /drʌŋk/ *see* **drink.** —*a.* ivre. **get ~,** s'enivrer. —*n.*, **~ard** *n.* ivrogne(sse) *m.* (*f.*). **~en** *a.* ivre; (*habitually*) ivrogne. **~enness** *n.* ivresse *f.*
dry /draɪ/ *a.* (**drier, driest**) sec; (*day*) sans pluie. —*v.t./i.* sécher. **be** *or* **feel ~,** avoir soif. **~-clean** *v.t.* nettoyer à sec. **~-cleaner** *n.* teinturier *m.* **~ up,** (*dry dishes*) essuyer la vaisselle; (*of supplies*) (se) tarir; (*be silent*: *fam.*) se taire. **~ness** *n.* sécheresse *f.*
dual /ˈdjuːəl/ *a.* double. **~ carriageway,** route à quatre voies *f.*
dub /dʌb/ *v.t.* (*p.t.* **dubbed**) (*film*) doubler; (*nickname*) surnommer.
dubious /ˈdjuːbɪəs/ *a.* douteux. **be ~ about sth.,** (*person*) douter de qch.
duchess /ˈdʌtʃɪs/ *n.* duchesse *f.*
duck /dʌk/ *n.* canard *m.* —*v.i.* se baisser subitement. —*v.t.* (*head*) baisser; (*person*) plonger dans l'eau. **~ling** *n.* caneton *m.*
duct /dʌkt/ *n.* conduit *m.*
dud /dʌd/ *a.* (*tool etc.*: *sl.*) mal fichu; (*coin*: *sl.*) faux; (*cheque*: *sl.*) sans provision. —*n.* **be a ~,** (*not work*: *sl.*) ne pas marcher.
dude /duːd/ *n.* (*Amer.*) dandy *m.*
due /djuː/ *a.* (*owing*) dû; (*expected*) attendu; (*proper*) qui convient. —*adv.* **~ east**/*etc.*, droit vers l'est/*etc.* —*n.* dû *m.* **~s,** droits *m. pl.*; (*of club*) cotisation *f.* **~ to,** à cause de; (*caused by*) dû à.
duel /ˈdjuːəl/ *n.* duel *m.*
duet /djuːˈet/ *n.* duo *m.*

duffel /ˈdʌfl/ *a.* **~ bag,** sac de marin *m.* **~ coat,** duffel-coat *m.*
dug /dʌg/ *see* **dig.**
duke /djuːk/ *n.* duc *m.*
dull /dʌl/ *a.* (**-er, -est**) ennuyeux; (*colour*) terne; (*weather*) morne; (*sound*) sourd; (*stupid*) bête. —*v.t.* (*pain*) amortir; (*mind*) engourdir.
duly /ˈdjuːlɪ/ *adv.* comme il convient; (*in due time*) en temps voulu.
dumb /dʌm/ *a.* (**-er, -est**) muet; (*stupid*: *fam.*) bête.
dumbfound /dʌmˈfaʊnd/ *v.t.* sidérer, ahurir.
dummy /ˈdʌmɪ/ *n.* (*comm.*) article factice *m.*; (*of tailor*) mannequin *m.*; (*of baby*) sucette *f.* —*a.* factice. **~ run,** essai *m.*
dump /dʌmp/ *v.t.* déposer; (*abandon*: *fam.*) se débarrasser de. —*n.* tas d'ordures *m.*; (*refuse tip*) décharge *f.*; (*mil.*) dépôt *m.*; (*dull place*: *fam.*) trou *m.* **be in the ~s,** (*fam.*) avoir le cafard.
dumpling /ˈdʌmplɪŋ/ *n.* boulette de pâte *f.*
dumpy /ˈdʌmpɪ/ *a.* (**-ier, -iest**) boulot, rondelet.
dunce /dʌns/ *n.* cancre *m.*, âne *m.*
dune /djuːn/ *n.* dune *f.*
dung /dʌŋ/ *n.* (*excrement*) bouse *f.*, crotte *f.*; (*manure*) fumier *m.*
dungarees /dʌŋgəˈriːz/ *n. pl.* (*overalls*) salopette *f.*; (*jeans*: *Amer.*) jean *m.*
dungeon /ˈdʌndʒən/ *n.* cachot *m.*
dunk /dʌŋk/ *v.t.* tremper.
duo /ˈdjuːəʊ/ *n.* duo *m.*
dupe /djuːp/ *v.t.* duper. —*n.* dupe *f.*
duplicate[1] /ˈdjuːplɪkət/ *n.* double *m.* —*a.* identique.
duplicat|e[2] /ˈdjuːplɪkeɪt/ *v.t.* faire un double de; (*on machine*) polycopier. **~or** *n.* duplicateur *m.*
duplicity /djuːˈplɪsətɪ/ *n.* duplicité *f.*
durable /ˈdjʊərəbl/ *a.* (*tough*) résistant; (*enduring*) durable.
duration /djʊˈreɪʃn/ *n.* durée *f.*
duress /djʊˈres/ *n.* contrainte *f.*
during /ˈdjʊərɪŋ/ *prep.* pendant.
dusk /dʌsk/ *n.* crépuscule *m.*
dusky /ˈdʌskɪ/ *a.* (**-ier, -iest**) foncé.
dust /dʌst/ *n.* poussière *f.* —*v.t.* épousseter; (*sprinkle*) saupoudrer. **~-jacket** *n.* jaquette *f.*
dustbin /ˈdʌstbɪn/ *n.* poubelle *f.*
duster /ˈdʌstə(r)/ *n.* chiffon *m.*
dustman /ˈdʌstmən/ *n.* (*pl.* **-men**) éboueur *m.*, boueux *m.*
dustpan /ˈdʌstpæn/ *n.* pelle à poussière *f.*
dusty /ˈdʌstɪ/ *a.* (**-ier, -iest**) poussiéreux.
Dutch /dʌtʃ/ *a.* hollandais. —*n.* (*lang.*) hollandais *m.* **go ~,** partager les frais. **~man** *n.* Hollandais *m.* **~woman** *n.* Hollandaise *f.*
dutiful /ˈdjuːtɪfl/ *a.* obéissant.
dut|y /ˈdjuːtɪ/ *n.* devoir *m.*; (*tax*) droit *m.* **~ies,** (*of official etc.*) fonctions *f. pl.* **~y-free** *a.* hors-taxe. **on ~y,** de service.
duvet /ˈduːveɪ/ *n.* couette *f.*, courtepointe *f.*
dwarf /dwɔːf/ *n.* (*pl.* **-fs**) nain(e) *m.* (*f.*). —*v.t.* rapetisser.
dwell /dwel/ *v.i.* (*p.t.* **dwelt**) demeurer. **~ on,** s'étendre sur. **~er** *n.* habitant(e) *m.* (*f.*). **~ing** *n.* habitation *f.*
dwindle /ˈdwɪndl/ *v.i.* diminuer.
dye /daɪ/ *v.t.* (*pres. p.* **dyeing**) teindre. —*n.* teinture *f.*
dying /ˈdaɪɪŋ/ *see* **die**[1].
dynamic /daɪˈnæmɪk/ *a.* dynamique.
dynamism /ˈdaɪnəmɪzəm/ *n.* dynamisme *m.*
dynamite /ˈdaɪnəmaɪt/ *n.* dynamite *f.* —*v.t.* dynamiter.
dynasty /ˈdɪnəstɪ, *Amer.* ˈdaɪnəstɪ/ *n.* dynastie *f.*
dysentery /ˈdɪsəntrɪ/ *n.* dysenterie *f.*

E

each /iːtʃ/ *a.* chaque. *—pron.* chacun(e). **~ one,** chacun(e). **~ other,** l'un(e) l'autre, les un(e)s les autres. **know ~ other,** se connaître. **love ~ other,** s'aimer.

eager /'iːgə(r)/ *a.* impatient (**to,** de); (*supporter, desire*) ardent. **be ~ to,** (*want*) avoir envie de. **~ for,** avide de. **~ly** *adv.* avec impatience *or* ardeur. **~ness** *n.* impatience *f.*, désir *m.*, ardeur *f.*

eagle /'iːgl/ *n.* aigle *m.*

ear[1] /ɪə(r)/ *n.* oreille *f.* **~-drum** *n.* tympan *m.* **~-ring** *n.* boucle d'oreille *f.*

ear[2] /ɪə(r)/ *n.* (*of corn*) épi *m.*

earache /'ɪəreɪk/ *n.* mal à l'oreille *m.*, mal d'oreille *m.*

earl /ɜːl/ *n.* comte *m.*

early /'ɜːlɪ/ (**-ier, -iest**) *adv.* tôt, de bonne heure; (*ahead of time*) en avance. *—a.* premier; (*hour*) matinal; (*fruit*) précoce; (*retirement*) anticipé. **have an ~ dinner,** dîner tôt. **in ~ summer,** au début de l'été.

earmark /'ɪəmɑːk/ *v.t.* destiner, réserver (**for,** à).

earn /ɜːn/ *v.t.* gagner; (*interest: comm.*) rapporter. **~ s.o. sth.,** (*bring*) valoir qch. à qn.

earnest /'ɜːnɪst/ *a.* sérieux. **in ~,** sérieusement.

earnings /'ɜːnɪŋz/ *n. pl.* salaire *m.*; (*profits*) bénéfices *m. pl.*

earphone /'ɪəfəʊn/ *n.* écouteur *m.*

earshot /'ɪəʃɒt/ *n.* **within ~,** à portée de voix.

earth /ɜːθ/ *n.* terre *f.* *—v.t.* (*electr.*) mettre à la terre. **why/how/where on ~? . . .,** pourquoi/comment/où diable? . . . **~ly** *a.* terrestre.

earthenware /'ɜːθnweə(r)/ *n.* faïence *f.*

earthquake /'ɜːθkweɪk/ *n.* tremblement de terre *m.*

earthy /'ɜːθɪ/ *a.* (*of earth*) terreux; (*coarse*) grossier.

earwig /'ɪəwɪg/ *n.* perce-oreille *m.*

ease /iːz/ *n.* aisance *f.*, facilité *f.*; (*comfort*) bien-être *m.* *—v.t./i.* (se) calmer; (*relax*) (se) détendre; (*slow down*) ralentir; (*slide*) glisser. **at ~,** à l'aise; (*mil.*) au repos. **with ~,** aisément.

easel /'iːzl/ *n.* chevalet *m.*

east /iːst/ *n.* est *m.* *—a.* d'est. *—adv.* vers l'est. **the E~,** (*Orient*) l'Orient *m.* **~erly** *a.* d'est. **~ern** *a.* de l'est, oriental. **~ward** *a.* à l'est. **~wards** *adv.* vers l'est.

Easter /'iːstə(r)/ *n.* Pâques *f. pl.* (*or m. sing.*). **~ egg,** œuf de Pâques *m.*

easy /'iːzɪ/ *a.* (**-ier, -iest**) facile; (*relaxed*) aisé. **~ chair,** fauteuil *m.* **go ~ with,** (*fam.*) y aller doucement avec. **take it ~,** ne pas se fatiguer. **easily** *adv.* facilement.

easygoing /iːzɪ'gəʊɪŋ/ *a.* (*with people*) accommodant; (*relaxed*) décontracté.

eat /iːt/ *v.t./i.* (*p.t.* **ate,** *p.p.* **eaten**) manger. **~ into,** ronger. **~able** *a.* mangeable. **~er** *n.* mangeu|r, -se *m., f.*

eau-de-Cologne /əʊdəkə'ləʊn/ *n.* eau de Cologne *f.*

eaves /iːvz/ *n. pl.* avant-toit *m.*

eavesdrop /'iːvzdrɒp/ *v.i.* (*p.t.* **-dropped**). **~ (on),** écouter en cachette.

ebb /eb/ *n.* reflux *m.* *—v.i.* refluer; (*fig.*) décliner.

ebony /'ebənɪ/ *n.* ébène *f.*

ebullient /ɪ'bʌlɪənt/ *a.* exubérant.

eccentric /ɪk'sentrɪk/ *a.* & *n.* excentrique (*m./f.*). **~ity** /eksen'trɪsətɪ/ *n.* excentricité *f.*

ecclesiastical /ɪkliːzɪ'æstɪkl/ *a.* ecclésiastique.

echo /ˈekəʊ/ *n.* (*pl.* **-oes**) écho *m.* —*v.t./i.* (*p.t.* **echoed,** *pres. p.* **echoing**) (se) répercuter; (*fig.*) répéter.
eclipse /ɪˈklɪps/ *n.* éclipse *f.* —*v.t.* éclipser.
ecology /iːˈkɒlədʒɪ/ *n.* écologie *f.*
economic /iːkəˈnɒmɪk/ *a.* économique; (*profitable*) rentable. **~al** *a.* économique; (*person*) économe. **~s** *n.* économie politique *f.*
economist /ɪˈkɒnəmɪst/ *n.* économiste *m./f.*
econom|y /ɪˈkɒnəmɪ/ *n.* économie *f.* **~ize** *v.i.* **~ (on),** économiser.
ecstasy /ˈekstəsɪ/ *n.* extase *f.*
ecstatic /ɪkˈstætɪk/ *a.* extasié. **~ally** *adv.* avec extase.
ecumenical /iːkjuːˈmenɪkl/ *a.* œcuménique.
eddy /ˈedɪ/ *n.* tourbillon *m.*
edge /edʒ/ *n.* bord *m.*; (*of town*) abords *m. pl.*; (*of knife*) tranchant *m.* —*v.t.* border. —*v.i.* (*move*) se glisser. **have the ~ on,** (*fam.*) l'emporter sur. **on ~,** énervé.
edging /ˈedʒɪŋ/ *n.* bordure *f.*
edgy /ˈedʒɪ/ *a.* énervé.
edible /ˈedɪbl/ *a.* mangeable; (*not poisonous*) comestible.
edict /ˈiːdɪkt/ *n.* décret *m.*
edifice /ˈedɪfɪs/ *n.* édifice *m.*
edify /ˈedɪfaɪ/ *v.t.* édifier.
edit /ˈedɪt/ *v.t.* (*p.t.* **edited**) (*newspaper*) diriger; (*prepare text of*) mettre au point, préparer; (*write*) rédiger; (*cut*) couper.
edition /ɪˈdɪʃn/ *n.* édition *f.*
editor /ˈedɪtə(r)/ *n.* (*writer*) rédac|teur, -trice *m., f.*; (*annotator*) édi|teur, -trice *m., f.* **the ~ (in chief),** le rédacteur en chef. **~ial** /-ˈtɔːrɪəl/ *a.* de la rédaction; *n.* éditorial *m.*
educat|e /ˈedʒʊkeɪt/ *v.t.* instruire; (*mind, public*) éduquer. **~ed** *a.* instruit. **~ion** /-ˈkeɪʃn/ *n.* éducation *f.*; (*schooling*) enseignement *m.* **~ional** /-ˈkeɪʃənl/ *a.* pédagogique, éducatif.
EEC *abbr.* (*European Economic Community*) CEE *f.*
eel /iːl/ *n.* anguille *f.*
eerie /ˈɪərɪ/ *a.* (**-ier, -iest**) sinistre.
effect /ɪˈfekt/ *n.* effet *m.* —*v.t.* effectuer. **come into ~,** entrer en vigueur. **take ~,** agir.
effective /ɪˈfektɪv/ *a.* efficace; (*striking*) frappant; (*actual*) effectif. **~ly** *adv.* efficacement; de manière frappante; effectivement. **~ness** *n.* efficacité *f.*
effeminate /ɪˈfemɪnət/ *a.* efféminé.
effervescent /efəˈvesnt/ *a.* effervescent.
efficien|t /ɪˈfɪʃnt/ *a.* efficace; (*person*) compétent. **~cy** *n.* efficacité *f.*; compétence *f.* **~tly** *adv.* efficacement.
effigy /ˈefɪdʒɪ/ *n.* effigie *f.*
effort /ˈefət/ *n.* effort *m.* **~less** *a.* facile.
effrontery /ɪˈfrʌntərɪ/ *n.* effronterie *f.*
effusive /ɪˈfjuːsɪv/ *a.* expansif.
e.g. /iːˈdʒiː/ *abbr.* par exemple.
egalitarian /ɪgælɪˈteərɪən/ *a.* égalitaire. —*n.* égalitariste *m./f.*
egg[1] /eg/ *n.* œuf *m.* **~-cup** *n.* coquetier *m.* **~-plant** *n.* aubergine *f.*
egg[2] /eg/ *v.t.* **~ on,** (*fam.*) inciter.
eggshell /ˈegʃel/ *n.* coquille d'œuf *f.*
ego /ˈegəʊ/ *n.* (*pl.* **-os**) moi *m.* **~(t)ism** *n.* égoïsme *m.* **~(t)ist** *n.* égoïste *m./f.*
Egypt /ˈiːdʒɪpt/ *n.* Égypte *f.* **~ian** /ɪˈdʒɪpʃn/ *a.* & *n.* égyptien(ne) (*m.* (*f.*)).
eh /eɪ/ *int.* (*fam.*) hein.
eiderdown /ˈaɪdədaʊn/ *n.* édredon *m.*
eight /eɪt/ *a.* & *n.* huit (*m.*). **eighth** /eɪtθ/ *a.* & *n.* huitième (*m./f*).
eighteen /eɪˈtiːn/ *a.* & *n.* dix-huit

(*m.*). **~th** *a.* & *n.* dix-huitième (*m./f.*).
eight|y /'eɪtɪ/ *a.* & *n.* quatre-vingts (*m.*) **~ieth** *a.* & *n.* quatre-vingtième (*m./f.*).
either /'aɪðə(r)/ *a.* & *pron.* l'un(e) ou l'autre; (*with negative*) ni l'un(e) ni l'autre; (*each*) chaque. —*adv.* non plus. —*conj.* **~ . . . or,** ou (bien) . . . ou (bien); (*with negative*) ni . . . ni.
eject /ɪ'dʒekt/ *v.t.* éjecter.
eke /iːk/ *v.t.* **~ out,** faire durer; (*living*) gagner difficilement.
elaborate[1] /ɪ'læbərət/ *a.* compliqué, recherché.
elaborate[2] /ɪ'læbəreɪt/ *v.t.* élaborer. —*v.i.* préciser. **~ on,** s'étendre sur.
elapse /ɪ'læps/ *v.i.* s'écouler.
elastic /ɪ'læstɪk/ *a.* & *n.* élastique (*m.*). **~ band,** élastique *m.* **~ity** /elæ'stɪsətɪ/ *n.* élasticité *f.*
elated /ɪ'leɪtɪd/ *a.* fou de joie.
elbow /'elbəʊ/ *n.* coude *m.*
elder[1] /'eldə(r)/ *a.* & *n.* aîné(e) (*m.* (*f.*)).
elder[2] /'eldə(r)/ *n.* (*tree*) sureau *m.*
elderly /'eldəlɪ/ *a.* (assez) âgé.
eldest /'eldɪst/ *a.* & *n.* aîné(e) (*m.* (*f.*)).
elect /ɪ'lekt/ *v.t.* élire. —*a.* (*president etc.*) futur. **~ to do,** choisir de faire. **~ion** /-kʃn/ *n.* élection *f.*
elector /ɪ'lektə(r)/ *n.* élec|teur, -trice *m., f.* **~al** *a.* électoral. **~ate** *n.* électorat *m.*
electric /ɪ'lektrɪk/ *a.* électrique. **~ blanket,** couverture chauffante *f.* **~al** *a.* électrique.
electrician /ɪlek'trɪʃn/ *n.* électricien *m.*
electricity /ɪlek'trɪsətɪ/ *n.* électricité *f.*
electrify /ɪ'lektrɪfaɪ/ *v.t.* électrifier.
electrocute /ɪ'lektrəkjuːt/ *v.t.* électrocuter.
electron /ɪ'lektrɒn/ *n.* électron *m.*
electronic /ɪlek'trɒnɪk/ *a.* électronique. **~s** *n.* électronique *f.*
elegan|t /'elɪgənt/ *a.* élégant. **~ce** *n.* élégance *f.* **~tly** *adv.* élégamment.
element /'elɪmənt/ *n.* élément *m.*; (*of heater etc.*) résistance *f.* **~ary** /-'mentrɪ/ *a.* élémentaire.
elephant /'elɪfənt/ *n.* éléphant *m.*
elevat|e /'elɪveɪt/ *v.t.* élever. **~ion** /-'veɪʃn/ *n.* élévation *f.*
elevator /'eləveɪtə(r)/ *n.* (*Amer.*) ascenseur *m.*
eleven /ɪ'levn/ *a.* & *n.* onze (*m.*). **~th** *a.* & *n.* onzième (*m./f.*).
elf /elf/ (*pl.* **elves**) lutin *m.*
elicit /ɪ'lɪsɪt/ *v.t.* obtenir (**from,** de).
eligible /'elɪdʒəbl/ *a.* admissible (**for,** à). **be ~ for,** (*entitled to*) avoir droit à.
eliminat|e /ɪ'lɪmɪneɪt/ *v.t.* éliminer. **~ion** /-'neɪʃn/ *n.* élimination *f.*
élite /eɪ'liːt/ *n.* élite *f.*
ellip|se /ɪ'lɪps/ *n.* ellipse *f.* **~tical** *a.* elliptique.
elm /elm/ *n.* orme *m.*
elocution /elə'kjuːʃn/ *n.* élocution *f.*
elongate /'iːlɒŋgeɪt/ *v.t.* allonger.
elope /ɪ'ləʊp/ *v.i.* s'enfuir. **~ment** *n.* fugue (amoureuse) *f.*
eloquen|t /'eləkwənt/ *a.* éloquent. **~ce** *n.* éloquence *f.* **~tly** *adv.* avec éloquence.
else /els/ *adv.* d'autre. **everybody ~,** tous les autres. **nobody ~,** personne d'autre. **nothing ~,** rien d'autre. **or ~,** ou bien. **somewhere ~,** autre part. **~where** *adv.* ailleurs.
elucidate /ɪ'luːsɪdeɪt/ *v.t.* élucider.
elude /ɪ'luːd/ *v.t.* échapper à; (*question*) éluder.
elusive /ɪ'luːsɪv/ *a.* insaisissable.
emaciated /ɪ'meɪʃɪeɪtɪd/ *a.* émacié.
emanate /'eməneɪt/ *v.i.* émaner.
emancipat|e /ɪ'mænsɪpeɪt/ *v.t.*

émanciper. **~ion** /-ˈpeɪʃn/ *n.* émancipation *f.*
embalm /ɪmˈbɑːm/ *v.t.* embaumer.
embankment /ɪmˈbæŋkmənt/ *n.* (*of river*) quai *m.*; (*of railway*) remblai *m.*, talus *m.*
embargo /ɪmˈbɑːgəʊ/ *n.* (*pl.* **-oes**) embargo *m.*
embark /ɪmˈbɑːk/ *v.t./i.* (s')embarquer. **~ on,** (*business etc.*) se lancer dans; (*journey*) commencer. **~ation** /embɑːˈkeɪʃn/ *n.* embarquement *m.*
embarrass /ɪmˈbærəs/ *v.t.* embarrasser, gêner. **~ment** *n.* embarras *m.*, gêne *f.*
embassy /ˈembəsɪ/ *n.* ambassade *f.*
embed /ɪmˈbed/ *v.t.* (*p.t.* **embedded**) encastrer.
embellish /ɪmˈbelɪʃ/ *v.t.* embellir. **~ment** *n.* enjolivement *m.*
embers /ˈembəz/ *n. pl.* braise *f.*
embezzle /ɪmˈbezl/ *v.t.* détourner. **~ment** *n.* détournement de fonds *m.* **~r** /-ə(r)/ *n.* escroc *m.*
embitter /ɪmˈbɪtə(r)/ *v.t.* (*person*) aigrir; (*situation*) envenimer.
emblem /ˈembləm/ *n.* emblème *m.*
embod|y /ɪmˈbɒdɪ/ *v.t.* incarner, exprimer; (*include*) contenir. **~iment** *n.* incarnation *f.*
emboss /ɪmˈbɒs/ *v.t.* (*metal*) repousser; (*paper*) gaufrer.
embrace /ɪmˈbreɪs/ *v.t./i.* (s')embrasser. —*n.* étreinte *f.*
embroider /ɪmˈbrɔɪdə(r)/ *v.t.* broder. **~y** *n.* broderie *f.*
embroil /ɪmˈbrɔɪl/ *v.t.* mêler (**in, à**).
embryo /ˈembrɪəʊ/ *n.* (*pl.* **-os**) embryon *m.* **~nic** /-ˈɒnɪk/ *a.* embryonnaire.
emend /ɪˈmend/ *v.t.* corriger.
emerald /ˈemərəld/ *n.* émeraude *f.*
emerge /ɪˈmɜːdʒ/ *v.i.* apparaître. **~nce** /-əns/ *n.* apparition *f.*
emergency /ɪˈmɜːdʒənsɪ/ *n.* (*crisis*) crise *f.*; (*urgent case: med.*) urgence *f.* **~ exit,** sortie de secours *f.* **in an ~,** en cas d'urgence.
emery /ˈemərɪ/ *n.* émeri *m.*
emigrant /ˈemɪgrənt/ *n.* émigrant(e) *m.* (*f.*).
emigrat|e /ˈemɪgreɪt/ *v.i.* émigrer. **~ion** /-ˈgreɪʃn/ *n.* émigration *f.*
eminen|t /ˈemɪnənt/ *a.* éminent. **~ce** *n.* éminence *f.* **~tly** *adv.* éminemment, parfaitement.
emissary /ˈemɪsərɪ/ *n.* émissaire *m.*
emi|t /ɪˈmɪt/ *v.t.* (*p.t.* **emitted**) émettre. **~ssion** *n.* émission *f.*
emotion /ɪˈməʊʃn/ *n.* émotion *f.* **~al** *a.* (*person, shock*) émotif; (*speech, scene*) émouvant.
emotive /ɪˈməʊtɪv/ *a.* émotif.
emperor /ˈempərə(r)/ *n.* empereur *m.*
emphasis /ˈemfəsɪs/ *n.* (*on word*) accent *m.* **lay ~ on,** mettre l'accent sur, accorder une importance à.
emphasize /ˈemfəsaɪz/ *v.t.* souligner; (*syllable*) insister sur.
emphatic /ɪmˈfætɪk/ *a.* catégorique; (*manner*) énergique.
empire /ˈempaɪə(r)/ *n.* empire *m.*
empirical /ɪmˈpɪrɪkl/ *a.* empirique.
employ /ɪmˈplɔɪ/ *v.t.* employer. **~er** *n.* employeu|r, -se *m., f.* **~ment** *n.* emploi *m.* **~ment agency,** agence de placement *f.*
employee /emplɔɪˈiː/ *n.* employé(e) *m.* (*f.*).
empower /ɪmˈpaʊə(r)/ *v.t.* autoriser (**to do,** à faire).
empress /ˈemprɪs/ *n.* impératrice *f.*
empt|y /ˈemptɪ/ *a.* (**-ier, -iest**) vide; (*promise*) vain. —*v.t./i.* (se) vider. **on an ~y stomach,** à jeun. **~ies** *n. pl.* bouteilles vides *f. pl.* **~iness** *n.* vide *m.*
emulate /ˈemjʊleɪt/ *v.t.* imiter.
emulsion /ɪˈmʌlʃn/ *n.* émulsion *f.*
enable /ɪˈneɪbl/ *v.t.* **~ s.o. to,** permettre à qn. de.

enamel /ɪ'næml/ *n.* émail *m.* —*v.t.* (*p.t.* **enamelled**) émailler.

enamoured /ɪ'næməd/ *a.* **be ~ of,** aimer beaucoup, être épris de.

encampment /ɪn'kæmpmənt/ *n.* campement *m.*

encase /ɪn'keɪs/ *v.t.* (*cover*) recouvrir (**in,** de); (*enclose*) enfermer (**in,** dans).

enchant /ɪn'tʃɑːnt/ *v.t.* enchanter. **~ing** *a.* enchanteur. **~ment** *n.* enchantement *m.*

encircle /ɪn'sɜːkl/ *v.t.* encercler.

enclave /'enkleɪv/ *n.* enclave *f.*

enclose /ɪn'kləʊz/ *v.t.* (*land*) clôturer; (*with letter*) joindre. **~d** *a.* (*space*) clos; (*market*) couvert; (*with letter*) ci-joint.

enclosure /ɪn'kləʊʒə(r)/ *n.* enceinte *f.*; (*comm.*) pièce jointe *f.*

encompass /ɪn'kʌmpəs/ *v.t.* (*include*) inclure.

encore /'ɒŋkɔː(r)/ *int.* & *n.* bis (*m.*).

encounter /ɪn'kaʊntə(r)/ *v.t.* rencontrer. —*n.* rencontre *f.*

encourage /ɪn'kʌrɪdʒ/ *v.t.* encourager. **~ment** *n.* encouragement *m.*

encroach /ɪn'krəʊtʃ/ *v.i.* **~ upon,** empiéter sur.

encumber /ɪn'kʌmbə(r)/ *v.t.* encombrer.

encyclical /ɪn'sɪklɪkl/ *n.* encyclique *f.*

encyclopaed|ia /ɪnsaɪklə'piːdɪə/ *n.* encyclopédie *f.* **~ic** *a.* encyclopédique.

end /end/ *n.* fin *f.*; (*farthest part*) bout *m.* —*v.t.*/*i.* (se) terminer. **~ up doing,** finir par faire. **come to an ~,** prendre fin. **no ~ of,** (*fam.*) énormément de. **on ~,** (*upright*) debout; (*in a row*) de suite.

endanger /ɪn'deɪndʒə(r)/ *v.t.* mettre en danger.

endear|ing /ɪn'dɪərɪŋ/ *a.* attachant. **~ment** *n.* parole tendre *f.*

endeavour /ɪn'devə(r)/ *n.* effort *m.* —*v.i.* s'efforcer (**to,** de).

ending /'endɪŋ/ *n.* fin *f.*

endive /'endɪv/ *n.* chicorée *f.*

endless /'endlɪs/ *a.* interminable; (*times*) innombrable; (*patience*) infini.

endorse /ɪn'dɔːs/ *v.t.* (*document*) endosser; (*action*) approuver. **~ment** *n.* (*auto.*) contravention *f.*

endow /ɪn'daʊ/ *v.t.* doter. **~ment** *n.* dotation *f.* (**of,** de).

endur|e /ɪn'djʊə(r)/ *v.t.* supporter. —*v.i.* durer. **~able** *a.* supportable. **~ance** *n.* endurance *f.* **~ing** *a.* durable.

enemy /'enəmɪ/ *n.* & *a.* ennemi(e) (*m.* (*f.*)).

energetic /enə'dʒetɪk/ *a.* énergique.

energy /'enədʒɪ/ *n.* énergie *f.*

enforce /ɪn'fɔːs/ *v.t.* appliquer, faire respecter; (*impose*) imposer (**on,** à). **~d** *a.* forcé.

engage /ɪn'geɪdʒ/ *v.t.* engager. —*v.i.* **~ in,** se lancer dans. **~d** *a.* fiancé; (*busy*) occupé. **get ~d,** se fiancer. **~ment** *n.* fiançailles *f. pl.*; (*meeting*) rendez-vous *m.*; (*undertaking*) engagement *m.*

engaging /ɪn'geɪdʒɪŋ/ *a.* engageant, séduisant.

engender /ɪn'dʒendə(r)/ *v.t.* engendrer.

engine /'endʒɪn/ *n.* moteur *m.*; (*of train*) locomotive *f.*; (*of ship*) machine *f.* **~-driver** *n.* mécanicien *m.*

engineer /'endʒɪ'nɪə(r)/ *n.* ingénieur *m.*; (*apliance repairman*) dépanneur *m.* —*v.t.* (*contrive*: *fam.*) machiner. **~ing** *n.* (*mechanical*) mécanique *f.*; (*roadbuilding etc.*) génie *m.*

England /'ɪŋglənd/ *n.* Angleterre *f.*

English /'ɪŋglɪʃ/ *a.* anglais. —*n.* (*lang.*) anglais *m.* **~-speaking** *a.* anglophone. **the ~,** les Anglais *m. pl.* **~man** *n.* Anglais *m.* **~woman** *n.* Anglaise *f.*

engrav|e /ɪn'greɪv/ *v.t.* graver. **~ing** *n.* gravure *f.*

engrossed /ɪn'grəʊst/ *a.* absorbé (**in,** par).

engulf /ɪn'gʌlf/ *v.t.* engouffrer.

enhance /ɪn'hɑːns/ *v.t.* rehausser; (*price, value*) augmenter.

enigma /ɪ'nɪgmə/ *n.* énigme *f.* **~tic** /enɪg'mætɪk/ *a.* énigmatique.

enjoy /ɪn'dʒɔɪ/ *v.t.* aimer (*doing,* faire); (*benefit from*) jouir de. **~ o.s.,** s'amuser. **~able** *a.* agréable. **~ment** *n.* plaisir *m.*

enlarge /ɪn'lɑːdʒ/ *v.t./i.* (s')agrandir. **~ upon,** s'étendre sur. **~ment** *n.* agrandissement *m.*

enlighten /ɪn'laɪtn/ *v.t.* éclairer. **~ment** *n.* édification *f.*; (*information*) éclaircissements *m. pl.*

enlist /ɪn'lɪst/ *v.t.* (*person*) recruter; (*fig.*) obtenir. *—v.i.* s'engager.

enliven /ɪn'laɪvn/ *v.t.* animer.

enmity /'enmətɪ/ *n.* inimitié *f.*

enormity /ɪ'nɔːmətɪ/ *n.* énormité *f.*

enormous /ɪ'nɔːməs/ *a.* énorme. **~ly** *adv.* énormément.

enough /ɪ'nʌf/ *adv.* & *n.* assez. *—a.* assez de. **~ glasses/time**/*etc.,* assez de verres/de temps/*etc.* **have ~ of,** en avoir assez de.

enquir|e /ɪn'kwaɪə(r)/ *v.t./i.* demander. **~e about,** se renseigner sur. **~y** *n.* demande de renseignements *f.*

enrage /ɪn'reɪdʒ/ *v.t.* mettre en rage, rendre furieux.

enrich /ɪn'rɪtʃ/ *v.t.* enrichir.

enrol /ɪn'rəʊl/ *v.t./i.* (*p.t.* **enrolled**) (s')inscrire. **~ment** *n.* inscription *f.*

ensconce /ɪn'skɒns/ *v.t.* **~ o.s.,** bien s'installer.

ensemble /ɒn'sɒmbl/ *n.* (*clothing* & *mus.*) ensemble *m.*

ensign /'ensən, 'ensaɪn/ *n.* (*flag*) pavillon *m.*

enslave /ɪn'sleɪv/ *v.t.* asservir.

ensue /ɪn'sjuː/ *v.i.* s'ensuivre.

ensure /ɪn'ʃʊə(r)/ *v.t.* assurer. **~ that,** (*ascertain*) s'assurer que.

entail /ɪn'teɪl/ *v.t.* entraîner.

entangle /ɪn'tæŋgl/ *v.t.* emmêler.

enter /'entə(r)/ *v.t.* (*room, club, etc.*) entrer dans; (*note down, register*) inscrire. *—v.i.* entrer (**into,** dans). **~ for,** s'inscrire à.

enterprise /'entəpraɪz/ *n.* entreprise *f.*; (*boldness*) initiative *f.*

enterprising /'entəpraɪzɪŋ/ *a.* entreprenant.

entertain /entə'teɪn/ *v.t.* amuser, divertir; (*guests*) recevoir; (*ideas*) considérer. **~er** *n.* artiste *m./f.* **~ment** *n.* amusement *m.,* divertissement *m.*; (*performance*) spectacle *m.*

enthral /ɪn'θrɔːl/ *v.t.* (*p.t.* **enthralled**) captiver.

enthuse /ɪn'θjuːz/ *v.i.* **~ over,** s'enthousiasmer pour.

enthusias|m /ɪn'θjuːzɪæzəm/ *n.* enthousiasme *m.* **~tic** /-'æstɪk/ *a.* enthousiaste. **~tically** *adv.* /-'æstɪklɪ/ *adv.* avec enthousiasme.

enthusiast /ɪn'θjuːzɪæst/ *n.* fervent(e) *m.(f.)*, passionné(e) *m.(f.)* (**for,** de).

entice /ɪn'taɪs/ *v.t.* attirer. **~ to do,** entraîner à faire. **~ment** *n.* (*attraction*) attrait *m.*

entire /ɪn'taɪə(r)/ *a.* entier. **~ly** *adv.* entièrement.

entirety /ɪn'taɪərətɪ/ *n.* **in its ~,** en entier.

entitle /ɪn'taɪtl/ *v.t.* donner droit à (**to sth.,** à qch.; **to do,** de faire). **~d** *a.* (*book*) intitulé. **be ~d to sth.,** avoir droit à qch. **~ment** *n.* droit *m.*

entity /'entətɪ/ *n.* entité *f.*

entrails /'entreɪlz/ *n. pl.* entrailles *f. pl.*

entrance[1] /'entrəns/ *n.* (*entering, way in*) entrée *f.* (**to,** de); (*right to enter*) admission *f.*

entrance[2] /ɪn'trɑːns/ *v.t.* transporter.

entrant /'entrənt/ *n.* (*sport*) concurrent(e) *m.* (*f.*); (*in exam*) candidat(e) *m.* (*f.*).
entreat /ɪn'triːt/ *v.t.* supplier.
entrench /ɪn'trentʃ/ *v.t.* (*mil.*) retrancher; (*fig.*) ancrer.
entrust /ɪn'trʌst/ *v.t.* confier.
entry /'entrɪ/ *n.* (*entrance*) entrée *f.*; (*word on list*) mot inscrit *m.* **~ form,** feuille d'inscription *f.*
entwine /ɪn'twaɪn *v.t.* entrelacer.
enumerate /ɪ'njuːməreɪt/ *v.t.* énumérer.
enunciate /ɪ'nʌnsɪeɪt/ *v.t.* (*word*) articuler; (*ideas*) énoncer.
envelop /ɪn'veləp/ *v.t.* (*p.t.* **enveloped**) envelopper.
envelope /'envələʊp/ *n.* enveloppe *f.*
enviable /'envɪəbl/ *a.* enviable.
envious /'envɪəs/ *a.* envieux (**of sth.,** de qch.). **~ of s.o.,** jaloux de qn. **~ly** *adv.* avec envie.
environment /ɪn'vaɪərənmənt/ *n.* milieu *m.*; (*ecological*) environnement *m.* **~al** /-'mentl/ *a.* du milieu; de l'environnement.
envisage /ɪn'vɪzɪdʒ/ *v.t.* envisager.
envoy /'envɔɪ/ *n.* envoyé(e) *m.* (*f.*).
envy /'envɪ/ *n.* envie *f.* —*v.t.* envier.
enzyme /'enzaɪm/ *n.* enzyme *m.*
ephemeral /ɪ'femərəl/ *a.* éphémère.
epic /'epɪk/ *n.* épopée *f.* —*a.* épique.
epidemic /epɪ'demɪk/ *n.* épidémie *f.*
epilep|sy /'epɪlepsɪ/ *n.* épilepsie *f.* **~tic** /-'leptɪk/ *a.* & *n.* épileptique (*m.*/*f.*).
epilogue /'epɪlɒg/ *n.* épilogue *m.*
episode /'epɪsəʊd/ *n.* épisode *m.*
epistle /ɪ'pɪsl/ *n.* épître *f.*
epitaph /'epɪtɑːf/ *n.* épitaphe *f.*
epithet /'epɪθet/ *n.* épithète *f.*
epitom|e /ɪ'pɪtəmɪ/ *n.* (*embodiment*) modèle *m.*; (*summary*) résumé *m.* **~ize** *v.t.* incarner.
epoch /'iːpɒk/ *n.* époque *f.* **~-making** *a.* qui fait époque.
equal /'iːkwəl/ *a.* égal. —*n.* égal(e) *m.* (*f.*). —*v.t.* (*p.t.* **equalled**) égaler. **~ to,** (*task*) à la hauteur de. **~ity** /ɪ'kwɒlətɪ/ *n.* égalité *f.* **~ly** *adv.* également; (*just as*) tout aussi.
equalize /'iːkwəlaɪz/ *v.t./i.* égaliser. **~r** /-ə(r)/ *n.* (*goal*) but égalisateur *m.*
equanimity /ekwə'nɪmətɪ/ *n.* égalité d'humeur *f.*, calme *m.*
equate /ɪ'kweɪt/ *v.t.* assimiler, égaler (**with,** à).
equation /ɪ'kweɪʒn/ *n.* équation *f.*
equator /ɪ'kweɪtə(r)/ *n.* équateur *m.* **~ial** /ekwə'tɔːrɪəl/ *a.* équatorial.
equilibrium /iːkwɪ'lɪbrɪəm/ *n.* équilibre *m.*
equinox /'iːkwɪnɒks/ *n.* équinoxe *m.*
equip /ɪ'kwɪp/ *v.t.* (*p.t.* **equipped**) équiper (**with,** de). **~ment** *n.* équipement *m.*
equitable /'ekwɪtəbl/ *a.* équitable.
equity /'ekwətɪ/ *n.* équité *f.*
equivalen|t /ɪ'kwɪvələnt/ *a.* & *n.* équivalent (*m.*). **~ce** *n.* équivalence *f.*
equivocal /ɪ'kwɪvəkl/ *a.* équivoque.
era /'ɪərə/ *n.* ère *f.*, époque *f.*
eradicate /ɪ'rædɪkeɪt/ *v.t.* supprimer, éliminer.
erase /ɪ'reɪz/ *v.t.* effacer. **~r** /-ə(r)/ *n.* (*rubber*) gomme *f.*
erect /ɪ'rekt/ *a.* droit. —*v.t.* ériger. **~ion** /-kʃn/ *n.* érection *f.*
ermine /'ɜːmɪn/ *n.* hermine *f.*
ero|de /ɪ'rəʊd/ *v.t.* ronger. **~sion** *n.* érosion *f.*
erotic /ɪ'rɒtɪk/ *a.* érotique. **~ism** /-sɪzəm/ *n.* érotisme *m.*
err /ɜː(r)/ *v.i.* (*be mistaken*) se tromper; (*sin*) pécher.
errand /'erənd/ *n.* course *f.*
erratic /ɪ'rætɪk/ *a.* (*uneven*) irrégulier; (*person*) capricieux.
erroneous /ɪ'rəʊnɪəs/ *a.* erroné.

error /'erə(r)/ *n.* erreur *f.*

erudit|e /'eru:daɪt, *Amer.* 'erjʊdaɪt/ *a.* érudit. **~ion** /-'dɪʃn/ *n.* érudition *f.*

erupt /ɪ'rʌpt/ *v.i.* (*volcano*) entrer en éruption; (*fig.*) éclater. **~ion** /-pʃn/ *n.* éruption *f.*

escalat|e /'eskəleɪt/ *v.t./i.* (s')intensifier; (*of prices*) monter en flèche. **~ion** /-'leɪʃn/ *n.* escalade *f.*

escalator /'eskəleɪtə(r)/ *n.* escalier mécanique *m.*, escalator *m.*

escapade /eskə'peɪd/ *n.* fredaine *f.*

escape /ɪ'skeɪp/ *v.i.* s'échapper (**from a place,** d'un lieu). *—v.t.* échapper à. *—n.* fuite *f.*, évasion *f.*; (*of gas etc.*) fuite *f.* **~ from s.o.,** échapper à qn. **~ to,** s'enfuir dans. **have a lucky** *or* **narrow ~,** l'échapper belle.

escapism /ɪ'skeɪpɪzəm/ *n.* évasion (de la réalité) *f.*

escort[1] /'eskɔ:t/ *n.* (*guard*) escorte *f.*; (*of lady*) cavalier *m.*

escort[2] /ɪ'skɔ:t/ *v.t.* escorter.

Eskimo /'eskɪməʊ/ *n.* (*pl.* **-os**) Esquimau(de) *m.* (*f.*).

especial /ɪ'speʃl/ *a.* particulier. **~ly** *adv.* particulièrement.

espionage /'espɪənɑ:ʒ/ *n.* espionnage *m.*

esplanade /esplə'neɪd/ *n.* esplanade *f.*

espresso /e'spresəʊ/ *n.* (*pl.* **-os**) (café) express *m.*

essay /'eseɪ/ *n.* essai *m.*; (*schol.*) rédaction *f.*; (*univ.*) dissertation *f.*

essence /'esns/ *n.* essence *f.*; (*main point*) essentiel *m.*

essential /ɪ'senʃl/ *a.* essentiel. *—n. pl.* **the ~s,** l'essentiel *m.* **~ly** *adv.* essentiellement.

establish /ɪ'stæblɪʃ/ *v.t.* établir; (*business, state*) fonder. **~ment** *n.* établissement *m.*; fondation *f.* **the E~ment,** les pouvoirs établis.

estate /ɪ'steɪt/ *n.* (*land*) propriété *f.*; (*possessions*) biens *m. pl.*; (*inheritance*) succession *f.*; (*district*) cité *f.*, complexe *m.* **~ agent,** agent immobilier *m.* **~ car,** break *m.*

esteem /ɪ'sti:m/ *v.t.* estimer. *—n.* estime *f.*

estimate[1] /'estɪmət/ *n.* (*calculation*) estimation *f.*; (*comm.*) devis *m.*

estimat|e[2] /'estɪmeɪt/ *v.t.* estimer. **~ion** /-'meɪʃn/ *n.* jugement *m.*; (*high regard*) estime *f.*

estuary /'estʃʊərɪ/ *n.* estuaire *m.*

etc. /et'setərə/ *adv.* etc.

etching /'etʃɪŋ/ *n.* eau-forte *f.*

eternal /ɪ'tɜ:nl/ *a.* éternel.

eternity /ɪ'tɜ:nətɪ/ *n.* éternité *f.*

ether /'i:θə(r)/ *n.* éther *m.*

ethereal /ɪ'θɪərɪəl/ *a.* éthéré.

ethic /'eθɪk/ *n.* éthique *f.* **~s,** moralité *f.* **~al** *a.* éthique.

Ethiopia /i:θɪ'əʊpɪə/ *n.* Éthiopie *f.* **~n** *a.* & *n.* éthiopien(ne) (*m.*(*f.*)).

ethnic /'eθnɪk/ *a.* ethnique.

ethos /'i:θɒs/ *n.* génie *m.*

etiquette /'etɪket/ *n.* étiquette *f.*

etymology /etɪ'mɒlədʒɪ/ *n.* étymologie *f.*

eucalyptus /ju:kə'lɪptəs/ *n.* (*pl.* **-tuses**) eucalyptus *m.*

eulogy /'ju:lədʒɪ/ *n.* éloge *m.*

euphemism /'ju:fəmɪzəm/ *n.* euphémisme *m.*

euphoria /ju:'fɔ:rɪə/ *n.* euphorie *f.*

Europe /'jʊərəp/ *n.* Europe *f.* **~an** /-'pɪən/ *a.* & *n.* européen(ne) (*m.* (*f.*)).

euthanasia /ju:θə'neɪzɪə/ *n.* euthanasie *f.*

evacuat|e /ɪ'vækjʊeɪt/ *v.t.* évacuer. **~ion** /-'eɪʃn/ *n.* évacuation *f.*

evade /ɪ'veɪd/ *v.t.* esquiver.

evaluate /ɪ'væljʊeɪt/ *v.t.* évaluer.

evangelical /i:væn'dʒelɪkl/ *a.* évangélique.

evangelist /ɪ'vændʒəlɪst/ *n.* évangéliste *m.*

evaporat|e /ɪ'væpəreɪt/ *v.i.* s'évaporer. **~ed milk,** lait concentré *m.* **~ion** /-'reɪʃn/ *n.* évaporation *f.*

evasion /ɪ'veɪʒn/ *n.* fuite *f.* (**of,** devant; (*excuse*) subterfuge *m.*
evasive /ɪ'veɪsɪv/ *a.* évasif.
eve /iːv/ *n.* veille *f.* (**of,** de).
even /'iːvn/ *a.* régulier; (*surface*) uni; (*equal, unvarying*) égal; (*number*) pair. —*v.t./i.* **~ (out** *or* **up),** (s')égaliser. —*adv.* même. **~ better**/*etc.*, (*still*) encore mieux/*etc.* **get ~ with,** se venger de. **~ly** *adv.* régulièrement; (*equally*) de manière égale.
evening /'iːvnɪŋ/ *n.* soir *m.*; (*whole evening, event*) soirée *f.*
event /ɪ'vent/ *n.* événement *m.*; (*sport*) épreuve *f.* **in the ~ of,** en cas de. **~ful** *a.* mouvementé.
eventual /ɪ'ventʃʊəl/ *a.* final, définitif. **~ity** /-'ælətɪ/ *n.* éventualité *f.* **~ly** *adv.* en fin de compte; (*in future*) un jour ou l'autre.
ever /'evə(r)/ *adv.* jamais; (*at all times*) toujours. **~ since** *prep.* & *adv.* depuis; *conj.* depuis que. **~ so,** (*fam.*) vraiment.
evergreen /'evəgriːn/ *n.* arbre à feuilles persistantes *m.*
everlasting /evə'lɑːstɪŋ/ *a.* éternel.
every /'evrɪ/ *a.* chaque. **~ one,** chacun(e). **~ other day,** un jour sur deux, tous les deux jours.
everybody /'evrɪbɒdɪ/ *pron.* tout le monde.
everyday /'evrɪdeɪ/ *a.* quotidien.
everyone /'evrɪwʌn/ *pron.* tout le monde.
everything /'evrɪθɪŋ/ *pron.* tout.
everywhere /'evrɪweə(r)/ *adv.* partout. **~ he goes,** partout où il va.
evict /ɪ'vɪkt/ *v.t.* expulser. **~ion** /-kʃn/ *n.* expulsion *f.*
evidence /'evɪdəns/ *n.* (*proof*) preuve(s) *f.* (*pl.*).; (*certainty*) évidence *f.*; (*signs*) signes *m. pl.*; (*testimony*) témoignage *m.* **give ~,** témoigner. **in ~,** en vue.
evident /'evɪdənt/ *a.* évident. **~ly** *adv.* de toute évidence.
evil /'iːvl/ *a.* mauvais. —*n.* mal *m.*
evo|ke /ɪ'vəʊk/ *v.t.* évoquer. **~cative** /ɪ'vɒkətɪv/ *a.* évocateur.
evolution /iːvə'luːʃn/ *n.* évolution *f.*
evolve /ɪ'vɒlv/ *v.i.* se développer, évoluer. —*v.t.* développer.
ewe /juː/ *n.* brebis *f.*
ex- /eks/ *pref.* ex-, ancien.
exacerbate /ɪg'zæsəbeɪt/ *v.t.* exacerber.
exact[1] /ɪg'zækt/ *a.* exact. **~ly** *adv.* exactement. **~ness** *n.* exactitude *f.*
exact[2] /ɪg'zækt/ *v.t.* exiger (**from,** de). **~ing** *a.* exigeant.
exaggerat|e /ɪg'zædʒəreɪt/ *v.t./i.* exagérer. **~ion** /-'reɪʃn/ *n.* exagération *f.*
exalt /ɪg'zɔːlt/ *v.t.* (*in rank*) élever; (*praise*) exalter.
exam /ɪg'zæm/ *n.* (*fam.*) examen *m.*
examination /ɪgzæmɪ'neɪʃn/ *n.* examen *m.*
examine /ɪg'zæmɪn/ *v.t.* examiner; (*witness etc.*) interroger. **~r** /-ə(r)/ *n.* examina|teur, -trice *m., f.*
example /ɪg'zɑːmpl/ *n.* exemple *m.* **for ~,** par exemple. **make an ~ of,** punir pour l'exemple.
exasperat|e /ɪg'zæspəreɪt/ *v.t.* exaspérer. **~ion** /-'reɪʃn/ *n.* exaspération *f.*
excavat|e /'ekskəveɪt/ *v.t.* creuser; (*uncover*) déterrer. **~ions** /-'veɪʃnz/ *n. pl.* (*archaeol.*) fouilles *f. pl.*
exceed /ɪk'siːd/ *v.t.* dépasser. **~ingly** *adv.* extrêmement.
excel /ɪk'sel/ *v.i.* (*p.t.* **excelled**) exceller. —*v.t.* surpasser.
excellen|t /'eksələnt/ *a.* excellent. **~ce** *n.* excellence *f.* **~tly** *adv.* admirablement, parfaitement.
except /ɪk'sept/ *prep.* sauf, excepté. —*v.t.* excepter. **~ for,** à part. **~ing** *prep.* sauf, excepté.
exception /ɪk'sepʃn/ *n.* exception *f.* **take ~ to,** s'offenser de.

exceptional /ɪk'sepʃənl/ *a.* exceptionnel. **~ly** *adv.* exceptionnellement.
excerpt /'eksɜːpt/ *n.* extrait *m.*
excess[1] /ɪk'ses/ *n.* excès *m.*
excess[2] /'ekses/ *a.* excédentaire. **~ fare,** supplément *m.* **~ luggage,** excédent de bagages *m.*
excessive /ɪk'sesɪv/ *a.* excessif. **~ly** *adv.* excessivement.
exchange /ɪks'tʃeɪndʒ/ *v.t.* échanger. *—n.* échange *m.*; (*between currencies*) change *m.* **(telephone) ~,** central (téléphonique) *m.*
exchequer /ɪks'tʃekə(r)/ *n.* (*British pol.*) Échiquier *m.*
excise /'eksaɪz/ *n.* impôt (indirect) *m.*
excit|e /ɪk'saɪt/ *v.t.* exciter; (*enthuse*) enthousiasmer. **~able** *a.* excitable. **~ed** *a.* excité. **get ~ed,** s'exciter. **~ement** *n.* excitation *f.* **~ing** *a.* passionnant.
exclaim /ɪk'skleɪm/ *v.t./i.* exclamer, s'écrier.
exclamation /ekskləˈmeɪʃn/ *n.* exclamation *f.* **~ mark** *or* **point** (*Amer.*), point d'exclamation *m.*
exclu|de /ɪk'skluːd/ *v.t.* exclure. **~sion** *n.* exclusion *f.*
exclusive /ɪk'skluːsɪv/ *a.* (*rights etc.*) exclusif; (*club etc.*) sélect; (*news item*) en exclusivité. **~ of service**/*etc.*, service/*etc.* non compris. **~ly** *adv.* exclusivement.
excommunicate /ekskə'mjuːnɪkeɪt/ *v.t.* excommunier.
excrement /'ekskrəmənt/ *n.* excrément(s) *m.* (*pl.*).
excruciating /ɪk'skruːʃɪeɪtɪŋ/ *a.* atroce, insupportable.
excursion /ɪk'skɜːʃn/ *n.* excursion *f.*
excus|e[1] /ɪk'skjuːz/ *v.t.* excuser. **~e from,** (*exempt*) dispenser de. **~e me!,** excusez-moi!, pardon! **~able** *a.* excusable.
excuse[2] /ɪk'skjuːs/ *n.* excuse *f.*
ex-directory /eksdɪ'rektərɪ/ *a.* qui n'est pas dans l'annuaire.
execute /'eksɪkjuːt/ *v.t.* exécuter.
execution /eksɪ'kjuːʃn/ *n.* exécution *f.* **~er** *n.* bourreau *m.*
executive /ɪg'zekjʊtɪv/ *n.* (pouvoir) exécutif *m.*; (*person*) cadre *m.* *—a.* exécutif.
exemplary /ɪg'zemplərɪ/ *a.* exemplaire.
exemplify /ɪg'zemplɪfaɪ/ *v.t.* illustrer.
exempt /ɪg'zempt/ *a.* exempt **(from,** de). *—v.t.* exempter. **~ion** /-pʃn/ *n.* exemption *f.*
exercise /'eksəsaɪz/ *n.* exercice *m.* *—v.t.* exercer; (*restraint, patience*) faire preuve de. *—v.i.* prendre de l'exercice. **~ book,** cahier *m.*
exert /ɪg'zɜːt/ *v.t.* exercer. **~ o.s.,** se dépenser, faire des efforts. **~ion** /-ʃn/ *n.* effort *m.*
exhaust /ɪg'zɔːst/ *v.t.* épuiser. *—n.* (*auto.*) (pot d')échappement *m.* **~ed** *a.* épuisé. **~ion** /-stʃən/ *n.* épuisement *m.*
exhaustive /ɪg'zɔːstɪv/ *a.* complet.
exhibit /ɪg'zɪbɪt/ *v.t.* exposer; (*fig.*) faire preuve de. *—n.* objet exposé *m.* **~or** *n.* exposant(e) *m.* (*f.*).
exhibition /eksɪ'bɪʃn/ *n.* exposition *f.*; (*act of showing*) démonstration *f.* **~ist** *n.* exhibitionniste *m./f.*
exhilarat|e /ɪg'zɪləreɪt/ *v.t.* transporter de joie; (*invigorate*) stimuler. **~ion** /-'reɪʃn/ *n.* joie *f.*
exhort /ɪg'zɔːt/ *v.t.* exhorter **(to,** à).
exhume /eks'hjuːm/ *v.t.* exhumer.
exile /'eksaɪl/ *n.* exil *m.*; (*person*) exilé(e) *m.* (*f.*). *—v.t.* exiler.
exist /ɪg'zɪst/ *v.i.* exister. **~ence** *n.* existence *f.* **be in ~ence,** exister.
exit /'eksɪt/ *n.* sortie *f.*
exodus /'eksədəs/ *n.* exode *m.*
exonerate /ɪg'zɒnəreɪt/ *v.t.* disculper, innocenter.
exorbitant /ɪg'zɔːbɪtənt/ *a.* exorbitant.

exorcize /ˈeksɔːsaɪz/ *v.t.* exorciser.
exotic /ɪgˈzɒtɪk/ *a.* exotique.
expan|d /ɪkˈspænd/ *v.t./i.* (*develop*) (se) développer; (*extend*) (s')étendre; (*metal, liquid*) (se) dilater. **~sion** *n.* développement *m.*; dilatation *f.*; (*pol., comm.*) expansion *f.*
expanse /ɪkˈspæns/ *n.* étendue *f.*
expatriate /eksˈpætrɪət, *Amer.* eksˈpeɪtrɪət/ *a.* & *n.* expatrié(e) (*m.* (*f.*)).
expect /ɪkˈspekt/ *v.t.* attendre, s'attendre à; (*suppose*) supposer; (*demand*) exiger; (*baby*) attendre. **~ to do,** compter faire. **~ation** /ekspekˈteɪʃn/ *n.* attente *f.*
expectan|t /ɪkˈspektənt/ *a.* **~t look,** air d'attente *m.* **~t mother,** future mère *f.* **~cy** *n.* attente *f.*
expedient /ɪkˈspiːdɪənt/ *a.* opportun. —*n.* expédient *m.*
expedite /ˈekspɪdaɪt/ *v.t.* hâter.
expedition /ekspɪˈdɪʃn/ *n.* expédition *f.*
expel /ɪkˈspel/ *v.t.* (*p.t.* **expelled**) expulser; (*from school*) renvoyer.
expend /ɪkˈspend/ *v.t.* dépenser. **~able** *a.* remplaçable.
expenditure /ɪkˈspendɪtʃə(r)/ *n.* dépense(s) *f.* (*pl.*).
expense /ɪkˈspens/ *n.* dépense *f.*, frais *m. pl.* **at s.o.'s ~,** aux dépens de qn.
expensive /ɪkˈspensɪv/ *a.* cher, coûteux; (*tastes, habits*) de luxe. **~ly** *adv.* coûteusement.
experience /ɪkˈspɪərɪəns/ *n.* expérience *f.*; (*adventure*) aventure *f.* —*v.t.* (*undergo*) connaître; (*feel*) éprouver. **~d** *a.* expérimenté.
experiment /ɪkˈsperɪmənt/ *n.* expérience *f.* —*v.i.* faire une expérience. **~al** /-ˈmentl/ *a.* expérimental.
expert /ˈekspɜːt/ *n.* expert(e) *m.* (*f.*). —*a.* expert. **~ly** *adv.* habilement.
expertise /ekspɜːˈtiːz/ *n.* compétence *f.* (**in,** en).
expir|e /ɪkˈspaɪə(r)/ *v.i.* expirer. **~ed** *a.* périmé. **~y** *n.* expiration *f.*
expl|ain /ɪkˈspleɪn/ *v.t.* expliquer. **~anation** /ekspləˈneɪʃn/ *n.* explication *f.* **~anatory** /-ænətərɪ/ *a.* explicatif.
expletive /ɪkˈspliːtɪv, *Amer.* ˈeksplətɪv/ *n.* juron *m.*
explicit /ɪkˈsplɪsɪt/ *a.* explicite.
explo|de /ɪkˈspləʊd/ *v.t./i.* (faire) exploser. **~sion** *n.* explosion *f.* **~sive** *a.* & *n.* explosif (*m.*).
exploit[1] /ˈeksplɔɪt/ *n.* exploit *m.*
exploit[2] /ɪkˈsplɔɪt/ *v.t.* exploiter. **~ation** /eksplɔɪˈteɪʃn/ *n.* exploitation *f.*
exploratory /ɪkˈsplɒrətrɪ/ *a.* (*talks: pol.*) exploratoire.
explor|e /ɪkˈsplɔː(r)/ *v.t.* explorer; (*fig.*) examiner. **~ation** /ekspləˈreɪʃn/ *n.* exploration *f.* **~er** *n.* explora|teur, -trice *m., f.*
exponent /ɪkˈspəʊnənt/ *n.* interprète *m.* (**of,** de).
export[1] /ɪkˈspɔːt/ *v.t.* exporter. **~er** *n.* exportateur *m.*
export[2] /ˈekspɔːt/ *n.* exportation *f.*
expos|e /ɪkˈspəʊz/ *v.t.* exposer; (*disclose*) dévoiler. **~ure** /-ʒə(r)/ *n.* exposition *f.*; (*photo.*) pose *f.* **die of ~ure,** mourir de froid.
expound /ɪkˈspaʊnd/ *v.t.* exposer.
express[1] /ɪkˈspres/ *a.* formel, exprès; (*letter*) exprès *invar.* —*adv.* (*by express post*) (par) exprès. —*n.* (*train*) rapide *m.*; (*less fast*) express *m.* **~ly** *adv.* expressément.
express[2] /ɪkˈspres/ *v.t.* exprimer. **~ion** /-ʃn/ *n.* expression *f.* **~ive** *a.* expressif.
expulsion /ɪkˈspʌlʃn/ *n.* expulsion *f.*; (*from school*) renvoi *m.*
expurgate /ˈekspəgeɪt/ *v.t.* expurger.
exquisite /ˈekskwɪzɪt/ *a.* exquis. **~ly** *adv.* d'une façon exquise.

ex-serviceman /eks'sɜːvɪsmən/ *n.* (*pl.* **-men**) ancien combattant *m.*
extant /ek'stænt/ *a.* existant.
extempore /ek'stempərɪ/ *a.* & *adv.* impromptu.
exten|d /ɪk'stend/ *v.t.* (*increase*) étendre, agrandir; (*arm, leg*) étendre; (*prolong*) prolonger; (*house*) agrandir; (*grant*) offrir. —*v.i.* (*stretch*) s'étendre; (*in time*) se prolonger. **~sion** *n.* (*of line, road*) prolongement *m.*; (*in time*) prolongation *f.*; (*building*) annexe *f.*; (*of phone*) appareil supplémentaire *m.*; (*phone number*) poste *m.*
extensive /ɪk'stensɪv/ *a.* vaste; (*study*) profond; (*damage etc.*) important. **~ly** *adv.* (*much*) beaucoup; (*very*) très.
extent /ɪk'stent/ *n.* (*size, scope*) étendue *f.*; (*degree*) mesure *f.* **to such an ~ that,** à tel point que.
extenuate /ɪk'stenjʊeɪt/ *v.t.* atténuer.
exterior /ɪk'stɪərɪə(r)/ *a.* & *n.* extérieur (*m.*).
exterminat|e /ɪk'stɜːmɪneɪt/ *v.t.* exterminer. **~ion** /-'neɪʃn/ *n.* extermination *f.*
external /ɪk'stɜːnl/ *a.* extérieur; (*cause, medical use*) externe. **~ly** *adv.* extérieurement.
extinct /ɪk'stɪŋkt/ *a.* (*species*) disparu; (*volcano, passion*) éteint. **~ion** /-kʃn/ *n.* extinction *f.*
extinguish /ɪk'stɪŋgwɪʃ/ *v.t.* éteindre. **~er** *n.* extincteur *m.*
extol /ɪk'stəʊl/ *v.t.* (*p.t.* **extolled**) exalter, chanter les louanges de.
extort /ɪk'stɔːt/ *v.t.* extorquer **(from,** à). **~ion** /-ʃn/ *n.* (*jurid.*) extorsion (de fonds) *f.*
extortionate /ɪk'stɔːʃənət/ *a.* exorbitant.
extra /'ekstrə/ *a.* de plus, supplémentaire. —*adv.* plus (que d'habitude). **~ strong,** extra-fort. —*n.* (*additional thing*) supplément *m.*; (*cinema*) figurant(e) *m.* (*f.*). **~ charge,** supplément *m.* **~ time,** (*football*) prolongation *f.*
extra- /'ekstrə/ *pref.* extra-.
extract¹ /ɪk'strækt/ *v.t.* extraire; (*promise, tooth*) arracher; (*fig.*) obtenir. **~ion** /-kʃn/ *n.* extraction *f.*
extract² /'ekstrækt/ *n.* extrait *m.*
extra-curricular /ekstrəkə'rɪkjʊlə(r)/ *a.* hors programme.
extradit|e /'ekstrədaɪt/ *v.t.* extrader. **~ion** /-'dɪʃn/ *n.* extradition *f.*
extramarital /ekstrə'mærɪtl/ *a.* extra-conjugal.
extramural /ekstrə'mjʊərəl/ *a.* (*univ.*) hors faculté.
extraordinary /ɪk'strɔːdnrɪ/ *a.* extraordinaire.
extravagan|t /ɪk'strævəgənt/ *a.* extravagant; (*wasteful*) prodigue. **~ce** *n.* extravagance *f.*; prodigalité *f.*
extrem|e /ɪk'striːm/ *a.* & *n.* extrême (*m.*). **~ely** *adv.* extrêmement. **~ist** *n.* extrémiste *m./f.*
extremity /ɪk'stremətɪ/ *n.* extrémité *f.*
extricate /'ekstrɪkeɪt/ *v.t.* dégager.
extrovert /'ekstrəvɜːt/ *n.* extraverti(e) *m.* (*f.*).
exuberan|t /ɪg'zjuːbərənt/ *a.* exubérant. **~ce** *n.* exubérance *f.*
exude /ɪg'zjuːd/ *v.t.* (*charm etc.*) manifester libéralement.
exult /ɪg'zʌlt/ *v.i.* exulter.
eye /aɪ/ *n.* œil *m.* (*pl.* yeux). —*v.t.* (*p.t.* **eyed,** *pres. p.* **eyeing**) regarder. **keep an ~ on,** surveiller. **~-opener** *n.* révélation *f.* **~-shadow** *n.* fard à paupières *m.*
eyeball /'aɪbɔːl/ *n.* globe oculaire *m.*
eyebrow /'aɪbraʊ/ *n.* sourcil *m.*
eyeful /'aɪfʊl/ *n.* **get an ~,** (*fam.*) se rincer l'œil.
eyelash /'aɪlæʃ/ *n.* cil *m.*
eyelet /'aɪlɪt/ *n.* œillet *m.*
eyelid /'aɪlɪd/ *n.* paupière *f.*

eyesight /ˈaɪsaɪt/ *n.* vue *f.*
eyesore /ˈaɪsɔː(r)/ *n.* horreur *f.*
eyewitness /ˈaɪwɪtnɪs/ *n.* témoin oculaire *m.*

F

fable /ˈfeɪbl/ *n.* fable *f.*
fabric /ˈfæbrɪk/ *n.* (*cloth*) tissu *m.*
fabrication /fæbrɪˈkeɪʃn/ *n.* (*invention*) invention *f.*
fabulous /ˈfæbjʊləs/ *a.* fabuleux; (*marvellous*: *fam.*) formidable.
façade /fəˈsɑːd/ *n.* façade *f.*
face /feɪs/ *n.* visage *m.*, figure *f.*; (*aspect*) face *f.*; (*of clock*) cadran *m.* —*v.t.* être en face de; (*confront*) faire face à, affronter. —*v.i.* se tourner; (*of house*) être exposé. **~-flannel** *n.* gant de toilette *m.* **~-lift** *n.* lifting *m.* **~ to face,** face à face. **~ up to,** faire face à. **in the ~ of, ~d with,** face à. **make a (funny) ~,** faire une grimace.
faceless /ˈfeɪslɪs/ *a.* anonyme.
facet /ˈfæsɪt/ *n.* facette *f.*
facetious /fəˈsiːʃəs/ *a.* facétieux.
facial /ˈfeɪʃl/ *a.* de la face, facial. —*n.* soin du visage *m.*
facile /ˈfæsaɪl, *Amer.* ˈfæsl/ *a.* facile, superficiel.
facilitate /fəˈsɪlɪteɪt/ *v.t.* faciliter.
facilit|y /fəˈsɪlətɪ/ *n.* facilité *f.* **~ies,** (*equipment*) équipements *m. pl.*
facing /ˈfeɪsɪŋ/ *n.* parement *m.*
facsimile /fækˈsɪməlɪ/ *n.* facsimilé *m.*
fact /fækt/ *n.* fait *m.* **as a matter of ~, in ~,** en fait.
faction /ˈfækʃn/ *n.* faction *f.*
factor /ˈfæktə(r)/ *n.* facteur *m.*
factory /ˈfæktərɪ/ *n.* usine *f.*
factual /ˈfæktʃʊəl/ *a.* basé sur les faits.
faculty /ˈfæklti/ *n.* faculté *f.*
fad /fæd/ *n.* manie *f.*, folie *f.*
fade /feɪd/ *v.i.* (*sound*) s'affaiblir; (*memory*) s'évanouir; (*flower*) se faner; (*material*) déteindre; (*colour*) passer.
fag /fæg/ *n.* (*chore*: *fam.*) corvée *f.*; (*cigarette*: *sl.*) sèche *f.*; (*homosexual*: *Amer.*, *sl.*) pédé *m.*
fagged /fægd/ *a.* (*tired*) éreinté.
fail /feɪl/ *v.i.* échouer; (*grow weak*) (s'af)faiblir; (*run short*) manquer; (*engine etc.*) tomber en panne. —*v.t.* (*exam*) échouer à; (*candidate*) refuser, recaler; (*disappoint*) décevoir. **~ s.o.,** (*of words etc.*) manquer à qn. **~ to do,** (*not do*) ne pas faire; (*not be able*) ne pas réussir à faire. **without ~,** à coup sûr.
failing /ˈfeɪlɪŋ/ *n.* défaut *m.* —*prep.* à défaut de.
failure /ˈfeɪljə(r)/ *n.* échec *m.*; (*person*) raté(e) *m.* (*f.*).; (*breakdown*) panne *f.* **~ to do,** (*inability*) incapacité de faire *f.*
faint /feɪnt/ *a.* (**-er, -est**) léger, faible. —*v.i.* s'évanouir. —*n.* évanouissement *m.* **feel ~,** (*ill*) se trouver mal. **the ~est idea,** la moindre idée. **~-hearted** *a.* timide. **~ly** *adv.* (*weakly*) faiblement; (*slightly*) légèrement. **~ness** *n.* faiblesse *f.*
fair[1] /feə(r)/ *n.* foire *f.* **~-ground** *n.* champ de foire *m.*
fair[2] /feə(r)/ *a.* (**-er, -est**) (*hair, person*) blond; (*skin etc.*) clair; (*just*) juste, équitable; (*weather*) beau; (*amount*) raisonnable. —*adv.* (*play*) loyalement. **~ play,** le fair-play. **~ly** *adv.* (*justly*) équitablement; (*rather*) assez. **~ness** *n.* justice *f.*
fairy /ˈfeərɪ/ *n.* fée *f.* **~ story, ~-tale** *n.* conte de fées *m.*
faith /feɪθ/ *n.* foi. *f.* **~-healer** *n.* guérisseu|r, -se *m.*, *f.*
faithful /ˈfeɪθfl/ *a.* fidèle. **~ly** *adv.* fidèlement. **~ness** *n.* fidélité *f.*
fake /feɪk/ *n.* (*forgery*) faux *m.*;

(*person*) imposteur *m*. **it is a ~,** c'est faux. —*a*. faux. —*v.t*. (*copy*) faire un faux de; (*alter*) falsifier, truquer; (*illness*) simuler.

falcon /'fɔːlkən/ *n*. faucon *m*.

fall /fɔːl/ *v.i*. (*p.t*. **fell,** *p.p*. **fallen**) tomber. —*n*. chute *f*.; (*autumn*: *Amer*.) automne *m*. **~ back on,** se rabattre sur. **~ down** *or* **off,** tomber. **~ for,** (*person*: *fam*.) tomber amoureux de; (*a trick*: *fam*.) se laisser prendre à. **~ in,** (*mil*.) se mettre en rangs. **~ off,** (*decrease*) diminuer. **~ out,** se brouiller (**with,** avec). **~-out** *n*. retombées *f. pl*. **~ over,** tomber (par terre). **~ short,** être insuffisant. **~ through,** (*plans*) tomber à l'eau.

fallacy /'fæləsɪ/ *n*. erreur *f*.

fallible /'fæləbl/ *a*. faillible.

fallow /'fæləʊ/ *a*. en jachère.

false /fɔːls/ *a*. faux. **~hood** *n*. mensonge *m*. **~ly** *adv*. faussement. **~ness** *n*. fausseté *f*.

falsetto /fɔːl'setəʊ/ *n*. (*pl*. **-os**) fausset *m*.

falsify /'fɔːlsɪfaɪ/ *v.t*. falsifier.

falter /'fɔːltə(r)/ *v.i*. vaciller.

fame /feɪm/ *n*. renommée *f*.

famed /feɪmd/ *a*. renommé.

familiar /fə'mɪlɪə(r)/ *a*. familier. **be ~ with,** connaître. **~ity** /-'ærətɪ/ *n*. familiarité *f*. **~ize** *v.t*. familiariser.

family /'fæməlɪ/ *n*. famille *f*. —*a*. de famille, familial.

famine /'fæmɪn/ *n*. famine *f*.

famished /'fæmɪʃt/ *a*. affamé.

famous /'feɪməs/ *a*. célèbre. **~ly** *adv*. (*very well*: *fam*.) à merveille.

fan[1] /fæn/ *n*. ventilateur *m*.; (*hand-held*) éventail *m*. —*v.t*. (*p.t*. **fanned**) éventer; (*fig*.) attiser. —*v.i*. **~ out,** se déployer en éventail. **~ belt,** courroie de ventilateur *f*.

fan[2] /fæn/ *n*. (*of person*) admira|teur, -trice *m*., *f*.; (*enthusiast*) fervent(e) *m*. (*f*.), passionné(e) *m*. (*f*.).

fanatic /fə'nætɪk/ *n*. fanatique *m*./*f*. **~al** *a*. fanatique. **~ism** /-sɪzəm/ *n*. fanatisme *m*.

fancier /'fænsɪə(r)/ *n*. (**dog**/*etc*.) **~,** amateur (de chiens/*etc*.) *m*.

fanciful /'fænsɪfl/ *a*. fantaisiste.

fancy /'fænsɪ/ *n*. (*whim, fantasy*) fantaisie *f*.; (*liking*) goût *m*. —*a*. (*buttons etc*.) fantaisie *invar*.; (*prices*) extravagant; (*impressive*) impressionnant. —*v.t*. s'imaginer; (*want*: *fam*.) avoir envie de; (*like*: *fam*.) aimer. **take a ~ to s.o.,** se prendre d'affection pour qn. **it took my ~,** ça m'a plu. **~ dress,** travesti *m*.

fanfare /'fænfeə(r)/ *n*. fanfare *f*.

fang /fæŋ/ *n*. (*of dog etc*.) croc *m*.; (*of snake*) crochet *m*.

fanlight /'fænlaɪt/ *n*. imposte *f*.

fantastic /fæn'tæstɪk/ *a*. fantastique.

fantas|y /'fæntəsɪ/ *n*. fantaisie *f*.; (*day-dream*) fantasme *m*. **~ize** *v.i*. faire des fantasmes.

far /fɑː(r)/ *adv*. loin; (*much*) beaucoup; (*very*) très. —*a*. lointain; (*end, side*) autre. **~ away, ~ off,** au loin. **as ~ as,** (*up to*) jusqu'à. **as ~ as I know,** autant que je sache. **~-away** *a*. lointain. **the Far East,** l'Extrême-Orient *m*. **~-fetched** *a*. bizarre, exagéré. **~-reaching** *a*. de grande portée.

farc|e /fɑːs/ *n*. farce *f*. **~ical** *a*. ridicule, grotesque.

fare /feə(r)/ *n*. (prix du) billet *m*.; (*food*) nourriture *f*. —*v.i*. (*progress*) aller; (*manage*) se débrouiller.

farewell /feə'wel/ *int*. & *n*. adieu (*m*.).

farm /fɑːm/ *n*. ferme *f*. —*v.t*. cultiver. —*v.i*. être fermier. **~ out,** céder en sous-traitance. **~er** *n*. fermier *m*. **~ing** *n*. agriculture *f*.

farmhouse /'fɑːmhaʊs/ *n*. ferme *f*.

farmyard /ˈfɑːmjɑːd/ *n.* basse-cour *f.*

farth|er /ˈfɑːðə(r)/ *adv.* plus loin. —*a.* plus éloigné. **~est** *adv.* le plus loin; *a.* le plus éloigné.

fascinat|e /ˈfæsɪneɪt/ *v.t.* fasciner. **~ion** /-ˈneɪʃn/ *n.* fascination *f.*

Fascis|t /ˈfæʃɪst/ *n.* fasciste *m./f.* **~m** /-zəm/ *n.* fascisme *m.*

fashion /ˈfæʃn/ *n.* (*current style*) mode *f.*; (*manner*) façon *f.* —*v.t.* façonner. **~ designer,** couturier *m.* **~able** *a.*, **~ably** *adv.* à la mode.

fast[1] /fɑːst/ *a.* (**-er, -est**) rapide; (*colour*) grand teint *invar.*, fixe; (*firm*) fixe, solide. —*adv.* vite; (*firmly*) ferme. **be ~,** (*clock etc.*) avancer. **~ asleep,** profondément endormi.

fast[2] /fɑːst/ *v.i.* (*go without food*) jeûner. —*n.* jeûne *m.*

fasten /ˈfɑːsn/ *v.t./i.* (s')attacher. **~er, ~ing** *ns.* attache *f.*, fermeture *f.*

fastidious /fəˈstɪdɪəs/ *a.* difficile.

fat /fæt/ *n.* graisse *f.*; (*on meat*) gras *m.* —*a.* (**fatter, fattest**) gros, gras; (*meat*) gras; (*sum, volume*: *fig.*) gros. **a ~ lot,** (*sl.*) bien peu (**of,** de). **~-head** *n.* (*fam.*) imbécile *m., f.* **~ness** *n.* corpulence *f.*

fatal /ˈfeɪtl/ *a.* mortel; (*fateful, disastrous*) fatal. **~ity** /fəˈtælətɪ/ *n.* mort *m.* **~ly** *adv.* mortellement.

fatalist /ˈfeɪtəlɪst/ *n.* fataliste *m./f.*

fate /feɪt/ *n.* (*controlling power*) destin *m.*, sort *m.*; (*one's lot*) sort *m.* **~ful** *a.* fatidique.

fated /ˈfeɪtɪd/ *a.* destiné (**to,** à).

father /ˈfɑːðə(r)/ *n.* père *m.* **~-in-law** *n.* (*pl.* **~s-in-law**) beau-père *m.* **~hood** *n.* paternité *f.* **~ly** *a.* paternel.

fathom /ˈfæðəm/ *n.* brasse *f.* (*= 1,8 m.*). —*v.t.* **~ (out),** comprendre.

fatigue /fəˈtiːg/ *n.* fatigue *f.* —*v.t.* fatiguer.

fatten /ˈfætn/ *v.t./i.* engraisser. **~ing** *a.* qui fait grossir.

fatty /ˈfætɪ/ *a.* gras; (*tissue*) adipeux. —*n.* (*person*: *fam.*) gros(se) *m.* (*f.*).

fatuous /ˈfætʃʊəs/ *a.* stupide.

faucet /ˈfɔːsɪt/ *n.* (*Amer.*) robinet *m.*

fault /fɔːlt/ *n.* (*defect, failing*) défaut *m.*; (*blame*) faute *f.*; (*geol.*) faille *f.* —*v.t.* **~ sth./s.o.,** trouver des défauts à qch./chez qn. **at ~,** fautif. **~less** *a.* irréprochable. **~y** *a.* défectueux.

fauna /ˈfɔːnə/ *n.* faune *f.*

favour /ˈfeɪvə(r)/ *n.* faveur *f.* —*v.t.* favoriser; (*support*) être en faveur de; (*prefer*) préférer. **do s.o. a ~,** rendre service à qn. **~able** *a.* favorable. **~ably** *adv.* favorablement.

favourit|e /ˈfeɪvərɪt/ *a.* & *n.* favori(te) (*m.* (*f.*)). **~ism** *n.* favoritisme *m.*

fawn[1] /fɔːn/ *n.* faon *m.* —*a.* fauve.

fawn[2] /fɔːn/ *v.i.* **~ on,** flatter bassement, flagorner.

FBI *abbr.* (*Federal Bureau of Investigation*) (*Amer.*) service d'enquêtes du Ministère de la Justice *m.*

fear /fɪə(r)/ *n.* crainte *f.*, peur *f.*; (*fig.*) risque *m.* —*v.t.* craindre. **for ~ of/that,** de peur de/que. **~ful** *a.* (*terrible*) affreux; (*timid*) craintif. **~less** *a.* intrépide. **~lessness** *n.* intrépidité *f.*

fearsome /ˈfɪəsəm/ *a.* redoutable.

feasib|le /ˈfiːzəbl/ *a.* faisable; (*likely*) plausible. **~ility** /-ˈbɪlətɪ/ *n.* possibilité *f.*; plausibilité *f.*

feast /fiːst/ *n.* festin *m.*; (*relig.*) fête *f.* —*v.i.* festoyer. —*v.t.* régaler. **~ on,** se régaler de.

feat /fiːt/ *n.* exploit *m.*

feather /ˈfeðə(r)/ *n.* plume *f.* —*v.t.* **~ one's nest,** s'enrichir. **~ duster,** plumeau *m.*

featherweight /ˈfeðəweɪt/ *n.* poids plume *m. invar.*

feature /ˈfiːtʃə(r)/ *n.* caractéristique *f.*; (*of person, face*) trait *m.*; (*film*) long métrage *m.*; (*article*) article vedette *m.* —*v.t.* représenter; (*give prominence to*) mettre en vedette. —*v.i.* figurer (**in,** dans).

February /ˈfebrʊərɪ/ *n.* février *m.*

feckless /ˈfeklɪs/ *a.* inepte.

fed /fed/ *see* **feed.** —*a.* **be ~ up,** (*fam.*) en avoir marre (**with,** de).

federa|l /ˈfedərəl/ *a.* fédéral. **~tion** /-ˈreɪʃn/ *n.* fédération *f.*

fee /fiː/ *n.* (*for entrance*) prix *m.* **~(s),** (*of doctor etc.*) honoraires *m. pl.*; (*of actor, artist*) cachet *m.*; (*for tuition*) frais *m. pl.*; (*for enrolment*) droits *m. pl.*

feeble /fiːbl/ *a.* (**-er, -est**) faible. **~-minded** *a.* faible d'esprit.

feed /fiːd/ *v.t.* (*p.t.* **fed**) nourrir, donner à manger à; (*suckle*) allaiter; (*supply*) alimenter. —*v.i.* se nourrir (**on,** de). —*n.* nourriture *f.*; (*of baby*) tétée *f.*

feedback /ˈfiːdbæk/ *n.* réaction(s) *f.* (*pl.*).

feel /fiːl/ *v.t.* (*p.t.* **felt**) (*touch*) tâter; (*be conscious of*) sentir; (*experience*) éprouver; (*think*) estimer. —*v.i.* (*tired, lonely, etc.*) se sentir. **~ hot/thirsty**/*etc.*, avoir chaud/soif/*etc.* **~ as if,** avoir l'impression que. **~ awful,** (*ill*) se sentir malade. **~ like,** (*want: fam.*) avoir envie de.

feeler /ˈfiːlə(r)/ *n.* antenne *f.* **put out a ~,** lancer un ballon d'essai.

feeling /ˈfiːlɪŋ/ *n.* sentiment *m.*; (*physical*) sensation *f.*

feet /fiːt/ *see* **foot.**

feign /feɪn/ *v.t.* feindre.

feint /feɪnt/ *n.* feinte *f.*

felicitous /fəˈlɪsɪtəs/ *a.* heureux.

feline /ˈfiːlaɪn/ *a.* félin.

fell[1] /fel/ *v.t.* (*cut down*) abattre.

fell[2] /fel/ *see* **fall.**

fellow /ˈfeləʊ/ *n.* compagnon *m.*, camarade *m.*; (*of society*) membre *m.*; (*man: fam.*) type *m.* **~-countryman** *n.* compatriote *m.* **~-passenger, ~-traveller** *n.* compagnon de voyage *m.* **~ship** *n.* camaraderie *f.*; (*group*) association *f.*

felony /ˈfelənɪ/ *n.* crime *m.*

felt[1] /felt/ *n.* feutre *m.*

felt[2] /felt/ *see* **feel.**

female /ˈfiːmeɪl/ *a.* (*animal etc.*) femelle; (*voice, sex, etc.*) féminin. —*n.* femme *f.*; (*animal*) femelle *f.*

feminin|e /ˈfemənɪn/ *a.* & *n.* féminin (*m.*). **~ity** /-ˈnɪnətɪ/ *n.* féminité *f.*

feminist /ˈfemɪnɪst/ *n.* féministe *m.*/*f.*

fenc|e /fens/ *n.* barrière *f.*; (*person: jurid.*) receleu|r, -se *m.*, *f.* —*v.t.* **~e (in),** clôturer. —*v.i.* (*sport*) faire de l'escrime. **~er** *n.* escrimeu|r, -se *m.*, *f.* **~ing** *n.* escrime *f.*

fend /fend/ *v.i.* **~ for o.s.,** se débrouiller tout seul. —*v.t.* **~ off,** (*blow, attack*) parer.

fender /ˈfendə(r)/ *n.* (*for fireplace*) garde-feu *m. invar.*; (*mudguard: Amer.*) garde-boue *m. invar.*

fennel /ˈfenl/ *n.* (*culin.*) fenouil *m.*

ferment[1] /fəˈment/ *v.t.*/*i.* (faire) fermenter. **~ation** /fɜːmenˈteɪʃn/ *n.* fermentation *f.*

ferment[2] /ˈfɜːment/ *n.* ferment *m.*; (*excitement: fig.*) agitation *f.*

fern /fɜːn/ *n.* fougère *f.*

feroc|ious /fəˈrəʊʃəs/ *a.* féroce. **~ity** /-ˈrɒsətɪ/ *n.* férocité *f.*

ferret /ˈferɪt/ *n.* (*animal*) furet *m.* —*v.i.* (*p.t.* **ferreted**) fureter. —*v.t.* **~ out,** dénicher.

ferry /ˈferɪ/ *n.* ferry(-boat) *m.*, bac *m.* —*v.t.* transporter.

fertil|e /ˈfɜːtaɪl, *Amer.* ˈfɜːtl/ *a.* fertile; (*person, animal*) fécond. **~ity** /fəˈtɪlətɪ/ *n.* fertilité *f.*; fécondité *f.* **~ize** /-əlaɪz/ *v.t.* fertiliser; féconder.

fertilizer /ˈfɜːtəlaɪzə(r)/ *n.* engrais *m.*

fervent /'fɜːvənt/ *a.* fervent.
fervour /'fɜːvə(r)/ *n.* ferveur *f.*
fester /'festə(r)/ *v.i.* (*wound*) suppurer; (*fig.*) rester sur le cœur.
festival /'festɪvl/ *n.* festival *m.*; (*relig.*) fête *f.*
festiv|e /'festɪv/ *a.* de fête, gai. **~e season,** période des fêtes *f.* **~ity** /fe'stɪvətɪ/ *n.* réjouissances *f. pl.*
festoon /fe'stuːn/ *v.i.* **~ with,** orner de.
fetch /fetʃ/ *v.t.* (*go for*) aller chercher; (*bring person*) amener; (*bring thing*) apporter; (*be sold for*) rapporter.
fête /feɪt/ *n.* fête *f.* —*v.t.* fêter.
fetid /'fetɪd/ *a.* fétide.
fetish /'fetɪʃ/ *n.* (*object*) fétiche *m.*; (*psych.*) obsession *f.*
fetter /'fetə(r)/ *v.t.* enchaîner. **~s** *n. pl.* chaînes *f. pl.*
feud /fjuːd/ *n.* querelle *f.*
feudal /'fjuːdl/ *a.* féodal.
fever /'fiːvə(r)/ *n.* fièvre *f.* **~ish** *a.* fiévreux.
few /fjuː/ *a.* & *n.* peu (de). **~ books,** peu de livres. **they are ~,** ils sont peu nombreux. **a ~** *a.* quelques; *n.* quelques-un(e)s. **a good ~, quite a ~,** (*fam.*) bon nombre (de). **~er** *a.* & *n.* moins (de). **be ~er,** être moins nombreux (**than,** que). **~est** *a.* & *n.* le moins (de).
fiancé /fɪ'ɒnseɪ/ *n.* fiancé *m.*
fiancée /fɪ'ɒnseɪ/ *n.* fiancée *f.*
fiasco /fɪ'æskəʊ/ *n.* (*pl.* **-os**) fiasco *m.*
fib /fɪb/ *n.* mensonge *m.* **~ber** *n.* menteu|r, -se *m., f.*
fibre /'faɪbə(r)/ *n.* fibre *f.*
fibreglass /'faɪbəglɑːs/ *n.* fibre de verre *f.*
fickle /'fɪkl/ *a.* inconstant.
fiction /'fɪkʃn/ *n.* fiction *f.* (**works of**) **~,** romans *m. pl.* **~al** *a.* fictif.
fictitious /fɪk'tɪʃəs/ *a.* fictif.
fiddle /'fɪdl/ *n.* (*fam.*) violon *m.*; (*swindle*: *sl.*) combine *f.* —*v.i.* (*sl.*) frauder. —*v.t.* (*sl.*) falsifier. **~ with,** (*fam.*) tripoter. **~r** /-ə(r)/ *n.* (*fam.*) violoniste *m./f.*
fidelity /fɪ'delətɪ/ *n.* fidélité *f.*
fidget /'fɪdʒɪt/ *v.i.* (*p.t.* **fidgeted**) remuer sans cesse. —*n.* **be a ~,** être remuant. **~ with,** tripoter. **~y** *a.* remuant.
field /fiːld/ *n.* champ *m.*; (*sport*) terrain *m.*; (*fig.*) domaine *m.* —*v.t.* (*ball*: *cricket*) bloquer. **~-day** *n.* grande occasion *f.* **~-glasses** *n. pl.* jumelles *f. pl.* **F~ Marshal,** maréchal *m.*
fieldwork /'fiːldwɜːk/ *n.* travaux pratiques *m. pl.*
fiend /fiːnd/ *n.* démon *m.* **~ish** *a.* diabolique.
fierce /fɪəs/ *a.* (**-er, -est**) féroce; (*storm, attack*) violent. **~ness** *n.* férocité *f.*; violence *f.*
fiery /'faɪərɪ/ *a.* (**-ier, -iest**) (*hot*) ardent; (*spirited*) fougueux.
fiesta /fɪ'estə/ *n.* fiesta *f.*
fifteen /fɪf'tiːn/ *a.* & *n.* quinze (*m.*). **~th** *a.* & *n.* quinzième (*m./f.*).
fifth /fɪfθ/ *a.* & *n.* cinquième (*m./f.*). **~ column,** cinquième colonne *f.*
fift|y /'fɪftɪ/ *a.* & *n.* cinquante (*m.*). **~ieth** *a.* & *n.* cinquantième (*m./f.*). **a ~y-fifty chance,** (*equal*) une chance sur deux.
fig /fɪg/ *n.* figue *f.*
fight /faɪt/ *v.i.* (*p.t.* **fought**) se battre; (*struggle*: *fig.*) lutter; (*quarrel*) se disputer. —*v.t.* se battre avec; (*evil etc.*: *fig.*) lutter contre. —*n.* (*struggle*) lutte *f.*; (*quarrel*) dispute *f.*; (*brawl*) bagarre *f.*; (*mil.*) combat *m.* **~ back,** se défendre. **~ over sth.,** se disputer qch. **~ shy of,** fuir devant. **~er** *n.* (*brawler, soldier*) combattant *m.*; (*fig.*) battant *m.*; (*aircraft*) chasseur *m.* **~ing** *n.* combats *m. pl.*
figment /'fɪgmənt/ *n.* invention *f.*
figurative /'fɪgjərətɪv/ *a.* figuré.
figure /'fɪgə(r)/ *n.* (*number*) chiffre

m.; (*diagram*) figure *f.*; (*shape*) forme *f.*; (*of woman*) ligne *f.* **~s,** arithmétique *f.* —*v.t.* s'imaginer. —*v.i.* (*appear*) figurer. **~ out,** comprendre. **~-head** *n.* (*person with no real power*) prête-nom *m.* **~ of speech,** façon de parler *f.* **that ~s,** (*Amer., fam.*) c'est logique.

filament /'fɪləmənt/ *n.* filament *m.*

filch /fɪltʃ/ *v.t.* voler, piquer.

fil|e[1] /faɪl/ *n.* (*tool*) lime *f.* —*v.t.* limer. **~ings** *n. pl.* limaille *f.*

file[2] /faɪl/ *n.* dossier *m.*, classeur *m.*; (*row*) file *f.* —*v.t.* (*papers*) classer. —*v.i.* **~ in,** entrer en file. **~ past,** défiler devant.

fill /fɪl/ *v.t./i.* (se) remplir. —*n.* **eat one's ~,** manger à sa faim. **have had one's ~,** en avoir assez. **~ in,** (*form*) remplir. **~ out,** (*get fat*) grossir. **~ up,** (*auto.*) faire le plein (d'essence).

fillet /'fɪlɪt, *Amer.* fɪ'leɪ/ *n.* filet *m.* —*v.t.* (*p.t.* **filleted**) découper en filets.

filling /'fɪlɪŋ/ *n.* (*of tooth*) plombage *m.* **~ station,** station-service *f.*

filly /'fɪlɪ/ *n.* pouliche *f.*

film /fɪlm/ *n.* film *m.*; (*photo.*) pellicule *f.* —*v.t.* filmer. **~-goer** *n.* cinéphile *m.*/*f.* **~ star,** vedette de cinéma *f.*

filter /'fɪltə(r)/ *n.* filtre *m.*; (*traffic signal*) flèche *f.* —*v.t./i.* filtrer; (*of traffic*) suivre la flèche. **~-tip** *n.* bout filtre *m.*

filth /fɪlθ/ *n.* saleté *f.* **~iness** *n.* saleté *f.* **~y** *a.* sale.

fin /fɪn/ *n.* (*of fish, seal*) nageoire *f.*; (*of shark*) aileron *m.*

final /'faɪnl/ *a.* dernier; (*conclusive*) définitif. —*n.* (*sport*) finale *f.* **~ist** *n.* finaliste *m.*/*f.* **~ly** *adv.* (*lastly, at last*) enfin, finalement; (*once and for all*) définitivement.

finale /fɪ'nɑːlɪ/ *n.* (*mus.*) final(e) *m.*

finalize /'faɪnəlaɪz/ *v.t.* mettre au point, fixer.

financ|e /'faɪnæns/ *n.* finance *f.* —*a.* financier. —*v.t.* financer. **~ier** /-'nænsɪə(r)/ *n.* financier *m.*

financial /faɪ'nænʃl/ *a.* financier. **~ly** *adv.* financièrement.

find /faɪnd/ *v.t.* (*p.t.* **found**) trouver; (*sth. lost*) retrouver. —*n.* trouvaille *f.* **~ out** *v.t.* découvrir; *v.i.* se renseigner (**about,** sur). **~ings** *n. pl.* conclusions *f. pl.*

fine[1] /faɪn/ *n.* amende *f.* —*v.t.* condamner à une amende.

fine[2] /faɪn/ *a.* (**-er, -est**) fin; (*excellent*) beau. —*adv.* (très) bien; (*small*) fin. **~ arts,** beaux-arts *m. pl.* **~ly** *adv.* (*admirably*) magnifiquement; (*cut*) fin.

finery /'faɪnərɪ/ *n.* atours *m. pl.*

finesse /fɪ'nes/ *n.* finesse *f.*

finger /'fɪŋgə(r)/ *n.* doigt *m.* —*v.t.* palper. **~-nail** *n.* ongle *m.* **~-stall** *n.* doigtier *m.*

fingerprint /'fɪŋgəprɪnt/ *n.* empreinte digitale *f.*

fingertip /'fɪŋgətɪp/ *n.* bout du doigt *m.*

finicking, finicky /'fɪnɪkɪŋ, 'fɪnɪkɪ/ *adjs.* méticuleux.

finish /'fɪnɪʃ/ *v.t./i.* finir. —*n.* fin *f.*; (*of race*) arrivée *f.*; (*appearance*) finition *f.* **~ doing,** finir de faire. **~ up doing,** finir par faire. **~ up in,** (*land up in*) se retrouver à.

finite /'faɪnaɪt/ *a.* fini.

Fin|land /'fɪnlənd/ *n.* Finlande *f.* **~n** *n.* Finlandais(e) *m.* (*f.*). **~nish** *a.* finlandais; *n.* (*lang.*) finnois *m.*

fir /fɜː(r)/ *n.* sapin *m.*

fire /'faɪə(r)/ *n.* feu *m.*; (*conflagration*) incendie *m.* —*v.t.* (*bullet etc.*) tirer; (*dismiss*) renvoyer; (*fig.*) enflammer. —*v.i.* tirer (**at,** sur). **~ a gun,** tirer un coup de revolver *or* de fusil. **~ brigade,** pompiers *m. pl.* **~-engine** *n.* voiture de pompiers *f.* **~-escape** *n.* escalier de secours *m.* **~ station,** caserne de pompiers *f.*

firearm /'faɪərɑːm/ *n.* arme à feu *f.*

firecracker /ˈfaɪəkrækə(r)/ *n.* (*Amer.*) pétard *m.*
firelight /ˈfaɪəlaɪt/ *n.* lueur du feu *f.*
fireman /ˈfaɪəmən/ *n.* (*pl.* **-men**) pompier *m.*
fireplace /ˈfaɪəpleɪs/ *n.* cheminée *f.*
fireside /ˈfaɪəsaɪd/ *n.* coin du feu *m.*
firewood /ˈfaɪəwʊd/ *n.* bois de chauffage *m.*
firework /ˈfaɪəwɜːk/ *n.* feu d'artifice *m.*
firing-squad /ˈfaɪərɪŋskwɒd/ *n.* peloton d'exécution *m.*
firm[1] /fɜːm/ *n.* firme *f.*, société *f.*
firm[2] /fɜːm/ *a.* (**-er, -est**) ferme; (*belief*) solide. **~ly** *adv.* fermement. **~ness** *n.* fermeté *f.*
first /fɜːst/ *a.* premier. —*n.* prem|ier, -ière *m., f.* —*adv.* d'abord, premièrement; (*arrive etc.*) le premier, la première. **at ~,** d'abord. **at ~ hand,** de première main. **at ~ sight,** à première vue. **~ aid,** premiers soins *m. pl.* **~-class** *a.* de première classe. **~ floor,** (*Amer.*) rez-de-chaussée *m. invar.* **F~ Lady,** (*Amer.*) épouse du Président *f.* **~ name,** prénom *m.* **~ of all,** tout d'abord. **~-rate** *a.* excellent. **~ly** *adv.* premièrement.
fiscal /ˈfɪskl/ *a.* fiscal.
fish /fɪʃ/ *n.* (*usually invar.*) poisson *m.* —*v.i.* pêcher. **~ for,** (*cod etc.*) pêcher. **~ out,** (*from water*) repêcher; (*take out: fam.*) sortir. **~ shop,** poissonnerie *f.* **~ing** *n.* pêche *f.* **go ~ing,** aller à la pêche. **~ing rod,** canne à pêche *f.* **~y** *a.* de poisson; (*fig.*) louche.
fisherman /ˈfɪʃəmən/ *n.* (*pl.* **-men**) *n.* pêcheur *m.*
fishmonger /ˈfɪʃmʌŋgə(r)/ *n.* poissonn|ier, -ière *m., f.*
fission /ˈfɪʃn/ *n.* fission *f.*
fist /fɪst/ *n.* poing *m.*
fit[1] /fɪt/ *n.* (*bout*) accès *m.*, crise *f.*
fit[2] /fɪt/ *a.* (**fitter, fittest**) en bonne santé; (*proper*) convenable; (*good enough*) bon; (*able*) capable. —*v.t./i.* (*p.t.* **fitted**) (*clothes*) aller (à); (*match*) s'accorder (avec); (*put or go in or on*) (s')adapter (**to,** à); (*install*) poser. —*n.* **be a good ~,** (*dress*) être à la bonne taille. **~ out, ~ up,** équiper. **~ness** *n.* santé *f.*; (*of remark*) justesse *f.*
fitful /ˈfɪtfl/ *a.* irrégulier.
fitment /ˈfɪtmənt/ *n.* meuble fixe *m.*
fitting /ˈfɪtɪŋ/ *a.* approprié.
fittings /ˈfɪtɪŋz/ *n. pl.* (*in house*) installations *f. pl.*
five /faɪv/ *a.* & *n.* cinq (*m.*).
fiver /ˈfaɪvə(r)/ *n.* (*fam.*) billet de cinq livres *m.*
fix /fɪks/ *v.t.* (*make firm, attach, decide*) fixer; (*mend*) réparer; (*deal with*) arranger. —*n.* **in a ~,** dans le pétrin. **~ s.o. up with sth.,** trouver qch. à qn. **~ed** *a.* fixe.
fixation /fɪkˈseɪʃn/ *n.* fixation *f.*
fixture /ˈfɪkstʃə(r)/ *n.* (*sport*) match *m.* **~s,** (*in house*) installations *f. pl.*
fizz /fɪz/ *v.i.* pétiller. —*n.* pétillement *m.* **~y** *a.* gazeux.
fizzle /ˈfɪzl/ *v.i.* pétiller. **~ out,** (*plan etc.*) finir en queue de poisson.
flab /flæb/ *n.* (*fam.*) corpulence *f.* **~by** /ˈflæbɪ/ *a.* flasque.
flabbergast /ˈflæbəgɑːst/ *v.t.* sidérer, ahurir.
flag[1] /flæg/ *n.* drapeau *m.*; (*naut.*) pavillon *m.* —*v.t.* (*p.t.* **flagged**). **~ (down),** faire signe de s'arrêter à. **~-pole** *n.* mât *m.*
flag[2] /flæg/ *v.i.* (*p.t.* **flagged**) (*weaken*) faiblir; (*sick person*) s'affaiblir; (*droop*) dépérir.
flagon /ˈflægən/ *n.* bouteille *f.*
flagrant /ˈfleɪgrənt/ *a.* flagrant.
flagstone /ˈflægstəʊn/ *n.* dalle *f.*
flair /fleə(r)/ *n.* flair *m.*
flak|e /fleɪk/ *n.* flocon *m.*; (*of paint, metal*) écaille *f.* —*v.i.* s'écailler. **~y** *a.* (*paint*) écailleux.
flamboyant /flæmˈbɔɪənt/ *a.*

(*colour*) éclatant; (*manner*) extravagant.
flame /fleɪm/ *n.* flamme *f.* —*v.i.* flamber.
flamingo /flə'mɪŋgəʊ/ *n.* (*pl.* **-os**) flamant (rose) *m.*
flammable /'flæməbl/ *a.* inflammable.
flan /flæn/ *n.* tarte *f.*; (*custard tart*) flan *m.*
flank /flæŋk/ *n.* flanc *m.* —*v.t.* flanquer.
flannel /'flænl/ *n.* flannelle *f.*; (*for face*) gant de toilette *m.*
flannelette /flænə'let/ *n.* pilou *m.*
flap /flæp/ *v.i.* (*p.t.* **flapped**) battre. —*v.t.* **~ its wings,** battre des ailes. —*n.* (*of pocket*) rabat *m.*; (*of table*) abattant *m.* **get into a ~,** (*fam.*) s'affoler.
flare /fleə(r)/ *v.i.* **~ up,** s'enflammer, flamber; (*fighting*) éclater; (*person*) s'emporter. —*n.* flamboiement *m.*; (*mil.*) fusée éclairante *f.*; (*in skirt*) évasement *m.* **~d** *a.* (*skirt*) évasé.
flash /flæʃ/ *v.i.* briller; (*on and off*) clignoter. —*v.t.* faire briller; (*aim torch*) diriger (**at,** sur); (*flaunt*) étaler. —*n.* éclair *m.*, éclat *m.*; (*of news, camera*) flash *m.* **~ past,** passer à toute vitesse.
flashback /'flæʃbæk/ *n.* retour en arrière *m.*
flashlight /'flæʃlaɪt/ *n.* (*torch*) lampe électrique *f.*
flashy /'flæʃɪ/ *a.* voyant.
flask /flɑːsk/ *n.* flacon *m.*; (*vacuum flask*) thermos *m.*/*f. invar.* (P.).
flat /flæt/ *a.* (**flatter, flattest**) plat; (*tyre*) à plat; (*refusal*) catégorique; (*fare, rate*) fixe. —*adv.* (*say*) carrément. —*n.* (*rooms*) appartement *m.*; (*tyre*: *fam.*) crevaison *f.*; (*mus.*) bémol *m.* **~ out,** à toute vitesse. **~ly** *adv.* catégoriquement. **~ness** *n.* égalité *f.*
flatten /'flætn/ *v.t.*/*i.* (s')aplatir.
flatter /'flaetə(r)/ *v.t.* flatter. **~er** *n.* flatteu|r, -se *m.*, *f.* **~ing** *a.* flatteur. **~y** *n.* flatterie *f.*
flatulence /'flætjʊləns/ *n.* flatulence *f.*
flaunt /flɔːnt/ *v.t.* étaler, afficher.
flautist /'flɔːtɪst/ *n.* flûtiste *m.*/*f.*
flavour /'fleɪvə(r)/ *n.* goût *m.*; (*of ice-cream etc.*) parfum *m.* —*v.t.* parfumer, assaisonner. **~ing** *n.* arôme synthétique *m.*
flaw /flɔː/ *n.* défaut *m.* **~ed** *a.* imparfait. **~less** *a.* parfait.
flax /flæks/ *n.* lin *m.* **~en** *a.* de lin.
flea /fliː/ *n.* puce *f.* **~ market,** (*hum.*) marché aux puces *m.*
fleck /flek/ *n.* petite tache *f.*
fled /fled/ *see* **flee.**
fledged /fledʒd/ *a.* **fully-~,** (*doctor etc.*) diplômé; (*member, citizen*) à part entière.
flee /fliː/ *v.i.* (*p.t.* **fled**) s'enfuir. —*v.t.* s'enfuir de; (*danger*) fuir.
fleece /fliːs/ *n.* toison *f.* —*v.t.* voler.
fleet /fliːt/ *n.* (*naut., aviat.*) flotte *f.* **a ~ of vehicles,** un parc automobile.
fleeting /'fliːtɪŋ/ *a.* très bref.
Flemish /'flemɪʃ/ *a.* flamand. —*n.* (*lang.*) flamand *m.*
flesh /fleʃ/ *n.* chair *f.* **one's (own) ~ and blood,** les siens *m. pl.* **~y** *a.* charnu.
flew /fluː/ *see* **fly**[2].
flex[1] /fleks/ *v.t.* (*knee etc.*) fléchir; (*muscle*) faire jouer.
flex[2] /fleks/ *n.* (*electr.*) fil souple *m.*
flexib|le /'fleksəbl/ *a.* flexible. **~ility** /-'bɪlətɪ/ *n.* flexibilité *f.*
flexitime /'fleksɪtaɪm/ *n.* horaire variable *m.*
flick /flɪk/ *n.* petit coup *m.* —*v.t.* donner un petit coup à. **~-knife** *n.* couteau à cran d'arrêt *m.*
flicker /'flɪkə(r)/ *v.i.* vaciller. —*n.* vacillement *m.*; (*light*) lueur *f.*
flier /'flaɪə(r)/ *n.* = **flyer.**
flies /flaɪz/ *n. pl.* (*on trousers*: *fam.*) braguette *f.*
flight[1] /flaɪt/ *n.* (*of bird, plane, etc.*)

vol *m.* **~-deck** *n.* poste de pilotage *m.* **~ of stairs,** escalier *m.*
flight[2] /flaɪt/ *n.* (*fleeing*) fuite *f.* **put to ~,** mettre en fuite. **take (to) ~,** prendre la fuite.
flighty /ˈflaɪtɪ/ *a.* (**-ier, -iest**) frivole, volage.
flimsy /ˈflɪmzɪ/ *a.* (**-ier, -iest**) (*pej.*) mince, peu solide.
flinch /flɪntʃ/ *v.i.* (*wince*) broncher; (*draw back*) reculer.
fling /flɪŋ/ *v.t.* (*p.t.* **flung**) jeter. —*n.* **have a ~,** faire la fête.
flint /flɪnt/ *n.* silex *m.*; (*for lighter*) pierre *f.*
flip /flɪp/ *v.t.* (*p.t.* **flipped**) donner un petit coup à. —*n.* chiquenaude *f.* **~ through,** feuilleter. **the ~ side,** (*of record*) l'autre face *f.*
flippant /ˈflɪpənt/ *a.* désinvolte.
flipper /ˈflɪpə(r)/ *n.* (*of seal etc.*) nageoire *f.*; (*of swimmer*) palme *f.*
flirt /flɜːt/ *v.i.* flirter. —*n.* flirteu|r, -se *m., f.* **~ation** /-ˈteɪʃn/ *n.* flirt *m.*
flit /flɪt/ *v.i.* (*p.t.* **flitted**) voltiger.
float /fləʊt/ *v.t./i.* (faire) flotter. —*n.* flotteur *m.*; (*cart*) char *m.*
flock /flɒk/ *n.* (*of sheep etc.*) troupeau *m.*; (*of people*) foule *f.* —*v.i.* venir en foule.
flog /flɒg/ *v.t.* (*p.t.* **flogged**) (*beat*) fouetter; (*sell*: *sl.*) vendre.
flood /flʌd/ *n.* inondation *f.*; (*fig.*) flot *m.* —*v.t.* inonder. —*v.i.* (*building etc.*) être inondé; (*river*) déborder; (*people*: *fig.*) affluer.
floodlight /ˈflʌdlaɪt/ *n.* projecteur *m.* —*v.t.* (*p.t.* **floodlit**) illuminer.
floor /flɔː(r)/ *n.* sol *m.*, plancher *m.*; (*for dancing*) piste *f.*; (*storey*) étage *m.* —*v.t.* (*knock down*) terrasser; (*baffle*) stupéfier.
flop /flɒp/ *v.i.* (*p.t.* **flopped**) s'agiter faiblement; (*drop*) s'affaler; (*fail*: *sl.*) échouer. —*n.* (*sl.*) échec *m.*, fiasco *m.* **~py** *a.* lâche, flasque.
flora /ˈflɔːrə/ *n.* flore *f.*
floral /ˈflɔːrəl/ *a.* floral.
florid /ˈflɒrɪd/ *a.* fleuri.
florist /ˈflɒrɪst/ *n.* fleuriste *m.*/*f.*
flounce /flaʊns/ *n.* volant *m.*
flounder[1] /ˈflaʊndə(r)/ *v.i.* patauger (avec difficulté).
flounder[2] /ˈflaʊndə(r)/ *n.* (*fish*: *Amer.*) flet *m.*, plie *f.*
flour /ˈflaʊə(r)/ *n.* farine *f.* **~y** *a.* farineux.
flourish /ˈflʌrɪʃ/ *v.i.* prospérer. —*v.t.* brandir. —*n.* geste élégant *m.*; (*curve*) fioriture *f.*
flout /flaʊt/ *v.t.* faire fi de.
flow /fləʊ/ *v.i.* couler; (*circulate*) circuler; (*traffic*) s'écouler; (*hang loosely*) flotter. —*n.* (*of liquid, traffic*) écoulement *m.*; (*of tide*) flux *m.*; (*of orders, words*: *fig.*) flot *m.* **~ chart,** organigramme *m.* **~ in,** affluer. **~ into,** (*of river*) se jeter dans.
flower /ˈflaʊə(r)/ *n.* fleur *f.* —*v.i.* fleurir. **~-bed** *n.* plate-bande *f.* **~ed** *a.* à fleurs. **~y** *a.* fleuri.
flown /fləʊn/ *see* **fly**[2].
flu /fluː/ *n.* (*fam.*) grippe *f.*
fluctuat|e /ˈflʌktʃʊeɪt/ *v.i.* varier. **~ion** /-ˈeɪʃn/ *n.* variation *f.*
flue /fluː/ *n.* (*duct*) tuyau *m.*
fluen|t /ˈfluːənt/ *a.* (*style*) aisé. **be ~t (in a language),** parler (une langue) couramment. **~cy** *n.* facilité *f.* **~tly** *adv.* avec facilité; (*lang.*) couramment.
fluff /flʌf/ *n.* peluche(s) *f.* (*pl.*); (*down*) duvet *m.* **~y** *a.* pelucheux.
fluid /ˈfluːɪd/ *a.* & *n.* fluide (*m.*).
fluke /fluːk/ *n.* coup de chance *m.*
flung /flʌŋ/ *see* **fling.**
flunk /flʌŋk/ *v.t./i.* (*Amer., fam.*) être collé (à).
fluorescent /flʊəˈresnt/ *a.* fluorescent.
fluoride /ˈflʊəraɪd/ *n.* (*in toothpaste, water*) fluor *m.*
flurry /ˈflʌrɪ/ *n.* (*squall*) rafale *f.*; (*fig.*) agitation *f.*
flush[1] /flʌʃ/ *v.i.* rougir. —*v.t.* nettoyer à grande eau. —*n.* (*blush*) rougeur *f.*; (*fig.*) excitation *f.* —*a.*

~ with, (*level with*) au ras de. **~ the toilet,** tirer la chasse d'eau.

flush[2] /flʌʃ/ *v.t.* **~ out,** chasser.

fluster /'flʌstə(r)/ *v.t.* énerver.

flute /fluːt/ *n.* flûte *f.*

flutter /'flʌtə(r)/ *v.i.* voleter; (*of wings*) battre. *—n.* (*of wings*) battement *m.*; (*fig.*) agitation *f.*

flux /flʌks/ *n.* changement continuel *m.*

fly[1] /flaɪ/ *n.* mouche *f.*

fly[2] /flaɪ/ *v.i.* (*p.t.* **flew,** *p.p.* **flown**) voler; (*of passengers*) voyager en avion; (*of flag*) flotter; (*rush*) aller à toute vitesse. *—v.t.* (*aircraft*) piloter; (*passengers, goods*) transporter par avion; (*flag*) arborer. *—n.* (*of trousers*) braguette *f.*

flyer /'flaɪə(r)/ *n.* aviateur *m.*; (*circular: Amer.*) prospectus *m.*

flying /'flaɪɪŋ/ *a.* (*saucer etc.*) volant. *—n.* (*activity*) aviation *f.* **~ buttress,** arc-boutant *m.* **with ~ colours,** haut la main. **~ start,** excellent départ *m.* **~ visit,** visite éclair *f.* (*a. invar.*).

flyover /'flaɪəʊvə(r)/ *n.* (*road*) toboggan *m.*, saut-de-mouton *m.*

flyweight /'flaɪweɪt/ *n.* poids mouche *m.*

foal /fəʊl/ *n.* poulain *m.*

foam /fəʊm/ *n.* écume *f.*, mousse *f.* *—v.i.* écumer, mousser. **~ (rubber)** *n.* caoutchouc mousse *m.*

fob /fɒb/ *v.t.* (*p.t.* **fobbed**). **~ off on (to) s.o.,** (*palm off*) refiler à qn. **~ s.o. off with,** amener qn. à accepter par la ruse.

focal /'fəʊkl/ *a.* focal.

focus /'fəʊkəs/ *n.* (*pl.* **-cuses** *or* **-ci** /-saɪ/) foyer *m.*; (*fig.*) centre *m.* *—v.t./i.* (*p.t.* **focused**) (faire) converger; (*instrument*) mettre au point; (*fig.*) (se) concentrer. **be in/out of ~,** être/ne pas être au point.

fodder /'fɒdə(r)/ *n.* fourrage *m.*

foe /fəʊ/ *n.* ennemi(e) *m.(f.).*

foetus /'fiːtəs/ *n.* (*pl.* **-tuses**) fœtus *m.*

fog /fɒg/ *n.* brouillard *m.* *—v.t./i.* (*p.t.* **fogged**) (*window etc.*) (s')embuer. **~-horn** *n.* (*naut.*) corne de brume *f.* **~gy** *a.* brumeux. **it is ~gy,** il fait du brouillard.

fog(e)y /'fəʊgɪ/ *n.* **(old) ~,** vieille baderne *f.*

foible /'fɔɪbl/ *n.* faiblesse *f.*

foil[1] /fɔɪl/ *n.* (*tin foil*) papier d'aluminium *m.*; (*fig.*) repoussoir *m.*

foil[2] /fɔɪl/ *v.t.* (*thwart*) déjouer.

foist /fɔɪst/ *v.t.* imposer **(on,** à).

fold[1] /fəʊld/ *v.t./i.* (se) plier; (*arms*) croiser; (*fail*) s'effondrer. *—n.* pli *m.* **~er** *n.* (*file*) chemise *f.*; (*leaflet*) dépliant *m.* **~ing** *a.* pliant.

fold[2] /fəʊld/ *n.* (*for sheep*) parc à moutons *m.*; (*relig.*) bercail *m.*

foliage /'fəʊlɪɪdʒ/ *n.* feuillage *m.*

folk /fəʊk/ *n.* gens *m. pl.* **~s,** parents *m. pl.* *—a.* folklorique.

folklore /'fəʊklɔː(r)/ *n.* folklore *m.*

follow /'fɒləʊ/ *v.t./i.* suivre. **it ~s that,** il s'ensuit que. **~ suit,** en faire autant. **~ up,** (*letter etc.*) donner suite à. **~er** *n.* partisan *m.* **~ing** *n.* partisans *m. pl.*; *a.* suivant; *prep.* à la suite de.

folly /'fɒlɪ/ *n.* sottise *f.*

foment /fəʊ'ment/ *v.t.* fomenter.

fond /fɒnd/ *a.* **(-er, -est)** (*loving*) affectueux; (*hope*) cher. **be ~ of,** aimer. **~ness** *n.* affection *f.*; (*for things*) attachement *m.*

fondle /'fɒndl/ *v.t.* caresser.

food /fuːd/ *n.* nourriture *f.* *—a.* alimentaire. **~ processor,** robot (ménager) *m.*

fool /fuːl/ *n.* idiot(e) *m.* (*f.*). *—v.t.* duper. *—v.i.* faire l'idiot.

foolhardy /'fuːlhɑːdɪ/ *a.* téméraire.

foolish /'fuːlɪʃ/ *a.* idiot. **~ly** *adv.* sottement. **~ness** *n.* sottise *f.*

foolproof /'fuːlpruːf/ *a.* infaillible.

foot /fʊt/ *n.* (*pl.* **feet**) pied *m.*; (*measure*) pied *m.* (= *30.48cm.*); (*of stairs, page*) bas *m.* —*v.t.* (*bill*) payer. **~-bridge** *n.* passerelle *f.* **on ~,** à pied. **on** *or* **to one's feet,** debout. **under s.o.'s feet,** dans les jambes de qn.

footage /'fʊtɪdʒ/ *n.* (*of film*) métrage *m.*

football /'fʊtbɔːl/ *n.* (*ball*) ballon *m.*; (*game*) football *m.* **~ pools,** paris sur les matchs de football *m. pl.* **~er** *n.* footballeur *m.*

foothills /'fʊthɪlz/ *n. pl.* contreforts *m. pl.*

foothold /'fʊthəʊld/ *n.* prise *f.*

footing /'fʊtɪŋ/ *n.* prise (de pied) *f.*, équilibre *m.*; (*fig.*) situation *f.* **on an equal ~,** sur un pied d'égalité.

footlights /'fʊtlaɪts/ *n. pl.* rampe *f.*

footman /'fʊtmən/ *n.* (*pl.* **-men**) valet de pied *m.*

footnote /'fʊtnəʊt/ *n.* note (en bas de la page) *f.*

footpath /'fʊtpɑːθ/ *n.* sentier *m.*; (*at the side of the road*) chemin *m.*

footprint /'fʊtprɪnt/ *n.* empreinte (de pied) *f.*

footsore /'fʊtsɔː(r)/ *a.* **be ~,** avoir les pieds douloureux.

footstep /'fʊtstep/ *n.* pas *m.*

footwear /'fʊtweə(r)/ *n.* chaussures *f. pl.*

for /fɔː(r), *unstressed* fə(r)/ *prep.* pour; (*in spite of*) malgré; (*during*) pendant; (*before*) avant. —*conj.* car. **a liking ~,** le goût de. **he has been away ~,** il est absent depuis. **~ ever,** pour toujours. **~ good,** pour de bon.

forage /'fɒrɪdʒ/ *v.i.* fourrager. —*n.* fourrage *m.*

foray /'fɒreɪ/ *n.* incursion *f.*

forbade /fə'bæd/ *see* **forbid.**

forbear /fɔː'beə(r)/ *v.t./i.* (*p.t.* **forbore,** *p.p.* **forborne**) s'abstenir. **~ance** *n.* patience *f.*

forbid /fə'bɪd/ *v.t.* (*p.t.* **forbade,** *p.p.* **forbidden**) interdire, défendre (**s.o. to do,** à qn. de faire). **~ s.o. sth.,** interdire *or* défendre qch. à qn. **you are ~den to leave,** il vous est interdit de partir.

forbidding /fə'bɪdɪŋ/ *a.* menaçant.

force /fɔːs/ *n.* force *f.* —*v.t.* forcer. **~ into,** faire entrer de force. **~ on,** imposer à. **come into ~,** entrer en vigueur. **the ~s,** les forces armées *f. pl.* **~d** *a.* forcé. **~ful** *a.* énergique.

force-feed /'fɔːsfiːd/ *v.t.* (*p.t.* **-fed**) nourrir de force.

forceps /'fɔːseps/ *n. invar.* forceps *m.*

forcibl|e /'fɔːsəbl/ *a.*, **~y** *adv.* de force.

ford /fɔːd/ *n.* gué *m.* —*v.t.* passer à gué.

fore /fɔː(r)/ *a.* antérieur. —*n.* **to the ~,** en évidence.

forearm /'fɔːrɑːm/ *n.* avant-bras *m. invar.*

foreboding /fɔː'bəʊdɪŋ/ *n.* pressentiment *m.*

forecast /'fɔːkɑːst/ *v.t.* (*p.t.* **forecast**) prévoir. —*n.* prévision *f.*

forecourt /'fɔːkɔːt/ *n.* (*of garage*) devant *m.*; (*of station*) cour *f.*

forefathers /'fɔːfɑːðəz/ *n. pl.* aïeux *m. pl.*

forefinger /'fɔːfɪŋgə(r)/ *n.* index *m.*

forefront /'fɔːfrʌnt/ *n.* premier rang *m.*

foregone /'fɔːgɒn/ *a.* **~ conclusion,** résultat à prévoir *m.*

foreground /'fɔːgraʊnd/ *n.* premier plan *m.*

forehead /'fɒrɪd/ *n.* front *m.*

foreign /'fɒrən/ *a.* étranger; (*trade*) extérieur; (*travel*) à l'étranger. **~er** *n.* étrang|er, -ère *m., f.*

foreman /'fɔːmən/ *n.* (*pl.* **-men**) contremaître *m.*

foremost /'fɔːməʊst/ *a.* le plus éminent. —*adv.* **first and ~,** tout d'abord.

forensic /fə'rensɪk/ *a.* médico-légal. ~ **medicine,** médecine légale *f.*
forerunner /'fɔːrʌnə(r)/ *n.* précurseur *m.*
foresee /fɔː'siː/ *v.t.* (*p.t.* **-saw,** *p.p.* **-seen**) prévoir. ~**able** *a.* prévisible.
foreshadow /fɔː'ʃædəʊ/ *v.t.* présager, laisser prévoir.
foresight /'fɔːsaɪt/ *n.* prévoyance *f.*
forest /'fɒrɪst/ *n.* forêt *f.*
forestall /fɔː'stɔːl/ *v.t.* devancer.
forestry /'fɒrɪstrɪ/ *n.* sylviculture *f.*
foretaste /'fɔːteɪst/ *n.* avant-goût *m.*
foretell /fɔː'tel/ *v.t.* (*p.t.* **foretold**) prédire.
forever /fə'revə(r)/ *adv.* toujours.
forewarn /fɔː'wɔːn/ *v.t.* avertir.
foreword /'fɔːwɜːd/ *n.* avant-propos *m. invar.*
forfeit /'fɔːfɪt/ *n.* (*penalty*) peine *f.*; (*in game*) gage *m.* —*v.t.* perdre.
forgave /fə'geɪv/ *see* **forgive.**
forge[1] /fɔːdʒ/ *v.i.* ~ **ahead,** aller de l'avant, avancer.
forge[2] /fɔːdʒ/ *n.* forge *f.* —*v.t.* (*metal, friendship*) forger; (*copy*) contrefaire, falsifier. ~**r** /-ə(r)/ *n.* faussaire *m.* ~**ry** /-ərɪ/ *n.* faux *m.*, contrefaçon *f.*
forget /fə'get/ *v.t./i.* (*p.t.* **forgot,** *p.p.* **forgotten**) oublier. ~**-me-not** *n.* myosotis *m.* ~ **o.s.,** s'oublier. ~**ful** *a.* distrait. ~**ful of,** oublieux de.
forgive /fə'gɪv/ *v.t.* (*p.t.* **forgave,** *p.p.* **forgiven**) pardonner (**s.o. for sth.,** qch. à qn.). ~**ness** *n.* pardon *m.*
forgo /fɔː'gəʊ/ *v.t.* (*p.t.* **forwent,** *p.p.* **forgone**) renoncer à.
fork /fɔːk/ *n.* fourchette *f.*; (*for digging etc.*) fourche *f.*; (*in road*) bifurcation *f.* —*v.i.* (*road*) bifurquer. ~**-lift truck,** chariot élévateur *m.* ~ **out,** (*sl.*) payer. ~**ed** *a.* fourchu.
forlorn /fə'lɔːn/ *a.* triste, abandonné. ~ **hope,** mince espoir *m.*
form /fɔːm/ *n.* forme *f.*; (*document*) formulaire *m.*; (*schol.*) classe *f.* —*v.t./i.* (se) former.
formal /'fɔːml/ *a.* officiel, en bonne et due forme; (*person*) compassé, cérémonieux; (*dress*) de cérémonie; (*denial, grammar*) formel. ~**ity** /-'mælətɪ/ *n.* cérémonial *m.*; (*requirement*) formalité *f.* ~**ly** *adv.* officiellement.
format /'fɔːmæt/ *n.* format *m.*
formation /fɔː'meɪʃn/ *n.* formation *f.*
formative /'fɔːmətɪv/ *a.* formateur.
former /'fɔːmə(r)/ *a.* ancien; (*first of two*) premier. —*n.* **the** ~, celui-là, celle-là. ~**ly** *adv.* autrefois.
formidable /'fɔːmɪdəbl/ *a.* redoutable, terrible.
formula /'fɔːmjʊlə/ *n.* (*pl.* **-ae** /-iː/ *or* **-as**) formule *f.*
formulate /'fɔːmjʊleɪt/ *v.t.* formuler.
forsake /fə'seɪk/ *v.t.* (*p.t.* **forsook,** *p.p.* **forsaken**) abandonner.
fort /fɔːt/ *n.* (*mil.*) fort *m.*
forte /'fɔːteɪ/ *n.* (*talent*) fort *m.*
forth /fɔːθ/ *adv.* en avant. **go back and** ~, aller et venir.
forthcoming /fɔːθ'kʌmɪŋ/ *a.* à venir, prochain; (*sociable: fam.*) communicatif.
forthright /'fɔːθraɪt/ *a.* direct.
forthwith /fɔːθ'wɪθ/ *adv.* sur-le-champ.
fortif|y /'fɔːtɪfaɪ/ *v.t.* fortifier. ~**ication** /-ɪ'keɪʃn/ *n.* fortification *f.*
fortitude /'fɔːtɪtjuːd/ *n.* courage *m.*
fortnight /'fɔːtnaɪt/ *n.* quinze jours *m. pl.*, quinzaine *f.* ~**ly** *a.* bimensuel; *adv.* tous les quinze jours.
fortress /'fɔːtrɪs/ *n.* forteresse *f.*
fortuitous /fɔː'tjuːɪtəs/ *a.* fortuit.
fortunate /'fɔːtʃənət/ *a.* heureux.

be ~, avoir de la chance. **~ly** *adv.* heureusement.
fortune /ˈfɔːtʃuːn/ *n.* fortune *f.* **~-teller** *n.* diseuse de bonne aventure *f.* **have the good ~ to,** avoir la chance de.
fort|y /ˈfɔːtɪ/ *a.* & *n.* quarante (*m.*). **~y winks,** un petit somme. **~ieth** *a.* & *n.* quarantième (*m.*/*f.*).
forum /ˈfɔːrəm/ *n.* forum *m.*
forward /ˈfɔːwəd/ *a.* en avant; (*advanced*) précoce; (*pert*) effronté. —*n.* (*sport*) avant *m.* —*adv.* en avant. —*v.t.* (*letter*) faire suivre; (*goods*) expédier; (*fig.*) favoriser. **come ~,** se présenter. **go ~,** avancer. **~ness** *n.* précocité *f.*
forwards /ˈfɔːwədz/ *adv.* en avant.
fossil /ˈfɒsl/ *n.* & *a.* fossile (*m.*).
foster /ˈfɒstə(r)/ *v.t.* (*promote*) encourager; (*child*) élever. **~-child** *n.* enfant adoptif *m.* **~-mother** *n.* mère adoptive *f.*
fought /fɔːt/ *see* **fight.**
foul /faʊl/ *a.* (**-er, -est**) (*smell, weather, etc.*) infect; (*place, action*) immonde; (*language*) ordurier. —*n.* (*football*) faute *f.* —*v.t.* souiller, encrasser. **~-mouthed** *a.* au langage ordurier. **~ play,** jeu irrégulier *m.*; (*crime*) acte criminel *m.* **~ up,** (*sl.*) gâcher.
found[1] /faʊnd/ *see* **find.**
found[2] /faʊnd/ *v.t.* fonder. **~ation** /-ˈdeɪʃn/ *n.* fondation *f.*; (*basis*) fondement *m.* **~er**[1] *n.* fonda|teur, -trice *m., f.*
founder[2] /ˈfaʊndə(r)/ *v.i.* sombrer.
foundry /ˈfaʊndrɪ/ *n.* fonderie *f.*
fountain /ˈfaʊntɪn/ *n.* fontaine *f.* **~-pen** *n.* stylo à encre *m.*
four /fɔː(r)/ *a.* & *n.* quatre (*m.*). **~fold** *a.* quadruple; *adv.* au quadruple. **~th** *a.* & *n.* quatrième (*m.*/*f.*).
foursome /ˈfɔːsəm/ *n.* partie à quatre *f.*
fourteen /fɔːˈtiːn/ *a.* & *n.* quatorze (*m.*). **~th** *a.* & *n.* quatorzième (*m.*/*f.*).
fowl /faʊl/ *n.* volaille *f.*
fox /fɒks/ *n.* renard *m.* —*v.t.* (*baffle*) mystifier; (*deceive*) tromper.
foyer /ˈfɔɪeɪ/ *n.* (*hall*) foyer *m.*
fraction /ˈfrækʃn/ *n.* fraction *f.*
fracture /ˈfræktʃə(r)/ *n.* fracture *f.* —*v.t.*/*i.* (se) fracturer.
fragile /ˈfrædʒaɪl, *Amer.* ˈfrædʒəl/ *a.* fragile.
fragment /ˈfrægmənt/ *n.* fragment *m.* **~ary** *a.* fragmentaire.
fragran|t /ˈfreɪgrənt/ *a.* parfumé. **~ce** *n.* parfum *m.*
frail /freɪl/ *a.* (**-er, -est**) frêle.
frame /freɪm/ *n.* charpente *f.*; (*of picture*) cadre *m.*; (*of window*) châssis *m.*; (*of spectacles*) monture *f.* —*v.t.* encadrer; (*fig.*) formuler; (*jurid., sl.*) monter un coup contre. **~ of mind,** humeur *f.*
framework /ˈfreɪmwɜːk/ *n.* structure *f.*; (*context*) cadre *m.*
franc /fræŋk/ *n.* franc *m.*
France /frɑːns/ *n.* France *f.*
franchise /ˈfræntʃaɪz/ *n.* (*pol.*) droit de vote *m.*; (*comm.*) concession *f.*
Franco- /ˈfræŋkəʊ/ *pref.* franco-.
frank[1] /fræŋk/ *a.* franc. **~ly** *adv.* franchement. **~ness** *n.* franchise *f.*
frank[2] /fræŋk/ *v.t.* affranchir.
frantic /ˈfræntɪk/ *a.* frénétique. **~ with,** fou de.
fratern|al /frəˈtɜːnl/ *a.* fraternel. **~ity** *n.* (*bond*) fraternité *f.*; (*group, club*) confrérie *f.*
fraternize /ˈfrætənaɪz/ *v.i.* fraterniser (**with,** avec).
fraud /frɔːd/ *n.* (*deception*) fraude *f.*; (*person*) imposteur *m.* **~ulent** *a.* frauduleux.
fraught /frɔːt/ *a.* (*tense*) tendu. **~ with,** chargé de.
fray[1] /freɪ/ *n.* rixe *f.*
fray[2] /freɪ/ *v.t.*/*i.* (s')effilocher.

freak /friːk/ *n.* phénomène *m.* —*a.* anormal. **~ish** *a.* anormal.

freckle /ˈfrekl/ *n.* tache de rousseur *f.* **~d** *a.* couvert de taches de rousseur.

free /friː/ *a.* (**freer** /ˈfriːə(r)/, **freest** /ˈfriːɪst/) libre; (*gratis*) gratuit; (*lavish*) généreux. —*v.t.* (*p.t.* **freed**) libérer; (*clear*) dégager. **a ~ hand,** carte blanche *f.* **~ kick,** coup franc *m.* **~ lance,** collabora|teur, -trice indépendant(e) *m., f.* **~ of charge,** gratuit(ement). **~-range** *a.* (*eggs*) de ferme. **~ly** *adv.* librement.

freedom /ˈfriːdəm/ *n.* liberté *f.*

Freemason /ˈfriːmeɪsn/ *n.* franc-maçon *m.* **~ry** *n.* franc-maçonnerie *f.*

freeway /ˈfriːweɪ/ *n.* (*Amer.*) autoroute *f.*

freez|e /friːz/ *v.t./i.* (*p.t.* **froze,** *p.p.* **frozen**) geler; (*culin.*) (se) congeler; (*wages etc.*) bloquer. —*n.* gel *m.*; blocage *m.* **~er** *n.* congélateur *m.* **~ing** *a.* glacial. **below ~ing,** au-dessous de zéro.

freight /freɪt/ *n.* fret *m.* **~er** *n.* (*ship*) cargo *m.*

French /frentʃ/ *a.* français. —*n.* (*lang.*) français *m.* **~-speaking** *a.* francophone. **~ window** *n.* porte-fenêtre *f.* **the ~,** les Français *m. pl.* **~man** *n.* Français *m.* **~woman** *n.* Française *f.*

frenz|y /ˈfrenzɪ/ *n.* frénésie *f.* **~ied** *a.* frénétique.

frequen|t[1] /ˈfriːkwənt/ *a.* fréquent. **~cy** *n.* fréquence *f.* **~tly** *adv.* fréquemment.

frequent[2] /frɪˈkwent/ *v.t.* fréquenter.

fresco /ˈfreskəʊ/ *n.* (*pl.* **-os**) fresque *f.*

fresh /freʃ/ *a.* (**-er, -est**) frais; (*different, additional*) nouveau; (*cheeky: fam.*) culotté. **~ water,** eau douce *f.* **~ly** *adv.* nouvellement. **~ness** *n.* fraîcheur *f.*

freshen /ˈfreʃn/ *v.i.* (*weather*) fraîchir. **~ up,** (*person*) se rafraîchir.

fret /fret/ *v.i.* (*p.t.* **fretted**) se tracasser. **~ful** *a.* ronchon, insatisfait.

friar /ˈfraɪə(r)/ *n.* moine *m.*, frère *m.*

friction /ˈfrɪkʃn/ *n.* friction *f.*

Friday /ˈfraɪdɪ/ *n.* vendredi *m.*

fridge /frɪdʒ/ *n.* frigo *m.*

fried /fraɪd/ *see* **fry.** —*a.* frit.

friend /frend/ *n.* ami(e) *m.* (*f.*). **~ship** *n.* amitié *f.*

friendl|y /ˈfrendlɪ/ *a.* (**-ier, -iest**) amical, gentil. **F~y Society,** mutuelle *f.*, société de prévoyance *f.* **~iness** *n.* gentillesse *f.*

frieze /friːz/ *n.* frise *f.*

frigate /ˈfrɪgət/ *n.* frégate *f.*

fright /fraɪt/ *n.* peur *f.*; (*person, thing*) horreur *f.* **~ful** *a.* affreux. **~fully** *adv.* affreusement.

frighten /ˈfraɪtn/ *v.t.* effrayer. **~ off,** faire fuir. **~ed** *a.* effrayé. **be ~ed,** avoir peur (**of,** de).

frigid /ˈfrɪdʒɪd/ *a.* froid, glacial; (*psych.*) frigide. **~ity** /-ˈdʒɪdətɪ/ *n.* frigidité *f.*

frill /frɪl/ *n.* (*trimming*) fanfreluche *f.* **with no ~s,** très simple.

fringe /frɪndʒ/ *n.* (*edging, hair*) frange *f.*; (*of area*) bordure *f.*; (*of society*) marge *f.* **~ benefits,** avantages sociaux *m. pl.*

frisk /frɪsk/ *v.t.* (*search*) fouiller.

frisky /ˈfrɪskɪ/ *a.* (**-ier, -iest**) fringant, frétillant.

fritter[1] /ˈfrɪtə(r)/ *n.* beignet *m.*

fritter[2] /ˈfrɪtə(r)/ *v.t.* **~ away,** gaspiller.

frivol|ous /ˈfrɪvələs/ *a.* frivole. **~ity** /-ˈvɒlətɪ/ *n.* frivolité *f.*

frizzy /ˈfrɪzɪ/ *a.* crépu, crêpelé.

fro /frəʊ/ *see* **to and fro.**

frock /frɒk/ *n.* robe *f.*

frog /frɒg/ *n.* grenouille *f.* **a ~ in one's throat,** un chat dans la gorge.

frogman /'frɒgmən/ *n.* (*pl.* **-men**) homme-grenouille *m.*

frolic /'frɒlɪk/ *v.i.* (*p.t.* **frolicked**) s'ébattre. —*n.* ébats *m. pl.*

from /frɒm, *unstressed* frəm/ *prep.* de; (*with time, prices, etc.*) à partir de, de; (*out of*) dans; (*habit, conviction, etc.*) par; (*according to*) d'après. **take ~,** (*away from*) prendre à.

front /frʌnt/ *n.* (*of car, train, etc.*) avant *m.*; (*of garment, building*) devant *m.*; (*mil., pol.*) front *m.*; (*of book, pamphlet, etc.*) début *m.*; (*appearance: fig.*) façade *f.* —*a.* de devant, avant *invar.*; (*first*) premier. **~ door,** porte d'entrée *f.* **in ~ (of),** devant. **~age** *n.* façade *f.* **~al** *a.* frontal; (*attack*) de front.

frontier /'frʌntɪə(r)/ *n.* frontière *f.*

frost /frɒst/ *n.* gel *m.*, gelée *f.*; (*on glass etc.*) givre *m.* —*v.t./i.* (se) givrer. **~-bite** *n.* gelure *f.* **~-bitten** *a.* gelé. **~ed** *a.* (*glass*) dépoli. **~ing** *n.* (*icing: Amer.*) glace *f.* **~y** *a.* (*weather, welcome*) glacial; (*window*) givré.

froth /frɒθ/ *n.* mousse *f.*, écume *f.* —*v.i.* mousser, écumer. **~y** *a.* mousseux.

frown /fraʊn/ *v.i.* froncer les sourcils. —*n.* froncement de sourcils *m.* **~ on,** désapprouver.

froze, frozen /frəʊz, 'frəʊzn/ *see* **freeze.**

frugal /'fru:gl/ *a.* (*person*) économe; (*meal, life*) frugal. **~ly** *adv.* (*live*) simplement.

fruit /fru:t/ *n.* fruit *m.*; (*collectively*) fruits *m. pl.* **~ machine,** machine à sous *f.* **~ salad,** salade de fruits *f.* **~erer** *n.* fruit|ier, -ière *m., f.* **~y** *a.* (*taste*) fruité.

fruit|ful /'fru:tfl/ *a.* fécond; (*fig.*) fructueux. **~less** *a.* stérile.

fruition /fru:'ɪʃn/ *n.* **come to ~,** se réaliser.

frustrat|e /frʌ'streɪt/ *v.t.* (*plan*) faire échouer; (*person: psych.*) frustrer; (*upset: fam.*) exaspérer. **~ion** /-ʃn/ *n.* (*psych.*) frustration *f.*; (*disappointment*) déception *f.*

fry[1] /fraɪ/ *v.t./i.* (*p.t.* **fried**) (faire) frire. **~ing-pan** *n.* poêle (à frire) *f.*

fry[2] /fraɪ/ *n.* **the small ~,** le menu fretin.

fuddy-duddy /'fʌdɪdʌdɪ/ *n.* **be a ~,** (*sl.*) être vieux jeu *invar.*

fudge /fʌdʒ/ *n.* fondant *m.*

fuel /'fju:əl/ *n.* combustible *m.*; (*for car engine*) carburant *m.* —*v.t.* (*p.t.* **fuelled**) alimenter en combustible.

fugitive /'fju:dʒətɪv/ *n.* & *a.* fugiti|f, -ve (*m., f.*).

fugue /fju:g/ *n.* (*mus.*) fugue *f.*

fulfil /fʊl'fɪl/ *v.t.* (*p.t.* **fulfilled**) accomplir, réaliser; (*condition*) remplir. **~ o.s.,** s'épanouir. **~ling** *a.* satisfaisant. **~ment** *n.* réalisation *f.*; épanouissement *m.*

full /fʊl/ *a.* (**-er, -est**) plein; (*bus, hotel*) complet; (*programme*) chargé; (*price*) entier; (*skirt*) ample. —*n.* **in ~,** intégral(ement). **write in ~,** écrire en toutes lettres. **to the ~,** complètement. **be ~ (up),** n'avoir plus faim. **~ back,** (*sport*) arrière *m.* **~ moon,** pleine lune *f.* **~-scale** *a.* (*drawing etc.*) grandeur nature *invar.*; (*fig.*) de grande envergure. **at ~ speed,** à toute vitesse. **~ stop,** point *m.* **~-time** *a.* & *adv.* à plein temps. **~y** *adv.* complètement.

fulsome /'fʊlsəm/ *a.* excessif.

fumble /'fʌmbl/ *v.i.* tâtonner, fouiller. **~ with,** tripoter.

fume /fju:m/ *v.i.* rager. **~s** *n. pl.* exhalaisons *f. pl.*, vapeurs *f. pl.*

fumigate /'fju:mɪgeɪt/ *v.t.* désinfecter.

fun /fʌn/ *n.* amusement *m.* **for ~,** pour rire. **~-fair** *n.* fête foraine *f.* **make ~ of,** se moquer de.

function /ˈfʌŋkʃn/ *n.* (*purpose, duty*) fonction *f.*; (*event*) réunion *f.*, cérémonie *f.* —*v.i.* fonctionner. **~al** *a.* fonctionnel.
fund /fʌnd/ *n.* fonds *m.* —*v.t.* fournir les fonds pour.
fundamental /fʌndəˈmentl/ *a.* fondamental.
funeral /ˈfjuːnərəl/ *n.* enterrement *m.*, funérailles *f. pl.* —*a.* funèbre.
fungus /ˈfʌŋgəs/ *n.* (*pl.* **-gi** /-gaɪ/) (*plant*) champignon *m.*; (*mould*) moisissure *f.*
funicular /fjuːˈnɪkjʊlə(r)/ *n.* funiculaire *m.*
funk /fʌŋk/ *m.* **be in a ~,** (*afraid*: *sl.*) avoir la frousse; (*depressed*: *Amer.*, *sl.*) être déprimé.
funnel /ˈfʌnl/ *n.* (*for pouring*) entonnoir *m.*; (*of ship*) cheminée *f.*
funn|y /ˈfʌnɪ/ *a.* (**-ier, -iest**) drôle; (*odd*) bizarre. **~y business,** affaire louche *f.* **~ily** *adv.* drôlement; bizarrement.
fur /fɜː(r)/ *n.* fourrure *f.*; (*in kettle*) tartre *m.*
furious /ˈfjʊərɪəs/ *a.* furieux. **~ly** *adv.* furieusement.
furnace /ˈfɜːnɪs/ *n.* fourneau *m.*
furnish /ˈfɜːnɪʃ/ *v.t.* (*with furniture*) meubler; (*supply*) fournir. **~ings** *n. pl.* ameublement *m.*
furniture /ˈfɜːnɪtʃə(r)/ *n.* meubles *m. pl.*, mobilier *m.*
furrier /ˈfʌrɪə(r)/ *n.* fourreur *m.*
furrow /ˈfʌrəʊ/ *n.* sillon *m.*
furry /ˈfɜːrɪ/ *a.* (*animal*) à fourrure; (*toy*) en peluche.
furth|er /ˈfɜːðə(r)/ *a.* plus éloigné; (*additional*) supplémentaire. —*adv.* plus loin; (*more*) davantage. —*v.t.* avancer. **~est** *a.* le plus éloigné; *adv.* le plus loin.
furthermore /ˈfɜːðəmɔː(r)/ *adv.* en outre, de plus.
furtive /ˈfɜːtɪv/ *a.* furtif.
fury /ˈfjʊərɪ/ *n.* fureur *f.*
fuse[1] /fjuːz/ *v.t./i.* (*melt*) fondre; (*unite*: *fig.*) fusionner. —*n.* fusible *m.*, plomb *m.* **~ the lights** *etc.*, faire sauter les plombs.
fuse[2] /fjuːz/ *n.* (*of bomb*) amorce *f.*
fuselage /ˈfjuːzəlɑːʒ/ *n.* fuselage *m.*
fusion /ˈfjuːʒn/ *n.* fusion *f.*
fuss /fʌs/ *n.* histoire(s) *f.* (*pl.*), agitation *f.* —*v.i.* s'agiter. **make a ~ of,** faire grand cas de. **~y** *a.* (*finicky*) tatillon; (*hard to please*) difficile.
fusty /ˈfʌstɪ/ *a.* (**-ier, -iest**) qui sent le renfermé.
futile /ˈfjuːtaɪl/ *a.* futile, vain.
future /ˈfjuːtʃə(r)/ *a.* futur. —*n.* avenir *m.*; (*gram.*) futur *m.* **in ~,** à l'avenir.
fuzz /fʌz/ *n.* (*fluff, growth*) duvet *m.*; (*police*: *sl.*) flics *m. pl.*
fuzzy /ˈfʌzɪ/ *a.* (*hair*) crépu; (*photograph*) flou; (*person*: *fam.*) à l'esprit confus.

G

gabardine /gæbəˈdiːn/ *n.* gabardine *f.*
gabble /ˈgæbl/ *v.t./i.* bredouiller. —*n.* baragouin *m.*
gable /ˈgeɪbl/ *n.* pignon *m.*
gad /gæd/ *v.i.* (*p.t.* **gadded**). **~ about,** se promener, aller çà et là.
gadget /ˈgædʒɪt/ *n.* gadget *m.*
Gaelic /ˈgeɪlɪk/ *n.* gaélique *m.*
gaffe /gæf/ *n.* (*blunder*) gaffe *f.*
gag /gæg/ *n.* bâillon *m.*; (*joke*) gag *m.* —*v.t.* (*p.t.* **gagged**) bâillonner.
gaiety /ˈgeɪətɪ/ *n.* gaieté *f.*
gaily /ˈgeɪlɪ/ *adv.* gaiement.
gain /geɪn/ *v.t.* gagner; (*speed, weight*) prendre. —*v.i.* (*of clock*) avancer. —*n.* acquisition *f.*; (*profit*) gain *m.* **~ful** *a.* profitable.
gainsay /geɪnˈseɪ/ *v.t.* (*p.t.* **gainsaid**) (*formal*) contredire.
gait /geɪt/ *n.* démarche *f.*
gala /ˈgɑːlə/ *n.* (*festive occasion*) gala *m.*; (*sport*) concours *m.*
galaxy /ˈgæləksɪ/ *n.* galaxie *f.*

gale /geɪl/ *n.* forte rafale de vent *f.*, tempête *f.*

gall /gɔːl/ *n.* bile *f.*; (*fig.*) fiel *m.*; (*impudence*: *sl.*) culot *m.* **~-bladder** *n.* vésicule biliaire *f.*

gallant /ˈgælənt/ *a.* (*brave*) courageux; (*chivalrous*) galant. **~ry** *n.* courage *m.*

galleon /ˈgælɪən/ *n.* galion *m.*

gallery /ˈgælərɪ/ *n.* galerie *f.*

galley /ˈgælɪ/ *n.* (*ship*) galère *f.*

Gallic /ˈgælɪk/ *a.* français. **~ism** /-sɪzəm/ *n.* gallicisme *m.*

gallivant /gælɪˈvænt/ *v.i.* (*fam.*) se promener, aller çà et là.

gallon /ˈgælən/ *n.* gallon *m.* (*imperial = 4.546 litres*; *Amer. = 3.785 litres*).

gallop /ˈgæləp/ *n.* galop *m.* —*v.i.* (*p.t.* **galloped**) galoper.

gallows /ˈgæləʊz/ *n.* potence *f.*

galore /gəˈlɔː(r)/ *adv.* en abondance, à gogo.

galosh /gəˈlɒʃ/ *n.* (*overshoe*) caoutchouc *m.*

galvanize /ˈgælvənaɪz/ *v.t.* galvaniser.

gambit /ˈgæmbɪt/ *n.* (**opening**) **~**, (*move*) première démarche *f.*; (*ploy*) stratagème *m.*

gambl|e /ˈgæmbl/ *v.t./i.* jouer. —*n.* (*venture*) entreprise risquée *f.*; (*bet*) pari *m.*; (*risk*) risque *m.* **~e on,** miser sur. **~er** *n.* joueu|r, -se *m., f.* **~ing** *n.* jeu *m.*

game[1] /geɪm/ *n.* jeu *m.*; (*football*) match *m.*; (*tennis*) partie *f.*; (*animals, birds*) gibier *m.* —*a.* (*brave*) brave. **~ for,** prêt à.

game[2] /geɪm/ *a.* (*lame*) estropié.

gamekeeper /ˈgeɪmkiːpə(r)/ *n.* garde-chasse *m.*

gammon /ˈgæmən/ *n.* jambon fumé *m.*

gamut /ˈgæmət/ *n.* gamme *f.*

gamy /ˈgeɪmɪ/ *a.* faisandé.

gang /gæŋ/ *n.* bande *f.*; (*of workmen*) équipe *f.* —*v.i.* **~ up,** se liguer (**on, against,** contre).

gangling /ˈgæŋglɪŋ/ *a.* dégingandé, grand et maigre.

gangrene /ˈgæŋgriːn/ *n.* gangrène *f.*

gangster /ˈgæŋstə(r)/ *n.* gangster *m.*

gangway /ˈgæŋweɪ/ *n.* passage *m.*; (*aisle*) allée *f.*; (*of ship*) passerelle *f.*

gaol /dʒeɪl/ *n.* prison *f.* —*v.t.* mettre en prison. **~er** *n.* geôlier *m.*

gaolbird /ˈdʒeɪlbɜːd/ *n.* récidiviste *m./f.*

gap /gæp/ *n.* trou *m.*, vide *m.*; (*in time*) intervalle *m.*; (*in education*) lacune *f.*; (*difference*) écart *m.*

gap|e /geɪp/ *v.i.* rester bouche bée. **~ing** *a.* béant.

garage /ˈgærɑːʒ, *Amer.* gəˈrɑːʒ/ *n.* garage *m.* —*v.t.* mettre au garage.

garb /gɑːb/ *n.* costume *m.*

garbage /ˈgɑːbɪdʒ/ *n.* ordures *f. pl.*

garble /ˈgɑːbl/ *v.t.* déformer.

garden /ˈgɑːdn/ *n.* jardin *m.* —*v.i.* jardiner. **~er** *n.* jardin|ier, -ière *m., f.* **~ing** *n.* jardinage *m.*

gargle /ˈgɑːgl/ *v.i.* se gargariser. —*n.* gargarisme *m.*

gargoyle /ˈgɑːgɔɪl/ *n.* gargouille *f.*

garish /ˈgeərɪʃ/ *a.* voyant, criard.

garland /ˈgɑːlənd/ *n.* guirlande *f.*

garlic /ˈgɑːlɪk/ *n.* ail *m.*

garment /ˈgɑːmənt/ *n.* vêtement *m.*

garnish /ˈgɑːnɪʃ/ *v.t.* garnir (**with,** de). —*n.* garniture *f.*

garret /ˈgærət/ *n.* mansarde *f.*

garrison /ˈgærɪsn/ *n.* garnison *f.*

garrulous /ˈgærələs/ *a.* loquace.

garter /ˈgɑːtə(r)/ *n.* jarretière *f.*

gas /gæs/ *n.* (*pl.* **gases**) gaz *m.*; (*med.*) anesthésique *m.*; (*petrol*: *Amer., fam.*) essence *f.* —*a.* (*mask, pipe*) à gaz. —*v.t.* asphyxier; (*mil.*) gazer. —*v.i.* (*fam.*) bavarder.

gash /gæʃ/ *n.* entaille *f.* —*v.t.* entailler.

gasoline /ˈgæsəliːn/ *n.* (*petrol*: *Amer.*) essence *f.*

gasometer /gəˈsɒmɪtə(r)/ n. gazomètre m.

gasp /ɡɑːsp/ v.i. haleter; (in surprise: fig.) avoir le souffle coupé. —n. halètement m.

gassy /ˈɡæsɪ/ a. gazeux.

gastric /ˈɡæstrɪk/ a. gastrique.

gastronomy /ɡæˈstrɒnəmɪ/ n. gastronomie f.

gate /ɡeɪt/ n. porte f.; (of metal) grille f.; (barrier) barrière f.

gatecrash /ˈɡeɪtkræʃ/ v.t./i. venir sans invitation (à).

gateway /ˈɡeɪtweɪ/ n. porte f.

gather /ˈɡæðə(r)/ v.t. (people, objects) rassembler; (pick up) ramasser; (flowers) cueillir; (fig.) comprendre; (sewing) froncer. —v.i. (people) se rassembler; (crowd) se former; (pile up) s'accumuler. ~ speed, prendre de la vitesse. ~ing n. rassemblement m.

gaudy /ˈɡɔːdɪ/ a. (-ier, -iest) voyant, criard.

gauge /ɡeɪdʒ/ n. jauge f., indicateur m. —v.t. jauger, évaluer.

gaunt /ɡɔːnt/ a. (lean) émacié; (grim) lugubre.

gauntlet /ˈɡɔːntlɪt/ n. run the ~ of, subir (l'assaut de).

gauze /ɡɔːz/ n. gaze f.

gave /ɡeɪv/ see give.

gawky /ˈɡɔːkɪ/ a. (-ier, -iest) gauche, maladroit.

gawp (or **gawk**) /ɡɔːp, ɡɔːk/ v.i. ~ (at), regarder bouche bée.

gay /ɡeɪ/ a. (-er, -est) (joyful) gai; (fam.) homosexuel.

gaze /ɡeɪz/ v.i. ~ (at), regarder (fixement). —n. regard (fixe) m.

gazelle /ɡəˈzel/ n. gazelle f.

gazette /ɡəˈzet/ n. journal (officiel) m.

GB abbr. see **Great Britain**.

gear /ɡɪə(r)/ n. équipement m.; (techn.) engrenage m.; (auto.) vitesse f. —v.t. adapter. **in ~,** en prise. **out of ~,** au point mort.

gearbox /ˈɡɪəbɒks/ n. (auto.) boîte de vitesses f.

geese /ɡiːs/ see **goose**.

geezer /ˈɡiːzə(r)/ n. (sl.) type m.

gel /dʒel/ n. gelée f.

gelatine /ˈdʒelətiːn/ n. gélatine f.

gelignite /ˈdʒelɪɡnaɪt/ n. nitroglycérine f.

gem /dʒem/ n. pierre précieuse f.

gender /ˈdʒendə(r)/ n. genre m.

gene /dʒiːn/ n. gène m.

genealogy /dʒiːnɪˈælədʒɪ/ n. généalogie f.

general /ˈdʒenrəl/ a. général. —n. général m. ~ **election,** élections législatives f. pl. ~ **practitioner,** (med.) généraliste m. **in ~,** en général. ~**ly** adv. généralement.

generaliz|e /ˈdʒenrəlaɪz/ v.t./i. généraliser. ~**ation** /-ˈzeɪʃn/ n. généralisation f.

generate /ˈdʒenəreɪt/ v.t. produire.

generation /dʒenəˈreɪʃn/ n. génération f.

generator /ˈdʒenəreɪtə(r)/ n. (electr.) groupe électrogène m.

gener|ous /ˈdʒenərəs/ a. généreux; (plentiful) copieux. ~**osity** /-ˈrɒsətɪ/ n. générosité f.

genetic /dʒɪˈnetɪk/ a. génétique. ~**s** n. génétique f.

Geneva /dʒɪˈniːvə/ n. Genève m./f.

genial /ˈdʒiːnɪəl/ a. affable, sympathique; (climate) doux.

genital /ˈdʒenɪtl/ a. génital. ~**s** n. pl. organes génitaux m. pl.

genius /ˈdʒiːnɪəs/ n. (pl. -uses) génie m.

genocide /ˈdʒenəsaɪd/ n. génocide m.

gent /dʒent/ n. (sl.) monsieur m.

genteel /dʒenˈtiːl/ a. distingué.

gentl|e /ˈdʒentl/ a. (-er, -est) (mild, kind) doux; (slight) léger; (hint) discret. ~**eness** n. douceur f. ~**y** adv. doucement.

gentleman /ˈdʒentlmən/ n. (pl. -men) (man) monsieur m.; (well-bred) gentleman m.

genuine /ˈdʒenjʊɪn/ *a*. (*true*) véritable; (*person, belief*) sincère.

geograph|y /dʒɪˈɒgrəfɪ/ *n*. géographie *f*. **~er** *n*. géographe *m*./*f*. **~ical** /dʒɪəˈgræfɪkl/ *a*. géographique.

geolog|y /dʒɪˈɒlədʒɪ/ *n*. géologie *f*. **~ical** /dʒɪəˈlɒdʒɪkl/ *a*. géologique. **~ist** *n*. géologue *m*./*f*.

geometr|y /dʒɪˈɒmətrɪ/ *n*. géométrie *f*. **~ic(al)** /dʒɪəˈmetrɪk(l)/ *a*. géométrique.

geranium /dʒəˈreɪnɪəm/ *n*. géranium *m*.

geriatric /dʒerɪˈætrɪk/ *a*. gériatrique.

germ /dʒɜːm/ *n*. (*rudiment, seed*) germe *m*.; (*med*.) microbe *m*.

German /ˈdʒɜːmən/ *a*. & *n*. allemand(e) (*m*. (*f*.)); (*lang*.) allemand *m*. **~ measles,** rubéole *f*. **~ shepherd,** (*dog*: *Amer*.) berger allemand *m*. **~ic** /dʒəˈmænɪk/ *a*. germanique. **~y** *n*. Allemagne *f*.

germinate /ˈdʒɜːmɪneɪt/ *v.t./i*. (faire) germer.

gestation /dʒeˈsteɪʃn/ *n*. gestation *f*.

gesticulate /dʒeˈstɪkjʊleɪt/ *v.i*. gesticuler.

gesture /ˈdʒestʃə(r)/ *n*. geste *m*.

get /get/ *v.t*. (*p.t*. & *p.p*. **got,** *p.p*. *Amer*. **gotten,** *pres. p*. **getting**) avoir, obtenir, recevoir; (*catch*) prendre; (*buy*) acheter, prendre; (*find*) trouver; (*fetch*) aller chercher; (*understand*: *sl*.) comprendre. **~ s.o. to do sth.,** faire faire qch. à qn. —*v.i*. aller, arriver (**to,** à); (*become*) devenir; (*start*) se mettre (**to,** à); (*manage*) parvenir (**to,** à). **~ married/ready**/*etc*., se marier/se préparer/*etc*. **~ about,** (*person*) se déplacer. **~ across,** (*cross*) traverser. **~ along** *or* **by,** (*manage*) se débrouiller. **~ along** *or* **on,** (*progress*) avancer. **~ along** *or* **on with,** s'entendre avec. **~ at,** (*reach*) parvenir à. **what are you ~ting at?,** où veux-tu en venir? **~ away,** partir; (*escape*) s'échapper. **~ back** *v.i*. revenir; *v.t*. (*recover*) récupérer. **~ by** *or* **through,** (*pass*) passer. **~ down** *v.t./i*. descendre; (*depress*) déprimer. **~ in,** entrer, arriver. **~ off** *v.i*. (*from car etc*.) descendre; (*leave*) partir; (*jurid*.) être acquitté; *v.t*. (*remove*) enlever. **~ on,** (*on train etc*.) monter; (*succeed*) réussir. **~ on with,** continuer. **~ out,** sortir. **~ out of,** (*fig*.) se soustraire à. **~ over,** (*illness*) se remettre de. **~ round,** (*rule*) contourner; (*person*) entortiller. **~ through,** (*finish*) finir. **~ up** *v.i*. se lever; *v.t*. (*climb, bring*) monter. **~-up** *n*. (*clothes*: *fam*.) mise *f*.

getaway /ˈgetəweɪ/ *n*. fuite *f*.

geyser /ˈgiːzə(r)/ *n*. chauffe-eau *m. invar*.; (*geol*.) geyser *m*.

Ghana /ˈgɑːnə/ *n*. Ghana *m*.

ghastly /ˈgɑːstlɪ/ *a*. (**-ier, -iest**) affreux; (*pale*) blême.

gherkin /ˈgɜːkɪn/ *n*. cornichon *m*.

ghetto /ˈgetəʊ/ *n*. (*pl*. **-os**) ghetto *m*.

ghost /gəʊst/ *n*. fantôme *m*. **~ly** *a*. spectral.

ghoulish /ˈguːlɪʃ/ *a*. morbide.

giant /ˈdʒaɪənt/ *n*. & *a*. géant (*m*.).

gibberish /ˈdʒɪbərɪʃ/ *n*. baragouin *m*., charabia *m*.

gibe /dʒaɪb/ *n*. raillerie *f*. —*v.i*. **~ (at),** railler.

giblets /ˈdʒɪblɪts/ *n. pl*. abattis *m. pl*., abats *m. pl*.

gidd|y /ˈgɪdɪ/ *a*. (**-ier, -iest**) vertigineux. **be** *or* **feel ~y,** avoir le vertige. **~iness** *n*. vertige *m*.

gift /gɪft/ *n*. cadeau *m*.; (*ability*) don *m*. **~-wrap** *v.t*. (*p.t*. **-wrapped**) faire un paquet-cadeau de.

gifted /ˈgɪftɪd/ *a*. doué.

gig /gɪg/ *n*. (*fam*.) séance de jazz *f*.

gigantic /dʒaɪˈgæntɪk/ *a*. gigantesque.

giggle /'gɪgl/ *v.i.* ricaner (sottement), glousser. —*n.* ricanement *m.* **the ~s,** le fou rire.
gild /gɪld/ *v.t.* dorer.
gills /gɪlz/ *n. pl.* ouïes *f. pl.*
gilt /gɪlt/ *a.* doré. —*n.* dorure *f.* **~-edged** *a.* (*comm.*) de tout repos.
gimmick /'gɪmɪk/ *n.* truc *m.*
gin /dʒɪn/ *n.* gin *m.*
ginger /'dʒɪndʒə(r)/ *n.* gingembre *m.* —*a.* roux. **~ ale, ~ beer,** boisson gazeuse au gingembre *f.*
gingerbread /'dʒɪndʒəbred/ *n.* pain d'épice *m.*
gingerly /'dʒɪndʒəlɪ/ *adv.* avec précaution.
gipsy /'dʒɪpsɪ/ *n.* = **gypsy.**
giraffe /dʒɪ'rɑːf/ *n.* girafe *f.*
girder /'gɜːdə(r)/ *n.* poutre *f.*
girdle /'gɜːdl/ *n.* (*belt*) ceinture *f.*; (*corset*) gaine *f.*
girl /gɜːl/ *n.* (petite) fille *f.*; (*young woman*) (jeune) fille *f.* **~-friend** *n.* amie *f.*; (*of boy*) petite amie *f.* **~hood** *n.* enfance *f.*, jeunesse *f.* **~ish** *a.* de (jeune) fille.
giro /'dʒaɪərəʊ/ *n.* (*pl.* **-os**) virement bancaire *m.*
girth /gɜːθ/ *n.* circonférence *f.*
gist /dʒɪst/ *n.* essentiel *m.*
give /gɪv/ *v.t.* (*p.t.* **gave,** *p.p.* **given**) donner; (*gesture*) faire; (*laugh, sigh, etc.*) pousser. —*v.i.* donner; (*yield*) céder; (*stretch*) se détendre. —*n.* élasticité *f.* **~ away,** donner; (*secret*) trahir. **~ back,** rendre. **~ in,** (*yield*) se rendre. **~ off,** dégager. **~ out** *v.t.* distribuer; *v.i.* (*become used up*) s'épuiser. **~ over,** (*devote*) consacrer; (*stop*: *fam.*) cesser. **~ up** *v.t./i.* (*renounce*) renoncer (à); (*yield*) céder. **~ o.s. up,** se rendre. **~ way,** céder; (*collapse*) s'effondrer.
given /'gɪvn/ *see* **give.** —*a.* donné. **~ name,** prénom *m.*
glacier /'glæsɪə(r), *Amer.* 'gleɪʃə(r)/ *n.* glacier *m.*
glad /glæd/ *a.* content. **~ly** *adv.* avec plaisir.
gladden /'glædn/ *v.t.* réjouir.
glade /gleɪd/ *n.* clairière *f.*
gladiolus /glædɪ'əʊləs/ *n.* (*pl.* **-li** /-laɪ/) glaïeul *m.*
glam|our /'glæmə(r)/ *n.* enchantement *m.*, séduction *f.* **~orize** *v.t.* rendre séduisant. **~orous** *a.* séduisant, ensorcelant.
glance /glɑːns/ *n.* coup d'œil *m.* —*v.i.* **~ at,** jeter un coup d'œil à.
gland /glænd/ *n.* glande *f.*
glar|e /gleə(r)/ *v.i.* briller très fort. —*n.* éclat (aveuglant) *m.*; (*stare*: *fig.*) regard furieux *m.* **~e at,** regarder d'un air furieux. **~ing** *a.* éblouissant; (*obvious*) flagrant.
glass /glɑːs/ *n.* verre *m.*; (*mirror*) miroir *m.* **~es,** (*spectacles*) lunettes *f. pl.* **~y** *a.* vitreux.
glaze /gleɪz/ *v.t.* (*door etc.*) vitrer; (*pottery*) vernisser. —*n.* vernis *m.*
gleam /gliːm/ *n.* lueur *f.* —*v.i.* luire.
glean /gliːn/ *v.t.* glaner.
glee /gliː/ *n.* joie *f.* **~ club,** chorale *f.* **~ful** *a.* joyeux.
glen /glen/ *n.* vallon *m.*
glib /glɪb/ *a.* (*person*: *pej.*) qui a la parole facile *or* du bagou; (*reply, excuse*) désinvolte, spécieux. **~ly** *adv.* avec désinvolture.
glide /glaɪd/ *v.i.* glisser; (*of plane*) planer. **~r** /-ə(r)/ *n.* planeur *m.*
glimmer /'glɪmə(r)/ *n.* lueur *f.* —*v.i.* luire.
glimpse /glɪmps/ *n.* aperçu *m.* **catch a ~ of,** entrevoir.
glint /glɪnt/ *n.* éclair *m.* —*v.i.* étinceler.
glisten /'glɪsn/ *v.i.* briller, luire.
glitter /'glɪtə(r)/ *v.i.* scintiller. —*n.* scintillement *m.*
gloat /gləʊt/ *v.i.* jubiler (**over,** à l'idée de).
global /'gləʊbl/ *a.* (*world-wide*) mondial; (*all-embracing*) global.
globe /gləʊb/ *n.* globe *m.*
gloom /gluːm/ *n.* obscurité *f.*; (*sad-*

ness: *fig*.) tristesse *f*. **~y** *a*. triste; (*pessimistic*) pessimiste.
glorif|y /ˈglɔːrɪfaɪ/ *v.t.* glorifier. **a ~ied waitress**/*etc*., à peine plus qu'une serveuse/*etc*.
glorious /ˈglɔːrɪəs/ *a*. splendide; (*deed, hero, etc*.) glorieux.
glory /ˈglɔːrɪ/ *n*. gloire *f*.; (*beauty*) splendeur *f*. —*v.i.* **~ in**, s'enorgueillir de.
gloss /glɒs/ *n*. lustre *m*., brillant *m*. —*a*. brillant. —*v.i.* **~ over**, (*make light of*) glisser sur; (*cover up*) dissimuler. **~y** *a*. brillant.
glossary /ˈglɒsərɪ/ *n*. glossaire *m*.
glove /glʌv/ *n*. gant *m*. **~ compartment**, (*auto*.) vide-poches *m*. *invar*. **~d** *a*. ganté.
glow /gləʊ/ *v.i.* rougeoyer; (*person, eyes*) rayonner. —*n*. rougeoiement *m*., éclat *m*. **~ing** *a*. (*account etc*.) enthousiaste.
glucose /ˈgluːkəʊs/ *n*. glucose *m*.
glue /gluː/ *n*. colle *f*. —*v.t.* (*pres. p*. **gluing**) coller.
glum /glʌm/ *a*. (**glummer, glummest**) triste, morne.
glut /glʌt/ *n*. surabondance *f*.
glutton /ˈglʌtn/ *n*. glouton(ne) *m*. (*f*.). **~ous** *a*. glouton. **~y** *n*. gloutonnerie *f*.
glycerine /ˈglɪsəriːn/ *n*. glycérine *f*.
gnarled /nɑːld/ *a*. noueux.
gnash /næʃ/ *v.t.* **~ one's teeth**, grincer des dents.
gnat /næt/ *n*. (*fly*) cousin *m*.
gnaw /nɔː/ *v.t./i.* ronger.
gnome /nəʊm/ *n*. gnome *m*.
go /gəʊ/ *v.i.* (*p.t.* **went**, *p.p.* **gone**) aller; (*leave*) partir; (*work*) marcher; (*become*) devenir; (*be sold*) se vendre; (*vanish*) disparaître. **~ riding/shopping/***etc*., faire du cheval/les courses/*etc*. —*n*. (*pl*. **goes**) (*try*) coup *m*.; (*success*) réussite *f*.; (*turn*) tour *m*.; (*energy*) dynamisme *m*. **be ~ing to do**, aller faire. **~ across**, traverser. **~ ahead!**, allez-y! **~-ahead** *n*. feu vert *m*.; *a*. dynamique. **~ away**, s'en aller. **~ back**, retourner; (*go home*) rentrer. **~ back on**, (*promise etc*.) revenir sur. **~ bad** *or* **off**, se gâter. **~-between** *n*. intermédiaire *m*./*f*. **~ by**, (*pass*) passer. **~ down**, descendre; (*sun*) se coucher. **~ for**, aller chercher; (*like*) aimer; (*attack*: *sl*.) attaquer. **~ in**, (r)entrer. **~ in for**, (*exam*) se présenter à. **~-kart** *n*. kart *m*. **~ off**, partir; (*explode*) sauter; (*ring*) sonner. **~ on**, continuer; (*happen*) se passer. **~ out**, sortir; (*light, fire*) s'éteindre. **~ over**, (*cross*) traverser; (*pass*) passer. **~ over** *or* **through**, (*check*) examiner; (*search*) fouiller. **~ round**, (*be enough*) suffire. **~-slow** *n*. grève perlée *f*. **~ through**, (*suffer*) subir. **~ under**, (*sink*) couler; (*fail*) échouer. **~ up**, monter. **~ without**, se passer de. **on the ~**, actif.
goad /gəʊd/ *v.t.* aiguillonner.
goal /gəʊl/ *n*. but *m*. **~-post** *n*. poteau de but *m*.
goalkeeper /ˈgəʊlkiːpə(r)/ *n*. gardien de but *m*.
goat /gəʊt/ *n*. chèvre *f*.
goatee /gəʊˈtiː/ *n*. barbiche *f*.
gobble /ˈgɒbl/ *v.t.* engouffrer.
goblet /ˈgɒblɪt/ *n*. verre à pied *m*.
goblin /ˈgɒblɪn/ *n*. lutin *m*.
God /gɒd/ *n*. Dieu *m*. **~-forsaken** *a*. perdu.
god /gɒd/ *n*. dieu *m*. **~dess** *n*. déesse *f*. **~ly** *a*. dévot.
god|child /ˈgɒdtʃaɪld/ *n*. (*pl*. **-children**) filleul(e) *m*. (*f*.). **~-daughter** *n*. filleule *f*. **~father** *n*. parrain *m*. **~mother** *n*. marraine *f*. **~son** *n*. filleul *m*.
godsend /ˈgɒdsend/ *n*. aubaine *f*.
goggle /ˈgɒgl/ *v.i.* **~ (at)**, regarder avec de gros yeux.
goggles /ˈgɒglz/ *n*. *pl*. lunettes (protectrices) *f*. *pl*.

going /ˈgəʊɪŋ/ *n.* **it is slow/hard ~,** c'est lent/difficile. —*a.* (*price, rate*) actuel. **~s-on** *n. pl.* activités (bizarres) *f. pl.*

gold /gəʊld/ *n.* or *m.* —*a.* en or, d'or. **~-mine** *n.* mine d'or *f.*

golden /ˈgəʊldən/ *a.* d'or; (*in colour*) doré; (*opportunity*) unique. **~ wedding,** noces d'or *f. pl.*

goldfish /ˈgəʊldfɪʃ/ *n. invar.* poisson rouge *m.*

gold-plated /gəʊldˈpleɪtɪd/ *a.* plaqué or.

goldsmith /ˈgəʊldsmɪθ/ *n.* orfèvre *m.*

golf /gɒlf/ *n.* golf *m.* **~-course** *n.* terrain de golf *m.* **~er** *n.* joueu|r, -se de golf *m., f.*

golly /ˈgɒlɪ/ *int.* mince, zut.

gondol|a /ˈgɒndələ/ *n.* gondole *f.* **~ier** /-ˈlɪə(r)/ *n.* gondolier *m.*

gone /gɒn/ *see* **go.** —*a.* parti. **~ six o'clock,** six heures passées.

gong /gɒŋ/ *n.* gong *m.*

good /gʊd/ *a.* (**better, best**) bon; (*weather*) beau; (*well-behaved*) sage. —*n.* bien *m.* **as ~ as,** (*almost*) pratiquement. **be ~ with,** savoir s'y prendre avec. **do ~,** faire du bien. **feel ~,** se sentir bien. **~-for-nothing** *a.* & *n.* propre à rien (*m./f.*). **G~ Friday,** Vendredi saint *m.* **~-afternoon, ~-morning** *ints.* bonjour. **~-evening** *int.* bonsoir. **~-looking** *a.* joli. **~ name,** réputation *f.* **~-night** *int.* bonsoir, bonne nuit. **it is ~ for you,** ça vous fait du bien. **it is no ~ shouting/***etc.*, ça ne sert à rien de crier/*etc.* **~ness** *n.* bonté *f.* **my ~ness!,** mon Dieu!

goodbye /gʊdˈbaɪ/ *int.* & *n.* au revoir (*m. invar.*).

goods /gʊdz/ *n. pl.* marchandises *f. pl.*

goodwill /gʊdˈwɪl/ *n.* bonne volonté *f.*

goody /ˈgʊdɪ/ *n.* (*fam.*) bonne chose *f.* **~-goody** *n.* petit(e) saint(e) *m.* (*f.*).

gooey /ˈguːɪ/ *a.* (*sl.*) poisseux.

goof /guːf/ *v.i.* (*Amer.*) gaffer.

goose /guːs/ *n.* (*pl.* **geese**) oie *f.* **~-flesh, ~-pimples** *ns.* chair de poule *f.*

gooseberry /ˈgʊzbərɪ/ *n.* groseille à maquereau *f.*

gore[1] /gɔː(r)/ *n.* (*blood*) sang *m.*

gore[2] /gɔː(r)/ *v.t.* encorner.

gorge /gɔːdʒ/ *n.* (*geog.*) gorge *f.* —*v.t.* **~ o.s.,** se gorger.

gorgeous /ˈgɔːdʒəs/ *a.* magnifique, splendide, formidable.

gorilla /gəˈrɪlə/ *n.* gorille *m.*

gormless /ˈgɔːmlɪs/ *a.* (*sl.*) stupide.

gorse /gɔːs/ *n. invar.* ajonc(s) *m.* (*pl.*).

gory /ˈgɔːrɪ/ *a.* (**-ier, -iest**) sanglant; (*horrific: fig.*) horrible.

gosh /gɒʃ/ *int.* mince (alors).

gospel /ˈgɒspl/ *n.* évangile *m.* **the G~,** l'Évangile *m.*

gossip /ˈgɒsɪp/ *n.* bavardage(s) *m.* (*pl.*), commérage(s) *m.* (*pl.*); (*person*) bavard(e) *m.* (*f.*). —*v.i.* (*p.t.* **gossiped**) bavarder. **~y** *a.* bavard.

got /gɒt/ *see* **get.** —**have ~,** avoir. **have ~ to do,** devoir faire.

Gothic /ˈgɒθɪk/ *a.* gothique.

gouge /gaʊdʒ/ *v.t.* **~ out,** arracher.

gourmet /ˈgʊəmeɪ/ *n.* gourmet *m.*

gout /gaʊt/ *n.* (*med.*) goutte *f.*

govern /ˈgʌvn/ *v.t./i.* gouverner. **~ess** /-ənɪs/ *n.* gouvernante *f.* **~or** /-ənə(r)/ *n.* gouverneur *m.*

government /ˈgʌvənmənt/ *n.* gouvernement *m.* **~al** /-ˈmentl/ *a.* gouvernemental.

gown /gaʊn/ *n.* robe *f.*; (*of judge, teacher*) toge *f.*

GP *abbr. see* **general practitioner.**

grab /græb/ *v.t.* (*p.t.* **grabbed**) saisir.

grace /greɪs/ *n.* grâce *f.* —*v.t.*

(*honour*) honorer; (*adorn*) orner. **~ful** *a.* gracieux.

gracious /ˈgreɪʃəs/ *a.* (*kind*) bienveillant; (*elegant*) élégant.

gradation /grəˈdeɪʃn/ *n.* gradation *f.*

grade /greɪd/ *n.* catégorie *f.*; (*of goods*) qualité *f.*; (*on scale*) grade *m.*; (*school mark*) note *f.*; (*class: Amer.*) classe *f.* —*v.t.* classer; (*school work*) noter. **~ school,** (*Amer.*) école primaire *f.*

gradient /ˈgreɪdɪənt/ *n.* (*slope*) inclinaison *f.*

gradual /ˈgrædʒʊəl/ *a.* progressif, graduel. **~ly** *adv.* progressivement, peu à peu.

graduate[1] /ˈgrædʒʊət/ *n.* (*univ.*) licencié(e) *m.* (*f.*), diplômé(e) *m.* (*f.*).

graduat|e[2] /ˈgrædʒʊeɪt/ *v.i.* obtenir son diplôme. —*v.t.* graduer. **~ion** /-ˈeɪʃn/ *n.* remise de diplômes *f.*

graffiti /grəˈfiːtiː/ *n. pl.* graffiti *m. pl.*

graft[1] /grɑːft/ *n.* (*med.*; *bot.*) greffe *f.* —*v.t.* greffer.

graft[2] /grɑːft/ *n.* (*bribery: fam.*) corruption *f.*

grain /greɪn/ *n.* (*seed, quantity, texture*) grain *m.*; (*in wood*) fibre *f.*

gram /græm/ *n.* gramme *m.*

gramm|ar /ˈgræmə(r)/ *n.* grammaire *f.* **~atical** /grəˈmætɪkl/ *a.* grammatical.

gramophone /ˈgræməfəʊn/ *n.* phonographe *m.*

grand /grænd/ *a.* (**-er, -est**) magnifique; (*duke, chorus*) grand. **~ piano,** piano à queue *m.*

grand|child /ˈgræn(d)tʃaɪld/ *n.* (*pl.* **-children**) petit(e)-enfant *m.* (*f.*). **~daughter** *n.* petite-fille *f.* **~father** *n.* grand-père *m.* **~-mother** *n.* grand-mère *f.* **~-parents** *n. pl.* grands-parents *m. pl.* **~son** *n.* petit-fils *m.*

grandeur /ˈgrændʒə(r)/ *n.* grandeur *f.*

grandiose /ˈgrændɪəʊs/ *a.* grandiose.

grandstand /ˈgræn(d)stænd/ *n.* tribune *f.*

granite /ˈgrænɪt/ *n.* granit *m.*

granny /ˈgrænɪ/ *n.* (*fam.*) grand-maman *f.*, mémé *f.*, mamie *f.*

grant /grɑːnt/ *v.t.* (*give*) accorder; (*request*) accéder à; (*admit*) admettre (**that,** que). —*n.* subvention *f.*; (*univ.*) bourse *f.* **take sth. for ~ed,** considérer qch. comme une chose acquise.

granulated /ˈgrænjʊleɪtɪd/ *a.* **~ sugar,** sucre semoule *m.*

granule /ˈgrænjuːl/ *n.* granule *m.*

grape /greɪp/ *n.* grain de raisin *m.* **~s,** raisin(s) *m.* (*pl.*).

grapefruit /ˈgreɪpfruːt/ *n. invar.* pamplemousse *m.*

graph /grɑːf/ *n.* graphique *m.*

graphic /ˈgræfɪk/ *a.* (*arts etc.*) graphique; (*fig.*) vivant, explicite.

grapple /græpl/ *v.i.* **~ with,** affronter, être aux prises avec.

grasp /grɑːsp/ *v.t.* saisir. —*n.* (*hold*) prise *f.*; (*strength of hand*) poigne *f.*; (*reach*) portée *f.*; (*fig.*) compréhension *f.*

grasping /ˈgrɑːspɪŋ/ *a.* rapace.

grass /grɑːs/ *n.* herbe *f.* **~ roots,** peuple *m.*; (*pol.*) base *f.* **~-roots** *a.* populaire. **~y** *a.* herbeux.

grasshopper /ˈgrɑːshɒpə(r)/ *n.* sauterelle *f.*

grassland /ˈgrɑːslænd/ *n.* prairie *f.*

grate[1] /greɪt/ *n.* (*fireplace*) foyer *m.*; (*frame*) grille *f.*

grate[2] /greɪt/ *v.t.* râper. —*v.i.* grincer. **~ one's teeth,** grincer des dents. **~r** /-ə(r)/ *n.* râpe *f.*

grateful /ˈgreɪtfl/ *a.* reconnaissant. **~ly** *adv.* avec reconnaissance.

gratif|y /ˈgrætɪfaɪ/ *v.t.* satisfaire; (*please*) faire plaisir à. **~ied** *a.* très heureux. **~ying** *a.* agréable.

grating /'greɪtɪŋ/ *n.* grille *f.*
gratis /'greɪtɪs, 'grætɪs/ *a.* & *adv.* gratis (*a. invar.*).
gratitude /'grætɪtju:d/ *n.* gratitude *f.*
gratuitous /grə'tju:ɪtəs/ *a.* gratuit.
gratuity /grə'tju:ətɪ/ *n.* (*tip*) pourboire *m.*; (*bounty*: *mil.*) prime *f.*
grave[1] /greɪv/ *n.* tombe *f.* **~-digger** *n.* fossoyeur *m.*
grave[2] /greɪv/ *a.* (**-er, -est**) (*serious*) grave. **~ly** *adv.* gravement.
grave[3] /grɑ:v/ *a.* **~ accent,** accent grave *m.*
gravel /'grævl/ *n.* gravier *m.*
gravestone /'greɪvstəʊn/ *n.* pierre tombale *f.*
graveyard /'greɪvjɑ:d/ *n.* cimetière *m.*
gravitat|e /'grævɪteɪt/ *v.i.* graviter. **~ion** /-'teɪʃn/ *n.* gravitation *f.*
gravity /'grævətɪ/ *n.* (*seriousness*) gravité *f.*; (*force*) pesanteur *f.*
gravy /'greɪvɪ/ *n.* jus (de viande) *m.*
graze[1] /greɪz/ *v.t./i.* (*eat*) paître.
graze[2] /greɪz/ *v.t.* (*touch*) frôler; (*scrape*) écorcher. *—n.* écorchure *f.*
greas|e /gri:s/ *n.* graisse *f.* *—v.t.* graisser. **~e-proof paper,** papier sulfurisé *m.* **~y** *a.* graisseux.
great /greɪt/ *a.* (**-er, -est**) grand; (*very good*: *fam.*) magnifique. **~ Britain,** Grande-Bretagne *f.* **~-grandfather** *n.* arrière-grand-père *m.* **~-grandmother** *n.* arrière-grand-mère *f.* **~ly** *adv.* (*very*) très; (*much*) beaucoup. **~ness** *n.* grandeur *f.*
Greece /gri:s/ *n.* Grèce *f.*
greed /gri:d/ *n.* avidité *f.*; (*for food*) gourmandise *f.* **~y** *a.* avide; gourmand.
Greek /gri:k/ *a.* & *n.* grec(que) (*m.* (*f.*)); (*lang.*) grec *m.*
green /gri:n/ *a.* (**-er, -est**) vert; (*fig.*) naïf. *—n.* vert *m.*; (*grass*) pelouse *f.* **~s,** légumes verts *m. pl.* **~ belt,** zone de verdure *f.* **~ light,** feu vert *m.* **the ~ pound,** la livre verte. **~ery** *n.* verdure *f.*
greengage /'gri:ngeɪdʒ/ *n.* (*plum*) reine-claude *f.*
greengrocer /'gri:ngrəʊsə(r)/ *n.* marchand(e) de fruits et légumes *m.* (*f.*).
greenhouse /'gri:nhaʊs/ *n.* serre *f.*
greet /gri:t/ *v.t.* (*receive*) accueillir; (*address politely*) saluer. **~ing** *n.* accueil *m.* **~ings** *n. pl.* compliments *m. pl.*; (*wishes*) vœux *m. pl.*
gregarious /grɪ'geərɪəs/ *a.* (*instinct*) grégaire; (*person*) sociable.
grenade /grɪ'neɪd/ *n.* grenade *f.*
grew /gru:/ *see* **grow.**
grey /greɪ/ *a.* (**-er, -est**) gris; (*fig.*) triste. *—n.* gris *m.* *—v.i.* (*hair, person*) grisonner.
greyhound /'greɪhaʊnd/ *n.* lévrier *m.*
grid /grɪd/ *n.* grille *f.*; (*network*: *electr.*) réseau *m.*; (*culin.*) gril *m.*
grief /gri:f/ *n.* chagrin *m.* **come to ~,** (*person*) avoir un malheur; (*fail*) tourner mal.
grievance /'gri:vns/ *n.* grief *m.*
grieve /gri:v/ *v.t./i.* (s')affliger. **~ for,** pleurer.
grill /grɪl/ *n.* (*cooking device*) gril *m.*; (*food*) grillade *f.* *—v.t./i.* griller; (*interrogate*) cuisiner.
grille /grɪl/ *n.* grille *f.*
grim /grɪm/ *a.* (**grimmer, grimmest**) sinistre.
grimace /grɪ'meɪs/ *n.* grimace *f.* *—v.i.* grimacer.
grim|e /graɪm/ *n.* crasse *f.* **~y** *a.* crasseux.
grin /grɪn/ *v.i.* (*p.t.* **grinned**) sourire. *—n.* (large) sourire *m.*
grind /graɪnd/ *v.t.* (*p.t.* **ground**) écraser; (*coffee*) moudre; (*sharpen*) aiguiser. *—n.* corvée *f.* **~ one's teeth,** grincer des dents.
grip /grɪp/ *v.t.* (*p.t.* **gripped**) saisir; (*interest*) passionner. *—n.*

prise *f.*; (*strength of hand*) poigne *f.* **come to ~s,** en venir aux prises.

gripe /graɪp/ *n.* **~s,** (*med.*) coliques *f. pl.* —*v.i.* (*grumble*: *sl.*) râler.

grisly /ˈgrɪzlɪ/ *a.* (**-ier, -iest**) macabre, horrible.

gristle /ˈgrɪsl/ *n.* cartilage *m.*

grit /grɪt/ *n.* gravillon *m.*, sable *m.*; (*fig.*) courage *m.* —*v.t.* (*p.t.* **gritted**) (*road*) sabler; (*teeth*) serrer.

grizzle /ˈgrɪzl/ *v.i.* (*cry*) pleurnicher.

groan /grəʊn/ *v.i.* gémir. —*n.* gémissement *m.*

grocer /ˈgrəʊsə(r)/ *n.* épic|ier, -ière *m.*, *f.* **~ies** *n. pl.* (*goods*) épicerie *f.* **~y** *n.* (*shop*) épicerie *f.*

grog /grɒg/ *n.* grog *m.*

groggy /ˈgrɒgɪ/ *a.* (*weak*) faible; (*unsteady*) chancelant; (*ill*) mal fichu.

groin /grɔɪn/ *n.* aine *f.*

groom /gruːm/ *n.* marié *m.*; (*for horses*) valet d'écurie *m.* —*v.t.* (*horse*) panser; (*fig.*) préparer.

groove /gruːv/ *n.* (*for door etc.*) rainure *f.*; (*in record*) sillon *m.*

grope /grəʊp/ *v.i.* tâtonner. **~ for,** chercher à tâtons.

gross /grəʊs/ *a.* (**-er, -est**) (*coarse*) grossier; (*comm.*) brut. —*n. invar.* grosse *f.* **~ly** *adv.* grossièrement; (*very*) extrêmement.

grotesque /grəʊˈtesk/ *a.* grotesque, horrible.

grotto /ˈgrɒtəʊ/ *n.* (*pl.* **-oes**) grotte *f.*

grotty /ˈgrɒtɪ/ *a.* (*sl.*) moche.

grouch /graʊtʃ/ *v.i.* (*grumble*: *fam.*) rouspéter, râler.

ground[1] /graʊnd/ *n.* terre *f.*, sol *m.*; (*area*) terrain *m.*; (*reason*) raison *f.*; (*electr.*, *Amer.*) masse *f.* **~s,** terres *f. pl.*, parc *m.*; (*of coffee*) marc *m.* —*v.t.*/*i.* (*naut.*) échouer; (*aircraft*) retenir au sol. **~ floor,** rez-de-chaussée *m. invar.* **~less** *a.* sans fondement. **~ swell,** lame de fond *f.*

ground[2] /graʊnd/ *see* **grind.**

grounding /ˈgraʊndɪŋ/ *n.* connaissances (de base) *f. pl.*

groundsheet /ˈgraʊndʃiːt/ *n.* tapis de sol *m.*

groundwork /ˈgraʊndwɜːk/ *n.* travail préparatoire *m.*

group /gruːp/ *n.* groupe *m.* —*v.t.*/*i.* (se) grouper.

grouse[1] /graʊs/ *n. invar.* (*bird*) coq de bruyère *m.*, grouse *f.*

grouse[2] /graʊs/ *v.i.* (*grumble*: *fam.*) rouspéter, râler.

grove /grəʊv/ *n.* bocage *m.*

grovel /ˈgrɒvl/ *v.i.* (*p.t.* **grovelled**) ramper. **~ling** *a.* rampant.

grow /grəʊ/ *v.i.* (*p.t.* **grew,** *p.p.* **grown**) grandir; (*of plant*) pousser; (*become*) devenir. —*v.t.* cultiver. **~ up,** devenir adulte. **~er** *n.* cultiva|teur, -trice *m.*, *f.*

growl /graʊl/ *v.i.* grogner. —*n.* grognement *m.*

grown /grəʊn/ *see* **grow.** —*a.* adulte. **~-up** *a.* & *n.* adulte (*m.*/*f.*).

growth /grəʊθ/ *n.* croissance *f.*; (*in numbers*) accroissement *m.*; (*of hair, tooth*) pousse *f.*; (*med.*) tumeur *f.*

grub /grʌb/ *n.* (*larva*) larve *f.*; (*food*: *sl.*) bouffe *f.*

grubby /ˈgrʌbɪ/ *a.* (**-ier, -iest**) sale.

grudge /grʌdʒ/ *v.t.* **~ doing,** faire à contrecœur. **~ s.o. sth.,** (*success, wealth*) en vouloir à qn. de qch. —*n.* rancune *f.* **have a ~ against,** en vouloir à. **grudgingly** *adv.* à contrecœur.

gruelling /ˈgruːəlɪŋ/ *a.* exténuant.

gruesome /ˈgruːsəm/ *a.* macabre.

gruff /grʌf/ *a.* (**-er, -est**) bourru.

grumble /ˈgrʌmbl/ *v.i.* ronchonner, grogner (**at,** après).

grumpy /ˈgrʌmpɪ/ *a.* (**-ier, -iest**) grincheux, grognon.

grunt /grʌnt/ *v.i.* grogner. —*n.* grognement *m.*

guarant|ee /gærən'tiː/ *n.* garantie *f.* —*v.t.* garantir. **~or** *n.* garant(e) *m.* (*f.*).

guard /gɑːd/ *v.t.* protéger; (*watch*) surveiller. —*v.i.* **~ against,** se protéger contre. —*n.* (*vigilance, mil. group*) garde *f.*; (*person*) garde *m.*; (*on train*) chef de train *m.* **~ian** *n.* gardien(ne) *m.* (*f.*); (*of orphan*) tu|teur, -trice *m.*, *f.*

guarded /'gɑːdɪd/ *a.* prudent.

guerrilla /gə'rɪlə/ *n.* guérillero *m.* **~ warfare,** guérilla *f.*

guess /ges/ *v.t./i.* deviner; (*suppose*) penser. —*n.* conjecture *f.*

guesswork /'geswɜːk/ *n.* conjectures *f. pl.*

guest /gest/ *n.* invité(e) *m.* (*f.*); (*in hotel*) client(e) *m.* (*f.*). **~-house** *n.* pension *f.*

guffaw /gə'fɔː/ *n.* gros rire *m.* —*v.i.* s'esclaffer, rire bruyamment.

guidance /'gaɪdns/ *n.* (*advice*) conseils *m. pl.*; (*information*) information *f.*

guide /gaɪd/ *n.* (*person, book*) guide *m.* —*v.t.* guider. **~d** /-ɪd/ *a.* **~d missile,** missile téléguidé *m.* **~-lines** *n. pl.* grandes lignes *f. pl.*

Guide /gaɪd/ *n.* (*girl*) guide *f.*

guidebook /'gaɪdbʊk/ *n.* guide *m.*

guild /gɪld/ *n.* corporation *f.*

guile /gaɪl/ *n.* ruse *f.*

guillotine /'gɪlətiːn/ *n.* guillotine *f.*; (*for paper*) massicot *m.*

guilt /gɪlt/ *n.* culpabilité *f.* **~y** *a.* coupable.

guinea-pig /'gɪnɪpɪg/ *n.* cobaye *m.*

guise /gaɪz/ *n.* apparence *f.*

guitar /gɪ'tɑː(r)/ *n.* guitare *f.* **~ist** *n.* guitariste *m.*/*f.*

gulf /gʌlf/ *n.* (*part of sea*) golfe *m.*; (*hollow*) gouffre *m.*

gull /gʌl/ *n.* mouette *f.*, goéland *m.*

gullet /'gʌlɪt/ *n.* gosier *m.*

gullible /'gʌləbl/ *a.* crédule.

gully /'gʌlɪ/ *n.* (*ravine*) ravine *f.*; (*drain*) rigole *f.*

gulp /gʌlp/ *v.t.* **~ (down),** avaler en vitesse. —*v.i.* (*from fear etc.*) avoir un serrement de gorge. —*n.* gorgée *f.*

gum[1] /gʌm/ *n.* (*anat.*) gencive *f.*

gum[2] /gʌm/ *n.* (*from tree*) gomme *f.*; (*glue*) colle *f.*; (*for chewing*) chewing-gum *m.* —*v.t.* (*p.t.* **gummed**) gommer.

gumboil /'gʌmbɔɪl/ *n.* abcès dentaire *m.*

gumboot /'gʌmbuːt/ *n.* botte de caoutchouc *f.*

gumption /'gʌmpʃn/ *n.* (*fam.*) initiative *f.*, courage *m.*, audace *f.*

gun /gʌn/ *n.* (*pistol*) pistolet *m.*; (*rifle*) fusil *m.*; (*large*) canon *m.* —*v.t.* (*p.t.* **gunned**). **~ down,** abattre. **~ner** *n.* artilleur *m.*

gunfire /'gʌnfaɪə(r)/ *n.* fusillade *f.*

gunge /gʌndʒ/ *n.* (*sl.*) crasse *f.*

gunman /'gʌnmən/ *n.* (*pl.* **-men**) bandit armé *m.*

gunpowder /'gʌnpaʊdə(r)/ *n.* poudre à canon *f.*

gunshot /'gʌnʃɒt/ *n.* coup de feu *m.*

gurgle /'gɜːgl/ *n.* glouglou *m.* —*v.i.* glouglouter.

guru /'gʊruː/ *n.* (*pl.* **-us**) gourou *m.*

gush /gʌʃ/ *v.i.* **~ (out),** jaillir. —*n.* jaillissement *m.*

gust /gʌst/ *n.* rafale *f.*; (*of smoke*) bouffée *f.* **~y** *a.* venteux.

gusto /'gʌstəʊ/ *n.* enthousiasme *m.*

gut /gʌt/ *n.* boyau *m.* **~s,** boyaux *m. pl.*, ventre *m.*; (*courage: fam.*) cran *m.* —*v.t.* (*p.t.* **gutted**) (*fish*) vider; (*of fire*) dévaster.

gutter /'gʌtə(r)/ *n.* (*on roof*) gouttière *f.*; (*in street*) caniveau *m.*

guttural /'gʌtərəl/ *a.* guttural.

guy /gaɪ/ *n.* (*man: fam.*) type *m.*

guzzle /'gʌzl/ *v.t./i.* (*eat*) bâfrer; (*drink: Amer.*) boire d'un trait.

gym /dʒɪm/ *n.* (*fam.*) gymnase *m.*; (*fam.*) gym(nastique) *f.* **~-slip** *n.* tunique *f.* **~nasium** *n.* gymnase *m.*

gymnast /'dʒɪmnæst/ *n.* gymnaste

m./f. **~ics** /-'næstɪks/ *n. pl.* gymnastique *f.*

gynaecolog|y /gaɪnɪ'kɒlədʒɪ/ *n.* gynécologie *f.* **~ist** *n.* gynécologue *m./f.*

gypsy /'dʒɪpsɪ/ *n.* bohémien(ne) *m.* (*f.*).

gyrate /dʒaɪ'reɪt/ *v.i.* tournoyer.

H

haberdashery /hæbə'dæʃərɪ/ *n.* mercerie *f.*

habit /'hæbɪt/ *n.* habitude *f.*; (*costume: relig.*) habit *m.* **be in/get into the ~ of,** avoir/prendre l'habitude de.

habit|able /'hæbɪtəbl/ *a.* habitable. **~ation** /-'teɪʃn/ *n.* habitation *f.*

habitat /'hæbɪtæt/ *n.* habitat *m.*

habitual /hə'bɪtʃʊəl/ *a.* (*usual*) habituel; (*smoker, liar*) invétéré. **~ly** *adv.* habituellement.

hack[1] /hæk/ *n.* (*old horse*) haridelle *f.*; (*writer*) nègre *m.*, écrivailleu|r, -se *m., f.*

hack[2] /hæk/ *v.t.* hacher, tailler.

hackneyed /'hæknɪd/ *a.* rebattu.

had /hæd/ *see* **have.**

haddock /'hædək/ *n. invar.* églefin *m.* **smoked ~,** haddock *m.*

haemorrhage /'hemərɪdʒ/ *n.* hémorragie *f.*

haemorrhoids /'hemərɔɪdz/ *n. pl.* hémorroïdes *f. pl.*

hag /hæg/ *n.* (vieille) sorcière *f.*

haggard /'hægəd/ *a.* (*person*) qui a le visage défait; (*face, look*) défait, hagard.

haggle /'hægl/ *v.i.* marchander. **~ over,** (*object*) marchander; (*price*) discuter.

Hague (The) /(ðə)'heɪg/ *n.* La Haye.

hail[1] /heɪl/ *v.t.* (*greet*) saluer; (*taxi*) héler. —*v.i.* **~ from,** venir de.

hail[2] /heɪl/ *n.* grêle *f.* —*v.i.* grêler.

hailstone /'heɪlstəʊn/ *n.* grêlon *m.*

hair /heə(r)/ *n.* (*on head*) cheveux *m. pl.*; (*on body, of animal*) poils *m. pl.*; (*single strand on head*) cheveu *m.*; (*on body*) poil *m.* **~-do** *n.* (*fam.*) coiffure *f.* **~-raising** *a.* horrifique. **~-style** *n.* coiffure *f.*

hairbrush /'heəbrʌʃ/ *n.* brosse à cheveux *f.*

haircut /'heəkʌt/ *n.* coupe de cheveux *f.* **have a ~,** se faire couper les cheveux.

hairdresser /'heədresə(r)/ *n.* coiffeu|r, -se *m., f.*

hairpin /'heəpɪn/ *n.* épingle à cheveux *f.*

hairy /'heərɪ/ *a.* (**-ier, -iest**) poilu; (*terrifying: sl.*) horrifique.

hake /heɪk/ *n. invar.* colin *m.*

hale /heɪl/ *a.* vigoureux.

half /hɑːf/ *n.* (*pl.* **halves**) moitié *f.*, demi(e) *m.* (*f.*). —*a.* demi. —*adv.* à moitié. **~ a dozen,** une demi-douzaine. **~ an hour,** une demi-heure. **~-back** *n.* (*sport*) demi *m.* **~-caste** *n.* métis(se) *m.* (*f.*). **~-hearted** *a.* tiède. **at ~-mast** *adv.* en berne. **~-term** *n.* congé de (de)mi-trimestre *m.* **~-time** *n.* mi-temps *f.* **~-way** *adv.* à mi-chemin. **~-wit** *n.* imbécile *m./f.*

halibut /'hælɪbət/ *n. invar.* (*fish*) flétan *m.*

hall /hɔːl/ *n.* (*room*) salle *f.*; (*entrance*) vestibule *m.*; (*mansion*) manoir *m.*; (*corridor*) couloir *m.* **~ of residence,** foyer d'étudiants *m.*

hallelujah /hælɪ'luːjə/ *int.* & *n.* = **alleluia.**

hallmark /'hɔːlmɑːk/ *n.* (*on gold etc.*) poinçon *m.*; (*fig.*) sceau *m.*

hallo /hə'ləʊ/ *int.* & *n.* bonjour (*m.*). **~!,** (*telephone*) allô!; (*surprise*) tiens!

hallow /'hæləʊ/ *v.t.* sanctifier.

Hallowe'en /hæləʊ'iːn/ *n.* la veille de la Toussaint.

hallucination /həlu:sɪˈneɪʃn/ *n.* hallucination *f.*

halo /ˈheɪləʊ/ *n.* (*pl.* **-oes**) auréole *f.*

halt /hɔ:lt/ *n.* halte *f.* —*v.t./i.* (s')arrêter.

halve /hɑ:v/ *v.t.* diviser en deux; (*time etc.*) réduire de moitié.

ham /hæm/ *n.* jambon *m.*; (*theatre*: *sl.*) cabotin(e) *m.* (*f.*).

hamburger /ˈhæmbɜ:gə(r)/ *n.* hamburger *m.*

hamlet /ˈhæmlɪt/ *n.* hameau *m.*

hammer /ˈhæmə(r)/ marteau *m.* —*v.t./i.* marteler, frapper; (*defeat*) battre à plate couture.

hammock /ˈhæmək/ *n.* hamac *m.*

hamper¹ /ˈhæmpə(r)/ *n.* panier *m.*

hamper² /ˈhæmpə(r)/ *v.t.* gêner.

hamster /ˈhæmstə(r)/ *n.* hamster *m.*

hand /hænd/ *n.* main *f.*; (*of clock*) aiguille *f.*; (*writing*) écriture *f.*; (*worker*) ouvr|ier, -ière *m.*, *f.*; (*cards*) jeu *m.* (**helping**) ~, coup de main *m.* —*v.t.* donner. **at** ~, proche. **~-luggage** *n.* bagages à main *m. pl.* **~ in** *or* **over**, remettre. **~ out**, distribuer. **~-out** *n.* prospectus *m.*; (*money*) aumône *f.* **on** ~, disponible. **on one's ~s**, (*fig.*) sur les bras. **on the one** ~ **. . . on the other** ~, d'une part . . . d'autre part. **to** ~, à portée de la main.

handbag /ˈhændbæg/ *n.* sac à main *m.*

handbook /ˈhændbʊk/ *n.* manuel *m.*

handcuffs /ˈhændkʌfs/ *n. pl.* menottes *f. pl.*

handful /ˈhændfʊl/ *n.* poignée *f.*; (*person*: *fam.*) personne difficile *f.*

handicap /ˈhændɪkæp/ *n.* handicap *m.* —*v.t.* (*p.t.* **handicapped**) handicaper.

handicraft /ˈhændɪkrɑ:ft/ *n.* travaux manuels *m. pl.*, artisanat *m.*

handiwork /ˈhændɪwɜ:k/ *n.* ouvrage *m.*

handkerchief /ˈhæŋkətʃɪf/ *n.* (*pl.* **-fs**) mouchoir *m.*

handle /ˈhændl/ *n.* (*of door etc.*) poignée *f.*; (*of implement*) manche *m.*; (*of cup etc.*) anse *f.*; (*of pan etc.*) queue *f.* —*v.t.* manier; (*deal with*) s'occuper de; (*touch*) toucher à.

handlebar /ˈhændlbɑ:(r)/ *n.* guidon *m.*

handshake /ˈhændʃeɪk/ *n.* poignée de main *f.*

handsome /ˈhænsəm/ *a.* (*good-looking*) beau; (*generous*) généreux; (*large*) considérable.

handwriting /ˈhændraɪtɪŋ/ *n.* écriture *f.*

handy /ˈhændɪ/ *a.* (**-ier, -iest**) (*useful*) commode, utile; (*person*) adroit; (*near*) accessible.

handyman /ˈhændɪmæn/ *n.* (*pl.* **-men**) bricoleur *m.*; (*servant*) homme à tout faire *m.*

hang /hæŋ/ *v.t.* (*p.t.* **hung**) suspendre, accrocher; (*p.t.* **hanged**) (*criminal*) pendre. —*v.i.* pendre. —*n.* **get the ~ of doing**, trouver le truc pour faire. **~ about**, traîner. **~-gliding** *n.* vol libre *m.* **~ on**, (*hold out*) tenir bon; (*wait*: *sl.*) attendre. **~ out** *v.i.* pendre; (*live*: *sl.*) crécher; *v.t.* (*washing*) étendre. **~ up**, (*telephone*) raccrocher. **~-up** *n.* (*sl.*) complexe *m.*

hangar /ˈhæŋə(r)/ *n.* hangar *m.*

hanger /ˈhæŋə(r)/ *n.* (*for clothes*) cintre *m.* **~-on** *n.* parasite *m.*

hangover /ˈhæŋəʊvə(r)/ *n.* (*after drinking*) gueule de bois *f.*

hanker /ˈhæŋkə(r)/ *v.i.* **~ after**, avoir envie de. **~ing** *n.* envie *f.*

hanky-panky /ˈhæŋkɪpæŋkɪ/ *n.* (*trickery*: *sl.*) manigances *f. pl.*

haphazard /hæpˈhæzəd/ *a.*, **~ly** *adv.* au petit bonheur, au hasard.

hapless /ˈhæplɪs/ *a.* infortuné.

happen /ˈhæpən/ *v.i.* arriver, se passer. **he ~s (often) to do**, il lui arrive (souvent) de faire. **he**

~s to know that, il se trouve qu'il sait que. **~ing** *n.* événement *m.*

happ|y /ˈhæpɪ/ *a.* (**-ier, -iest**) heureux. **~y medium** *or* **mean,** juste milieu *m.* **~ily** *adv.* joyeusement; (*fortunately*) heureusement. **~iness** *n.* bonheur *m.* **~y-go-lucky** *a.* insouciant.

harass /ˈhærəs/ *v.t.* harceler. **~ment** *n.* harcèlement *m.*

harbour /ˈhɑːbə(r)/ *n.* port *m.* —*v.t.* (*shelter*) héberger.

hard /hɑːd/ *a.* (**-er, -est**) dur; (*difficult*) difficile, dur. —*adv.* dur; (*think*) sérieusement; (*pull*) fort. **~-boiled egg,** œuf dur *m.* **~ by,** tout près. **~ done by,** mal traité. **~-headed** *a.* réaliste. **~ of hearing,** dur d'oreille. **~ shoulder,** accotement stabilisé *m.* **~ up,** (*fam.*) fauché. **~-working** *a.* travailleur. **~ness** *n.* dureté *f.*

hardboard /ˈhɑːdbɔːd/ *n.* Isorel *m.* (P.).

harden /ˈhɑːdn/ *v.t./i.* durcir.

hardly /ˈhɑːdlɪ/ *adv.* à peine. **~ ever,** presque jamais.

hardship /ˈhɑːdʃɪp/ *n.* **~(s),** épreuves *f. pl.*, souffrance *f.*

hardware /ˈhɑːdweə(r)/ *n.* (*metal goods*) quincaillerie *f.*; (*machinery, of computer*) matériel *m.*

hardy /ˈhɑːdɪ/ *a.* (**-ier, -iest**) résistant.

hare /heə(r)/ *n.* lièvre *m.* **~-brained** *a.* écervelé.

hark /hɑːk/ *v.i.* écouter. **~ back to,** revenir sur.

harm /hɑːm/ *n.* (*hurt*) mal *m.*; (*wrong*) tort *m.* —*v.t.* (*hurt*) faire du mal à; (*wrong*) faire du tort à; (*object*) endommager. **there is no ~ in,** il n'y a pas de mal à. **~ful** *a.* nuisible. **~less** *a.* inoffensif.

harmonica /hɑːˈmɒnɪkə/ *n.* harmonica *m.*

harmon|y /ˈhɑːmənɪ/ *n.* harmonie *f.* **~ious** /-ˈməʊnɪəs/ *a.* harmonieux. **~ize** *v.t./i.* (s')harmoniser.

harness /ˈhɑːnɪs/ *n.* harnais *m.* —*v.t.* (*horse*) harnacher; (*control*) maîtriser; (*use*) exploiter.

harp /hɑːp/ *n.* harpe *f.* —*v.i.* **~ on (about),** rabâcher. **~ist** *n.* harpiste *m./f.*

harpoon /hɑːˈpuːn/ *n.* harpon *m.*

harpsichord /ˈhɑːpsɪkɔːd/ *n.* clavecin *m.*

harrowing /ˈhærəʊɪŋ/ *a.* déchirant, qui déchire le cœur.

harsh /hɑːʃ/ *a.* (**-er, -est**) dur, rude; (*taste*) âpre; (*sound*) rude, âpre. **~ly** *adv.* durement. **~ness** *n.* dureté *f.*

harvest /ˈhɑːvɪst/ *n.* moisson *f.*, récolte *f.* —*v.t.* moissonner, récolter. **~er** *n.* moissonneuse *f.*

has /hæz/ *see* **have.**

hash /hæʃ/ *n.* (*culin.*) hachis *m.*; (*fig.*) gâchis *m.* **make a ~ of,** (*bungle*: *sl.*) saboter.

hashish /ˈhæʃiːʃ/ *n.* ha(s)chisch *m.*

hassle /ˈhæsl/ *n.* (*fam.*) difficulté(s) *f.* (*pl.*); (*bother, effort*: *fam.*) mal *m.*, peine *f.*; (*quarrel*: *fam.*) chamaillerie *f.* —*v.t.* (*harass*: *fam.*) harceler.

haste /heɪst/ *n.* hâte *f.* **in ~,** à la hâte. **make ~,** se hâter.

hasten /ˈheɪsn/ *v.t./i.* (se) hâter.

hast|y /ˈheɪstɪ/ *a.* (**-ier, -iest**) précipité. **~ily** *adv.* à la hâte.

hat /hæt/ *n.* chapeau *m.* **a ~ trick,** trois succès consécutifs.

hatch[1] /hætʃ/ *n.* (*for food*) passe-plat *m.*; (*naut.*) écoutille *f.*

hatch[2] /hætʃ/ *v.t./i.* (faire) éclore.

hatchback /ˈhætʃbæk/ *n.* voiture avec hayon arrière *f.*

hatchet /ˈhætʃɪt/ *n.* hachette *f.*

hate /heɪt/ *n.* haine *f.* —*v.t.* haïr. **~ful** *a.* haïssable.

hatred /ˈheɪtrɪd/ *n.* haine *f.*

haughty /ˈhɔːtɪ/ *a.* (**-ier, -iest**) hautain.

haul /hɔːl/ *v.t.* traîner, tirer;

(*goods*) camionner. —*n.* (*of thieves*) butin *m.*; (*catch*) prise *f.*; (*journey*) voyage *m.* **~age** *n.* camionnage *m.* **~ier** *n.* camionneur *m.*

haunt /hɔːnt/ *v.t.* hanter. —*n.* endroit favori *m.*

have /hæv/ *v.t.* (*3 sing. present tense* **has**; *p.t.* **had**) avoir; (*meal, bath, etc.*) prendre; (*walk, dream, etc.*) faire. —*v. aux.* avoir; (*with aller, partir, etc. & pronominal verbs*) être. **~ it out with,** s'expliquer avec. **~ just done,** venir de faire. **~ sth. done,** faire faire qch. **~ to do,** devoir faire. **the ~s and have-nots,** les riches et les pauvres *m. pl.*

haven /ˈheɪvn/ *n.* havre *m.*, abri *m.*

haversack /ˈhævəsæk/ *n.* musette *f.*

havoc /ˈhævək/ *n.* ravages *m. pl.*

haw /hɔː/ *see* **hum.**

hawk[1] /hɔːk/ *n.* faucon *m.*

hawk[2] /hɔːk/ *v.t.* colporter. **~er** *n.* colporteu|r, -se *m., f.*

hawthorn /ˈhɔːθɔːn/ *n.* aubépine *f.*

hay /heɪ/ *n.* foin *m.* **~ fever,** rhume des foins *m.*

haystack /ˈheɪstæk/ *n.* meule de foin *f.*

haywire /ˈheɪwaɪə(r)/ *a.* **go ~,** (*plans*) se désorganiser; (*machine*) se détraquer.

hazard /ˈhæzəd/ *n.* risque *m.* —*v.t.* risquer, hasarder. **~ous** *a.* hasardeux, risqué.

haze /heɪz/ *n.* brume *f.*

hazel /ˈheɪzl/ *n.* (*bush*) noisetier *m.* **~-nut** *n.* noisette *f.*

hazy /ˈheɪzɪ/ *a.* (**-ier, -iest**) (*misty*) brumeux; (*fig.*) flou, vague.

he /hiː/ *pron.* il; (*emphatic*) lui. —*n.* mâle *m.*

head /hed/ *n.* tête *f.*; (*leader*) chef *m.*; (*of beer*) mousse *f.* —*a.* principal. —*v.t.* être à la tête de. —*v.i.* **~ for,** se diriger vers. **~-dress** *n.* coiffure *f.*; (*lady's*) coiffe *f.* **~-on** *a.* & *adv.* de plein fouet. **~s or tails?,** pile ou face? **~ the ball,** faire une tête. **~ waiter,** maître d'hôtel *m.* **~er** *n.* (*football*) tête *f.*

headache /ˈhedeɪk/ *n.* mal de tête *m.*

heading /ˈhedɪŋ/ *n.* titre *m.*; (*subject category*) rubrique *f.*

headlamp /ˈhedlæmp/ *n.* phare *m.*

headland /ˈhedlənd/ *n.* cap *m.*

headlight /ˈhedlaɪt/ *n.* phare *m.*

headline /ˈhedlaɪn/ *n.* titre *m.*

headlong /ˈhedlɒŋ/ *adv.* (*in a rush*) à toute allure.

head|master /hedˈmɑːstə(r)/ *n.* (*of school*) directeur *m.* **~mistress** *n.* directrice *f.*

headphone /ˈhedfəʊn/ *n.* écouteur *m.* **~s,** casque (à écouteurs) *m.*

headquarters /ˈhedkwɔːtəz/ *n. pl.* siège *m.*, bureau central *m.*; (*mil.*) quartier général *m.*

headstrong /ˈhedstrɒŋ/ *a.* têtu.

headway /ˈhedweɪ/ *n.* progrès *m.* (*pl.*). **make ~,** faire des progrès.

heady /ˈhedɪ/ *a.* (**-ier, -iest**) (*wine*) capiteux; (*exciting*) grisant.

heal /hiːl/ *v.t./i.* guérir.

health /helθ/ *n.* santé *f.* **~y** *a.* sain; (*person*) en bonne santé.

heap /hiːp/ *n.* tas *m.* —*v.t.* entasser. **~s of,** (*fam.*) des tas de.

hear /hɪə(r)/ *v.t./i.* (*p.t.* **heard** /hɜːd/) entendre. **hear, hear!,** bravo! **~ from,** recevoir des nouvelles de. **~ of** *or* **about,** entendre parler de. **not ~ of,** (*refuse to allow*) ne pas entendre parler de. **~ing** *n.* ouïe *f.*; (*of witness*) audition *f.* **~ing-aid** *n.* appareil acoustique *m.*

hearsay /ˈhɪəseɪ/ *n.* ouï-dire *m. invar.* **from ~,** par ouï-dire.

hearse /hɜːs/ *n.* corbillard *m.*

heart /hɑːt/ *n.* cœur *m.* **~s,** (*cards*) cœur *m.* **at ~,** au fond. **by ~,** par cœur. **~ attack,** crise cardiaque *f.* **~-break** *n.* chagrin *m.* **~-breaking** *a.* navrant. **be ~-**

broken, avoir le cœur brisé. **~-to-heart** *a.* à cœur ouvert. **lose ~,** perdre courage.

heartache /ˈhɑːteɪk/ *n.* chagrin *m.*

heartburn /ˈhɑːtbɜːn/ *n.* brûlures d'estomac *f. pl.*

hearten /ˈhɑːtn/ *v.t.* encourager.

heartfelt /ˈhɑːtfelt/ *a.* sincère.

hearth /hɑːθ/ *n.* foyer *m.*

heartless /ˈhɑːtlɪs/ *a.* cruel.

heart|y /ˈhɑːtɪ/ *a.* (**-ier, -iest**) (*sincere*) chaleureux; (*meal*) gros. **~ily** *adv.* (*eat*) avec appétit.

heat /hiːt/ *n.* chaleur *f.*; (*excitement*: *fig.*) feu *m.*; (*contest*) éliminatoire *f.* —*v.t./i.* chauffer. **~ stroke,** insolation *f.* **~ wave,** vague de chaleur *f.* **~er** *n.* radiateur *m.* **~ing** *n.* chauffage *m.*

heated /ˈhiːtɪd/ *a.* (*fig.*) passionné.

heath /hiːθ/ *n.* (*area*) lande *f.*

heathen /ˈhiːðn/ *n.* païen(ne) *m.* (*f.*).

heather /ˈheðə(r)/ *n.* bruyère *f.*

heave /hiːv/ *v.t./i.* (*lift*) (se) soulever; (*a sigh*) pousser; (*throw*: *fam.*) lancer; (*retch*) avoir des nausées.

heaven /ˈhevn/ *n.* ciel *m.* **~ly** *a.* céleste; (*pleasing*: *fam.*) divin.

heav|y /ˈhevɪ/ *a.* (**-ier, -iest**) lourd; (*cold, work, etc.*) gros; (*traffic*) dense. **~ily** *adv.* lourdement; (*smoke, drink*) beaucoup.

heavyweight /ˈhevɪweɪt/ *n.* poids lourd *m.*

Hebrew /ˈhiːbruː/ *a.* hébreu (*m. only*), hébraïque. —*n.* (*lang.*) hébreu *m.*

heckle /ˈhekl/ *v.t.* (*speaker*) interrompre, interpeller.

hectic /ˈhektɪk/ *a.* très bousculé, trépidant, agité.

hedge /hedʒ/ *n.* haie *f.* —*v.t.* entourer. —*v.i.* (*in answering*) répondre évasivement.

hedgehog /ˈhedʒhɒg/ *n.* hérisson *m.*

heed /hiːd/ *v.t.* faire attention à. —*n.* **pay ~ to,** faire attention à. **~less** *a.* **~less of,** inattentif à.

heel /hiːl/ *n.* talon *m.*; (*man*: *sl.*) salaud *m.* **down at ~,** (*Amer.*) **down at the ~s,** miteux.

hefty /ˈheftɪ/ *a.* (**-ier, -iest**) gros, lourd.

heifer /ˈhefə(r)/ *n.* génisse *f.*

height /haɪt/ *n.* hauteur *f.*; (*of person*) taille *f.*; (*of plane, mountain*) altitude *f.*; (*of fame, glory*) apogée *m.*; (*of joy, folly, pain*) comble *m.*

heighten /ˈhaɪtn/ *v.t.* (*raise*) rehausser; (*fig.*) augmenter.

heinous /ˈheɪnəs/ *a.* atroce.

heir /eə(r)/ *n.* héritier *m.* **~ess** *n.* héritière *f.*

heirloom /ˈeəluːm/ *n.* bijou (meuble, tableau, *etc.*) de famille *m.*

held /held/ *see* **hold**[1].

helicopter /ˈhelɪkɒptə(r)/ *n.* hélicoptère *m.*

heliport /ˈhelɪpɔːt/ *n.* héliport *m.*

hell /hel/ *n.* enfer *m.* **~-bent** *a.* acharné **(on,** à). **~ish** *a.* infernal.

hello /həˈləʊ/ *int.* & *n.* = **hallo.**

helm /helm/ *n.* (*of ship*) barre *f.*

helmet /ˈhelmɪt/ *n.* casque *m.*

help /help/ *v.t./i.* aider. —*n.* aide *f.*; (*employees*) personnel *m.*; (*charwoman*) femme de ménage *f.* **~ o.s. to,** se servir de. **he cannot ~ laughing,** il ne peut pas s'empêcher de rire. **~er** *n.* aide *m./f.* **~ful** *a.* utile; (*person*) serviable. **~less** *a.* impuissant.

helping /ˈhelpɪŋ/ *n.* portion *f.*

helter-skelter /heltəˈskeltə(r)/ *n.* toboggan *m.* —*adv.* pêle-mêle.

hem /hem/ *n.* ourlet *m.* —*v.t.* (*p.t.* **hemmed**) ourler. **~ in,** enfermer.

hemisphere /ˈhemɪsfɪə(r)/ *n.* hémisphère *m.*

hemp /hemp/ *n.* chanvre *m.*

hen /hen/ *n.* poule *f.*

hence /hens/ *adv.* (*for this reason*)

d'où; (*from now*) d'ici. **~forth** *adv.* désormais.

henchman /ˈhentʃmən/ *n.* (*pl.* **-men**) acolyte *m.*, homme de main *m.*

henpecked /ˈhenpekt/ *a.* dominé *or* harcelé par sa femme.

her /hɜː(r)/ *pron.* la, l'*; (*after prep.*) elle. **(to) ~,** lui. **I know ~,** je la connais. —*a.* son, sa, *pl.* ses.

herald /ˈherəld/ *v.t.* annoncer.

heraldry /ˈherəldrɪ/ *n.* héraldique *f.*

herb /hɜːb, *Amer.* ɜːb/ *n.* herbe *f.* **~s,** (*culin.*) fines herbes *f. pl.*

herd /hɜːd/ *n.* troupeau *m.* —*v.t./i.* **~ together,** (s')entasser.

here /hɪə(r)/ *adv.* ici. **~!,** (*take this*) tenez! **~ is, ~ are,** voici. **~abouts** *adv.* par ici.

hereafter /hɪərˈɑːftə(r)/ *adv.* après; (*in book*) ci-après.

hereby /hɪəˈbaɪ/ *adv.* par le présent acte; (*in letter*) par la présente.

hereditary /həˈredɪtərɪ/ *a.* héréditaire.

heredity /həˈredətɪ/ *n.* hérédité *f.*

here|sy /ˈherəsɪ/ *n.* hérésie *f.* **~tic** *n.* hérétique *m./f.*

herewith /hɪəˈwɪð/ *adv.* (*comm.*) avec ceci, ci-joint.

heritage /ˈherɪtɪdʒ/ *n.* patrimoine *m.*, héritage *m.*

hermetic /hɜːˈmetɪk/ *a.* hermétique.

hermit /ˈhɜːmɪt/ *n.* ermite *m.*

hernia /ˈhɜːnɪə/ *n.* hernie *f.*

hero /ˈhɪərəʊ/ *n.* (*pl.* **-oes**) héros *m.* **~ine** /ˈherəʊɪn/ *n.* héroïne *f.* **~ism** /ˈherəʊɪzəm/ *n.* héroïsme *m.*

heroic /hɪˈrəʊɪk/ *a.* héroïque.

heroin /ˈherəʊɪn/ *n.* héroïne *f.*

heron /ˈherən/ *n.* héron *m.*

herring /ˈherɪŋ/ *n.* hareng *m.*

hers /hɜːz/ *poss. pron.* le sien, la sienne, les sien(ne)s. **it is ~,** c'est à elle *or* le sien.

herself /hɜːˈself/ *pron.* elle-même; (*reflexive*) se; (*after prep.*) elle.

hesitant /ˈhezɪtənt/ *a.* hésitant.

hesitat|e /ˈhezɪteɪt/ *v.i.* hésiter. **~ion** /-ˈteɪʃn/ *n.* hésitation *f.*

het /het/ *a.* **~ up,** (*sl.*) énervé.

heterogeneous /hetərəˈdʒiːmɪəs/ *a.* hétérogène.

hew /hjuː/ *v.t.* (*p.p.* **hewn**) tailler.

hexagon /ˈheksəgən/ *n.* hexagone *m.* **~al** /-ˈægənl/ *a.* hexagonal.

hey /heɪ/ *int.* dites donc.

heyday /ˈheɪdeɪ/ *n.* apogée *m.*

hi /haɪ/ *int.* (*greeting: Amer.*) salut.

hibernat|e /ˈhaɪbəneɪt/ *v.i.* hiberner. **~ion** /-ˈneɪʃn/ *n.* hibernation *f.*

hiccup /ˈhɪkʌp/ *n.* hoquet *m.* —*v.i.* hoqueter. **(the) ~s,** le hoquet.

hide[1] /haɪd/ *v.t.* (*p.t.* **hid,** *p.p.* **hidden**) cacher (**from,** à). —*v.i.* se cacher (**from,** de). **go into hiding,** se cacher. **~-out** *n.* (*fam.*) cachette *f.*

hide[2] /haɪd/ *n.* (*skin*) peau *f.*

hideous /ˈhɪdɪəs/ *a.* (*dreadful*) atroce; (*ugly*) hideux.

hiding /ˈhaɪdɪŋ/ *n.* (*thrashing: fam.*) correction *f.*

hierarchy /ˈhaɪərɑːkɪ/ *n.* hiérarchie *f.*

hi-fi /haɪˈfaɪ/ *a.* & *n.* hi-fi *a.* & *f. invar.*; (*gramophone*) chaîne hi-fi *f.*

high /haɪ/ *a.* (**-er, -est**) haut; (*price, number*) élevé; (*priest, speed*) grand; (*voice*) aigu. —*n.* **a (new) ~,** (*recorded level*) un record. —*adv.* haut. **~-handed** *a.* autoritaire. **~-jump,** saut en hauteur *m.* **~-rise building,** tour *f.* **~ road,** grand-route *f.* **~ school,** lycée *m.* **in the ~ season,** en pleine saison. **~-speed** *a.* ultra-rapide. **~ spot,** (*fam.*) point culminant *m.* **~ street,** grand-rue *f.* **~-strung** *a.* (*Amer.*) nerveux. **~ tea,** goûter dînatoire *m.* **~er education,** enseignement supérieur *m.*

highbrow /ˈhaɪbraʊ/ *a.* & *n.* intellectuel(le) (*m.* (*f.*)).

highlight /ˈhaɪlaɪt/ *n.* (*vivid moment*) instant remarquable *m.* —*v.t.* (*emphasize*) souligner.

highly /ˈhaɪlɪ/ *adv.* extrêmement; (*paid*) très bien. **~-strung** *a.* nerveux. **speak/think ~ of,** dire/penser du bien de.

Highness /ˈhaɪnɪs/ *n.* Altesse *f.*

highway /ˈhaɪweɪ/ *n.* route nationale *f.*

hijack /ˈhaɪdʒæk/ *v.t.* détourner. —*n.* détournement *m.* **~er** *n.* pirate (de l'air) *m.*

hike /haɪk/ *n.* excursion à pied *f.* —*v.i.* aller à pied. **~r** /-ə(r)/ *n.* excursionniste *m.*/*f.*

hilarious /hɪˈleərɪəs/ *a.* (*funny*) désopilant.

hill /hɪl/ *n.* colline *f.*; (*slope*) côte *f.* **~-billy** *n.* (*Amer.*) péquenaud(e) *m.* (*f.*). **~y** *a.* accidenté.

hillside /ˈhɪlsaɪd/ *n.* coteau *m.*

hilt /hɪlt/ *n.* (*of sword*) garde *f.* **to the ~,** tout à fait, au maximum.

him /hɪm/ *pron.* le, l'*; (*after prep.*) lui. **(to) ~,** lui. **I know ~,** je le connais.

himself /hɪmˈself/ *pron.* lui-même; (*reflexive*) se; (*after prep.*) lui.

hind /haɪnd/ *a.* de derrière.

hind|er /ˈhɪndə(r)/ *v.t.* (*hamper*) gêner; (*prevent*) empêcher. **~rance** *n.* obstacle *m.*, gêne *f.*

hindsight /ˈhaɪndsaɪt/ *n.* **with ~,** rétrospectivement.

Hindu /hɪnˈduː/ *n.* & *a.* hindou(e) (*m.* (*f.*)). **~ism** /ˈhɪnduːɪzəm/ *n.* hindouisme *m.*

hinge /hɪndʒ/ *n.* charnière *f.* —*v.i.* **~ on,** (*depend on*) dépendre de.

hint /hɪnt/ *n.* allusion *f.*; (*advice*) conseil *m.* —*v.t.* laisser entendre. —*v.i.* **~ at,** faire allusion à.

hip /hɪp/ *n.* hanche *f.*

hippie /ˈhɪpɪ/ *n.* hippie *m.*/*f.*

hippopotamus /hɪpəˈpɒtəməs/ *n.* (*pl.* **-muses**) hippopotame *m.*

hire /ˈhaɪə(r)/ *v.t.* (*thing*) louer; (*person*) engager. —*n.* location *f.* **~-purchase** *n.* achat à crédit *m.*, vente à crédit. *f.*

hirsute /ˈhɜːsjuːt/ *a.* hirsute.

his /hɪz/ *a.* son, sa, *pl.* ses. —*poss. pron.* le sien, la sienne, les sien(ne)s. **it is ~,** c'est à lui *or* le sien.

hiss /hɪs/ *n.* sifflement *m.* —*v.t.*/*i.* siffler.

historian /hɪˈstɔːrɪən/ *n.* historien(ne) *m.* (*f.*).

histor|y /ˈhɪstərɪ/ *n.* histoire *f.* **make ~y,** entrer dans l'histoire. **~ic(al)** /hɪˈstɒrɪk(l)/ *a.* historique.

histrionic /hɪstrɪˈɒnɪk/ *a.* théâtral.

hit /hɪt/ *v.t.* (*p.t.* **hit,** *pres. p.* **hitting**) frapper; (*knock against, collide with*) heurter; (*find*) trouver; (*affect*) toucher. —*v.i.* **~ on,** (*find*) tomber sur. —*n.* (*blow*) coup *m.*; (*fig.*) succès *m.* **~ it off,** s'entendre bien (**with,** avec). **~-or-miss** *a.* fait au petit bonheur.

hitch /hɪtʃ/ *v.t.* (*fasten*) accrocher. —*n.* (*snag*) anicroche *f.* **~ a lift, ~-hike** *v.i.* faire de l'auto-stop. **~-hiker** *n.* auto-stoppeu|r, -se *m.*, *f.* **~ up,** (*pull up*) remonter.

hitherto /hɪðəˈtuː/ *adv.* jusqu'ici.

hive /haɪv/ *n.* ruche *f.* —*v.t.* **~ off,** séparer; (*industry*) dénationaliser.

hoard /hɔːd/ *v.t.* amasser. —*n.* réserve(s) *f.* (*pl.*); (*of money*) magot *m.*, trésor *m.*

hoarding /ˈhɔːdɪŋ/ *n.* panneau d'affichage *m.*

hoar-frost /ˈhɔːfrɒst/ *n.* givre *m.*

hoarse /hɔːs/ *a.* (**-er, -est**) enroué. **~ness** *n.* enrouement *m.*

hoax /həʊks/ *n.* canular *m.* —*v.t.* faire un canular à.

hob /hɒb/ *n.* plaque chauffante *f.*

hobble /ˈhɒbl/ *v.i.* clopiner.

hobby /ˈhɒbɪ/ *n.* passe-temps *m.* *invar.* **~-horse** *n.* (*fig.*) dada *m.*

hob-nob /ˈhɒbnɒb/ *v.i.* (*p.t.* **hob-nobbed**). **~ with,** frayer avec.
hock[1] /hɒk/ *n.* vin du Rhin *m.*
hock[2] /hɒk/ *v.t.* (*pawn*: *sl.*) mettre au clou.
hockey /ˈhɒkɪ/ *n.* hockey *m.*
hodgepodge /ˈhɒdʒpɒdʒ/ *n.* fatras *m.*
hoe /həʊ/ *n.* binette *f.* —*v.t.* (*pres. p.* **hoeing**) biner.
hog /hɒg/ *n.* cochon *m.* —*v.t.* (*p.t.* **hogged**) (*fam.*) accaparer.
hoist /hɔɪst/ *v.t.* hisser. —*n.* palan *m.*
hold[1] /həʊld/ *v.t.* (*p.t.* **held**) tenir; (*contain*) contenir; (*interest, breath, etc.*) retenir; (*possess*) avoir; (*believe*) maintenir. —*v.i.* (*of rope, weather, etc.*) tenir. —*n.* prise *f.* **get ~ of,** saisir; (*fig.*) trouver. **~ back,** (*contain*) retenir; (*hide*) cacher. **~ on,** (*stand firm*) tenir bon; (*wait*) attendre. **~ on to,** (*keep*) garder; (*cling to*) se cramponner à. **~ one's tongue,** se taire. **~ out** *v.t.* (*offer*) offrir; *v.i.* (*resist*) tenir le coup. **~ up,** (*support*) soutenir; (*delay*) retarder; (*rob*) attaquer. **~-up** *n.* retard *m.*; (*of traffic*) bouchon *m.*; (*robbery*) hold-up *m. invar.* **~ with,** approuver. **~er** *n.* déten|teur, -trice *m., f.*; (*of post*) titulaire *m.*/*f.*; (*for object*) support *m.*
hold[2] /həʊld/ *n.* (*of ship*) cale *f.*
holdall /ˈhəʊldɔːl/ *n.* (*bag*) fourre-tout *m. invar.*
holding /ˈhəʊldɪŋ/ *n.* (*possession, land*) possession *f.*
hole /həʊl/ *n.* trou *m.* —*v.t.* trouer.
holiday /ˈhɒlədeɪ/ *n.* vacances *f. pl.*; (*public*) jour férié *m.*; (*day off*) congé *m.* —*v.i.* passer ses vacances. **~-maker** *n.* vacanc|ier, -ière *m., f.*
holiness /ˈhəʊlɪnɪs/ *n.* sainteté *f.*
Holland /ˈhɒlənd/ *n.* Hollande *f.*
hollow /ˈhɒləʊ/ *a.* creux; (*fig.*) faux. —*n.* creux *m.* —*v.t.* creuser.
holly /ˈhɒlɪ/ *n.* houx *m.*
holster /ˈhəʊlstə(r)/ *n.* étui de revolver *m.*
holy /ˈhəʊlɪ/ *a.* (**-ier, -iest**) saint, sacré; (*water*) bénit. **H~ Ghost, H~ Spirit,** Saint-Esprit *m.*
homage /ˈhɒmɪdʒ/ *n.* hommage *m.*
home /həʊm/ *n.* maison *f.*, foyer *m.*; (*institution*) maison *f.*; (*for soldiers, workers*) foyer *m.*; (*country*) pays natal *m.* —*a.* de la maison, du foyer; (*of family*) de famille; (*pol.*) national, intérieur; (*match, visit*) à domicile. —*adv.* (**at**) **~,** à la maison, chez soi. **come** *or* **go ~,** rentrer; (*from abroad*) rentrer dans son pays. **feel at ~ with,** être à l'aise avec. **H~ Counties,** région autour de Londres *f.* **H~ Office,** ministère de l'Intérieur *m.* **H~ Secretary,** ministre de l'Intérieur *m.* **~ town,** ville natale *f.* **~ truth,** vérité bien sentie *f.* **~less** *a.* sans abri.
homeland /ˈhəʊmlænd/ *n.* patrie *f.*
homely /ˈhəʊmlɪ/ *a.* (**-ier, -iest**) simple; (*person*: *Amer.*) assez laid.
homesick /ˈhəʊmsɪk/ *a.* **be ~,** avoir le mal du pays.
homeward /ˈhəʊmwəd/ *a.* (*journey*) de retour.
homework /ˈhəʊmwɜːk/ *n.* devoirs *m. pl.*
homicide /ˈhɒmɪsaɪd/ *n.* homicide *m.*
homogeneous /hɒməˈdʒiːmɪəs/ *a.* homogène.
homosexual /hɒməˈsekʃʊəl/ *a.* & *n.* homosexuel(le) (*m.* (*f.*)).
honest /ˈɒnɪst/ *a.* honnête; (*frank*) franc. **~ly** *adv.* honnêtement; franchement. **~y** *n.* honnêteté *f.*
honey /ˈhʌnɪ/ *n.* miel *m.*; (*person*: *fam.*) chéri(e) *m.* (*f.*).
honeycomb /ˈhʌnɪkəʊm/ *n.* rayon de miel *m.*

honeymoon /ˈhʌnɪmuːn/ *n.* lune de miel *f.*
honk /hɒŋk/ *v.i.* klaxonner.
honorary /ˈɒnərərɪ/ *a.* (*person*) honoraire; (*duties*) honorifique.
honour /ˈɒnə(r)/ *n.* honneur *m.* —*v.t.* honorer. **~able** *a.* honorable.
hood /hʊd/ *n.* capuchon *m.*; (*car roof*) capote *f.*; (*car engine cover: Amer.*) capot *m.*
hoodlum /ˈhuːdləm/ *n.* voyou *m.*
hoodwink /ˈhʊdwɪŋk/ *v.t.* tromper.
hoof /huːf/ *n.* (*pl.* **-fs**) sabot *m.*
hook /hʊk/ *n.* crochet *m.*; (*on garment*) agrafe *f.*; (*for fishing*) hameçon *m.* —*v.t./i.* (s')accrocher; (*garment*) (s')agrafer. **off the ~,** tiré d'affaire; (*phone*) décroché.
hooked /hʊkt/ *a.* crochu. **~ on,** (*sl.*) adonné à.
hooker /ˈhʊkə(r)/ *n.* (*rugby*) talonneur *m.*; (*Amer., sl.*) prostituée *f.*
hookey /ˈhʊkɪ/ *n.* **play ~,** (*Amer., sl.*) faire l'école buissonnière.
hooligan /ˈhuːlɪɡən/ *n.* voyou *m.*
hoop /huːp/ *n.* (*toy etc.*) cerceau *m.*
hooray /huːˈreɪ/ *int.* & *n.* = **hurrah.**
hoot /huːt/ *n.* (h)ululement *m.*; coup de klaxon *m.*; huée *f.* —*v.i.* (*owl*) (h)ululer; (*of car*) klaxonner; (*jeer*) huer. **~er** *n.* klaxon *m.* (P.); (*of factory*) sirène *f.*
Hoover /ˈhuːvə(r)/ *n.* (P.) aspirateur *m.* —*v.t.* passer à l'aspirateur.
hop[1] /hɒp/ *v.i.* (*p.t.* **hopped**) sauter (à cloche-pied). —*n.* saut *m.*; (*flight*) étape *f.* **~ in,** (*fam.*) monter. **~ it,** (*sl.*) décamper. **~ out,** (*fam.*) descendre.
hop[2] /hɒp/ *n.* **~(s),** houblon *m.*
hope /həʊp/ *n.* espoir *m.* —*v.t./i.* espérer. **~ for,** espérer (avoir). **~ful** *a.* encourageant. **be ~ful (that),** avoir bon espoir (que). **~fully** *adv.* avec espoir; (*it is hoped*) on l'espère. **~less** *a.* sans espoir; (*useless: fig.*) nul. **~lessly** *adv.* sans espoir *m.*
hopscotch /ˈhɒpskɒtʃ/ *n.* marelle *f.*
horde /hɔːd/ *n.* horde *f.*, foule *f.*
horizon /həˈraɪzn/ *n.* horizon *m.*
horizontal /hɒrɪˈzɒntl/ *a.* horizontal.
hormone /ˈhɔːməʊn/ *n.* hormone *f.*
horn /hɔːn/ *n.* corne *f.*; (*of car*) klaxon *m.* (P.); (*mus.*) cor *m.* —*v.i.* **~ in,** (*sl.*) interrompre. **~y** *a.* (*hands*) calleux.
hornet /ˈhɔːnɪt/ *n.* frelon *m.*
horoscope /ˈhɒrəskəʊp/ *n.* horoscope *m.*
horrible /ˈhɒrəbl/ *a.* horrible.
horrid /ˈhɒrɪd/ *a.* horrible.
horrific /həˈrɪfɪk/ *a.* horrifiant.
horr|or /ˈhɒrə(r)/ *n.* horreur *f.* —*a.* (*film etc.*) d'épouvante. **~ify** *v.t.* horrifier.
hors-d'œuvre /ɔːˈdɜːvrə/ *n.* hors-d'œuvre *m. invar.*
horse /hɔːs/ *n.* cheval *m.* **~-chestnut** *n.* marron (d'Inde) *m.* **~-radish** *n.* raifort *m.* **~ sense,** (*fam.*) bon sens *m.*
horseback /ˈhɔːsbæk/ *n.* **on ~,** à cheval.
horseman /ˈhɔːsmən/ *n.* (*pl.* **-men**) cavalier *m.*
horsepower /ˈhɔːspaʊə(r)/ *n.* (*unit*) cheval (vapeur) *m.*
horseshoe /ˈhɔːsʃuː/ *n.* fer à cheval *m.*
horsy /ˈhɔːsɪ/ *a.* (*face etc.*) chevalin.
horticultur|e /ˈhɔːtɪkʌltʃə(r)/ *n.* horticulture *f.* **~al** /-ˈkʌltʃərəl/ *a.* horticole.
hose /həʊz/ *n.* (*tube*) tuyau *m.* —*v.t.* arroser. **~-pipe** *n.* tuyau *m.*
hosiery /ˈhəʊzɪərɪ/ *n.* bonneterie *f.*
hospice /ˈhɒspɪs/ *n.* hospice *m.*
hospit|able /hɒˈspɪtəbl/ *a.* hospitalier. **~ably** *adv.* avec hospitalité. **~ality** /-ˈtælətɪ/ *n.* hospitalité *f.*
hospital /ˈhɒspɪtl/ *n.* hôpital *m.*

host[1] /həʊst/ *n.* (*master of house*) hôte *m.* **~ess** *n.* hôtesse *f.*
host[2] /həʊst/ *n.* **a ~ of,** une foule de.
host[3] /həʊst/ *n.* (*relig.*) hostie *f.*
hostage /ˈhɒstɪdʒ/ *n.* otage *m.*
hostel /ˈhɒstl/ *n.* foyer *m.*
hostil|e /ˈhɒstaɪl/ *a.* hostile. **~ity** /hɒˈstɪlətɪ/ *n.* hostilité *f.*
hot /hɒt/ *a.* (**hotter, hottest**) chaud; (*culin.*) épicé; (*news*) récent. **be** *or* **feel ~,** avoir chaud. **it is ~,** il fait chaud. *—v.t./i.* (*p.t.* **hotted**). **~ up,** (*fam.*) chauffer. **~ dog,** hot-dog *m.* **~ line,** téléphone rouge *m.* **~ shot,** (*Amer., sl.*) crack *m.* **~-water bottle,** bouillotte *f.* **in ~ water,** (*fam.*) dans le pétrin. **~ly** *adv.* vivement.
hotbed /ˈhɒtbed/ *n.* foyer *m.*
hotchpotch /ˈhɒtʃpɒtʃ/ *n.* fatras *m.*
hotel /həʊˈtel/ *n.* hôtel *m.* **~ier** /-ɪeɪ/ *n.* hôtel|ier, -ière *m., f.*
hothead /ˈhɒthed/ *n.* tête brûlée *f.* **~ed** *a.* impétueux.
hotplate /ˈhɒtpleɪt/ *n.* plaque chauffante *f.*
hound /haʊnd/ *n.* chien courant *m.* *—v.t.* poursuivre.
hour /ˈaʊə(r)/ *n.* heure *f.* **~ly** *a.* & *adv.* toutes les heures. **~ly pay,** salaire horaire *m.* **paid ~ly,** payé à l'heure.
house[1] /haʊs/ *n.* (*pl.* **-s** /ˈhaʊzɪz/) *n.* maison *f.*; (*theatre*) salle *f.*; (*pol.*) chambre *f.* **~-proud** *a.* méticuleux. **~-warming** *n.* pendaison de la crémaillère *f.*
house[2] /haʊz/ *v.t.* loger; (*of building*) abriter; (*keep*) garder.
housebreaking /ˈhaʊsbreɪkɪŋ/ *n.* cambriolage *m.*
household /ˈhaʊshəʊld/ *n.* (*house, family*) ménage *m.* **~er** *n.* occupant(e) *m.* (*f.*); (*owner*) propriétaire *m./f.*
housekeep|er /ˈhaʊskiːpə(r)/ *n.* gouvernante *f.* **~ing** *n.* ménage *m.*
housewife /ˈhaʊswaɪf/ *n.* (*pl.* **-wives**) ménagère *f.*
housework /ˈhaʊswɜːk/ *n.* ménage *m.*, travaux de ménage *m. pl.*
housing /ˈhaʊzɪŋ/ *n.* logement *m.*
hovel /ˈhɒvl/ *n.* taudis *m.*
hover /ˈhɒvə(r)/ *v.i.* (*bird, threat, etc.*) planer; (*loiter*) rôder.
hovercraft /ˈhɒvəkrɑːft/ *n.* aéroglisseur *m.*
how /haʊ/ *adv.* comment. **~ long/tall is . . .?,** quelle est la longueur/hauteur de . . .? **~ pretty!,** comme *or* que c'est joli! **~ about a walk?,** si on faisait une promenade? **~ are you?,** comment allez-vous? **~ do you do?,** (*introduction*) enchanté. **~ many?, ~ much?,** combien?
however /haʊˈevə(r)/ *adv.* de quelque manière que; (*nevertheless*) cependant. **~ small/delicate/***etc.* **it may be,** quelque petit/délicat/*etc.* que ce soit.
howl /haʊl/ *n.* hurlement *m.* *—v.i.* hurler.
howler /ˈhaʊlə(r)/ *n.* (*fam.*) bévue *f.*
HP *abbr. see* **hire-purchase.**
hp *abbr. see* **horsepower.**
hub /hʌb/ *n.* moyeu *m.*; (*fig.*) centre *m.* **~-cap** *n.* enjoliveur *m.*
hubbub /ˈhʌbʌb/ *n.* vacarme *m.*
huddle /ˈhʌdl/ *v.i.* se blottir.
hue[1] /hjuː/ *n.* (*colour*) teinte *f.*
hue[2] /hjuː/ *n.* **~ and cry,** clameur *f.*
huff /hʌf/ *n.* **in a ~,** fâché, vexé.
hug /hʌg/ *v.t.* (*p.t.* **hugged**) serrer dans ses bras; (*keep close to*) serrer. *—n.* étreinte *f.*
huge /hjuːdʒ/ *a.* énorme. **~ly** *adv.* énormément.
hulk /hʌlk/ *n.* (*of ship*) épave *f.*; (*person*) mastodonte *m.*
hull /hʌl/ *n.* (*of ship*) coque *f.*
hullo /həˈləʊ/ *int.* & *n.* = **hallo.**
hum /hʌm/ *v.t./i.* (*p.t.* **hummed**) (*person*) fredonner; (*insect*) bour-

donner; (*engine*) vrombir. —*n.* bourdonnement *m.*; vrombissement *m.* **~** (*or* **hem**) **and haw** (*or* **ha**), bafouiller.

human /'hju:mən/ *a.* humain. —*n.* être humain *m.* **~itarian** /-mænɪ'teərɪən/ *a.* humanitaire.

humane /hju:'meɪn/ *a.* humain, plein d'humanité.

humanity /hju:'mænətɪ/ *n.* humanité *f.*

humbl|e /'hʌmbl/ *a.* (**-er, -est**) humble. —*v.t.* humilier. **~y** *adv.* humblement.

humbug /'hʌmbʌg/ *n.* (*false talk*) charlatanisme *m.*

humdrum /'hʌmdrʌm/ *a.* monotone.

humid /'hju:mɪd/ *a.* humide. **~ity** /-'mɪdətɪ/ *n.* humidité *f.*

humiliat|e /hju:'mɪlɪeɪt/ *v.t.* humilier. **~ion** /-'eɪʃn/ *n.* humiliation *f.*

humility /hju:'mɪlətɪ/ *n.* humilité *f.*

humorist /'hju:mərɪst/ humoriste *m./f.*

hum|our /'hju:mə(r)/ *n.* humour *m.*; (*mood*) humeur *f.* —*v.t.* ménager. **~orous** *a.* humoristique; (*person*) plein d'humour. **~orously** *adv.* avec humour.

hump /hʌmp/ *n.* bosse *f.* —*v.t.* voûter. **the ~,** (*sl.*) le cafard.

hunch[1] /hʌntʃ/ *v.t.* voûter.

hunch[2] /hʌntʃ/ *n.* petite idée *f.*

hunchback /'hʌntʃbæk/ *n.* bossu(e) *m.* (*f.*).

hundred /'hʌndrəd/ *a.* & *n.* cent (*m.*). **~s of,** des centaines de. **~fold** *a.* centuple; *adv.* au centuple. **~th** *a.* & *n.* centième (*m./f.*).

hundredweight /'hʌndrədweɪt/ *n.* 50.8 kg.; (*Amer.*) 45.36 kg.

hung /hʌŋ/ *see* **hang.**

Hungar|y /'hʌŋgərɪ/ *n.* Hongrie *f.* **~ian** /-'geərɪən/ *a.* & *n.* hongrois(e) (*m.* (*f.*)).

hunger /'hʌŋgə(r)/ *n.* faim *f.* —*v.i.* **~ for,** avoir faim de. **~-strike** *n.* grève de la faim *f.*

hungr|y /'hʌŋgrɪ/ *a.* (**-ier, -iest**) affamé. **be ~y,** avoir faim. **~ily** *adv.* avidement.

hunk /hʌŋk/ *n.* gros morceau *m.*

hunt /hʌnt/ *v.t./i.* chasser. —*n.* chasse *f.* **~ for,** chercher. **~er** *n.* chasseur *m.* **~ing** *n.* chasse *f.*

hurdle /'hɜ:dl/ *n.* (*sport*) haie *f.*; (*fig.*) obstacle *m.*

hurl /hɜ:l/ *v.t.* lancer.

hurrah, hurray /hʊ'rɑ:, hʊ'reɪ/ *int.* & *n.* hourra (*m.*).

hurricane /'hʌrɪkən, *Amer.* 'hʌrɪkeɪn/ *n.* ouragan *m.*

hurried /'hʌrɪd/ *a.* précipité. **~ly** *adv.* précipitamment.

hurry /'hʌrɪ/ *v.i.* se dépêcher, se presser. —*v.t.* presser, activer. —*n.* hâte *f.* **in a ~,** pressé.

hurt /hɜ:t/ *v.t./i.* (*p.t.* **hurt**) faire mal (à); (*injure, offend*) blesser. —*a.* blessé. —*n.* mal *m.* **~ful** *a.* blessant.

hurtle /'hɜ:tl/ *v.t.* lancer. —*v.i.* **~ along,** avancer à toute vitesse.

husband /'hʌzbənd/ *n.* mari *m.*

hush /hʌʃ/ *v.t.* faire taire. —*n.* silence *m.* **~-hush** *a.* (*fam.*) ultra-secret. **~ up,** (*news etc.*) étouffer.

husk /hʌsk/ *n.* (*of grain*) enveloppe *f.*

husky /'hʌskɪ/ *a.* (**-ier, -iest**) (*hoarse*) enroué; (*burly*) costaud.

hustle /'hʌsl/ *v.t.* (*push, rush*) bousculer. —*v.i.* (*work busily*: *Amer.*) se démener. —*n.* bousculade *f.* **~ and bustle,** agitation *f.*

hut /hʌt/ *n.* cabane *f.*

hutch /hʌtʃ/ *n.* clapier *m.*

hyacinth /'haɪəsɪnθ/ *n.* jacinthe *f.*

hybrid /'haɪbrɪd/ *a.* & *n.* hybride (*m.*).

hydrangea /haɪ'dreɪndʒə/ *n.* hortensia *m.*

hydrant /'haɪdrənt/ *n.* (**fire**) **~,** bouche d'incendie *f.*

hydraulic /haɪ'drɔːlɪk/ *a.* hydraulique.
hydroelectric /haɪdrəʊɪ'lektrɪk/ *a.* hydro-électrique.
hydrogen /'haɪdrədʒən/ *n.* hydrogène *m.* **~ bomb,** bombe à hydrogène *f.*
hyena /haɪ'iːnə/ *n.* hyène *f.*
hygiene /'haɪdʒiːn/ *n.* hygiène *f.*
hygienic /haɪ'dʒiːnɪk/ *a.* hygiénique.
hymn /hɪm/ *n.* cantique *m.*, hymne *m.*
hyper- /'haɪpə(r)/ *pref.* hyper-.
hypermarket /'haɪpəmɑːkɪt/ *n.* hypermarché *m.*
hyphen /'haɪfn/ *n.* trait d'union *m.* **~ate** *v.t.* mettre un trait d'union à.
hypno|sis /hɪp'nəʊsɪs/ *n.* hypnose *f.* **~tic** /-'nɒtɪk/ *a.* hypnotique.
hypnot|ize /'hɪpnətaɪz/ *v.t.* hypnotiser. **~ism** *n.* hypnotisme *m.*
hypochondriac /haɪpə'kɒndrɪæk/ *n.* malade imaginaire *m.*/*f.*
hypocrisy /hɪ'pɒkrəsɪ/ *n.* hypocrisie *f.*
hypocrit|e /'hɪpəkrɪt/ *n.* hypocrite *m.*/*f.* **~ical** /-'krɪtɪkl/ *a.* hypocrite.
hypodermic /haɪpə'dɜːmɪk/ *a.* hypodermique. *—n.* seringue hypodermique *f.*
hypothe|sis /haɪ'pɒθəsɪs/ *n.* (*pl.* **-theses** /-siːz/) hypothèse *f.* **~tical** /-ə'θetɪkl/ *a.* hypothétique.
hyster|ia /hɪ'stɪərɪə/ *n.* hystérie *f.* **~ical** /-erɪkl/ *a.* hystérique; (*person*) surexcité.
hysterics /hɪ'sterɪks/ *n. pl.* crise de nerfs *or* de rire *f.*

I

I /aɪ/ *pron.* je, j'*; (*stressed*) moi.
ice /aɪs/ *n.* glace *f.*; (*on road*) verglas *m.* *—v.t.* (*cake*) glacer. *—v.i.* **~ (up),** (*window*) se givrer; (*river*) geler. **~-cream** *n.* glace *f.* **~-cube** *n.* glaçon *m.* **~ hockey,** hockey sur glace *m.* **~ lolly,** glace (sur bâtonnet) *f.*
iceberg /'aɪsbɜːg/ *n.* iceberg *m.*
Iceland /'aɪslənd/ *n.* Islande *f.* **~er** *n.* Islandais(e) *m.* (*f.*). **~ic** /-'lændɪk/ *a.* islandais; *n.* (*lang.*) islandais *m.*
icicle /'aɪsɪkl/ *n.* glaçon *m.*
icing /'aɪsɪŋ/ *n.* (*sugar*) glace *f.*
icon /'aɪkɒn/ *n.* icône *f.*
icy /'aɪsɪ/ *a.* (**-ier, -iest**) (*hands, wind*) glacé; (*road*) verglacé; (*manner, welcome*) glacial.
idea /aɪ'dɪə/ *n.* idée *f.*
ideal /aɪ'dɪəl/ *a.* idéal. *—n.* idéal *m.* **~ize** *v.t.* idéaliser. **~ly** *adv.* idéalement.
idealis|t /aɪ'dɪəlɪst/ *n.* idéaliste *m.*/*f.* **~m** /-zəm/ *n.* idéalisme *m.* **~tic** /-'lɪstɪk/ *a.* idéaliste.
identical /aɪ'dentɪkl/ *a.* identique.
identif|y /aɪ'dentɪfaɪ/ *v.t.* identifier. *—v.i.* **~y with,** s'identifier à. **~ication** /-ɪ'keɪʃn/ *n.* identification *f.*
identikit /aɪ'dentɪkɪt/ *n.* portrait-robot *m.*
identity /aɪ'dentətɪ/ *n.* identité *f.*
ideolog|y /aɪdɪ'ɒlədʒɪ/ *n.* idéologie *f.* **~ical** /-ə'lɒdʒɪkl/ *a.* idéologique.
idiocy /'ɪdɪəsɪ/ *n.* idiotie *f.*
idiom /'ɪdɪəm/ *n.* expression idiomatique *f.*; (*language*) idiome *m.* **~atic** /-'mætɪk/ *a.* idiomatique.
idiosyncrasy /ɪdɪə'sɪŋkrəsɪ/ *n.* particularité *f.*
idiot /'ɪdɪət/ *n.* idiot(e) *m.* (*f.*). **~ic** /-'ɒtɪk/ *a.* idiot.
idle /'aɪdl/ *a.* (**-er, -est**) désœuvré, oisif; (*lazy*) paresseux; (*unemployed*) sans travail; (*machine*) au repos; (*fig.*) vain. *—v.i.* (*engine*) tourner au ralenti. *—v.t.* **~ away,** gaspiller. **~ness** *n.* oisiveté *f.* **~r** /-ə(r)/ *n.* oisi|f, -ve *m.*, *f.*

idol /'aɪdl/ *n.* idole *f.* **~ize** *v.t.* idolâtrer.

idyllic /ɪ'dɪlɪk, *Amer.* aɪ'dɪlɪk/ *a.* idyllique.

i.e. *abbr.* c'est-à-dire.

if /ɪf/ *conj.* si.

igloo /'ɪgluː/ *n.* igloo *m.*

ignite /ɪg'naɪt/ *v.t./i.* (s')enflammer.

ignition /ɪg'nɪʃn/ *n.* (*auto.*) allumage *m.* **~ (switch)**, contact *m.*

ignoramus /ɪgnə'reɪməs/ *n.* (*pl.* **-muses**) ignare *m./f.*

ignoran|t /'ɪgnərənt/ *a.* ignorant (**of**, de). **~ce** *n.* ignorance *f.* **~tly** *adv.* par ignorance.

ignore /ɪg'nɔː(r)/ *v.t.* ne faire *or* prêter aucune attention à; (*person in street etc.*) faire semblant de ne pas voir.

ilk /ɪlk/ *n.* (*kind: fam.*) acabit *m.*

ill /ɪl/ *a.* malade; (*bad*) mauvais. —*adv.* mal. —*n.* mal *m.* **~-advised** *a.* peu judicieux. **~ at ease**, mal à l'aise. **~-bred** *a.* mal élevé. **~-fated** *a.* malheureux. **~-gotten** *a.* mal acquis. **~-natured** *a.* désagréable. **~-treat** *v.t.* maltraiter. **~ will**, malveillance *f.*

illegal /ɪ'liːgl/ *a.* illégal.

illegible /ɪ'ledʒəbl/ *a.* illisible.

illegitima|te /ɪlɪ'dʒɪtɪmət/ *a.* illégitime. **~cy** *n.* illégitimité *f.*

illitera|te /ɪ'lɪtərət/ *a.* & *n.* illettré(e) (*m.* (*f.*)), analphabète *m./f.* **~cy** *n.* analphabétisme *m.*

illness /'ɪlnɪs/ *n.* maladie *f.*

illogical /ɪ'lɒdʒɪkl/ *a.* illogique.

illuminat|e /ɪ'luːmɪneɪt/ *v.t.* éclairer; (*decorate with lights*) illuminer. **~ion** /-'neɪʃn/ *n.* éclairage *m.*; illumination *f.*

illusion /ɪ'luːʒn/ *n.* illusion *f.*

illusory /ɪ'luːsərɪ/ *a.* illusoire.

illustrat|e /'ɪləstreɪt/ *v.t.* illustrer. **~ion** /-'streɪʃn/ *n.* illustration *f.* **~ive** /-ətɪv/ *a.* qui illustre.

illustrious /ɪ'lʌstrɪəs/ *a.* illustre.

image /'ɪmɪdʒ/ *n.* image *f.* **(public) ~**, (*of firm, person*) image de marque *f.* **~ry** /-ərɪ/ *n.* images *f. pl.*

imaginary /ɪ'mædʒɪnərɪ/ *a.* imaginaire.

imaginat|ion /ɪmædʒɪ'neɪʃn/ *n.* imagination *f.* **~ive** /ɪ'mædʒɪnətɪv/ *a.* plein d'imagination.

imagin|e /ɪ'mædʒɪn/ *v.t.* (*picture to o.s.*) (s')imaginer; (*suppose*) imaginer. **~able** *a.* imaginable.

imbalance /ɪm'bæləns/ *n.* déséquilibre *m.*

imbecil|e /'ɪmbəsiːl/ *n.* & *a.* imbécile (*m./f.*). **~ity** /-'sɪlətɪ/ *n.* imbécillité *f.*

imbibe /ɪm'baɪb/ *v.t.* absorber.

imbue /ɪm'bjuː/ *v.t.* imprégner.

imitat|e /'ɪmɪteɪt/ *v.t.* imiter. **~ion** /-'teɪʃn/ *n.* imitation *f.* **~or** *n.* imita|teur, -trice *m., f.*

immaculate /ɪ'mækjʊlət/ *a.* (*room, dress, etc.*) impeccable.

immaterial /ɪmə'tɪərɪəl/ *a.* sans importance (**to**, pour; **that**, que).

immature /ɪmə'tjʊə(r)/ *a.* pas mûr.

immediate /ɪ'miːdɪət/ *a.* immédiat. **~ly** *adv.* immédiatement; *conj.* dès que.

immens|e /ɪ'mens/ *a.* immense. **~ely** *adv.* extrêmement, immensément. **~ity** *n.* immensité *f.*

immers|e /ɪ'mɜːs/ *v.t.* plonger, immerger. **~ion** /-ɜːʃn/ *n.* immersion *f.* **~ion heater**, chauffe-eau (électrique) *m. invar.*

immigr|ate /'ɪmɪgreɪt/ *v.i.* immigrer. **~ant** *n.* & *a.* immigré(e) (*m.* (*f.*)); (*newly-arrived*) immigrant(e) (*m.* (*f.*)). **~ation** /-'greɪʃn/ *n.* immigration *f.*

imminen|t /'ɪmɪnənt/ *a.* imminent. **~ce** *n.* imminence *f.*

immobil|e /ɪ'məʊbaɪl, *Amer.* ɪ'məʊbl/ *a.* immobile. **~ize** /-əlaɪz/ *v.t.* immobiliser.

immoderate /ɪ'mɒdərət/ *a.* immodéré.

immodest /ɪ'mɒdɪst/ *a.* impudique.

immoral /ɪ'mɒrəl/ *a.* immoral. **~ity** /ɪmə'rælətɪ/ *n.* immoralité *f.*

immortal /ɪ'mɔːtl/ *a.* immortel. **~ity** /-'tælətɪ/ *n.* immortalité *f.* **~ize** *v.t.* immortaliser.

immun|e /ɪ'mjuːn/ *a.* immunisé (**from, to,** contre). **~ity** *n.* immunité *f.*

immuniz|e /'ɪmjʊnaɪz/ *v.t.* immuniser. **~ation** /-'zeɪʃn/ *n.* immunisation *f.*

imp /ɪmp/ *n.* lutin *m.*

impact /'ɪmpækt/ *n.* impact *m.*

impair /ɪm'peə(r)/ *v.t.* détériorer.

impale /ɪm'peɪl/ *v.t.* empaler.

impart /ɪm'pɑːt/ *v.t.* communiquer, transmettre.

impartial /ɪm'pɑːʃl/ *a.* impartial. **~ity** /-ɪ'ælətɪ/ *n.* impartialité *f.*

impassable /ɪm'pɑːsəbl/ *a.* (*barrier etc.*) infranchissable; (*road*) impraticable.

impasse /'æmpɑːs, *Amer.* 'ɪmpæs/ *n.* impasse *f.*

impassioned /ɪm'pæʃnd/ *a.* passionné.

impassive /ɪm'pæsɪv/ *a.* impassible.

impatien|t /ɪm'peɪʃnt/ *a.* impatient. **~ce** *n.* impatience *f.* **~tly** *adv.* impatiemment.

impeach /ɪm'piːtʃ/ *v.t.* mettre en accusation.

impeccable /ɪm'pekəbl/ *a.* impeccable.

impede /ɪm'piːd/ *v.t.* gêner.

impediment /ɪm'pedɪmənt/ *n.* obstacle *m.* (**speech**) **~**, défaut d'élocution *m.*

impel /ɪm'pel/ *v.t.* (*p.t.* **impelled**) pousser, forcer (**to do,** à faire).

impending /ɪm'pendɪŋ/ *a.* imminent.

impenetrable /ɪm'penɪtrəbl/ *a.* impénétrable.

imperative /ɪm'perətɪv/ *a.* nécessaire; (*need etc.*) impérieux. —*n.* (*gram.*) impératif *m.*

imperceptible /ɪmpə'septəbl/ *a.* imperceptible.

imperfect /ɪm'pɜːfɪkt/ *a.* imparfait; (*faulty*) défectueux. **~ion** /-ə'fekʃn/ *n.* imperfection *f.*

imperial /ɪm'pɪərɪəl/ *a.* impérial; (*measure*) légal (au Royaume-Uni). **~ism** *n.* impérialisme *m.*

imperil /ɪm'perəl/ *v.t.* (*p.t.* **imperilled**) mettre en péril.

imperious /ɪm'pɪərɪəs/ *a.* impérieux.

impersonal /ɪm'pɜːsənl/ *a.* impersonnel.

impersonat|e /ɪm'pɜːsəneɪt/ *v.t.* se faire passer pour; (*mimic*) imiter. **~ion** /-'neɪʃn/ *n.* imitation *f.* **~or** *n.* imita|teur, -trice *m.*, *f.*

impertinen|t /ɪm'pɜːtɪnənt/ *a.* impertinent. **~ce** *n.* impertinence *f.* **~tly** *adv.* avec impertinence.

impervious /ɪm'pɜːvɪəs/ *a.* **~ to,** imperméable à.

impetuous /ɪm'petʃʊəs/ *a.* impétueux.

impetus /'ɪmpɪtəs/ *n.* impulsion *f.*

impinge /ɪm'pɪndʒ/ *v.i.* **~ on,** affecter; (*encroach*) empiéter sur.

impish /'ɪmpɪʃ/ *a.* espiègle.

implacable /ɪm'plækəbl/ *a.* implacable.

implant /ɪm'plɑːnt/ *v.t.* implanter.

implement[1] /'ɪmplɪmənt/ *n.* (*tool*) outil *m.*; (*utensil*) ustensile *m.*

implement[2] /'ɪmplɪment/ *v.t.* exécuter, mettre en pratique.

implicat|e /'ɪmplɪkeɪt/ *v.t.* impliquer. **~ion** /-'keɪʃn/ *n.* implication *f.*

implicit /ɪm'plɪsɪt/ *a.* (*implied*) implicite; (*unquestioning*) absolu.

implore /ɪm'plɔː(r)/ *v.t.* implorer.

impl|y /ɪm'plaɪ/ *v.t.* (*assume, mean*) impliquer; (*insinuate*) laisser entendre. **~ied** *a.* implicite.

impolite /ɪmpə'laɪt/ *a.* impoli.

imponderable /ɪm'pɒndərəbl/ *a.* & *n.* impondérable (*m.*).

import[1] /ɪm'pɔːt/ *v.t.* importer.

~ation /-ˈteɪʃn/ *n.* importation *f.* **~er** *n.* importa|teur, -trice *m., f.*

import² /ˈɪmpɔːt/ *n.* (*article*) importation *f.*; (*meaning*) sens *m.*

importan|t /ɪmˈpɔːtnt/ *a.* important. **~ce** *n.* importance *f.*

impos|e /ɪmˈpəʊz/ *v.t.* imposer. —*v.i.* **~e on,** abuser de l'amabilité de. **~ition** /-əˈzɪʃn/ *n.* imposition *f.*; (*fig.*) dérangement *m.*

imposing /ɪmˈpəʊzɪŋ/ *a.* imposant.

impossib|le /ɪmˈpɒsəbl/ *a.* impossible. **~ility** /-ˈbɪlətɪ/ *n.* impossibilité *f.*

impostor /ɪmˈpɒstə(r)/ *n.* imposteur *m.*

impoten|t /ˈɪmpətənt/ *a.* impuissant. **~ce** *n.* impuissance *f.*

impound /ɪmˈpaʊnd/ *v.t.* confisquer, saisir.

impoverish /ɪmˈpɒvərɪʃ/ *v.t.* appauvrir.

impracticable /ɪmˈpræktɪkəbl/ *a.* impraticable.

impractical /ɪmˈpræktɪkl/ *a.* (*Amer.*) peu pratique.

imprecise /ɪmprɪˈsaɪs/ *a.* imprécis.

impregnable /ɪmˈpregnəbl/ *a.* imprenable; (*fig.*) inattaquable.

impregnate /ˈɪmpregneɪt/ *v.t.* imprégner (**with,** de).

impresario /ɪmprɪˈsɑːrɪəʊ/ *n.* (*pl.* **-os**) impresario *m.*

impress /ɪmˈpres/ *v.t.* impressionner; (*imprint*) imprimer. **~ on s.o.,** faire comprendre à qn.

impression /ɪmˈpreʃn/ *n.* impression *f.* **~able** *a.* impressionnable.

impressive /ɪmˈpresɪv/ *a.* impressionnant.

imprint¹ /ˈɪmprɪnt/ *n.* empreinte *f.*

imprint² /ɪmˈprɪnt/ *v.t.* imprimer.

imprison /ɪmˈprɪzn/ *v.t.* emprisonner. **~ment** *n.* emprisonnement *m.*, prison *f.*

improbab|le /ɪmˈprɒbəbl/ *a.* (*not likely*) improbable; (*incredible*) invraisemblable. **~ility** /-ˈbɪlətɪ/ *n.* improbabilité *f.*

impromptu /ɪmˈprɒmptjuː/ *a.* & *adv.* impromptu.

improp|er /ɪmˈprɒpə(r)/ *a.* inconvenant, indécent; (*wrong*) incorrect. **~riety** /-əˈpraɪətɪ/ *n.* inconvenance *f.*

improve /ɪmˈpruːv/ *v.t./i.* (s')améliorer. **~ment** *n.* amélioration *f.*

improvis|e /ˈɪmprəvaɪz/ *v.t./i.* improviser. **~ation** /-ˈzeɪʃn/ *n.* improvisation *f.*

imprudent /ɪmˈpruːdnt/ *a.* imprudent.

impuden|t /ˈɪmpjʊdənt/ *a.* impudent. **~ce** *n.* impudence *f.*

impulse /ˈɪmpʌls/ *n.* impulsion *f.* **on ~,** sur un coup de tête.

impulsive /ɪmˈpʌlsɪv/ *a.* impulsif. **~ly** *adv.* par impulsion.

impunity /ɪmˈpjuːnətɪ/ *n.* impunité *f.* **with ~,** impunément.

impur|e /ɪmˈpjʊə(r)/ *a.* impur. **~ity** *n.* impureté *f.*

impute /ɪmˈpjuːt/ *v.t.* imputer.

in /ɪn/ *prep.* dans, à, en. —*adv.* (*inside*) dedans; (*at home*) là, à la maison; (*in fashion*) à la mode. **~ the box/garden,** dans la boîte/le jardin. **~ Paris/school,** à Paris/l'école. **~ winter/English,** en hiver/anglais. **~ India,** en Inde. **~ Japan,** au Japon. **~ a firm manner/voice,** d'une manière/voix ferme. **~ an hour,** (*at end of*) au bout d'une heure. **~ an hour('s time),** dans une heure. **in (the space of) an hour,** en une heure. **~ doing,** en faisant. **~ the evening,** le soir. **one ~ ten,** un sur dix. **the best ~,** le meilleur de. **we are ~ for,** on va avoir. **~-laws** *n. pl.* (*fam.*) beaux-parents *m. pl.* **~-patient** *n.* malade hospitalisé(e) *m./f.* **the ~s and outs of,** les tenants et aboutissants de. **~ so far as,** dans la mesure où.

inability /ɪnəˈbɪlətɪ/ *n.* incapacité *f.* (**to do,** de faire).

inaccessible /ɪnæk'sesəbl/ *a.* inaccessible.
inaccurate /ɪn'ækjərət/ *a.* inexact.
inaction /ɪn'ækʃn/ *n.* inaction *f.*
inactiv|e /ɪn'æktɪv/ *a.* inactif. **~ity** /-'tɪvətɪ/ *n.* inaction *f.*
inadequa|te /ɪn'ædɪkwət/ *a.* insuffisant. **~cy** *n.* insuffisance *f.*
inadmissible /ɪnəd'mɪsəbl/ *a.* inadmissible.
inadvertently /ɪnəd'vɜːtəntlɪ/ *adv.* par mégarde.
inadvisable /ɪnəd'vaɪzəbl/ *a.* déconseillé, pas recommandé.
inane /ɪ'neɪn/ *a.* inepte.
inanimate /ɪn'ænɪmət/ *a.* inanimé.
inappropriate /ɪnə'prəʊprɪət/ *a.* inopportun.
inarticulate /ɪnɑː'tɪkjʊlət/ *a.* qui a du mal à s'exprimer.
inasmuch as /ɪnəz'mʌtʃəz/ *adv.* en ce sens que; (*because*) vu que.
inattentive /ɪnə'tentɪv/ *a.* inattentif.
inaugural /ɪ'nɔːgjʊrəl/ *a.* inaugural.
inaugurat|e /ɪ'nɔːgjʊreɪt/ *v.t.* (*open, begin*) inaugurer; (*person*) investir. **~ion** /-'reɪʃn/ *n.* inauguration *f.*; investiture *f.*
inauspicious /ɪnɔː'spɪʃəs/ *a.* peu propice.
inborn /ɪn'bɔːn/ *a.* inné.
inbred /ɪn'bred/ *a.* (*inborn*) inné.
incalculable /ɪn'kælkjʊləbl/ *a.* incalculable.
incapable /ɪn'keɪpəbl/ *a.* incapable.
incapacit|y /ɪnkə'pæsətɪ/ *n.* incapacité *f.* **~ate** *v.t.* rendre incapable (*de travailler etc.*).
incarcerate /ɪn'kɑːsəreɪt/ *v.t.* incarcérer.
incarnat|e /ɪn'kɑːneɪt/ *a.* incarné. **~ion** /-'neɪʃn/ *n.* incarnation *f.*
incendiary /ɪn'sendɪərɪ/ *a.* incendiaire. —*n.* (*bomb*) bombe incendiaire *f.*
incense[1] /'ɪnsens/ *n.* encens *m.*
incense[2] /ɪn'sens/ *v.t.* mettre en fureur.
incentive /ɪn'sentɪv/ *n.* motivation *f.*; (*payment*) prime (d'encouragement) *f.*
inception /ɪn'sepʃn/ *n.* début *m.*
incessant /ɪn'sesnt/ *a.* incessant. **~ly** *adv.* sans cesse.
incest /'ɪnsest/ *n.* inceste *m.* **~uous** /ɪn'sestjʊəs/ *a.* incestueux.
inch /ɪntʃ/ *n.* pouce *m.* (= *2.54 cm.*). —*v.i.* avancer doucement.
incidence /'ɪnsɪdəns/ *n.* fréquence *f.*
incident /'ɪnsɪdənt/ *n.* incident *m.*; (*in play, film, etc.*) épisode *m.*
incidental /ɪnsɪ'dentl/ *a.* accessoire. **~ly** *adv.* accessoirement; (*by the way*) à propos.
incinerat|e /ɪn'sɪnəreɪt/ *v.t.* incinérer. **~or** *n.* incinérateur *m.*
incipient /ɪn'sɪpɪənt/ *a.* naissant.
incision /ɪn'sɪʒn/ *n.* incision *f.*
incisive /ɪn'saɪsɪv/ *a.* incisif.
incite /ɪn'saɪt/ *v.t.* inciter, pousser. **~ment** *n.* incitation *f.*
inclement /ɪn'klemənt/ *a.* inclément, rigoureux.
inclination /ɪnklɪ'neɪʃn/ *n.* (*propensity, bowing*) inclination *f.*
incline[1] /ɪn'klaɪn/ *v.t./i.* incliner. **be ~d to,** avoir tendance à.
incline[2] /'ɪnklaɪn/ *n.* pente *f.*
inclu|de /ɪn'kluːd/ *v.t.* comprendre, inclure. **~ding** *prep.* (y) compris. **~sion** *n.* inclusion *f.*
inclusive /ɪn'kluːsɪv/ *a.* & *adv.* inclus, compris. **be ~ of,** comprendre, inclure.
incognito /ɪnkɒg'niːtəʊ/ *adv.* incognito.
incoherent /ɪnkəʊ'hɪərənt/ *a.* incohérent.
income /'ɪnkʌm/ *n.* revenu *m.* **~ tax,** impôt sur le revenu *m.*
incoming /'ɪnkʌmɪŋ/ *a.* (*tide*) montant; (*tenant etc.*) nouveau.

incomparable /ɪn'kɒmprəbl/ *a.* incomparable.
incompatible /ɪnkəm'pætəbl/ *a.* incompatible.
incompeten/t /ɪn'kɒmpɪtənt/ *a.* incompétent. **~ce** *n.* incompétence *f.*
incomplete /ɪnkəm'pliːt/ *a.* incomplet.
incomprehensible /ɪnkɒmprɪ'hensəbl/ *a.* incompréhensible.
inconceivable /ɪnkən'siːvəbl/ *a.* inconcevable.
inconclusive /ɪnkən'kluːsɪv/ *a.* peu concluant.
incongruous /ɪn'kɒŋgrʊəs/ *a.* déplacé, incongru.
inconsequential /ɪnkɒnsɪ'kwenʃl/ *a.* sans importance.
inconsiderate /ɪnkən'sɪdərət/ *a.* (*person*) qui ne se soucie pas des autres; (*act*) irréfléchi.
inconsisten|t /ɪnkən'sɪstənt/ *a.* sans cohérence, inconséquent; (*at variance*) contradictoire. **~t with,** incompatible avec. **~cy** *n.* inconséquence *f.* **~cies,** contradictions *f. pl.*
inconspicuous /ɪnkən'spɪkjʊəs *a.* peu en évidence.
incontinen|t /ɪn'kɒntɪnənt/ *a.* incontinent. **~ce** *n.* incontinence *f.*
inconvenien|t /ɪnkən'viːnɪənt/ *a.* incommode, peu pratique; (*time*) mal choisi. **be ~t for,** ne pas convenir à. **~ce** *n.* dérangement *m.*; (*drawback*) inconvénient *m.*; *v.t.* déranger.
incorporate /ɪn'kɔːpəreɪt/ *v.t.* incorporer; (*include*) contenir.
incorrect /ɪnkə'rekt/ *a.* inexact.
incorrigible /ɪn'kɒrɪdʒəbl/ *a.* incorrigible.
incorruptible /ɪnkə'rʌptəbl/ *a.* incorruptible.
increas|e¹ /ɪn'kriːs/ *v.t./i.* augmenter. **~ing** *a.* croissant. **~ingly** *adv.* de plus en plus.
increase² /'ɪnkriːs/ *n.* augmentation *f.* **(in, of,** de).
incredible /ɪn'kredəbl/ *a.* incroyable.
incredulous /ɪn'kredjʊləs/ *a.* incrédule.
increment /'ɪnkrəmənt/ *n.* augmentation *f.*
incriminat|e /ɪn'krɪmɪneɪt/ *v.t.* incriminer. **~ing** *a.* compromettant.
incubat|e /'ɪnkjʊbeɪt/ *v.t.* (*eggs*) couver. **~ion** /-'beɪʃn/ *n.* incubation *f.* **~or** *n.* couveuse *f.*
inculcate /'ɪnkʌlkeɪt/ *v.t.* inculquer.
incumbent /ɪn'kʌmbənt/ *n.* (*pol., relig.*) titulaire *m./f.*
incur /ɪn'kɜː/ *v.t.* (*p.t.* **incurred**) encourir; (*debts*) contracter.
incurable /ɪn'kjʊərəbl/ *a.* incurable.
incursion /ɪn'kɜːʃn/ *n.* incursion *f.*
indebted /ɪn'detɪd/ *a.* **~ to s.o.,** redevable à qn. **(for,** de).
indecen|t /ɪn'diːsnt/ *a.* indécent. **~cy** *n.* indécence *f.*
indecision /ɪndɪ'sɪʒn/ *n.* indécision *f.*
indecisive /ɪndɪ'saɪsɪv/ *a.* indécis.
indeed /ɪn'diːd/ *adv.* en effet, vraiment.
indefinable /ɪndɪ'faɪnəbl/ *a.* indéfinissable.
indefinite /ɪn'defɪnɪt/ *a.* indéfini; (*time*) indéterminé. **~ly** *adv.* indéfiniment.
indelible /ɪn'deləbl/ *a.* indélébile.
indemni|fy /ɪn'demnɪfaɪ/ *v.t.* (*compensate*) indemniser **(for,** de); (*safeguard*) garantir. **~ty** /-nətɪ/ *n.* indemnité *f.*; garantie *f.*
indent /ɪn'dent/ *v.t.* (*text*) renfoncer. **~ation** /-'teɪʃn/ *n.* (*outline*) découpure *f.*
independen|t /ɪndɪ'pendənt/ *a.* indépendant. **~ce** *n.* indépendance *f.* **~tly** *adv.* de façon

indépendante. **~tly of,** indépendamment de.

indescribable /ɪndɪ'skraɪbəbl/ *a.* indescriptible.

indestructible /ɪndɪ'strʌktəbl/ *a.* indestructible.

indeterminate /ɪndɪ'tɜːmɪnət/ *a.* indéterminé.

index /'ɪndeks/ *n.* (*pl.* **indexes**) (*figure*) indice *m.*; (*in book*) index *m.*; (*in library*) catalogue *m.* —*v.t.* classer. **~ finger** index *m.* **~-linked** *a.* indexé.

India /'ɪndɪə/ *n.* Inde *f.* **~n** *a.* & *n.* indien(ne) (*m.* (*f.*)). **~n summer,** été de la Saint-Martin *m.*

indicat|e /'ɪndɪkeɪt/ *v.t.* indiquer. **~ion** /-'keɪʃn/ *n.* indication *f.* **~or** *n.* (*device*) indicateur *m.*; (*on vehicle*) clignotant *m.*; (*board*) tableau *m.*

indicative /ɪn'dɪkətɪv/ *a.* indicatif. —*n.* (*gram.*) indicatif *m.*

indict /ɪn'daɪt/ *v.t.* accuser. **~ment** *n.* accusation *f.*

indifferen|t /ɪn'dɪfrənt/ *a.* indifférent; (*not good*) médiocre. **~ce** *n.* indifférence *f.*

indigenous /ɪn'dɪdʒɪnəs/ *a.* indigène.

indigest|ion /ɪndɪ'dʒestʃən/ *n.* indigestion *f.* **~ible** /-təbl/ *a.* indigeste.

indign|ant /ɪn'dɪgnənt/ *a.* indigné. **~ation** /-'neɪʃn/ *n.* indignation *f.*

indigo /'ɪndɪgəʊ/ *n.* indigo *m.*

indirect /ɪndɪ'rekt/ *a.* indirect. **~ly** *adv.* indirectement.

indiscr|eet /ɪndɪ'skriːt/ *a.* indiscret; (*not wary*) imprudent. **~etion** /-eʃn/ *n.* indiscrétion *f.*

indiscriminate /ɪndɪ'skrɪmɪnət/ *a.* qui manque de discernement; (*random*) fait au hasard. **~ly** *adv.* sans discernement; au hasard.

indispensable /ɪndɪ'spensəbl/ *a.* indispensable.

indispos|ed /ɪndɪ'spəʊzd/ *a.* indisposé, souffrant. **~ition** /-ə'zɪʃn/ *n.* indisposition *f.*

indisputable /ɪndɪ'spjuːtəbl/ *a.* incontestable.

indistinct /ɪndɪ'stɪŋkt/ *a.* indistinct.

indistinguishable /ɪndɪ'stɪŋgwɪʃəbl/ *a.* indifférenciable.

individual /ɪndɪ'vɪdʒʊəl/ *a.* individuel. —*n.* individu *m.* **~ist** *n.* individualiste *m./f.* **~ity** /-'ælətɪ/ *n.* individualité *f.* **~ly** *adv.* individuellement.

indivisible /ɪndɪ'vɪzəbl/ *a.* indivisible.

Indo-China /ɪndəʊ'tʃaɪnə/ *n.* Indochine *f.*

indoctrinat|e /ɪn'dɒktrɪneɪt/ *v.t.* endoctriner. **~ion** /-'neɪʃn/ *n.* endoctrinement *m.*

indolen|t /'ɪndələnt/ *a.* indolent. **~ce** *n.* indolence *f.*

indomitable /ɪn'dɒmɪtəbl/ *a.* indomptable.

Indonesia /ɪndəʊ'niːzɪə/ *n.* Indonésie *f.* **~n** *a.* & *n.* indonésien(ne) (*m.* (*f.*)).

indoor /'ɪndɔː(r)/ *a.* (*clothes etc.*) d'intérieur; (*under cover*) couvert. **~s** /ɪn'dɔːz/ *adv.* à l'intérieur.

induce /ɪn'djuːs/ *v.t.* (*influence*) persuader; (*cause*) provoquer. **~ment** *n.* encouragement *m.*

induct /ɪn'dʌkt/ *v.t.* investir, installer; (*mil., Amer.*) incorporer.

indulge /ɪn'dʌldʒ/ *v.t.* (*desires*) satisfaire; (*person*) se montrer indulgent pour, gâter. —*v.i.* **~ in,** se livrer à, s'offrir.

indulgen|t /ɪn'dʌldʒənt/ *a.* indulgent. **~ce** *n.* indulgence *f.*

industrial /ɪn'dʌstrɪəl/ *a.* industriel; (*unrest etc.*) ouvrier; (*action*) revendicatif. **~ist** *n.* industriel *m.* **~ized** *a.* industrialisé.

industrious /ɪn'dʌstrɪəs/ *a.* travailleur, appliqué.

industry /'ɪndəstrɪ/ *n.* industrie *f.*; (*zeal*) application *f.*

inebriated /ɪ'ni:brɪeɪtɪd/ *a.* ivre.
inedible /ɪn'edɪbl/ *a.* (*food*) immangeable.
ineffective /ɪnɪ'fektɪv/ *a.* inefficace; (*person*) incapable.
ineffectual /ɪnɪ'fektʃʊəl/ *a.* inefficace; (*person*) incapable.
inefficien|t /ɪnɪ'fɪʃnt/ *a.* inefficace; (*person*) incompétent. **~cy** *n.* inefficacité *f.*; incompétence *f.*
ineligible /ɪn'elɪdʒəbl/ *a.* inéligible. **be ~ for,** ne pas avoir droit à.
inept /ɪ'nept/ *a.* (*absurd*) inepte; (*out of place*) mal à propos.
inequality /ɪnɪ'kwɒlətɪ/ *n.* inégalité *f.*
inert /ɪ'nɜ:t/ *a.* inerte.
inertia /ɪ'nɜ:ʃə/ *n.* inertie *f.*
inescapable /ɪnɪ'skeɪpəbl/ *a.* inéluctable.
inevitabl|e /ɪn'evɪtəbl/ *a.* inévitable. **~y** *adv.* inévitablement.
inexact /ɪnɪg'zækt/ *a.* inexact.
inexcusable /ɪnɪk'skju:zəbl/ *a.* inexcusable.
inexhaustible /ɪnɪg'zɔ:stəbl/ *a.* inépuisable.
inexorable /ɪn'eksərəbl/ *a.* inexorable.
inexpensive /ɪnɪk'spensɪv/ *a.* bon marché *invar.*, pas cher.
inexperience /ɪnɪk'spɪərɪəns/ *n.* inexpérience *f.* **~d** *a.* inexpérimenté.
inexplicable /ɪnɪk'splɪkəbl/ *a.* inexplicable.
inextricable /ɪnɪk'strɪkəbl/ *a.* inextricable.
infallib|le /ɪn'fæləbl/ *a.* infaillible. **~ility** /-'bɪlətɪ/ *n.* infaillibilité *f.*
infam|ous /'ɪnfəməs/ *a.* infâme. **~y** *n.* infamie *f.*
infan|t /'ɪnfənt/ *n.* nourrisson *m.*, petit(e) enfant *m./f.* **~cy** *n.* petite enfance *f.*; (*fig.*) enfance *f.*
infantile /'ɪnfəntaɪl/ *a.* infantile.
infantry /'ɪnfəntrɪ/ *n.* infanterie *f.*
infatuat|ed /ɪn'fætʃʊeɪtɪd/ *a.* **~ed with,** engoué de. **~ion** /-'eɪʃn/ *n.* engouement *m.*, béguin *m.*
infect /ɪn'fekt/ *v.t.* infecter. **~ s.o. with,** communiquer à qn. **~ion** /-kʃn/ *n.* infection *f.*
infectious /ɪn'fekʃəs/ *a.* (*person, disease & fig.*) contagieux.
infer /ɪn'fɜ:(r)/ *v.t.* (*p.t.* **inferred**) déduire. **~ence** /'ɪnfərəns/ *n.* déduction *f.*
inferior /ɪn'fɪərɪə(r)/ *a.* inférieur (**to,** à); (*work, product*) de qualité inférieure. —*n.* inférieur(e) *m.* (*f.*). **~ity** /-'ɒrətɪ/ *n.* infériorité *f.*
infernal /ɪn'fɜ:nl/ *a.* infernal. **~ly** *adv.* (*fam.*) atrocement.
inferno /ɪn'fɜ:nəʊ/ *n.* (*pl.* **-os**) (*hell*) enfer *m.*; (*blaze*) incendie *m.*
infertil|e /ɪn'fɜ:taɪl, *Amer.* ɪn'fɜ:tl/ *a.* infertile. **~ity** /-ə'tɪlətɪ/ *n.* infertilité *f.*
infest /ɪn'fest/ *v.t.* infester.
infidelity /ɪnfɪ'delətɪ/ *n.* infidélité *f.*
infighting /'ɪnfaɪtɪŋ/ *n.* querelles internes *f. pl.*
infiltrat|e /'ɪnfɪltreɪt/ *v.t./i.* s'infiltrer (dans). **~ion** /-'treɪʃn/ *n.* infiltration *f.*
infinite /'ɪnfɪnɪt/ *a.* infini. **~ly** *adv.* infiniment.
infinitesimal /ɪnfɪnɪ'tesɪml/ *a.* infinitésimal.
infinitive /ɪn'fɪnətɪv/ *n.* infinitif *m.*
infinity /ɪn'fɪnətɪ/ *n.* infinité *f.*
infirm /ɪn'fɜ:m/ *a.* infirme. **~ity** *n.* infirmité *f.*
infirmary /ɪn'fɜ:mərɪ/ *n.* hôpital *m.*; (*sick-bay*) infirmerie *f.*
inflam|e /ɪn'fleɪm/ *v.t.* enflammer. **~mable** /-æməbl/ *a.* inflammable. **~mation** /-ə'meɪʃn/ *n.* inflammation *f.*
inflammatory /ɪn'flæmətrɪ/ *a.* incendiaire.
inflate /ɪn'fleɪt/ *v.t.* (*balloon, prices, etc.*) gonfler.
inflation /ɪn'fleɪʃn/ *n.* inflation *f.* **~ary** *a.* inflationniste.

inflection /ɪnˈflekʃn/ *n.* inflexion *f.*; (*suffix*: *gram.*) désinence *f.*
inflexible /ɪnˈfleksəbl/ *a.* inflexible.
inflict /ɪnˈflɪkt/ *v.t.* infliger (**on,** à).
influence /ˈɪnflʊəns/ *n.* influence *f.* —*v.t.* influencer. **under the ~,** (*drunk*: *fam.*) en état d'ivresse.
influential /ɪnflʊˈenʃl/ *a.* influent.
influenza /ɪnflʊˈenzə/ *n.* grippe *f.*
influx /ˈɪnflʌks/ *n.* afflux *m.*
inform /ɪnˈfɔːm/ *v.t.* informer. **keep ~ed,** tenir au courant. **~ant** *n.* informa|teur, -trice *m., f.* **~er** *n.* indica|teur, -trice *m., f.*
informal /ɪnˈfɔːml/ *a.* (*simple*) simple, sans cérémonie; (*unofficial*) officieux; (*colloquial*) familier. **~ity** /-ˈmælətɪ/ *n.* simplicité *f.* **~ly** *adv.* sans cérémonie.
information /ɪnfəˈmeɪʃn/ *n.* renseignement(s) *m.* (*pl.*), information(s) *f.* (*pl.*).
informative /ɪnˈfɔːmətɪv/ *a.* instructif.
infra-red /ɪnfrəˈred/ *a.* infrarouge.
infrequent /ɪnˈfriːkwənt/ *a.* peu fréquent. **~ly** *adv.* rarement.
infringe /ɪnˈfrɪndʒ/ *v.t.* contrevenir à. **~ on,** empiéter sur. **~ment** *n.* infraction *f.*
infuriate /ɪnˈfjʊərɪeɪt/ *v.t.* exaspérer, rendre furieux.
infus|e /ɪnˈfjuːz/ *v.t.* infuser. **~ion** /-ʒn/ *n.* infusion *f.*
ingen|ious /ɪnˈdʒiːnɪəs/ *a.* ingénieux. **~uity** /-ɪˈnjuːətɪ/ *n.* ingéniosité *f.*
ingenuous /ɪnˈdʒenjʊəs/ *a.* ingénu.
ingot /ˈɪŋgət/ *n.* lingot *m.*
ingrained /ɪnˈgreɪnd/ *a.* enraciné.
ingratiate /ɪnˈgreɪʃɪeɪt/ *v.t.* **~ o.s. with,** gagner les bonnes grâces de.
ingratitude /ɪnˈgrætɪtjuːd/ *n.* ingratitude *f.*
ingredient /ɪnˈgriːdɪənt/ *n.* ingrédient *m.*
inhabit /ɪnˈhæbɪt/ *v.t.* habiter. **~able** *a.* habitable. **~ant** *n.* habitant(e) *m.* (*f.*).
inhale /ɪnˈheɪl/ *v.t.* inhaler; (*tobacco smoke*) avaler.
inherent /ɪnˈhɪərənt/ *a.* inhérent. **~ly** *adv.* en soi, intrinsèquement.
inherit /ɪnˈherɪt/ *v.t.* hériter (de). **~ance** *n.* héritage *m.*
inhibit /ɪnˈhɪbɪt/ *v.t.* (*hinder*) gêner; (*prevent*) empêcher. **be ~ed,** avoir des inhibitions. **~ion** /-ˈbɪʃn/ *n.* inhibition *f.*
inhospitable /ɪnhɒˈspɪtəbl/ *a.* inhospitalier.
inhuman /ɪnˈhjuːmən/ *a.* (*brutal, not human*) inhumain. **~ity** /-ˈmænətɪ/ *n.* inhumanité *f.*
inhumane /ɪnhjuːˈmeɪn/ *a.* (*unkind*) inhumain.
inimitable /ɪˈnɪmɪtəbl/ *a.* inimitable.
iniquit|ous /ɪˈnɪkwɪtəs/ *a.* inique. **~y** /-ətɪ/ *n.* iniquité *f.*
initial /ɪˈnɪʃl/ *n.* initiale *f.* —*v.t.* (*p.t.* **initialled**) parapher. —*a.* initial. **~ly** *adv.* initialement.
initiat|e /ɪˈnɪʃɪeɪt/ *v.t.* (*begin*) amorcer; (*scheme*) lancer; (*person*) initier (**into,** à). **~ion** /-ˈeɪʃn/ *n.* initiation *f.*; (*start*) amorce *f.*
initiative /ɪˈnɪʃətɪv/ *n.* initiative *f.*
inject /ɪnˈdʒekt/ *v.t.* injecter; (*new element*: *fig.*) insuffler. **~ion** /-kʃn/ *n.* injection *f.*, piqûre *f.*
injunction /ɪnˈdʒʌŋkʃn/ *n.* (*court order*) ordonnance *f.*
injure /ˈɪndʒə(r)/ *v.t.* blesser; (*do wrong to*) nuire à.
injury /ˈɪndʒərɪ/ *n.* (*physical*) blessure *f.*; (*wrong*) préjudice *m.*
injustice /ɪnˈdʒʌstɪs/ *n.* injustice *f.*
ink /ɪŋk/ *n.* encre *f.* **~-well** *n.* encrier *m.* **~y** *a.* taché d'encre.
inkling /ˈɪŋklɪŋ/ *n.* petite idée *f.*
inland /ˈɪnlənd/ *a.* intérieur. —*adv.* à l'intérieur. **I~ Revenue,** fisc *m.*

inlay[1] /ɪn'leɪ/ *v.t.* (*p.t.* **inlaid**) incruster.
inlay[2] /'ɪnleɪ/ *n.* incrustation *f.*
inlet /'ɪnlet/ *n.* bras de mer *m.*; (*techn.*) arrivée *f.*
inmate /'ɪnmeɪt/ *n.* (*of asylum*) interné(e) *m.* (*f.*); (*of prison*) détenu(e) *m.* (*f.*).
inn /ɪn/ *n.* auberge *f.*
innards /'ɪnədz/ *n. pl.* (*fam.*) entrailles *f. pl.*
innate /ɪ'neɪt/ *a.* inné.
inner /'ɪnə(r)/ *a.* intérieur, interne; (*fig.*) profond, intime. **~most** *a.* le plus profond.
innings /'ɪnɪŋz/ *n. invar.* tour de batte *m.*; (*fig.*) tour *m.*
innkeeper /'ɪnkiːpə(r)/ *n.* aubergiste *m./f.*
innocen|t /'ɪnəsnt/ *a.* & *n.* innocent(e) (*m.* (*f.*)). **~ce** *n.* innocence *f.*
innocuous /ɪ'nɒkjʊəs/ *a.* inoffensif.
innovat|e /'ɪnəveɪt/ *v.i.* innover. **~ion** /-'veɪʃn/ *n.* innovation *f.* **~or** *n.* innova|teur, -trice *m.*, *f.*
innuendo /ɪnjuː'endəʊ/ *n.* (*pl.* **-oes**) insinuation *f.*
innumerable /ɪ'njuːmərəbl/ *a.* innombrable.
inoculat|e /ɪ'nɒkjʊleɪt/ *v.t.* inoculer. **~ion** /-'leɪʃn/ *n.* inoculation *f.*
inoffensive /ɪnə'fensɪv/ *a.* inoffensif.
inoperative /ɪn'ɒpərətɪv/ *a.* inopérant.
inopportune /ɪn'ɒpətjuːn/ *a.* inopportun.
inordinate /ɪ'nɔːdɪnət/ *a.* excessif. **~ly** *adv.* excessivement.
input /'ɪnpʊt/ *n.* (*data*) données *f. pl.*; (*computer process*) entrée *f.*; (*power: electr.*) énergie *f.*
inquest /'ɪnkwest/ *n.* enquête *f.*
inquir|e /ɪn'kwaɪə(r)/ *v.i.* faire une enquête. **~y** *n.* enquête *f.*
inquisition /ɪnkwɪ'zɪʃn/ *n.* inquisition *f.*
inquisitive /ɪn'kwɪzətɪv/ *a.* curieux; (*prying*) indiscret.
inroad /'ɪnrəʊd/ *n.* incursion *f.*
insan|e /ɪn'seɪn/ *a.* fou. **~ity** /ɪn'sænətɪ/ *n.* folie *f.*, démence *f.*
insanitary /ɪn'sænɪtrɪ/ *a.* insalubre, malsain.
insatiable /ɪn'seɪʃəbl/ *a.* insatiable.
inscri|be /ɪn'skraɪb/ *v.t.* inscrire; (*book*) dédicacer. **~ption** /-ɪpʃn/ *n.* inscription *f.*; dédicace *f.*
inscrutable /ɪn'skruːtəbl/ *a.* impénétrable.
insect /'ɪnsekt/ *n.* insecte *m.*
insecticide /ɪn'sektɪsaɪd/ *n.* insecticide *m.*
insecur|e /ɪnsɪ'kjʊə(r)/ *a.* (*not firm*) peu solide; (*unsafe*) peu sûr; (*worried*) anxieux. **~ity** *n.* insécurité *f.*
insemination /ɪnsemɪ'neɪʃn/ *n.* insémination *f.*
insensible /ɪn'sensəbl/ *a.* insensible; (*unconscious*) inconscient.
insensitive /ɪn'sensətɪv/ *a.* insensible.
inseparable /ɪn'seprəbl/ *a.* inséparable.
insert[1] /ɪn'sɜːt/ *v.t.* insérer. **~ion** /-ʃn/ *n.* insertion *f.*
insert[2] /'ɪnsɜːt/ *n.* insertion *f.*
inshore /ɪn'ʃɔː(r)/ *a.* côtier.
inside /ɪn'saɪd/ *n.* intérieur *m.* **~(s)**, (*fam.*) entrailles *f. pl.* —*a.* intérieur. —*adv.* à l'intérieur, dedans. —*prep.* à l'intérieur de; (*of time*) en moins de. **~ out**, à l'envers; (*thoroughly*) à fond.
insidious /ɪn'sɪdɪəs/ *a.* insidieux.
insight /'ɪnsaɪt/ *n.* (*perception*) perspicacité *f.*; (*idea*) aperçu *m.*
insignia /ɪn'sɪgnɪə/ *n. pl.* insignes *m. pl.*
insignificant /ɪnsɪg'nɪfɪkənt/ *a.* insignifiant.
insincer|e /ɪnsɪn'sɪə(r)/ *a.* peu

sincère. **~ity** /-'serətɪ/ *n.* manque de sincérité *m.*

insinuat|e /ɪn'sɪnjʊeɪt/ *v.t.* insinuer. **~ion** /-'eɪʃn/ *n.* insinuation *f.*

insipid /ɪn'sɪpɪd/ *a.* insipide.

insist /ɪn'sɪst/ *v.t./i.* insister. **~ on,** affirmer; (*demand*) exiger. **~ on doing,** insister pour faire.

insisten|t /ɪn'sɪstənt/ *a.* insistant. **~ce** *n.* insistance *f.* **~tly** *adv.* avec insistance.

insolen|t /'ɪnsələnt/ *a.* insolent. **~ce** *n.* insolence *f.*

insoluble /ɪn'sɒljʊbl/ *a.* insoluble.

insolvent /ɪn'sɒlvənt/ *a.* insolvable.

insomnia /ɪn'sɒmnɪə/ *n.* insomnie *f.* **~c** /-ɪæk/ *n.* insomniaque *m./f.*

inspect /ɪn'spekt/ *v.t.* inspecter; (*tickets*) contrôler. **~ion** /-kʃn/ *n.* inspection *f.*; contrôle *m.* **~or** *n.* inspec|teur, -trice *m., f.*; (*on train, bus*) contrôleu|r, -se *m., f.*

inspir|e /ɪn'spaɪə(r)/ *v.t.* inspirer. **~ation** /-ə'reɪʃn/ *n.* inspiration *f.*

instability /ɪnstə'bɪlətɪ/ *n.* instabilité *f.*

install /ɪn'stɔːl/ *v.t.* installer. **~ation** /-ə'leɪʃn/ *n.* installation *f.*

instalment /ɪn'stɔːlmənt/ *n.* (*payment*) acompte *m.*, versement *m.*; (*of serial*) épisode *m.*

instance /'ɪnstəns/ *n.* exemple *m.*; (*case*) cas *m.* **for ~,** par exemple. **in the first ~,** en premier lieu.

instant /'ɪnstənt/ *a.* immédiat; (*food*) instantané. —*n.* instant *m.* **~ly** *adv.* immédiatement.

instantaneous /ɪnstən'teɪnɪəs/ *a.* instantané.

instead /ɪn'sted/ *adv.* plutôt. **~ of doing,** au lieu de faire. **~ of s.o.,** à la place de qn.

instep /'ɪnstep/ *n.* cou-de-pied *m.*

instigat|e /'ɪnstɪgeɪt/ *v.t.* provoquer. **~ion** /-'geɪʃn/ *n.* instigation *f.* **~or** *n.* instiga|teur, -trice *m., f.*

instil /ɪn'stɪl/ *v.t.* (*p.t.* **instilled**) inculquer; (*inspire*) insuffler.

instinct /'ɪnstɪŋkt/ *n.* instinct *m.* **~ive** /ɪn'stɪŋktɪv/ *a.* instinctif.

institut|e /'ɪnstɪtjuːt/ *n.* institut *m.* —*v.t.* instituer; (*inquiry etc.*) entamer. **~ion** /-'tjuːʃn/ *n.* institution *f.*; (*school, hospital*) établissement *m.*

instruct /ɪn'strʌkt/ *v.t.* instruire; (*order*) ordonner. **~ s.o. in sth.,** enseigner qch. à qn. **~ion** /-kʃn/ *n.* instruction *f.* **~ions** /-kʃnz/ *n. pl.* (*for use*) mode d'emploi *m.* **~ive** *a.* instructif. **~or** *n.* instructeur *m.*, professeur *m.*

instrument /'ɪnstrʊmənt/ *n.* instrument *m.*

instrumental /ɪnstrʊ'mentl/ *a.* instrumental. **be ~ in,** contribuer à. **~ist** *n.* instrumentaliste *m./f.*

insubordinat|e /ɪnsə'bɔːdɪnət/ *a.* insubordonné. **~ion** /-'neɪʃn/ *n.* insubordination *f.*

insufferable /ɪn'sʌfrəbl/ *a.* intolérable, insupportable.

insufficient /ɪnsə'fɪʃnt/ *a.* insuffisant. **~ly** *adv.* insuffisamment.

insular /'ɪnsjʊlə(r)/ *a.* insulaire; (*mind, person: fig.*) borné.

insulat|e /'ɪnsjʊleɪt/ *v.t.* (*room, wire, etc.*) isoler. **~ing tape,** chatterton *m.* **~ion** /-'leɪʃn/ *n.* isolation *f.*

insulin /'ɪnsjʊlɪn/ *n.* insuline *f.*

insult¹ /ɪn'sʌlt/ *v.t.* insulter.

insult² /'ɪnsʌlt/ *n.* insulte *f.*

insuperable /ɪn'sjuːprəbl/ *a.* insurmontable.

insur|e /ɪn'ʃʊə(r)/ *v.t.* assurer. **~e that,** (*ensure: Amer.*) s'assurer que. **~ance** *n.* assurance *f.*

insurmountable /ɪnsə'maʊntəbl/ *a.* insurmontable.

insurrection /ɪnsə'rekʃn/ *n.* insurrection *f.*

intact /ɪn'tækt/ *a.* intact.

intake /ˈɪnteɪk/ *n.* admission(s) *f.* (*pl.*); (*techn.*) prise *f.*
intangible /ɪnˈtændʒəbl/ *a.* intangible.
integral /ˈɪntɪgrəl/ *a.* intégral. **be an ~ part of,** faire partie intégrante de.
integrat|e /ˈɪntɪgreɪt/ *v.t./i.* (s')intégrer. **~ion** /-ˈgreɪʃn/ *n.* intégration *f.*; (*racial*) déségrégation *f.*
integrity /ɪnˈtegrətɪ/ *n.* intégrité *f.*
intellect /ˈɪntəlekt/ *n.* intelligence *f.* **~ual** /-ˈlektʃʊəl/ *a.* & *n.* intellectuel(le) (*m.* (*f.*)).
intelligen|t /ɪnˈtelɪdʒənt/ *a.* intelligent. **~ce** *n.* intelligence *f.*; (*mil.*) renseignements *m. pl.* **~tly** *adv.* intelligemment.
intelligentsia /ɪntelɪˈdʒentsɪə/ *n.* intelligentsia *f.*
intelligible /ɪnˈtelɪdʒəbl/ *a.* intelligible.
intemperance /ɪnˈtempərəns/ *n.* (*drunkenness*) ivrognerie *f.*
intend /ɪnˈtend/ *v.t.* destiner. **~ to do,** avoir l'intention de faire. **~ed** *a.* intentionnel; *n.* (*future spouse*: *fam.*) promis(e) *m.* (*f.*).
intens|e /ɪnˈtens/ *a.* intense; (*person*) passionné. **~ely** *adv.* (*to live etc.*) intensément; (*very*) extrêmement. **~ity** *n.* intensité *f.*
intensif|y /ɪnˈtensɪfaɪ/ *v.t.* intensifier. **~ication** /-ɪˈkeɪʃn/ *n.* intensification *f.*
intensive /ɪnˈtensɪv/ *a.* intensif. **in ~ care,** en réanimation.
intent /ɪnˈtent/ *n.* intention *f.* —*a.* attentif. **~ on,** absorbé par. **~ on doing,** résolu à faire. **~ly** *adv.* attentivement.
intention /ɪnˈtenʃn/ *n.* intention *f.* **~al** *a.* intentionnel.
inter /ɪnˈtɜː(r)/ *v.t.* (*p.t.* **interred**) enterrer.
inter- /ˈɪntə(r)/ *pref.* inter-.
interact /ɪntəˈrækt/ *v.i.* avoir une action réciproque. **~ion** /-kʃn/ *n.* interaction *f.*
intercede /ɪntəˈsiːd/ *v.i.* intercéder.
intercept /ɪntəˈsept/ *v.t.* intercepter. **~ion** /-pʃn/ *n.* interception *f.*
interchange /ˈɪntətʃeɪndʒ/ *n.* (*road junction*) échangeur *m.*
interchangeable /ɪntəˈtʃeɪndʒəbl/ *a.* interchangeable.
intercom /ˈɪntəkɒm/ *n.* interphone *m.*
interconnected /ɪntəkəˈnektɪd/ *a.* (*facts, events, etc.*) lié.
intercourse /ˈɪntəkɔːs/ *n.* (*sexual, social*) rapports *m. pl.*
interest /ˈɪntrəst/ *n.* intérêt *m.*; (*stake*) intérêts *m. pl.* —*v.t.* intéresser. **~ed** *a.* intéressé. **be ~ed in,** s'intéresser à. **~ing** *a.* intéressant.
interfer|e /ɪntəˈfɪə(r)/ *v.i.* se mêler des affaires des autres. **~e in,** s'ingérer dans. **~ence** *n.* ingérence *f.*; (*radio*) parasites *m. pl.*
interim /ˈɪntərɪm/ *n.* intérim *m.* —*a.* intérimaire.
interior /ɪnˈtɪərɪə(r)/ *n.* intérieur *m.* —*a.* intérieur.
interjection /ɪntəˈdʒekʃn/ *n.* interjection *f.*
interlock /ɪntəˈlɒk/ *v.t./i.* (*techn.*) (s')emboîter, (s')enclencher.
interloper /ˈɪntələʊpə(r)/ *n.* intrus(e) *m.* (*f.*).
interlude /ˈɪntəluːd/ *n.* intervalle *m.*; (*theatre, mus.*) intermède *m.*
intermarr|iage /ɪntəˈmærɪdʒ/ *n.* mariage entre membres de races différentes *m.* **~y** *v.i.* se marier (entre eux).
intermediary /ɪntəˈmiːdɪərɪ/ *a.* & *n.* intermédiaire (*m.*/*f.*).
intermediate /ɪntəˈmiːdɪət/ *a.* intermédiaire; (*exam etc.*) moyen.
interminable /ɪnˈtɜːmɪnəbl/ *a.* interminable.

intermission /ɪntə'mɪʃn/ *n.* pause *f.*; (*theatre etc.*) entracte *m.*

intermittent /ɪntə'mɪtnt/ *a.* intermittent. **~ly** *adv.* par intermittence.

intern[1] /ɪn'tɜːn/ *v.t.* interner. **~ee** /-'niː/ *n.* interné(e) *m.* (*f.*). **~ment** *n.* internement *m.*

intern[2] /'ɪntɜːn/ *n.* (*doctor: Amer.*) interne *m.*/*f.*

internal /ɪn'tɜːnl/ *a.* interne; (*domestic: pol.*) intérieur. **~ly** *adv.* intérieurement.

international /ɪntə'næʃnəl/ *a.* & *n.* international (*m.*).

interplay /'ɪntəpleɪ/ *n.* jeu *m.*, interaction *f.*

interpolate /ɪn'tɜːpəleɪt/ *v.t.* interpoler.

interpret /ɪn'tɜːprɪt/ *v.t./i.* interpréter. **~ation** /-'teɪʃn/ *n.* interprétation *f.* **~er** *n.* interprète *m.*/*f.*

interrelated /ɪntərɪ'leɪtɪd/ *a.* en corrélation, lié.

interrogat|e /ɪn'terəgeɪt/ *v.t.* interroger. **~ion** /-'geɪʃn/ *n.* interrogation *f.* **(of, de)**; (*session of questions*) interrogatoire *m.*

interrogative /ɪntə'rɒgətɪv/ *a.* & *n.* interrogatif (*m.*).

interrupt /ɪntə'rʌpt/ *v.t.* interrompre. **~ion** /-pʃn/ *n.* interruption *f.*

intersect /ɪntə'sekt/ *v.t./i.* (*lines, roads*) (se) couper. **~ion** /-kʃn/ *n.* intersection *f.*; (*crossroads*) croisement *m.*

interspersed /ɪntə'spɜːst/ *a.* (*scattered*) dispersé. **~ with,** parsemé de.

intertwine /ɪntə'twaɪn/ *v.t./i.* (s')entrelacer.

interval /'ɪntəvl/ *n.* intervalle *m.*; (*theatre*) entracte *m.* **at ~s,** par intervalles.

interven|e /ɪntə'viːn/ *v.i.* intervenir; (*of time*) s'écouler (**between,** entre). **~tion** /-'venʃn/ *n.* intervention *f.*

interview /'ɪntəvjuː/ *n.* (*with reporter*) interview *f.*; (*for job etc.*) entrevue *f.* —*v.t.* interviewer. **~er** *n.* interviewer *m.*

intestin|e /ɪn'testɪn/ *n.* intestin *m.* **~al** *a.* intestinal.

intima|te[1] /'ɪntɪmət/ *a.* intime; (*detailed*) profond. **~cy** *n.* intimité *f.* **~tely** *adv.* intimement.

intimate[2] /'ɪntɪmeɪt/ *v.t.* (*state*) annoncer; (*imply*) suggérer.

intimidat|e /ɪn'tɪmɪdeɪt/ *v.t.* intimider. **~ion** /-'deɪʃn/ *n.* intimidation *f.*

into /'ɪntuː, *unstressed* 'ɪntə/ *prep.* (*put, go, fall, etc.*) dans; (*divide, translate, etc.*) en.

intolerable /ɪn'tɒlərəbl/ *a.* intolérable.

intoleran|t /ɪn'tɒlərənt/ *a.* intolérant. **~ce** *n.* intolérance *f.*

intonation /ɪntə'neɪʃn/ *n.* intonation *f.*

intoxicat|e /ɪn'tɒksɪkeɪt/ *v.t.* enivrer. **~ed** *a.* ivre. **~ion** /-'keɪʃn/ *n.* ivresse *f.*

intra- /'ɪntrə/ *pref.* intra-.

intractable /ɪn'træktəbl/ *a.* très difficile.

intransigent /ɪn'trænsɪdʒənt/ *a.* intransigeant.

intransitive /ɪn'trænsətɪv/ *a.* (*verb*) intransitif.

intravenous /ɪntrə'viːnəs/ *a.* (*med.*) intraveineux.

intrepid /ɪn'trepɪd/ *a.* intrépide.

intrica|te /'ɪntrɪkət/ *a.* complexe. **~cy** *n.* complexité *f.*

intrigu|e /ɪn'triːg/ *v.t./i.* intriguer. —*n.* intrigue *f.* **~ing** *a.* très intéressant; (*curious*) curieux.

intrinsic /ɪn'trɪnsɪk/ *a.* intrinsèque. **~ally** /-klɪ/ *adv.* intrinsèquement.

introduce /ɪntrə'djuːs/ *v.t.* (*bring in, insert*) introduire; (*programme, question*) présenter. **~ s.o. to,** (*person*) présenter qn. à.

introduct|ion /ɪntrə'dʌkʃn/ *n.*

introduction *f.*; (*to person*) présentation *f.* **~ory** /-tərɪ/ *a.* (*letter, words*) d'introduction.
introspective /ɪntrə'spektɪv/ *a.* introspectif.
introvert /'ɪntrəvɜːt/ *n.* introverti(e) *m.* (*f.*).
intru|de /ɪn'truːd/ *v.i.* (*person*) s'imposer (**on s.o.,** à qn.), déranger. **~der** *n.* intrus(e) *m.* (*f.*). **~sion** *n.* intrusion *f.*
intuit|ion /ɪntjuː'ɪʃn/ *n.* intuition *f.* **~ive** /ɪn'tjuːɪtɪv/ *a.* intuitif.
inundat|e /'ɪnʌndeɪt/ *v.t.* inonder. **~ion** /-'deɪʃn/ *n.* inondation *f.*
invade /ɪn'veɪd/ *v.t.* envahir. **~r** /-ə(r)/ *n.* envahisseu|r, -se *m., f.*
invalid[1] /'ɪnvəlɪd/ *n.* malade *m./f.*; (*disabled*) infirme *m./f.*
invalid[2] /ɪn'vælɪd/ *a.* non valable. **~ate** *v.t.* invalider.
invaluable /ɪn'væljʊəbl/ *a.* inestimable.
invariabl|e /ɪn'veərɪəbl/ *a.* invariable. **~y** *adv.* invariablement.
invasion /ɪn'veɪʒn/ *n.* invasion *f.*
invective /ɪn'vektɪv/ *n.* invective *f.*
inveigh /ɪn'veɪ/ *v.i.* invectiver.
inveigle /ɪn'veɪgl/ *v.t.* persuader.
invent /ɪn'vent/ *v.t.* inventer. **~ion** /-enʃn/ *n.* invention *f.* **~ive** *a.* inventif. **~or** *n.* inven|teur, -trice *m., f.*
inventory /'ɪnvəntrɪ/ *n.* inventaire *m.*
inverse /ɪn'vɜːs/ *a.* & *n.* inverse (*m.*). **~ly** *adv.* inversement.
inver|t /ɪn'vɜːt/ *v.t.* intervertir. **~ted commas,** guillemets *m. pl.* **~sion** *n.* inversion *f.*
invest /ɪn'vest/ *v.t.* investir; (*time, effort*: *fig.*) consacrer. —*v.i.* faire un investissement. **~ in,** (*buy*: *fam.*) se payer. **~ment** *n.* investissement *m.* **~or** *n.* actionnaire *m./f.*
investigat|e /ɪn'vestɪgeɪt/ *v.t.* étudier; (*crime etc.*) enquêter sur. **~ion** /-'geɪʃn/ *n.* investigation *f.* **under ~ion,** à l'étude. **~or** *n.* (*police*) enquêteu|r, -se *m., f.*
inveterate /ɪn'vetərət/ *a.* invétéré.
invidious /ɪn'vɪdɪəs/ *a.* (*hateful*) odieux; (*unfair*) injuste.
invigilat|e /ɪn'vɪdʒɪleɪt/ *v.i.* (*schol.*) être de surveillance. **~or** *n.* surveillant(e) *m.* (*f.*).
invigorate /ɪn'vɪgəreɪt/ *v.t.* vivifier; (*encourage*) stimuler.
invincible /ɪn'vɪnsəbl/ *a.* invincible.
invisible /ɪn'vɪzəbl/ *a.* invisible.
invit|e /ɪn'vaɪt/ *v.t.* inviter; (*ask for*) demander. **~ation** /ɪnvɪ'teɪʃn/ *n.* invitation *f.* **~ing** *a.* (*meal, smile, etc.*) engageant.
invoice /'ɪnvɔɪs/ *n.* facture *f.* —*v.t.* facturer.
invoke /ɪn'vəʊk/ *v.t.* invoquer.
involuntary /ɪn'vɒləntrɪ/ *a.* involontaire.
involve /ɪn'vɒlv/ *v.t.* entraîner. **~d** *a.* (*complex*) compliqué; (*at stake*) en jeu. **~d in,** mêlé à. **~ment** *n.* participation *f.* (**in,** à).
invulnerable /ɪn'vʌlnərəbl/ *a.* invulnérable.
inward /'ɪnwəd/ *a.* & *adv.* vers l'intérieur; (*feeling etc.*) intérieur. **~ly** *adv.* intérieurement. **~s** *adv.* vers l'intérieur.
iodine /'aɪədiːn/ *n.* iode *m.*; (*antiseptic*) teinture d'iode *f.*
iota /aɪ'əʊtə/ *n.* (*amount*) brin *m.*
IOU /aɪəʊ'juː/ *abbr.* (*I owe you*) reconnaissance de dette *f.*
IQ /aɪ'kjuː/ *abbr.* (*intelligence quotient*) QI *m.*
Iran /ɪ'rɑːn/ *n.* Iran *m.* **~ian** /ɪ'reɪnɪən/ *a.* & *n.* iranien(ne) (*m.* (*f.*)).
Iraq /ɪ'rɑːk/ *n.* Irak *m.* **~i** *a.* & *n.* irakien(ne) (*m.* (*f.*)).
irascible /ɪ'ræsəbl/ *a.* irascible.
irate /aɪ'reɪt/ *a.* en colère, furieux.
ire /'aɪə(r)/ *n.* courroux *m.*
Ireland /'aɪələnd/ *n.* Irlande *f.*
iris /'aɪərɪs/ *n.* (*anat., bot.*) iris *m.*

Irish /ˈaɪərɪʃ/ *a.* irlandais. —*n.* (*lang.*) irlandais *m.* **~man** *n.* Irlandais *m.* **~woman** *n.* Irlandaise *f.*

irk /ɜːk/ *v.t.* ennuyer. **~some** *a.* ennuyeux.

iron /ˈaɪən/ *n.* fer *m.*; (*appliance*) fer (à repasser) *m.* —*a.* de fer. —*v.t.* repasser. **I~ Curtain,** rideau de fer *m.* **~ out,** faire disparaître. **~ing-board** *n.* planche à repasser *f.*

ironic(al) /aɪˈrɒnɪk(l)/ *a.* ironique.

ironmonger /ˈaɪənmʌŋgə(r)/ *n.* quincaillier *m.* **~y** *n.* quincaillerie *f.*

ironwork /ˈaɪənwɜːk/ *n.* ferronnerie *f.*

irony /ˈaɪərənɪ/ *n.* ironie *f.*

irrational /ɪˈræʃənl/ *a.* irrationnel; (*person*) pas rationnel.

irreconcilable /ɪrekənˈsaɪləbl/ *a.* irréconciliable; (*incompatible*) inconciliable.

irrefutable /ɪˈrefjʊtəbl/ *a.* irréfutable.

irregular /ɪˈregjʊlə(r)/ *a.* irrégulier. **~ity** /-ˈlærətɪ/ *n.* irrégularité *f.*

irrelevan|t /ɪˈreləvənt/ *a.* sans rapport (**to,** avec). **~ce** *n.* manque de rapport *m.*

irreparable /ɪˈrepərəbl/ *a.* irréparable, irrémédiable.

irreplaceable /ɪrɪˈpleɪsəbl/ *a.* irremplaçable.

irrepressible /ɪrɪˈpresəbl/ *a.* irrépressible.

irresistible /ɪrɪˈzɪstəbl/ *a.* irrésistible.

irresolute /ɪˈrezəluːt/ *a.* irrésolu.

irrespective /ɪrɪˈspektɪv/ *a.* **~ of,** sans tenir compte de.

irresponsible /ɪrɪˈspɒnsəbl/ *a.* irresponsable.

irretrievable /ɪrɪˈtriːvəbl/ *a.* irréparable.

irreverent /ɪˈrevərənt/ *a.* irrévérencieux.

irreversible /ɪrɪˈvɜːsəbl/ *a.* irréversible; (*decision*) irrévocable.

irrevocable /ɪˈrevəkəbl/ *a.* irrévocable.

irrigat|e /ˈɪrɪgeɪt/ *v.t.* irriguer. **~ion** /-ˈgeɪʃn/ *n.* irrigation *f.*

irritable /ˈɪrɪtəbl/ *a.* irritable.

irritat|e /ˈɪrɪteɪt/ *v.t.* irriter. **~ion** /-ˈteɪʃn/ *n.* irritation *f.*

is /ɪz/ *see* **be.**

Islam /ˈɪzlɑːm/ *n.* Islam *m.* **~ic** /ɪzˈlæmɪk/ *a.* islamique.

island /ˈaɪlənd/ *n.* île *f.* **traffic ~,** refuge *m.* **~er** *n.* insulaire *m.*/*f.*

isle /aɪl/ *n.* île *f.*

isolat|e /ˈaɪsəleɪt/ *v.t.* isoler. **~ion** /-ˈleɪʃn/ *n.* isolement *m.*

isotope /ˈaɪsətəʊp/ *n.* isotope *m.*

Israel /ˈɪzreɪl/ *n.* Israël *m.* **~i** /ɪzˈreɪlɪ/ *a.* & *n.* israélien(ne) (*m.* (*f.*)).

issue /ˈɪʃuː/ *n.* question *f.*; (*outcome*) résultat *m.*; (*of magazine etc.*) numéro *m.*; (*of stamps etc.*) émission *f.*; (*offspring*) descendance *f.* —*v.t.* distribuer, donner; (*stamps etc.*) émettre; (*book*) publier. —*v.i.* **~ from,** sortir de. **at ~,** en cause. **take ~,** engager une controverse.

isthmus /ˈɪsməs/ *n.* isthme *m.*

it /ɪt/ *pron.* (*subject*) il, elle; (*object*) le, la, l'*; (*impersonal subject*) il; (*non-specific*) ce, c'*, cela, ça. **~ is,** (*quiet, my book, etc.*) c'est. **~ is cold/warm/late**/*etc.*, il fait froid/chaud/tard/*etc.* **that's ~,** c'est ça. **who is ~?,** qui est-ce? **of ~, from ~,** en. **in ~, at ~, to ~,** y.

italic /ɪˈtælɪk/ *a.* italique. **~s** *n. pl.* italique *m.*

Ital|y /ˈɪtəlɪ/ *n.* Italie *f.* **~ian** /ɪˈtælɪən/ *a.* & *n.* italien(ne) (*m.* (*f.*)); (*lang.*) italien *m.*

itch /ɪtʃ/ *n.* démangeaison *f.* —*v.i.* démanger. **my arm ~es,** mon bras me démange. **I am ~ing to,** ça me démange de. **~y** *a.* qui démange.

item /ˈaɪtəm/ *n.* article *m.*, chose *f.*; (*on agenda*) question *f.* **news ~,** fait divers *m.* **~ize** *v.t.* détailler.
itinerant /aɪˈtɪnərənt/ *a.* itinérant; (*musician, actor*) ambulant.
itinerary /aɪˈtɪnərərɪ/ *n.* itinéraire *m.*
its /ɪts/ *a.* son, sa, *pl.* ses.
it's /ɪts/ = **it is, it has.**
itself /ɪtˈself/ *pron.* lui-même, elle-même; (*reflexive*) se.
ivory /ˈaɪvərɪ/ *n.* ivoire *m.* **~ tower,** tour d'ivoire *f.*
ivy /ˈaɪvɪ/ *n.* lierre *m.*

J

jab /dʒæb/ *v.t.* (*p.t.* **jabbed**) (*thrust*) enfoncer; (*prick*) piquer. —*n.* coup *m.*; (*injection*) piqûre *f.*
jabber /ˈdʒæbə(r)/ *v.i.* jacasser, bavarder; (*indistinctly*) bredouiller. —*n.* bavardage *m.*
jack /dʒæk/ *n.* (*techn.*) cric *m.*; (*cards*) valet *m.* —*v.t.* **~ up,** soulever (avec un cric).
jackal /ˈdʒækɔːl/ *n.* chacal *m.*
jackass /ˈdʒækæs/ *n.* âne *m.*
jackdaw /ˈdʒækdɔː/ *n.* choucas *m.*
jacket /ˈdʒækɪt/ *n.* veste *f.*, veston *m.*; (*of book*) jaquette *f.*
jack-knife /ˈdʒæknaɪf/ *n.* couteau pliant *m.*—*v.i.* (*lorry*) faire un tête-à-queue.
jackpot /ˈdʒækpɒt/ *n.* gros lot *m.* **hit the ~,** gagner le gros lot.
jade /dʒeɪd/ *n.* (*stone*) jade *m.*
jaded /ˈdʒeɪdɪd/ *a.* blasé.
jagged /ˈdʒægɪd/ *a.* dentelé.
jail /dʒeɪl/ *n.* & *v.t.* = **gaol.**
jalopy /dʒəˈlɒpɪ/ *n.* vieux tacot *m.*
jam¹ /dʒæm/ *n.* confiture *f.*
jam² /dʒæm/ *v.t./i.* (*p.t.* **jammed**) (*wedge, become wedged*) coincer; (*cram*) (s')entasser; (*street etc.*) encombrer; (*thrust*) enfoncer; (*radio*) brouiller. —*n.* foule *f.*; (*of traffic*) embouteillage *m.*; (*situation: fam.*) pétrin *m.* **~-packed** *a.* (*fam.*) bourré.
Jamaica /dʒəˈmeɪkə/ *n.* Jamaïque *f.*
jangle /ˈdʒæŋgl/ *n.* cliquetis *m.* —*v.t./i.* (faire) cliqueter.
janitor /ˈdʒænɪtə(r)/ *n.* concierge *m.*
January /ˈdʒænjʊərɪ/ *n.* janvier *m.*
Japan /dʒəˈpæn/ *n.* Japon *m.* **~ese** /dʒæpəˈniːz/ *a.* & *n.* japonais(e) (*m.* (*f.*)); (*lang.*) japonais *m.*
jar¹ /dʒɑː(r)/ *n.* pot *m.*, bocal *m.*
jar² /dʒɑː(r)/ *v.i.* (*p.t.* **jarred**) grincer; (*of colours etc.*) détonner. —*v.t.* ébranler. —*n.* son discordant *m.* **~ring** *a.* discordant.
jar³ /dʒɑː(r)/ *n.* **on the ~,** (*ajar*) entrouvert.
jargon /ˈdʒɑːgən/ *n.* jargon *m.*
jasmine /ˈdʒæsmɪn/ *n.* jasmin *m.*
jaundice /ˈdʒɔːndɪs/ *n.* jaunisse *f.*
jaundiced /ˈdʒɔːndɪst/ *a.* (*envious*) envieux; (*bitter*) aigri.
jaunt /dʒɔːnt/ *n.* (*trip*) balade *f.*
jaunty /ˈdʒɔːntɪ/ *a.* (**-ier, -iest**) (*cheerful, sprightly*) allègre.
javelin /ˈdʒævlɪn/ *n.* javelot *m.*
jaw /dʒɔː/ *n.* mâchoire *f.* —*v.i.* (*talk: sl.*) jacasser.
jay /dʒeɪ/ *n.* geai *m.* **~-walk** *v.i.* traverser la chaussée imprudemment.
jazz /dʒæz/ *n.* jazz *m.* —*v.t.* **~ up,** animer. **~y** *a.* tape-à-l'œil *invar.*
jealous /ˈdʒeləs/ *a.* jaloux. **~y** *n.* jalousie *f.*
jeans /dʒiːnz/ *n. pl.* (blue-)jean *m.*
jeep /dʒiːp/ *n.* jeep *f.*
jeer /dʒɪə(r)/ *v.t./i.* **~ (at),** railler; (*boo*) huer. —*n.* raillerie *f.*; huée *f.*
jell /dʒel/ *v.i.* (*set: fam.*) prendre. **~ied** *a.* en gelée.
jelly /ˈdʒelɪ/ *n.* gelée *f.*
jellyfish /ˈdʒelɪfɪʃ/ *n.* méduse *f.*
jeopard|y /ˈdʒepədɪ/ *n.* péril *m.* **~ize** *v.t.* mettre en péril.
jerk /dʒɜːk/ *n.* secousse *f.*; (*fool: sl.*)

idiot *m.*; (*creep: sl.*) salaud *m.* —*v.t.* donner une secousse à. **~ily** *adv.* par saccades. **~y** *a.* saccadé.

jersey /ˈdʒɜːzɪ/ *n.* (*garment*) chandail *m.*, tricot *m.*; (*fabric*) jersey *m.*

jest /dʒest/ *n.* plaisanterie *f.* —*v.i.* plaisanter. **~er** *n.* bouffon *m.*

Jesus /ˈdʒiːzəs/ *n.* Jésus *m.*

jet[1] /dʒet/ *n.* (*mineral*) jais *m.* **~-black** *a.* de jais.

jet[2] /dʒet/ *n.* (*stream*) jet *m.*; (*plane*) avion à réaction *m.*, jet *m.* **~ lag**, fatigue due au décalage horaire *f.* **~-propelled** *a.* à réaction.

jettison /ˈdʒetɪsn/ *v.t.* jeter à la mer; (*aviat.*) larguer; (*fig.*) abandonner.

jetty /ˈdʒetɪ/ *n.* (*breakwater*) jetée *f.*

Jew /dʒuː/ *n.* Juif *m.* **~ess** *n.* Juive *f.*

jewel /ˈdʒuːəl/ *n.* bijou *m.* **~led** *a.* orné de bijoux. **~ler** *n.* bijout|ier, -ière *m.*, *f.* **~lery** *n.* bijoux *m. pl.*

Jewish /ˈdʒuːɪʃ/ *a.* juif.

Jewry /ˈdʒʊərɪ/ *n.* les Juifs *m. pl.*

jib /dʒɪb/ *v.i.* (*p.t.* **jibbed**) regimber (**at**, devant). —*n.* (*sail*) foc *m.*

jiffy /ˈdʒɪfɪ/ *n.* (*fam.*) instant *m.*

jig /dʒɪg/ *n.* (*dance*) gigue *f.*

jiggle /ˈdʒɪgl/ *v.t.* secouer légèrement.

jigsaw /ˈdʒɪgsɔː/ *n.* puzzle *m.*

jilt /dʒɪlt/ *v.t.* laisser tomber.

jingle /ˈdʒɪŋgl/ *v.t.*/*i.* (faire) tinter. —*n.* tintement *m.*

jinx /dʒɪŋks/ *n.* (*person: fam.*) porte-malheur *m. invar.*; (*spell: fig.*) mauvais sort *m.*

jitter|s /ˈdʒɪtəz/ *n. pl.* **the ~s**, (*fam.*) la frousse *f.* **~y** /-ərɪ/ *a.* **be ~y**, (*fam.*) avoir la frousse.

job /dʒɒb/ *n.* travail *m.*; (*post*) poste *m.* **have a ~ doing**, avoir du mal à faire. **it is a good ~ that**, heureusement que. **~less** *a.* sans travail, au chômage.

jobcentre /ˈdʒɒbsentə(r)/ *n.* agence (nationale) pour l'emploi *f.*

jockey /ˈdʒɒkɪ/ *n.* jockey *m.* —*v.i.* (*manœuvre*) manœuvrer.

jocular /ˈdʒɒkjʊlə(r)/ *a.* jovial.

jog /dʒɒg/ *v.t.* (*p.t.* **jogged**) pousser; (*memory*) rafraîchir. —*v.i.* faire du jogging. **~ging** *n.* jogging *m.*

join /dʒɔɪn/ *v.t.* joindre, unir; (*club*) devenir membre de; (*political group*) adhérer à; (*army*) s'engager dans. **~ s.o.**, (*in activity*) se joindre à qn.; (*meet*) rejoindre qn. —*v.i.* (*roads etc.*) se rejoindre. —*n.* joint *m.* **~ in**, participer (à). **~ up**, (*mil.*) s'engager.

joiner /ˈdʒɔɪnə(r)/ *n.* menuisier *m.*

joint /dʒɔɪnt/ *a.* commun. —*n.* (*join*) joint *m.*; (*anat.*) articulation *f.*; (*culin.*) rôti *m.*; (*place: sl.*) boîte *f.* **~ author**, coauteur *m.* **out of ~**, déboîté. **~ly** *adv.* conjointement.

joist /dʒɔɪst/ *n.* solive *f.*

jok|e /dʒəʊk/ *n.* plaisanterie *f.*; (*trick*) farce *f.* —*v.i.* plaisanter. **~er** *n.* blagueu|r, -se *m.*, *f.*; (*cards*) joker *m.* **~ingly** *adv.* pour rire.

joll|y /ˈdʒɒlɪ/ *a.* (**-ier, -iest**) gai. —*adv.* (*fam.*) rudement. **~ification** /-fɪˈkeɪʃn/, **~ity** *ns.* réjouissances *f. pl.*

jolt /dʒəʊlt/ *v.t.*/*i.* (*vehicle, passenger*) cahoter; (*shake*) secouer. —*n.* cahot *m.*; secousse *f.*

Jordan /ˈdʒɔːdn/ *n.* Jordanie *f.*

jostle /ˈdʒɒsl/ *v.t.*/*i.* (*push*) bousculer; (*push each other*) se bousculer.

jot /dʒɒt/ *n.* brin *m.* —*v.t.* (*p.t.* **jotted**) noter. **~ter** *n.* (*pad*) bloc-notes *m.*

journal /ˈdʒɜːnl/ *n.* journal *m.* **~ism** *n.* journalisme *m.* **~ist** *n.* journaliste *m.*/*f.* **~ese** /əˈliːz/ *n.* jargon des journalistes *m.*

journey /ˈdʒɜːnɪ/ *n.* voyage *m.*; (*distance*) trajet *m.* —*v.i.* voyager.

jovial /ˈdʒəʊvɪəl/ *a.* jovial.

joy /dʒɔɪ/ *n.* joie *f.* **~-ride** *n.* balade

en voiture *f.* **~ful, ~ous** *adjs.* joyeux.
jubil|ant /'dʒuːbɪlənt/ *a.* débordant de joie. **be ~ant,** jubiler. **~ation** /-'leɪʃn/ *n.* jubilation *f.*
jubilee /'dʒuːbɪliː/ *n.* jubilé *m.*
Judaism /'dʒuːdeɪɪzəm/ *n.* judaïsme *m.*
judder /'dʒʌdə(r)/ *v.i.* vibrer. —*n.* vibration *f.*
judge /dʒʌdʒ/ *n.* juge *m.* —*v.t.* juger. **~ment** *n.* jugement *m.*
judic|iary /dʒuː'dɪʃərɪ/ *n.* magistrature *f.* **~ial** *a.* judiciaire.
judicious /dʒuː'dɪʃəs/ *a.* judicieux.
judo /'dʒuːdəʊ/ *n.* judo *m.*
jug /dʒʌg/ *n.* cruche *f.*, pichet *m.*
juggernaut /'dʒʌgənɔːt/ *n.* (*lorry*) poids lourd *m.*, mastodonte *m.*
juggle /'dʒʌgl/ *v.t./i.* jongler (avec). **~r** /-ə(r)/ *n.* jongleu|r, -se *m., f.*
juic|e /dʒuːs/ *n.* jus *m.* **~y** *a.* juteux; (*details etc.: fam.*) croustillant.
juke-box /'dʒuːkbɒks/ *n.* juke-box *m.*
July /dʒuː'laɪ/ *n.* juillet *m.*
jumble /'dʒʌmbl/ *v.t.* mélanger. —*n.* (*muddle*) mélange *m.* **~ sale,** vente (de charité) *f.*
jumbo /'dʒʌmbəʊ/ *a.* **~ jet,** avion géant *m.*, jumbo-jet *m.*
jump /dʒʌmp/ *v.t./i.* sauter; (*start*) sursauter; (*of price etc.*) faire un bond. —*n.* saut *m.*; sursaut *m.*; (*increase*) hausse *f.* **~ at,** sauter sur. **~ the gun,** agir prématurément. **~ the queue,** resquiller.
jumper /'dʒʌmpə(r)/ *n.* pull(-over) *m.*; (*dress: Amer.*) robe chasuble *f.*
jumpy /'dʒʌmpɪ/ *a.* nerveux.
junction /'dʒʌŋkʃn/ *n.* jonction *f.*; (*of roads etc.*) embranchement *m.*
juncture /'dʒʌŋktʃə(r)/ *n.* moment *m.*; (*state of affairs*) conjoncture *f.*
June /dʒuːn/ *n.* juin *m.*
jungle /'dʒʌŋgl/ *n.* jungle *f.*
junior /'dʒuːnɪə(r)/ *a.* (*in age*) plus jeune (**to,** que); (*in rank*) subalterne; (*school*) élémentaire; (*executive, doctor*) jeune. —*n.* cadet(te) *m.* (*f.*); (*schol.*) petit(e) élève *m./f.*; (*sport*) junior *m./f.*
junk /dʒʌŋk/ *n.* bric-à-brac *m. invar.*; (*poor material*) camelote *f.* —*v.t.* (*Amer., sl.*) balancer. **~-shop** *n.* boutique de brocanteur *f.*
junkie /'dʒʌŋkɪ/ *n.* (*sl.*) drogué(e) *m.* (*f.*).
junta /'dʒʌntə/ *n.* junte *f.*
jurisdiction /dʒʊərɪs'dɪkʃn/ *n.* juridiction *f.*
jurisprudence /dʒʊərɪs'pruːdəns/ *n.* jurisprudence *f.*
juror /'dʒʊərə(r)/ *n.* juré *m.*
jury /'dʒʊərɪ/ *n.* jury *m.*
just /dʒʌst/ *a.* (*fair*) juste. —*adv.* juste, exactement; (*only, slightly*) juste; (*simply*) tout simplement. **he has/had ~ left**/*etc.*, il vient/venait de partir/*etc.* **have ~ missed,** avoir manqué de peu. **~ as tall**/*etc.*, tout aussi grand/*etc.* (**as,** que). **~ listen!,** écoutez donc! **~ly** *adv.* avec justice.
justice /'dʒʌstɪs/ *n.* justice *f.* **J~ of the Peace,** juge de paix *m.*
justifiabl|e /dʒʌstɪ'faɪəbl/ *a.* justifiable. **~y** *adv.* avec raison.
justif|y /'dʒʌstɪfaɪ/ *v.t.* justifier. **~ication** /-ɪ'keɪʃn/ *n.* justification *f.*
jut /dʒʌt/ *v.i.* (*p.t.* **jutted**). **~ out,** faire saillie, dépasser.
juvenile /'dʒuːvənaɪl/ *a.* (*youthful*) juvénile; (*childish*) puéril; (*delinquent*) jeune; (*court*) pour enfants. —*n.* jeune *m./f.*
juxtapose /dʒʌkstə'pəʊz/ *v.t.* juxtaposer.

K

kaleidoscope /kə'laɪdəskəʊp/ *n.* kaléidoscope *m.*

kangaroo /kæŋgəˈruː/ *n.* kangourou *m.*
karate /kəˈrɑːtɪ/ *n.* karaté *m.*
kebab /kəˈbæb/ *n.* brochette *f.*
keel /kiːl/ *n.* (*of ship*) quille *f.* —*v.i.* **~ over,** chavirer.
keen /kiːn/ *a.* (**-er, -est**) (*interest, wind, feeling, etc.*) vif; (*mind, analysis*) pénétrant; (*edge, appetite*) aiguisé; (*eager*) enthousiaste. **be ~ on,** (*person, thing*: *fam.*) aimer beaucoup. **be ~ to do** *or* **on doing,** tenir beaucoup à faire. **~ly** *adv.* vivement; avec enthousiasme. **~ness** *n.* vivacité *f.*; enthousiasme *m.*
keep /kiːp/ *v.t.* (*p.t.* **kept**) garder; (*promise, shop, etc.*) tenir; (*family*) entretenir; (*animals*) élever; (*rule etc.*) respecter; (*celebrate*) célébrer; (*delay*) retenir; (*prevent*) empêcher; (*conceal*) cacher. —*v.i.* (*food*) se garder; (*remain*) rester. **~ (on),** continuer (**doing, à** faire). —*n.* subsistance *f.*; (*of castle*) donjon *m.* **for ~s,** (*fam.*) pour toujours. **~ back** *v.t.* retenir; *v.i.* ne pas s'approcher. **~ in/out,** empêcher d'entrer/de sortir. **~ up,** (se) maintenir. **~ up (with),** suivre. **~er** *n.* gardien(ne) *m.* (*f.*).
keeping /ˈkiːpɪŋ/ *n.* garde *f.* **in ~ with,** en accord avec.
keepsake /ˈkiːpseɪk/ *n.* (*thing*) souvenir *m.*
keg /keg/ *n.* tonnelet *m.*
kennel /ˈkenl/ *n.* niche *f.*
Kenya /ˈkenjə/ *n.* Kenya *m.*
kept /kept/ *see* **keep.**
kerb /kɜːb/ *n.* bord du trottoir *m.*
kerfuffle /kəˈfʌfl/ *n.* (*fuss*: *fam.*) histoire(s) *f.* (*pl.*).
kernel /ˈkɜːnl/ *n.* amande *f.*
kerosene /ˈkerəsiːn/ *n.* (*aviation fuel*) kérosène *m.*; (*paraffin*) pétrole (lampant) *m.*
ketchup /ˈketʃəp/ *n.* ketchup *m.*
kettle /ˈketl/ *n.* bouilloire *f.*
key /kiː/ *n.* clef *f.*; (*of piano etc.*) touche *f.* —*a.* clef (*f. invar.*). **~-ring** *n.* porte-clefs *m. invar.* —*v.t.* **~ up,** surexciter.
keyboard /ˈkiːbɔːd/ *n.* clavier *m.*
keyhole /ˈkiːhəʊl/ *n.* trou de la serrure *m.*
keynote /ˈkiːnəʊt/ *n.* (*of speech etc.*) note dominante *f.*
keystone /ˈkiːstəʊn/ *n.* (*archit., fig.*) clef de voûte *f.*
khaki /ˈkɑːkɪ/ *a.* kaki *invar.*
kibbutz /kɪˈbʊts/ *n.* (*pl.* **-im** /-iːm/) *n.* kibboutz *m.*
kick /kɪk/ *v.t./i.* donner un coup de pied (à); (*of horse*) ruer. —*n.* coup de pied *m.*; ruade *f.*; (*of gun*) recul *m.*; (*thrill*: *fam.*) (malin) plaisir *m.* **~-off** *n.* coup d'envoi *m.* **~ out,** (*fam.*) flanquer dehors. **~ up,** (*fuss, racket*: *fam.*) faire.
kid /kɪd/ *n.* (*goat, leather*) chevreau *m.*; (*child*: *sl.*) gosse *m./f.* —*v.t./i.* (*p.t.* **kidded**) blaguer.
kidnap /ˈkɪdnæp/ *v.t.* (*p.t.* **kidnapped**) enlever, kidnapper. **~ping** *n.* enlèvement *m.*
kidney /ˈkɪdnɪ/ *n.* rein *m.*; (*culin.*) rognon *m.*
kill /kɪl/ *v.t.* tuer; (*fig.*) mettre fin à. —*n.* mise à mort *f.* **~er** *n.* tueu|r, -se *m., f.* **~ing** *n.* massacre *m.*, meurtre *m.*; *a.* (*funny*: *fam.*) tordant; (*tiring*: *fam.*) tuant.
killjoy /ˈkɪldʒɔɪ/ *n.* rabat-joie *m. invar.*, trouble-fête *m./f. invar.*
kiln /kɪln/ *n.* four *m.*
kilo /ˈkiːləʊ/ *n.* (*pl.* **-os**) kilo *m.*
kilogram /ˈkɪləgræm/ *n.* kilogramme *m.*
kilohertz /ˈkɪləhɜːts/ *n.* kilohertz *m.*
kilometre /ˈkɪləmiːtə(r)/ *n.* kilomètre *m.*
kilowatt /ˈkɪləwɒt/ *n.* kilowatt *m.*
kilt /kɪlt/ *n.* kilt *m.*
kin /kɪn/ *n.* parents *m. pl.*
kind[1] /kaɪnd/ *n.* genre *m.*, sorte *f.*, espèce *f.* **in ~,** en nature *f.* **~ of,**

(*somewhat*: *fam.*) un peu. **be two of a ~,** se rassembler.

kind² /kaɪnd/ *a.* (**-er, -est**) gentil, bon. **~-hearted** *a.* bon. **~ness** *n.* bonté *f.*

kindergarten /'kɪndəgɑːtn/ *n.* jardin d'enfants *m.*

kindle /'kɪndl/ *v.t./i.* (s')allumer.

kindly /'kaɪndlɪ/ *a.* (**-ier, -iest**) bienveillant. —*adv.* avec bonté. **~ wait**/*etc.*, voulez-vous avoir la bonté d'attendre/*etc.*

kindred /'kɪndrɪd/ *a.* apparenté. **~ spirit,** personne qui a les mêmes goûts *f.*, âme sœur *f.*

kinetic /kɪ'netɪk/ *a.* cinétique.

king /kɪŋ/ *n.* roi *m.* **~-size(d)** *a.* extra-long, géant.

kingdom /'kɪŋdəm/ *n.* royaume *m.*; (*bot.*) règne *m.*

kink /kɪŋk/ *n.* (*in rope*) entortillement *m.*, déformation *f.*; (*fig.*) perversion *f.* **~y** *a.* (*fam.*) perverti.

kiosk /'kiːɒsk/ *n.* kiosque *m.* **telephone ~,** cabine téléphonique *f.*

kip /kɪp/ *n.* (*sl.*) roupillon *m.* —*v.i.* (*p.t.* **kipped**) (*sl.*) roupiller.

kipper /'kɪpə(r)/ *n.* hareng fumé *m.*

kiss /kɪs/ *n.* baiser *m.* —*v.t./i.* (s')embrasser.

kit /kɪt/ *n.* équipement *m.*; (*clothing*) affaires *f. pl.*; (*set of tools etc.*) trousse *f.*; (*for assembly*) kit *m.* —*v.t.* (*p.t.* **kitted**). **~ out,** équiper.

kitbag /'kɪtbæg/ *n.* sac *m.* (*de marin etc.*).

kitchen /'kɪtʃɪn/ *n.* cuisine *f.* **~ garden,** jardin potager *m.*

kitchenette /kɪtʃɪ'net/ *n.* kitchenette *f.*

kite /kaɪt/ *n.* (*toy*) cerf-volant *m.*

kith /kɪθ/ *n.* **~ and kin,** parents et amis *m. pl.*

kitten /'kɪtn/ *n.* chaton *m.*

kitty /'kɪtɪ/ *n.* (*fund*) cagnotte *f.*

knack /næk/ *n.* truc *m.*, chic *m.*

knapsack /'næpsæk/ *n.* sac à dos *m.*

knave /neɪv/ *n.* (*cards*) valet *m.*

knead /niːd/ *v.t.* pétrir.

knee /niː/ *n.* genou *m.* **~s-up** *n.* (*fam.*) fête *f.*, soirée (dansante) *f.*

kneecap /'niːkæp/ *n.* rotule *f.*

kneel /niːl/ *v.i.* (*p.t.* **knelt**). **~ (down),** s'agenouiller.

knell /nel/ *n.* glas *m.*

knew /njuː/ *see* **know.**

knickers /'nɪkəz/ *n. pl.* (*woman's undergarment*) culotte *f.*, slip *m.*

knife /naɪf/ *n.* (*pl.* **knives**) couteau *m.* —*v.t.* poignarder.

knight /naɪt/ *n.* chevalier *m.*; (*chess*) cavalier *m.* —*v.t.* faire *or* armer chevalier. **~hood** *n.* titre de chevalier *m.*

knit /nɪt/ *v.t./i.* (*p.t.* **knitted** *or* **knit**) tricoter; (*bones etc.*) (se) souder. **~ one's brow,** froncer les sourcils. **~ting** *n.* tricot *m.*

knitwear /'nɪtweə(r)/ *n.* tricots *m. pl.*

knob /nɒb/ *n.* bouton *m.*

knock /nɒk/ *v.t./i.* frapper, cogner; (*criticize*: *sl.*) critiquer. —*n.* coup *m.* **~ about** *v.t.* malmener; *v.i.* vadrouiller. **~ down,** (*chair, pedestrian*) renverser; (*demolish*) abattre; (*reduce*) baisser. **~-down** *a.* (*price*) très bas. **~-kneed** *a.* cagneux. **~ off** *v.t.* faire tomber; (*fam.*) expédier; *v.i.* (*fam.*) s'arrêter de travailler. **~ out,** (*by blow*) assommer; (*tire*) épuiser. **~-out** *n.* (*boxing*) knock-out *m.* **~ over,** renverser. **~ up,** (*meal etc.*) préparer en vitesse. **~er** *n.* heurtoir *m.*

knot /nɒt/ *n.* nœud *m.* —*v.t.* (*p.t.* **knotted**) nouer. **~ty** /'nɒtɪ/ *a.* noueux; (*problem*) épineux.

know /nəʊ/ *v.t./i.* (*p.t.* **knew,** *p.p.* **known**) savoir (**that,** que); (*person, place*) connaître. —*n.* **in the ~,** (*fam.*) dans le secret, au courant. **~ about,** (*cars etc.*) s'y connaître en. **~-all,** (*Amer.*) **~-it-all** *n.* je-sais-tout *m./f.* **~-how**

n. technique *f.* ~ **of,** connaître, avoir entendu parler de. **~ingly** *adv.* (*consciously*) sciemment.
knowledge /ˈnɒlɪdʒ/ *n.* connaissance *f.*; (*learning*) connaissances *f. pl.* **~able** *a.* bien informé.
known /nəʊn/ *see* **know.** —*a.* connu; (*recognized*) reconnu.
knuckle /ˈnʌkl/ *n.* articulation du doigt *f.* —*v.i.* ~ **under,** céder.
Koran /kəˈrɑːn/ *n.* Coran *m.*
Korea /kəˈrɪə/ *n.* Corée *f.*
kosher /ˈkəʊʃə(r)/ *a.* kascher *invar.*
kowtow /kaʊˈtaʊ/ *v.i.* se prosterner (**to,** devant).
kudos /ˈkjuːdɒs/ *n.* (*fam.*) gloire *f.*

L

lab /læb/ *n.* (*fam.*) labo *m.*
label /ˈleɪbl/ *n.* étiquette *f.* —*v.t.* (*p.t.* **labelled**) étiqueter.
laboratory /ləˈbɒrətrɪ, *Amer.* ˈlæbrətɔːrɪ/ *n.* laboratoire *m.*
laborious /ləˈbɔːrɪəs/ *a.* laborieux.
labour /ˈleɪbə(r)/ *n.* travail *m.*; (*workers*) main-d'œuvre *f.* —*v.i.* peiner. —*v.t.* insister sur. **in** ~, en train d'accoucher, en couches. **~ed** *a.* laborieux.
Labour /ˈleɪbə(r)/ *n.* le parti travailliste *m.* —*a.* travailliste.
labourer /ˈleɪbərə(r)/ *n.* manœuvre *m.*; (*on farm*) ouvrier agricole *m.*
labyrinth /ˈlæbərɪnθ/ *n.* labyrinthe *m.*
lace /leɪs/ *n.* dentelle *f.*; (*of shoe*) lacet *m.* —*v.t.* (*fasten*) lacer; (*drink*) arroser.
lacerate /ˈlæsəreɪt/ *v.t.* lacérer.
lack /læk/ *n.* manque *m.* —*v.t.* manquer de. **be ~ing,** manquer (**in,** de). **for** ~ **of,** à défaut de.
lackadaisical /lækəˈdeɪzɪkl/ *a.* indolent, apathique.
lackey /ˈlækɪ/ *n.* laquais *m.*
laconic /ləˈkɒnɪk/ *a.* laconique.
lacquer /ˈlækə(r)/ *n.* laque *f.*
lad /læd/ *n.* garçon *m.*, gars *m.*
ladder /ˈlædə(r)/ *n.* échelle *f.*; (*in stocking*) maille filée *f.* —*v.t./i.* (*stocking*) filer.
laden /ˈleɪdn/ *a.* chargé (**with,** de).
ladle /ˈleɪdl/ *n.* louche *f.*
lady /ˈleɪdɪ/ *n.* dame *f.* ~ **friend,** amie *f.* **~-in-waiting** *n.* dame d'honneur *f.* **young** ~, jeune femme *or* fille *f.* **~like** *a.* distingué.
lady|bird /ˈleɪdɪbɜːd/ *n.* coccinelle *f.* **~bug** *n.* (*Amer.*) coccinelle *f.*
lag[1] /læg/ *v.i.* (*p.t.* **lagged**) traîner. —*n.* (*interval*) décalage *m.*
lag[2] /læg/ *v.t.* (*p.t.* **lagged**) (*pipes*) calorifuger.
lager /ˈlɑːgə(r)/ *n.* bière blonde *f.*
lagoon /ləˈguːn/ *n.* lagune *f.*
laid /leɪd/ *see* **lay**[2].
lain /leɪn/ *see* **lie**[2].
lair /leə(r)/ *n.* tanière *f.*
laity /ˈleɪətɪ/ *n.* laïques *m. pl.*
lake /leɪk/ *n.* lac *m.*
lamb /læm/ *n.* agneau *m.*
lambswool /ˈlæmzwʊl/ *n.* laine d'agneau *f.*
lame /leɪm/ *a.* (**-er, -est**) boiteux; (*excuse*) faible. **~ly** *adv.* (*argue*) sans conviction.
lament /ləˈment/ *n.* lamentation *f.* —*v.t./i.* se lamenter (sur). **~able** *a.* lamentable.
laminated /ˈlæmɪneɪtɪd/ *a.* laminé.
lamp /læmp/ *n.* lampe *f.*
lamppost /ˈlæmppəʊst/ *n.* réverbère *m.*
lampshade /ˈlæmpʃeɪd/ *n.* abat-jour *m. invar.*
lance /lɑːns/ *n.* lance *f.* —*v.t.* (*med.*) inciser.
lancet /ˈlɑːnsɪt/ *n.* bistouri *m.*
land /lænd/ *n.* terre *f.*; (*plot*) terrain *m.*; (*country*) pays *m.* —*a.* terrestre; (*policy, reform*) agraire. —*v.t./i.* débarquer; (*aircraft*) (se)

poser, (faire) atterrir; (*fall*) tomber; (*obtain*) décrocher; (*put*) mettre; (*a blow*) porter. **~-locked** *a.* sans accès à la mer. **~ up,** se retrouver.
landed /ˈlændɪd/ *a.* foncier.
landing /ˈlændɪŋ/ *n.* débarquement *m.*; (*aviat.*) atterrissage *m.*; (*top of stairs*) palier *m.* **~-stage** *n.* débarcadère *m.*
land|lady /ˈlændleɪdɪ/ *n.* propriétaire *f.*; (*of inn*) patronne *f.* **~lord** *n.* propriétaire *m.*; patron *m.*
landmark /ˈlændmɑːk/ *n.* (point de) repère *m.*
landscape /ˈlæn(d)skeɪp/ *n.* paysage *m.* —*v.t.* aménager.
landslide /ˈlændslaɪd/ *n.* glissement de terrain *m.*; (*pol.*) raz-de-marée (électoral) *m. invar.*
lane /leɪn/ *n.* (*path, road*) chemin *m.*; (*strip of road*) voie *f.*; (*of traffic*) file *f.*; (*aviat.*) couloir *m.*
language /ˈlæŋgwɪdʒ/ *n.* langue *f.*; (*speech, style*) langage *m.*
languid /ˈlæŋgwɪd/ *a.* languissant.
languish /ˈlæŋgwɪʃ/ *v.i.* languir.
lank /læŋk/ *a.* grand et maigre.
lanky /ˈlæŋkɪ/ *a.* (**-ier, -iest**) dégingandé, grand et maigre.
lantern /ˈlæntən/ *n.* lanterne *f.*
lap[1] /læp/ *n.* genoux *m. pl.*; (*sport*) tour (de piste) *m.* —*v.t./i.* (*p.t.* **lapped**). **~ over,** (se) chevaucher.
lap[2] /læp/ *v.t.* (*p.t.* **lapped**). **~ up,** laper. —*v.i.* (*waves*) clapoter.
lapel /ləˈpel/ *n.* revers *m.*
lapse /læps/ *v.i.* (*decline*) se dégrader; (*expire*) se périmer. —*n.* défaillance *f.*, erreur *f.*; (*of time*) intervalle *m.* **~ into,** retomber dans.
larceny /ˈlɑːsənɪ/ *n.* vol simple *m.*
lard /lɑːd/ *n.* saindoux *m.*
larder /ˈlɑːdə(r)/ *n.* garde-manger *m. invar.*
large /lɑːdʒ/ *a.* (**-er, -est**) grand, gros. **at ~,** en liberté; (*as a whole*) en général. **~ly** *adv.* en grande mesure. **~ness** *n.* grandeur *f.*
lark[1] /lɑːk/ *n.* (*bird*) alouette *f.*
lark[2] /lɑːk/ *n.* (*bit of fun: fam.*) rigolade *f.* —*v.i.* (*fam.*) rigoler.
larva /ˈlɑːvə/ *n.* (*pl.* **-vae** /-viː/) larve *f.*
laryngitis /lærɪnˈdʒaɪtɪs/ *n.* laryngite *f.*
larynx /ˈlærɪŋks/ *n.* larynx *m.*
lascivious /ləˈsɪvɪəs/ *a.* lascif.
laser /ˈleɪzə(r)/ *n.* laser *m.*
lash /læʃ/ *v.t.* fouetter. —*n.* coup de fouet *m.*; (*eyelash*) cil *m.* **~ out,** (*spend*) dépenser follement. **~ out against,** attaquer.
lashings /ˈlæʃɪŋz/ *n. pl.* **~ of,** (*cream etc.: sl.*) des masses de.
lass /læs/ *n.* jeune fille *f.*
lasso /læˈsuː/ *n.* (*pl.* **-os**) lasso *m.*
last[1] /lɑːst/ *a.* dernier. —*adv.* en dernier; (*most recently*) la dernière fois. —*n.* dern|ier, -ière *m.*, *f.*; (*remainder*) reste *m.* **at (long) ~,** enfin. **~ night,** hier soir. **the ~ straw,** le comble. **the ~ word,** le mot de la fin. **on its ~ legs,** sur le point de rendre l'âme. **~ly** *adv.* en dernier lieu.
last[2] /lɑːst/ *v.i.* durer. **~ing** *a.* durable.
latch /lætʃ/ *n.* loquet *m.*
late /leɪt/ *a.* (**-er, -est**) (*not on time*) en retard; (*recent*) récent; (*former*) ancien; (*hour, fruit, etc.*) tardif; (*deceased*) défunt. **the late Mrs X,** feu Mme X. **~st** /-ɪst/, (*last*) dernier. —*adv.* (*not early*) tard; (*not on time*) en retard. **in ~ July,** fin juillet. **of ~,** dernièrement. **~ness** *n.* retard *m.*; (*of event*) heure tardive *f.*
lately /ˈleɪtlɪ/ *adv.* dernièrement.
latent /ˈleɪtnt/ *a.* latent.
lateral /ˈlætərəl/ *a.* latéral.
lathe /leɪð/ *n.* tour *m.*
lather /ˈlɑːðə(r)/ *n.* mousse *f.* —*v.t.* savonner. —*v.i.* mousser.

Latin /ˈlætɪn/ *n.* (*lang.*) latin *m.* —*a.* latin.
latitude /ˈlætɪtjuːd/ *n.* latitude *f.*
latrine /ləˈtriːn/ *n.* latrines *f. pl.*
latter /ˈlætə(r)/ *a.* dernier. —*n.* **the ~,** celui-ci, celle-ci. **~-day** *a.* moderne. **~ly** *adv.* dernièrement.
lattice /ˈlætɪs/ *n.* treillage *m.*
laudable /ˈlɔːdəbl/ *a.* louable.
laugh /lɑːf/ *v.i.* rire (**at,** de). —*n.* rire *m.* **~able** *a.* ridicule. **~ing-stock** *n.* objet de risée *m.*
laughter /ˈlɑːftə(r)/ *n.* (*act*) rire *m.*; (*sound of laughs*) rires *m. pl.*
launch¹ /lɔːntʃ/ *v.t.* lancer. —*n.* lancement *m.* **~ (out) into,** se lancer dans.
launch² /lɔːntʃ/ *n.* (*boat*) vedette *f.*
laund|er /ˈlɔːndə(r)/ *v.t.* blanchir. **~ress** *n.* blanchisseuse *f.*
launderette /lɔːnˈdret/ *n.* laverie automatique *f.*
laundry /ˈlɔːndrɪ/ *n.* (*place*) blanchisserie *f.*; (*clothes*) linge *m.*
laurel /ˈlɒrəl/ *n.* laurier *m.*
lava /ˈlɑːvə/ *n.* lave *f.*
lavatory /ˈlævətrɪ/ *n.* cabinets *m. pl.*
lavender /ˈlævəndə(r)/ *n.* lavande *f.*
lavish /ˈlævɪʃ/ *a.* (*person*) prodigue; (*plentiful*) copieux; (*lush*) somptueux. —*v.t.* prodiguer (**on,** à). **~ly** *adv.* copieusement.
law /lɔː/ *n.* loi *f.*; (*profession, subject of study*) droit *m.* **~-abiding** *a.* respectueux des lois. **~ and order,** l'ordre public. **~ful** *a.* légal. **~fully** *adv.* légalement. **~less** *a.* sans loi.
lawcourt /ˈlɔːkɔːt/ *n.* tribunal *m.*
lawn /lɔːn/ *n.* pelouse *f.*, gazon *m.* **~-mower** *n.* tondeuse à gazon *f.* **~ tennis,** tennis (sur gazon) *m.*
lawsuit /ˈlɔːsuːt/ *n.* procès *m.*
lawyer /ˈlɔːjə(r)/ *n.* avocat *m.*
lax /læks/ *a.* négligent; (*morals etc.*) relâché. **~ity** *n.* négligence *f.*
laxative /ˈlæksətɪv/ *n.* laxatif *m.*
lay¹ /leɪ/ *a.* (*non-clerical*) laïque; (*opinion etc.*) d'un profane.
lay² /leɪ/ *v.t.* (*p.t.* **laid**) poser, mettre; (*trap*) tendre; (*table*) mettre; (*plan*) former; (*eggs*) pondre. —*v.i.* pondre. **~ down,** (dé)poser; (*condition*) (im)poser. **~ hold of,** saisir. **~ off** *v.t.* (*worker*) licencier; *v.i.* (*fam.*) arrêter. **~-off** *n.* licenciement *m.* **~ on,** (*provide*) fournir. **~ out,** (*design*) dessiner; (*display*) disposer; (*money*) dépenser. **~ up,** (*store*) amasser. **~ waste,** ravager.
lay³ /leɪ/ *see* **lie**².
layabout /ˈleɪəbaʊt/ *n.* fainéant(e) *m.* (*f.*).
lay-by /ˈleɪbaɪ/ *n.* (*pl.* **-bys**) petite aire de stationnement *f.*
layer /ˈleɪə(r)/ *n.* couche *f.*
layman /ˈleɪmən/ *n.* (*pl.* **-men**) profane *m.*
layout /ˈleɪaʊt/ *n.* disposition *f.*
laze /leɪz/ *v.i.* paresser.
laz|y /ˈleɪzɪ/ *a.* (**-ier, -iest**) paresseux. **~iness** *n.* paresse *f.* **~y-bones** *n.* flemmard(e) *m.* (*f.*).
lead¹ /liːd/ *v.t./i.* (*p.t.* **led**) mener; (*team etc.*) diriger; (*life*) mener; (*induce*) amener. **~ to,** conduire à, mener à. —*n.* avance *f.*; (*clue*) indice *m.*; (*leash*) laisse *f.*; (*theatre*) premier rôle *m.*; (*wire*) fil *m.*; (*example*) exemple *m.* **in the ~,** en tête. **~ away,** emmener. **~ up to,** (*come to*) en venir à; (*precede*) précéder.
lead² /led/ *n.* plomb *m.*; (*of pencil*) mine *f.* **~en** *a.* de plomb.
leader /ˈliːdə(r)/ *n.* chef *m.*; (*of country, club, etc.*) dirigeant(e) *m.* (*f.*); (*leading article*) éditorial *m.* **~ship** *n.* direction *f.*
leading /ˈliːdɪŋ/ *a.* principal. **~ article,** éditorial *m.*
leaf /liːf/ *n.* (*pl.* **leaves**) feuille *f.*; (*of table*) rallonge *f.* —*v.i.* **~ through,** feuilleter. **~y** *a.* feuillu.

leaflet /'li:flɪt/ *n.* prospectus *m.*
league /li:g/ *n.* ligue *f.*; (*sport*) championnat *m.* **in ~ with,** de mèche avec.
leak /li:k/ *n.* fuite *f.* —*v.i.* fuir; (*news*: *fig.*) s'ébruiter. —*v.t.* répandre; (*fig.*) divulguer. **~age** *n.* fuite *f.* **~y** *a.* qui a une fuite.
lean[1] /li:n/ *a.* (**-er, -est**) maigre. —*n.* (*of meat*) maigre *m.* **~ness** *n.* maigreur *f.*
lean[2] /li:n/ *v.t./i.* (*p.t.* **leaned** *or* **leant** /lent/) (*rest*) (s')appuyer; (*slope*) pencher. **~ over,** (*of person*) se pencher. **~-to** *n.* appentis *m.*
leaning /'li:nɪŋ/ *a.* penché. —*n.* tendance *f.*
leap /li:p/ *v.i.* (*p.t.* **leaped** *or* **leapt** /lept/) bondir. —*n.* bond *m.* **~-frog** *n.* saute-mouton *m. invar.*; *v.i.* (*p.t.* **-frogged**) sauter (**over,** par-dessus). **~ year,** année bissextile *f.*
learn /lɜ:n/ *v.t./i.* (*p.t.* **learned** *or* **learnt**) apprendre (**to do,** à faire). **~er** *n.* débutant(e) *m.* (*f.*).
learn|ed /'lɜ:nɪd/ *a.* érudit. **~ing** *n.* érudition *f.*, connaissances *f. pl.*
lease /li:s/ *n.* bail *m.* —*v.t.* louer à bail.
leash /li:ʃ/ *n.* laisse *f.*
least /li:st/ *a.* **the ~,** (*smallest amount of*) le moins de; (*slightest*) le *or* la moindre. —*n.* le moins. —*adv.* le moins; (*with adjective*) le *or* la moins. **at ~,** au moins.
leather /'leðə(r)/ *n.* cuir *m.*
leave /li:v/ *v.t.* (*p.t.* **left**) laisser; (*depart from*) quitter. —*n.* (*holiday*) congé *m.*; (*consent*) permission *f.* **be left (over),** rester. **~ alone,** (*thing*) ne pas toucher à; (*person*) laisser tranquille. **~ out,** omettre. **on ~,** (*mil.*) en permission. **take one's ~,** prendre congé (**of,** de).
leavings /'li:vɪŋz/ *n. pl.* restes *m. pl.*
Leban|on /'lebənən/ *n.* Liban *m.* **~ese** /-'ni:z/ *a.* & *n.* libanais(e) (*m.* (*f.*)).
lecher /'letʃə(r)/ *n.* débauché *m.* **~ous** *a.* lubrique. **~y** *n.* lubricité *f.*
lectern /'lektən/ *n.* lutrin *m.*
lecture /'lektʃə(r)/ *n.* cours *m.*, conférence *f.*; (*rebuke*) réprimande *f.* —*v.t./i.* faire un cours *or* une conférence (à); (*rebuke*) réprimander. **~r** /-ə(r)/ *n.* conférenc|ier, -ière *m.*, *f.*, (*univ.*) enseignant(e) *m.* (*f.*).
led /led/ *see* **lead**[1].
ledge /ledʒ/ *n.* rebord *m.*, saillie *f.*
ledger /'ledʒə(r)/ *n.* grand livre *m.*
lee /li:/ *n.* côté sous le vent *m.*
leech /li:tʃ/ *n.* sangsue *f.*
leek /li:k/ *n.* poireau *m.*
leer /lɪə(r)/ *v.i.* **~ (at),** lorgner. —*n.* regard sournois *m.*
leeway /'li:weɪ/ *n.* (*naut.*) dérive *f.*; (*fig.*) liberté d'action *f.* **make up ~,** rattraper le retard.
left[1] /left/ *see* **leave. ~ luggage (office),** consigne *f.* **~-overs** *n. pl.* restes *m. pl.*
left[2] /left/ *a.* gauche. —*adv.* à gauche. —*n.* gauche *f.* **~-hand** *a.* à *or* de gauche. **~-handed** *a.* gaucher. **~-wing** *a.* (*pol.*) de gauche.
leftist /'leftɪst/ *n.* gauchiste *m./f.*
leg /leg/ *n.* jambe *f.*; (*of animal*) patte *f.*; (*of table*) pied *m.*; (*of chicken*) cuisse *f.*; (*of lamb*) gigot *m.*; (*of journey*) étape *f.*
legacy /'legəsɪ/ *n.* legs *m.*
legal /'li:gl/ *a.* légal; (*affairs etc.*) juridique. **~ity** /li:'gælətɪ/ *n.* légalité *f.* **~ly** *adv.* légalement.
legalize /'li:gəlaɪz/ *v.t.* légaliser.
legation /lɪ'geɪʃn/ *n.* légation *f.*
legend /'ledʒənd/ *n.* légende *f.* **~ary** *a.* légendaire.
leggings /'legɪŋz/ *n. pl.* jambières *f. pl.*
legib|le /'ledʒəbl/ *a.* lisible. **~ility**

/-ˈbɪlətɪ/ *n.* lisibilité *f.* **~ly** *adv.* lisiblement.
legion /ˈliːdʒən/ *n.* légion *f.*
legislat|e /ˈledʒɪsleɪt/ *v.i.* légiférer. **~ion** /-ˈleɪʃn/ *n.* (*body of laws*) législation *f.*; (*law*) loi *f.*
legislat|ive /ˈledʒɪslətɪv/ *a.* législatif. **~ure** /-eɪtʃə(r)/ *n.* corps législatif *m.*
legitima|te /lɪˈdʒɪtɪmət/ *a.* légitime. **~cy** *n.* légitimité *f.*
leisure /ˈleʒə(r)/ *n.* loisir(s) *m.* (*pl.*). **at one's ~**, à tête reposée. **~ly** *a.* lent; *adv.* sans se presser.
lemon /ˈlemən/ *n.* citron *m.*
lemonade /leməˈneɪd/ *n.* (*fizzy*) limonade *f.*; (*still*) citronnade *f.*
lend /lend/ *v.t.* (*p.t.* **lent**) prêter; (*contribute*) donner. **~ itself to,** se prêter à. **~er** *n.* prêteu|r, -se *m.*, *f.* **~ing** *n.* prêt *m.*
length /leŋθ/ *n.* longueur *f.*; (*in time*) durée *f.*; (*section*) morceau *m.* **at ~,** (*at last*) enfin. **at (great) ~,** longuement. **~y** *a.* long.
lengthen /ˈleŋθən/ *v.t./i.* (s')allonger.
lengthways /ˈleŋθweɪz/ *adv.* dans le sens de la longueur.
lenien|t /ˈliːnɪənt/ *a.* indulgent. **~cy** *n.* indulgence *f.* **~tly** *adv.* avec indulgence.
lens /lenz/ *n.* lentille *f.*; (*of spectacles*) verre *m.*; (*photo.*) objectif *m.*
lent /lent/ *see* **lend.**
Lent /lent/ *n.* Carême *m.*
lentil /ˈlentl/ *n.* (*bean*) lentille *f.*
leopard /ˈlepəd/ *n.* léopard *m.*
leotard /ˈliːəʊtɑːd/ *n.* collant *m.*
leper /ˈlepə(r)/ *n.* lépreu|x, -se *m.*, *f.*
leprosy /ˈleprəsɪ/ *n.* lèpre *f.*
lesbian /ˈlezbɪən/ *n.* lesbienne *f.* —*a.* lesbien.
lesion /ˈliːʒn/ *n.* lésion *f.*
less /les/ *a.* (*in quantity etc.*) moins de (**than,** que). —*adv., n. & prep.* moins. **~ than,** (*with numbers*) moins de. **work**/*etc.* **~ than,** travailler/*etc.* moins que. **ten pounds**/*etc.* **~,** dix livres/*etc.* de moins. **~ and less,** de moins en moins. **~er** *a.* moindre.
lessen /ˈlesn/ *v.t./i.* diminuer.
lesson /ˈlesn/ *n.* leçon *f.*
lest /lest/ *conj.* de peur que *or* de.
let /let/ *v.t.* (*p.t.* **let,** *pres. p.* **letting**) laisser; (*lease*) louer. —*v. aux.* **~ us do, ~'s do,** faisons. **~ him do,** qu'il fasse. —*n.* location *f.* **~ alone,** (*thing*) ne pas toucher à; (*person*) laisser tranquille. **~ down,** baisser; (*deflate*) dégonfler; (*fig.*) décevoir. **~-down** *n.* déception *f.* **~ go** *v.t.* lâcher; *v.i.* lâcher prise. **~ in/out,** laisser *or* faire entrer/sortir. **~ o.s. in for,** (*task*) s'engager à; (*trouble*) s'attirer. **~ off,** (*explode, fire*) faire éclater *or* partir; (*excuse*) dispenser. **~ up,** (*fam.*) s'arrêter. **~-up** *n.* répit *m.*
lethal /ˈliːθl/ *a.* mortel; (*weapon*) meurtrier.
letharg|y /ˈleθədʒɪ/ *n.* léthargie *f.* **~ic** /lɪˈθɑːdʒɪk/ *a.* léthargique.
letter /ˈletə(r)/ *n.* lettre *f.* **~-box** *n.* boîte à *or* aux lettres *f.* **~ing** *n.* (*letters*) caractères *m. pl.*
lettuce /ˈletɪs/ *n.* laitue *f.*, salade *f.*
leukaemia /luːˈkiːmɪə/ *n.* leucémie *f.*
level /ˈlevl/ *a.* plat, uni; (*on surface*) horizontal; (*in height*) au même niveau (**with,** que); (*in score*) à égalité. —*n.* niveau *m.* —*v.t.* (*p.t.* **levelled**) niveler; (*aim*) diriger. **be on the ~,** (*fam.*) être franc. **~ crossing,** passage à niveau *m.* **~-headed** *a.* équilibré.
lever /ˈliːvə(r)/ *n.* levier *m.* —*v.t.* soulever au moyen d'un levier.
leverage /ˈliːvərɪdʒ/ *n.* influence *f.*
levity /ˈlevətɪ/ *n.* légèreté *f.*
levy /ˈlevɪ/ *v.t.* (*tax*) (pré)lever. —*n.* impôt *m.*
lewd /ljuːd/ *a.* (**-er, -est**) obscène.

lexicography /leksɪ'kɒgrəfɪ/ *n.* lexicographie *f.*

lexicon /'leksɪkən/ *n.* lexique *m.*

liable /'laɪəbl/ *a.* **be ~ to do,** avoir tendance à faire, pouvoir faire. **~ to,** (*illness etc.*) sujet à; (*fine*) passible de. **~ for,** responsable de.

liabilit|y /laɪə'bɪlətɪ/ *n.* responsabilité *f.*; (*fam.*) handicap *m.* **~ies,** (*debts*) dettes *f. pl.*

liais|e /lɪ'eɪz/ *v.i.* (*fam.*) faire la liaison. **~on** /-ɒn/ *n.* liaison *f.*

liar /'laɪə(r)/ *n.* menteu|r, -se *m., f.*

libel /'laɪbl/ *n.* diffamation *f.* —*v.t.* (*p.t.* **libelled**) diffamer.

liberal /'lɪbərəl/ *a.* libéral; (*generous*) généreux, libéral. **~ly** *adv.* libéralement.

Liberal /'lɪbərəl/ *a.* & *n.* (*pol.*) libéral(e) (*m.* (*f.*)).

liberat|e /'lɪbəreɪt/ *v.t.* libérer. **~ion** /-'reɪʃn/ *n.* libération *f.*

libert|y /'lɪbətɪ/ *n.* liberté *f.* **at ~y to,** libre de. **take ~ies,** prendre des libertés.

librar|y /'laɪbrərɪ/ *n.* bibliothèque *f.* **~ian** /-'breərɪən/ *n.* bibliothécaire *m.*/*f.*

libretto /lɪ'bretəʊ/ *n.* (*pl.* **-os**) (*mus.*) livret *m.*

Libya /'lɪbɪə/ *n.* Libye *f.* **~n** *a.* & *n.* libyen(ne) (*m.* (*f.*)).

lice /laɪs/ *see* **louse.**

licence /'laɪsns/ *n.* permis *m.*; (*for television*) redevance *f.*; (*comm.*) licence *f.*; (*liberty*: *fig.*) licence *f.* **~ plate,** plaque minéralogique *f.*

license /'laɪsns/ *v.t.* accorder un permis à, autoriser.

licentious /laɪ'senʃəs/ *a.* licencieux.

lichen /'laɪkən/ *n.* lichen *m.*

lick /lɪk/ *v.t.* lécher; (*defeat*: *sl.*) rosser. —*n.* coup de langue *m.* **~ one's chops,** se lécher les babines.

licorice /'lɪkərɪs/ *n.* (*Amer.*) réglisse *f.*

lid /lɪd/ *n.* couvercle *m.*

lido /'laɪdəʊ/ *n.* (*pl.* **-os**) piscine en plein air *f.*

lie[1] /laɪ/ *n.* mensonge *m.* —*v.i.* (*p.t.* **lied,** *pres. p.* **lying**) (*tell lies*) mentir. **give the ~ to,** démentir.

lie[2] /laɪ/ *v.i.* (*p.t.* **lay,** *p.p.* **lain,** *pres. p.* **lying**) s'allonger; (*remain*) rester; (*be*) se trouver, être; (*in grave*) reposer. **be lying,** être allongé. **~ down,** s'allonger. **~ in, have a ~-in,** faire la grasse matinée. **~ low,** se cacher.

lieu /lju:/ *n.* **in ~ of,** au lieu de.

lieutenant /lef'tenənt, *Amer.* lu:'tenənt/ *n.* lieutenant *m.*

life /laɪf/ *n.* (*pl.* **lives**) vie *f.* **~ cycle,** cycle de vie *m.* **~-guard** *n.* sauveteur *m.* **~-jacket** *n.* gilet de sauvetage *m.* **~-size(d)** *a.* grandeur nature *invar.*

lifebelt /'laɪfbelt/ *n.* bouée de sauvetage *f.*

lifeboat /'laɪfbəʊt/ *n.* canot de sauvetage *m.*

lifebuoy /'laɪfbɔɪ/ *n.* bouée de sauvetage *f.*

lifeless /'laɪflɪs/ *a.* sans vie.

lifelike /'laɪflaɪk/ *a.* très ressemblant.

lifelong /'laɪflɒŋ/ *a.* de toute la vie.

lifetime /'laɪftaɪm/ *n.* vie *f.* **in one's ~,** de son vivant.

lift /lɪft/ *v.t.* lever; (*steal*: *fam.*) voler. —*v.i.* (*of fog*) se lever. —*n.* (*in building*) ascenseur *m.* **give a ~ to,** emmener (en voiture). **~-off** *n.* (*aviat.*) décollage *m.*

ligament /'lɪgəmənt/ *n.* ligament *m.*

light[1] /laɪt/ *n.* lumière *f.*; (*lamp*) lampe *f.*; (*for fire, on vehicle, etc.*) feu *m.*; (*headlight*) phare *m.* —*a.* (*not dark*) clair. —*v.t.* (*p.t.* **lit** *or* **lighted**) allumer; (*room etc.*) éclairer; (*match*) frotter. **bring to ~,** révéler. **come to ~,** être révélé. **~ up** *v.i.* s'allumer; *v.t.* (*room*) éclairer. **~-year** *n.* année-lumière *f.*

light² /laɪt/ *a.* **(-er, -est)** (*not heavy*) léger. **~-fingered** *a.* chapardeur. **~-headed** *a.* (*dizzy*) qui a un vertige; (*frivolous*) étourdi. **~-hearted** *a.* gai. **~ly** *adv.* légèrement. **~ness** *n.* légèreté *f.*

lighten¹ /ˈlaɪtn/ *v.t.* (*give light to*) éclairer; (*make brighter*) éclaircir.

lighten² /ˈlaɪtn/ *v.t.* (*make less heavy*) alléger.

lighter /ˈlaɪtə(r)/ *n.* briquet *m.*; (*for stove*) allume-gaz *m. invar.*

lighthouse /ˈlaɪthaʊs/ *n.* phare *m.*

lighting /ˈlaɪtɪŋ/ *n.* éclairage *m.*

lightning /ˈlaɪtnɪŋ/ *n.* éclair(s) *m.* (*pl.*), foudre *f.* —*a.* éclair *invar.*

lightweight /ˈlaɪtweɪt/ *a.* léger. —*n.* (*boxing*) poids léger *m.*

like¹ /laɪk/ *a.* semblable, pareil. —*prep.* comme. —*conj.* (*fam.*) comme. —*n.* pareil *m.* **be ~-minded,** avoir les mêmes sentiments. **the ~s of you,** des gens comme vous.

like² /laɪk/ *v.t.* aimer (bien). **~s** *n. pl.* goûts *m. pl.* **I should ~,** je voudrais, j'aimerais. **would you ~?,** voulez-vous? **~able** *a.* sympathique.

likel|y /ˈlaɪklɪ/ *a.* **(-ier, -iest)** probable. —*adv.* probablement. **he is ~y to do,** il fera probablement. **not ~y!,** (*fam.*) pas question! **~ihood** *n.* probabilité *f.*

liken /ˈlaɪkən/ *v.t.* comparer.

likeness /ˈlaɪknɪs/ *n.* ressemblance *f.*

likewise /ˈlaɪkwaɪz/ *adv.* de même.

liking /ˈlaɪkɪŋ/ *n.* (*for thing*) penchant *m.*; (*for person*) affection *f.*

lilac /ˈlaɪlək/ *n.* lilas *m.* —*a.* lilas *invar.*

lily /ˈlɪlɪ/ *n.* lis *m.*, lys *m.* **~ of the valley,** muguet *m.*

limb /lɪm/ *n.* membre *m.* **out on a ~,** isolé (et vulnérable).

limber /ˈlɪmbə(r)/ *v.i.* **~ up,** faire des exercices d'assouplissement.

limbo /ˈlɪmbəʊ/ *n.* **be in ~,** (*forgotten*) être tombé dans l'oubli.

lime¹ /laɪm/ *n.* chaux *f.*

lime² /laɪm/ *n.* (*fruit*) lime *f.*, citron vert *m.*

lime³ /laɪm/ *n.* **~(-tree),** tilleul *m.*

limelight /ˈlaɪmlaɪt/ *n.* **in the ~,** en vedette.

limerick /ˈlɪmərɪk/ *n.* poème humoristique *m.* (*de cinq vers*).

limit /ˈlɪmɪt/ *n.* limite *f.* —*v.t.* limiter. **~ed company,** société anonyme *f.* **~ation** /-ˈteɪʃn/ *n.* limitation *f.*

limousine /ˈlɪməziːn/ *n.* (*car*) limousine *f.*

limp¹ /lɪmp/ *v.i.* boiter. —*n.* **have a ~,** boiter.

limp² /lɪmp/ *a.* **(-er, -est)** mou.

limpid /ˈlɪmpɪd/ *a.* limpide.

linctus /ˈlɪŋktəs/ *n.* sirop *m.*

line¹ /laɪn/ *n.* ligne *f.*; (*track*) voie *f.*; (*wrinkle*) ride *f.*; (*row*) rangée *f.*, file *f.*; (*of poem*) vers *m.*; (*rope*) corde *f.*; (*of goods*) gamme *f.*; (*queue*: *Amer.*) queue *f.* —*v.t.* (*paper*) régler; (*streets etc.*) border. **in ~ for,** sur le point de recevoir. **in ~ with,** en accord avec. **~ up,** (s')aligner; (*in queue*) faire la queue.

line² /laɪn/ *v.t.* (*garment*) doubler; (*fill*) remplir, garnir.

lineage /ˈlɪnɪɪdʒ/ *n.* lignée *f.*

linear /ˈlɪnɪə(r)/ *a.* linéaire.

linen /ˈlɪnɪn/ *n.* (*sheets etc.*) linge *m.*; (*material*) lin *m.*, toile de lin *f.*

liner /ˈlaɪnə(r)/ *n.* paquebot *m.*

linesman /ˈlaɪnzmən/ *n.* (*football*) juge de touche *m.*

linger /ˈlɪŋgə(r)/ *v.i.* s'attarder; (*smells etc.*) persister.

lingerie /ˈlænʒərɪ/ *n.* lingerie *f.*

lingo /ˈlɪŋgəʊ/ *n.* (*pl.* **-os**) (*hum.*, *fam.*) jargon *m.*

linguist /ˈlɪŋgwɪst/ *n.* linguiste *m.*/*f.*

linguistic /lɪŋˈgwɪstɪk/ *a.* linguistique. **~s** *n.* linguistique *f.*

lining /'laɪnɪŋ/ *n.* doublure *f.*
link /lɪŋk/ *n.* lien *m.*; (*of chain*) maillon *m.* —*v.t.* relier; (*relate*) (re)lier. **~ up,** (*of roads*) se rejoindre. **~age** *n.* lien *m.*
links /'lɪŋks/ *n. invar.* terrain de golf *m.*
lino /'laɪnəʊ/ *n.* (*pl.* **-os**) lino *m.*
linoleum /lɪ'nəʊlɪəm/ *n.* linoléum *m.*
lint /lɪnt/ *n.* (*med.*) tissu ouaté *m.*; (*fluff*) peluche(s) *f.* (*pl.*).
lion /'laɪən/ *n.* lion *m.* **take the ~'s share,** se tailler la part du lion. **~ess** *n.* lionne *f.*
lip /lɪp/ *n.* lèvre *f.*; (*edge*) rebord *m.* **~-read** *v.t./i.* lire sur les lèvres. **pay ~-service to,** n'approuver que pour la forme.
lipstick /'lɪpstɪk/ *n.* rouge (à lèvres) *m.*
liquefy /'lɪkwɪfaɪ/ *v.t./i.* (se) liquéfier.
liqueur /lɪ'kjʊə(r)/ *n.* liqueur *f.*
liquid /'lɪkwɪd/ *n.* & *a.* liquide (*m.*). **~ize** *v.t.* passer au mixeur. **~izer** *n.* mixeur *m.*
liquidat|e /'lɪkwɪdeɪt/ *v.t.* liquider. **~ion** /-'deɪʃn/ *n.* liquidation *f.*
liquor /'lɪkə(r)/ *n.* alcool *m.*
liquorice /'lɪkərɪs/ *n.* réglisse *f.*
lira /'lɪərə/ *n.* (*pl.* **lire** /'lɪəreɪ/ *or* **liras**) lire *f.*
lisp /lɪsp/ *n.* zézaiement *m.* —*v.i.* zézayer. **with a ~,** en zézayant.
list[1] /lɪst/ *n.* liste *f.* —*v.t.* inscrire, dresser la liste de.
list[2] /lɪst/ *v.i.* (*ship*) gîter.
listen /'lɪsn/ *v.i.* écouter. **~ to, ~ in (to),** écouter. **~er** *n.* audi|teur, -trice *m.*/*f.*
listless /'lɪstlɪs/ *a.* apathique.
lit /lɪt/ *see* **light**[1].
litany /'lɪtənɪ/ *n.* litanie *f.*
literal /'lɪtərəl/ *a.* littéral; (*person*) prosaïque. **~ly** *adv.* littéralement.
literary /'lɪtərərɪ/ *a.* littéraire.
litera|te /'lɪtərət/ *a.* qui sait lire et écrire. **~cy** *n.* capacité de lire et écrire *f.*
literature /'lɪtrətʃə(r)/ *n.* littérature *f.*; (*fig.*) documentation *f.*
lithe /laɪð/ *a.* souple, agile.
litigation /lɪtɪ'geɪʃn/ *n.* litige *m.*
litre /'li:tə(r)/ *n.* litre *m.*
litter /'lɪtə(r)/ *n.* détritus *m. pl.*, papiers *m. pl.*; (*animals*) portée *f.* —*v.t.* éparpiller; (*make untidy*) laisser des détritus dans. **~-bin** *n.* poubelle *f.* **~ed with,** jonché de.
little /'lɪtl/ *a.* petit; (*not much*) peu de. —*n.* peu *m.* —*adv.* peu. **a ~,** un peu (de).
liturgy /'lɪtədʒɪ/ *n.* liturgie *f.*
live[1] /laɪv/ *a.* vivant; (*wire*) sous tension; (*broadcast*) en direct. **be a ~ wire,** être très dynamique.
live[2] /lɪv/ *v.t./i.* vivre; (*reside*) habiter, vivre. **~ down,** faire oublier. **~ it up,** mener la belle vie. **~ on,** (*feed o.s. on*) vivre de; (*continue*) survivre. **~ up to,** se montrer à la hauteur de.
livelihood /'laɪvlɪhʊd/ *n.* moyens d'existence *m. pl.*
livel|y /'laɪvlɪ/ *a.* (**-ier, -iest**) vif, vivant. **~iness** *n.* vivacité *f.*
liven /'laɪvn/ *v.t./i.* **~ up,** (s')animer; (*cheer up*) (s')égayer.
liver /'lɪvə(r)/ *n.* foie *m.*
livery /'lɪvərɪ/ *n.* livrée *f.*
livestock /'laɪvstɒk/ *n.* bétail *m.*
livid /'lɪvɪd/ *a.* livide; (*angry*: *fam.*) furieux.
living /'lɪvɪŋ/ *a.* vivant. —*n.* vie *f.* **~-room** *n.* salle de séjour *f.*
lizard /'lɪzəd/ *n.* lézard *m.*
llama /'lɑ:mə/ *n.* lama *m.*
load /ləʊd/ *n.* charge *f.*; (*loaded goods*) chargement *m.*, charge *f.*; (*weight, strain*) poids *m.* **~s of,** (*fam.*) des masses de. —*v.t.* charger. **~ed** *a.* (*dice*) pipé; (*wealthy*: *sl.*) riche.
loaf[1] /ləʊf/ *n.* (*pl.* **loaves**) pain *m.*
loaf[2] /ləʊf/ *v.i.* **~ (about),** fainéanter. **~er** *n.* fainéant(e) *m.* (*f.*).

loam /ləʊm/ *n.* terreau *m.*

loan /ləʊn/ *n.* prêt *m.*; (*money borrowed*) emprunt *m.* —*v.t.* (*lend: fam.*) prêter.

loath /ləʊθ/ *a.* peu disposé (**to,** à).

loath|e /ləʊð/ *v.t.* détester. **~ing** *n.* dégoût *m.* **~some** *a.* dégoûtant.

lobby /ˈlɒbɪ/ *n.* entrée *f.*, vestibule *m.*; (*pol.*) lobby *m.*, groupe de pression *m.* —*v.t.* faire pression sur.

lobe /ləʊb/ *n.* lobe *m.*

lobster /ˈlɒbstə(r)/ *n.* homard *m.*

local /ˈləʊkl/ *a.* local; (*shops etc.*) du quartier. —*n.* personne du coin *f.*; (*pub: fam.*) pub du coin *m.* **~ government,** administration locale *f.* **~ly** *adv.* localement; (*nearby*) dans les environs.

locale /ləʊˈkɑːl/ *n.* lieu *m.*

locality /ləʊˈkælətɪ/ *n.* (*district*) région *f.*; (*position*) lieu *m.*

localized /ˈləʊkəlaɪzd/ *a.* localisé.

locat|e /ləʊˈkeɪt/ *v.t.* (*situate*) situer; (*find*) repérer. **~ion** /-ʃn/ *n.* emplacement *m.* **on ~ion,** (*cinema*) en extérieur.

lock[1] /lɒk/ *n.* mèche (de cheveux) *f.*

lock[2] /lɒk/ *n.* (*of door etc.*) serrure *f.*; (*on canal*) écluse *f.* —*v.t./i.* fermer à clef; (*wheels: auto.*) (se) bloquer. **~ in** *or* **up,** (*person*) enfermer. **~ out,** (*by mistake*) enfermer dehors. **~-out** *n.* lock-out *m. invar.*

locker /ˈlɒkə(r)/ *n.* casier *m.*

locket /ˈlɒkɪt/ *n.* médaillon *m.*

locksmith /ˈlɒksmɪθ/ *n.* serrurier *m.*

locomotion /ləʊkəˈməʊʃn/ *n.* locomotion *f.*

locomotive /ˈləʊkəməʊtɪv/ *n.* locomotive *f.*

locum /ˈləʊkəm/ *n.* (*doctor etc.*) remplaçant(e) *m.* (*f.*).

locust /ˈləʊkəst/ *n.* criquet *m.*, sauterelle *f.*

lodge /lɒdʒ/ *n.* (*house*) pavillon (de gardien *or* de chasse) *m.*; (*of porter*) loge *f.* —*v.t.* loger; (*money, complaint*) déposer. —*v.i.* être logé (**with,** chez); (*become fixed*) se loger. **~r** /-ə(r)/ *n.* locataire *m.*/*f.*, pensionnaire *m.*/*f.*

lodgings /ˈlɒdʒɪŋz/ *n.* chambre (meublée) *f.*; (*flat*) logement *m.*

loft /lɒft/ *n.* grenier *m.*

lofty /ˈlɒftɪ/ *a.* (**-ier, -iest**) (*tall, noble*) élevé; (*haughty*) hautain.

log /lɒg/ *n.* (*of wood*) bûche *f.* **~(-book),** (*naut.*) journal de bord *m.* —*v.t.* (*p.t.* **logged**) noter; (*distance*) parcourir.

logarithm /ˈlɒgərɪðəm/ *n.* logarithme *m.*

loggerheads /ˈlɒgəhedz/ *n. pl.* **at ~,** en désaccord.

logic /ˈlɒdʒɪk/ *a.* logique. **~al** *a.* logique. **~ally** *adv.* logiquement.

logistics /ləˈdʒɪstɪks/ *n.* logistique *f.*

logo /ˈləʊgəʊ/ *n.* (*pl.* **-os**) (*fam.*) emblème *m.*

loin /lɔɪn/ *n.* (*culin.*) filet *m.* **~s,** reins *m. pl.*

loiter /ˈlɔɪtə(r)/ *v.i.* traîner.

loll /lɒl/ *v.i.* se prélasser.

loll|ipop /ˈlɒlɪpɒp/ *n.* sucette *f.* **~y** *n.* (*fam.*) sucette *f.*; (*sl.*) fric *m.*

London /ˈlʌndən/ *n.* Londres *m.*/*f.* **~er** *n.* Londonien(ne) *m.* (*f.*).

lone /ləʊn/ *a.* solitaire. **~r** /-ə(r)/ *n.* solitaire *m.*/*f.* **~some** *a.* solitaire.

lonely /ˈləʊnlɪ/ *a.* (**-ier, -iest**) solitaire; (*person*) seul, solitaire.

long[1] /lɒŋ/ *a.* (**-er, -est**) long. —*adv.* longtemps. **how ~ is?,** quelle est la longueur de?; (*in time*) quelle est la durée de? **how ~?,** combien de temps? **he will not be ~,** il n'en a pas pour longtemps. **a ~ time,** longtemps. **as** *or* **so ~ as,** pourvu que. **before ~,** avant peu. **do no ~er,** ne plus faire. **~-distance** *a.* (*flight*) sur long parcours; (*phone call*) interurbain. **~ face,** grimace *f.* **~ johns,** (*fam.*) caleçon long *m.* **~ jump,**

saut en longueur *m.* **~-playing record,** microsillon *m.* **~-range** *a.* à longue portée; (*forecast*) à long terme. **~-sighted** *a.* presbyte. **~-standing** *a.* de longue date. **~-suffering** *a.* très patient. **~-term** *a.* à long terme. **~ wave,** grandes ondes *f. pl.* **~-winded** *a.* (*speaker etc.*) verbeux.

long[2] /lɒŋ/ *v.i.* avoir bien *or* très envie (**for, to,** de). **~ for s.o.,** (*pine for*) languir après qn. **~ing** *n.* envie *f.*; (*nostalgia*) nostalgie *f.*

longevity /lɒnˈdʒevətɪ/ *n.* longévité *f.*

longhand /ˈlɒŋhænd/ *n.* écriture courante *f.*

longitude /ˈlɒndʒɪtjuːd/ *n.* longitude *f.*

loo /luː/ *n.* (*fam.*) toilettes *f. pl.*

look /lʊk/ *v.t./i.* regarder; (*seem*) avoir l'air. —*n.* regard *m.*; (*appearance*) air *m.*, aspect *m.* **(good) ~s,** beauté *f.* **~ after,** s'occuper de, soigner. **~ at,** regarder. **~ down on,** mépriser. **~ for,** chercher. **~ forward to,** attendre avec impatience. **~ in on,** passer voir. **~ into,** examiner. **~ like,** ressembler à, avoir l'air de. **~ out,** faire attention. **~ out for,** chercher; (*watch*) guetter. **~-out** *n.* (*mil.*) poste de guet *m.*; (*person*) guetteur *m.* **~ round,** se retourner. **~ up,** (*word*) chercher; (*visit*) passer voir. **~ up to,** respecter. **~ing-glass** *n.* glace *f.*

loom[1] /luːm/ *n.* métier à tisser *m.*

loom[2] /luːm/ *v.i.* surgir; (*event etc.*: *fig.*) paraître imminent.

loony /ˈluːnɪ/ *n.* & *a.* (*sl.*) fou, folle (*m.*, *f.*).

loop /luːp/ *n.* boucle *f.* —*v.t.* boucler.

loophole /ˈluːphəʊl/ *n.* (*in rule*) échappatoire *f.*

loose /luːs/ *a.* (**-er, -est**) (*knot etc.*) desserré; (*page etc.*) détaché; (*clothes*) ample, lâche; (*lax*) relâché; (*not packed*) en vrac; (*inexact*) vague; (*pej.*) immoral. **at a ~ end,** (*Amer.*) **at ~ ends,** désœuvré. **~ly** *adv.* sans serrer; (*roughly*) vaguement.

loosen /ˈluːsn/ *v.t.* (*slacken*) desserrer; (*untie*) défaire.

loot /luːt/ *n.* butin *m.* —*v.t.* piller. **~er** *n.* pillard(e) *m.* (*f.*). **~ing** *n.* pillage *m.*

lop /lɒp/ *v.t.* (*p.t.* **lopped**). **~ off,** couper.

lop-sided /lɒpˈsaɪdɪd/ *a.* de travers.

lord /lɔːd/ *n.* seigneur *m.*; (*British title*) lord *m.* **the L~,** le Seigneur. **(good) L~!,** mon Dieu! **~ly** *a.* noble; (*haughty*) hautain.

lore /lɔː(r)/ *n.* traditions *f. pl.*

lorry /ˈlɒrɪ/ *n.* camion *m.*

lose /luːz/ *v.t./i.* (*p.t.* **lost**) perdre. **get lost,** se perdre. **~r** /-ə(r)/ *n.* perdant(e) *m.* (*f.*).

loss /lɒs/ *n.* perte *f.* **be at a ~,** être perplexe. **be at a ~ to,** être incapable de.

lost /lɒst/ *see* **lose.** —*a.* perdu. **~ property,** (*Amer.*) **~ and found,** objets trouvés *m. pl.*

lot[1] /lɒt/ *n.* (*fate*) sort *m.*; (*at auction*) lot *m.*; (*land*) lotissement *m.*

lot[2] /lɒt/ *n.* **the ~,** (le) tout *m.*; (*people*) tous *m. pl.*, toutes *f. pl.* **a ~ (of), ~s (of),** (*fam.*) beaucoup (de). **quite a ~ (of),** (*fam.*) pas mal (de).

lotion /ˈləʊʃn/ *n.* lotion *f.*

lottery /ˈlɒtərɪ/ *n.* loterie *f.*

loud /laʊd/ *a.* (**-er, -est**) bruyant, fort. —*adv.* fort. **~ hailer,** porte-voix *m. invar.* **out ~,** tout haut. **~ly** *adv.* fort.

loudspeaker /laʊdˈspiːkə(r)/ *n.* haut-parleur *m.*

lounge /laʊndʒ/ *v.i.* paresser. —*n.* salon *m.* **~ suit,** complet *m.*

louse /laʊs/ *n.* (*pl.* **lice**) pou *m.*

lousy /ˈlaʊzɪ/ *a.* (**-ier, -iest**) pouilleux; (*bad*: *sl.*) infect.

lout /laʊt/ *n.* rustre *m.*

lovable /ˈlʌvəbl/ *a.* adorable.
love /lʌv/ *n.* amour *m.*; (*tennis*) zéro *m.* —*v.t.* aimer; (*like greatly*) aimer (beaucoup) (**to do,** faire). **in ~,** amoureux (**with,** de). **~ affair,** liaison amoureuse *f.*
lovely /ˈlʌvlɪ/ *a.* (**-ier, -iest**) joli; (*delightful: fam.*) très agréable.
lover /ˈlʌvə(r)/ *n.* amant *m.*; (*devotee*) amateur *m.* (**of,** de).
lovesick /ˈlʌvsɪk/ *a.* amoureux.
loving /ˈlʌvɪŋ/ *a.* affectueux.
low[1] /ləʊ/ *v.i.* meugler.
low[2] /ləʊ/ *a.* & *adv.* (**-er, -est**) bas. —*n.* (*low pressure*) dépression *f.* **reach a (new) ~,** atteindre son niveau le plus bas. **~-cut** *a.* décolleté. **~-down** *a.* méprisable; *n.* (*fam.*) renseignements *m. pl.* **~-key** *a.* modéré; (*discreet*) discret.
lowbrow /ˈləʊbraʊ/ *a.* peu intellectuel.
lower /ˈləʊə(r)/ *a.* & *adv. see* **low**[2]. —*v.t.* baisser. **~ o.s.,** s'abaisser.
lowlands /ˈləʊləndz/ *n. pl.* plaine(s) *f.* (*pl.*).
lowly /ˈləʊlɪ/ *a.* (**-ier, -iest**) humble.
loyal /ˈlɔɪəl/ *a.* loyal. **~ly** *adv.* loyalement. **~ty** *n.* loyauté *f.*
lozenge /ˈlɒzɪndʒ/ *n.* (*shape*) losange *m.*; (*tablet*) pastille *f.*
LP *abbr. see* **long-playing record.**
Ltd. *abbr.* (*Limited*) SA.
lubric|ate /ˈluːbrɪkeɪt/ *v.t.* graisser, lubrifier. **~ant** *n.* lubrifiant *m.* **~ation** /-ˈkeɪʃn/ *n.* graissage *m.*
lucid /ˈluːsɪd/ *a.* lucide. **~ity** /luːˈsɪdətɪ/ *n.* lucidité *f.*
luck /lʌk/ *n.* chance *f.* **bad ~,** malchance *f.*
luck|y /ˈlʌkɪ/ *a.* (**-ier, -iest**) qui a de la chance, heureux; (*event*) heureux; (*number*) qui porte bonheur. **~ily** *adv.* heureusement.
lucrative /ˈluːkrətɪv/ *a.* lucratif.
lucre /ˈluːkə(r)/ *n.* (*pej.*) lucre *m.*
ludicrous /ˈluːdɪkrəs/ *a.* ridicule.
lug /lʌg/ *v.t.* (*p.t.* **lugged**) traîner.
luggage /ˈlʌgɪdʒ/ *n.* bagages *m. pl.* **~-rack** *n.* porte-bagages *m. invar.*
lukewarm /ˈluːkwɔːm/ *a.* tiède.
lull /lʌl/ *v.t.* (*soothe, send to sleep*) endormir. —*n.* accalmie *f.*
lullaby /ˈlʌləbaɪ/ *n.* berceuse *f.*
lumbago /lʌmˈbeɪgəʊ/ *n.* lumbago *m.*
lumber /ˈlʌmbə(r)/ *n.* bric-à-brac *m. invar.*; (*wood*) bois de charpente *m.* —*v.t.* **~ s.o. with,** (*chore etc.*) coller à qn.
lumberjack /ˈlʌmbədʒæk/ *n.* (*Amer.*) bûcheron *m.*
luminous /ˈluːmɪnəs/ *a.* lumineux.
lump /lʌmp/ *n.* morceau *m.*; (*swelling on body*) grosseur *f.*; (*in liquid*) grumeau *m.* —*v.t.* **~ together,** réunir. **~ sum,** somme globale *f.* **~y** *a.* (*sauce*) grumeleux; (*bumpy*) bosselé.
lunacy /ˈluːnəsɪ/ *n.* folie *f.*
lunar /ˈluːnə(r)/ *a.* lunaire.
lunatic /ˈluːnətɪk/ *n.* fou, folle *m., f.*
lunch /lʌntʃ/ *n.* déjeuner *m.* —*v.i.* déjeuner.
luncheon /ˈlʌntʃən/ *n.* déjeuner *m.* **~ meat,** (*approx.*) saucisson *m.* **~ voucher,** chèque-repas *m.*
lung /lʌŋ/ *n.* poumon *m.*
lunge /lʌndʒ/ *n.* mouvement brusque en avant *m.* —*v.i.* s'élancer (**at,** sur).
lurch[1] /lɜːtʃ/ *n.* **leave in the ~,** planter là, laisser en plan.
lurch[2] /lɜːtʃ/ *v.i.* (*person*) tituber.
lure /lʊə(r)/ *v.t.* appâter, attirer. —*n.* (*attraction*) attrait *m.*, appât *m.*
lurid /ˈlʊərɪd/ *a.* choquant, affreux; (*gaudy*) voyant.
lurk /lɜːk/ *v.i.* se cacher; (*in ambush*) s'embusquer; (*prowl*) rôder.
luscious /ˈlʌʃəs/ *a.* appétissant.
lush /lʌʃ/ *a.* luxuriant. —*n.* (*Amer., fam.*) ivrogne(sse) *m.* (*f.*).

lust /lʌst/ *n.* luxure *f.*; (*fig.*) convoitise *f.* —*v.i.* ~ **after,** convoiter.
lustre /'lʌstə(r)/ *n.* lustre *m.*
lusty /'lʌstɪ/ *a.* (**-ier, -iest**) robuste.
lute /luːt/ *n.* (*mus.*) luth *m.*
Luxemburg /'lʌksəmbɜːg/ *n.* Luxembourg *m.*
luxuriant /lʌg'ʒʊərɪənt/ *a.* luxuriant.
luxurious /lʌg'ʒʊərɪəs/ *a.* luxueux.
luxury /'lʌkʃərɪ/ *n.* luxe *m.* —*a.* de luxe.
lye /laɪ/ *n.* lessive (alcaline) *f.*
lying /'laɪɪŋ/ *see* **lie**[1], **lie**[2]. —*n.* le mensonge *m.*
lynch /lɪntʃ/ *v.t.* lyncher.
lynx /lɪŋks/ *n.* lynx *m.*
lyre /'laɪə(r)/ *n.* (*mus.*) lyre *f.*
lyric /'lɪrɪk/ *a.* lyrique. **~s** *n. pl.* paroles *f. pl.* **~al** *a.* lyrique. **~ism** /-sɪzəm/ *n.* lyrisme *m.*

M

MA *abbr. see* **Master of Arts.**
mac /mæk/ *n.* (*fam.*) imper *m.*
macabre /mə'kɑːbrə/ *a.* macabre.
macaroni /mækə'rəʊnɪ/ *n.* macaronis *m. pl.*
macaroon /mækə'ruːn/ *n.* macaron *m.*
mace /meɪs/ *n.* (*staff*) masse *f.*
Mach /mɑːk/ *n.* ~ **(number),** (nombre de) Mach *m.*
machiavellian /mækɪə'velɪən/ *a.* machiavélique.
machinations /mækɪ'neɪʃnz/ *n. pl.* machinations *f. pl.*
machine /mə'ʃiːn/ *n.* machine *f.* —*v.t.* (*sew*) coudre à la machine; (*techn.*) usiner. **~-gun** *n.* mitrailleuse *f.*; *v.t.* (*p.t.* **-gunned**) mitrailler. **~-readable** *a.* en langage machine. **~ tool,** machine-outil *f.*
machinery /mə'ʃiːnərɪ/ *n.* machinerie *f.*; (*working parts & fig.*) mécanisme(s) *m.* (*pl.*).
machinist /mə'ʃiːnɪst/ *n.* (*operator*) opéra|teur, -trice sur machine *m.*, *f.*; (*on sewing-machine*) piqueu/r, -se *m.*, *f.*
macho /'mætʃəʊ/ *n.* (*pl.* **-os**) macho *m.*
mackerel /'mækrəl/ *n. invar.* (*fish*) maquereau *m.*
mackintosh /'mækɪntɒʃ/ *n.* imperméable *m.*
macrobiotic /mækrəʊbaɪ'ɒtɪk/ *a.* macrobiotique.
mad /mæd/ *a.* (**madder, maddest**) fou; (*foolish*) insensé; (*dog etc.*) enragé; (*angry*: *fam.*) furieux. **be ~ about,** se passionner pour; (*person*) être fou de. **like ~,** comme un fou. **~ly** *adv.* (*interested, in love, etc.*) follement; (*frantically*) comme un fou. **~ness** *n.* folie *f.*
Madagascar /mædə'gæskə(r)/ *n.* Madagascar *f.*
madam /'mædəm/ *n.* madame *f.*; (*unmarried*) mademoiselle *f.*
madcap /'mædkæp/ *a.* & *n.* écervelé(e) (*m.* (*f.*)).
madden /'mædn/ *v.t.* exaspérer.
made /meɪd/ *see* **make. ~ to measure,** fait sur mesure.
Madeira /mə'dɪərə/ *n.* (*wine*) madère *m.*
madhouse /'mædhaʊs/ *n.* (*fam.*) maison de fous *f.*
madman /'mædmən/ *n.* (*pl.* **-men**) fou *m.*
madonna /mə'dɒnə/ *n.* madone *f.*
madrigal /'mædrɪgl/ *n.* madrigal *m.*
maestro /'maɪstrəʊ/ *n.* (*pl.* **maestri** /-striː/) maestro *m.*
Mafia /'mæfɪə/ *n.* maf(f)ia *f.*
magazine /mægə'ziːn/ *n.* revue *f.*, magazine *m.*; (*of gun*) magasin *m.*
magenta /mə'dʒentə/ *a.* rouge violacé.

maggot /'mægət/ *n.* ver *m.*, asticot *m.* **~y** *a.* véreux.

Magi /'meɪdʒaɪ/ *n. pl.* **the ~,** les Rois mages *m. pl.*

magic /'mædʒɪk/ *n.* magie *f.* —*a.* magique. **~al** *a.* magique.

magician /mə'dʒɪʃn/ *n.* magicien(ne) *m.* (*f.*).

magistrate /'mædʒɪstreɪt/ *n.* magistrat *m.*

magnanim|ous /mæg'nænɪməs/ *a.* magnanime. **~ity** /-ə'nɪmətɪ/ *n.* magnanimité *f.*

magnate /'mægneɪt/ *n.* magnat *m.*

magnesia /mæg'ni:ʃə/ *n.* magnésie *f.*

magnet /'mægnɪt/ *n.* aimant *m.* **~ic** /-'netɪk/ *a.* magnétique. **~ism** *n.* magnétisme *m.* **~ize** *v.t.* magnétiser.

magnificen|t /mæg'nɪfɪsnt/ *a.* magnifique. **~ce** *n.* magnificence *f.*

magnif|y /'mægnɪfaɪ/ *v.t.* grossir; (*sound*) amplifier; (*fig.*) exagérer. **~ication** /-ɪ'keɪʃn/ *n.* grossissement *m.*; amplification *f.* **~ier** *n.*, **~ying glass,** loupe *f.*

magnitude /'mægnɪtju:d/ *n.* (*importance*) ampleur *f.*; (*size*) grandeur *f.*

magnolia /mæg'nəʊlɪə/ *n.* magnolia *m.*

magnum /'mægnəm/ *n.* magnum *m.*

magpie /'mægpaɪ/ *n.* pie *f.*

mahogany /mə'hɒgənɪ/ *n.* acajou *m.*

maid /meɪd/ *n.* (*servant*) bonne *f.*; (*girl*: *old use*) jeune fille *f.*

maiden /'meɪdn/ *n.* (*old use*) jeune fille *f.* —*a.* (*aunt*) célibataire; (*voyage*) premier. **~ name,** nom de jeune fille *m.* **~hood** *n.* virginité *f.* **~ly** *a.* virginal.

mail[1] /meɪl/ *n.* poste *f.*; (*letters*) courrier *m.* —*a.* (*bag, van*) postal. —*v.t.* envoyer par la poste. **~ing list,** liste d'adresses *f.* **~ order,** vente par correspondance *f.*

mail[2] /meɪl/ *n.* (*armour*) cotte de mailles *f.*

mailman /'meɪlmæn/ *n.* (*pl.* **-men**) (*Amer.*) facteur *m.*

maim /meɪm/ *v.t.* mutiler.

main[1] /meɪn/ *a.* principal. —*n.* **in the ~,** en général. **a ~ road,** une grande route. **~ly** *adv.* principalement, surtout.

main[2] /meɪn/ *n.* **(water/gas) ~,** conduite d'eau/de gaz *f.* **the ~s,** (*electr.*) le secteur.

mainland /'meɪnlənd/ *n.* continent *m.*

mainspring /'meɪnsprɪŋ/ *n.* ressort principal *m.*; (*motive*: *fig.*) mobile principal *m.*

mainstay /'meɪnsteɪ/ *n.* soutien *m.*

mainstream /'meɪnstri:m/ *n.* tendance principale *f.*, ligne *f.*

maintain /meɪn'teɪn/ *v.t.* (*continue, keep, assert*) maintenir; (*house, machine, family*) entretenir; (*rights*) soutenir.

maintenance /'meɪntənəns/ *n.* (*care*) entretien *m.*; (*continuation*) maintien *m.*; (*allowance*) pension alimentaire *f.*

maisonette /meɪzə'net/ *n.* duplex *m.*

maize /meɪz/ *n.* maïs *m.*

majestic /mə'dʒestɪk/ *a.* majestueux.

majesty /'mædʒəstɪ/ *n.* majesté *f.*

major /'meɪdʒə(r)/ *a.* majeur. —*n.* commandant *m.* —*v.i.* **~ in,** (*univ., Amer.*) se spécialiser en. **~ road,** route à priorité *f.*

Majorca /mə'dʒɔ:kə/ *n.* Majorque *f.*

majority /mə'dʒɒrətɪ/ *n.* majorité *f.* —*a.* majoritaire. **the ~ of people,** la plupart des gens.

make /meɪk/ *v.t./i.* (*p.t.* **made**) faire; (*manufacture*) fabriquer; (*friends*) se faire; (*money*) gagner, se faire; (*decision*) prendre; (*destination) arriver à; (*cause to be*) rendre. **~ s.o. do sth.,** obliger qn. à faire qch., faire faire qch. à qn. —*n.* fabrication *f.*; (*brand*) marque *f.* **be made of,** être fait de. **~ o.s. at home,** se mettre à l'aise. **~ it,** arriver; (*succeed*) réussir. **I ~ it two o'clock,** j'ai deux heures. **I cannot ~ anything of it,** je n'y comprends rien. **~ as if to,** faire mine de. **~ believe,** faire semblant. **~-believe** *a.* feint, illusoire; *n.* fantaisie *f.* **~ do,** (*manage*) se débrouiller (**with,** avec). **~ do with,** (*content o.s.*) se contenter de. **~ for,** se diriger vers. **~ good** *v.i.* réussir; *v.t.* compenser; (*repair*) réparer. **~ off,** filer (**with,** avec). **~ out** *v.t.* distinguer; (*understand*) comprendre; (*draw up*) faire; (*assert*) prétendre; *v.i.* (*fam.*) se débrouiller. **~ over,** céder (**to,** à); (*convert*) transformer. **~ up** *v.t.* faire, former; (*story*) inventer; (*deficit*) combler; *v.i.* se réconcilier. **~ up (one's face),** se maquiller. **~-up** *n.* maquillage *m.*; (*of object*) constitution *f.*; (*psych.*) caractère *m.* **~ up for,** compenser; (*time*) rattraper. **~ up one's mind,** se décider. **~ up to,** se concilier les bonnes grâces de.

maker /'meɪkə(r)/ *n.* fabricant *m.*

makeshift /'meɪkʃɪft/ *n.* expédient *m.* —*a.* provisoire.

making /'meɪkɪŋ/ *n.* **be the ~ of,** faire le succès de. **he has the ~s of,** il a l'étoffe de.

maladjusted /mælə'dʒʌstɪd/ *a.* inadapté.

maladministration /mælədmɪnɪ'streɪʃn/ *n.* mauvaise gestion *f.*

malaise /mæ'leɪz/ *n.* malaise *m.*

malaria /mə'leərɪə/ *n.* malaria *f.*

Malay /mə'leɪ/ *a.* & *n.* malais(e) (*m.* (*f.*)). **~sia** *n.* Malaysia *f.*

male /meɪl/ *a.* (*voice, sex*) masculin; (*bot., techn.*) mâle. —*n.* mâle *m.*

malevolen|t /mə'levələnt/ *a.* malveillant. **~ce** *n.* malveillance *f.*

malform|ation /mælfɔː'meɪʃn/ *n.* malformation *f.* **~ed** *a.* difforme.

malfunction /mæl'fʌŋkʃn/ *n.* mauvais fonctionnement *m.* —*v.i.* mal fonctionner.

malice /'mælɪs/ *n.* méchanceté *f.*

malicious /mə'lɪʃəs/ *a.* méchant. **~ly** *adv.* méchamment.

malign /mə'laɪn/ *a.* pernicieux. —*v.t.* calomnier.

malignan|t /mə'lɪgnənt/ *a.* malveillant; (*tumour*) malin. **~cy** *n.* malveillance *f.*; malignité *f.*

malinger /mə'lɪŋgə(r)/ *v.i.* feindre la maladie. **~er** *n.* simula|teur, -trice *m., f.*

malleable /'mælɪəbl/ *a.* malléable.

mallet /'mælɪt/ *n.* maillet *m.*

malnutrition /mælnjuː'trɪʃn/ *n.* sous-alimentation *f.*

malpractice /mæl'præktɪs/ *n.* faute professionnelle *f.*

malt /mɔːlt/ *n.* malt *m.* **~ whisky,** whisky pur malt *m.*

Malt|a /'mɔːltə/ *n.* Malte *f.* **~ese** /-'tiːz/ *a.* & *n.* maltais(e) (*m.* (*f.*)).

maltreat /mæl'triːt/ *v.t.* maltraiter. **~ment** *n.* mauvais traitement *m.*

mammal /'mæml/ *n.* mammifère *m.*

mammoth /'mæməθ/ *n.* mammouth *m.* —*a.* monstre.

man /mæn/ *n.* (*pl.* **men**) homme *m.*; (*in sports team*) joueur *m.*; (*chess*) pièce *f.* —*v.t.* (*p.t.* **manned**) pourvoir en hommes; (*ship*) armer; (*guns*) servir; (*be on duty at*) être de service à. **~-hour** *n.* heure de main-d'œuvre *f.* **~-hunt** *n.* chasse à l'homme *f.* **~ in the street,** homme de la rue *m.* **~-made** *a.* artificiel. **~-of-war** *n.* navire de guerre *m.* **~-sized** *a.* grand. **~ to man,** d'homme à homme.

manage /'mænɪdʒ/ *v.t.* diriger;

(*shop, affairs*) gérer; (*handle*) manier. **I could ~ another drink,** (*fam.*) je prendrais bien encore un verre. —*v.i.* se débrouiller. **~ to do,** réussir à faire. **~able** *a.* (*tool, size, person, etc.*) maniable; (*job*) faisable. **~ment** *n.* direction *f.*; (*of shop*) gestion *f.* **managing director,** directeur général *m.*

manager /ˈmænɪdʒə(r)/ *n.* directeur *m.*; (*of shop*) gérant *m.*; (*of actor*) impresario *m.* **~ess** /-ˈres/ *n.* directrice *f.*; gérante *f.* **~ial** /-ˈdʒɪərɪəl/ *a.* directorial. **~ial staff,** cadres *m. pl.*

mandarin /ˈmændərɪn/ *n.* mandarin *m.*; (*orange*) mandarine *f.*

mandate /ˈmændeɪt/ *n.* mandat *m.*

mandatory /ˈmændətrɪ/ *a.* obligatoire.

mane /meɪn/ *n.* crinière *f.*

manful /ˈmænfl/ *a.* courageux.

mangle[1] /ˈmæŋgl/ *n.* (*for wringing*) essoreuse *f.*; (*for smoothing*) calandre *f.*

mangle[2] /ˈmæŋgl/ *v.t.* mutiler.

mango /ˈmæŋgəʊ/ *n.* (*pl.* **-oes**) mangue *f.*

mangy /ˈmeɪndʒɪ/ *a.* galeux.

manhandle /ˈmænhændl/ *v.t.* maltraiter, malmener.

manhole /ˈmænhəʊl/ *n.* trou d'homme *m.*, regard *m.*

manhood /ˈmænhʊd/ *n.* âge d'homme *m.*; (*quality*) virilité *f.*

mania /ˈmeɪnɪə/ *n.* manie *f.* **~c** /-ɪæk/ *n.* maniaque *m./f.*, fou *m.*, folle *f.*

manicur|e /ˈmænɪkjʊə(r)/ *n.* soin des mains *m.* —*v.t.* soigner, manucurer. **~ist** *n.* manucure *m./f.*

manifest /ˈmænɪfest/ *a.* manifeste. —*v.t.* manifester. **~ation** /-ˈsteɪʃn/ *n.* manifestation *f.*

manifesto /mænɪˈfestəʊ/ *n.* (*pl.* **-os**) manifeste *m.*

manifold /ˈmænɪfəʊld/ *a.* multiple.

manipulat|e /məˈnɪpjʊleɪt/ *v.t.* (*tool, person*) manipuler. **~ion** /-ˈleɪʃn/ *n.* manipulation *f.*

mankind /mænˈkaɪnd/ *n.* genre humain *m.*

manly /ˈmænlɪ/ *a.* viril.

manner /ˈmænə(r)/ *n.* manière *f.*; (*attitude*) attitude *f.*; (*kind*) sorte *f.* **~s,** (*social behaviour*) manières *f. pl.* **~ed** *a.* maniéré.

mannerism /ˈmænərɪzəm/ *n.* trait particulier *m.*

manœuvre /məˈnuːvə(r)/ *n.* manœuvre *f.* —*v.t./i.* manœuvrer.

manor /ˈmænə(r)/ *n.* manoir *m.*

manpower /ˈmænpaʊə(r)/ *n.* main-d'œuvre *f.*

manservant /ˈmænsɜːvənt/ *n.* (*pl.* **menservants**) domestique *m.*

mansion /ˈmænʃn/ *n.* château *m.*

manslaughter /ˈmænslɔːtə(r)/ *n.* homicide involontaire *m.*

mantelpiece /ˈmæntlpiːs/ *n.* (*shelf*) cheminée *f.*

manual /ˈmænjʊəl/ *a.* manuel. —*n.* (*handbook*) manuel *m.*

manufacture /mænjʊˈfæktʃə(r)/ *v.t.* fabriquer. —*n.* fabrication *f.* **~r** /-ə(r)/ *n.* fabricant *m.*

manure /məˈnjʊə(r)/ *n.* fumier *m.*

manuscript /ˈmænjʊskrɪpt/ *n.* manuscrit *m.*

many /ˈmenɪ/ *a.* & *n.* beaucoup (de). **a great** *or* **good ~,** un grand nombre (de). **~ a,** bien des.

map /mæp/ *n.* carte *f.*; (*of streets etc.*) plan *m.* —*v.t.* (*p.t.* **mapped**) faire la carte de. **~ out,** (*route*) tracer; (*arrange*) organiser.

maple /ˈmeɪpl/ *n.* érable *m.*

mar /mɑː(r)/ *v.t.* (*p.t.* **marred**) gâter; (*spoil beauty of*) déparer.

marathon /ˈmærəθən/ *n.* marathon *m.*

marauding /məˈrɔːdɪŋ/ *a.* pillard.

marble /ˈmɑːbl/ *n.* marbre *m.*; (*for game*) bille *f.*

March /mɑːtʃ/ *n.* mars *m.*

march /mɑːtʃ/ *v.i.* (*mil.*) marcher

(au pas). **~ off**/*etc.*, partir/*etc.* allégrement. *—v.t.* **~ off,** (*lead away*) emmener. *—n.* marche *f.* **~-past** *n.* défilé *m.*

mare /'meə(r)/ *n.* jument *f.*

margarine /mɑːdʒə'riːn/ *n.* margarine *f.*

margin /'mɑːdʒɪn/ *n.* marge *f.* **~al** *a.* marginal; (*increase etc.*) léger, faible. **~al seat,** (*pol.*) siège chaudement disputé *m.* **~ally** *adv.* très peu.

marigold /'mærɪgəʊld/ *n.* souci *m.*

marijuana /mærɪ'wɑːnə/ *n.* marijuana *f.*

marina /mə'riːnə/ *n.* marina *f.*

marinate /'mærɪneɪt/ *v.t.* mariner.

marine /mə'riːn/ *a.* marin. *—n.* (*shipping*) marine *f.*; (*sailor*) fusilier marin *m.*

marionette /mærɪə'net/ *n.* marionnette *f.*

marital /'mærɪtl/ *a.* conjugal. **~ status,** situation de famille *f.*

maritime /'mærɪtaɪm/ *a.* maritime.

mark[1] /mɑːk/ *n.* (*currency*) mark *m.*

mark[2] /mɑːk/ *n.* marque *f.*; (*trace*) trace *f.*, marque *f.*; (*schol.*) note *f.*; (*target*) but *m.* *—v.t.* marquer; (*exam*) corriger. **~ out,** délimiter; (*person*) désigner. **~ time,** marquer le pas. **~er** *n.* marque *f.* **~ing** *n.* (*marks*) marques *f. pl.*

marked /mɑːkt/ *a.* marqué. **~ly** /-ɪdlɪ/ *adv.* visiblement.

market /'mɑːkɪt/ *n.* marché *m.* *—v.t.* (*sell*) vendre; (*launch*) commercialiser. **~ garden,** jardin maraîcher *m.* **on the ~,** en vente. **~ing** *n.* marketing *m.*

marksman /'mɑːksmən/ *n.* (*pl.* **-men**) tireur d'élite *m.*

marmalade /'mɑːməleɪd/ *n.* confiture d'oranges *f.*

maroon /mə'ruːn/ *n.* bordeaux *m. invar.* *—a.* bordeaux *invar.*

marooned /mə'ruːnd/ *a.* abandonné; (*snow-bound etc.*) bloqué.

marquee /mɑː'kiː/ *n.* grande tente *f.*; (*awning: Amer.*) marquise *f.*

marquis /'mɑːkwɪs/ *n.* marquis *m.*

marriage /'mærɪdʒ/ *n.* mariage *m.* **~able** *a.* nubile, mariable.

marrow /'mærəʊ/ *n.* (*of bone*) moelle *f.*; (*vegetable*) courge *f.*

marr|y /'mærɪ/ *v.t.* épouser; (*give or unite in marriage*) marier. *—v.i.* se marier. **~ied** *a.* marié; (*life*) conjugal. **get ~ied,** se marier.

marsh /mɑːʃ/ *n.* marais *m.* **~y** *a.* marécageux.

marshal /'mɑːʃl/ *n.* maréchal *m.*; (*at event*) membre du service d'ordre *m.* *—v.t.* (*p.t.* **marshalled**) rassembler.

marshmallow /mɑːʃ'mæləʊ/ *n.* guimauve *f.*

martial /'mɑːʃl/ *a.* martial. **~ law,** loi martiale *f.*

Martian /'mɑːʃn/ *a.* & *n.* martien(ne) (*m.* (*f.*)).

martyr /'mɑːtə(r)/ *n.* martyr(e) *m.* (*f.*). *—v.t.* martyriser. **~dom** *n.* martyre *m.*

marvel /'mɑːvl/ *n.* merveille *f.* *—v.i.* (*p.t.* **marvelled**) s'émerveiller (**at,** de).

marvellous /'mɑːvələs/ *a.* merveilleux.

Marxis|t /'mɑːksɪst/ *a.* & *n.* marxiste (*m.*/*f.*). **~m** /-zəm/ *n.* marxisme *m.*

marzipan /'mɑːzɪpæn/ *n.* pâte d'amandes *f.*

mascara /mæ'skɑːrə/ *n.* mascara *m.*

mascot /'mæskət/ *n.* mascotte *f.*

masculin|e /'mæskjʊlɪn/ *a.* & *n.* masculin (*m.*). **~ity** /-'lɪnətɪ/ *n.* masculinité *f.*

mash /mæʃ/ *n.* pâtée *f.*; (*potatoes: fam.*) purée *f.* *—v.t.* écraser. **~ed potatoes,** purée (de pommes de terre) *f.*

mask /mɑːsk/ *n.* masque *m.* *—v.t.* masquer.

masochis|t /ˈmæsəkɪst/ *n.* masochiste *m.*/*f.* **~m** /-zəm/ *n.* masochisme *m.*
mason /ˈmeɪsn/ *n.* (*builder*) maçon *m.* **~ry** *n.* maçonnerie *f.*
Mason /ˈmeɪsn/ *n.* maçon *m.* **~ic** /məˈsɒnɪk/ *a.* maçonnique.
masquerade /mɑːskəˈreɪd/ *n.* mascarade *f.* —*v.i.* **~ as,** se faire passer pour.
mass[1] /mæs/ *n.* (*relig.*) messe *f.*
mass[2] /mæs/ *n.* masse *f.* —*v.t.*/*i.* (se) masser. **~-produce** *v.t.* fabriquer en série. **the ~es,** les masses *f. pl.*
massacre /ˈmæsəkə(r)/ *n.* massacre *m.* —*v.t.* massacrer.
massage /ˈmæsɑːʒ, *Amer.* məˈsɑːʒ/ *n.* massage *m.* —*v.t.* masser.
masseu|r /mæˈsɜː(r)/ *n.* masseur *m.* **~se** /-ɜːz/ *n.* masseuse *f.*
massive /ˈmæsɪv/ *a.* (*large*) énorme; (*heavy*) massif.
mast /mɑːst/ *n.* mât *m.*; (*for radio, TV*) pylône *m.*
master /ˈmɑːstə(r)/ *n.* maître *m.*; (*in secondary school*) professeur *m.* —*v.t.* maîtriser, dominer. **~-key** *n.* passe-partout *m. invar.* **~-mind** *n.* (*of scheme etc.*) cerveau *m.*; *v.t.* diriger. **M~ of Arts**/*etc.*, titulaire d'une maîtrise ès lettres/*etc. m.*/*f.* **~-stroke** *n.* coup de maître *m.* **~y** *n.* maîtrise *f.*
masterly /ˈmɑːstəlɪ/ *a.* magistral.
masterpiece /ˈmɑːstəpiːs/ *n.* chef-d'œuvre *m.*
masturbat|e /ˈmæstəbeɪt/ *v.i.* se masturber. **~ion** /-ˈbeɪʃn/ *n.* masturbation *f.*
mat /mæt/ *n.* (petit) tapis *m.*, natte *f.*; (*at door*) paillasson *m.*
match[1] /mætʃ/ *n.* allumette *f.*
match[2] /mætʃ/ *n.* (*sport*) match *m.*; (*equal*) égal(e) *m.* (*f.*); (*marriage*) mariage *m.*; (*s.o. to marry*) parti *m.* —*v.t.* opposer; (*go with*) aller avec; (*cups etc.*) assortir; (*equal*) égaler. —*v.i.* (*be alike*) être assorti. **~ing** *a.* assorti.
matchbox /ˈmætʃbɒks/ *n.* boîte à allumettes *f.*
mate[1] /meɪt/ *n.* camarade *m.*/*f.*; (*of animal*) compagnon *m.*, compagne *f.*; (*assistant*) aide *m.*/*f* —*v.t.*/*i.* (s')accoupler (**with,** avec).
mate[2] /meɪt/ *n.* (*chess*) mat *m.*
material /məˈtɪərɪəl/ *n.* matière *f.*; (*fabric*) tissu *m.*; (*for building*) matériau(x) *m.* (*pl.*). **~s,** (*equipment*) matériel *m.* —*a.* matériel; (*fig.*) important. **~istic** /-ˈlɪstɪk/ *a.* matérialiste.
materialize /məˈtɪərɪəlaɪz/ *v.i.* se matérialiser, se réaliser.
maternal /məˈtɜːnl/ *a.* maternel.
maternity /məˈtɜːnətɪ/ *n.* maternité *f.* —*a.* (*clothes*) de grossesse. **~ hospital,** maternité *f.*
mathematic|s /mæθəˈmætɪks/ *n.* & *n. pl.* mathématiques *f. pl.* **~ian** /-əˈtɪʃn/ *n.* mathématicien(ne) *m.* (*f.*). **~al** *a.* mathématique.
maths /mæθs/ (*Amer.* **math** /mæθ/) *n.* & *n. pl.* (*fam.*) maths *f. pl.*
matinée /ˈmætɪneɪ/ *n.* matinée *f.*
matriculat|e /məˈtrɪkjʊleɪt/ *v.t.*/*i.* (s')inscrire. **~ion** /-ˈleɪʃn/ *n.* inscription *f.*
matrimon|y /ˈmætrɪmənɪ/ *n.* mariage *m.* **~ial** /-ˈməʊnɪəl/ *a.* matrimonial.
matrix /ˈmeɪtrɪks/ *n.* (*pl.* **matrices** /-ɪsiːz/) matrice *f.*
matron /ˈmeɪtrən/ *n.* (*married, elderly*) dame âgée *f.*; (*in hospital: former use*) infirmière-major *f.* **~ly** *a.* d'âge mûr; (*manner*) très digne.
matt /mæt/ *a.* mat.
matted /ˈmætɪd/ *a.* (*hair*) emmêlé.
matter /ˈmætə(r)/ *n.* (*substance*) matière *f.*; (*affair*) affaire *f.*; (*pus*) pus *m.* —*v.i.* importer. **as a ~ of fact,** en fait. **it does not ~,** ça ne fait rien. **~-of-fact** *a.* terre à terre *invar.* **no ~,** peu importe. **what is the ~?,** qu'est-ce qu'il y a?

matting /'mætɪŋ/ *n.* natte(s) *f.* (*pl.*).
mattress /'mætrɪs/ *n.* matelas *m.*
matur|e /mə'tjʊə(r)/ *a.* mûr. —*v.t./i.* (se) mûrir. **~ity** *n.* maturité *f.*
maul /mɔːl/ *v.t.* déchiqueter.
Mauritius /mə'rɪʃəs/ *n.* île Maurice *f.*
mausoleum /mɔːsə'lɪəm/ *n.* mausolée *m.*
mauve /məʊv/ *a.* & *n.* mauve (*m.*).
mawkish /'mɔːkɪʃ/ *a.* mièvre.
maxim /'mæksɪm/ *n.* maxime *f.*
maxim|um /'mæksɪməm/ *a.* & *n.* (*pl.* **-ima**) maximum (*m.*). **~ize** *v.t.* porter au maximum.
may /meɪ/ *v. aux.* (*p.t.* **might**) pouvoir. **he ~/might come,** il peut/pourrait venir. **you might have,** vous auriez pu. **you ~ leave,** vous pouvez partir. **~ I smoke?,** puis-je fumer? **~ he be happy,** qu'il soit heureux. **I ~** *or* **might as well stay,** je ferais aussi bien de rester.
May /meɪ/ *n.* mai *m.* **~ Day,** le Premier Mai.
maybe /'meɪbiː/ *adv.* peut-être.
mayhem /'meɪhem/ *n.* (*havoc*) ravages *m. pl.*
mayonnaise /meɪə'neɪz/ *n.* mayonnaise *f.*
mayor /meə(r)/ *n.* maire *m.* **~ess** *n.* (*wife*) femme du maire *f.*
maze /meɪz/ *n.* labyrinthe *m.*
me /miː/ *pron.* me, m'*; (*after prep.*) moi. **(to) ~,** me, m'*. **he knows ~,** il me connaît.
meadow /'medəʊ/ *n.* pré *m.*
meagre /'miːgə(r)/ *a.* maigre.
meal[1] /miːl/ *n.* repas *m.*
meal[2] /miːl/ *n.* (*grain*) farine *f.*
mealy-mouthed /miːlɪ'maʊðd/ *a.* mielleux.
mean[1] /miːn/ *a.* (**-er, -est**) (*poor*) misérable; (*miserly*) avare; (*unkind*) méchant. **~ness** *n.* avarice *f.*; méchanceté *f.*
mean[2] /miːn/ *a.* moyen. —*n.* milieu *m.*; (*average*) moyenne *f.* **in the ~ time,** en attendant.
mean[3] /miːn/ *v.t.* (*p.t.* **meant**) vouloir dire, signifier; (*involve*) entraîner. **be meant for,** être destiné à. **~ to do,** avoir l'intention de faire.
meander /mɪ'ændə(r)/ *v.i.* faire des méandres.
meaning /'miːnɪŋ/ *n.* sens *m.*, signification *f.* **~ful** *a.* significatif. **~less** *a.* dénué de sens.
means /miːnz/ *n.* moyen(s) *m.* (*pl.*). —*n. pl.* (*wealth*) moyens financiers *m. pl.* **by all ~,** certainement. **by no ~,** nullement.
meant /ment/ *see* **mean**[3].
mean|time /'miːntaɪm/, **~while** *advs.* en attendant.
measles /'miːzlz/ *n.* rougeole *f.*
measly /'miːzlɪ/ *a.* (*sl.*) minable.
measurable /'meʒərəbl/ *a.* mesurable.
measure /'meʒə(r)/ *n.* mesure *f.*; (*ruler*) règle *f.* —*v.t./i.* mesurer. **~ up to,** être à la hauteur de. **~d** *a.* mesuré. **~ment** *n.* mesure *f.*
meat /miːt/ *n.* viande *f.* **~y** *a.* de viande; (*fig.*) substantiel.
mechanic /mɪ'kænɪk/ *n.* mécanicien(ne) *m.* (*f.*).
mechanic|al /mɪ'kænɪkl/ *a.* mécanique. **~s** *n.* (*science*) mécanique *f.*; *n. pl.* mécanisme *m.*
mechan|ism /'mekənɪzəm/ *n.* mécanisme *m.* **~ize** *v.t.* mécaniser.
medal /'medl/ *n.* médaille *f.* **~list** *n.* médaillé(e) *m.* (*f.*). **be a gold ~list,** être médaille d'or.
medallion /mɪ'dælɪən/ *n.* (*medal, portrait, etc.*) médaillon *m.*
meddle /'medl/ *v.i.* (*interfere*) se mêler (**in,** de); (*tinker*) toucher (**with,** à). **~some** *a.* importun.
media /'miːdɪə/ *see* **medium.** —*n. pl.* **the ~,** les media *m. pl.*
mediat|e /'miːdɪeɪt/ *v.i.* servir d'intermédiaire. **~ion** /-'eɪʃn/ *n.*

médiation *f.* **~or** *n.* média|teur, -trice *m., f.*
medical /ˈmedɪkl/ *a.* médical; (*student*) en médecine. —*n.* (*fam.*) visite médicale *f.*
medicat|ed /ˈmedɪkeɪtɪd/ *a.* médical. **~ion** /-ˈkeɪʃn/ *n.* médicaments *m. pl.*
medicin|e /ˈmedsn/ *n.* (*science*) médecine *f.*; (*substance*) médicament *m.* **~al** /mɪˈdɪsɪnl/ *a.* médicinal.
medieval /medɪˈiːvl/ *a.* médiéval.
mediocr|e /miːdɪˈəʊkə(r)/ *a.* médiocre. **~ity** /-ˈɒkrətɪ/ *n.* médiocrité *f.*
meditat|e /ˈmedɪteɪt/ *v.t./i.* méditer. **~ion** /-ˈteɪʃn/ *n.* méditation *f.*
Mediterranean /medɪtəˈreɪnɪən/ *a.* méditerranéen. —*n.* **the ~,** la Méditerranée *f.*
medium /ˈmiːdɪəm/ *n.* (*pl.* **media**) milieu *m.*; (*for transmitting data etc.*) support *m.*; (*pl.* **mediums**) (*person*) médium *m.* —*a.* moyen.
medley /ˈmedlɪ/ *n.* mélange *m.*; (*mus.*) pot-pourri *m.*
meek /miːk/ *a.* (**-er, -est**) doux.
meet /miːt/ *v.t.* (*p.t.* **met**) rencontrer; (*see again*) retrouver; (*fetch*) (aller) chercher; (*be introduced to*) faire la connaissance de; (*face, satisfy*) faire face à. —*v.i.* se rencontrer; (*see each other again*) se retrouver; (*in session*) se réunir.
meeting /ˈmiːtɪŋ/ *n.* réunion *f.*; (*between two people*) rencontre *f.*
megaphone /ˈmegəfəʊn/ *n.* porte-voix *m. invar.*
melanchol|y /ˈmelənkəlɪ/ *n.* mélancolie *f.* —*a.* mélancolique. **~ic** /-ˈkɒlɪk/ *a.* mélancolique.
mellow /ˈmeləʊ/ *a.* (**-er, -est**) (*fruit*) mûr; (*sound, colour*) moelleux, doux; (*person*) mûri. —*v.t./i.* (*mature*) mûrir; (*soften*) (s')adoucir.
melodious /mɪˈləʊdɪəs/ *a.* mélodieux.
melodrama /ˈmelədrɑːmə/ *n.* mélodrame *m.* **~tic** /-əˈmætɪk/ *a.* mélodramatique.
melod|y /ˈmelədɪ/ *n.* mélodie *f.* **~ic** /mɪˈlɒdɪk/ *a.* mélodique.
melon /ˈmelən/ *n.* melon *m.*
melt /melt/ *v.t./i.* (faire) fondre. **~ing-pot** *n.* creuset *m.*
member /ˈmembə(r)/ *n.* membre *m.* **M~ of Parliament,** député *m.* **~ship** *n.* adhésion *f.*; (*members*) membres *m. pl.*; (*fee*) cotisation *f.*
membrane /ˈmembreɪn/ *n.* membrane *f.*
memento /mɪˈmentəʊ/ *n.* (*pl.* **-oes**) (*object*) souvenir *m.*
memo /ˈmeməʊ/ *n.* (*pl.* **-os**) (*fam.*) note *f.*
memoir /ˈmemwɑː(r)/ *n.* (*record, essay*) mémoire *m.*
memorable /ˈmemərəbl/ *a.* mémorable.
memorandum /meməˈrændəm/ *n.* (*pl.* **-ums**) note *f.*
memorial /mɪˈmɔːrɪəl/ *n.* monument *m.* —*a.* commémoratif.
memorize /ˈmeməraɪz/ *v.t.* apprendre par cœur.
memory /ˈmemərɪ/ *n.* (*faculty*) mémoire *f.*; (*thing remembered*) souvenir *m.* **from ~,** de mémoire. **in ~ of,** à la mémoire de.
men /men/ *see* **man.**
menac|e /ˈmenəs/ *n.* menace *f.*; (*nuisance*) peste *f.* —*v.t.* menacer. **~ingly** *adv.* d'un ton menaçant.
menagerie /mɪˈnædʒərɪ/ *n.* ménagerie *f.*
mend /mend/ *v.t.* réparer; (*darn*) raccommoder. —*n.* raccommodage *m.* **~ one's ways,** s'amender. **on the ~,** en voie de guérison.
menfolk /ˈmenfəʊk/ *n.* hommes *m. pl.*
menial /ˈmiːnɪəl/ *a.* servile.
meningitis /menɪnˈdʒaɪtɪs/ *n.* méningite *f.*
menopause /ˈmenəpɔːz/ *n.* ménopause *f.*

menstruation /menstrʊˈeɪʃn/ *n.* menstruation *f.*
mental /ˈmentl/ *a.* mental; (*hospital*) psychiatrique.
mentality /menˈtælətɪ/ *n.* mentalité *f.*
menthol /ˈmenθɒl/ *n.* menthol *m.* —*a.* mentholé.
mention /ˈmenʃn/ *v.t.* mentionner. —*n.* mention *f.* **don't ~ it!**, il n'y a pas de quoi!, je vous en prie!
mentor /ˈmentɔː(r)/ *n.* mentor *m.*
menu /ˈmenjuː/ *n.* menu *m.*
mercantile /ˈmɜːkəntaɪl/ *a.* commercial.
mercenary /ˈmɜːsɪnərɪ/ *a.* & *n.* mercenaire (*m.*).
merchandise /ˈmɜːtʃəndaɪz/ *n.* marchandises *f. pl.*
merchant /ˈmɜːtʃənt/ *n.* marchand *m.* —*a.* (*ship, navy*) marchand. **~ bank,** banque de commerce *f.*
merciful /ˈmɜːsɪfl/ *a.* miséricordieux. **~ly** *adv.* (*fortunately: fam.*) Dieu merci.
merciless /ˈmɜːsɪlɪs/ *a.* impitoyable, implacable.
mercury /ˈmɜːkjʊrɪ/ *n.* mercure *m.*
mercy /ˈmɜːsɪ/ *n.* pitié *f.* **at the ~ of,** à la merci de.
mere /mɪə(r)/ *a.* simple. **~ly** *adv.* simplement.
merest /ˈmɪərɪst/ *a.* moindre.
merge /mɜːdʒ/ *v.t./i.* (se) mêler (**with,** à); (*companies: comm.*) fusionner. **~r** /-ə(r)/ *n.* fusion *f.*
meridian /məˈrɪdɪən/ *n.* méridien *m.*
meringue /məˈræŋ/ *n.* meringue *f.*
merit /ˈmerɪt/ *n.* mérite *m.* —*v.t.* (*p.t.* **merited**) mériter.
mermaid /ˈmɜːmeɪd/ *n.* sirène *f.*
merriment /ˈmerɪmənt/ *n.* gaieté *f.*
merry /ˈmerɪ/ *a.* (**-ier, -iest**) gai. **make ~,** faire la fête. **~-go-round** *n.* manège *m.* **~-making** *n.* réjouissances *f. pl.* **merrily** *adv.* gaiement.
mesh /meʃ/ *n.* maille *f.*; (*fabric*) tissu à mailles *m.*; (*network*) réseau *m.*
mesmerize /ˈmezməraɪz/ *v.t.* hypnotiser.
mess /mes/ *n.* désordre *m.*, gâchis *m.*; (*dirt*) saleté *f.*; (*mil.*) mess *m.* —*v.t.* **~ up,** gâcher. —*v.i.* **~ about,** s'amuser; (*dawdle*) traîner. **~ with,** (*tinker with*) tripoter. **make a ~ of,** gâcher.
message /ˈmesɪdʒ/ *n.* message *m.*
messenger /ˈmesɪndʒə(r)/ *n.* messager *m.*
Messiah /mɪˈsaɪə(r)/ *n.* Messie *m.*
Messrs /ˈmesəz/ *n. pl.* **~ Smith,** Messieurs *or* MM. Smith.
messy /ˈmesɪ/ *a.* (**-ier, -iest**) en désordre; (*dirty*) sale.
met /met/ *see* **meet.**
metabolism /mɪˈtæbəlɪzəm/ *n.* métabolisme *m.*
metal /ˈmetl/ *n.* métal *m.* —*a.* de métal. **~lic** /mɪˈtælɪk/ *a.* métallique; (*paint, colour*) métallisé.
metallurgy /mɪˈtælədʒɪ, *Amer.* ˈmetəlɜːdʒɪ/ *n.* métallurgie *f.*
metamorphosis /metəˈmɔːfəsɪs/ *n.* (*pl.* **-phoses** /-siːz/) métamorphose *f.*
metaphor /ˈmetəfə(r)/ *n.* métaphore *f.* **~ical** /-ˈfɒrɪkl/ *a.* métaphorique.
mete /miːt/ *v.t.* **~ out,** donner, distribuer; (*justice*) rendre.
meteor /ˈmiːtɪə(r)/ *n.* météore *m.*
meteorolog|y /miːtɪəˈrɒlədʒɪ/ *n.* météorologie *f.* **~ical** /-əˈlɒdʒɪkl/ *a.* météorologique.
meter[1] /ˈmiːtə(r)/ *n.* compteur *m.*
meter[2] /ˈmiːtə(r)/ *n.* (*Amer.*) = **metre.**
method /ˈmeθəd/ *n.* méthode *f.*
methodical /mɪˈθɒdɪkl/ *a.* méthodique.
Methodist /ˈmeθədɪst/ *n.* & *a.* méthodiste (*m./f.*).
methylated /ˈmeθɪleɪtɪd/ *a.* **~ spirit,** alcool à brûler *m.*

meticulous /mɪ'tɪkjʊləs/ *a.* méticuleux.
metre /'mi:tə(r)/ *n.* mètre *m.*
metric /'metrɪk/ *a.* métrique. **~ation** /-'keɪʃn/ *n.* adoption du système métrique *f.*
metropol|is /mə'trɒpəlɪs/ *n.* (*city*) métropole *f.* **~itan** /metrə'pɒlɪtən/ *a.* métropolitain.
mettle /'metl/ *n.* courage *m.*
mew /mju:/ *n.* miaulement *m.* —*v.i.* miauler.
mews /mju:z/ *n. pl.* (*dwellings*) appartements chic aménagés dans des anciennes écuries *m. pl.*
Mexic|o /'meksɪkəʊ/ *n.* Mexique *m.* **~an** *a.* & *n.* mexicain(e) (*m.* (*f.*)).
miaow /mi:'aʊ/ *n.* & *v.i.* = **mew.**
mice /maɪs/ *see* **mouse.**
mickey /'mɪkɪ/ *n.* **take the ~ out of,** (*sl.*) se moquer de.
micro- /'maɪkrəʊ/ *pref.* micro-.
microbe /'maɪkrəʊb/ *n.* microbe *m.*
microchip /'maɪkrəʊtʃɪp/ *n.* microplaquette *f.*, puce *f.*
microfilm /'maɪkrəʊfɪlm/ *n.* microfilm *m.*
microphone /'maɪkrəfəʊn/ *n.* microphone *m.*
microprocessor /maɪkrəʊ'prəʊsesə(r)/ *n.* microprocesseur *m.*
microscop|e /'maɪkrəskəʊp/ *n.* microscope *m.* **~ic** /-'skɒpɪk/ *a.* microscopique.
microwave /'maɪkrəʊweɪv/ *n.* micro-onde *f.* **~ oven,** four à micro-ondes *m.*
mid /mɪd/ *a.* **in ~ air**/*etc.*, en plein ciel/*etc.* **in ~ March**/*etc.*, à la mi-mars/*etc.* **in ~ ocean**/*etc.*, au milieu de l'océan/*etc.*
midday /mɪd'deɪ/ *n.* midi *m.*
middle /'mɪdl/ *a.* du milieu; (*quality*) moyen. —*n.* milieu *m.* **in the ~ of,** au milieu de. **~-aged** *a.* d'un certain âge. **M~ Ages,** moyen âge *m.* **~ class,** classe moyenne *f.* **~-class** *a.* bourgeois. **M~ East,** Proche-Orient *m.*
middleman /'mɪdlmæn/ *n.* (*pl.* **-men**) intermédiaire *m.*
middling /'mɪdlɪŋ/ *a.* moyen.
midge /mɪdʒ/ *n.* moucheron *m.*
midget /'mɪdʒɪt/ *n.* nain(e) *m.* (*f.*). —*a.* minuscule.
Midlands /'mɪdləndz/ *n. pl.* région du centre de l'Angleterre *f.*
midnight /'mɪdnaɪt/ *n.* minuit *f.*
midriff /'mɪdrɪf/ *n.* ventre *m.*
midst /mɪdst/ *n.* **in the ~ of,** au milieu de. **in our ~,** parmi nous.
midsummer /mɪd'sʌmə(r)/ *n.* milieu de l'été *m.*; (*solstice*) solstice d'été *m.*
midway /mɪd'weɪ/ *adv.* à mi-chemin.
midwife /'mɪdwaɪf/ *n.* (*pl.* **-wives**) sage-femme *f.*
midwinter /mɪd'wɪntə(r)/ *n.* milieu de l'hiver *m.*
might[1] /maɪt/ *n.* puissance *f.* **~y** *a.* puissant; (*very great*: *fam.*) très grand; *adv.* (*fam.*) rudement.
might[2] /maɪt/ *see* **may.**
migraine /'mi:greɪn, *Amer.* 'maɪgreɪn/ *n.* migraine *f.*
migrant /'maɪgrənt/ *a.* & *n.* (*bird*) migrateur (*m.*); (*worker*) migrant(e) (*m.* (*f.*)).
migrat|e /maɪ'greɪt/ *v.i.* émigrer. **~ion** /-ʃn/ *n.* migration *f.*
mike /maɪk/ *n.* (*fam.*) micro *m.*
mild /maɪld/ *a.* (**-er, -est**) doux; (*illness*) bénin. **~ly** *adv.* doucement. **~ness** *n.* douceur *f.*
mildew /'mɪldju:/ *n.* moisissure *f.*
mile /maɪl/ *n.* mille *m.* (= *1.6 km.*). **~s too big**/*etc.*, (*fam.*) beaucoup trop grand/*etc.* **~age** *n.* (*loosely*) kilométrage *m.*
milestone /'maɪlstəʊn/ *n.* borne *f.*; (*event, stage*: *fig.*) jalon *m.*
militant /'mɪlɪtənt/ *a.* & *n.* militant(e) (*m.* (*f.*)).
military /'mɪlɪtrɪ/ *a.* militaire.
militate /'mɪlɪteɪt/ *v.i.* militer.
militia /mɪ'lɪʃə/ *n.* milice *f.*
milk /mɪlk/ *n.* lait *m.* —*a.* (*product*)

laitier. —*v.t.* (*cow etc.*) traire; (*fig.*) exploiter. ~ **shake,** milk-shake *m.* **~y** *a.* (*diet*) lacté; (*colour*) laiteux; (*tea etc.*) au lait. **M~y Way,** Voie lactée *f.*

milkman /ˈmɪlkmən, *Amer.* ˈmɪlkmæn/ *n.* (*pl.* **-men**) laitier *m.*

mill /mɪl/ *n.* moulin *m.*; (*factory*) usine *f.* —*v.t.* moudre. —*v.i.* ~ **around,** tourner en rond; (*crowd*) grouiller. **~er** *n.* meunier *m.*

millennium /mɪˈlenɪəm/ *n.* (*pl.* **-ums**) millénaire *m.*

millet /ˈmɪlɪt/ *n.* millet *m.*

milli- /ˈmɪlɪ/ *pref.* milli-.

millimetre /ˈmɪlɪmiːtə(r)/ *n.* millimètre *m.*

milliner /ˈmɪlɪnə(r)/ *n.* modiste *f.*

million /ˈmɪljən/ *n.* million *m.* **a ~ pounds,** un million de livres. **~aire** /-ˈneə(r)/ *n.* millionnaire *m.*

millstone /ˈmɪlstəʊn/ *n.* meule *f.*; (*burden: fig.*) boulet *m.*

mime /maɪm/ *n.* (*actor*) mime *m./f.*; (*art*) (art du) mime *m.* —*v.t./i.* mimer.

mimic /ˈmɪmɪk/ *v.t.* (*p.t.* **mimicked**) imiter. —*n.* imita|teur, -trice *m., f.* **~ry** *n.* imitation *f.*

minaret /mɪnəˈret/ *n.* minaret *m.*

mince /mɪns/ *v.t.* hacher. —*n.* viande hachée *f.* ~ **pie,** tarte aux fruits confits *f.* **not to ~ matters,** ne pas mâcher ses mots. **~r** /-ə(r)/ *n.* (*machine*) hachoir *m.*

mincemeat /ˈmɪnsmiːt/ *n.* hachis de fruits confits *m.* **make ~ of,** anéantir, pulvériser.

mind /maɪnd/ *n.* esprit *m.*; (*sanity*) raison *f.*; (*opinion*) avis *m.* —*v.t.* (*have charge of*) s'occuper de; (*heed*) faire attention à. **be on s.o.'s ~,** préoccuper qn. **I do not ~ the noise**/*etc.*, le bruit/*etc.* ne me dérange pas. **I do not ~,** ça m'est égal. **~ful** *a.* attentif (**of,** à). **~less** *a.* irréfléchi.

minder /ˈmaɪndə(r)/ *n.* gardien(ne) *m.* (*f.*).

mine[1] /maɪn/ *poss. pron.* le mien, la mienne, les mien(ne)s. **it is ~,** c'est à moi *or* le mien.

min|e[2] /maɪn/ *n.* mine *f.* —*v.t.* extraire; (*mil.*) miner. **~er** *n.* mineur *m.* **~ing** *n.* exploitation minière *f.*; *a.* minier.

minefield /ˈmaɪnfiːld/ *n.* champ de mines *m.*

mineral /ˈmɪnərəl/ *n.* & *a.* minéral (*m.*). ~ **(water),** (*fizzy soft drink*) boisson gazeuse *f.* ~ **water,** (*natural*) eau minérale *f.*

minesweeper /ˈmaɪnswiːpə(r)/ *n.* (*ship*) dragueur de mines *m.*

mingle /ˈmɪŋgl/ *v.t./i.* (se) mêler (**with,** à).

mingy /ˈmɪndʒɪ/ *a.* (*fam.*) radin.

mini- /ˈmɪnɪ/ *pref.* mini-.

miniature /ˈmɪnɪtʃə(r)/ *a.* & *n.* miniature (*f.*).

minibus /ˈmɪnɪbʌs/ *n.* minibus *m.*

minicab /ˈmɪnɪkæb/ *n.* taxi *m.*

minim /ˈmɪnɪm/ *n.* blanche *f.*

minim|um /ˈmɪnɪməm/ *a.* & *n.* (*pl.* **-ima**) minimum (*m.*). **~al** *a.* minimal. **~ize** *v.t.* minimiser.

minist|er /ˈmɪnɪstə(r)/ *n.* ministre *m.* **~erial** /-ˈstɪərɪəl/ *a.* ministériel. **~ry** *n.* ministère *m.*

mink /mɪŋk/ *n.* vison *m.*

minor /ˈmaɪnə(r)/ *a.* petit, mineur. —*n.* (*jurid.*) mineur(e) *m.* (*f.*).

minority /maɪˈnɒrətɪ/ *n.* minorité *f.* —*a.* minoritaire.

minster /ˈmɪnstə(r)/ *n.* église abbatiale *f.*

minstrel /ˈmɪnstrəl/ *n.* ménestrel *m.*, jongleu|r, -se *m., f.*

mint[1] /mɪnt/ *n.* **the M~,** l'Hôtel de la Monnaie *m.* **a ~,** une fortune. —*v.t.* frapper. **in ~ condition,** à l'état neuf.

mint[2] /mɪnt/ *n.* (*plant*) menthe *f.*; (*sweet*) pastille de menthe *f.*

minus /ˈmaɪnəs/ *prep.* moins;

(*without*: *fam.*) sans. —*n.* (*sign*) moins *m.* **~ sign,** moins *m.*

minute[1] /ˈmɪnɪt/ *n.* minute *f.* **~s,** (*of meeting*) procès-verbal *m.*

minute[2] /maɪˈnjuːt/ *a.* (*tiny*) minuscule; (*detailed*) minutieux.

mirac|le /ˈmɪrəkl/ *n.* miracle *m.* **~ulous** /mɪˈrækjʊləs/ *a.* miraculeux.

mirage /ˈmɪrɑːʒ/ *n.* mirage *m.*

mire /maɪə(r)/ *n.* fange *f.*

mirror /ˈmɪrə(r)/ *n.* miroir *m.*, glace *f.* —*v.t.* refléter.

mirth /mɜːθ/ *n.* gaieté *f.*

misadventure /mɪsədˈventʃə(r)/ *n.* mésaventure *f.*

misanthropist /mɪsˈænθrəpɪst/ *n.* misanthrope *m./f.*

misapprehension /mɪsæprɪˈhenʃn/ *n.* malentendu *m.*

misbehav|e /mɪsbɪˈheɪv/ *v.i.* se conduire mal. **~iour** *n.* mauvaise conduite *f.*

miscalculat|e /mɪsˈkælkjʊleɪt/ *v.t.* mal calculer. —*v.i.* se tromper. **~ion** /-ˈleɪʃn/ *n.* erreur de calcul *f.*

miscarr|y /mɪsˈkærɪ/ *v.i.* faire une fausse couche. **~iage** /-ɪdʒ/ *n.* fausse couche *f.* **~iage of justice,** erreur judiciaire *f.*

miscellaneous /mɪsəˈleɪnɪəs/ *a.* divers.

mischief /ˈmɪstʃɪf/ *n.* (*foolish conduct*) espièglerie *f.*; (*harm*) mal *m.* **get into ~,** faire des sottises.

mischievous /ˈmɪstʃɪvəs/ *a.* espiègle; (*malicious*) méchant.

misconception /mɪskənˈsepʃn/ *n.* idée fausse *f.*

misconduct /mɪsˈkɒndʌkt/ *n.* mauvaise conduite *f.*

misconstrue /mɪskənˈstruː/ *v.t.* mal interpréter.

misdeed /mɪsˈdiːd/ *n.* méfait *m.*

misdemeanour /mɪsdɪˈmiːnə(r)/ *n.* (*jurid.*) délit *m.*

misdirect /mɪsdɪˈrekt/ *v.t.* (*person*) mal renseigner.

miser /ˈmaɪzə(r)/ *n.* avare *m./f.* **~ly** *a.* avare.

miserable /ˈmɪzrəbl/ *a.* (*sad*) malheureux; (*wretched*) misérable; (*unpleasant*) affreux.

misery /ˈmɪzərɪ/ *n.* (*unhappiness*) malheur *m.*; (*pain*) souffrances *f. pl.*; (*poverty*) misère *f.*; (*person*: *fam.*) grincheu|x, -se *m., f.*

misfire /mɪsˈfaɪə(r)/ *v.i.* (*plan etc.*) rater; (*engine*) avoir des ratés.

misfit /ˈmɪsfɪt/ *n.* inadapté(e) *m.* (*f.*).

misfortune /mɪsˈfɔːtʃuːn/ *n.* malheur *m.*

misgiving /mɪsˈgɪvɪŋ/ *n.* (*doubt*) doute *m.*; (*apprehension*) crainte *f.*

misguided /mɪsˈgaɪdɪd/ *a.* (*foolish*) imprudent; (*mistaken*) erroné. **be ~,** (*person*) se tromper.

mishap /ˈmɪshæp/ *n.* mésaventure *f.*, contretemps *m.*

misinform /mɪsɪnˈfɔːm/ *v.t.* mal renseigner.

misinterpret /mɪsɪnˈtɜːprɪt/ *v.t.* mal interpréter.

misjudge /mɪsˈdʒʌdʒ/ *v.t.* mal juger.

mislay /mɪsˈleɪ/ *v.t.* (*p.t.* **mislaid**) égarer.

mislead /mɪsˈliːd/ *v.t.* (*p.t.* **misled**) tromper. **~ing** *a.* trompeur.

mismanage /mɪsˈmænɪdʒ/ *v.t.* mal gérer. **~ment** *n.* mauvaise gestion *f.*

misnomer /mɪsˈnəʊmə(r)/ *n.* terme impropre *m.*

misplace /mɪsˈpleɪs/ *v.t.* mal placer; (*lose*) égarer.

misprint /ˈmɪsprɪnt/ *n.* faute d'impression *f.*, coquille *f.*

misrepresent /mɪsreprɪˈzent/ *v.t.* présenter sous un faux jour.

miss[1] /mɪs/ *v.t./i.* manquer; (*deceased person etc.*) regretter. **he ~es her/Paris/***etc.*, elle/Paris/*etc.* lui manque. **I ~ you,** tu me manques. —*n.* coup manqué *m.* **it was a near ~,** on l'a échappé belle *or* de peu. **~ out,** omettre.

miss[2] /mɪs/ *n.* (*pl.* **misses**) mademoiselle *f.* (*pl.* mesdemoiselles). **M~ Smith,** Mademoiselle *or* Mlle Smith.

misshapen /mɪsˈʃeɪpən/ *a.* difforme.

missile /ˈmɪsaɪl/ *n.* (*mil.*) missile *m.*; (*object thrown*) projectile *m.*

missing /ˈmɪsɪŋ/ *a.* (*after disaster*) disparu. **be ~,** (*not present, lost*) manquer.

mission /ˈmɪʃn/ *n.* mission *f.*

missionary /ˈmɪʃənrɪ/ *n.* missionnaire *m.*/*f.*

missive /ˈmɪsɪv/ *n.* missive *f.*

misspell /mɪsˈspel/ *v.t.* (*p.t.* **misspelt** *or* **misspelled**) mal écrire.

mist /mɪst/ *n.* brume *f.*; (*on window*) buée *f.* —*v.t.*/*i.* (s')embuer.

mistake /mɪˈsteɪk/ *n.* erreur *f.*, faute *f.* —*v.t.* (*p.t.* **mistook,** *p.p.* **mistaken**) mal comprendre; (*choose wrongly*) se tromper de. **~ for,** prendre pour. **~n** /-ən/ *a.* erroné. **be ~n,** se tromper. **~nly** /-ənlɪ/ *adv.* par erreur.

mistletoe /ˈmɪsltəʊ/ *n.* gui *m.*

mistreat /mɪsˈtriːt/ *v.t.* maltraiter.

mistress /ˈmɪstrɪs/ *n.* maîtresse *f.*

mistrust /mɪsˈtrʌst/ *v.t.* se méfier de. —*n.* méfiance *f.*

misty /ˈmɪstɪ/ *a.* (**-ier, -iest**) brumeux; (*window*) embué.

misunderstand /mɪsʌndəˈstænd/ *v.t.* (*p.t.* **-stood**) mal comprendre. **~ing** *n.* malentendu *m.*

misuse[1] /mɪsˈjuːz/ *v.t.* mal employer; (*power etc.*) abuser de.

misuse[2] /mɪsˈjuːs/ *n.* mauvais emploi *m.*; (*unfair use*) abus *m.*

mite /maɪt/ *n.* (*child*) pauvre petit(e) *m.* (*f.*).

mitigate /ˈmɪtɪgeɪt/ *v.t.* atténuer.

mitten /ˈmɪtn/ *n.* moufle *f.*

mix /mɪks/ *v.t.*/*i.* (se) mélanger. —*n.* mélange *m.* **~ up,** mélanger; (*bewilder*) embrouiller; (*mistake, confuse*) confondre (**with,** avec). **~-up** *n.* confusion *f.* **~ with,** (*people*) fréquenter. **~er** *n.* (*culin.*) mélangeur *m.* **be a good ~er,** être sociable.

mixed /mɪkst/ *a.* (*school etc.*) mixte; (*assorted*) assorti. **be ~-up,** (*fam.*) avoir des problèmes.

mixture /ˈmɪkstʃə(r)/ *n.* mélange *m.*; (*for cough*) sirop *m.*

moan /məʊn/ *n.* gémissement *m.* —*v.i.* gémir; (*complain*) grogner. **~er** *n.* (*grumbler*) grognon *m.*

moat /məʊt/ *n.* douve(s) *f.* (*pl.*).

mob /mɒb/ *n.* (*crowd*) cohue *f.*; (*gang*: *sl.*) bande *f.* —*v.t.* (*p.t.* **mobbed**) assiéger.

mobil|e /ˈməʊbaɪl/ *a.* mobile. **~e home,** caravane *f.* —*n.* mobile *m.* **~ity** /-ˈbɪlətɪ/ *n.* mobilité *f.*

mobiliz|e /ˈməʊbɪlaɪz/ *v.t.*/*i.* mobiliser. **~ation** /-ˈzeɪʃn/ *n.* mobilisation *f.*

moccasin /ˈmɒkəsɪn/ *n.* mocassin *m.*

mocha /ˈməʊkə/ *n.* moka *m.*

mock /mɒk/ *v.t.*/*i.* se moquer (de). —*a.* faux. **~-up** *n.* maquette *f.*

mockery /ˈmɒkərɪ/ *n.* moquerie *f.* **a ~ of,** une parodie de.

mode /məʊd/ *n.* (*way, method*) mode *m.*; (*fashion*) mode *f.*

model /ˈmɒdl/ *n.* modèle *m.*; (*of toy*) modèle réduit *m.*; (*artist's*) modèle *m.*; (*for fashion*) mannequin *m.* —*a.* modèle; (*car etc.*) modèle réduit *invar.* —*v.t.* (*p.t.* **modelled**) modeler; (*clothes*) présenter. —*v.i.* être mannequin; (*pose*) poser. **~ling** *n.* métier de mannequin *m.*

moderate[1] /ˈmɒdərət/ *a.* & *n.* modéré(e) (*m.* (*f.*)). **~ly** *adv.* (*in moderation*) modérément; (*fairly*) moyennement.

moderat|e[2] /ˈmɒdəreɪt/ *v.t.*/*i.* (se) modérer. **~ion** /-ˈreɪʃn/ *n.* modération *f.* **in ~ion,** avec modération.

modern /ˈmɒdn/ *a.* moderne. **~ languages,** langues vivantes *f. pl.* **~ize** *v.t.* moderniser.
modest /ˈmɒdɪst/ *a.* modeste. **~y** *n.* modestie *f.*
modicum /ˈmɒdɪkəm/ *n.* **a ~ of,** un peu de.
modif|y /ˈmɒdɪfaɪ/ *v.t.* modifier. **~ication** /-ɪˈkeɪʃn/ *n.* modification *f.*
modulat|e /ˈmɒdjʊleɪt/ *v.t./i.* moduler. **~ion** /-ˈleɪʃn/ *n.* modulation *f.*
module /ˈmɒdjuːl/ *n.* module *m.*
mohair /ˈməʊheə(r)/ *n.* mohair *m.*
moist /mɔɪst/ *a.* (**-er, -est**) humide, moite. **~ure** /ˈmɔɪstʃə(r)/ *n.* humidité *f.*
moisten /ˈmɔɪsn/ *v.t.* humecter.
molar /ˈməʊlə(r)/ *n.* molaire *f.*
molasses /məˈlæsɪz/ *n.* mélasse *f.*
mold /məʊld/ (*Amer.*) = **mould.**
mole[1] /məʊl/ *n.* grain de beauté *m.*
mole[2] /məʊl/ *n.* (*animal*) taupe *f.*
molecule /ˈmɒlɪkjuːl/ *n.* molécule *f.*
molest /məˈlest/ *v.t.* (*pester*) importuner; (*ill-treat*) molester.
mollusc /ˈmɒləsk/ *n.* mollusque *m.*
mollycoddle /ˈmɒlɪkɒdl/ *v.t.* dorloter, chouchouter.
molten /ˈməʊltən/ *a.* en fusion.
mom /mɒm/ *n.* (*Amer.*) maman *f.*
moment /ˈməʊmənt/ *n.* moment *m.*
momentar|y /ˈməʊməntrɪ, *Amer.* -terɪ/ *a.* momentané. **~ily** /*Amer.* məʊmənˈterəlɪ/ *adv.* momentanément; (*soon*: *Amer.*) très bientôt.
momentous /məˈmentəs/ *a.* important.
momentum /məˈmentəm/ *n.* élan *m.*
Monaco /ˈmɒnəkəʊ/ *n.* Monaco *f.*
monarch /ˈmɒnək/ *n.* monarque *m.* **~y** *n.* monarchie *f.*
monast|ery /ˈmɒnəstrɪ/ *n.* monastère *m.* **~ic** /məˈnæstɪk/ *a.* monastique.
Monday /ˈmʌndɪ/ *n.* lundi *m.*
monetarist /ˈmʌnɪtərɪst/ *n.* monétariste *m./f.*
monetary /ˈmʌnɪtrɪ/ *a.* monétaire.
money /ˈmʌnɪ/ *n.* argent *m.* **~s,** sommes d'argent *f. pl.* **~-box** *n.* tirelire *f.* **~-lender** *n.* prêteu|r, -se *m., f.* **~ order,** mandat *m.* **~-spinner** *n.* mine d'or *f.*
mongol /ˈmɒŋgl/ *n.* & *a.* (*med.*) mongolien(ne) (*m.* (*f.*)).
mongrel /ˈmʌŋgrəl/ *n.* (chien) bâtard *m.*
monitor /ˈmɒnɪtə(r)/ *n.* (*pupil*) chef de classe *m.*; (*techn.*) moniteur *m.* —*v.t.* contrôler; (*a broadcast*) écouter.
monk /mʌŋk/ *n.* moine *m.*
monkey /ˈmʌŋkɪ/ *n.* singe *m.* **~-nut** *n.* cacahuète *f.* **~-wrench** *n.* clef à molette *f.*
mono /ˈmɒnəʊ/ *n.* (*pl.* **-os**) mono *f.* —*a.* mono *invar.*
monocle /ˈmɒnəkl/ *n.* monocle *m.*
monogram /ˈmɒnəgræm/ *n.* monogramme *m.*
monologue /ˈmɒnəlɒg/ *n.* monologue *m.*
monopol|y /məˈnɒpəlɪ/ *n.* monopole *m.* **~ize** *v.t.* monopoliser.
monosyllab|le /ˈmɒnəsɪləbl/ *n.* monosyllabe *m.* **~ic** /-ˈlæbɪk/ *a.* monosyllabique.
monotone /ˈmɒnətəʊn/ *n.* ton uniforme *m.*
monoton|ous /məˈnɒtənəs/ *a.* monotone. **~y** *n.* monotonie *f.*
monsoon /mɒnˈsuːn/ *n.* mousson *f.*
monst|er /ˈmɒnstə(r)/ *n.* monstre *m.* **~rous** *a.* monstrueux.
monstrosity /mɒnˈstrɒsətɪ/ *n.* monstruosité *f.*
month /mʌnθ/ *n.* mois *m.*
monthly /ˈmʌnθlɪ/ *a.* mensuel. —*adv.* mensuellement. —*n.* (*periodical*) mensuel *m.*
monument /ˈmɒnjʊmənt/ *n.* monument *m.* **~al** /-ˈmentl/ *a.* monumental.

moo /muː/ *n.* meuglement *m.* —*v.i.* meugler.
mooch /muːtʃ/ *v.i.* (*sl.*) flâner. —*v.t.* (*Amer., sl.*) se procurer.
mood /muːd/ *n.* humeur *f.* **in a good/bad ~,** de bonne/mauvaise humeur. **~y** *a.* d'humeur changeante; (*sullen*) maussade.
moon /muːn/ *n.* lune *f.*
moon|light /ˈmuːnlaɪt/ *n.* clair de lune *m.* **~lit** *a.* éclairé par la lune.
moonlighting /ˈmuːnlaɪtɪŋ/ *n.* (*fam.*) travail noir *m.*
moor[1] /mʊə(r)/ *n.* lande *f.*
moor[2] /mʊə(r)/ *v.t.* amarrer. **~ings** *n. pl.* (*chains etc.*) amarres *f. pl.*; (*place*) mouillage *m.*
moose /muːs/ *n. invar.* élan *m.*
moot /muːt/ *a.* discutable. —*v.t.* (*question*) soulever.
mop /mɒp/ *n.* balai à franges *m.* —*v.t.* (*p.t.* **mopped**). **~ (up),** éponger. **~ of hair,** tignasse *f.*
mope /məʊp/ *v.i.* se morfondre.
moped /ˈməʊped/ *n.* cyclomoteur *m.*
moral /ˈmɒrəl/ *a.* moral. —*n.* morale *f.* **~s,** moralité *f.* **~ize** *v.i.* moraliser. **~ly** *adv.* moralement.
morale /məˈrɑːl/ *n.* moral *m.*
morality /məˈrælətɪ/ *n.* moralité *f.*
morass /məˈræs/ *n.* marais *m.*
morbid /ˈmɔːbɪd/ *a.* morbide.
more /mɔː(r)/ *a.* (*a greater amount of*) plus de (**than,** que). —*n.* & *adv.* plus (**than,** que). (**some**) **~ tea/pens**/*etc.*, (*additional*) encore du thé/des stylos/*etc.* **no ~ bread**/*etc.*, plus de pain/*etc.* **I want no ~, I do not want any ~,** je n'en veux plus. **~ or less,** plus ou moins.
moreover /mɔːˈrəʊvə(r)/ *adv.* de plus, en outre.
morgue /mɔːg/ *n.* morgue *f.*
moribund /ˈmɒrɪbʌnd/ *a.* moribond.
morning /ˈmɔːnɪŋ/ *n.* matin *m.*; (*whole morning*) matinée *f.*
Moroc|co /məˈrɒkəʊ/ *n.* Maroc *m.* **~an** *a.* & *n.* marocain(e) (*m.* (*f.*)).
moron /ˈmɔːrɒn/ *n.* crétin(e) *m.* (*f.*).
morose /məˈrəʊs/ *a.* morose.
morphine /ˈmɔːfiːn/ *n.* morphine *f.*
Morse /mɔːs/ *n.* **~ (code),** morse *m.*
morsel /ˈmɔːsl/ *n.* petit morceau *m.*; (*of food*) bouchée *f.*
mortal /ˈmɔːtl/ *a.* & *n.* mortel(le) (*m.* (*f.*)). **~ity** /mɔːˈtælətɪ/ *n.* mortalité *f.*
mortar /ˈmɔːtə(r)/ *n.* mortier *m.*
mortgage /ˈmɔːgɪdʒ/ *n.* prêt hypothécaire *m.*, emprunt-logement *m.* —*v.t.* hypothéquer.
mortify /ˈmɔːtɪfaɪ/ *v.t.* mortifier.
mortuary /ˈmɔːtʃərɪ/ *n.* morgue *f.*
mosaic /məʊˈzeɪɪk/ *n.* mosaïque *f.*
Moscow /ˈmɒskəʊ/ *n.* Moscou *m.*/*f.*
Moses /ˈməʊzɪz/ *a.* **~ basket,** couffin *m.*
mosque /mɒsk/ *n.* mosquée *f.*
mosquito /məˈskiːtəʊ/ *n.* (*pl.* **-oes**) moustique *m.*
moss /mɒs/ *n.* mousse *f.* **~y** *a.* moussu.
most /məʊst/ *a.* (*the greatest amount of*) le plus de; (*the majority of*) la plupart de. —*n.* le plus. —*adv.* (le) plus; (*very*) fort. **~ of,** la plus grande partie de; (*majority*) la plupart de. **at ~,** tout au plus. **for the ~ part,** pour la plupart. **make the ~ of,** profiter de. **~ly** *adv.* surtout.
motel /məʊˈtel/ *n.* motel *m.*
moth /mɒθ/ *n.* papillon de nuit *m.*; (*in cloth*) mite *f.* **~-ball** *n.* boule de naphtaline *f.* **~-eaten** *a.* mité.
mother /ˈmʌðə(r)/ *n.* mère *f.* —*v.t.* entourer de soins maternels, materner. **~hood** *n.* maternité *f.* **~-in-law** *n.* (*pl.* **~s-in-law**) belle-mère *f.* **~-of-pearl** *n.* nacre *f.* **M~'s Day,** la fête des mères. **~-to-be** *n.* future maman *f.* **~ tongue,** langue maternelle *f.*
motherly /ˈmʌðəlɪ/ *a.* maternel.

motif /məʊ'ti:f/ *n.* motif *m.*
motion /'məʊʃn/ *n.* mouvement *m.*; (*proposal*) motion *f.* —*v.t./i.* **~** (to) **s.o. to,** faire signe à qn. de. **~less** *a.* immobile.
motivat|e /'məʊtɪveɪt/ *v.t.* motiver. **~ion** /-'veɪʃn/ *n.* motivation *f.*
motive /'məʊtɪv/ *n.* motif *m.*
motley /'mɒtlɪ/ *a.* bigarré.
motor /'məʊtə(r)/ *n.* moteur *m.*; (*car*) auto *f.* —*a.* (*anat.*) moteur; (*boat*) à moteur. —*v.i.* aller en auto. **~ bike,** (*fam.*) moto *f.* **~ car,** auto *f.* **~ cycle,** motocyclette *f.* **~-cyclist** *n.* motocycliste *m./f.* **~ing** *n.* (*sport*) l'automobile *f.* **~ized** *a.* motorisé. **~ vehicle,** véhicule automobile *m.*
motorist /'məʊtərɪst/ *n.* automobiliste *m./f.*
motorway /'məʊtəweɪ/ *n.* autoroute *f.*
mottled /'mɒtld/ *a.* tacheté.
motto /'mɒtəʊ/ *n.* (*pl.* **-oes**) devise *f.*
mould[1] /məʊld/ *n.* moule *m.* —*v.t.* mouler; (*influence*) former. **~ing** *n.* (*on wall etc.*) moulure *f.*
mould[2] /məʊld/ *n.* (*fungus, rot*) moisissure *f.* **~y** *a.* moisi.
moult /məʊlt/ *v.i.* muer.
mound /maʊnd/ *n.* monticule *m.*, tertre *m.*; (*pile*: *fig.*) tas *m.*
mount[1] /maʊnt/ *n.* (*hill*) mont *m.*
mount[2] /maʊnt/ *v.t./i.* monter. —*n.* monture *f.* **~ up,** s'accumuler; (*add up*) chiffrer (**to,** à).
mountain /'maʊntɪn/ *n.* montagne *f.* **~ous** *a.* montagneux.
mountaineer /maʊntɪ'nɪə(r)/ *n.* alpiniste *m./f.* **~ing** *n.* alpinisme *m.*
mourn /mɔ:n/ *v.t./i.* **~ (for),** pleurer. **~er** *n.* personne qui suit le cortège funèbre *f.* **~ing** *n.* deuil *m.*
mournful /'mɔ:nfl/ *a.* triste.
mouse /maʊs/ *n.* (*pl.* **mice**) souris *f.*
mousetrap /'maʊstræp/ *n.* souricière *f.*
mousse /mu:s/ *n.* (*dish*) mousse *f.*
moustache /mə'stɑ:ʃ, *Amer.* 'mʌstæʃ/ *n.* moustache *f.*
mousy /'maʊsɪ/ *a.* (*hair*) d'un brun terne; (*fig.*) timide.
mouth[1] /maʊθ/ *n.* bouche *f.*; (*of dog, cat, etc.*) gueule *f.* **~-organ** *n.* harmonica *m.*
mouth[2] /maʊð/ *v.t.* dire.
mouthful /'maʊθfʊl/ *n.* bouchée *f.*
mouthpiece /'maʊθpi:s/ *n.* (*mus.*) embouchure *f.*; (*person*: *fig.*) porte-parole *m. invar.*
mouthwash /'maʊθwɒ:ʃ/ *n.* eau dentifrice *f.*
movable /'mu:vəbl/ *a.* mobile.
move /mu:v/ *v.t./i.* remuer, (se) déplacer, bouger; (*incite*) pousser; (*emotionally*) émouvoir; (*propose*) proposer; (*depart*) partir; (*act*) agir. **~ (out),** déménager. —*n.* mouvement *m.*; (*in game*) coup *m.*; (*player's turn*) tour *m.*; (*procedure*: *fig.*) démarche *f.*; (*house change*) déménagement *m.* **~ back,** (faire) reculer. **~ forward** *or* **on,** (faire) avancer. **~ in,** emménager. **~ over,** se pousser. **on the ~,** en marche.
movement /'mu:vmənt/ *n.* mouvement *m.*
movie /'mu:vɪ/ *n.* (*Amer.*) film *m.* **the ~s,** le cinéma.
moving /'mu:vɪŋ/ *a.* en mouvement; (*touching*) émouvant.
mow /məʊ/ *v.t.* (*p.p.* **mowed** *or* **mown**) (*corn etc.*) faucher; (*lawn*) tondre. **~ down,** faucher. **~er** *n.* (*for lawn*) tondeuse *f.*
MP *abbr. see* **Member of Parliament.**
Mr /'mɪstə(r)/ *n.* (*pl.* **Messrs**). **~ Smith,** Monsieur *or* M. Smith.
Mrs /'mɪsɪz/ *n.* (*pl.* **Mrs**). **~ Smith,** Madame *or* Mme Smith. **the ~ Smith,** Mesdames *or* Mmes Smith.

Ms /mɪz/ *n.* (*title of married or unmarried woman*). ~ **Smith,** Madame *or* Mme Smith.

much /mʌtʃ/ *a.* beaucoup de. —*adv.* & *n.* beaucoup.

muck /mʌk/ *n.* fumier *m.*; (*dirt*: *fam.*) saleté *f.* —*v.i.* ~ **about,** (*sl.*) s'amuser. ~ **about with,** (*sl.*) tripoter. ~ **in,** (*sl.*) participer. —*v.t.* ~ **up,** (*sl.*) gâcher. ~**y** *a.* sale.

mucus /'mju:kəs/ *n.* mucus *m.*

mud /mʌd/ *n.* boue *f.* ~**dy** *a.* couvert de boue.

muddle /'mʌdl/ *v.t.* embrouiller. —*v.i.* ~ **through,** se débrouiller. —*n.* désordre *m.*, confusion *f.*; (*mix-up*) confusion *f.*

mudguard /'mʌdgɑ:d/ *n.* garde-boue *m. invar.*

muff /mʌf/ *n.* manchon *m.*

muffin /'mʌfɪn/ *n.* muffin *m.* (*petit pain rond et plat*).

muffle /'mʌfl/ *v.t.* emmitoufler; (*sound*) assourdir. ~**r** /-ə(r)/ *n.* (*scarf*) cache-nez *m. invar.*

mug /mʌg/ *n.* tasse *f.*; (*in plastic, metal*) gobelet *m.*; (*for beer*) chope *f.*; (*face*: *sl.*) gueule *f.*; (*fool*: *sl.*) idiot(e) *m.* (*f.*) —*v.t.* (*p.t.* **mugged**) agresser. ~**ger** *n.* agresseur *m.* ~**ging** *n.* agression *f.*

muggy /'mʌgɪ/ *a.* lourd.

Muhammadan /mə'hæmɪdən/ *a.* & *n.* mahométan(e) (*m.*(*f.*)).

mule /mju:l/ *n.* (*male*) mulet *m.*; (*female*) mule *f.*

mull[1] /mʌl/ *v.t.* (*wine*) chauffer.

mull[2] /mʌl/ *v.t.* ~ **over,** ruminer.

multi- /'mʌltɪ/ *pref.* multi-.

multicoloured /'mʌltɪkʌləd/ *a.* multicolore.

multifarious /mʌltɪ'feərɪəs/ *a.* divers.

multinational /mʌltɪ'næʃnəl/ *a.* & *n.* multinational(e) (*f.*).

multiple /'mʌltɪpl/ *a.* & *n.* multiple (*m.*).

multipl|y /'mʌltɪplaɪ/ *v.t./i.* (se) multiplier. ~**ication** /-ɪ'keɪʃn/ *n.* multiplication *f.*

multitude /'mʌltɪtju:d/ *n.* multitude *f.*

mum[1] /mʌm/ *a.* **keep** ~, (*fam.*) garder le silence.

mum[2] /mʌm/ *n.* (*fam.*) maman *f.*

mumble /'mʌmbl/ *v.t./i.* marmotter, marmonner.

mummy[1] /'mʌmɪ/ *n.* (*embalmed body*) momie *f.*

mummy[2] /'mʌmɪ/ *n.* (*mother*: *fam.*) maman *f.*

mumps /mʌmps/ *n.* oreillons *m. pl.*

munch /mʌntʃ/ *v.t./i.* mastiquer.

mundane /mʌn'deɪn/ *a.* banal.

municipal /mju:'nɪsɪpl/ *a.* municipal. ~**ity** /-'pæləti/ *n.* municipalité *f.*

munitions /mju:'nɪʃnz/ *n. pl.* munitions *f. pl.*

mural /'mjʊərəl/ *a.* mural. —*n.* peinture murale *f.*

murder /'mɜ:də(r)/ *n.* meurtre *m.* —*v.t.* assassiner; (*ruin*: *fam.*) massacrer. ~**er** *n.* meurtrier *m.*, assassin *m.* ~**ess** *n.* meurtrière *f.* ~**ous** *a.* meurtrier.

murky /'mɜ:kɪ/ *a.* (**-ier, -iest**) (*night, plans, etc.*) sombre, ténébreux; (*liquid*) épais, sale.

murmur /'mɜ:mə(r)/ *n.* murmure *m.* —*v.t./i.* murmurer.

muscle /'mʌsl/ *n.* muscle *m.* —*v.i.* ~ **in,** (*Amer.*, *sl.*) s'introduire de force (**on,** dans).

muscular /'mʌskjʊlə(r)/ *a.* musculaire; (*brawny*) musclé.

muse /mju:z/ *v.i.* méditer.

museum /mju:'zɪəm/ *n.* musée *m.*

mush /mʌʃ/ *n.* (*pulp, soft food*) bouillie *f.* ~**y** *a.* mou.

mushroom /'mʌʃrʊm/ *n.* champignon *m.* —*v.i.* pousser comme des champignons.

music /'mju:zɪk/ *n.* musique *f.* ~**al** *a.* musical; (*instrument*) de musique; (*talented*) doué pour la musique; *n.* comédie musicale *f.*

musician /mjuː'zɪʃn/ *n.* musicien(ne) *m.* (*f.*).
musk /mʌsk/ *n.* musc *m.*
Muslim /'mʊzlɪm/ *a.* & *n.* musulman(e) (*m.* (*f.*)).
muslin /'mʌzlɪn/ *n.* mousseline *f.*
mussel /'mʌsl/ *n.* moule *f.*
must /mʌst/ *v. aux.* devoir. **you ~ go,** vous devez partir, il faut que vous partiez. **he ~ be old,** il doit être vieux. **I ~ have done it,** j'ai dû le faire. —*n.* **be a ~,** (*fam.*) être obligatoire.
mustard /'mʌstəd/ *n.* moutarde *f.*
muster /'mʌstə(r)/ *v.t./i.* (se) rassembler.
musty /'mʌstɪ/ *a.* (**-ier, -iest**) (*room, etc.*) qui sent le moisi; (*smell, taste*) de moisi.
mutation /mjuː'teɪʃn/ *n.* mutation *f.*
mute /mjuːt/ *a.* & *n.* muet(te) (*m.* (*f.*)). **~d** /-ɪd/ *a.* (*colour, sound*) sourd, atténué; (*criticism*) voilé.
mutilat|e /'mjuːtɪleɪt/ *v.t.* mutiler. **~ion** /-'leɪʃn/ *n.* mutilation *f.*
mutin|y /'mjuːtɪnɪ/ *n.* mutinerie *f.* —*v.i.* se mutiner. **~ous** *a.* (*sailor etc.*) mutiné; (*fig.*) rebelle.
mutter /'mʌtə(r)/ *v.t./i.* marmonner, murmurer.
mutton /'mʌtn/ *n.* mouton *m.*
mutual /'mjuːtʃʊəl/ *a.* mutuel; (*common to two or more: fam.*) commun. **~ly** *adv.* mutuellement.
muzzle /'mʌzl/ *n.* (*snout*) museau *m.*; (*device*) muselière *f.*; (*of gun*) gueule *f.* —*v.t.* museler.
my /maɪ/ *a.* mon, ma, *pl.* mes.
myopic /maɪ'ɒpɪk/ *a.* myope.
myriad /'mɪrɪəd/ *n.* myriade *f.*
myself /maɪ'self/ *pron.* moi-même; (*reflexive*) me, m'*; (*after prep.*) moi.
mysterious /mɪ'stɪərɪəs/ *a.* mystérieux.
mystery /'mɪstərɪ/ *n.* mystère *m.*
mystic /'mɪstɪk/ *a.* & *n.* mystique (*m./f.*). **~al** *a.* mystique. **~ism** /-sɪzəm/ *n.* mysticisme *m.*
mystif|y /'mɪstɪfaɪ/ *v.t.* laisser perplexe. **~ication** /-ɪ'keɪʃn/ *n.* perplexité *f.*
mystique /mɪ'stiːk/ *n.* mystique *f.*
myth /mɪθ/ *n.* mythe *m.* **~ical** *a.* mythique.
mythology /mɪ'θɒlədʒɪ/ *n.* mythologie *f.*

N

nab /næb/ *v.t.* (*p.t.* **nabbed**) (*arrest: sl.*) épingler, attraper.
nag /næg/ *v.t./i.* (*p.t.* **nagged**) critiquer; (*pester*) harceler.
nagging /'nægɪŋ/ *a.* persistant.
nail /neɪl/ *n.* clou *m.*; (*of finger, toe*) ongle *m.* —*v.t.* clouer. **~ polish,** vernis à ongles *m.* **on the ~,** (*pay*) sans tarder, tout de suite.
naïve /naɪ'iːv/ *a.* naïf.
naked /'neɪkɪd/ *a.* nu. **to the ~ eye,** à l'œil nu. **~ly** *adv.* à nu. **~ness** *n.* nudité *f.*
name /neɪm/ *n.* nom *m.*; (*fig.*) réputation *f.* —*v.t.* nommer; (*fix*) fixer. **be ~d after,** porter le nom de. **~less** *a.* sans nom, anonyme.
namely /'neɪmlɪ/ *adv.* à savoir.
namesake /'neɪmseɪk/ *n.* (*person*) homonyme *m.*
nanny /'nænɪ/ *n.* bonne d'enfants *f.* **~-goat** *n.* chèvre *f.*
nap /næp/ *n.* somme *m.* —*v.i.* (*p.t.* **napped**) faire un somme. **catch ~ping,** prendre au dépourvu.
nape /neɪp/ *n.* nuque *f.*
napkin /'næpkɪn/ *n.* (*at meals*) serviette *f.*; (*for baby*) couche *f.*
nappy /'næpɪ/ *n.* couche *f.*
narcotic /nɑː'kɒtɪk/ *a.* & *n.* narcotique (*m.*).
narrat|e /nə'reɪt/ *v.t.* raconter. **~ion** /-ʃn/ *n.* narration *f.* **~or** *n.* narra|teur, -trice *m., f.*

narrative /ˈnærətɪv/ *n.* récit *m.*

narrow /ˈnærəʊ/ *a.* (**-er, -est**) étroit. *—v.t./i.* (se) rétrécir; (*limit*) (se) limiter. **~ly** *adv.* étroitement; (*just*) de justesse. **~-minded** *a.* à l'esprit étroit; (*ideas etc.*) étroit. **~ness** *n.* étroitesse *f.*

nasal /ˈneɪzl/ *a.* nasal.

nast|y /ˈnɑːstɪ/ *a.* (**-ier, -iest**) mauvais, désagréable; (*malicious*) méchant. **~ily** *adv.* désagréablement; méchamment. **~iness** *n.* (*malice*) méchanceté *f.*

nation /ˈneɪʃn/ *n.* nation *f.* **~-wide** *a.* dans l'ensemble du pays.

national /ˈnæʃnəl/ *a.* national. *—n.* ressortissant(e) *m.* (*f.*). **~ anthem,** hymne national *m.* **~ism** *n.* nationalisme *m.* **~ize** *v.t.* nationaliser. **~ly** *adv.* à l'échelle nationale.

nationality /næʃəˈnælətɪ/ *n.* nationalité *f.*

native /ˈneɪtɪv/ *n.* (*local inhabitant*) autochtone *m.*/*f.*; (*non-European*) indigène *m.*/*f.* *—a.* indigène; (*country*) natal; (*inborn*) inné. **be a ~ of,** être originaire de. **~ language,** langue maternelle *f.* **~ speaker of French,** personne de langue maternelle française *f.*

Nativity /nəˈtɪvətɪ/ *n.* **the ~,** la Nativité *f.*

natter /ˈnætə(r)/ *v.i.* bavarder.

natural /ˈnætʃrəl/ *a.* naturel. **~ history,** histoire naturelle *f.* **~ist** *n.* naturaliste *m.*/*f.* **~ly** *adv.* (*normally, of course*) naturellement; (*by nature*) de nature.

naturaliz|e /ˈnætʃrəlaɪz/ *v.t.* naturaliser. **~ation** /-ˈzeɪʃn/ *n.* naturalisation *f.*

nature /ˈneɪtʃə(r)/ *n.* nature *f.*

naught /nɔːt/ *n.* (*old use*) rien *m.*

naught|y /ˈnɔːtɪ/ *a.* (**-ier, -iest**) vilain, méchant; (*indecent*) grivois. **~ily** *adv.* mal.

nause|a /ˈnɔːsɪə/ *n.* nausée *f.* **~ous** *a.* nauséabond.

nauseate /ˈnɔːsɪeɪt/ *v.t.* écœurer.

nautical /ˈnɔːtɪkl/ *a.* nautique.

naval /ˈneɪvl/ *a.* (*battle etc.*) naval; (*officer*) de marine.

nave /neɪv/ *n.* (*of church*) nef *f.*

navel /ˈneɪvl/ *n.* nombril *m.*

navigable /ˈnævɪgəbl/ *a.* navigable.

navigat|e /ˈnævɪgeɪt/ *v.t.* (*sea etc.*) naviguer sur; (*ship*) piloter. *—v.i.* naviguer. **~ion** /-ˈgeɪʃn/ *n.* navigation *f.* **~or** *n.* navigateur *m.*

navvy /ˈnævɪ/ *n.* terrassier *m.*

navy /ˈneɪvɪ/ *n.* marine *f.* **~ (blue),** bleu marine *invar.*

near /nɪə(r)/ *adv.* près. *—prep.* près de. *—a.* proche. *—v.t.* approcher de. **draw ~,** (s')approcher (**to,** de). **~ by** *adv.* tout près. **N~ East,** Proche-Orient *m.* **~ to,** près de. **~ness** *n.* proximité *f.*

nearby /nɪəˈbaɪ/ *a.* proche.

nearly /ˈnɪəlɪ/ *adv.* presque. **not ~ as pretty**/*etc.* **as,** loin d'être aussi joli/*etc.* que.

neat /niːt/ *a.* (**-er, -est**) soigné, net; (*room etc.*) bien rangé; (*clever*) habile; (*whisky, brandy, etc.*) sec. **~ly** *adv.* avec soin; habilement. **~ness** *n.* netteté *f.*

nebulous /ˈnebjʊləs/ *a.* nébuleux.

necessar|y /ˈnesəsərɪ/ *a.* nécessaire. **~ies** *n. pl.* nécessaire *m.* **~ily** *adv.* nécessairement.

necessitate /nɪˈsesɪteɪt/ *v.t.* nécessiter.

necessity /nɪˈsesətɪ/ *n.* nécessité *f.*; (*thing*) chose indispensable *f.*

neck /nek/ *n.* cou *m.*; (*of dress*) encolure *f.* **~ and neck,** à égalité.

necklace /ˈneklɪs/ *n.* collier *m.*

neckline /ˈneklaɪn/ *n.* encolure *f.*

necktie /ˈnektaɪ/ *n.* cravate *f.*

nectarine /ˈnektərɪn/ *n.* brugnon *m.*, nectarine *f.*

need /niːd/ *n.* besoin *m.* *—v.t.* avoir besoin de; (*demand*) demander. **you ~ not come,** vous n'êtes pas obligé de venir. **~less** *a.*

inutile. **~lessly** *adv.* inutilement.

needle /ˈniːdl/ *n.* aiguille *f.* —*v.t.* (*annoy: fam.*) asticoter, agacer.

needlework /ˈniːdlwɜːk/ *n.* couture *f.*; (*object*) ouvrage (à l'aiguille) *m.*

needy /ˈniːdɪ/ *a.* (**-ier, -iest**) nécessiteux, indigent.

negation /nɪˈgeɪʃn/ *n.* négation *f.*

negative /ˈnegətɪv/ *a.* négatif. —*n.* (*of photograph*) négatif *m.*; (*word: gram.*) négation *f.* **in the ~,** (*answer*) par la négative; (*gram.*) à la forme négative. **~ly** *adv.* négativement.

neglect /nɪˈglekt/ *v.t.* négliger, laisser à l'abandon. —*n.* manque de soins *m.* **(state of) ~,** abandon *m.* **~ to do,** négliger de faire. **~ful** *a.* négligent.

négligé /ˈneglɪʒeɪ/ *n.* négligé *m.*

negligen|t /ˈneglɪdʒənt/ *a.* négligent. **~ce** *n.* négligence *f.*

negligible /ˈneglɪdʒəbl/ *a.* négligeable.

negotiable /nɪˈgəʊʃəbl/ *a.* négociable.

negotiat|e /nɪˈgəʊʃɪeɪt/ *v.t./i.* négocier. **~ion** /-ˈeɪʃn/ *n.* négociation *f.* **~or** *n.* négocia|teur, -trice *m., f.*

Negr|o /ˈniːgrəʊ/ *n.* (*pl.* **-oes**) Noir *m.* —*a.* noir; (*art, music*) nègre. **~ess** *n.* Noire *f.*

neigh /neɪ/ *n.* hennissement *m.* —*v.i.* hennir.

neighbour /ˈneɪbə(r)/ *n.* voisin(e) *m.* (*f.*). **~hood** *n.* voisinage *m.*, quartier *m.* **in the ~hood of,** aux alentours de. **~ing** *a.* voisin.

neighbourly /ˈneɪbəlɪ/ *a.* amical.

neither /ˈnaɪðə(r)/ *a.* & *pron.* aucun(e) des deux, ni l'un(e) ni l'autre. —*adv.* ni. —*conj.* (ne) non plus. **~ big nor small,** ni grand ni petit. **~ shall I come,** je ne viendrai pas non plus.

neon /ˈniːɒn/ *n.* néon *m.* —*a.* (*lamp etc.*) au néon.

nephew /ˈnevjuː, *Amer.* ˈnefjuː/ *n.* neveu *m.*

nerve /nɜːv/ *n.* nerf *m.*; (*courage*) courage *m.*; (*calm*) sang-froid *m.*; (*impudence: fam.*) culot *m.* **~s,** (*before exams etc.*) le trac *m.* **~-racking** *a.* éprouvant.

nervous /ˈnɜːvəs/ *a.* nerveux. **be** *or* **feel ~,** (*afraid*) avoir peur. **~ly** *adv.* (*tensely*) nerveusement; (*timidly*) craintivement. **~ness** *n.* nervosité *f.*; (*fear*) crainte *f.*

nervy /ˈnɜːvɪ/ *a.* = **nervous;** (*Amer., fam.*) effronté.

nest /nest/ *n.* nid *m.* —*v.i.* nicher. **~-egg** *n.* pécule *m.*

nestle /ˈnesl/ *v.i.* se blottir.

net[1] /net/ *n.* filet *m.* —*v.t.* (*p.t.* **netted**) prendre au filet. **~ting** *n.* (*nets*) filets *m. pl.*; (*wire*) treillis *m.*; (*fabric*) voile *m.*

net[2] /net/ *a.* (*weight etc.*) net.

netball /ˈnetbɔːl/ *n.* netball *m.*

Netherlands /ˈneðələndz/ *n. pl.* **the ~,** les Pays-Bas *m. pl.*

nettle /ˈnetl/ *n.* ortie *f.*

network /ˈnetwɜːk/ *n.* réseau *m.*

neuro|sis /njʊəˈrəʊsɪs/ *n.* (*pl.* **-oses** /-siːz/) névrose *f.* **~tic** /-ˈrɒtɪk/ *a.* & *n.* névrosé(e) (*m.* (*f.*)).

neuter /ˈnjuːtə(r)/ *a.* & *n.* neutre (*m.*). —*v.t.* (*castrate*) châtrer.

neutral /ˈnjuːtrəl/ *a.* neutre. **~ (gear),** (*auto.*) point mort *m.* **~ity** /-ˈtrælətɪ/ *n.* neutralité *f.*

neutron /ˈnjuːtrɒn/ *n.* neutron *m.* **~ bomb,** bombe à neutrons *f.*

never /ˈnevə(r)/ *adv.* (ne) jamais; (*not: fam.*) (ne) pas. **he ~ refuses,** il ne refuse jamais. **I ~ saw him,** (*fam.*) je ne l'ai pas vu. **~ again,** plus jamais. **~ mind,** (*don't worry*) ne vous en faites pas; (*it doesn't matter*) peu importe. **~-ending** *a.* interminable.

nevertheless /nevəðəˈles/ *adv.* néanmoins, toutefois.

new /njuː/ *a.* (**-er, -est**) nouveau; (*brand-new*) neuf. **~-born** *a.*

nouveau-né. **~-laid egg,** œuf frais *m.* **~ moon,** nouvelle lune *f.* **~ year,** nouvel an *m.* **N~ Year's Day,** le jour de l'an. **N~ Year's Eve,** la Saint-Sylvestre. **N~ Zealand,** Nouvelle-Zélande *f.* **N~ Zealander,** Néo-Zélandais(e) *m.* (*f.*). **~ness** *n.* nouveauté *f.*

newcomer /ˈnjuːkʌmə(r)/ *n.* nouveau venu *m.*, nouvelle venue *f.*

newfangled /njuːˈfæŋgld/ *a.* (*pej.*) moderne, neuf.

newly /ˈnjuːlɪ/ *adv.* nouvellement. **~-weds** *n. pl.* nouveaux mariés *m. pl.*

news /njuːz/ *n.* nouvelle(s) *f.* (*pl.*); (*radio, press*) informations *f. pl.*; (*TV*) actualités *f. pl.*, informations *f. pl.* **~caster, ~-reader** *ns.* speaker(ine) *m.* (*f.*).

newsagent /ˈnjuːzeɪdʒənt/ *n.* marchand(e) de journaux *m.* (*f.*).

newsletter /ˈnjuːzletə(r)/ *n.* bulletin *m.*

newspaper /ˈnjuːspeɪpə(r)/ *n.* journal *m.*

newsreel /ˈnjuːzriːl/ *n.* actualités *f. pl.*

newt /njuːt/ *n.* triton *m.*

next /nekst/ *a.* prochain; (*adjoining*) voisin; (*following*) suivant. —*adv.* la prochaine fois; (*afterwards*) ensuite. —*n.* suivant(e) *m.* (*f.*). **~ door,** à côté (**to,** de). **~-door** *a.* d'à côté. **~ of kin,** parent le plus proche *m.* **~ to,** à côté de.

nib /nɪb/ *n.* bec *m.*, plume *f.*

nibble /ˈnɪbl/ *v.t./i.* grignoter.

nice /naɪs/ *a.* (**-er, -est**) agréable, bon; (*kind*) gentil; (*pretty*) joli; (*respectable*) bien *invar.*; (*subtle*) délicat. **~ly** *adv.* agréablement; gentiment; (*well*) bien.

nicety /ˈnaɪsətɪ/ *n.* subtilité *f.*

niche /nɪtʃ, niːʃ/ *n.* (*recess*) niche *f.*; (*fig.*) place *f.*, situation *f.*

nick /nɪk/ *n.* petite entaille *f.* —*v.t.* (*steal, arrest: sl.*) piquer. **in the ~ of time,** juste à temps.

nickel /ˈnɪkl/ *n.* nickel *m.*; (*Amer.*) pièce de cinq cents *f.*

nickname /ˈnɪkneɪm/ *n.* surnom *m.*; (*short form*) diminutif *m.* —*v.t.* surnommer.

nicotine /ˈnɪkətiːn/ *n.* nicotine *f.*

niece /niːs/ *n.* nièce *f.*

nifty /ˈnɪftɪ/ *a.* (*sl.*) chic *invar.*

Nigeria /naɪˈdʒɪərɪə/ *n.* Nigéria *m.*/*f.* **~n** *a.* & *n.* nigérian(e) (*m.* (*f.*)).

niggardly /ˈnɪgədlɪ/ *a.* chiche.

niggling /ˈnɪglɪŋ/ *a.* (*person*) tatillon; (*detail*) insignifiant.

night /naɪt/ *n.* nuit *f.*; (*evening*) soir *m.* —*a.* de nuit. **~-cap** *n.* boisson *f.* (*avant d'aller se coucher*). **~-club** *n.* boîte de nuit *f.* **~-dress, ~-gown** *ns.* chemise de nuit *f.* **~-life** *n.* vie nocturne *f.* **~-school** *n.* cours du soir *m. pl.* **~-time** *n.* nuit *f.* **~-watchman** *n.* veilleur de nuit *m.*

nightfall /ˈnaɪtfɔːl/ *n.* tombée de la nuit *f.*

nightingale /ˈnaɪtɪŋgeɪl/ *n.* rossignol *m.*

nightly /ˈnaɪtlɪ/ *a.* & *adv.* (de) chaque nuit *or* soir.

nightmare /ˈnaɪtmeə(r)/ *n.* cauchemar *m.*

nil /nɪl/ *n.* rien *m.*; (*sport*) zéro *m.* —*a.* (*chances, risk, etc.*) nul.

nimble /ˈnɪmbl/ *a.* (**-er, -est**) agile.

nin|e /naɪn/ *a.* & *n.* neuf (*m.*). **~th** *a.* & *n.* neuvième (*m.*/*f.*).

nineteen /naɪnˈtiːn/ *a.* & *n.* dix-neuf (*m.*). **~th** *a.* & *n.* dix-neuvième (*m.*/*f.*).

ninet|y /ˈnaɪntɪ/ *a.* & *n.* quatre-vingt-dix (*m.*). **~ieth** *a.* & *n.* quatre-vingt-dixième (*m.*/*f.*).

nip /nɪp/ *v.t./i.* (*p.t.* **nipped**) (*pinch*) pincer; (*rush: sl.*) courir. —*n.* pincement *m.*; (*cold*) fraîcheur *f.*

nipper /ˈnɪpə(r)/ *n.* (*sl.*) gosse *m.*/*f.*

nipple /ˈnɪpl/ *n.* bout de sein *m.*; (*of baby's bottle*) tétine *f.*

nippy /ˈnɪpɪ/ *a.* (**-ier, -iest**) (*fam.*) alerte; (*chilly: fam.*) frais.
nitrogen /ˈnaɪtrədʒən/ *n.* azote *m.*
nitwit /ˈnɪtwɪt/ *n.* (*fam.*) imbécile *m./f.*
no /nəʊ/ *a.* aucun(e); pas de. —*adv.* non. —*n.* (*pl.* **noes**) non *m. invar.* **~ man**/*etc.*, aucun homme/*etc.* **~ money**/**time**/*etc.*, pas d'argent/de temps/*etc.* **~ man's land,** no man's land *m.* **~ one** = **nobody. ~ smoking**/**entry,** défense de fumer/d'entrer. **~ way!,** (*Amer., fam.*) pas question!
nob|le /ˈnəʊbl/ *a.* (**-er, -est**) noble. **~ility** /-ˈbɪlətɪ/ *n.* noblesse *f.*
nobleman /ˈnəʊblmən/ *n.* (*pl.* **-men**) noble *m.*
nobody /ˈnəʊbədɪ/ *pron.* (ne) personne. —*n.* nullité *f.* **he knows ~,** il ne connaît personne. **~ is there,** personne n'est là.
nocturnal /nɒkˈtɜːnl/ *a.* nocturne.
nod /nɒd/ *v.t./i.* (*p.t.* **nodded**). **~ (one's head),** faire un signe de tête. —*n.* signe de tête *m.*
noise /nɔɪz/ *n.* bruit *m.* **~less** *a.* silencieux.
nois|y /ˈnɔɪzɪ/ *a.* (**-ier, -iest**) bruyant. **~ily** *adv.* bruyamment.
nomad /ˈnəʊmæd/ *n.* nomade *m./f.* **~ic** /-ˈmædɪk/ *a.* nomade.
nominal /ˈnɒmɪnl/ *a.* symbolique, nominal; (*value*) nominal.
nominat|e /ˈnɒmɪneɪt/ *v.t.* nommer; (*put forward*) proposer. **~ion** /-ˈneɪʃn/ *n.* nomination *f.*
non- /nɒn/ *pref.* non-.
non-commissioned /nɒnkəˈmɪʃnd/ *a.* **~ officer,** sous-officier *m.*
non-committal /nɒnkəˈmɪtl/ *a.* évasif.
nondescript /ˈnɒndɪskrɪpt/ *a.* indéfinissable.
none /nʌn/ *pron.* aucun(e). **~ of us,** aucun de nous. **I have ~,** je n'en ai pas. **~ of,** pas une seule partie de. —*adv.* **~ too,** (ne) pas tellement. **he is ~ the happier,** il n'en est pas plus heureux.
nonentity /nɒˈnentətɪ/ *n.* nullité *f.*
non-existent /nɒnɪgˈzɪstənt/ *a.* inexistant.
nonplussed /nɒnˈplʌst/ *a.* perplexe, déconcerté.
nonsens|e /ˈnɒnsəns/ *n.* absurdités *f. pl.* **~ical** /-ˈsensɪkl/ *a.* absurde.
non-smoker /nɒnˈsməʊkə(r)/ *n.* non-fumeur *m.*
non-stop /nɒnˈstɒp/ *a.* (*train, flight*) direct. —*adv.* sans arrêt.
noodles /ˈnuːdlz/ *n. pl.* nouilles *f. pl.*
nook /nʊk/ *n.* (re)coin *m.*
noon /nuːn/ *n.* midi *m.*
noose /nuːs/ *n.* nœud coulant *m.*
nor /nɔː(r)/ *adv.* ni. —*conj.* (ne) non plus. **~ shall I come,** je ne viendrai pas non plus.
norm /nɔːm/ *n.* norme *f.*
normal /ˈnɔːml/ *a.* normal. **~ity** /nɔːˈmælətɪ/ *n.* normalité *f.* **~ly** *adv.* normalement.
Norman /ˈnɔːmən/ *a.* & *n.* normand(e) (*m., f.*). **~dy** *n.* Normandie *f.*
north /nɔːθ/ *n.* nord *m.* —*a.* nord *invar.*, du nord. —*adv.* vers le nord. **N~ America,** Amérique du Nord *f.* **N~ American** *a.* & *n.* nord-américain(e) (*m.* (*f.*)). **~-east** *n.* nord-est *m.* **~erly** /ˈnɔːðəlɪ/ *a.* du nord. **~ward** *a.* au nord. **~wards** *adv.* vers le nord. **~-west** *n.* nord-ouest *m.*
northern /ˈnɔːðən/ *a.* du nord. **~er** *n.* habitant(e) du nord *m.* (*f.*).
Norw|ay /ˈnɔːweɪ/ *n.* Norvège *f.* **~egian** /nɔːˈwiːdʒən/ *a.* & *n.* norvégien(ne) (*m.* (*f.*)).
nose /nəʊz/ *n.* nez *m.* —*v.i.* **~ about,** fouiner.
nosebleed /ˈnəʊzbliːd/ *n.* saignement de nez *m.*
nosedive /ˈnəʊzdaɪv/ *n.* piqué *m.*
nostalg|ia /nɒˈstældʒə/ *n.* nostalgie *f.* **~ic** *a.* nostalgique.

nostril /ˈnɒstrəl/ *n.* narine *f.*; (*of horse*) naseau *m.*
nosy /ˈnəʊzɪ/ *a.* (**-ier, -iest**) (*fam.*) curieux, indiscret.
not /nɒt/ *adv.* (ne) pas. **I do ~ know,** je ne sais pas. **~ at all,** pas du tout. **~ yet,** pas encore. **I suppose ~,** je suppose que non.
notable /ˈnəʊtəbl/ *a.* notable. —*n.* (*person*) notable *m.*
notably /ˈnəʊtəblɪ/ *adv.* notamment.
notary /ˈnəʊtərɪ/ *n.* notaire *m.*
notation /nəʊˈteɪʃn/ *n.* notation *f.*
notch /nɒtʃ/ *n.* entaille *f.* —*v.t.* **~ up,** (*score etc.*) marquer.
note /nəʊt/ *n.* note *f.*; (*banknote*) billet *m.*; (*short letter*) mot *m.* —*v.t.* noter; (*notice*) remarquer.
notebook /ˈnəʊtbʊk/ *n.* carnet *m.*
noted /ˈnəʊtɪd/ *a.* éminent.
notepaper /ˈnəʊtpeɪpə(r)/ *n.* papier à lettres *m.*
noteworthy /ˈnəʊtwɜːðɪ/ *a.* remarquable.
nothing /ˈnʌθɪŋ/ *pron.* (ne) rien. —*n.* rien *m.*; (*person*) nullité *f.* —*adv.* nullement. **he eats ~,** il ne mange rien. **~ big**/*etc.*, rien de grand/*etc.* **~ else,** rien d'autre. **~ much,** pas grand-chose.
notice /ˈnəʊtɪs/ *n.* avis *m.*, annonce *f.*; (*poster*) affiche *f.* (**advance**) **~,** préavis *m.* **~** (**of dismissal**), congé *m.* —*v.t.* remarquer, observer. **~-board** *n.* tableau d'affichage *m.* **take ~,** faire attention (**of,** à).
noticeabl|e /ˈnəʊtɪsəbl/ *a.* visible. **~y** *adv.* visiblement.
notif|y /ˈnəʊtɪfaɪ/ *v.t.* (*inform*) aviser; (*make known*) notifier. **~ication** /-ɪˈkeɪʃn/ *n.* avis *m.*
notion /ˈnəʊʃn/ *n.* notion *f.* **~s,** (*sewing goods etc.*: *Amer.*) mercerie *f.*
notor|ious /nəʊˈtɔːrɪəs/ *a.* (tristement) célèbre. **~iety** /-əˈraɪətɪ/ *n.* notoriété *f.* **~iously** *adv.* notoirement.
notwithstanding /nɒtwɪθˈstændɪŋ/ *prep.* malgré. —*adv.* néanmoins.
nougat /ˈnuːgɑː/ *n.* nougat *m.*
nought /nɔːt/ *n.* zéro *m.*
noun /naʊn/ *n.* nom *m.*
nourish /ˈnʌrɪʃ/ *v.t.* nourrir. **~ment** *n.* nourriture *f.*
novel /ˈnɒvl/ *n.* roman *m.* —*a.* nouveau. **~ist** *n.* romanc|ier, -ière *m., f.* **~ty** *n.* nouveauté *f.*
November /nəʊˈvembə(r)/ *n.* novembre *m.*
novice /ˈnɒvɪs/ *n.* novice *m./f.*
now /naʊ/ *adv.* maintenant. —*conj.* maintenant que. **just ~,** maintenant; (*a moment ago*) tout à l'heure. **~ and again, ~ and then,** de temps à autre.
nowadays /ˈnaʊədeɪz/ *adv.* de nos jours.
nowhere /ˈnəʊweə(r)/ *adv.* nulle part.
nozzle /ˈnɒzl/ *n.* (*tip*) embout *m.*; (*of hose*) lance *f.*
nuance /ˈnjuːɑːns/ *n.* nuance *f.*
nuclear /ˈnjuːklɪə(r)/ *a.* nucléaire.
nucleus /ˈnjuːklɪəs/ *n.* (*pl.* **-lei** /-lɪaɪ/) noyau *m.*
nud|e /njuːd/ *a.* nu. —*n.* nu *m.* **in the ~e,** tout nu. **~ity** *n.* nudité *f.*
nudge /nʌdʒ/ *v.t.* pousser du coude. —*n.* coup de coude *m.*
nudis|t /ˈnjuːdɪst/ *n.* nudiste *m./f.* **~m** /-zəm/ *n.* nudisme *m.*
nuisance /ˈnjuːsns/ *n.* (*thing, event*) ennui *m.*; (*person*) peste *f.* **be a ~,** être ennuyeux.
null /nʌl/ *a.* nul. **~ify** *v.t.* infirmer.
numb /nʌm/ *a.* engourdi. —*v.t.* engourdir.
number /ˈnʌmbə(r)/ *n.* nombre *m.*; (*of ticket, house, page, etc.*) numéro *m.* —*v.t.* numéroter; (*count, include*) compter. **~-plate** *n.* plaque d'immatriculation *f.*
numerate /ˈnjuːmərət/ *a.* qui a

une bonne connaissance des mathématiques.
numeral /ˈnjuːmərəl/ *n.* chiffre *m.*
numerical /njuːˈmerɪkl/ *a.* numérique.
numerous /ˈnjuːmərəs/ *a.* nombreux.
nun /nʌn/ *n.* religieuse *f.*
nurs|e /nɜːs/ *n.* infirmière *f.*, infirmier *m.*; (*nanny*) nurse *f.* —*v.t.* soigner; (*hope etc.*) nourrir. **~ing home,** clinique *f.*
nursemaid /ˈnɜːsmeɪd/ *n.* bonne d'enfants *f.*
nursery /ˈnɜːsərɪ/ *n.* chambre d'enfants *f.*; (*for plants*) pépinière *f.* **(day) ~,** crèche *f.* **~ rhyme,** chanson enfantine *f.*, comptine *f.* **~ school,** (école) maternelle *f.*
nurture /ˈnɜːtʃə(r)/ *v.t.* élever.
nut /nʌt/ *n.* (*walnut, Brazil nut, etc.*) noix *f.*; (*hazelnut*) noisette *f.*; (*peanut*) cacahuète *f.*; (*techn.*) écrou *m.*; (*sl.*) idiot(e) *m.* (*f.*).
nutcrackers /ˈnʌtkrækəz/ *n. pl.* casse-noix *m. invar.*
nutmeg /ˈnʌtmeg/ *n.* muscade *f.*
nutrient /ˈnjuːtrɪənt/ *n.* substance nutritive *f.*
nutrit|ion /njuːˈtrɪʃn/ *n.* nutrition *f.* **~ious** *a.* nutritif.
nuts /nʌts/ *a.* (*crazy: sl.*) cinglé.
nutshell /ˈnʌtʃel/ *n.* coquille de noix *f.* **in a ~,** en un mot.
nylon /ˈnaɪlɒn/ *n.* nylon *m.* **~s,** bas nylon *m. pl.*

O

oaf /əʊf/ *n.* (*pl.* **oafs**) lourdaud(e) *m.* (*f.*).
oak /əʊk/ *n.* chêne *m.*
OAP *abbr.* (*old-age pensioner*) retraité(e) *m.* (*f.*), personne âgée *f.*
oar /ɔː(r)/ *n.* aviron *m.*, rame *f.*
oasis /əʊˈeɪsɪs/ *n.* (*pl.* **oases** /-siːz/) oasis *f.*
oath /əʊθ/ *n.* (*promise*) serment *m.*; (*swear-word*) juron *m.*
oatmeal /ˈəʊtmiːl/ *n.* farine d'avoine *f.*, flocons d'avoine *m. pl.*
oats /əʊts/ *n. pl.* avoine *f.*
obedien|t /əˈbiːdɪənt/ *a.* obéissant. **~ce** *n.* obéissance *f.* **~tly** *adv.* docilement, avec soumission.
obes|e /əʊˈbiːs/ *a.* obèse. **~ity** *n.* obésité *f.*
obey /əˈbeɪ/ *v.t./i.* obéir (à).
obituary /əˈbɪtʃʊərɪ/ *n.* nécrologie *f.*
object[1] /ˈɒbdʒɪkt/ *n.* (*thing*) objet *m.*; (*aim*) but *m.*, objet *m.*; (*gram.*) complément (d'objet) *m.* **money/ etc. is no ~,** l'argent/*etc.* ne pose pas de problèmes.
object[2] /əbˈdʒekt/ *v.i.* protester. —*v.t.* **~ that,** objecter que. **~ to,** désapprouver, protester contre. **~ion** /-kʃn/ *n.* objection *f.*; (*drawback*) inconvénient *m.*
objectionable /əbˈdʒekʃnəbl/ *a.* désagréable.
objectiv|e /əbˈdʒektɪv/ *a.* objectif. —*n.* objectif *m.* **~ity** /ɒbdʒekˈtɪvətɪ/ *n.* objectivité *f.*
obligat|e /ˈɒblɪgeɪt/ *v.t.* obliger. **~ion** /-ˈgeɪʃn/ *n.* obligation *f.* **under an ~ion to s.o.,** redevable à qn. **(for,** de).
obligatory /əˈblɪgətrɪ/ *a.* obligatoire.
oblig|e /əˈblaɪdʒ/ *v.t.* obliger. **~e to do,** obliger à faire. **~ed** *a.* obligé (**to,** de). **~ed to s.o.,** redevable à qn. **~ing** *a.* obligeant. **~ingly** *adv.* obligeamment.
oblique /əˈbliːk/ *a.* oblique; (*reference etc.: fig.*) indirect.
obliterat|e /əˈblɪtəreɪt/ *v.t.* effacer. **~ion** /-ˈreɪʃn/ *n.* effacement *m.*
oblivion /əˈblɪvɪən/ *n.* oubli *m.*
oblivious /əˈblɪvɪəs/ *a.* (*unaware*) inconscient (**to, of,** de).
oblong /ˈɒblɒŋ/ *a.* oblong. —*n.* rectangle *m.*
obnoxious /əbˈnɒkʃəs/ *a.* odieux.

oboe /ˈəʊbəʊ/ *n.* hautbois *m.*
obscen|e /əbˈsiːn/ *a.* obscène. **~ity** /-enətɪ/ *n.* obscénité *f.*
obscur|e /əbˈskjʊə(r)/ *a.* obscur. —*v.t.* obscurcir; (*conceal*) cacher. **~ely** *adv.* obscurément. **~ity** *n.* obscurité *f.*
obsequious /əbˈsiːkwɪəs/ *a.* obséquieux.
observan|t /əbˈzɜːvənt/ *a.* observateur. **~ce** *n.* observance *f.*
observatory /əbˈzɜːvətrɪ/ *n.* observatoire *m.*
observ|e /əbˈzɜːv/ *v.t.* observer; (*remark*) remarquer. **~ation** /ɒbzəˈveɪʃn/ *n.* observation *f.* **~er** *n.* observa|teur, -trice *m., f.*
obsess /əbˈses/ *v.t.* obséder. **~ion** /-ʃn/ *n.* obsession *f.* **~ive** *a.* obsédant; (*psych.*) obsessionnel.
obsolete /ˈɒbsəliːt/ *a.* dépassé.
obstacle /ˈɒbstəkl/ *n.* obstacle *m.*
obstetric|s /əbˈstetrɪks/ *n.* obstétrique *f.* **~ian** /ɒbstɪˈtrɪʃn/ *n.* médecin accoucheur *m.*
obstina|te /ˈɒbstɪnət/ *a.* obstiné. **~cy** *n.* obstination *f.* **~tely** *adv.* obstinément.
obstruct /əbˈstrʌkt/ *v.t.* (*block*) boucher; (*congest*) encombrer; (*hinder*) entraver. **~ion** /-kʃn/ *n.* (*act*) obstruction *f.*; (*thing*) obstacle *m.*; (*traffic jam*) encombrement *m.*
obtain /əbˈteɪn/ *v.t.* obtenir. —*v.i.* avoir cours. **~able** *a.* disponible.
obtrusive /əbˈtruːsɪv/ *a.* importun; (*thing*) trop en évidence.
obtuse /əbˈtjuːs/ *a.* obtus.
obviate /ˈɒbvɪeɪt/ *v.t.* éviter.
obvious /ˈɒbvɪəs/ *a.* évident, manifeste. **~ly** *adv.* manifestement.
occasion /əˈkeɪʒn/ *n.* occasion *f.*; (*big event*) événement *m.* —*v.t.* occasionner. **on ~,** à l'occasion.
occasional /əˈkeɪʒənl/ *a.* fait, pris, *etc.* de temps en temps; (*visitor etc.*) qui vient de temps en temps. **~ly** *adv.* de temps en temps. **very ~ly,** rarement.
occult /ɒˈkʌlt/ *a.* occulte.
occupation /ɒkjʊˈpeɪʃn/ *n.* (*activity, occupying*) occupation *f.*; (*job*) métier *m.*, profession *f.* **~al** *a.* professionnel, du métier.
occup|y /ˈɒkjʊpaɪ/ *v.t.* occuper. **~ant, ~ier** *ns.* occupant(e) *m.* (*f.*).
occur /əˈkɜː(r)/ *v.i.* (*p.t.* **occurred**) se produire; (*arise*) se présenter. **~ to s.o.,** venir à l'esprit de qn.
occurrence /əˈkʌrəns/ *n.* événement *m.* **the ~ of,** l'existence de. **of frequent ~,** qui arrive souvent.
ocean /ˈəʊʃn/ *n.* océan *m.*
o'clock /əˈklɒk/ *adv.* **it is six ~**/*etc.*, il est six heures/*etc.*
octagon /ˈɒktəgən/ *n.* octogone *m.*
octane /ˈɒkteɪn/ *n.* octane *m.*
octave /ˈɒktɪv/ *n.* octave *f.*
October /ɒkˈtəʊbə(r)/ *n.* octobre *m.*
octopus /ˈɒktəpəs/ *n.* (*pl.* **-puses**) pieuvre *f.*
odd /ɒd/ *a.* (**-er, -est**) bizarre; (*number*) impair; (*left over*) qui reste; (*not of set*) dépareillé; (*occasional*) fait, pris, *etc.* de temps en temps. **~ jobs,** menus travaux *m. pl.* **twenty ~,** vingt et quelques. **~ity** *n.* bizarrerie *f.*; (*thing*) curiosité *f.* **~ly** *adv.* bizarrement.
oddment /ˈɒdmənt/ *n.* fin de série *f.*
odds /ɒdz/ *n. pl.* chances *f. pl.*; (*in betting*) cote *f.* **at ~,** en désaccord. **it makes no ~,** ça ne fait rien. **~ and ends,** des petites choses.
ode /əʊd/ *n.* ode *f.*
odious /ˈəʊdɪəs/ *a.* odieux.
odour /ˈəʊdə(r)/ *n.* odeur *f.* **~less** *a.* inodore.
of /ɒv, *unstressed* əv/ *prep.* de. **~ the,** du, de la, *pl.* des. **~ it, ~ them,** en. **a friend ~ mine,** un de mes amis. **six ~ them,** six d'entre eux. **the fifth ~ June**/*etc.*, le cinq juin/*etc.*

off /ɒf/ *adv.* parti, absent; (*switched off*) fermé, éteint; (*taken off*) enlevé, détaché; (*cancelled*) annulé; (*food*) mauvais. —*prep.* de; (*distant from*) éloigné de. **be ~,** (*leave*) partir. **be better ~,** (*in a better position, richer*) être mieux. **a day ~,** un jour de congé. **20% ~,** une réduction de 20%. **take sth. ~,** (*a surface*) prendre qch. sur. **on the ~ chance (that),** au cas où. **~ colour,** (*ill*) patraque. **~ color,** (*improper: Amer.*) scabreux. **~-licence** *n.* débit de vins *m.* **~-load** *v.t.* décharger. **~-putting** *a.* (*fam.*) rebutant. **~-stage** *a.* & *adv.* dans les coulisses. **~-white** *a.* blanc cassé *invar.*
offal /'ɒfl/ *n.* abats *m. pl.*
offence /ə'fens/ *n.* délit *m.* **give ~ to,** offenser. **take ~,** s'offenser (**at,** de).
offend /ə'fend/ *v.t.* offenser; (*fig.*) choquer. **be ~ed,** s'offenser (**at,** de). **~er** *n.* délinquant(e) *m.* (*f.*).
offensive /ə'fensɪv/ *a.* offensant; (*disgusting*) dégoûtant; (*weapon*) offensif. —*n.* offensive *f.*
offer /'ɒfə(r)/ *v.t.* (*p.t.* **offered**) offrir. —*n.* offre *f.* **on ~,** en promotion. **~ing** *n.* offrande *f.*
offhand /ɒf'hænd/ *a.* désinvolte. —*adv.* à l'improviste.
office /'ɒfɪs/ *n.* bureau *m.*; (*duty*) fonction *f.*; (*surgery: Amer.*) cabinet *m.* **good ~s,** bons offices *m. pl.* **in ~,** au pouvoir.
officer /'ɒfɪsə(r)/ *n.* (*army etc.*) officier *m.*; (*policeman*) agent *m.*
official /ə'fɪʃl/ *a.* officiel. —*n.* officiel *m.*; (*civil servant*) fonctionnaire *m.*/*f.* **~ly** *adv.* officiellement.
officiate /ə'fɪʃɪeɪt/ *v.i.* (*priest*) officier; (*president*) présider. **~ as,** faire fonction de.
officious /ə'fɪʃəs/ *a.* trop zélé.
offing /'ɒfɪŋ/ *n.* **in the ~,** en perspective.
offset /'ɒfset/ *v.t.* (*p.t.* **-set,** *pres. p.* **-setting**) compenser.
offshoot /'ɔfʃuːt/ *n.* rejeton *m.*
offshore /ɒf'ʃɔː(r)/ *a.* côtier.
offside /ɒf'saɪd/ *a.* (*sport*) hors jeu *invar.*
offspring /'ɒfsprɪŋ/ *n. invar.* progéniture *f.*
often /'ɒfn/ *adv.* souvent. **how ~?,** combien de fois? **every so ~,** de temps en temps.
ogle /'əʊgl/ *v.t.* lorgner.
ogre /'əʊgə(r)/ *n.* ogre *m.*
oh /əʊ/ *int.* oh, ah.
oil /ɔɪl/ *n.* huile *f.*; (*petroleum*) pétrole *m.*; (*for heating*) mazout *m.* —*v.t.* graisser. **~-painting** *n.* peinture à l'huile *f.* **~-tanker** *n.* pétrolier *m.* **~y** *a.* graisseux.
oilfield /'ɔɪlfiːld/ *n.* gisement pétrolifère *m.*
oilskins /'ɔɪlskɪnz/ *n. pl.* ciré *m.*
ointment /'ɔɪntmənt/ *n.* pommade *f.*, onguent *m.*
OK /əʊ'keɪ/ *a.* & *adv.* (*fam.*) bien.
old /əʊld/ *a.* (**-er, -est**) vieux; (*person*) vieux, âgé; (*former*) ancien. **how ~ is he?,** quel âge a-t-il? **he is eight years ~,** il a huit ans. **of ~,** jadis. **~ age,** vieillesse *f.* **~ boy,** ancien élève *m.*; (*fellow: fam.*) vieux *m.* **~er, ~est,** (*son etc.*) aîné. **~-fashioned** *a.* démodé; (*person*) vieux jeu *invar.* **~ maid,** vieille fille *f.* **~ man,** vieillard *m.*, vieux *m.* **~-time** *a.* ancien. **~ woman,** vieille *f.*
olive /'ɒlɪv/ *n.* olive *f.* —*a.* olive *invar.* **~ oil,** huile d'olive *f.*
Olympic /ə'lɪmpɪk/ *a.* olympique. **~s** *n. pl.*, **~ Games,** Jeux olympiques *m. pl.*
omelette /'ɒmlɪt/ *n.* omelette *f.*
omen /'əʊmen/ *n.* augure *m.*
ominous /'ɒmɪnəs/ *a.* de mauvais augure; (*fig.*) menaçant.

omi|t /ə'mɪt/ *v.t.* (*p.t.* **omitted**) omettre. **~ssion** *n.* omission *f.*

omnipotent /ɒm'nɪpətənt/ *a.* omnipotent.

on /ɒn/ *prep.* sur. —*adv.* en avant; (*switched on*) allumé, ouvert; (*machine*) en marche; (*put on*) mis; (*happening*) en cours. **~ foot/time/***etc.*, à pied/l'heure/*etc.* **~ doing,** en faisant. **~ Tuesday,** mardi. **~ Tuesdays,** le mardi. **walk/***etc.* **~,** continuer à marcher/*etc.* **be ~,** (*of film*) passer. **be ~ at,** (*fam.*) être après. **~ and off,** de temps en temps.

once /wʌns/ *adv.* une fois; (*formerly*) autrefois. —*conj.* une fois que. **all at ~,** tout à coup. **~-over** *n.* (*fam.*) coup d'œil rapide *m.*

oncoming /'ɒnkʌmɪŋ/ *a.* (*vehicle etc.*) qui approche.

one /wʌn/ *a.* & *n.* un(e) (*m.* (*f.*)). —*pron.* un(e) *m.* (*f.*); (*impersonal*) on. **~ (and only),** seul (et unique). **a big/red/***etc.* **~,** un(e) grand(e)/rouge/*etc.* **this/that ~,** celui-ci/-là, celle-ci/-là. **~ another,** l'un(e) l'autre. **~-eyed,** borgne. **~-off** *a.* (*fam.*), **~ of a kind,** (*Amer.*) unique, exceptionnel. **~-sided** *a.* (*biased*) partial; (*unequal*) inégal. **~-way** *a.* (*street*) à sens unique; (*ticket*) simple.

oneself /wʌn'self/ *pron.* soi-même; (*reflexive*) se.

onion /'ʌnjən/ *n.* oignon *m.*

onlooker /'ɒnlʊkə(r)/ *n.* spectа|teur, -trice *m.*, *f.*

only /'əʊnlɪ/ *a.* seul. **an ~ son/***etc.*, un fils/*etc.* unique. —*adv.* & *conj.* seulement. **he ~ has six,** il n'en a que six, il en a six seulement. **~ too,** extrêmement.

onset /'ɒnset/ *n.* début *m.*

onslaught /'ɒnslɔːt/ *n.* attaque *f.*

onus /'əʊnəs/ *n.* **the ~ is on me/***etc.*, c'est ma/*etc.* responsabilité (**to,** de).

onward(s) /'ɒnwəd(z)/ *adv.* en avant.

onyx /'ɒnɪks/ *n.* onyx *m.*

ooze /uːz/ *v.i.* suinter.

opal /'əʊpl/ *n.* opale *f.*

opaque /əʊ'peɪk/ *a.* opaque.

open /'əʊpən/ *a.* ouvert; (*view*) dégagé; (*free to all*) public; (*undisguised*) manifeste; (*question*) en attente. —*v.t.*/*i.* (s')ouvrir; (*of shop, play*) ouvrir. **in the ~ air,** en plein air. **~-ended** *a.* sans limite (*de durée etc.*); (*system*) qui peut évoluer. **~-heart** *a.* (*surgery*) à cœur ouvert. **keep ~ house,** tenir table ouverte. **~ out** *or* **up,** (s')ouvrir. **~-plan** *a.* sans cloisons. **~ secret,** secret de Polichinelle *m.*

opener /'əʊpənə(r)/ *n.* ouvre-boîte(s) *m.*, ouvre-bouteille(s) *m.*

opening /'əʊpənɪŋ/ *n.* ouverture *f.*; (*job*) débouché *m.*, poste vacant *m.*

openly /'əʊpənlɪ/ *adv.* ouvertement.

opera /'ɒpərə/ *n.* opéra *m.* **~-glasses** *n. pl.* jumelles *f. pl.* **~tic** /ɒpə'rætɪk/ *a.* d'opéra.

operat|e /'ɒpəreɪt/ *v.t.*/*i.* opérer; (*techn.*) (faire) fonctionner. **~e on,** (*med.*) opérer. **~ion** /-'reɪʃn/ *n.* opération *f.* **in ~ion,** en vigueur; (*techn.*) en service. **~or** *n.* opéra|teur, -trice *m.*, *f.*; (*telephonist*) standardiste *m.*/*f.*

operational /ɒpə'reɪʃənl/ *a.* opérationnel.

operative /'ɒpərətɪv/ *a.* (*med.*) opératoire; (*law etc.*) en vigueur.

operetta /ɒpə'retə/ *n.* opérette *f.*

opinion /ə'pɪnjən/ *n.* opinion *f.*, avis *m.* **~ated** *a.* dogmatique.

opium /'əʊpɪəm/ *n.* opium *m.*

opponent /ə'pəʊnənt/ *n.* adversaire *m.*/*f.*

opportune /'ɒpətjuːn/ *a.* opportun.

opportunist /ɒpə'tjuːnɪst/ *n.* opportuniste *m.*/*f.*

opportunity /ɒpə'tjuːnətɪ/ *n.* occasion *f.* (**to do,** de faire).
oppos|e /ə'pəʊz/ *v.t.* s'opposer à. **~ed to,** opposé à. **~ing** *a.* opposé.
opposite /'ɒpəzɪt/ *a.* opposé. —*n.* contraire *m.*, opposé *m.* —*adv.* en face. —*prep.* **~ (to),** en face de. **one's ~ number,** son homologue *m.*/*f.*
opposition /ɒpə'zɪʃn/ *n.* opposition *f.*; (*mil.*) résistance *f.*
oppress /ə'pres/ *v.t.* opprimer. **~ion** /-ʃn/ *n.* oppression *f.* **~ive** *a.* (*cruel*) oppressif; (*heat*) oppressant. **~or** *n.* oppresseur *m.*
opt /ɒpt/ *v.i.* **~ for,** opter pour. **~ out,** refuser de participer (**of,** à). **~ to do,** choisir de faire.
optical /'ɒptɪkl/ *a.* optique. **~ illusion,** illusion d'optique *f.*
optician /ɒp'tɪʃn/ *n.* opticien(ne) *m.* (*f.*).
optimis|t /'ɒptɪmɪst/ *n.* optimiste *m.*/*f.* **~m** /-zəm/ *n.* optimisme *m.* **~tic** /-'mɪstɪk/ *a.* optimiste. **~tically** /-'mɪstɪklɪ/ *adv.* avec optimisme.
optimum /'ɒptɪməm/ *a.* & *n.* (*pl.* **-ima**) optimum (*m.*).
option /'ɒpʃn/ *n.* choix *m.*, option *f.*
optional /'ɒpʃənl/ *a.* facultatif.
opulen|t /'ɒpjʊlənt/ *a.* opulent. **~ce** *n.* opulence *f.*
or /ɔː(r)/ *conj.* ou; (*with negative*) ni.
oracle /'ɒrəkl/ *n.* oracle *m.*
oral /'ɔːrəl/ *a.* oral. —*n.* (*examination*: *fam.*) oral *m.*
orange /'ɒrɪndʒ/ *n.* (*fruit*) orange *f.* —*a.* (*colour*) orange *invar.*
orangeade /ɒrɪndʒ'eɪd/ *n.* orangeade *f.*
orator /'ɒrətə(r)/ *n.* ora|teur, -trice *m.*, *f.* **~y** /-trɪ/ *n.* rhétorique *f.*
oratorio /ɒrə'tɔːrɪəʊ/ *n.* (*pl.* **-os**) oratorio *m.*
orbit /'ɔːbɪt/ *n.* orbite *f.* —*v.t.* graviter autour de, orbiter.
orchard /'ɔːtʃəd/ *n.* verger *m.*
orchestra /'ɔːkɪstrə/ *n.* orchestre *m.* **~l** /-'kestrəl/ *a.* orchestral.
orchestrate /'ɔːkɪstreɪt/ *v.t.* orchestrer.
orchid /'ɔːkɪd/ *n.* orchidée *f.*
ordain /ɔː'deɪn/ *v.t.* décréter (**that,** que); (*relig.*) ordonner.
ordeal /ɔː'diːl/ *n.* épreuve *f.*
order /'ɔːdə(r)/ *n.* ordre *m.*; (*comm.*) commande *f.* —*v.t.* ordonner; (*goods etc.*) commander. **in ~,** (*tidy*) en ordre; (*document*) en règle; (*fitting*) de règle. **in ~ that,** pour que. **in ~ to,** pour. **~ s.o. to,** ordonner à qn. de.
orderly /'ɔːdəlɪ/ *a.* (*tidy*) ordonné; (*not unruly*) discipliné. —*n.* (*mil.*) planton *m.*; (*med.*) garçon de salle *m.*
ordinary /'ɔːdɪnrɪ/ *a.* (*usual*) ordinaire; (*average*) moyen.
ordination /ɔːdɪ'neɪʃn/ *n.* (*relig.*) ordination *f.*
ore /ɔː(r)/ *n.* minerai *m.*
organ /'ɔːgən/ *n.* organe *m.*; (*mus.*) orgue *m.* **~ist** *n.* organiste *m.*/*f.*
organic /ɔː'gænɪk/ *a.* organique.
organism /'ɔːgənɪzəm/ *n.* organisme *m.*
organiz|e /'ɔːgənaɪz/ *v.t.* organiser. **~ation** /-'zeɪʃn/ *n.* organisation *f.* **~er** *n.* organisa|teur, -trice *m.*, *f.*
orgasm /'ɔːgæzəm/ *n.* orgasme *m.*
orgy /'ɔːdʒɪ/ *n.* orgie *f.*
Orient /'ɔːrɪənt/ *n.* **the ~,** l'Orient *m.* **~al** /-'entl/ *n.* Oriental(e) *m.* (*f.*).
oriental /ɔːrɪ'entl/ *a.* oriental.
orient(at|e) /'ɔːrɪənt(eɪt)/ *v.t.* orienter. **~ion** /-'teɪʃn/ *n.* orientation *f.*
orifice /'ɒrɪfɪs/ *n.* orifice *m.*
origin /'ɒrɪdʒɪn/ *n.* origine *f.*
original /ə'rɪdʒənl/ *a.* (*first*) originel; (*not copied*) original. **~ity** /-'nælətɪ/ *n.* originalité *f.* **~ly** *adv.* (*at the outset*) à l'origine; (*write etc.*) originalement.
originat|e /ə'rɪdʒɪneɪt/ *v.i.* prendre

naissance. *—v.t.* être l'auteur de. **~e from,** provenir de; (*person*) venir de. **~or** *n.* auteur *m.*

ornament /'ɔːnəmənt/ *n.* (*decoration*) ornement *m.*; (*object*) objet décoratif *m.* **~al** /-'mentl/ *a.* ornemental. **~ation** /-en'teɪʃn/ *n.* ornementation *f.*

ornate /ɔː'neɪt/ *a.* richement orné.

ornithology /ɔːnɪ'θɒlədʒɪ/ *n.* ornithologie *f.*

orphan /'ɔːfn/ *n.* orphelin(e) *m.* (*f.*). *—v.t.* rendre orphelin. **~age** *n.* orphelinat *m.*

orthodox /'ɔːθədɒks/ *a.* orthodoxe. **~y** *n.* orthodoxie *f.*

orthopaedic /ɔːθə'piːdɪk/ *a.* orthopédique.

oscillate /'ɒsɪleɪt/ *v.i.* osciller.

ostensibl|e /ɒs'tensəbl/ *a.* apparent, prétendu. **~y** *adv.* apparemment, prétendument.

ostentati|on /ɒsten'teɪʃn/ *n.* ostentation *f.* **~ous** *a.* prétentieux.

osteopath /'ɒstɪəpæθ/ *n.* chiropracteur *m.*

ostracize /'ɒstrəsaɪz/ *v.t.* frapper d'ostracisme.

ostrich /'ɒstrɪtʃ/ *n.* autruche *f.*

other /'ʌðə(r)/ *a.* autre. *—n.* & *pron.* autre *m./f.* *—adv.* **~ than,** autrement que. **(some) ~s,** d'autres. **the ~ one,** l'autre *m./f.*

otherwise /'ʌðəwaɪz/ *adv.* autrement.

otter /'ɒtə(r)/ *n.* loutre *f.*

ouch /aʊtʃ/ *int.* aïe!

ought /ɔːt/ *v. aux.* devoir. **you ~ to stay,** vous devriez rester. **he ~ to succeed,** il devrait réussir. **I ~ to have done it,** j'aurais dû le faire.

ounce /aʊns/ *n.* once *f.* (*= 28.35 g.*).

our /'aʊə(r)/ *a.* notre, *pl.* nos.

ours /'aʊəz/ *poss. pron.* le *or* la nôtre, les nôtres.

ourselves /aʊə'selvz/ *pron.* nous-mêmes; (*reflexive & after prep.*) nous.

oust /aʊst/ *v.t.* évincer.

out /aʊt/ *adv.* dehors; (*gone out*) sorti; (*light*) éteint; (*in blossom*) épanoui; (*tide*) bas; (*secret*) révélé; (*sun*) levé. **be ~,** (*wrong*) se tromper. **be ~ to,** être résolu à. **run**/*etc.* **~,** sortir en courant/*etc.* **~-and-out** *a.* absolu. **~ of,** hors de; (*without*) sans, à court de. **~ of pity**/*etc.*, par pitié/*etc.* **made ~ of,** fait en *or* de. **take ~ of,** prendre dans. **5 ~ of 6,** 5 sur 6. **~ of date,** démodé; (*not valid*) périmé. **~ of doors,** dehors. **~ of hand,** (*situation*) dont on n'est plus maître. **~ of line,** (*impertinent*: *Amer.*) incorrect. **~ of one's mind,** dément. **~ of order,** (*broken*) en panne. **~ of place,** (*object, remark*) déplacé. **~ of the way,** écarté. **~-patient** *n.* malade en consultation externe *m./f.*

outbid /aʊt'bɪd/ *v.t.* (*p.t.* **-bid,** *pres. p.* **-bidding**) enchérir sur.

outboard /'aʊtbɔːd/ *a.* (*motor*) hors-bord *invar.*

outbreak /'aʊtbreɪk/ *n.* (*of war etc.*) début *m.*; (*of violence, boils*) éruption *f.*

outburst /'aʊtbɜːst/ *n.* explosion *f.*

outcast /'aʊtkɑːst/ *n.* paria *m.*

outcome /'aʊtkʌm/ *n.* résultat *m.*

outcry /'aʊtkraɪ/ *n.* tollé *m.*

outdated /aʊt'deɪtɪd/ *a.* démodé.

outdo /aʊt'duː/ *v.t.* (*p.t.* **-did,** *p.p.* **-done**) surpasser.

outdoor /'aʊtdɔː(r)/ *a.* de *or* en plein air. **~s** /-'dɔːz/ *adv.* dehors.

outer /'aʊtə(r)/ *a.* extérieur. **~ space,** espace (cosmique) *m.*

outfit /'aʊtfɪt/ *n.* (*articles*) équipement *m.*; (*clothes*) tenue *f.*; (*group*: *fam.*) équipe *f.* **~ter** *n.* spécialiste de confection *m./f.*

outgoing /'aʊtgəʊɪŋ/ *a.* (*minister, tenant*) sortant; (*sociable*) ouvert. **~s** *n. pl.* dépenses *f. pl.*

outgrow /aʊt'grəʊ/ *v.t.* (*p.t.* **-grew,**

p.p. **-grown**) (*person*) grandir plus vite que; (*clothes*) devenir trop grand pour.
outhouse /ˈaʊthaʊs/ *n.* appentis *m.*; (*of mansion*) dépendance *f.*; (*Amer.*) cabinets extérieurs *m. pl.*
outing /ˈaʊtɪŋ/ *n.* sortie *f.*
outlandish /aʊtˈlændɪʃ/ *a.* bizarre, étrange.
outlaw /ˈaʊtlɔː/ *n.* hors-la-loi *m. invar.* —*v.t.* proscrire.
outlay /ˈaʊtleɪ/ *n.* dépenses *f. pl.*
outlet /ˈaʊtlet/ *n.* (*for water, gases*) sortie *f.*; (*for goods*) débouché *m.*; (*for feelings*) exutoire *m.*
outline /ˈaʊtlaɪn/ *n.* contour *m.*; (*summary*) esquisse *f.* (**main**) **~s,** grandes lignes *f. pl.* —*v.t.* tracer le contour de; (*summarize*) exposer sommairement.
outlive /aʊtˈlɪv/ *v.t.* survivre à.
outlook /ˈaʊtlʊk/ *n.* perspective *f.*
outlying /ˈaʊtlaɪɪŋ/ *a.* écarté.
outmoded /aʊtˈməʊdɪd/ *a.* démodé.
outnumber /aʊtˈnʌmbə(r)/ *v.t.* surpasser en nombre.
outpost /ˈaʊtpəʊst/ *n.* avant-poste *m.*
output /ˈaʊtpʊt/ *n.* rendement *m.*; (*of computer*) sortie *f.*
outrage /ˈaʊtreɪdʒ/ *n.* atrocité *f.*; (*scandal*) scandale *m.* —*v.t.* (*morals*) outrager; (*person*) scandaliser.
outrageous /aʊtˈreɪdʒəs/ *a.* scandaleux, atroce.
outright /aʊtˈraɪt/ *adv.* complètement; (*at once*) sur le coup; (*frankly*) carrément. —*a.* /ˈaʊtraɪt/ complet; (*refusal*) net.
outset /ˈaʊtset/ *n.* début *m.*
outside[1] /aʊtˈsaɪd/ *n.* extérieur *m.* —*adv.* (au) dehors. —*prep.* en dehors de; (*in front of*) devant.
outside[2] /ˈaʊtsaɪd/ *a.* extérieur.
outsider /aʊtˈsaɪdə(r)/ *n.* étrang|er, -ère *m., f.*; (*sport*) outsider *m.*
outsize /ˈaʊtsaɪz/ *a.* grande taille *invar.*
outskirts /ˈaʊtskɜːts/ *n. pl.* banlieue *f.*
outspoken /aʊtˈspəʊkən/ *a.* franc.
outstanding /aʊtˈstændɪŋ/ *a.* exceptionnel; (*not settled*) en suspens.
outstretched /aʊtˈstretʃt/ *a.* (*arm*) tendu.
outstrip /aʊtˈstrɪp/ *v.t.* (*p.t.* **-stripped**) devancer, surpasser.
outward /ˈaʊtwəd/ *a.* & *adv.* vers l'extérieur; (*sign etc.*) extérieur; (*journey*) d'aller. **~ly** *adv.* extérieurement. **~s** *adv.* vers l'extérieur.
outweigh /aʊtˈweɪ/ *v.t.* (*exceed in importance*) l'emporter sur.
outwit /aʊtˈwɪt/ *v.t.* (*p.t.* **-witted**) duper, être plus malin que.
oval /ˈəʊvl/ *n.* & *a.* ovale (*m.*).
ovary /ˈəʊvərɪ/ *n.* ovaire *m.*
ovation /əˈveɪʃn/ *n.* ovation *f.*
oven /ˈʌvn/ *n.* four *m.*
over /ˈəʊvə(r)/ *prep.* sur, au-dessus de; (*across*) de l'autre côté de; (*during*) pendant; (*more than*) plus de. —*adv.* (par-)dessus; (*ended*) fini; (*past*) passé; (*too*) trop; (*more*) plus. **jump**/*etc.* **~,** sauter/*etc.* par-dessus. **~ the radio,** à la radio. **ask ~,** inviter chez soi. **he has some ~,** il lui en reste. **all ~ (the table),** partout (sur la table). **~ and over,** à maintes reprises. **~ here,** par ici. **~ there,** là-bas.
over- /ˈəʊvə(r)/ *pref.* sur-, trop.
overall[1] /ˈəʊvərɔːl/ *n.* blouse *f.* **~s,** bleu(s) de travail *m.* (*pl.*).
overall[2] /əʊvərˈɔːl/ *a.* global, d'ensemble; (*length, width*) total. —*adv.* globalement.
overawe /əʊvərˈɔː/ *v.t.* intimider.
overbalance /əʊvəˈbæləns/ *v.t./i.* (faire) basculer.
overbearing /əʊvəˈbeərɪŋ/ *a.* autoritaire.

overboard /'əʊvəbɔːd/ *adv.* par-dessus bord.
overbook /əʊvə'bʊk/ *v.t.* accepter trop de réservations pour.
overcast /'əʊvəkɑːst/ *a.* couvert.
overcharge /əʊvə'tʃɑːdʒ/ *v.t.* ~ **s.o. (for)**, faire payer trop cher à qn.
overcoat /'əʊvəkəʊt/ *n.* pardessus *m.*
overcome /əʊvə'kʌm/ *v.t.* (*p.t.* **-came**, *p.p.* **-come**) triompher de; (*difficulty*) surmonter, triompher de. ~ **by**, accablé de.
overcrowded /əʊvə'kraʊdɪd/ *a.* bondé; (*country*) surpeuplé.
overdo /əʊvə'duː/ *v.t.* (*p.t.* **-did**, *p.p.* **-done**) exagérer; (*culin.*) trop cuire. ~ **it**, (*overwork*) se surmener.
overdose /'əʊvədəʊs/ *n.* dose excessive *f.*
overdraft /'əʊvədrɑːft/ *n.* découvert *m.*
overdraw /əʊvə'drɔː/ *v.t.* (*p.t.* **-drew**, *p.p.* **-drawn**) (*one's account*) mettre à découvert.
overdue /əʊvə'djuː/ *a.* en retard; (*belated*) tardif; (*bill*) impayé.
overestimate /əʊvər'estɪmeɪt/ *v.t.* surestimer.
overflow¹ /əʊvə'fləʊ/ *v.i.* déborder.
overflow² /'əʊvəfləʊ/ *n.* (*outlet*) trop-plein *m.*
overgrown /əʊvə'grəʊn/ *a.* (*garden etc.*) envahi par la végétation.
overhang /əʊvə'hæŋ/ *v.t.* (*p.t.* **-hung**) surplomber. —*v.i.* faire saillie.
overhaul¹ /əʊvə'hɔːl/ *v.t.* réviser.
overhaul² /'əʊvəhɔːl/ *n.* révision *f.*
overhead¹ /əʊvə'hed/ *adv.* au-dessus; (*in sky*) dans le ciel.
overhead² /'əʊvəhed/ *a.* aérien. ~**s** *n. pl.* frais généraux *m. pl.*
overhear /əʊvə'hɪə(r)/ *v.t.* (*p.t.* **-heard**) surprendre, entendre.
overjoyed /əʊvə'dʒɔɪd/ *a.* ravi.
overland *a.* /'əʊvəlænd/, *adv.* /əʊvə'lænd/ par voie de terre.
overlap /əʊvə'læp/ *v.t./i.* (*p.t.* **-lapped**) (se) chevaucher.
overleaf /əʊvə'liːf/ *adv.* au verso.
overload /əʊvə'ləʊd/ *v.t.* surcharger.
overlook /əʊvə'lʊk/ *v.t.* oublier, négliger; (*of window, house*) donner sur; (*of tower*) dominer.
overly /'əʊvəlɪ/ *adv.* excessivement.
overnight /əʊvə'naɪt/ *adv.* (pendant) la nuit; (*instantly*: *fig.*) du jour au lendemain. —*a.* /'əʊvənaɪt/ (*train etc.*) de nuit; (*stay etc.*) d'une nuit; (*fig.*) soudain.
overpay /əʊvə'peɪ/ *v.t.* (*p.t.* **-paid**) (*person*) surpayer.
overpower /əʊvə'paʊə(r)/ *v.t.* subjuguer; (*opponent*) maîtriser; (*fig.*) accabler. ~**ing** *a.* irrésistible; (*heat, smell*) accablant.
overpriced /əʊvə'praɪst/ *a.* trop cher.
overrate /əʊvə'reɪt/ *v.t.* surestimer. ~**d** /-ɪd/ *a.* surfait.
overreact /əʊvərɪ'ækt/ *v.i.* réagir excessivement.
overreach /əʊvə'riːtʃ/ *v. pr.* ~ **o.s.**, trop entreprendre.
overrid|e /əʊvə'raɪd/ *v.t.* (*p.t.* **-rode**, *p.p.* **-ridden**) passer outre à. ~**ing** *a.* prépondérant; (*importance*) majeur.
overripe /'əʊvəraɪp/ *a.* trop mûr.
overrule /əʊvə'ruːl/ *v.t.* rejeter.
overrun /əʊvə'rʌn/ *v.t.* (*p.t.* **-ran**, *p.p.* **-run**, *pres. p.* **-running**) envahir; (*a limit*) aller au-delà de.
overseas /əʊvə'siːz/ *a.* d'outre-mer, étranger. —*adv.* outre-mer, à l'étranger.
oversee /əʊvə'siː/ *v.t.* (*p.t.* **-saw**, *p.p.* **-seen**) surveiller. ~**r** /'əʊvəsɪə(r)/ *n.* contremaître *m.*
overshadow /əʊvə'ʃædəʊ/ *v.t.* (*darken*) assombrir; (*fig.*) éclipser.

overshoot /əʊvəˈʃuːt/ *v.t.* (*p.t.* **-shot**) dépasser.
oversight /ˈəʊvəsaɪt/ *n.* omission *f.*
oversleep /əʊvəˈsliːp/ *v.i.* (*p.t.* **-slept**) se réveiller trop tard.
overstep /əʊvəˈstep/ *v.t.* (*p.t.* **-stepped**) dépasser.
overt /ˈəʊvɜːt/ *a.* manifeste.
overtake /əʊvəˈteɪk/ *v.t./i.* (*p.t.* **-took,** *p.p.* **-taken**) dépasser; (*vehicle*) doubler, dépasser; (*surprise*) surprendre.
overtax /əʊvəˈtæks/ *v.t.* (*strain*) fatiguer; (*taxpayer*) surimposer.
overthrow /əʊvəˈθrəʊ/ *v.t.* (*p.t.* **-threw,** *p.p.* **-thrown**) renverser.
overtime /ˈəʊvətaɪm/ *n.* heures supplémentaires *f. pl.*
overtone /ˈəʊvətəʊn/ *n.* nuance *f.*
overture /ˈəʊvətjʊə(r)/ *n.* ouverture *f.*
overturn /əʊvəˈtɜːn/ *v.t./i.* (se) renverser.
overweight /əʊvəˈweɪt/ *a.* **be ~,** peser trop, excéder le poids normal.
overwhelm /əʊvəˈwelm/ *v.t.* accabler; (*defeat*) écraser; (*amaze*) bouleverser. **~ing** *a.* accablant; (*victory*) écrasant; (*urge*) irrésistible.
overwork /əʊvəˈwɜːk/ *v.t./i.* (se) surmener. —*n.* surmenage *m.*
ow|e /əʊ/ *v.t.* devoir. **~ing** *a.* dû. **~ing to,** à cause de.
owl /aʊl/ *n.* hibou *m.*
own[1] /əʊn/ *a.* propre. **a house**/*etc.* **of one's ~,** sa propre maison/*etc.*, une maison/*etc.* à soi. **get one's ~ back,** (*fam.*) prendre sa revanche. **hold one's ~,** bien se défendre. **on one's ~,** tout seul.
own[2] /əʊn/ *v.t.* posséder. **~ up (to),** (*fam.*) avouer. **~er** *n.* propriétaire *m./f.* **~ership** *n.* possession *f.* (**of,** de); (*right*) propriété *f.*
ox /ɒks/ *n.* (*pl.* **oxen**) bœuf *m.*
oxygen /ˈɒksɪdʒən/ *n.* oxygène *m.*
oyster /ˈɔɪstə(r)/ *n.* huître *f.*

P

pace /peɪs/ *n.* pas *m.* —*v.t.* (*room etc.*) arpenter. —*v.i.* **~ (up and down),** faire les cent pas. **keep ~ with,** suivre.
Pacific /pəˈsɪfɪk/ *a.* pacifique. —*n.* **~ (Ocean),** Pacifique *m.*
pacifist /ˈpæsɪfɪst/ *n.* pacifiste *m./f.*
pacify /ˈpæsɪfaɪ/ *v.t.* (*country*) pacifier; (*person*) apaiser.
pack /pæk/ *n.* paquet *m.*; (*mil.*) sac *m.*; (*of hounds*) meute *f.*; (*of thieves*) bande *f.*; (*of lies*) tissu *m.* —*v.t.* emballer; (*suitcase*) faire; (*box, room*) remplir; (*press down*) tasser. —*v.i.* **~ (one's bags),** faire ses valises. **~ into,** (*cram*) (s')entasser dans. **~ off,** expédier. **send ~ing,** envoyer promener. **~ed** *a.* (*crowded*) bondé. **~ed lunch,** repas froid *m.* **~ing** *n.* (*action, material*) emballage *m.*
package /ˈpækɪdʒ/ *n.* paquet *m.* —*v.t.* empaqueter. **~ deal,** marché global *m.*, ensemble de propositions (à accepter) *m.* **~ tour,** voyage organisé *m.*
packet /ˈpækɪt/ *n.* paquet *m.*
pact /pækt/ *n.* pacte *m.*
pad[1] /pæd/ *n.* bloc(-notes) *m.*; (*for ink*) tampon *m.* **(launching) ~,** rampe (de lancement) *f.* —*v.t.* (*p.t.* **padded**) rembourrer; (*text: fig.*) délayer. **~ding** *n.* rembourrage *m.*; délayage *m.*
pad[2] /pæd/ *v.i.* (*p.t.* **padded**) (*walk*) marcher à pas feutrés.
paddle[1] /ˈpædl/ *n.* pagaie *f.* —*v.t.* **~ a canoe,** pagayer. **~-steamer** *n.* bateau à roues *m.*
paddle[2] /ˈpædl/ *v.i.* barboter, se mouiller les pieds.
paddock /ˈpædək/ *n.* paddock *m.*
paddy(-field) /ˈpædɪ(fiːld)/ *n.* rizière *f.*
padlock /ˈpædlɒk/ *n.* cadenas *m.* —*v.t.* cadenasser.

paediatrician /piːdɪəˈtrɪʃn/ *n.* pédiatre *m./f.*
pagan /ˈpeɪgən/ *a.* & *n.* païen(ne) (*m.* (*f.*)).
page[1] /peɪdʒ/ *n.* (*of book etc.*) page *f.*
page[2] /peɪdʒ/ *n.* (*in hotel*) chasseur *m.* —*v.t.* (faire) appeler.
pageant /ˈpædʒənt/ *n.* spectacle (historique) *m.* **~ry** *n.* pompe *f.*
pagoda /pəˈgəʊdə/ *n.* pagode *f.*
paid /peɪd/ *see* **pay.** —*a.* **put ~ to,** (*fam.*) mettre fin à.
pail /peɪl/ *n.* seau *m.*
pain /peɪn/ *n.* douleur *f.* **~s,** efforts *m. pl.* —*v.t.* (*grieve*) peiner. **be in ~,** souffrir. **take ~s to,** se donner du mal pour. **~-killer** *n.* analgésique *m.* **~less** *a.* indolore.
painful /ˈpeɪnfl/ *a.* douloureux; (*laborious*) pénible.
painstaking /ˈpeɪnzteɪkɪŋ/ *a.* assidu, appliqué.
paint /peɪnt/ *n.* peinture *f.* **~s,** (*in tube, box*) couleurs *f. pl.* —*v.t./i.* peindre. **~er** *n.* peintre *m.* **~ing** *n.* peinture *f.*
paintbrush /ˈpeɪntbrʌʃ/ *n.* pinceau *m.*
pair /peə(r)/ *n.* paire *f.*; (*of people*) couple *m.* **a ~ of trousers,** un pantalon. —*v.i.* **~ off,** (*at dance etc.*) former un couple.
pajamas /pəˈdʒɑːməz/ *n.pl.* (*Amer.*) pyjama *m.*
Pakistan /pɑːkɪˈstɑːn/ *n.* Pakistan *m.* **~i** *a.* & *n.* pakistanais(e) (*m.*(*f.*)).
pal /pæl/ *n.* (*fam.*) cop|ain, -ine *m.*, *f.*
palace /ˈpælɪs/ *n.* palais *m.*
palat|e /ˈpælət/ *n.* (*of mouth*) palais *m.* **~able** *a.* agréable au goût.
palatial /pəˈleɪʃl/ *a.* somptueux.
palaver /pəˈlɑːvə(r)/ *n.* (*fuss: fam.*) histoire(s) *f.* (*pl.*).
pale[1] /peɪl/ *a.* (**-er, -est**) pâle. —*v.i.* pâlir. **~ness** *n.* pâleur *f.*
pale[2] /peɪl/ *n.* (*stake*) pieu *m.*
Palestin|e /ˈpælɪstaɪn/ *n.* Palestine *f.* **~ian** /-ˈstɪnɪən/ *a.* & *n.* palestinien(ne) (*m.* (*f.*)).
palette /ˈpælɪt/ *n.* palette *f.*
pall /pɔːl/ *v.i.* devenir insipide.
pallid /ˈpælɪd/ *a.* pâle.
palm /pɑːm/ *n.* (*of hand*) paume *f.*; (*tree*) palmier *m.*; (*symbol*) palme *f.* —*v.t.* **~ off,** (*thing*) refiler, coller (**on,** à); (*person*) coller. **P~ Sunday,** dimanche des Rameaux *m.*
palmist /ˈpɑːmɪst/ *n.* chiromancien(ne) *m.* (*f.*).
palpable /ˈpælpəbl/ *a.* manifeste.
palpitat|e /ˈpælpɪteɪt/ *v.i.* palpiter. **~ion** /-ˈteɪʃn/ *n.* palpitation *f.*
paltry /ˈpɔːltrɪ/ *a.* (**-ier, -iest**) dérisoire, piètre.
pamper /ˈpæmpə(r)/ *v.t.* dorloter.
pamphlet /ˈpæmflɪt/ *n.* brochure *f.*
pan /pæn/ *n.* casserole *f.*; (*for frying*) poêle *f.*; (*of lavatory*) cuvette *f.* —*v.t.* (*p.t.* **panned**) (*fam.*) critiquer.
panacea /pænəˈsɪə/ *n.* panacée *f.*
panache /pəˈnæʃ/ *n.* panache *m.*
pancake /ˈpænkeɪk/ *n.* crêpe *f.*
pancreas /ˈpæŋkrɪəs/ *n.* pancréas *m.*
panda /ˈpændə/ *n.* panda *m.* **~ car,** voiture pie (de la police) *f.*
pandemonium /pændɪˈməʊnɪəm/ *n.* tumulte *m.*, chaos *m.*
pander /ˈpændə(r)/ *v.i.* **~ to,** (*person, taste*) flatter bassement.
pane /peɪn/ *n.* carreau *m.*, vitre *f.*
panel /ˈpænl/ *n.* (*of door etc.*) panneau *m.*; (*jury*) jury *m.*; (*speakers: TV*) invités *m. pl.* (**instrument**) **~,** tableau de bord *m.* **~ of experts,** groupe d'experts *m.* **~led** *a.* lambrissé. **~ling** *n.* lambrissage *m.* **~list** *n.* (*TV*) invité(e) (de tribune) *m.* (*f.*).
pang /pæŋ/ *n.* pincement au cœur *m.* **~s,** (*of hunger, death*) affres *f. pl.* **~s of conscience,** remords *m.pl.*
panic /ˈpænɪk/ *n.* panique *f.*

—*v.t./i.* (*p.t.* **panicked**) (s')affoler, paniquer. **~-stricken** *a.* pris de panique, affolé.
panorama /pænə'rɑːmə/ *n.* panorama *m.*
pansy /'pænzɪ/ *n.* (*bot.*) pensée *f.*
pant /pænt/ *v.i.* haleter.
panther /'pænθə(r)/ *n.* panthère *f.*
panties /'pæntɪz/ *n. pl.* (*fam.*) slip *m.*, culotte *f.* (*de femme*).
pantomime /'pæntəmaɪm/ *n.* (*show*) spectacle de Noël *m.*; (*mime*) pantomime *f.*
pantry /'pæntrɪ/ *n.* office *m.*
pants /pænts/ *n. pl.* (*underwear*: *fam.*) slip *m.*; (*trousers*: *fam.* & *Amer.*) pantalon *m.*
papacy /'peɪpəsɪ/ *n.* papauté *f.*
papal /'peɪpl/ *a.* papal.
paper /'peɪpə(r)/ *n.* papier *m.*; (*newspaper*) journal *m.*; (*exam*) épreuve *f.*; (*essay*) exposé *m.* —*v.t.* (*room*) tapisser. **on ~,** par écrit. **~-clip** *n.* trombone *m.*
paperback /'peɪpəbæk/ *a.* & *n.* **~** (**book**), livre broché *m.*
paperweight /'peɪpəweɪt/ *n.* presse-papiers *m. invar.*
paperwork /'peɪpəwɜːk/ *n.* paperasserie *f.*
paprika /'pæprɪkə/ *n.* paprika *m.*
par /pɑː(r)/ *n.* **be below ~,** ne pas être en forme. **on a ~ with,** à égalité avec.
parable /'pærəbl/ *n.* parabole *f.*
parachut|e /'pærəʃuːt/ *n.* parachute *m.* —*v.i.* descendre en parachute. **~ist** *n.* parachutiste *m./f.*
parade /pə'reɪd/ *n.* (*procession*) défilé *m.*; (*ceremony, display*) parade *f.*; (*street*) avenue *f.* —*v.i.* défiler. —*v.t.* faire parade de.
paradise /'pærədaɪs/ *n.* paradis *m.*
paradox /'pærədɒks/ *n.* paradoxe *m.* **~ical** /-'dɒksɪkl/ *a.* paradoxal.
paraffin /'pærəfɪn/ *n.* pétrole (lampant) *m.*; (*wax*) paraffine *f.*
paragon /'pærəgən/ *n.* modèle *m.*
paragraph /'pærəgrɑːf/ *n.* paragraphe *m.*
parallel /'pærəlel/ *a.* parallèle. —*n.* (*line*) parallèle *f.*; (*comparison* & *geog.*) parallèle *m.* —*v.t.* (*p.t.* **paralleled**) être semblable à.
paralyse /'pærəlaɪz/ *v.t.* paralyser.
paraly|sis /pə'ræləsɪs/ *n.* paralysie *f.* **~tic** /pærə'lɪtɪk/ *a.* & *n.* paralytique (*m./f.*).
parameter /pə'ræmɪtə(r)/ *n.* paramètre *m.*
paramount /'pærəmaʊnt/ *a.* primordial, fondamental.
paranoia /pærə'nɔɪə/ *n.* paranoïa *f.*
parapet /'pærəpɪt/ *n.* parapet *m.*
paraphernalia /pærəfə'neɪlɪə/ *n.* attirail *m.*, équipement *m.*
paraphrase /'pærəfreɪz/ *n.* paraphrase *f.* —*v.t.* paraphraser.
parasite /'pærəsaɪt/ *n.* parasite *m.*
parasol /'pærəsɒl/ *n.* ombrelle *f.*; (*on table, at beach*) parasol *m.*
paratrooper /'pærətruːpə(r)/ *n.* (*mil.*) parachutiste *m/f.*
parcel /'pɑːsl/ *n.* colis *m.*, paquet *m.* —*v.t.* (*p.t.* **parcelled**). **~ out,** diviser en parcelles.
parch /pɑːtʃ/ *v.t.* dessécher. **be ~ed,** (*person*) avoir très soif.
parchment /'pɑːtʃmənt/ *n.* parchemin *m.*
pardon /'pɑːdn/ *n.* pardon *m.*; (*jurid.*) grâce *m.* —*v.t.* (*p.t.* **pardoned**) pardonner (**s.o. for sth.,** qch. à qn.); gracier. **I beg your ~,** pardon.
pare /peə(r)/ *v.t.* (*clip*) rogner; (*peel*) éplucher.
parent /'peərənt/ *n.* père *m.*, mère *f.* **~s,** parents *m. pl.* **~al** /pə'rentl/ *a.* des parents. **~hood** *n.* paternité *f.*, maternité *f.*
parenthesis /pə'renθəsɪs/ *n.* (*pl.* **-theses** /-siːz/) parenthèse *f.*
Paris /'pærɪs/ *n.* Paris *m./f.* **~ian** /pə'rɪzɪən, *Amer.* pə'riːʒn/ *a.* & *n.* parisien(ne) (*m.* (*f.*)).

parish /ˈpærɪʃ/ *n.* (*relig.*) paroisse *f.*; (*municipal*) commune *f.* **~ioner** /pəˈrɪʃənə(r)/ *n.* paroissien(ne) *m.* (*f.*).

parity /ˈpærətɪ/ *n.* parité *f.*

park /pɑːk/ *n.* parc *m.* —*v.t./i.* (se) garer; (*remain parked*) stationner. **~ing-lot** *n.* (*Amer.*) parking *m.* **~ing-meter** *n.* parcmètre *m.*

parka /ˈpɑːkə/ *n.* parka *m./f.*

parliament /ˈpɑːləmənt/ *n.* parlement *m.* **~ary** /-ˈmentrɪ/ *a.* parlementaire.

parlour /ˈpɑːlə(r)/ *n.* salon *m.*

parochial /pəˈrəʊkɪəl/ *a.* (*relig.*) paroissial; (*fig.*) borné, provincial.

parody /ˈpærədɪ/ *n.*. parodie *f.* —*v.t.* parodier.

parole /pəˈrəʊl/ *n.* **on ~,** en liberté conditionnelle.

parquet /ˈpɑːkeɪ/ *n.* parquet *m.*

parrot /ˈpærət/ *n.* perroquet *m.*

parry /ˈpærɪ/ *v.t.* (*sport*) parer; (*question etc.*) esquiver. —*n.* parade *f.*

parsimonious /pɑːsɪˈməʊnɪəs/ *a.* parcimonieux.

parsley /ˈpɑːslɪ/ *n.* persil *m.*

parsnip /ˈpɑːsnɪp/ *n.* panais *m.*

parson /ˈpɑːsn/ *n.* (*fam.*) pasteur *m.*

part /pɑːt/ *n.* partie *f.*; (*of serial*) épisode *m.*; (*of machine*) pièce *f.*; (*theatre*) rôle *m.*; (*side in dispute*) parti *m.* —*a.* partiel. —*adv.* en partie. —*v.t./i.* (*separate*) (se) séparer. **in ~,** en partie. **on the ~ of,** de la part de. **~-exchange** *n.* reprise *f.* **~ of speech,** catégorie grammaticale *f.* **~-time** *a.* & *adv.* à temps partiel. **~ with,** se séparer de. **these ~s,** cette région, ce coin.

partake /pɑːˈteɪk/ *v.i.* (*p.t.* **-took,** *p.p.* **-taken**) participer (**in,** à).

partial /ˈpɑːʃl/ *a.* partiel; (*biased*) partial. **be ~ to,** avoir une prédilection pour. **~ity** /-ɪˈælətɪ/ *n.* (*bias*) partialité *f.*; (*fondness*) prédilection *f.* **~ly** *adv.* partiellement.

particip|ate /pɑːˈtɪsɪpeɪt/ *v.i.* participer (**in,** à). **~ant** *n.* participant(e) *m.* (*f.*). **~ation** /-ˈpeɪʃn/ *n.* participation *f.*

participle /ˈpɑːtɪsɪpl/ *n.* participe *m.*

particle /ˈpɑːtɪkl/ *n.* particule *f.*

particular /pəˈtɪkjʊlə(r)/ *a.* particulier; (*fussy*) difficile; (*careful*) méticuleux. **that ~ man,** cet homme-là en particulier. **~s** *n. pl.* détails *m. pl.* **in ~,** en particulier. **~ly** *adv.* particulièrement.

parting /ˈpɑːtɪŋ/ *n.* séparation *f.*; (*in hair*) raie *f.* —*a.* d'adieu.

partisan /pɑːtɪˈzæn, *Amer.* ˈpɑːtɪzn/ *n.* partisan(e) *m.* (*f.*).

partition /pɑːˈtɪʃn/ *n.* (*of room*) cloison *f.*; (*pol.*) partage *m.*, partition *f.* —*v.t.* (*room*) cloisonner; (*country*) partager.

partly /ˈpɑːtlɪ/ *adv.* en partie.

partner /ˈpɑːtnə(r)/ *n.* associé(e) *m.* (*f.*); (*sport*) partenaire *m./f.* **~ship** *n.* association *f.*

partridge /ˈpɑːtrɪdʒ/ *n.* perdrix *f.*

party /ˈpɑːtɪ/ *n.* réception *f.*; (*informal*) surprise-partie *f.*; (*for birthday*) fête *f.*; (*group*) groupe *m.*, équipe *f.*; (*pol.*) parti *m.*; (*jurid.*) partie *f.* **~ line,** (*telephone*) ligne commune *f.*

pass /pɑːs/ *v.t./i.* (*p.t.* **passed**) passer; (*overtake*) dépasser; (*in exam*) être reçu (à); (*approve*) accepter, autoriser; (*remark*) faire; (*judgement*) prononcer; (*law, bill*) voter. **~ (by),** (*building*) passer devant; (*person*) croiser. —*n.* (*permit*) laissez-passer *m. invar.*; (*ticket*) carte (d'abonnement) *f.*; (*geog.*) col *m.*; (*sport*) passe *f.* **~ (mark),** (*in exam*) moyenne *f.* **make a ~ at,** (*fam.*) faire des avances à. **~ away,** mourir. **~ out** *or* **round,** distribuer. **~ out,** (*faint: fam.*)

s'évanouir. **~ over,** (*overlook*) passer sur. **~ up,** (*forego*: *fam.*) laisser passer.

passable /ˈpɑːsəbl/ *a.* (*adequate*) passable; (*road*) praticable.

passage /ˈpæsɪdʒ/ *n.* (*way through, text, etc.*) passage *m.*; (*voyage*) traversée *f.*; (*corridor*) couloir *m.*

passenger /ˈpæsɪndʒə(r)/ *n.* passag|er, -ère *m.*, *f.*; (*in train*) voyageu|r, -se *m.*, *f.*

passer-by /pɑːsəˈbaɪ/ *n.* (*pl.* **passers-by**) passant(e) *m.* (*f.*).

passing /ˈpɑːsɪŋ/ *a.* (*fleeting*) fugitif, passager.

passion /ˈpæʃn/ *n.* passion *f.* **~ate** *a.* passionné. **~ately** *adv.* passionnément.

passive /ˈpæsɪv/ *a.* passif. **~ness** *n.* passivité *f.*

Passover /ˈpɑːsəʊvə(r)/ *n.* Pâque *f.*

passport /ˈpɑːspɔːt/ *n.* passeport *m.*

password /ˈpɑːswɜːd/ *n.* mot de passe *m.*

past /pɑːst/ *a.* passé; (*former*) ancien. —*n.* passé *m.* —*prep.* au-delà de; (*in time*) plus de; (*in front of*) devant. —*adv.* devant. **the ~ months,** ces derniers mois.

pasta /ˈpæstə/ *n.* pâtes *f. pl.*

paste /peɪst/ *n.* (*glue*) colle *f.*; (*dough*) pâte *f.*; (*of fish, meat*) pâté *m.*; (*jewellery*) strass *m.* —*v.t.* coller.

pastel /ˈpæstl/ *n.* pastel *m.* —*a.* pastel *invar.*

pasteurize /ˈpæstʃəraɪz/ *v.t.* pasteuriser.

pastiche /pæˈstiːʃ/ *n.* pastiche *m.*

pastille /ˈpæstɪl/ *n.* pastille *f.*

pastime /ˈpɑːstaɪm/ *n.* passe-temps *m. invar.*

pastoral /ˈpɑːstərəl/ *a.* pastoral.

pastry /ˈpeɪstrɪ/ *n.* (*dough*) pâte *f.*; (*tart*) pâtisserie *f.*

pasture /ˈpɑːstʃə(r)/ *n.* pâturage *m.*

pasty[1] /ˈpæstɪ/ *n.* petit pâté *m.*

pasty[2] /ˈpeɪstɪ/ *a.* pâteux.

pat /pæt/ *v.t.* (*p.t.* **patted**) tapoter. —*n.* petite tape *f.* —*adv.* & *a.* à propos; (*ready*) tout prêt.

patch /pætʃ/ *n.* pièce *f.*; (*over eye*) bandeau *m.*; (*spot*) tache *f.*; (*of vegetables*) carré *m.* —*v.t.* **~ up,** rapiécer; (*fig.*) régler. **bad ~,** période difficile *f.* **not be a ~ on,** ne pas arriver à la cheville de. **~y** *a.* inégal.

patchwork /ˈpætʃwɜːk/ *n.* patchwork *m.*

pâté /ˈpæteɪ/ *n.* pâté *m.*

patent /ˈpeɪtnt/ *a.* patent. —*n.* brevet (d'invention) *m.* —*v.t.* breveter. **~ leather,** cuir verni *m.* **~ly** *adv.* manifestement.

paternal /pəˈtɜːnl/ *a.* paternel.

paternity /pəˈtɜːnətɪ/ *n.* paternité *f.*

path /pɑːθ/ *n.* (*pl.* **-s** /pɑːðz/) sentier *m.*, chemin *m.*; (*in park*) allée *f.*; (*of rocket*) trajectoire *f.*

pathetic /pəˈθetɪk/ *a.* pitoyable.

pathology /pəˈθɒlədʒɪ/ *n.* pathologie *f.*

pathos /ˈpeɪθɒs/ *n.* pathétique *m.*

patience /ˈpeɪʃns/ *n.* patience *f.*

patient /ˈpeɪʃnt/ *a.* patient. —*n.* malade *m.*/*f.*, patient(e) *m.* (*f.*). **~ly** *adv.* patiemment.

patio /ˈpætɪəʊ/ *n.* (*pl.* **-os**) patio *m.*

patriot /ˈpætrɪət, ˈpeɪtrɪət/ *n.* patriote *m.*/*f.* **~ic** /-ˈɒtɪk/ *a.* patriotique; (*person*) patriote. **~ism** *n.* patriotisme *m.*

patrol /pəˈtrəʊl/ *n.* patrouille *f.* —*v.t.*/*i.* patrouiller (dans).

patron /ˈpeɪtrən/ *n.* (*of the arts etc.*) protec|teur, -trice *m.*, *f.*; (*customer*) client(e) *m.* (*f.*). **~ saint,** saint(e) patron(ne) *m.* (*f.*).

patron|age /ˈpætrənɪdʒ/ *n.* clientèle *f.*; (*support*) patronage *m.* **~ize** *v.t.* être client de; (*fig.*) traiter avec condescendance.

patter[1] /ˈpætə(r)/ *n.* (*of steps*) bruit *m.*; (*of rain*) crépitement *m.*

patter[2] /ˈpætə(r)/ *n.* (*speech*) baratin *m.*

pattern /ˈpætn/ *n.* motif *m.*, dessin *m.*; (*for sewing*) patron *m.*; (*procedure, type*) schéma *m.*; (*example*) exemple *m.*

paunch /pɔːntʃ/ *n.* panse *f.*

pauper /ˈpɔːpə(r)/ *n.* indigent(e) *m.* (*f.*), pauvre *m.*, pauvresse *f.*

pause /pɔːz/ *n.* pause *f.* —*v.i.* faire une pause; (*hesitate*) hésiter.

pav|e /peɪv/ *v.t.* paver. **~e the way,** ouvrir la voie (**for,** à). **~ing-stone** *n.* pavé *m.*

pavement /ˈpeɪvmənt/ *n.* trottoir *m.*; (*Amer.*) chaussée *f.*

pavilion /pəˈvɪljən/ *n.* pavillon *m.*

paw /pɔː/ *n.* patte *f.* —*v.t.* (*of animal*) donner des coups de patte à; (*touch*: *fam.*) tripoter.

pawn[1] /pɔːn/ *n.* (*chess & fig.*) pion *m.*

pawn[2] /pɔːn/ *v.t.* mettre en gage. —*n.* **in ~,** en gage. **~-shop** *n.* mont-de-piété *m.*

pawnbroker /ˈpɔːnbrəʊkə(r)/ *n.* prêteur sur gages *m.*

pay /peɪ/ *v.t./i.* (*p.t.* **paid**) payer; (*yield*: *comm.*) rapporter; (*compliment, visit*) faire. —*n.* salaire *m.*, paie *f.* **in the ~ of,** à la solde de. **~ back,** rembourser. **~ for,** payer. **~ homage,** rendre hommage (**to,** à). **~ in,** verser (**to,** à). **~ off** *or* **out** *or* **up,** payer. **~ off,** (*succeed*: *fam.*) être payant. **~-off** *n.* (*sl.*) règlement de comptes *m.*

payable /ˈpeɪəbl/ *a.* payable.

payment /ˈpeɪmənt/ *n.* paiement *m.*; (*reward*) récompense *f.*

payroll /ˈpeɪrəʊl/ *n.* registre du personnel *m.* **be on the ~ of,** être membre du personnel de.

pea /piː/ *n.* (petit) pois *m.* **~-shooter** *n.* sarbacane *f.*

peace /piːs/ *n.* paix *f.* **~ of mind,** tranquillité d'esprit *f.* **~able** *a.* pacifique.

peaceful /ˈpiːsfl/ *a.* paisible; (*intention, measure*) pacifique.

peacemaker /ˈpiːsmeɪkə(r)/ *n.* concilia|teur, -trice *m., f.*

peach /piːtʃ/ *n.* pêche *f.*

peacock /ˈpiːkɒk/ *n.* paon *m.*

peak /piːk/ *n.* sommet *m.*; (*of mountain*) pic *m.*; (*maximum*) maximum *m.* **~ hours,** heures de pointe *f. pl.* **~ed cap,** casquette *f.*

peaky /ˈpiːkɪ/ *a.* (*pale*) pâlot; (*puny*) chétif; (*off colour*) patraque.

peal /piːl/ *n.* (*of bells*) carillon *m.*; (*of laughter*) éclat *m.*

peanut /ˈpiːnʌt/ *n.* cacahuète *f.* **~s,** (*money*: *sl.*) une bagatelle.

pear /peə(r)/ *n.* poire *f.*

pearl /pɜːl/ *n.* perle *f.* **~y** *a.* nacré.

peasant /ˈpeznt/ *n.* paysan(ne) *m.* (*f.*).

peat /piːt/ *n.* tourbe *f.*

pebble /ˈpebl/ *n.* caillou *m.*; (*on beach*) galet *m.*

peck /pek/ *v.t./i.* (*food etc.*) picorer; (*attack*) donner des coups de bec (à). —*n.* coup de bec *m.*

peckish /ˈpekɪʃ/ *a.* **be ~,** (*fam.*) avoir faim.

peculiar /pɪˈkjuːlɪə(r)/ *a.* (*odd*) bizarre; (*special*) particulier (**to,** à). **~ity** /-ˈærətɪ/ *n.* bizarrerie *f.*; (*feature*) particularité *f.*

pedal /ˈpedl/ *n.* pédale *f.* —*v.i.* pédaler.

pedantic /pɪˈdæntɪk/ *a.* pédant.

peddle /ˈpedl/ *v.t.* colporter.

pedestal /ˈpedɪstl/ *n.* piédestal *m.*

pedestrian /pɪˈdestrɪən/ *n.* piéton *m.* —*a.* (*precinct, street*) piétonnier; (*fig.*) prosaïque. **~ crossing,** passage pour piétons *m.*

pedigree /ˈpedɪgriː/ *n.* (*of person*) ascendance *f.*; (*of animal*) pedigree *m.* —*a.* (*cattle etc.*) de race.

pedlar /ˈpedlə(r)/ *n.* camelot *m.*; (*door-to-door*) colporteu|r, -se *m., f.*

peek /piːk/ *v.i.* & *n.* = **peep**[1].

peel /piːl/ *n.* épluchure(s) *f.* (*pl.*);

(*of orange*) écorce *f.* —*v.t.* (*fruit, vegetables*) éplucher. —*v.i.* (*of skin*) peler; (*of paint*) s'écailler. **~ings** *n. pl.* épluchures *f. pl.*

peep[1] /piːp/ *v.i.* jeter un coup d'œil (furtif) (**at,** à). —*n.* coup d'œil (furtif) *m.* **~-hole** *n.* judas *m.* **P~ing Tom,** voyeur *m.*

peep[2] /piːp/ *v.i.* (*chirp*) pépier.

peer[1] /pɪə(r)/ *v.i.* **~ (at),** regarder attentivement, scruter.

peer[2] /pɪə(r)/ *n.* (*equal, noble*) pair *m.* **~age** *n.* pairie *f.*

peeved /piːvd/ *a.* (*sl.*) irrité.

peevish /ˈpiːvɪʃ/ *a.* grincheux.

peg /peg/ *n.* cheville *f.*; (*for clothes*) pince à linge *f.*; (*to hang coats etc.*) patère *f.*; (*for tent*) piquet *m.* —*v.t.* (*p.t.* **pegged**) (*prices*) stabiliser. **buy off the ~,** acheter en prêt-à-porter.

pejorative /pɪˈdʒɒrətɪv/ *a.* péjoratif.

pelican /ˈpelɪkən/ *n.* pélican *m.* **~ crossing,** passage clouté (avec feux de signalisation) *m.*

pellet /ˈpelɪt/ *n.* (*round mass*) boulette *f.*; (*for gun*) plomb *m.*

pelt[1] /pelt/ *n.* (*skin*) peau *f.*

pelt[2] /pelt/ *v.t.* bombarder (**with,** de). —*v.i.* pleuvoir à torrents.

pelvis /ˈpelvɪs/ *n.* (*anat.*) bassin *m.*

pen[1] /pen/ *n.* (*for sheep etc.*) enclos *m.*; (*for baby, cattle*) parc *m.*

pen[2] /pen/ *n.* stylo *m.*; (*to be dipped in ink*) plume *f.* —*v.t.* (*p.t.* **penned**) écrire. **~-friend** *n.* correspondant(e) *m.* (*f.*). **~-name** *n.* pseudonyme *m.*

penal /ˈpiːnl/ *a.* pénal. **~ize** *v.t.* pénaliser; (*fig.*) handicaper.

penalty /ˈpenltɪ/ *n.* peine *f.*; (*fine*) amende *f.*; (*sport*) pénalité *f.*

penance /ˈpenəns/ *n.* pénitence *f.*

pence /pens/ *see* **penny.**

pencil /ˈpensl/ *n.* crayon *m.* —*v.t.* (*p.t.* **pencilled**) crayonner. **~-sharpener** *n.* taille-crayon(s) *m.*

pendant /ˈpendənt/ *n.* pendentif *m.*

pending /ˈpendɪŋ/ *a.* en suspens. —*prep.* (*until*) en attendant.

pendulum /ˈpendjʊləm/ *n.* pendule *m.*; (*of clock*) balancier *m.*

penetrat|e /ˈpenɪtreɪt/ *v.t.* (*enter*) pénétrer dans; (*understand, permeate*) pénétrer. —*v.i.* pénétrer. **~ing** *a.* pénétrant. **~ion** /-ˈtreɪʃn/ *n.* pénétration *f.*

penguin /ˈpeŋgwɪn/ *n.* manchot *m.*, pingouin *m.*

penicillin /penɪˈsɪlɪn/ *n.* pénicilline *f.*

peninsula /pəˈnɪnsjʊlə/ *n.* péninsule *f.*

penis /ˈpiːnɪs/ *n.* pénis *m.*

peniten|t /ˈpenɪtənt/ *a.* & *n.* pénitent(e) (*m.* (*f.*)). **~ce** *n.* pénitence *f.*

penitentiary /penɪˈtenʃərɪ/ *n.* (*Amer.*) prison *f.*, pénitencier *m.*

penknife /ˈpennaɪf/ *n.* (*pl.* **-knives**) canif *m.*

pennant /ˈpenənt/ *n.* flamme *f.*

penniless /ˈpenɪlɪs/ *a.* sans le sou.

penny /ˈpenɪ/ *n.* (*pl.* **pennies** *or* **pence**) penny *m.*; (*fig.*) sou *m.*

pension /ˈpenʃn/ *n.* pension *f.*; (*for retirement*) retraite *f.* —*v.t.* **~ off,** mettre à la retraite. **~able** *a.* qui a droit à une retraite. **~er** *n.* (**old-age**) **~er,** retraité(e) *m.* (*f.*), personne âgée *f.*

pensive /ˈpensɪv/ *a.* pensif.

Pentecost /ˈpentɪkɒst/ *n.* Pentecôte *f.*

penthouse /ˈpenthaʊs/ *n.* appartement de luxe *m.* (*sur le toit d'un immeuble*).

pent-up /pentˈʌp/ *a.* refoulé.

penultimate /penˈʌltɪmət/ *a.* avant-dernier.

people /ˈpiːpl/ *n. pl.* gens *m. pl.*, personnes *f. pl.* —*n.* peuple *m.* —*v.t.* peupler. **English**/*etc.* **~,** les Anglais/*etc. m. pl.* **~ say,** on dit.

pep /pep/ *n.* entrain *m.* **~ talk,** discours d'encouragement *m.*

pepper /ˈpepə(r)/ *n.* poivre *m.*;

(*vegetable*) poivron *m.* —*v.t.* (*culin.*) poivrer. **~y** *a.* poivré.
peppermint /'pepəmɪnt/ *n.* (*plant*) menthe poivrée *f.*; (*sweet*) bonbon à la menthe *m.*
per /pɜː(r)/ *prep.* par. **~ annum,** par an. **~ cent,** pour cent. **~ kilo**/*etc.*, le kilo/*etc.* **ten km. ~ hour,** dix km à l'heure.
perceive /pə'siːv/ *v.t.* percevoir; (*notice*) s'apercevoir de. **~ that,** s'apercevoir que.
percentage /pə'sentɪdʒ/ *n.* pourcentage *m.*
perceptible /pə'septəbl/ *a.* perceptible.
percept|ion /pə'sepʃn/ *n.* perception *f.* **~ive** /-tɪv/ *a.* pénétrant.
perch /pɜːtʃ/ *n.* (*of bird*) perchoir *m.* —*v.i.* (se) percher.
percolat|e /'pɜːkəleɪt/ *v.t.* passer. —*v.i.* filtrer. **~or** *n.* cafetière *f.*
percussion /pə'kʌʃn/ *n.* percussion *f.*
peremptory /pə'remptərɪ/ *a.* péremptoire.
perennial /pə'renɪəl/ *a.* perpétuel; (*plant*) vivace.
perfect[1] /'pɜːfɪkt/ *a.* parfait. **~ly** *adv.* parfaitement.
perfect[2] /pə'fekt/ *v.t.* parfaire, mettre au point. **~ion** /-kʃn/ *n.* perfection *f.* **to ~ion,** à la perfection. **~ionist** /-kʃənɪst/ *n.* perfectionniste *m.*/*f.*
perforat|e /'pɜːfəreɪt/ *v.t.* perforer. **~ion** /-'reɪʃn/ *n.* perforation *f.*; (*line of holes*) pointillé *m.*
perform /pə'fɔːm/ *v.t.* exécuter, faire; (*a function*) remplir; (*mus.*, *theatre*) interpréter, jouer. —*v.i.* jouer; (*behave, function*) se comporter. **~ance** *n.* exécution *f.*; interprétation *f.*; (*of car, team*) performance *f.*; (*show*) représentation *f.*; séance *f.*; (*fuss*) histoire *f.* **~er** *n.* artiste *m.*/*f.*
perfume /'pɜːfjuːm/ *n.* parfum *m.*
perfunctory /pə'fʌŋktərɪ/ *a.* négligent, superficiel.
perhaps /pə'hæps/ *adv.* peut-être.
peril /'perəl/ *n.* péril *m.* **~ous** *a.* périlleux.
perimeter /pə'rɪmɪtə(r)/ *n.* périmètre *m.*
period /'pɪərɪəd/ *n.* période *f.*, époque *f.*; (*era*) époque *f.*; (*lesson*) cours *m.*; (*gram.*) point *m.*; (*med.*) règles *f. pl.* —*a.* d'époque. **~ic** /-'ɒdɪk/ *a.* périodique. **~ically** /-'ɒdɪklɪ/ *adv.* périodiquement.
periodical /pɪərɪ'ɒdɪkl/ *n.* périodique *m.*
peripher|y /pə'rɪfərɪ/ *n.* périphérie *f.* **~al** *a.* périphérique; (*of lesser importance*: *fig.*) accessoire.
periscope /'perɪskəʊp/ *n.* périscope *m.*
perish /'perɪʃ/ *v.i.* périr; (*rot*) se détériorer. **~able** *a.* périssable. **~ing** *a.* (*cold*: *fam.*) glacial.
perjur|e /'pɜːdʒə(r)/ *v. pr.* **~e o.s.,** se parjurer. **~y** *n.* parjure *m.*
perk[1] /pɜːk/ *v.t.*/*i.* **~ up,** (*fam.*) (se) remonter. **~y** *a.* (*fam.*) gai.
perk[2] /pɜːk/ *n.* (*fam.*) avantage *m.*
perm /pɜːm/ *n.* permanente *f.* —*v.t.* **have one's hair ~ed,** se faire faire une permanente.
permanen|t /'pɜːmənənt/ *a.* permanent. **~ce** *n.* permanence *f.* **~tly** *adv.* à titre permanent.
permeable /'pɜːmɪəbl/ *a.* perméable.
permeate /'pɜːmɪeɪt/ *v.t.* imprégner, se répandre dans.
permissible /pə'mɪsəbl/ *a.* permis.
permission /pə'mɪʃn/ *n.* permission *f.*
permissive /pə'mɪsɪv/ *a.* tolérant, laxiste. **~ness** *n.* laxisme *m.*
permit[1] /pə'mɪt/ *v.t.* (*p.t.* **permitted**) permettre (**s.o. to,** à qn. de), autoriser (**s.o. to,** qn. à).
permit[2] /'pɜːmɪt/ *n.* permis *m.*; (*pass*) laissez-passer *m. invar.*

permutation /pɜːmjuːˈteɪʃn/ *n.* permutation *f.*
pernicious /pəˈnɪʃəs/ *a.* nocif, pernicieux; (*med.*) pernicieux.
peroxide /pəˈrɒksaɪd/ *n.* eau oxygénée *f.*
perpendicular /pɜːpənˈdɪkjʊlə(r)/ *a.* & *n.* perpendiculaire (*f.*).
perpetrat|e /ˈpɜːpɪtreɪt/ *v.t.* perpétrer. **~or** *n.* auteur *m.*
perpetual /pəˈpetʃʊəl/ *a.* perpétuel.
perpetuate /pəˈpetʃʊeɪt/ *v.t.* perpétuer.
perplex /pəˈpleks/ *v.t.* rendre perplexe. **~ed** *a.* perplexe. **~ing** *a.* déroutant. **~ity** *n.* perplexité *f.*
persecut|e /ˈpɜːsɪkjuːt/ *v.t.* persécuter. **~ion** /-ˈkjuːʃn/ *n.* persécution *f.*
persever|e /pɜːsɪˈvɪə(r)/ *v.i.* persévérer. **~ance** *n.* persévérance *f.*
Persian /ˈpɜːʃn/ *a.* & *n.* (*lang.*) persan (*m.*).
persist /pəˈsɪst/ *v.i.* persister (**in doing,** à faire). **~ence** *n.* persistance *f.* **~ent** *a.* (*cough, snow, etc.*) persistant; (*obstinate*) obstiné; (*continual*) continuel. **~ently** *adv.* avec persistance.
person /ˈpɜːsn/ *n.* personne *f.* **in ~,** en personne. **~able** *a.* beau.
personal /ˈpɜːsənl/ *a.* personnel; (*hygiene, habits*) intime; (*secretary*) particulier. **~ly** *adv.* personnellement.
personality /pɜːsəˈnælətɪ/ *n.* personnalité *f.*; (*on TV*) vedette *f.*
personify /pəˈsɒnɪfaɪ/ *v.t.* personnifier.
personnel /pɜːsəˈnel/ *n.* personnel *m.*
perspective /pəˈspektɪv/ *n.* perspective *f.*
perspir|e /pəˈspaɪə(r)/ *v.i.* transpirer. **~ation** /-əˈreɪʃn/ *n.* transpiration *f.*
persua|de /pəˈsweɪd/ *v.t.* persuader (**to,** de). **~sion** /-eɪʒn/ *n.* persuasion *f.*
persuasive /pəˈsweɪsɪv/ *a.* (*person, speech, etc.*) persuasif. **~ly** *adv.* d'une manière persuasive.
pert /pɜːt/ *a.* (*saucy*) impertinent; (*lively*) plein d'entrain. **~ly** *adv.* avec impertinence.
pertain /pəˈteɪn/ *v.i.* **~ to,** se rapporter à.
pertinent /ˈpɜːtɪnənt/ *a.* pertinent. **~ly** *adv.* pertinemment.
perturb /pəˈtɜːb/ *v.t.* troubler.
Peru /pəˈruː/ *n.* Pérou *m.* **~vian** *a.* & *n.* péruvien(ne) (*m.* (*f.*)).
perus|e /pəˈruːz/ *v.t.* lire (attentivement). **~al** *n.* lecture *f.*
perva|de /pəˈveɪd/ *v.t.* imprégner, envahir. **~sive** *a.* envahissant.
pervers|e /pəˈvɜːs/ *a.* (*stubborn*) entêté; (*wicked*) pervers. **~ity** *n.* perversité *f.*
perver|t[1] /pəˈvɜːt/ *v.t.* pervertir. **~sion** *n.* perversion *f.*
pervert[2] /ˈpɜːvɜːt/ *n.* perverti(e) *m.* (*f.*), dépravé(e) *m.*(*f.*).
peseta /pəˈseɪtə/ *n.* peseta *f.*
pessimis|t /ˈpesɪmɪst/ *n.* pessimiste *m.*/*f.* **~m** /-zəm/ *n.* pessimisme *m.* **~tic** /-ˈmɪstɪk/ *a.* pessimiste. **~tically** /-ˈmɪstɪklɪ/ *adv.* avec pessimisme.
pest /pest/ *n.* insecte *or* animal nuisible *m.*; (*person: fam.*) enquiquineu|r, -se *m.*, *f.*
pester /ˈpestə(r)/ *v.t.* harceler.
pesticide /ˈpestɪsaɪd/ *n.* pesticide *m.*, insecticide *m.*
pet /pet/ *n.* animal (domestique) *m.*; (*favourite*) chouchou(te) *m.* (*f.*). —*a.* (*tame*) apprivoisé. —*v.t.* (*p.t.* **petted**) caresser; (*sexually*) peloter. **~ hate,** bête noire *f.* **~ name,** diminutif *m.*
petal /ˈpetl/ *n.* pétale *m.*
peter /ˈpiːtə(r)/ *v.i.* **~ out,** (*supplies*) s'épuiser; (*road*) finir.
petite /pəˈtiːt/ *a.* (*woman*) menue.

petition /pɪ'tɪʃn/ *n.* pétition *f.* —*v.t.* adresser une pétition à.

petrify /'petrɪfaɪ/ *v.t.* pétrifier; (*scare*: *fig.*) pétrifier de peur.

petrol /'petrəl/ *n.* essence *f.* ~ **station,** station-service *f.*

petroleum /pɪ'trəʊlɪəm/ *n.* pétrole *m.*

petticoat /'petɪkəʊt/ *n.* jupon *m.*

petty /'petɪ/ *a.* (**-ier, -iest**) (*minor*) petit; (*mean*) mesquin. ~ **cash,** petite monnaie *f.*

petulan|t /'petjʊlənt/ *a.* irritable. **~ce** *n.* irritabilité *f.*

pew /pjuː/ *n.* banc (d'église) *m.*

pewter /'pjuːtə(r)/ *n.* étain *m.*

phallic /'fælɪk/ *a.* phallique.

phantom /'fæntəm/ *n.* fantôme *m.*

pharmaceutical /fɑːmə'sjuːtɪkl/ *a.* pharmaceutique.

pharmac|y /'fɑːməsɪ/ *n.* pharmacie *f.* **~ist** *n.* pharmacien(ne) *m.* (*f.*).

pharyngitis /færɪn'dʒaɪtɪs/ *n.* pharyngite *f.*

phase /feɪz/ *n.* phase *f.* —*v.t.* ~ **in/out,** introduire/retirer progressivement.

pheasant /'feznt/ *n.* faisan *m.*

phenomen|on /fɪ'nɒmɪnən/ *n.* (*pl.* **-ena**) phénomène *m.* **~al** *a.* phénoménal.

phew /fjuː/ *int.* ouf.

phial /'faɪəl/ *n.* fiole *f.*

philanderer /fɪ'lændərə(r)/ *n.* coureur (de femmes) *m.*

philanthrop|ist /fɪ'lænθrəpɪst/ *n.* philanthrope *m.*/*f.* **~ic** /-ən'θrɒpɪk/ *a.* philanthropique.

philatel|y /fɪ'lætəlɪ/ *n.* philatélie *f.* **~ist** *n.* philatéliste *m.*/*f.*

philharmonic /fɪlɑː'mɒnɪk/ *a.* philharmonique.

Philippines /'fɪlɪpiːnz/ *n. pl.* **the ~,** les Philippines *f. pl.*

philistine /'fɪlɪstaɪn, *Amer.* 'fɪlɪstiːn/ *n.* philistin *m.*

philosoph|y /fɪ'lɒsəfɪ/ *n.* philosophie *f.* **~er** *n.* philosophe *m.*/*f.* **~ical** /-ə'sɒfɪkl/ *a.* philosophique; (*resigned*) philosophe.

phlegm /flem/ *n.* (*med.*) mucosité *f.*

phlegmatic /fleg'mætɪk/ *a.* flegmatique.

phobia /'fəʊbɪə/ *n.* phobie *f.*

phone /fəʊn/ *n.* téléphone *m.* —*v.t.* (*person*) téléphoner à; (*message*) téléphoner. —*v.i.* téléphoner. ~ **back,** rappeler. ~ **book,** annuaire *m.* ~ **box,** ~ **booth,** cabine téléphonique *f.* ~ **call,** coup de fil *m.*

phonetic /fə'netɪk/ *a.* phonétique.

phoney /'fəʊnɪ/ *a.* (**-ier, -iest**) (*sl.*) faux. —*n.* (*person*: *sl.*) charlatan *m.* **it is a ~,** (*sl.*) c'est faux.

phosphate /'fɒsfeɪt/ *n.* phosphate *m.*

phosphorus /'fɒsfərəs/ *n.* phosphore *m.*

photo /'fəʊtəʊ/ *n.* (*pl.* **-os**) (*fam.*) photo *f.*

photocopy /'fəʊtəʊkɒpɪ/ *n.* photocopie *f.* —*v.t.* photocopier.

photogenic /fəʊtəʊ'dʒenɪk/ *a.* photogénique.

photograph /'fəʊtəgrɑːf/ *n.* photographie *f.* —*v.t.* photographier. **~er** /fə'tɒgrəfə(r)/ *n.* photographe *m.*/*f.* **~ic** /-'græfɪk/ *a.* photographique. **~y** /fə'tɒgrəfɪ/ *n.* (*activity*) photographie *f.*

phrase /freɪz/ *n.* expression *f.*; (*idiom & gram.*) locution *f.* —*v.t.* exprimer, formuler. **~-book** *n.* recueil de locutions *m.*

physical /'fɪzɪkl/ *a.* physique. **~ly** *adv.* physiquement.

physician /fɪ'zɪʃn/ *n.* médecin *m.*

physicist /'fɪzɪsɪst/ *n.* physicien(ne) *m.* (*f.*).

physics /'fɪzɪks/ *n.* physique *f.*

physiology /fɪzɪ'ɒlədʒɪ/ *n.* physiologie *f.*

physiotherap|y /fɪzɪəʊ'θerəpɪ/ *n.* kinésithérapie *f.* **~ist** *n.* kinésithérapeute *m.*/*f.*

physique /fɪ'ziːk/ *n.* constitution *f.*; (*appearance*) physique *m.*

pian|o /pɪ'ænəʊ/ *n.* (*pl.* **-os**) piano *m.* **~ist** /'pɪənɪst/ *n.* pianiste *m./f.*

piazza /pɪ'ætsə/ *n.* (*square*) place *f.*

pick[1] /pɪk/ (*tool*) *n.* pioche *f.*

pick[2] /pɪk/ *v.t.* choisir; (*flower etc.*) cueillir; (*lock*) crocheter; (*nose*) se curer; (*pockets*) faire. **~ (off),** enlever. *—n.* choix *m.*; (*best*) meilleur(e) *m.* (*f.*). **~ a quarrel with,** chercher querelle à. **~ holes in,** relever les défauts de. **~ on,** harceler. **~ out,** choisir; (*identify*) distinguer. **~ up** *v.t.* ramasser; (*sth. fallen*) relever; (*weight*) soulever; (*habit, passenger, speed, etc.*) prendre; (*learn*) apprendre; *v.i.* s'améliorer. **~-me-up** *n.* remontant *m.* **~-up** *n.* partenaire de rencontre *m./f.*; (*truck, stylus-holder*) pick-up *m.*

pickaxe /'pɪkæks/ *n.* pioche *f.*

picket /'pɪkɪt/ *n.* (*single striker*) gréviste *m./f.*; (*stake*) piquet *m.* **~ (line),** piquet de grève *m.* *—v.t.* (*p.t.* **picketed**) mettre un piquet de grève devant.

pickings /'pɪkɪŋz/ *n. pl.* restes *m. pl.*

pickle /'pɪkl/ *n.* vinaigre *m.*; (*brine*) saumure *f.* **~s,** pickles *m. pl.*; (*Amer.*) concombres *m.pl.* *—v.t.* conserver dans du vinaigre *or* de la saumure. **in a ~,** (*fam.*) dans le pétrin.

pickpocket /'pɪkpɒkɪt/ *n.* (*thief*) pickpocket *m.*

picnic /'pɪknɪk/ *n.* pique-nique *m.* *—v.i.* (*p.t.* **picnicked**) pique-niquer.

pictorial /pɪk'tɔːrɪəl/ *a.* illustré.

picture /'pɪktʃə(r)/ *n.* image *f.*; (*painting*) tableau *m.*; (*photograph*) photo *f.*; (*drawing*) dessin *m.*; (*film*) film *m.*; (*fig.*) description *f.*, tableau *m.* *—v.t.* s'imaginer; (*describe*) dépeindre. **the ~s,** (*cinema*) le cinéma.

picturesque /pɪktʃə'resk/ *a.* pittoresque.

piddling /'pɪdlɪŋ/ *a.* (*fam.*) dérisoire.

pidgin /'pɪdʒɪn/ *a.* **~ English,** pidgin *m.*

pie /paɪ/ *n.* tarte *f.*; (*of meat*) pâté en croûte *m.*

piebald /'paɪbɔːld/ *a.* pie *invar.*

piece /piːs/ *n.* morceau *m.*; (*of currency, machine, etc.*) pièce *f.* *—v.t.* **~ (together),** (r)assembler. **a ~ of advice/furniture/***etc.*, un conseil/meuble/*etc.* **~-work** *n.* travail à la pièce *m.* **take to ~s,** démonter.

piecemeal /'piːsmiːl/ *a.* par bribes.

pier /pɪə(r)/ *n.* (*promenade*) jetée *f.*

pierc|e /pɪəs/ *v.t.* percer. **~ing** *a.* perçant; (*cold*) glacial.

piety /'paɪətɪ/ *n.* piété *f.*

piffl|e /'pɪfl/ *n.* (*sl.*) fadaises *f. pl.* **~ing** *a.* (*sl.*) insignifiant.

pig /pɪg/ *n.* cochon *m.* **~-headed** *a.* entêté.

pigeon /'pɪdʒən/ *n.* pigeon *m.* **~-hole** *n.* casier *m.*

piggy /'pɪgɪ/ *a.* porcin; (*greedy: fam.*) goinfre. **~-back** *adv.* sur le dos. **~ bank,** tirelire *f.*

pigment /'pɪgmənt/ *n.* pigment *m.* **~ation** /-en'teɪʃn/ *n.* pigmentation *f.*

pigsty /'pɪgstaɪ/ *n.* porcherie *f.*

pigtail /'pɪgteɪl/ *n.* natte *f.*

pike /paɪk/ *n. invar.* (*fish*) brochet *m.*

pilchard /'pɪltʃəd/ *n.* pilchard *m.*

pile /paɪl/ *n.* pile *f.*, tas *m.*; (*of* carpet) poils *m.pl.* *—v.t.* **~ (up),** (*stack*) empiler. *—v.i.* **~ into,** s'empiler dans. **~ up,** (*accumulate*) (s')accumuler. **a ~ of,** (*fam.*) un tas de. **~-up** *n.* (*auto*) carambolage *m.*

piles /paɪlz/ *n. pl.* hémorroïdes *f. pl.*

pilfer /'pɪlfə(r)/ *v.t.* chaparder. **~age** *n.* chapardage *m.*

pilgrim /ˈpɪlgrɪm/ *n.* pèlerin *m.* **~age** *n.* pèlerinage *m.*

pill /pɪl/ *n.* pilule *f.*

pillage /ˈpɪlɪdʒ/ *n.* pillage *m.* —*v.t.* piller. —*v.i.* se livrer au pillage.

pillar /ˈpɪlə(r)/ *n.* pilier *m.* **~-box** *n.* boîte à *or* aux lettres *f.*

pillion /ˈpɪljən/ *n.* siège arrière *m.* **ride ~,** monter derrière.

pillory /ˈpɪlərɪ/ *n.* pilori *m.*

pillow /ˈpɪləʊ/ *n.* oreiller *m.*

pillowcase /ˈpɪləʊkeɪs/ *n.* taie d'oreiller *f.*

pilot /ˈpaɪlət/ *n.* pilote *m.* —*a.* pilote. —*v.t.* (*p.t.* **piloted**) piloter. **~-light** *n.* veilleuse *f.*

pimento /pɪˈmentəʊ/ *n.* (*pl.* **-os**) piment *m.*

pimp /pɪmp/ *n.* souteneur *m.*

pimpl|e /ˈpɪmpl/ *n.* bouton *m.* **~y** *a.* boutonneux.

pin /pɪn/ *n.* épingle *f.*; (*techn.*) goupille *f.* —*v.t.* (*p.t.* **pinned**) épingler, attacher; (*hold down*) clouer. **have ~s and needles,** avoir des fourmis. **~ s.o. down,** (*fig.*) forcer qn. à se décider. **~-point** *v.t.* repérer, définir. **~ up,** afficher. **~-up** *n.* (*fam.*) pin-up *f. invar.*

pinafore /ˈpɪnəfɔː(r)/ *n.* tablier *m.*

pincers /ˈpɪnsəz/ *n. pl.* tenailles *f. pl.*

pinch /pɪntʃ/ *v.t.* pincer; (*steal: sl.*) piquer. —*v.i.* (*be too tight*) serrer. —*n.* (*mark*) pinçon *m.*; (*of salt*) pincée *f.* **at a ~,** au besoin.

pincushion /ˈpɪnkʊʃn/ *n.* pelote à épingles *f.*

pine[1] /paɪn/ *n.* (*tree*) pin *m.*

pine[2] /paɪn/ *v.i.* **~ away,** dépérir. **~ for,** languir après.

pineapple /ˈpaɪnæpl/ *n.* ananas *m.*

ping /pɪŋ/ *n.* bruit métallique *m.*

ping-pong /ˈpɪŋpɒŋ/ *n.* ping-pong *m.*

pink /pɪŋk/ *a.* & *n.* rose (*m.*).

pinnacle /ˈpɪnəkl/ *n.* pinacle *m.*

pint /paɪnt/ *n.* pinte *f.* (*imperial = 0.57 litre*; *Amer.* = *0.47 litre*).

pioneer /paɪəˈnɪə(r)/ *n.* pionnier *m.* —*v.t.* être le premier à faire, utiliser, étudier, *etc.*

pious /ˈpaɪəs/ *a.* pieux.

pip[1] /pɪp/ *n.* (*seed*) pépin *m.*

pip[2] /pɪp/ *n.* (*sound*) top *m.*

pipe /paɪp/ *n.* tuyau *m.*; (*of smoker*) pipe *f.*; (*mus.*) pipeau *m.* —*v.t.* transporter par tuyau. **~-cleaner** *n.* cure-pipe *m.* **~ down,** se taire. **~-dream** *n.* chimère *f.*

pipeline /ˈpaɪplaɪn/ *n.* pipeline *m.* **in the ~,** en route.

piping /ˈpaɪpɪŋ/ *n.* tuyau(x) *m.* (*pl.*). **~ hot,** très chaud.

piquant /ˈpiːkənt/ *a.* piquant.

pique /piːk/ *n.* dépit *m.*

pira|te /ˈpaɪərət/ *n.* pirate *m.* **~cy** *n.* piraterie *f.*

pistachio /pɪˈstæʃɪəʊ/ *n.* (*pl.* **-os**) pistache *f.*

pistol /ˈpɪstl/ *n.* pistolet *m.*

piston /ˈpɪstən/ *n.* piston *m.*

pit /pɪt/ *n.* fosse *f.*, trou *m.*; (*mine*) puits *m.*; (*quarry*) carrière *f.*; (*of stomach*) creux *m.*; (*of cherry etc.*: *Amer.*) noyau *m.* —*v.t.* (*p.t.* **pitted**) trouer; (*fig.*) opposer. **~ o.s. against,** se mesurer à.

pitch[1] /pɪtʃ/ *n.* (*tar*) poix *f.* **~-black** *a.* d'un noir d'ébène.

pitch[2] /pɪtʃ/ *v.t.* lancer; (*tent*) dresser. —*v.i.* (*of ship*) tanguer. —*n.* degré *m.*; (*of voice*) hauteur *f.*; (*mus.*) ton *m.*; (*sport*) terrain *m.* **~ed battle,** bataille rangée *f.* **~ in,** (*fam.*) contribuer. **~ into,** (*fam.*) s'attaquer à.

pitcher /ˈpɪtʃə(r)/ *n.* cruche *f.*

pitchfork /ˈpɪtʃfɔːk/ *n.* fourche à foin *f.*

piteous /ˈpɪtɪəs/ *a.* pitoyable.

pitfall /ˈpɪtfɔːl/ *n.* piège *m.*

pith /pɪθ/ *n.* (*of orange*) peau blanche *f.*; (*essence*: *fig.*) moelle *f.*

pithy /ˈpɪθɪ/ *a.* (**-ier, -iest**) (*terse*) concis; (*forceful*) vigoureux.

piti|ful /ˈpɪtɪfl/ *a.* pitoyable. **~less** *a.* impitoyable.
pittance /ˈpɪtns/ *n.* revenu *or* salaire dérisoire *m.*
pity /ˈpɪtɪ/ *n.* pitié *f.*; (*regrettable fact*) dommage *m.* —*v.t.* plaindre. **take ~ on,** avoir pitié de.
pivot /ˈpɪvət/ *n.* pivot *m.* —*v.i.* (*p.t.* **pivoted**) pivoter.
pixie /ˈpɪksɪ/ *n.* lutin *m.*
pizza /ˈpiːtsə/ *n.* pizza *f.*
placard /ˈplækɑːd/ *n.* affiche *f.*
placate /pləˈkeɪt, *Amer.* ˈpleɪkeɪt/ *v.t.* calmer.
place /pleɪs/ *n.* endroit *m.*, lieu *m.*; (*house*) maison *f.*; (*seat, rank, etc.*) place *f.* —*v.t.* placer; (*an order*) passer; (*remember*) situer. **at** *or* **to my ~,** chez moi. **be ~d,** (*in race*) se placer. **~-mat** *n.* set *m.*
placid /ˈplæsɪd/ *a.* placide.
plagiar|ize /ˈpleɪdʒəraɪz/ *v.t.* plagier. **~ism** *n.* plagiat *m.*
plague /pleɪg/ *n.* peste *f.*; (*nuisance: fam.*) fléau *m.* —*v.t.* harceler.
plaice /pleɪs/ *n. invar.* carrelet *m.*
plaid /plæd/ *n.* tissu écossais *m.*
plain /pleɪn/ *a.* (**-er, -est**) clair; (*candid*) franc; (*simple*) simple; (*not pretty*) sans beauté; (*not patterned*) uni. —*adv.* franchement. —*n.* plaine *f.* **in ~ clothes,** en civil. **~ly** *adv.* clairement; franchement; simplement. **~ness** *n.* simplicité *f.*
plaintiff /ˈpleɪntɪf/ *n.* plaignant(e) *m.* (*f.*).
plaintive /ˈpleɪntɪv/ *a.* plaintif.
plait /plæt/ *v.t.* tresser, natter. —*n.* tresse *f.*, natte *f.*
plan /plæn/ *n.* projet *m.*, plan *m.*; (*diagram*) plan *m.* —*v.t.* (*p.t.* **planned**) prévoir, projeter; (*arrange*) organiser; (*design*) concevoir; (*economy, work*) planifier. —*v.i.* faire des projets. **~ to do,** avoir l'intention de faire.
plane[1] /pleɪn/ *n.* (*tree*) platane *m.*
plane[2] /pleɪn/ *n.* (*level*) plan *m.*; (*aeroplane*) avion *m.* —*a.* plan.
plane[3] /pleɪn/ *n.* (*tool*) rabot *m.* —*v.t.* raboter.
planet /ˈplænɪt/ *n.* planète *f.* **~ary** *a.* planétaire.
plank /plæŋk/ *n.* planche *f.*
planning /ˈplænɪŋ/ *n.* (*pol., comm.*) planification *f.* **family ~,** planning familial *m.*
plant /plɑːnt/ *n.* plante *f.*; (*techn.*) matériel *m.*; (*factory*) usine *f.* —*v.t.* planter; (*bomb*) (dé)poser. **~ation** /-ˈteɪʃn/ *n.* plantation *f.*
plaque /plɑːk/ *n.* plaque *f.*
plasma /ˈplæzmə/ *n.* plasma *m.*
plaster /ˈplɑːstə(r)/ *n.* plâtre *m.*; (*adhesive*) sparadrap *m.* —*v.t.* plâtrer; (*cover*) tapisser (**with,** de). **~ of Paris,** plâtre à mouler *m.* **~er** *n.* plâtrier *m.*
plastic /ˈplæstɪk/ *a.* en plastique; (*art, substance*) plastique. —*n.* plastique *m.* **~ surgery,** chirurgie esthétique *f.*
Plasticine /ˈplæstɪsiːn/ *n.* (P.) pâte à modeler *f.*
plate /pleɪt/ *n.* assiette *f.*; (*of metal*) plaque *f.*; (*gold or silver dishes*) vaisselle plate *f.*; (*in book*) gravure *f.* —*v.t.* (*metal*) plaquer. **~ful** *n.* (*pl.* **-fuls**) assiettée *f.*
plateau /ˈplætəʊ/ *n.* (*pl.* **-eaux** /-əʊz/) plateau *m.*
platform /ˈplætfɔːm/ *n.* (*in classroom, hall, etc.*) estrade *f.*; (*for speaking*) tribune *f.*; (*rail.*) quai *m.*; (*of bus & pol.*) plate-forme *f.*
platinum /ˈplætɪnəm/ *n.* platine *m.*
platitude /ˈplætɪtjuːd/ *n.* platitude *f.*
platonic /pləˈtɒnɪk/ *a.* platonique.
platoon /pləˈtuːn/ *n.* (*mil.*) section *f.*
platter /ˈplætə(r)/ *n.* plat *m.*
plausible /ˈplɔːzəbl/ *a.* plausible.
play /pleɪ/ *v.t./i.* jouer; (*instrument*) jouer de; (*game*) jouer à; (*opponent*) jouer contre; (*match*) disputer. —*n.* jeu *m.*; (*theatre*)

pièce *f.* **~-act** *v.i.* jouer la comédie. **~ down,** minimiser. **~-group, ~-school** *ns.* garderie *f.* **~ on,** (*take advantage of*) jouer sur. **~ on words,** jeu de mots *m.* **~ed out,** épuisé. **~-pen** *n.* parc *m.* **~ safe,** ne pas prendre de risques. **~ up,** (*fam.*) créer des problèmes (à). **~ up to,** flatter. **~er** *n.* joueu|r, -se *m.*, *f.*

playboy /ˈpleɪbɔɪ/ *n.* play-boy *m.*

playful /ˈpleɪfl/ *a.* enjoué; (*child*) joueur. **~ly** *adv.* avec espièglerie.

playground /ˈpleɪgraʊnd/ *n.* cour de récréation *f.*

playing /ˈpleɪɪŋ/ *n.* jeu *m.* **~-card** *n.* carte à jouer *f.* **~-field** *n.* terrain de sport *m.*

playmate /ˈpleɪmeɪt/ *n.* camarade *m.*/*f.*, cop|ain, -ine *m.*, *f.*

plaything /ˈpleɪθɪŋ/ *n.* jouet *m.*

playwright /ˈpleɪraɪt/ *n.* dramaturge *m.*/*f.*

plc *abbr.* (*public limited company*) SA.

plea /pliː/ *n.* (*entreaty*) supplication *f.*; (*reason*) excuse *f.*; (*jurid.*) défense *f.*

plead /pliːd/ *v.t.*/*i.* (*jurid.*) plaider; (*as excuse*) alléguer. **~ for,** (*beg for*) implorer. **~ with,** (*beg*) implorer.

pleasant /ˈpleznt/ *a.* agréable. **~ly** *adv.* agréablement.

please /pliːz/ *v.t.*/*i.* plaire (à), faire plaisir (à). —*adv.* s'il vous *or* te plaît. **~ o.s., do as one ~s,** faire ce qu'on veut. **~d** *a.* content (**with,** de). **pleasing** *a.* agréable.

pleasur|e /ˈpleʒə(r)/ *n.* plaisir *m.* **~able** *a.* très agréable.

pleat /pliːt/ *n.* pli *m.* —*v.t.* plisser.

plebiscite /ˈplebɪsɪt/ *n.* plébiscite *m.*

pledge /pledʒ/ *n.* (*token*) gage *m.*; (*fig.*) promesse *f.* —*v.t.* promettre; (*pawn*) engager.

plentiful /ˈplentɪfl/ *a.* abondant.

plenty /ˈplentɪ/ *n.* abondance *f.* **~ (of),** (*a great deal*) beaucoup (de); (*enough*) assez (de).

pleurisy /ˈplʊərəsɪ/ *n.* pleurésie *f.*

pliable /ˈplaɪəbl/ *a.* souple.

pliers /ˈplaɪəz/ *n. pl.* pince(s) *f.* (*pl.*).

plight /plaɪt/ *n.* triste situation *f.*

plimsoll /ˈplɪms(ə)l/ *n.* chaussure de gym *f.*

plinth /plɪnθ/ *n.* socle *m.*

plod /plɒd/ *v.i.* (*p.t.* **plodded**) avancer péniblement *or* d'un pas lent; (*work*) bûcher. **~der** *n.* bûcheu|r, -se *m.*, *f.* **~ding** *a.* lent.

plonk /plɒŋk/ *n.* (*sl.*) pinard *m.*

plot /plɒt/ *n.* complot *m.*; (*of novel etc.*) intrigue *f.* **~ (of land),** terrain *m.* —*v.t.*/*i.* (*p.t.* **plotted**) comploter; (*mark out*) tracer.

plough /plaʊ/ *n.* charrue *f.* —*v.t.*/*i.* labourer. **~ into,** rentrer dans. **~ through,** avancer péniblement dans.

plow /plaʊ/ *n.* & *v.t.*/*i.* (*Amer.*) = **plough.**

ploy /plɔɪ/ *n.* (*fam.*) stratagème *m.*

pluck /plʌk/ *v.t.* cueillir; (*bird*) plumer; (*eyebrows*) épiler. —*n.* courage *m.* **~ up courage,** prendre son courage à deux mains. **~y** *a.* courageux.

plug /plʌg/ *n.* (*of cloth, paper, etc.*) tampon *m.*; (*for sink etc.*) bonde *f.*; (*electr.*) fiche *f.*, prise *f.* —*v.t.* (*p.t.* **plugged**) (*hole*) boucher; (*publicize*: *fam.*) faire du battage autour de. —*v.i.* **~ away,** (*work*: *fam.*) bosser. **~ in,** brancher. **~-hole** *n.* vidange *f.*

plum /plʌm/ *n.* prune *f.* **~ job,** travail en or *m.* **~ pudding,** (plum-)pudding *m.*

plumb /plʌm/ *adv.* tout à fait. —*v.t.* (*probe*) sonder.

plumb|er /ˈplʌmə(r)/ *n.* plombier *m.* **~ing** *n.* plomberie *f.*

plume /pluːm/ *n.* plume(s) *f.* (*pl.*).

plummet /ˈplʌmɪt/ *v.i.* (*p.t.* **plummeted**) tomber, plonger.

plump /plʌmp/ *a.* (**-er, -est**) potelé,

dodu. —*v.i.* ~ **for**, choisir. ~**ness** *n.* rondeur *f.*

plunder /ˈplʌndə(r)/ *v.t.* piller. —*n.* (*act*) pillage *m.*; (*goods*) butin *m.*

plunge /plʌndʒ/ *v.t./i.* (*dive, thrust*) plonger; (*fall*) tomber. —*n.* plongeon *m.*; (*fall*) chute *f.*

plunger /ˈplʌndʒə(r)/ *n.* (*for sink etc.*) ventouse *f.*, déboucheur *m.*

plural /ˈplʊərəl/ *a.* pluriel; (*noun*) au pluriel. —*n.* pluriel *m.*

plus /plʌs/ *prep.* plus. —*a.* (*electr.* & *fig.*) positif. —*n.* signe plus *m.*; (*fig.*) atout *m.* **ten** ~, plus de dix.

plush(y) /ˈplʌʃ(ɪ)/ *a.* somptueux.

ply /plaɪ/ *v.t.* (*tool*) manier; (*trade*) exercer. —*v.i.* faire la navette. ~ **s.o. with drink**, offrir continuellement à boire à qn.

plywood /ˈplaɪwʊd/ *n.* contreplaqué *m.*

p.m. /piːˈem/ *adv.* de l'après-midi *or* du soir.

pneumatic /njuːˈmætɪk/ *a.* pneumatique.

pneumonia /njuːˈməʊnɪə/ *n.* pneumonie *f.*

PO *abbr. see* **Post Office.**

poach /pəʊtʃ/ *v.t./i.* (*steal*) braconner; (*culin.*) pocher. ~**er** *n.* braconnier *m.*

pocket /ˈpɒkɪt/ *n.* poche *f.* —*a.* de poche. —*v.t.* empocher. **be £5 in/out of** ~, avoir empoché/déboursé £5. ~**-book** *n.* (*notebook*) carnet *m.*; (*purse: Amer.*) porte-monnaie *m.invar.*; (*handbag: Amer.*) sac à main *m.* ~**-money** *n.* argent de poche *m.*

pock-marked /ˈpɒkmɑːkt/ *a.* (*face etc.*) grêlé.

pod /pɒd/ *n.* cosse *f.*

podgy /ˈpɒdʒɪ/ *a.* (**-ier, -iest**) dodu.

poem /ˈpəʊɪm/ *n.* poème *m.*

poet /ˈpəʊɪt/ *n.* poète *m.* ~**ic** /-ˈetɪk/ *a.* poétique.

poetry /ˈpəʊɪtrɪ/ *n.* poésie *f.*

poignant /ˈpɔɪnjənt/ *a.* poignant.

point /pɔɪnt/ *n.* point *m.*; (*tip*) pointe *f.*; (*decimal point*) virgule *f.*; (*meaning*) sens *m.*, intérêt *m.*; (*remark*) remarque *f.* ~**s**, (*rail.*) aiguillage *m.* —*v.t.* (*aim*) braquer; (*show*) indiquer. —*v.i.* indiquer du doigt (**at** *or* **to s.o.**, qn.). **good** ~**s**, qualités *f. pl.* **on the** ~ **of**, sur le point de. ~**-blank** *a.* & *adv.* à bout portant. ~ **in time**, moment *m.* ~ **of view**, point de vue *m.* ~ **out**, signaler. **to the** ~, pertinent. **what is the** ~**?**, à quoi bon?

pointed /ˈpɔɪntɪd/ *a.* pointu; (*remark*) lourd de sens.

pointer /ˈpɔɪntə(r)/ *n.* (*indicator*) index *m.*; (*dog*) chien d'arrêt *m.*; (*advice: fam.*) tuyau *m.*

pointless /ˈpɔɪntlɪs/ *a.* inutile.

poise /pɔɪz/ *n.* équilibre *m.*; (*carriage*) maintien *m.*; (*fig.*) assurance *f.* ~**d** *a.* en équilibre; (*confident*) assuré. ~**d for**, prêt à.

poison /ˈpɔɪzn/ *n.* poison *m.* —*v.t.* empoisonner. ~**ous** *a.* (*substance etc.*) toxique; (*plant*) vénéneux; (*snake*) venimeux.

poke /pəʊk/ *v.t./i.* (*push*) pousser; (*fire*) tisonner; (*thrust*) fourrer. —*n.* (petit) coup *m.* ~ **about**, fureter. ~ **fun at**, se moquer de. ~ **out**, (*head*) sortir.

poker[1] /ˈpəʊkə(r)/ *n.* tisonnier *m.*

poker[2] /ˈpəʊkə(r)/ *n.* (*cards*) poker *m.*

poky /ˈpəʊkɪ/ *a.* (**-ier, -iest**) (*small*) exigu; (*slow: Amer.*) lent.

Poland /ˈpəʊlənd/ *n.* Pologne *f.*

polar /ˈpəʊlə(r)/ *a.* polaire. ~ **bear**, ours blanc *m.*

polarize /ˈpəʊləraɪz/ *v.t.* polariser.

pole[1] /pəʊl/ *n.* (*fixed*) poteau *m.*; (*rod*) perche *f.*; (*for flag*) mât *m.*

pole[2] /pəʊl/ *n.* (*geog.*) pôle *m.*

Pole /pəʊl/ *n.* Polonais(e) *m.* (*f.*).

polemic /pəˈlemɪk/ *n.* polémique *f.*

police /pəˈliːs/ *n.* police *f.* —*v.t.* faire la police dans. ~ **state**, état policier *m.* ~ **station**, commissariat de police *m.*

police|man /pə'liːsmən/ *n.* (*pl.* **-men**) agent de police *m.* **~woman** (*pl.* **-women**) femme-agent *f.*
policy[1] /'pɒlɪsɪ/ *n.* politique *f.*
policy[2] /'pɒlɪsɪ/ *n.* (*insurance*) police (d'assurance) *f.*
polio(myelitis) /'pəʊlɪəʊ(maɪə'laɪtɪs)/ *n.* polio(myélite) *f.*
polish /'pɒlɪʃ/ *v.t.* polir; (*shoes, floor*) cirer. —*n.* (*for shoes*) cirage *m.*; (*for floor*) encaustique *f.*; (*for nails*) vernis *m.*; (*shine*) poli *m.*; (*fig.*) raffinement *m.* **~ off,** finir en vitesse. **~ up,** (*language*) perfectionner. **~ed** *a.* raffiné.
Polish /'pəʊlɪʃ/ *a.* polonais. —*n.* (*lang.*) polonais *m.*
polite /pə'laɪt/ *a.* poli. **~ly** *adv.* poliment. **~ness** *n.* politesse *f.*
political /pə'lɪtɪkl/ *a.* politique.
politician /pɒlɪ'tɪʃn/ *n.* homme politique *m.*, femme politique *f.*
politics /'pɒlətɪks/ *n.* politique *f.*
polka /'pɒlkə, *Amer.* 'pəʊlkə/ *n.* polka *f.* **~ dots,** pois *m. pl.*
poll /pəʊl/ *n.* scrutin *m.*; (*survey*) sondage *m.* —*v.t.* (*votes*) obtenir. **go to the ~s,** aller aux urnes. **~ing-booth** *n.* isoloir *m.*
pollen /'pɒlən/ *n.* pollen *m.*
pollut|e /pə'luːt/ *v.t.* polluer. **~ion** /-ʃn/ *n.* pollution *f.*
polo /'pəʊləʊ/ *n.* polo *m.* **~ neck,** col roulé *m.*
polygamy /pə'lɪgəmɪ/ *n.* polygamie *f.*
polytechnic /pɒlɪ'teknɪk/ *n.* institut universitaire de technologie *m.*
polythene /'pɒlɪθiːn/ *n.* polythène *m.*, polyéthylène *m.*
pomegranate /'pɒmɪgrænɪt/ *n.* (*fruit*) grenade *f.*
pomp /pɒmp/ *n.* pompe *f.*
pompon /'pɒmpɒn/ *n.* pompon *m.*
pomp|ous /'pɒmpəs/ *a.* pompeux. **~osity** /-'pɒsətɪ/ *n.* solennité *f.*
pond /pɒnd/ *n.* étang *m.*; (*artificial*) bassin *m.*; (*stagnant*) mare *f.*
ponder /'pɒndə(r)/ *v.t./i.* réfléchir (à), méditer (sur).
ponderous /'pɒndərəs/ *a.* pesant.
pong /pɒŋ/ *n.* (*stink*: *sl.*) puanteur *f.* —*v.i.* (*sl.*) puer.
pony /'pəʊnɪ/ *n.* poney *m.* **~-tail** *n.* queue de cheval *f.*
poodle /'puːdl/ *n.* caniche *m.*
pool[1] /puːl/ *n.* (*puddle*) flaque *f.*; (*pond*) étang *m.*; (*of blood*) mare *f.*; (*for swimming*) piscine *f.*
pool[2] /puːl/ *n.* (*fund*) fonds commun *m.*, (*of ideas*) réservoir *m.*; (*of typists*) pool *m.*; (*snooker*) billard américain *m.* **~s,** pari mutuel sur le football *m.* —*v.t.* mettre en commun.
poor /pʊə(r)/ *a.* (**-er, -est**) pauvre; (*not good*) médiocre, mauvais. **~ly** *adv.* mal; *a.* malade.
pop[1] /pɒp/ *n.* (*noise*) bruit sec *m.* —*v.t./i.* (*p.t.* **popped**) (*burst*) crever; (*put*) mettre. **~ in/out/off,** entrer/sortir/partir. **~ over,** faire un saut (**to see s.o.,** chez qn.). **~ up,** surgir.
pop[2] /pɒp/ *n.* (*mus.*) musique pop *f.* —*a.* pop *invar.*
popcorn /'pɒpkɔːn/ *n.* pop-corn *m.*
pope /pəʊp/ *n.* pape *m.*
poplar /'pɒplə(r)/ *n.* peuplier *m.*
poppy /'pɒpɪ/ *n.* pavot *m.*; (*wild*) coquelicot *m.*
popular /'pɒpjʊlə(r)/ *a.* populaire; (*in fashion*) en vogue. **be ~ with,** plaire à. **~ity** /-'lærətɪ/ *n.* popularité *f.* **~ize** *v.t.* populariser. **~ly** *adv.* communément.
populat|e /'pɒpjʊleɪt/ *v.t.* peupler. **~ion** /-'leɪʃn/ *n.* population *f.*
populous /'pɒpjʊləs/ *a.* populeux.
porcelain /'pɔːsəlɪn/ *n.* porcelaine *f.*
porch /pɔːtʃ/ *n.* porche *m.*
porcupine /'pɔːkjʊpaɪn/ *n.* (*rodent*) porc-épic *m.*
pore[1] /pɔː(r)/ *n.* pore *m.*

pore² /pɔː(r)/ *v.i.* **~ over,** étudier minutieusement.
pork /pɔːk/ *n.* (*food*) porc *m.*
pornograph|y /pɔːˈnɒgrəfɪ/ *n.* pornographie *f.* **~ic** /-əˈgræfɪk/ *a.* pornographique.
porous /ˈpɔːrəs/ *a.* poreux.
porpoise /ˈpɔːpəs/ *n.* marsouin *m.*
porridge /ˈpɒrɪdʒ/ *n.* porridge *m.*
port¹ /pɔːt/ *n.* (*harbour*) port *m.* **~ of call,** escale *f.*
port² /pɔːt/ *n.* (*left: naut.*) bâbord *m.*
port³ /pɔːt/ *n.* (*wine*) porto *m.*
portable /ˈpɔːtəbl/ *a.* portatif.
portal /ˈpɔːtl/ *n.* portail *m.*
porter¹ /ˈpɔːtə(r)/ *n.* (*carrier*) porteur *m.*
porter² /ˈpɔːtə(r)/ *n.* (*door-keeper*) portier *m.*
portfolio /pɔːtˈfəʊlɪəʊ/ *n.* (*pl.* **-os**) (*pol., comm.*) portefeuille *m.*
porthole /ˈpɔːthəʊl/ *n.* hublot *m.*
portico /ˈpɔːtɪkəʊ/ *n.* (*pl.* **-oes**) portique *m.*
portion /ˈpɔːʃn/ *n.* (*share, helping*) portion *f.*; (*part*) partie *f.*
portly /ˈpɔːtlɪ/ *a.* (**-ier, -iest**) corpulent (et digne).
portrait /ˈpɔːtrɪt/ *n.* portrait *m.*
portray /pɔːˈtreɪ/ *v.t.* représenter. **~al** *n.* portrait *m.*, peinture *f.*
Portug|al /ˈpɔːtjʊgl/ *n.* Portugal *m.* **~uese** /-ˈgiːz/ *a.* & *n. invar.* portugais(e) (*m.* (*f.*)).
pose /pəʊz/ *v.t./i.* poser. —*n.* pose *f.* **~ as,** (*expert etc.*) se poser en.
poser /ˈpəʊzə(r)/ *n.* colle *f.*
posh /pɒʃ/ *a.* (*sl.*) chic *invar.*
position /pəˈzɪʃn/ *n.* position *f.*; (*job, state*) situation *f.* —*v.t.* placer.
positive /ˈpɒzətɪv/ *a.* (*test, help, etc.*) positif; (*sure*) sûr, certain; (*real*) réel, vrai. **~ly** *adv.* positivement; (*absolutely*) complètement.
possess /pəˈzes/ *v.t.* posséder. **~ion** /-ʃn/ *n.* possession *f.* **take ~ion of,** prendre possession de. **~or** *n.* possesseur *m.*
possessive /pəˈzesɪv/ *a.* possessif.
possib|le /ˈpɒsəbl/ *a.* possible. **~ility** /-ˈbɪlətɪ/ *n.* possibilité *f.*
possibly /ˈpɒsəblɪ/ *adv.* peut-être. **if I ~ can,** si cela m'est possible. **I cannot ~ leave,** il m'est impossible de partir.
post¹ /pəʊst/ *n.* (*pole*) poteau *m.* —*v.t.* **~ (up),** (*a notice*) afficher.
post² /pəʊst/ *n.* (*station, job*) poste *m.* —*v.t.* poster; (*appoint*) affecter.
post³ /pəʊst/ *n.* (*mail service*) poste *f.*; (*letters*) courrier *m.* —*a.* postal. —*v.t.* (*put in box*) poster; (*send*) envoyer (par la poste). **keep ~ed,** tenir au courant. **~-box** *n.* boîte à *or* aux lettres *f.* **~-code** *n.* code postal *m.* **P~ Office,** postes *f. pl.*; (*in France*) Postes et Télécommunications *f. pl.* **~ office,** bureau de poste *m.*, poste *f.*
post- /pəʊst/ *pref.* post-.
postage /ˈpəʊstɪdʒ/ *n.* tarif postal *m.*, frais de port *m.pl.*
postal /ˈpəʊstl/ *a.* postal. **~ order,** mandat *m.* **~ worker,** employé(e) des postes *m.*(*f.*)
postcard /ˈpəʊstkɑːd/ *n.* carte postale *f.*
poster /ˈpəʊstə(r)/ *n.* affiche *f.*
posterior /pɒˈstɪərɪə(r)/ *n.* postérieur *m.*
posterity /pɒˈsterətɪ/ *n.* postérité *f.*
postgraduate /pəʊstˈgrædʒʊət/ *n.* étudiant(e) de troisième cycle *m.*(*f.*).
posthumous /ˈpɒstjʊməs/ *a.* posthume. **~ly** *adv.* à titre posthume.
postman /ˈpəʊstmən/ *n.* (*pl.* **-men**) facteur *m.*
postmark /ˈpəʊstmɑːk/ *n.* cachet de la poste *m.*
postmaster /ˈpəʊstmɑːstə(r)/ *n.* receveur des postes *m.*
post-mortem /pəʊstˈmɔːtəm/ *n.* autopsie *f.*
postpone /pəˈspəʊn/ *v.t.* remettre. **~ment** *n.* ajournement *m.*

postscript /ˈpəʊsskrɪpt/ *n.* (*to letter*) post-scriptum *m. invar.*
postulate /ˈpɒstjʊleɪt/ *v.t.* postuler.
posture /ˈpɒstʃə(r)/ *n.* posture *f.* —*v.i.* (*affectedly*) poser.
post-war /ˈpəʊstwɔː(r)/ *a.* d'après-guerre.
pot /pɒt/ *n.* pot *m.*; (*for cooking*) marmite *f.*; (*drug*: *sl.*) marie-jeanne *f.* **go to ~,** (*sl.*) aller à la ruine. **~-belly** *n.* gros ventre *m.* **take ~ luck,** tenter sa chance. **take a ~-shot at,** faire un carton sur.
potato /pəˈteɪtəʊ/ *n.* (*pl.* **-oes**) pomme de terre *f.*
poten|t /ˈpəʊtnt/ *a.* puissant; (*drink*) fort. **~cy** *n.* puissance *f.*
potential /pəˈtenʃl/ *a.* & *n.* potentiel (*m.*). **~ly** *adv.* potentiellement.
pot-hol|e /ˈpɒthəʊl/ *n.* (*in rock*) caverne *f.*; (*in road*) nid de poule *m.* **~ing** *n.* spéléologie *f.*
potion /ˈpəʊʃn/ *n.* potion *f.*
potted /ˈpɒtɪd/ *a.* (*plant etc.*) en pot; (*preserved*) en conserve; (*abridged*) condensé.
potter[1] /ˈpɒtə(r)/ *n.* potier *m.* **~y** *n.* (*art*) poterie *f.*; (*objects*) poteries *f.pl.*
potter[2] /ˈpɒtə(r)/ *v.i.* bricoler.
potty /ˈpɒtɪ/ *a.* (**-ier, -iest**) (*crazy*: *sl.*) toqué.
pouch /paʊtʃ/ *n.* poche *f.*; (*for tobacco*) blague *f.*
pouffe /puːf/ *n.* pouf *m.*
poultice /ˈpəʊltɪs/ *n.* cataplasme *m.*
poult|ry /ˈpəʊltrɪ/ *n.* volaille *f.* **~erer** *n.* marchand de volailles *m.*
pounce /paʊns/ *v.i.* bondir (**on,** sur). —*n.* bond *m.*
pound[1] /paʊnd/ *n.* (*weight*) livre *f.* (*= 454 g.*); (*money*) livre *f.*
pound[2] /paʊnd/ *n.* (*for dogs, cars*) fourrière *f.*
pound[3] /paʊnd/ *v.t.* (*crush*) piler; (*bombard*) pilonner. —*v.i.* frapper fort; (*of heart*) battre fort; (*walk*) marcher à pas lourds.
pour /pɔː(r)/ *v.t.* verser. —*v.i.* couler, ruisseler (**from,** de); (*rain*) pleuvoir à torrents. **~ in/out,** (*people*) arriver/sortir en masse. **~ off** *or* **out,** vider. **~ing rain,** pluie torrentielle *f.*
pout /paʊt/ *v.t./i.* **~ (one's lips),** faire la moue. —*n.* moue *f.*
poverty /ˈpɒvətɪ/ *n.* misère *f.*, pauvreté *f.*
powder /ˈpaʊdə(r)/ *n.* poudre *f.* —*v.t.* poudrer. **~ed** *a.* en poudre. **~y** *a.* poudreux.
power /ˈpaʊə(r)/ *n.* puissance *f.*; (*ability, authority*) pouvoir *m.*; (*energy*) énergie *f.*; (*electr.*) courant *m.* **~ cut,** coupure de courant *f.* **~ed by,** fonctionnant à; (*jet etc.*) propulsé par. **~less** *a.* impuissant. **~-station** *n.* centrale électrique *f.*
powerful /ˈpaʊəfl/ *a.* puissant. **~ly** *adv.* puissamment.
practicable /ˈpræktɪkəbl/ *a.* praticable.
practical /ˈpræktɪkl/ *a.* pratique. **~ joke,** farce *f.*
practically /ˈpræktɪklɪ/ *adv.* pratiquement.
practice /ˈpræktɪs/ *n.* pratique *f.*; (*of profession*) exercice *m.*; (*sport*) entraînement *m.*; (*clients*) clientèle *f.* **be in ~,** (*doctor, lawyer*) exercer. **in ~,** (*in fact*) en pratique; (*well-trained*) en forme. **out of ~,** rouillé. **put into ~,** mettre en pratique.
practis|e /ˈpræktɪs/ *v.t./i.* (*musician, typist, etc.*) s'exercer (à); (*sport*) s'entraîner (à); (*put into practice*) pratiquer; (*profession*) exercer. **~ed** *a.* expérimenté. **~ing** *a.* (*Catholic etc.*) pratiquant.
practitioner /prækˈtɪʃənə(r)/ *n.* praticien(ne) *m.* (*f.*).

pragmatic /præg'mætɪk/ *a.* pragmatique.
prairie /'preərɪ/ *n.* (*in North America*) prairie *f.*
praise /preɪz/ *v.t.* louer. —*n.* éloge(s) *m.* (*pl.*), louange(s) *f.*(*pl.*).
praiseworthy /'preɪzwɜ:ðɪ/ *a.* digne d'éloges.
pram /præm/ *n.* voiture d'enfant *f.*, landau *m.*
prance /prɑ:ns/ *v.i.* caracoler.
prank /præŋk/ *n.* farce *f.*
prattle /'prætl/ *v.i.* jaser.
prawn /prɔ:n/ *n.* crevette rose *f.*
pray /preɪ/ *v.i.* prier.
prayer /preə(r)/ *n.* prière *f.*
pre- /pri:/ *pref.* pré-.
preach /pri:tʃ/ *v.t./i.* prêcher. **~ at** *or* **to,** prêcher. **~er** *n.* prédicateur *m.*
preamble /pri:'æmbl/ *n.* préambule *m.*
pre-arrange /pri:ə'reɪndʒ/ *v.t.* fixer à l'avance.
precarious /prɪ'keərɪəs/ *a.* précaire.
precaution /prɪ'kɔ:ʃn/ *n.* précaution *f.* **~ary** *a.* de précaution.
preced|e /prɪ'si:d/ *v.t.* précéder. **~ing** *a.* précédent.
precedence /'presɪdəns/ *n.* priorité *f.*; (*in rank*) préséance *f.*
precedent /'presɪdənt/ *n.* précédent *m.*
precept /'pri:sept/ *n.* précepte *m.*
precinct /'pri:sɪŋkt/ *n.* enceinte *f.*; (*pedestrian area*) zone *f.*; (*district: Amer.*) circonscription *f.*
precious /'preʃəs/ *a.* précieux. —*adv.* (*very: fam.*) très.
precipice /'presɪpɪs/ *n.* (*geog.*) à-pic *m. invar.*; (*fig.*) précipice *m.*
precipitat|e /prɪ'sɪpɪteɪt/ *v.t.* (*person, event, chemical*) précipiter. **~ion** /-'teɪʃn/ *n.* précipitation *f.*
précis /'preɪsi:/ *n. invar.* précis *m.*
precis|e /prɪ'saɪs/ *a.* précis; (*careful*) méticuleux. **~ely** *adv.* précisément. **~ion** /-'sɪʒn/ *n.* précision *f.*
preclude /prɪ'klu:d/ *v.t.* (*prevent*) empêcher; (*rule out*) exclure.
precocious /prɪ'kəʊʃəs/ *a.* précoce.
preconc|eived /pri:kən'si:vd/ *a.* préconçu. **~eption** *n.* préconception *f.*
pre-condition /pri:kən'dɪʃn/ *n.* condition requise *f.*
predator /'predətə(r)/ *n.* prédateur *m.* **~y** *a.* rapace.
predecessor /'pri:dɪsesə(r)/ *n.* prédécesseur *m.*
predicament /prɪ'dɪkəmənt/ *n.* mauvaise situation *or* passe *f.*
predict /prɪ'dɪkt/ *v.t.* prédire. **~able** *a.* prévisible. **~ion** /-kʃn/ *n.* prédiction *f.*
predispose /pri:dɪ'spəʊz/ *v.t.* prédisposer (**to do,** à faire).
predominant /prɪ'dɒmɪnənt/ *a.* prédominant. **~ly** *adv.* pour la plupart.
predominate /prɪ'dɒmɪneɪt/ *v.i.* prédominer.
pre-eminent /pri:'emɪnənt/ *a.* prééminent.
pre-empt /pri:'empt/ *v.t.* acquérir d'avance.
preen /pri:n/ *v.t.* (*bird*) lisser. **~ o.s.,** (*person*) se bichonner.
prefab /'pri:fæb/ *n.* (*fam.*) bâtiment préfabriqué *m.* **~ricated** /-'fæbrɪkeɪtɪd/ *a.* préfabriqué.
preface /'prefɪs/ *n.* préface *f.*
prefect /'pri:fekt/ *n.* (*pupil*) élève chargé(e) de la discipline *m./f.*; (*official*) préfet *m.*
prefer /prɪ'fɜ:(r)/ *v.t.* (*p.t.* **preferred**) préférer (**to do,** faire). **~able** /'prefrəbl/ *a.* préférable.
preferen|ce /'prefrəns/ *n.* préférence *f.* **~tial** /-ə'renʃl/ *a.* préférentiel.
prefix /'pri:fɪks/ *n.* préfixe *m.*
pregnan|t /'pregnənt/ *a.* (*woman*)

enceinte; (*animal*) pleine. **~cy** *n.* (*of woman*) grossesse *f.*

prehistoric /priːhɪˈstɒrɪk/ *a.* préhistorique.

prejudge /priːˈdʒʌdʒ/ *v.t.* préjuger de; (*person*) juger d'avance.

prejudice /ˈpredʒʊdɪs/ *n.* préjugé(s) *m.* (*pl.*); (*harm*) préjudice *m.* —*v.t.* (*claim*) porter préjudice à; (*person*) prévenir. **~d** *a.* partial; (*person*) qui a des préjugés.

preliminar|y /prɪˈlɪmɪnərɪ/ *a.* préliminaire. **~ies** *n. pl.* préliminaires *m. pl.*

prelude /ˈpreljuːd/ *n.* prélude *m.*

pre-marital /priːˈmærɪtl/ *a.* avant le mariage.

premature /ˈpremətjʊə(r)/ *a.* prématuré.

premeditated /priːˈmedɪteɪtɪd/ *a.* prémédité.

premier /ˈpremɪə(r)/ *a.* premier. —*n.* premier ministre *m.*

première /ˈpremɪeə(r)/ *n.* première *f.*

premises /ˈpremɪsɪz/ *n. pl.* locaux *m. pl.* **on the ~,** sur les lieux.

premiss /ˈpremɪs/ *n.* prémisse *f.*

premium /ˈpriːmɪəm/ *n.* prime *f.* **be at a ~,** faire prime.

premonition /priːməˈnɪʃn/ *n.* prémonition *f.*, pressentiment *m.*

preoccup|ation /priːɒkjʊˈpeɪʃn/ *n.* préoccupation *f.* **~ied** /-ˈɒkjʊpaɪd/ *a.* préoccupé.

prep /prep/ *n.* (*work*) devoirs *m.pl.* **~ school** = **preparatory school.**

preparation /prepəˈreɪʃn/ *n.* préparation *f.* **~s,** préparatifs *m. pl.*

preparatory /prɪˈpærətrɪ/ *a.* préparatoire. **~ school,** école primaire privée *f.*; (*Amer.*) école secondaire privée *f.*

prepare /prɪˈpeə(r)/ *v.t./i.* (se) préparer (**for,** à). **be ~d for,** (*expect*) s'attendre à. **~d to,** prêt à.

prepay /priːˈpeɪ/ *v.t.* (*p.t.* **-paid**) payer d'avance.

preponderance /prɪˈpɒndərəns/ *n.* prédominance *f.*

preposition /prepəˈzɪʃn/ *n.* préposition *f.*

preposterous /prɪˈpɒstərəs/ *a.* absurde, ridicule.

prerequisite /priːˈrekwɪzɪt/ *n.* condition préalable *f.*

prerogative /prɪˈrɒgətɪv/ *n.* prérogative *f.*

Presbyterian /prezbɪˈtɪərɪən/ *a.* & *n.* presbytérien(ne) (*m.* (*f.*)).

prescri|be /prɪˈskraɪb/ *v.t.* prescrire. **~ption** /-ɪpʃn/ *n.* prescription *f.*; (*med.*) ordonnance *f.*

presence /ˈprezns/ *n.* présence *f.* **~ of mind,** présence d'esprit *f.*

present¹ /ˈpreznt/ *a.* présent. —*n.* présent *m.* **at ~,** à présent. **for the ~,** pour le moment.

present² /ˈpreznt/ *n.* (*gift*) cadeau *m.*

present³ /prɪˈzent/ *v.t.* présenter; (*film, concert, etc.*) donner. **~ s.o. with,** offrir à qn. **~able** *a.* présentable. **~ation** /preznˈteɪʃn/ *n.* présentation *f.*

presently /ˈprezntlɪ/ *adv.* bientôt; (*now: Amer.*) en ce moment.

preservative /prɪˈzɜːvətɪv/ *n.* (*culin.*) agent de conservation *m.*

preserv|e /prɪˈzɜːv/ *v.t.* préserver; (*maintain & culin.*) conserver. —*n.* réserve *f.*; (*fig.*) domaine *m.*; (*jam*) confiture *f.* **~ation** /prezəˈveɪʃn/ *n.* conservation *f.*

preside /prɪˈzaɪd/ *v.i.* présider. **~ over,** présider.

presiden|t /ˈprezɪdənt/ *n.* président(e) *m.* (*f.*). **~cy** *n.* présidence *f.* **~tial** /-ˈdenʃl/ *a.* présidentiel.

press /pres/ *v.t./i.* (*button etc.*) appuyer (sur); (*squeeze, urge*) presser; (*iron*) repasser; (*pursue*) poursuivre. —*n.* (*newspapers, machine*) presse *f.*; (*for wine*) pressoir *m.* **be ~ed for,** (*time etc.*) manquer de. **~ conference/cutting,** conférence/coupure de

presse *f.* ~ **on,** continuer (**with sth.,** qch.). ~**-stud** *n.* bouton-pression *m.* ~**-up** *n.* traction *f.*
pressing /'presɪŋ/ *a.* pressant.
pressure /'preʃə(r)/ *n.* pression *f.* —*v.t.* faire pression sur. ~**-cooker** *n.* cocotte-minute *f.* ~ **group,** groupe de pression *m.*
pressurize /'preʃəraɪz/ *v.t.* (*cabin etc.*) pressuriser; (*person*) faire pression sur.
prestige /pre'stiːʒ/ *n.* prestige *m.*
prestigious /pre'stɪdʒəs/ *a.* prestigieux.
presumably /prɪ'zjuːməblɪ/ *adv.* vraisemblablement.
presum|e /prɪ'zjuːm/ *v.t.* (*suppose*) présumer. ~**e to,** (*venture*) se permettre de. ~**ption** /-'zʌmpʃn/ *n.* présomption *f.*
presumptuous /prɪ'zʌmptʃʊəs/ *a.* présomptueux.
pretence /prɪ'tens/ *n.* feinte *f.*, simulation *f.*; (*claim*) prétention *f.*; (*pretext*) prétexte *m.*
pretend /prɪ'tend/ *v.t./i.* faire semblant (**to do,** de faire). ~ **to,** (*lay claim to*) prétendre à.
pretentious /prɪ'tenʃəs/ *a.* prétentieux.
pretext /'priːtekst/ *n.* prétexte *m.*
pretty /'prɪtɪ/ *a.* (**-ier, -iest**) joli. —*adv.* assez. ~ **much,** presque.
prevail /prɪ'veɪl/ *v.i.* prédominer; (*win*) prévaloir. ~ **on,** persuader.
prevalen|t /'prevələnt/ *a.* répandu. ~**ce** *n.* fréquence *f.*
prevent /prɪ'vent/ *v.t.* empêcher (**from doing,** de faire). ~**able** *a.* évitable. ~**ion** /-enʃn/ *n.* prévention *f.* ~**ive** *a.* préventif.
preview /'priːvjuː/ *n.* avant-première *f.*; (*fig.*) aperçu *m.*
previous /'priːvɪəs/ *a.* précédent, antérieur. ~ **to,** avant. ~**ly** *adv.* précédemment, auparavant.
pre-war /'priːwɔː(r)/ *a.* d'avant-guerre.
prey /preɪ/ *n.* proie *f.* —*v.i.* ~ **on,** faire sa proie de; (*worry*) préoccuper. **bird of** ~, rapace *m.*
price /praɪs/ *n.* prix *m.* —*v.t.* fixer le prix de. ~**less** *a.* inestimable; (*amusing*: *sl.*) impayable.
pricey /'praɪsɪ/ *a.* (*fam.*) coûteux.
prick /prɪk/ *v.t.* (*with pin etc.*) piquer. —*n.* piqûre *f.* ~ **up one's ears,** dresser l'oreille.
prickl|e /'prɪkl/ *n.* piquant *m.*; (*sensation*) picotement *m.* ~**y** *a.* piquant; (*person*) irritable.
pride /praɪd/ *n.* orgueil *m.*; (*satisfaction*) fierté *f.* —*v. pr.* ~ **o.s. on,** s'enorgueillir de. ~ **of place,** place d'honneur *f.*
priest /priːst/ *n.* prêtre *m.* ~**hood** *n.* sacerdoce *m.* ~**ly** *a.* sacerdotal.
prig /prɪg/ *n.* petit saint *m.*, pharisien(ne) *m.*(*f.*). ~**gish** *a.* hypocrite.
prim /prɪm/ *a.* (**primmer, primmest**) guindé, méticuleux.
primar|y /'praɪmərɪ/ *a.* (*school, elections, etc.*) primaire; (*chief, basic*) premier, fondamental. ~**ily** /*Amer.* -'merɪlɪ/ *adv.* essentiellement.
prime[1] /praɪm/ *a.* principal, premier; (*first-rate*) excellent. **P~ Minister,** Premier Ministre *m.* **the ~ of life,** la force de l'âge.
prime[2] /praɪm/ *v.t.* (*pump, gun*) amorcer; (*surface*) apprêter. ~**r**[1] /-ə(r)/ *n.* (*paint etc.*) apprêt *m.*
primer[2] /'praɪmə(r)/ *n.* (*school-book*) premier livre *m.*
primeval /praɪ'miːvl/ *a.* primitif.
primitive /'prɪmɪtɪv/ *a.* primitif.
primrose /'prɪmrəʊz/ *n.* primevère (jaune) *f.*
prince /prɪns/ *n.* prince *m.* ~**ly** *a.* princier.
princess /prɪn'ses/ *n.* princesse *f.*
principal /'prɪnsəpl/ *a.* principal. —*n.* (*of school etc.*) direc|teur, -trice *m., f.* ~**ly** *adv.* principalement.

principle /'prɪnsəpl/ *n.* principe *m.* **in/on ~,** en/par principe.

print /prɪnt/ *v.t.* imprimer; (*write in capitals*) écrire en majuscules. —*n.* (*of foot etc.*) empreinte *f.*; (*letters*) caractères *m. pl.*; (*photograph*) épreuve *f.*; (*engraving*) gravure *f.* **in ~,** disponible. **out of ~,** épuisé. **~-out** *n.* listage *m.* **~ed matter,** imprimés *m. pl.*

print|er /'prɪntə(r)/ *n.* (*person*) imprimeur *m.*; (*computer device*) imprimante *f.* **~ing** *n.* impression *f.*

prior[1] /'praɪə(r)/ *a.* précédent. **~ to,** *prep.* avant (de).

prior[2] /'praɪə(r)/ *n.* (*relig.*) prieur *m.* **~y** *n.* prieuré *m.*

priority /praɪ'ɒrətɪ/ *n.* priorité *f.*

prise /praɪz/ *v.t.* forcer. **~ open,** ouvrir en forçant.

prism /'prɪzəm/ *n.* prisme *m.*

prison /'prɪzn/ *n.* prison *f.* **~er** *n.* prisonn|ier, -ière *m., f.* **~ officer,** gardien(ne) de prison *m.* (*f.*).

pristine /'prɪstiːn/ *a.* primitif; (*condition*) parfait.

privacy /'praɪvəsɪ/ *n.* intimité *f.*, solitude *f.*

private /'praɪvɪt/ *a.* privé; (*confidential*) personnel; (*lessons, house, etc.*) particulier; (*ceremony*) intime. —*n.* (*soldier*) simple soldat *m.* **in ~,** en privé; (*of ceremony*) dans l'intimité. **~ly** *adv.* en privé; dans l'intimité; (*inwardly*) intérieurement.

privet /'prɪvɪt/ *n.* (*bot.*) troène *m.*

privilege /'prɪvəlɪdʒ/ *n.* privilège *m.* **~d** *a.* privilégié. **be ~d to,** avoir le privilège de.

privy /'prɪvɪ/ *a.* **~ to,** au fait de.

prize /praɪz/ *n.* prix *m.* —*a.* (*entry etc.*) primé; (*fool etc.*) parfait. —*v.t.* (*value*) priser. **~-fighter** *n.* boxeur professionnel *m.* **~-winner** *n.* lauréat(e) *m.*(*f.*); (*in lottery etc.*) gagnant(e) *m.* (*f.*).

pro /prəʊ/ *n.* **the ~s and cons,** le pour et le contre.

pro- /prəʊ/ *pref.* pro-.

probab|le /'prɒbəbl/ *a.* probable. **~ility** /-'bɪlətɪ/ *n.* probabilité *f.* **~ly** *adv.* probablement.

probation /prə'beɪʃn/ *n.* (*testing*) essai *m.*; (*jurid.*) liberté surveillée *f.* **~ary** *a.* d'essai.

probe /prəʊb/ *n.* (*device*) sonde *f.*; (*fig.*) enquête *f.* —*v.t.* sonder. —*v.i.* **~ into,** sonder.

problem /'prɒbləm/ *n.* problème *m.* —*a.* difficile. **~atic** /-'mætɪk/ *a.* problématique.

procedure /prə'siːdʒə(r)/ *n.* procédure *f.*

proceed /prə'siːd/ *v.i.* (*go*) aller, avancer; (*pass*) passer (**to,** à); (*act*) procéder. **~ (with),** (*continue*) continuer. **~ to do,** se mettre à faire. **~ing** *n.* procédé *m.*

proceedings /prə'siːdɪŋz/ *n. pl.* (*discussions*) débats *m. pl.*; (*meeting*) réunion *f.*; (*report*) actes *m. pl.*; (*jurid.*) poursuites *f. pl.*

proceeds /'prəʊsiːdz/ *n. pl.* (*profits*) produit *m.*, bénéfices *m. pl.*

process /'prəʊses/ *n.* processus *m.*; (*method*) procédé *m.* —*v.t.* (*material, data*) traiter. **in ~,** en cours. **in the ~ of doing,** en train de faire.

procession /prə'seʃn/ *n.* défilé *m.*

procl|aim /prə'kleɪm/ *v.t.* proclamer. **~amation** /prɒklə'meɪʃn/ *n.* proclamation *f.*

procrastinate /prə'kræstɪneɪt/ *v.i.* différer, tergiverser.

procreation /prəʊkrɪ'eɪʃn/ *n.* procréation *f.*

procure /prə'kjʊə(r)/ *v.t.* obtenir.

prod /prɒd/ *v.t./i.* (*p.t.* **prodded**) pousser. —*n.* poussée *f.*, coup *m.*

prodigal /'prɒdɪgl/ *a.* prodigue.

prodigious /prə'dɪdʒəs/ *a.* prodigieux.

prodigy /'prɒdɪdʒɪ/ *n.* prodige *m.*

produc|e[1] /prə'djuːs/ *v.t./i.* produire; (*bring out*) sortir; (*show*) présenter; (*cause*) provoquer;

(*theatre, TV*) mettre en scène; (*radio*) réaliser. **~er** *n.* metteur en scène *m.*; réalisateur *m.* **~tion** /-'dʌkʃn/ *n.* production *f.*; mise en scène *f.*; réalisation *f.*

produce[2] /'prɒdjuːs/ *n.* (*food etc.*) produits *m. pl.*

product /'prɒdʌkt/ *n.* produit *m.*

productiv|e /prə'dʌktɪv/ *a.* productif. **~ity** /prɒdʌk'tɪvətɪ/ *n.* productivité *f.*

profan|e /prə'feɪn/ *a.* sacrilège; (*secular*) profane. **~ity** /-'fænətɪ/ *n.* (*oath*) juron *m.*

profess /prə'fes/ *v.t.* professer. **~ to do,** prétendre faire.

profession /prə'feʃn/ *n.* profession *f.* **~al** *a.* professionnel; (*of high quality*) de professionnel; (*person*) qui exerce une profession libérale; *n.* professionnel(le) *m.* (*f.*).

professor /prə'fesə(r)/ *n.* professeur (titulaire d'une chaire) *m.*

proficien|t /prə'fɪʃnt/ *a.* compétent. **~cy** *n.* compétence *f.*

profile /'prəʊfaɪl/ *n.* profil *m.*

profit /'prɒfɪt/ *n.* profit *m.*, bénéfice *m.* —*v.i.* (*p.t.* **profited**). **~ by,** tirer profit de. **~able** *a.* rentable.

profound /prə'faʊnd/ *a.* profond. **~ly** *adv.* profondément.

profus|e /prə'fjuːs/ *a.* abondant. **~e in,** (*lavish in*) prodigue de. **~ely** *adv.* en abondance. **~ion** /-ʒn/ *n.* profusion *f.*

progeny /'prɒdʒənɪ/ *n.* progéniture *f.*

program /'prəʊgræm/ *n.* (*Amer.*) = **programme. (computer) ~,** programme *m.* —*v.t.* (*p.t.* **programmed**) programmer. **~mer** *n.* programmeu|r, -se *m.*, *f.* **~ming** *n.* (*on computer*) programmation *f.*

programme /'prəʊgræm/ *n.* programme *m.*; (*broadcast*) émission *f.*

progress[1] /'prəʊgres/ *n.* progrès *m.* (*pl.*). **in ~,** en cours.

progress[2] /prə'gres/ *v.i.* (*advance, improve*) progresser. **~ion** /-ʃn/ *n.* progression *f.*

progressive /prə'gresɪv/ *a.* progressif; (*reforming*) progressiste. **~ly** *adv.* progressivement.

prohibit /prə'hɪbɪt/ *v.t.* interdire (**s.o. from doing,** à qn. de faire).

prohibitive /prə'hɪbətɪv/ *a.* (*price etc.*) prohibitif.

project[1] /prə'dʒekt/ *v.t.* projeter. —*v.i.* (*jut out*) être en saillie. **~ion** /-kʃn/ *n.* projection *f.*; saillie *f.*

project[2] /'prɒdʒekt/ *n.* (*plan*) projet *m.*; (*undertaking*) entreprise *f.*

projectile /prə'dʒektaɪl/ *n.* projectile *m.*

projector /prə'dʒektə(r)/ *n.* (*cinema etc.*) projecteur *m.*

proletari|at /prəʊlɪ'teərɪət/ *n.* prolétariat *m.* **~an** *a.* prolétarien; *n.* prolétaire *m.*/*f.*

proliferat|e /prə'lɪfəreɪt/ *v.i.* proliférer. **~ion** /-'reɪʃn/ *n.* prolifération *f.*

prolific /prə'lɪfɪk/ *a.* prolifique.

prologue /'prəʊlɒg/ *n.* prologue *m.*

prolong /prə'lɒŋ/ *v.t.* prolonger.

promenade /prɒmə'nɑːd/ *n.* promenade *f.* —*v.t.*/*i.* (se) promener.

prominen|t /'prɒmɪnənt/ *a.* (*projecting*) proéminent; (*conspicuous*) bien en vue; (*fig.*) important. **~ce** *n.* proéminence *f.*; importance *f.* **~tly** *adv.* bien en vue.

promiscu|ous /prə'mɪskjʊəs/ *a.* de mœurs faciles. **~ity** /prɒmɪ'skjuːətɪ/ *n.* liberté de mœurs *f.*

promis|e /'prɒmɪs/ *n.* promesse *f.* —*v.t.*/*i.* promettre. **~ing** *a.* prometteur; (*person*) qui promet.

promot|e /prə'məʊt/ *v.t.* promouvoir. **~ion** /-'məʊʃn/ *n.* (*of person, sales, etc.*) promotion *f.*

prompt /prɒmpt/ *a.* rapide; (*punctual*) à l'heure, ponctuel. —*adv.* (*on the dot*) pile. —*v.t.* inciter; (*cause*) provoquer; (*theatre*) souffler (son rôle) à. **~er**

n. souffleu|r, -se *m.*, *f.* **~ly** *adv.* rapidement; ponctuellement. **~ness** *n.* rapidité *f.*

prone /prəʊn/ *a.* couché sur le ventre. **~ to,** prédisposé à.

prong /prɒŋ/ *n.* (*of fork*) dent *f.*

pronoun /'prəʊnaʊn/ *n.* pronom *m.*

pron|ounce /prə'naʊns/ *v.t.* prononcer. **~ouncement** *n.* déclaration *f.* **~unciation** /-ʌnsɪ'eɪʃn/ *n.* prononciation *f.*

pronounced /prə'naʊnst/ *a.* (*noticeable*) prononcé.

proof /pruːf/ *n.* (*evidence*) preuve *f.*; (*test, trial copy*) épreuve *f.*; (*of liquor*) teneur en alcool *f.* —*a.* **~ against,** à l'épreuve de.

prop[1] /prɒp/ *n.* support *m.* —*v.t.* (*p.t.* **propped**). **~ (up),** (*support*) étayer; (*lean*) appuyer.

prop[2] /prɒp/ *n.* (*theatre, fam.*) accessoire *m.*

propaganda /prɒpə'gændə/ *n.* propagande *f.*

propagat|e /'prɒpəgeɪt/ *v.t./i.* (se) propager. **~ion** /-'geɪʃn/ *n.* propagation *f.*

propel /prə'pel/ *v.t.* (*p.t.* **propelled**) propulser.

propeller /prə'pelə(r)/ *n.* hélice *f.*

proper /'prɒpə(r)/ *a.* correct, bon; (*seemly*) convenable; (*real*) vrai; (*thorough: fam.*) parfait. **~ noun,** nom propre *m.* **~ly** *adv.* correctement, comme il faut; (*rightly*) avec raison.

property /'prɒpətɪ/ *n.* propriété *f.*; (*things owned*) biens *m. pl.*, propriété *f.* —*a.* immobilier, foncier.

prophecy /'prɒfəsɪ/ *n.* prophétie *f.*

prophesy /'prɒfɪsaɪ/ *v.t./i.* prophétiser. **~ that,** prédire que.

prophet /'prɒfɪt/ *n.* prophète *m.* **~ic** /prə'fetɪk/ *a.* prophétique.

proportion /prə'pɔːʃn/ *n.* (*ratio, dimension*) proportion *f.*; (*amount*) partie *f.* **~al, ~ate** *adjs.* proportionnel.

proposal /prə'pəʊzl/ *n.* proposition *f.*; (*of marriage*) demande en mariage *f.*

propos|e /prə'pəʊz/ *v.t.* proposer. —*v.i.* **~e to,** faire une demande en mariage à. **~e to do,** se proposer de faire. **~ition** /prɒpə'zɪʃn/ *n.* proposition *f.*; (*matter: fam.*) affaire *f.*; *v.t.* (*fam.*) faire des propositions malhonnêtes à.

propound /prə'paʊnd/ *v.t.* (*theory etc.*) proposer.

proprietor /prə'praɪətə(r)/ *n.* propriétaire *m./f.*

propriety /prə'praɪətɪ/ *n.* (*correct behaviour*) bienséance *f.*

propulsion /prə'pʌlʃn/ *n.* propulsion *f.*

prosaic /prə'zeɪɪk/ *a.* prosaïque.

proscribe /prə'skraɪb/ *v.t.* proscrire.

prose /prəʊz/ *n.* prose *f.*; (*translation*) thème *m.*

prosecut|e /'prɒsɪkjuːt/ *v.t.* poursuivre. **~ion** /-'kjuːʃn/ *n.* poursuites *f. pl.* **~or** *n.* procureur *m.*

prospect[1] /'prɒspekt/ *n.* perspective *f.*; (*chance*) espoir *m.*

prospect[2] /prə'spekt/ *v.t./i.* prospecter. **~or** *n.* prospecteur *m.*

prospective /prə'spektɪv/ *a.* (*future*) futur; (*possible*) éventuel.

prospectus /prə'spektəs/ *n.* prospectus *m.*; (*univ.*) guide *m.*

prosper /'prɒspə(r)/ *v.i.* prospérer.

prosper|ous /'prɒspərəs/ *a.* prospère. **~ity** /-'sperətɪ/ *n.* prospérité *f.*

prostitut|e /'prɒstɪtjuːt/ *n.* prostituée *f.* **~ion** /-'tjuːʃn/ *n.* prostitution *f.*

prostrate /'prɒstreɪt/ *a.* (*prone*) à plat ventre; (*submissive*) prosterné; (*exhausted*) prostré.

protagonist /prə'tægənɪst/ *n.* protagoniste *m.*

protect /prə'tekt/ *v.t.* protéger. **~ion** /-kʃn/ *n.* protection *f.* **~or** *n.* protec|teur, -trice *m.*, *f.*

protective /prəˈtektɪv/ *a.* protecteur; (*clothes*) de protection.
protégé /ˈprɒtɪʒeɪ/ *n.* protégé *m.* **~e** *n.* protégée *f.*
protein /ˈprəʊtiːn/ *n.* protéine *f.*
protest¹ /ˈprəʊtest/ *n.* protestation *f.* **under ~**, en protestant.
protest² /prəˈtest/ *v.t./i.* protester. **~er** *n.* (*pol.*) contestataire *m./f.*
Protestant /ˈprɒtɪstənt/ *a.* & *n.* protestant(e) (*m.* (*f.*)).
protocol /ˈprəʊtəkɒl/ *n.* protocole *m.*
prototype /ˈprəʊtətaɪp/ *n.* prototype *m.*
protract /prəˈtrækt/ *v.t.* prolonger, faire traîner.
protractor /prəˈtræktə(r)/ *n.* (*for measuring*) rapporteur *m.*
protrude /prəˈtruːd/ *v.i.* dépasser.
proud /praʊd/ *a.* (**-er**, **-est**) fier, orgueilleux. **~ly** *adv.* fièrement.
prove /pruːv/ *v.t.* prouver. —*v.i.* **~ (to be) easy**/*etc.*, se révéler facile/*etc.* **~ o.s.**, faire ses preuves. **~n** *a.* prouvé.
proverb /ˈprɒvɜːb/ *n.* proverbe *m.* **~ial** /prəˈvɜːbɪəl/ *a.* proverbial.
provide /prəˈvaɪd/ *v.t.* fournir (**s.o. with sth.**, qch. à qn.). —*v.i.* **~ for**, (*allow for*) prévoir; (*guard against*) parer à; (*person*) pourvoir aux besoins de.
provided /prəˈvaɪdɪd/ *conj.* **~ that**, à condition que.
providence /ˈprɒvɪdəns/ *n.* providence *f.*
providing /prəˈvaɪdɪŋ/ *conj.* = **provided.**
provinc|e /ˈprɒvɪns/ *n.* province *f.*; (*fig.*) compétence *f.* **~ial** /prəˈvɪnʃl/ *a.* & *n.* provincial(e) (*m.*(*f.*)).
provision /prəˈvɪʒn/ *n.* (*stock*) provision *f.*; (*supplying*) fourniture *f.*; (*stipulation*) disposition *f.* **~s**, (*food*) provisions *f. pl.*
provisional /prəˈvɪʒənl/ *a.* provisoire. **~ly** *adv.* provisoirement.
proviso /prəˈvaɪzəʊ/ *n.* (*pl.* **-os**) condition *f.*, stipulation *f.*
provo|ke /prəˈvəʊk/ *v.t.* provoquer. **~cation** /prɒvəˈkeɪʃn/ *n.* provocation *f.* **~cative** /-ˈvɒkətɪv/ *a.* provocant.
prow /praʊ/ *n.* proue *f.*
prowess /ˈpraʊɪs/ *n.* prouesse *f.*
prowl /praʊl/ *v.i.* rôder. —*n.* **be on the ~**, rôder. **~er** *n.* rôdeu|r, -se *m.*, *f.*
proximity /prɒkˈsɪmətɪ/ *n.* proximité *f.*
proxy /ˈprɒksɪ/ *n.* **by ~**, par procuration.
prud|e /pruːd/ *n.* prude *f.* **~ish** *a.* prude.
pruden|t /ˈpruːdnt/ *a.* prudent. **~ce** *n.* prudence *f.* **~tly** *adv.* prudemment.
prune¹ /pruːn/ *n.* pruneau *m.*
prune² /pruːn/ *v.t.* (*cut*) tailler.
pry¹ /praɪ/ *v.i.* être indiscret. **~ into**, fourrer son nez dans.
pry² /praɪ/ *v.t.* (*Amer.*) = **prise.**
psalm /sɑːm/ *n.* psaume *m.*
pseudo- /ˈsjuːdəʊ/ *pref.* pseudo-.
pseudonym /ˈsjuːdənɪm/ *n.* pseudonyme *m.*
psychiatr|y /saɪˈkaɪətrɪ/ *n.* psychiatrie *f.* **~ic** /-ɪˈætrɪk/ *a.* psychiatrique. **~ist** *n.* psychiatre *m./f.*
psychic /ˈsaɪkɪk/ *a.* (*phenomenon etc.*) métapsychique; (*person*) doué de télépathie.
psychoanalys|e /saɪkəʊˈænəlaɪz/ *v.t.* psychanalyser. **~t** /-ɪst/ *n.* psychanalyste *m./f.*
psychoanalysis /saɪkəʊəˈnæləsɪs/ *n.* psychanalyse *f.*
psycholog|y /saɪˈkɒlədʒɪ/ *n.* psychologie *f.* **~ical** /-əˈlɒdʒɪkl/ *a.* psychologique. **~ist** *n.* psychologue *m./f.*
pyschopath /ˈsaɪkəʊpæθ/ *n.* psychopathe *m./f.*
pub /pʌb/ *n.* pub *m.*
puberty /ˈpjuːbətɪ/ *n.* puberté *f.*

public /'pʌblɪk/ *a.* public; (*library etc.*) municipal. **in ~,** en public. **~ house,** pub *m.* **~ school,** école privée *f.*; (*Amer.*) école publique *f.* **~ servant,** fonctionnaire *m./f.* **~-spirited** *a.* dévoué au bien public. **~ly** *adv.* publiquement.
publican /'pʌblɪkən/ *n.* patron(ne) de pub *m.*(*f.*).
publication /pʌblɪ'keɪʃn/ *n.* publication *f.*
publicity /pʌb'lɪsətɪ/ *n.* publicité *f.*
publicize /'pʌblɪsaɪz/ *v.t.* faire connaître au public.
publish /'pʌblɪʃ/ *v.t.* publier. **~er** *n.* éditeur *m.* **~ing** *n.* publication *f.* (**of,** de); (*profession*) édition *f.*
puck /pʌk/ *n.* (*ice hockey*) palet *m.*
pucker /'pʌkə(r)/ *v.t./i.* (se) plisser.
pudding /'pʊdɪŋ/ *n.* dessert *m.*; (*steamed*) pudding *m.* **black ~,** boudin *m.* **rice ~,** riz au lait *m.*
puddle /'pʌdl/ *n.* flaque d'eau *f.*
pudgy /'pʌdʒɪ/ *a.* (**-ier, -iest**) dodu.
puerile /'pjʊəraɪl/ *a.* puéril.
puff /pʌf/ *n.* bouffée *f.* —*v.t./i.* souffler. **~ at,** (*cigar*) tirer sur. **~ out,** (*swell*) (se) gonfler.
puffy /'pʌfɪ/ *a.* gonflé.
pugnacious /pʌg'neɪʃəs/ *a.* batailleur, combatif.
pug-nosed /'pʌgnəʊzd/ *a.* camus.
pull /pʊl/ *v.t./i.* tirer; (*muscle*) se froisser. —*n.* traction *f.*; (*fig.*) attraction *f.*; (*influence*) influence *f.* **give a ~,** tirer. **~ a face,** faire une grimace. **~ one's weight,** faire sa part du travail. **~ s.o.'s leg,** faire marcher qn. **~ away,** (*auto.*) démarrer. **~ back** *or* **out,** (*withdraw*) (se) retirer. **~ down,** baisser; (*building*) démolir. **~ in,** (*enter*) entrer; (*stop*) s'arrêter. **~ off,** enlever; (*fig.*) réussir. **~ out,** (*from bag etc.*) sortir; (*extract*) arracher; (*auto.*) déboîter. **~ over,** (*auto.*) se ranger. **~ round** *or* **through,** s'en tirer. **~ o.s. together,** se ressaisir. **~ up,** remonter; (*uproot*) déraciner; (*auto.*) (s')arrêter.
pulley /'pʊlɪ/ *n.* poulie *f.*
pullover /'pʊləʊvə(r)/ *n.* pull (-over) *m.*
pulp /pʌlp/ *n.* (*of fruit*) pulpe *f.*; (*for paper*) pâte à papier *f.*
pulpit /'pʊlpɪt/ *n.* chaire *f.*
pulsate /pʌl'seɪt/ *v.i.* battre.
pulse /pʌls/ *n.* (*med.*) pouls *m.*
pulverize /'pʌlvəraɪz/ *v.t.* (*grind, defeat*) pulvériser.
pummel /'pʌml/ *v.t.* (*p.t.* **pummelled**) bourrer de coups.
pump[1] /pʌmp/ *n.* pompe *f.* —*v.t./i.* pomper; (*person*) soutirer des renseignements à. **~ up,** gonfler.
pump[2] /pʌmp/ *n.* (*plimsoll*) tennis *m.*; (*for dancing*) escarpin *m.*
pumpkin /'pʌmpkɪn/ *n.* potiron *m.*
pun /pʌn/ *n.* jeu de mots *m.*
punch[1] /pʌntʃ/ *v.t.* donner un coup de poing à; (*perforate*) poinçonner; (*a hole*) faire. —*n.* coup de poing *m.*; (*vigour*: *sl.*) punch *m.*; (*device*) poinçonneuse *f.* **~-drunk** *a.* sonné. **~-up** *n.* (*fam.*) bagarre *f.*
punch[2] /pʌntʃ/ *n.* (*drink*) punch *m.*
punctual /'pʌŋktʃʊəl/ *a.* à l'heure; (*habitually*) ponctuel. **~ity** /-'ælətɪ/ *n.* ponctualité *f.* **~ly** *adv.* à l'heure; ponctuellement.
punctuat|e /'pʌŋktʃʊeɪt/ *v.t.* ponctuer. **~ion** /-'eɪʃn/ *n.* ponctuation *f.*
puncture /'pʌŋktʃə(r)/ *n.* (*in tyre*) crevaison *f.* —*v.t./i.* crever.
pundit /'pʌndɪt/ *n.* expert *m.*
pungent /'pʌndʒənt/ *a.* âcre.
punish /'pʌnɪʃ/ *v.t.* punir (**for sth.,** de qch.). **~able** *a.* punissable (**by,** de). **~ment** *n.* punition *f.*
punitive /'pjuːmɪtɪv/ *a.* punitif.
punk /pʌŋk/ *n.* (*music, fan*) punk *m.*; (*person*: *Amer., fam.*) salaud *m.*
punt[1] /pʌnt/ *n.* (*boat*) bachot *m.*
punt[2] /pʌnt/ *v.i.* (*bet*) parier.
puny /'pjuːnɪ/ *a.* (**-ier, -iest**) chétif.

pup(py) /ˈpʌp(ɪ)/ *n.* chiot *m.*
pupil /ˈpjuːpl/ *n.* (*person*) élève *m.*/*f.*; (*of eye*) pupille *f.*
puppet /ˈpʌpɪt/ *n.* marionnette *f.*
purchase /ˈpɜːtʃəs/ *v.t.* acheter (**from s.o.,** à qn.). —*n.* achat *m.* **~r** /-ə(r)/ *n.* acheteu|r, -se *m., f.*
pur|e /pjʊə(r)/ *a.* (**-er, -est**) pur. **~ely** *adv.* purement. **~ity** *n.* pureté *f.*
purgatory /ˈpɜːgətrɪ/ *n.* purgatoire *m.*
purge /pɜːdʒ/ *v.t.* purger (**of,** de). —*n.* purge *f.*
purif|y /ˈpjʊərɪfaɪ/ *v.t.* purifier. **~ication** /-ɪˈkeɪʃn/ *n.* purification *f.*
purist /ˈpjʊərɪst/ *n.* puriste *m.*/*f.*
puritan /ˈpjʊərɪtən/ *n.* puritain(e) *m.* (*f.*). **~ical** /-ˈtænɪkl/ *a.* puritain.
purple /ˈpɜːpl/ *a.* & *n.* violet (*m.*).
purport /pəˈpɔːt/ *v.t.* **~ to be,** (*claim*) prétendre être.
purpose /ˈpɜːpəs/ *n.* but *m.*; (*fig.*) résolution *f.* **on ~,** exprès. **~-built** *a.* construit spécialement. **to no ~,** sans résultat.
purposely /ˈpɜːpəslɪ/ *adv.* exprès.
purr /pɜː(r)/ *n.* ronronnement *m.* —*v.i.* ronronner.
purse /pɜːs/ *n.* porte-monnaie *m. invar.*; (*handbag*: *Amer.*) sac à main *m.* —*v.t.* (*lips*) pincer.
pursue /pəˈsjuː/ *v.t.* poursuivre. **~r** /-ə(r)/ *n.* poursuivant(e) *m.* (*f.*).
pursuit /pəˈsjuːt/ *n.* poursuite *f.*; (*fig.*) activité *f.*, occupation *f.*
purveyor /pəˈveɪə(r)/ *n.* fournisseur *m.*
pus /pʌs/ *n.* pus *m.*
push /pʊʃ/ *v.t.*/*i.* pousser; (*button*) appuyer sur; (*thrust*) enfoncer. —*n.* poussée *f.*; (*effort*) gros effort *m.*; (*drive*) dynamisme *m.* **be ~ed for,** (*time etc.*) manquer de. **be ~ing thirty**/*etc.*, (*fam.*) friser la trentaine/*etc.* **give the ~ to,** (*sl.*) flanquer à la porte. **~ back,** repousser. **~-chair** *n.* poussette *f.* **~ off,** (*sl.*) filer. **~ on,** continuer. **~ up,** (*lift, increase*) relever. **~-up** *n.* (*Amer.*) traction *f.*
pushing /ˈpʊʃɪŋ/ *a.* arriviste.
puss /pʊs/ *n.* (*cat*) minet(te) *m.* (*f.*).
put /pʊt/ *v.t.*/*i.* (*p.t.* **put,** *pres. p.* **putting**) mettre, placer, poser; (*say*) dire; (*estimate*) évaluer; (*question*) poser. **~ across,** communiquer. **~ away,** ranger; (*fig.*) enfermer. **~ back,** remettre; (*delay*) retarder. **~ by,** mettre de côté. **~ down,** (dé)poser; (*write*) inscrire; (*pay*) verser; (*suppress*) réprimer. **~ in,** (*insert*) introduire; (*submit*) soumettre. **~ in for,** faire une demande de. **~ off,** (*postpone*) renvoyer à plus tard; (*disconcert*) déconcerter. **~ s.o. off sth.,** dégoûter qn. de qch. **~ on,** (*clothes, light, radio*) mettre; (*speed, accent*) prendre. **~ out,** sortir; (*stretch*) (é)tendre; (*extinguish*) éteindre; (*disconcert*) déconcerter; (*inconvenience*) déranger. **~ up,** lever, remonter; (*building*) construire; (*notice*) mettre; (*price*) augmenter; (*guest*) héberger; (*offer*) offrir. **~-up job,** coup monté *m.* **~ up with,** supporter.
putrefy /ˈpjuːtrɪfaɪ/ *v.i.* se putréfier.
putt /pʌt/ *n.* (*golf*) putt *m.*
putter /ˈpʌtə(r)/ *v.i.* (*Amer.*) bricoler.
putty /ˈpʌtɪ/ *n.* mastic *m.*
puzzle /ˈpʌzl/ *n.* énigme *f.*; (*game*) casse-tête *m. invar.* —*v.t.* rendre perplexe. —*v.i.* se creuser la tête.
pygmy /ˈpɪgmɪ/ *n.* pygmée *m.*
pyjamas /pəˈdʒɑːməz/ *n. pl.* pyjama *m.*
pylon /ˈpaɪlɒn/ *n.* pylône *m.*
pyramid /ˈpɪrəmɪd/ *n.* pyramide *f.*
Pyrenees /pɪrəˈniːz/ *n. pl.* **the ~,** les Pyrénées *f. pl.*
python /ˈpaɪθn/ *n.* python *m.*

Q

quack[1] /kwæk/ *n.* (*of duck*) coin-coin *m. invar*.
quack[2] /kwæk/ *n.* charlatan *m.*
quad /kwɒd/ (*fam.*) = **quadrangle, quadruplet.**
quadrangle /ˈkwɒdræŋgl/ (*of college*) *n.* cour *f.*
quadruped /ˈkwɒdrʊped/ *n.* quadrupède *m.*
quadruple /kwɒˈdruːpl/ *a.* & *n.* quadruple (*m.*). —*v.t./i.* quadrupler. **~ts** /-plɪts/ *n. pl.* quadruplé(e)s *m.* (*f.*) *pl.*
quagmire /ˈkwægmaɪə(r)/ *n.* (*bog*) bourbier *m.*
quail /kweɪl/ *n.* (*bird*) caille *f.*
quaint /kweɪnt/ *a.* (**-er, -est**) pittoresque; (*old*) vieillot; (*odd*) bizarre. **~ness** *n.* pittoresque *m.*
quake /kweɪk/ *v.i.* trembler. —*n.* (*fam.*) tremblement de terre *m.*
Quaker /ˈkweɪkə(r)/ *n.* quaker(esse) *m.* (*f.*).
qualification /kwɒlɪfɪˈkeɪʃn/ *n.* diplôme *m.*; (*ability*) compétence *f.*; (*fig.*) réserve *f.*, restriction *f.*
qualif|y /ˈkwɒlɪfaɪ/ *v.t.* qualifier; (*modify*: *fig.*) mettre des réserves à; (*statement*) nuancer. —*v.i.* obtenir son diplôme (**as**, de); (*sport*) se qualifier; (*fig.*) remplir les conditions requises. **~ied** *a.* diplômé; (*able*) qualifié (**to do,** pour faire); (*fig.*) conditionnel; (*success*) modéré.
qualit|y /ˈkwɒlətɪ/ *n.* qualité *f.* **~ative** /-ɪtətɪv/ *a.* qualitatif.
qualm /kwɑːm/ *n.* scrupule *m.*
quandary /ˈkwɒndərɪ/ *n.* embarras *m.*, dilemme *m.*
quantit|y /ˈkwɒntətɪ/ *n.* quantité *f.* **~ative** /-ɪtətɪv/ *a.* quantitatif.
quarantine /ˈkwɒrəntiːn/ *n.* (*isolation*) quarantaine *f.*
quarrel /ˈkwɒrəl/ *n.* dispute *f.*, querelle *f.* —*v.i.* (*p.t.* **quarrelled**) se disputer. **~some** *a.* querelleur.
quarry[1] /ˈkwɒrɪ/ *n.* (*prey*) proie *f.*
quarry[2] /ˈkwɒrɪ/ *n.* (*excavation*) carrière *f.*
quart /kwɔːt/ *n.* (*approx.*) litre *m.*
quarter /ˈkwɔːtə(r)/ *n.* quart *m.*; (*of year*) trimestre *m.*; (*25 cents*: *Amer.*) quart de dollar *m.*; (*district*) quartier *m.* **~s,** logement(s) *m.* (*pl.*). —*v.t.* diviser en quatre; (*mil.*) cantonner. **from all ~s,** de toutes parts. **~-final** *n.* quart de finale *m.* **~ly** *a.* trimestriel; *adv.* trimestriellement.
quartermaster /ˈkwɔːtəmɑːstə(r)/ *n.* (*mil.*) intendant *m.*
quartet /kwɔːˈtet/ *n.* quatuor *m.*
quartz /kwɔːts/ *n.* quartz *m.* —*a.* (*watch etc.*) à quartz.
quash /kwɒʃ/ *v.t.* (*suppress*) étouffer; (*jurid.*) annuler.
quasi- /ˈkweɪsaɪ/ *pref.* quasi-.
quaver /ˈkweɪvə(r)/ *v.i.* trembler, chevroter. —*n.* (*mus.*) croche *f.*
quay /kiː/ *n.* (*naut.*) quai *m.* **~side** *n.* (*edge of quay*) quai *m.*
queasy /ˈkwiːzɪ/ *a.* (*stomach*) délicat. **feel ~,** avoir mal au cœur.
queen /kwiːn/ *n.* reine *f.*; (*cards*) dame *f.* **~ mother,** reine mère *f.*
queer /kwɪə(r)/ *a.* (**-er, -est**) étrange; (*dubious*) louche; (*ill*) patraque. —*n.* (*sl.*) homosexuel *m.*
quell /kwel/ *v.t.* réprimer.
quench /kwentʃ/ *v.t.* éteindre; (*thirst*) étancher; (*desire*) étouffer.
query /ˈkwɪərɪ/ *n.* question *f.* —*v.t.* mettre en question.
quest /kwest/ *n.* recherche *f.*
question /ˈkwestʃən/ *n.* question *f.* —*v.t.* interroger; (*doubt*) mettre en question, douter de. **in ~,** en question. **no ~ of,** pas question de. **out of the ~,** hors de question. **~ mark,** point d'interrogation *m.*
questionable /ˈkwestʃənəbl/ *a.* discutable.
questionnaire /kwestʃəˈneə(r)/ *n.* questionnaire *m.*

queue /kjuː/ *n.* queue *f.* —*v.i.* (*pres. p.* **queuing**) faire la queue.
quibble /ˈkwɪbl/ *v.i.* ergoter.
quick /kwɪk/ *a.* (**-er, -est**) rapide. —*adv.* vite. —*n.* **cut to the ~,** piquer au vif. **be ~,** (*hurry*) se dépêcher. **have a ~ temper,** s'emporter facilement. **~ly** *adv.* rapidement, vite.
quicken /ˈkwɪkən/ *v.t./i.* (s')accélérer.
quicksand /ˈkwɪksænd/ *n.* **~(s),** sables mouvants *m. pl.*
quid /kwɪd/ *n. invar.* (*sl.*) livre *f.*
quiet /ˈkwaɪət/ *a.* (**-er, -est**) (*calm, still*) tranquille; (*silent*) silencieux; (*gentle*) doux; (*discreet*) discret. —*n.* tranquillité *f.* **keep ~,** se taire. **on the ~,** en cachette. **~ly** *adv.* tranquillement; silencieusement; doucement; discrètement. **~ness** *n.* tranquillité *f.*
quieten /ˈkwaɪətn/ *v.t./i.* (se) calmer.
quill /kwɪl/ *n.* plume (d'oie) *f.*
quilt /kwɪlt/ *n.* édredon *m.* (**continental**) **~,** couette *f.* —*v.t.* matelasser.
quinine /ˈkwɪniːn, *Amer.* ˈkwaɪnaɪn/ *n.* quinine *f.*
quintet /kwɪnˈtet/ *n.* quintette *m.*
quintuplets /kwɪnˈtjuːplɪts/ *n. pl.* quintuplé(e)s *m.* (*f.*) *pl.*
quip /kwɪp/ *n.* mot piquant *m.*
quirk /kwɜːk/ *n.* bizarrerie *f.*
quit /kwɪt/ *v.t.* (*p.t.* **quitted**) quitter. —*v.i.* abandonner; (*resign*) démissionner. **~ doing,** (*cease*: *Amer.*) cesser de faire.
quite /kwaɪt/ *adv.* tout à fait, vraiment; (*rather*) assez. **~ (so)!,** parfaitement! **~ a few,** un assez grand nombre (de).
quits /kwɪts/ *a.* quitte (**with,** envers). **call it ~,** en rester là.
quiver /ˈkwɪvə(r)/ *v.i.* trembler.
quiz /kwɪz/ *n.* (*pl.* **quizzes**) test *m.*; (*game*) jeu-concours *m.* —*v.t.* (*p.t.* **quizzed**) questionner.
quizzical /ˈkwɪzɪkl/ *a.* moqueur.
quorum /ˈkwɔːrəm/ *n.* quorum *m.*
quota /ˈkwəʊtə/ *n.* quota *m.*
quotation /kwəʊˈteɪʃn/ *n.* citation *f.*; (*price*) devis *m.*; (*stock exchange*) cotation *f.* **~ marks,** guillemets *m. pl.*
quote /kwəʊt/ *v.t.* citer; (*reference*: *comm.*) rappeler; (*price*) indiquer; (*share price*) coter. —*v.i.* **~ from,** citer. —*n.* (*fam.*) = **quotation. in ~s,** (*fam.*) entre guillemets.
quotient /ˈkwəʊʃnt/ *n.* quotient *m.*

R

rabbi /ˈræbaɪ/ *n.* rabbin *m.*
rabbit /ˈræbɪt/ *n.* lapin *m.*
rabble /ˈræbl/ *n.* (*crowd*) cohue *f.* **the ~,** (*pej.*) la populace.
rabid /ˈræbɪd/ *a.* enragé.
rabies /ˈreɪbiːz/ *n.* (*disease*) rage *f.*
race[1] /reɪs/ *n.* course *f.* —*v.t.* (*horse*) faire courir; (*engine*) emballer. **~ (against),** faire la course à. —*v.i.* courir; (*rush*) foncer. **~-track** *n.* piste *f.*; (*for horses*) champ de courses *m.* **racing** *n.* courses *f. pl.* **racing car,** voiture de course *f.*
race[2] /reɪs/ *n.* (*group*) race *f.* —*a.* racial; (*relations*) entre les races.
racecourse /ˈreɪskɔːs/ *n.* champ de courses *m.*
racehorse /ˈreɪshɔːs/ *n.* cheval de course *m.*
racial /ˈreɪʃl/ *a.* racial.
racis|t /ˈreɪsɪst/ *a.* & *n.* raciste (*m./f.*). **~m** /-zəm/ *n.* racisme *m.*
rack[1] /ræk/ *n.* (*shelf*) étagère *f.*; (*pigeon-holes*) casier *m.*; (*for luggage*) porte-bagages *m. invar.*; (*for dishes*) égouttoir *m.*; (*on car roof*) galerie *f.* —*v.t.* **~ one's brains,** se creuser la cervelle.
rack[2] /ræk/ *n.* **go to ~ and ruin,** aller à la ruine; (*building*) tomber en ruine.

racket[1] /'rækɪt/ *n.* raquette *f.*
racket[2] /'rækɪt/ *n.* (*din*) tapage *m.*; (*dealings*) combine *f.*; (*crime*) racket *m.* **~eer** /-ə'tɪə(r)/ *n.* racketteur *m.*
racy /'reɪsɪ/ *a.* (**-ier, -iest**) fougueux, piquant; (*Amer.*) risqué.
radar /'reɪdɑː(r)/ *n.* radar *m.* —*a.* (*system etc.*) radar *invar.*
radian|t /'reɪdɪənt/ *a.* rayonnant. **~ce** *n.* éclat *m.* **~tly** *adv.* avec éclat.
radiat|e /'reɪdɪeɪt/ *v.t.* dégager. —*v.i.* rayonner (**from,** de). **~ion** /-'eɪʃn/ *n.* rayonnement *m.*; (*radioactivity*) radiation *f.*
radiator /'reɪdɪeɪtə(r)/ *n.* radiateur *m.*
radical /'rædɪkl/ *a.* radical. —*n.* (*person: pol.*) radical(e) *m.*(*f.*).
radio /'reɪdɪəʊ/ *n.* (*pl.* **-os**) radio *f.* —*v.t.* (*message*) envoyer par radio; (*person*) appeler par radio.
radioactiv|e /reɪdɪəʊ'æktɪv/ *a.* radioactif. **~ity** /-'tɪvətɪ/ *n.* radioactivité *f.*
radiographer /reɪdɪ'ɒgrəfə(r)/ *n.* radiologue *m.*/*f.*
radish /'rædɪʃ/ *n.* radis *m.*
radius /'reɪdɪəs/ *n.* (*pl.* **-dii** /-dɪaɪ/) rayon *m.*
raffish /'ræfɪʃ/ *a.* libertin.
raffle /'ræfl/ *n.* tombola *f.*
raft /rɑːft/ *n.* radeau *m.*
rafter /'rɑːftə(r)/ *n.* chevron *m.*
rag[1] /ræg/ *n.* lambeau *m.*, loque *f.*; (*for wiping*) chiffon *m.*; (*newspaper*) torchon *m.* **in ~s,** (*person*) en haillons; (*clothes*) en lambeaux.
rag[2] /ræg/ *v.t.* (*p.t.* **ragged**) (*tease: sl.*) taquiner. —*n.* (*univ., sl.*) carnaval *m.* (*pour une œuvre de charité*).
ragamuffin /'rægəmʌfɪn/ *n.* va-nu-pieds *m. invar.*
rage /reɪdʒ/ *n.* rage *f.*, fureur *f.* —*v.i.* rager; (*storm, battle*) faire rage. **be all the ~,** faire fureur. **raging** *a.* (*storm, fever, etc.*) violent.
ragged /'rægɪd/ *a.* (*clothes, person*) loqueteux; (*edge*) déchiqueté.
raid /reɪd/ *n.* (*mil.*) raid *m.*; (*by police*) rafle *f.*; (*by criminals*) hold-up *m. invar.* —*v.t.* faire un raid *or* une rafle *or* un hold-up dans. **~er** *n.* (*person*) bandit *m.*, pillard *m.* **~ers** *n. pl.* (*mil.*) commando *m.*
rail /reɪl/ *n.* (*on balcony*) balustrade *f.*; (*stairs*) main courante *f.*, rampe *f.*; (*for train*) rail *m.*; (*for curtain*) tringle *f.* **by ~,** par chemin de fer.
railing /'reɪlɪŋ/ *n.* **~(s),** grille *f.*
railroad /'reɪlrəʊd/ *n.* (*Amer.*) = **railway.**
railway /'reɪlweɪ/ *n.* chemin de fer *m.* **~man** *n.* (*pl.* **-men**) cheminot *m.* **~ station,** gare *f.*
rain /reɪn/ *n.* pluie *f.* —*v.i.* pleuvoir. **~-storm** *n.* trombe d'eau *f.* **~-water** *n.* eau de pluie *f.*
rainbow /'reɪnbəʊ/ *n.* arc-en-ciel *m.*
raincoat /'reɪnkəʊt/ *n.* imperméable *m.*
rainfall /'reɪnfɔːl/ *n.* précipitation *f.*
rainy /'reɪnɪ/ *a.* (**-ier, -iest**) pluvieux; (*season*) des pluies.
raise /reɪz/ *v.t.* lever; (*breed, build*) élever; (*question etc.*) soulever; (*price etc.*) relever; (*money etc.*) obtenir; (*voice*) élever. —*n.* (*Amer.*) augmentation *f.*
raisin /'reɪzn/ *n.* raisin sec *m.*
rake[1] /reɪk/ *n.* râteau *m.* —*v.t.* (*garden*) ratisser; (*search*) fouiller dans. **~ in,** (*money*) amasser. **~-off** *n.* (*fam.*) profit *m.* **~ up,** (*memories, past*) remuer.
rake[2] /reɪk/ *n.* (*man*) débauché *m.*
rally /'rælɪ/ *v.t./i.* (se) rallier; (*strength*) reprendre. —*n.* rassemblement *m.*; (*auto.*) rallye *m.*
ram /ræm/ *n.* bélier *m.* —*v.t.*

(*p.t.* **rammed**) (*thrust*) enfoncer; (*crash into*) emboutir, percuter.

rambl|e /'ræmbl/ *n.* randonnée *f.* —*v.i.* faire une randonnée. **~e on,** parler (sans cesse), divaguer. **~ing** *a.* (*speech*) décousu.

ramification /ræmɪfɪ'keɪʃn/ *n.* ramification *f.*

ramp /ræmp/ *n.* (*slope*) rampe *f.*; (*in garage*) pont de graissage *m.*

rampage[1] /ræm'peɪdʒ/ *v.i.* se livrer à des actes de violence, se déchaîner.

rampage[2] /'ræmpeɪdʒ/ *n.* **go on the ~ = rampage**[1].

rampant /'ræmpənt/ *a.* **be ~,** (*disease etc.*) sévir, être répandu.

rampart /'ræmpɑːt/ *n.* rempart *m.*

ramshackle /'ræmʃækl/ *a.* délabré.

ran /ræn/ *see* **run.**

ranch /rɑːntʃ/ *n.* ranch *m.*

rancid /'rænsɪd/ *a.* rance.

rancour /'ræŋkə(r)/ *n.* rancœur *f.*

random /'rændəm/ *a.* fait, pris, *etc.* au hasard. —*n.* **at ~,** au hasard.

randy /'rændɪ/ *a.* (**-ier, -iest**) (*fam.*) lascif, voluptueux.

rang /ræŋ/ *see* **ring**[2].

range /reɪndʒ/ *n.* (*distance*) portée *f.*; (*of aircraft etc.*) rayon d'action *m.*; (*series*) gamme *f.*; (*scale*) échelle *f.*; (*choice*) choix *m.*; (*domain*) champ *m.*; (*of mountains*) chaîne *f.*; (*stove*) cuisinière *f.* —*v.i.* s'étendre; (*vary*) varier.

ranger /'reɪndʒə(r)/ *n.* garde forestier *m.*

rank[1] /ræŋk/ *n.* rang *m.*; (*grade: mil.*) grade *m.*, rang *m.* —*v.t./i.* **~ among,** compter parmi. **the ~ and file,** les gens ordinaires.

rank[2] /ræŋk/ *a.* (**-er, -est**) (*plants: pej.*) luxuriant; (*smell*) fétide; (*complete*) absolu.

ransack /'rænsæk/ *v.t.* (*search*) fouiller; (*pillage*) saccager.

ransom /'rænsəm/ *n.* rançon *f.* —*v.t.* rançonner; (*redeem*) racheter. **hold to ~,** rançonner.

rant /rænt/ *v.i.* tempêter.

rap /ræp/ *n.* petit coup sec *m.* —*v.t./i.* (*p.t.* **rapped**) frapper.

rape /reɪp/ *v.t.* violer. —*n.* viol *m.*

rapid /'ræpɪd/ *a.* rapide. **~ity** /rə'pɪdətɪ/ *n.* rapidité *f.* **~s** *n. pl.* (*of river*) rapides *m. pl.*

rapist /'reɪpɪst/ *n.* violeur *m.*

rapport /ræ'pɔː(r)/ *n.* rapport *m.*

rapt /ræpt/ *a.* (*attention*) profond. **~ in,** plongé dans.

raptur|e /'ræptʃə(r)/ *n.* extase *f.* **~ous** *a.* (*person*) en extase; (*welcome etc.*) frénétique.

rar|e[1] /reə(r)/ *a.* (**-er, -est**) rare. **~ely** *adv.* rarement. **~ity** *n.* rareté *f.*

rare[2] /reə(r)/ *a.* (**-er, -est**) (*culin.*) saignant.

rarefied /'reərɪfaɪd/ *a.* raréfié.

raring /'reərɪŋ/ *a.* **~ to,** (*fam.*) impatient de.

rascal /'rɑːskl/ *n.* coquin(e) *m.*(*f.*).

rash[1] /ræʃ/ *n.* (*med.*) éruption *f.*, rougeurs *f. pl.*

rash[2] /ræʃ/ *a.* (**-er, -est**) imprudent. **~ly** *adv.* imprudemment. **~ness** *n.* imprudence *f.*

rasher /'ræʃə(r)/ *n.* tranche (de lard) *f.*

rasp /rɑːsp/ *n.* (*file*) râpe *f.*

raspberry /'rɑːzbrɪ/ *n.* framboise *f.*

rasping /'rɑːspɪŋ/ *a.* grinçant.

rat /ræt/ *n.* rat *m.* —*v.i.* (*p.t.* **ratted**). **~ on,** (*desert*) lâcher; (*inform on*) dénoncer. **~ race,** jungle *f.*, course au bifteck *f.*, lutte acharnée pour réussir *f.*

rate /reɪt/ *n.* (*ratio, level*) taux *m.*; (*speed*) allure *f.*; (*price*) tarif *m.* **~s,** (*taxes*) impôts locaux *m. pl.* —*v.t.* évaluer; (*consider*) considérer; (*deserve: Amer.*) mériter. **at any ~,** en tout cas. **at the ~ of,** (*on the basis of*) à raison de.

rateable /'reɪtəbl/ *a.* **~ value,** valeur locative imposable *f.*

ratepayer /ˈreɪtpeɪə(r)/ *n.* contribuable *m./f.*

rather /ˈrɑːðə(r)/ *adv.* (*by preference*) plutôt; (*fairly*) assez, plutôt; (*a little*) un peu. **I would ~ go,** j'aimerais mieux partir.

ratif|y /ˈrætɪfaɪ/ *v.t.* ratifier. **~ication** /-ɪˈkeɪʃn/ *n.* ratification *f.*

rating /ˈreɪtɪŋ/ *n.* classement *m.*; (*sailor*) matelot *m.* (*number*) indice *m.*; (*TV*) popularité *f.*

ratio /ˈreɪʃɪəʊ/ *n.* (*pl.* **-os**) proportion *f.*

ration /ˈræʃn/ *n.* ration *f.* —*v.t.* rationner.

rational /ˈræʃənl/ *a.* rationnel; (*person*) raisonnable.

rationalize /ˈræʃənəlaɪz/ *v.t.* donner une explication rationnelle à; (*organize*) rationaliser.

rattle /ˈrætl/ *v.i.* faire du bruit; (*of bottles*) cliqueter. —*v.t.* secouer; (*sl.*) déconcerter. —*n.* bruit (de ferraille) *m.*; cliquetis *m.*; (*toy*) hochet *m.* **~ off,** débiter en vitesse.

rattlesnake /ˈrætlsneɪk/ *n.* serpent à sonnette *m.*, crotale *m.*

raucous /ˈrɔːkəs/ *a.* rauque.

raunchy /ˈrɔːntʃɪ/ *a.* (**-ier, -iest**) (*Amer., sl.*) grossier, cochon.

ravage /ˈrævɪdʒ/ *v.t.* ravager. **~s** /-ɪz/ *n. pl.* ravages *m. pl.*

rav|e /reɪv/ *v.i.* divaguer; (*in anger*) tempêter. **~e about,** s'extasier sur. **~ings** *n. pl.* divagations *f. pl.*

raven /ˈreɪvn/ *n.* corbeau *m.*

ravenous /ˈrævənəs/ *a.* vorace. **I am ~,** je meurs de faim.

ravine /rəˈviːn/ *n.* ravin *m.*

raving /ˈreɪvɪŋ/ *a.* **~ lunatic,** fou furieux *m.*, folle furieuse *f.*

ravioli /rævɪˈəʊlɪ/ *n.* ravioli *m. pl.*

ravish /ˈrævɪʃ/ *v.t.* (*rape*) ravir. **~ing** *a.* (*enchanting*) ravissant.

raw /rɔː/ *a.* (**-er, -est**) cru; (*not processed*) brut; (*wound*) à vif; (*immature*) inexpérimenté. **get a ~ deal,** être mal traité. **~ material,** matière première *f.*

ray /reɪ/ *n.* (*of light etc.*) rayon *m.* **~ of hope,** lueur d'espoir *f.*

raze /reɪz/ *v.t.* (*destroy*) raser.

razor /ˈreɪzə(r)/ *n.* rasoir *m.*

re /riː/ *prep.* concernant.

re- /riː/ *pref.* re-, ré-, r-.

reach /riːtʃ/ *v.t.* atteindre, arriver à; (*contact*) joindre; (*hand over*) passer. —*v.i.* s'étendre. —*n.* portée *f.* **~ for,** tendre la main pour prendre. **within ~ of,** à portée de; (*close to*) à proximité de.

react /rɪˈækt/ *v.i.* réagir.

reaction /rɪˈækʃn/ *n.* réaction *f.* **~ary** *a.* & *n.* réactionnaire (*m./f.*).

reactor /rɪˈæktə(r)/ *n.* réacteur *m.*

read /riːd/ *v.t./i.* (*p.t.* **read** /red/) lire; (*fig.*) comprendre; (*study*) étudier; (*of instrument*) indiquer. —*n.* (*fam.*) lecture *f.* **~ about s.o.,** lire un article sur qn. **~able** *a.* agréable *or* facile à lire. **~ing** *n.* lecture *f.*; indication *f.* **~ing-lamp** *n.* lampe de bureau *f.*

reader /ˈriːdə(r)/ *n.* lec|teur, -trice *m., f.* **~ship** *n.* lecteurs *m. pl.*

readily /ˈredɪlɪ/ *adv.* (*willingly*) volontiers; (*easily*) facilement.

readiness /ˈredɪnɪs/ *n.* empressement *m.* **in ~,** prêt (**for,** à).

readjust /riːəˈdʒʌst/ *v.t.* rajuster. —*v.i.* se réadapter (**to,** à).

ready /ˈredɪ/ *a.* (**-ier, -iest**) prêt; (*quick*) prompt. —*n.* **at the ~,** tout prêt. **~-made** *a.* tout fait. **~ money,** (argent) liquide *m.* **~ reckoner,** barème *m.*

real /rɪəl/ *a.* vrai, véritable, réel. —*adv.* (*Amer., fam.*) vraiment. **~ estate,** biens fonciers *m. pl.*

realis|t /ˈrɪəlɪst/ *n.* réaliste *m./f.* **~m** /-zəm/ *n.* réalisme *m.* **~tic** /-ˈlɪstɪk/ *a.* réaliste. **~tically** /-ˈlɪstɪklɪ/ *adv.* avec réalisme.

reality /rɪˈælətɪ/ *n.* réalité *f.*

realiz|e /ˈrɪəlaɪz/ *v.t.* se rendre compte de, comprendre; (*fulfil,*

turn into cash) réaliser; (*price*) atteindre. **~ation** /-ˈzeɪʃn/ *n.* prise de conscience *f.*; réalisation *f.*
really /ˈrɪəlɪ/ *adv.* vraiment.
realm /relm/ *n.* royaume *m.*
reap /riːp/ *v.t.* (*crop, field*) moissonner; (*fig.*) récolter.
reappear /riːəˈpɪə(r)/ *v.i.* réapparaître, reparaître.
reappraisal /riːəˈpreɪzl/ *n.* réévaluation *f.*
rear[1] /rɪə(r)/ *n.* arrière *m.*, derrière *m.* —*a.* arrière *invar.*, de derrière.
rear[2] /rɪə(r)/ *v.t.* (*bring up, breed*) élever. —*v.i.* (*horse*) se cabrer. **~ one's head,** dresser la tête.
rearguard /ˈrɪəgɑːd/ *n.* (*mil.*) arrière-garde *f.*
rearm /riːˈɑːm/ *v.t./i.* réarmer.
rearrange /riːəˈreɪndʒ/ *v.t.* réarranger.
reason /ˈriːzn/ *n.* raison *f.* —*v.i.* raisonner. **~ with,** raisonner. **within ~,** avec modération. **~ing** *n.* raisonnement *m.*
reasonable /ˈriːznəbl/ *a.* raisonnable.
reassur|e /riːəˈʃʊə(r)/ *v.t.* rassurer. **~ance** *n.* réconfort *m.*
rebate /ˈriːbeɪt/ *n.* remboursement (partiel) *m.*; (*discount*) rabais *m.*
rebel[1] /ˈrebl/ *n.* & *a.* rebelle (*m./f.*).
rebel[2] /rɪˈbel/ *v.i.* (*p.t.* **rebelled**) se rebeller. **~lion** *n.* rébellion *f.* **~lious** *a.* rebelle.
rebound /rɪˈbaʊnd/ *v.i.* rebondir. **~ on,** (*backfire*) se retourner contre. —*n.* /ˈriːbaʊnd/ *n.* rebond *m.*
rebuff /rɪˈbʌf/ *v.t.* repousser. —*n.* rebuffade *f.*
rebuild /riːˈbɪld/ *v.t.* reconstruire.
rebuke /rɪˈbjuːk/ *v.t.* réprimander. —*n.* réprimande *f.*, reproche *m.*
rebuttal /rɪˈbʌtl/ *n.* réfutation *f.*
recall /rɪˈkɔːl/ *v.t.* (*to s.o., call back*) rappeler; (*remember*) se rappeler. —*n.* rappel *m.*
recant /rɪˈkænt/ *v.i.* se rétracter.
recap /ˈriːkæp/ *v.t./i.* (*p.t.* **recapped**) (*fam.*) récapituler. —*n.* (*fam.*) récapitulation *f.*
recapitulat|e /riːkəˈpɪtʃʊleɪt/ *v.t./i.* récapituler. **~ion** /-ˈleɪʃn/ *n.* récapitulation *f.*
recapture /riːˈkæptʃə(r)/ *v.t.* reprendre; (*recall*) recréer.
reced|e /rɪˈsiːd/ *v.i.* s'éloigner. **his hair is ~ing,** son front se dégarnit. **~ing** *a.* (*forehead*) fuyant.
receipt /rɪˈsiːt/ *n.* (*written*) reçu *m.*; (*receiving*) réception *f.* **~s,** (*money: comm.*) recettes *f. pl.*
receive /rɪˈsiːv/ *v.t.* recevoir. **~r** /-ə(r)/ *n.* (*of stolen goods*) receleu|r, -se *m., f.*; (*telephone*) récepteur *m.*
recent /ˈriːsnt/ *a.* récent. **~ly** *adv.* récemment.
receptacle /rɪˈseptəkl/ *n.* récipient *m.*
reception /rɪˈsepʃn/ *n.* réception *f.* **~ist** *n.* réceptionniste *m./f.*
receptive /rɪˈseptɪv/ *a.* réceptif.
recess /rɪˈses/ *n.* (*alcove*) renfoncement *m.*; (*nook*) recoin *m.*; (*holiday*) vacances *f. pl.*; (*schol., Amer.*) récréation *f.*
recession /rɪˈseʃn/ *n.* récession *f.*
recharge /riːˈtʃɑːdʒ/ *v.t.* recharger.
recipe /ˈresəpɪ/ *n.* recette *f.*
recipient /rɪˈsɪpɪənt/ *n.* (*of honour*) récipiendaire *m.*; (*of letter*) destinataire *m./f.*
reciprocal /rɪˈsɪprəkl/ *a.* réciproque.
reciprocate /rɪˈsɪprəkeɪt/ *v.t.* offrir en retour. —*v.i.* en faire autant.
recital /rɪˈsaɪtl/ *n.* récital *m.*
recite /rɪˈsaɪt/ *v.t.* (*poem, lesson, etc.*) réciter; (*list*) énumérer.
reckless /ˈreklɪs/ *a.* imprudent. **~ly** *adv.* imprudemment.
reckon /ˈrekən/ *v.t./i.* calculer; (*judge*) considérer; (*think*) penser. **~ on/with,** compter sur/avec. **~ing** *n.* calcul(s) *m.* (*pl.*).
reclaim /rɪˈkleɪm/ *v.t.* (*seek return of*) réclamer; (*land*) défricher; (*flooded land*) assécher.

reclin|e /rɪ'klaɪn/ *v.i.* être étendu. **~ing** *a.* (*person*) étendu.
recluse /rɪ'kluːs/ *n.* reclus(e) *m.* (*f.*), ermite *m.*
recognition /rekəg'nɪʃn/ *n.* reconnaissance *f.* **beyond ~,** méconnaissable. **gain ~,** être reconnu.
recognize /'rekəgnaɪz/ *v.t.* reconnaître.
recoil /rɪ'kɔɪl/ *v.i.* reculer.
recollect /rekə'lekt/ *v.t.* se souvenir de, se rappeler. **~ion** /-kʃn/ *n.* souvenir *m.*
recommend /rekə'mend/ *v.t.* recommander. **~ation** /-'deɪʃn/ *n.* recommandation *f.*
recompense /'rekəmpens/ *v.t.* (ré)compenser. —*n.* récompense *f.*
reconcil|e /'rekənsaɪl/ *v.t.* (*people*) réconcilier; (*facts*) concilier. **~e o.s. to,** se résigner à. **~iation** /-sɪlɪ'eɪʃn/ *n.* réconciliation *f.*
recondition /riːkən'dɪʃn/ *v.t.* remettre à neuf, réviser.
reconn|oitre /rekə'nɔɪtə(r)/ *v.t.* (*pres. p.* **-tring**) (*mil.*) reconnaître. **~aissance** /rɪ'kɒnɪsns/ *n.* reconnaissance *f.*
reconsider /riːkən'sɪdə(r)/ *v.t.* reconsidérer. —*v.i.* se déjuger.
reconstruct /riːkən'strʌkt/ *v.t.* reconstruire; (*crime*) reconstituer.
record¹ /rɪ'kɔːd/ *v.t./i.* (*in register, on tape, etc.*) enregistrer; (*in diary*) noter. **~ that,** rapporter que. **~ing** *n.* enregistrement *m.*
record² /'rekɔːd/ *n.* (*report*) rapport *m.*; (*register*) registre *m.*; (*mention*) mention *f.*; (*file*) dossier *m.*; (*fig.*) résultats *m. pl.*; (*mus.*) disque *m.*; (*sport*) record *m.* **(criminal) ~,** casier judiciaire *m.* —*a.* record *invar.* **off the ~,** officieusement. **~-player** *n.* électrophone *m.*
recorder /rɪ'kɔːdə(r)/ *n.* (*mus.*) flûte à bec *f.*
recount /rɪ'kaʊnt/ *v.t.* raconter.
re-count /riː'kaʊnt/ *v.t.* recompter.
recoup /rɪ'kuːp/ *v.t.* récupérer.
recourse /rɪ'kɔːs/ *n.* recours *m.* **have ~ to,** avoir recours à.
recover /rɪ'kʌvə(r)/ *v.t.* récupérer. —*v.i.* se remettre; (*med.*) se rétablir; (*economy*) se redresser. **~y** *n.* récupération *f.*; (*med.*) rétablissement *m.*
recreation /rekrɪ'eɪʃn/ *n.* récréation *f.* **~al** *a.* de récréation.
recrimination /rɪkrɪmɪ'neɪʃn/ *n.* contre-accusation *f.*
recruit /rɪ'kruːt/ *n.* recrue *f.* —*v.t.* recruter. **~ment** *n.* recrutement *m.*
rectang|le /'rektæŋgl/ *n.* rectangle *m.* **~ular** /-'tæŋgjʊlə(r)/ *a.* rectangulaire.
rectif|y /'rektɪfaɪ/ *v.t.* rectifier. **~ication** /-ɪ'keɪʃn/ *n.* rectification *f.*
recuperate /rɪ'kjuːpəreɪt/ *v.t.* récupérer. —*v.i.* (*med.*) se rétablir.
recur /rɪ'kɜː(r)/ *v.i.* (*p.t.* **recurred**) revenir, se répéter.
recurren|t /rɪ'kʌrənt/ *a.* fréquent. **~ce** *n.* répétition *f.*, retour *m.*
recycle /riː'saɪkl/ *v.t.* recycler.
red /red/ *a.* **(redder, reddest)** rouge; (*hair*) roux. —*n.* rouge *m.* **in the ~,** en déficit. **~ carpet,** réception solennelle *f.* **R~ Cross,** Croix-Rouge *f.* **~-handed** *a.* en flagrant délit. **~ herring,** fausse piste *f.* **~-hot** *a.* brûlant. **R~ Indian,** Peau-Rouge *m./f.* **~ light,** feu rouge *m.* **~ tape,** paperasserie *f.*, bureaucratie *f.*
redd|en /'redn/ *v.t./i.* rougir. **~ish** *a.* rougeâtre.
redecorate /riː'dekəreɪt/ *v.t.* (*repaint etc.*) repeindre, refaire.
redeem /rɪ'diːm/ *v.t.* racheter. **~ing quality,** qualité qui rachète les défauts *f.* **redemption** *n.* /rɪ'dempʃn/ rachat *m.*
redeploy /riːdɪ'plɔɪ/ *v.t.* réorganiser; (*troops*) répartir.

redirect /riːdaɪə'rekt/ *v.t.* (*letter*) faire suivre.

redness /'rednɪs/ *n.* rougeur *f.*

redo /riː'duː/ *v.t.* (*p.t.* **-did,** *p.p.* **-done**) refaire.

redouble /rɪ'dʌbl/ *v.t.* redoubler.

redress /rɪ'dres/ *v.t.* (*wrong etc.*) redresser. —*n.* réparation *f.*

reduc|e /rɪ'djuːs/ *v.t.* réduire; (*temperature etc.*) faire baisser. **~tion** /rɪ'dʌkʃn/ *n.* réduction *f.*

redundan|t /rɪ'dʌndənt/ *a.* superflu; (*worker*) mis au chômage. **~cy** *n.* mise au chômage *f.*; (*word, phrase*) pléonasme *m.*

reed /riːd/ *n.* (*plant*) roseau *m.*; (*mus.*) anche *f.*

reef /riːf/ *n.* récif *m.*, écueil *m.*

reek /riːk/ *n.* puanteur *f.* —*v.i.* **~** **(of),** puer.

reel /riːl/ *n.* (*of thread*) bobine *f.*; (*of film*) bande *f.*; (*winding device*) dévidoir *m.* —*v.i.* chanceler. —*v.t.* **~ off,** réciter.

refectory /rɪ'fektərɪ/ *n.* réfectoire *m.*

refer /rɪ'fɜː(r)/ *v.t./i.* (*p.t.* **referred**). **~ to,** (*allude to*) faire allusion à; (*concern*) s'appliquer à; (*consult*) consulter; (*submit*) soumettre à; (*direct*) renvoyer à.

referee /refə'riː/ *n.* arbitre *m.*; (*for job*) répondant(e) *m.* (*f.*). —*v.t.* (*p.t.* **refereed**) arbitrer.

reference /'refrəns/ *n.* référence *f.*; (*mention*) allusion *f.*; (*person*) répondant(e) *m.* (*f.*). **in** *or* **with ~ to,** en ce qui concerne; (*comm.*) suite à. **~ book,** ouvrage de référence *m.*

referendum /refə'rendəm/ *n.* (*pl.* **-ums**) référendum *m.*

refill[1] /riː'fɪl/ *v.t.* remplir (à nouveau); (*pen etc.*) recharger.

refill[2] /'riːfɪl/ *n.* (*of pen, lighter, lipstick*) recharge *f.*

refine /rɪ'faɪn/ *v.t.* raffiner. **~d** *a.* raffiné. **~ment** *n.* raffinement *m.*; (*techn.*) raffinage *m.* **~ry** /-ərɪ/ *n.* raffinerie *f.*

reflate /riː'fleɪt/ *v.t.* relancer.

reflect /rɪ'flekt/ *v.t.* refléter; (*of mirror*) réfléchir, refléter. —*v.i.* réfléchir (**on,** à). **~ on s.o.,** (*glory etc.*) (faire) rejaillir sur qn. **~ion** /-kʃn/ *n.* réflexion *f.*; (*image*) reflet *m.* **~or** *n.* réflecteur *m.*

reflective /rɪ'flektɪv/ *a.* réfléchi.

reflex /'riːfleks/ *a.* & *n.* réflexe (*m.*).

reflexive /rɪ'fleksɪv/ *a.* (*gram.*) réfléchi.

reform /rɪ'fɔːm/ *v.t.* réformer. —*v.i.* (*person*) s'amender. —*n.* réforme *f.* **~er** *n.* réforma|teur, -trice *m., f.*

refract /rɪ'frækt/ *v.t.* réfracter.

refrain[1] /rɪ'freɪn/ *n.* refrain *m.*

refrain[2] /rɪ'freɪn/ *v.i.* s'abstenir (**from,** de).

refresh /rɪ'freʃ/ *v.t.* rafraîchir; (*of rest etc.*) ragaillardir, délasser. **~ing** *a.* (*drink*) rafraîchissant; (*sleep*) réparateur. **~ments** *n. pl.* rafraîchissements *m. pl.*

refresher /rɪ'freʃə(r)/ *a.* (*course*) de perfectionnement.

refrigerat|e /rɪ'frɪdʒəreɪt/ *v.t.* réfrigérer. **~or** *n.* réfrigérateur *m.*

refuel /riː'fjuːəl/ *v.t./i.* (*p.t.* **refuelled**) (se) ravitailler.

refuge /'refjuːdʒ/ *n.* refuge *m.* **take ~,** se réfugier.

refugee /refjʊ'dʒiː/ *n.* réfugié(e) *m.* (*f.*).

refund /rɪ'fʌnd/ *v.t.* rembourser. —*n.* /'riːfʌnd/ remboursement *m.*

refurbish /riː'fɜːbɪʃ/ *v.t.* remettre à neuf.

refus|e[1] /rɪ'fjuːz/ *v.t./i.* refuser. **~al** *n.* refus *m.*

refuse[2] /'refjuːs/ *n.* détritus *m. pl.*

refute /rɪ'fjuːt/ *v.t.* réfuter.

regain /rɪ'geɪn/ *v.t.* retrouver; (*lost ground*) regagner.

regal /'riːgl/ *a.* royal, majestueux.

regalia /rɪ'geɪlɪə/ *n. pl.* (*insignia*) insignes (royaux) *m. pl.*

regard /rɪ'gɑːd/ *v.t.* regarder,

considérer. —*n.* considération *f.*, estime *f.* **~s,** amitiés *f. pl.* **in this ~,** à cet égard. **as ~s, ~ing** *prep.* en ce qui concerne.
regardless /rɪ'gɑːdlɪs/ *adv.* quand même. **~ of,** sans tenir compte de.
regatta /rɪ'gætə/ *n.* régates *f. pl.*
regenerate /rɪ'dʒenəreɪt/ *v.t.* régénérer.
regen|t /'riːdʒənt/ *n.* régent(e) *m.* (*f.*). **~cy** *n.* régence *f.*
regime /reɪ'ʒiːm/ *n.* régime *m.*
regiment /'redʒɪmənt/ *n.* régiment *m.* **~al** /-'mentl/ *a.* d'un régiment. **~ation** /-en'teɪʃn/ *n.* discipline excessive *f.*
region /'riːdʒən/ *n.* région *f.* **in the ~ of,** environ. **~al** *a.* régional.
regist|er /'redʒɪstə(r)/ *n.* registre *m.* —*v.t.* enregistrer; (*vehicle*) immatriculer; (*birth*) déclarer; (*letter*) recommander; (*indicate*) indiquer; (*express*) exprimer. —*v.i.* (*enrol*) s'inscrire; (*fig.*) être compris. **~er office,** bureau d'état civil *m.* **~ration** /-'streɪʃn/ *n.* enregistrement *m.*; inscription *f.*; (*vehicle document*) carte grise *f.* **~ration (number),** (*auto.*) numéro d'immatriculation *m.*
registrar /redʒɪ'strɑː(r)/ *n.* officier de l'état civil *m.*; (*univ.*) secrétaire général *m.*
regret /rɪ'gret/ *n.* regret *m.* —*v.t.* (*p.t.* **regretted**) regretter **(to do,** de faire). **~fully** *adv.* à regret. **~table** *a.* regrettable, fâcheux. **~tably** *adv.* malheureusement; (*small, poor, etc.*) fâcheusement.
regroup /riː'gruːp/ *v.t./i.* (se) regrouper.
regular /'regjʊlə(r)/ *a.* régulier; (*usual*) habituel; (*thorough*: *fam.*) vrai. —*n.* (*fam.*) habitué(e) *m.* (*f.*). **~ity** /-'lærətɪ/ *n.* régularité *f.* **~ly** *adv.* régulièrement.
regulat|e /'regjʊleɪt/ *v.t.* régler. **~ion** /-'leɪʃn/ *n.* réglage *m.*; (*rule*) règlement *m.*
rehabilitat|e /riːə'bɪlɪteɪt/ *v.t.* réadapter; (*in public esteem*) réhabiliter. **~ion** /-'teɪʃn/ *n.* réadaptation *f.*; réhabilitation *f.*
rehash[1] /riː'hæʃ/ *v.t.* remanier.
rehash[2] /'riːhæʃ/ *n.* réchauffé *m.*
rehears|e /rɪ'hɜːs/ *v.t./i* (*theatre*) répéter. **~al** *n.* répétition *f.*
reign /reɪn/ *n.* règne *m.* —*v.i.* régner **(over,** sur).
reimburse /riːɪm'bɜːs/ *v.t.* rembourser.
rein /reɪn/ *n.* rêne *f.*
reindeer /'reɪndɪə(r)/ *n. invar.* renne *m.*
reinforce /riːɪn'fɔːs/ *v.t.* renforcer. **~ment** *n.* renforcement *m.* **~ments** *n. pl.* renforts *m. pl.*
reinstate /riːɪn'steɪt/ *v.t.* réintégrer, rétablir.
reiterate /riː'ɪtəreɪt/ *v.t.* réitérer.
reject[1] /rɪ'dʒekt/ *v.t.* (*offer, plea, etc.*) rejeter; (*book, goods, etc.*) refuser. **~ion** /-kʃn/ *n.* rejet *m.*; refus *m.*
reject[2] /'riːdʒekt/ *n.* (article de) rebut *m.*
rejoic|e /rɪ'dʒɔɪs/ *v.i.* se réjouir. **~ing** *n.* réjouissance *f.*
rejoin /rɪ'dʒɔɪn/ *v.t.* rejoindre.
rejuvenate /rɪ'dʒuːvəneɪt/ *v.t.* rajeunir.
relapse /rɪ'læps/ *n.* rechute *f.* —*v.i.* rechuter. **~ into,** retomber dans.
relate /rɪ'leɪt/ *v.t.* raconter; (*associate*) rapprocher. —*v.i.* **~ to,** se rapporter à; (*get on with*) s'entendre avec. **~d** /-ɪd/ *a.* (*ideas etc.*) lié. **~d to s.o.,** parent(e) de qn.
relation /rɪ'leɪʃn/ *n.* rapport *m.*; (*person*) parent(e) *m.* (*f.*). **~ship** *n.* lien de parenté *m.*; (*link*) rapport *m.*; (*affair*) liaison *f.*
relative /'relətɪv/ *n.* parent(e) *m.* (*f.*). —*a.* relatif; (*respective*) respectif. **~ly** *adv.* relativement.
relax /rɪ'læks/ *v.t./i.* (se) relâcher; (*fig.*) (se) détendre. **~ation**

/riːlæk'seɪʃn/ *n.* relâchement *m.*; détente *f.* **~ing** *a.* délassant.
relay[1] /'riːleɪ/ *n.* relais *m.* **~ race,** course de relais *f.*
relay[2] /rɪ'leɪ/ *v.t.* relayer.
release /rɪ'liːs/ *v.t.* libérer; (*bomb*) lâcher; (*film*) sortir; (*news*) publier; (*smoke*) dégager; (*spring*) déclencher. —*n.* libération *f.*; sortie *f.*; (*record*) nouveau disque *m.*
relegate /'relɪgeɪt/ *v.t.* reléguer.
relent /rɪ'lent/ *v.i.* se laisser fléchir. **~less** *a.* impitoyable.
relevan|t /'reləvənt/ *a.* pertinent. **be ~t to,** avoir rapport à. **~ce** *n.* pertinence *f.*, rapport *m.*
reliab|le /rɪ'laɪəbl/ *a.* sérieux, sûr; (*machine*) fiable. **~ility** /-'bɪlətɪ/ *n.* sérieux *m.*; fiabilité *f.*
reliance /rɪ'laɪəns/ *n.* dépendance *f.*; (*trust*) confiance *f.*
relic /'relɪk/ *n.* relique *f.* **~s,** (*of past*) vestiges *m. pl.*
relief /rɪ'liːf/ *n.* soulagement *m.* (**from,** à); (*assistance*) secours *m.*; (*outline, design*) relief *m.* **~ road,** route de délestage *f.*
relieve /rɪ'liːv/ *v.t.* soulager; (*help*) secourir; (*take over from*) relayer.
religion /rɪ'lɪdʒən/ *n.* religion *f.*
religious /rɪ'lɪdʒəs/ *a.* religieux.
relinquish /rɪ'lɪŋkwɪʃ/ *v.t.* abandonner; (*relax hold of*) lâcher.
relish /'relɪʃ/ *n.* plaisir *m.*, goût *m.*; (*culin.*) assaisonnement *m.* —*v.t.* savourer; (*idea etc.*) aimer.
relocate /riːləʊ'keɪt/ *v.t.* muter. —*v.i.* se déplacer, déménager.
reluctan|t /rɪ'lʌktənt/ *a.* fait, donné, *etc.* à contrecœur. **~t to,** peu disposé à. **~ce** *n.* répugnance *f.* **~tly** *adv.* à contrecœur.
rely /rɪ'laɪ/ *v.i.* **~ on,** compter sur; (*financially*) dépendre de.
remain /rɪ'meɪn/ *v.i.* rester. **~s** *n. pl.* restes *m. pl.*
remainder /rɪ'meɪndə(r)/ *n.* reste *m.*; (*book*) invendu soldé *m.*
remand /rɪ'mɑːnd/ *v.t.* mettre en détention préventive. —*n.* **on ~,** en détention préventive.
remark /rɪ'mɑːk/ *n.* remarque *f.* —*v.t.* remarquer. —*v.i.* **~ on,** faire des commentaires sur. **~able** *a.* remarquable.
remarry /riː'mærɪ/ *v.i.* se remarier.
remed|y /'remədɪ/ *n.* remède *m.* —*v.t.* remédier à. **~ial** /rɪ'miːdɪəl/ *a.* (*class etc.*) de rattrapage; (*treatment: med.*) curatif.
rememb|er /rɪ'membə(r)/ *v.t.* se souvenir de, se rappeler. **~er to do,** ne pas oublier de faire. **~rance** *n.* souvenir *m.*
remind /rɪ'maɪnd/ *v.t.* rappeler (**s.o. of sth.,** qch. à qn.). **~ s.o. to do,** rappeler à qn. qu'il doit faire. **~er** *n.* (*letter, signal*) rappel *m.*
reminisce /remɪ'nɪs/ *v.i.* évoquer ses souvenirs. **~nces** *n. pl.* réminiscences *f. pl.*
reminiscent /remɪ'nɪsnt/ *a.* **~ of,** qui rappelle, qui évoque.
remiss /rɪ'mɪs/ *a.* négligent.
remission /rɪ'mɪʃn/ *n.* rémission *f.*; (*jurid.*) remise (de peine) *f.*
remit /rɪ'mɪt/ *v.t.* (*p.t.* **remitted**) (*money*) envoyer; (*debt*) remettre. **~tance** *n.* paiement *m.*
remnant /'remnənt/ *n.* reste *m.*, débris *m.*; (*trace*) vestige *m.*; (*of cloth*) coupon *m.*
remorse /rɪ'mɔːs/ *n.* remords *m.* (*pl.*). **~ful** *a.* plein de remords. **~less** *a.* implacable.
remote /rɪ'məʊt/ *a.* (*place, time*) lointain; (*person*) distant; (*slight*) vague. **~ control,** télécommande *f.* **~ly** *adv.* au loin; vaguement. **~ness** *n.* éloignement *m.*
removable /rɪ'muːvəbl/ *a.* (*detachable*) amovible.
remov|e /rɪ'muːv/ *v.t.* enlever; (*lead away*) emmener; (*dismiss*) renvoyer; (*do away with*) supprimer. **~al** *n.* enlèvement *m.*; renvoi *m.*; suppression *f.*; (*from*

house) déménagement *m.* **~er** *n.* (*for paint*) décapant *m.*
remunerat|e /rɪ'mjuːnəreɪt/ *v.t.* rémunérer. **~ion** /-'reɪʃn/ *n.* rémunération *f.*
rename /riː'neɪm/ *v.t.* rebaptiser.
rend /rend/ *v.t.* (*p.t.* **rent**) déchirer.
render /'rendə(r)/ *v.t.* (*give, make*) rendre; (*mus.*) interpréter. **~ing** *n.* interprétation *f.*
rendezvous /'rɒndɪvuː/ *n.* (*pl.* **-vous** /-vuːz/) rendez-vous *m. invar.*
renegade /'renɪgeɪd/ *n.* renégat(e) *m.* (*f.*).
renew /rɪ'njuː/ *v.t.* renouveler; (*resume*) reprendre. **~able** *a.* renouvelable. **~al** *n.* renouvellement *m.*; reprise *f.*
renounce /rɪ'naʊns/ *v.t.* renoncer à; (*disown*) renier.
renovat|e /'renəveɪt/ *v.t.* rénover. **~ion** /-'veɪʃn/ *n.* rénovation *f.*
renown /rɪ'naʊn/ *n.* renommée *f.* **~ed** *a.* renommé.
rent[1] /rent/ *see* **rend.**
rent[2] /rent/ *n.* loyer *m.* —*v.t.* louer. **~al** *n.* prix de location *m.*
renunciation /rɪnʌnsɪ'eɪʃn/ *n.* renonciation *f.*
reopen /riː'əʊpən/ *v.t./i.* rouvrir. **~ing** *n.* réouverture *f.*
reorganize /riː'ɔːgənaɪz/ *v.t.* réorganiser.
rep /rep/ *n.* (*comm., fam.*) représentant(e) *m.* (*f.*).
repair /rɪ'peə(r)/ *v.t.* réparer. —*n.* réparation *f.* **in good/bad ~,** en bon/mauvais état.
repartee /repɑː'tiː/ *n.* repartie *f.*
repatriat|e /riː'pætrɪeɪt/ *v.t.* rapatrier. **~ion** /-'eɪʃn/ *n.* rapatriement *m.*
repay /riː'peɪ/ *v.t.* (*p.t.* **repaid**) rembourser; (*reward*) récompenser. **~ment** *n.* remboursement *m.*; récompense *f.*
repeal /rɪ'piːl/ *v.t.* abroger, annuler. —*n.* abrogation *f.*
repeat /rɪ'piːt/ *v.t./i.* répéter; (*renew*) renouveler. —*n.* répétition *f.*; (*broadcast*) reprise *f.* **~ itself, ~ o.s.,** se répéter.
repeatedly /rɪ'piːtɪdlɪ/ *adv.* à maintes reprises.
repel /rɪ'pel/ *v.t.* (*p.t.* **repelled**) repousser. **~lent** *a.* repoussant.
repent /rɪ'pent/ *v.i.* se repentir (**of,** de). **~ance** *n.* repentir *m.* **~ant** *a.* repentant.
repercussion /riːpə'kʌʃn/ *n.* répercussion *f.*
repertoire /'repətwɑː(r)/ *n.* répertoire *m.*
repertory /'repətrɪ/ *n.* répertoire *m.* **~ (theatre),** théâtre de répertoire *m.*
repetit|ion /repɪ'tɪʃn/ *n.* répétition *f.* **~ious** /-'tɪʃəs/, **~ive** /rɪ'petətɪv/ *adjs.* plein de répétitions.
replace /rɪ'pleɪs/ *v.t.* remettre; (*take the place of*) remplacer. **~ment** *n.* remplacement *m.* (**of,** de); (*person*) remplaçant(e) *m.* (*f.*); (*new part*) pièce de rechange *f.*
replay /'riːpleɪ/ *n.* (*sport*) match rejoué *m.*; (*recording*) répétition immédiate *f.*
replenish /rɪ'plenɪʃ/ *v.t.* (*refill*) remplir; (*renew*) renouveler.
replete /rɪ'pliːt/ *a.* (*with food*) rassasié. **~ with,** rempli de.
replica /'replɪkə/ *n.* copie exacte *f.*
reply /rɪ'plaɪ/ *v.t./i.* répondre. —*n.* réponse *f.*
report /rɪ'pɔːt/ *v.t.* rapporter, annoncer (**that,** que); (*notify*) signaler; (*denounce*) dénoncer. —*v.i.* faire un rapport. **~ (on),** (*news item*) faire un reportage sur. **~ to,** (*go*) se présenter chez. —*n.* rapport *m.*; (*in press*) reportage *m.*; (*schol.*) bulletin *m.*; (*sound*) détonation *f.* **~edly** *adv.* selon ce qu'on dit.
reporter /rɪ'pɔːtə(r)/ *n.* reporter *m.*
repose /rɪ'pəʊz/ *n.* repos *m.*

repossess /riːpə'zes/ *v.t.* reprendre possession de.

represent /reprɪ'zent/ *v.t.* représenter. **~ation** /-'teɪʃn/ *n.* représentation *f.* **~ations** /-'teɪʃnz/ *n. pl.* remontrances *f. pl.*

representative /reprɪ'zentətɪv/ *a.* représentatif, typique (**of,** de). —*n.* représentant(e) *m.* (*f.*).

repress /rɪ'pres/ *v.t.* réprimer. **~ion** /-ʃn/ *n.* répression *f.* **~ive** *a.* répressif.

reprieve /rɪ'priːv/ *n.* (*delay*) sursis *m.*; (*pardon*) grâce *f.* —*v.t.* accorder un sursis à; gracier.

reprimand /'reprɪmɑːnd/ *v.t.* réprimander. —*n.* réprimande *f.*

reprint /'riːprɪnt/ *n.* réimpression *f.*; (*offprint*) tiré à part *m.*

reprisals /rɪ'praɪzlz/ *n. pl.* représailles *f. pl.*

reproach /rɪ'prəʊtʃ/ *v.t.* reprocher (**s.o. for sth.,** qch. à qn.). —*n.* reproche *m.* **~ful** *a.* de reproche, réprobateur. **~fully** *adv.* avec reproche.

reproduc|e /riːprə'djuːs/ *v.t./i.* (se) reproduire. **~tion** /-'dʌkʃn/ *n.* reproduction *f.* **~tive** /-'dʌktɪv/ *a.* reproducteur.

reptile /'reptaɪl/ *n.* reptile *m.*

republic /rɪ'pʌblɪk/ *n.* république *f.* **~an** *a.* & *n.* républicain(e) (*m.* (*f.*)).

repudiate /rɪ'pjuːdɪeɪt/ *v.t.* répudier; (*treaty*) refuser d'honorer.

repugnan|t /rɪ'pʌgnənt/ *a.* répugnant. **~ce** *n.* répugnance *f.*

repuls|e /rɪ'pʌls/ *v.t.* repousser. **~ion** /-ʃn/ *n.* répulsion *f.* **~ive** *a.* repoussant.

reputable /'repjʊtəbl/ *a.* honorable, de bonne réputation.

reputation /repjʊ'teɪʃn/ *n.* réputation *f.*

repute /rɪ'pjuːt/ *n.* réputation *f.* **~d** /-ɪd/ *a.* réputé. **~dly** /-ɪdlɪ/ *adv.* d'après ce qu'on dit.

request /rɪ'kwest/ *n.* demande *f.* —*v.t.* demander (**of, from,** à). **~ stop,** arrêt facultatif *m.*

requiem /'rekwɪem/ *n.* requiem *m.*

require /rɪ'kwaɪə(r)/ *v.t.* (*of thing*) demander; (*of person*) avoir besoin de; (*demand, order*) exiger. **~d** *a.* requis. **~ment** *n.* exigence *f.*; (*condition*) condition (requise) *f.*

requisite /'rekwɪzɪt/ *a.* nécessaire. —*n.* chose nécessaire *f.* **~s,** (*for travel etc.*) articles *m. pl.*

requisition /rekwɪ'zɪʃn/ *n.* réquisition *f.* —*v.t.* réquisitionner.

re-route /riː'ruːt/ *v.t.* dérouter.

resale /'riːseɪl/ *n.* revente *f.*

rescind /rɪ'sɪnd/ *v.t.* annuler.

rescue /'reskjuː/ *v.t.* sauver. —*n.* sauvetage *m.* (**of,** de); (*help*) secours *m.* **~r** /-ə(r)/ *n.* sauveteur *m.*

research /rɪ'sɜːtʃ/ *n.* recherche(s) *f.* (*pl.*). —*v.t./i.* faire des recherches (sur). **~er** *n.* chercheu|r, -se *m., f.*

resembl|e /rɪ'zembl/ *v.t.* ressembler à. **~ance** *n.* ressemblance *f.*

resent /rɪ'zent/ *v.t.* être indigné de, s'offenser de. **~ful** *a.* plein de ressentiment, indigné. **~ment** *n.* ressentiment *m.*

reservation /rezə'veɪʃn/ *n.* réserve *f.*; (*booking*) réservation *f.*; (*Amer.*) réserve (indienne) *f.*

reserve /rɪ'zɜːv/ *v.t.* réserver. —*n.* (*reticence, stock, land*) réserve *f.*; (*sport*) remplaçant(e) *m.* (*f.*). **in ~,** en réserve. **the ~s,** (*mil.*) les réserves *f. pl.* **~d** *a.* (*person, room*) réservé.

reservist /rɪ'zɜːvɪst/ *n.* (*mil.*) réserviste *m.*

reservoir /'rezəvwɑː(r)/ *n.* (*lake, supply, etc.*) réservoir *m.*

reshape /riː'ʃeɪp/ *v.t.* remodeler.

reshuffle /riː'ʃʌfl/ *v.t.* (*pol.*) remanier. —*n.* (*pol.*) remaniement (ministériel) *m.*

reside /rɪ'zaɪd/ *v.i.* résider.

residen|t /'rezɪdənt/ *a.* résidant. **be ~t,** résider. —*n.* habitant(e) *m.* (*f.*); (*foreigner*) résident(e) *m.* (*f.*);

(*in hotel*) pensionnaire *m.*/*f.* **~ce** *n.* résidence *f.*; (*of students*) foyer *m.* **in ~ce,** (*doctor*) résidant; (*students*) au foyer.

residential /rezɪ'denʃl/ *a.* résidentiel.

residue /'rezɪdjuː/ *n.* résidu *m.*

resign /rɪ'zaɪn/ *v.t.* abandonner; (*job*) démissionner de. —*v.i.* démissionner. **~ o.s. to,** se résigner à. **~ation** /rezɪg'neɪʃn/ *n.* résignation *f.*; (*from job*) démission *f.* **~ed** *a.* résigné.

resilien|t /rɪ'zɪlɪənt/ *a.* élastique; (*person*) qui a du ressort. **~ce** *n.* élasticité *f.*; ressort *m.*

resin /'rezɪn/ *n.* résine *f.*

resist /rɪ'zɪst/ *v.t.*/*i.* résister (à). **~ance** *n.* résistance *f.* **~ant** *a.* (*med.*) rebelle; (*metal*) résistant.

resolut|e /'rezəluːt/ *a.* résolu. **~ion** /-'luːʃn/ *n.* résolution *f.*

resolve /rɪ'zɒlv/ *v.t.* résoudre (**to do,** de faire). —*n.* résolution *f.* **~d** *a.* résolu (**to do,** à faire).

resonan|t /'rezənənt/ *a.* résonnant. **~ce** *n.* résonance *f.*

resort /rɪ'zɔːt/ *v.i.* **~ to,** avoir recours à. —*n.* (*recourse*) recours *m.*; (*place*) station *f.* **in the last ~,** en dernier ressort.

resound /rɪ'zaʊnd/ *v.i.* retentir (**with,** de). **~ing** *a.* retentissant.

resource /rɪ'sɔːs/ *n.* (*expedient*) ressource *f.* **~s,** (*wealth etc.*) ressources *f. pl.* **~ful** *a.* ingénieux. **~fulness** *n.* ingéniosité *f.*

respect /rɪ'spekt/ *n.* respect *m.*; (*aspect*) égard *m.* —*v.t.* respecter. **with ~ to,** à l'égard de, relativement à. **~ful** *a.* respectueux.

respectab|le /rɪ'spektəbl/ *a.* respectable. **~ility** /-'bɪlətɪ/ *n.* respectabilité *f.* **~ly** *adv.* convenablement.

respective /rɪ'spektɪv/ *a.* respectif. **~ly** *adv.* respectivement.

respiration /respə'reɪʃn/ *n.* respiration *f.*

respite /'resp(a)ɪt/ *n.* répit *m.*

resplendent /rɪ'splendənt/ *a.* resplendissant.

respond /rɪ'spɒnd/ *v.i.* répondre (**to,** à). **~ to,** (*react to*) réagir à.

response /rɪ'spɒns/ *n.* réponse *f.*

responsib|le /rɪ'spɒnsəbl/ *a.* responsable; (*job*) qui comporte des responsabilités. **~ility** /-'bɪlətɪ/ *n.* responsabilité *f.* **~ly** *adv.* de façon responsable.

responsive /rɪ'spɒnsɪv/ *a.* qui réagit bien. **~ to,** sensible à.

rest[1] /rest/ *v.t.*/*i.* (se) reposer; (*lean*) (s')appuyer (**on,** sur); (*be buried, lie*) reposer. —*n.* (*repose*) repos *m.*; (*support*) support *m.*

rest[2] /rest/ *v.i.* (*remain*) demeurer. —*n.* (*remainder*) reste *m.* (**of,** de). **the ~ (of the),** (*others, other*) les autres. **it ~s with him to,** il lui appartient de.

restaurant /'restərɒnt/ *n.* restaurant *m.*

restful /'restfl/ *a.* reposant.

restitution /restɪ'tjuːʃn/ *n.* (*for injury*) compensation *f.*

restive /'restɪv/ *a.* rétif.

restless /'restlɪs/ *a.* agité. **~ly** *adv.* avec agitation, fébrilement.

restor|e /rɪ'stɔː(r)/ *v.t.* rétablir; (*building*) restaurer. **~ation** /restə'reɪʃn/ *n.* rétablissement *m.*

restrain /rɪ'streɪn/ *v.t.* contenir. **~ s.o. from,** retenir qn. de. **~ed** *a.* (*moderate*) mesuré; (*in control of self*) maître de soi. **~t** *n.* contrainte *f.*; (*moderation*) retenue *f.*

restrict /rɪ'strɪkt/ *v.t.* restreindre. **~ion** /-kʃn/ *n.* restriction *f.* **~ive** *a.* restrictif.

restructure /riː'strʌktʃə(r)/ *v.t.* restructurer.

result /rɪ'zʌlt/ *n.* résultat *m.* —*v.i.* résulter. **~ in,** aboutir à.

resum|e /rɪ'zjuːm/ *v.t.*/*i.* reprendre. **~ption** /rɪ'zʌmpʃn/ *n.* reprise *f.*

résumé /'rezjuːmeɪ/ *n.* résumé *m.*

resurgence /rɪ'sɜːdʒəns/ *n.* réapparition *f.*
resurrect /rezə'rekt/ *v.t.* ressusciter. **~ion** /-kʃn/ *n.* résurrection *f.*
resuscitate /rɪ'sʌsɪteɪt/ *v.t.* réanimer.
retail /'riːteɪl/ *n.* détail *m.* —*a.* & *adv.* au détail. —*v.t./i.* (se) vendre au détail. **~er** *n.* détaillant(e) *m.* (*f.*).
retain /rɪ'teɪn/ *v.t.* (*hold back, remember*) retenir; (*keep*) conserver.
retainer /rɪ'teɪnə(r)/ *n.* (*fee to lawyer etc.*) provision *f.*
retaliat|e /rɪ'tælɪeɪt/ *v.i.* riposter. **~ion** /-'eɪʃn/ *n.* représailles *f. pl.*
retarded /rɪ'tɑːdɪd/ *a.* arriéré.
retch /retʃ/ *v.i.* avoir un haut-le-cœur.
retentive /rɪ'tentɪv/ *a.* (*memory*) fidèle. **~ of,** qui retient.
rethink /riː'θɪŋk/ *v.t.* (*p.t.* **rethought**) repenser.
reticen|t /'retɪsnt/ *a.* réticent. **~ce** *n.* réticence *f.*
retina /'retɪnə/ *n.* rétine *f.*
retinue /'retɪnjuː/ *n.* suite *f.*
retire /rɪ'taɪə(r)/ *v.i.* (*from work*) prendre sa retraite; (*withdraw*) se retirer; (*go to bed*) se coucher. —*v.t.* mettre à la retraite. **~d** *a.* retraité. **~ment** *n.* retraite *f.*
retiring /rɪ'taɪərɪŋ/ *a.* réservé.
retort /rɪ'tɔːt/ *v.t./i.* répliquer. —*n.* réplique *f.*
retrace /riː'treɪs/ *v.t.* revenir sur.
retract /rɪ'trækt/ *v.t./i.* (se) rétracter.
retrain /riː'treɪn/ *v.t./i.* (se) recycler.
retreat /rɪ'triːt/ *v.i.* (*mil.*) battre en retraite. —*n.* retraite *f.*
retrial /riː'traɪəl/ *n.* nouveau procès *m.*
retribution /retrɪ'bjuːʃn/ *n.* châtiment *m.*; (*vengeance*) vengeance *f.*
retriev|e /rɪ'triːv/ *v.t.* (*recover*) récupérer; (*restore*) rétablir; (*put right*) réparer. **~al** *n.* récupération *f.*; (*of information*) recherche documentaire *f.* **~er** *n.* (*dog*) chien d'arrêt *m.*
retrograde /'retrəgreɪd/ *a.* rétrograde —*v.i.* rétrograder.
retrospect /'retrəspekt/ *n.* **in ~,** rétrospectivement.
return /rɪ'tɜːn/ *v.i.* (*come back*) revenir; (*go back*) retourner; (*go home*) rentrer. —*v.t.* (*give back*) rendre; (*bring back*) rapporter; (*send back*) renvoyer; (*put back*) remettre. —*n.* retour *m.*; (*yield*) rapport *m.* **~s,** (*comm.*) bénéfices *m. pl.* **in ~ for,** en échange de. **~ match,** match retour *m.* **~ ticket,** aller et retour *m.*
reunion /riː'juːnɪən/ *n.* réunion *f.*
reunite /riːjuː'naɪt/ *v.t.* réunir.
rev /rev/ *n.* (*auto., fam.*) tour *m.* —*v.t./i.* (*p.t.* **revved**). **~ (up),** (*engine: fam.*) (s')emballer.
revamp /riː'væmp/ *v.t.* rénover.
reveal /rɪ'viːl/ *v.t.* révéler; (*allow to appear*) laisser voir. **~ing** *a.* révélateur.
revel /'revl/ *v.i.* (*p.t.* **revelled**) faire bombance. **~ in,** se délecter de. **~ry** *n.* festivités *f. pl.*
revelation /revə'leɪʃn/ *n.* révélation *f.*
revenge /rɪ'vendʒ/ *n.* vengeance *f.*; (*sport*) revanche *f.* —*v.t.* venger.
revenue /'revənjuː/ *n.* revenu *m.*
reverberate /rɪ'vɜːbəreɪt/ *v.i.* (*sound, light*) se répercuter.
revere /rɪ'vɪə(r)/ *v.t.* révérer. **~nce** /'revərəns/ *n.* vénération *f.*
reverend /'revərənd/ *a.* révérend.
reverent /'revərənt/ *a.* respectueux.
reverie /'revərɪ/ *n.* rêverie *f.*
revers|e /rɪ'vɜːs/ *a.* contraire, inverse. —*n.* contraire *m.*; (*back*) revers *m.*, envers *m.*; (*gear*) marche arrière *f.* —*v.t.* (*situation, bucket, etc.*) renverser; (*order*) in-

verser; (*decision*) annuler. —*v.i.* (*auto.*) faire marche arrière. **~al** *n.* renversement *m.*; (*of view*) revirement *m.*

revert /rɪˈvɜːt/ *v.i.* **~ to,** revenir à.

review /rɪˈvjuː/ *n.* (*inspection, magazine*) revue *f.*; (*of book etc.*) critique *f.* —*v.t.* passer en revue; (*situation*) réexaminer; faire la critique de. **~er** *n.* critique *m.*

revile /rɪˈvaɪl/ *v.t.* injurier.

revis|e /rɪˈvaɪz/ *v.t.* réviser. **~ion** /-ɪʒn/ *n.* révision *f.*

revitalize /riːˈvaɪtəlaɪz/ *v.t.* revitaliser, revivifier.

reviv|e /rɪˈvaɪv/ *v.t./i.* ressusciter, (se) ranimer. **~al** *n.* (*resumption*) reprise *f.*; (*of faith*) renouveau *m.*

revoke /rɪˈvəʊk/ *v.t.* révoquer.

revolt /rɪˈvəʊlt/ *v.t./i.* (se) révolter. —*n.* révolte *f.*

revolting /rɪˈvəʊltɪŋ/ *a.* dégoûtant.

revolution /revəˈluːʃn/ *n.* révolution *f.* **~ary** *a.* & *n.* révolutionnaire (*m./f.*). **~ize** *v.t.* révolutionner.

revolv|e /rɪˈvɒlv/ *v.i.* tourner. **~ing door,** tambour *m.*

revolver /rɪˈvɒlvə(r)/ *n.* revolver *m.*

revulsion /rɪˈvʌlʃn/ *n.* dégoût *m.*

reward /rɪˈwɔːd/ *n.* récompense *f.* —*v.t.* récompenser. **~ing** *a.* rémunérateur; (*worthwhile*) qui (en) vaut la peine.

rewrite /riːˈraɪt/ *v.t.* récrire.

rhapsody /ˈræpsədɪ/ *n.* rhapsodie *f.*

rhetoric /ˈretərɪk/ *n.* rhétorique *f.* **~al** /rɪˈtɒrɪkl/ *a.* (de) rhétorique; (*question*) de pure forme.

rheumati|c /ruːˈmætɪk/ *a.* (*pain*) rhumatismal; (*person*) rhumatisant. **~sm** /ˈruːmətɪzəm/ *n.* rhumatisme *m.*

rhinoceros /raɪˈnɒsərəs/ *n.* (*pl.* **-oses**) rhinocéros *m.*

rhubarb /ˈruːbɑːb/ *n.* rhubarbe *f.*

rhyme /raɪm/ *n.* rime *f.*; (*poem*) vers *m. pl.* —*v.t./i.* (faire) rimer.

rhythm /ˈrɪðəm/ *n.* rythme *m.* **~ic(al)** /ˈrɪðmɪk(l)/ *a.* rythmique.

rib /rɪb/ *n.* côte *f.*

ribald /ˈrɪbld/ *a.* grivois.

ribbon /ˈrɪbən/ *n.* ruban *m.* **in ~s,** (*torn pieces*) en lambeaux.

rice /raɪs/ *n.* riz *m.*

rich /rɪtʃ/ *a.* (**-er, -est**) riche. **~es** *n. pl.* richesses *f. pl.* **~ly** *adv.* richement. **~ness** *n.* richesse *f.*

rickety /ˈrɪkətɪ/ *a.* branlant.

ricochet /ˈrɪkəʃeɪ/ *n.* ricochet *m.* —*v.i.* (*p.t.* **ricocheted** /-ʃeɪd/) ricocher.

rid /rɪd/ *v.t.* (*p.t.* **rid,** *pres. p.* **ridding**) débarrasser (**of,** de). **get ~ of,** se débarrasser de.

riddance /ˈrɪdns/ *n.* **good ~!,** bon débarras!

ridden /ˈrɪdn/ *see* **ride.** —*a.* **~ by,** plein de; (*fear*) hanté par. **debt-~** *a.* criblé de dettes.

riddle[1] /ˈrɪdl/ *n.* énigme *f.*

riddle[2] /ˈrɪdl/ *v.t.* **~ with,** (*bullets*) cribler de; (*mistakes*) bourrer de.

ride /raɪd/ *v.i.* (*p.t.* **rode,** *p.p.* **ridden**) aller (à bicyclette, à cheval, *etc.*); (*in car*) rouler. **~ (a horse),** (*go riding as sport*) monter (à cheval). —*v.t.* (*a particular horse*) monter; (*distance*) parcourir. —*n.* promenade *f.*, tour *m.*; (*distance*) trajet *m.* **~r** /-ə(r)/ *n.* caval|ier, -ière *m., f.*; (*cyclist*) cycliste *m./f.*; (*in document*) annexe *f.*

ridge /rɪdʒ/ *n.* arête *f.*, crête *f.*

ridicule /ˈrɪdɪkjuːl/ *n.* ridicule *m.* —*v.t.* ridiculiser.

ridiculous /rɪˈdɪkjʊləs/ *a.* ridicule.

riding /ˈraɪdɪŋ/ *n.* équitation *f.*

rife /raɪf/ *a.* **be ~,** être répandu, sévir. **~ with,** abondant en.

riff-raff /ˈrɪfræf/ *n.* canaille *f.*

rifle /ˈraɪfl/ *n.* fusil *m.* —*v.t.* (*rob*) dévaliser.

rift /rɪft/ *n.* (*crack*) fissure *f.*; (*between people*) désaccord *m.*

rig[1] /rɪg/ *v.t.* (*p.t.* **rigged**) (*equip*) équiper. —*n.* (*for oil*) derrick *m.* **~ out,** habiller. **~-out** *n.* (*fam.*) tenue *f.* **~ up,** (*arrange*) arranger.

rig[2] /rɪg/ *v.t.* (*p.t.* **rigged**) (*election, match, etc.*) truquer.

right /raɪt/ *a.* (*correct*) exact, juste; (*morally*) bon; (*fair*) juste; (*not mistaken*) bon, qu'il faut; (*not left*) droit. **be ~,** (*person*) avoir raison (**to,** de). —*n.* (*entitlement*) droit *m.*; (*not left*) droite *f.*; (*not evil*) le bien —*v.t.* (*a wrong, sth. fallen, etc.*) redresser. —*adv.* (*not left*) à droite; (*directly*) tout droit; (*exactly*) bien, juste; (*completely*) tout (à fait). **be in the ~,** avoir raison. **put ~,** arranger, rectifier. **~ angle,** angle droit *m.* **~ away,** tout de suite. **~-hand** *a.* à *or* de droite. **~-hand man,** bras droit *m.* **~-handed** *a.* droitier. **~ of way,** (*auto.*) priorité *f.* **~-wing** *a.* (*pol.*) de droite.

righteous /ˈraɪtʃəs/ *a.* (*person*) vertueux; (*cause, anger*) juste.

rightful /ˈraɪtfl/ *a.* légitime. **~ly** *adv.* à juste titre.

rightly /ˈraɪtlɪ/ *adv.* correctement; (*with reason*) à juste titre.

rigid /ˈrɪdʒɪd/ *a.* rigide. **~ity** /rɪˈdʒɪdətɪ/ *n.* rigidité *f.*

rigmarole /ˈrɪgmərəʊl/ *n.* charabia *m.*; (*procedure*) comédie *f.*

rig|our /ˈrɪgə(r)/ *n.* rigueur *f.* **~orous** *a.* rigoureux.

rile /raɪl/ *v.t.* (*fam.*) agacer.

rim /rɪm/ *n.* bord *m.*; (*of wheel*) jante *f.* **~med** *a.* bordé.

rind /raɪnd/ *n.* (*on cheese*) croûte *f.*; (*on bacon*) couenne *f.*; (*on fruit*) écorce *f.*

ring[1] /rɪŋ/ *n.* anneau *m.*; (*on finger, with stone*) bague *f.*; (*circle*) cercle *m.*; (*boxing*) ring *m.*; (*arena*) piste *f.* —*v.t.* entourer; (*word in text etc.*) entourer d'un cercle.

ring[2] /rɪŋ/ *v.t./i.* (*p.t.* **rang,** *p.p.* **rung**) sonner; (*of words etc.*) retentir. —*n.* sonnerie *f.*; (*fam.*) coup de téléphone *m.* **~ the bell,** sonner. **~ back,** rappeler. **~ off,** raccrocher. **~ up,** téléphoner (à). **~ing** *n.* (*of bell*) sonnerie *f.* **~ing tone,** tonalité *f.*

ringleader /ˈrɪŋliːdə(r)/ *n.* chef *m.*

rink /rɪŋk/ *n.* patinoire *f.*

rinse /rɪns/ *v.t.* rincer. **~ out,** rincer. —*n.* rinçage *m.*

riot /ˈraɪət/ *n.* émeute *f.*; (*of colours*) orgie *f.* —*v.i.* faire une émeute. **run ~,** se déchaîner. **~er** *n.* émeut|ier, -ière *m., f.*

riotous /ˈraɪətəs/ *a.* turbulent.

rip /rɪp/ *v.t./i.* (*p.t.* **ripped**) (se) déchirer. —*n.* déchirure *f.* **let ~,** (*not check*) laisser courir. **~ off,** (*sl.*) rouler. **~-off** *n.* (*sl.*) vol *m.*

ripe /raɪp/ *a.* (**-er, -est**) mûr. **~ness** *n.* maturité *f.*

ripen /ˈraɪpən/ *v.t./i.* mûrir.

ripple /ˈrɪpl/ *n.* ride *f.*, ondulation *f.*; (*sound*) murmure *m.* —*v.t./i.* (*water*) (se) rider.

rise /raɪz/ *v.i.* (*p.t.* **rose,** *p.p.* **risen**) (*go upwards, increase*) monter, s'élever; (*stand up, get up from bed*) se lever; (*rebel*) se soulever; (*sun, curtain*) se lever. —*n.* (*slope*) pente *f.*; (*of curtain*) lever *m.*; (*increase*) hausse *f.*; (*in pay*) augmentation *f.*; (*progress, boom*) essor *m.* **give ~ to,** donner lieu à. **~r** /-ə(r)/ *n.* **be an early ~r,** se lever tôt.

rising /ˈraɪzɪŋ/ *n.* (*revolt*) soulèvement *m.* —*a.* (*increasing*) croissant; (*price*) qui monte; (*tide*) montant; (*sun*) levant. **~ generation,** nouvelle génération *f.*

risk /rɪsk/ *n.* risque *m.* —*v.t.* risquer. **at ~,** menacé. **~ doing,** (*venture*) se risquer à faire. **~y** *a.* risqué.

rissole /ˈrɪsəʊl/ *n.* croquette *f.*

rite /raɪt/ *n.* rite *m.* **last ~s,** derniers sacrements *m. pl.*
ritual /'rɪtʃʊəl/ *a.* & *n.* rituel (*m.*).
rival /'raɪvl/ *n.* rival(e) *m.* (*f.*). —*a.* rival; (*claim*) opposé. —*v.t.* (*p.t.* **rivalled**) rivaliser avec. **~ry** *n.* rivalité *f.*
river /'rɪvə(r)/ *n.* rivière *f.*; (*flowing into sea & fig.*) fleuve *m.* —*a.* (*fishing, traffic, etc.*) fluvial.
rivet /'rɪvɪt/ *n.* (*bolt*) rivet *m.* —*v.t.* (*p.t.* **riveted**) river, riveter. **~ing** *a.* fascinant.
Riviera /rɪvɪ'eərə/ *n.* **the (French) ~,** la Côte d'Azur.
road /rəʊd/ *n.* route *f.*; (*in town*) rue *f.*; (*small*) chemin *m.* **the ~ to,** (*glory etc.*: *fig.*) le chemin de. **~-hog** *n.* chauffard *m.* **~-map** *n.* carte routière *f.* **~-works** *n. pl.* travaux *m. pl.*
roadside /'rəʊdsaɪd/ *n.* bord de la route *m.*
roadway /'rəʊdweɪ/ *n.* chaussée *f.*
roadworthy /'rəʊdwɜːðɪ/ *a.* en état de marche.
roam /rəʊm/ *v.i.* errer. —*v.t.* (*streets, seas, etc.*) parcourir.
roar /rɔː(r)/ *n.* hurlement *m.*; rugissement *m.*; grondement *m.* —*v.t./i.* hurler; (*of lion, wind*) rugir; (*of lorry, thunder*) gronder.
roaring /'rɔːrɪŋ/ *a.* (*trade, success*) très gros. **~ fire,** belle flambée *f.*
roast /rəʊst/ *v.t./i.* rôtir. —*n.* (*roast or roasting meat*) rôti *m.* —*a.* rôti. **~ beef,** rôti de bœuf *m.*
rob /rɒb/ *v.t.* (*p.t.* **robbed**) voler (**s.o. of sth.,** qch. à qn.); (*bank, house*) dévaliser; (*deprive*) priver (**of,** de). **~ber** *n.* voleu|r, -se *m., f.* **~bery** *n.* vol *m.*
robe /rəʊb/ *n.* (*of judge etc.*) robe *f.*; (*dressing-gown*) peignoir *m.*
robin /'rɒbɪn/ *n.* rouge-gorge *m.*
robot /'rəʊbɒt/ *n.* robot *m.*
robust /rəʊ'bʌst/ *a.* robuste.
rock[1] /rɒk/ *n.* roche *f.*; (*rock face, boulder*) rocher *m.*; (*hurled stone*) pierre *f.*; (*sweet*) sucre d'orge *m.* **on the ~s,** (*drink*) avec des glaçons; (*marriage*) en crise. **~-bottom** *a.* (*fam.*) très bas.
rock[2] /rɒk/ *v.t./i.* (se) balancer; (*shake*) (faire) trembler; (*child*) bercer. —*n.* (*mus.*) rock *m.* **~ing-chair** *n.* fauteuil à bascule *m.*
rockery /'rɒkərɪ/ *n.* rocaille *f.*
rocket /'rɒkɪt/ *n.* fusée *f.*
rocky /'rɒkɪ/ *a.* (**-ier, -iest**) (*ground*) rocailleux; (*hill*) rocheux; (*shaky*: *fig.*) branlant.
rod /rɒd/ *n.* (*metal*) tige *f.*; (*for curtain*) tringle *f.*; (*wooden*) baguette *f.*; (*for fishing*) canne à pêche *f.*
rode /rəʊd/ *see* **ride.**
rodent /'rəʊdnt/ *n.* rongeur *m.*
rodeo /rəʊ'deɪəʊ, *Amer.* 'rəʊdɪəʊ/ *n.* (*pl.* **-os**) rodéo *m.*
roe[1] /rəʊ/ *n.* œufs de poisson *m. pl.*
roe[2] /rəʊ/ *n.* (*pl.* **roe** *or* **roes**) (*deer*) chevreuil *m.*
rogu|e /rəʊg/ *n.* (*dishonest*) bandit, voleu|r, -se *m.*; (*mischievous*) coquin(e) *m.* (*f.*). **~ish** *a.* coquin.
role /rəʊl/ *n.* rôle *m.*
roll /rəʊl/ *v.t./i.* rouler. **~ (about),** (*child, dog*) se rouler. —*n.* rouleau *m.*; (*list*) liste *f.*; (*bread*) petit pain *m.*; (*of drum, thunder*) roulement *m.*; (*of ship*) roulis *m.* **be ~ing (in money),** (*fam.*) rouler sur l'or. **~-call** *n.* appel *m.* **~ing-pin** *n.* rouleau à pâtisserie *m.* **~ over,** (*turn over*) se retourner. **~ up** *v.t.* (*sleeves*) retrousser; *v.i.* (*fam.*) s'amener.
roller /'rəʊlə(r)/ *n.* rouleau *m.* **~-coaster** *n.* montagnes russes *f. pl.* **~-skate** *n.* patin à roulettes *m.*
rollicking /'rɒlɪkɪŋ/ *a.* exubérant.
rolling /'rəʊlɪŋ/ *a.* onduleux.
Roman /'rəʊmən/ *a.* & *n.* romain(e) (*m.* (*f.*)). **~ Catholic** *a.* & *n.* catholique (*m./f.*). **~ numerals,** chiffres romains *m. pl.*
romance /rə'mæns/ *n.* roman

d'amour *m.*; (*love*) amour *m.*; (*affair*) idylle *f.*; (*fig.*) poésie *f.*
romantic /rə'mæntɪk/ *a.* (*of love etc.*) romantique; (*of the imagination*) romanesque. **~ally** *adv.* (*behave*) en romantique.
Romania /rəʊ'meɪnɪə/ *n.* Roumanie *f.* **~n** *a.* & *n.* roumain(e) (*m.* (*f.*)).
romp /rɒmp/ *v.i.* s'ébattre; (*fig.*) réussir. *—n.* ébats *m. pl.*
roof /ruːf/ *n.* (*pl.* **roofs**) toit *m.*; (*of tunnel*) plafond *m.*; (*of mouth*) palais *m.* *—v.t.* recouvrir. **~ing** *n.* toiture *f.* **~-rack** *n.* galerie *f.* **~-top** *n.* toit *m.*
rook[1] /rʊk/ *n.* (*bird*) corneille *f.*
rook[2] /rʊk/ *n.* (*chess*) tour *f.*
room /ruːm/ *n.* pièce *f.*; (*bedroom*) chambre *f.*; (*large hall*) salle *f.*; (*space*) place *f.* **~s,** meublé *m.* **~y** *a.* spacieux; (*clothes*) ample.
roost /ruːst/ *n.* perchoir *m.* *—v.i.* percher. **~er** /'ruːstə(r)/ *n.* coq *m.*
root[1] /ruːt/ *n.* racine *f.*; (*source*) origine *f.* *—v.t./i.* (s')enraciner. **~ out,** extirper. **take ~,** prendre racine. **~less** *a.* sans racines.
root[2] /ruːt/ *v.i.* **~ about,** fouiller. **~ for,** (*Amer., fam.*) encourager.
rope /rəʊp/ *n.* corde *f.* *—v.t.* attacher. **know the ~s,** être au courant. **~ in,** (*person*) enrôler.
rosary /'rəʊzərɪ/ *n.* chapelet *m.*
rose[1] /rəʊz/ *n.* (*flower*) rose *f.*; (*colour*) rose *m.*; (*nozzle*) pomme *f.*
rose[2] /rəʊz/ *see* **rise.**
rosé /'rəʊzeɪ/ *n.* rosé *m.*
rosette /rəʊ'zet/ *n.* (*sport*) cocarde *f.*; (*officer's*) rosette *f.*
roster /'rɒstə(r)/ *n.* liste (de service) *f.*, tableau (de service) *m.*
rostrum /'rɒstrəm/ *n.* (*pl.* **-tra**) tribune *f.*; (*sport*) podium *m.*
rosy /'rəʊzɪ/ *a.* (**-ier, -iest**) rose; (*hopeful*) plein d'espoir.
rot /rɒt/ *v.t./i.* (*p.t.* **rotted**) pourrir. *—n.* pourriture *f.*; (*nonsense: sl.*) bêtises *f. pl.*, âneries *f. pl.*
rota /'rəʊtə/ *n.* liste (de service) *f.*
rotary /'rəʊtərɪ/ *a.* rotatif.
rotat|e /rəʊ'teɪt/ *v.t./i.* (faire) tourner; (*change round*) alterner. **~ion** /-ʃn/ *n.* rotation *f.*
rote /rəʊt/ *n.* **by ~,** machinalement.
rotten /'rɒtn/ *a.* pourri; (*tooth*) gâté; (*bad: fam.*) mauvais, sale.
rotund /rəʊ'tʌnd/ *a.* rond.
rouge /ruːʒ/ *n.* rouge (à joues) *m.*
rough /rʌf/ *a.* (**-er, -est**) rude; (*to touch*) rugueux; (*ground*) accidenté; (*violent*) brutal; (*bad*) mauvais; (*estimate etc.*) approximatif; (*diamond*) brut. *—adv.* (*live*) à la dure; (*play*) brutalement. *—n.* (*ruffian*) voyou *m.* *—v.t.* **~ it,** vivre à la dure. **~-and-ready** *a.* (*solution etc.*) grossier (mais efficace). **~-and-tumble** *n.* mêlée *f.* **~ out,** ébaucher. **~ paper,** papier brouillon *m.* **~ly** *adv.* rudement; (*approximately*) à peu près. **~ness** *n.* rudesse *f.*; brutalité *f.*
roughage /'rʌfɪdʒ/ *n.* fibres (alimentaires) *f. pl.*
roulette /ruː'let/ *n.* roulette *f.*
round /raʊnd/ *a.* (**-er, -est**) rond. *—n.* (*circle*) rond *m.*; (*slice*) tranche *f.*; (*of visits, drinks*) tournée *f.*; (*mil.*) ronde *f.*; (*competition*) partie *f.*, manche *f.*; (*boxing*) round *m.*; (*of talks*) série *f.* *—prep.* autour de. *—adv.* autour. *—v.t.* (*object*) arrondir; (*corner*) tourner. **go** *or* **come ~ to,** (*a friend etc.*) passer chez. **~ about,** (*near by*) par ici; (*fig.*) à peu près. **~ of applause,** applaudissements *m. pl.* **~ off,** terminer. **~ the clock,** vingt-quatre heures sur vingt-quatre. **~ up,** rassembler. **~-up** *n.* rassemblement *m.*; (*of suspects*) rafle *f.*
roundabout /'raʊndəbaʊt/ *n.* manège *m.*; (*for traffic*) rond-point (à sens giratoire) *m.* *—a.* indirect.

rounders /ˈraʊndəz/ *n.* sorte de base-ball *f.*
roundly /ˈraʊndlɪ/ *adv.* (*bluntly*) franchement.
rous|e /raʊz/ *v.t.* éveiller. **be ~ed,** (*angry*) être en colère. **~ing** *a.* (*speech, music*) excitant; (*cheers*) frénétique.
rout /raʊt/ *n.* (*defeat*) déroute *f.* —*v.t.* mettre en déroute.
route /ruːt/ *n.* itinéraire *m.*, parcours *m.*; (*naut., aviat.*) route *f.*
routine /ruːˈtiːn/ *n.* routine *f.* —*a.* de routine. **daily ~,** travail quotidien *m.*
rov|e /rəʊv/ *v.t./i.* errer (dans). **~ing** *a.* (*life*) vagabond.
row[1] /rəʊ/ *n.* rangée *f.*, rang *m.* **in a ~,** (*consecutive*) consécutif.
row[2] /rəʊ/ *v.i.* ramer. —*v.t.* faire aller à la rame. **~ing** *n.* canotage *m.* **~(ing)-boat** *n.* bateau à rames *m.*
row[3] /raʊ/ *n.* (*noise: fam.*) tapage *m.*; (*quarrel: fam.*) engueulade *f.* —*v.i.* (*fam.*) s'engueuler.
rowdy /ˈraʊdɪ/ *a.* **(-ier, -iest)** tapageur. —*n.* voyou *m.*
royal /ˈrɔɪəl/ *a.* royal. **~ly** *adv.* (*treat, live, etc.*) royalement.
royalty /ˈrɔɪəltɪ/ *n.* famille royale *f.*; (*payment*) droits d'auteur *m. pl.*
rub /rʌb/ *v.t./i.* (*p.t.* **rubbed**) frotter. —*n.* friction *f.* **~ it in,** insister là-dessus. **~ off on,** déteindre sur. **~ out,** (s')effacer.
rubber /ˈrʌbə(r)/ *n.* caoutchouc *m.*; (*eraser*) gomme *f.* **~ band,** élastique *m.* **~ stamp,** tampon *m.* **~-stamp** *v.t.* approuver. **~y** *a.* caoutchouteux.
rubbish /ˈrʌbɪʃ/ *n.* (*refuse*) ordures *f. pl.*; (*junk*) saletés *f. pl.*; (*fig.*) bêtises *f. pl.* **~y** *a.* sans valeur.
rubble /ˈrʌbl/ *n.* décombres *m. pl.*
ruby /ˈruːbɪ/ *n.* rubis *m.*
rucksack /ˈrʌksæk/ *n.* sac à dos *m.*
rudder /ˈrʌdə(r)/ *n.* gouvernail *m.*
ruddy /ˈrʌdɪ/ *a.* **(-ier, -iest)** coloré, rougeâtre; (*damned: sl.*) fichu.
rude /ruːd/ *a.* **(-er, -est)** impoli, grossier; (*improper*) indécent; (*shock, blow*) brutal. **~ly** *adv.* impoliment. **~ness** *n.* impolitesse *f.*; indécence *f.*; brutalité *f.*
rudiment /ˈruːdɪmənt/ *n.* rudiment *m.* **~ary** /-ˈmentrɪ/ *a.* rudimentaire.
rueful /ˈruːfl/ *a.* triste.
ruffian /ˈrʌfɪən/ *n.* voyou *m.*
ruffle /ˈrʌfl/ *v.t.* (*hair*) ébouriffer; (*clothes*) froisser; (*person*) contrarier. —*n.* (*frill*) ruche *f.*
rug /rʌg/ *n.* petit tapis *m.*
Rugby /ˈrʌgbɪ/ *n.* **~ (football),** rugby *m.*
rugged /ˈrʌgɪd/ *a.* (*surface*) rude, rugueux; (*ground*) accidenté; (*character, features*) rude.
ruin /ˈruːɪn/ *n.* ruine *f.* —*v.t.* (*destroy*) ruiner; (*damage*) abîmer; (*spoil*) gâter. **~ous** *a.* ruineux.
rule /ruːl/ *n.* règle *f.*; (*regulation*) règlement *m.*; (*pol.*) gouvernement *m.* —*v.t.* gouverner; (*master*) dominer; (*decide*) décider. —*v.i.* régner. **as a ~,** en règle générale. **~ out,** exclure. **~d paper,** papier réglé *m.* **~r** /-ə(r)/ *n.* dirigeant(e) *m.* (*f.*), gouvernant *m.*; (*measure*) règle *f.* **ruling** *a.* (*class*) dirigeant; *n.* décision *f.*
rum /rʌm/ *n.* rhum *m.*
rumble /ˈrʌmbl/ *v.i.* gronder; (*stomach*) gargouiller. —*n.* grondement *m.*; gargouillement *m.*
rummage /ˈrʌmɪdʒ/ *v.i.* fouiller.
rumour /ˈruːmə(r)/ *n.* bruit *m.*, rumeur *f.* —*v.t.* **it is ~ed that,** le bruit court que.
rump /rʌmp/ *n.* (*of horse etc.*) croupe *f.*; (*of fowl*) croupion *m.*
rumpus /ˈrʌmpəs/ *n.* (*uproar: fam.*) chahut *m.*
run /rʌn/ *v.i.* (*p.t.* **ran,** *p.p.* **run,** *pres. p.* **running**) courir; (*flow*)

couler; (*pass*) passer; (*function*) marcher; (*melt*) fondre; (*extend*) s'étendre; (*of bus etc.*) circuler; (*of play*) se jouer; (*last*) durer; (*of colour in washing*) déteindre; (*in election*) être candidat. —*v.t.* (*manage*) diriger; (*risk, race*) courir; (*house*) tenir; (*blockade*) forcer; (*temperature, errand*) faire; (*drive*) conduire, transporter; (*pass*) passer; (*present*) présenter. —*n.* course *f.*; (*journey*) parcours *m.*; (*outing*) promenade *f.*; (*rush*) ruée *f.*; (*series*) série *f.*; (*in cricket*) point *m.* **have the ~ of,** avoir à sa disposition. **in the long ~,** avec le temps. **on the ~,** en fuite. **~ across,** rencontrer par hasard. **~ away,** s'enfuir. **~ down,** descendre en courant; (*of vehicle*) renverser; (*belittle*) dénigrer. **be ~ down,** (*weak etc.*) être sans forces *or* mal fichu. **~ in,** (*vehicle*) roder. **~ into,** (*hit*) heurter. **~ off,** (*copies*) tirer. **~-of-the-mill** *a.* ordinaire. **~ out,** (*be used up*) s'épuiser; (*of lease*) expirer. **~ out of,** manquer de. **~ over,** (*of vehicle*) écraser. **~ up,** (*bill*) laisser accumuler. **the ~-up to,** la période qui précède.

runaway /'rʌnəweɪ/ *n.* fugiti|f, -ve *m., f.* —*a.* fugitif; (*horse, vehicle*) fou; (*inflation*) galopant.

rung[1] /rʌŋ/ *n.* (*of ladder*) barreau *m.*

rung[2] /rʌŋ/ *see* **ring**[2].

runner /'rʌnə(r)/ *n.* coureu|r, -se *m., f.* **~ bean,** haricot (grimpant) *m.* **~-up** *n.* second(e) *m.* (*f.*).

running /'rʌnɪŋ/ *n.* course *f.* —*a.* (*commentary*) suivi; (*water*) courant. **be in the ~,** avoir des chances de réussir. **four days**/*etc.* **~,** quatre jours/*etc.* de suite.

runny /'rʌnɪ/ *a.* (*nose*) qui coule.

runt /rʌnt/ *n.* avorton *m.*

runway /'rʌnweɪ/ *n.* piste *f.*

rupture /'rʌptʃə(r)/ *n.* (*breaking, breach*) rupture *f.*; (*med.*) hernie *f.* —*v.t./i.* (se) rompre. **~ o.s.,** se donner une hernie.

rural /'rʊərəl/ *a.* rural.

ruse /ruːz/ *n.* (*trick*) ruse *f.*

rush[1] /rʌʃ/ *n.* (*plant*) jonc *m.*

rush[2] /rʌʃ/ *v.i.* (*move*) se précipiter; (*be in a hurry*) se dépêcher. —*v.t.* faire, envoyer, *etc.* en vitesse; (*person*) bousculer; (*mil.*) prendre d'assaut. —*n.* ruée *f.*; (*haste*) bousculade *f.* **in a ~,** pressé. **~-hour** *n.* heure de pointe *f.*

rusk /rʌsk/ *n.* biscotte *f.*

russet /'rʌsɪt/ *a.* roussâtre, roux.

Russia /'rʌʃə/ *n.* Russie *f.* **~n** *a.* & *n.* russe (*m.*/*f.*); (*lang.*) russe *m.*

rust /rʌst/ *n.* rouille *f.* —*v.t./i.* rouiller. **~-proof** *a.* inoxydable. **~y** *a.* (*tool, person, etc.*) rouillé.

rustic /'rʌstɪk/ *a.* rustique.

rustle /'rʌsl/ *v.t./i.* (*leaves*) (faire) bruire; (*steal*: *Amer.*) voler. **~ up,** (*food etc.*: *fam.*) préparer.

rut /rʌt/ *n.* ornière *f.* **be in a ~,** rester dans l'ornière.

ruthless /'ruːθlɪs/ *a.* impitoyable. **~ness** *n.* cruauté *f.*

rye /raɪ/ *n.* seigle *m.*; (*whisky*) whisky *m.* (*à base de seigle*).

S

sabbath /'sæbəθ/ *n.* (*Jewish*) sabbat *m.*; (*Christian*) dimanche *m.*

sabbatical /sə'bætɪkl/ *a.* (*univ.*) sabbatique.

sabot|age /'sæbətɑːʒ/ *n.* sabotage *m.* —*v.t.* saboter. **~eur** /-'tɜː(r)/ *n.* saboteu|r, -se *m., f.*

saccharin /'sækərɪn/ *n.* saccharine *f.*

sachet /'sæʃeɪ/ *n.* sachet *m.*

sack[1] /sæk/ *n.* (*bag*) sac *m.* —*v.t.* (*fam.*) renvoyer. **get the ~,** (*fam.*) être renvoyé. **~ing** *n.* toile à sac *f.*; (*dismissal*: *fam.*) renvoi *m.*

sack² /sæk/ *v.t.* (*plunder*) saccager.
sacrament /'sækrəmənt/ *n.* sacrement *m.*
sacred /'seɪkrɪd/ *a.* sacré.
sacrifice /'sækrɪfaɪs/ *n.* sacrifice *m.* —*v.t.* sacrifier.
sacrileg|e /'sækrɪlɪdʒ/ *n.* sacrilège *m.* **~ious** /-'lɪdʒəs/ *a.* sacrilège.
sacrosanct /'sækrəʊsæŋkt/ *a.* sacro-saint.
sad /sæd/ *a.* **(sadder, saddest)** triste. **~ly** *adv.* tristement; (*unfortunately*) malheureusement. **~ness** *n.* tristesse *f.*
sadden /'sædn/ *v.t.* attrister.
saddle /'sædl/ *n.* selle *f.* —*v.t.* (*horse*) seller. **~ s.o. with,** (*task, person*) coller à qn. **in the ~,** bien en selle. **~-bag** *n.* sacoche *f.*
sadis|t /'seɪdɪst/ *n.* sadique *m./f.* **~m** /-zəm/ *n.* sadisme *m.* **~tic** /sə'dɪstɪk/ *a.* sadique.
safari /sə'fɑːrɪ/ *n.* safari *m.*
safe /seɪf/ *a.* **(-er, ~est)** (*not dangerous*) sans danger; (*reliable*) sûr; (*out of danger*) en sécurité; (*after accident*) sain et sauf; (*wise: fig.*) prudent. —*n.* coffre-fort *m.* **in ~ keeping,** en sécurité. **~ conduct,** sauf-conduit *m.* **~ from,** à l'abri de. **~ly** *adv.* sans danger; (*in safe place*) en sûreté.
safeguard /'seɪfgɑːd/ *n.* sauvegarde *f.* —*v.t.* sauvegarder.
safety /'seɪftɪ/ *n.* sécurité *f.* **~-pin** *n.* épingle de sûreté *f.* **~-valve** *n.* soupape de sûreté *f.*
saffron /'sæfrən/ *n.* safran *m.*
sag /sæg/ *v.i.* (*p.t.* **sagged**) s'affaisser, fléchir. **~ging** *a.* affaissé.
saga /'sɑːgə/ *n.* saga *f.*
sage¹ /seɪdʒ/ *n.* (*herb*) sauge *f.*
sage² /seɪdʒ/ *a.* & *n.* sage (*m.*).
sago /'seɪgəʊ/ *n.* (*pl.* **-os**) sagou *m.*
said /sed/ *see* **say.**
sail /seɪl/ *n.* voile *f.*; (*journey*) tour en bateau *m.* —*v.i.* naviguer; (*leave*) partir; (*sport*) faire de la voile; (*glide*) glisser. —*v.t.* (*boat*) piloter. **~ing-boat, ~ing-ship** *ns.* bateau à voiles *m.*
sailor /'seɪlə(r)/ *n.* marin *m.*
saint /seɪnt/ *n.* saint(e) *m.* (*f.*). **~ly** *a.* (*person, act, etc.*) saint.
sake /seɪk/ *n.* **for the ~ of,** pour, pour l'amour de.
salad /'sæləd/ *n.* salade *f.* **~-dressing** *n.* sauce de salade *f.*
salami /sə'lɑːmɪ/ *n.* salami *m.*
salar|y /'sælərɪ/ *n.* traitement *m.*, salaire *m.* **~ied** *a.* salarié.
sale /seɪl/ *n.* vente *f.* **~s,** (*at reduced prices*) soldes *m. pl.* **for ~,** à vendre. **on ~,** en vente; (*at a reduced price: Amer.*) en solde.
saleable /'seɪləbl/ *a.* vendable.
sales|man /'seɪlzmən/ *n.* (*pl.* **-men**) (*in shop*) vendeur *m.*; (*traveller*) représentant *m.* **~woman** *n.* (*pl.* **-women**) vendeuse *f.*; représentante *f.*
salient /'seɪlɪənt/ *a.* saillant.
saliva /sə'laɪvə/ *n.* salive *f.*
sallow /'sæləʊ/ *a.* **(-er, -est)** (*complexion*) jaunâtre.
salmon /'sæmən/ *n. invar.* saumon *m.*
salon /'sælɒn/ *n.* salon *m.*
saloon /sə'luːn/ *n.* (*on ship*) salon *m.*; (*bar: Amer.*) bar *m.*, saloon *m.* **~ (car),** berline *f.*
salt /sɔːlt/ *n.* sel *m.* —*a.* (*culin.*) salé. —*v.t.* saler. **~-cellar** *n.* salière *f.* **~y** *a.* salé.
salutary /'sæljʊtrɪ/ *a.* salutaire.
salute /sə'luːt/ *n.* (*mil.*) salut *m.* —*v.t.* saluer. —*v.i.* faire un salut.
salvage /'sælvɪdʒ/ *n.* sauvetage *m.*; (*of waste*) récupération *f.*; (*goods*) objets sauvés *m. pl.* —*v.t.* sauver; (*for re-use*) récupérer.
salvation /sæl'veɪʃn/ *n.* salut *m.*
salvo /'sælvəʊ/ *n.* (*pl.* **-oes**) salve *f.*
same /seɪm/ *a.* même **(as,** que). —*pron.* **the ~,** le *or* la même, les mêmes. **at the ~ time,** en même temps. **the ~ (thing),** la même chose.

sample /'sɑːmpl/ *n.* échantillon *m.* —*v.t.* essayer; (*food*) goûter.

sanatorium /sænə'tɔːrɪəm/ *n.* (*pl.* **-iums**) sanatorium *m.*

sanctify /'sæŋktɪfaɪ/ *v.t.* sanctifier.

sanctimonious /sæŋktɪ'məʊnɪəs/ *a.* (*person*) bigot; (*air, tone*) de petit saint.

sanction /'sæŋkʃn/ *n.* sanction *f.* —*v.t.* sanctionner.

sanctity /'sæŋktətɪ/ *n.* sainteté *f.*

sanctuary /'sæŋktʃʊərɪ/ *n.* (*relig.*) sanctuaire *m.*; (*for animals*) réserve *f.*; (*refuge*) asile *m.*

sand /sænd/ *n.* sable *m.* **~s,** (*beach*) plage *f.* —*v.t.* sabler. **~-castle** *n.* château de sable *m.*

sandal /'sændl/ *n.* sandale *f.*

sandpaper /'sændpeɪpə(r)/ *n.* papier de verre *m.* —*v.t.* poncer.

sandwich /'sænwɪdʒ/ *n.* sandwich *m.* —*v.t.* **~ed between,** pris en sandwich entre.

sandy /'sændɪ/ *a.* sablonneux, de sable; (*hair*) blond roux *invar.*

sane /seɪn/ *a.* (**-er, -est**) (*view etc.*) sain; (*person*) sain d'esprit. **~ly** *adv.* sainement.

sang /sæŋ/ *see* **sing.**

sanitary /'sænɪtrɪ/ *a.* (*clean*) hygiénique; (*system etc.*) sanitaire.

sanitation /sænɪ'teɪʃn/ *n.* hygiène (publique) *f.*; (*drainage etc.*) système sanitaire *m.*

sanity /'sænətɪ/ *n.* santé mentale *f.*; (*good sense: fig.*) bon sens *m.*

sank /sæŋk/ *see* **sink.**

Santa Claus /'sæntəklɔːz/ *n.* le père Noël *m.*

sap /sæp/ *n.* (*of plants*) sève *f.* —*v.t.* (*p.t.* **sapped**) (*undermine*) saper.

sapphire /'sæfaɪə(r)/ *n.* saphir *m.*

sarcas|m /'sɑːkæzəm/ *n.* sarcasme *m.* **~tic** /sɑː'kæstɪk/ *a.* sarcastique.

sardine /sɑː'diːn/ *n.* sardine *f.*

Sardinia /sɑː'dɪnɪə/ *n.* Sardaigne *f.*

sardonic /sɑː'dɒnɪk/ *a.* sardonique.

sash /sæʃ/ *n.* (*on uniform*) écharpe *f.*; (*on dress*) ceinture *f.*

sat /sæt/ *see* **sit.**

satanic /sə'tænɪk/ *a.* satanique.

satchel /'sætʃl/ *n.* cartable *m.*

satellite /'sætəlaɪt/ *n.* & *a.* satellite (*m.*).

satiate /'seɪʃɪeɪt/ *v.t.* rassasier.

satin /'sætɪn/ *n.* satin *m.*

satir|e /'sætaɪə(r)/ *n.* satire *f.* **~ical** /sə'tɪrɪkl/ *a.* satirique.

satiri|ze /'sætəraɪz/ *v.t.* faire la satire de. **~st** /-ɪst/ *n.* écrivain satirique *m.*

satisfactor|y /sætɪs'fæktərɪ/ *a.* satisfaisant. **~ily** *adv.* d'une manière satisfaisante.

satisf|y /'sætɪsfaɪ/ *v.t.* satisfaire; (*convince*) convaincre. **~action** /-'fækʃn/ *n.* satisfaction *f.* **~ying** *a.* satisfaisant.

satsuma /sæt'suːmə/ *n.* mandarine *f.*

saturat|e /'sætʃəreɪt/ *v.t.* saturer. **~ed** *a.* (*wet*) trempé. **~ion** /-'reɪʃn/ *n.* saturation *f.*

Saturday /'sætədɪ/ *n.* samedi *m.*

sauce /sɔːs/ *n.* sauce *f.*; (*impudence: sl.*) toupet *m.*

saucepan /'sɔːspən/ *n.* casserole *f.*

saucer /'sɔːsə(r)/ *n.* soucoupe *f.*

saucy /'sɔːsɪ/ *a.* (**-ier, -iest**) impertinent; (*boldly smart*) coquin.

Saudi Arabia /saʊdɪə'reɪbɪə/ *n.* Arabie Séoudite *f.*

sauerkraut /'saʊəkraʊt/ *n.* choucroute *f.*

sauna /'sɔːnə/ *n.* sauna *m.*

saunter /'sɔːntə(r)/ *v.i.* flâner.

sausage /'sɒsɪdʒ/ *n.* saucisse *f.*; (*pre-cooked*) saucisson *m.*

savage /'sævɪdʒ/ *a.* (*fierce*) féroce; (*wild*) sauvage. —*n.* sauvage *m./f.* —*v.t.* attaquer férocement. **~ry** *n.* sauvagerie *f.*

sav|e /seɪv/ *v.t.* sauver; (*money, time*) économiser, épargner; (*keep*) garder; (*prevent*) éviter (**from,** de). —*n.* (*football*) arrêt *m.*

—*prep.* sauf. **~er** *n.* épargnant(e) *m.* (*f.*). **~ing** *n.* (*of time, money*) économie *f.* **~ings** *n. pl.* économies *f. pl.*

saviour /ˈseɪvɪə(r)/ *n.* sauveur *m.*

savour /ˈseɪvə(r)/ *n.* saveur *f.* —*v.t.* savourer. **~y** *a.* (*tasty*) savoureux; (*culin.*) salé.

saw[1] /sɔː/ *see* **see**[1].

saw[2] /sɔː/ *n.* scie *f.* —*v.t.* (*p.t.* **sawed,** *p.p.* **sawn** /sɔːn/ *or* **sawed**) scier.

sawdust /ˈsɔːdʌst/ *n.* sciure *f.*

saxophone /ˈsæksəfəʊn/ *n.* saxophone *m.*

say /seɪ/ *v.t./i.* (*p.t.* **said** /sed/) dire; (*prayer*) faire. —*n.* **have a ~,** dire son mot; (*in decision*) avoir voix au chapitre. **I ~!,** dites donc!

saying /ˈseɪɪŋ/ *n.* proverbe *m.*

scab /skæb/ *n.* (*on sore*) croûte *f.*; (*blackleg: fam.*) jaune *m.*

scaffold /ˈskæfəʊld/ *n.* (*gallows*) échafaud *m.* **~ing** /-əldɪŋ/ *n.* (*for workmen*) échafaudage *m.*

scald /skɔːld/ *v.t.* (*injure, cleanse*) ébouillanter. —*n.* brûlure *f.*

scale[1] /skeɪl/ *n.* (*of fish*) écaille *f.*

scale[2] /skeɪl/ *n.* (*for measuring, size, etc.*) échelle *f.*; (*mus.*) gamme *f.* —*v.t.* (*climb*) escalader. **~ down,** réduire (proportionnellement).

scales /skeɪlz/ *n. pl.* (*for weighing*) balance *f.*

scallop /ˈskɒləp/ *n.* coquille Saint-Jacques *f.*

scalp /skælp/ *n.* cuir chevelu *m.* —*v.t.* (*mutilate*) scalper.

scalpel /ˈskælp(ə)l/ *n.* scalpel *m.*

scamp /skæmp/ *n.* coquin(e) *m.*(*f.*).

scamper /ˈskæmpə(r)/ *v.i.* courir, trotter. **~ away,** détaler.

scampi /ˈskæmpɪ/ *n. pl.* grosses crevettes *f. pl.*, gambas *f. pl.*

scan /skæn/ *v.t.* (*p.t.* **scanned**) scruter; (*quickly*) parcourir; (*poetry*) scander; (*of radar*) balayer.

scandal /ˈskændl/ *n.* (*disgrace, outrage*) scandale *m.*; (*gossip*) cancans *m. pl.* **~ous** *a.* scandaleux.

scandalize /ˈskændəlaɪz/ *v.t.* scandaliser.

Scandinavia /skændɪˈneɪvɪə/ *n.* Scandinavie *f.* **~n** *a.* & *n.* scandinave (*m.*/*f.*).

scant /skænt/ *a.* insuffisant.

scant|y /ˈskæntɪ/ *a.* (**-ier, -iest**) insuffisant; (*clothing*) sommaire. **~ily** *adv.* insuffisamment. **~ily dressed,** à peine vêtu.

scapegoat /ˈskeɪpgəʊt/ *n.* bouc émissaire *m.*

scar /skɑː(r)/ *n.* cicatrice *f.* —*v.t.* (*p.t.* **scarred**) marquer d'une cicatrice; (*fig.*) marquer.

scarc|e /skeəs/ *a.* (**-er, -est**) rare. **make o.s. ~e,** (*fam.*) se sauver. **~ity** *n.* rareté *f.*, pénurie *f.*

scarcely /ˈskeəslɪ/ *adv.* à peine.

scare /ˈskeə(r)/ *v.t.* faire peur à. —*n.* peur *f.* **be ~d,** avoir peur. **bomb ~,** alerte à la bombe *f.*

scarecrow /ˈskeəkrəʊ/ *n.* épouvantail *m.*

scaremonger /ˈskeəmʌŋgə(r)/ *n.* alarmiste *m.*/*f.*

scarf /skɑːf/ *n.* (*pl.* **scarves**) écharpe *f.*; (*over head*) foulard *m.*

scarlet /ˈskɑːlət/ *a.* écarlate. **~ fever,** scarlatine *f.*

scary /ˈskeərɪ/ *a.* (**-ier, -iest**) (*fam.*) qui fait peur, effrayant.

scathing /ˈskeɪðɪŋ/ *a.* cinglant.

scatter /ˈskætə(r)/ *v.t.* (*throw*) éparpiller, répandre; (*disperse*) disperser. —*v.i.* se disperser. **~-brain** *n.* écervelé(e) *m.* (*f.*).

scatty /ˈskætɪ/ *a.* (**-ier, -iest**) (*sl.*) écervelé, farfelu.

scavenge /ˈskævɪndʒ/ *v.i.* fouiller (dans les ordures). **~r** /-ə(r)/ *n.* (*vagrant*) personne qui fouille dans les ordures *f.*

scenario /sɪˈnɑːrɪəʊ/ *n.* (*pl.* **-os**) scénario *m.*

scene /siːn/ *n.* scène *f.*; (*of accident, crime*) lieu(x) *m.* (*pl.*).; (*sight*) spectacle *m.*; (*incident*) incident *m.* **behind the ~s,** en coulisse.

scenery /ˈsiːnərɪ/ *n.* paysage *m.*; (*theatre*) décor(s) *m.* (*pl.*).

scenic /ˈsiːnɪk/ *a.* pittoresque.

scent /sent/ *n.* (*perfume*) parfum *m.*; (*trail*) piste *f.* —*v.t.* flairer; (*make fragrant*) parfumer.

sceptic /ˈskeptɪk/ *n.* sceptique *m.*/*f.* **~al** *a.* sceptique. **~ism** /-sɪzəm/ *n.* scepticisme *m.*

sceptre /ˈseptə(r)/ *n.* sceptre *m.*

schedule /ˈʃedjuːl, *Amer.* /ˈskedʒʊl/ *n.* programme *m.*, horaire *m.* —*v.t.* prévoir. **behind ~,** en retard. **on ~,** (*train*) à l'heure; (*work*) à jour.

scheme /skiːm/ *n.* plan *m.*; (*dishonest*) combine *f.*; (*fig.*) arrangement *m.* —*v.i.* intriguer. **~r** /-ə(r)/ *n.* intrigant(e) *m.* (*f.*).

schism /ˈsɪzəm/ *n.* schisme *m.*

schizophrenic /skɪtsəʊˈfrenɪk/ *a.* & *n.* schizophrène (*m.*/*f.*).

scholar /ˈskɒlə(r)/ *n.* érudit(e) *m.* (*f.*) **~ly** *a.* érudit. **~ship** *n.* érudition *f.*; (*grant*) bourse *f.*

scholastic /skəˈlæstɪk/ *a.* scolaire.

school /skuːl/ *n.* école *f.*; (*of university*) faculté *f.* —*a.* (*age, year, holidays*) scolaire. —*v.t.* (*person*) éduquer; (*animal*) dresser. **~ing** *n.* (*education*) instruction *f.*; (*attendance*) scolarité *f.*

school|boy /ˈskuːlbɔɪ/ *n.* écolier *m.* **~girl** *n.* écolière *f.*

school|master /ˈskuːlmɑːstə(r)/, **~mistress, ~teacher** *ns.* (*primary*) institu|teur, -trice *m.*, *f.*; (*secondary*) professeur *m.*

schooner /ˈskuːnə(r)/ *n.* goélette *f.*

sciatica /saɪˈætɪkə/ *n.* sciatique *f.*

scien|ce /ˈsaɪəns/ *n.* science *f.* **~ce fiction,** science-fiction *f.* **~tific** /-ˈtɪfɪk/ *a.* scientifique.

scientist /ˈsaɪəntɪst/ *n.* scientifique *m.*/*f.*

scintillate /ˈsɪntɪleɪt/ *v.i.* scintiller; (*person*: *fig.*) briller.

scissors /ˈsɪzəz/ *n. pl.* ciseaux *m. pl.*

sclerosis /skləˈrəʊsɪs/ *n.* sclérose *f.*

scoff[1] /skɒf/ *v.i.* **~ at,** se moquer de.

scoff[2] /skɒf/ *v.t.* (*eat*: *sl.*) bouffer.

scold /skəʊld/ *v.t.* réprimander. **~ing** *n.* réprimande *f.*

scone /skɒn/ *n.* petit pain au lait *m.*, galette *f.*

scoop /skuːp/ *n.* (*for grain, sugar*) pelle (à main) *f.*; (*for food*) cuiller *f.*; (*news*) exclusivité *f.* —*v.t.* (*pick up*) ramasser. **~ out,** creuser.

scoot /skuːt/ *v.i.* (*fam.*) filer.

scooter /ˈskuːtə(r)/ *n.* (*child's*) trottinette *f.*; (*motor cycle*) scooter *m.*

scope /skəʊp/ *n.* étendue *f.*; (*competence*) compétence *f.*; (*opportunity*) possibilité(s) *f.* (*pl.*).

scorch /skɔːtʃ/ *v.t.* brûler, roussir. **~ing** *a.* brûlant, très chaud.

score /skɔː(r)/ *n.* score *m.*; (*mus.*) partition *f.* —*v.t.* marquer; (*success*) remporter. —*v.i.* marquer un point; (*football*) marquer un but; (*keep score*) compter les points. **a ~ (of),** (*twenty*) vingt. **on that ~,** à cet égard. **~ out,** rayer. **~r** /-ə(r)/ *n.* (*sport*) marqueur *m.*

scorn /skɔːn/ *n.* mépris *m.* —*v.t.* mépriser. **~ful** *a.* méprisant. **~fully** *adv.* avec mépris.

scorpion /ˈskɔːpɪən/ *n.* scorpion *m.*

Scot /skɒt/ *n.* Écossais(e) *m.* (*f.*). **~tish** *a.* écossais.

Scotch /skɒtʃ/ *a.* écossais. —*n.* whisky *m.*, scotch *m.*

scotch /skɒtʃ/ *v.t.* mettre fin à.

scot-free /skɒtˈfriː/ *a.* & *adv.* sans être puni; (*gratis*) sans payer.

Scotland /ˈskɒtlənd/ *n.* Écosse *f.*

Scots /skɒts/ *a.* écossais. **~man** *n.* Écossais *m.* **~woman** *n.* Écossaise *f.*

scoundrel /ˈskaʊndrəl/ *n.* vaurien *m.*, bandit *m.*, gredin(e) *m.*(*f.*).

scour[1] /ˈskaʊə(r)/ *v.t.* (*pan*) récurer. **~er** *n.* tampon à récurer *m.*

cour² /'skaʊə(r)/ *v.t.* (*search*) parcourir.
courge /skɜːdʒ/ *n.* fléau *m.*
cout /skaʊt/ *n.* (*mil.*) éclaireur *m.* —*v.i.* **~ (for)**, chercher.
cout /skaʊt/ *n.* (*boy*) scout *m.*, éclaireur *m.* **~ing** *n.* scoutisme *n.*
cowl /skaʊl/ *n.* air renfrogné *m.* —*v.i.* se renfrogner.
craggy /'skrægɪ/ *a.* (**-ier, -iest**) décharné, efflanqué.
cram /skræm/ *v.i.* (*sl.*) se tirer.
cramble /'skræmbl/ *v.i.* (*clamber*) grimper. —*v.t.* (*eggs*) brouiller. —*n.* bousculade *f.*, ruée *f.* **~ for,** se bousculer pour avoir.
crap¹ /skræp/ *n.* petit morceau *m.* **~s,** (*of metal, fabric, etc.*) déchets *n. pl.*; (*of food*) restes *m. pl.* —*v.t.* (*p.t.* **scrapped**) mettre au rebut; *plan etc.*) abandonner. **~-book** *n.* album *m.* **~-iron** *n.* ferraille *f.* **~-paper** *n.* brouillon *m.* **~py** *a.* fragmentaire.
rap² /skræp/ *n.* (*fight*: *fam.*) bagarre *f.*, dispute *f.*
rape /skreɪp/ *v.t.* racler, gratter; *graze*) érafler. —*v.i.* (*rub*) frotter. —*n.* raclement *m.*; éraflure *f.*; *fig.*) mauvais pas *m.* **~ through,** réussir de justesse. **~ together,** réunir. **~r** /-ə(r)/ *n.* racloir *m.*
ratch /skrætʃ/ *v.t./i.* (se) gratter; *with claw, nail*) griffer; (*graze*) érafler. —*n.* éraflure *f.* **start from ~,** partir de zéro. **up to ~,** au niveau voulu.
rawl /skrɔːl/ *n.* gribouillage *m.* —*v.t./i.* gribouiller.
rawny /'skrɔːnɪ/ *a.* (**-ier, -iest**) décharné, émacié.
ream /skriːm/ *v.t./i.* crier, hurler. —*n.* cri (perçant) *m.*
reech /skriːtʃ/ *v.i.* (*scream*) hurler; (*of brakes*) grincer. —*n.* hurlement *m.*; grincement *m.*
reen /skriːn/ *n.* écran *m.*; (*folding*) paravent *m.* —*v.t.* masquer; (*protect*) protéger; (*film*) projeter; (*candidates*) filtrer.
screw /skruː/ *n.* vis *f.* —*v.t.* visser. **~ up,** (*eyes*) plisser; (*ruin*: *sl.*) bousiller.
screwdriver /'skruːdraɪvə(r)/ *n.* tournevis *m.*
screwy /'skruːɪ/ *a.* (**-ier, -iest**) (*crazy*: *sl.*) cinglé.
scribble /'skrɪbl/ *v.t./i.* griffonner. —*n.* griffonnage *m.*
scribe /skraɪb/ *n.* scribe *m.*
script /skrɪpt/ *n.* écriture *f.*; (*of film*) scénario *m.*; (*of play*) texte *m.* **~-writer** *n.* scénariste *m./f.*
Scriptures /'skrɪptʃəz/ *n. pl.* **the ~,** l'Écriture (sainte) *f.*
scroll /skrəʊl/ *n.* rouleau *m.*
scrounge /skraʊndʒ/ *v.t.* (*meal*) se faire payer; (*steal*) chiper. —*v.i.* (*beg*) quémander. **~ money from,** taper. **~r** /-ə(r)/ *n.* parasite *m.*; (*of money*) tapeu|r, -se *m., f.*
scrub¹ /skrʌb/ *n.* (*land*) broussailles *f. pl.*
scrub² /skrʌb/ *v.t./i.* (*p.t.* **scrubbed**) nettoyer (à la brosse), frotter. —*n.* nettoyage *m.*
scruff /skrʌf/ *n.* **by the ~ of the neck,** par la peau du cou.
scruffy /'skrʌfɪ/ *a.* (**-ier, -iest**) (*fam.*) miteux, sale.
scrum /skrʌm/ *n.* (*Rugby*) mêlée *f.*
scruple /'skruːpl/ *n.* scrupule *m.*
scrupulous /'skruːpjʊləs/ *a.* scrupuleux. **~ly** *adv.* scrupuleusement. **~ly clean,** impeccable.
scrutin|y /'skruːtɪnɪ/ *n.* examen minutieux *m.* **~ize** *v.t.* scruter.
scuff /skʌf/ *v.t.* (*scratch*) érafler.
scuffle /'skʌfl/ *n.* bagarre *f.*
sculpt /skʌlpt/ *v.t./i.* (*fam.*) sculpter. **~or** *n.* sculpteur *m.* **~ure** /-tʃə(r)/ *n.* sculpture *f.*; *v.t./i.* sculpter.
scum /skʌm/ *n.* (*on liquid*) écume *f.*; (*people*: *pej.*) racaille *f.*
scurf /skɜːf/ *n.* pellicules *f. pl.*

scurrilous /ˈskʌrɪləs/ *a.* grossier, injurieux, venimeux.

scurry /ˈskʌrɪ/ *v.i.* courir (**for,** pour chercher). **~ off,** filer.

scurvy /ˈskɜːvɪ/ *n.* scorbut *m.*

scuttle[1] /ˈskʌtl/ *v.t.* (*ship*) saborder.

scuttle[2] /ˈskʌtl/ *v.i.* **~ away,** se sauver, filer.

scythe /saɪð/ *n.* faux *f.*

sea /siː/ *n.* mer *f.* —*a.* de (la) mer, marin. **at ~,** en mer. **by ~,** par mer. **~-green** *a.* vert glauque *invar.* **~-level** *n.* niveau de la mer *m.* **~ shell,** coquillage *m.* **~-shore** *n.* rivage *m.*

seaboard /ˈsiːbɔːd/ *n.* littoral *m.*

seafarer /ˈsiːfeərə(r)/ *n.* marin *m.*

seafood /ˈsiːfuːd/ *n.* fruits de mer *m. pl.*

seagull /ˈsiːgʌl/ *n.* mouette *f.*

seal[1] /siːl/ *n.* (*animal*) phoque *m.*

seal[2] /siːl/ *n.* sceau *m.*; (*with wax*) cachet *m.* —*v.t.* sceller; cacheter; (*stick down*) coller. **~ing-wax** *n.* cire à cacheter *f.* **~ off,** (*area*) boucler.

seam /siːm/ *n.* (*in cloth etc.*) couture *f.*; (*of coal*) veine *f.*

seaman /ˈsiːmən/ *n.* (*pl.* **-men**) marin *m.*

seamy /ˈsiːmɪ/ *a.* **~ side,** côté sordide *m.*

seance /ˈseɪɑːns/ *n.* séance de spiritisme *f.*

seaplane /ˈsiːpleɪn/ *n.* hydravion *m.*

seaport /ˈsiːpɔːt/ *n.* port de mer *m.*

search /sɜːtʃ/ *v.t./i.* fouiller; (*study*) examiner. —*n.* fouille *f.*; (*quest*) recherche(s) *f.* (*pl.*). **in ~ of,** à la recherche de. **~ for,** chercher. **~-party** *n.* équipe de secours *f.* **~ing** *a.* (*piercing*) pénétrant.

searchlight /ˈsɜːtʃlaɪt/ *n.* projecteur *m.*

seasick /ˈsiːsɪk/ *a.* **be ~,** avoir le mal de mer.

seaside /ˈsiːsaɪd/ *n.* bord de mer *m.*

season /ˈsiːzn/ *n.* saison *f.* —*v* assaisonner. **~able** *a.* qui c vient à la saison. **~al** *a.* saiso nier. **~ing** *n.* assaisonnement **~-ticket** *n.* carte d'abonnemen

seasoned /ˈsiːznd/ *a.* expérimen

seat /siːt/ *n.* siège *m.*; (*place*) pla *f.*; (*of trousers*) fond *m.* —*v* (*put*) placer; (*have seats for*) av des places assises pour. **be ~e** **take a ~,** s'asseoir. **~-belt** ceinture de sécurité *f.*

seaweed /ˈsiːwiːd/ *n.* algues *f. pl.*

seaworthy /ˈsiːwɜːðɪ/ *a.* en ét de naviguer.

sece|de /sɪˈsiːd/ *v.i.* faire sécessio **~ssion** /-eʃn/ *n.* sécession *f.*

seclu|de /sɪˈkluːd/ *v.t.* isoler. **~d** *a.* isolé. **~sion** /-ʒn/ *n.* solitude

second[1] /ˈsekənd/ *a.* deuxièm second. —*n.* deuxième *m.* second(e) *m.* (*f.*); (*unit of tim* seconde *f.* **~s,** (*goods*) articl de second choix *m. pl.* —*adv.* (*race etc.*) en seconde place. —*v* (*proposal*) appuyer. **~-best** de second choix, numéro de *invar.* **~-class** *a.* de deuxièn classe. **at ~ hand,** de secon main. **~-hand** *a.* d'occasion; (*on clock*) trotteuse *f.* **~-rate** médiocre. **have ~ thought** avoir des doutes, changer d'av **on ~ thoughts,** (*Amer.*) **on thought,** à la réflexion. **~ly** *a* deuxièmement.

second[2] /sɪˈkɒnd/ *v.t.* (*transfe* détacher (**to,** à).

secondary /ˈsekəndrɪ/ *a.* seco daire. **~ school,** lycée *m.*, c lège *m.*

secrecy /ˈsiːkrəsɪ/ *n.* secret *m.*

secret /ˈsiːkrɪt/ *a.* secret. — secret *m.* **in ~,** en secret. **~** *adv.* en secret, secrètement.

secretariat /sekrəˈteərɪət/ secrétariat *m.*

secretar|y /ˈsekrətrɪ/ *n.* secrétaire *m./f.* **S~y of State,** ministre *m.*; (*Amer.*) ministre des Affaires étrangères *m.* **~ial** /-ˈteərɪəl/ *a.* (*work etc.*) de secrétaire.
secret|e /sɪˈkriːt/ *v.t.* (*med.*) sécréter. **~ion** /-ʃn/ *n.* sécrétion *f.*
secretive /ˈsiːkrətɪv/ *a.* cachottier.
sect /sekt/ *n.* secte *f.* **~arian** /-ˈteərɪən/ *a.* sectaire.
section /ˈsekʃn/ *n.* section *f.*; (*of country, town*) partie *f.*; (*in store*) rayon *m.*; (*newspaper column*) rubrique *f.*
sector /ˈsektə(r)/ *n.* secteur *m.*
secular /ˈsekjʊlə(r)/ *a.* (*school etc.*) laïque; (*art, music, etc.*) profane.
secure /sɪˈkjʊə(r)/ *a.* (*safe*) en sûreté; (*in mind*) tranquille; (*firm*) solide; (*window etc.*) bien fermé. —*v.t.* attacher; (*obtain*) s'assurer; (*ensure*) assurer. **~ly** *adv.* solidement; (*safely*) en sûreté.
security /sɪˈkjʊərətɪ/ *n.* (*safety*) sécurité *f.*; (*for loan*) caution *f.*
sedate[1] /sɪˈdeɪt/ *a.* calme.
sedat|e[2] /sɪˈdeɪt/ *v.t.* donner un sédatif à. **~ion** /-ʃn/ *n.* sédation *f.*
sedative /ˈsedətɪv/ *n.* sédatif *m.*
sedentary /ˈsedntrɪ/ *a.* sédentaire.
sediment /ˈsedɪmənt/ *n.* sédiment *m.*
sedition /sɪˈdɪʃn/ *n.* sédition *f.*
seduce /sɪˈdjuːs/ *v.t.* séduire. **~r** /-ə(r)/ *n.* séduc|teur, -trice *m., f.*
seduct|ion /sɪˈdʌkʃn/ *n.* séduction *f.* **~ive** /-tɪv/ *a.* séduisant.
see[1] /siː/ *v.t./i.* (*p.t.* **saw,** *p.p.* **seen**) voir; (*escort*) (r)accompagner. **~ about** *or* **to,** s'occuper de. **~ through,** (*task*) mener à bonne fin; (*person*) deviner (le jeu de). **~ (to it) that,** veiller à ce que. **~ing that,** vu que.
see[2] /siː/ *n.* (*of bishop*) évêché *m.*
seed /siːd/ *n.* graine *f.*; (*collectively*) graines *f. pl.*; (*origin: fig.*) germe *m.*; (*tennis*) tête de série *f.* **go to ~,** (*plant*) monter en graine; (*person*) se laisser aller. **~ling** *n.* plant *m.*
seedy /ˈsiːdɪ/ *a.* (**-ier, -iest**) miteux.
seek /siːk/ *v.t.* (*p.t.* **sought**) chercher. **~ out,** aller chercher.
seem /siːm/ *v.i.* sembler. **~ingly** *adv.* apparemment.
seemly /ˈsiːmlɪ/ *adv.* convenable.
seen /siːn/ *see* **see**[1].
seep /siːp/ *v.i.* (*ooze*) suinter. **~ into,** s'infiltrer dans. **~age** *n.* suintement *m.*; infiltration *f.*
see-saw /ˈsiːsɔː/ *n.* bascule *f.*
seethe /siːð/ *v.i.* **~ with,** (*anger*) bouillir de; (*people*) grouiller de.
segment /ˈsegmənt/ *n.* segment *m.*
segregat|e /ˈsegrɪgeɪt/ *v.t.* séparer. **~ion** /-ˈgeɪʃn/ *n.* ségrégation *f.*
seize /siːz/ *v.t.* saisir; (*take possession of*) s'emparer de. —*v.i.* **~ on,** (*chance etc.*) saisir. **~ up,** (*engine etc.*) se gripper.
seizure /ˈsiːʒə(r)/ *n.* (*med.*) crise *f.*
seldom /ˈseldəm/ *adv.* rarement.
select /sɪˈlekt/ *v.t.* choisir, sélectionner. —*a.* choisi; (*exclusive*) sélect. **~ion** /-kʃn/ *n.* sélection *f.*
selective /sɪˈlektɪv/ *a.* sélectif.
self /self/ *n.* (*pl.* **selves**) (*on cheque*) moi-même. **the ~,** le moi *m. invar.* **your good ~,** vous-même.
self- /self/ *pref.* **~-assurance** *n.* assurance *f.* **~-assured** *a.* sûr de soi. **~-catering** *a.* où l'on fait la cuisine soi-même. **~-centred** *a.* égocentrique. **~-confidence** *n.* confiance en soi *f.* **~-confident** *a.* sûr de soi. **~-conscious** *a.* gêné, timide. **~-contained** *a.* (*flat*) indépendant. **~-control** *n.* maîtrise de soi *f.* **~-defence** *n.* légitime défense *f.* **~-denial** *n.* abnégation *f.* **~-employed** *a.* qui travaille à son compte. **~-esteem** *n.* amour-propre *m.* **~-evident** *a.* évident. **~-government** *n.* autonomie *f.* **~-indulgent** *a.* qui se permet

tout. **~-interest** *n.* intérêt personnel *m.* **~-portrait** *n.* autoportrait *m.* **~-possessed** *a.* assuré. **~-reliant** *a.* indépendant. **~-respect** *n.* respect de soi *m.*, dignité *f.* **~-righteous** *a.* satisfait de soi. **~-sacrifice** *n.* abnégation *f.* **~-satisfied** *a.* content de soi. **~-seeking** *a.* égoïste. **~-service** *n.* & *a.* libre-service (*m.*). **~-styled** *a.* soi-disant. **~-sufficient** *a.* indépendant. **~-willed** *a.* entêté.

selfish /'selfɪʃ/ *a.* égoïste; (*motive*) intéressé. **~ness** *n.* égoïsme *m.*

selfless /'selflɪs/ *a.* désintéressé.

sell /sel/ *v.t./i.* (*p.t.* **sold**) (se) vendre. **be sold out of,** n'avoir plus de. **~ off,** liquider. **~-out,** *n.* trahison *f.* **it was a ~-out,** on a vendu tous les billets. **~ up,** vendre son fonds, sa maison, *etc.* **~er** *n.* vendeu|r, -se *m., f.*

Sellotape /'seləʊteɪp/ *n.* (P.) scotch *m.* (P.).

semantic /sɪ'mæntɪk/ *a.* sémantique. **~s** *n.* sémantique *f.*

semaphore /'seməfɔː(r)/ *n.* signaux à bras *m. pl.*; (*device*: *rail.*) sémaphore *m.*

semblance /'sembləns/ *n.* semblant *m.*

semen /'siːmən/ *n.* sperme *m.*

semester /sɪ'mestə(r)/ *n.* (*univ., Amer.*) semestre *m.*

semi- /'semɪ/ *pref.* semi-, demi-.

semibreve /'semɪbriːv/ *n.* (*mus.*) ronde *f.*

semicirc|le /'semɪsɜːkl/ *n.* demi-cercle *m.* **~ular** /-'sɜːkjʊlə(r)/ *a.* en demi-cercle.

semicolon /semɪ'kəʊlən/ *n.* point-virgule *m.*

semi-detached /semɪ'dɪtætʃt/ *a.* **~ house,** maison jumelle *f.*

semifinal /semɪ'faɪnl/ *n.* demi-finale *f.*

seminar /'semɪnɑː(r)/ *n.* séminaire *m.*

seminary /'semɪnərɪ/ *n.* séminaire *m.*

semiquaver /'semɪkweɪvə(r)/ (*mus.*) double croche *f.*

Semit|e /'siːmaɪt, *Amer.* 'sema *n.* Sémite *m./f.* **~ic** /sɪ'mɪtɪk/ sémite; (*lang.*) sémitique.

semolina /semə'liːnə/ *n.* semoule

senat|e /'senɪt/ *n.* sénat *m.* **~** /-ətə(r)/ *n.* sénateur *m.*

send /send/ *v.t./i.* (*p.t.* **sen** envoyer. **~ away,** (*dismiss*) re voyer. **~ (away *or* off) fo** commander (par lettre). **back,** renvoyer. **~ for,** (*perso help*) envoyer chercher. **~-o** *n.* adieux chaleureux *m. pl.* **up,** (*fam.*) parodier. **~er** *n.* e pédi|teur, -trice *m., f.*

senil|e /'siːnaɪl/ *a.* sénile. **~it** /sɪ'nɪlətɪ/ *n.* sénilité *f.*

senior /'siːnɪə(r)/ *a.* plus â **(to,** que); (*in rank*) supérieu (*teacher, partner*) principal. — aîné(e) *m.* (*f.*); (*schol.*) grand(*m.* (*f.*). **~ citizen,** personne âg *f.* **~ity** /-'ɒrətɪ/ *n.* priorité d'â *f.*; supériorité *f.*; (*in servic* ancienneté *f.*

sensation /sen'seɪʃn/ *n.* sensatic *f.* **~al** *a.* (*event*) qui fait sensatio (*wonderful*) sensationnel.

sense /sens/ *n.* sens *m.*; (*sensatio* sensation *f.*; (*mental impressio* sentiment *m.*; (*common sense*) bo sens *m.* **~s,** raison *f.* —*v.t.* (pres sentir. **make ~,** avoir du sen **make ~ of,** comprendre. **~less** stupide; (*med.*) sans connaissanc

sensibilit|y /sensə'bɪlətɪ/ *n.* se sibilité *f.* **~ies,** susceptibilité *f.*

sensible /'sensəbl/ *a.* raisonnabl sensé; (*clothing*) fonctionnel.

sensitiv|e /'sensətɪv/ *a.* sensib **(to,** à); (*touchy*) susceptible. **~it** /-'tɪvətɪ/ *n.* sensibilité *f.*

sensory /'sensərɪ/ *a.* sensoriel.

sensual /'senʃʊəl/ *a.* sensuel. **~it** /-'ælətɪ/ *n.* sensualité *f.*

sensuous /'senʃʊəs/ *a.* sensuel.
sent /sent/ *see* **send.**
sentence /'sentəns/ *n.* phrase *f.*; (*decision*: *jurid.*) jugement *m.*, condamnation *f.*; (*punishment*) peine *f.* —*v.t.* ~ **to,** condamner à.
sentiment /'sentɪmənt/ *n.* sentiment *m.*
sentimental /sentɪ'mentl/ *a.* sentimental. **~ity** /-'tælətɪ/ *n.* sentimentalité *f.*
sentry /'sentrɪ/ *n.* sentinelle *f.*
separable /'sepərəbl/ *a.* séparable.
separate[1] /'seprət/ *a.* séparé, différent; (*independent*) indépendant. **~s** *n. pl.* coordonnés *m. pl.* **~ly** *adv.* séparément.
separat|e[2] /'sepəreɪt/ *v.t./i.* (se) séparer. **~ion** /-'reɪʃn/ *n.* séparation *f.*
September /sep'tembə(r)/ *n.* septembre *m.*
septic /'septɪk/ *a.* (*wound*) infecté. ~ **tank,** fosse septique *f.*
sequel /'siːkwəl/ *n.* suite *f.*
sequence /'siːkwəns/ *n.* (*order*) ordre *m.*; (*series*) suite *f.*; (*of film*) séquence *f.*
sequin /'siːkwɪn/ *n.* paillette *f.*
serenade /serə'neɪd/ *n.* sérénade *f.* —*v.t.* donner une sérénade à.
seren|e /sɪ'riːn/ *a.* serein. **~ity** /-enətɪ/ *n.* sérénité *f.*
sergeant /'sɑːdʒənt/ *n.* (*mil.*) sergent *m.*; (*policeman*) brigadier *m.*
serial /'sɪərɪəl/ *n.* (*story*) feuilleton *m.* —*a.* (*number*) de série.
series /'sɪərɪz/ *n. invar.* série *f.*
serious /'sɪərɪəs/ *a.* sérieux; (*very bad, critical*) grave, sérieux. **~ly** *adv.* sérieusement, gravement. **take ~ly,** prendre au sérieux. **~ness** *n.* sérieux *m.*
sermon /'sɜːmən/ *n.* sermon *m.*
serpent /'sɜːpənt/ *n.* serpent *m.*
serrated /sɪ'reɪtɪd/ *a.* (*edge*) en dents de scie.
serum /'sɪərəm/ *n.* (*pl.* **-a**) sérum *m.*
servant /'sɜːvənt/ *n.* domestique *m./f.*; (*of God etc.*) serviteur *m.*
serve /sɜːv/ *v.t./i.* servir; (*undergo, carry out*) faire; (*of transport*) desservir. —*n.* (*tennis*) service *m.* ~ **as/to,** servir de/à. ~ **its purpose,** remplir sa fonction.
service /'sɜːvɪs/ *n.* service *m.*; (*maintenance*) révision *f.* **~s,** (*mil.*) forces armées *f. pl.* —*v.t.* (*car etc.*) réviser. **of ~ to,** utile à. ~ **area,** (*auto.*) aire de services *f.* ~ **charge,** service *m.* ~ **station,** station-service *f.*
serviceable /'sɜːvɪsəbl/ *a.* (*usable*) utilisable; (*useful*) commode; (*durable*) solide.
serviceman /'sɜːvɪsmən/ *n.* (*pl.* **-men**) militaire *m.*
serviette /sɜːvɪ'et/ *n.* serviette *f.*
servile /'sɜːvaɪl/ *a.* servile.
session /'seʃn/ *n.* séance *f.*; (*univ.*) année (universitaire) *f.*; (*univ., Amer.*) semestre *m.*
set /set/ *v.t.* (*p.t.* **set,** *pres. p.* **setting**) mettre; (*put down*) poser, mettre; (*limit etc.*) fixer; (*watch, clock*) régler; (*example, task*) donner; (*in plaster*) plâtrer. —*v.i.* (*of sun*) se coucher; (*of jelly*) prendre. —*n.* (*of chairs, stamps, etc.*) série *f.*; (*of knives, keys, etc.*) jeu *m.*; (*of people*) groupe *m.*; (*TV, radio*) poste *m.*; (*style of hair*) mise en plis *f.*; (*theatre*) décor *m.*; (*tennis*) set *m.*; (*mathematics*) ensemble *m.* —*a.* fixe; (*in habits*) régulier; (*opposed*) opposé; (*meal*) à prix fixe; (*book*) au programme. **be ~ on doing,** être résolu à faire. ~ **about** *or* **to,** se mettre à. ~ **back,** (*delay*) retarder; (*cost*: *sl.*) coûter. **~-back** *n.* revers *m.* ~ **fire to,** mettre le feu à. ~ **in,** (*take hold*) s'installer, commencer. ~ **off** *or* **out,** partir. ~ **off,** (*mechanism, activity*) déclencher; (*bomb*) faire éclater. ~ **out,** (*state*) exposer; (*arrange*) disposer. ~ **sail,** partir.

~ square, équerre *f.* **~ to,** (*about to*) sur le point de. **~-to** *n.* querelle *f.* **~ up,** (*establish*) fonder, établir; (*launch*) lancer. **~-up** *n.* (*fam.*) affaire *f.*

settee /se'tiː/ *n.* canapé *m.*

setting /'setɪŋ/ *n.* cadre *m.*

settle /'setl/ *v.t.* (*arrange, pay*) régler; (*date*) fixer; (*nerves*) calmer. —*v.i.* (*come to rest*) se poser; (*live*) s'installer. **~ down,** se calmer; (*become orderly*) se ranger. **~ for,** accepter. **~ up (with),** régler. **~r** /-ə(r)/ *n.* colon *m.*

settlement /'setlmənt/ *n.* règlement *m.* **(of,** de); (*agreement*) accord *m.*; (*place*) colonie *f.*

seven /'sevn/ *a.* & *n.* sept (*m.*). **~th** *a.* & *n.* septième (*m./f.*).

seventeen /sevn'tiːn/ *a.* & *n.* dix-sept (*m.*). **~th** *a.* & *n.* dix-septième (*m./f.*).

sevent|y /'sevntɪ/ *a.* & *n.* soixante-dix (*m.*). **~ieth** *a.* & *n.* soixante-dixième (*m./f.*).

sever /'sevə(r)/ *v.t.* (*cut*) couper; (*relations*) rompre. **~ance** *n.* (*breaking off*) rupture *f.*

several /'sevrəl/ *a.* & *pron.* plusieurs.

sever|e /sɪ'vɪə(r)/ *a.* **(-er, -est)** sévère; (*violent*) violent; (*serious*) grave. **~ely** *adv.* sévèrement; gravement. **~ity** /sɪ'verətɪ/ *n.* sévérité *f.*; violence *f.*; gravité *f.*

sew /səʊ/ *v.t./i.* (*p.t.* **sewed,** *p.p.* **sewn** *or* **sewed**) coudre. **~ing** *n.* couture *f.* **~ing-machine** *n.* machine à coudre *f.*

sewage /'sjuːɪdʒ/ *n.* eaux d'égout *f. pl.*, vidanges *f. pl.*

sewer /'sjuːə(r)/ *n.* égout *m.*

sewn /səʊn/ *see* **sew.**

sex /seks/ *n.* sexe *m.* —*a.* sexuel. **have ~,** avoir des rapports (sexuels). **~ maniac,** obsédé(e) sexuel(le) *m.(f.).* **~y** *a.* sexy *invar.*

sexist /'seksɪst/ *a.* & *n.* sexist (*m./f.*).

sextet /seks'tet/ *n.* sextuor *m.*

sexual /'sekʃʊəl/ *a.* sexuel. ~ **intercourse,** rapports sexuels *n pl.* **~ity** /-'ælətɪ/ *n.* sexualité *f.*

shabb|y /'ʃæbɪ/ *a.* **(-ier, -iest)** (*place, object*) minable, miteux (*person*) pauvrement vêtu; (*mear* mesquin. **~ily** *adv.* (*dres* pauvrement; (*act*) mesquinemen

shack /ʃæk/ *n.* cabane *f.*

shackles /'ʃæklz/ *n. pl.* chaîne *f. pl.*

shade /ʃeɪd/ *n.* ombre *f.*; (*of colou opinion*) nuance *f.*; (*for lamp* abat-jour *m.*; (*blind: Amer.*) stor *m.* **a ~ bigger**/*etc.*, légèremen plus grand/*etc.* —*v.t.* (*of perso etc.*) abriter; (*of tree*) ombrager.

shadow /'ʃædəʊ/ *n.* ombre *f.* —*v.* (*follow*) filer. **S~ Cabinet,** cab net fantôme *m.* **~y** *a.* ombragé (*fig.*) vague.

shady /'ʃeɪdɪ/ *a.* **(-ier, -iest** ombragé; (*dubious: fig.*) louche.

shaft /ʃɑːft/ *n.* (*of arrow*) hampe *f.* (*axle*) arbre *m.*; (*of mine*) puits *m*

shaggy /'ʃægɪ/ *a.* **(-ier, -iest** (*beard*) hirsute; (*hair*) brous sailleux; (*animal*) à longs poils.

shake /ʃeɪk/ *v.t.* (*p.t.* **shook,** *p.p* **shaken**) secouer; (*bottle*) agiter (*house, belief, etc.*) ébranler. —*v.i* trembler. —*n.* secousse *f.* **~ hands with,** serrer la main à. **~ off,** (*get rid of*) se débarrasser de **~ one's head,** (*in refusal*) dir non de la tête. **~ up,** (*disturb rouse, mix contents of*) secouer **~-up** *n.* (*upheaval*) remanie ment *m.*

shaky /'ʃeɪkɪ/ *a.* **(-ier, -iest)** (*hand voice*) tremblant; (*table etc.*) bran lant; (*weak: fig.*) faible.

shall /ʃæl, *unstressed* ʃ(ə)l/ *v. aux* **I ~ do,** je ferai. **we ~ do,** nous ferons.

shallot /ʃə'lɒt/ *n.* échalote *f.*

shallow /ˈʃæləʊ/ *a.* (**-er, -est**) peu profond; (*fig.*) superficiel.

sham /ʃæm/ *n.* comédie *f.*; (*person*) imposteur *m.*; (*jewel*) imitation *f.* —*a.* faux; (*affected*) feint. —*v.t.* (*p.t.* **shammed**) feindre.

shambles /ˈʃæmblz/ *n. pl.* (*mess*: *fam.*) désordre *m.*, pagaille *f.*

shame /ʃeɪm/ *n.* honte *f.* —*v.t.* faire honte à. **it is a ~,** c'est dommage. **~ful** *a.* honteux. **~fully** *adv.* honteusement. **~less** *a.* éhonté.

shamefaced /ˈʃeɪmfeɪst/ *a.* honteux.

shampoo /ʃæmˈpuː/ *n.* shampooing *m.* —*v.t.* faire un shampooing à, shampooiner.

shandy /ˈʃændɪ/ *n.* panaché *m.*

shan't /ʃɑːnt/ = **shall not.**

shanty /ˈʃæntɪ/ *n.* (*shack*) baraque *f.* **~ town,** bidonville *m.*

shape /ʃeɪp/ *n.* forme *f.* —*v.t.* (*fashion, mould*) façonner; (*future etc.*: *fig.*) déterminer. —*v.i.* **~ up,** (*plan etc.*) prendre tournure *or* forme; (*person etc.*) faire des progrès. **~less** *a.* informe.

shapely /ˈʃeɪplɪ/ *a.* (**-ier, -iest**) (*leg, person*) bien tourné.

share /ʃeə(r)/ *n.* part *f.*; (*comm.*) action *f.* —*v.t./i.* partager. **~-out** *n.* partage *m.*

shareholder /ˈʃeəhəʊldə(r)/ *n.* actionnaire *m./f.*

shark /ʃɑːk/ *n.* requin *m.*

sharp /ʃɑːp/ *a.* (**-er, -est**) (*knife etc.*) tranchant; (*pin etc.*) pointu; (*point*) aigu; (*acute*) vif; (*sudden*) brusque; (*dishonest*) peu scrupuleux. —*adv.* (*stop*) net. **six o'clock**/*etc.* **~,** six heures/*etc.* pile. —*n.* (*mus.*) dièse *m.* **~ly** *adv.* (*harshly*) vivement; (*suddenly*) brusquement.

sharpen /ˈʃɑːpən/ *v.t.* aiguiser; (*pencil*) tailler. **~er** *n.* (*for pencil*) taille-crayon(s) *m.*

shatter /ˈʃætə(r)/ *v.t./i.* (*glass etc.*) (faire) voler en éclats, (se) briser; (*upset, ruin*) anéantir.

shav|e /ʃeɪv/ *v.t./i.* (se) raser. —*n.* **have a ~e,** se raser. **~en** *a.* rasé. **~er** *n.* rasoir électrique *m.* **~ing-brush** *n.* blaireau *m.* **~ing-cream** *n.* crème à raser *f.*

shaving /ˈʃeɪvɪŋ/ *n.* copeau *m.*

shawl /ʃɔːl/ *n.* châle *m.*

she /ʃiː/ *pron.* elle. —*n.* femelle *f.*

sheaf /ʃiːf/ *n.* (*pl.* **sheaves**) gerbe *f.*

shear /ʃɪə(r)/ *v.t.* (*p.p.* **shorn** *or* **sheared**) (*sheep etc.*) tondre.

shears /ʃɪəz/ *n. pl.* cisaille(s) *f.* (*pl.*).

sheath /ʃiːθ/ *n.* (*pl.* **-s** /ʃiːðz/) gaine *f.*, fourreau *m.*; (*contraceptive*) préservatif *m.*

sheathe /ʃiːð/ *v.t.* rengainer.

shed[1] /ʃed/ *n.* remise *f.*

shed[2] /ʃed/ *v.t.* (*p.t.* **shed,** *pres. p.* **shedding**) perdre; (*light, tears*) répandre.

sheen /ʃiːn/ *n.* lustre *m.*

sheep /ʃiːp/ *n. invar.* mouton *m.* **~-dog** *n.* chien de berger *m.*

sheepish /ˈʃiːpɪʃ/ *a.* penaud. **~ly** *adv.* d'un air penaud.

sheepskin /ˈʃiːpskɪn/ *n.* peau de mouton *f.*

sheer /ʃɪə(r)/ *a.* pur (et simple); (*steep*) à pic; (*fabric*) très fin. —*adv.* à pic, verticalement.

sheet /ʃiːt/ *n.* drap *m.*; (*of paper*) feuille *f.*; (*of glass, ice*) plaque *f.*

sheikh /ʃeɪk/ *n.* cheik *m.*

shelf /ʃelf/ *n.* (*pl.* **shelves**) rayon *m.*, étagère *f.* **on the ~,** (*person*) laissé pour compte.

shell /ʃel/ *n.* coquille *f.*; (*on beach*) coquillage *m.*; (*of building*) carcasse *f.*; (*explosive*) obus *m.* —*v.t.* (*nut etc.*) décortiquer; (*peas*) écosser; (*mil.*) bombarder.

shellfish /ˈʃelfɪʃ/ *n. invar.* (*lobster etc.*) crustacé(s) *m.* (*pl.*); (*mollusc*) coquillage(s) *m.* (*pl.*).

shelter /ˈʃeltə(r)/ *n.* abri *m.* —*v.t./i.* (s')abriter; (*give lodging to*) donner asile à. **~ed** *a.* (*life etc.*) protégé.

shelve /ʃelv/ *v.t.* (*plan etc.*) laisser en suspens, remettre à plus tard.

shelving /ˈʃelvɪŋ/ *n.* (*shelves*) rayonnage(s) *m.* (*pl.*).

shepherd /ˈʃepəd/ *n.* berger *m.* —*v.t.* (*people*) guider. **~ess** /-ˈdes/ *n.* bergère *f.* **~'s pie,** hachis Parmentier *m.*

sherbet /ˈʃɜːbət/ *n.* jus de fruits *m.*; (*powder*) poudre acidulée *f.*; (*water-ice*: *Amer.*) sorbet *m.*

sheriff /ˈʃerɪf/ *n.* shérif *m.*

sherry /ˈʃerɪ/ *n.* xérès *m.*

shield /ʃiːld/ *n.* bouclier *m.*; (*screen*) écran *m.* —*v.t.* protéger.

shift /ʃɪft/ *v.t./i.* (se) déplacer, bouger; (*exchange, alter*) changer de. —*n.* changement *m.*; (*workers*) équipe *f.*; (*work*) poste *m.* **make ~,** se débrouiller.

shiftless /ˈʃɪftlɪs/ *a.* paresseux.

shifty /ˈʃɪftɪ/ *a.* (**-ier, -iest**) louche.

shilling /ˈʃɪlɪŋ/ *n.* shilling *m.*

shilly-shally /ˈʃɪlɪʃælɪ/ *v.i.* hésiter, balancer.

shimmer /ˈʃɪmə(r)/ *v.i.* chatoyer. —*n.* chatoiement *m.*

shin /ʃɪn/ *n.* tibia *m.*

shine /ʃaɪn/ *v.t./i.* (*p.t.* **shone** /ʃɒn/) (faire) briller. —*n.* éclat *m.*, brillant *m.* **~ one's torch** *or* **the light (on),** éclairer.

shingle /ˈʃɪŋgl/ *n.* (*pebbles*) galets *m. pl.*; (*on roof*) bardeau *m.*

shingles /ˈʃɪŋglz/ *n. pl.* (*med.*) zona *m.*

shiny /ˈʃaɪnɪ/ *a.* (**-ier, -iest**) brillant.

ship /ʃɪp/ *n.* bateau *m.*, navire *m.* —*v.t.* (*p.t.* **shipped**) transporter; (*send*) expédier; (*load*) embarquer. **~ment** *n.* cargaison *f.*, envoi *m.* **~per** *n.* expéditeur *m.* **~ping** *n.* (*ships*) navigation *f.*, navires *m. pl.*

shipbuilding /ˈʃɪpbɪldɪŋ/ *n.* construction navale *f.*

shipshape /ˈʃɪpʃeɪp/ *adv.* & *a.* parfaitement en ordre.

shipwreck /ˈʃɪprek/ *n.* naufrage *m.* **~ed** *a.* naufragé. **be ~ed,** faire naufrage.

shipyard /ˈʃɪpjɑːd/ *n.* chantier naval *m.*

shirk /ʃɜːk/ *v.t.* esquiver. **~er** *n.* tire-au-flanc *m. invar.*

shirt /ʃɜːt/ *n.* chemise *f.*; (*of woman*) chemisier *m.* **in ~-sleeves,** en bras de chemise.

shiver /ˈʃɪvə(r)/ *v.i.* frissonner. —*n.* frisson *m.*

shoal /ʃəʊl/ *n.* (*of fish*) banc *m.*

shock /ʃɒk/ *n.* choc *m.*, sécousse *f.*; (*electr.*) décharge *f.*; (*med.*) choc *m.* —*a.* (*result*) choc *invar.*; (*tactics*) de choc. —*v.t.* choquer. **be a ~er,** (*fam.*) être affreux. **~ing** *a.* choquant; (*bad*: *fam.*) affreux. **~ingly** *adv.* (*fam.*) affreusement.

shodd|y /ˈʃɒdɪ/ *a.* (**-ier, -iest**) mal fait, mauvais. **~ily** *adv.* mal.

shoe /ʃuː/ *n.* chaussure *f.*, soulier *m.*; (*of horse*) fer (à cheval) *m.*; (*in vehicle*) sabot (de frein) *m.* —*v.t.* (*p.t.* **shod** /ʃɒd/, *pres. p.* **shoeing**) (*horse*) ferrer. **be well shod,** être bien chaussé. **on a ~-string,** avec très peu d'argent.

shoehorn /ˈʃuːhɔːn/ *n.* chausse-pied *m.*

shoelace /ˈʃuːleɪs/ *n.* lacet *m.*

shoemaker /ˈʃuːmeɪkə(r)/ *n.* cordonnier *m.*

shone /ʃɒn/ *see* **shine.**

shoo /ʃuː/ *v.t.* chasser.

shook /ʃʊk/ *see* **shake.**

shoot /ʃuːt/ *v.t.* (*p.t.* **shot**) (*gun*) tirer un coup de; (*missile, glance*) lancer; (*kill, wound*) tuer, blesser (d'un coup de fusil, de pistolet, *etc.*); (*execute*) fusiller; (*hunt*) chasser; (*film*) tourner. —*v.i.* tirer (**at,** sur). —*n.* (*bot.*) pousse *f.* **~ down,** abattre. **~ out,** (*rush*) sortir en vitesse. **~ up,** (*spurt*) jaillir; (*grow*) pousser vite. **~ing-range** *n.* stand de tir *m.*

shop /ʃɒp/ *n.* magasin *m.*, boutique *f.*; (*workshop*) atelier *m.* —*v.i.* (*p.t.* **shopped**) faire ses courses. **~ around,** comparer les prix. **~ assistant,** vendeu|r, -se *m.*, *f.* **~-floor** *n.* (*workers*) ouvriers *m. pl.* **~per** *n.* acheteu|r, -se *m.*, *f.* **~-soiled,** (*Amer.*) **~-worn** *adjs.* abîmé. **~ steward,** délégué(e) syndical(e) *m.* (*f.*). **~ window,** vitrine *f.*

shopkeeper /ˈʃɒpkiːpə(r)/ *n.* commerçant(e) *m.* (*f.*).

shoplift|er /ˈʃɒplɪftə(r)/ *n.* voleu|r, -se à l'étalage *m.*, *f.* **~ing** *n.* vol à l'étalage *m.*

shopping /ˈʃɒpɪŋ/ *n.* (*goods*) achats *m. pl.* **go ~,** faire ses courses. **~ bag,** sac à provisions *m.* **~ centre,** centre commercial *m.*

shore /ʃɔː(r)/ *n.* rivage *m.*

shorn /ʃɔːn/ *see* **shear.** —*a.* **~ of,** dépouillé de.

short /ʃɔːt/ *a.* (**-er, -est**) court; (*person*) petit; (*brief*) court, bref; (*curt*) brusque. **be ~ (of),** (*lack*) manquer (de). —*adv.* (*stop*) net. —*n.* (*electr.*) court-circuit *m.* **~s,** (*trousers*) short *m.* **he is called Tom for ~,** son diminutif est Tom. **in ~,** en bref. **~-change** *v.t.* (*cheat*) rouler. **~ circuit,** court-circuit *m.* **~-circuit** *v.t.* court-circuiter. **~ cut,** raccourci *m.* **~-handed** *a.* à court de personnel. **~ list,** liste des candidats choisis *f.* **~-lived** *a.* éphémère. **~-sighted** *a.* myope. **~ story,** nouvelle *f.* **~ wave,** ondes courtes *f. pl.*

shortage /ˈʃɔːtɪdʒ/ *n.* manque *m.*

shortbread /ˈʃɔːtbred/ *n.* sablé *m.*

shortcoming /ˈʃɔːtkʌmɪŋ/ *n.* défaut *m.*

shorten /ˈʃɔːtn/ *v.t.* raccourcir.

shorthand /ˈʃɔːthænd/ *n.* sténo(graphie) *f.* **~ typist,** sténodactylo *f.*

shortly /ˈʃɔːtlɪ/ *adv.* bientôt.

shot /ʃɒt/ *see* **shoot.** —*n.* (*firing, attempt, etc.*) coup *m.*; (*person*) tireur *m.*; (*bullet*) balle *f.*; (*photograph*) photo *f.*; (*injection*) piqûre *f.* **like a ~,** comme une flèche. **~-gun** *n.* fusil de chasse *m.*

should /ʃʊd, *unstressed* ʃəd/ *v. aux.* devoir. **you ~ help me,** vous devriez m'aider. **I ~ have stayed,** j'aurais dû rester. **I ~ like to,** j'aimerais bien. **if he ~ come,** s'il vient.

shoulder /ˈʃəʊldə(r)/ *n.* épaule *f.* —*v.t.* (*responsibility*) endosser; (*burden*) se charger de. **~-blade** *n.* omoplate *f.*

shout /ʃaʊt/ *n.* cri *m.* —*v.t./i.* crier. **~ at,** engueuler. **~ down,** huer.

shove /ʃʌv/ *n.* poussée *f.* —*v.t./i.* pousser; (*put*: *fam.*) ficher. **~ off,** (*depart*: *fam.*) se tirer.

shovel /ˈʃʌvl/ *n.* pelle *f.* —*v.t.* (*p.t.* **shovelled**) pelleter.

show /ʃəʊ/ *v.t.* (*p.t.* **showed,** *p.p.* **shown**) montrer; (*of dial, needle*) indiquer; (*put on display*) exposer; (*film*) donner; (*conduct*) conduire. —*v.i.* (*be visible*) se voir. —*n.* démonstration *f.*; (*ostentation*) parade *f.*; (*exhibition*) exposition *f.*, salon *m.*; (*theatre*) spectacle *m.*; (*cinema*) séance *f.* **for ~,** pour l'effet. **on ~,** exposé. **~-down** *n.* épreuve de force *f.* **~-jumping** *n.* concours hippique *m.* **~ in,** faire entrer. **~ off** *v.t.* étaler; *v.i.* poser, crâner. **~-off** *n.* poseu|r, -se *m.*, *f.* **~-piece** *n.* modèle du genre *m.* **~ up,** (faire) ressortir; (*appear*: *fam.*) se montrer. **~ing** *n.* performance *f.*; (*cinema*) séance *f.*

shower /ˈʃaʊə(r)/ *n.* (*of rain*) averse *f.*; (*of blows etc.*) grêle *f.*; (*for washing*) douche *f.* —*v.t.* **~ with,** couvrir de. —*v.i.* se doucher. **~y** *a.* pluvieux.

showerproof /ˈʃaʊəpruːf/ *a.* imperméable.

showmanship /ˈʃəʊmənʃɪp/ *n.* art de la mise en scène *m.*

shown /ʃəʊn/ *see* **show.**

showroom /ˈʃəʊrʊm/ *n.* salle d'exposition *f.*

showy /ˈʃəʊɪ/ *a.* (**-ier, -iest**) voyant; (*manner*) prétentieux.

shrank /ʃræŋk/ *see* **shrink.**

shrapnel /ˈʃræpn(ə)l/ *n.* éclats d'obus *m. pl.*

shred /ʃred/ *n.* lambeau *m.*; (*least amount: fig.*) parcelle *f.* —*v.t.* (*p.t.* **shredded**) déchiqueter; (*culin.*) râper.

shrew /ʃruː/ *n.* (*woman*) mégère *f.*

shrewd /ʃruːd/ *a.* (**-er, -est**) astucieux. **~ness** *n.* astuce *f.*

shriek /ʃriːk/ *n.* hurlement *m.* —*v.t./i.* hurler.

shrift /ʃrɪft/ *n.* **give s.o. short ~,** traiter qn. sans ménagement.

shrill /ʃrɪl/ *a.* strident, aigu.

shrimp /ʃrɪmp/ *n.* crevette *f.*

shrine /ʃraɪn/ *n.* (*place*) lieu saint *m.*; (*tomb*) châsse *f.*

shrink /ʃrɪŋk/ *v.t./i.* (*p.t.* **shrank,** *p.p.* **shrunk**) rétrécir; (*lessen*) diminuer. **~ from,** reculer devant. **~age** *n.* rétrécissement *m.*

shrivel /ˈʃrɪvl/ *v.t./i.* (*p.t.* **shrivelled**) (se) ratatiner.

shroud /ʃraʊd/ *n.* linceul *m.* —*v.t.* (*veil*) envelopper.

Shrove /ʃrəʊv/ *n.* **~ Tuesday,** Mardi gras *m.*

shrub /ʃrʌb/ *n.* arbuste *m.*

shrug /ʃrʌg/ *v.t.* (*p.t.* **shrugged**). **~ one's shoulders,** hausser les épaules. —*n.* haussement d'épaules *m.*

shrunk /ʃrʌŋk/ *see* **shrink. ~en** *a.* rétréci; (*person*) ratatiné.

shudder /ˈʃʌdə(r)/ *v.i.* frémir. —*n.* frémissement *m.*

shuffle /ˈʃʌfl/ *v.t.* (*feet*) traîner; (*cards*) battre. —*v.i.* traîner les pieds. —*n.* démarche traînante *f.*

shun /ʃʌn/ *v.t.* (*p.t.* **shunned**) éviter, fuir.

shunt /ʃʌnt/ *v.t.* (*train*) aiguiller.

shush /ʃʊʃ/ *int.* (*fam.*) chut.

shut /ʃʌt/ *v.t.* (*p.t.* **shut,** *pres. p.* **shutting**) fermer. —*v.i.* se fermer; (*of shop, bank, etc.*) fermer. **~ down** *or* **up,** fermer. **~-down** *n.* fermeture *f.* **~ in** *or* **up,** enfermer. **~ up** *v.i.* (*fam.*) se taire; *v.t.* (*fam.*) faire taire.

shutter /ˈʃʌtə(r)/ *n.* volet *m.*; (*photo.*) obturateur *m.*

shuttle /ˈʃʌtl/ *n.* (*bus etc.*) navette *f.* —*v.i.* faire la navette. —*v.t.* transporter. **~ service,** navette *f.*

shuttlecock /ˈʃʌtlkɒk/ *n.* (*badminton*) volant *m.*

shy /ʃaɪ/ *a.* (**-er, -est**) timide. —*v.i.* reculer. **~ness** *n.* timidité *f.*

Siamese /saɪəˈmiːz/ *a.* siamois.

sibling /ˈsɪblɪŋ/ *n.* frère *m.*, sœur *f.*

Sicily /ˈsɪsɪlɪ/ *n.* Sicile *f.*

sick /sɪk/ *a.* malade; (*humour*) macabre. **be ~,** (*vomit*) vomir. **be ~ of,** en avoir assez *or* marre de. **feel ~,** avoir mal au cœur. **~-room** *n.* chambre de malade *f.*

sicken /ˈsɪkən/ *v.t.* écœurer. —*v.i.* **be ~ing for,** (*illness*) couver.

sickle /ˈsɪkl/ *n.* faucille *f.*

sickly /ˈsɪklɪ/ *a.* (**-ier, -iest**) (*person*) maladif; (*taste, smell, etc.*) écœurant.

sickness /ˈsɪknɪs/ *n.* maladie *f.*

side /saɪd/ *n.* côté *m.*; (*of road, river*) bord *m.*; (*of hill*) flanc *m.*; (*sport*) équipe *f.* —*a.* latéral. —*v.i.* **~ with,** se ranger du côté de. **on the ~,** (*extra*) en plus; (*secretly*) en catimini. **~ by side,** côte à côte. **~-car** *n.* side-car *m.* **~-effect** *n.* effet secondaire *m.* **~-saddle** *adv.* en amazone. **~-show** *n.* petite attraction *f.* **~-step** *v.t.* (*p.t.* **-stepped**) éviter. **~-track** *v.t.* faire dévier de son sujet. **~-whiskers** *n. pl.* favoris *m. pl.*

sideboard /ˈsaɪdbɔːd/ *n.* buffet *m.* **~s,** (*whiskers*: *sl.*) pattes *f. pl.*
sideburns /ˈsaɪdbɜːnz/ *n. pl.* pattes *f. pl.*, rouflaquettes *f. pl.*
sidelight /ˈsaɪdlaɪt/ *n.* (*auto.*) veilleuse *f.*, lanterne *f.*
sideline /ˈsaɪdlaɪn/ *n.* activité secondaire *f.*
sidewalk /ˈsaɪdwɔːk/ *n.* (*Amer.*) trottoir *m.*
side|ways /ˈsaɪdweɪz/, **~long** *adv.* & *a.* de côté.
siding /ˈsaɪdɪŋ/ *n.* voie de garage *f.*
sidle /ˈsaɪdl/ *v.i.* avancer furtivement (**up to,** vers).
siege /siːdʒ/ *n.* siège *m.*
siesta /sɪˈestə/ *n.* sieste *f.*
sieve /sɪv/ *n.* tamis *m.*; (*for liquids*) passoire *f.* —*v.t.* tamiser.
sift /sɪft/ *v.t.* tamiser. —*v.i.* **~ through,** examiner.
sigh /saɪ/ *n.* soupir *m.* —*v.t./i.* soupirer.
sight /saɪt/ *n.* vue *f.*; (*scene*) spectacle *m.*; (*on gun*) mire *f.* —*v.t.* apercevoir. **at** *or* **on ~,** à vue. **catch ~ of,** apercevoir. **in ~,** visible. **lose ~ of,** perdre de vue.
sightsee|ing /ˈsaɪtsiːɪŋ/ *n.* tourisme *m.* **~r** /-ə(r)/ *n.* touriste *m./f.*
sign /saɪn/ *n.* signe *m.*; (*notice*) panneau *m.* —*v.t./i.* signer. **~ on** *or* **up,** (s')enrôler.
signal /ˈsɪgnəl/ *n.* signal *m.* —*v.t.* (*p.t.* **signalled**) communiquer (par signaux); (*person*) faire signe à. **~-box** *n.* poste d'aiguillage *m.*
signalman /ˈsɪgnəlmən/ *n.* (*pl.* **-men**) (*rail.*) aiguilleur *m.*
signatory /ˈsɪgnətrɪ/ *n.* signataire *m./f.*
signature /ˈsɪgnətʃə(r)/ *n.* signature *f.* **~ tune,** indicatif musical *m.*
signet-ring /ˈsɪgnɪtrɪŋ/ *n.* chevalière *f.*
significan|t /sɪgˈnɪfɪkənt/ *a.* important; (*meaningful*) significatif. **~ce** *n.* importance *f.*; (*meaning*) signification *f.* **~tly** *adv.* (*much*) sensiblement.
signify /ˈsɪgnɪfaɪ/ *v.t.* signifier.
signpost /ˈsaɪnpəʊst/ *n.* poteau indicateur *m.*
silence /ˈsaɪləns/ *n.* silence *m.* —*v.t.* faire taire. **~r** /-ə(r)/ *n.* (*on gun, car*) silencieux *m.*
silent /ˈsaɪlənt/ *a.* silencieux; (*film*) muet. **~ly** *adv.* silencieusement.
silhouette /sɪluːˈet/ *n.* silhouette *f.* —*v.t.* **be ~d against,** se profiler contre.
silicon /ˈsɪlɪkən/ *n.* silicium *m.* **~ chip,** microplaquette *f.*
silk /sɪlk/ *n.* soie *f.* **~en, ~y** *adjs.* soyeux.
sill /sɪl/ *n.* rebord *m.*
silly /ˈsɪlɪ/ *a.* (**-ier, -iest**) bête, idiot. **~(-billy)** *n.* (*fam.*) idiot(e) *m.* (*f.*).
silo /ˈsaɪləʊ/ *n.* (*pl.* **-os**) silo *m.*
silt /sɪlt/ *n.* vase *f.*
silver /ˈsɪlvə(r)/ *n.* argent *m.*; (*silverware*) argenterie *f.* —*a.* en argent, d'argent. **~ wedding,** noces d'argent *f. pl.* **~y** *a.* argenté; (*sound*) argentin.
silversmith /ˈsɪlvəsmɪθ/ *n.* orfèvre *m.*
silverware /ˈsɪlvəweə(r)/ *n.* argenterie *f.*
similar /ˈsɪmɪlə(r)/ *a.* semblable (**to,** à). **~ity** /-əˈlærətɪ/ *n.* ressemblance *f.* **~ly** *adv.* de même.
simile /ˈsɪmɪlɪ/ *n.* comparaison *f.*
simmer /ˈsɪmə(r)/ *v.t./i.* (*soup etc.*) mijoter; (*water*) (laisser) frémir; (*smoulder*: *fig.*) couver. **~ down,** se calmer.
simpl|e /ˈsɪmpl/ *a.* (**-er, -est**) simple. **~e-minded** *a.* simple d'esprit. **~icity** /-ˈplɪsətɪ/ *n.* simplicité *f.* **~y** *adv.* simplement; (*absolutely*) absolument.
simpleton /ˈsɪmpltən/ *n.* niais(e) *m.* (*f.*).
simplif|y /ˈsɪmplɪfaɪ/ *v.t.* simplifier. **~ication** /-ɪˈkeɪʃn/ *n.* simplification *f.*

simulat|e /ˈsɪmjʊleɪt/ *v.t.* simuler. **~ion** /-ˈleɪʃn/ *n.* simulation *f.*

simultaneous /sɪmlˈteɪnɪəs, *Amer.* saɪmlˈteɪnɪəs/ *a.* simultané. **~ly** *adv.* simultanément.

sin /sɪn/ *n.* péché *m.* —*v.i.* (*p.t.* **sinned**) pécher.

since /sɪns/ *prep.* & *adv.* depuis. —*conj.* depuis que; (*because*) puisque. **~ then,** depuis.

sincer|e /sɪnˈsɪə(r)/ *a.* sincère. **~ely** *adv.* sincèrement. **~ity** /-ˈserətɪ/ *n.* sincérité *f.*

sinew /ˈsɪnjuː/ *n.* tendon *m.* **~s,** muscles *m. pl.*

sinful /ˈsɪnfl/ *a.* (*act*) coupable, qui constitue un péché; (*shocking*) scandaleux. **~ person,** péch|eur, -eresse *m., f.*

sing /sɪŋ/ *v.t./i.* (*p.t.* **sang,** *p.p.* **sung**) chanter. **~er** *n.* chanteu|r, -se *m., f.*

singe /sɪndʒ/ *v.t.* (*pres. p.* **singeing**) brûler légèrement, roussir.

single /ˈsɪŋgl/ *a.* seul; (*not double*) simple; (*unmarried*) célibataire; (*room, bed*) pour une personne; (*ticket*) simple. —*n.* (*ticket*) aller simple *m.*; (*record*) 45 tours *m. invar.* **~s,** (*tennis*) simple *m.* —*v.t.* **~ out,** choisir. **~-handed** *a.* sans aide. **~-minded** *a.* tenace. **singly** *adv.* un à un.

singlet /ˈsɪŋglɪt/ *n.* maillot de corps *m.*

singsong /ˈsɪŋsɒŋ/ *n.* **have a ~,** chanter en chœur. —*a.* (*voice*) monotone.

singular /ˈsɪŋgjʊlə(r)/ *n.* singulier *m.* —*a.* (*uncommon & gram.*) singulier; (*noun*) au singulier. **~ly** *adv.* singulièrement.

sinister /ˈsɪnɪstə(r)/ *a.* sinistre.

sink /sɪŋk/ *v.t./i.* (*p.t.* **sank,** *p.p.* **sunk**) (faire) couler; (*of ground, person*) s'affaisser; (*well*) creuser; (*money*) investir. —*n.* (*in kitchen*) évier *m.*; (*wash-basin*) lavabo *m.* **~ in,** (*fig.*) être compris. **~ into** *v.t.* (*thrust*) enfoncer dans; *v.i.* (*go deep*) s'enfoncer dans.

sinner /ˈsɪnə(r)/ *n.* péch|eur, -eresse *m., f.*

sinuous /ˈsɪnjʊəs/ *a.* sinueux.

sinus /ˈsaɪnəs/ *n.* (*pl.* **-uses**) (*anat.*) sinus *m.*

sip /sɪp/ *n.* petite gorgée *f.* —*v.t.* (*p.t.* **sipped**) boire à petites gorgées.

siphon /ˈsaɪfn/ *n.* siphon *m.* —*v.t.* **~ off,** siphonner.

sir /sɜː(r)/ *n.* monsieur *m.* **S~,** (*title*) Sir *m.*

siren /ˈsaɪərən/ *n.* sirène *f.*

sirloin /ˈsɜːlɔɪn/ *n.* faux-filet *m.*, aloyau *m.*; (*Amer.*) romsteck *m.*

sissy /ˈsɪsɪ/ *n.* personne efféminée *f.*; (*coward*) dégonflé(e) *m.* (*f.*).

sister /ˈsɪstə(r)/ *n.* sœur *f.*; (*nurse*) infirmière en chef *f.* **~-in-law** (*pl.* **~s-in-law**) belle-sœur *f.* **~ly** *a.* fraternel.

sit /sɪt/ *v.t./i.* (*p.t.* **sat,** *pres. p.* **sitting**) (s')asseoir; (*of committee etc.*) siéger. **~ (for),** (*exam*) se présenter à. **be ~ting,** être assis. **~ around,** ne rien faire. **~ down,** s'asseoir. **~-in** *n.* sit-in *m. invar.* **~ting** *n.* séance *f.*; (*in restaurant*) service *m.* **~ting-room** *n.* salon *m.*

site /saɪt/ *n.* emplacement *m.* (**building**) **~,** chantier *m.* —*v.t.* placer, construire, situer.

situat|e /ˈsɪtʃʊeɪt/ *v.t.* situer. **be ~ed,** être situé. **~ion** /-ˈeɪʃn/ *n.* situation *f.*

six /sɪks/ *a.* & *n.* six (*m.*). **~th** *a.* & *n.* sixième (*m./f.*).

sixteen /sɪkˈstiːn/ *a.* & *n.* seize (*m.*). **~th** *a.* & *n.* seizième (*m./f.*).

sixt|y /ˈsɪkstɪ/ *a.* & *n.* soixante (*m.*). **~ieth** *a.* & *n.* soixantième (*m./f.*).

size /saɪz/ *n.* dimension *f.*; (*of person, garment, etc.*) taille *f.*; (*of shoes*) pointure *f.*; (*of sum, salary*) montant *m.*; (*extent*) ampleur *f.* —*v.t.* **~ up,** (*fam.*) jauger, juger. **~able** *a.* assez grand.

sizzle /sɪzl/ *v.i.* grésiller.
skate[1] /skeɪt/ *n. invar.* (*fish*) raie *f.*
skat|e[2] /skeɪt/ *n.* patin *m.* —*v.i.* patiner. **~er** *n.* patineu|r, -se *m., f.* **~ing** *n.* patinage *m.* **~ing-rink** *n.* patinoire *f.*
skateboard /ˈskeɪtbɔːd/ *n.* skateboard *m.*, planche à roulettes *f.*
skelet|on /ˈskelɪtən/ *n.* squelette *m.* **~on crew** *or* **staff,** effectifs minimums *m. pl.* **~al** *a.* squelettique.
sketch /sketʃ/ *n.* esquisse *f.*, croquis *m.*; (*theatre*) sketch *m.* —*v.t.* (*portrait, idea, etc.*) esquisser. —*v.i.* faire des esquisses.
sketchy /ˈsketʃɪ/ *a.* (**-ier, -iest**) sommaire, incomplet.
skew /skjuː/ *n.* **on the ~,** de travers. **~-whiff** *a.* (*fam.*) de travers.
skewer /ˈskjʊə(r)/ *n.* brochette *f.*
ski /skiː/ *n.* (*pl.* **-is**) ski *m.* —*v.i.* (*p.t.* **ski'd** *or* **skied,** *pres. p.* **skiing**) skier; (*go skiing*) faire du ski. **~er** *n.* skieu|r, -se *m., f.* **~ing** *n.* ski *m.*
skid /skɪd/ *v.i.* (*p.t.* **skidded**) déraper. —*n.* dérapage *m.*
skilful /ˈskɪlfl/ *a.* habile.
skill /skɪl/ *n.* habileté *f.*; (*craft*) métier *m.* **~s,** aptitudes *f. pl.* **~ed** *a.* habile; (*worker*) qualifié.
skim /skɪm/ *v.t.* (*p.t.* **skimmed**) écumer; (*milk*) écrémer; (*pass or glide over*) effleurer. —*v.i.* **~ through,** parcourir.
skimp /skɪmp/ *v.t./i.* lésiner (sur).
skimpy /ˈskɪmpɪ/ *a.* (**-ier, -iest**) (*clothes*) étriqué; (*meal*) chiche.
skin /skɪn/ *n.* peau *f.* —*v.t.* (*p.t.* **skinned**) (*animal*) écorcher; (*fruit*) éplucher. **~-diving** *n.* plongée sous-marine *f.*
skinflint /ˈskɪnflɪnt/ *n.* avare *m./f.*
skinny /ˈskɪnɪ/ *a.* (**-ier, -iest**) maigre, maigrichon.
skint /skɪnt/ *a.* (*sl.*) fauché.
skip[1] /skɪp/ *v.i.* (*p.t.* **skipped**) sautiller; (*with rope*) sauter à la corde. —*v.t.* (*page, class, etc.*) sauter. —*n.* petit saut *m.* **~ping-rope** *n.* corde à sauter *f.*
skip[2] /skɪp/ *n.* (*container*) benne *f.*
skipper /ˈskɪpə(r)/ *n.* capitaine *m.*
skirmish /ˈskɜːmɪʃ/ *n.* escarmouche *f.*, accrochage *m.*
skirt /skɜːt/ *n.* jupe *f.* —*v.t.* contourner. **~ing-board** *n.* plinthe *f.*
skit /skɪt/ *n.* sketch satirique *m.*
skittle /ˈskɪtl/ *n.* quille *f.*
skive /skaɪv/ *v.i.* (*sl.*) tirer au flanc.
skivvy /ˈskɪvɪ/ *n.* (*fam.*) boniche *f.*
skulk /skʌlk/ *v.i.* (*move*) rôder furtivement; (*hide*) se cacher.
skull /skʌl/ *n.* crâne *m.* **~-cap** *n.* calotte *f.*
skunk /skʌŋk/ *n.* (*animal*) mouffette *f.*; (*person*: *sl.*) salaud *m.*
sky /skaɪ/ *n.* ciel *m.* **~-blue** *a.* & *n.* bleu ciel *a.* & *m. invar.*
skylight /ˈskaɪlaɪt/ *n.* lucarne *f.*
skyscraper /ˈskaɪskreɪpə(r)/ *n.* gratte-ciel *m. invar.*
slab /slæb/ *n.* plaque *f.*, bloc *m.*; (*of paving-stone*) dalle *f.*
slack /slæk/ *a.* (**-er, -est**) (*rope*) lâche; (*person*) négligent; (*business*) stagnant; (*period*) creux. —*n.* **the ~,** (*in rope*) du mou —*v.t./i.* (se) relâcher.
slacken /ˈslækən/ *v.t./i.* (se) relâcher; (*slow*) (se) ralentir.
slacks /slæks/ *n. pl.* pantalon *m.*
slag /slæg/ *n.* scories *f. pl.*
slain /sleɪn/ *see* **slay.**
slake /sleɪk/ *v.t.* étancher.
slalom /ˈslɑːləm/ *n.* slalom *m.*
slam /slæm/ *v.t./i.* (*p.t.* **slammed**) (*door etc.*) claquer; (*throw*) flanquer; (*criticize*: *sl.*) critiquer. —*n.* (*noise*) claquement *m.*
slander /ˈslɑːndə(r)/ *n.* diffamation *f.*, calomnie *f.* —*v.t.* diffamer, calomnier. **~ous** *a.* diffamatoire.
slang /slæŋ/ *n.* argot *m.* **~y** *a.* argotique.
slant /slɑːnt/ *v.t./i.* (faire) pencher; (*news*) présenter sous un certain

jour. —*n.* inclinaison *f.*; (*bias*) angle *m.* **be ~ing,** être penché.

slap /slæp/ *v.t.* (*p.t.* **slapped**) (*strike*) donner une claque à; (*face*) gifler; (*put*) flanquer. —*n.* claque *f.*; gifle *f.* —*adv.* tout droit. **~-happy** *a.* (*carefree*: *fam.*) insouciant; (*dazed*: *fam.*) abruti. **~-up meal,** (*sl.*) gueuleton *m.*

slapdash /ˈslæpdæʃ/ *a.* négligent.

slapstick /ˈslæpstɪk/ *n.* grosse farce *f.*

slash /slæʃ/ *v.t.* (*cut*) taillader; (*sever*) trancher; (*fig.*) réduire (radicalement). —*n.* taillade *f.*

slat /slæt/ *n.* (*in blind*) lamelle *f.*

slate /sleɪt/ *n.* ardoise *f.* —*v.t.* (*fam.*) critiquer, éreinter.

slaughter /ˈslɔːtə(r)/ *v.t.* massacrer; (*animals*) abattre. —*n.* massacre *m.*; abattage *m.*

slaughterhouse /ˈslɔːtəhaʊs/ *n.* abattoir *m.*

Slav /slɑːv/ *a.* & *n.* slave (*m.*/*f.*). **~onic** /sləˈvɒnɪk/ *a.* (*lang.*) slave.

slave /sleɪv/ *n.* esclave *m.*/*f.* —*v.i.* trimer. **~-driver** *n.* négr|ier, -ière *m.*, *f.* **~ry** /-ərɪ/ *n.* esclavage *m.*

slavish /ˈsleɪvɪʃ/ *a.* servile.

slay /sleɪ/ *v.t.* (*p.t.* **slew,** *p.p.* **slain**) tuer.

sleazy /ˈsliːzɪ/ *a.* (**-ier, -iest**) (*fam.*) sordide, miteux.

sledge /sledʒ/ *n.* luge *f.*; (*horse-drawn*) traîneau *m.* **~-hammer** *n.* marteau de forgeron *m.*

sleek /sliːk/ *a.* (**-er, -est**) lisse, brillant; (*manner*) onctueux.

sleep /sliːp/ *n.* sommeil *m.* —*v.i.* (*p.t.* **slept**) dormir; (*spend the night*) coucher. —*v.t.* loger. **go to ~,** s'endormir. **~er** *n.* dormeu|r, -se *m.*, *f.*; (*beam*: *rail.*) traverse *f.*; (*berth*) couchette *f.* **~ing-bag** *n.* sac de couchage *m.* **~less** *a.* sans sommeil. **~-walker** *n.* somnambule *m.*/*f.*

sleep|y /ˈsliːpɪ/ *a.* (**-ier, -iest**) somnolent. **be ~y,** avoir sommeil. **~ily** *adv.* à moitié endormi.

sleet /sliːt/ *n.* neige fondue *f.*; (*coat of ice*: *Amer.*) verglas *m.* —*v.i.* tomber de la neige fondue.

sleeve /sliːv/ *n.* manche *f.*; (*of record*) pochette *f.* **up one's ~,** en réserve. **~less** *a.* sans manches.

sleigh /sleɪ/ *n.* traîneau *m.*

sleight /slaɪt/ *n.* **~ of hand,** prestidigitation *f.*

slender /ˈslendə(r)/ *a.* mince, svelte; (*scanty*: *fig.*) faible.

slept /slept/ *see* **sleep.**

sleuth /sluːθ/ *n.* limier *m.*

slew[1] /sluː/ *v.i.* (*turn*) virer.

slew[2] /sluː/ *see* **slay.**

slice /slaɪs/ *n.* tranche *f.* —*v.t.* couper (en tranches).

slick /slɪk/ *a.* (*unctuous*) mielleux; (*cunning*) astucieux. —*n.* **(oil) ~,** nappe de pétrole *f.*, marée noire *f.*

slide /slaɪd/ *v.t.*/*i.* (*p.t.* **slid**) glisser. —*n.* glissade *f.*; (*fall*: *fig.*) baisse *f.*; (*in playground*) toboggan *m.*; (*for hair*) barrette *f.*; (*photo.*) diapositive *f.* **~ into,** (*go silently*) se glisser dans. **~-rule** *n.* règle à calcul *f.* **sliding** *a.* (*door, panel*) à glissière, à coulisse. **sliding scale,** échelle mobile *f.*

slight /slaɪt/ *a.* (**-er, -est**) petit, léger; (*slender*) mince; (*frail*) frêle. —*v.t.* (*insult*) offenser. —*n.* affront *m.* **~est** *a.* moindre. **~ly** *adv.* légèrement, un peu.

slim /slɪm/ *a.* (**slimmer, slimmest**) mince. —*v.i.* (*p.t.* **slimmed**) maigrir. **~ness** *n.* minceur *f.*

slim|e /slaɪm/ *n.* boue (visqueuse) *f.*; (*on river-bed*) vase *f.* **~y** *a.* boueux; vaseux; (*sticky, servile*) visqueux.

sling /slɪŋ/ *n.* (*weapon, toy*) fronde *f.*; (*bandage*) écharpe *f.* —*v.t.* (*p.t.* **slung**) jeter, lancer.

slip /slɪp/ *v.t.*/*i.* (*p.t.* **slipped**) glisser. —*n.* faux pas *m.*; (*mistake*) erreur *f.*; (*petticoat*) combinaison *f.*; (*paper*) fiche *f.* **give the ~ to,** fausser compagnie à. **~ away,** s'esquiver. **~-cover** *n.* (*Amer.*) housse *f.* **~ into,** (*go*) se glisser dans; (*clothes*) mettre. **~ of the tongue,** lapsus *m.* **~-road** *n.* bretelle *f.* **~ s.o.'s mind,** échapper à qn. **~ up,** (*fam.*) gaffer. **~-up** *n.* (*fam.*) gaffe *f.*

slipper /'slɪpə(r)/ *n.* pantoufle *f.*

slippery /'slɪpərɪ/ *a.* glissant.

slipshod /'slɪpʃɒd/ *a.* (*person*) négligent; (*work*) négligé.

slit /slɪt/ *n.* fente *f.* —*v.t.* (*p.t.* **slit,** *pres. p.* **slitting**) couper, fendre.

slither /'slɪðə(r)/ *v.i.* glisser.

sliver /'slɪvə(r)/ *n.* (*of cheese etc.*) lamelle *f.*; (*splinter*) éclat *m.*

slob /slɒb/ *n.* (*fam.*) rustre *m.*

slobber /'slɒbə(r)/ *v.i.* baver.

slog /slɒg/ *v.t.* (*p.t.* **slogged**) (*hit*) frapper dur. —*v.i.* (*work*) trimer. —*n.* (*work*) travail dur *m.*; (*effort*) gros effort *m.*

slogan /'sləʊgən/ *n.* slogan *m.*

slop /slɒp/ *v.t./i.* (*p.t.* **slopped**) (se) répandre. **~s** *n. pl.* eaux sales *f. pl.*

slop|e /sləʊp/ *v.i.* être en pente; (*of handwriting*) pencher. —*n.* pente *f.*; (*of mountain*) flanc *m.* **~ing** *a.* en pente.

sloppy /'slɒpɪ/ *a.* (**-ier, -iest**) (*ground*) détrempé; (*food*) liquide; (*work*) négligé; (*person*) négligent; (*fig.*) sentimental.

slosh /slɒʃ/ *v.t.* (*fam.*) répandre; (*hit*: *sl.*) frapper. —*v.i.* patauger.

slot /slɒt/ *n.* fente *f.* —*v.t./i.* (*p.t.* **slotted**) (s')insérer. **~-machine** *n.* distributeur automatique *m.*; (*for gambling*) machine à sous *f.*

sloth /sləʊθ/ *n.* paresse *f.*

slouch /slaʊtʃ/ *v.i.* avoir le dos voûté; (*move*) marcher le dos voûté.

slovenl|y /'slʌvnlɪ/ *a.* débraillé. **~iness** *n.* débraillé *m.*

slow /sləʊ/ *a.* (**-er, -est**) lent. —*adv.* lentement. —*v.t./i.* ralentir. **be ~,** (*clock etc.*) retarder. **in ~ motion,** au ralenti. **~ly** *adv.* lentement. **~ness** *n.* lenteur *f.*

slow|coach /'sləʊkəʊtʃ/, (*Amer.*) **~poke** *ns.* lambin(e) *m.* (*f.*).

sludge /slʌdʒ/ *n.* gadoue *f.*, boue *f.*

slug /slʌg/ *n.* (*mollusc*) limace *f.*; (*bullet*) balle *f.*; (*blow*) coup *m.*

sluggish /'slʌgɪʃ/ *a.* lent, mou.

sluice /sluːs/ *n.* (*gate*) vanne *f.*

slum /slʌm/ *n.* taudis *m.*

slumber /'slʌmbə(r)/ *n.* sommeil. *m.* —*v.i.* dormir.

slump /slʌmp/ *n.* effondrement *m.*; baisse *f.*; (*in business*) marasme *m.* —*v.i.* (*collapse, fall limply*) s'effondrer; (*decrease*) baisser.

slung /slʌŋ/ *see* **sling.**

slur /slɜː(r)/ *v.t./i.* (*p.t.* **slurred**) (*spoken words*) mal articuler. —*n.* bredouillement *m.*; (*discredit*) atteinte *f.* (**on,** à).

slush /slʌʃ/ *n.* (*snow*) neige fondue *f.* **~ fund,** fonds servant à des pots-de-vin *m.* **~y** *a.* (*road*) couvert de neige fondue.

slut /slʌt/ *n.* (*dirty*) souillon *f.*; (*immoral*) dévergondée *f.*

sly /slaɪ/ *a.* (**slyer, slyest**) (*crafty*) rusé; (*secretive*) sournois. —*n.* **on the ~,** en cachette. **~ly** *adv.* sournoisement.

smack[1] /smæk/ *n.* tape *f.*; (*on face*) gifle *f.* —*v.t.* donner une tape à; gifler. —*adv.* (*fam.*) tout droit.

smack[2] /smæk/ *v.i.* **~ of sth.,** (*have flavour*) sentir qch.

small /smɔːl/ *a.* (**-er, -est**) petit. —*n.* **~ of the back,** creux des reins *m.* —*adv.* (*cut etc.*) menu. **~ness** *n.* petitesse *f.* **~ talk,** menus propos *m. pl.* **~-time** *a.* petit, peu important.

smallholding /'smɔːlhəʊldɪŋ/ *n.* petite ferme *f.*

smallpox /'smɔːlpɒks/ *n.* variole *f.*

smarmy /'smɑːmɪ/ *a.* (**-ier, -iest**) (*fam.*) obséquieux, patelin.

smart /smɑːt/ *a.* (**-er, -est**) élégant; (*clever*) astucieux, intelligent; (*brisk*) rapide. —*v.i.* (*of wound etc.*) brûler. **~ly** *adv.* élégamment. **~ness** *n.* élégance *f.*
smarten /ˈsmɑːtn/ *v.t./i.* **~ (up)**, embellir. **~ (o.s.) up**, se faire beau; (*tidy*) s'arranger.
smash /smæʃ/ *v.t./i.* (se) briser, (se) fracasser; (*opponent, record*) pulvériser. —*n.* (*noise*) fracas *m.*; (*blow*) coup *m.*; (*fig.*) collision *f.*
smashing /ˈsmæʃɪŋ/ *a.* (*fam.*) formidable, épatant.
smattering /ˈsmætərɪŋ/ *n.* connaissances vagues *f. pl.*
smear /smɪə(r)/ *v.t.* (*stain*) tacher; (*coat*) enduire; (*discredit: fig.*) entacher. —*n.* tache *f.*
smell /smel/ *n.* odeur *f.*; (*sense*) odorat *m.* —*v.t./i.* (*p.t.* **smelt** *or* **smelled**) sentir. **~ of**, sentir. **~y** *a.* malodorant.
smelt[1] /smelt/ *see* **smell.**
smelt[2] /smelt/ *v.t.* (*ore*) fondre.
smil|e /smaɪl/ *n.* sourire. —*v.i.* sourire. **~ing** *a.* souriant.
smirk /smɜːk/ *n.* sourire affecté *m.*
smite /smaɪt/ *v.t.* (*p.t.* **smote,** *p.p.* **smitten**) (*old use*) frapper.
smith /smɪθ/ *n.* forgeron *m.*
smithereens /smɪðəˈriːnz/ *n. pl.* **to** *or* **in ~,** en mille morceaux.
smitten /ˈsmɪtn/ *see* **smite.** —*a.* (*in love*) épris (**with,** de).
smock /smɒk/ *n.* blouse *f.*
smog /smɒg/ *n.* brouillard mélangé de fumée *m.*, smog *m.*
smoke /sməʊk/ *n.* fumée *f.* —*v.t./i.* fumer. **have a ~,** fumer. **~less** *a.* (*fuel*) non polluant. **~r** /-ə(r)/ *n.* fumeu|r, -se *m., f.* **~-screen** *n.* écran de fumée *m.*; (*fig.*) manœuvre de diversion *f.* **smoky** *a.* (*air*) enfumé.
smooth /smuːð/ *a.* (**-er, -est**) lisse; (*movement*) régulier; (*manners, cream*) onctueux. —*v.t.* lisser. **~ out,** (*fig.*) faire disparaître. **~ly** *adv.* facilement, doucement.
smother /ˈsmʌðə(r)/ *v.t.* (*stifle*) étouffer; (*cover*) couvrir.
smoulder /ˈsməʊldə(r)/ *v.i.* (*fire, discontent, etc.*) couver.
smudge /smʌdʒ/ *n.* tache *f.* —*v.t./i.* (se) salir, (se) tacher.
smug /smʌg/ *a.* (**smugger, smuggest**) suffisant. **~ly** *adv.* avec suffisance. **~ness** *n.* suffisance *f.*
smuggl|e /ˈsmʌgl/ *v.t.* passer (en contrebande). **~er** *n.* contreband|ier, -ière *m., f.* **~ing** *n.* contrebande *f.*
smut /smʌt/ *n.* saleté *f.* **~ty** *a.* sale.
snack /snæk/ *n.* casse-croûte *m. invar.* **~-bar** *n.* snack(-bar) *m.*
snag /snæg/ *n.* difficulté *f.*, inconvénient *m.*; (*in cloth*) accroc *m.*
snail /sneɪl/ *n.* escargot *m.* **at a ~'s pace,** à un pas de tortue.
snake /sneɪk/ *n.* serpent *m.*
snap /snæp/ *v.t./i.* (*p.t.* **snapped**) (*whip, fingers, etc.*) (faire) claquer; (*break*) (se) casser net; (*say*) dire sèchement. —*n.* claquement *m.*; (*photograph*) instantané *m.*; (*press-stud: Amer.*) bouton-pression *m.* —*a.* soudain. **~ at,** (*bite*) happer. **~ up,** (*buy*) sauter sur.
snappy /ˈsnæpɪ/ *a.* (**-ier, -iest**) (*brisk: fam.*) prompt, rapide. **make it ~,** (*fam.*) se dépêcher.
snapshot /ˈsnæpʃɒt/ *n.* instantané *m.*, photo *f.*
snare /sneə(r)/ *n.* piège *m.*
snarl /snɑːl/ *v.i.* gronder (en montrant les dents). —*n.* grondement *m.*
snatch /snætʃ/ *v.t.* (*grab*) saisir; (*steal*) voler. **~ from s.o.,** arracher à qn. —*n.* (*theft*) vol *m.*; (*short part*) fragment *m.*
sneak /sniːk/ *v.i.* aller furtivement. —*n.* (*schol., sl.*) rapporteu|r, -se *m., f.* **~y** *a.* sournois.

sneakers /ˈsniːkəz/ *n. pl.* (*shoes*) tennis *m. pl.*
sneaking /ˈsniːkɪŋ/ *a.* caché.
sneer /snɪə(r)/ *n.* ricanement *m.* —*v.i.* ricaner.
sneeze /sniːz/ *n.* éternuement *m.* —*v.i.* éternuer.
snide /snaɪd/ *a.* (*fam.*) narquois.
sniff /snɪf/ *v.t./i.* renifler. —*n.* reniflement *m.*
snigger /ˈsnɪgə(r)/ *n.* ricanement *m.* —*v.i.* ricaner.
snip /snɪp/ *v.t.* (*p.t.* **snipped**) couper. —*n.* morceau coupé *m.*; (*bargain*: *sl.*) bonne affaire *f.*
snipe /snaɪp/ *v.i.* canarder. **~r** /-ə(r)/ *n.* tireur embusqué *m.*
snippet /ˈsnɪpɪt/ *n.* bribe *f.*
snivel /ˈsnɪvl/ *v.i.* (*p.t.* **snivelled**) pleurnicher.
snob /snɒb/ *n.* snob *m./f.* **~bery** *n.* snobisme *m.* **~bish** *a.* snob *invar.*
snooker /ˈsnuːkə(r)/ *n.* (*sorte de*) jeu de billard *m.*
snoop /snuːp/ *v.i.* (*fam.*) fourrer son nez partout. **~ on,** espionner.
snooty /ˈsnuːtɪ/ *a.* (**-ier, -iest**) (*fam.*) snob *invar.*, hautain.
snooze /snuːz/ *n.* petit somme *m.* —*v.i.* faire un petit somme.
snore /snɔː(r)/ *n.* ronflement *m.* —*v.i.* ronfler.
snorkel /ˈsnɔːkl/ *n.* tuba *m.*
snort /snɔːt/ *n.* grognement *m.* —*v.i.* (*person*) grogner; (*horse*) s'ébrouer.
snout /snaʊt/ *n.* museau *m.*
snow /snəʊ/ *n.* neige *f.* —*v.i.* neiger. **be ~ed under with,** être submergé de. **~-drift** *n.* congère *f.* **~-plough** *n.* chasse-neige *m. invar.* **~y** *a.* neigeux.
snowball /ˈsnəʊbɔːl/ *n.* boule de neige *f.*
snowdrop /ˈsnəʊdrɒp/ *n.* perce-neige *m./f. invar.*
snowfall /ˈsnəʊfɔːl/ *n.* chute de neige *f.*
snowflake /ˈsnəʊfleɪk/ *n.* flocon de neige *m.*
snowman /ˈsnəʊmæn/ *n.* (*pl.* **-men**) bonhomme de neige *m.*
snowstorm /ˈsnəʊstɔːm/ *n.* tempête de neige *f.*
snub /snʌb/ *v.t.* (*p.t.* **snubbed**) (*person*) snober; (*offer*) repousser. —*n.* rebuffade *f.*
snub-nosed /ˈsnʌbnəʊzd/ *a.* au nez retroussé.
snuff¹ /snʌf/ *n.* tabac à priser *m.*
snuff² /snʌf/ *v.t.* (*candle*) moucher.
snuffle /ˈsnʌfl/ *v.i.* renifler.
snug /snʌg/ *a.* (**snugger, snuggest**) (*cosy*) confortable; (*tight*) bien ajusté; (*safe*) sûr.
snuggle /ˈsnʌgl/ *v.i.* se pelotonner.
so /səʊ/ *adv.* si, tellement; (*thus*) ainsi. —*conj.* donc, alors. **~ am I,** moi aussi. **~ does he,** lui aussi. **that is ~,** c'est ça. **I think ~,** je pense que oui. **five or ~,** environ cinq. **~-and-so** *n.* un(e) tel(le) *m.* (*f.*). **~ as to,** de manière à. **~-called** *a.* soi-disant *invar.* **~ far,** jusqu'ici. **~ long!,** (*fam.*) à bientôt! **~ many, ~ much,** tant (de). **~-so** *a.* & *adv.* comme ci comme ça. **~ that,** pour que.
soak /səʊk/ *v.t./i.* (faire) tremper (**in,** dans). **~ in** *or* **up,** absorber. **~ing** *a.* trempé.
soap /səʊp/ *n.* savon *m.* —*v.t.* savonner. **~ opera,** feuilleton mélo *m.* **~ powder,** lessive *f.* **~y** *a.* savonneux.
soar /sɔː(r)/ *v.i.* monter (en flèche).
sob /sɒb/ *n.* sanglot *m.* —*v.i.* (*p.t.* **sobbed**) sangloter.
sober /ˈsəʊbə(r)/ *a.* qui n'est pas ivre; (*serious*) sérieux; (*colour*) sobre. —*v.t./i.* **~ up,** dessoûler.
soccer /ˈsɒkə(r)/ *n.* (*fam.*) football *m.*
sociable /ˈsəʊʃəbl/ *a.* sociable.
social /ˈsəʊʃl/ *a.* social; (*gathering, life*) mondain. —*n.* réunion (amicale) *f.*, fête *f.* **~ly** *adv.*

socialement; (*meet*) en société. **~ security,** aide sociale *f.*; (*for old age*: *Amer.*) pension (de retraite) *f.* **~ worker,** assistant(e) social(e) *m.* (*f.*).
socialis|t /ˈsəʊʃəlɪst/ *n.* socialiste *m.*/*f.* **~m** /-zəm/ *n.* socialisme *m.*
socialize /ˈsəʊʃəlaɪz/ *v.i.* se mêler aux autres. **~ with,** fréquenter.
society /səˈsaɪətɪ/ *n.* société *f.*
sociolog|y /səʊsɪˈɒlədʒɪ/ *n.* sociologie *f.* **~ical** /-əˈlɒdʒɪkl/ *a.* sociologique. **~ist** *n.* sociologue *m.*/*f.*
sock[1] /sɒk/ *n.* chaussette *f.*
sock[2] /sɒk/ *v.t.* (*hit*: *sl.*) flanquer un coup (de poing) à.
socket /ˈsɒkɪt/ *n.* cavité *f.*; (*for lamp*) douille *f.*; (*wall plug*) prise de courant *f.*; (*of tooth*) alvéole *f.*
soda /ˈsəʊdə/ *n.* soude *f.* **~(-pop),** (*Amer.*) soda *m.* **~(-water),** soda *m.*, eau de Seltz *f.*
sodden /ˈsɒdn/ *a.* détrempé.
sodium /ˈsəʊdɪəm/ *n.* sodium *m.*
sofa /ˈsəʊfə/ *n.* sofa *m.*
soft /sɒft/ *a.* (**-er, -est**) (*gentle, lenient*) doux; (*not hard*) doux, mou; (*heart, wood*) tendre; (*silly*) ramolli; (*easy*: *sl.*) facile. **~ drink,** boisson non alcoolisée *f.* **~ly** *adv.* doucement. **~ness** *n.* douceur *f.* **~ spot,** faible *m.*
soften /ˈsɒfn/ *v.t.*/*i.* (se) ramollir; (*tone down, lessen*) (s')adoucir.
software /ˈsɒftweə(r)/ *n.* (*for computer*) logiciel *m.*
soggy /ˈsɒgɪ/ *a.* (**-ier, -iest**) détrempé; (*bread etc.*) ramolli.
soil[1] /sɔɪl/ *n.* sol *m.*, terre *f.*
soil[2] /sɔɪl/ *v.t.*/*i.* (se) salir.
solar /ˈsəʊlə(r)/ *a.* solaire.
sold /səʊld/ *see* **sell.** —*a.* **~ out,** épuisé.
solder /ˈsɒldə(r), *Amer.* ˈsɒdə(r)/ *n.* soudure *f.* —*v.t.* souder.
soldier /ˈsəʊldʒə(r)/ *n.* soldat *m.* —*v.i.* **~ on,** (*fam.*) persévérer.
sole[1] /səʊl/ *n.* (*of foot*) plante *f.*; (*of shoe*) semelle *f.*
sole[2] /səʊl/ *n.* (*fish*) sole *f.*
sole[3] /səʊl/ *a.* unique, seul. **~ly** *adv.* uniquement.
solemn /ˈsɒləm/ *a.* (*formal*) solennel; (*not cheerful*) grave. **~ity** /səˈlemnətɪ/ *n.* solennité *f.* **~ly** *adv.* solennellement; gravement.
solicit /səˈlɪsɪt/ *v.t.* (*seek*) solliciter. —*v.i.* (*of prostitute*) racoler.
solicitor /səˈlɪsɪtə(r)/ *n.* avoué *m.*
solid /ˈsɒlɪd/ *a.* solide; (*not hollow*) plein; (*gold*) massif; (*mass*) compact; (*meal*) substantiel. —*n.* solide *m.* **~s,** (*food*) aliments solides *m. pl.* **~ity** /səˈlɪdətɪ/ *n.* solidité *f.* **~ly** *adv.* solidement.
solidarity /sɒlɪˈdærətɪ/ *n.* solidarité *f.*
solidify /səˈlɪdɪfaɪ/ *v.t.*/*i.* (se) solidifier.
soliloquy /səˈlɪləkwɪ/ *n.* monologue *m.*, soliloque *m.*
solitary /ˈsɒlɪtrɪ/ *a.* (*alone, lonely*) solitaire; (*only, single*) seul.
solitude /ˈsɒlɪtjuːd/ *n.* solitude *f.*
solo /ˈsəʊləʊ/ *n.* (*pl.* **-os**) solo *m.* —*a.* (*mus.*) solo *invar.*; (*flight*) en solitaire. **~ist** *n.* soliste *m.*/*f.*
solstice /ˈsɒlstɪs/ *n.* solstice *m.*
soluble /ˈsɒljʊbl/ *a.* soluble.
solution /səˈluːʃn/ *n.* solution *f.*
solv|e /sɒlv/ *v.t.* résoudre. **~able** *a.* soluble.
solvent /ˈsɒlvənt/ *a.* (*comm.*) solvable. —*n.* (dis)solvant *m.*
sombre /ˈsɒmbə(r)/ *a.* sombre.
some /sʌm/ *a.* (*quantity, number*) du, de l'*, de la, des; (*unspecified, some or other*) un(e), quelque; (*a little*) un peu de; (*a certain*) un(e) certain(e), quelque; (*contrasted with others*) quelques, certain(e)s. —*pron.* quelques-un(e)s; (*certain quantity of it or them*) en; (*a little*) un peu. —*adv.* (*approximately*) quelque. **pour ~ milk,** versez du lait. **he wants ~,** il en veut. **~ book (or other),** un livre (quelconque), quelque livre.

somebody /ˈsʌmbədɪ/ *pron.* quelqu'un. —*n.* **be a ~,** être quelqu'un.
somehow /ˈsʌmhaʊ/ *adv.* d'une manière ou d'une autre; (*for some reason*) je ne sais pas pourquoi.
someone /ˈsʌmwʌn/ *pron.* & *n.* = **somebody.**
somersault /ˈsʌməsɔːlt/ *n.* culbute *f.* —*v.i.* faire la culbute.
something /ˈsʌmθɪŋ/ *pron.* & *n.* quelque chose (*m.*). **~ good**/*etc.*, quelque chose de bon/*etc.* **~ like,** un peu comme.
sometime /ˈsʌmtaɪm/ *adv.* un jour. —*a.* (*former*) ancien.
sometimes /ˈsʌmtaɪmz/ *adv.* quelquefois, parfois.
somewhat /ˈsʌmwɒt/ *adv.* quelque peu, un peu.
somewhere /ˈsʌmweə(r)/ *adv.* quelque part.
son /sʌn/ *n.* fils *m.* **~-in-law** *n.* (*pl.* **~s-in-law**) beau-fils *m.*, gendre *m.*
Sonar /ˈsəʊnɑː(r)/ *n.* sonar *m.*
sonata /səˈnɑːtə/ *n.* sonate *f.*
song /sɒŋ/ *n.* chanson *f.* **going for a ~,** à vendre pour une bouchée de pain.
sonic /ˈsɒnɪk/ *a.* **~ boom,** bang supersonique *m.*
sonnet /ˈsɒnɪt/ *n.* sonnet *m.*
sonny /ˈsʌnɪ/ *n.* (*fam.*) fiston *m.*
soon /suːn/ *adv.* (**-er, -est**) bientôt; (*early*) tôt. **I would ~er stay,** j'aimerais mieux rester. **~ after,** peu après. **~er or later,** tôt ou tard.
soot /sʊt/ *n.* suie *f.* **~y** *a.* couvert de suie.
sooth|e /suːð/ *v.t.* calmer. **~ing** *a.* (*remedy, words, etc.*) calmant.
sophisticated /səˈfɪstɪkeɪtɪd/ *a.* raffiné; (*machine etc.*) sophistiqué.
sophomore /ˈsɒfəmɔː(r)/ *n.* (*Amer.*) étudiant(e) de seconde année *m.* (*f.*).
soporific /sɒpəˈrɪfɪk/ *a.* soporifique.
sopping /ˈsɒpɪŋ/ *a.* trempé.
soppy /ˈsɒpɪ/ *a.* (**-ier, -iest**) (*fam.*) sentimental; (*silly: fam.*) bête.
soprano /səˈprɑːnəʊ/ *n.* (*pl.* **-os**) (*voice*) soprano *m.*; (*singer*) soprano *m.*/*f.*
sorcerer /ˈsɔːsərə(r)/ *n.* sorcier *m.*
sordid /ˈsɔːdɪd/ *a.* sordide.
sore /ˈsɔː(r)/ *a.* (**-er, -est**) douloureux; (*vexed*) en rogne (**at, with,** contre). —*n.* plaie *f.*
sorely /ˈsɔːlɪ/ *adv.* fortement.
sorrow /ˈsɒrəʊ/ *n.* chagrin *m.* **~ful** *a.* triste.
sorry /ˈsɒrɪ/ *a.* (**-ier, -iest**) (*regretful*) désolé (**to,** de; **that,** que); (*wretched*) triste. **feel ~ for,** plaindre. **~!,** pardon!
sort /sɔːt/ *n.* genre *m.*, sorte *f.*, espèce *f.*; (*person: fam.*) type *m.* —*v.t.* **~ (out),** (*classify*) trier. **be out of ~s,** ne pas être dans son assiette. **~ out,** (*tidy*) ranger; (*arrange*) arranger; (*problem*) régler.
soufflé /ˈsuːfleɪ/ *n.* soufflé *m.*
sought /sɔːt/ *see* **seek.**
soul /səʊl/ *n.* âme *f.*
soulful /ˈsəʊlfl/ *a.* plein de sentiment, très expressif.
sound[1] /saʊnd/ *n.* son *m.*, bruit *m.* —*v.t.*/*i.* sonner; (*seem*) sembler (**as if,** que). **~ a horn,** klaxonner. **~ barrier,** mur du son *m.* **~ like,** sembler être. **~-proof** *a.* insonorisé; *v.t.* insonoriser.
sound[2] /saʊnd/ *a.* (**-er, -est**) solide; (*healthy*) sain; (*sensible*) sensé. **~ asleep,** profondément endormi. **~ly** *adv.* solidement; (*sleep*) profondément.
sound[3] /saʊnd/ *v.t.* (*test*) sonder.
soup /suːp/ *n.* soupe *f.*, potage *m.* **in the ~,** (*sl.*) dans le pétrin.
sour /ˈsaʊə(r)/ *a.* (**-er, -est**) aigre. —*v.t.*/*i.* (s')aigrir.
source /sɔːs/ *n.* source *f.*

south /saʊθ/ *n.* sud *m.* —*a.* sud *invar.*, du sud. —*adv.* vers le sud. **S~ Africa/America,** Afrique/ Amérique du Sud *f.* **S~ African** *a.* & *n.* sud-africain(e) (*m.* (*f.*)). **S~ American** *a.* & *n.* sud-américain(e) (*m.* (*f.*)). **~-east** *n.* sud-est *m.* **~erly** /ˈsʌðəlɪ/ *a.* du sud. **~ward** *a.* au sud. **~wards** *adv.* vers le sud. **~-west** *n.* sud-ouest *m.*

southern /ˈsʌðən/ *a.* du sud. **~er** *n.* habitant(e) du sud *m.* (*f.*).

souvenir /suːvəˈnɪə(r)/ *n.* (*thing*) souvenir *m.*

sovereign /ˈsɒvrɪn/ *n.* & *a.* souverain(e) (*m.* (*f.*)). **~ty** *n.* souveraineté *f.*

Soviet /ˈsəʊvɪət/ *a.* soviétique. **the ~ Union,** l'Union soviétique *f.*

sow[1] /səʊ/ *v.t.* (*p.t.* **sowed,** *p.p.* **sowed** *or* **sown**) (*seed etc.*) semer; (*land*) ensemencer.

sow[2] /saʊ/ *n.* (*pig*) truie *f.*

soya /ˈsɔɪə/ *n.* **~ bean,** graine de soja *f.*

spa /spɑː/ *n.* station thermale *f.*

space /speɪs/ *n.* espace *m.*; (*room*) place *f.*; (*period*) période *f.* —*a.* (*research etc.*) spatial. —*v.t.* **~ (out),** espacer.

space|craft /ˈspeɪskrɑːft/ *n. invar.*, **~ship** *n.* engin spatial *m.*

spacesuit /ˈspeɪss(j)uːt/ *n.* scaphandre *m.*

spacious /ˈspeɪʃəs/ *a.* spacieux.

spade[1] /speɪd/ *n.* (*large, for garden*) bêche *f.*; (*child's*) pelle *f.*

spade[2] /speɪd/ *n.* (*cards*) pique *m.*

spadework /ˈspeɪdwɜːk/ *n.* (*fig.*) travail préparatoire *m.*

spaghetti /spəˈgetɪ/ *n.* spaghetti *m. pl.*

Spa|in /speɪn/ *n.* Espagne *f.* **~niard** /ˈspænɪəd/ *n.* Espagnol(e) *m.* (*f.*). **~nish** /ˈspænɪʃ/ *a.* espagnol; *n.* (*lang.*) espagnol *m.*

span[1] /spæn/ *n.* (*of arch*) portée *f.*; (*of wings*) envergure *f.*; (*of time*) durée *f.* —*v.t.* (*p.t.* **spanned**) enjamber; (*in time*) embrasser.

span[2] /spæn/ *see* **spick.**

spaniel /ˈspænɪəl/ *n.* épagneul *m.*

spank /spæŋk/ *v.t.* donner une fessée à. **~ing** *n.* fessée *f.*

spanner /ˈspænə(r)/ *n.* (*tool*) clé (plate) *f.*; (*adjustable*) clé à molette *f.*

spar /spɑː(r)/ *v.i.* (*p.t.* **sparred**) s'entraîner (à la boxe).

spare /speə(r)/ *v.t.* épargner; (*do without*) se passer de; (*afford to give*) donner, accorder; (*use with restraint*) ménager. —*a.* (*surplus*) de trop; (*tyre, shoes, etc.*) de rechange; (*room, bed*) d'ami. —*n.* **~ (part),** pièce de rechange *f.* **~ time,** loisirs *m. pl.*

sparing /ˈspeərɪŋ/ *a.* frugal. **~ of,** avare de. **~ly** *adv.* frugalement.

spark /spɑːk/ *n.* étincelle *f.* —*v.t.* **~ off,** (*initiate*) provoquer. **~(ing)-plug** *n.* bougie *f.*

sparkle /ˈspɑːkl/ *v.i.* étinceler. —*n.* étincellement *m.*

sparkling /ˈspɑːklɪŋ/ *a.* (*wine*) mousseux, pétillant.

sparrow /ˈspærəʊ/ *n.* moineau *m.*

sparse /spɑːs/ *a.* clairsemé. **~ly** *adv.* (*furnished etc.*) peu.

spartan /ˈspɑːtn/ *a.* spartiate.

spasm /ˈspæzəm/ *n.* (*of muscle*) spasme *m.*; (*of coughing, anger, etc.*) accès *m.*

spasmodic /spæzˈmɒdɪk/ *a.* intermittent.

spastic /ˈspæstɪk/ *n.* handicapé(e) moteur *m.* (*f.*).

spat /spæt/ *see* **spit**[1].

spate /speɪt/ *n.* **a ~ of,** (*letters etc.*) une avalanche de.

spatter /ˈspætə(r)/ *v.t.* éclabousser (**with,** de).

spatula /ˈspætjʊlə/ *n.* spatule *f.*

spawn /spɔːn/ *n.* frai *m.*, œufs *m. pl.* —*v.t.* pondre. —*v.i.* frayer.

speak /spiːk/ *v.i.* (*p.t.* **spoke,** *p.p.* **spoken**) parler. —*v.t.* (*say*) dire;

(*language*) parler. ~ **up,** parler plus fort.

speaker /'spiːkə(r)/ *n.* (*in public*) orateur *m.*; (*loudspeaker*) haut-parleur *m.* **be a French/a good/** *etc.* **~,** parler français/bien/ *etc.*

spear /spɪə(r)/ *n.* lance *f.*

spearhead /'spɪəhed/ *n.* fer de lance *m.* —*v.t.* (*lead*) mener.

spearmint /'spɪəmɪnt/ *n.* menthe verte *f.* —*a.* à la menthe.

spec /spek/ *n.* **on ~,** (*as speculation: fam.*) à tout hasard.

special /'speʃl/ *a.* spécial; (*exceptional*) exceptionnel. **~ity** /-ɪ'ælətɪ/ *n.* spécialité *f.* **~ly** *adv.* spécialement. **~ty** *n.* spécialité *f.*

specialist /'speʃəlɪst/ *n.* spécialiste *m./f.*

specialize /'speʃəlaɪz/ *v.i.* se spécialiser (**in,** en). **~d** *a.* spécialisé.

species /'spiːʃɪz/ *n. invar.* espèce *f.*

specific /spə'sɪfɪk/ *a.* précis, explicite. **~ally** *adv.* explicitement; (*exactly*) précisément.

specif|y /'spesɪfaɪ/ *v.t.* spécifier. **~ication** /-ɪ'keɪʃn/ *n.* spécification *f.*; (*details*) prescriptions *f. pl.*

specimen /'spesɪmɪn/ *n.* spécimen *m.*, échantillon *m.*

speck /spek/ *n.* (*stain*) (petite) tache *f.*; (*particle*) grain *m.*

speckled /'spekld/ *a.* tacheté.

specs /speks/ *n. pl.* (*fam.*) lunettes *f. pl.*

spectacle /'spektəkl/ *n.* spectacle *m.* **~s,** lunettes *f. pl.*

spectacular /spek'tækjʊlə(r)/ *a.* spectaculaire.

spectator /spek'teɪtə(r)/ *n.* specta|teur, -trice *m., f.*

spectre /'spektə(r)/ *n.* spectre *m.*

spectrum /'spektrəm/ *n.* (*pl.* **-tra**) spectre *m.*; (*of ideas etc.*) gamme *f.*

speculat|e /'spekjʊleɪt/ *v.i.* s'interroger (**about,** sur); (*comm.*) spéculer. **~ion** /-'leɪʃn/ *n.* conjectures *f. pl.*; (*comm.*) spéculation *f.* **~or** *n.* spécula|teur, -trice *m., f.*

speech /spiːtʃ/ *n.* (*faculty*) parole *f.*; (*diction*) élocution *f.*; (*dialect*) langage *m.*; (*address*) discours *m.* **~less** *a.* muet (**with,** de).

speed /spiːd/ *n.* (*of movement*) vitesse *f.*; (*swiftness*) rapidité *f.* —*v.i.* (*p.t.* **sped** /sped/) aller vite; (*p.t.* **speeded**) (*drive too fast*) aller trop vite. **~ up,** accélérer; (*of pace*) s'accélérer. **~ing** *n.* excès de vitesse *m.*

speedometer /spiː'dɒmɪtə(r)/ *n.* compteur (de vitesse) *m.*

speedway /'spiːdweɪ/ *n.* piste pour motos *f.*; (*Amer.*) autodrome *m.*

speed|y /'spiːdɪ/ *a.* (**-ier, -iest**) rapide. **~ily** *adv.* rapidement.

spell[1] /spel/ *n.* (*magic*) charme *m.*, sortilège *m.*; (*curse*) sort *m.*

spell[2] /spel/ *v.t./i.* (*p.t.* **spelled** *or* **spelt**) écrire; (*mean*) signifier. **~ out,** épeler; (*explain*) expliquer. **~ing** *n.* orthographe *f.*

spell[3] /spel/ *n.* (courte) période *f.*

spend /spend/ *v.t.* (*p.t.* **spent**) (*money*) dépenser (**on,** pour); (*time, holiday*) passer; (*energy*) consacrer (**on,** à). —*v.i.* dépenser.

spendthrift /'spendθrɪft/ *n.* dépens|ier, -ière *m., f.*

spent /spent/ *see* **spend.** —*a.* (*used*) utilisé; (*person*) épuisé.

sperm /spɜːm/ *n.* (*pl.* **sperms** *or* **sperm**) (*semen*) sperme *m.*; (*cell*) spermatozoïde *m.*

spew /spjuː/ *v.t./i.* vomir.

sphere /sfɪə(r)/ *n.* sphère *f.*

spherical /'sferɪkl/ *a.* sphérique.

sphinx /sfɪŋks/ *n.* sphinx *m.*

spic|e /spaɪs/ *n.* épice *f.*; (*fig.*) piquant *m.* **~y** *a.* épicé; piquant.

spick /spɪk/ *a.* **~ and span,** impeccable, d'une propreté parfaite.

spider /'spaɪdə(r)/ *n.* araignée *f.*

spik|e /spaɪk/ *n.* (*of metal etc.*) pointe *f.* **~y** *a.* garni de pointes.

spill /spɪl/ *v.t.* (*p.t.* **spilled** *or* **spilt**) renverser, répandre. —*v.i.* se répandre. **~ over,** déborder.

spin /spɪn/ *v.t./i.* (*p.t.* **spun,** *pres. p.* **spinning**) (*wool, web, of spinner*) filer; (*turn*) (faire) tourner; (*story*) débiter. —*n.* (*movement, excursion*) tour *m.* **~-drier** *n.* essoreuse *f.* **~ning-wheel** *n.* rouet *m.* **~-off** *n.* avantage accessoire *m.*; (*by-product*) dérivé *m.*

spinach /'spɪnɪdʒ/ *n.* (*plant*) épinard *m.*; (*as food*) épinards *m. pl.*

spinal /'spaɪnl/ *a.* vertébral. **~ cord,** moelle épinière *f.*

spindl|e /'spɪndl/ *n.* fuseau *m.* **~y** *a.* filiforme, grêle.

spine /spaɪn/ *n.* colonne vertébrale *f.*; (*prickle*) piquant *m.*

spineless /'spaɪnlɪs/ *a.* (*fig.*) sans caractère, mou, lâche.

spinster /'spɪnstə(r)/ *n.* célibataire *f.*; (*pej.*) vieille fille *f.*

spiral /'spaɪərəl/ *a.* en spirale; (*staircase*) en colimaçon. —*n.* spirale *f.* —*v.i.* (*p.t.* **spiralled**) monter (en spirale).

spire /'spaɪə(r)/ *n.* flèche *f.*

spirit /'spɪrɪt/ *n.* esprit *m.*; (*boldness*) courage *m.* **~s,** (*morale*) moral *m.*; (*drink*) spiritueux *m. pl.* —*v.t.* **~ away,** faire disparaître. **~-lamp** *n.* lampe à alcool *f.* **~-level** *n.* niveau à bulle *m.*

spirited /'spɪrɪtɪd/ *a.* fougueux.

spiritual /'spɪrɪtʃʊəl/ *a.* spirituel. —*n.* (*song*) (negro-)spiritual *m.*

spiritualis|t /'spɪrɪtʃʊəlɪst/ *n.* spirite *m./f.* **~m** /-zəm/ *n.* spiritisme *m.*

spit[1] /spɪt/ *v.t./i.* (*p.t.* **spat** *or* **spit,** *pres. p.* **spitting**) cracher; (*of rain*) crachiner. —*n.* crachat(s) *m.* (*pl.*). **the ~ting image of,** le portrait craché *or* vivant de.

spit[2] /spɪt/ *n.* (*for meat*) broche *f.*

spite /spaɪt/ *n.* rancune *f.* —*v.t.* contrarier. **in ~ of,** malgré. **~ful** *a.* méchant, rancunier. **~fully** *adv.* méchamment.

spittle /'spɪtl/ *n.* crachat(s) *m.* (*pl.*).

splash /splæʃ/ *v.t.* éclabousser. —*v.i.* faire des éclaboussures. **~ (about),** patauger. —*n.* (*act, mark*) éclaboussure *f.*; (*sound*) plouf *m.*; (*of colour*) tache *f.*

spleen /spliːn/ *n.* (*anat.*) rate *f.*

splendid /'splendɪd/ *a.* magnifique, splendide.

splendour /'splendə(r)/ *n.* splendeur *f.*, éclat *m.*

splint /splɪnt/ *n.* (*med.*) éclisse *f.*

splinter /'splɪntə(r)/ *n.* éclat *m.*; (*in finger*) écharde *f.* **~ group,** groupe dissident *m.*

split /splɪt/ *v.t./i.* (*p.t.* **split,** *pres. p.* **splitting**) (se) fendre; (*tear*) (se) déchirer; (*divide*) (se) diviser; (*share*) partager; (*of friends*) rompre. —*n.* fente *f.*; déchirure *f.*; (*share: fam.*) part *f.*, partage *m.*; (*quarrel*) rupture *f.*; (*pol.*) scission *f.* **a ~ second,** un rien de temps. **~ one's sides,** se tordre (de rire).

splurge /splɜːdʒ/ *v.i.* (*fam.*) faire de folles dépenses.

splutter /'splʌtə(r)/ *v.i.* crachoter; (*stammer*) bafouiller; (*engine*) tousser; (*fat*) crépiter.

spoil /spɔɪl/ *v.t.* (*p.t.* **spoilt** *or* **spoiled**) (*pamper*) gâter; (*ruin*) abîmer; (*mar*) gâcher, gâter. —*n.* **~(s),** (*plunder*) butin *m.* **~-sport** *n.* trouble-fête *m./f. invar.*

spoke[1] /spəʊk/ *n.* rayon *m.*

spoke[2], **spoken** /spəʊk, 'spəʊkən/ *see* **speak.**

spokesman /'spəʊksmən/ *n.* (*pl.* **-men**) porte-parole *m. invar.*

sponge /spʌndʒ/ *n.* éponge *f.* —*v.t.* éponger. —*v.i.* **~ on,** vivre aux crochets de. **~-cake** *n.* gâteau de Savoie *m.* **~r** /-ə(r)/ *n.* parasite *m.*

spongy *a.* spongieux.

sponsor /'spɒnsə(r)/ *n.* personne qui assure le patronage *f.*; (*surety*) garant *m.*; (*for membership*) parrain *m.*, marraine *f.* —*v.t.* patronner; (*member*) parrainer. **~ship** *n.* patronage *m.*; parrainage *m.*

spontane|ous /spɒn'teɪnɪəs/ *a.* spontané. **~ity** /-tə'niːətɪ/ *n.* spontanéité *f.* **~ously** *adv.* spontanément.

spoof /spuːf/ *n.* (*fam.*) parodie *f.*

spooky /'spuːkɪ/ *a.* (**-ier, -iest**) (*fam.*) qui donne des frissons.

spool /spuːl/ *n.* bobine *f.*

spoon /spuːn/ *n.* cuiller *f.* **~-feed** *v.t.* (*p.t.* **-fed**) nourrir à la cuiller; (*help*: *fig.*) mâcher la besogne à. **~ful** *n.* (*pl.* **-fuls**) cuillerée *f.*

sporadic /spə'rædɪk/ *a.* sporadique.

sport /spɔːt/ *n.* sport *m.* (**good**) **~,** (*person*: *sl.*) chic type *m.* —*v.t.* (*display*) exhiber, arborer. **~s car/coat,** voiture/veste de sport *f.* **~y** *a.* (*fam.*) sportif.

sporting /'spɔːtɪŋ/ *a.* sportif. **a ~ chance,** une assez bonne chance.

sports|man /'spɔːtsmən/ *n.* (*pl.* **-men**) sportif *m.* **~manship** *n.* sportivité *f.* **~woman** *n.* (*pl.* **-women**) sportive *f.*

spot /spɒt/ *n.* (*mark, stain*) tache *f.*; (*dot*) point *m.*; (*in pattern*) pois *m.*; (*drop*) goutte *f.*; (*place*) endroit *m.*; (*pimple*) bouton *m.* —*v.t.* (*p.t.* **spotted**) (*fam.*) apercevoir. **a ~ of,** (*fam.*) un peu de. **be in a ~,** (*fam.*) avoir des problèmes. **on the ~,** sur place; (*without delay*) sur le coup. **~ check,** contrôle à l'improviste *m.* **~ted** *a.* tacheté; (*fabric*) à pois. **~ty** *a.* (*skin*) boutonneux.

spotless /'spɒtlɪs/ *a.* impeccable.

spotlight /'spɒtlaɪt/ *n.* (*lamp*) projecteur *m.*, spot *m.*

spouse /spaʊz/ *n.* époux *m.*, épouse *f.*

spout /spaʊt/ *n.* (*of vessel*) bec *m.*; (*of liquid*) jet *m.* —*v.i.* jaillir. **up the ~,** (*ruined*: *sl.*) fichu.

sprain /spreɪn/ *n.* entorse *f.*, foulure *f.* —*v.t.* **~ one's wrist**/*etc.*, se fouler le poignet/*etc.*

sprang /spræŋ/ *see* **spring.**

sprawl /sprɔːl/ *v.i.* (*town, person, etc.*) s'étaler. —*n.* étalement *m.*

spray[1] /spreɪ/ *n.* (*of flowers*) gerbe *f.*

spray[2] /spreɪ/ *n.* (*water*) gerbe d'eau *f.*; (*from sea*) embruns *m. pl.*; (*device*) bombe *f.*, atomiseur *m.* —*v.t.* (*surface, insecticide*) vaporiser; (*plant etc.*) arroser.

spread /spred/ *v.t./i.* (*p.t.* **spread**) (*stretch, extend*) (s')étendre; (*news, fear, etc.*) (se) répandre; (*illness*) (se) propager; (*butter etc.*) (s')étaler. —*n.* propagation *f.*; (*paste*) pâte à tartiner *f.* **~-eagled** *a.* bras et jambes écartés.

spree /spriː/ *n.* **go on a ~,** (*have fun*: *fam.*) faire la noce.

sprig /sprɪg/ *n.* (*shoot*) brin *m.*; (*twig*) brindille *f.*

sprightly /'spraɪtlɪ/ *a.* (**-ier, -iest**) alerte, vif.

spring /sprɪŋ/ *v.i.* (*p.t.* **sprang,** *p.p.* **sprung**) bondir. —*v.t.* faire, annoncer, *etc.* à l'improviste (**on,** à). —*n.* bond *m.*; (*device*) ressort *m.*; (*season*) printemps *m.*; (*of water*) source *f.* **~-clean** *v.t.* nettoyer de fond en comble. **~ from,** provenir de. **~ up,** surgir.

springboard /'sprɪŋbɔːd/ *n.* tremplin *m.*

springtime /'sprɪŋtaɪm/ *n.* printemps *m.*

springy /'sprɪŋɪ/ *a.* (**-ier, -iest**) élastique.

sprinkle /'sprɪŋkl/ *v.t.* (*with liquid*) arroser (**with,** de); (*with salt, flour*) saupoudrer (**with,** de). **~ sand**/*etc.*, répandre du sable/*etc.*

sprinkling /'sprɪŋklɪŋ/ *n.* (*amount*) petite quantité *f.*

sprint /sprɪnt/ *v.i.* (*sport*) sprinter. —*n.* sprint *m.* **~er** *n.* sprinteu|r, -se *m., f.*

sprite /spraɪt/ *n.* lutin *m.*

sprout /spraʊt/ *v.t./i.* pousser. —*n.* (*on plant etc.*) pousse *f.* (**Brussels**) **~s,** choux de Bruxelles *m. pl.*

spruce[1] /spru:s/ *a.* pimpant. *—v.t.* **~ o.s. up,** se faire beau.
spruce[2] /spru:s/ *n.* (*tree*) épicéa *m.*
sprung /sprʌŋ/ *see* **spring.** *—a.* (*mattress etc.*) à ressorts.
spry /spraɪ/ *a.* **(spryer, spryest)** alerte, vif.
spud /spʌd/ *n.* (*sl.*) patate *f.*
spun /spʌn/ *see* **spin.**
spur /spɜ:(r)/ *n.* (*of rider, cock, etc.*) éperon *m.*; (*stimulus*) aiguillon *m.* *—v.t.* (*p.t.* **spurred**) éperonner. **on the ~ of the moment,** sous l'impulsion du moment.
spurious /ˈspjʊərɪəs/ *a.* faux.
spurn /spɜ:n/ *v.t.* repousser.
spurt /spɜ:t/ *v.i.* jaillir; (*fig.*) accélérer. *—n.* jet *m.*; (*fig.*) élan *m.*
spy /spaɪ/ *n.* espion(ne) *m.* (*f.*). *—v.i.* espionner. *—v.t.* apercevoir. **~ on,** espionner. **~ out,** reconnaître.
squabble /ˈskwɒbl/ *v.i.* se chamailler. *—n.* chamaillerie *f.*
squad /skwɒd/ *n.* (*of soldiers etc.*) escouade *f.*; (*sport*) équipe *f.*
squadron /ˈskwɒdrən/ *n.* (*mil.*) escadron *m.*; (*aviat.*) escadrille *f.*; (*naut.*) escadre *f.*
squal|id /ˈskwɒlɪd/ *a.* sordide. **~or** *n.* conditions sordides *f. pl.*
squall /skwɔ:l/ *n.* rafale *f.*
squander /ˈskwɒndə(r)/ *v.t.* (*money, time, etc.*) gaspiller.
square /skweə(r)/ *n.* carré *m.*; (*open space in town*) place *f.*; (*instrument*) équerre *f.* *—a.* carré; (*honest*) honnête; (*meal*) solide. **(all) ~,** (*quits*) quitte. *—v.t.* (*settle*) régler. *—v.i.* (*agree*) s'accorder. **~ up to,** faire face à. **~ly** *adv.* carrément.
squash /skwɒʃ/ *v.t.* écraser; (*crowd*) serrer. *—n.* (*game*) squash *m.*; (*marrow*: *Amer.*) courge *f.* **lemon ~,** citronnade *f.* **orange ~,** orangeade *f.* **~y** *a.* mou.
squat /skwɒt/ *v.i.* (*p.t.* **squatted**) s'accroupir. *—a.* (*dumpy*) trapu.
squatter /ˈskwɒtə(r)/ *n.* squatter *m.*
squawk /skwɔ:k/ *n.* cri rauque *m.* *—v.i.* pousser un cri rauque.
squeak /skwi:k/ *n.* petit cri *m.*; (*of door etc.*) grincement *m.* *—v.i.* crier; grincer. **~y** *a.* grinçant.
squeal /skwi:l/ *n.* cri aigu *m.* *—v.i.* pousser un cri aigu. **~ on,** (*inform on*: *sl.*) dénoncer.
squeamish /ˈskwi:mɪʃ/ *a.* (trop) délicat, facilement dégoûté.
squeeze /skwi:z/ *v.t.* presser; (*hand, arm*) serrer; (*extract*) exprimer **(from,** de); (*extort*) soutirer **(from,** à). *—v.i.* (*force one's way*) se glisser. *—n.* pression *f.*; (*comm.*) restrictions de crédit *f. pl.*
squelch /skweltʃ/ *v.i.* faire flic flac. *—v.t.* (*suppress*) supprimer.
squid /skwɪd/ *n.* calmar *m.*
squiggle /ˈskwɪgl/ *n.* ligne onduleuse *f.*
squint /skwɪnt/ *v.i.* loucher; (*with half-shut eyes*) plisser les yeux. *—n.* (*med.*) strabisme *m.*
squire /ˈskwaɪə(r)/ *n.* propriétaire terrien *m.*
squirm /skwɜ:m/ *v.i.* se tortiller.
squirrel /ˈskwɪrəl, *Amer.* ˈskwɜ:rəl/ *n.* écureuil *m.*
squirt /skwɜ:t/ *v.t./i.* (faire) jaillir. *—n.* jet *m.*
stab /stæb/ *v.t.* (*p.t.* **stabbed**) (*with knife etc.*) poignarder. *—n.* coup (de couteau) *m.*
stabilize /ˈsteɪbəlaɪz/ *v.t.* stabiliser.
stab|le[1] /ˈsteɪbl/ *a.* **(-er, -est)** stable. **~ility** /stəˈbɪlətɪ/ *n.* stabilité *f.*
stable[2] /ˈsteɪbl/ *n.* écurie *f.* **~-boy** *n.* lad *m.*
stack /stæk/ *n.* tas *m.* *—v.t.* **~ (up),** entasser, empiler.
stadium /ˈsteɪdɪəm/ *n.* stade *m.*
staff /stɑ:f/ *n.* personnel *m.*; (*in school*) professeurs *m. pl.*; (*mil.*) état-major *m.*; (*stick*) bâton *m.* *—v.t.* pourvoir en personnel.

stag /stæg/ *n.* cerf *m.* **~-party** *n.* réunion d'hommes *f.*
stage /steɪdʒ/ *n.* (*theatre*) scène *f.*; (*phase*) stade *m.*, étape *f.*; (*platform in hall*) estrade *f.* —*v.t.* mettre en scène; (*fig.*) organiser. **go on the ~,** faire du théâtre. **~-coach** *n.* (*old use*) diligence *f.* **~ fright,** trac *m.*
stagger /ˈstægə(r)/ *v.i.* chanceler. —*v.t.* (*shock*) stupéfier; (*holidays etc.*) étaler. **~ing** *a.* stupéfiant.
stagnant /ˈstægnənt/ *a.* stagnant.
stagnat|e /stægˈneɪt/ *v.i.* stagner. **~ion** /-ʃn/ *n.* stagnation *f.*
staid /steɪd/ *a.* sérieux.
stain /steɪn/ *v.t.* tacher; (*wood etc.*) colorer. —*n.* tache *f.*; (*colouring*) colorant *m.* **~ed glass window,** vitrail *m.* **~less steel,** acier inoxydable *m.*
stair /steə(r)/ *n.* marche *f.* **~s,** escalier *m.*
stair|case /ˈsteəkeɪs/, **~way** *ns.* escalier *m.*
stake /steɪk/ *n.* (*post*) pieu *m.*; (*wager*) enjeu *m.* —*v.t.* (*area*) jalonner; (*wager*) jouer. **at ~,** en jeu. **~ a claim to,** revendiquer.
stale /steɪl/ *a.* (**-er, -est**) pas frais; (*bread*) rassis; (*smell*) rance; (*news*) vieux. **~ness** *n.* manque de fraîcheur *m.*
stalemate /ˈsteɪlmeɪt/ *n.* (*chess*) pat *m.*; (*fig.*) impasse *f.*
stalk[1] /stɔːk/ *n.* (*of plant*) tige *f.*
stalk[2] /stɔːk/ *v.i.* marcher dignement. —*v.t.* (*prey*) traquer.
stall /stɔːl/ *n.* (*in stable*) stalle *f.*; (*in market*) éventaire *m.* **~s,** (*theatre*) orchestre *m.* —*v.t./i.* (*auto.*) caler. **~ (for time),** temporiser.
stallion /ˈstæljən/ *n.* étalon *m.*
stalwart /ˈstɔːlwət/ *n.* (*supporter*) partisan(e) fidèle *m.* (*f.*).
stamina /ˈstæmɪnə/ *n.* résistance *f.*
stammer /ˈstæmə(r)/ *v.t./i.* bégayer. —*n.* bégaiement *m.*
stamp /stæmp/ *v.t./i.* **~ (one's foot),** taper du pied. —*v.t.* (*letter etc.*) timbrer. —*n.* (*for postage, marking*) timbre *m.*; (*mark: fig.*) sceau *m.* **~-collecting** *n.* philatélie *f.* **~ out,** supprimer.
stampede /stæmˈpiːd/ *n.* fuite désordonnée *f.*; (*rush: fig.*) ruée *f.* —*v.i.* s'enfuir en désordre; se ruer.
stance /stæns/ *n.* position *f.*
stand /stænd/ *v.i.* (*p.t.* **stood**) être *or* se tenir (debout); (*rise*) se lever; (*be situated*) se trouver; (*rest*) reposer; (*pol.*) être candidat (**for,** à). —*v.t.* mettre (debout); (*tolerate*) supporter. —*n.* position *f.*; (*mil.*) résistance *f.*; (*for lamp etc.*) support *m.*; (*at fair*) stand *m.*; (*in street*) kiosque *m.*; (*for spectators*) tribune *f.*; (*jurid., Amer.*) barre *f.* **~ a chance,** avoir une chance. **~ back,** reculer. **~ by** *or* **around,** ne rien faire. **~ by,** (*be ready*) se tenir prêt; (*promise, person*) rester fidèle à. **~-by** *a.* de réserve; *n.* **be a ~-by,** être de réserve. **~ down,** se désister. **~ for,** représenter; (*fam.*) supporter. **~ in for,** remplacer. **~-in** *n.* remplaçant(e) *m.* (*f.*). **~ in line,** (*Amer.*) faire la queue. **~-offish** *a.* (*fam.*) distant. **~ out,** (*be conspicuous*) ressortir. **~ to reason,** être logique. **~ up,** se lever. **~ up for,** défendre. **~ up to,** résister à.
standard /ˈstændəd/ *n.* norme *f.*; (*level*) niveau (voulu) *m.*; (*flag*) étendard *m.* **~s,** (*morals*) principes *m. pl.* —*a.* ordinaire. **~ lamp,** lampadaire *m.* **~ of living,** niveau de vie *m.*
standardize /ˈstændədaɪz/ *v.t.* standardiser.
standing /ˈstændɪŋ/ *a.* debout *invar.*; (*army, offer*) permanent. —*n.* position *f.*, réputation *f.*; (*duration*) durée *f.*
standpoint /ˈstændpɔɪnt/ *n.* point de vue *m.*

standstill /'stændstɪl/ *n.* **at a ~,** immobile. **bring/come to a ~,** (s')immobiliser.
stank /stæŋk/ *see* **stink.**
stanza /'stænzə/ *n.* strophe *f.*
staple[1] /'steɪpl/ *n.* agrafe *f.* —*v.t.* agrafer. **~r** /-ə(r)/ *n.* agrafeuse *f.*
staple[2] /'steɪpl/ *a.* principal, de base. —*n.* (*comm.*) article de base *m.*
star /stɑː(r)/ *n.* étoile *f.*; (*famous person*) vedette *f.* —*v.t.* (*p.t.* **starred**) (*of film*) avoir pour vedette. —*v.i.* **~ in,** être la vedette de. **~dom** *n.* célébrité *f.*
starboard /'stɑːbəd/ *n.* tribord *m.*
starch /stɑːtʃ/ *n.* amidon *m.*; (*in food*) fécule *f.* —*v.t.* amidonner. **~y** *a.* féculent; (*stiff*) guindé.
stare /steə(r)/ *v.i.* **~ at,** regarder fixement. —*n.* regard fixe *m.*
starfish /'stɑːfɪʃ/ *n.* étoile de mer *f.*
stark /stɑːk/ *a.* **(-er, -est)** (*desolate*) désolé; (*severe*) austère; (*utter*) complet; (*fact etc.*) brutal. —*adv.* complètement.
starling /'stɑːlɪŋ/ *n.* étourneau *m.*
starlit /'stɑːlɪt/ *a.* étoilé.
starry /'stɑːrɪ/ *a.* étoilé. **~-eyed** *a.* naïf, (trop) optimiste.
start /stɑːt/ *v.t./i.* commencer; (*machine*) (se) mettre en marche; (*fashion etc.*) lancer; (*leave*) partir; (*cause*) provoquer; (*jump*) sursauter; (*of vehicle*) démarrer. —*n.* commencement *m.*, début *m.*; (*of race*) départ *m.*; (*lead*) avance *f.*; (*jump*) sursaut *m.* **~ to do,** commencer *or* se mettre à faire. **~er** *n.* (*auto.*) démarreur *m.*; (*runner*) partant *m.*; (*culin.*) entrée *f.*
startle /'stɑːtl/ *v.t.* (*make jump*) faire tressaillir; (*shock*) alarmer.
starv|e /stɑːv/ *v.i.* mourir de faim. —*v.t.* affamer; (*deprive*) priver. **~ation** /-'veɪʃn/ *n.* faim *f.*
stash /stæʃ/ *v.t.* (*hide*: *sl.*) cacher.
state /steɪt/ *n.* état *m.*; (*pomp*) apparat *m.* **S~,** (*pol.*) État *m.* —*a.* d'État, de l'État; (*school*) public. —*v.t.* affirmer (**that,** que) (*views*) exprimer; (*fix*) fixer.
stateless /'steɪtlɪs/ *a.* apatride.
stately /'steɪtlɪ/ *a.* **(-ier, -iest)** majestueux. **~ home,** château *m.*
statement /'steɪtmənt/ *n.* déclaration *f.*; (*of account*) relevé *m.*
statesman /'steɪtsmən/ *n.* (*pl.* **-men**) homme d'État *m.*
static /'stætɪk/ *a.* statique. —*n.* (*radio, TV*) parasites *m. pl.*
station /'steɪʃn/ *n.* station *f.*; (*rail.*) gare *f.*; (*mil.*) poste *m.*; (*rank*) condition *f.* —*v.t.* poster, placer. **~ed at** *or* **in,** (*mil.*) en garnison à.
stationary /'steɪʃənrɪ/ *a.* immobile, stationnaire; (*vehicle*) à l'arrêt.
stationer /'steɪʃnə(r)/ *n.* papet|ier, -ière *m., f.* **~'s shop,** papeterie *f.* **~y** *n.* papeterie *f.*
statistic /stə'tɪstɪk/ *n.* statistique *f.* **~s,** statistique *f.* **~al** *a.* statistique.
statue /'stætʃuː/ *n.* statue *f.*
statuesque /stætʃʊ'esk/ *a.* sculptural.
stature /'stætʃə(r)/ *n.* stature *f.*
status /'steɪtəs/ *n.* (*pl.* **-uses**) situation *f.*, statut *m.*; (*prestige*) standing *m.* **~ quo,** statu quo *m.*
statut|e /'stætʃuːt/ *n.* loi *f.* **~es,** (*rules*) statuts *m. pl.* **~ory** /-ʊtrɪ/ *a.* statutaire; (*holiday*) légal.
staunch /stɔːntʃ/ *a.* **(-er, -est)** (*friend etc.*) loyal, fidèle.
stave /steɪv/ *n.* (*mus.*) portée *f.* —*v.t.* **~ off,** éviter, conjurer.
stay /steɪ/ *v.i.* rester; (*spend time*) séjourner; (*reside*) loger. —*v.t.* (*hunger*) tromper. —*n.* séjour *m.* **~ away from,** (*school etc.*) ne pas aller à. **~ in,** rester à la maison. **~ up (late),** veiller, se coucher tard.
stead /sted/ *n.* **in my/your/***etc.* **~,** à ma/votre/*etc.* place.
steadfast /'stedfɑːst/ *a.* ferme.

stead|y /ˈstedɪ/ *a.* (**-ier, -iest**) stable; (*hand, voice*) ferme; (*regular*) régulier; (*staid*) sérieux. —*v.t.* maintenir, assurer; (*calm*) calmer. **~ily** *adv.* fermement; régulièrement.
steak /steɪk/ *n.* steak *m.*, bifteck *m.*
steal /stiːl/ *v.t./i.* (*p.t.* **stole,** *p.p.* **stolen**) voler (**from s.o.,** à qn.).
stealth /stelθ/ *n.* **by ~,** furtivement. **~y** *a.* furtif.
steam /stiːm/ *n.* vapeur *f.*; (*on glass*) buée *f.* —*v.t.* (*cook*) cuire à la vapeur; (*window*) embuer. —*v.i.* fumer. **~-engine** *n.* locomotive à vapeur *f.* **~y** *a.* humide.
steam|er /ˈstiːmə(r)/, **~ship** *ns.* (bateau à) vapeur *m.*
steamroller /ˈstiːmrəʊlə(r)/ *n.* rouleau compresseur *m.*
steel /stiːl/ *n.* acier *m.* —*v. pr.* **~ o.s.,** s'endurcir, se cuirasser. **~ industry,** sidérurgie *f.*
steep[1] /stiːp/ *v.t.* (*soak*) tremper. **~ed in,** (*fig.*) imprégné de.
steep[2] /stiːp/ *a.* (**-er, -est**) raide, rapide. (*price*: *fam.*) excessif. **~ly** *adv.* **rise ~ly,** (*slope, price*) monter rapidement.
steeple /ˈstiːpl/ *n.* clocher *m.*
steeplechase /ˈstiːpltʃeɪs/ *n.* (*race*) steeple(-chase) *m.*
steer[1] /stɪə(r)/ *n.* (*ox*) bouvillon *m.*
steer[2] /stɪə(r)/ *v.t.* diriger; (*ship*) gouverner; (*fig.*) guider. —*v.i.* (*in ship*) gouverner. **~ clear of,** éviter. **~ing** *n.* (*auto.*) direction *f.* **~ing-wheel** *n.* volant *m.*
stem[1] /stem/ *n.* tige *f.* —*v.i.* (*p.t.* **stemmed**). **~ from,** provenir de.
stem[2] /stem/ *v.t.* (*p.t.* **stemmed**) (*check, stop*) endiguer, contenir.
stench /stentʃ/ *n.* puanteur *f.*
stencil /ˈstensl/ *n.* pochoir *m.*; (*for typing*) stencil *m.* —*v.t.* (*p.t.* **stencilled**) (*document*) polycopier.
stenographer /steˈnɒgrəfə(r)/ *n.* (*Amer.*) sténodactylo *f.*
step /step/ *v.i.* (*p.t.* **stepped**) marcher, aller. —*v.t.* **~ up,** augmenter. —*n.* pas *m.*; (*stair*) marche *f.*; (*of train*) marchepied *m.*; (*action*) mesure *f.* **~s,** (*ladder*) escabeau *m.* **in ~,** au pas; (*fig.*) conforme (**with,** à). **~ down,** (*resign*) démissionner. **~ in,** (*intervene*) intervenir. **~-ladder** *n.* escabeau *m.* **~ping-stone** *n.* (*fig.*) tremplin *m.*
step|brother /ˈstepbrʌðə(r)/ *n.* demi-frère *m.* **~daughter** *n.* belle-fille *f.* **~father** *n.* beau-père *m.* **~mother** *n.* belle-mère *f.* **~sister** *n.* demi-sœur *f.* **~son** *n.* beau-fils *m.*
stereo /ˈsterɪəʊ/ *n.* (*pl.* **-os**) stéréo *f.*; (*record-player*) chaîne stéréo *f.* —*a.* stéréo *invar.* **~phonic** /-əˈfɒnɪk/ *a.* stéréophonique.
stereotype /ˈsterɪətaɪp/ *n.* stéréotype *m.* **~d** *a.* stéréotypé.
steril|e /ˈsteraɪl, *Amer.* ˈsterəl/ *a.* stérile. **~ity** /stəˈrɪlətɪ/ *n.* stérilité *f.*
steriliz|e /ˈsterəlaɪz/ *v.t.* stériliser. **~ation** /-ˈzeɪʃn/ *n.* stérilisation *f.*
sterling /ˈstɜːlɪŋ/ *n.* livre(s) sterling *f.* (*pl.*). —*a.* sterling *invar.*; (*silver*) fin; (*fig.*) excellent.
stern[1] /stɜːn/ *a.* (**-er, -est**) sévère.
stern[2] /stɜːn/ *n.* (*of ship*) arrière *m.*
stethoscope /ˈsteθəskəʊp/ *n.* stéthoscope *m.*
stew /stjuː/ *v.t./i.* cuire à la casserole. —*n.* ragoût *m.* **~ed fruit,** compote *f.* **~ed tea,** thé trop infusé *m.* **~-pan** *n.* cocotte *f.*
steward /stjʊəd/ *n.* (*of club etc.*) intendant *m.*; (*on ship etc.*) steward *m.* **~ess** /-ˈdes/ *n.* hôtesse *f.*
stick[1] /stɪk/ *n.* bâton *m.*; (*for walking*) canne *f.*
stick[2] /stɪk/ *v.t.* (*p.t.* **stuck**) (*glue*) coller; (*thrust*) enfoncer; (*put*: *fam.*) mettre; (*endure*: *sl.*) supporter. —*v.i.* (*adhere*) coller, adhérer; (*to pan*) attacher; (*remain*: *fam.*) rester; (*be jammed*) être

coincé. **be stuck with s.o.,** (*fam.*) se farcir qn. **~-in-the-mud** *n.* encroûté(e) *m.* (*f.*). **~ out** *v.t.* (*head etc.*) sortir; (*tongue*) tirer; *v.i.* (*protrude*) dépasser. **~ to,** (*promise etc.*) rester fidèle à. **~ up for,** (*fam.*) défendre. **~ing-plaster** *n.* sparadrap *m.*

sticker /'stɪkə(r)/ *n.* autocollant *m.*

stickler /'stɪklə(r)/ *n.* **be a ~ for,** insister sur.

sticky /'stɪkɪ/ *a.* (**-ier, -iest**) poisseux; (*label, tape*) adhésif.

stiff /stɪf/ *a.* (**-er, -est**) raide; (*limb, joint*) ankylosé; (*tough*) dur; (*drink*) fort; (*price*) élevé; (*manner*) guindé. **~ neck,** torticolis *m.* **~ness** *n.* raideur *f.*

stiffen /'stɪfn/ *v.t./i.* (se) raidir.

stifle /'staɪfl/ *v.t./i.* étouffer.

stigma /'stɪgmə/ *n.* (*pl.* **-as**) stigmate *m.* **~tize** *v.t.* stigmatiser.

stile /staɪl/ *n.* échalier *m.*

still[1] /stɪl/ *a.* immobile; (*quiet*) calme, tranquille. —*n.* silence *m.* —*adv.* encore, toujours; (*even*) encore; (*nevertheless*) tout de même. **~ life,** nature morte *f.*

still[2] /stɪl/ *n.* (*apparatus*) alambic *m.*

stillborn /'stɪlbɔːn/ *a.* mort-né.

stilted /'stɪltɪd/ *a.* guindé.

stilts /stɪlts/ *n. pl.* échasses *f. pl.*

stimul|ate /'stɪmjʊleɪt/ *v.t.* stimuler. **~ant** *n.* stimulant *m.* **~ation** /-'leɪʃn/ *n.* stimulation *f.*

stimulus /'stɪmjʊləs/ *n.* (*pl.* **-li** /-laɪ/) (*spur*) stimulant *m.*

sting /stɪŋ/ *n.* piqûre *f.*; (*organ*) dard *m.* —*v.t./i.* (*p.t.* **stung**) piquer. **~ing** *a.* (*fig.*) cinglant.

stingy /'stɪndʒɪ/ *a.* (**-ier, -iest**) avare (**with,** de).

stink /stɪŋk/ *n.* puanteur *f.* —*v.i.* (*p.t.* **stank** *or* **stunk,** *p.p.* **stunk**). **~ (of),** puer. —*v.t.* **~ out,** (*room etc.*) empester.

stinker /'stɪŋkə(r)/ *n.* (*thing: sl.*) vacherie *f.*; (*person: sl.*) vache *f.*

stint /stɪnt/ *v.i.* **~ on,** lésiner sur. —*n.* (*work*) part de travail *f.*

stipend /'staɪpend/ *n.* (*of clergyman*) traitement *m.*

stipulat|e /'stɪpjʊleɪt/ *v.t.* stipuler. **~ion** /-'leɪʃn/ *n.* stipulation *f.*

stir /stɜː(r)/ *v.t./i.* (*p.t.* **stirred**) (*move*) remuer; (*excite*) exciter. —*n.* agitation *f.* **~ up,** (*trouble etc.*) provoquer.

stirrup /'stɪrəp/ *n.* étrier *m.*

stitch /stɪtʃ/ *n.* point *m.*; (*in knitting*) maille *f.*; (*med.*) point de suture *m.* —*v.t.* coudre. **be in ~es,** (*fam.*) avoir le fou rire.

stoat /stəʊt/ *n.* hermine *f.*

stock /stɒk/ *n.* réserve *f.*; (*comm.*) stock *m.*; (*financial*) valeurs *f. pl.*; (*family*) souche *f.*; (*soup*) bouillon *m.* —*a.* (*goods*) courant. —*v.t.* (*shop etc.*) approvisionner; (*sell*) vendre. —*v.i.* **~ up,** s'approvisionner (**with,** de). **~-car** *n.* stock-car *m.* **S~ Exchange, ~ market,** Bourse *f.* **~ phrase,** cliché *m.* **~-taking** *n.* (*comm.*) inventaire *m.* **take ~,** (*fig.*) faire le point.

stockbroker /'stɒkbrəʊkə(r)/ *n.* agent de change *m.*

stocking /'stɒkɪŋ/ *n.* bas *m.*

stockist /'stɒkɪst/ *n.* stockiste *m.*

stockpile /'stɒkpaɪl/ *n.* stock *m.* —*v.t.* stocker; (*arms*) amasser.

stocky /'stɒkɪ/ *a.* (**-ier, -iest**) trapu.

stodg|e /stɒdʒ/ *n.* (*fam.*) aliment(s) lourd(s) *m.* (*pl.*). **~y** *a.* lourd.

stoic /'stəʊɪk/ *n.* stoïque *m./f.* **~al** *a.* stoïque. **~ism** /-sɪzəm/ *n.* stoïcisme *m.*

stoke /stəʊk/ *v.t.* (*boiler, fire*) garnir, alimenter.

stole[1] /stəʊl/ *n.* (*garment*) étole *f.*

stole[2], **stolen** /stəʊl, 'stəʊlən/ *see* **steal.**

stolid /'stɒlɪd/ *a.* flegmatique.

stomach /'stʌmək/ *n.* estomac *m.*; (*abdomen*) ventre *m.* —*v.t.* (*put up*

with) supporter. **~-ache** *n.* mal à l'estomac *or* au ventre *m.*
ston|e /stəʊn/ *n.* pierre *f.*; (*pebble*) caillou *m.*; (*in fruit*) noyau *m.*; (*weight*) 6.350 kg. —*a.* de pierre. —*v.t.* lapider; (*fruit*) dénoyauter. **~y** *a.* pierreux. **~y-broke** *a.* (*sl.*) fauché.
stone- /stəʊn/ *pref.* complètement.
stonemason /'stəʊnmeɪsn/ *n.* maçon *m.*, tailleur de pierre *m.*
stood /stʊd/ *see* **stand.**
stooge /stuːdʒ/ *n.* (*actor*) comparse *m.*/*f.*; (*fig.*) fantoche *m.*, laquais *m.*
stool /stuːl/ *n.* tabouret *m.*
stoop /stuːp/ *v.i.* (*bend*) se baisser; (*condescend*) s'abaisser. —*n.* **have a ~,** être voûté.
stop /stɒp/ *v.t./i.* (*p.t.* **stopped**) (s')arrêter; (*prevent*) empêcher (**from,** de); (*hole, leak, etc.*) boucher; (*of pain, noise, etc.*) cesser; (*stay*: *fam.*) rester. —*n.* arrêt *m.*; (*full stop*) point *m.* **~(-over),** halte *f.*; (*port of call*) escale *f.* **~-light** *n.* (*on vehicle*) stop *m.* **~-watch** *n.* chronomètre *m.*
stopgap /'stɒpgæp/ *n.* bouche-trou *m.* —*a.* intérimaire.
stoppage /'stɒpɪdʒ/ *n.* arrêt *m.*; (*of work*) arrêt de travail *m.*; (*of pay*) retenue *f.*
stopper /'stɒpə(r)/ *n.* bouchon *m.*
storage /'stɔːrɪdʒ/ *n.* (*of goods, food, etc.*) emmagasinage *m.*
store /stɔː(r)/ *n.* réserve *f.*; (*warehouse*) entrepôt *m.*; (*shop*) grand magasin *m.*; (*Amer.*) magasin *m.* —*v.t.* (*for future*) mettre en réserve; (*in warehouse, mind*) emmagasiner. **have in ~ for,** réserver à. **set ~ by,** attacher du prix à. **~-room** *n.* réserve *f.*
storey /'stɔːrɪ/ *n.* étage *m.*
stork /stɔːk/ *n.* cigogne *f.*
storm /stɔːm/ *n.* tempête *f.*, orage *m.* —*v.t.* prendre d'assaut. —*v.i.* (*rage*) tempêter. **~y** *a.* orageux.
story /'stɔːrɪ/ *n.* histoire *f.*; (*in press*) article *m.*; (*storey*: *Amer.*) étage *m.* **~-teller** *n.* conteu|r, -se *m.*, *f.*; (*liar*: *fam.*) menteu|r, -se *m.*, *f.*
stout /staʊt/ *a.* (**-er, -est**) corpulent; (*strong*) solide. —*n.* bière brune *f.* **~ness** *n.* corpulence *f.*
stove /stəʊv/ *n.* (*for cooking*) cuisinière *f.*; (*heater*) poêle *m.*
stow /stəʊ/ *v.t.* **~ away,** (*put away*) ranger; (*hide*) cacher. —*v.i.* voyager clandestinement.
stowaway /'stəʊəweɪ/ *n.* passag|er, -ère clandestin(e) *m.*, *f.*
straddle /'strædl/ *v.t.* être à cheval sur, enjamber.
straggle /'strægl/ *v.i.* (*lag behind*) traîner en désordre. **~r** /-ə(r)/ *n.* traînard(e) *m.* (*f.*).
straight /streɪt/ *a.* (**-er, -est**) droit; (*tidy*) en ordre; (*frank*) franc. —*adv.* (*in straight line*) droit; (*direct*) tout droit. —*n.* ligne droite *f.* **~ ahead** *or* **on,** tout droit. **~ away,** tout de suite. **~ face,** visage sérieux *m.* **~ off,** (*fam.*) sans hésiter.
straighten /'streɪtn/ *v.t.* (*nail, situation, etc.*) redresser; (*tidy*) arranger.
straightforward /streɪt'fɔːwəd/ *a.* honnête; (*easy*) simple.
strain[1] /streɪn/ *n.* (*breed*) race *f.*; (*streak*) tendance *f.*
strain[2] /streɪn/ *v.t.* (*rope, ears*) tendre; (*limb*) fouler; (*eyes*) fatiguer; (*muscle*) froisser; (*filter*) passer; (*vegetables*) égoutter; (*fig.*) mettre à l'épreuve. —*v.i.* fournir des efforts. —*n.* tension *f.*; (*fig.*) effort *m.* **~s,** (*tune*: *mus.*) accents *m. pl.* **~ed** *a.* forcé; (*relations*) tendu. **~er** *n.* passoire *f.*
strait /streɪt/ *n.* détroit *m.* **~s,** détroit *m.*; (*fig.*) embarras *m.* **~-jacket** *n.* camisole de force *f.* **~-laced** *a.* collet monté *invar.*
strand /strænd/ *n.* (*thread*) fil *m.*, brin *m.*; (*lock of hair*) mèche *f.*

stranded /ˈstrændɪd/ *a.* (*person*) en rade; (*ship*) échoué.

strange /streɪndʒ/ *a.* (-**er**, -**est**) étrange; (*unknown*) inconnu. **~ly** *adv.* étrangement. **~ness** *n.* étrangeté *f.*

stranger /ˈstreɪndʒə(r)/ *n.* inconnu(e) *m.* (*f.*).

strangle /ˈstræŋgl/ *v.t.* étrangler.

stranglehold /ˈstræŋglhəʊld/ *n.* **have a ~ on,** tenir à la gorge.

strap /stræp/ *n.* (*of leather etc.*) courroie *f.*; (*of dress*) bretelle *f.*; (*of watch*) bracelet *m.* —*v.t.* (*p.t.* **strapped**) attacher.

strapping /ˈstræpɪŋ/ *a.* costaud.

stratagem /ˈstrætədʒəm/ *n.* stratagème *m.*

strategic /strəˈtiːdʒɪk/ *a.* stratégique.

strategy /ˈstrætədʒɪ/ *n.* stratégie *f.*

stratum /ˈstrɑːtəm/ *n.* (*pl.* **strata**) couche *f.*

straw /strɔː/ *n.* paille *f.*

strawberry /ˈstrɔːbrɪ/ *n.* fraise *f.*

stray /streɪ/ *v.i.* s'égarer; (*deviate*) s'écarter. —*a.* perdu; (*isolated*) isolé. —*n.* animal perdu *m.*

streak /striːk/ *n.* raie *f.*, bande *f.*; (*trace*) trace *f.*; (*period*) période *f.*; (*tendency*) tendance *f.* —*v.t.* (*mark*) strier. **~y** *a.* strié.

stream /striːm/ *n.* ruisseau *m.*; (*current*) courant *m.*; (*flow*) flot *m.*; (*in schools*) classe (de niveau) *f.* —*v.i.* ruisseler (**with,** de).

streamer /ˈstriːmə(r)/ *n.* (*of paper*) serpentin *m.*; (*flag*) banderole *f.*

streamline /ˈstriːmlaɪn/ *v.t.* rationaliser. **~d** *a.* (*shape*) aérodynamique.

street /striːt/ *n.* rue *f.* **~ lamp,** réverbère *m.*

streetcar /ˈstriːtkɑː(r)/ *n.* (*Amer.*) tramway *m.*

strength /streŋθ/ *n.* force *f.*: (*of wall, fabric, etc.*) solidité *f.* **on the ~ of,** en vertu de.

strengthen /ˈstreŋθn/ *v.t.* renforcer, fortifier.

strenuous /ˈstrenjʊəs/ *a.* énergique; (*arduous*) ardu; (*tiring*) fatigant. **~ly** *adv.* énergiquement.

stress /stres/ *n.* accent *m.*; (*pressure*) pression *f.*; (*med.*) stress *m.* —*v.t.* souligner, insister sur.

stretch /stretʃ/ *v.t.* (*pull taut*) tendre; (*arm, leg*) étendre; (*neck*) tendre; (*clothes*) étirer; (*truth etc.*) forcer. —*v.i.* s'étendre; (*of person, clothes*) s'étirer. —*n.* étendue *f.*; (*period*) période *f.*; (*of road*) tronçon *m.* —*a.* (*fabric*) extensible. **at a ~,** d'affilée.

stretcher /ˈstretʃə(r)/ *n.* brancard *m.*

strew /struː/ *v.t.* (*p.t.* **strewed,** *p.p.* **strewed** *or* **strewn**) (*scatter*) répandre; (*cover*) joncher.

stricken /ˈstrɪkən/ *a.* **~ with,** frappé *or* atteint de.

strict /strɪkt/ *a.* (-**er**, -**est**) strict. **~ly** *adv.* strictement. **~ness** *n.* sévérité *f.*

stride /straɪd/ *v.i.* (*p.t.* **strode,** *p.p.* **stridden**) faire de grands pas. —*n.* grand pas *m.*

strident /ˈstraɪdnt/ *a.* strident.

strife /straɪf/ *n.* conflit(s) *m.* (*pl.*).

strike /straɪk/ *v.t.* (*p.t.* **struck**) frapper; (*blow*) donner; (*match*) frotter; (*gold etc.*) trouver; (*of clock*) sonner. —*v.i.* faire grève; (*attack*) attaquer. —*n.* (*of workers*) grève *f.*; (*mil.*) attaque *f.*; (*find*) découverte *f.* **on ~,** en grève. **~ off** *or* **out,** rayer. **~ up a friendship,** lier amitié (**with,** avec).

striker /ˈstraɪkə(r)/ *n.* gréviste *m*/*f.*; (*football*) buteur *m.*

striking /ˈstraɪkɪŋ/ *a.* frappant.

string /strɪŋ/ *n.* ficelle *f.*; (*of violin, racket, etc.*) corde *f.*; (*of pearls*) collier *m.*; (*of lies etc.*) chapelet *m.* —*v.t.* (*p.t.* **strung**) (*thread*) enfiler. **pull ~s,** faire jouer ses relations. **~ out,** (s')échelonner. **~ed** *a.* (*instrument*) à cordes.

stringent /'strɪndʒənt/ *a.* rigoureux, strict.

stringy /'strɪŋɪ/ *a.* filandreux.

strip[1] /strɪp/ *v.t./i.* (*p.t.* **stripped**) (*undress*) (se) déshabiller; (*machine*) démonter; (*deprive*) dépouiller. **~per** *n.* strip-teaseuse *f.*; (*solvent*) décapant *m.* **~-tease** *n.* strip-tease *m.*

strip[2] /strɪp/ *n.* bande *f.* **comic ~,** bande dessinée *f.*

stripe /straɪp/ *n.* rayure *f.*, raie *f.* **~d** *a.* rayé.

strive /straɪv/ *v.i.* (*p.t.* **strove,** *p.p.* **striven**) s'efforcer (**to,** de).

strode /strəʊd/ *see* **stride.**

stroke[1] /strəʊk/ *n.* coup *m.*; (*of pen*) trait *m.*; (*swimming*) nage *f.*; (*med.*) attaque *f.*, congestion *f.*

stroke[2] /strəʊk/ *v.t.* (*with hand*) caresser. *—n.* caresse *f.*

stroll /strəʊl/ *v.i.* flâner. *—n.* petit tour *m.* **~ in**/*etc.*, entrer/*etc.* tranquillement.

strong /strɒŋ/ *a.* (**-er, -est**) fort; (*shoes, fabric, etc.*) solide. **be fifty**/*etc.* **~,** être au nombre de cinquante/*etc.* **~-box** *n.* coffre-fort *m.* **~ language,** propos grossiers *m. pl.* **~-minded** *a.* résolu. **~-room** *n.* chambre forte *f.* **~ly** *adv.* (*greatly*) fortement; (*with energy*) avec force; (*deeply*) profondément.

stronghold /'strɒŋhəʊld/ *n.* bastion *m.*

strove /strəʊv/ *see* **strive.**

struck /strʌk/ *see* **strike.** *—a.* **~ on,** (*sl.*) impressionné par.

structur|e /'strʌktʃə(r)/ *n.* (*of cell, poem, etc.*) structure *f.*; (*building*) construction *f.* **~al** *a.* structural; de (la) construction.

struggle /'strʌgl/ *v.i.* lutter, se battre. *—n.* lutte *f.*; (*effort*) effort *m.* **have a ~ to,** avoir du mal à.

strum /strʌm/ *v.t.* (*p.t.* **strummed**) (*banjo etc.*) gratter de.

strung /strʌŋ/ *see* **string.** *—a.* **~ up,** (*tense*) nerveux.

strut /strʌt/ *n.* (*support*) étai *m.* *—v.i.* (*p.t.* **strutted**) se pavaner.

stub /stʌb/ *n.* bout *m.*; (*of tree*) souche *f.*; (*counterfoil*) talon *m.* *—v.t.* (*p.t.* **stubbed**). **~ out,** écraser.

stubble /'stʌbl/ *n.* (*on chin*) barbe de plusieurs jours *f.*; (*remains of wheat*) chaume *m.*

stubborn /'stʌbən/ *a.* opiniâtre, obstiné. **~ly** *adv.* obstinément. **~ness** *n.* opiniâtreté *f.*

stubby /'stʌbɪ/ *a.* (**-ier, -iest**) (*finger*) épais; (*person*) trapu.

stuck /stʌk/ *see* **stick**[2]. *—a.* (*jammed*) coincé; (*in difficulties*) en panne. **~-up** *a.* (*sl.*) prétentieux.

stud[1] /stʌd/ *n.* clou *m.*; (*for collar*) bouton *m.* *—v.t.* (*p.t.* **studded**) clouter. **~ded with,** parsemé de.

stud[2] /stʌd/ *n.* (*horses*) écurie *f.* **~(-farm)** *n.* haras *m.*

student /'stjuːdnt/ *n.* (*univ.*) étudiant(e) *m.* (*f.*); (*schol.*) élève *m./f.* *—a.* (*restaurant, life, residence*) universitaire.

studied /'stʌdɪd/ *a.* étudié.

studio /'stjuːdɪəʊ/ *n.* (*pl.* **-os**) studio *m.* **~ flat,** studio *m.*

studious /'stjuːdɪəs/ *a.* (*person*) studieux; (*deliberate*) étudié. **~ly** *adv.* (*carefully*) avec soin.

study /'stʌdɪ/ *n.* étude *f.*; (*office*) bureau *m.* *—v.t./i.* étudier.

stuff /stʌf/ *n.* substance *f.*; (*sl.*) chose(s) *f.* (*pl.*). *—v.t.* rembourrer; (*animal*) empailler; (*cram*) bourrer; (*culin.*) farcir; (*block up*) boucher; (*put*) fourrer. **~ing** *n.* bourre *f.*; (*culin.*) farce *f.*

stuffy /'stʌfɪ/ *a.* (**-ier, -iest**) mal aéré; (*dull: fam.*) vieux jeu *invar.*

stumbl|e /'stʌmbl/ *v.i.* trébucher. **~e across** *or* **on,** tomber sur.

~ing-block *n.* pierre d'achoppement *f.*
stump /stʌmp/ *n.* (*of tree*) souche *f.*; (*of limb*) moignon *m.*; (*of pencil*) bout *m.*
stumped /stʌmpt/ *a.* (*baffled*: *fam.*) embarrassé.
stun /stʌn/ *v.t.* (*p.t.* **stunned**) étourdir; (*bewilder*) stupéfier.
stung /stʌŋ/ *see* **sting.**
stunk /stʌŋk/ *see* **stink.**
stunning /ˈstʌnɪŋ/ *a.* (*delightful*: *fam.*) sensationnel.
stunt[1] /stʌnt/ *v.t.* (*growth*) retarder. **~ed** *a.* (*person*) rabougri.
stunt[2] /stʌnt/ *n.* (*feat*: *fam.*) tour de force *m.*; (*trick*: *fam.*) truc *m.*
stupefy /ˈstjuːpɪfaɪ/ *v.t.* abrutir; (*amaze*) stupéfier.
stupendous /stjuːˈpendəs/ *a.* prodigieux, formidable.
stupid /ˈstjuːpɪd/ *a.* stupide, bête. **~ity** /-ˈpɪdətɪ/ *n.* stupidité *f.* **~ly** *adv.* stupidement, bêtement.
stupor /ˈstjuːpə(r)/ *n.* stupeur *f.*
sturd|y /ˈstɜːdɪ/ *a.* (**-ier, -iest**) robuste. **~iness** *n.* robustesse *f.*
sturgeon /ˈstɜːdʒən/ *n. invar.* (*fish*) esturgeon *m.*
stutter /ˈstʌtə(r)/ *v.i.* bégayer. —*n.* bégaiement *m.*
sty[1] /staɪ/ *n.* (*pigsty*) porcherie *f.*
sty[2] /staɪ/ *n.* (*on eye*) orgelet *m.*
styl|e /staɪl/ *n.* style *m.*; (*fashion*) mode *f.*; (*sort*) genre *m.*; (*pattern*) modèle *m.* —*v.t.* (*design*) créer. **in ~e,** (*live etc.*) dans le luxe. **~e s.o.'s hair,** coiffer qn. **~ist** *n.* (*of hair*) coiffeu|r, -se *m., f.*
stylish /ˈstaɪlɪʃ/ *a.* élégant.
stylized /ˈstaɪlaɪzd/ *a.* stylisé.
stylus /ˈstaɪləs/ *n.* (*pl.* **-uses**) (*of record-player*) saphir *m.*
suave /swɑːv/ *a.* (*urbane*) courtois; (*smooth*: *pej.*) doucereux.
sub- /sʌb/ *pref.* sous-, sub-.
subconscious /sʌbˈkɒnʃəs/ *a.* & *n.* subconscient (*m.*).
subcontract /sʌbkənˈtrækt/ *v.t.* sous-traiter.
subdivide /sʌbdɪˈvaɪd/ *v.t.* subdiviser.
subdue /səbˈdjuː/ *v.t.* (*feeling*) maîtriser; (*country*) subjuguer. **~d** *a.* (*weak*) faible; (*light*) tamisé.
subject[1] /ˈsʌbdʒɪkt/ *a.* (*state etc.*) soumis. —*n.* sujet *m.*; (*schol., univ.*) matière *f.*; (*citizen*) ressortissant(e) *m.* (*f.*), sujet(te) *m.* (*f.*). **~-matter** *n.* contenu *m.* **~ to,** soumis à; (*liable to*) sujet à.
subject[2] /səbˈdʒekt/ *v.t.* soumettre. **~ion** /-kʃn/ *n.* soumission *f.*
subjective /səbˈdʒektɪv/ *a.* subjectif.
subjunctive /səbˈdʒʌŋktɪv/ *a.* & *n.* subjonctif (*m.*).
sublimate /ˈsʌblɪmeɪt/ *v.t.* (*emotion etc.*) sublimer.
sublime /səˈblaɪm/ *a.* sublime.
submarine /sʌbməˈriːn/ *n.* sous-marin *m.*
submerge /səbˈmɜːdʒ/ *v.t.* submerger. —*v.i.* plonger.
submissive /səbˈmɪsɪv/ *a.* soumis.
submi|t /səbˈmɪt/ *v.t./i.* (*p.t.* **submitted**) (se) soumettre (**to,** à). **~ssion** *n.* soumission *f.*
subordinate[1] /səˈbɔːdɪnət/ *a.* subalterne; (*gram.*) subordonné. —*n.* subordonné(e) *m.* (*f.*).
subordinate[2] /səˈbɔːdɪneɪt/ *v.t.* subordonner (**to,** à).
subpoena /səbˈpiːnə/ *n.* (*pl.* **-as**) (*jurid.*) citation *f.*, assignation *f.*
subscribe /səbˈskraɪb/ *v.t./i.* verser (de l'argent) (**to,** à). **~ to,** (*loan, theory*) souscrire à; (*newspaper*) s'abonner à, être abonné à. **~r** /-ə(r)/ *n.* abonné(e) *m.* (*f.*).
subscription /-ɪpʃn/ *n.* souscription *f.*; abonnement *m.*; (*membership dues*) cotisation *f.*
subsequent /ˈsʌbsɪkwənt/ *a.* (*later*) ultérieur; (*next*) suivant. **~ly** *adv.* par la suite.
subside /səbˈsaɪd/ *v.i.* (*land etc.*)

s'affaisser; (*flood, wind*) baisser. **~nce** /-əns/ *n.* affaissement *m.*

subsidiary /səb'sɪdɪərɪ/ *a.* accessoire. —*n.* (*comm.*) filiale *f.*

subsid|y /'sʌbsədɪ/ *n.* subvention *f.* **~ize** /-ɪdaɪz/ *v.t.* subventionner.

subsist /səb'sɪst/ *v.i.* subsister. **~ence** *n.* subsistance *f.*

substance /sʌbstəns/ *n.* substance *f.*

substandard /sʌb'stændəd/ *a.* de qualité inférieure.

substantial /səb'stænʃl/ *a.* considérable; (*meal*) substantiel. **~ly** *adv.* considérablement.

substantiate /səb'stænʃɪeɪt/ *v.t.* justifier, prouver.

substitut|e /'sʌbstɪtjuːt/ *n.* succédané *m.*; (*person*) remplaçant(e) *m.* (*f.*). —*v.t.* substituer (**for,** à). **~ion** /-'tjuːʃn/ *n.* substitution *f.*

subterfuge /'sʌbtəfjuːdʒ/ *n.* subterfuge *m.*

subterranean /sʌbtə'reɪnɪən/ *a.* souterrain.

subtitle /'sʌbtaɪtl/ *n.* sous-titre *m.*

subtle /'sʌtl/ *a.* (**-er, -est**) subtil. **~ty** *n.* subtilité *f.*

subtotal /sʌb'təʊtl/ *n.* total partiel *m.*

subtract /səb'trækt/ *v.t.* soustraire. **~ion** /-kʃn/ *n.* soustraction *f.*

suburb /'sʌbɜːb/ *n.* faubourg *m.*, banlieue *f.* **~s,** banlieue *f.* **~an** /sə'bɜːbən/ *a.* de banlieue.

suburbia /sə'bɜːbɪə/ *n.* la banlieue *f.*

subversive /səb'vɜːsɪv/ *a.* subversif.

subver|t /səb'vɜːt/ *v.t.* renverser. **~sion** /-ʃn/ *n.* subversion *f.*

subway /'sʌbweɪ/ *n.* passage souterrain *m.*; (*Amer.*) métro *m.*

succeed /sək'siːd/ *v.i.* réussir (**in doing,** à faire). —*v.t.* (*follow*) succéder à. **~ing** *a.* suivant.

success /sək'ses/ *n.* succès *m.*, réussite *f.*

successful /sək'sesfl/ *a.* réussi, couronné de succès; (*favourable*) heureux; (*in exam*) reçu. **be ~ in doing,** réussir à faire. **~ly** *adv.* avec succès.

succession /sək'seʃn/ *n.* succession *f.* **in ~,** de suite.

successive /sək'sesɪv/ *a.* successif. **six ~ days,** six jours consécutifs.

successor /sək'sesə(r)/ *n.* successeur *m.*

succinct /sək'sɪŋkt/ *a.* succinct.

succulent /'sʌkjʊlənt/ *a.* succulent.

succumb /sə'kʌm/ *v.i.* succomber.

such /sʌtʃ/ *a.* & *pron.* tel(le), tel(le)s; (*so much*) tant (de). —*adv.* si. **~ a book**/*etc.*, un tel livre/*etc.* **~ books**/*etc.*, de tels livres/*etc.* **~ courage**/*etc.*, tant de courage/*etc.* **~ a big house,** une si grande maison. **~ as,** comme, tel que. **~-and-such** *a.* tel ou tel.

suck /sʌk/ *v.t.* sucer. **~ in** *or* **up,** aspirer. **~er** *n.* (*rubber pad*) ventouse *f.*; (*person: sl.*) dupe *f.*

suckle /'sʌkl/ *v.t.* allaiter.

suction /'sʌkʃn/ *n.* succion *f.*

sudden /'sʌdn/ *a.* soudain, subit. **all of a ~,** tout à coup. **~ly** *adv.* subitement, brusquement. **~ness** *n.* soudaineté *f.*

suds /sʌdz/ *n. pl.* (*froth*) mousse de savon *f.*

sue /s(j)uː/ *v.t.* (*pres. p.* **suing**) poursuivre (en justice).

suede /sweɪd/ *n.* daim *m.*

suet /'suːɪt/ *n.* graisse de rognon *f.*

suffer /'sʌfə(r)/ *v.t./i.* souffrir; (*loss, attack, etc.*) subir. **~er** *n.* victime *f.*, malade *m./f.* **~ing** *n.* souffrance(s) *f.* (*pl.*).

suffice /sə'faɪs/ *v.i.* suffire.

sufficient /sə'fɪʃnt/ *a.* (*enough*) suffisamment de; (*big enough*) suffisant. **~ly** *adv.* suffisamment.

suffix /'sʌfɪks/ *n.* suffixe *m.*

suffocat|e /'sʌfəkeɪt/ *v.t./i.* suffoquer. **~ion** /-'keɪʃn/ *n.* suffocation *f.*; (*med.*) asphyxie *f.*
suffused /sə'fjuːzd/ *a.* **~ with,** (*light, tears*) baigné de.
sugar /'ʃʊgə(r)/ *n.* sucre *m.* —*v.t.* sucrer. **~y** *a.* sucré.
suggest /sə'dʒest/ *v.t.* suggérer. **~ion** /-tʃn/ *n.* suggestion *f.*
suggestive /sə'dʒestɪv/ *a.* suggestif. **be ~ of,** suggérer.
suicid|e /'s(j)uːɪsaɪd/ *n.* suicide *m.* **commit ~e,** se suicider. **~al** /-'saɪdl/ *a.* suicidaire.
suit /s(j)uːt/ *n.* complet *m.*, costume *m.*; (*woman's*) tailleur *m.*; (*cards*) couleur *f.* —*v.t.* convenir à; (*of garment, style, etc.*) aller à; (*adapt*) adapter. **~ability** *n.* (*of action etc.*) à-propos *m.*; (*of candidate*) aptitude(s) *f.* (*pl.*). **~able** *a.* qui convient (**for,** à), convenable. **~ably** *adv.* convenablement. **~ed** *a.* (**well**) **~ed,** (*matched*) bien assorti. **~ed to,** fait pour, apte à.
suitcase /'s(j)uːtkeɪs/ *n.* valise *f.*
suite /swiːt/ *n.* (*rooms, retinue*) suite *f.*; (*furniture*) mobilier *m.*
suitor /'s(j)uːtə(r)/ *n.* soupirant *m.*
sulk /sʌlk/ *v.i.* bouder. **~y** *a.* boudeur, maussade.
sullen /'sʌlən/ *a.* maussade. **~ly** *adv.* d'un air maussade.
sulphur /'sʌlfə(r)/ *n.* soufre *m.* **~ic** /-'fjʊərɪk/ *a.* **~ic acid,** acide sulfurique *m.*
sultan /'sʌltən/ *n.* sultan *m.*
sultana /sʌl'tɑːnə/ raisin de Smyrne *m.*, raisin sec *m.*
sultry /'sʌltrɪ/ *a.* (**-ier, -iest**) étouffant, lourd; (*fig.*) sensuel.
sum /sʌm/ *n.* somme *f.*; (*in arithmetic*) calcul *m.* —*v.t./i.* (*p.t.* **summed**). **~ up,** résumer, récapituler; (*assess*) évaluer.
summar|y /'sʌmərɪ/ *n.* résumé *m.* —*a.* sommaire. **~ize** *v.t.* résumer.
summer /'sʌmə(r)/ *n.* été *m.* —*a.* d'été. **~-time** *n.* été *m.* **~y** *a.* estival.
summit /'sʌmɪt/ *n.* sommet *m.* **~ conference,** (*pol.*) conférence au sommet *f.*
summon /'sʌmən/ *v.t.* appeler; (*meeting, s.o. to meeting*) convoquer. **~ up,** (*strength, courage, etc.*) rassembler.
summons /'sʌmənz/ *n.* (*jurid.*) assignation *f.* —*v.t.* assigner.
sump /sʌmp/ *n.* (*auto.*) carter *m.*
sumptuous /'sʌmptʃʊəs/ *a.* somptueux, luxueux.
sun /sʌn/ *n.* soleil *m.* —*v.t.* (*p.t.* **sunned**). **~ o.s.,** se chauffer au soleil. **~-glasses** *n. pl.* lunettes de soleil *f. pl.* **~-tan** *n.* bronzage *m.* **~-tanned** *a.* bronzé.
sunbathe /'sʌnbeɪð/ *v.i.* prendre un bain de soleil.
sunburn /'sʌnbɜːn/ *n.* coup de soleil *m.* **~t** *a.* brûlé par le soleil.
Sunday /'sʌndɪ/ *n.* dimanche *m.* **~ school,** catéchisme *m.*
sundial /'sʌndaɪəl/ *n.* cadran solaire *m.*
sundown /'sʌndaʊn/ *n.* = **sunset.**
sundr|y /'sʌndrɪ/ *a.* divers. **~ies** *n. pl.* articles divers *m. pl.* **all and ~y,** tout le monde.
sunflower /'sʌnflaʊə(r)/ *n.* tournesol *m.*
sung /sʌŋ/ *see* **sing.**
sunk /sʌŋk/ *see* **sink.**
sunken /'sʌŋkən/ *a.* (*ship etc.*) submergé; (*eyes*) creux.
sunlight /'sʌnlaɪt/ *n.* soleil *m.*
sunny /'sʌnɪ/ *a.* (**-ier, -iest**) (*room, day, etc.*) ensoleillé.
sunrise /'sʌnraɪz/ *n.* lever du soleil *m.*
sunset /'sʌnset/ *n.* coucher du soleil *m.*
sunshade /'sʌnʃeɪd/ *n.* (*lady's*) ombrelle *f.*; (*awning*) parasol *m.*
sunshine /'sʌnʃaɪn/ *n.* soleil *m.*
sunstroke /'sʌnstrəʊk/ *n.* insolation *f.*

super /'su:pə(r)/ *a.* (*sl.*) formidable.
superb /su:'pɜ:b/ *a.* superbe.
supercilious /su:pə'sɪlɪəs/ *a.* hautain, dédaigneux.
superficial /su:pə'fɪʃl/ *a.* superficiel. **~ity** /-ɪ'æləti/ *n.* caractère superficiel *m.* **~ly** *adv.* superficiellement.
superfluous /su:'pɜ:fluəs/ *a.* superflu.
superhuman /su:pə'hju:mən/ *a.* surhumain.
superimpose /su:pərɪm'pəʊz/ *v.t.* superposer (**on,** à).
superintendent /su:pərɪn'tendənt/ *n.* direc|teur, -trice *m., f.*; (*of police*) commissaire *m.*
superior /su:'pɪərɪə(r)/ *a.* & *n.* supérieur(e) (*m.* (*f.*)). **~ity** /-'ɒrəti/ *n.* supériorité *f.*
superlative /su:'pɜ:lətɪv/ *a.* suprême. —*n.* (*gram.*) superlatif *m.*
superman /'su:pəmæn/ *n.* (*pl.* **-men**) surhomme *m.*
supermarket /'su:pəmɑ:kɪt/ *n.* supermarché *m.*
supernatural /su:pə'nætʃrəl/ *a.* surnaturel.
superpower /'su:pəpaʊə(r)/ *n.* superpuissance *f.*
supersede /su:pə'si:d/ *v.t.* remplacer, supplanter.
supersonic /su:pə'sɒnɪk/ *a.* supersonique.
superstiti|on /su:pə'stɪʃn/ *n.* superstition *f.* **~ous** *a.* superstitieux.
supertanker /'su:pətæŋkə(r)/ *n.* pétrolier géant *m.*
supervis|e /'su:pəvaɪz/ *v.t.* surveiller, diriger. **~ion** /-'vɪʒn/ *n.* surveillance *f.* **~or** *n.* surveillant(e) *m.* (*f.*); (*shop*) chef de rayon *m.*; (*firm*) chef de service *m.* **~ory** /-'vaɪzərɪ/ *a.* de surveillance.
supper /'sʌpə(r)/ *n.* dîner *m.*; (*late at night*) souper *m.*
supple /'sʌpl/ *a.* souple.
supplement¹ /'sʌplɪmənt/ *n.* supplément *m.* **~ary** /-'mentrɪ/ *a.* supplémentaire.
supplement² /'sʌplɪment/ *v.t.* compléter.
supplier /sə'plaɪə(r)/ *n.* fournisseur *m.*
suppl|y /sə'plaɪ/ *v.t.* fournir; (*equip*) pourvoir; (*feed*) alimenter (**with,** en). —*n.* provision *f.*; (*of gas etc.*) alimentation *f.* **~ies,** (*food*) vivres *m. pl.*; (*material*) fournitures *f. pl.*
support /sə'pɔ:t/ *v.t.* soutenir; (*family*) assurer la subsistance de; (*endure*) supporter. —*n.* soutien *m.*, appui *m.*; (*techn.*) support *m.* **~er** *n.* partisan(e) *m.* (*f.*).; (*sport*) supporter *m.*
suppos|e /sə'pəʊz/ *v.t./i.* supposer. **be ~ed to do,** être censé faire, devoir faire. **~ition** /sʌpə'zɪʃn/ *n.* supposition *f.*
supposedly /sə'pəʊzɪdlɪ/ *adv.* soi-disant, prétendument.
suppress /sə'pres/ *v.t.* (*put an end to*) supprimer; (*restrain*) réprimer; (*stifle*) étouffer. **~ion** /-ʃn/ *n.* suppression *f.*; répression *f.*
suprem|e /su:'pri:m/ *a.* suprême. **~acy** /-eməsɪ/ *n.* suprématie *f.*
surcharge /'sɜ:tʃɑ:dʒ/ *n.* prix supplémentaire *m.*; (*tax*) surtaxe *f.*; (*on stamp*) surcharge *f.*
sure /ʃʊə(r)/ *a.* (**-er, -est**) sûr. —*adv.* (*Amer., fam.*) pour sûr. **make ~ of,** s'assurer de. **~ly** *adv.* sûrement.
surety /'ʃʊərəti/ *n.* caution *f.*
surf /sɜ:f/ *n.* (*waves*) ressac *m.* **~-riding** *n.* surf *m.*
surfboard /'sɜ:fbɔ:d/ *n.* planche de surf *f.*
surface /'sɜ:fɪs/ *n.* surface *f.* —*a.* superficiel. —*v.t.* revêtir. —*v.i.* faire surface; (*fig.*) réapparaître. **~ mail,** courrier maritime *m.*
surfeit /'sɜ:fɪt/ *n.* excès *m.* (**of,** de).
surge /sɜ:dʒ/ *v.i.* (*of crowd*) déferler;

(*of waves*) s'enfler; (*increase*) monter. —*n.* (*wave*) vague *f.*; (*rise*) montée *f.*

surgeon /'sɜːdʒən/ *n.* chirurgien *m.*

surg|ery /'sɜːdʒərɪ/ *n.* chirurgie *f.*; (*office*) cabinet *m.*; (*session*) consultation *f.* **~ical** *a.* chirurgical.

surly /'sɜːlɪ/ *a.* (**-ier, -iest**) bourru.

surmise /sə'maɪz/ *v.t.* conjecturer. —*n.* conjecture *f.*

surmount /sə'maʊnt/ *v.t.* (*overcome, cap*) surmonter.

surname /'sɜːneɪm/ *n.* nom de famille *m.*

surpass /sə'pɑːs/ *v.t.* surpasser.

surplus /'sɜːpləs/ *n.* surplus *m.* —*a.* en surplus.

surpris|e /sə'praɪz/ *n.* surprise *f.* —*v.t.* surprendre. **~ed** *a.* surpris (**at,** de). **~ing** *a.* surprenant. **~ingly** *adv.* étonnamment.

surrealism /sə'rɪəlɪzəm/ *n.* surréalisme *m.*

surrender /sə'rendə(r)/ *v.i.* se rendre. —*v.t.* (*hand over*) remettre; (*mil.*) rendre. —*n.* (*mil.*) reddition *f.*; (*of passport etc.*) remise *f.*

surreptitious /sʌrəp'tɪʃəs/ *a.* subreptice, furtif.

surround /sə'raʊnd/ *v.t.* entourer; (*mil.*) encercler. **~ing** *a.* environnant. **~ings** *n. pl.* environs *m. pl.*; (*setting*) cadre *m.*

surveillance /sɜː'veɪləns/ *n.* surveillance *f.*

survey[1] /sə'veɪ/ *v.t.* (*review*) passer en revue; (*inquire into*) enquêter sur; (*building*) inspecter. **~or** *n.* expert (géomètre) *m.*

survey[2] /'sɜːveɪ/ *n.* (*inquiry*) enquête *f.*; inspection *f.*; (*general view*) vue d'ensemble *f.*

survival /sə'vaɪvl/ *n.* survie *f.*; (*relic*) vestige *m.*

surviv|e /sə'vaɪv/ *v.t./i.* survivre (à). **~or** *n.* survivant(e) *m.* (*f.*).

susceptib|le /sə'septəbl/ *a.* sensible (**to,** à). **~le to,** (*prone to*) prédisposé à. **~ility** /-'bɪlətɪ/ *n.* sensibilité *f.*; prédisposition *f.*

suspect[1] /sə'spekt/ *v.t.* soupçonner; (*doubt*) douter de.

suspect[2] /'sʌspekt/ *n.* & *a.* suspect(e) (*m.* (*f.*)).

suspen|d /sə'spend/ *v.t.* (*hang, stop*) suspendre; (*licence*) retirer provisoirement. **~sion** *n.* suspension *f.*; retrait provisoire *m.* **~sion bridge,** pont suspendu *m.*

suspender /sə'spendə(r)/ *n.* jarretelle *f.* **~s,** (*braces: Amer.*) bretelles *f. pl.*

suspense /sə'spens/ *n.* attente *f.*; (*in book etc.*) suspense *m.*

suspicion /sə'spɪʃn/ *n.* soupçon *m.*; (*distrust*) méfiance *f.*

suspicious /səs'pɪʃəs/ *a.* soupçonneux; (*causing suspicion*) suspect. **be ~ of,** (*distrust*) se méfier de. **~ly** *adv.* de façon suspecte.

sustain /səs'teɪn/ *v.t.* supporter; (*effort etc.*) soutenir; (*suffer*) subir.

sustenance /'sʌstɪnəns/ *n.* (*food*) nourriture *f.*; (*quality*) valeur nutritive *f.*

swab /swɒb/ *n.* (*pad*) tampon *m.*

swagger /'swægə(r)/ *v.i.* (*walk*) se pavaner, parader.

swallow[1] /'swɒləʊ/ *v.t./i.* avaler. **~ up,** (*absorb, engulf*) engloutir.

swallow[2] /'swɒləʊ/ *n.* hirondelle *f.*

swam /swæm/ *see* **swim.**

swamp /swɒmp/ *n.* marais *m.* —*v.t.* (*flood, overwhelm*) submerger. **~y** *a.* marécageux.

swan /swɒn/ *n.* cygne *m.* **~-song** *n.* (*fig.*) chant du cygne *m.*

swank /swæŋk/ *n.* (*behaviour: fam.*) épate *f.*, esbroufe *f.*; (*person: fam.*) crâneu|r, -se *m.*, *f.* —*v.i.* (*show off: fam.*) crâner.

swap /swɒp/ *v.t./i.* (*p.t.* **swapped**) (*fam.*) échanger. —*n.* (*fam.*) échange *m.*

swarm /swɔːm/ *n.* (*of insects, people*) essaim *m.* —*v.i.* fourmiller. ~ **into** *or* … *wd*) envahir.

swarthy /'swɔːðɪ/ *a.* (-ier, -iest) noiraud; (*complexion*) basané.

swastika /'swɒstɪkə/ *n.* (*Nazi*) croix gammée *f.*

swat /swɒt/ *v.t.* (*p.t.* **swatted**) (*fly etc.*) écraser.

sway /sweɪ/ *v.t./i.* (se) balancer; (*influence*) influencer. —*n.* balancement *m.*; (*rule*) empire *m.*

swear /sweə(r)/ *v.t./i.* (*p.t.* **swore,** *p.p.* **sworn**) jurer (**to sth.,** de qch.). ~ **by sth.,** (*fam.*) ne jurer que par qch. ~**-word** *n.* juron *m.*

sweat /swet/ *n.* sueur *f.* —*v.i.* suer. ~**y** *a.* en sueur.

sweater /'swetə(r)/ *n.* pull-over *m.*

swede /swiːd/ *n.* rutabaga *m.*

Swed|e /swiːd/ *n.* Suédois(e) *m.* (*f.*). ~**en** *n.* Suède *f.* ~**ish** *a.* suédois; *n.* (*lang.*) suédois *m.*

sweep /swiːp/ *v.t./i.* (*p.t.* **swept**) balayer; (*go*) aller rapidement *or* majestueusement; (*carry away*) emporter, entraîner. —*n.* coup de balai *m.*; (*curve*) courbe *f.*; (*mouvement*) geste *m.*, mouvement *m.* ~**ing** *a.* (*gesture*) large; (*action*) qui va loin; (*statement*) trop général.

sweet /swiːt/ *a.* (-er, -est) (*not sour, pleasant*) doux; (*not savoury*) sucré; (*charming*: *fam.*) gentil. —*n.* bonbon *m.*; (*dish*) dessert *m.*; (*person*) chéri(e) *m.* (*f.*). **have a** ~ **tooth,** aimer les sucreries. ~ **shop,** confiserie *f.* ~**ly** *adv.* gentiment. ~**ness** *n.* douceur *f.*; goût sucré *m.*

sweeten /'swiːtn/ *v.t.* sucrer; (*fig.*) adoucir. ~**er** *n.* édulcorant *m.*

sweetheart /'swiːthɑːt/ *n.* petit(e) ami(e) *m.* (*f.*).; (*term of endearment*) chéri(e) *m.* (*f.*).

swell /swel/ *v.t./i.* (*p.t.* **swelled,** *p.p.* **swollen** *or* **swelled**) (*increase*) grossir; (*expand*) (se) gonfler; (*of hand, face*) enfler. —*n.* (*of sea*) houle *f.* —*a.* (*fam.*) formidable. ~**ing** *n.* (*med.*) enflure *f.*

swelter /'sweltə(r)/ *v.i.* étouffer.

swept /swept/ *see* **sweep.**

swerve /swɜːv/ *v.i.* faire un écart.

swift /swɪft/ *a.* (-**er**, -**est**) rapide. —*n.* (*bird*) martinet *m.* ~**ly** *adv.* rapidement. ~**ness** *n.* rapidité *f.*

swig /swɪg/ *v.t.* (*p.t.* **swigged**) (*drink*: *fam.*) lamper. —*n.* (*fam.*) lampée *f.*, coup *m.*

swill /swɪl/ *v.t.* rincer; (*drink*) lamper. —*n.* (*pig-food*) pâtée *f.*

swim /swɪm/ *v.i.* (*p.t.* **swam,** *p.p.* **swum,** *pres. p.* **swimming**) nager; (*be dizzy*) tourner. —*v.t.* traverser à la nage; (*distance*) nager. —*n.* baignade *f.* ~**mer** *n.* nageu|r, -se *m.*, *f.* ~**ming** *n.* natation *f.* ~**ming-bath,** ~**ming-pool** *ns.* piscine *f.* ~**-suit** *n.* maillot (de bain) *m.*

swindle /'swɪndl/ *v.t.* escroquer. —*n.* escroquerie *f.* ~**r** /-ə(r)/ *n.* escroc *m.*

swine /swaɪn/ *n. pl.* (*pigs*) pourceaux *m. pl.* —*n. invar.* (*person*: *fam.*) cochon *m.*

swing /swɪŋ/ *v.t./i.* (*p.t.* **swung**) (se) balancer; (*turn round*) tourner; (*of pendulum*) osciller. —*n.* balancement *m.*; (*seat*) balançoire *f.*; (*of opinion*) revirement *m.*; (*mus.*) rythme *m.* **be in full** ~, battre son plein. ~ **round,** (*of person*) se retourner.

swingeing /'swɪndʒɪŋ/ *a.* écrasant.

swipe /swaɪp/ *v.t.* (*hit*: *fam.*) frapper; (*steal*: *fam.*) piquer. —*n.* (*hit*: *fam.*) grand coup *m.*

swirl /swɜːl/ *v.i.* tourbillonner. —*n.* tourbillon *m.*

swish /swɪʃ/ *v.i.* (*hiss*) siffler, cingler l'air. —*a.* (*fam.*) chic *invar.*

Swiss /swɪs/ *a.* suisse. —*n. invar.* Suisse(sse) *m.* (*f.*).

switch /swɪtʃ/ *n.* bouton (électrique) *m.*, interrupteur *m.*; (*shift*) changement *m.*, revirement *m.*

—*v.t.* (*transfer*) transférer; (*exchange*) échanger (**for,** contre); (*reverse positions of*) changer de place. **~ trains**/*etc.*, (*change*) changer de train/*etc.* —*v.i.* (*go over*) passer. **~ off,** éteindre, fermer. **~ on,** mettre, allumer.

switchback /ˈswɪtʃbæk/ *n.* montagnes russes *f. pl.*

switchboard /ˈswɪtʃbɔːd/ *n.* (*telephone*) standard *m.*

Switzerland /ˈswɪtsələnd/ *n.* Suisse *f.*

swivel /ˈswɪvl/ *v.t./i.* (*p.t.* **swivelled**) (faire) pivoter.

swollen /ˈswəʊlən/ *see* **swell.**

swoon /swuːn/ *v.i.* se pâmer.

swoop /swuːp/ *v.i.* (*bird*) fondre; (*police*) faire une descente, foncer. —*n.* (*police raid*) descente *f.*

sword /sɔːd/ *n.* épée *f.*

swore /swɔː(r)/ *see* **swear.**

sworn /swɔːn/ *see* **swear.** —*a.* (*enemy*) juré; (*ally*) dévoué.

swot /swɒt/ *v.t./i.* (*p.t.* **swotted**) (*study*: *sl.*) bûcher. —*n.* (*sl.*) bûcheu|r, -se *m., f.*

swum /swʌm/ *see* **swim.**

swung /swʌŋ/ *see* **swing.**

sycamore /ˈsɪkəmɔː(r)/ *n.* (*maple*) sycomore *m.*; (*Amer.*) platane *m.*

syllable /ˈsɪləbl/ *n.* syllabe *f.*

syllabus /ˈsɪləbəs/ *n.* (*pl.* **-uses**) (*schol.*, *univ.*) programme *m.*

symbol /ˈsɪmbl/ *n.* symbole *m.* **~ic(al)** /-ˈbɒlɪk(l)/ *a.* symbolique. **~ism** *n.* symbolisme *m.*

symbolize /ˈsɪmbəlaɪz/ *v.t.* symboliser.

symmetr|y /ˈsɪmətrɪ/ *n.* symétrie *f.* **~ical** /sɪˈmetrɪkl/ *a.* symétrique.

sympathize /ˈsɪmpəθaɪz/ *v.i.* **~ with,** (*pity*) plaindre; (*fig.*) comprendre les sentiments de.

sympath|y /ˈsɪmpəθɪ/ *n.* (*pity*) compassion *f.*; (*fig.*) compréhension *f.*; (*solidarity*) solidarité *f.*; (*condolences*) condoléances *f. pl.* **be in ~y with,** comprendre, être en accord avec. **~etic** /-ˈθetɪk/ *a.* compatissant; (*fig.*) compréhensif. **~etically** /-ˈθetɪklɪ/ *adv.* avec compassion; (*fig.*) avec compréhension.

symphon|y /ˈsɪmfənɪ/ *n.* symphonie *f.* —*a.* symphonique. **~ic** /-ˈfɒnɪk/ *a.* symphonique.

symposium /sɪmˈpəʊzɪəm/ *n.* (*pl.* **-ia**) symposium *m.*

symptom /ˈsɪmptəm/ *n.* symptôme *m.* **~atic** /-ˈmætɪk/ *a.* symptomatique (**of,** de).

synagogue /ˈsɪnəgɒg/ *n.* synagogue *f.*

synchronize /ˈsɪŋkrənaɪz/ *v.t.* synchroniser.

syncopat|e /ˈsɪŋkəpeɪt/ *v.t.* syncoper. **~ion** /-ˈpeɪʃn/ *n.* syncope *f.*

syndicate /ˈsɪndɪkət/ *n.* syndicat *m.*

syndrome /ˈsɪndrəʊm/ *n.* syndrome *m.*

synonym /ˈsɪnənɪm/ *n.* synonyme *m.* **~ous** /sɪˈnɒnɪməs/ *a.* synonyme.

synopsis /sɪˈnɒpsɪs/ *n.* (*pl.* **-opses** /-siːz/) résumé *m.*

syntax /ˈsɪntæks/ *n.* syntaxe *f.*

synthesis /ˈsɪnθəsɪs/ *n.* (*pl.* **-theses** /-siːz/) synthèse *f.*

synthetic /sɪnˈθetɪk/ *a.* synthétique.

syphilis /ˈsɪfɪlɪs/ *n.* syphilis *f.*

Syria /ˈsɪrɪə/ *n.* Syrie *f.* **~n** *a.* & *n.* syrien(ne) (*m.* (*f.*)).

syringe /sɪˈrɪndʒ/ *n.* seringue *f.*

syrup /ˈsɪrəp/ *n.* (*liquid*) sirop *m.*; (*treacle*) mélasse raffinée *f.* **~y** *a.* sirupeux.

system /ˈsɪstəm/ *n.* système *m.*; (*body*) organisme *m.*; (*order*) méthode *f.* **~s analyst,** analyste-programmeu|r, -se *m., f.*

systematic /sɪstəˈmætɪk/ *a.* systématique.

T

tab /tæb/ *n.* (*flap*) languette *f.*, patte *f.*; (*loop*) attache *f.*; (*label*) étiquette *f.*; (*Amer., fam.*) addition *f.* **keep ~s on,** (*fam.*) surveiller.

tabernacle /ˈtæbənækl/ *n.* tabernacle *m.*

table /ˈteɪbl/ *n.* table *f.* —*v.t.* présenter; (*postpone*) ajourner. **at ~,** à table. **lay** *or* **set the ~,** mettre la table. **~-cloth** *n.* nappe *f.* **~-mat** *n.* dessous-de-plat *m. invar.* **~ of contents,** table des matières *f.* **~ tennis,** ping-pong *m.*

tablespoon /ˈteɪblspuːn/ *n.* cuiller à soupe *f.* **~ful** *n.* (*pl.* **~fuls**) cuillerée à soupe *f.*

tablet /ˈtæblɪt/ *n.* (*of stone*) plaque *f.*; (*drug*) comprimé *m.*

tabloid /ˈtæblɔɪd/ *n.* tabloïd *m.*

taboo /təˈbuː/ *n.* & *a.* tabou (*m.*).

tabulator /ˈtæbjʊleɪtə(r)/ *n.* (*on typewriter*) tabulateur *m.*

tacit /ˈtæsɪt/ *a.* tacite.

taciturn /ˈtæsɪtɜːn/ *a.* taciturne.

tack /tæk/ *n.* (*nail*) broquette *f.*; (*stitch*) point de bâti *m.*; (*course of action*) voie *f.* —*v.t.* (*nail*) clouer; (*stitch*) bâtir; (*add*) ajouter. —*v.i.* (*naut.*) louvoyer.

tackle /ˈtækl/ *n.* équipement *m.*, matériel *m.*; (*football*) plaquage *m.* —*v.t.* (*problem etc.*) s'attaquer à; (*football player*) plaquer.

tacky /ˈtækɪ/ *a.* (**-ier, -iest**) poisseux, pas sec; (*shabby, mean*: *Amer.*) moche.

tact /tækt/ *n.* tact *m.* **~ful** *a.* plein de tact. **~fully** *adv.* avec tact. **~less** *a.* qui manque de tact. **~lessly** *adv.* sans tact.

tactic /ˈtæktɪk/ *n.* tactique *f.* **~s** *n.* & *n. pl.* tactique *f.* **~al** *a.* tactique.

tactile /ˈtæktaɪl/ *a.* tactile.

tadpole /ˈtædpəʊl/ *n.* têtard *m.*

tag /tæg/ *n.* (*label*) étiquette *f.*; (*end piece*) bout *m.*; (*phrase*) cliché *m.* —*v.t.* (*p.t.* **tagged**) étiqueter; (*join*) ajouter. —*v.i.* **~ along,** (*fam.*) suivre.

tail /teɪl/ *n.* queue *f.*; (*of shirt*) pan *m.* **~s,** (*coat*) habit *m.* **~s!,** (*tossing coin*) pile! —*v.t.* (*follow*) filer. —*v.i.* **~ away** *or* **off,** diminuer. **~-back** *n.* (*traffic*) bouchon *m.* **~-end** *n.* fin *f.*, bout *m.*

tailcoat /ˈteɪlkəʊt/ *n.* habit *m.*

tailor /ˈteɪlə(r)/ *n.* tailleur *m.* —*v.t.* (*garment*) façonner; (*fig.*) adapter. **~-made** *a.* fait sur mesure. **~-made for,** (*fig.*) fait pour.

tainted /ˈteɪntɪd/ *a.* (*infected*) infecté; (*decayed*) gâté; (*fig.*) souillé.

take /teɪk/ *v.t./i.* (*p.t.* **took,** *p.p.* **taken**) prendre; (*carry*) (ap)porter (**to,** à); (*escort*) accompagner, amener; (*contain*) contenir; (*tolerate*) supporter; (*prize*) remporter; (*exam*) passer; (*choice*) faire; (*precedence*) avoir. **be ~n by** *or* **with,** être impressionné par. **be ~n ill,** tomber malade. **it ~s time to,** il faut du temps pour. **~ after,** ressembler à. **~ away,** (*object*) emporter; (*person*) emmener; (*remove*) enlever (**from,** à). **~ back,** reprendre; (*return*) rendre; (*accompany*) raccompagner; (*statement*) retirer. **~ down,** (*object*) descendre; (*notes*) prendre. **~ in,** (*object*) rentrer; (*include*) inclure; (*cheat*) tromper; (*grasp*) saisir. **~ it that,** supposer que. **~ off** *v.t.* enlever; (*mimic*) imiter; *v.i.* (*aviat.*) décoller. **~-off** *n.* imitation *f.*; (*aviat.*) décollage *m.* **~ on,** (*task, staff, passenger, etc.*) prendre. **~ out,** sortir; (*stain etc.*) enlever. **~ over** *v.t.* (*factory, country, etc.*) prendre la direction de; (*firm*: *comm.*) racheter; *v.i.* (*of dictator*) prendre le pouvoir. **~ over from,** (*relieve*) prendre la relève de; (*succeed*) prendre la succession de. **~-over** *n.* (*pol.*) prise de pouvoir *f.*; (*comm.*) rachat

m. ~ **part,** participer (**in,** à). ~ **place,** avoir lieu. ~ **sides,** prendre parti (**with,** pour). ~ **to,** se prendre d'amitié pour; (*activity*) prendre goût à. ~ **to doing,** se mettre à faire. ~ **up,** (*object*) monter; (*hobby*) se mettre à; (*occupy*) prendre; (*resume*) reprendre. ~ **up with,** se lier avec.
takings /'teɪkɪŋz/ *n. pl.* recette *f.*
talcum /'tælkəm/ *n.* talc *m.* ~ **powder,** talc *m.*
tale /teɪl/ *n.* conte *m.*; (*report*) récit *m.*; (*lie*) histoire *f.*
talent /'tælənt/ *n.* talent *m.* **~ed** *a.* doué, qui a du talent.
talk /tɔːk/ *v.t./i.* parler; (*say*) dire; (*chat*) bavarder. —*n.* conversation *f.*, entretien *m.*; (*words*) propos *m. pl.*; (*lecture*) exposé *m.* ~ **into doing,** persuader de faire. ~ **over,** discuter (de). **~er** *n.* causeu|r, -se *m., f.* **~ing-to** *n.* (*fam.*) réprimande *f.*
talkative /'tɔːkətɪv/ *a.* bavard.
tall /tɔːl/ *a.* (**-er, -est**) (*high*) haut; (*person*) grand. ~ **story,** (*fam.*) histoire invraisemblable *f.*
tallboy /'tɔːlbɔɪ/ *n.* commode *f.*
tally /'tælɪ/ *v.i.* correspondre (**with,** à), s'accorder (**with,** avec).
tambourine /tæmbə'riːn/ *n.* tambourin *m.*
tame /teɪm/ *a.* (**-er, -est**) apprivoisé; (*dull*) insipide. —*v.t.* apprivoiser; (*lion*) dompter. **~r** /-ə(r)/ *n.* dompteu|r, -se *m., f.*
tamper /'tæmpə(r)/ *v.i.* ~ **with,** toucher à, tripoter; (*text*) altérer.
tampon /'tæmpən/ *n.* (*med.*) tampon hygiénique *m.*
tan /tæn/ *v.t./i.* (*p.t.* **tanned**) bronzer; (*hide*) tanner. —*n.* bronzage *m.* —*a.* marron clair *invar.*
tandem /'tændəm/ *n.* (*bicycle*) tandem *m.* **in** ~, en tandem.
tang /tæŋ/ *n.* (*taste*) saveur forte *f.*; (*smell*) odeur forte *f.*
tangent /'tændʒənt/ *n.* tangente *f.*
tangerine /tændʒə'riːn/ *n.* mandarine *f.*
tangible /'tændʒəbl/ *a.* tangible.
tangle /'tæŋgl/ *v.t.* enchevêtrer. —*n.* enchevêtrement *m.* **become ~d,** s'enchevêtrer.
tango /'tæŋgəʊ/ *n.* (*pl.* **-os**) tango *m.*
tank /tæŋk/ *n.* réservoir *m.*; (*vat*) cuve *f.*; (*for fish*) aquarium *m.*; (*mil.*) char *m.*, tank *m.*
tankard /'tæŋkəd/ *n.* chope *f.*
tanker /'tæŋkə(r)/ *n.* camion-citerne *m.*; (*ship*) pétrolier *m.*
tantaliz|e /'tæntəlaɪz/ *v.t.* tourmenter. **~ing** *a.* tentant.
tantamount /'tæntəmaʊnt/ *a.* **be** ~ **to,** équivaloir à.
tantrum /'tæntrəm/ *n.* crise de colère *or* de rage *f.*
tap[1] /tæp/ *n.* (*for water etc.*) robinet *m.* —*v.t.* (*p.t.* **tapped**) (*resources*) exploiter; (*telephone*) mettre sur table d'écoute.
tap[2] /tæp/ *v.t./i.* (*p.t.* **tapped**) frapper (doucement). —*n.* petit coup *m.* **on** ~, (*fam.*) disponible. **~-dance** *n.* claquettes *f. pl.*
tape /teɪp/ *n.* ruban *m.*; (*sticky*) ruban adhésif *m.* (**magnetic**) ~, bande (magnétique) *f.* —*v.t.* (*tie*) attacher; (*stick*) coller; (*record*) enregistrer. **~-measure** *n.* mètre (à) ruban *m.* ~ **recorder,** magnétophone *m.*
taper /'teɪpə(r)/ *n.* (*for lighting*) bougie *f.* —*v.t./i.* (s')effiler. ~ **off,** (*diminish*) diminuer. **~ed, ~ing** *adjs.* (*fingers etc.*) effilé, fuselé; (*trousers*) étroit du bas.
tapestry /'tæpɪstrɪ/ *n.* tapisserie *f.*
tapioca /tæpɪ'əʊkə/ *n.* tapioca *m.*
tar /tɑː(r)/ *n.* goudron *m.* —*v.t.* (*p.t.* **tarred**) goudronner.
tardy /'tɑːdɪ/ *a.* (**-ier, -iest**) (*slow*) lent; (*belated*) tardif.
target /'tɑːgɪt/ *n.* cible *f.*; (*objective*) objectif *m.*

tariff /ˈtærɪf/ *n.* (*charges*) tarif *m.*; (*on imports*) tarif douanier *m.*
Tarmac /ˈtɑːmæk/ *n.* (P.) macadam (goudronné) *m.*; (*runway*) piste *f.*
tarnish /ˈtɑːnɪʃ/ *v.t./i.* (se) ternir.
tarpaulin /tɑːˈpɔːlɪn/ *n.* bâche goudronnée *f.*
tarry /ˈtærɪ/ *v.i.* (*old use*) s'attarder.
tart[1] /tɑːt/ *a.* (**-er, -est**) acide.
tart[2] /tɑːt/ *n.* tarte *f.*; (*prostitute*: *sl.*) poule *f.* —*v.t.* ~ **up,** (*pej.*, *sl.*) embellir (sans le moindre goût).
tartan /ˈtɑːtn/ *n.* tartan *m.* —*a.* écossais.
tartar /ˈtɑːtə(r)/ *n.* tartre *m.* ~ **sauce,** sauce tartare *f.*
task /tɑːsk/ *n.* tâche *f.*, travail *m.* **take to ~,** réprimander. ~ **force,** détachement spécial *m.*
tassel /ˈtæsl/ *n.* gland *m.*, pompon *m.*
taste /teɪst/ *n.* goût *m.* —*v.t.* (*eat, enjoy*) goûter; (*try*) goûter à; (*perceive taste of*) sentir le goût de. —*v.i.* ~ **of** *or* **like,** avoir un goût de. **have a ~ of,** (*experience*) goûter de. **~less** *a.* sans goût; (*fig.*) de mauvais goût.
tasteful /ˈteɪstfl/ *a.* de bon goût. **~ly** *adv.* avec goût.
tasty /ˈteɪstɪ/ *a.* (**-ier, -iest**) délicieux, savoureux.
tat /tæt/ *see* **tit**[2].
tatter|s /ˈtætəz/ *n. pl.* lambeaux *m. pl.* **~ed** /-əd/ *a.* en lambeaux.
tattoo[1] /təˈtuː/ *n.* (*mil.*) spectacle militaire *m.*
tattoo[2] /təˈtuː/ *v.t.* tatouer. —*n.* tatouage *m.*
tatty /ˈtætɪ/ *a.* (**-ier, -iest**) (*shabby*: *fam.*) miteux, minable.
taught /tɔːt/ *see* **teach.**
taunt /tɔːnt/ *v.t.* railler. —*n.* raillerie *f.* **~ing** *a.* railleur.
taut /tɔːt/ *a.* tendu.
tavern /ˈtævn/ *n.* taverne *f.*
tawdry /ˈtɔːdrɪ/ *a.* (**-ier, -iest**) (*showy*) tape-à-l'œil *invar.*
tax /tæks/ *n.* taxe *f.*, impôt *m.*; (*on income*) impôts *m. pl.* —*v.t.* imposer; (*put to test*: *fig.*) mettre à l'épreuve. **~able** *a.* imposable. **~ation** /-ˈseɪʃn/ *n.* imposition *f.*; (*taxes*) impôts *m. pl.* **~-collector** *n.* percepteur *m.* **~ing** *a.* (*fig.*) éprouvant.
taxi /ˈtæksɪ/ *n.* (*pl.* **-is**) taxi *m.* —*v.i.* (*p.t.* **taxied,** *pres. p.* **taxiing**) (*aviat.*) rouler au sol. **~-cab** *n.* taxi *m.* ~ **rank,** (*Amer.*) ~ **stand,** station de taxi *f.*
taxpayer /ˈtækspeɪə(r)/ *n.* contribuable *m./f.*
tea /tiː/ *n.* thé *m.*; (*snack*) goûter *m.* **~-bag** *n.* sachet de thé *m.* **~-break** *n.* pause-thé *f.* **~-leaf** *n.* feuille de thé *f.* **~-set** *n.* service à thé *m.* **~-shop** *n.* salon de thé *m.* **~-towel** *n.* torchon *m.*
teach /tiːtʃ/ *v.t.* (*p.t.* **taught**) apprendre (**s.o. sth.,** qch. à qn.); (*in school*) enseigner (**s.o. sth.,** qch. à qn.). —*v.i.* enseigner. **~er** *n.* professeur *m.*; (*primary*) institu|teur, -trice *m.*, *f.*; (*member of teaching profession*) enseignant(e) *m.* (*f.*). **~ing** *n.* enseignement *m.*; *a.* pédagogique; (*staff*) enseignant.
teacup /ˈtiːkʌp/ *n.* tasse à thé *f.*
teak /tiːk/ *n.* (*wood*) teck *m.*
team /tiːm/ *n.* équipe *f.*; (*of animals*) attelage *m.* —*v.i.* ~ **up,** faire équipe (**with,** avec). **~-work** *n.* travail d'équipe *m.*
teapot /ˈtiːpɒt/ *n.* théière *f.*
tear[1] /teə(r)/ *v.t./i.* (*p.t.* **tore,** *p.p.* **torn**) (se) déchirer; (*snatch*) arracher (**from,** à); (*rush*) aller à toute vitesse. —*n.* déchirure *f.*
tear[2] /tɪə(r)/ *n.* larme *f.* **in ~s,** en larmes. **~-gas** *n.* gaz lacrymogène *m.*
tearful /ˈtɪəfl/ *a.* (*voice*) larmoyant; (*person*) en larmes. **~ly** *adv.* en pleurant, les larmes aux yeux.

tease /tiːz/ *v.t.* taquiner. —*n.* (*person: fam.*) taquin(e) *m.* (*f.*).
teaser /ˈtiːzə(r)/ *n.* (*fam.*) colle *f.*
teaspoon /ˈtiːspuːn/ *n.* petite cuiller *f.* **~ful** *n.* (*pl.* **-fuls**) cuillerée à café *f.*
teat /tiːt/ *n.* (*of bottle, animal*) tétine *f.*
technical /ˈteknɪkl/ *a.* technique. **~ity** /-ˈkælətɪ/ *n.* détail technique *m.* **~ly** *adv.* techniquement.
technician /tekˈnɪʃn/ *n.* technicien(ne) *m.* (*f.*).
technique /tekˈniːk/ *n.* technique *f.*
technolog|y /tekˈnɒlədʒɪ/ *n.* technologie *f.* **~ical** /-əˈlɒdʒɪkl/ *a.* technologique.
teddy /ˈtedɪ/ *a.* **~ bear**, ours en peluche *m.*
tedious /ˈtiːdɪəs/ *a.* fastidieux.
tedium /ˈtiːdɪəm/ *n.* ennui *m.*
tee /tiː/ *n.* (*golf*) tee *m.*
teem[1] /tiːm/ *v.i.* (*swarm*) grouiller (**with**, de).
teem[2] /tiːm/ *v.i.* **~ (with rain)**, pleuvoir à torrents.
teenage /ˈtiːneɪdʒ/ *a.* (d')adolescent. **~d** *a.* adolescent. **~r** /-ə(r)/ *n.* adolescent(e) *m.* (*f.*).
teens /tiːnz/ *n. pl.* **in one's ~**, adolescent.
teeny /ˈtiːnɪ/ *a.* (**-ier, -iest**) (*tiny: fam.*) minuscule.
teeter /ˈtiːtə(r)/ *v.i.* chanceler.
teeth /tiːθ/ *see* **tooth.**
teeth|e /tiːð/ *v.i.* faire ses dents. **~ing troubles**, (*fig.*) difficultés initiales *f. pl.*
teetotaller /tiːˈtəʊtlə(r)/ *n.* personne qui ne boit pas d'alcool *f.*
telecommunications /telɪkəmjuːnɪˈkeɪʃnz/ *n. pl.* télécommunications *f. pl.*
telegram /ˈtelɪgræm/ *n.* télégramme *m.*
telegraph /ˈtelɪgrɑːf/ *n.* télégraphe *m.* —*a.* télégraphique. **~ic** /-ˈgræfɪk/ *a.* télégraphique.
telepath|y /tɪˈlepəθɪ/ *n.* télépathie *f.* **~ic** /telɪˈpæθɪk/ *a.* télépathique.
telephone /ˈtelɪfəʊn/ *n.* téléphone *m.* —*v.t.* (*person*) téléphoner à; (*message*) téléphoner. —*v.i.* téléphoner. **~ book**, annuaire *m.* **~-box** *n.*, **~ booth**, cabine téléphonique *f.* **~ call**, coup de téléphone *m.*
telephonist /tɪˈlefənɪst/ *n.* (*in exchange*) téléphoniste *m.*/*f.*
telescop|e /ˈtelɪskəʊp/ *n.* télescope *m.* —*v.t.*/*i.* (se) télescoper. **~ic** /-ˈskɒpɪk/ *a.* télescopique.
televise /ˈtelɪvaɪz/ *v.t.* téléviser.
television /ˈtelɪvɪʒn/ *n.* télévision *f.* **~ set**, poste de télévision *m.*
telex /ˈteleks/ *n.* télex *m.* —*v.t.* envoyer par télex.
tell /tel/ *v.t.* (*p.t.* **told**) dire (**s.o. sth**, qch. à qn.); (*story*) raconter; (*distinguish*) distinguer. —*v.i.* avoir un effet; (*know*) savoir. **~ of**, parler de. **~ off**, (*fam.*) gronder. **~-tale** *n.* rapporteu|r, -se *m.*, *f.* **~ tales**, rapporter.
teller /ˈtelə(r)/ *n.* (*in bank*) caiss|ier, -ière *m.*, *f.*
telling /ˈtelɪŋ/ *a.* révélateur.
telly /ˈtelɪ/ *n.* (*fam.*) télé *f.*
temerity /tɪˈmerətɪ/ *n.* témérité *f.*
temp /temp/ *n.* (*temporary employee: fam.*) intérimaire *m.*/*f.*
temper /ˈtempə(r)/ *n.* humeur *f.*; (*anger*) colère *f.* —*v.t.* (*metal*) tremper; (*fig.*) tempérer. **lose one's ~**, se mettre en colère.
temperament /ˈtemprəmənt/ *n.* tempérament *m.* **~al** /-ˈmentl/ *a.* capricieux; (*innate*) inné.
temperance /ˈtempərəns/ *n.* (*in drinking*) tempérance *f.*
temperate /ˈtempərət/ *a.* tempéré.
temperature /ˈtemprətʃə(r)/ *n.* température *f.* **have a ~**, avoir (de) la fièvre *or* de la température.
tempest /ˈtempɪst/ *n.* tempête *f.*
tempestuous /temˈpestʃʊəs/ *a.* (*meeting etc.*) orageux.

template /ˈtempl(e)ɪt/ *n.* patron *m.*
temple[1] /ˈtempl/ *n.* temple *m.*
temple[2] /ˈtempl/ *n.* (*of head*) tempe *f.*
tempo /ˈtempəʊ/ *n.* (*pl.* **-os**) tempo *m.*
temporal /ˈtempərəl/ *a.* temporel.
temporar|y /ˈtemprərɪ/ *a.* temporaire, provisoire. **~ily** *adv.* temporairement, provisoirement.
tempt /tempt/ *v.t.* tenter. **~ s.o. to do,** donner envie à qn. de faire. **~ation** /-ˈteɪʃn/ *n.* tentation *f.* **~ing** *a.* tentant.
ten /ten/ *a.* & *n.* dix (*m.*).
tenable /ˈtenəbl/ *a.* défendable.
tenac|ious /tɪˈneɪʃəs/ *a.* tenace. **~ity** /-æsətɪ/ *n.* ténacité *f.*
tenancy /ˈtenənsɪ/ *n.* location *f.*
tenant /ˈtenənt/ *n.* locataire *m./f.*
tend[1] /tend/ *v.t.* s'occuper de.
tend[2] /tend/ *v.i.* **~ to,** (*be apt to*) avoir tendance à.
tendency /ˈtendənsɪ/ *n.* tendance *f.*
tender[1] /ˈtendə(r)/ *a.* tendre; (*sore, painful*) sensible. **~ly** *adv.* tendrement. **~ness** *n.* tendresse *f.*
tender[2] /ˈtendə(r)/ *v.t.* offrir, donner. —*n.* (*comm.*) soumission *f.* **be legal ~,** (*money*) avoir cours.
tendon /ˈtendən/ *n.* tendon *m.*
tenement /ˈtenəmənt/ *n.* maison de rapport *f.*, H.L.M. *m./f.*; (*slum: Amer.*) taudis *m.*
tenet /ˈtenɪt/ *n.* principe *m.*
tenfold /ˈtenfəʊld/ *a.* décuple. —*adv.* au décuple.
tenner /ˈtenə(r)/ *n.* (*fam.*) billet de dix livres *m.*
tennis /ˈtenɪs/ *n.* tennis *m.*
tenor /ˈtenə(r)/ *n.* (*meaning*) sens général *m.*; (*mus.*) ténor *m.*
tense[1] /tens/ *n.* (*gram.*) temps *m.*
tense[2] /tens/ *a.* (**-er, -est**) tendu. —*v.t.* (*muscles*) tendre, raidir. —*v.i.* (*of face*) se crisper. **~ness** *n.* tension *f.*
tension /ˈtenʃn/ *n.* tension *f.*
tent /tent/ *n.* tente *f.*
tentacle /ˈtentəkl/ *n.* tentacule *m.*
tentative /ˈtentətɪv/ *a.* provisoire; (*hesitant*) timide. **~ly** *adv.* provisoirement; timidement.
tenterhooks /ˈtentəhʊks/ *n. pl.* **on ~,** sur des charbons ardents.
tenth /tenθ/ *a.* & *n.* dixième (*m./f.*).
tenuous /ˈtenjʊəs/ *a.* ténu.
tenure /ˈtenjʊə(r)/ *n.* (*in job, office*) (période de) jouissance *f.*
tepid /ˈtepɪd/ *a.* tiède.
term /tɜːm/ *n.* (*word, limit*) terme *m.*; (*of imprisonment*) temps; (*in school etc.*) trimestre *m.*; (*Amer.*) semestre *m.* **~s,** conditions *f. pl.* —*v.t.* appeler. **on good/bad ~s,** en bons/mauvais termes. **~ of office,** (*pol.*) mandat *m.*
terminal /ˈtɜːmɪnl/ *a.* terminal, final. —*n.* (*oil, computer*) terminal *m.*; (*rail.*) terminus *m.*; (*electr.*) borne *f.* (**air**) **~,** aérogare *f.*
terminat|e /ˈtɜːmɪneɪt/ *v.t.* mettre fin à. —*v.i.* prendre fin. **~ion** /-ˈneɪʃn/ *n.* fin *f.*
terminology /tɜːmɪˈnɒlədʒɪ/ *n.* terminologie *f.*
terminus /ˈtɜːmɪnəs/ *n.* (*pl.* **-ni** /-naɪ/) (*station*) terminus *m.*
terrace /ˈterəs/ *n.* terrasse *f.*; (*houses*) rangée de maisons contiguës *f.* **the ~s,** (*sport*) les gradins *m. pl.*
terrain /teˈreɪn/ *n.* terrain *m.*
terrestrial /tɪˈrestrɪəl/ *a.* terrestre.
terribl|e /ˈterəbl/ *a.* affreux, atroce. **~y** *adv.* affreusement; (*very*) terriblement.
terrier /ˈterɪə(r)/ *n.* (*dog*) terrier *m.*
terrific /təˈrɪfɪk/ *a.* (*fam.*) terrible. **~ally** /-klɪ/ *adv.* (*very: fam.*) terriblement; (*very well: fam.*) terriblement bien.
terrif|y /ˈterɪfaɪ/ *v.t.* terrifier. **be ~ied of,** avoir très peur de.
territorial /terɪˈtɔːrɪəl/ *a.* territorial.
territory /ˈterɪtərɪ/ *n.* territoire *m.*

terror /'terə(r)/ *n.* terreur *f.*
terroris|t /'terərɪst/ *n.* terroriste *m./f.* **~m** /-zəm/ *n.* terrorisme *m.*
terrorize /'terəraɪz/ *v.t.* terroriser.
terse /tɜːs/ *a.* concis, laconique.
test /test/ *n.* examen *m.*, analyse *f.*; (*of goods*) contrôle *m.*; (*of machine etc.*) essai *m.*; (*in school*) interrogation *f.*; (*of strength etc.*: *fig.*) épreuve *f.* —*v.t.* examiner, analyser; (*check*) contrôler; (*try*) essayer; (*pupil*) donner une interrogation à; (*fig.*) éprouver. **~ match,** match international *m.* **~-tube** *n.* éprouvette *f.*
testament /'testəmənt/ *n.* testament *m.* **Old/New T~,** Ancien/Nouveau Testament *m.*
testicle /'testɪkl/ *n.* testicule *m.*
testify /'testɪfaɪ/ *v.t./i.* témoigner (**to,** de). **~ that,** témoigner que.
testimonial /testɪ'məʊnɪəl/ *n.* recommendation *f.*
testimony /'testɪmənɪ/ *n.* témoignage *m.*
testy /'testɪ/ *a.* grincheux.
tetanus /'tetənəs/ *n.* tétanos *m.*
tetchy /'tetʃɪ/ *a.* grincheux.
tether /'teðə(r)/ *v.t.* attacher. —*n.* **at the end of one's ~,** à bout.
text /tekst/ *n.* texte *m.*
textbook /'tekstbʊk/ *n.* manuel *m.*
textile /'tekstaɪl/ *n.* & *a.* textile (*m.*).
texture /'tekstʃə(r)/ *n.* (*of paper etc.*) grain *m.* (*of fabric*) texture *f.*
Thai /taɪ/ *a.* & *n.* thaïlandais(e) (*m.* (*f.*)). **~land** *n.* Thaïlande *f.*
Thames /temz/ *n.* Tamise *f.*
than /ðæn, *unstressed* ðən/ *conj.* que, qu'*; (*with numbers*) de. **more/less ~ ten,** plus/moins de dix.
thank /θæŋk/ *v.t.* remercier. **~s** *n. pl.* remerciements *m. pl.* **~ you!,** merci! **~s!,** (*fam.*) merci! **~s to,** grâce à. **T~sgiving (Day),** (*Amer.*) jour d'action de grâces *m.* (*fête nationale*).
thankful /'θæŋkfl/ *a.* reconnaissant (**for,** de). **~ly** *adv.* (*happily*) heureusement.
thankless /'θæŋklɪs/ *a.* ingrat.
that /ðæt, *unstressed* ðət/ *a.* (*pl.* **those**) ce *or* cet*, cette. **those,** ces. —*pron.* ce *or* c'*, cela, ça. **~ (one),** celui-là, celle-là. **those (ones),** ceux-là, celles-là. —*adv.* si, aussi. —*rel. pron.* (*subject*) qui; (*object*) que, qu'*. —*conj.* que, qu'*. **~ boy,** ce garçon; (*with emphasis*) ce garçon-là. **~ is,** c'est. **~ is (to say),** c'est-à-dire. **after ~,** après ça *or* cela. **the day ~,** le jour où. **~ much,** autant que ça.
thatch /θætʃ/ *n.* chaume *m.* **~ed** *a.* en chaume. **~ed cottage,** chaumière *f.*
thaw /θɔː/ *v.t./i.* (faire) dégeler; (*snow*) (faire) fondre. —*n.* dégel *m.*
the /*before vowel* ðɪ, *before consonant* ðə, *stressed* ðiː/ *a.* le *or* l'*, la *or* l'*, *pl.* les. **of ~, from ~,** du, de l'*, de la, *pl.* des. **to ~, at ~,** au, à l'*, à la, *pl.* aux.
theatre /'θɪətə(r)/ *n.* théâtre *m.*
theatrical /θɪ'ætrɪkl/ *a.* théâtral.
theft /θeft/ *n.* vol *m.*
their /ðeə(r)/ *a.* leur, *pl.* leurs.
theirs /ðeəz/ *poss. pron.* le *or* la leur, les leurs.
them /ðem, *unstressed* ðəm/ *pron.* les; (*after prep.*) eux, elles. **(to) ~,** leur. **I know ~,** je les connais.
theme /θiːm/ *n.* thème *m.* **~ song,** (*in film etc.*) chanson principale *f.*
themselves /ðəm'selvz/ *pron.* eux-mêmes, elles-mêmes; (*reflexive*) se; (*after prep.*) eux, elles.
then /ðen/ *adv.* alors; (*next*) ensuite, puis; (*therefore*) alors, donc. —*a.* d'alors. **from ~ on,** dès lors.
theolog|y /θɪ'ɒlədʒɪ/ *n.* théologie *f.* **~ian** /θɪə'ləʊdʒən/ *n.* théologien(ne) *m.* (*f.*).
theorem /'θɪərəm/ *n.* théorème *m.*
theor|y /'θɪərɪ/ *n.* théorie *f.* **~etical** /-'retɪkl/ *a.* théorique.

therapeutic /θerəˈpjuːtɪk/ *a.* thérapeutique.
therapy /ˈθerəpɪ/ *n.* thérapie *f.*
there /ðeə(r)/ *adv.* là; (*with verb*) y; (*over there*) là-bas. —*int.* allez. **he goes ~,** il y va. **on ~,** là-dessus. **~ is, ~ are,** il y a; (*pointing*) voilà. **~, ~!,** allons, allons! **~abouts** *adv.* par là. **~after** *adv.* par la suite. **~by** *adv.* de cette manière.
therefore /ˈðeəfɔː(r)/ *adv.* donc.
thermal /ˈθɜːml/ *a.* thermique.
thermometer /θəˈmɒmɪtə(r)/ *n.* thermomètre *m.*
thermonuclear /θɜːməʊˈnjuːklɪə(r)/ *a.* thermonucléaire.
Thermos /ˈθɜːməs/ *n.* (P.) thermos *m./f. invar.* (P.).
thermostat /ˈθɜːməstæt/ *n.* thermostat *m.*
thesaurus /θɪˈsɔːrəs/ *n.* (*pl.* **-ri** /-raɪ/) dictionnaire de synonymes *m.*
these /ðiːz/ *see* **this.**
thesis /ˈθiːsɪs/ *n.* (*pl.* **theses** /-siːz/) thèse *f.*
they /ðeɪ/ *pron.* ils, elles; (*emphatic*) eux, elles; (*people in general*) on.
thick /θɪk/ *a.* (**-er, -est**) épais; (*stupid*) bête; (*friends: fam.*) très lié. —*adv.* = **thickly.** —*n.* **in the ~ of,** au plus gros de. **~ly** *adv.* (*grow*) dru; (*spread*) en couche épaisse. **~ness** *n.* épaisseur *f.* **~-skinned** *a.* peu sensible.
thicken /ˈθɪkən/ *v.t./i.* (s')épaissir.
thickset /θɪkˈset/ *a.* trapu.
thief /θiːf/ *n.* (*pl.* **thieves**) voleu|r, -se *m., f.*
thiev|e /θiːv/ *v.t./i.* voler. **~ing** *a.* voleur.
thigh /θaɪ/ *n.* cuisse *f.*
thimble /ˈθɪmbl/ *n.* dé (à coudre) *m.*
thin /θɪn/ *a.* (**thinner, thinnest**) mince; (*person*) maigre, mince; (*sparse*) clairsemé; (*fine*) fin. —*adv.* = **thinly.** —*v.t./i.* (*p.t.* **thinned**) (*liquid*) (s')éclaircir. **~ out,** (*in quantity*) (s')éclaircir. **~ly** *adv.* (*slightly*) légèrement. **~ness** *n.* minceur *f.*; maigreur *f.*
thing /θɪŋ/ *n.* chose *f.* **~s,** (*belongings*) affaires *f. pl.* **the best ~ is to,** le mieux est de. **the (right) ~,** ce qu'il faut (**for s.o.,** à qn.).
think /θɪŋk/ *v.t./i.* (*p.t.* **thought**) penser (**about, of,** à); (*carefully*) réfléchir (**about, of,** à). **~ better of it,** se raviser. **~ nothing of,** trouver naturel de. **~ of,** (*hold opinion of*) penser de. **~ over,** bien réfléchir à. **~-tank** *n.* comité d'experts *m.* **~ up,** inventer. **~er** *n.* penseu|r, -se *m., f.*
third /θɜːd/ *a.* troisième. —*n.* troisième *m./f.*; (*fraction*) tiers *m.* **~ly** *adv.* troisièmement. **~-rate** *a.* très inférieur. **T~ World,** Tiers-Monde *m.*
thirst /θɜːst/ *n.* soif *f.* **~y** *a.* **be ~y,** avoir soif. **make ~y,** donner soif à.
thirteen /θɜːˈtiːn/ *a.* & *n.* treize (*m.*). **~th** *a.* & *n.* treizième (*m./f.*).
thirt|y /ˈθɜːtɪ/ *a.* & *n.* trente (*m.*). **~ieth** *a.* & *n.* trentième (*m./f.*).
this /ðɪs/ *a.* (*pl.* **these**) ce *or* cet*, cette. **these,** ces. —*pron.* ce *or* c'*, ceci. **~ (one),** celui-ci, celle-ci. **these (ones),** ceux-ci, celles-ci. **~ boy,** ce garçon; (*with emphasis*) ce garçon-ci. **~ is,** c'est. **after ~,** après ceci.
thistle /ˈθɪsl/ *n.* chardon *m.*
thorn /θɔːn/ *n.* épine *f.* **~y** *a.* épineux.
thorough /ˈθʌrə/ *a.* consciencieux; (*deep*) profond; (*cleaning, washing*) à fond. **~ly** *adv.* (*clean, study, etc.*) à fond; (*very*) tout à fait.
thoroughbred /ˈθʌrəbred/ *n.* (*horse etc.*) pur-sang *m. invar.*
thoroughfare /ˈθʌrəfeə(r)/ *n.* grande artère *f.*
those /ðəʊz/ *see* **that.**
though /ðəʊ/ *conj.* bien que. —*adv.* (*fam.*) cependant.

thought /θɔːt/ *see* **think.** —*n.* pensée *f.*; (*idea*) idée *f.*
thoughtful /ˈθɔːtfl/ *a.* pensif; (*considerate*) attentionné. **~ly** *adv.* pensivement; avec considération.
thoughtless /ˈθɔːtlɪs/ *a.* étourdi. **~ly** *adv.* étourdiment.
thousand /ˈθaʊznd/ *a.* & *n.* mille (*m. invar.*). **~s of,** des milliers de.
thrash /θræʃ/ *v.t.* rosser; (*defeat*) écraser. **~ out,** discuter à fond.
thread /θred/ *n.* (*yarn & fig.*) fil *m.*; (*of screw*) pas *m.* —*v.t.* enfiler. **~ one's way,** se faufiler.
threadbare /ˈθredbeə(r)/ *a.* râpé.
threat /θret/ *n.* menace *f.*
threaten /ˈθretn/ *v.t./i.* menacer. **~ingly** *adv.* d'un air menaçant.
three /θriː/ *a.* & *n.* trois (*m.*). **~fold** *a.* triple; *adv.* trois fois (autant).
thresh /θreʃ/ *v.t.* (*corn etc.*) battre.
threshold /ˈθreʃəʊld/ *n.* seuil *m.*
threw /θruː/ *see* **throw.**
thrift /θrɪft/ *n.* économie *f.* **~y** *a.* économe.
thrill /θrɪl/ *n.* émotion *f.*, frisson *m.* —*v.t.* transporter (de joie). —*v.i.* frissonner (de joie). **be ~ed,** être ravi. **~ing** *a.* excitant.
thriller /ˈθrɪlə(r)/ *n.* livre *or* film à suspense *m.*
thriv|e /θraɪv/ *v.i.* (*p.t.* **thrived** *or* **throve,** *p.p.* **thrived** *or* **thriven**) prospérer. **he ~es on it,** cela lui réussit. **~ing** *a.* prospère.
throat /θrəʊt/ *n.* gorge *f.* **have a sore ~,** avoir mal à la gorge.
throb /θrɒb/ *v.i.* (*p.t.* **throbbed**) (*wound*) causer des élancements; (*heart*) palpiter; (*fig.*) vibrer. —*n.* (*pain*) élancement *m.*; palpitation *f.* **~bing** *a.* (*pain*) lancinant.
throes /θrəʊz/ *n. pl.* **in the ~ of,** au milieu de, aux prises avec.
thrombosis /θrɒmˈbəʊsɪs/ *n.* thrombose *f.*
throne /θrəʊn/ *n.* trône *m.*
throng /θrɒŋ/ *n.* foule *f.* —*v.t.* (*streets etc.*) se presser dans. —*v.i.* (*arrive*) affluer.
throttle /ˈθrɒtl/ *n.* (*auto.*) accélérateur *m.* —*v.t.* étrangler.
through /θruː/ *prep.* à travers; (*during*) pendant; (*by means or way of, out of*) par; (*by reason of*) grâce à, à cause de. —*adv.* à travers; (*entirely*) jusqu'au bout. —*a.* (*train etc.*) direct. **be ~,** (*finished*) avoir fini. **come** *or* **go ~,** (*cross, pierce*) traverser.
throughout /θruːˈaʊt/ *prep.* **~ the country**/*etc.*, dans tout le pays/*etc.* **~ the day**/*etc.*, pendant toute la journée/*etc.* —*adv.* (*place*) partout; (*time*) tout le temps.
throw /θrəʊ/ *v.t.* (*p.t.* **threw,** *p.p.* **thrown**) jeter, lancer; (*baffle: fam.*) déconcerter. —*n.* jet *m.*; (*of dice*) coup *m.* **~ a party,** (*fam.*) donner une réception. **~ away,** jeter. **~-away** *a.* à jeter. **~ off,** (*get rid of*) se débarrasser de. **~ out,** jeter; (*person*) expulser; (*reject*) rejeter. **~ over,** (*desert*) plaquer. **~ up,** (*one's arms*) lever; (*resign from*) abandonner; (*vomit*) vomir.
thrush /θrʌʃ/ *n.* (*bird*) grive *f.*
thrust /θrʌst/ *v.t.* (*p.t.* **thrust**) pousser. —*n.* poussée *f.* **~ into,** (*put*) enfoncer dans, mettre dans. **~ upon,** (*force on*) imposer à.
thud /θʌd/ *n.* bruit sourd *m.*
thug /θʌg/ *n.* voyou *m.*, bandit *m.*
thumb /θʌm/ *n.* pouce *m.* —*v.t.* (*book*) feuilleter. **~ a lift,** faire de l'auto-stop. **~-index,** répertoire à onglets *m.*
thumbtack /ˈθʌmtæk/ *n.* (*Amer.*) punaise *f.*
thump /θʌmp/ *v.t./i.* cogner (sur); (*of heart*) battre fort. —*n.* grand coup *m.* **~ing** *a.* (*fam.*) énorme.
thunder /ˈθʌndə(r)/ *n.* tonnerre *m.* —*v.i.* (*weather, person, etc.*) tonner. **~ past,** passer dans un bruit de tonnerre. **~y** *a.* orageux.

thunderbolt /ˈθʌndəbəʊlt/ *n.* coup de foudre *m.*; (*event*: *fig.*) coup de tonnerre *m.*
thunderstorm /ˈθʌndəstɔːm/ *n.* orage *m.*
Thursday /ˈθɜːzdɪ/ *n.* jeudi *m.*
thus /ðʌs/ *adv.* ainsi.
thwart /θwɔːt/ *v.t.* contrecarrer.
thyme /taɪm/ *n.* thym *m.*
thyroid /ˈθaɪrɔɪd/ *n.* thyroïde *f.*
tiara /tɪˈɑːrə/ *n.* diadème *m.*
tic /tɪk/ *n.* tic (nerveux) *m.*
tick[1] /tɪk/ *n.* (*sound*) tic-tac *m.*; (*mark*) coche *f.*; (*moment*: *fam.*) instant *m.* —*v.i.* faire tic-tac. —*v.t.* **~ (off)**, cocher. **~ off,** (*sl.*) réprimander. **~ over,** (*engine, factory*) tourner au ralenti.
tick[2] /tɪk/ *n.* (*insect*) tique *f.*
ticket /ˈtɪkɪt/ *n.* billet *m.*; (*for bus, cloakroom, etc*) ticket *m.*; (*label*) étiquette *f.* **~-collector** *n.* contrôleu|r, -se *m., f.* **~-office** *n.* guichet *m.*
tickle /ˈtɪkl/ *v.t.* chatouiller; (*amuse*: *fig.*) amuser. —*n.* chatouillement *m.*
ticklish /ˈtɪklɪʃ/ *a.* chatouilleux.
tidal /ˈtaɪdl/ *a.* qui a des marées. **~ wave,** raz-de-marée *m. invar.*
tiddly-winks /ˈtɪdlɪwɪŋks/ *n.* (*game*) jeu de puce *m.*
tide /taɪd/ *n.* marée *f.*; (*of events*) cours *m.* —*v.t.* **~ over,** dépanner.
tidings /ˈtaɪdɪŋz/ *n. pl.* nouvelles *f. pl.*
tid|y /ˈtaɪdɪ/ *a.* (**-ier, -iest**) (*room*) bien rangé; (*appearance, work*) soigné; (*methodical*) ordonné; (*amount*: *fam.*) joli. —*v.t./i.* ranger. **~y o.s.,** s'arranger. **~ily** *adv.* avec soin. **~iness** *n.* ordre *m.*
tie /taɪ/ *v.t.* (*pres. p.* **tying**) attacher, nouer; (*a knot*) faire; (*link*) lier. —*v.i.* (*darts etc.*) finir à égalité de points; (*football*) faire match nul; (*in race*) être ex aequo. —*n.* attache *f.*; (*necktie*) cravate *f.*; (*link*) lien *m.*; égalité (de points) *f.*; match nul *m.* **~ in with,** être lié à. **~ up,** attacher; (*money*) immobiliser; (*occupy*) occuper. **~-up** *n.* (*link*) lien *m.*; (*auto., Amer.*) bouchon *m.*
tier /tɪə(r)/ *n.* étage *m.*, niveau *m.*; (*in stadium etc.*) gradin *m.*
tiff /tɪf/ *n.* petite querelle *f.*
tiger /ˈtaɪgə(r)/ *n.* tigre *m.*
tight /taɪt/ *a.* (**-er, -est**) (*clothes*) étroit, juste; (*rope*) tendu; (*lid*) solidement fixé; (*control*) strict; (*knot, collar, schedule*) serré; (*drunk*: *fam.*) ivre. —*adv.* (*hold, sleep, etc.*) bien; (*squeeze*) fort. **~ corner,** situation difficile *f.* **~-fisted** *a.* avare. **~ly** *adv.* bien; (*squeeze*) fort.
tighten /ˈtaɪtn/ *v.t./i.* (se) tendre; (*bolt etc.*) (se) resserrer; (*control etc.*) renforcer. **~ up on,** se montrer plus strict à l'égard de.
tightrope /ˈtaɪtrəʊp/ *n.* corde raide *f.* **~ walker,** funambule *m./f.*
tights /taɪts/ *n. pl.* collant *m.*
tile /taɪl/ *n.* (*on wall, floor*) carreau *m.*; (*on roof*) tuile *f.* —*v.t.* carreler; couvrir de tuiles.
till[1] /tɪl/ *v.t.* (*land*) cultiver.
till[2] /tɪl/ *prep.* & *conj.* = **until.**
till[3] /tɪl/ *n.* caisse (enregistreuse) *f.*
tilt /tɪlt/ *v.t./i.* pencher. —*n.* (*slope*) inclinaison *f.* **(at) full ~,** à toute vitesse.
timber /ˈtɪmbə(r)/ *n.* bois (de construction) *m.*; (*trees*) arbres *m. pl.*
time /taɪm/ *n.* temps *m.*; (*moment*) moment *m.*; (*epoch*) époque *f.*; (*by clock*) heure *f.*; (*occasion*) fois *f.*; (*rhythm*) mesure *f.* **~s,** (*multiplying*) fois *f. pl.* —*v.t.* choisir le moment de; (*measure*) minuter; (*sport*) chronométrer. **behind the ~s,** en retard sur son temps. **for the ~ being,** pour le moment. **from ~ to time,** de temps en temps. **have a good ~,** s'amuser. **in no ~,** en un rien de temps. **in**

~, à temps; (*eventually*) avec le temps. **on ~,** à l'heure. **~ bomb,** bombe à retardement *f*. **~-honoured** *a*. consacré (par l'usage). **~-lag** *n*. décalage *m*. **~ off,** du temps libre. **~ zone,** fuseau horaire *m*.

timeless /ˈtaɪmlɪs/ *a*. éternel.

timely /ˈtaɪmlɪ/ *a*. à propos.

timer /ˈtaɪmə(r)/ *n*. (*techn*.) minuterie *f*.; (*culin*.) compte-minutes *m*. *invar*.; (*with sand*) sablier *m*.

timetable /ˈtaɪmteɪbl/ *n*. horaire *m*.

timid /ˈtɪmɪd/ *a*. timide; (*fearful*) peureux. **~ly** *adv*. timidement.

timing /ˈtaɪmɪŋ/ *n*. (*measuring*) minutage *m*.; (*moment*) moment *m*.; (*of artist*) rythme *m*.

tin /tɪn/ *n*. étain *m*.; (*container*) boîte *f*. **~(plate),** fer-blanc *m*. —*v.t*. (*p.t*. **tinned**) mettre en boîte. **~ foil,** papier d'aluminium *m*. **~ny** *a*. métallique. **~-opener** *n*. ouvre-boîte(s) *m*.

tinge /tɪndʒ/ *v.t*. teinter (**with,** de). —*n*. teinte *f*.

tingle /ˈtɪŋgl/ *v.i*. (*prickle*) picoter. —*n*. picotement *m*.

tinker /ˈtɪŋkə(r)/ *n*. rétameur *m*. —*v.i*. **~ (with),** bricoler.

tinkle /ˈtɪŋkl/ *n*. tintement *m*.; (*fam*.) coup de téléphone *m*.

tinsel /ˈtɪnsl/ *n*. cheveux d'ange *m*. *pl*., guirlandes de Noël *f*. *pl*.

tint /tɪnt/ *n*. teinte *f*.; (*for hair*) shampooing colorant *m*. —*v.t*. (*glass, paper*) teinter.

tiny /ˈtaɪnɪ/ *a*. (**-ier, -iest**) minuscule, tout petit.

tip[1] /tɪp/ *n*. bout *m*. **~ped cigarette,** cigarette (à bout) filtre *f*.

tip[2] /tɪp/ *v.t./i*. (*p.t*. **tipped**) (*tilt*) pencher; (*overturn*) (faire) basculer; (*pour*) verser; (*empty*) déverser. —*n*. (*money*) pourboire *m*.; (*advice*) tuyau *m*.; (*for rubbish*) décharge *f*. **~ off,** prévenir. **~-off** *n*. tuyau *m*. (*pour prévenir*).

tipple /ˈtɪpl/ *v.i*. (*drink*) picoler.

tipsy /ˈtɪpsɪ/ *a*. un peu ivre, gris.

tiptoe /ˈtɪptəʊ/ *n*. **on ~,** sur la pointe des pieds.

tiptop /ˈtɪptɒp/ *a*. (*fam*.) excellent.

tir|e[1] /ˈtaɪə(r)/ *v.t./i*. (se) fatiguer. **~e of,** se lasser de. **~eless** *a*. infatigable. **~ing** *a*. fatigant.

tire[2] /ˈtaɪə(r)/ *n*. (*Amer*.) pneu *m*.

tired /taɪəd/ *a*. fatigué. **be ~ of,** en avoir assez de.

tiresome /ˈtaɪəsəm/ *a*. ennuyeux.

tissue /ˈtɪʃuː/ *n*. tissu *m*.; (*handkerchief*) mouchoir en papier *m*. **~-paper** *n*. papier de soie *m*.

tit[1] /tɪt/ *n*. (*bird*) mésange *f*.

tit[2] /tɪt/ *n*. **give ~ for tat,** rendre coup pour coup.

titbit /ˈtɪtbɪt/ *n*. friandise *f*.

titillate /ˈtɪtɪleɪt/ *v.t*. exciter.

title /ˈtaɪtl/ *n*. titre *m*. **~-deed** *n*. titre de propriété *m*. **~-role** *n*. rôle principal *m*.

titled /ˈtaɪtld/ *a*. (*person*) titré.

tittle-tattle /ˈtɪtltætl/ *n*. commérages *m*. *pl*., potins *m*. *pl*.

titular /ˈtɪtjʊlə(r)/ *a*. (*ruler etc*.) nominal.

to /tuː, *unstressed* tə/ *prep*. à; (*towards*) vers; (*of attitude*) envers. —*adv*. **push** *or* **pull ~,** (*close*) fermer. **~ France**/*etc*., en France/*etc*. **~ town,** en ville. **~ Canada**/*etc*., au Canada/*etc*. **~ the baker's**/*etc*., chez le boulanger/*etc*. **the road**/**door**/*etc*. **~,** la route/porte/*etc*. de. **~ me**/**her**/*etc*., me/lui/*etc*. **~ do**/**sit**/*etc*., faire/s'asseoir/*etc*. **ten ~ six,** (*by clock*) six heures moins dix. **go ~ and fro,** aller et venir. **husband-**/*etc*. **~-be** *n*. mari/*etc*. futur *m*. **~-do** *n*. (*fuss*) chichi(s) *m*. (*pl*.).

toad /təʊd/ *n*. crapaud *m*.

toadstool /ˈtəʊdstuːl/ *n*. champignon (vénéneux) *m*.

toast /təʊst/ *n*. pain grillé *m*., toast *m*.; (*drink*) toast *m*. —*v.t*.

(*bread*) faire griller; (*drink to*) porter un toast à; (*event*) arroser. **~er** *n.* grille-pain *m. invar.*

tobacco /təˈbækəʊ/ *n.* tabac *m.*

tobacconist /təˈbækənɪst/ *n.* marchand(e) de tabac *m.* (*f.*). **~'s shop,** tabac *m.*

toboggan /təˈbɒgən/ *n.* toboggan *m.*, luge *f.*

today /təˈdeɪ/ *n.* & *adv.* aujourd'hui (*m.*).

toddler /ˈtɒdlə(r)/ *n.* tout(e) petit(e) enfant *m./f.*

toddy /ˈtɒdɪ/ *n.* (*drink*) grog *m.*

toe /təʊ/ *n.* orteil *m.*; (*of shoe*) bout *m.* —*v.t.* **~ the line,** se conformer. **on one's ~s,** vigilant. **~-hold** *n.* prise (précaire) *f.*

toff /tɒf/ *n.* (*sl.*) dandy *m.*, aristo *m.*

toffee /ˈtɒfɪ/ *n.* caramel *m.* **~-apple** *n.* pomme caramélisée *f.*

together /təˈgeðə(r)/ *adv.* ensemble; (*at same time*) en même temps. **~ with,** avec. **~ness** *n.* camaraderie *f.*

toil /tɔɪl/ *v.i.* peiner. —*n.* labeur *m.*

toilet /ˈtɔɪlɪt/ *n.* toilettes *f. pl.*; (*grooming*) toilette *f.* **~-paper** *n.* papier hygiénique *m.* **~-roll** *n.* rouleau de papier hygiénique *m.* **~ water,** eau de toilette *f.*

toiletries /ˈtɔɪlɪtrɪz/ *n. pl.* articles de toilette *m. pl.*

token /ˈtəʊkən/ *n.* témoignage *m.*, marque *f.*; (*voucher*) bon *m.*; (*coin*) jeton *m.* —*a.* symbolique.

told /təʊld/ *see* **tell.** —*a.* **all ~,** (*all in all*) en tout.

tolerabl|e /ˈtɒlərəbl/ *a.* tolérable; (*not bad*) passable. **~y** *adv.* (*work, play, etc.*) passablement.

toleran|t /ˈtɒlərənt/ *a.* tolérant (**of,** à l'égard de). **~ce** *n.* tolérance *f.* **~tly** *adv.* avec tolérance.

tolerate /ˈtɒləreɪt/ *v.t.* tolérer.

toll[1] /təʊl/ *n.* péage *m.* **death ~,** nombre de morts *m.* **take its ~,** (*of age*) faire sentir son poids.

toll[2] /təʊl/ *v.i.* (*of bell*) sonner.

tom /tɒm/, **~-cat** *ns.* matou *m.*

tomato /təˈmɑːtəʊ, *Amer.* təˈmeɪtəʊ/ *n.* (*pl.* **~oes**) tomate *f.*

tomb /tuːm/ *n.* tombeau *m.*

tombola /tɒmˈbəʊlə/ *n.* tombola *f.*

tomboy /ˈtɒmbɔɪ/ *n.* garçon manqué *m.*

tombstone /ˈtuːmstəʊn/ *n.* pierre tombale *f.*

tomfoolery /tɒmˈfuːlərɪ/ *n.* âneries *f. pl.*, bêtises *f. pl.*

tomorrow /təˈmɒrəʊ/ *n.* & *adv.* demain (*m.*). **~ morning/night,** demain matin/soir.

ton /tʌn/ *n.* tonne *f.* (= *1016 kg.*). (**metric**) **~,** tonne *f.* (= *1000 kg.*). **~s of,** (*fam.*) des masses de.

tone /təʊn/ *n.* ton *m.*; (*of radio, telephone, etc.*) tonalité *f.* —*v.t.* **~ down,** atténuer. —*v.i.* **~ in,** s'harmoniser (**with,** avec). **~-deaf** *a.* qui n'a pas d'oreille. **~ up,** (*muscles*) tonifier.

tongs /tɒŋz/ *n. pl.* pinces *f. pl.*; (*for sugar*) pince *f.*; (*for hair*) fer *m.*

tongue /tʌŋ/ *n.* langue *f.* **~-tied** *a.* muet. **~-twister** *n.* phrase difficile à prononcer *f.* **with one's ~ in one's cheek,** ironiquement.

tonic /ˈtɒnɪk/ *n.* (*med.*) tonique *m.* —*a.* (*effect, water, accent*) tonique.

tonight /təˈnaɪt/ *n.* & *adv.* cette nuit (*f.*); (*evening*) ce soir (*m.*).

tonne /tʌn/ *n.* (*metric*) tonne *f.*

tonsil /ˈtɒnsl/ *n.* amygdale *f.*

tonsillitis /tɒnsɪˈlaɪtɪs/ *n.* angine *f.*

too /tuː/ *adv.* trop; (*also*) aussi. **~ many** *a.* trop de; *n.* trop. **~ much** *a.* trop de; *adv.* & *n.* trop.

took /tʊk/ *see* **take.**

tool /tuːl/ *n.* outil *m.* **~-bag** *n.* trousse à outils *f.*

toot /tuːt/ *n.* coup de klaxon *m.* —*v.t./i.* **~ (the horn),** klaxonner.

tooth /tuːθ/ *n.* (*pl.* **teeth**) dent *f.* **~less** *a.* édenté.

toothache /ˈtuːθeɪk/ *n.* mal de dents *m.*

toothbrush /ˈtuːθbrʌʃ/ *n.* brosse à dents *f.*
toothcomb /ˈtuːθkəʊm/ *n.* peigne fin *m.*
toothpaste /ˈtuːθpeɪst/ *n.* dentifrice *m.*, pâte dentifrice *f.*
toothpick /ˈtuːθpɪk/ *n.* cure-dent *m.*
top[1] /tɒp/ *n.* (*highest point*) sommet *m.*; (*upper part*) haut *m.*; (*upper surface*) dessus *m.*; (*lid*) couvercle *m.*; (*of bottle, tube*) bouchon *m.*; (*of beer bottle*) capsule *f.*; (*of list*) tête *f.* —*a.* (*shelf etc.*) du haut; (*in rank*) premier; (*best*) meilleur; (*distinguished*) éminent; (*maximum*) maximum. —*v.t.* (*p.t.* **topped**) (*exceed*) dépasser. **from ~ to bottom,** de fond en comble. **on ~ of,** sur; (*fig.*) en plus de. **~ hat,** haut-de-forme *m.* **~-heavy** *a.* trop lourd du haut. **~-notch** *a.* excellent. **~ secret,** ultra-secret. **~ up,** remplir. **~ped with,** surmonté de; (*cream etc.*: *culin.*) nappé de.
top[2] /tɒp/ *n.* (*toy*) toupie *f.*
topic /ˈtɒpɪk/ *n.* sujet *m.*
topical /ˈtɒpɪkl/ *a.* d'actualité.
topless /ˈtɒplɪs/ *a.* aux seins nus.
topple /ˈtɒpl/ *v.t./i.* (faire) tomber, (faire) basculer.
topsy-turvy /tɒpsɪˈtɜːvɪ/ *adv.* & *a.* sens dessus dessous.
torch /tɔːtʃ/ *n.* (*electric*) lampe de poche *f.*; (*flaming*) torche *f.*
tore /tɔː(r)/ *see* **tear**[1].
torment[1] /ˈtɔːmənt/ *n.* tourment *m.*
torment[2] /tɔːˈment/ *v.t.* tourmenter; (*annoy*) agacer.
torn /tɔːn/ *see* **tear**[1].
tornado /tɔːˈneɪdəʊ/ *n.* (*pl.* **-oes**) tornade *f.*
torpedo /tɔːˈpiːdəʊ/ *n.* (*pl.* **-oes**) torpille *f.* —*v.t.* torpiller.
torrent /ˈtɒrənt/ *n.* torrent *m.* **~ial** /təˈrenʃl/ *a.* torrentiel.
torrid /ˈtɒrɪd/ *a.* (*climate etc.*) torride; (*fig.*) passionné.
torso /ˈtɔːsəʊ/ *n.* (*pl.* **-os**) torse *m.*
tortoise /ˈtɔːtəs/ *n.* tortue *f.*
tortoiseshell /ˈtɔːtəsʃel/ *n.* (*for ornaments etc.*) écaille *f.*
tortuous /ˈtɔːtʃʊəs/ *a.* tortueux.
torture /ˈtɔːtʃə(r)/ *n.* torture *f.*, supplice *m.* —*v.t.* torturer. **~r** /-ə(r)/ *n.* tortionnaire *m.*
Tory /ˈtɔːrɪ/ *n.* tory *m.* —*a.* tory (*f. invar.*).
toss /tɒs/ *v.t.* jeter, lancer; (*shake*) agiter. —*v.i.* s'agiter. **~ a coin, ~ up,** tirer à pile ou face (**for,** pour).
tot[1] /tɒt/ *n.* petit(e) enfant *m./f.*; (*glass*: *fam.*) petit verre *m.*
tot[2] /tɒt/ *v.t.* (*p.t.* **totted**). **~ up,** (*fam.*) additionner.
total /ˈtəʊtl/ *a.* total. —*n.* total *m.* —*v.t.* (*p.t.* **totalled**) (*find total of*) totaliser; (*amount to*) s'élever à. **~ity** /-ˈtælətɪ/ *n.* totalité *f.* **~ly** *adv.* totalement.
totalitarian /təʊtælɪˈteərɪən/ *a.* totalitaire.
totter /ˈtɒtə(r)/ *v.i.* chanceler.
touch /tʌtʃ/ *v.t./i.* toucher; (*of ends, gardens, etc.*) se toucher; (*tamper with*) toucher à. —*n.* (*sense*) toucher *m.*; (*contact*) contact *m.*; (*of colour*) touche *f.*; (*football*) touche *f.* **a ~ of,** (*small amount*) un peu de. **get in ~ with,** contacter. **~-and-go** *a.* douteux. **~ down,** (*aviat.*) atterrir. **~-line** *n.* (ligne de) touche *f.* **~ off,** (*explode*) faire partir; (*cause*) déclencher. **~ on,** (*mention*) aborder. **~ up,** retoucher.
touching /ˈtʌtʃɪŋ/ *a.* touchant.
touchstone /ˈtʌtʃstəʊn/ *n.* pierre de touche *f.*
touchy /ˈtʌtʃɪ/ *a.* susceptible.
tough /tʌf/ *a.* (**-er, -est**) (*hard, difficult*) dur; (*strong*) solide; (*relentless*) acharné. —*n.* **~ (guy),** dur *m.* **~ luck!,** (*fam.*) tant pis! **~ness** *n.* dureté *f.*; solidité *f.*
toughen /ˈtʌfn/ *v.t.* (*strengthen*) renforcer; (*person*) endurcir.

toupee /'tu:peɪ/ *n.* postiche *m.*

tour /tʊə(r)/ *n.* voyage *m.*; (*visit*) visite *f.*; (*by team etc.*) tournée *f.* —*v.t.* visiter. **on ~,** en tournée.

tourism /'tʊərɪzəm/ *n.* tourisme *m.*

tourist /'tʊərɪst/ *n.* touriste *m.*/*f.* —*a.* touristique. **~ office,** syndicat d'initiative *m.*

tournament /'tɔ:nəmənt/ *n.* (*sport & medieval*) tournoi *m.*

tousle /'taʊzl/ *v.t.* ébouriffer.

tout /taʊt/ *v.i.* **~ (for),** racoler. —*v.t.* (*sell*) revendre. —*n.* racoleu|r, -se *m.f.*; revendeu|r, -se *m.,f.*

tow /təʊ/ *v.t.* remorquer. —*n.* remorque *f.* **on ~,** en remorque. **~ away,** (*vehicle*) (faire) enlever. **~-path** *n.* chemin de halage *m.*

toward(s) /tə'wɔ:d(z), *Amer.* tɔ:d(z)/ *prep.* vers; (*of attitude*) envers.

towel /'taʊəl/ *n.* serviette *f.*; (*tea-towel*) torchon *m.* **~ling** *n.* tissu-éponge *m.*

tower /'taʊə(r)/ *n.* tour *f.* —*v.i.* **~ above,** dominer. **~ block,** tour *f.*, immeuble *m.* **~ing** *a.* très haut.

town /taʊn/ *n.* ville *f.* **go to ~,** (*fam.*) mettre le paquet. **~ council,** conseil municipal *m.* **~ hall,** hôtel de ville *m.*

toxic /'tɒksɪk/ *a.* toxique.

toxin /'tɒksɪn/ *n.* toxine *f.*

toy /tɔɪ/ *n.* jouet *m.* —*v.i.* **~ with,** (*object*) jouer avec; (*idea*) caresser.

toyshop /'tɔɪʃɒp/ *n.* magasin de jouets *m.*

trace /treɪs/ *n.* trace *f.* —*v.t.* suivre *or* retrouver la trace de; (*draw*) tracer; (*with tracing-paper*) décalquer; (*relate*) retracer.

tracing /'treɪsɪŋ/ *n.* calque *m.* **~-paper** *n.* papier-calque *m. invar.*

track /træk/ *n.* (*of person etc.*) trace *f.*, piste *f.*; (*path, race-track & of tape*) piste *f.*; (*of rocket etc.*) trajectoire *f.*; (*rail.*) voie *f.* —*v.t.* suivre la trace *or* la trajectoire de. **keep ~ of,** suivre. **~ down,** (*find*) retrouver; (*hunt*) traquer. **~ suit,** survêtement *m.*

tract[1] /trækt/ *n.* (*land*) étendue *f.*; (*anat.*) appareil *m.*

tract[2] /trækt/ *n.* (*pamphlet*) tract *m.*

tractor /'træktə(r)/ *n.* tracteur *m.*

trade /treɪd/ *n.* commerce *m.*; (*job*) métier *m.*; (*swap*) échange *m.* —*v.i.* faire du commerce. —*v.t.* échanger. **~ in,** (*used article*) faire reprendre. **~-in** *n.* reprise *f.* **~ mark,** marque de fabrique *f.* **~ on,** (*exploit*) abuser de. **~ union,** syndicat *m.* **~-unionist** *n.* syndicaliste *m.*/*f.* **~r** /-ə(r)/ *n.* négociant(e) *m.* (*f.*), commerçant(e) *m.* (*f.*).

tradesman /'treɪdzmən/ *n.* (*pl.* **-men**) commerçant *m.*

trading /'treɪdɪŋ/ *n.* commerce *m.* **~ estate,** zone industrielle *f.*

tradition /trə'dɪʃn/ *n.* tradition *f.* **~al** *a.* traditionnel.

traffic /'træfɪk/ *n.* trafic *m.*; (*on road*) circulation *f.* —*v.i.* (*p.t.* **trafficked**) trafiquer (**in,** de). **~ circle,** (*Amer.*) rond-point *m.* **~ jam,** embouteillage *m.* **~-lights** *n. pl.* feux (de circulation) *m. pl.* **~ warden,** contractuel(le) *m.* (*f.*).

tragedy /'trædʒədɪ/ *n.* tragédie *f.*

tragic /'trædʒɪk/ *a.* tragique.

trail /treɪl/ *v.t.*/*i.* traîner; (*of plant*) ramper; (*track*) suivre. —*n.* (*of powder etc.*) traînée *f.*; (*track*) piste *f.*; (*beaten path*) sentier *m.*

trailer /'treɪlə(r)/ *n.* remorque *f.*; (*caravan*: *Amer.*) caravane *f.*; (*film*) bande-annonce *f.*

train /treɪn/ *n.* (*rail.*) train *m.*; (*procession*) file *f.*; (*of dress*) traîne *f.* —*v.t.* (*instruct, develop*) former; (*sportsman*) entraîner; (*animal*) dresser; (*ear*) exercer; (*aim*) braquer. —*v.i.* recevoir une formation; s'entraîner. **~ed** *a.* (*skilled*) qualifié; (*doctor etc.*) diplômé.

~er *n.* (*sport*) entraîneu|r, -se *m.*, *f.* **~ing** *n.* formation *f.*; entraînement *m.*; dressage *m.*
trainee /treɪ'niː/ *n.* stagiaire *m./f.*
traipse /treɪps/ *v.i.* (*fam.*) traîner.
trait /treɪ(t)/ *n.* trait *m.*
traitor /'treɪtə(r)/ *n.* traître *m.*
tram /træm/ *n.* tram(way) *m.*
tramp /træmp/ *v.i.* marcher (d'un pas lourd). —*v.t.* parcourir. —*n.* pas lourds *m. pl.*; (*vagrant*) clochard(e) *m.* (*f.*); (*Amer., sl.*) dévergondée *f.*; (*hike*) randonnée *f.*
trample /'træmpl/ *v.t./i.* **~ (on),** piétiner; (*fig.*) fouler aux pieds.
trampoline /'træmpəliːn/ *n.* (*canvas sheet*) trampoline *m.*
trance /trɑːns/ *n.* transe *f.*
tranquil /'træŋkwɪl/ *a.* tranquille. **~lity** /-'kwɪlətɪ/ *n.* tranquillité *f.*
tranquillizer /'træŋkwɪlaɪzə(r)/ *n.* (*drug*) tranquillisant *m.*
transact /træn'zækt/ *v.t.* traiter. **~ion** /-kʃn/ *n.* transaction *f.*
transatlantic /trænzət'læntɪk/ *a.* transatlantique.
transcend /træn'send/ *v.t.* transcender. **~ent** *a.* transcendant.
transcri|be /træn'skraɪb/ *v.t.* transcrire. **~ption** /-ɪpʃn/ *n.* transcription *f.*
transcript /'trænskrɪpt/ *n.* (*written copy*) transcription *f.*
transfer[1] /træns'fɜː(r)/ *v.t.* (*p.t.* **transferred**) transférer; (*power*) faire passer. —*v.i.* être transféré. **~ the charges,** (*telephone*) téléphoner en PCV.
transfer[2] /'trænsfɜː(r)/ *n.* transfert *m.*; (*of power*) passation *f.*; (*image*) décalcomanie *f.*
transform /træns'fɔːm/ *v.t.* transformer. **~ation** /-ə'meɪʃn/ *n.* transformation *f.* **~er** *n.* (*electr.*) transformateur *m.*
transfusion /træns'fjuːʒn/ *n.* (*of blood*) transfusion *f.*
transient /'trænzɪənt/ *a.* transitoire, éphémère.
transistor /træn'zɪstə(r)/ *n.* (*device, radio set*) transistor *m.*
transit /'trænsɪt/ *n.* transit *m.*
transition /træn'zɪʃn/ *n.* transition *f.* **~al** *a.* transitoire.
transitive /'trænsətɪv/ *a.* transitif.
transitory /'trænsɪtərɪ/ *a.* transitoire.
translat|e /trænz'leɪt/ *v.t.* traduire. **~ion** /-ʃn/ *n.* traduction *f.* **~or** *n.* traduc|teur, -trice *m., f.*
translucent /trænz'luːsnt/ *a.* translucide.
transmi|t /trænz'mɪt/ *v.t.* (*p.t.* **transmitted**) (*pass on etc.*) transmettre; (*broadcast*) émettre. **~ssion** *n.* transmission *f.*; émission *f.* **~tter** *n.* émetteur *m.*
transparen|t /træns'pærənt/ *a.* transparent. **~cy** *n.* transparence *f.*; (*photo.*) diapositive *f.*
transpire /træn'spaɪə(r)/ *v.i.* s'avérer; (*happen: fam.*) arriver.
transplant[1] /træns'plɑːnt/ *v.t.* transplanter; (*med.*) greffer.
transplant[2] /'trænsplɑːnt/ *n.* transplantation *f.*; greffe *f.*
transport[1] /træn'spɔːt/ *v.t.* (*carry, delight*) transporter. **~ation** /-'teɪʃn/ *n.* transport *m.*
transport[2] /'trænspɔːt/ *n.* (*of goods, delight, etc.*) transport *m.*
transpose /træn'spəʊz/ *v.t.* transposer.
transverse /'trænzvɜːs/ *a.* transversal.
transvestite /trænz'vestaɪt/ *n.* travesti(e) *m.* (*f.*).
trap /træp/ *n.* piège *m.* —*v.t.* (*p.t.* **trapped**) (*jam, pin down*) coincer; (*cut off*) bloquer; (*snare*) prendre au piège. **~per** *n.* trappeur *m.*
trapdoor /træp'dɔː(r)/ *n.* trappe *f.*
trapeze /trə'piːz/ *n.* trapèze *m.*
trappings /'træpɪŋz/ *n. pl.* (*fig.*) signes extérieurs *m. pl.*, apparat *m.*
trash /træʃ/ *n.* (*junk*) saleté(s) *f.* (*pl.*); (*refuse*) ordures *f. pl.*; (*non-*

sense) idioties *f. pl.* **~-can** *n.* (*Amer.*) poubelle *f.* **~y** *a.* qui ne vaut rien, de mauvaise qualité.

trauma /ˈtrɔːmə/ *n.* traumatisme *m.* **~tic** /-ˈmætɪk/ *a.* traumatisant.

travel /ˈtrævl/ *v.i.* (*p.t.* **travelled,** *Amer.* **traveled**) voyager; (*of vehicle, bullet, etc.*) aller. *—v.t.* parcourir. *—n.* voyage(s) *m.* (*pl.*). **~ler** *n.* voyageu|r, -se *m., f.* **~ler's cheque,** chèque de voyage *m.* **~ling** *n.* voyage(s) *m.* (*pl.*).

travesty /ˈtrævəstɪ/ *n.* parodie *f.*, simulacre *m.* *—v.t.* travestir.

trawler /ˈtrɔːlə(r)/ *n.* chalutier *m.*

tray /treɪ/ *n.* plateau *m.*; (*on office desk*) corbeille *f.*

treacherous /ˈtretʃərəs/ *a.* traître. **~ly** *adv.* traîtreusement.

treachery /ˈtretʃərɪ/ *n.* traîtrise *f.*

treacle /ˈtriːkl/ *n.* mélasse *f.*

tread /tred/ *v.i.* (*p.t.* **trod,** *p.p.* **trodden**) marcher. *—v.t.* parcourir (à pied); (*soil: fig.*) fouler. *—n.* pas *m.*; (*of tyre*) chape *f.* **~ sth. into,** (*carpet*) étaler qch. sur (avec les pieds).

treason /ˈtriːzn/ *n.* trahison *f.*

treasure /ˈtreʒə(r)/ *n.* trésor *m.* *—v.t.* attacher une grande valeur à; (*store*) conserver. **~r** /-ə(r)/ *n.* trésor|ier, -ière *m., f.*

treasury /ˈtreʒərɪ/ *n.* trésorerie *f.* **the T~,** le ministère des Finances.

treat /triːt/ *v.t.* traiter; (*consider*) considérer. *—n.* (*pleasure*) plaisir *m.*, régal *m.*; (*present*) gâterie *f.*; (*food*) régal *m.* **~ s.o. to sth.,** offrir qch. à qn.

treatise /ˈtriːtɪz/ *n.* traité *m.*

treatment /ˈtriːtmənt/ *n.* traitement *m.*

treaty /ˈtriːtɪ/ *n.* (*pact*) traité *m.*

trebl|e /ˈtrebl/ *a.* triple. *—v.t./i.* tripler. *—n.* (*voice: mus.*) soprano *m.* **~y** *adv.* triplement.

tree /triː/ *n.* arbre *m.* **~-top** *n.* cime (d'un arbre) *f.*

trek /trek/ *n.* voyage pénible *m.*; (*sport*) randonnée *f.* *—v.i.* (*p.t.* **trekked**) voyager (péniblement); (*sport*) faire une randonnée.

trellis /ˈtrelɪs/ *n.* treillage *m.*

tremble /ˈtrembl/ *v.i.* trembler.

tremendous /trɪˈmendəs/ *a.* énorme; (*excellent: fam.*) fantastique. **~ly** *adv.* fantastiquement.

tremor /ˈtremə(r)/ *n.* tremblement *m.* (**earth**) **~,** secousse (sismique) *f.*

trench /trentʃ/ *n.* tranchée *f.*

trend /trend/ *n.* tendance *f.*; (*fashion*) mode *f.* **~-setter** *n.* lanceu|r, -se de mode *m., f.* **~y** *a.* (*fam.*) dans le vent.

trepidation /trepɪˈdeɪʃn/ *n.* (*fear*) inquiétude *f.*

trespass /ˈtrespəs/ *v.i.* s'introduire sans autorisation (**on,** dans). **~er** *n.* intrus(e) *m.* (*f.*).

trestle /ˈtresl/ *n.* tréteau *m.* **~-table** *n.* table à tréteaux *f.*

tri- /traɪ/ *pref.* tri-.

trial /ˈtraɪəl/ *n.* (*jurid.*) procès *m.*; (*test*) essai *m.*; (*ordeal*) épreuve *f.* **go on ~,** passer en jugement. **~ and error,** tâtonnements *m. pl.*

triang|le /ˈtraɪæŋgl/ *n.* triangle *m.* **~ular** /-ˈæŋgjʊlə(r)/ *a.* triangulaire.

trib|e /traɪb/ *n.* tribu *f.* **~al** *a.* tribal.

tribulation /trɪbjʊˈleɪʃn/ *n.* tribulation *f.*

tribunal /traɪˈbjuːnl/ *n.* tribunal *m.*; (*mil.*) commission *f.*

tributary /ˈtrɪbjʊtərɪ/ *n.* affluent *m.*

tribute /ˈtrɪbjuːt/ *n.* tribut *m.* **pay ~ to,** rendre hommage à.

trick /trɪk/ *n.* astuce *f.*, ruse *f.*; (*joke, feat of skill*) tour *m.*; (*habit*) manie *f.* *—v.t.* tromper. **do the ~,** (*fam.*) faire l'affaire.

trickery /ˈtrɪkərɪ/ *n.* ruse *f.*

trickle /ˈtrɪkl/ *v.i.* dégouliner; (*fig.*)

arriver *or* partir en petit nombre. —*n.* filet *m.*; (*fig.*) petit nombre *m.*
tricky /'trɪkɪ/ *a.* (*crafty*) rusé; (*problem*) délicat, difficile.
tricycle /'traɪsɪkl/ *n.* tricycle *m.*
trifle /'traɪfl/ *n.* bagatelle *f.*; (*cake*) diplomate *m.* —*v.i.* **~ with,** jouer avec. **a ~,** (*small amount*) un peu.
trifling /'traɪflɪŋ/ *a.* insignifiant.
trigger /'trɪgə(r)/ *n.* (*of gun*) gâchette *f.*, détente *f.* —*v.t.* **~ (off),** (*initiate*) déclencher.
trilby /'trɪlbɪ/ *n.* (*hat*) feutre *m.*
trilogy /'trɪlədʒɪ/ *n.* trilogie *f.*
trim /trɪm/ *a.* (**trimmer, trimmest**) net, soigné. —*v.t.* (*p.t.* **trimmed**) (*cut*) couper légèrement; (*hair*) rafraîchir. —*n.* (*cut*) coupe légère *f.*; (*decoration*) garniture *f.* **in ~,** en bon ordre; (*fit*) en forme. **~ with,** (*decorate*) orner de. **~ming(s)** *n.* (*pl.*) garniture(s) *f.* (*pl.*).
Trinity /'trɪnətɪ/ *n.* (*feast*) Trinité *f.* **the ~,** (*dogma*) la Trinité.
trinket /'trɪŋkɪt/ *n.* colifichet *m.*
trio /'triːəʊ/ *n.* (*pl.* **-os**) trio *m.*
trip /trɪp/ *v.t./i.* (*p.t.* **tripped**) (faire) trébucher; (*go lightly*) marcher d'un pas léger. —*n.* (*journey*) voyage *m.*; (*outing*) excursion *f.*; (*stumble*) faux pas *m.*
tripe /traɪp/ *n.* (*food*) tripes *f. pl.*; (*nonsense*: *sl.*) bêtises *f. pl.*
triple /'trɪpl/ *a.* triple. —*v.t./i.* tripler. **~ts** /-plɪts/ *n. pl.* triplé(e)s *m.* (*f.*) *pl.*
triplicate /'trɪplɪkət/ *n.* **in ~,** en trois exemplaires.
tripod /'traɪpɒd/ *n.* trépied *m.*
tripper /'trɪpə(r)/ *n.* (*on day trip etc.*) excursionniste *m./f.*
trite /traɪt/ *a.* banal.
triumph /'traɪəmf/ *n.* triomphe *m.* —*v.i.* triompher (**over,** de). **~al** /-'ʌmfl/ *a.* triomphal. **~ant** /-'ʌmfənt/ *a.* triomphant, triomphal. **~antly** /-'ʌmfəntlɪ/ *adv.* en triomphe.
trivial /'trɪvɪəl/ *a.* insignifiant. **~ity** /-'ælətɪ/ *n.* insignifiance *f.*
trod, trodden /trɒd, 'trɒdn/ *see* **tread.**
trolley /'trɒlɪ/ *n.* chariot *m.* **(tea-)~,** table roulante *f.* **~-bus** *n.* trolleybus *m.*
trombone /trɒm'bəʊn/ *n.* (*mus.*) trombone *m.*
troop /truːp/ *n.* bande *f.* **~s,** (*mil.*) troupes *f. pl.* —*v.i.* **~ in/out,** entrer/sortir en bande. **~er** *n.* soldat de cavalerie *m.* **~ing the colour,** le salut au drapeau.
trophy /'trəʊfɪ/ *n.* trophée *m.*
tropic /'trɒpɪk/ *n.* tropique *m.* **~s,** tropiques *m. pl.* **~al** *a.* tropical.
trot /trɒt/ *n.* trot *m.* —*v.i.* (*p.t.* **trotted**) trotter. **on the ~,** (*fam.*) de suite. **~ out,** (*produce*: *fam.*) sortir; (*state*: *fam.*) formuler.
trouble /'trʌbl/ *n.* ennui(s) *m.* (*pl.*), difficulté(s) *f.* (*pl.*); (*pains, effort*) mal *m.*, peine *f.* **~(s),** (*unrest*) conflits *m. pl.* —*v.t./i.* (*bother*) (se) déranger; (*worry*) ennuyer. **be in ~,** avoir des ennuis. **~d** *a.* inquiet; (*period*) agité. **~-maker** *n.* provoca|teur, -trice *m., f.*
troublesome /'trʌblsəm/ *a.* ennuyeux, pénible.
trough /trɒf/ *n.* (*drinking*) abreuvoir *m.*; (*feeding*) auge *f.* **~ (of low pressure),** dépression *f.*
trounce /traʊns/ *v.t.* (*defeat*) écraser; (*thrash*) rosser.
troupe /truːp/ *n.* (*theatre*) troupe *f.*
trousers /'traʊzəz/ *n. pl.* pantalon *m.* **short ~,** culotte courte *f.*
trousseau /'truːsəʊ/ *n.* (*pl.* **-s** /-əʊz/) (*of bride*) trousseau *m.*
trout /traʊt/ *n. invar.* truite *f.*
trowel /'traʊəl/ *n.* (*garden*) déplantoir *m.*; (*for mortar*) truelle *f.*
truan|t /'truːənt/ *n.* absentéiste *m./f.*; (*schol.*) élève absent(e) sans permission *m./f.* **play ~t,** sécher les cours. **~cy** *n.* absentéisme *m.*
truce /truːs/ *n.* trêve *f.*

truck /trʌk/ *n.* (*lorry*) camion *m.*; (*cart*) chariot *m.*; (*rail.*) wagon *m.*, plateforme *f.* **~-driver** *n.* camionneur *m.*

truculent /ˈtrʌkjʊlənt/ *a.* agressif.

trudge /trʌdʒ/ *v.i.* marcher péniblement, se traîner.

true /truː/ *a.* (**-er, -est**) vrai; (*accurate*) exact; (*faithful*) fidèle.

truffle /ˈtrʌfl/ *n.* truffe *f.*

truly /ˈtruːlɪ/ *adv.* vraiment; (*faithfully*) fidèlement; (*truthfully*) sincèrement.

trump /trʌmp/ *n.* atout *m.* —*v.t.* **~ up,** inventer. **~ card,** atout *m.*

trumpet /ˈtrʌmpɪt/ *n.* trompette *f.*

truncheon /ˈtrʌntʃən/ *n.* matraque *f.*

trundle /ˈtrʌndl/ *v.t./i.* rouler bruyamment.

trunk /trʌŋk/ *n.* (*of tree, body*) tronc *m.*; (*of elephant*) trompe *f.*; (*box*) malle *f.*; (*auto., Amer.*) coffre *m.* **~s,** (*for swimming*) slip de bain *m.* **~-call** *n.* communication interurbaine *f.* **~-road** *n.* route nationale *f.*

truss /trʌs/ *n.* (*med.*) bandage herniaire *m.* —*v.t.* (*fowl*) trousser.

trust /trʌst/ *n.* confiance *f.*; (*association*) trust *m.* —*v.t.* avoir confiance en. —*v.i.* **~ in** *or* **to,** s'en remettre à. **in ~,** en dépôt. **on ~,** de confiance. **~ s.o. with,** confier à qn. **~ed** *a.* (*friend etc.*) éprouvé, sûr. **~ful, ~ing** *adjs.* confiant. **~y** *a.* fidèle.

trustee /trʌsˈtiː/ *n.* administra|teur, -trice *m., f.*

trustworthy /ˈtrʌstwɜːðɪ/ *a.* digne de confiance.

truth /truːθ/ *n.* (*pl.* **-s** /truːðz/) vérité *f.* **~ful** *a.* (*account etc.*) véridique; (*person*) qui dit la vérité. **~fully** *adv.* sincèrement.

try /traɪ/ *v.t./i.* (*p.t.* **tried**) essayer; (*be a strain on*) éprouver; (*jurid.*) juger. —*n.* (*attempt*) essai *m.*; (*Rugby*) essai *m.* **~ on** *or* **out,** essayer. **~ to do,** essayer de faire. **~ing** *a.* éprouvant.

tsar /zɑː(r)/ *n.* tsar *m.*

T-shirt /ˈtiːʃɜːt/ *n.* tee-shirt *m.*

tub /tʌb/ *n.* baquet *m.*, cuve *f.*; (*bath: fam.*) baignoire *f.*

tuba /ˈtjuːbə/ *n.* tuba *m.*

tubby /ˈtʌbɪ/ *a.* (**-ier, -iest**) dodu.

tub|e /tjuːb/ *n.* tube *m.*; (*railway: fam.*) métro *m.* **~ing** *n.* tubes *m. pl.*

tuberculosis /tjuːbɜːkjʊˈləʊsɪs/ *n.* tuberculose *f.*

tubular /ˈtjuːbjʊlə(r)/ *a.* tubulaire.

tuck /tʌk/ *n.* (*fold*) rempli *m.*, (re)pli *m.* —*v.t.* (*put away, place*) ranger; (*hide*) cacher. —*v.i.* **~ in** *or* **into,** (*eat: sl.*) attaquer. **~ in,** (*shirt*) rentrer; (*blanket, person*) border. **~-shop** *n.* (*schol.*) boutique à provisions *f.*

Tuesday /ˈtjuːzdɪ/ *n.* mardi *m.*

tuft /tʌft/ *n.* (*of hair etc.*) touffe *f.*

tug /tʌg/ *v.t.* (*p.t.* **tugged**) tirer fort (sur). —*v.i.* tirer fort. —*n.* (*boat*) remorqueur *m.*

tuition /tjuːˈɪʃn/ *n.* cours *m. pl.*; (*fee*) frais de scolarité *m. pl.*

tulip /ˈtjuːlɪp/ *n.* tulipe *f.*

tumble /ˈtʌmbl/ *v.i.* (*fall*) dégringoler. —*n.* chute *f.* **~-drier** *n.* séchoir à linge (à air chaud) *m.* **~ to,** (*realize: fam.*) piger.

tumbledown /ˈtʌmbldaʊn/ *a.* délabré, en ruine.

tumbler /ˈtʌmblə(r)/ *n.* gobelet *m.*

tummy /ˈtʌmɪ/ *n.* (*fam.*) ventre *m.*

tumour /ˈtjuːmə(r)/ *n.* tumeur *f.*

tumult /ˈtjuːmʌlt/ *n.* tumulte *m.* **~uous** /-ˈmʌltʃʊəs/ *a.* tumultueux.

tuna /ˈtjuːnə/ *n.* *invar.* thon *m.*

tune /tjuːn/ *n.* air *m.* —*v.t.* (*engine*) régler; (*mus.*) accorder. —*v.i.* **~ in (to),** (*radio, TV*) écouter. **be in ~/out of ~,** (*instrument*) être accordé/désaccordé; (*singer*) chanter juste/faux. **~ful** *a.*

mélodieux. **tuning-fork** *n.* diapason *m.*

tunic /ˈtjuːmɪk/ *n.* tunique *f.*

Tunisia /tjuːˈnɪzɪə/ *n.* Tunisie *f.* **~n** *a.* & *n.* tunisien(ne) (*m.* (*f.*)).

tunnel /ˈtʌnl/ *n.* tunnel *m.* —*v.i.* (*p.t.* **tunnelled**) creuser un tunnel (**into,** dans).

turban /ˈtɜːbən/ *n.* turban *m.*

turbine /ˈtɜːbaɪn/ *n.* turbine *f.*

turbulen|t /ˈtɜːbjʊlənt/ *a.* turbulent. **~ce** *n.* turbulence *f.*

tureen /tjʊˈriːn/ *n.* soupière *f.*

turf /tɜːf/ *n.* (*pl.* **turf** *or* **turves**) gazon *m.* —*v.t.* **~ out,** (*sl.*) jeter dehors. **the ~,** (*racing*) le turf.

turgid /ˈtɜːdʒɪd/ *a.* (*speech, style*) boursouflé, ampoulé.

Turk /tɜːk/ *n.* Turc *m.*, Turque *f.* **~ey** *n.* Turquie *f.* **~ish** *a.* turc; *n.* (*lang.*) turc *m.*

turkey /ˈtɜːkɪ/ *n.* dindon *m.*, dinde *f.*; (*as food*) dinde *f.*

turmoil /ˈtɜːmɔɪl/ *n.* trouble *m.*, chaos *m.* **in ~,** en ébullition.

turn /tɜːn/ *v.t./i.* tourner; (*of person*) se tourner; (*change*) (se) transformer (**into,** en); (*become*) devenir; (*deflect*) détourner. —*n.* tour *m.*; (*in road*) tournant *m.*; (*of mind, events*) tournure *f.*; (*illness: fam.*) crise *f.* **do a good ~,** rendre service. **in ~,** à tour de rôle. **speak out of ~,** commettre une indiscrétion. **take ~s,** se relayer. **~ against,** se retourner contre. **~ away** *v.i.* se détourner; *v.t.* (*avert*) détourner; (*refuse*) refuser; (*send back*) renvoyer. **~ back** *v.i.* (*return*) retourner; (*vehicle*) faire demi-tour; *v.t.* (*fold*) rabattre. **~ down,** refuser; (*fold*) rabattre; (*reduce*) baisser. **~ in,** (*go to bed: fam.*) se coucher. **~ off,** (*light etc.*) éteindre, fermer; (*tap*) fermer; (*of driver*) tourner. **~ on,** (*light etc.*) mettre, allumer; (*tap*) ouvrir. **~ out** *v.t.* (*light*) éteindre; (*empty*) vider; (*produce*) produire; *v.i.* (*transpire*) s'avérer; (*come: fam.*) venir. **~-out** *n.* assistance *f.* **~ round,** (*person*) se retourner. **~ up** *v.i.* arriver; (*be found*) se retrouver; *v.t.* (*find*) déterrer; (*collar*) remonter. **~-up** *n.* (*of trousers*) revers *m.*

turning /ˈtɜːnɪŋ/ *n.* rue (latérale) *f.*; (*bend*) tournant *m.* **~-point** *n.* tournant *m.*

turnip /ˈtɜːnɪp/ *n.* navet *m.*

turnover /ˈtɜːnəʊvə(r)/ *n.* (*pie, tart*) chausson *m.*; (*money*) chiffre d'affaires *m.*

turnpike /ˈtɜːnpaɪk/ *n.* (*Amer.*) autoroute à péage *f.*

turnstile /ˈtɜːnstaɪl/ *n.* (*gate*) tourniquet *m.*

turntable /ˈtɜːnteɪbl/ *n.* (*for record*) platine *f.*, plateau *m.*

turpentine /ˈtɜːpəntaɪn/ *n.* térébenthine *f.*

turquoise /ˈtɜːkwɔɪz/ *a.* turquoise *invar.*

turret /ˈtʌrɪt/ *n.* tourelle *f.*

turtle /ˈtɜːtl/ *n.* tortue de mer *f.* **~-neck** *a.* à col montant, roulé.

tusk /tʌsk/ *n.* (*tooth*) défense *f.*

tussle /ˈtʌsl/ *n.* bagarre *f.*, lutte *f.*

tutor /ˈtjuːtə(r)/ *n.* précep|teur, -trice *m.*, *f.*; (*univ.*) direc|teur, -trice d'études *m.*, *f.*

tutorial /tjuːˈtɔːrɪəl/ *n.* (*univ.*) séance d'études *or* de travaux pratiques *f.*

tuxedo /tʌkˈsiːdəʊ/ *n.* (*pl.* **-os**) (*Amer.*) smoking *m.*

TV /tiːˈviː/ *n.* télé *f.*

twaddle /ˈtwɒdl/ *n.* fadaises *f. pl.*

twang /twæŋ/ *n.* (*son: mus.*) pincement *m.*; (*in voice*) nasillement *m.* —*v.t./i.* (faire) vibrer.

tweed /twiːd/ *n.* tweed *m.*

tweezers /ˈtwiːzəz/ *n. pl.* pince (à épiler) *f.*

twel|ve /twelv/ *a.* & *n.* douze (*m.*). **~fth** *a.* & *n.* douzième (*m.*/*f.*).

twent|y /ˈtwentɪ/ *a.* & *n.* vingt (*m.*). **~ieth** *a.* & *n.* vingtième (*m.*/*f.*).

twerp /twɜːp/ *n.* (*sl.*) idiot(e) *m.* (*f.*).
twice /twaɪs/ *adv.* deux fois.
twiddle /'twɪdl/ *v.t./i.* ~ **(with),** (*fiddle with*) tripoter.
twig[1] /twɪg/ *n.* brindille *f.*
twig[2] /twɪg/ *v.t./i.* (*p.t.* **twigged**) (*understand*: *fam.*) piger.
twilight /'twaɪlaɪt/ *n.* crépuscule *m.* —*a.* crépusculaire.
twin /twɪn/ *n.* & *a.* jum|eau, -elle (*m.*, *f.*). —*v.t.* (*p.t.* **twinned**) jumeler. **~ning** *n.* jumelage *m.*
twine /twaɪn/ *n.* ficelle *f.* —*v.t./i.* (*wind*) (s')enlacer.
twinge /twɪndʒ/ *n.* petite douleur aiguë *f.*; (*remorse*) remords *m.*
twinkle /'twɪŋkl/ *v.i.* (*star etc.*) scintiller; (*eye*) pétiller. —*n.* scintillement *m.*; pétillement *m.*
twirl /twɜːl/ *v.t./i.* (faire) tournoyer.
twist /twɪst/ *v.t.* tordre; (*weave together*) entortiller; (*roll*) enrouler; (*distort*) déformer. —*v.i.* (*rope etc.*) s'entortiller; (*road*) zigzaguer. —*n.* torsion *f.*; (*in rope*) tortillon *m.*; (*in road*) tournant *m.*; (*of events*) tournure *f.*, tour *m.*
twit /twɪt/ *n.* (*fam.*) idiot(e) *m.* (*f.*).
twitch /twɪtʃ/ *v.t./i.* (se) contracter nerveusement. —*n.* (*tic*) tic *m.*; (*jerk*) secousse *f.*
two /tuː/ *a.* & *n.* deux (*m.*). **in** *or* **of ~ minds,** indécis. **~-faced** *a.* hypocrite. **~fold** *a.* double; *adv.* au double. **~-piece** *n.* (*garment*) deux-pièces *m. invar.*
twosome /'tuːsəm/ *n.* couple *m.*
tycoon /taɪ'kuːn/ *n.* magnat *m.*
tying /'taɪɪŋ/ *see* **tie.**
type /taɪp/ *n.* (*example*) type *m.*; (*kind*) genre *m.*, sorte *f.*; (*person*: *fam.*) type *m.*; (*print*) caractères *m. pl.* —*v.t./i.* (*write*) taper (à la machine).
typescript /'taɪpskrɪpt/ *n.* manuscrit dactylographié *m.*
typewrit|er /'taɪpraɪtə(r)/ *n.* machine à écrire *f.* **~ten** /-ɪtn/ *a.* dactylographié.
typhoid /'taɪfɔɪd/ *n.* ~ **(fever),** typhoïde *f.*
typhoon /taɪ'fuːn/ *n.* typhon *m.*
typhus /'taɪfəs/ *n.* typhus *m.*
typical /'tɪpɪkl/ *a.* typique. **~ly** *adv.* typiquement.
typify /'tɪpɪfaɪ/ *v.t.* être typique de.
typing /'taɪpɪŋ/ *n.* dactylo(graphie) *f.*
typist /'taɪpɪst/ *n.* dactylo *f.*
tyrann|y /'tɪrənɪ/ *n.* tyrannie *f.* **~ical** /tɪ'rænɪkl/ *a.* tyrannique.
tyrant /taɪərənt/ *n.* tyran *m.*
tyre /'taɪə(r)/ *n.* pneu *m.*

U

ubiquitous /juː'bɪkwɪtəs/ *a.* omniprésent, qu'on trouve partout.
udder /'ʌdər/ *n.* pis *m.*, mamelle *f.*
ugl|y /'ʌglɪ/ *a.* (**-ier, -iest**) laid. **~iness** *n.* laideur *f.*
UK *abbr. see* **United Kingdom.**
ulcer /'ʌlsə(r)/ *n.* ulcère *m.*
ulterior /ʌl'tɪərɪə(r)/ *a.* ultérieur. **~ motive,** arrière-pensée *f.*
ultimate /'ʌltɪmət/ *a.* dernier, ultime; (*definitive*) définitif; (*basic*) fondamental. **~ly** *adv.* à la fin; (*in the last analysis*) en fin de compte.
ultimatum /ʌltɪ'meɪtəm/ *n.* (*pl.* **-ums**) ultimatum *m.*
ultra- /'ʌltrə/ *pref.* ultra-.
ultraviolet /ʌltrə'vaɪələt/ *a.* ultraviolet.
umbrella /ʌm'brelə/ *n.* parapluie *m.*
umpire /'ʌmpaɪə(r)/ *n.* (*sport*) arbitre *m.* —*v.t.* arbitrer.
umpteen /'ʌmptiːn/ *a.* (*many*: *sl.*) un tas de. **~th** *a.* (*sl.*) énième.
un- /ʌn/ *pref.* in-, dé(s)-, non, peu, mal, sans.
unabated /ʌnə'beɪtɪd/ *a.* non diminué, aussi fort qu'avant.

unable /ʌn'eɪbl/ *a.* incapable (**to do,** de faire).
unabridged /ʌnə'brɪdʒd/ *a.* (*text*) intégral.
unacceptable /ʌnək'septəbl/ *a.* inacceptable, inadmissible.
unaccountable /ʌnə'kaʊntəbl/ *a.* (*strange*) inexplicable.
unaccustomed /ʌnə'kʌstəmd/ *a.* inaccoutumé. **~ to,** peu habitué à.
unadulterated /ʌnə'dʌltəreɪtɪd/ *a.* (*pure, sheer*) pur.
unaided /ʌn'eɪdɪd/ *a.* sans aide.
unanim|ous /juː'nænɪməs/ *a.* unanime. **~ity** /-ə'nɪmətɪ/ *n.* unanimité *f.* **~ously** *adv.* à l'unanimité.
unarmed /ʌn'ɑːmd/ *a.* non armé.
unashamed /ʌnə'ʃeɪmd/ *a.* éhonté. **~ly** /-ɪdlɪ/ *adv.* sans vergogne.
unassuming /ʌnə'sjuːmɪŋ/ *a.* modeste, sans prétention.
unattached /ʌnə'tætʃt/ *a.* libre.
unattainable /ʌnə'teɪnəbl/ *a.* inaccessible.
unattended /ʌnə'tendɪd/ *a.* (laissé) sans surveillance.
unattractive /ʌnə'træktɪv/ *a.* peu séduisant, laid; (*offer*) peu intéressant.
unavoidabl|e /ʌnə'vɔɪdəbl/ *a.* inévitable. **~y** *adv.* inévitablement.
unaware /ʌnə'weə(r)/ *a.* **be ~ of,** ignorer. **~s** /-eəz/ *adv.* au dépourvu.
unbalanced /ʌn'bælənst/ *a.* (*mind, person*) déséquilibré.
unbearable /ʌn'beərəbl/ *a.* insupportable.
unbeat|able /ʌn'biːtəbl/ *a.* imbattable. **~en** *a.* non battu.
unbeknown(st) /ʌnbɪ'nəʊn(st)/ *a.* **~(st) to,** (*fam.*) à l'insu de.
unbelievable /ʌnbɪ'liːvəbl/ *a.* incroyable.
unbend /ʌn'bend/ *v.i.* (*p.t.* **unbent**) (*relax*) se détendre.
unbiased /ʌn'baɪəst/ *a.* impartial.
unblock /ʌn'blɒk/ *v.t.* déboucher.
unborn /ʌn'bɔːn/ *a.* futur, à venir.
unbounded /ʌn'baʊndɪd/ *a.* illimité.
unbreakable /ʌn'breɪkəbl/ *a.* incassable.
unbridled /ʌn'braɪdld/ *a.* débridé.
unbroken /ʌn'brəʊkən/ *a.* (*intact*) intact; (*continuous*) continu.
unburden /ʌn'bɜːdn/ *v. pr.* **~ o.s.,** (*open one's heart*) s'épancher.
unbutton /ʌn'bʌtn/ *v.t.* déboutonner.
uncalled-for /ʌn'kɔːldfɔː(r)/ *a.* injustifié, superflu.
uncanny /ʌn'kænɪ/ *a.* (**-ier, -iest**) étrange, mystérieux.
unceasing /ʌn'siːsɪŋ/ *a.* incessant.
unceremonious /ʌnserɪ'məʊnɪəs/ *a.* sans façon, brusque.
uncertain /ʌn'sɜːtn/ *a.* incertain. **be ~ whether,** ne pas savoir exactement si (**to do,** on doit faire). **~ty** *n.* incertitude *f.*
unchang|ed /ʌn'tʃeɪndʒd/ *a.* inchangé. **~ing** *a.* immuable.
uncivilized /ʌn'sɪvɪlaɪzd/ *a.* barbare.
uncle /'ʌŋkl/ *n.* oncle *m.*
uncomfortable /ʌn'kʌmftəbl/ *a.* (*thing*) peu confortable; (*unpleasant*) désagréable. **feel** *or* **be ~,** (*person*) être mal à l'aise.
uncommon /ʌn'kɒmən/ *a.* rare. **~ly** *adv.* remarquablement.
uncompromising /ʌn'kɒmprəmaɪzɪŋ/ *a.* intransigeant.
unconcerned /ʌnkən'sɜːnd/ *a.* (*indifferent*) indifférent (**by, à**).
unconditional /ʌnkən'dɪʃənl/ *a.* inconditionnel.
unconscious /ʌn'kɒnʃəs/ *a.* sans connaissance, inanimé; (*not aware*) inconscient (**of,** de). **~ly** *adv.* inconsciemment.
unconventional /ʌnkən'venʃənl/ *a.* peu conventionnel.
uncooperative /ʌnkəʊ'ɒpərətɪv/ *a.* peu coopératif.

uncork /ʌnˈkɔːk/ *v.t.* déboucher.
uncouth /ʌnˈkuːθ/ *a.* grossier.
uncover /ʌnˈkʌvə(r)/ *v.t.* découvrir.
unctuous /ˈʌŋktʃʊəs/ *a.* onctueux.
undecided /ʌndɪˈsaɪdɪd/ *a.* indécis.
undefinable /ʌndɪˈfaɪnəbl/ *a.* indéfinissable.
undeniable /ʌndɪˈnaɪəbl/ *a.* indéniable, incontestable.
under /ˈʌndə(r)/ *prep.* sous; (*less than*) moins de; (*according to*) selon. —*adv.* au-dessous. **~ age,** mineur. **~-side** *n.* dessous *m.* **~ way,** (*in progress*) en cours; (*on the way*) en route.
under- /ˈʌndə(r)/ *pref.* sous-.
undercarriage /ˈʌndəkærɪdʒ/ *n.* (*aviat.*) train d'atterrissage *m.*
underclothes /ˈʌndəkləʊðz/ *n. pl.* sous-vêtements *m. pl.*
undercoat /ˈʌndəkəʊt/ *n.* (*of paint*) couche de fond *f.*
undercover /ʌndəˈkʌvə(r)/ (*agent, operation*) *a.* secret.
undercurrent /ˈʌndəkʌrənt/ *n.* courant (profond) *m.*
undercut /ʌndəˈkʌt/ *v.t.* (*p.t.* **undercut,** *pres.p.* **undercutting**) (*comm.*) vendre moins cher que.
underdog /ˈʌndədɒg/ *n.* (*pol.*) opprimé(e) *m.* (*f.*); (*socially*) déshérité(e) *m.* (*f.*).
underdone /ˈʌndədʌn/ *a.* pas assez cuit; (*steak*) saignant.
underestimate /ʌndəˈrestɪmeɪt/ *v.t.* sous-estimer.
underfed /ˈʌndəfed/ *a.* sous-alimenté.
underfoot /ʌndəˈfʊt/ *adv.* sous les pieds.
undergo /ʌndəˈgəʊ/ *v.t.* (*p.t.* **-went,** *pp.* **-gone**) subir.
undergraduate /ʌndəˈgrædʒʊət/ *n.* étudiant(e) (qui prépare la licence) *m.* (*f.*).
underground[1] /ʌndəˈgraʊnd/ *adv.* sous terre.
underground[2] /ˈʌndəgraʊnd/ *a.* souterrain; (*secret*) clandestin. —*n.* (*rail*) métro *m.*
undergrowth /ˈʌndəgrəʊθ/ *n.* sous-bois *m. invar.*
underhand /ˈʌndəhænd/ *a.* (*deceitful*) sournois.
under|lie /ʌndəˈlaɪ/ *v.t.* (*p.t.* **-lay,** *p.p.* **-lain,** *pres. p.* **-lying**) sous-tendre. **~lying** *a.* fondamental.
underline /ʌndəˈlaɪn/ *v.t.* souligner.
undermine /ʌndəˈmaɪn/ *v.t.* (*cliff, society, etc.*) miner, saper.
underneath /ʌndəˈniːθ/ *prep.* sous. —*adv.* (en) dessous.
underpaid /ʌndəˈpeɪd/ *a.* sous-payé.
underpants /ˈʌndəpænts/ *n. pl.* (*man's*) slip *m.*
underpass /ˈʌndəpɑːs/ *n.* (*for cars, people*) passage souterrain *m.*
underprivileged /ʌndəˈprɪvəlɪdʒd/ *a.* défavorisé.
underrate /ʌndəˈreɪt/ *v.t.* sous-estimer.
undersized /ʌndəˈsaɪzd/ *a.* trop petit; (*stunted, puny*) chétif.
understand /ʌndəˈstænd/ *v.t./i.* (*p.t.* **-stood**) comprendre. **~able** *a.* compréhensible. **~ing** *a.* compréhensif; *n.* compréhension *f.*; (*agreement*) entente *f.*
understatement /ˈʌndəsteɪtmənt/ *n.* affirmation au-dessous de la vérité *f.*
understudy /ˈʌndəstʌdɪ/ *n.* (*theatre*) doublure *f.*
undertak|e /ʌndəˈteɪk/ *v.t.* (*p.t.* **-took,** *p.p.* **-taken**) entreprendre; (*responsibility*) assumer. **~e to,** s'engager à. **~ing** *n.* (*task*) entreprise *f.*; (*promise*) promesse *f.*
undertaker /ˈʌndəteɪkə(r)/ *n.* entrepreneur de pompes funèbres *m.*
undertone /ˈʌndətəʊn/ *n.* **in an ~,** à mi-voix.
undervalue /ʌndəˈvæljuː/ *v.t.* sous-évaluer.

underwater /ʌndəˈwɔːtə(r)/ *a.* sous-marin. —*adv.* sous l'eau.
underwear /ˈʌndəweə(r)/ *n.* sous-vêtements *m. pl.*
underweight /ˈʌndəweɪt/ *a.* (*person*) qui ne pèse pas assez.
underwent /ʌndəˈwent/ *see* **undergo.**
underworld /ˈʌndəwɜːld/ *n.* (*of crime*) milieu *m.*, pègre *f.*
undeserved /ʌndɪˈzɜːvd/ *a.* immérité.
undesirable /ʌndɪˈzaɪərəbl/ *a.* peu souhaitable; (*person*) indésirable.
undies /ˈʌndɪz/ *n. pl.* (*female underwear: fam.*) dessous *m. pl.*
undignified /ʌnˈdɪgnɪfaɪd/ *a.* qui manque de dignité, sans dignité.
undisputed /ʌndɪˈspjuːtɪd/ *a.* incontesté.
undistinguished /ʌndɪˈstɪŋgwɪʃt/ *a.* médiocre.
undo /ʌnˈduː/ *v.t.* (*p.t.* **-did,** *p.p.* **-done** /-dʌn/) défaire, détacher; (*a wrong*) réparer. **leave ~ne,** ne pas faire.
undoubted /ʌnˈdaʊtɪd/ *a.* indubitable. **~ly** *adv.* indubitablement.
undreamt /ʌnˈdremt/ *a.* **~ of,** insoupçonné, inimaginable.
undress /ʌnˈdres/ *v.t./i.* (se) déshabiller. **get ~ed,** se déshabiller.
undu|e /ʌnˈdjuː/ *a.* excessif. **~ly** *adv.* excessivement.
undulate /ˈʌndjʊleɪt/ *v.i.* onduler.
undying /ʌnˈdaɪɪŋ/ *a.* éternel.
unearth /ʌnˈɜːθ/ *v.t.* déterrer.
unearthly /ʌnˈɜːθlɪ/ *a.* mystérieux. **~ hour,** (*fam.*) heure indue *f.*
uneasy /ʌnˈiːzɪ/ *a.* (*ill at ease*) mal à l'aise; (*worried*) inquiet; (*situation*) difficile.
uneducated /ʌnˈedʒʊkeɪtɪd/ *a.* (*person*) inculte; (*speech*) populaire.
unemploy|ed /ʌnɪmˈplɔɪd/ *a.* en chômage. **~ment** *n.* chômage *m.*
unending /ʌnˈendɪŋ/ *a.* interminable, sans fin.
unequal /ʌnˈiːkwəl/ *a.* inégal. **~led** *a.* inégalé.
unerring /ʌnˈɜːrɪŋ/ *a.* infaillible.
uneven /ʌnˈiːvn/ *a.* inégal.
unexpected /ʌnɪkˈspektɪd/ *a.* inattendu. **~ly** *adv.* subitement; (*arrive*) à l'improviste.
unfailing /ʌnˈfeɪlɪŋ/ *a.* constant, continuel; (*loyal*) fidèle.
unfair /ʌnˈfeə(r)/ *a.* injuste. **~ness** *n.* injustice *f.*
unfaithful /ʌnˈfeɪθfl/ *a.* infidèle.
unfamiliar /ʌnfəˈmɪlɪə(r)/ *a.* inconnu, peu familier. **be ~ with,** ne pas connaître.
unfasten /ʌnˈfɑːsn/ *v.t.* défaire.
unfavourable /ʌnˈfeɪvərəbl/ *a.* défavorable.
unfeeling /ʌnˈfiːlɪŋ/ *a.* insensible.
unfinished /ʌnˈfɪnɪʃt/ *a.* inachevé.
unfit /ʌnˈfɪt/ *a.* (*med.*) peu en forme; (*unsuitable*) impropre (**for,** à). **~ to,** (*unable*) pas en état de.
unflinching /ʌnˈflɪntʃɪŋ/ *a.* (*fearless*) intrépide.
unfold /ʌnˈfəʊld/ *v.t.* déplier; (*expose*) exposer. —*v.i.* se dérouler.
unforeseen /ʌnfɔːˈsiːn/ *a.* imprévu.
unforgettable /ʌnfəˈgetəbl/ *a.* inoubliable.
unforgivable /ʌnfəˈgɪvəbl/ *a.* impardonnable, inexcusable.
unfortunate /ʌnˈfɔːtʃʊnət/ *a.* malheureux; (*event*) fâcheux. **~ly** *adv.* malheureusement.
unfounded /ʌnˈfaʊndɪd/ *a.* (*rumour etc.*) sans fondement.
unfriendly /ʌnˈfrendlɪ/ *a.* peu amical, froid.
ungainly /ʌnˈgeɪnlɪ/ *a.* gauche.
ungodly /ʌnˈgɒdlɪ/ *a.* impie. **~ hour,** (*fam.*) heure indue *f.*
ungrateful /ʌnˈgreɪtfl/ *a.* ingrat.
unhapp|y /ʌnˈhæpɪ/ *a.* (**-ier, -iest**) malheureux, triste; (*not pleased*) mécontent (**with,** de). **~ily** *adv.* malheureusement. **~iness** *n.* tristesse *f.*

unharmed /ʌnˈhɑːmd/ *a.* indemne, sain et sauf.
unhealthy /ʌnˈhelθɪ/ *a.* (**-ier, -iest**) (*climate etc.*) malsain; (*person*) en mauvaise santé.
unheard-of /ʌnˈhɜːdɒv/ *a.* inouï.
unhinge /ʌnˈhɪndʒ/ *v.t.* (*person, mind*) déséquilibrer.
unholy /ʌnˈhəʊlɪ/ *a.* (**-ier, -iest**) (*person, act, etc.*) impie; (*great: fam.*) invraisemblable.
unhook /ʌnˈhʊk/ *v.t.* décrocher; (*dress*) dégrafer.
unhoped /ʌnˈhəʊpt/ *a.* **~ for,** inespéré.
unhurt /ʌnˈhɜːt/ *a.* indemne.
unicorn /ˈjuːnɪkɔːn/ *n.* licorne *f.*
uniform /ˈjuːnɪfɔːm/ *n.* uniforme *m.* —*a.* uniforme. **~ity** /-ˈfɔːmətɪ/ *n.* uniformité *f.* **~ly** *adv.* uniformément.
unif|y /ˈjuːnɪfaɪ/ *v.t.* unifier. **~ication** /-ɪˈkeɪʃn/ *n.* unification *f.*
unilateral /juːnɪˈlætrəl/ *a.* unilatéral.
unimaginable /ʌnɪˈmædʒɪnəbl/ *a.* inimaginable.
unimportant /ʌnɪmˈpɔːtnt/ *a.* peu important.
uninhabited /ʌnɪnˈhæbɪtɪd/ *a.* inhabité.
unintentional /ʌnɪnˈtenʃənl/ *a.* involontaire.
uninterest|ed /ʌnˈɪntrəstɪd/ *a.* indifférent (**in,** à). **~ing** *a.* peu intéressant.
union /ˈjuːnɪən/ *n.* union *f.*; (*trade union*) syndicat *m.* **~ist** *n.* syndiqué(e) *m.* (*f.*). **U~ Jack,** drapeau britannique *m.*
unique /juːˈniːk/ *a.* unique. **~ly** *adv.* exceptionnellement.
unisex /ˈjuːnɪseks/ *a.* unisexe.
unison /ˈjuːnɪsn/ *n.* **in ~,** à l'unisson.
unit /ˈjuːnɪt/ *n.* unité *f.*; (*of furniture etc.*) élément *m.*, bloc *m.*
unite /juːˈnaɪt/ *v.t./i.* (s')unir. **U~d Kingdom,** Royaume-Uni *m.* **U~d States (of America),** États-Unis (d'Amérique) *m. pl.*
unity /ˈjuːnətɪ/ *n.* unité *f.*; (*harmony: fig.*) harmonie *f.*
universal /juːnɪˈvɜːsl/ *a.* universel.
universe /ˈjuːnɪvɜːs/ *n.* univers *m.*
university /juːnɪˈvɜːsətɪ/ *n.* université *f.* —*a.* universitaire; (*student, teacher*) d'université.
unjust /ʌnˈdʒʌst/ *a.* injuste.
unkempt /ʌnˈkempt/ *a.* négligé.
unkind /ʌnˈkaɪnd/ *a.* pas gentil, méchant. **~ly** *adv.* méchamment.
unknowingly /ʌnˈnəʊɪŋlɪ/ *adv.* sans le savoir, inconsciemment.
unknown /ʌnˈnəʊn/ *a.* inconnu. —*n.* **the ~,** l'inconnu *m.*
unleash /ʌnˈliːʃ/ *v.t.* déchaîner.
unless /ənˈles/ *conj.* à moins que.
unlike /ʌnˈlaɪk/ *a.* (*brothers etc.*) différents. —*prep.* à la différence de; (*different from*) très différent de.
unlikel|y /ʌnˈlaɪklɪ/ *a.* improbable. **~ihood** *n.* improbabilité *f.*
unlimited /ʌnˈlɪmɪtɪd/ *a.* illimité.
unload /ʌnˈləʊd/ *v.t.* décharger.
unlock /ʌnˈlɒk/ *v.t.* ouvrir.
unluck|y /ʌnˈlʌkɪ/ *a.* (**-ier, -iest**) malheureux; (*number*) qui porte malheur. **~ily** *adv.* malheureusement.
unmarried /ʌnˈmærɪd/ *a.* célibataire, qui n'est pas marié.
unmask /ʌnˈmɑːsk/ *v.t.* démasquer.
unmentionable /ʌnˈmenʃənəbl/ *a.* dont il ne faut pas parler; (*shocking*) innommable.
unmistakable /ʌnmɪˈsteɪkəbl/ *a.* (*voice etc.*) facilement reconnaissable; (*clear*) très net.
unmitigated /ʌnˈmɪtɪgeɪtɪd/ *a.* (*absolute*) absolu.
unmoved /ʌnˈmuːvd/ *a.* indifférent (**by,** à), insensible (**by,** à).
unnatural /ʌnˈnætʃrəl/ *a.* pas naturel, anormal.

unnecessary /ʌn'nesəsərɪ/ *a.* inutile; (*superfluous*) superflu.
unnerve /ʌn'nɜːv/ *v.t.* troubler.
unnoticed /ʌn'nəʊtɪst/ *a.* inaperçu.
unobtrusive /ʌnəb'truːsɪv/ *a.* (*person, object*) discret.
unofficial /ʌnə'fɪʃl/ *a.* officieux.
unorthodox /ʌn'ɔːθədɒks/ *a.* peu orthodoxe.
unpack /ʌn'pæk/ *v.t.* (*suitcase etc.*) défaire; (*contents*) déballer. —*v.i.* défaire sa valise.
unpalatable /ʌn'pælətəbl/ *a.* (*food, fact, etc.*) désagréable.
unparalleled /ʌn'pærəleld/ *a.* incomparable.
unpleasant /ʌn'pleznt/ *a.* désagréable (**to,** avec).
unplug /ʌn'plʌg/ *v.t.* (*electr.*) débrancher; (*unblock*) déboucher.
unpopular /ʌn'pɒpjʊlə(r)/ *a.* impopulaire.
unprecedented /ʌn'presɪdentɪd/ *a.* sans précédent.
unpredictable /ʌnprɪ'dɪktəbl/ *a.* imprévisible.
unprepared /ʌnprɪ'peəd/ *a.* non préparé; (*person*) qui n'a rien préparé. **be ~ for,** (*not expect*) ne pas s'attendre à.
unpretentious /ʌnprɪ'tenʃəs/ *a.* sans prétention(s).
unprincipled /ʌn'prɪnsəpld/ *a.* sans scrupules.
unprofessional /ʌnprə'feʃənl/ *a.* (*work*) d'amateur; (*conduct*) contraire au code professionnel.
unpublished /ʌn'pʌblɪʃt/ *a.* inédit.
unqualified /ʌn'kwɒlɪfaɪd/ *a.* non diplômé; (*success etc.*) total. **be ~ to,** ne pas être qualifié pour.
unquestionabl|e /ʌn'kwestʃənəbl/ *a.* incontestable. **~y** *adv.* incontestablement.
unravel /ʌn'rævl/ *v.t.* (*p.t.* **unravelled**) démêler, débrouiller.
unreal /ʌn'rɪəl/ *a.* irréel.
unreasonable /ʌn'riːznəbl/ *a.* déraisonnable, peu raisonnable.
unrecognizable /ʌnrekəg'naɪzəbl/ *a.* méconnaissable.
unrelated /ʌnrɪ'leɪtɪd/ *a.* (*facts*) sans rapport (**to,** avec).
unreliable /ʌnrɪ'laɪəbl/ *a.* peu sérieux; (*machine*) peu fiable.
unrelieved /ʌnrɪ'liːvd/ *a.* perpétuel; (*colour*) uniforme.
unreservedly /ʌnrɪ'zɜːvɪdlɪ/ *adv.* sans réserve.
unrest /ʌn'rest/ *n.* troubles *m. pl.*
unrivalled /ʌn'raɪvld/ *a.* sans égal, incomparable.
unroll /ʌn'rəʊl/ *v.t.* dérouler.
unruffled /ʌn'rʌfld/ *a.* (*person*) qui n'a pas perdu son calme.
unruly /ʌn'ruːlɪ/ *a.* indiscipliné.
unsafe /ʌn'seɪf/ *a.* (*dangerous*) dangereux; (*person*) en danger.
unsaid /ʌn'sed/ *a.* **leave ~,** passer sous silence.
unsatisfactory /ʌnsætɪs'fæktərɪ/ *a.* peu satisfaisant.
unsavoury /ʌn'seɪvərɪ/ *a.* désagréable, répugnant.
unscathed /ʌn'skeɪðd/ *a.* indemne.
unscrew /ʌn'skruː/ *v.t.* dévisser.
unscrupulous /ʌn'skruːpjʊləs/ *a.* sans scrupules, malhonnête.
unseemly /ʌn'siːmlɪ/ *a.* inconvenant, incorrect, incongru.
unseen /ʌn'siːn/ *a.* inaperçu. —*n.* (*translation*) version *f.*
unsettle /ʌn'setl/ *v.t.* troubler. **~d** *a.* (*weather*) instable.
unshakeable /ʌn'ʃeɪkəbl/ *a.* (*person, belief, etc.*) inébranlable.
unshaven /ʌn'ʃeɪvn/ *a.* pas rasé.
unsightly /ʌn'saɪtlɪ/ *a.* laid.
unskilled /ʌn'skɪld/ *a.* inexpert; (*worker*) non qualifié.
unsociable /ʌn'səʊʃəbl/ *a.* insociable, farouche.
unsophisticated /ʌnsə'fɪstɪkeɪtɪd/ *a.* simple.

unsound /ʌn'saʊnd/ *a.* peu solide. **of ~ mind,** fou.
unspeakable /ʌn'spi:kəbl/ *a.* indescriptible; (*bad*) innommable.
unspecified /ʌn'spesɪfaɪd/ *a.* indéterminé.
unstable /ʌn'steɪbl/ *a.* instable.
unsteady /ʌn'stedɪ/ *a.* (*step*) chancelant; (*ladder*) instable; (*hand*) mal assuré.
unstuck /ʌn'stʌk/ *a.* décollé. **come ~,** (*fail: fam.*) échouer.
unsuccessful /ʌnsək'sesfl/ *a.* (*result, candidate*) malheureux; (*attempt*) infructueux. **be ~,** ne pas réussir (**in doing,** à faire).
unsuit|able /ʌn's(j)u:təbl/ *a.* qui ne convient pas (**for,** à), peu approprié. **~ed** *a.* inapte (**to,** à).
unsure /ʌn'ʃʊə(r)/ *a.* incertain.
unsuspecting /ʌnsə'spektɪŋ/ *a.* qui ne se doute de rien.
untangle /ʌn'tæŋgl/ *v.t.* démêler.
unthinkable /ʌn'θɪŋkəbl/ *a.* impensable, inconcevable.
untid|y /ʌn'taɪdɪ/ *a.* (**-ier, -iest**) désordonné; (*clothes, hair*) mal soigné. **~ily** *adv.* sans soin.
untie /ʌn'taɪ/ *v.t.* (*knot, parcel*) défaire; (*person*) détacher.
until /ən'tɪl/ *prep.* jusqu'à. **not ~,** pas avant. *—conj.* jusqu'à ce que; (*before*) avant que.
untimely /ʌn'taɪmlɪ/ *a.* inopportun; (*death*) prématuré.
untold /ʌn'təʊld/ *a.* incalculable.
untoward /ʌntə'wɔ:d/ *a.* fâcheux.
untrue /ʌn'tru:/ *a.* faux.
unused[1] /ʌn'ju:zd/ *a.* (*new*) neuf; (*not in use*) inutilisé.
unused[2] /ʌn'ju:st/ *a.* **~ to,** peu habitué à.
unusual /ʌn'ju:ʒʊəl/ *a.* exceptionnel; (*strange*) insolite, étrange. **~ly** *adv.* exceptionnellement.
unveil /ʌn'veɪl/ *v.t.* dévoiler.
unwanted /ʌn'wɒntɪd/ *a.* (*useless*) superflu; (*child*) non souhaité.
unwelcome /ʌn'welkəm/ *a.* fâcheux; (*guest*) importun.
unwell /ʌn'wel/ *a.* indisposé.
unwieldy /ʌn'wi:ldɪ/ *a.* difficile à manier.
unwilling /ʌn'wɪlɪŋ/ *a.* peu disposé (**to,** à); (*victim*) récalcitrant. **~ly** *adv.* à contrecœur.
unwind /ʌn'waɪnd/ *v.t./i.* (*p.t.* **unwound** /ʌn'waʊnd/) (se) dérouler; (*relax: fam.*) se détendre.
unwise /ʌn'waɪz/ *a.* imprudent.
unwittingly /ʌn'wɪtɪŋlɪ/ *adv.* involontairement.
unworkable /ʌn'wɜ:kəbl/ *a.* (*plan etc.*) irréalisable.
unworthy /ʌn'wɜ:ðɪ/ *a.* indigne.
unwrap /ʌn'ræp/ *v.t.* (*p.t.* **unwrapped**) ouvrir, défaire.
unwritten /ʌn'rɪtn/ *a.* (*agreement*) verbal, tacite.
up /ʌp/ *adv.* en haut, en l'air; (*sun, curtain*) levé; (*out of bed*) levé, debout; (*finished*) fini. **be ~,** (*level, price*) avoir monté. *—prep.* (*a hill*) en haut de; (*a tree*) dans; (*a ladder*) sur. *—v.t.* (*p.t.* **upped**) augmenter. **come** *or* **go ~,** monter. **~ to,** jusqu'à; (*task*) à la hauteur de. **it is ~ to you,** ça dépend de vous (**to,** de). **be ~ to sth.,** (*do*) faire qch.; (*plot*) préparer qch. **be ~ to,** (*in book*) en être à. **be ~ against,** faire face à. **be ~ in,** (*fam.*) s'y connaître en. **feel ~ to doing,** (*able*) être de taille à faire. **have ~s and downs,** connaître des hauts et des bas. **~ to date,** moderne; (*news*) récent.
upbringing /'ʌpbrɪŋɪŋ/ *n.* éducation *f.*
update /ʌp'deɪt/ *v.t.* mettre à jour.
upgrade /ʌp'greɪd/ *v.t.* (*person*) promouvoir; (*job*) revaloriser.
upheaval /ʌp'hi:vl/ *n.* bouleversement *m.*
uphill /ʌp'hɪl/ *a.* qui monte; (*fig.*) difficile. *—adv.* **go ~,** monter.

uphold /ʌp'həʊld/ *v.t.* (*p.t.* **upheld**) maintenir.
upholster /ʌp'həʊlstə(r)/ *v.t.* (*pad*) rembourrer; (*cover*) recouvrir. **~y** *n.* (*in vehicle*) garniture *f.*
upkeep /'ʌpki:p/ *n.* entretien *m.*
upon /ə'pɒn/ *prep.* sur.
upper /'ʌpə(r)/ *a.* supérieur. —*n.* (*of shoe*) empeigne *f.* **have the ~ hand,** avoir le dessus. **~ class,** aristocratie *f.* **~most** *a.* (*highest*) le plus haut.
upright /'ʌpraɪt/ *a.* droit. —*n.* (*post*) montant *m.*
uprising /'ʌpraɪzɪŋ/ *n.* soulèvement *m.*, insurrection *f.*
uproar /'ʌprɔ:(r)/ *n.* tumulte *m.*
uproot /ʌp'ru:t/ *v.t.* déraciner.
upset[1] /ʌp'set/ *v.t.* (*p.t.* **upset,** *pres. p.* **upsetting**) (*overturn*) renverser; (*plan, stomach*) déranger; (*person*) contrarier, affliger.
upset[2] /'ʌpset/ *n.* dérangement *m.*; (*distress*) chagrin *m.*
upshot /'ʌpʃɒt/ *n.* résultat *m.*
upside-down /ʌpsaɪd'daʊn/ *adv.* (*in position, in disorder*) à l'envers, sens dessus dessous.
upstairs /ʌp'steəz/ *adv.* en haut. —*a.* (*flat etc.*) d'en haut.
upstart /'ʌpstɑ:t/ *n.* (*pej.*) parvenu(e) *m.* (*f.*).
upstream /ʌp'stri:m/ *adv.* en amont.
upsurge /'ʌpsɜ:dʒ/ *n.* recrudescence *f.*; (*of anger*) accès *m.*
uptake /'ʌpteɪk/ *n.* **be quick on the ~,** comprendre vite.
uptight /'ʌptaɪt/ *a.* (*tense: fam.*) crispé; (*angry: fam.*) en colère.
upturn /'ʌptɜ:n/ *n.* amélioration *f.*
upward /'ʌpwəd/ *a.* & *adv.*, **~s** *adv.* vers le haut.
uranium /jʊ'reɪnɪəm/ *n.* uranium *m.*
urban /'ɜ:bən/ *a.* urbain.
urbane /ɜ:'beɪn/ *a.* courtois.
urchin /'ɜ:tʃɪn/ *n.* garnement *m.*
urge /ɜ:dʒ/ *v.t.* conseiller vivement (**to do,** de faire). —*n.* forte envie *f.* **~ on,** (*impel*) encourager.
urgen|t /'ɜ:dʒənt/ *a.* urgent; (*request*) pressant. **~cy** *n.* urgence *f.*; (*of request, tone*) insistance *f.* **~tly** *adv.* d'urgence.
urinal /jʊə'raɪnl/ *n.* urinoir *m.*
urin|e /'jʊərɪn/ *n.* urine *f.* **~ate** *v.i.* uriner.
urn /ɜ:n/ *n.* urne *f.*; (*for tea, coffee*) fontaine *f.*
us /ʌs, *unstressed* əs/ *pron.* nous. (**to**) **~,** nous.
US *abbr. see* **United States.**
USA *abbr. see* **United States of America.**
usable /'ju:zəbl/ *a.* utilisable.
usage /'ju:sɪdʒ/ *n.* usage *m.*
use[1] /ju:z/ *v.t.* se servir de, utiliser; (*consume*) consommer. **~ up,** épuiser. **~r** /-ə(r)/ *n.* usager *m.*
use[2] /ju:s/ *n.* usage *m.*, emploi *m.* **in ~,** en usage. **it is no ~ shouting/*etc.***, ça ne sert à rien de crier/*etc.* **make ~ of,** se servir de. **of ~,** utile.
used[1] /ju:zd/ *a.* (*second-hand*) d'occasion.
used[2] /ju:st/ *p.t.* **he ~ to do,** il faisait (autrefois), il avait l'habitude de faire. —*a.* **~ to,** habitué à.
use|ful /'ju:sfl/ *a.* utile. **~fully** *adv.* utilement. **~less** *a.* inutile; (*person*) incompétent.
usher /'ʌʃə(r)/ *n.* (*in theatre, hall*) placeur *m.* —*v.t.* **~ in,** faire entrer. **~ette** *n.* ouvreuse *f.*
USSR *abbr.* (*Union of Soviet Socialist Republics*) URSS *f.*
usual /'ju:ʒʊəl/ *a.* habituel, normal. **as ~,** comme d'habitude. **~ly** *adv.* d'habitude.
usurp /ju:'zɜ:p/ *v.t.* usurper.
utensil /ju:'tensl/ *n.* ustensile *m.*
uterus /'ju:tərəs/ *n.* utérus *m.*
utilitarian /ju:tɪlɪ'teərɪən/ *a.* utilitaire.
utility /ju:'tɪlətɪ/ *n.* utilité *f.* (**public**) **~,** service public *m.*

utilize /'juːtɪlaɪz/ *v.t.* utiliser.
utmost /'ʌtməʊst/ *a.* (*furthest, most intense*) extrême. **the ~ care**/*etc.*, (*greatest*) le plus grand soin/*etc.* —*n.* **do one's ~,** faire tout son possible.
Utopia /juː'təʊpɪə/ *n.* utopie *f.* **~n** *a.* utopique.
utter[1] /'ʌtə(r)/ *a.* complet, absolu. **~ly** *adv.* complètement.
utter[2] /'ʌtə(r)/ *v.t.* proférer; (*sigh, shout*) pousser. **~ance** *n.* déclaration *f.* **give ~ance to,** exprimer.
U-turn /'juːtɜːn/ *n.* demi-tour *m.*

V

vacan|t /'veɪkənt/ *a.* (*post*) vacant; (*seat etc.*) libre; (*look*) vague. **~cy** *n.* (*post*) poste vacant *m.*; (*room*) chambre disponible *f.*
vacate /və'keɪt, *Amer.* 'veɪkeɪt/ *v.t.* quitter.
vacation /veɪ'keɪʃn/ *n.* (*Amer.*) vacances *f. pl.*
vaccinat|e /'væksɪneɪt/ *v.t.* vacciner. **~ion** /-'neɪʃn/ *n.* vaccination *f.*
vaccine /'væksiːn/ *n.* vaccin *m.*
vacuum /'vækjʊəm/ *n.* (*pl.* **-cuums** *or* **-cua**) vide *m.* **~ cleaner,** aspirateur *m.* **~ flask,** bouteille thermos *f.* (P.).
vagabond /'vægəbɒnd/ *n.* vagabond(e) *m.* (*f.*).
vagina /və'dʒaɪnə/ *n.* vagin *m.*
vagrant /'veɪgrənt/ *n.* vagabond(e) *m.* (*f.*), clochard(e) *m.* (*f.*).
vague /veɪg/ *a.* (**-er, -est**) vague; (*outline*) flou. **be ~ about,** ne pas préciser. **~ly** *adv.* vaguement.
vain /veɪn/ *a.* (**-er, -est**) (*conceited*) vaniteux; (*useless*) vain. **in ~,** en vain. **~ly** *adv.* en vain.
valentine /'væləntaɪn/ *n.* (*card*) carte de la Saint-Valentin *f.*
valet /'vælɪt, 'væleɪ/ *n.* (*manservant*) valet de chambre *m.*
valiant /'vælɪənt/ *a.* courageux.
valid /'vælɪd/ *a.* valable. **~ity** /və'lɪdətɪ/ *n.* validité *f.*
validate /'vælɪdeɪt/ *v.t.* valider.
valley /'vælɪ/ *n.* vallée *f.*
valuable /'væljʊəbl/ *a.* (*object*) de valeur; (*help etc.*) précieux. **~s** *n. pl.* objets de valeur *m. pl.*
valuation /væljʊ'eɪʃn/ *n.* expertise *f.*; (*of house*) évaluation *f.*
value /'væljuː/ *n.* valeur *f.* —*v.t.* (*appraise*) évaluer; (*cherish*) attacher de la valeur à. **~ added tax,** taxe à la valeur ajoutée *f.*, TVA *f.* **~r** /-ə(r)/ *n.* expert *m.*
valve /vælv/ *n.* (*techn.*) soupape *f.*; (*of tyre*) valve *f.*; (*radio*) lampe *f.*
vampire /'væmpaɪə(r)/ *n.* vampire *m.*
van /væn/ *n.* (*vehicle*) camionnette *f.*; (*rail.*) fourgon *m.*
vandal /'vændl/ *n.* vandale *m.*/*f.* **~ism** /-əlɪzəm/ *n.* vandalisme *m.*
vandalize /'vændəlaɪz/ *v.t.* abîmer, détruire, saccager.
vanguard /'vængɑːd/ *n.* (*of army, progress, etc.*) avant-garde *f.*
vanilla /və'nɪlə/ *n.* vanille *f.*
vanish /'vænɪʃ/ *v.i.* disparaître.
vanity /'vænətɪ/ *n.* vanité *f.* **~ case,** mallette de toilette *f.*
vantage-point /'vɑːntɪdʒpɔɪnt/ *n.* (*place*) excellent point de vue *m.*
vapour /'veɪpə(r)/ *n.* vapeur *f.*
vari|able /'veərɪəbl/ *a.* variable. **~ation** /-'eɪʃn/ *n.* variation *f.* **~ed** /-ɪd/ *a.* varié.
variance /'veərɪəns/ *n.* **at ~,** en désaccord (**with,** avec).
variant /'veərɪənt/ *a.* différent. —*n.* variante *f.*
varicose /'værɪkəʊs/ *a.* **~ veins,** varices *f. pl.*
variety /və'raɪətɪ/ *n.* variété *f.*; (*entertainment*) variétés *f. pl.*
various /'veərɪəs/ *a.* divers. **~ly** *adv.* diversement.

varnish /ˈvɑːnɪʃ/ *n.* vernis *m.* —*v.t.* vernir.
vary /ˈveərɪ/ *v.t./i.* varier.
vase /vɑːz, *Amer.* veɪs/ *n.* vase *m.*
vast /vɑːst/ *a.* vaste, immense. **~ly** *adv.* infiniment, extrêmement. **~ness** *n.* immensité *f.*
vat /væt/ *n.* cuve *f.*
VAT /viːeɪˈtiː, væt/ *abbr.* (*value added tax*) TVA *f.*
vault[1] /vɔːlt/ *n.* (*roof*) voûte *f.*; (*in bank*) chambre forte *f.*; (*tomb*) caveau *m.*; (*cellar*) cave *f.*
vault[2] /vɔːlt/ *v.t./i.* sauter. —*n.* saut *m.*
vaunt /vɔːnt/ *v.t.* vanter.
veal /viːl/ *n.* (*meat*) veau *m.*
veer /vɪə(r)/ *v.i.* tourner, virer.
vegan /ˈviːgən/ *n.* végétaliste *m./f.*, végétarien(ne) *m.* (*f.*).
vegetable /ˈvedʒtəbl/ *n.* légume *m.* —*a.* végétal. **~ garden,** (jardin) potager *m.*
vegetarian /vedʒɪˈteərɪən/ *n.* végétarien(ne) *m.* (*f.*).
vegetate /ˈvedʒɪteɪt/ *v.i.* végéter.
vegetation /vedʒɪˈteɪʃn/ *n.* végétation *f.*
vehement /ˈviːəmənt/ *a.* véhément. **~ly** *adv.* avec véhémence.
vehicle /ˈviːɪkl/ *n.* véhicule *m.*
veil /veɪl/ *n.* voile *m.* —*v.t.* voiler.
vein /veɪn/ *n.* (*in body, rock*) veine *f.*; (*mood*) esprit *m.*
velocity /vɪˈlɒsətɪ/ *n.* vélocité *f.*
velvet /ˈvelvɪt/ *n.* velours *m.*
vendetta /venˈdetə/ *n.* vendetta *f.*
vending-machine /ˈvendɪŋməʃiːn/ *n.* distributeur automatique *m.*
vendor /ˈvendə(r)/ *n.* vendeu|r, -se *m., f.*
veneer /vəˈnɪə(r)/ *n.* placage *m.*; (*appearance: fig.*) vernis *m.*
venerable /ˈvenərəbl/ *a.* vénérable.
venereal /vəˈnɪərɪəl/ *a.* vénérien.
venetian /vəˈniːʃn/ *a.* **~ blind,** jalousie *f.*
vengeance /ˈvendʒəns/ *n.* vengeance *f.* **with a ~,** furieusement.
venison /ˈvenɪzn/ *n.* venaison *f.*
venom /ˈvenəm/ *n.* venin *m.* **~ous** /ˈvenəməs/ *a.* venimeux.
vent[1] /vent/ *n.* (*in coat*) fente *f.*
vent[2] /vent/ *n.* (*hole*) orifice *m.*; (*for air*) bouche d'aération *f.* —*v.t.* (*anger*) décharger (**on,** sur). **give ~ to,** donner libre cours à.
ventilat|e /ˈventɪleɪt/ *v.t.* ventiler. **~ion** /-ˈleɪʃn/ *n.* ventilation *f.* **~or** *n.* ventilateur *m.*
ventriloquist /venˈtrɪləkwɪst/ *n.* ventriloque *m./f.*
venture /ˈventʃə(r)/ *n.* entreprise (risquée) *f.* —*v.t./i.* (se) risquer.
venue /ˈvenjuː/ *n.* lieu de rencontre *or* de rendez-vous *m.*
veranda /vəˈrændə/ *n.* véranda *f.*
verb /vɜːb/ *n.* verbe *m.*
verbal /ˈvɜːbl/ *a.* verbal.
verbatim /vɜːˈbeɪtɪm/ *adv.* textuellement, mot pour mot.
verbose /vɜːˈbəʊs/ *a.* verbeux.
verdict /ˈvɜːdɪkt/ *n.* verdict *m.*
verge /vɜːdʒ/ *n.* bord *m.* —*v.i.* **~ on,** friser, frôler. **on the ~ of doing,** sur le point de faire.
verif|y /ˈverɪfaɪ/ *v.t.* vérifier. **~ication** /-ɪˈkeɪʃn/ *n.* vérification *f.*
vermicelli /vɜːmɪˈselɪ/ *n.* vermicelle(s) *m.* (*pl.*).
vermin /ˈvɜːmɪn/ *n.* vermine *f.*
vermouth /ˈvɜːməθ/ *n.* vermouth *m.*
vernacular /vəˈnækjʊlə(r)/ *n.* langue *f.*; (*regional*) dialecte *m.*
versatil|e /ˈvɜːsətaɪl, *Amer.* ˈvɜːsətl/ *a.* (*person*) aux talents variés; (*mind*) souple. **~ity** /-ˈtɪlətɪ/ *n.* souplesse *f.* **her ~ity,** la variété de ses talents.
verse /vɜːs/ *n.* strophe *f.*; (*of Bible*) verset *m.*; (*poetry*) vers *m. pl.*
versed /vɜːst/ *a.* **~ in,** versé dans.
version /ˈvɜːʃn/ *n.* version *f.*
versus /ˈvɜːsəs/ *prep.* contre.

vertebra /ˈvɜːtɪbrə/ *n.* (*pl.* **-brae** /-briː/) vertèbre *f.*
vertical /ˈvɜːtɪkl/ *a.* vertical. **~ly** *adv.* verticalement.
vertigo /ˈvɜːtɪgəʊ/ *n.* vertige *m.*
verve /vɜːv/ *n.* fougue *f.*
very /ˈverɪ/ *adv.* très. —*a.* (*actual*) même. **the ~ day**/*etc.*, le jour/*etc.* même. **at the ~ end,** tout à la fin. **the ~ first,** le tout premier. **~ much,** beaucoup.
vessel /ˈvesl/ *n.* (*duct, ship*) vaisseau *m.*
vest /vest/ *n.* tricot de corps *m.*; (*waistcoat: Amer.*) gilet *m.*
vested /ˈvestɪd/ *a.* **~ interests,** droits acquis *m. pl.*, intérêts *m. pl.*
vestige /ˈvestɪdʒ/ *n.* vestige *m.*
vestry /ˈvestrɪ/ *n.* sacristie *f.*
vet /vet/ *n.* (*fam.*) vétérinaire *m./f.* —*v.t.* (*p.t.* **vetted**) (*candidate etc.*) examiner (de près).
veteran /ˈvetərən/ *n.* vétéran *m.* **(war) ~,** ancien combattant *m.*
veterinary /ˈvetərɪnərɪ/ *a.* vétérinaire. **~ surgeon,** vétérinaire *m./f.*
veto /ˈviːtəʊ/ *n.* (*pl.* **-oes**) veto *m.*; (*right*) droit de veto *m.* —*v.t.* mettre son veto à.
vex /veks/ *v.t.* contrarier, irriter. **~ed question,** question controversée *f.*
via /ˈvaɪə/ *prep.* via, par.
viable /ˈvaɪəbl/ *a.* (*baby, plan, firm*) viable.
viaduct /ˈvaɪədʌkt/ *n.* viaduc *m.*
vibrant /ˈvaɪbrənt/ *a.* vibrant.
vibrat|e /vaɪˈbreɪt/ *v.t./i.* (faire) vibrer. **~ion** /-ʃn/ *n.* vibration *f.*
vicar /ˈvɪkə(r)/ *n.* pasteur *m.* **~age** *n.* presbytère *m.*
vicarious /vɪˈkeərɪəs/ *a.* (*emotion*) ressenti indirectement.
vice[1] /vaɪs/ *n.* (*depravity*) vice *m.*
vice[2] /vaɪs/ *n.* (*techn.*) étau *m.*
vice- /vaɪs/ *pref.* vice-.
vice versa /ˈvaɪsɪ ˈvɜːsə/ *adv.* vice versa.
vicinity /vɪˈsɪnətɪ/ *n.* environs *m. pl.* **in the ~ of,** aux environs de.
vicious /ˈvɪʃəs/ *a.* (*spiteful*) méchant; (*violent*) brutal. **~ circle,** cercle vicieux *m.* **~ly** *adv.* méchamment; brutalement.
victim /ˈvɪktɪm/ *n.* victime *f.*
victimiz|e /ˈvɪktɪmaɪz/ *v.t.* persécuter, martyriser. **~ation** /-ˈzeɪʃn/ *n.* persécution *f.*
victor /ˈvɪktə(r)/ *n.* vainqueur *m.*
Victorian /vɪkˈtɔːrɪən/ *a.* & *n.* victorien(ne) (*m.* (*f.*)).
victor|y /ˈvɪktərɪ/ *n.* victoire *f.* **~ious** /-ˈtɔːrɪəs/ *a.* victorieux.
video /ˈvɪdɪəʊ/ *a.* vidéo *invar.* —*n.* (*fam.*) magnétoscope *m.*
videotape /ˈvɪdɪəʊteɪp/ *n.* bande vidéo *f.* **~ recorder,** magnétoscope *m.*
vie /vaɪ/ *v.i.* (*pres. p.* **vying**) rivaliser (**with,** avec).
view /vjuː/ *n.* vue *f.* —*v.t.* regarder; (*house*) visiter. **in my ~,** à mon avis. **in ~ of,** compte tenu de. **on ~,** exposé. **with a ~ to,** dans le but de. **~er** *n.* (*TV*) téléspecta|teur, -trice *m., f.*
viewpoint /ˈvjuːpɔɪnt/ *n.* point de vue *m.*
vigil /ˈvɪdʒɪl/ *n.* veille *f.*; (*over sick person, corpse*) veillée *f.*
vigilan|t /ˈvɪdʒɪlənt/ *a.* vigilant. **~ce** *n.* vigilance *f.*
vig|our /ˈvɪgə(r)/ *n.* vigueur *f.* **~orous** *a.* vigoureux.
vile /vaɪl/ *a.* (*base*) infâme, vil; (*bad*) abominable, exécrable.
vilify /ˈvɪlɪfaɪ/ *v.t.* diffamer.
villa /ˈvɪlə/ *n.* villa *f.*, pavillon *m.*
village /ˈvɪlɪdʒ/ *n.* village *m.* **~r** /-ə(r)/ *n.* villageois(e) *m.* (*f.*).
villain /ˈvɪlən/ *n.* scélérat *m.*, bandit *m.*; (*in story etc.*) traître *m.* **~y** *n.* infamie *f.*
vindicat|e /ˈvɪndɪkeɪt/ *v.t.* justifier. **~ion** /-ˈkeɪʃn/ *n.* justification *f.*
vindictive /vɪnˈdɪktɪv/ *a.* vindicatif.

vine /vaɪn/ *n.* vigne *f.*
vinegar /ˈvɪnɪɡə(r)/ *n.* vinaigre *m.*
vineyard /ˈvɪnjəd/ *n.* vignoble *m.*
vintage /ˈvɪntɪdʒ/ *n.* (*year*) année *f.*, millésime *m.* —*a.* (*wine*) de grand cru; (*car*) d'époque.
vinyl /ˈvaɪnɪl/ *n.* vinyle *m.*
viola /vɪˈəʊlə/ *n.* (*mus.*) alto *m.*
violat|e /ˈvaɪəleɪt/ *v.t.* violer. **~ion** /-ˈleɪʃn/ *n.* violation *f.*
violen|t /ˈvaɪələnt/ *a.* violent. **~ce** *n.* violence *f.* **~tly** *adv.* violemment, avec violence.
violet /ˈvaɪələt/ *n.* (*bot.*) violette *f.*; (*colour*) violet *m.* —*a.* violet.
violin /vaɪəˈlɪn/ *n.* violon *m.* **~ist** *n.* violoniste *m.*/*f.*
VIP /viːaɪˈpiː/ *abbr.* (*very important person*) personnage de marque *m.*
viper /ˈvaɪpə(r)/ *n.* vipère *f.*
virgin /ˈvɜːdʒɪn/ *n.* (*woman*) vierge *f.* —*a.* vierge. **be a ~**, (*woman, man*) être vierge. **~ity** /vəˈdʒɪnətɪ/ *n.* virginité *f.*
viril|e /ˈvɪraɪl, *Amer.* ˈvɪrəl/ *a.* viril. **~ity** /vɪˈrɪlətɪ/ *n.* virilité *f.*
virtual /ˈvɜːtʃʊəl/ *a.* vrai. **a ~ failure**/*etc.*, pratiquement un échec/*etc.* **~ly** *adv.* pratiquement.
virtue /ˈvɜːtʃuː/ *n.* (*goodness, chastity*) vertu *f.*; (*merit*) mérite *m.* **by** *or* **in ~ of**, en raison de.
virtuos|o /vɜːtʃʊˈəʊsəʊ/ *n.* (*pl.* **-si** /-siː/) virtuose *m.*/*f.* **~ity** /-ˈɒsətɪ/ *n.* virtuosité *f.*
virtuous /ˈvɜːtʃʊəs/ *a.* vertueux.
virulent /ˈvɪrʊlənt/ *a.* virulent.
virus /ˈvaɪərəs/ *n.* (*pl.* **-uses**) virus *m.*
visa /ˈviːzə/ *n.* visa *m.*
viscount /ˈvaɪkaʊnt/ *n.* vicomte *m.*
viscous /ˈvɪskəs/ *a.* visqueux.
vise /vaɪs/ *n.* (*Amer.*) étau *m.*
visib|le /ˈvɪzəbl/ *a.* (*discernible, obvious*) visible. **~ility** /-ˈbɪlətɪ/ *n.* visibilité *f.* **~ly** *adv.* visiblement.
vision /ˈvɪʒn/ *n.* vision *f.*
visionary /ˈvɪʒənərɪ/ *a.* & *n.* visionnaire (*m.*/*f.*).
visit /ˈvɪzɪt/ *v.t.* (*p.t.* **visited**) (*person*) rendre visite à; (*place*) visiter. —*v.i.* être en visite. —*n.* (*tour, call*) visite *f.*; (*stay*) séjour *m.* **~or** *n.* visiteu|r, -se *m.*, *f.*; (*guest*) invité(e) *m.* (*f.*); (*in hotel*) client(e) *m.* (*f.*).
visor /ˈvaɪzə(r)/ *n.* visière *f.*
vista /ˈvɪstə/ *n.* perspective *f.*
visual /ˈvɪʒʊəl/ *a.* visuel. **~ly** *adv.* visuellement.
visualize /ˈvɪʒʊəlaɪz/ *v.t.* se représenter; (*foresee*) envisager.
vital /ˈvaɪtl/ *a.* vital. **~ statistics**, (*fam.*) mensurations *f. pl.*
vitality /vaɪˈtælətɪ/ *n.* vitalité *f.*
vitally /ˈvaɪtəlɪ/ *adv.* extrêmement.
vitamin /ˈvɪtəmɪn/ *n.* vitamine *f.*
vivac|ious /vɪˈveɪʃəs/ *a.* plein d'entrain, animé. **~ity** /-æsətɪ/ *n.* vivacité *f.*, entrain *m.*
vivid /ˈvɪvɪd/ *a.* vif; (*graphic*) vivant. **~ly** *adv.* vivement; (*describe*) de façon vivante.
vivisection /vɪvɪˈsekʃn/ *n.* vivisection *f.*
vocabulary /vəˈkæbjʊlərɪ/ *n.* vocabulaire *m.*
vocal /ˈvəʊkl/ *a.* vocal; (*person*: *fig.*) qui s'exprime franchement. **~ cords**, cordes vocales *f. pl.* **~ist** *n.* chanteu|r, -se *m.*, *f.*
vocation /vəˈkeɪʃn/ *n.* vocation *f.* **~al** *a.* professionnel.
vociferous /vəˈsɪfərəs/ *a.* bruyant.
vodka /ˈvɒdkə/ *n.* vodka *f.*
vogue /vəʊɡ/ *n.* (*fashion, popularity*) vogue *f.* **in ~**, en vogue.
voice /vɔɪs/ *n.* voix *f.* —*v.t.* (*express*) formuler.
void /vɔɪd/ *a.* vide (**of**, de); (*not valid*) nul. —*n.* vide *m.*
volatile /ˈvɒlətaɪl, *Amer.* ˈvɒlətl/ *a.* (*person*) versatile; (*situation*) variable.
volcan|o /vɒlˈkeɪnəʊ/ *n.* (*pl.* **-oes**) volcan *m.* **~ic** /-ænɪk/ *a.* volcanique.

volition /vəˈlɪʃn/ *n.* **of one's own ~,** de son propre gré.
volley /ˈvɒlɪ/ *n.* (*of blows etc.*) volée *f.*; (*of gunfire*) salve *f.*
volt /vəʊlt/ *n.* (*electr.*) volt *m.* **~age** *n.* voltage *m.*
voluble /ˈvɒljʊbl/ *a.* volubile.
volume /ˈvɒljuːm/ *n.* volume *m.*
voluntar|y /ˈvɒləntərɪ/ *a.* volontaire; (*unpaid*) bénévole. **~ily** /-trəlɪ, *Amer.* -ˈterəlɪ/ *adv.* volontairement.
volunteer /vɒlənˈtɪə(r)/ *n.* volontaire *m./f.* —*v.i.* s'offrir (**to do,** pour faire); (*mil.*) s'engager comme volontaire. —*v.t.* offrir.
voluptuous /vəˈlʌptʃʊəs/ *a.* voluptueux.
vomit /ˈvɒmɪt/ *v.t./i.* (*p.t.* **vomited**) vomir. —*n.* vomi(ssement) *m.*
voracious /vəˈreɪʃəs/ *a.* vorace.
vot|e /vəʊt/ *n.* vote *m.*; (*right*) droit de vote *m.* —*v.t./i.* voter. **~ (in),** (*person*) élire. **~er** *n.* élec|teur, -trice *m., f.* **~ing** *n.* vote *m.* (**of,** de); (*poll*) scrutin *m.*
vouch /ˈvaʊtʃ/ *v.i.* **~ for,** se porter garant de, répondre de.
voucher /ˈvaʊtʃə(r)/ *n.* bon *m.*
vow /vaʊ/ *n.* vœu *m.* —*v.t.* (*loyalty etc.*) jurer (**to,** à). **~ to do,** jurer de faire.
vowel /ˈvaʊəl/ *n.* voyelle *f.*
voyage /ˈvɔɪɪdʒ/ *n.* voyage (par mer) *m.*
vulgar /ˈvʌlgə(r)/ *a.* vulgaire. **~ity** /-ˈgærətɪ/ *n.* vulgarité *f.*
vulnerab|le /ˈvʌlnərəbl/ *a.* vulnérable. **~ility** /-ˈbɪlətɪ/ *n.* vulnérabilité *f.*
vulture /ˈvʌltʃə(r)/ *n.* vautour *m.*

W

wad /wɒd/ *n.* (*pad*) tampon *m.*; (*bundle*) liasse *f.*
wadding /ˈwɒdɪŋ/ *n.* rembourrage *m.*, ouate *f.*
waddle /ˈwɒdl/ *v.i.* se dandiner.
wade /weɪd/ *v.i.* **~ through,** (*mud etc.*) patauger dans; (*book: fig.*) avancer péniblement dans.
wafer /ˈweɪfə(r)/ *n.* (*biscuit*) gaufrette *f.*; (*relig.*) hostie *f.*
waffle[1] /ˈwɒfl/ *n.* (*talk: fam.*) verbiage *m.* —*v.i.* (*fam.*) divaguer.
waffle[2] /ˈwɒfl/ *n.* (*cake*) gaufre *f.*
waft /wɒft/ *v.i.* flotter. —*v.t.* porter.
wag /wæg/ *v.t./i.* (*p.t.* **wagged**) (*tail*) remuer.
wage[1] /weɪdʒ/ *v.t.* (*campaign*) mener. **~ war,** faire la guerre.
wage[2] /weɪdʒ/ *n.* (*weekly, daily*) salaire *m.* **~s,** salaire *m.* **~-earner** *n.* salarié(e) *m.* (*f.*).
wager /ˈweɪdʒə(r)/ *n.* (*bet*) pari *m.* —*v.t.* parier (**that,** que).
waggle /ˈwægl/ *v.t./i.* remuer.
wagon /ˈwægən/ *n.* (*horse-drawn*) chariot *m.*; (*rail.*) wagon (de marchandises) *m.*
waif /weɪf/ *n.* enfant abandonné(e) *m./f.*
wail /weɪl/ *v.i.* (*utter cry or complaint*) gémir. —*n.* gémissement *m.*
waist /weɪst/ *n.* taille *f.*
waistcoat /ˈweɪskəʊt/ *n.* gilet *m.*
wait /weɪt/ *v.t./i.* attendre. —*n.* attente *f.* **~ for,** attendre. **~ on,** servir. **~ing-list** *n.* liste d'attente *f.* **~ing-room** *n.* salle d'attente *f.*
wait|er /ˈweɪtə(r)/ *n.* garçon *m.*, serveur *m.* **~ress** *n.* serveuse *f.*
waive /weɪv/ *v.t.* renoncer à.
wake[1] /weɪk/ *v.t./i.* (*p.t.* **woke,** *p.p.* **woken**). **~ (up),** (se) réveiller.
wake[2] /weɪk/ *n.* (*track*) sillage *m.* **in the ~ of,** (*after*) à la suite de.
waken /ˈweɪkən/ *v.t./i.* (se) réveiller, (s')éveiller.
Wales /weɪlz/ *n.* pays de Galles *m.*
walk /wɔːk/ *v.i.* marcher; (*not ride*) aller à pied; (*stroll*) se promener.

—*v.t.* (*streets*) parcourir; (*distance*) faire à pied; (*dog*) promener. —*n.* promenade *f.*, tour *m.*; (*gait*) (dé)marche *f.*; (*pace*) marche *f.*, pas *m.*; (*path*) allée *f.* **~ of life,** condition sociale *f.* **~ out,** (*go away*) partir; (*worker*) faire grève. **~-out** *n.* grève surprise *f.* **~ out on,** abandonner. **~-over** *n.* victoire facile *f.*

walker /'wɔːkə(r)/ *n.* (*person*) marcheu|r, -se *m.*, *f.*

walkie-talkie /wɔːkɪ'tɔːkɪ/ *n.* talkie-walkie *m.*

walking /'wɔːkɪŋ/ *n.* marche (à pied) *f.* —*a.* (*corpse, dictionary: fig.*) vivant. **~-stick** *n.* canne *f.*

wall /wɔːl/ *n.* mur *m.*; (*of tunnel, stomach, etc.*) paroi *f.* —*a.* mural. —*v.t.* (*city*) fortifier. **go to the ~,** (*firm*) faire faillite.

wallet /'wɒlɪt/ *n.* portefeuille *m.*

wallflower /'wɔːlflaʊə(r)/ *n.* (*bot.*) giroflée *f.*

wallop /'wɒləp/ *v.t.* (*p.t.* **walloped**) (*hit: sl.*) taper sur. —*n.* (*blow: sl.*) grand coup *m.*

wallow /'wɒləʊ/ *v.i.* se vautrer.

wallpaper /'wɔːlpeɪpə(r)/ *n.* papier peint *m.* —*v.t.* tapisser.

walnut /'wɔːlnʌt/ *n.* (*nut*) noix *f.*; (*tree*) noyer *m.*

walrus /'wɔːlrəs/ *n.* morse *m.*

waltz /wɔːls/ *n.* valse *f.* —*v.i.* valser.

wan /wɒn/ *a.* pâle, blême.

wand /wɒnd/ *n.* baguette (magique) *f.*

wander /'wɒndə(r)/ *v.i.* errer; (*stroll*) flâner; (*digress*) s'écarter. **~er** *n.* vagabond(e) *m.* (*f.*).

wane /weɪn/ *v.i.* décroître. —*n.* **on the ~,** (*strength, fame, etc.*) en déclin; (*person*) sur son déclin.

wangle /'wæŋgl/ *v.t.* (*obtain: sl.*) se débrouiller pour avoir.

want /wɒnt/ *v.t.* vouloir (**to do,** faire); (*need*) avoir besoin de; (*ask for*) demander. —*v.i.* **~ for,** manquer de. —*n.* (*need, poverty*) besoin *m.*; (*desire*) désir *m.*; (*lack*) manque *m.* **for ~ of,** faute de. **~ed** *a.* (*criminal*) recherché par la police.

wanting /'wɒntɪŋ/ *a.* **be ~,** manquer (**in,** de).

wanton /'wɒntən/ *a.* (*cruelty*) gratuit; (*woman*) impudique.

war /wɔː(r)/ *n.* guerre *f.* **at ~,** en guerre. **on the ~-path,** sur le sentier de la guerre.

ward /wɔːd/ *n.* (*in hospital*) salle *f.*; (*minor: jurid.*) pupille *m.*/*f.*; (*pol.*) division électorale *f.* —*v.t.* **~ off,** (*danger*) prévenir; (*blow, anger*) détourner.

warden /'wɔːdn/ *n.* direc|teur, -trice *m.*, *f.*; (*of park*) gardien(ne) *m.* (*f.*). **(traffic) ~,** contractuel(le) *m.* (*f.*).

warder /'wɔːdə(r)/ *n.* gardien (de prison) *m.*

wardrobe /'wɔːdrəʊb/ *n.* (*place*) armoire *f.*; (*clothes*) garde-robe *f.*

warehouse /'weəhaʊs/ *n.* (*pl.* **-s** /-haʊzɪz/) entrepôt *m.*

wares /weəz/ *n. pl.* (*goods*) marchandises *f. pl.*

warfare /'wɔːfeə(r)/ *n.* guerre *f.*

warhead /'wɔːhed/ *n.* ogive *f.*

warily /'weərɪlɪ/ *adv.* avec prudence.

warm /wɔːm/ *a.* (**-er, -est**) chaud; (*hearty*) chaleureux. **be** *or* **feel ~,** avoir chaud. **it is ~,** il fait chaud. —*v.t.*/*i.* **~ (up),** (se) réchauffer; (*food*) chauffer; (*liven up*) (s')animer. **~-hearted** *a.* chaleureux. **~ly** *adv.* (*wrap up etc.*) chaudement; (*heartily*) chaleureusement. **~th** *n.* chaleur *f.*

warn /wɔːn/ *v.t.* avertir, prévenir. **~ s.o. off sth.,** (*advise against*) mettre qn. en garde contre qch.; (*forbid*) interdire qch. à qn. **~ing** *n.* avertissement *m.*; (*notice*) avis *m.* **without ~ing,** sans prévenir.

warp /wɔːp/ *v.t./i.* (*wood etc.*) (se) voiler; (*pervert*) pervertir.

warrant /ˈwɒrənt/ *n.* (*for arrest*) mandat (d'arrêt) *m.*; (*comm.*) autorisation *f.* —*v.t.* justifier.

warranty /ˈwɒrəntɪ/ *n.* garantie *f.*

warring /ˈwɔːrɪŋ/ *a.* en guerre.

warrior /ˈwɒrɪə(r)/ *n.* guerr|ier, -ière *m., f.*

warship /ˈwɔːʃɪp/ *n.* navire de guerre *m.*

wart /wɔːt/ *n.* verrue *f.*

wartime /ˈwɔːtaɪm/ *n.* **in ~,** en temps de guerre.

wary /ˈweərɪ/ *a.* (**-ier, -iest**) prudent.

was /wɒz, *unstressed* wəz/ *see* **be.**

wash /wɒʃ/ *v.t./i.* (se) laver; (*flow over*) baigner. —*n.* lavage *m.*; (*clothes*) lessive *f.*; (*of ship*) sillage *m.* **have a ~,** se laver. **~-basin** *n.* lavabo *m.* **~-cloth** *n.* (*Amer.*) gant de toilette *m.* **~ down,** (*meal*) arroser. **~ one's hands of,** se laver les mains de. **~ out,** (*cup etc.*) laver; (*stain*) enlever. **~-out** *n.* (*sl.*) fiasco *m.* **~-room** *n.* (*Amer.*) toilettes *f. pl.* **~ up,** faire la vaisselle; (*Amer.*) se laver. **~able** *a.* lavable. **~ing** *n.* lessive *f.* **~ing-machine** *n.* machine à laver *f.* **~ing-powder** *n.* lessive *f.* **~ing-up** *n.* vaisselle *f.*

washed-out /wɒʃtˈaʊt/ *a.* (*faded*) délavé; (*tired*) lessivé; (*ruined*) anéanti.

washer /ˈwɒʃə(r)/ *n.* rondelle *f.*

wasp /wɒsp/ *n.* guêpe *f.*

wastage /ˈweɪstɪdʒ/ *n.* gaspillage *m.* **some ~,** (*in goods, among candidates, etc.*) du déchet.

waste /weɪst/ *v.t.* gaspiller; (*time*) perdre. —*v.i.* **~ away,** dépérir. —*a.* superflu; (*product*) de rebut. —*n.* gaspillage *m.*; (*of time*) perte *f.*; (*rubbish*) déchets *m. pl.* **~ (land),** (*desolate*) terre désolée *f.*; (*unused*) terre inculte *f.*; (*in town*) terrain vague *m.* **~ paper,** vieux papiers *m. pl.* **~-paper basket,** corbeille (à papier) *f.*

wasteful /ˈweɪstfl/ *a.* peu économique; (*person*) gaspilleur.

watch /wɒtʃ/ *v.t./i.* regarder, observer; (*guard, spy on*) surveiller; (*be careful about*) faire attention à. —*n.* surveillance *f.*; (*naut.*) quart *m.*; (*for telling time*) montre *f.* **be on the ~,** guetter. **~-dog** *n.* chien de garde *m.* **~ out,** (*be on the look-out*) guetter; (*take care*) faire attention (**for,** à). **~-tower** *n.* tour de guet *f.* **~ful** *a.* vigilant.

watchmaker /ˈwɒtʃmeɪkə(r)/ *n.* horlog|er, -ère *m., f.*

watchman /ˈwɒtʃmən/ *n.* (*pl.* **-men**) (*of building*) gardien *m.*

water /ˈwɔːtə(r)/ *n.* eau *f.* —*v.t.* arroser. —*v.i.* (*of eyes*) larmoyer. **my/his/***etc.* **mouth ~s,** l'eau me/lui/*etc.* vient à la bouche. **by ~,** en bateau. **~-closet** *n.* waters *m. pl.* **~-colour** *n.* couleur pour aquarelle *f.*; (*painting*) aquarelle *f.* **~ down,** couper (d'eau); (*tone down*) édulcorer. **~-ice** *n.* sorbet *m.* **~-lily** *n.* nénuphar *m.* **~-main** *n.* canalisation d'eau *f.* **~-melon** *n.* pastèque *f.* **~-pistol** *n.* pistolet à eau *m.* **~ polo,** water-polo *m.* **~ power,** énergie hydraulique *f.* **~-skiing** *n.* ski nautique *m.*

watercress /ˈwɔːtəkres/ *n.* cresson (de fontaine) *m.*

waterfall /ˈwɔːtəfɔːl/ *n.* chute d'eau *f.*, cascade *f.*

watering-can /ˈwɔːtərɪŋkæn/ *n.* arrosoir *m.*

waterlogged /ˈwɔːtəlɒgd/ *a.* imprégné d'eau; (*land*) détrempé.

watermark /ˈwɔːtəmɑːk/ *n.* (*in paper*) filigrane *m.*

waterproof /ˈwɔːtəpruːf/ *a.* (*material*) imperméable.

watershed /ˈwɔːtəʃed/ *n.* (*in affairs*) tournant décisif *m.*

watertight /ˈwɔːtətaɪt/ *a.* étanche.

waterway /ˈwɔːtəweɪ/ *n.* voie navigable *f.*

waterworks /ˈwɔːtəwɜːks/ *n.* (*place*) station hydraulique *f.*

watery /ˈwɔːtərɪ/ *a.* (*colour*) délavé; (*eyes*) humide; (*soup*) trop liquide; (*tea*) faible.

watt /wɒt/ *n.* watt *m.*

wav|e /weɪv/ *n.* vague *f.*; (*in hair*) ondulation *f.*; (*radio*) onde *f.*; (*sign*) signe *m.* —*v.t.* agiter. —*v.i.* faire signe (de la main); (*of flag, hair, etc.*) onduler. **~y** *a.* (*line*) onduleux; (*hair*) ondulé.

wavelength /ˈweɪvleŋθ/ *n.* (*radio & fig.*) longueur d'ondes *f.*

waver /ˈweɪvə(r)/ *v.i.* vaciller.

wax[1] /wæks/ *n.* cire *f.*; (*for skis*) fart *m.* —*v.t.* cirer; farter; (*car*) astiquer. **~en, ~y** *adjs.* cireux.

wax[2] /wæks/ *v.i.* (*of moon*) croître.

waxwork /ˈwækswɜːk/ *n.* (*dummy*) figure de cire *f.*

way /weɪ/ *n.* (*road, path*) chemin *m.* (to, de); (*distance*) distance *f.*; (*direction*) direction *f.*; (*manner*) façon *f.*; (*means*) moyen *m.*; (*particular*) égard *m.* **~s,** (*habits*) habitudes *f. pl.* —*adv.* (*fam.*) loin. **be in the ~,** bloquer le passage; (*hindrance*: *fig.*) gêner (qn.). **be on one's** *or* **the ~,** être en route. **by the ~,** à propos. **by the ~side,** au bord de la route. **by ~ of,** comme; (*via*) par. **go out of one's ~ to,** se donner du mal pour. **in a ~,** dans un sens. **that ~,** par là. **this ~,** par ici. **~ in,** entrée *f.* **~ out,** sortie *f.* **~-out** *a.* (*strange*: *fam.*) original.

wayfarer /ˈweɪfeərə(r)/ *n.* voyageu|r, -se *m., f.*

waylay /ˈweɪleɪ/ *v.t.* (*p.t.* **-laid**) (*assail, stop*) assaillir.

wayward /ˈweɪwəd/ *a.* capricieux.

WC /dʌb(ə)ljuːˈsiː/ *n.* w.-c. *m. pl.*

we /wiː/ *pron.* nous.

weak /wiːk/ *a.* (**-er, -est**) faible; (*delicate*) fragile. **~ly** *adv.* faiblement; *a.* faible. **~ness** *n.* faiblesse *f.*; (*fault*) point faible *m.* **a ~ness for,** (*liking*) un faible pour.

weaken /ˈwiːkən/ *v.t.* affaiblir —*v.i.* s'affaiblir, faiblir.

weakling /ˈwiːklɪŋ/ *n.* gringalet *m.*

wealth /welθ/ *n.* richesse *f.*; (*riches, resources*) richesses *f. pl.*; (*quantity*) profusion *f.*

wealthy /ˈwelθɪ/ *a.* (**-ier, -iest**) riche. —*n.* **the ~,** les riches *m. pl.*

wean /wiːn/ *v.t.* (*baby*) sevrer.

weapon /ˈwepən/ *n.* arme *f.*

wear /weə(r)/ *v.t.* (*p.t.* **wore,** *p.p.* **worn**) porter; (*put on*) mettre; (*expression etc.*) avoir. —*v.i.* (*last*) durer. **~ (out),** (s')user. —*n.* usage *m.*; (*damage*) usure *f.*; (*clothing*) vêtements *m. pl.* **~ down,** user. **~ off,** (*colour, pain*) passer. **~ on,** (*time*) passer. **~ out,** (*exhaust*) épuiser. **~er** *n.* **~er of,** personne vêtue de *f.*

wear|y /ˈwɪərɪ/ *a.* (**-ier, -iest**) fatigué, las; (*tiring*) fatigant. —*v.i.* **~y of,** se lasser de. **~ily** *adv.* avec lassitude. **~iness** *n.* lassitude *f.*, fatigue *f.*

weasel /ˈwiːzl/ *n.* belette *f.*

weather /ˈweðə(r)/ *n.* temps *m.* —*a.* météorologique. —*v.t.* (*survive*) réchapper de *or* à. **under the ~,** patraque. **~-beaten** *a.* tanné. **~-vane** *n.* girouette *f.*

weathercock /ˈweðəkɒk/ *n.* girouette *f.*

weave /wiːv/ *v.t./i.* (*p.t.* **wove,** *p.p.* **woven**) tisser; (*basket etc.*) tresser; (*move*) se faufiler. —*n.* (*style*) tissage *m.* **~r** /-ə(r)/ *n.* tisserand(e) *m.* (*f.*).

web /web/ *n.* (*of spider*) toile *f.*; (*fabric*) tissu *m.*; (*on foot*) palmure *f.* **~bed** *a.* (*foot*) palmé. **~bing** *n.* (*in chair*) sangles *f. pl.*

wed /wed/ *v.t.* (*p.t.* **wedded**) épouser. —*v.i.* se marier. **~ded to,** (*devoted to*: *fig.*) attaché à.

wedding /'wedɪŋ/ *n.* mariage *m.* **~-ring** *n.* alliance *f.*
wedge /wedʒ/ *n.* coin *m.*; (*under wheel etc.*) cale *f.* —*v.t.* caler; (*push*) enfoncer; (*crowd*) coincer.
wedlock /'wedlɒk/ *n.* mariage *m.*
Wednesday /'wenzdɪ/ *n.* mercredi *m.*
wee /wiː/ *a.* (*fam.*) tout petit.
weed /wiːd/ *n.* mauvaise herbe *f.* —*v.t./i.* désherber. **~-killer** *n.* désherbant *m.* **~ out,** extirper. **~y** *a.* (*person: fig.*) faible, maigre.
week /wiːk/ *n.* semaine *f.* **a ~ today/tomorrow,** aujourd'hui/demain en huit. **~ly** *adv.* toutes les semaines; *a.* & *n.* (*periodical*) hebdomadaire (*m.*).
weekday /'wiːkdeɪ/ *n.* jour de semaine *m.*
weekend /wiːk'end/ *n.* week-end *m.*, fin de semaine *f.*
weep /wiːp/ *v.t./i.* (*p.t.* **wept**) pleurer (**for s.o.,** qn.). **~ing willow,** saule pleureur *m.*
weigh /weɪ/ *v.t./i.* peser. **~ anchor,** lever l'ancre. **~ down,** lester (avec un poids); (*bend*) faire plier; (*fig.*) accabler. **~ up,** (*examine: fam.*) calculer.
weight /weɪt/ *n.* poids *m.* —*v.t.* **~ down = weigh down. ~-lifting** *n.* haltérophilie *f.* **~y** *a.* lourd; (*subject etc.*) de poids.
weighting /'weɪtɪŋ/ *n.* indemnité *f.*
weir /wɪə(r)/ *n.* barrage *m.*
weird /wɪəd/ *a.* (**-er, -est**) mystérieux; (*strange*) bizarre.
welcome /'welkəm/ *a.* agréable; (*timely*) opportun. **be ~,** être le *or* la bienvenu(e), être les bienvenu(e)s. **you're ~!,** (*after thank you*) il n'y a pas de quoi! **~ to do,** libre de faire. —*int.* soyez le *or* la bienvenu(e), soyez les bienvenu(e)s. —*n.* accueil *m.* —*v.t.* accueillir; (*as greeting*) souhaiter la bienvenue à; (*fig.*) se réjouir de.
weld /weld/ *v.t.* souder. —*n.* soudure *f.* **~er** *n.* soudeur *m.* **~ing** *n.* soudure *f.*
welfare /'welfeə(r)/ *n.* bien-être *m.*; (*aid*) aide sociale *f.* **W~ State,** État-providence *m.*
well[1] /wel/ *n.* (*for water, oil*) puits *m.*; (*of stairs*) cage *f.*
well[2] /wel/ *adv.* (**better, best**) bien. —*a.* bien *invar.* **be ~,** (*healthy*) aller bien. —*int.* eh bien; (*surprise*) tiens. **do ~,** (*succeed*) réussir. **~-behaved** *a.* sage. **~-being** *n.* bien-être *m.* **~-disposed** *a.* bien disposé. **~ done!,** bravo! **~-heeled** *a.* (*fam.*) nanti. **~-known** *a.* (bien) connu. **~-meaning** *a.* bien intentionné. **~ off,** aisé, riche. **~-read** *a.* instruit. **~-spoken** *a.* qui parle bien. **~-to-do** *a.* riche. **~-wisher** *n.* admira|teur, -trice *m., f.*
wellington /'welɪŋtən/ *n.* (*boot*) botte de caoutchouc *f.*
Welsh /welʃ/ *a.* gallois. —*n.* (*lang.*) gallois *m.* **~man** *n.* Gallois *m.* **~ rabbit,** croûte au fromage *f.* **~woman** *n.* Galloise *f.*
welsh /welʃ/ *v.i.* **~ on,** (*debt, promise*) ne pas honorer.
welterweight /'weltəweɪt/ *n.* poids mi-moyen *m.*
wench /wentʃ/ *n.* (*old use*) jeune fille *f.*
wend /wend/ *v.t.* **~ one's way,** se diriger, aller son chemin.
went /went/ *see* **go.**
wept /wept/ *see* **weep.**
were /wɜː(r), *unstressed* wə(r)/ *see* **be.**
west /west/ *n.* ouest *m.* **the W~,** (*pol.*) l'Occident *m.* —*a.* d'ouest. —*adv.* vers l'ouest. **W~ Germany,** Allemagne de l'Ouest *f.* **W~ Indian** *a.* & *n.* antillais(e) (*m.* (*f.*)). **the W~ Indies,** les Antilles *f. pl.* **~erly** *a.* d'ouest. **~ern** *a.* de l'ouest; (*pol.*) occidental; *n.* (*film*) western *m.* **~erner** *n.* occidental(e) *m.* (*f.*). **~ward** *a.*

à l'ouest. **~wards** *adv.* vers l'ouest.

westernize /'westənaɪz/ *v.t.* occidentaliser.

wet /wet/ *a.* **(wetter, wettest)** mouillé; (*damp, rainy*) humide. —*v.t.* (*p.t.* **wetted**) mouiller. —*n.* **the ~,** l'humidité *f.*; (*rain*) la pluie *f.* **~ blanket,** rabat-joie *m. invar.* **~ness** *n.* humidité *f.*

whack /wæk/ *n.* (*fam.*) grand coup *m.* —*v.t.* (*fam.*) taper sur.

whacked /wækt/ *a.* (*fam.*) claqué.

whacking /'wækɪŋ/ *a.* énorme.

whale /weɪl/ *n.* baleine *f.*

wham /wæm/ *int.* vlan.

wharf /wɔːf/ *n.* (*pl.* **wharfs**) (*for ships*) quai *m.*

what /wɒt/ *a.* (*in questions*) quel(le), quel(le)s. —*pron.* (*in questions*) qu'est-ce qui; (*object*) (qu'est-ce) que *or* qu'*; (*after prep.*) quoi; (*that which*) ce qui; (*object*) ce que, ce qu'*. —*int.* quoi, comment. **~ a fool**/*etc.*, quel idiot/*etc.* **~ about me/him**/*etc.***?**, et moi/lui/*etc.*? **~ about doing?,** si on faisait? **~ for?**, pourquoi? **~ is it?**, qu'est-ce que c'est? **~ you need,** ce dont vous avez besoin.

whatever /wɒt'evə(r)/ *a.* **~ book**/*etc.*, quel que soit le livre/ *etc.* —*pron.* (*no matter what*) quoi que, quoi qu'*; (*anything that*) tout ce qui; (*object*) tout ce que *or* qu'*. **nothing ~,** rien du tout.

whatsoever /wɒtsəʊ'evər/ *a.* & *pron.* = **whatever.**

wheat /wiːt/ *n.* blé *m.*, froment *m.*

wheedle /'wiːdl/ *v.t.* cajoler.

wheel /wiːl/ *n.* roue *f.* —*v.t.* pousser. —*v.i.* tourner. **at the ~,** (*of vehicle*) au volant; (*helm*) au gouvernail. **~ and deal,** (*Amer.*) faire des combines.

wheelbarrow /'wiːlbærəʊ/ *n.* brouette *f.*

wheelchair /'wiːltʃeə(r)/ *n.* fauteuil roulant *m.*

wheeze /wiːz/ *v.i.* siffler (en respirant). —*n.* sifflement *m.*

when /wen/ *adv.* & *pron.* quand. —*conj.* quand, lorsque. **the day/ moment ~,** le jour/moment où.

whenever /wen'evə(r)/ *conj.* & *adv.* (*at whatever time*) quand; (*every time that*) chaque fois que.

where /weə(r)/ *adv., conj.,* & *pron.* où; (*whereas*) alors que; (*the place that*) là où. **~abouts** *adv.* (à peu près) où; *n.* **s.o.'s ~abouts,** l'endroit où se trouve qn. **~by** *adv.* par quoi. **~upon** *adv.* sur quoi.

whereas /weər'æz/ *conj.* alors que.

wherever /weər'evə(r)/ *conj.* & *adv.* où que; (*everywhere*) partout où; (*anywhere*) (là) où; (*emphatic where*) où donc.

whet /wet/ *v.t.* (*p.t.* **whetted**) (*appetite, desire*) aiguiser.

whether /'weðə(r)/ *conj.* si. **not know ~,** ne pas savoir si. **~ I go or not,** que j'aille ou non.

which /wɪtʃ/ *a.* (*in questions*) quel(le), quel(le)s. —*pron.* (*in questions*) lequel, laquelle, lesquel(le)s; (*the one or ones that*) celui (celle, ceux, celles) qui; (*object*) celui (celle, ceux, celles) que *or* qu'*; (*referring to whole sentence,* = *and that*) ce qui; (*object*) ce que, ce qu'*; (*after prep.*) lequel/*etc.* —*rel. pron.* qui; (*object*) que, qu'*. **the bird ~ flies,** l'oiseau qui vole. **the hat ~ he wears,** le chapeau qu'il porte. **~ one,** lequel/*etc.* **of ~, from ~,** duquel/*etc.* **to ~, at ~,** auquel/*etc.* **the book of ~,** le livre dont *or* duquel. **after ~,** après quoi.

whichever /wɪtʃ'evə(r)/ *a.* **~ book**/*etc.*, quel que soit le livre/ *etc.* que *or* qui. **take ~ book you wish,** prenez le livre que vous voulez. —*pron.* celui (celle, ceux, celles) qui *or* que.

whiff /wɪf/ *n.* (*puff*) bouffée *f.*

while /waɪl/ *n.* moment *m.* —*conj.* (*when*) pendant que; (*although*) bien que; (*as long as*) tant que. —*v.t.* ~ **away,** (*time*) passer.

whilst /waɪlst/ *conj.* = **while.**

whim /wɪm/ *n.* caprice *m.*

whimper /'wɪmpə(r)/ *v.i.* geindre, pleurnicher. —*n.* pleurnichement *m.*

whimsical /'wɪmzɪkl/ *a.* (*person*) capricieux; (*odd*) bizarre.

whine /waɪn/ *v.i.* gémir, se plaindre. —*n.* gémissement *m.*

whip /wɪp/ *n.* fouet *m.* —*v.t.* (*p.t.* **whipped**) fouetter; (*culin.*) fouetter, battre; (*seize*) enlever brusquement. —*v.i.* (*move*) aller en vitesse. ~**-round** *n.* (*fam.*) collecte *f.* ~ **out,** (*gun etc.*) sortir. ~ **up,** exciter; (*cause*) provoquer; (*meal: fam.*) préparer.

whirl /wɜːl/ *v.t./i.* (faire) tourbillonner. —*n.* tourbillon *m.*

whirlpool /'wɜːlpuːl/ *n.* (*in sea etc.*) tourbillon *m.*

whirlwind /'wɜːlwɪnd/ *n.* tourbillon (de vent) *m.*

whirr /wɜː(r)/ *v.i.* vrombir.

whisk /wɪsk/ *v.t.* (*snatch*) enlever *or* emmener brusquement; (*culin.*) fouetter. —*n.* (*culin.*) fouet *m.*; (*broom, brush*) petit balai *m.* ~ **away,** (*brush away*) chasser.

whisker /'wɪskə(r)/ *n.* poil *m.* ~**s,** (*man's*) barbe *f.*, moustache *f.*; (*sideboards*) favoris *m. pl.*

whisky /'wɪskɪ/ *n.* whisky *m.*

whisper /'wɪspə(r)/ *v.t./i.* chuchoter. —*n.* chuchotement *m.*; (*rumour: fig.*) rumeur *f.*, bruit *m.*

whistle /'wɪsl/ *n.* sifflement *m.*; (*instrument*) sifflet *m.* —*v.t./i.* siffler. ~ **at** *or* **for,** siffler.

Whit /wɪt/ *a.* ~ **Sunday,** dimanche de Pentecôte *m.*

white /waɪt/ *a.* (-er, -est) blanc. —*n.* blanc *m.*; (*person*) blanc(he) *m.* (*f.*). ~ **coffee,** café au lait *m.* ~**-collar worker,** employé(e) de bureau *m.* (*f.*). ~ **elephant,** objet, projet, *etc.* inutile *m.* ~ **lie,** pieux mensonge *m.* **W**~ **Paper,** livre blanc *m.* ~**ness** *n.* blancheur *f.*

whiten /'waɪtn/ *v.t./i.* blanchir.

whitewash /'waɪtwɒʃ/ *n.* blanc de chaux *m.* —*v.t.* blanchir à la chaux; (*person: fig.*) blanchir.

whiting /'waɪtɪŋ/ *n. invar.* (*fish*) merlan *m.*

Whitsun /'wɪtsn/ *n.* la Pentecôte *f.*

whittle /wɪtl/ *v.t.* ~ **down,** tailler (au couteau); (*fig.*) réduire.

whiz /wɪz/ *v.i.* (*p.t.* **whizzed**) (*through air*) fendre l'air; (*hiss*) siffler; (*rush*) aller à toute vitesse. ~**-kid** *n.* jeune prodige *m.*

who /huː/ *pron.* qui.

whodunit /huː'dʌnɪt/ *n.* (*story: fam.*) roman policier *m.*

whoever /huː'evə(r)/ *pron.* (*no matter who*) qui que ce soit qui *or* que; (*the one who*) quiconque.

whole /həʊl/ *a.* entier; (*intact*) intact. **the** ~ **house**/*etc.*, toute la maison/*etc.* —*n.* totalité *f.*; (*unit*) tout *m.* **on the** ~**,** dans l'ensemble. ~**-hearted** *a.*, ~**-heartedly** *adv.* sans réserve.

wholemeal /'həʊlmiːl/ *a.* ~ **bread,** pain complet *m.*

wholesale /'həʊlseɪl/ *n.* gros *m.* —*a.* (*firm*) de gros; (*fig.*) systématique. —*adv.* (*in large quantities*) en gros; (*buy or sell one item*) au prix de gros; (*fig.*) en masse. ~**r** /-ə(r)/ *n.* grossiste *m./f.*

wholesome /'həʊlsəm/ *a.* sain.

wholewheat /'həʊlhwiːt/ *a.* (*Amer.*) = **wholemeal.**

wholly /'həʊlɪ/ *adv.* entièrement.

whom /huːm/ *pron.* (*that*) que, qu'*; (*after prep. & in questions*) qui. **of** ~**,** dont. **with** ~**,** avec qui.

whooping cough /'huːpɪŋkɒf/ *n.* coqueluche *f.*

whopping /'wɒpɪŋ/ *a.* (*sl.*) énorme.

whore /hɔː(r)/ *n.* putain *f.*

whose /huːz/ *pron.* & *a.* à qui, de

qui. **~ hat is this?, ~ is this hat?,** à qui est ce chapeau? **~ son are you?,** de qui êtes-vous le fils? **the man ~ hat I see,** l'homme dont *or* de qui je vois le chapeau.

why /waɪ/ *adv.* pourquoi. *—int.* eh bien, ma parole, tiens.

wick /wɪk/ *n.* (*of lamp etc.*) mèche *f.*

wicked /'wɪkɪd/ *a.* méchant, mauvais, vilain. **~ly** *adv.* méchamment. **~ness** *n.* méchanceté *f.*

wicker /'wɪkə(r)/ *n.* osier *m.* **~work** *n.* vannerie *f.*

wicket /'wɪkɪt/ *n.* guichet *m.*

wide /waɪd/ *a.* (**-er, -est**) large; (*ocean etc.*) vaste. *—adv.* (*fall etc.*) loin du but. **open ~,** ouvrir tout grand. **~ awake,** éveillé. **~ly** *adv.* (*spread, space*) largement; (*travel*) beaucoup; (*generally*) généralement; (*extremely*) extrêmement.

widen /'waɪdn/ *v.t./i.* (s')élargir.

widespread /'waɪdspred/ *a.* très répandu.

widow /'wɪdəʊ/ *n.* veuve *f.* **~ed** *a.* (*man*) veuf; (*woman*) veuve. **be ~ed,** (*become widower or widow*) devenir veuf *or* veuve. **~er** *n.* veuf *m.*

width /wɪdθ/ *n.* largeur *f.*

wield /wiːld/ *v.t.* (*axe etc.*) manier; (*power: fig.*) exercer.

wife /waɪf/ *n.* (*pl.* **wives**) femme *f.*, épouse *f.* **~ly** *a.* d'épouse.

wig /wɪg/ *n.* perruque *f.*

wiggle /'wɪgl/ *v.t./i.* remuer; (*hips*) tortiller; (*of worm*) se tortiller.

wild /waɪld/ *a.* (**-er, -est**) sauvage; (*sea, enthusiasm*) déchaîné; (*mad*) fou; (*angry*) furieux. *—adv.* (*grow*) à l'état sauvage. **~s** *n. pl.* régions sauvages *f. pl.* **run ~,** (*free*) courir en liberté. **~-goose chase,** fausse piste *f.* **~ly** *adv.* violemment; (*madly*) follement.

wildcat /'waɪldkæt/ *a.* **~ strike,** grève sauvage *f.*

wilderness /'wɪldənɪs/ *n.* désert *m.*

wildlife /'waɪldlaɪf/ *n.* faune *f.*

wile /waɪl/ *n.* ruse *f.*, artifice *m.*

wilful /'wɪlfl/ *a.* (*intentional, obstinate*) volontaire.

will[1] /wɪl/ *v. aux.* **he ~ do/you ~ sing/***etc.*, (*future tense*) il fera/tu chanteras/*etc.* **~ you have a coffee?,** voulez-vous prendre un café?

will[2] /wɪl/ *n.* volonté *f.*; (*document*) testament *m.* *—v.t.* (*wish*) vouloir. **at ~,** quand *or* comme on veut. **~-power** *n.* volonté *f.* **~ o.s. to do,** faire un effort de volonté pour faire.

willing /'wɪlɪŋ/ *a.* (*help, offer*) spontané; (*helper*) bien disposé. **~ to,** disposé à. **~ly** *adv.* (*with pleasure*) volontiers; (*not forced*) volontairement. **~ness** *n.* empressement *m.* (**to do,** à faire); (*goodwill*) bonne volonté *f.*

willow /'wɪləʊ/ *n.* saule *m.*

willowy /'wɪləʊɪ/ *a.* (*person*) svelte.

willy-nilly /wɪlɪ'nɪlɪ/ *adv.* bon gré mal gré.

wilt /wɪlt/ *v.i.* (*plant etc.*) dépérir.

wily /'waɪlɪ/ *a.* (**-ier, -iest**) rusé.

win /wɪn/ *v.t./i.* (*p.t.* **won,** *pres. p.* **winning**) gagner; (*victory, prize*) remporter; (*fame, fortune*) acquérir, trouver. *—n.* victoire *f.*

winc|e /wɪns/ *v.i.* se crisper, tressaillir. **without ~ing,** sans broncher.

winch /wɪntʃ/ *n.* treuil *m.* *—v.t.* hisser au treuil.

wind[1] /wɪnd/ *n.* vent *m.*; (*breath*) souffle *m.* **get ~ of,** avoir vent de. **in the ~,** dans l'air. **~-cheater,** (*Amer.*) **~breaker** *ns.* blouson *m.* **~ instrument,** instrument à vent *m.* **~-swept** *a.* balayé par les vents.

wind[2] /waɪnd/ *v.t./i.* (*p.t.* **wound**) (s')enrouler; (*of path, river*) serpenter. **~ (up),** (*clock etc.*) remonter. **~ up,** (*end*) (se) terminer. **~ing** *a.* (*path*) sinueux.

windfall /ˈwɪndfɔːl/ *n.* fruit tombé *m.*; (*money*: *fig.*) aubaine *f.*
windmill /ˈwɪndmɪl/ *n.* moulin à vent *m.*
window /ˈwɪndəʊ/ *n.* fenêtre *f.*; (*in vehicle, train*) vitre *f.*; (*in shop*) vitrine *f.*; (*counter*) guichet *m.* **~-box** *n.* jardinière *f.* **~-dresser** *n.* étalagiste *m.*/*f.* **~-ledge** *n.* rebord de (la) fenêtre *m.* **~-shopping** *n.* lèche-vitrines *m.* **~-sill** *n.* (*inside*) appui de (la) fenêtre *m.*; (*outside*) rebord de (la) fenêtre *m.*
windpipe /ˈwɪndpaɪp/ *n.* trachée *f.*
windscreen /ˈwɪndskriːn/ *n.* pare-brise *m. invar.*
windshield /ˈwɪndʃiːld/ *n.* (*Amer.*) pare-brise *m. invar.*
windy /ˈwɪndɪ/ *a.* (**-ier, -iest**) venteux. **it is ~,** il y a du vent.
wine /waɪn/ *n.* vin *m.* **~-cellar** *n.* cave (à vin) *f.* **~-grower** *n.* viticulteur *m.* **~-growing** *n.* viticulture *f.*; *a.* viticole. **~ list,** carte des vins *f.* **~-tasting** *n.* dégustation de vins *f.* **~ waiter,** sommelier *m.*
wineglass /ˈwaɪnglɑːs/ *n.* verre à vin *m.*
wing /wɪŋ/ *n.* aile *f.* **~s,** (*theatre*) coulisses *f. pl.* **under one's ~,** sous son aile. **~ed** *a.* ailé. **~er** *n.* (*sport*) ailier *m.*
wink /wɪŋk/ *v.i.* faire un clin d'œil; (*light, star*) clignoter. —*n.* clin d'œil *m.*; clignotement *m.*
winner /ˈwɪnə(r)/ *n.* (*of game*) gagnant(e) *m.* (*f.*); (*of fight*) vainqueur *m.*
winning /ˈwɪnɪŋ/ *see* **win.** —*a.* (*number, horse*) gagnant; (*team*) victorieux; (*smile*) engageant. **~s** *n. pl.* gains *m. pl.*
wint|er /ˈwɪntə(r)/ *n.* hiver *m.* —*v.i.* hiverner. **~ry** *a.* hivernal.
wipe /waɪp/ *v.t.* essuyer. —*v.i.* **~ up,** essuyer la vaisselle. —*n.* coup de torchon *or* d'éponge *m.* **~ off** *or* **out,** essuyer. **~ out,** (*destroy*) anéantir; (*remove*) effacer. **~r** /-ə(r)/ *n.* (*for windscreen*: *auto.*) essuie-glace *m. invar.*
wir|e /ˈwaɪə(r)/ *n.* fil *m.* **~e netting,** grillage *m.* **~ing** *n.* (*electr.*) installation électrique *f.*
wireless /ˈwaɪəlɪs/ *n.* radio *f.*
wiry /ˈwaɪərɪ/ *a.* (**-ier, -iest**) (*person*) nerveux et maigre.
wisdom /ˈwɪzdəm/ *n.* sagesse *f.*
wise /waɪz/ *a.* (**-er, -est**) prudent, sage; (*look*) averti. **~ guy,** (*fam.*) petit malin *m.* **~ man,** sage *m.* **~ly** *adv.* prudemment.
wisecrack /ˈwaɪzkræk/ *n.* (*fam.*) mot d'esprit *m.*, astuce *f.*
wish /wɪʃ/ *n.* (*specific*) souhait *m.*, vœu *m.*; (*general*) désir *m.* —*v.t.* souhaiter, vouloir, désirer (**to do,** faire); (*bid*) souhaiter. —*v.i.* **~ for,** souhaiter. **best ~es,** (*in letter*) amitiés *f. pl.*; (*on greeting card*) meilleurs vœux *m. pl.*
wishful /ˈwɪʃfl/ *a.* **it is ~ thinking,** on se fait des illusions.
wishy-washy /ˈwɪʃɪwɒʃɪ/ *a.* fade.
wisp /wɪsp/ *n.* (*of smoke*) volute *f.*
wistful /ˈwɪstfl/ *a.* mélancolique.
wit /wɪt/ *n.* intelligence *f.*; (*humour*) esprit *m.*; (*person*) homme d'esprit *m.*, femme d'esprit *f.* **be at one's ~'s** *or* **~s' end,** ne plus savoir que faire.
witch /wɪtʃ/ *n.* sorcière *f.* **~craft** *n.* sorcellerie *f.*
with /wɪð/ *prep.* avec; (*having*) à; (*because of*) de; (*at house of*) chez. **the man ~ the beard,** l'homme à la barbe. **fill**/*etc.* **~,** remplir/*etc.* de. **pleased/shaking**/*etc.* **~,** content/frémissant/*etc.* de. **~ it,** (*fam.*) dans le vent.
withdraw /wɪðˈdrɔː/ *v.t.*/*i.* (*p.t.* **withdrew,** *p.p.* **withdrawn**) (se) retirer. **~al** *n.* retrait *m.* **~n** *a.* (*person*) renfermé.
wither /ˈwɪðə(r)/ *v.t.*/*i.* (se) flétrir. **~ed** *a.* (*person*) desséché.
withhold /wɪðˈhəʊld/ *v.t.* (*p.t.* **withheld**) refuser (de donner);

(*retain*) retenir; (*conceal, not tell*) cacher (**from,** à).
within /wɪ'ðɪn/ *prep. & adv.* à l'intérieur (de); (*in distances*) à moins de. **~ a month,** (*before*) avant un mois. **~ sight,** en vue.
without /wɪ'ðaʊt/ *prep.* sans.
withstand /wɪð'stænd/ *v.t.* (*p.t.* **withstood**) résister à.
witness /'wɪtnɪs/ *n.* témoin *m.*; (*evidence*) témoignage *m.* —*v.t.* être le témoin de, voir; (*document*) signer. **bear ~ to,** témoigner de.
witticism /'wɪtɪsɪzəm/ *n.* bon mot *m.*
witt|y /'wɪtɪ/ *a.* (**-ier, -iest**) spirituel. **~iness** *n.* esprit *m.*
wives /waɪvz/ *see* **wife.**
wizard /'wɪzəd/ *n.* magicien *m.*; (*genius*: *fig.*) génie *m.*
wizened /'wɪznd/ *a.* ratatiné.
wobbl|e /'wɒbl/ *v.i.* (*of jelly, voice, hand*) trembler; (*stagger*) chanceler; (*of table, chair*) branler. **~y** *a.* tremblant; branlant.
woe /wəʊ/ *n.* malheur *m.*
woke, woken /wəʊk, 'wəʊkən/ *see* **wake**[1].
wolf /wʊlf/ *n.* (*pl.* **wolves**) loup *m.* —*v.t.* (*food*) engloutir. **cry ~,** crier au loup. **~-whistle** *n.* sifflement admiratif *m.*
woman /'wʊmən/ *n.* (*pl.* **women**) femme *f.* **~ doctor,** femme médecin *f.* **~ driver,** femme au volant *f.* **~ friend,** amie *f.* **~hood** *n.* féminité *f.* **~ly** *a.* féminin.
womanize /'wʊmənaɪz/ *v.i.* courir le jupon *or* les femmes.
womb /wu:m/ *n.* utérus *m.*
women /'wɪmɪn/ *see* **woman.**
won /wʌn/ *see* **win.**
wonder /'wʌndə(r)/ *n.* émerveillement *m.*; (*thing*) merveille *f.* —*v.t.* se demander (**if,** si). —*v.i.* s'étonner (**at,** de); (*reflect*) songer (**about,** à). **it is no ~,** ce *or* il n'est pas étonnant (**that,** que).
wonderful /'wʌndəfl/ *a.* merveilleux. **~ly** *adv.* merveilleusement; (*work, do, etc.*) à merveille.
won't /wəʊnt/ = **will not.**
woo /wu:/ *v.t.* (*woman*) faire la cour à; (*please*) chercher à plaire à.
wood /wʊd/ *n.* bois *m.* **~ed** *a.* boisé. **~en** *a.* en *or* de bois; (*stiff*: *fig.*) raide, comme du bois.
woodcut /'wʊdkʌt/ *n.* gravure sur bois *f.*
woodland /'wʊdlənd/ *n.* région boisée *f.*, bois *m. pl.*
woodpecker /'wʊdpekə(r)/ *n.* (*bird*) pic *m.*, pivert *m.*
woodwind /'wʊdwɪnd/ *n.* (*mus.*) bois *m. pl.*
woodwork /'wʊdwɜ:k/ *n.* (*craft, objects*) menuiserie *f.*
woodworm /'wʊdwɜ:m/ *n.* (*larvae*) vers (de bois) *m. pl.*
woody /'wʊdɪ/ *a.* (*wooded*) boisé; (*like wood*) ligneux.
wool /wʊl/ *n.* laine *f.* **~len** *a.* de laine. **~lens** *n. pl.* lainages *m. pl.* **~ly** *a.* laineux; (*vague*) nébuleux; *n.* (*garment*: *fam.*) lainage *m.*
word /wɜ:d/ *n.* mot *m.*; (*spoken*) parole *f.*, mot *m.*; (*promise*) parole *f.*; (*news*) nouvelles *f. pl.* —*v.t.* rédiger. **by ~ of mouth,** de vive voix. **have a ~ with,** parler à. **in other ~s,** autrement dit. **~ processor,** machine de traitement de texte *f.* **~ing** *n.* termes *m. pl.*
wordy /'wɜ:dɪ/ *a.* verbeux.
wore /wɔ:(r)/ *see* **wear.**
work /wɜ:k/ *n.* travail *m.*; (*product, book, etc.*) œuvre *f.*, ouvrage *m.*; (*building etc. work*) travaux *m. pl.* **~s,** (*techn.*) mécanisme *m.*; (*factory*) usine *f.* —*v.t./i.* (*of person*) travailler; (*shape, hammer, etc.*) travailler; (*techn.*) (faire) fonctionner, (faire) marcher; (*land, mine*) exploiter; (*of drug etc.*) agir. **~ s.o.,** (*make work*) faire travailler qn. **~ in,** (s')introduire. **~ off,** (*get rid of*) se débarrasser de. **~ out** *v.t.* (*solve*)

résoudre; (*calculate*) calculer; (*elaborate*) élaborer; *v.i.* (*succeed*) marcher; (*sport*) s'entraîner. **~-to-rule** *n.* grève du zèle *f.* **~ up** *v.t.* développer; *v.i.* (*to climax*) monter vers. **~ed up,** (*person*) énervé.

workable /'wɜːkəbl/ *a.* réalisable.

workaholic /wɜːkə'hɒlɪk/ *n.* (*fam.*) bourreau de travail *m.*

worker /'wɜːkə(r)/ *n.* travailleu|r, -se *m., f.*; (*manual*) ouvr|ier, -ière *m., f.*

working /'wɜːkɪŋ/ *a.* (*day, lunch, etc.*) de travail. **~s** *n. pl.* mécanisme *m.* **~ class,** classe ouvrière *f.* **~-class** *a.* ouvrier. **in ~ order,** en état de marche.

workman /'wɜːkmən/ *n.* (*pl.* **-men**) ouvrier *m.* **~ship** *n.* maîtrise *f.*

workshop /'wɜːkʃɒp/ *n.* atelier *m.*

world /wɜːld/ *n.* monde *m.* —*a.* (*power etc.*) mondial; (*record etc.*) du monde. **a ~ of,** énormément de. **~-wide** *a.* universel.

worldly /'wɜːldlɪ/ *a.* de ce monde, terrestre. **~-wise** *a.* qui a l'expérience du monde.

worm /wɜːm/ *n.* ver *m.* —*v.t.* **~ one's way into,** s'insinuer dans. **~-eaten** *a.* (*wood*) vermoulu; (*fruit*) véreux.

worn /wɔːn/ *see* **wear.** —*a.* usé. **~-out** *a.* (*thing*) complètement usé; (*person*) épuisé.

worr|y /'wʌrɪ/ *v.t./i.* (s')inquiéter. —*n.* souci *m.* **~ied** *a.* inquiet. **~ier** *n.* inqu|iet, -iète *m., f.*

worse /wɜːs/ *a.* pire, plus mauvais. —*adv.* plus mal. —*n.* pire *m.*

worsen /'wɜːsn/ *v.t./i.* empirer.

worship /'wɜːʃɪp/ *n.* (*adoration*) culte *m.* —*v.t.* (*p.t.* **worshipped**) adorer. —*v.i.* faire ses dévotions. **~per** *n.* (*in church*) fidèle *m./f.*

worst /wɜːst/ *a.* pire, plus mauvais. —*adv.* (**the**) **~,** (*sing etc.*) le plus mal. —*n.* **the ~ (one),** (*person, object*) le *or* la pire. **the ~ (thing),** le pire (**that,** que). **get the ~ of it,** (*be defeated*) avoir le dessous.

worth /wɜːθ/ *a.* **be ~,** valoir. **it is ~ waiting**/*etc.*, ça vaut la peine d'attendre/*etc.* —*n.* valeur *f.* **ten pence ~ of,** (pour) dix pence de. **it is ~ (one's) while,** ça (en) vaut la peine. **~less** *a.* qui ne vaut rien.

worthwhile /wɜːθ'waɪl/ *a.* qui (en) vaut la peine.

worthy /'wɜːðɪ/ *a.* (**-ier, -iest**) digne (**of,** de); (*laudable*) louable. —*n.* (*person*) notable *m.*

would /wʊd, *unstressed* wəd/ *v. aux.* **he ~ do**/**you ~ sing**/*etc.*, (*conditional tense*) il ferait/tu chanterais/*etc.* **he ~ have done,** il aurait fait. **I ~ come every day,** (*used to*) je venais chaque jour. **~ you come here?,** voulez-vous venir ici? **~-be** *a.* soi-disant.

wound[1] /wuːnd/ *n.* blessure *f.* —*v.t.* blesser. **the ~ed,** les blessés *m. pl.*

wound[2] /waʊnd/ *see* **wind**[2].

wove, woven /wəʊv, 'wəʊvn/ *see* **weave.**

wow /waʊ/ *int.* mince (alors).

wrangle /'ræŋgl/ *v.i.* se disputer. —*n.* dispute *f.*

wrap /ræp/ *v.t.* (*p.t.* **wrapped**). **~ (up),** envelopper. —*v.i.* **~ up,** (*dress warmly*) se couvrir. —*n.* châle *m.* **~ped up in,** (*engrossed*) absorbé par. **~per** *n.* (*of book*) jaquette *f.*; (*of sweet*) papier *m.* **~ping** *n.* emballage *m.*

wrath /rɒθ/ *n.* courroux *m.*

wreak /riːk/ *v.t.* **~ havoc,** (*of storm etc.*) faire des ravages.

wreath /riːθ/ *n.* (*pl.* **-s** /-ðz/) (*of flowers, leaves*) couronne *f.*

wreck /rek/ *n.* (*sinking*) naufrage *m.*; (*ship, remains, person*) épave *f.*; (*vehicle*) voiture accidentée *or* délabrée *f.* —*v.t.* détruire; (*ship*) provoquer le naufrage de. **~age** *n.* (*pieces*) débris *m. pl.*

wren /ren/ *n.* roitelet *m.*

wrench /rentʃ/ *v.t.* (*pull*) tirer sur;

(*twist*) tordre; (*snatch*) arracher (**from,** à). —*n.* (*tool*) clé *f.*
wrest /rest/ *v.t.* arracher (**from,** à).
wrestl|e /'resl/ *v.i.* lutter, se débattre (**with,** contre). **~er** *n.* lutteu|r, -se *m., f.*; catcheu|r, -se *m., f.* **~ing** *n.* lutte *f.* (**all-in**) **~ing,** catch *m.*
wretch /retʃ/ *n.* malheureu|x, -se *m., f.*; (*rascal*) misérable *m./f.*
wretched /'retʃɪd/ *a.* (*pitiful, poor*) misérable; (*bad*) affreux.
wriggle /'rɪgl/ *v.t./i.* (se) tortiller.
wring /rɪŋ/ *v.t.* (*p.t.* **wrung**) (*twist*) tordre; (*clothes*) essorer. **~ out of,** (*obtain from*) arracher à. **~ing wet,** trempé (jusqu'aux os).
wringer /'rɪŋə(r)/ *n.* essoreuse *f.*
wrinkle /'rɪŋkl/ *n.* (*crease*) pli *m.*; (*on skin*) ride *f.* —*v.t./i.* (se) rider.
wrist /rɪst/ *n.* poignet *m.* **~-watch** *n.* montre-bracelet *f.*
writ /rɪt/ *n.* acte judiciaire *m.*
write /raɪt/ *v.t./i.* (*p.t.* **wrote,** *p.p.* **written,** écrire. **~ back,** répondre. **~ down,** noter. **~ off,** (*debt*) annuler; (*vehicle*) considérer bon pour la casse. **~-off** *n.* perte totale *f.* **~ up,** (*from notes*) rédiger. **~-up** *n.* compte rendu *m.*
writer /'raɪtə(r)/ *n.* auteur *m.*, écrivain *m.* **~ of,** auteur de.
writhe /raɪð/ *v.i.* se tordre.
writing /'raɪtɪŋ/ *n.* écriture *f.* **~(s),** (*works*) écrits *m. pl.* **in ~,** par écrit. **~-paper** *n.* papier à lettres *m.*
written /'rɪtn/ *see* **write.**
wrong /rɒŋ/ *a.* (*incorrect, mistaken*) faux, mauvais; (*unfair*) injuste; (*amiss*) qui ne va pas; (*clock*) pas à l'heure. **be ~,** (*person*) avoir tort (**to,** de); (*be mistaken*) se tromper. —*adv.* mal. —*n.* injustice *f.*; (*evil*) mal *m.* —*v.t.* faire (du) tort à. **be in the ~,** avoir tort. **go ~,** (*err*) se tromper; (*turn out badly*) mal tourner; (*vehicle*) tomber en panne. **it is ~ to,** (*morally*) c'est mal de. **what is ~ with you?,** qu'est-ce que vous avez? **~ly** *adv.* mal; (*blame etc.*) à tort.
wrongful /'rɒŋfl/ *a.* injustifié, injuste. **~ly** *adv.* à tort.
wrote /rəʊt/ *see* **write.**
wrought /rɔːt/ *a.* **~ iron,** fer forgé *m.*
wrung /rʌŋ/ *see* **wring.**
wry /raɪ/ *a.* (**wryer, wryest**) (*smile*) désabusé, forcé. **~ face,** grimace *f.*

X

xerox /'zɪərɒks/ *v.t.* photocopier.
Xmas /'krɪsməs/ *n.* Noël *m.*
X-ray /'eksreɪ/ *n.* rayon X *m.*; (*photograph*) radio(graphie) *f.* —*v.t.* radiographier.
xylophone /'zaɪləfəʊn/ *n.* xylophone *m.*

Y

yacht /jɒt/ *n.* yacht *m.* **~ing** *n.* yachting *m.*
yank /jæŋk/ *v.t.* tirer brusquement. —*n.* coup brusque *m.*
Yank /jæŋk/ *n.* (*fam.*) Américain(e) *m.* (*f.*), Amerloque *m./f.*
yap /jæp/ *v.i.* (*p.t.* **yapped**) japper.
yard[1] /jɑːd/ *n.* (*measure*) yard *m.* (= *0.9144 metre*).
yard[2] /jɑːd/ *n.* (*of house etc.*) cour *f.*; (*garden*: *Amer.*) jardin *m.*; (*for storage*) chantier *m.*, dépôt *m.*
yardstick /'jɑːdstɪk/ *n.* mesure *f.*
yarn /jɑːn/ *n.* (*thread*) fil *m.*; (*tale*: *fam.*) (longue) histoire *f.*
yawn /jɔːn/ *v.i.* bâiller. —*n.* bâillement *m.* **~ing** *a.* (*gaping*) béant.
year /jɪə(r)/ *n.* an *m.*, année *f.* **school/tax/***etc.* **~,** année scolaire/fiscale/*etc.* **be ten/***etc.*

~s old, avoir dix/*etc.* ans. **~-book** *n.* annuaire *m.* **~ly** *a.* annuel; *adv.* annuellement.
yearn /jɜːn/ *v.i.* avoir bien *or* très envie (**for, to,** de). **~ing** *n.* envie *f.*
yeast /jiːst/ *n.* levure *f.*
yell /jel/ *v.t./i.* hurler. —*n.* hurlement *m.*
yellow /ˈjeləʊ/ *a.* jaune; (*cowardly*: *fam.*) froussard. —*n.* jaune *m.*
yelp /jelp/ *n.* (*of dog etc.*) jappement *m.* —*v.i.* japper.
yen /jen/ *n.* (*desire*) grande envie *f.*
yes /jes/ *adv.* oui; (*as answer to negative question*) si. —*n.* oui *m. invar.*
yesterday /ˈjestədɪ/ *n.* & *adv.* hier (*m.*).
yet /jet/ *adv.* encore; (*already*) déjà. —*conj.* pourtant, néanmoins.
yew /juː/ *n.* (*tree, wood*) if *m.*
Yiddish /ˈjɪdɪʃ/ *n.* yiddish *m.*
yield /jiːld/ *v.t.* (*produce*) produire, rendre; (*profit*) rapporter; (*surrender*) céder. —*v.i.* (*give way*) céder. —*n.* rendement *m.*
yoga /ˈjəʊgə/ *n.* yoga *m.*
yoghurt /ˈjɒgət, *Amer.* ˈjəʊgərt/ *n.* yaourt *m.*
yoke /jəʊk/ *n.* joug *m.*
yokel /ˈjəʊkl/ *n.* rustre *m.*
yolk /jəʊk/ *n.* jaune (d'œuf) *m.*
yonder /ˈjɒndə(r)/ *adv.* là-bas.
you /juː/ *pron.* (*familiar form*) tu, *pl.* vous; (*polite form*) vous; (*object*) te, t'*, *pl.* vous; (*polite*) vous; (*after prep.*) toi, *pl.* vous; (*polite*) vous; (*indefinite*) on; (*object*) vous. (**to**) **~**, te, t'*, *pl.* vous; (*polite*) vous. **I know ~,** je te connais; je vous connais.
young /jʌŋ/ *a.* (**-er, -est**) jeune. —*n.* (*people*) jeunes *m. pl.*; (*of animals*) petits *m. pl.* **~er** *a.* (*brother etc.*) cadet. **~est** *a.* **my ~est brother,** le cadet de mes frères.
youngster /ˈjʌŋstə(r)/ *n.* jeune *m./f.*
your /jɔː(r)/ *a.* (*familiar form*) ton, ta, *pl.* tes; (*polite form, & familiar form pl.*) votre, *pl.* vos.
yours /jɔːz/ *poss. pron.* (*familiar form*) le tien, la tienne, les tien(ne)s; (*polite form, & familiar form pl.*) le *or* la vôtre, les vôtres.
yoursel|f /jɔːˈself/ *pron.* (*familiar form*) toi-même; (*polite form*) vous-même; (*reflexive & after prep.*) te, t'*; vous. **~ves** *pron. pl.* vous-mêmes; (*reflexive*) vous.
youth /juːθ/ *n.* (*pl.* **-s** /-ðz/) jeunesse *f.*; (*young man*) jeune *m.* **~ club,** centre de jeunes *m.* **~ hostel,** auberge de jeunesse *f.* **~ful** *a.* juvénile, jeune.
yo-yo /ˈjəʊjəʊ/ *n.* (*pl.* **-os**) (P.) yo-yo *m. invar.* (P.).
Yugoslav /ˈjuːgəslɑːv/ *a.* & *n.* Yougoslave (*m./f.*). **~ia** /-ˈslɑːvɪə/ *n.* Yougoslavie *f.*

Z

zany /ˈzeɪnɪ/ *a.* (**-ier, -iest**) farfelu.
zeal /ziːl/ *n.* zèle *m.*
zealous /ˈzeləs/ *a.* zélé. **~ly** *adv.* avec zèle.
zebra /ˈzebrə, ˈziːbrə/ *n.* zèbre *m.* **~ crossing,** passage pour piétons *m.*
zenith /ˈzenɪθ/ *n.* zénith *m.*
zero /ˈzɪərəʊ/ *n.* (*pl.* **-os**) zéro *m.* **~ hour,** l'heure H *f.*
zest /zest/ *n.* (*gusto*) entrain *m.*; (*spice*: *fig.*) piment *m.*; (*of orange or lemon peel*) zeste *m.*
zigzag /ˈzɪgzæg/ *n.* zigzag *m.* —*a.* & *adv.* en zigzag. —*v.i.* (*p.t.* **zigzagged**) zigzaguer.
zinc /zɪŋk/ *n.* zinc *m.*
Zionism /ˈzaɪənɪzəm/ *n.* sionisme *m.*
zip /zɪp/ *n.* (*vigour*) allant *m.* **~(-fastener),** fermeture éclair *f.* (P.). —*v.t.* (*p.t.* **zipped**) fermer

avec une fermeture éclair (P.). —*v.i.* aller à toute vitesse. **Z~ code,** (*Amer.*) code postal *m.*
zipper /'zɪpə(r)/ *n.* (*Amer.*) = **zip (-fastener).**
zither /'zɪðə(r)/ *n.* cithare *f.*
zodiac /'zəʊdɪæk/ *n.* zodiaque *m.*
zombie /'zɒmbɪ/ *n.* mort(e) vivant(e) *m.* (*f.*); (*fam.*) automate *m.*
zone /zəʊn/ *n.* zone *f.*
zoo /zuː/ *n.* zoo *m.*
zoolog|y /zəʊ'ɒlədʒɪ/ *n.* zoologie *f.* **~ical** /-ə'lɒdʒɪkl/ *a.* zoologique. **~ist** *n.* zoologiste *m.*/*f.*
zoom /zuːm/ *v.i.* (*rush*) se précipiter. **~ lens,** zoom *m.* **~ off** *or* **past,** filer (comme une flèche).
zucchini /zuː'kiːmɪ/ *n.* *invar.* (*Amer.*) courgette *f.*

French Verb Tables

Notes The conditional may be formed by substituting the following endings for those of the future: *ais* for *ai* and *as*, *ait* for *a*, *ions* for *ons*, *iez* for *ez*, *aient* for *ont*. The present participle is formed (unless otherwise indicated) by substituting *ant* for *ons* in the first person plural of the present tense (e.g. *finissant* and *donnant* may be derived from *finissons* and *donnons*). The imperative forms are (unless otherwise indicated) the same as the second persons singular and plural and the first person plural of the present tense. The second person singular does not take *s* after *e* or *a* (e.g. *donne*, *va*), except when followed by *y* or *en* (e.g. *vas-y*).

Regular verbs:

1. in ***-er*** (e.g. **donn|er**)

Present. ~e, ~es, ~e, ~ons, ~ez, ~ent.
Imperfect. ~ais, ~ais, ~ait, ~ions, ~iez, ~aient.
Past historic. ~ai, ~as, ~a, ~âmes, ~âtes, ~èrent.
Future. ~erai, ~eras, ~era, ~erons, ~erez, ~eront.
Present subjunctive. ~e, ~es, ~e, ~ions, ~iez, ~ent.
Past participle. ~é.

2. in ***-ir*** (e.g. **fin|ir**)

Pres. ~is, ~is, ~it, ~issons, ~issez, ~issent.
Impf. ~issais, ~issais, ~issait, ~issions, ~issiez, ~issaient.
Past hist. ~is, ~is, ~it, ~îmes, ~îtes, ~irent.
Fut. ~irai, ~iras, ~ira, ~irons, ~irez, ~iront.
Pres. sub. ~isse, ~isses, ~isse, ~issions, ~issiez, ~issent.
Past part. ~i.

3. in ***-re*** (e.g. **vend|re**)

Pres. ~s, ~s, ~, ~ons, ~ez, ~ent.
Impf. ~ais, ~ais, ~ait, ~ions, ~iez, ~aient.
Past hist. ~is, ~is, ~it, ~îmes, ~îtes, ~irent.
Fut. ~rai, ~ras, ~ra, ~rons, ~rez, ~ront.
Pres. sub. ~e, ~es, ~e, ~ions, ~iez, ~ent.
Past part. ~u.

Peculiarities of *-er* verbs:

In verbs in *-cer* (e.g. **commencer**) and *-ger* (e.g. **manger**), *c* becomes *ç* and *g* becomes *ge* before *a* and *o* (e.g. commença, commençons; mangea, mangeons).

In verbs in *-yer* (e.g. **nettoyer**), *y* becomes *i* before mute *e* (e.g. nettoie, nettoierai). Verbs in *-ayer* (e.g. **payer**) may retain *y* before mute *e* (e.g. paye or paie, payerai or paierai).

In verbs in *-eler* (e.g. **appeler**) and in *-eter* (e.g. **jeter**), *l* becomes *ll* and *t* becomes *tt* before a syllable containing mute *e* (e.g. appelle, appellerai; jette, jetterai). In the verbs **celer, ciseler, congeler, déceler, démanteler, écarteler, geler, marteler, modeler** and **peler**, and in the verbs **acheter, crocheter, fureter, haleter** and **racheter**, *e* becomes *è* before a syllable containing mute *e* (e.g. cèle, cèlerai; achète, achèterai).

In verbs in which the penultimate syllable contains mute *e* (e.g. **semer**) or *é* (e.g. **révéler**), both *e* and *é* become *è* before a syllable containing mute *e* (e.g. sème, sèmerai; révèle). However, in the verbs in which the penultimate syllable contains *é*, *é* remains unchanged in the future and conditional (e.g. révélerai).

Irregular verbs:

At least the first persons singular and plural of the present tense are shown. Forms not listed may be derived from these. Though the base form of the imperfect, future, and present subjunctive may be irregular, the endings of these tenses are as shown in the regular verb section. Only the first person singular of these tenses is given in most cases. The base form of the past historic may also be irregular but the endings of this tense shown in the verbs below fall (with few exceptions) into the 'u' category, listed under **être** and **avoir**, and the 'i' category shown under **finir** and **vendre** in the regular verb section. Only the first person singular of the past historic is listed in most cases. Additional forms appear throughout when these cannot be derived from the forms given or when it is considered helpful to list them. Only those irregular verbs judged to be the most useful are shown in the tables.

abattre	*as* BATTRE.
accueillir	*as* CUEILLIR.
acquérir	• *Pres.* acquiers, acquérons, acquièrent. • *Impf.* acquérais. • *Past hist.* acquis. • *Fut.* acquerrai. • *Pres. sub.* acquière. • *Past part.* acquis.
admettre	*as* METTRE.
aller	• *Pres.* vais, vas, va, allons, allez, vont. • *Fut.* irai. • *Pres. sub.* aille, allions.
apercevoir	*as* RECEVOIR.
apparaître	*as* CONNAÎTRE.

appartenir *as* TENIR.

apprendre *as* PRENDRE.

asseoir • *Pres.* assieds, asseyons, asseyent. • *Impf.* asseyais. • *Past hist.* assis. • *Fut.* assiérai. • *Pres. sub.* asseye. • *Past part.* assis.

atteindre • *Pres.* atteins, atteignons, atteignent. • *Impf.* atteignais. • *Past hist.* atteignis. • *Fut.* atteindrai. • *Pres. sub.* atteigne. • *Past part.* atteint.

avoir • *Pres.* ai, as, a, avons, avez, ont. • *Impf.* avais. • *Past hist.* eus, eut, eûmes, eûtes, eurent. • *Fut.* aurai. • *Pres. sub.* aie, aies, ait, ayons, ayez, aient. • *Pres. part.* ayant. • *Past part.* eu. • *Imp.* aie, ayons, ayez.

battre • *Pres.* bats, bat, battons, battez, battent.

boire • *Pres.* bois, buvons, boivent. • *Impf.* buvais. • *Past hist.* bus. • *Pres. sub.* boive, buvions. • *Past part.* bu.

bouillir • *Pres.* bous, bouillons, bouillent. • *Impf.* bouillais. • *Pres. sub.* bouille.

combattre *as* BATTRE.

commettre *as* METTRE.

comprendre *as* PRENDRE.

concevoir *as* RECEVOIR.

conclure • *Pres.* conclus, concluons, concluent. • *Past hist.* conclus. • *Past part.* conclu.

conduire • *Pres.* conduis, conduisons, conduisent. • *Impf.* conduisais. • *Past hist.* conduisis. • *Pres. sub.* conduise. • *Past part.* conduit.

connaître • *Pres.* connais, connaît, connaissons. • *Impf.* connaissais. • *Past hist.* connus. • *Pres. sub.* connaisse. • *Past part.* connu.

construire *as* CONDUIRE.

contenir *as* TENIR.

contraindre *as* ATTEINDRE (except *ai* replaces *ei*).

contredire *as* DIRE, except • *Pres.* vous contredisez.

convaincre *as* VAINCRE.

convenir *as* TENIR.

corrompre *as* ROMPRE.

coudre • *Pres.* couds, cousons, cousent. • *Impf.* cousais. • *Past hist.* cousis. • *Pres. sub.* couse. • *Past part.* cousu.

courir • *Pres.* cours, courons, courent. • *Impf.* courais. • *Past hist.* courus. • *Fut.* courrai. • *Pres. sub.* coure. • *Past part.* couru.

couvrir	• *Pres.* couvre, couvrons. • *Impf.* couvrais. • *Pres. sub.* couvre. • *Past part.* couvert.
craindre	*as* ATTEINDRE (except *ai* replaces *ei*).
croire	• *Pres.* crois, croit, croyons, croyez, croient. • *Impf.* croyais. • *Past hist.* crus. • *Pres. sub.* croie, croyions. • *Past part.* cru.
croître	• *Pres.* crois, croît, croissons. • *Impf.* croissais. • *Past hist.* crûs. • *Pres. sub.* croisse. • *Past part.* crû, crue.
cueillir	• *Pres.* cueille, cueillons. • *Impf.* cueillais. • *Fut.* cueillerai. • *Pres. sub.* cueille.
débattre	*as* BATTRE.
décevoir	*as* RECEVOIR.
découvrir	*as* COUVRIR.
décrire	*as* ÉCRIRE.
déduire	*as* CONDUIRE.
défaire	*as* FAIRE.
détenir	*as* TENIR.
détruire	*as* CONDUIRE.
devenir	*as* TENIR.
devoir	• *Pres.* dois, devons, doivent. • *Impf.* devais. • *Past hist.* dus. • *Fut.* devrai. • *Pres. sub.* doive. • *Past part.* dû, due.
dire	• *Pres.* dis, dit, disons, dites, disent. • *Impf.* disais. • *Past hist.* dis. • *Past part.* dit.
disparaître	*as* CONNAÎTRE.
dissoudre	• *Pres.* dissous, dissolvons. • *Impf.* dissolvais. • *Pres. sub.* dissolve. • *Past part.* dissous, dissoute.
distraire	*as* EXTRAIRE.
dormir	• *Pres.* dors, dormons. • *Impf.* dormais. • *Pres. sub.* dorme.
écrire	• *Pres.* écris, écrivons. • *Impf.* écrivais. • *Past hist.* écrivis. • *Pres. sub.* écrive. • *Past part.* écrit.
élire	*as* LIRE.
émettre	*as* METTRE.
s'enfuir	*as* FUIR.
entreprendre	*as* PRENDRE.
entretenir	*as* TENIR.
envoyer	• *Fut.* enverrai.
éteindre	*as* ATTEINDRE.
être	• *Pres.* suis, es, est, sommes, êtes, sont. • *Impf.* étais. • *Past hist.* fus, fut, fûmes, fûtes, furent.

• *Fut.* serai. • *Pres. sub.* sois, soit, soyons, soyez, soient. • *Pres. part.* étant. • *Past part.* été. • *Imp.* sois, soyons, soyez.

exclure *as* CONCLURE.

extraire • *Pres.* extrais, extrayons. • *Impf.* extrayais. • *Pres. sub.* extraie. • *Past part.* extrait.

faire • *Pres.* fais, fait, faisons, faites, font. • *Impf.* faisais. • *Past hist.* fis. • *Fut.* ferai. • *Pres. sub.* fasse. • *Past part.* fait.

falloir (impersonal) • *Pres.* faut. • *Impf.* fallait. • *Past hist.* fallut. • *Fut.* faudra. • *Pres. sub.* faille. • *Past part.* fallu.

feindre *as* ATTEINDRE.

fuir • *Pres.* fuis, fuyons, fuient. • *Impf.* fuyais. • *Past hist.* fuis. • *Pres. sub.* fuie. • *Past part.* fui.

inscrire *as* ÉCRIRE.

instruire *as* CONDUIRE.

interdire *as* DIRE, except • *Pres.* vous interdisez.

interrompre *as* ROMPRE.

intervenir *as* TENIR.

introduire *as* CONDUIRE.

joindre *as* ATTEINDRE (except *oi* replaces *ei*).

lire • *Pres.* lis, lit, lisons, lisez, lisent. • *Impf.* lisais. • *Past hist.* lus. • *Pres. sub.* lise. • *Past part.* lu.

luire • *Pres.* luis, luisons. • *Impf.* luisais. • *Past hist.* luisis. • *Pres. sub.* luise. • *Past part.* lui.

maintenir *as* TENIR.

maudire • *Pres.* maudis, maudissons. • *Impf.* maudissais. • *Past hist.* maudis. • *Pres. sub.* maudisse. • *Past part.* maudit.

mentir *as* SORTIR (except *en* replaces *or*).

mettre • *Pres.* mets, met, mettons, mettez, mettent. • *Past hist.* mis. • *Past part.* mis.

mourir • *Pres.* meurs, mourons, meurent. • *Impf.* mourais. • *Past hist.* mourus. • *Fut.* mourrai. • *Pres. sub.* meure, mourions. • *Past part.* mort.

mouvoir • *Pres.* meus, mouvons, meuvent. • *Impf.* mouvais. • *Fut.* mouvrai. • *Pres. sub.* meuve, mouvions. • *Past part.* mû, mue.

naître • *Pres.* nais, naît, naissons. • *Impf.* naissais. • *Past hist.* naquis. • *Pres. sub.* naisse. • *Past part.* né.

nuire	*as* LUIRE.
obtenir	*as* TENIR.
offrir, ouvrir	*as* COUVRIR.
omettre	*as* METTRE.
paraître	*as* CONNAÎTRE.
parcourir	*as* COURIR.
partir	*as* SORTIR (except *ar* replaces *or*).
parvenir	*as* TENIR.
peindre	*as* ATTEINDRE.
percevoir	*as* RECEVOIR.
permettre	*as* METTRE.
plaindre	*as* ATTEINDRE (except *ai* replaces *ei*).
plaire	• *Pres.* plais, plaît, plaisons. • *Impf.* plaisais. • *Past hist.* plus. • *Pres. sub.* plaise. • *Past part.* plu.
pleuvoir	(impersonal) • *Pres.* pleut. • *Impf.* pleuvait. • *Past hist.* plut. • *Fut.* pleuvra. • *Pres. sub.* pleuve. • *Past part.* plu.
poursuivre	*as* SUIVRE.
pourvoir	*as* VOIR, except • *Fut.* pourvoirai.
pouvoir	• *Pres.* peux, peut, pouvons, pouvez, peuvent. • *Impf.* pouvais. • *Past hist.* pus. • *Fut.* pourrai. • *Pres. sub.* puisse. • *Past part.* pu.
prédire	*as* DIRE, except • *Pres.* vous prédisez.
prendre	• *Pres.* prends, prenons, prennent. • *Impf.* prenais. • *Past hist.* pris. • *Pres. sub.* prenne, prenions. • *Past part.* pris.
prescrire	*as* ÉCRIRE.
prévenir	*as* TENIR.
prévoir	*as* VOIR, except • *Fut.* prévoirai.
produire	*as* CONDUIRE.
promettre	*as* METTRE.
provenir	*as* TENIR.
recevoir	• *Pres.* reçois, recevons, reçoivent. • *Impf.* recevais. • *Past hist.* reçus. • *Fut.* recevrai. • *Pres. sub.* reçoive, recevions. • *Past part.* reçu.
reconduire	*as* CONDUIRE.
reconnaître	*as* CONNAÎTRE.
reconstruire	*as* CONDUIRE.
recouvrir	*as* COUVRIR.
recueillir	*as* CUEILLIR.
redire	*as* DIRE.
réduire	*as* CONDUIRE.
refaire	*as* FAIRE.

rejoindre *as* ATTEINDRE (except *oi* replaces *ei*).
remettre *as* METTRE.
renvoyer *as* ENVOYER.
repartir *as* SORTIR (except *ar* replaces *or*).
reprendre *as* PRENDRE.
reproduire *as* CONDUIRE.
résoudre • *Pres.* résous, résolvons. • *Impf.* résolvais. • *Past hist.* résolus. • *Pres. sub.* résolve. • *Past part.* résolu.
ressortir *as* SORTIR.
restreindre *as* ATTEINDRE.
retenir, revenir *as* TENIR.
revivre *as* VIVRE.
revoir *as* VOIR.
rire • *Pres.* ris, rit, rions, riez, rient. • *Impf.* riais. • *Past hist.* ris. • *Pres. sub.* rie, riions. • *Past part.* ri.
rompre *as* VENDRE (regular), except • *Pres.* il rompt.
satisfaire *as* FAIRE.
savoir • *Pres.* sais, sait, savons, savez, savent. • *Impf.* savais. • *Past hist.* sus. • *Fut.* saurai. • *Pres. sub.* sache, sachions. • *Pres. part.* sachant. • *Past part.* su. • *Imp.* sache, sachons, sachez.
séduire *as* CONDUIRE.
sentir *as* SORTIR (except *en* replaces *or*).
servir • *Pres.* sers, servons. • *Impf.* servais. • *Pres. sub.* serve.
sortir • *Pres.* sors, sortons. • *Impf.* sortais. • *Pres. sub.* sorte.
souffrir *as* COUVRIR.
soumettre *as* METTRE.
soustraire *as* EXTRAIRE.
soutenir *as* TENIR.
suffire • *Pres.* suffis, suffisons. • *Impf.* suffisais. • *Past hist.* suffis. • *Pres. sub.* suffise. • *Past part.* suffi.
suivre • *Pres.* suis, suivons. • *Impf.* suivais. • *Past hist.* suivis. • *Pres. sub.* suive. • *Past part.* suivi.
surprendre *as* PRENDRE.
survivre *as* VIVRE.
taire • *Pres.* tais, taisons. • *Impf.* taisais. • *Past hist.* tus. • *Pres. sub.* taise. • *Past part.* tu.
teindre *as* ATTEINDRE.

tenir • *Pres.* tiens, tenons, tiennent. • *Impf.* tenais. • *Past hist.* tins, tint, tînmes, tîntes, tinrent. • *Fut.* tiendrai. • *Pres. sub.* tienne. • *Past part.* tenu.

traduire *as* CONDUIRE.

traire *as* EXTRAIRE.

transmettre *as* METTRE.

vaincre • *Pres.* vaincs, vainc, vainquons. • *Impf.* vainquais. • *Past hist.* vainquis. • *Pres. sub.* vainque. • *Past part.* vaincu.

valoir • *Pres.* vaux, vaut, valons, valez, valent. • *Impf.* valais. • *Past hist.* valus. • *Fut.* vaudrai. • *Pres. sub.* vaille. • *Past part.* valu.

venir *as* TENIR.

vivre • *Pres.* vis, vit, vivons, vivez, vivent. • *Impf.* vivais. • *Past hist.* vécus. • *Pres. sub.* vive. • *Past part.* vécu.

voir • *Pres.* vois, voyons, voient. • *Impf.* voyais. • *Past hist.* vis. • *Fut.* verrai. • *Pres. sub.* voie, voyions. • *Past part.* vu.

vouloir • *Pres.* veux, veut, voulons, voulez, veulent. • *Impf.* voulais. • *Past hist.* voulus. • *Fut.* voudrai. • *Pres. sub.* veuille, voulions. • *Past part.* voulu. • *Imp.* veuille, veuillons, veuillez.

Numbers · Les Nombres

one (first)	1	un (premier)
two (second)	2	deux (deuxième)
three (third)	3	trois (troisième)
four (fourth)	4	quatre (quatrième)
five (fifth)	5	cinq (cinquième)
six (sixth)	6	six (sixième)
seven (seventh)	7	sept (septième)
eight (eighth)	8	huit (huitième)
nine (ninth)	9	neuf (neuvième)
ten (tenth)	10	dix (dixième)
eleven (eleventh)	11	onze (onzième)
twelve (twelfth)	12	douze (douzième)
thirteen (thirteenth)	13	treize (treizième)
fourteen (fourteenth)	14	quatorze (quatorzième)
fifteen (fifteenth)	15	quinze (quinzième)
sixteen (sixteenth)	16	seize (seizième)
seventeen (seventeenth)	17	dix-sept (dix-septième)
eighteen (eighteenth)	18	dix-huit (dix-huitième)
nineteen (nineteenth)	19	dix-neuf (dix-neuvième)
twenty (twentieth)	20	vingt (vingtième)
twenty-one (twenty-first)	21	vingt et un (vingt-et-unième)
twenty-two (twenty-second)	22	vingt-deux (vingt-deuxième)
thirty (thirtieth)	30	trente (trentième)
thirty-one (thirty-first)	31	trente et un (trente-et-unième)
forty (fortieth)	40	quarante (quarantième)
fifty (fiftieth)	50	cinquante (cinquantième)
sixty (sixtieth)	60	soixante (soixantième)
seventy (seventieth)	70	soixante-dix (soixante-dixième)
seventy-one (seventy-first)	71	soixante et onze (soixante-et-onzième)
seventy-three (seventy-third)	73	soixante-treize (soixante-treizième)
eighty (eightieth)	80	quatre-vingts (quatre-vingtième)
eighty-one (eighty-first)	81	quatre-vingt-un (quatre-vingt-unième)
ninety (ninetieth)	90	quatre-vingt-dix (quatre-vingt-dixième)
a *or* one hundred (hundredth)	100	cent (centième)
a hundred and one (hundred-and-first)	101	cent un (cent unième)
two hundred (two hundredth)	200	deux cents (deux centième)
a *or* one thousand (thousandth)	1,000	mille (millième)

Oxford Minidictionaries

Oxford's minidictionaries pack a large amount of up-to-date information into a small format. They offer a clear guide to and contain the essential information about a wide variety of subjects, in language readily comprehensible to the non-specialist. Excellent value, they fit easily into pocket, handbag, briefcase, or satchel, for use in your school, college, office, or home.

THE OXFORD MINIDICTIONARY

SECOND EDITION

Compiled by Joyce M. Hawkins

The Oxford Minidictionary contains over 40,000 entries covering the spelling and meaning of the commonest words of current English. Appendices list countries, chemical elements, metric units, and temperatures, and give helpful guidance on some points of correct English usage and punctuation.

THE OXFORD MINIGUIDE TO ENGLISH USAGE

E. S. C. Weiner

This reference book is for everyone who needs simple and direct guidance on spelling, pronunciation, meanings, and grammar. Points of usage are illustrated by quotations from good modern writers. Appendices list principles of punctuation and clichéd phrases, and describe the various forms of English overseas.

THE OXFORD MINIDICTIONARY OF SPELLING AND WORD-DIVISION

Compiled by R. E. Allen

This is a guide to the spelling and inflexion of over 60,000 words, including irregular and difficult plurals and parts of verbs, proper names, and clarification of confusable words. It also gives systematic advice on the division of words at the end of lines in printing and word processing.

THE OXFORD MINIDICTIONARY OF QUOTATIONS

Selected from the famous *Oxford Dictionary of Quotations*, this minidictionary contains nearly 4,000 quotations from more than 700 authors, and is served by an extensive and easy-to-use index.

THE OXFORD MINIDICTIONARY OF FIRST NAMES

Patrick Hanks and Flavia Hodges

This handy guide explains the meaning and origin of, and gives the correct pronunciation for, nearly 2,000 first names in common use in the English-speaking world. It also records bearers of the name, alternate spellings and forms, diminutives, and foreign-language variants.

THE OXFORD ITALIAN MINIDICTIONARY

Joyce Andrews

Designed for the needs of students, holiday-makers, and travellers, this minidictionary gives the meaning and pronunciation of 45,000 words and phrases, in entries arranged from both Italian to English and from English to Italian. It also includes tables of irregular verbs and useful technical jargon and slang.

MINIDICTIONARY OF COMPUTING

This handy reference book provides an explanatory guide, with diagrams and tables, to over 1,000 key words of computer terminology, covering terms encountered by users of home and small business computers. It also includes details of computer hardware, programming, and programme languages.

MINIDICTIONARY OF CHEMISTRY

With over 3,000 entries, this minidictionary provides an ideal source of reference for chemistry students and non-scientists wanting concise and accurate definitions of chemical terms. It contains invaluable background information and is illustrated with tables and diagrams.

MINIDICTIONARY OF PHYSICS

Providing clear and accurate definitions of key terms of physics and related subjects in nearly 2,500 entries, this minidictionary is further enhanced by tables and diagrams illustrating the material and extensive cross-references.